165.00

AFRICA

THE
GARLAND
ENCYCLOPEDIA
OF
WORLD MUSIC

VOLUME 1

THE GARLAND ENCYCLOPEDIA OF WORLD MUSIC

Volume 1
AFRICA
edited by Ruth M. Stone

Volume 2
**SOUTH AMERICA, MEXICO,
CENTRAL AMERICA, AND THE CARIBBEAN**
edited by Dale A. Olsen and Daniel E. Sheehy

Volume 3
THE UNITED STATES AND CANADA
edited by Ellen Koskoff

Volume 4
SOUTHEAST ASIA
edited by Terry E. Miller and Sean Williams

Volume 5
SOUTH ASIA: THE INDIAN SUBCONTINENT
edited by Alison Arnold

Volume 6
THE MIDDLE EAST
edited by Virginia Danielson, Scott Marcus, and Dwight Reynolds

Volume 7
EAST ASIA: CHINA, JAPAN, AND KOREA
edited by Robert C. Provine, Yosihiko Tokumaru, and J. Lawrence Witzleben

Volume 8
EUROPE
edited by Timothy Rice, Christopher Goertzen, and James Porter

Volume 9
AUSTRALIA AND THE PACIFIC ISLANDS
edited by Adrienne L. Kaeppler and J. Wainwright Love

Volume 10
THE WORLD'S MUSIC: GENERAL PERSPECTIVES AND REFERENCE TOOLS

Advisory Editors
Bruno Nettl and Ruth M. Stone

Founding Editors
James Porter and Timothy Rice

AFRICA

THE GARLAND ENCYCLOPEDIA OF WORLD MUSIC

VOLUME 1

Ruth M. Stone

Editor

GARLAND PUBLISHING, INC.

New York and London   1998

The initial planning of The Garland Encyclopedia of World Music was assisted by a grant from the National Endowment for the Humanities.

Library of Congress Cataloging-in-Publication Data

The Garland encyclopedia of world music / [advisory editors, Bruno Nettl and Ruth M. Stone ; founding editors, James Porter and Timothy Rice].
      p.   cm.
    Includes bibliographical references, discographies, and indexes.
    Contents: v. 1. Africa / Ruth M. Stone, editor.
    ISBN 0-8240-6035-0 (alk. paper)
      1. Music—Encyclopedias.   2. Folk music—Encyclopedias.
3. Popular music—Encyclopedias.   I. Nettl, Bruno, 1930–   .
II. Stone, Ruth M.   III. Porter, James, 1937–   . IV. Rice, Timothy, 1945–   .
ML100.G16   1998
780′.9—dc21   97-9671
                                                                     CIP
                                                                     MN

For Garland Publishing:

Vice-President: Leo Balk
Managing Editor: Richard Wallis
Director of Production: Anne Vinnicombe
Project Editor: Barbara Curialle Gerr
Copy Editor: J. Wainwright Love
Desktop publishing: Betty Probert (Special Projects Group)
Design: Lawrence Wolfson Design
Glossary and index: Marilyn Bliss
Music typesetting: Hyunjung Choi
Maps: Indiana University Graphic Services
Audio examples: Archives of Traditional Music, Indiana University

Cover illustration: Court musician plays traditional music outside the emir's palace, Kano, Nigeria.
© Robert Frerck/Odyssey/Chicago.

Unless otherwise noted, all interior illustrations were provided by the authors of articles and sections in this Encyclopedia.

"Time in African Performance" adapted from Ruth M. Stone, *Dried Millet Breaking*, 1988. Courtesy of Indiana University Press, Bloomington, Indiana.

Printed on acid-free, 250-year-life paper
Manufactured in the United States of America

Contents

Audio Examples

The following examples are included on the accompanying audio compact disc packaged with this volume. Track numbers are also indicated on the pages listed below for easy reference to text discussions. Complete descriptions of each example may be found on pages 823–825.

Track page reference

About *The Garland Encyclopedia of World Music*

Scholars have created many kinds of encyclopedias devoted to preserving and transmitting knowledge about the world. The study of music has itself been the subject of numerous encyclopedias in many languages. Yet until now the term music encyclopedia has been synonymous with surveys of the history, theory, and performance practice of European-based traditions.

In July 1988, the editors of *The Garland Encyclopedia of World Music* gathered for a meeting to determine the nature and scope of a massive new undertaking. For this, the first encyclopedia devoted to the music of all the world's peoples, the editors decided against the traditional alphabetic approach to compartmentalizing knowledge from A to Z. Instead, they chose a geographic approach, with each volume devoted to a single region and coverage assigned to the world's experts on specific music cultures.

For several decades, ethnomusicologists (following the practice of previous generations of comparative musicologists) have been documenting the music of the world through fieldwork, recording, and analysis. Now, for the first time, they have created an encyclopedia that summarizes in one place the major findings that have resulted from the explosion in such documentation since the 1960s. The volumes in this series comprise contributions from all those specialists who have from the start defined the field of ethnomusicology: anthropologists, linguists, dance ethnologists, cultural historians, folklorists, literary scholars, and—of course—musicologists, composers, and performers. This multidisciplinary approach continues to enrich the field, and future generations of students and scholars will find *The Garland Encyclopedia of World Music* to be an invaluable resource that contributes to knowledge in all its varieties.

Each volume has a similar design and organization: three large sections that cover the major topics of a region from broad general issues to specific music practices. Each section consists of articles written by leading researchers, and extensive glossaries and indexes give the reader easy access to terms, names, and places of interest.

Part 1: an introduction to the region, its culture, and its music as well as a survey of previous music scholarship and research

Part 2: major issues and processes that link the musics of the region

Part 3: detailed accounts of individual music cultures

The editors of each volume have determined how this three-part structure is to be constructed and applied depending on the nature of their regions of interest. The concepts covered in Part 2 will therefore differ from volume to volume; likewise, the articles in Part 3 might be about the music of nations, ethnic groups, islands, or subregions. The picture of music presented in each volume is thus comprehensive yet remains focused on critical ideas and issues.

Complementing the texts of the encyclopedia's articles are numerous illustrations: photographs, drawings, maps, charts, song texts, and music examples. At the end of each volume is a useful set of study and research tools, including a glossary of terms, lists of audio and visual resources, and an extensive bibliography. An audio compact disc will be found inside the back cover of each volume, with sound examples that are linked (with a in the margin) to discussions in the text.

The Garland Encyclopedia of World Music represents the work of hundreds of specialists guided by a team of distinguished editors. With a sense of pride, Garland Publishing offers this new series to readers everywhere.

Preface
Ruth M. Stone

This volume covers the making of African music, its performers and audiences, theories of musical conception, and the exchange of music among peoples on the continent and beyond. It presents a comprehensive view of the music of Africa from the perspectives of those who have studied it and those who make it.

The authors whose articles are gathered here come from Africa, Europe, Asia, and the United States. They have all conducted fieldwork in Africa, experiencing firsthand the artistry about which they write. Together, their articles—commissioned and written exclusively for this encyclopedia—reflect the current state of scholarship about music in Africa.

All these authors have met frequently at international conferences around the globe. Their ideas form a kind of dialogue with musicians, ritual specialists, and audiences. In some cases, direct quotes convey the performers' voices, and the compact disc brings an even more immediate experience of their creativity. Scholars and performers speak and make music with multiple voices, which at some points converge in consensus, and at others diverge into contrast. In this respect, the volume reflects the first of several definitions of the word *encyclopedia* in the *Oxford English Dictionary*: "the circle of learning."

Circles of learning

A circle of learning implies connections and relations from one area of knowledge to another, but not an exhaustive knowledge. Whatever any encyclopedia describing music on the continent of Africa may purport, a great deal is known to local musicians and specialists alone, and is yet to be studied by Western and African scholars. For all the published analyses of musical practices within the past two or three decades, no honest account can claim comprehensiveness. This volume celebrates the explosion of ideas that have been studied recently without unfairly promising to be an exhaustive representation of the universe of performance in Africa. As a written document, it sketches outlines that continue to unfold, and for which our knowledge must be considered emergent.

The organization of any encyclopedia speaks a great deal about the underlying orientations of the editors and the state of current scholarship. In this volume, we have decided to emphasize thematic issues and processes. As we realized, musical practices often transcend political boundaries, many of whose lines were drawn during the colonial period, dividing ethnic groups. While political divisions have influenced many things—like roads, which tend, particularly in West Africa, to lead from the coast inward, but not across national boundaries—some of those divisions are under challenge by armed struggles. Therefore, the potential choice of a political entity (like a country) as a descriptive unit would underline, even if implicitly, a kind of containment within the geographic space that echoes the colonial period. In this volume, themes that have emerged in the course of research became the focus of the organization.

Travel and exchange

This volume explores issues that transcend regional boundaries. Though such issues are anchored in specific examples and interpretation of local practice, their relevance is often not limited to a single political region. Furthermore, recognizing the streams of influence and exchange that have flowed within Africa, and to and from Africa, a number of articles consider the nature of this movement of people and musical practices.

This volume, then, deliberately highlights concepts of intra- and intercontinental movement. Beyond this, the goal is to emphasize Africans as individuals and groups who have initiated travel and action, and do not simply wait for outside forces to act upon them, as many colonial accounts either implicitly or explicitly narrate. By beginning with such assumptions, we seek to counteract the idea that only Westerners or outsiders were, and are, active travelers on the continent. About one hundred years before the oldest extant written report of a European voyage of discovery, the Egyptian pharaoh Necho hired Phoenicians to circumnavigate the continent, which they did in three years. The first Greek settlement on the continent, Cyrene, was founded about 631 B.C., on land that is now in Libya. Even today, Egypt remains a center of active intellectual life and architectural monuments of the Islamic world.

Among the significant streams of exchanges are the contacts of Arabs with Africans as caravans moved across the Sahara Desert, bringing musical instruments and ideas about musical performance with their salt, gold, and ivory. Along Africa's eastern coast, Arabs came in ships, carried by seasonal winds; the Omanis, in particular, set up city-states along the coast. Many Africans went to Arabia, some of them as slaves, where they performed music whose styles influence local practices today.

Europeans—including the Portuguese and later the British, the French, the Germans, the Dutch, and others—moved to colonize Africa, and social connections between Europe and Africa still accent musical life in Africa. The Americas became the residence of many West and Central Africans brought for slavery into the New World, and the impact of that institution continues. Long before Europeans "discovered" Africa, interchange with the Indian subcontinent, the Malay and Indonesian worlds, and the Far East also moved along the ocean highways.

HOW THIS VOLUME IS ORGANIZED

Encompassing a broad geographical span and a variety of musical practices, the volume treats a selection of the riches African culture offers. Part 1 profiles Africa as a whole, with two overview articles followed by an article on the representation of African music in early documents (McCall) and a historical review of the scholarly study of African music from an African viewpoint (Nketia).

Issues and processes

The articles in the first section of Part 2 focus on themes and issues that, crosscutting local practices and sensibilities, integrate the performance of music and other arts within Africa. Among these themes are the integration of music with other arts (Hampton), notation and oral tradition (Shelemay), timbral concepts (Fales), compositional practices (Mensah, Njoku), theory and technology (Arom and Voisin), music as healing (Friedson), and dance (Kwakwa).

The articles in the second section of Part 2 focus on themes that have emerged from the movement of peoples within and beyond Africa: intra-African streams of influence (Kubik), Islam and its effect on music in one part of West Africa (Monts), guitar music (Kaye), the Kru mariners of Liberia (Schmidt), effects of Latin American music in Zaïre (Mukuna), and interchanges that occur in local contexts, like Ghana (Avorgbedor) and Nigeria (Brooks). Part 2 concludes with a broad survey of African popular music (Impey).

Selected regional case studies

Part 3 presents five overview articles on regional musical practices in Africa: West (DjeDje), North (Wendt), East (Cooke), Central (Kubik), and Southern (Kaemmer). Then, within each of the regions, additional articles provide case studies that continue the themes raised in the earlier sections of the volume.

The topics for West Africa encompass Yoruba popular music (Waterman), genre definitions in praise singing in Northern Sierra Leone (Arntson), and the dynamics of social interaction in Hausa performance (Besmer). For North Africa, the essays explore the interface of poetic performance and music in Somalia (Johnson), the range of performances in Sudan (Simon), and Tuareg performance that crosses the borders of Algeria and Niger (Wendt). The East African articles comment on a range of issues from popular music to various religious musics for Kenya (Kavyu) and Tanzania (Martin). For Central Africa, the transitions of Pygmy music (Kisliuk) are studied. Finally, for Southern Africa, the authors describe the principles of harmony in Zambia (Tsukada), mbira music and other genres of the Shona of Zimbabwe (Kaemmer), popular musical practices in South Africa (Coplan), and the wonderful hybrid of traditions found on the island of Madagascar, 400 kilometers east of the continental coast (Rakotomalala).

Studies of Africa have sometimes separated the continent into the area north of the Sahara Desert and the area south of the Sahara. By statement or implication, the sub-Saharan region has been considered the more characteristically African. This volume, however, takes Africa as a whole, with the assumption that travel across the desert has carried musical practices with it; even farther afield, clearly sub-Saharan musical practices occur in the eastern coastal region of Arabia. The Sahara is not a neat dividing line of musical styles, and our choice of the continental borders as boundaries for this volume is more arbitrary than indicative of actual practice. The article on the Tuareg (Wendt) shows how the same group of people occupy two separate countries—Algeria and Niger—on the edges of the desert area.

Certain issues in music are accented by regional location. The case study articles, highlighting local issues, present rich descriptive detail to illuminate the analysis of these issues, grounding and anchoring them in data. For a variety of reasons, opportunities for equally intensive study throughout the various areas of Africa have not yet arisen.

Research tools

Readers will find research aids throughout the volume. Maps help locate the places and peoples mentioned in the text; references at the end of each article specify further readings and recordings. Cross-references to other articles in this volume are indicated with brackets [see ISLAM IN LIBERIA]. For readers seeking a general bibliographic guide to African music, John Gray's compilation *African Music: A Bibliographical Guide* (1991) is the most comprehensive recent source (see GUIDE TO PUBLICATIONS). In addition, there is a wealth of other illustrations including photographs, drawings, and graphs.

Musical examples

Throughout the encyclopedia, musical examples supplement the verbal representations of musical sound. In most cases, these appear as staff notation or some variation of it. Some authors, however, explore other forms of notation. Labanotation illustrates body-movement patterns (Hampton); the modified staff serves as a xylophone tablature (Arntson); graphs based on frequency of sound-wave vibration illustrate timbral issues (Fales); and symbols of poetic scansion (Johnson) reflect textual construction.

One article (Shelemay) explicitly addresses the concept of notation in the study of African music. It explores both indigenous and foreign forms of notation—written and aural—that have been applied to African music, including a music-notation system employed in Ethiopia.

Writing music, like writing in general (many would say or think), marks a high level of knowledge and sophistication. Yet most African peoples perpetuate their musical traditions through aural forms of notation (Shelemay). The value of the written is largely the researcher's value. Because most notation ignores indigenous concepts, we may fail to notice in it the intricacies of indigenous aural notations. Further, some African peoples have adopted other aural notations, such as Tonic Sol-fa, to supplement their own systems (Njoku).

Glossary

An extensive glossary of three thousand entries provides definitions or identifications for terms, concepts, instruments, ethnic groups, and musical genres. Readers will also find selected items from the glossary reproduced at the tops of many pages within the volume.

Discography

The discography provides reference to commercially produced sound recordings. These reflect the late-twentieth-century proliferation of tapes, compact discs, and other recordings of African music from across the continent. Many more recordings exist in archives around the world.

Compact disc

A selection of recorded examples is available on the compact disc that accompanies this volume. These examples are intended to supplement and illustrate the discussions found in the articles. Our goal has been to seek examples unavailable on commercial recordings. In the margins of the text, a circled number specifies the track of the recorded example illustrating a particular discussion. A booklet of notes on the recordings is packaged with the compact disc, and is duplicated on pages 823–826, preceding the index.

ACKNOWLEDGMENTS

An encyclopedia, more than most academic enterprises, is a team effort. I have been assisted by a host of people who helped to shape and complete this massive project. Since 1989, I have been assisted by an editorial assistant: Mary Dart served for several years in that capacity, followed by Susan Oehler. More recently, Nina Fales and Cathy Brigham helped with final details. To these people and to the College of Arts and Sciences at Indiana University, which funded much of their work, I am greatly indebted. They checked the many details, handled the correspondence, and worked out numerous problems such as converting computer files.

An ever-present companion in the editing process has been Jacob Love, who has served as copy editor and brought an eagle eye to the copy. I shall miss our nearly continuous e-mail and phone conversations as we worried over one or another of the texts.

The shape of the volume developed in a series of meetings in 1988 and 1989, during which the founding editors, James Porter and Tim Rice, facilitated discussions. Other Africanist ethnomusicologists who attended and contributed included J. H. Kwabena Nketia and Jacqueline Cogdell DjeDje. Finally, I am grateful to Gerhard Kubik, who spent several weeks in Bloomington in 1991 working with me on his contributions and making suggestions about the encyclopedia.

Colleagues at the Archives of Traditional Music who provided reference help include Mary Bucknum, Marilyn Graf, Karen Metelnick, and Suzanne Mudge.

I must thank Leo Balk and Richard Wallis, who have represented Garland Publishing and provided strong commitment to this project and sound advice at crucial moments.

Finally, my family—Verlon, my husband, and Angela, my daughter—have supported this project and the time I have devoted to it the last number of years, and this shared commitment is important.

In the end, though I am appreciative of much help, I take responsibility for errors that may have inadvertently crept into the manuscript.

—Ruth M. Stone

ORTHOGRAPHY

ε or ẹ   = "eh" as in **bet**

ɔ or ọ   = "aw" as in **awful**

ŋ or ṇ   = "ng" as in **sing**

γ or yg = "ch" as in German **ach**

ʃ or ṣ   = "sh" as in **shout**

6   = implosive "b"

ɗ   = implosive "d"

!   = click sound

ʹ   = high tone

ˋ   = low tone

ˆ   = high-low tone

˜   = nasalized sound

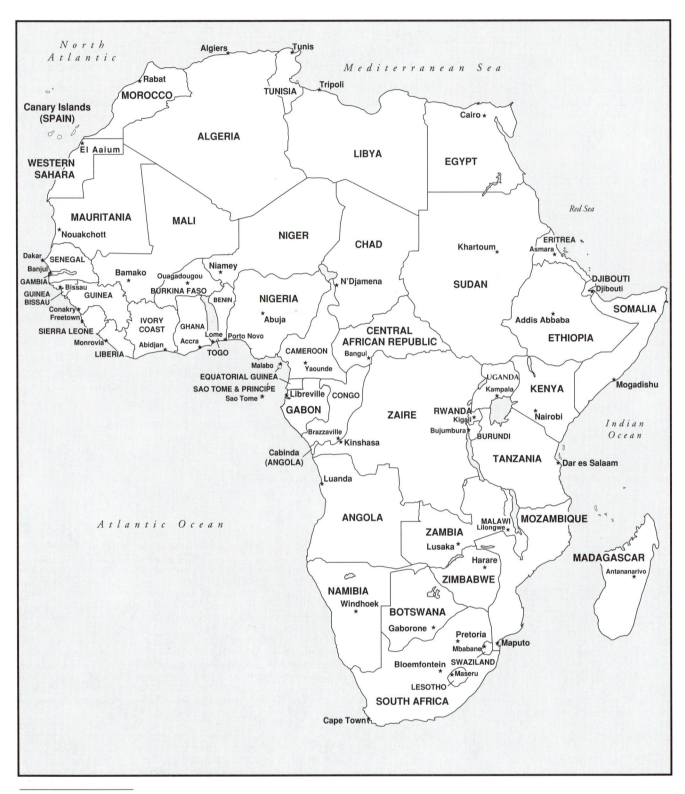

As this volume was going to press, a new government in Zaïre had changed the name of the nation to "Democratic Republic of the Congo."

Part 1
Introduction to African Music

Africa astounds with its geographic expanse and its regional diversities. Because of its rich cultural heritage, we see today an extraordinary vitality in the performing arts. We begin with an introduction to African artistic expression and a survey of the history of our knowledge about African music.

Profile of Africa
Ruth M. Stone

Peoples and Languages
Subsistence and Industry
Transport and Trade
Social and Political Formations
Religious Beliefs and Practices

The African continent first impresses by its size: the second-largest of the continents of the world, it encloses more than 28 million square kilometers, spanning 8,000 kilometers from north to south and 7,400 kilometers from east to west. Islands dot the coasts, with Madagascar in the southeast being the largest.

Bisected by the equator, lying predominantly within the tropical region where thick rainforests grow, the continent consists of a plateau that rises from rather narrow coastal plains. Vast expanses of grassland also characterize its inland regions. The Sahara Desert dominates northern Africa, and the Kalahari Desert southern Africa. Vast mineral resources (of iron, gold, diamonds, oil) and deep tropical forests enrich the continent.

PEOPLES AND LANGUAGES

The population of the continent constitutes only one-tenth of the world's people, though many urban areas and countries (like Nigeria) have a high density, counterbalancing vast regions of sparse population. Large urban areas have sprung up in nearly every country of Africa, with high-rise office buildings and computers part of the milieu. People cluster into nearly three thousand ethnic groups, each of which shares aspects of social identity. The most widely known reference work that classifies these groups is George Peter Murdock's *Africa: Its People and Their Culture History* (1959).

About one thousand distinct indigenous languages are spoken throughout Africa. Joseph Greenberg (1970) classifies them into four major divisions: Niger-Kordofanian, Nilo-Saharan, Hamito-Semitic, and Khoisan. The Niger-Kordofanian is the largest and most widespread of these, extending from West Africa to the southern tip of Africa; its geographical distribution points to the rapid movement of people from West Africa eastward and southward beginning about 2000 B.C. and extending into the 1600s of the common era.

Swahili, an East African trade language (with a Bantu grammar and much Arabic vocabulary), reflects the movements of peoples both within Africa and to and from Arabia. Bambara and Hausa, other trade languages (spoken across wide areas of

FIGURE 1   Playing technique of the *nkangala* mouth bow in Malawi. Photo by Gerhard Kubik.

West Africa), are but a few of the languages that show Arabic influence. In addition, the Austronesian family is represented by Malagasy, spoken on the island of Madagascar, and the Indo-European family by Afrikaans, spoken by descendants of seventeenth-century Dutch settlers in South Africa.

Following colonial rule in many countries, English, French, and Portuguese still serve as languages of commerce and education in the former colonies. Several languages of the Indian subcontinent are spoken by members of Asian communities that have arisen in many African countries, and numerous Lebanese traders throughout Africa speak a dialect of Arabic.

From the 1500s to the 1800s, trade in slaves produced a great outward movement of perhaps 10 million people from West and Central Africa to the Americas, and from East Africa to Arabia. A token return of ex-slaves and their descendants to Liberia during the 1800s represented a further disruption, as African-American settlers displaced portions of local populations. The long-term effects of this loss of manpower, and the attendant suffering it produced, have yet to be adequately understood. The movement of peoples, however, contributed to the formation of languages, such as the Krio of Sierra Leone and Liberian English of Liberia—hybrids of indigenous and foreign tongues.

Though indigenous systems of writing were not widespread in Africa, some peoples invented their own scripts. These peoples included some of the Tuareg and Berber groups in the Sahara and more than fifteen groups in West Africa, including the Vai and the Kpelle of Liberia, whose music is studied in this volume.

SUBSISTENCE AND INDUSTRY

A majority of Africans engage in farming for their employment. In many areas, farmers use shifting cultivation, in which they plant a portion of land for a time and leave it to regenerate, moving to another plot. This form of agriculture is characteristically tied to a complex system of communal ownership. Increasingly, however, people and corporations, by acquiring exclusive ownership of large areas of arable land, are changing African land-use patterns.

International commerce has resulted in a shift from subsistence to cash crops: cocoa, coffee, palm oil, rubber, sugarcane, tea, tobacco. The wage laborers who work

Typical of early African kingdoms were large retinues of royal musicians, who enhanced state occasions and provided musical commentary on events.

with the crops migrate from their home villages, settling permanently or temporarily on large farms. Grassland areas throughout the continent support flocks of camels, cattle, goats, and sheep, and people there are predominantly herders, who frequently live as nomads to find the best grazing for their animals.

In many areas of Africa, rich natural resources—coal, copper, diamonds, gold, iron, oil, uranium—contribute to employment for notable sectors of the population. Processing these materials provides wages for workers and exports for the resource-rich nations.

TRANSPORT AND TRADE

For trade and travel, people have long moved across African deserts and savannas, and through African forests, but the intensity and speed of their movement increased with the building of roads, railways, and airports, particularly since the 1950s in many parts of the continent.

Suddenly, perishable fruits and vegetables could be shipped from interior farms to coastal urban areas. Taxis and buses built a lively trade shuttling people and goods up and down roads, from local markets to urban areas and back again. Manufactured goods were more readily available from petty traders and shopkeepers alike, and foods like frozen fish became part of the daily diet.

Among all that activity, cassettes of the latest popular music of the local country and the world became part of the goods available for purchase. Feature films of East Asian karate, Indian loveplots, or American black heroes became available, first from itinerant film projectionists, and by the 1980s from video clubs. On a weekly and sometimes daily basis, maritime shipping was now supplemented with air travel to Europe and the rest of the world.

SOCIAL AND POLITICAL FORMATIONS

Several African kingdoms with large centralized governments emerged in the Middle Ages. Among these were Ghana in the West African grasslands area around the Niger River (A.D. 700–1200); Mali, which succeeded Ghana and became larger (1200–1500); and Songhai (1350–1600), which took over the territory of ancient Mali. Kanem-Bornu flourished further east in the interior (800–1800). In the forest region, Benin developed in parts of present-day Nigeria (1300–1800); Ashanti, in the area of contemporary Ghana (1700–1900); Kongo, along the Congo River (1400–1650); Luba-Lunda, in the Congo-Angola-Zambia grasslands (1400–1700); Zimbabwe, in southern Africa (1400–1800); and Buganda, in the area of present-day Uganda (1700–1900) (Davidson 1966:184–185).

Archaeological evidence is only now providing information about the full extent of indigenous African empires, fueled by long-distance trade in gold, ivory, salt, and other commodities. Typical of these kingdoms were large retinues of royal musicians, who enhanced state occasions and provided musical commentary on events. Benin bronze plaques, preserving visual images of some of these musicians, are in museums around the world.

Alongside large-scale political formations have been much smaller political units, known as stateless societies. Operating in smaller territories, inhabited by smaller numbers of people, these societies may have several levels in a hierarchy of chiefs, who in turn owe allegiance to a national government. At the lowest level in these societies, government is consensual in nature; at the upper levels, chiefs, in consultation with elders and ordinary citizens, make decisions.

West Africa supports Poro and Sande (called secret societies by Westerners), organizations to which adults belong, and through which they are enculturated about social mores and customs. Children of various ages leave the village and live apart in the forest, in enclosures known as Poro (for men) and Sande (for women). There, they learn dances and songs that they will perform upon emergence at the closing ceremonies. Required parts of their education, these songs and dances are displayed for community appreciation at the end of the educational period. It is during this seclusion that promising young soloists in dance and drumming may be identified and specially tutored.

Kinship, though long studied by anthropologists in Africa, has proved complex and often hard to interpret. Ancestors are noted in formal lineages, which may be recited in praise singing and often reinterpreted according to the occasion and its requirements. Residence may be patrilocal or matrilocal, depending on local customs. And the extended families that are ubiquitous in Africa become distanced through urban relocation and labor migration, even if formal ties continue.

Settlements may take the form of nomadic camps (moving with the season and pasture), cities, towns, or dispersed homesteads along motor roads. They may also develop around mines, rubber plantations, and other work sites. Camps for workers who periodically travel home may become permanent settlements, where families also reside.

RELIGIOUS BELIEFS AND PRACTICES

Though indigenous religious beliefs and practices exhibit many varieties of practice, they share some common themes. A high, supreme, and often distant creator god rules. Intermediate deities become the focus of worship, divination, and sacrificial offerings. Spirits live in water, trees, rocks, and other places, and these become the beings through whose mediation people maintain contact with the creator god.

Indigenous religious practices in Africa have been influenced and overlaid by Christian and Islamic practices, among other world religions. New religious movements, such as *aladura* groups [FOREIGN-INDIGENOUS INTERCHANGE], have skillfully linked Christian religious practices with indigenous ones.

Elsewhere, Islam penetrated the forest region and brought changes to local practices, even as it, too, underwent change [ISLAM IN LIBERIA]. The observance of Ramadan, the month of fasting, was introduced, certain musical practices were banned, and altered indigenous practices remained as compromises.

REFERENCES

Davidson, Basil. 1966. *African Kingdoms.* New York: Time-Life Books.

Greenberg, Joseph H. 1970. *The Languages of Africa.* Bloomington, Ind.: Research Center for the Language Sciences.

Murdock, George P. 1959. *Africa: Its People and Their Culture History.* New York: McGraw-Hill.

African Music in a Constellation of Arts
Ruth M. Stone

Concepts of Music
Concepts of Performance
Historic Preservation of African Music

African performance is a tightly wrapped bundle of arts that are sometimes difficult to separate, even for analysis. Singing, playing instruments, dancing, masquerading, and dramatizing are part of a conceptual package that many Africans think of as one and the same. The Kpelle people of Liberia use a single word, *sang*, to describe a well-danced movement, a well-sung phrase, or especially fine drumming. For them, the expressive acts that gives rise to these media are related and interlinked. The visual arts, the musical arts, the dramatic arts—all work together in the same domain and are conceptually treated as intertwined. To describe the execution of a sequence of dances, a Kpelle drummer might say, "The dance she spoke."

CONCEPTS OF MUSIC

Honest observers are hard pressed to find a single indigenous group in Africa that has a term congruent with the usual Western notion of "music." There are terms for more specific acts like singing, playing instruments, and more broadly performing (dance, games, music); but the isolation of musical sound from other arts proves a Western abstraction, of which we should be aware when we approach the study of performance in Africa.

The arts maintain a close link to the rest of social and political life. In performance, they both reflect upon that life and create it. Highlife songs are famous for having been employed in political campaigns in Ghana, poetry in Somalia has influenced political history, and work is both coordinated and enhanced as bush clearers follow the accompaniment of an instrumental ensemble. The arts are not an extra or separate expression to be enjoyed apart from the social and political ebb and flow. They emerge centrally in the course of life, vital to normal conduct.

While musical specialists in the West have often used notions of "folk," "popular," and "art" to categorize music, these concepts prove problematic in African settings. They often indicate more of the social formations associated with music than of musical sound. "Folk" is often equated with "traditional," or music performed in rural areas, "popular" is commonly associated with mass audiences and urban areas, and "art" is associated with elite, upper-class, written notation. These terms also imply a prejudicial tilt toward things written and reserved for a few, but in African

Instruments are more than material objects: they frequently take on human features and qualities. Certain solo instruments may have personal names, be kept in special houses, receive special sacrificial food or other offerings, and be regarded as quasi-human.

FIGURE I   Mpumpu, king of the masks among the Mbwela and Nkhangala of Southeastern Angola, 1965. Photo by Gerhard Kubik.

settings, aural traditions are highly developed and practiced forms of transmission, no less competent or effective in artistic creation.

A further complication is that African practices often mingle musics from apparently disparate idioms. African and Western elements may be codominant, as Akin Euba asserts (1992:308) is the case for J. H. Kwabena Nketia's composition *Volta Fantasy.* Djimo Kouyate, performer on the twenty-one-stringed harp-lute (*kora*) of Senegal, performs with Mamaya African Jazz, an eight-member ensemble, which performs a fusion of African music and worldbeat, the latter a form of international popular music (Brown 1994). The West African superstar Baaba Maal recorded an album, *Firin' in Fouta,* in three phases, each reflecting a different kind of music. He began by returning to his ancestral village (Podor, northern Senegal), where he recorded instruments and songs of everyday life. In Dakar, the capital, his band, Dande Lenol, transformed these sounds into rhythm tracks. Finally, he took those tracks to England, where he added vocals, synthesizers, and Celtic instruments. The resultant album draws on local African music to inform high-tech Western dance music (Himes 1995).

Some scholars have delineated musical style areas within Africa. Perhaps the most commented upon, and the most criticized, is that of Alan Lomax, who, using musical traits as discerned by Western listeners, divided Africa into fifteen regions: North Africa, Sahara, Western Sudan, Moslem Sudan, Eastern Sudan, Ethiopia, Guinea Coast, Equatorial Bantu, Upper Nile, Northeast Bantu, Central Bantu, African Hunters, South African Bantu, Madagascar, and Afro-American (Lomax 1968:91–95). But the limitations of such mapping derive from the interpretations of Western listeners, who may or may not know much about the conception of that sound.

CONCEPTS OF PERFORMANCE

Some generalizations can be drawn about performance in Africa, emphasizing the perspectives of the performers and their ideas about creating that performance. However, we must bear in mind that great variation exists, even about fundamental ideas.

Performers

To some extent, most people in African communities are expected to perform music and dance at a basic level. Performing is considered as normal as speaking. In many areas, social puberty is marked by singing and dancing, as young people display their accomplishments in token of their maturation. Solo performers may be trained to excel because they have shown aptitude for an instrument, or they may be selected because they come from a family whose occupation is to be musicians, as is frequently the case among the *griots* of West Africa.

Soloists develop their skills most often with the aid of a tutelary spirit or some form of supernatural assistance. At musical performances, spirits are sometimes present, forming an elusive audience, which certain human participants will sense. The elusive teacher can make a singer's voice particularly fine. The tutelary spirit makes high demands, however, and fame does not come easily. For aiding the singer, the spirit may exact much, even the singer's life.

The tragedy of Pona-wɛni

Such a relationship, always treacherous, can end in tragedy. My own fieldwork shows such a case. In 1970, I recorded Pona-wɛni, a fine female singer, as she performed with Wokpɛɛ, a male soloist. They sang "*Giing*," the favorite song of the year in central Bong County, Liberia; in 1972, it was included on a Folkways recording. In 1975, on my return, I gave the singer a copy of it.

On a market day in late 1988, I returned to Totota, where I met musicians from the town of Gbeyilataa, performers I had worked with at various times over the last eighteen years. As we sat under a tree and conversed about various people from their town, they talked easily of who was around and performing, and who had moved elsewhere. Of Pona-wɛni, they said nothing.

Eventually, I inquired if the musicians would like to hear some of the music some of them had performed in 1970. With eagerness, they responded that they would. By chance, I selected "*Giing*" to be played. Immediately on hearing its beginning, several people looked astonished, and one woman burst into tears. As I stopped the tape, the story of Pona-wɛni poured out.

During my absence, Pona-wɛni had excelled, become famous for her talent. But some villagers murmured that she had exceeded herself. One day, as she was crossing a log bridge over a swollen creek, a tutelary spirit pulled her down into the torrent, from which she never emerged. The special power that had helped her succeed and be admired had been responsible for balancing benefits with misfortune.

Performance as an engine of national policy

While ensembles of performers are formed and perform within a local region, often traveling to neighboring towns, some ensembles have been formed to represent contemporary nation-states. The ensembles may meld performers from various locations and teach them to adapt their performances to meet the requirements of the Western stage.

Some African countries have set up national training centers where musicians and dancers work together to create ensembles. These performers are often paid by the national government. They travel around the country or tour the world, representing a blend of musics from the particular region, adapted to outsiders' expectations for performance.

Musical instruments as human extensions

The people of Africa make and use a vast array of musical instruments. Beyond an expected variety of drums, musicians play harps, harp-lutes, lutes, lyres, and zithers, to name but a few of the stringed instruments found across the continent.

Within African contexts, instruments are more than material objects: they frequently take on human features and qualities. Certain solo instruments may have personal names, be kept in special houses, receive special sacrificial food or other offerings, and be regarded as quasi-human. To the musician playing them, these instruments provide power and sometimes special aid. A close, humanlike partnership sometimes develops between musician and instrument.

While ethnomusicologists categorize instruments as aerophones (bullroarers, flutes, horns, oboes), chordophones (harps, lutes, zithers), membranophones

Myths, legends, epics, oral histories, and life histories were only a few of the genres that embodied memories of performances.

(drums), and idiophones (rattles, lamellophones, xylophones), African peoples frequently employ other ways of grouping instruments. Among the Kpelle of Liberia, instruments are either blown (*fɛɛ*) or struck (*ngale*); all aerophones fit into the former category, and all other instruments fit into the latter. All Kpelle stringed instruments are plucked, and so the finger, from a Kpelle conception, "strikes" the string (Stone 1982:55–57).

Exchange among voices

Ethnomusicologists describe musical sounds according to pitches (labeled with numbers or letters of the alphabet), but peoples in Africa often conceive of these sounds as voices. People, instruments, and birds all employ voices, which, in performance, musicians imitate. Performers conceive of one voice singing a part and another voice responding, in a call-and-response kind of dialogue.

In the idea of call and response, the conversational metaphor captures many exchanges that are the fabric of the performance. Kpelle choral singing always has a counterpart to the solo or the first part. A master drummer may create the first part, and a vocal soloist may become the counterpart to the drum. But then, when the chorus members come in as a response to the soloist, the vocalist and master drummer function as a pair, to which the chorus answers. A web of balances is created, and interchanges abound at many levels. The voices that create these exchanges are frequently described in terms like *large* or *small*, implying certain aspects of pitch, timbre, and dynamics.

Some peoples stress the primacy of the transaction between paired performing parts (Stone 1985:139–148). Two players of the *mangwilo*, a xylophone of southeast Africa, sit at the same instrument facing one another. One is called the starting one (*opachera*) and the other the responding one (*wakulela*) (Kubik 1965:36). Similarly, among the Shona of Zimbabwe, a solo mbira player designates one part he or she plays as *kushaura* 'to lead the piece, to take the solo part' and the second as *kutsinhira* 'to exchange parts of a song, to interweave a second interlocking part' (Berliner 1978:73).

Motoric patterns in performance

In the early twentieth century, Erich M. von Hornbostel called for the study of patterns of human movement to aid our understanding of African rhythm (1928:30–62). Though many scholars have found fault with his conclusions, some, taking leads from his work, have explored issues of bodily movement.

Gerhard Kubik has underscored the importance of the acoustic, motoric, and visual elements of rhythm (1972:28–39; 1977:253–274). Moses Serwadda and Hewitt Pantaleoni have shown how drumming and dancing link: "A drummer will indicate the dance motions sometimes as a way of explaining and teaching a [drum] pattern" (1968:52).

In multipart textures, individual parts often interweave or interlock in short, repetitive motives (ostinatos), which become layered in complex ways. Certain of these motives are invariant; others subtly transform in variation as the performance develops. A sense of multiple layering emerges as the density increases, ideally with contrasting timbres among parts.

HISTORICAL PRESERVATION OF AFRICAN MUSIC

Documentation of African performances predates the arrival of the Europeans or sound recordings. Oral traditions served to preserve in dynamic ways the aspects of performance that people wanted to remember. Myths, legends, epics, oral histories, and life histories were only a few of the genres that embodied memories of performances.

Almost a thousand years before the phonograph was invented, Arab travelers wrote about their impressions of African music. Perhaps the most famous, Mohammed ibn Abdullah ibn Battuta, vividly described court music scenes in the kingdom of Mali in the 1100s (Gibb 1929). When first the Portuguese, and then other Europeans, arrived in Africa, Arabs had long been active in exploring the continent. We should beware of assuming that the "dark continent" (as Europeans unsubtly dubbed it) suddenly came to life with the arrival of the Europeans. African contacts with the outside world—especially with West, South, and Southeast Asia—were lively long before Europeans "discovered" the continent.

As Europeans began to study Africa, and in particular its music, their interpretations emphasized a music of rather monotonous stasis and inaction, discovered by ever-adventurous Europeans, who, conversely, associated themselves with music of change and development. Such interpretations are especially curious when we note that motion and action are central to the aesthetic principles of many African groups. The most charitable assessment is that European misperceptions came from a lack of appreciation of African musical subtleties, including the language of performance. Especially after the publication of Charles Darwin's *Origin of Species* (1859), theories of musical evolutionism, which ascribed a more limited development to Africans than to Europeans, fueled the outsiders' mistaken notions.

Before the twentieth century, African music was preserved for Western posterity in verbal descriptions and musical notation. These forms of writing froze and isolated moving sounds into static forms. As wax cylinders were etched with sound (beginning in Africa in the early 1900s), they opened up new horizons while fixing sound images, though perhaps not to the same extent (or in the same way) as written musical transcription.

Western adventurers collected examples of African sounds in much the same manner as they collected samples of African flora and fauna. These examples were transported back to archives and museums to be sorted, duplicated, and catalogued (Stone and Gillis 1976). Africans, in contrast, have over the years been more concerned with continuing their live performance traditions, and have paid less attention to acquiring and preserving samples of sounds.

REFERENCES

Berliner, Paul. 1978. *The Soul of Mbira*. Berkeley: University of California Press.

Brown, Joe. 1994. "Djimo Kouyate." *Washington Post,* 28 January.

Darwin, Charles. 1859. *Origin of Species*. London: British Museum.

Euba, Akin. 1992. "Creating Authentic Forms of New African Art Music." International Conference on African Music and Dance: Problems and Prospects. Working documents. Bellagio Study and Conference Center, Bellagio, Italy, 12–16 October.

Gibb, Hamilton A. R. 1929. *Ibn Battuta, Travels in Asia and Africa.* London: Darf.

Gray, John. 1991. *African Music: A Bibliographical Guide to the Traditional, Popular, Arts, and Liturgical Musics of Sub-Saharan Africa.* New York and Westport, Conn.: Greenwood Press.

Greenberg, Joseph. 1970. *The Languages of Africa,* 3rd ed. Bloomington and The Hague: Indiana University and Mouton.

Himes, Geoffrey. 1995. "Maal's African Dance Mix." *Washington Post,* 20 January.

Hornbostel, Erich M. von. 1928. "African Negro Music." *Africa* 1:30–62.

Kubik, Gerhard. 1965. "Transcription of Mangwilo Xylophone Music from Film Strips." *African Music* 3(4):35–41.

———. 1972. "Transcription of African Music from Silent Film: Theory and Methods." *African Music* 5(1):28–39.

———. 1977. "Patterns of Body Movement in the Music of Boys' Initiation in South-East Angola." In *The Anthropology of the Body,* ed. John Blacking, 253–274. London: Academic Press.

Serwadda, Moses, and Hewitt Pantaleoni. 1968. "A Possible Notation for African Dance Drumming." *African Music* 4(2):45–52.

Stone, Ruth M. 1982. *Let the Inside Be Sweet: The Interpretation of Music Event among the Kpelle of Liberia.* Bloomington: Indiana University Press.

———. 1985. "In Search of Time in African Music." *Music Theory Spectrum* 7:139–158.

Stone, Ruth M., and Frank J. Gillis. 1976. *African Music and Oral Data: A Catalog of Field Recordings, 1902–1975.* Bloomington and London: Indiana University Press.

The Scholarly Study of African Music: A Historical Review

J. H. Kwabena Nketia

The Goals of African Musicology
The Beginnings of African Scholarship in Music: 1920–1950
The Search for Broader Perspectives: 1950–1960
Profiles of Individual Research: 1950–1960
Scholarship in the Period of Institutional Development: 1960–1970
Trends in African Scholarship: 1970–1980
Western Scholars' Contribution to African Musicology
The Challenge of Sociopolitical Change
Challenges for the Future

In the early 1980s, African scholars at the University of Nairobi decided to found a journal devoted to the scholarly study of African music. They decided to call it *African Musicology*. Though the proposed title seemed attractive because of its apparent novelty, the reaction to it was mixed, for it seemed to suggest the existence of an African tradition of musicology distinctive and separate from musicology in the Western tradition. Nobody doubted, however, the founders' intention: to create a journal that would specialize in African materials, encouraging an Africa-centered approach to the presentation and interpretation of data.

The term *African musicology* is not new. Klaus P. Wachsmann, who worked in Uganda for twenty years (1937–1957), used it in articles between 1966 and 1971, when his awareness of institutional changes in Africa led him to take stock of the status and role musicology had assumed in the musical scene (Wachsmann 1966b, 1970). African scholars and composers had emerged, and ministries and departments of culture had begun to support music and musical research in ways that could not have been envisaged before political independence. Since research in African studies, and particularly in the music of Africa, had been done by Western scholars, a new era, calling for partnership in research and the cross-fertilization of ideas through dialogue, seemed to have dawned. African scholars saw they had much to gain from collaborating with their Western colleagues. Wachsmann believed a conceptual focus on "African musicology" would foster the development of a collective consciousness of goals and commitment.

Though this position resembled that of scholars in African history, linguistics, and archaeology, Wachsmann did not receive support for his proposal. Ethnomusicologists were more concerned with the unity of their discipline and what made it different from historical musicology, with theories and methods applicable to musical materials anywhere, rather than with the development of branches or areal studies; hence Claude Palisca's assertion—"There is only one musicology," and its branches include "European, Asiatic, Oceanic, African, North and South American" and their subgroups—was not taken seriously, perhaps because his concept of branches seemed amorphous, as it included so-called primitive music and folk music as separate branches (Palisca 1965:108).

Herbert Ogunde   Nigerian musician who developed musical drama with indigenous instruments in the 1940s

Nigerian Institute of Music   Founded at Onitsha in 1949 with the primary objective of promoting Nigerian music

pragmatic research   Rediscovering one's musical culture for immediate practical value

scholarly research   The analysis, classification, evaluation, and interpretation of evidence

THE GOALS OF AFRICAN MUSICOLOGY

Participation in musicological research by scholars from different geocultural areas who specialize in the music of their own societies will inevitably lead to a substantial increase in the number of scholars in areal studies—a situation already evident in African musicology, an area of activity in which scholars who share a common concern for understanding the music of Africa participate, each from unique perspectives, backgrounds, and interests, but linked by common topical interests and a common concern for the collection, analysis, and systematization of data.

The writings of African scholars and their colleagues show that African musicology embraces (1) critical and analytical studies, which examine or exemplify musicological issues in the light of field data; (2) investigations that take into account the history, archaeology, and ethnology of Africa, or of specific areas in which fieldwork is undertaken; (3) developmental studies, which respond to the environment in which music is cultivated and practiced; and (4) the dissemination of information and materials on African music, both within and outside Africa.

The goals of African musicology are thus scholarly and humanistic, not only in terms of its quest for knowledge and understanding of human beings in Africa as makers and users of music, but also in regard to practical issues related to music as a language or mode of communication, music as an object of aesthetic interest, and music as culture.

Creative musicians and performers have always shared in these goals. Thus, in 1945, when the Nigerian musician Herbert Ogunde started to develop his musical drama, his aim was "to revive Yoruba music," which colonialists had downgraded; accordingly, composing new songs for old stories, he "transformed Yoruba musical forms by mixing indigenous instruments with others from elsewhere in the country" (Etherton 1982:45). He, and others like him, described as research the activity of looking for the traditional music and dance of their own culture. To them, research meant something pragmatic, the process of rediscovering their culture, which did not seem to them to require elaborate scholarly preparation.

A report on the Nigerian Institute of Music showed a similar interest in promoting music and research. Founded at Onitsha, in 1949, the institute had the primary object of promoting music in Nigeria. Its secretary, Udemesuo Onyido (also the Anglican supervisor of music at Abor), reported:

> To stimulate public interest, the Institute organized an All-Eastern Nigeria Music Festival at Onitsha in October 1951, at which most of the best choirs in Eastern Nigeria took part. This festival proved such a success that in the following year, Music Festivals were organized in all the three regions of Nigeria (in the east, at Onitsha; in the west, at Ibadan; and in the north, at Zaria). In October 1954 an All-Nigerian Music Festival was held at Enugu under the auspices of the Institute. The success of these festivals, the most outstanding features of which are the indige-

nous music performed, has induced the Institute to organize annual music festivals for the whole of the Federation of Nigeria. (Onyido 1955:62)

Since this was the colonial period, the officers of the institute included both expatriates and prominent Nigerians. The institute had a director of research, Wilberforce Echezona, also director of music of the Anglican diocese of Niger.

Pragmatic and scholarly dimensions of study

These activities affirm the status that African music acquired in both the colonial and postcolonial periods, for in addition to its role and function in traditional societies, it became an avenue for expressing consciousness of identity, a source for exploring new directions in creativity, and an object of study and research.

In the period when consciousness of the African heritage of culture began to spread, scholars held two concepts of research. First, there was *pragmatic* research, the simple process of rediscovering one's musical culture in the social environment, or looking for materials that have immediate practical value because they enhance one's consciousness of identity, or because they can be used creatively. This kind of research, which can be random, differs from applied research, which uses the results of systematic research. Pragmatic research usually stops on the level of data. It is used by collectors and others looking for specific information in the field.

Second, there was *scholarly* research, which seeks not only to discover or rediscover, but also to analyze, classify, evaluate, and interpret evidence. Because it requires academic preparation, it becomes more and more evident in African writing as musicians turn their attention from collecting information about traditional music to investigating the material and contexts of music.

The history of African writings on music shows constant interaction between the purely pragmatic and the purely scholarly, between collecting songs for educational or creative purposes and studying them musicologically. That guided or determined the shift from one position to the other, or led some musicians to combine both approaches related not only to the goals they set themselves, but also to the pressures and challenges of the social, cultural, and political environment, or response to Western praxis.

The periods of African music scholarship, 1920–1980

The factors that have stimulated African interest in the study of African music and nurtured the growth of African scholarship naturally differ from those that brought Western observers and scholars to Africa in the colonial period, and from those that generate interest among scholars abroad.

The history of Western scholarship in Africa is substantially a part of the history of comparative musicology and ethnomusicology, whereas African scholarship began in response to the challenge of colonialism and the need for developing consciousness of identity. It went through a period in which African writers applied the positive scholarly skills acquired in the process of acculturation before it gradually integrated itself into international scholarship in music. Accordingly, African scholarship underwent four periods of development: colonial foundation, 1920–1950; cultural awakening and revival, 1950–1960; a great transition, 1960–1970; and cultural development and studies, 1970–1980.

In view of the circumstances under which African scholarship in music developed, this review begins with African writings. Never having been collated, they are little known to musicological readers; the works of Western scholars in African studies are more fully known. I hope this review will pave the way for dialogue and part-

Schools taught Western music of some sort, but ignored African music because it was "pagan" or "undeveloped."

nership in research, generating in younger scholars a consciousness of the need to build on the foundations laid by previous generations—by assessing their contributions, reinterpreting their data, reformulating their theories in the light of new data, and extending their fields of investigation.

Though this review could have been selective in respect to early African writings (highlighting only those that satisfy certain scholarly criteria), I have included almost everything that has come to my notice—first, because my interest has been principally in the subject matter, ideas, attitudes, and even the biases reflected in African writings; and second, because I believe that a historical view of African scholarship in music would be incomplete without the corroborative evidence in the sporadic writings of individuals who responded to the pressures and challenges that stimulated scholarly research. The history of a humanistic discipline cannot always be confined to the scholars' works, for many disciplines not only began in nonscholarly antecedents, but continue to be enriched by data provided by the interested public.

The observations on which the review is based are drawn not only from documentary sources, but also from personal knowledge of individuals, institutions, and cultural movements in Africa. Though I dwell now and then on individual scholars because of their contributions, my interest here lies in identifying significant developments in African musicology in sub-Saharan Africa as a whole, and not in reviewing the state of musical studies in individual African countries or regions (for which, see Arom 1976:2–4).

The focus of this study is on musical scholarship, rather than on composition. Therefore, it does not discuss Western composers and composers of new African music (Omibiyi 1979), or composers active in preparing African hymns (Jones 1976), except when they also happen to write on African music. Similarly, it omits active musical performers, teachers, and festival promoters, except where their work had a direct bearing on the development of perspectives on African musicology, or had programmatic consequences for the institution of courses in African music.

Since the present state of African musicology is the result of the contributions made by both African and Western scholars, the review of African scholarship (which inevitably combines perspectives from African cultural values past and present, traditional forms of musical knowledge, and musical practice with the humanistic and scientific approaches characteristic of Western praxis) leads into a review of the role played by Western scholars' contributions to African musicology. I then enumerate the areas in which Africanists' work exemplifies general ethnomusicological theories and approaches, and review the practical programs of recording and documentation that emerged.

THE BEGINNINGS OF AFRICAN SCHOLARSHIP IN MUSIC 1920–1950

In 1881, when Edward Wylmot Blyden addressed Liberia College on "the aims and methods of a liberal education for Africans," he strongly recommended that the cur-

riculum of higher education in Africa include the study of the customs and institutions of African societies. He urged that teachers interest themselves in

> the songs of our unsophisticated brethren as they sing of their history, as they tell of
> their traditions, of the wonderful and mysterious events of their tribal and national
> life, of the achievements of what we call their superstitions; we must lend a ready
> ear to the ditties of the Kroomen who pull our boats, of the Pesseh and Golah men
> who till our farms; we must read the compositions, rude as we may think them, of
> the Mandingoes and the Veys (Vai). (Blyden 1882)

Blyden was also concerned with the environment in which an institution of higher
education would be located. He preferred to have it sited where it could receive some
stimulus from the cultural activities of its environment, including indigenous music
and dance. This was one of the reasons he did not think studying overseas was
enough for Africans, for they would miss "the smell of the African ground."

Two factors made it difficult for these ideas to be taken seriously. As a result of
the activities of the early missionaries (who preached against African cultures, and
barred African converts from participating in their traditional music and dance),
some Africans felt a prejudice against African music and dance. Educators of the
colonial period looked at education largely as a tool of social change—which often
meant progressive westernization. Accordingly, schools taught Western music of
some sort, but ignored African music because it was "pagan" or "undeveloped."
Materials for courses in this music were not available in the form of textbooks. Thus,
institutional barriers blocked the study of African music in schools, and its use in
Christian worship—barriers that could be broken down only through research that
demonstrated the intrinsic values of this music and provided suitable instructional
materials, and the creation of music for Christian worship.

Blyden's recommendations therefore had to await the growth of "cultural nationalism," the liberalization of colonial educational policy, a change in Christian missionaries' attitudes toward African cultures, and the emergence of a generation of literate Africans, committed to research and education in African music.

Colonial development and music: 1920–1950

Important foundations for scholarship in music were laid in the period 1920–1950,
when the major colonial powers began to emphasize the development of human and
material resources in the colonies. This emphasis created the need for better knowledge and understanding of colonial peoples. Accordingly, journals and magazines—
including the *Gold Coast Review*, the *Gold Coast Teachers' Journal*, the *Uganda Journal*,
Tanganyika Notes and Records, *Sudan Notes and Records*, *The Nigerian Teacher*, and
The Nigerian Field—provided a forum for literary and scientific contributions by
colonial administrators, educators, missionaries, and local authors. This period saw
the founding of international journals devoted to African affairs, languages and cultures, education, and development, providing other outlets for African writers.

Most African writers who published articles on music adopted a journalistic
approach, reporting what they knew or felt as carriers of African traditions (Caluza
1931; Bansisa 1936). Others dealt with specific topics, like songs and lyrics
(Sempebbwa 1948; Azu 1949), drums and other instruments (Addo 1932, 1933,
1934; Djan 1942; Kaggwa 1934), presented their observations on some aspect of
music and dance (Traore 1942; Okeke 1936), or reported on the state of music in a
given territory or of an ethnic group (Margai 1926; Kintu 1940).

The significance of these writers lies in what they symbolize, the information
they provide, and their speculations and attitudes, rather than in their scholarly per-

In addition to taking private lessons from African musicians, literate African musicians unable to go abroad immediately could also take advantage of correspondence courses and external examinations in Western music.

---

spectives—for what most of them wrote was the outcome of their awareness of their musical environment, rather than the outcome of systematic inquiry. Some of them, and others who followed, were encouraged to share what they knew, or what they had collected from their community, because of the contribution they could make to scholarship and the growth of a positive attitude to African music and cultures. Such encouragement was given to Ugandans by the East African Music Research Scheme, funded by the Social Science Research Council of the United Kingdom and directed by Klaus Wachsmann, who, as educator and curator of the Uganda Museum (Kampala), involved African musicians and schoolteachers in his programs.

In this period, another development that stimulated African interest in traditional music was the opening of prospects for education abroad. In the late 1800s and early 1900s, a few enterprising individuals, with the sponsorship of certain bodies, had set a precedent for such studies. F. C. Coker (of Nigeria) studied music in Germany in 1874, followed by Ekundayo Phillips, who from 1911 to 1914 studied at Trinity College of Music (London), and in turn taught other aspiring musicians, including Fela Sowande, the eminent Nigerian composer and organist.

In the 1920s and 1930s, "native African youths . . . possessing intelligence and musical talent" studied in the United States. Among these were C. Kamba Simango (of Mozambique), an alumnus of Hampton Institute and Columbia University; Madikane Cole (of southeast Africa), also of Hampton Institute, who later revisited the United States with African musicians to give performances to benefit his missionary work on the East Coast; and Nicholas J. Ballanta (of Sierra Leone), a product of the Institute of Musical Art, New York (Cuney-Hare 1936:34–35).

In addition to taking private lessons from African musicians, literate African musicians unable to go abroad immediately could also take advantage of correspondence courses and external examinations in Western music offered by institutions in London, including the Victoria College of Music, Trinity College of Music, and the Associated Board of the Royal Schools of Music. The diploma-testing facilities of these bodies were made available to countries in the British Empire. Local representatives were appointed to supervise the written examinations, and visiting examiners were sent around for the practical examinations. An announcement in the *Gold Coast Teachers' Journal* (1933:230) shows that official recognition was eventually given to this arrangement:

All good teachers spend some of their spare time studying. It is natural that they should wish to test themselves by entering for some recognized public examination, so that they may know exactly how their studies are progressing. . . . The Associated Board has just opened its examinations to West Africa. The local secretary is Mr. W. E. Ward, Achimota, who will provide on application, free copies of the syllabus and full details of the examinations etc. At a small charge, he will also supply specimen papers, copies of prescribed music and other matter. For the present only written examinations will be held, the papers being sent and marked in England. Practical examinations may be held in future if there are enough candidates to justify the Board in sending an examiner from England—but not for a year or two. Nevertheless these examinations are easily the best available in the Gold Coast, and there are no better examinations available anywhere. They provide a regular, carefully graded course to the highest level; and they should be a means of improving the musicianship of the teachers and pupils of West Africa.

Facilities such as those provided by overseas examining bodies and tutorials available locally encouraged not only the systematic study of Western music and music theory, but also here and there some reflection on possible analogs of such theory in African music and areas of difference, and the sociocultural importance of music in Africa. Some ecclesiastical musicians—like Ransome-Kuti of Nigeria (who began to compose new Yoruba hymns about 1902), Ekundayo Phillips, Ola Olude, and T. A. Bankole—tried to develop theories of composition in the Yoruba idiom in the colonial period. A biographical note on T. A. Bankole, father of Ayo Bankole (the famous Nigerian composer and organist), shows that similar problems engaged his attention, for in 1924, when he was appointed assistant organist at the First Baptist Church in Lagos, he wanted to develop tonal Yoruba music for ecclesiastical use: in a book-length manuscript, "Yoruba Music and Pentatonality," he propounded techniques of composing with traditional words (Alájá-Browne 1981:7).

The contribution of George Ballanta

Of the trained African musicians who turned to the systematic study of their own music in this period, two deserve particular mention: Nicholas George Ballanta of Sierra Leone (born in 1894) and Ephraim Amu of Ghana (born in 1899).

A biographical note on George Ballanta, written by the editor of *Musical America* ("Mephisto's Musings" 1926:6), gives some idea of the preparation that enabled him to adopt a scholarly approach to African music. He

> began his study of music alone, and without any other aid than Sir John Stainer's book on harmony for which he sent to London, he acquired considerable knowledge of the art in his native country. He made such progress that he was able, prior to 1921, through submitting compositions by mail, to pass the intermediary examination of Durham University, England, for the degree of Bachelor of Music.

Music study and fieldwork in the United States

Ballanta began studying at the Institute of Musical Art in 1922, and received a diploma there in 1924. One of his compositions was played at a student recital in New York in 1923, and he had previously conducted some of his works at a "Negro pageant" in Symphony Hall, Boston. Sponsored by the Penn Normal Industrial and Agricultural School in St. Helena (South Carolina), he studied African-American music, not only in St. Helena, but also in Alabama, Georgia, and South Carolina. The editor of *Musical America* concludes his biographical sketch with the information that "while at Penn School, he recorded 103 spirituals of St. Helena which are now available in one volume." This book of transcriptions of spirituals was published in 1925.

Fieldwork in Africa

The knowledge that Ballanta gained from his study of African-American music and his experience in collecting and transcribing music in the United States prepared him

Ballanta's interest was clearly in comparative studies—in providing an overview of African music, rather than detailed ethnographic studies of individual musical cultures.

for similar activities in Africa under the sponsorship of the Guggenheim Foundation, which awarded him a fellowship in 1925, and a second grant in 1927. The purpose of the award was to enable him "to continue scientific studies of the musical conceptions of the African peoples and compare these with the musical conceptions of the older systems of European music" (Cuney-Hare 1936:260).

In a published report on his trip (1926), Ballanta claims to have traveled more than 11,000 kilometers during two years' research in West Africa. On this field trip, he collected more than two thousand examples of African songs from his own country (Sierra Leone), Liberia, Senegal, Guinea, Gold Coast (Ghana), and Nigeria. Because he was a composer, he took an interest in technical aspects of the music, such as scales, melody, rhythm, harmony, and form, the relationship between speech tones and melodic contours, and prosody and musical instruments. He observed the effect of social change on the music of West Africa, and tried to classify the region based on the presence or absence of "Western or Eastern influence." He claimed to have been objective, despite his background, for he noted "it is essential for an investigator to dispossess himself of his acquired conceptions if he is to appreciate African music."

Some of his observations—on form and structure (such as call and response, speech tone, and melodic contour) and the problems these pose in hymns translated into African languages, drum language, and the nature of African musical traditions—anticipate those made by subsequent scholars. It is evident from his report, however, that he was not able to achieve complete objectivity, for he makes inaccurate statements and assertions, like "All African melodies are constructed upon harmonic background," and "Duple time is the only time used by Africans" (Ballanta 1926:10–11).

Broad studies of sound structure

Ballanta's interest was clearly in comparative studies—in providing an overview of African music, rather than detailed ethnographic studies of individual musical cultures. Though he took note of the use of music in customary rites (like puberty festivals and funerals), he did not investigate any correlations between "use" and "structure."

In another brief article, "Music of the African Races," Ballanta elaborated on his observations on scales and melody, and modified his comments on harmony. He was particularly concerned with "the principles of tonal expression" in African music, with "tone progression and tone combination," which he believed "are determined by perception of a principal tone and an interval of association"—that is, "the interval which exists between the principal tone and the tone next in importance in the whole mass of tones used for tonal expression" and which "for all purposes is the perfect fourth in African music," opposed to "the perfect fifth in Western music" (1931–1932:441–444). It is obvious that he did not take heptatonic usages into account.

He found many scales in African music. The most important, he believed, was a five-tone scale, observable in "many inflections." He developed a theory to account for these inflections. Assuming a standard pentatonic scale existed, he believed each standard tone had a tone "in opposite phases with it," about a quarter tone above or below it; the tones in opposite phases were used "for and instead of the standard tones," which he believed rarely followed each other, so quarter tones were rare.

In addition to the quarter-tone inflections, Ballanta found half-tone inflections, which bridged two standard tones a major second apart, and two tones a minor third or greater interval apart: a "mean tone" divided this interval into two equal parts. Because of all these inflections and bridging tones,

> it is not easy to note down African music by existing musical notations, as the signs would convey a different idea from what they are intended to represent. A wholly different notation is necessary to do this properly. (Ballanta 1931–1932:442)

Unlike his previous article (in which he provides transcriptions in staff notation), this article has no musical quotations of songs.

On the question of harmony, Ballanta modifies his statement that "all African songs have a harmonic background." He points out that

> There is no perception of harmony as the term is understood in music. What enters into a musical expression by way of tone combination is a highly developed form of polyphony, which may embrace two, or at most three parts. This polyphonic form is freest from the point of view of concords and discords and it is preponderantly rhythmic; that is to say, each part preserves its individuality. (Ballanta 1931–1932:442)

In addition to these observations, he draws attention to changes observable in West African music as a result of contact from beyond Africa: (1) the substitution of a perfect fifth for a perfect fourth as an interval of association, (2) the use of a major third instead of a major second as an interval of harmonic definition, and (3) the exclusion of ternary metrical divisions and the retention of only duple divisions, grouped into 3+3+2 instead of 4+4.

Social contexts of music

Ballanta approaches the social categories of music more systematically, for he observes that "music is not cultivated in Africa for its own sake. It is always used in connection with dances or to accompany workmen." He sets up a hierarchy of categories of songs "in order of emotional content." In ascending order of structural complexity, these categories are work songs, play songs, dance songs, ceremonial songs, and love songs.

Though Ballanta's observations were not always accurate, his approach to African music was more theoretical and systematic than that of most writers of his time, for he believed his mission was to undertake "scientific studies of the musical conceptions" of African peoples and "to compare them with those of the West." His significance in the history of musical scholarship in Africa therefore lies in (1) his emphasis on extensive fieldwork; (2) his theoretical and descriptive approach to African music; and (3) his regional and comparative approach to African music (now favored by many African musicians).

In contrast to the musicians of his day, Ballanta addressed this task as an outsider, rather than an insider. His collection of songs seems to have had no significant programmatic effect on music in West Africa, or even in Sierra Leone, his home

Ephraim Amu Beginning in the 1930s, conducted fieldwork, taught performance, composed Ghanaian music

seperewa Harp-lute from West Africa on which Ephraim Amu apprenticed himself in developing teaching methods

country. Nor did he spearhead any movement against the institutional barriers that blocked the study and use of African music in Africa. Nevertheless, his research did make him aware of the need for change. In 1926, at a conference on African culture and the Christian church held in Le Zoute (Belgium) by the International Missionary Council, he stressed the importance of using African music, at least as a tool of evangelism. He said that because

> the African loves music intensely, . . . one way of approaching him is to get him to sing about the love of God in his own way. The songs you hear in Africa may not be suitable for use, but substitute other words and adopt the tunes. Fit words to his tunes telling the truth of the Gospel and you will do a great deal towards getting that truth into his mind. (Smith 1926:73)

The contribution of Ephraim Amu

A different picture emerges when one turns to Ephraim Amu (of Ghana), for his encounter with the traditional music of his people completely changed his stance and values. The challenge that issued from it created an identity crisis that steered him away from Western music to the traditional music of his people. He combined the interest in fieldwork that Ballanta developed with a determination to break institutional barriers in the way of traditional African music; however, unlike Ballanta, he became aware of traditional African music, not by studying abroad, but by facing local circumstances.

FIGURE 1 Ephraim Amu (extreme right) and his students perform Amu's incidental music to an African production of Shakespeare's *Merchant of Venice*, featuring indigenous drums, bamboo flutes, and voices; Achimota, Ghana, 1950. Photo by Atta Annan Mensah.

Amu acquired a basic knowledge of Western music locally when he attended elementary school in his hometown, Peki-Avetile (1902–1915), and then at the Basel Mission Seminary in Abetifi (1916–1920). After he graduated from the seminary, he continued to study on his own, and to take private lessons in harmony and counterpoint (1920–1924) from the Reverend Mr. Allotey-Pappoe, a Ghanaian musician. In 1926, after teaching for six years in an elementary school in his hometown, he was appointed to the staff of the Presbyterian Training College (Akropong), where he taught music and other subjects until 1933.

Amu's conversion from Western music to African music took place when he was on the faculty of the Training College. One day, a colleague—ironically, a missionary—asked about the songs he had heard laborers sing as they worked on campus. As the missionary believed in proceeding from the known to the unknown, he asked Amu why he was not writing those songs down to teach to students. The contrast in the enthusiasm and intensity with which Ghanaians sang their own traditional songs in the community on ceremonial and festive occasions, and how Christian hymns were sung in church, had long puzzled him. He had noticed differences in the extent of participation: every member of a traditional performing group sang, while many members of Christian congregations sat quietly through the hymns. He was convinced that something needed to be done about this.

Early attempts to transcribe indigenous music

The problems he encountered as he tried to write down those supposedly simple tunes were considerable, but they opened up a world of music to him, and made him conscious of his own people's traditions, which he set out to study seriously. He collected several traditional songs, and learned to sing them. He wrote down the texts, and became fascinated by their expressions and idioms, and by the relationship evident between their speech tones and rhythms and those of the tunes. His notebooks (which I have inspected) show that he wrote Tonic Sol-fa here and there above the texts, so he could remind himself of what he learned to sing. However, he omitted time values from the notation because readers could deduce them from the textual speech rhythms.

After collecting songs and learning about the traditions associated with them, Amu turned his attention to instrumental music. His father had given up drumming when he became a Christian, so Amu never learned it as a child, and was expressly forbidden to do so when he grew up. The first thing he did was to go back home and learn from another drummer. From there, he studied with a master drummer elsewhere, and with players of bamboo and cane flutes and the harp-lute (*seperewa*). He learned how to make some of these instruments, but later specialized in making bamboo flutes.

Though Amu did not write a treatise on the materials he collected or learned, there is evidence that he approached his task (1) as a creative person interested in understanding the musical culture of his people, and in using the traditional idioms in his own way; (2) as an educator, who with his students shared the knowledge he had acquired, including that of making bamboo flutes; and (3) as a scholar, who systematized knowledge of traditional music for himself, at least to the point of being able to give systematic instruction in rhythm to students at the Presbyterian Training College, and also in the courses he offered to teachers in the field.

The introduction to his volume of original compositions (1933) contains ninety graded exercises in African rhythms, some of them based on traditional and popular tunes he had collected. The volume opens with the statement that though the book is not a "full treatise" on the traits of African music,

Amu's curriculum was bimusical in approach, for it combined knowledge of African music (particularly African rhythms, drumming, and flute playing) with the study of Western harmony, counterpoint, and piano.

an attempt has been made to describe the rhythm. It consists of duple and triple time mixed, occurring either in alternate bars, or in a number of duple time bars followed by one or more triple time bars or vice versa. Once the regular alternation of those two times is understood, all other manifestations will be found easy. It must be borne in mind that in the alternation, the triple time bar is of the same length as the duple time. (Amu 1933:1)

Pedagogical publications

In 1934, to help teachers in the field to master African rhythms, Amu published an article in the *Gold Coast Teachers' Journal*. He attached importance to this, as he wanted teachers to be able to read his system of rhythmic notation and pass it on to their pupils.

Amu composed both sacred and secular songs for mixed voices and for male voices—the former for "singing bands" (choirs), which he helped establish throughout the country, and the latter for students of the Presbyterian Training College. The mixed choirs were intended to complement regular choirs in church, for they often sang Western anthems, but the singing bands performed Amu's songs, or songs written by other composers in the idiom Amu had established. This idiom became popular in both literate and illiterate communities, for Amu composed patriotic songs that received acclaim for what he said through them. One, "*Yen ara Asase Ni*" (with the English subtitle "This Land Is Our Own"), was so popular, and so widely known, that between 1948 and 1957 it served as an anthem in Ghana's struggle for political independence; on national occasions, it can still be heard.

Amu's interest did not stop with music making. Conscious of the culture in which the music was practiced, he responded in practical terms: (1) by changing certain aspects of his own way of life, and (2) by emphasizing certain concrete symbols of culture, including African traditional costume, which had no place in the pulpit, but which he insisted on wearing when he preached; traditional music and dance, barred from church and school, but in some form reintroduced by him into these institutions; and the use of indigenous languages in contexts where others would use English.

Conflict over the introduction of indigenous forms

Amu's radicalness brought him into conflict with the church, and he was dismissed in 1933 from his job at the Presbyterian Training College. But this setback did not stop him. Because of his reputation as teacher, composer, and nationalist, he was immediately offered a position at Achimota School, the most prestigious institution in the country, established by the colonial government.

This appointment gave Amu greater scope for propagating his ideas. Since Achimota was not an ecclesiastical institution, it was much more receptive to cultural innovations. For a mode of recreation and entertainment in which all students could participate on Saturday nights, it instituted "tribal drumming and dancing" (as it was then called).

Study of music in London

Though Amu had turned from Western music to African music with success, his compositional techniques and later events showed that what he was fighting was not Western music per se, but Western "cultural imperialism," which had downgraded African music. Accordingly, after much internal debate, he accepted the award of a scholarship in 1937 to do advanced studies in Western music at the Royal College of Music (London). He decided to study for the associate diploma, with advanced harmony and counterpoint as areas of concentration.

In 1942, when Amu returned from London, he went back to Achimota School; however, because teacher education had been his area of interest, he joined Achimota Teacher Training College (on the same campus) in 1948. His aspirations for a new approach to music education in Ghana were fulfilled in 1949, when he succeeded in setting up a program for training specialist teachers of music and making the practical study of African drumming and the playing of bamboo flutes compulsory for all students. His curriculum was bimusical in approach, for it combined knowledge of African music (particularly African rhythms, drumming, and flute playing) with the study of Western harmony, counterpoint, and piano. This syllabus virtually spelled out the experiences from which Amu's musical idiom had grown.

In 1952, the School of Music was transferred to the University of Science and Technology (Kumasi), where Amu taught for about ten more years. Subsequently, it became the basis of the National Academy of Music (Winneba, southern Ghana), with practically the same objective, training specialist teachers of music competent in both African and Western music for the Ghana Educational Service.

Fieldwork on local music

As Amu had no time to continue his research on the scale he had envisaged in the 1920s, he seized the opportunity of the transfer of his school to another location to give up its headship. His retirement was overdue, and he wanted to spend two years doing fieldwork (which he accomplished with the support of a grant from the Rockefeller Foundation) and recording music from selected societies in all regions of Ghana. He deposited copies of his tapes at the University of Science and Technology (Kumasi) and the University of Ghana (Legon). When he retired from his position in Kumasi, he was reemployed by the Institute of African Studies, University of Ghana, which had set up a new school of music, dance, and drama.

Amu influenced many people in Ghana through his work as composer, teacher, and scholar, and as someone who believed in African cultural values. Though he devoted himself to training teachers, the research on which he based his pedagogy laid the foundation for scholarly studies of African music in Ghana. In 1937, when I became a student in the Presbyterian Training College, Amu had already left, but his course on African rhythm was still an integral part of the musical curriculum offered there. It was taught by another Ghanaian, Robert Danso, whom Amu had privately tutored. As my own interests at this time were toward composition, linguistics, and creative writing, Amu advised me (in 1942) to collect and analyze traditional songs for my musical and textual models. Following his example and encouragement, I collected over 100 Akan songs between 1942 and 1944, when I was on the faculty of the Presbyterian Training College, in charge of music and Twi (a Ghanaian language). The text of this collection—with an introduction in Twi on the context of performance, aspects of performance, and responsorial techniques—was later published by Oxford University Press (1949).

Nissio Fiagbedzi   Ethnomusicologist of
Ghana who focuses on intrinsic values of
African music

Atta Annan Mensah   Music educator and
composer from Ghana who has studied
composition in other parts of Africa

Amu's impact as a teacher

Nearly all other Ghanaians who have turned to musicology as a field of specialization attended Amu's School of Music before proceeding for further training at the University of Ghana or institutions abroad. They include Ben Aning, Simeon Asiama, Nissio Fiagbedzi, Atta Annan Mensah, Nicholas Zinzendorf Nayo, and Patrick Ofei. Amu also influenced several of Ghana's contemporary composers, including Geoffrey Boateng, Otto Boateng, Robert Danso, Atta Annan Mensah, Nicholas Zinzendorf Nayo, and me. His influence extended from individuals to institutions.

Blessed with longevity, Amu lived to see not only the development of the programs he initiated in music education, but also the continuation of research on African music in Ghana on a wider scale. What he was able to achieve in the colonial period almost singlehandedly is remarkable. Unlike other musicians and writers of the period 1920–1950 (including George Ballanta), he made a tremendous impact on his country. He was interested in giving tradition recognition and some measure of continuity through the formal learning process.

As a composer, Amu was also interested in change, and in the selective use of new musical experiences and techniques. Because his goals were humanistic, he accommodated continuity and change by combining three complementary approaches to African music: (1) the analytical approach, which enabled him to explore the intrinsic values of African music; (2) the pedagogical approach, which enabled him to pass on what he knew or discovered in his research through formal instruction and public lectures; and (3) the creative approach, which enabled him to generate interest in the African idiom in contemporary institutions and raise the level of awareness of African cultural traditions among the literate community.

Turning points in the development of scholarship or in the perspectives of a discipline nearly always hinge on individual thinkers and innovators. This reason, and the programmatic consequence of Amu's research, set Amu apart as a pioneer. His story is hardly known in the musicological world. Though he was a great teacher of his time, he did not publish much. Working more in oral tradition, he never cultivated the international world of scholarship, for he was too occupied with the problem of cultural identity, though it had then not become a burning political issue. He influenced many generations of Ghanaian students, but did not have pupils who (like those of Ferdinand de Saussure) could compile a monumental book out of their lecture notes; nor did he have (like Samuel Johnson) the fortune to befriend a Boswell.

THE SEARCH FOR BROADER PERSPECTIVES: 1950–1960

The need for studies that, going beyond the sporadic writings of the period 1920–1950 and the initial efforts of George Ballanta and Ephraim Amu, would be more systematic and extensive in coverage (but with more clearly defined objectives) was recognized soon after 1948, when the University of Ghana was established as a college in special relation with the University of London.

On the initiative of Kofi Abrefa Busia, Ghanaian Professor of Sociology, I was offered a faculty appointment in 1952 as research fellow in African Studies, to set up in his department a program of research in African music, language, folklore, dance, and drama. Busia felt that what was needed was institutional sponsorship of research on African music and related arts, and that his department could make a small beginning. Such an arrangement would ensure not only that research would be carried out over an extended period, but that in the process, materials and theoretical perspectives would be developed, to a level that would permit the establishment of courses in African music and related arts at the degree level at the University of Ghana. He believed that the home he provided for the arts would be temporary, and that the timing of their formation into a separate department would depend on the progress of the research.

Lumping the arts together was deliberate, though it seemed at first sight to ask too much of one person. It was intended to emphasize the unity of the arts in African contexts, while giving the program some flexibility in topics of research. Since language, folklore, dance, and drama are integrated into music and musical performance, I interpreted the terms of reference as an invitation to develop an interdisciplinary approach to the study of African music, drawing not only from the materials and perspectives of these subjects, but also from cognate disciplines (history, linguistics, social anthropology), to which I had had some exposure in addition to my training in music.

Study of relationships in music making

The school of linguistics to which I was then drawn was that of J. R. Firth (University of London), who, using formal and contextual techniques, emphasized analysis and synthesis. His concept of prosodic phonology and levels of abstraction, and his principle of contextualization (inspired by the ethnographic approach of Malinowski) seemed pertinent to my materials. As Firth states in his "Techniques of Semantics" and other papers in which he elaborated on his approach (Firth 1951), when the principle of context of situation is applied in linguistic terms, it enables one to deal with meaning on an empirical basis, for "in that context are human participants, what they say and what is going on." He describes any study that proceeds this way as a situational and experiential study. I found that such an approach could also be applied to the study of music as an event, letting a musicologist deal, on different levels of abstraction, with formal and ethnographic materials related to music.

Another reason this approach appealed to me was that unlike my colleagues in sociology, I had as the subject of my research program music, not society or culture. The latter was the context in which I found and studied my material, not the object of my study; hence it was my task to search for a conceptual framework that would make music central in my thinking, rather than something on the periphery. Accordingly, while my colleagues looked at the network of social relations in individual societies in their totality, I looked at relationships in music making. Such relationships—not only those of kinship, but also those of musical relationships—demanded observation of the distribution of musical roles and responsibilities.

While my colleagues looked at different social groups or units of social organization, I looked at musical traditions. I was aware that musical studies could contribute to some extent to the understanding of culture and society, but I regarded this as a by-product, a secondary objective. It was something that would grow out of my research, since I was also concerned with social processes related to music, for my view of music was not limited to its perception as an aural phenomenon. Experience

"For purely practical and personal reasons, I had to begin with the study of topics in my own society, so that I could learn as much as possible from traditional musicians and other knowledgeable persons."

had taught me to view it also as a focus of interaction. My task was to harness social anthropology and linguistics to the service of studies in African musicology, just as Western musicians have harnessed history and the critical methods of literary criticism (and to some extent philology) to the service of Western musicology.

Nketia's early research objectives

Since the music I had planned to study did not exist in written form, and could be reached only through performance, I decided to pursue five objectives.

1. The focus of my field research would be on musical events, including any event that incorporated music. My primary data would be drawn from observing and documenting such events in selected societies.

2. The research program would be based on the study of selected topics that allow for particular formal and contextual problems or themes to be investigated in the field, and not on the detailed study of the musical cultures of individual societies in their totality.

3. The research program would document information about music and musical instruments available in oral tradition. This documentation would relate to specific topics being investigated, or to musical events and interviews. A distinction would thus be maintained between studies and documentation. The former would be intensive, while the latter would be extensive, involving recordings of the repertories of individual societies or events for archival purposes, rather than for immediate analysis and study. The building of such an archive of recordings would be a major part of the program. The documentation would also include transcriptions of music, lyrics, and drum language. Since such texts are created and used by musicians, they must be studied from the viewpoint of the linguistic skills traditionally required or expected of musicians. This was part of the rationale behind my *Funeral Dirges of the Akan People* (1974).

4. The program would explore other documentary sources of data, particularly descriptive and historical studies and observers' accounts—the accounts of travelers, anthropologists, and historians. As it is impossible for any single individual to undertake fieldwork that covers the whole of a country or region (let alone the whole of Africa), one cannot but use data from secondary sources, including unpublished materials at national radio stations, ministries, and departments of information. The last often maintain an archive of photographs that cover musical events, performers, and musical instruments. When research has to start virtually from scratch, every available source must be utilized.

5. The program would build up a collection of musical instruments, and would explore the possibility of establishing performing groups or extension courses on the university campus.

For purely practical and personal reasons, I had to begin with the study of topics in my own society, so that I could learn as much as possible from traditional musicians and other knowledgeable persons. I did not see anything wrong with this, since Western musicologists study Western music, the music of their own society. I tended to look at musical research not only as an approach to unchartered fields of knowledge, but also as a learning process that contributes to the intellectual and artistic development of individuals. I wanted to experience and know music in my own society, and in other societies in Ghana, West Africa, and other parts of Africa, and to share my knowledge with others.

African music as experienced reality

In developing an approach to the study of African music, I searched also for African orientations and reactions in the writings of authors of the previous decades and those of the early 1950s, because what Western scholars and collectors had to say about African music was evident enough. One of the African writers whose remarks I found useful was Simon Ngubane, though he did not contribute many published data to our knowledge of African music. He did not wish to minimize the importance of scientific analysis, but he believed "with that intellectual attitude, one must try to get the message and the feeling behind the sometimes unusual sounds that make up African music, which thing, after all, is the most important thing in any music." He emphasized his point with the following anecdote:

> I remember a non-African musical friend of mine who, some years ago, said to me that to him African music was interesting only in an impersonal sort of way, that is, it did not concern him and his personal feelings. He further said that African music could only arouse his curiosity and perhaps lead him to want to analyze its forms and all the scientific side of its make up; but that it could possibly be something he could love as he loved the music of Europe, was something very far from him. . . . I have since found that my friend of four years ago is not alone in this attitude towards African music. I must say that it is difficult for an African to imagine how any one can love music with only his mind. (Ngubane 1948:21–25)

I assumed that Ngubane intended this to serve as a caveat to the African musicologist who may be carried away by an acquired capacity for making abstractions, or lured by Western preoccupations with scales, tonal measurements, systems of tuning, modes, and so on—which, with certain types of analytical theory, constitute one particular world view of music. It is noteworthy to find his position underscored eighteen years later by Fela Sowande, the eminent Nigerian composer and organist, when he turned his attention to systematic research into African music. Sowande warns about the danger of establishing music-education programs that might "breed a race of artistic enuchs [sic], through submitting to planning from the outside on African music as a thing and not as an experienced reality." Quoting Bastide's comments on the literature on African religion (which sees it "from the outside as a thing," and does not feel it "from within as an experienced reality"), he suggests that this observation is valid for studies of African music, which Africans "tend to dissect as a thing," not "as an experienced reality" (1966:23–24).

Klaus Wachsmann also noticed similar attitudes among Africans during this period, but he interpreted their reaction to overanalysis as a reflection of "the criterion or aesthetic principle of the music of negritude,"

> a quality claimed by a Negro musician: he is a person whose body and soul respond to music as one, a man who is so sensitive to the totality of his world that he has immediate and total rapport with it. Negatively stated, it is the refusal to treat

The Ghana Broadcasting Service, which had long
introduced broadcasts of traditional music in its
programs in Ghanaian languages, now extended its
offering to include special music magazines and talks
on music.

music as an object that can be analysed, dissected, and compartmentalized.
(Wachsmann 1966a:16)

These observations explain the emphasis on "the situational and experiential"
approach to the period under consideration—an approach that made it possible not
only to reinterpret African music to the outside world, but also to communicate to
the musicological public what was emerging in Africa itself as a result of the cultural
awakening ushered in by nationalist movements. This movement used traditional
cultural expressions as a basis for creating consciousness of identity, and as leverage
for building a united front in the fight for political independence. By encouraging
the wearing of traditional costumes by the literate community (brought up to reject
aspects of traditional life-styles), the performance of traditional rites and ceremonies
hitherto branded as pagan or unworthy, and the performance of traditional music
and dance at political rallies, it set in motion new trends in cultural revival. People
felt that a new sense of history, anchored in African cultural expressions, needed to be
generated to foster pride in things African; hence, what was formerly regarded only as
the heritage of individual ethnic groups came to be identified as a national heritage,
an achievement that might be shared.

For the same reason, a national theater movement was launched in Ghana to
stimulate individual and group initiative in presenting or recreating African traditions, or in developing new directions. Traditional music and dance assumed a new
role in new contexts, like concert halls and theaters, or improvised substitutes as a
source of aesthetic enjoyment in their own right. Musicians were no longer to regard
traditional songs only as a source for developing contemporary idioms, a source for
themes for composition, or tunes to be set to new words for use in Christian churches. African dances were not merely things to watch in traditional settings, but things
to learn to perform.

Musicology at the University of Ghana
The program in musicology set up at the University of Ghana had to take note of all
these considerations and the philosophy of African personality (later both a political
and a cultural ideology), for I believed musicologists must respond to the milieu in
which they work—to emerging ideas, values, trends, and cultural movements.
Humanist scholars have a dual commitment, to their discipline, and to their society.

The program therefore had to face implications of contextual changes, new
habits of listening, new communities of taste, new concepts of performance, new
modes of presentation, and new perspectives in performer-audience relationships. In
March 1957, as political and cultural movements culminated in the achievement of
political independence, my task clearly became, not merely to collect, analyze, and
interpret musical types and idioms along the lines I had mapped out, but to cover all
forms of music and music making, both traditional and contemporary.

Another issue the program had to face was how to disseminate the information on music and related arts that would become available through research. The approach to African music and dance as a source of entertainment and aesthetic enjoyment in new contexts outside their traditional setting attracted spectators who did not always have a common background knowledge of everything presented— basic knowledge of musical instruments, traditional ensembles, categories of songs, musical types and dances, and oral traditions. Encounters with different musical traditions showed that in local newspapers, journals, and magazines, Ghanaians were ready to read about traditions of music and dance (their own, and those of other ethnic groups), and that Ghanaians were ready to listen to public lectures on music.

The Ghana Broadcasting Service, which had long introduced broadcasts of traditional music in its programs in Ghanaian languages, now extended its offering to include special music magazines and talks on music in Ghana and elsewhere in Africa. The position of program organizer for music was established, and Atta Annan Mensah, a former student of Amu's (just back from studies at Trinity College of Music, London), was appointed to fill the post. He was to be responsible for producing radio programs, recording indigenous music of the Gold Coast, and coordinating his efforts with the faculty of the University College of the Gold Coast, Kumasi College of Technology, and other involved institutions. Around the same time, the Nigerian Broadcasting Service created a similar position for Fela Sowande (just back from London) to become actively involved in collecting, presenting, and disseminating information on Nigerian music and musicians.

In the 1950s, "speech knowledge of music"—to use Charles Seeger's famous phrase—became as interesting to the literate community as "music knowledge of music." The program in musicology at the University of Ghana had to take note of this by (1) supporting, in 1958, the formation of the Ghana Music Society, a forum for musicians and aspiring musicologists to discuss their research and problems related to music and cultural development in Ghana; (2) contributing to radio programs on traditional and contemporary music and to local journals, and even newspapers; (3) publishing the results of research in forms and styles that, so far as possible, allowed musicologists to fulfill at once their commitment to their discipline and their commitment to their society.

Nketia's study in the United States

Opportunities for testing the validity of the approach that my African materials suggested arose at international conferences I attended, particularly those of the International Folk Music Council, at which I read papers based on my work in Ghana. Most important was the opportunity I received from the Rockefeller Foundation in 1958, when it awarded me a fellowship to study theory and composition at the Juilliard School of Music and Columbia University (principally with Henry Cowell), and to acquaint myself with American ethnomusicology and meet scholars I had long wanted to see—George Herzog, Mantle Hood, Mieczyslaw Kolinski, David P. McAllester, Alan P. Merriam, Willard Rhodes, Curt Sachs. In the course of a year, I met all of them, and had the privilege of auditing Curt Sachs's course on musical instruments at Columbia University. In Ghana, I had read his standard works on this and other subjects, so it was a delight to hear unwritten rationales behind statements he had made in his published works.

I also audited courses given at Northwestern University by Herskovits and Merriam, whom I had met in Ghana. The foundation arranged for me to visit the studio of Harry Partch and the Archive of Traditional Music (Indiana University), where I discussed my approach with Herzog, who approved the use I had made of social anthropology and linguistics in designing a framework that made music central

Institute of African Studies   Established at the University of Ghana; J. H. Kwabena Nketia developed the Music and Related Arts section

West African Cultural Society   For preservation and promotion of African culture; branches in various countries

Alick Nkhata   Program organizer of the Central African Broadcasting Station who supported local music preservation

Philip Gbeho   Master drummer, competent in Ewe tradition, who spearheaded music education in Ghana

to my thinking, a mode of presentation that distinguished my areas of emphasis from those of colleagues in cultural anthropology. I also had a delightful, inspiring two weeks' visit with Hood at the Institute of Ethnomusicology (University of California at Los Angeles)—which strengthened my conviction that music was central in the discipline of ethnomusicology.

I found, not a unified American school of ethnomusicology, but an array of distinct interests and approaches, with varying emphases on music and culture, and different analytical methods, with varying emphases on classification and attitudes toward history and change. What most scholars I met had in common—a trait they shared with scholars elsewhere—was a commitment to studies that integrated music, society, and culture from different conceptual and analytical perspectives, a commitment that enabled them to share in the knowledge and insight gained by individual scholars working on different musical materials and cultures, at home or abroad. The environment in which I worked in Ghana, and the approaches it suggested, had led me to a similar commitment, for in Africa, where music is an integral part of social life, musicology cannot but be an integrated study of music, society, and culture.

Return to Ghana

After my sojourn in the United States, I returned to Ghana, where I was charged with developing the Music and Related Arts section of the recently established Institute of African Studies. In addition, I became director of the new School of Music, Dance and Drama, opened for undergraduate study. A few years later, I assumed directorship of the institute, the school, and the newly created National Dance Company.

One of the prime directives of President Kwame Nkrumah in his inauguration of the Institute of African Studies (1961) had been to establish relationships—not only with scholars of African culture in Europe and the United States, but also, and especially, with scholars of African descent in the Caribbean and the Americas. In line with this directive, the institute hosted the first meeting of the International Folk Music Council outside of Europe or the United States, and began a series of American study groups and institutions. We also established links with the Institute of Jamaica and the African Caribbean Institute. During this period, many distinguished scholars and artists visited the institute, including Maya Angelou, William Carter (UCLA), and Neville Dawes (Institute of Jamaica); a conference on African and African-American music at the institute brought Eileen Southern and other distinguished scholars and musicians.

Meanwhile, as increasing interest in the importance of an African viewpoint on African art and culture spread throughout the scholarly world, I continued to participate in conferences and activities beyond Ghana. My belief in the need for communication between scholars led me to serve on the executive board of the International Folk Music Council, the board of directors of the International Society for Music

Education, the scientific board of the International Institute for Comparative Music Studies and Documentation, and the International Music Council. Eventually, I joined the senior faculty of the Department of Music at UCLA, where I stayed until 1983, when I received appointment as chair and Andrew Mellon professor of music at the University of Pittsburgh.

PROFILES OF INDIVIDUAL RESEARCH: 1950–1960

Formation of organizations to promote African arts

The popularization of traditional music and dance received similar attention in other African countries, for the cultural awakening that played an important part in the struggle for independence in Ghana appeared in varying forms in other parts of the continent. It led to the formation of societies for the preservation and promotion of African culture, such as the West African Cultural Society, which had branches in Ghana, Nigeria, and Sierra Leone, paralleling Présence Africaine in Paris.

It was in the spirit of this awakening that Alick Nkhata, program organizer of what was then known as Central African Broadcasting Station (Ludaka), appealed to people in Central Africa to form listeners' clubs to "deal with indigenous music," including *makwaya* and other contemporary forms, because "the time has come when we must take steps to preserve our music" (quoted in Nkhata 1952:17–20).

Phillip Gbeho: bimusical visionary

The development of a university-based program did not stifle individual research, for there was an expansion in individual contributions similar in perspectives to those of earlier decades. Stress continued to be laid on training specialist teachers of African music and educating the public through lecture-demonstrations.

In Ghana, public education was spearheaded by Phillip Gbeho, a master drummer, competent in the Ewe tradition. He believed in the unity of African expressive forms, and insisted that the concept of music in Africa includes singing, drumming, and dancing: "They are all one and the same thing, and must not be separated"; when he spoke of a person's "being musical," he meant that the person understood them all (1952:31).

As chair of an interim committee for an arts council set up by the government of Ghana, Gbeho organized performances of traditional music and dance on important state occasions, and gave lecture-demonstrations around the country, sometimes in collaboration with the Department of Extramural Studies (University of Ghana). What he had to say, however, was based on the analysis of his experience, rather than on new research. Since his objective was to whip up enthusiasm and appreciation for traditional music (an objective he had furthered during his sojourn in London, as a student at Trinity College of Music), he always spoke in a popular style. The texts of his lectures were essentially the same as those he delivered in London, published as a series of articles in *West African Review* (1952–1953) and the *African Music Society Newsletter* and *Journal*.

In lectures on the analysis and interpretation of the music of African drum ensembles, Gbeho recognized the importance of approaches that take into account the structural roles of not only bells, rattles, and masterdrum, but also cross-rhythms emerging from dancers' kinetic expressions. Consciousness of cross-rhythms, he said, is a

> serious point in our music. It enables us to dance effectively with grace and ease. To do this you must learn to hear the rhythms of the drums, the gongong, the rattles and so on, and combine them with handclapping. An African learns to be conscious

Wilberforce Echezona   Studied, taught, and broadcast music of the Ibo of eastern Nigeria

Seth Cudjoe   Physician who worked on a prescriptive notation system for Ewe drumming in Ghana

Ghana Music Society   Formed in 1958 for research, radio programming, and publishing results of music studies

cross-rhythms   Rhythms of two or more instruments that create distinctively different and opposing patterns

mentally of every instrument employed in an African orchestra and this has a tremendous effect on his dance; all the various muscles of the body act differently to the rhythms of the instruments. (1952:31)

Though a staunch supporter of traditional music, Gbeho never rebelled against Western music, or suggested that it should be deemphasized. He believed in bimusicality, because bimusicality made sense in terms of his background and experience. He did not believe in syncretism, however. His unbelief set him apart from Amu. He maintained this position for a long time, but changed toward the end of his career. He probably did not have the same creative vision as Amu, for the syncretic music he composed was unimaginative or technically uninteresting. He was more a performer than a composer.

In pursuit of the ideal of bimusicality, Gbeho turned his attention and energy in the 1960s to developing what might seem a paradox, a national symphony orchestra, with funds from a nationalist government that had made the assertion of African cultural identity its avowed aim. When he created a national anthem for Ghana, he wrote it in the Western idiom, and campaigned successfully for its acceptance by the government. In his mind, he could reconcile these contradictions because he believed musical cultures could coexist in the same environment—a coexistence tacitly but widely accepted by many institutions and individuals all over Africa, by church and school, by radio and television, by nightclubs and other places of entertainment, by foreign embassies and cultural centers (which arrange or sponsor concerts of Western music by visiting artists from their home countries). African musicology must find a way of dealing with this situation, in particular with the principles of accommodation that make the coexistence of these and the varieties of syncretic and ethnic musical expressions possible.

Wilberforce Echezona: radio broadcasting

In addition to those who worked on their own in response to growing interest in African music, others—associated with cultural institutions such as museums, schools, and colleges—responded in different ways to particular needs, or to the challenges and opportunities they met in the course of their work.

One such person was Wilberforce Echezona (of Nigeria), who applied his training in Western music to the study of the music of his own people, the Ibo. While he taught music at St. Marks Teacher Training College (Akwa), he did much for school music in Eastern Nigeria by organizing music festivals there. Ekwueme describes him as a pioneer, "not only in promoting the standard of music in churches and schools, but also in encouraging indigenous traditional music and compositions by local choirmasters" (1972:389).

For the Eastern Nigerian Radio Station, Echezona, drawing on his fieldwork, planned and produced regular radio programs on Ibo music and musical instruments. His scholarly contribution to African musicology was made, not in the 1950s, but in the early 1960s. For published information on Ibo music in this period, readers have to turn to Ibos who seemed less academically qualified: Madumere and Harcourt Whyte, widely known and acclaimed as a composer of a new type of Ibo music.

Seth Cudjoe: prescriptively notating Ewe drumming

Of the nonuniversity-based contributions in the list above, four deserve mention because of their efforts to provide substantial studies based on research. The first of these consists of two essays by the physician Seth Cudjoe, who as a collaborator of Phillip Gbeho set himself the task of providing a scholarly exposition of Ewe drumming (Cudjoe 1953, 1958). He distinguished the strokes and the tones they produce, and suggested a notation suitable for them, for he believed that notating orally transmitted African music is one of the important tasks of African musicians: African music, he felt, must be accessible to musicians, not only through recordings, but also through notation. His interest in this matter was not in descriptive notation per se, but in the possibility that musicians could learn Ewe drumming from prescriptive notation.

Other Ghanaians, including Gbeho (though he did not leave posterity any transcriptions of Ewe music), shared this point of view. He implored African musicians to take an active part in research in African music. To do this effectively, he suggested, African musicians should "learn to read and write music thoroughly, for it is not sufficient to write down the words of a piece of music and the history connected with it" (1952:32–33).

Interest in notation was high in Ghana at this time, for the possibility of using staff notation with one or two additional symbols had been demonstrated by Amu (1933) and Riverson (1933). Though everybody was aware that the pitches of African music did not quite match those of tempered tuning, this awareness did not deter African musicians from using Western notation (just as the Roman alphabet has served for writing African languages), for it was thought that Africans who knew their own tradition could interpret the pitches in their own terms. The notation of rhythm, however, gave rise to differences of opinion, leading Amu and Riverson to offer explications of their approach at a conference of the Ghana Music Society in 1958 (Nketia 1958b).

Unlike these musicians, however, Cudjoe was adventurous and innovative, for the notation he suggested for drum music was not staff notation, but a combination of pulse notation and numerical notation. In it, each pulse of the standard Ewe bell pattern is assigned a number from 1 to 12. Drum strokes that occur on each pulse are represented by symbols derived from the figure of a drumstick, the area of the drumhead hit by the stick, and the type of stroke (whether it is open or free, damped or muted, and so on).

Analytically minded, Cudjoe provided an exposition of cross-rhythms in Ewe drum music, particularly as exemplified in *agbadza* drumming. He recognized the "additive" nature of the rhythms by indicating on the pulseline the positions where the sounds of each drum pattern fell, but resolved them into divisive groups in relation to the hand clapping.

As an African art critic, Cudjoe appreciated the role the arts play in African societies; hence, though his main interest was in the analysis of Ewe drumming, he also drew attention to the social importance of music in Africa. He did not, however, follow up his interest in music, or supply further expositions of Ewe drumming. Because the exigencies of his medical practice did not afford him time for systematic research in other fields, he was content to play the role of catalyst and critic.

Joseph Kyagambiddwa　Studied and notated Baganda xylophone music of Uganda in the 1950s

miko　A transpositional technique in Baganda xylophone playing

Ekundayo Phillips　Composer and organist who noted similarities between Gregorian and Yoruba chant in the 1950s

Clement da Cruz　Focused on ethnographic information embedded in Dahomean musical instruments and oral traditions

Joseph Kyagambiddwa: analyzing Baganda xylophones

In the 1950s, another contributor who believed in making African music accessible to musicians through notation was Joseph Kygambiddwa. In his work on *African Music from the Source of the Nile*, he provided examples of Baganda scales and rhythms and discussed various categories of songs—religious songs, work songs, play songs, war songs, and "dramatic" songs.

He devoted the greater proportion of the monograph to the music of Baganda xylophones. He provided an analysis of its basic structure, the songs used as themes for each piece, the parts played by each of the three performers (squatting around one instrument), and an exposition of *miko*, a transpositional technique. In scores (using staff notation), he then published the repertory of the xylophones. Though his pitch notation was an approximation by Western standards, this incongruity did not bother him, for what he was providing was a blueprint for musicians, not analytical scores for musicologists.

It is also clear that Kyagambiddwa approached his study primarily as a musician, for what he had to say about history and culture was not so carefully thought out or investigated as the repertory of xylophone music, which he had learned to play from teachers at the Uganda Museum in Kampala (to which he was attached for two years). As Wachsmann stated in a review of this work, its scholarly pitfalls worried him because the book "hardly reflects credit on the advice given by his teachers"; nevertheless, Kyagambiddwa did make a notable contribution, for everyone agreed that the publication of 62 scores and the discovery of the *miko* were "major events in ethnomusicology" (Wachsmann 1956:80–81).

Ekundayo Phillips: composer, organist, evolutionist

The third notable contributor of this period is the organist and composer Ekundayo Phillips (of Nigeria). He approached his study of Yoruba music from a composer's viewpoint, his main interest being the creative use of Yoruba tunes in new religious music and the history of Christian music. While Kyagambiddwa's monograph is mainly descriptive, the first part of Phillips's monograph (1953) is mainly historical. As an organist, Phillips was familiar with Western ecclesiastical music. He was naturally impressed by seeming similarities between Gregorian chant and Yoruba chant—a point made later by Father Carrol, who lists similarities and differences between the two forms of cantillation (1956:45–47).

In the light of impressions, Phillips deduced that music evolves in stages—from impassioned speech, to songs with clearly defined scales. Supposing a missing link between plainchant and later forms of expression, he suggested that Yoruba music was that link. Like other contributions of this period, his Yoruba examples were in staff notation.

The evolutionary approach is outmoded; hence, Phillips's historical inferences can be rejected. The significance of his monograph lies in (1) his efforts to find a comparative framework for interpreting Yoruba music, and to bring an African perspective into a way of looking at music that had been current when he was a student of Western music (at Trinity College of Music, between 1910 and 1920); and (2) the exposition of his approach to syncretism as a compositional technique.

Clement da Cruz: musical instruments and oral traditions

The last of the four major contributors of this period, Clement da Cruz, brought a different dimension to the study of African music. The other writers focused their attention on structure, giving incidental information on sociocultural background, but he focused on ethnographic information embedded in music in Dahomean society. He paid close attention to musical instruments and relevant oral traditions, no doubt because he worked as a museum scientist.

His study (1954) considered the music of Dahomey (now Benin) in four contexts: work, politics, worship (ritual), and entertainment. He dealt with the musical instruments of the Aja, the Aizo, the Fon, the Kotafon, and the Peda, providing relevant information on particular instruments wherever he could. He mentioned the musical types performed in the areas of his investigation, giving in some cases the kings during whose reign they came into being, and the social contexts in which they were used. His work remains informative, but not critical.

Areas of research

Taken together, the topics covered in the contributions of the 1950s by African writers and scholars working in the two streams (institutional and individual) are more diversified than those of the previous era. They number at least thirteen:

1. General observations on (a) the music of Africa (Adande 1952; Nketia 1959b); (b) individual countries (Euba 1960); (c) individual societies, the Adangme and the Gã of Ghana (Nketia 1957b, 1958e, 1958g, 1958h), the Baganda of Uganda (Kygambiddwa 1955), the Ewe of Ghana (Gadzekpo 1952; Cudjoe 1953), the Ibo of Nigeria (Madumere 1953; Whyte 1953), and the Yoruba of Nigeria (Phillips 1953).
2. Observations on ceremonies and festivals as music events (Nketia 1958c; Twala 1952; Ukeje 1953).
3. Instrumental resources and oral traditions, and problems associated with the development of instrumental African music (da Cruz 1954; Nketia 1958b).
4. Drums, drum ensembles, and techniques of drumming (Cudjoe 1953, 1958; Nketia 1954, 1959b; Onwona-Safo 1957a; Tsala 1955).
5. Drum language (Adande and Verger 1953; Nketia 1958f; Onwona-Safo 1957b).
6. Musicians—Yoruba musicians in Accra, drummers' roles, professionalism (Mensah 1958a; Nketia 1954, 1958i).
7. Songs and song texts (Adali-Mortty 1958; Kagame 1951; Mensah 1960; Nketia 1955, 1958a, 1958d).
8. Music and religion (Nketia 1957c, 1959a).
9. Music and dance, including descriptions of traditional dances and African choreographers' interpretation of them or African choreographers' approaches to dance theater (Keita 1959; Nketia 1957c; Opoku 1958; Tidjani 1954; Tsibangu 1953).
10. African music and the technical media (Gadzekpo 1954; Mensah 1958b; Nketia 1956).

Culture assumed a new importance as an area of governmental action, and departments or ministries of culture or arts councils were created to plan and implement nationwide cultural programs.

11. New trends in music (Nketia 1957a).
12. Problems in notation (Nketia 1958b).
13. History of music education (Riverson 1955).

SCHOLARSHIP IN THE PERIOD OF INSTITUTIONAL DEVELOPMENT: 1960–1970

In the decade of transition from colonial rule to independence (when many new nation-states emerged in Africa), Africans' contributions to the study of African music continued to expand, for the cultural revival that had characterized the previous decade became institutionalized in many African countries. Culture assumed a new importance as an area of governmental action, and departments or ministries of culture (or sometimes of culture and youth, or of sports and tourism) or arts councils were created to plan and implement nationwide cultural programs. National occasions, including the celebration of independence and its anniversary, invariably featured performances of traditional music and dance in national capitals and cities, and the formation of national dance companies became a common practice.

As the new nations tried to establish political, economic, and cultural ties, pan-Africanism and African unity became important issues. Pan-African arts festivals and colloquia were organized to affirm the universality of African cultural experiences, to foster pride in African cultural heritages, and to encourage the scholarly study, promotion, preservation, and creative use of African traditions. Because of the colonial experience, and the realization that some of the best exponents of culture belonged to a generation that might pass away without leaving posterity their knowledge or expertise, emphasis was laid on preservation and continuity.

The long-term development of the musical life and cultural image of each country through the creation of appropriate institutions for promotion, education, and research in music and related arts became a matter of national concern. The period 1960–1970 was therefore a period of institutional development, in which musicology came to be accepted, as both an academic discipline and something that could be of practical value to cultural development. In some African societies, institutional support for programs of music therefore became a major concern.

Some countries, such as Senegal and Upper Volta, preferred to set up research units under the aegis of their ministries of culture or education. Though the lack of trained nationals was initially a problem, foreign experts were hired as an interim measure, solely to collect, document, and archive "the national patrimony" of music, dance, drama, and visual arts, ensuring that they had local assistants, who would receive on-the-job training and eventually take over from them.

Teaching and research interrelationships

For the interdisciplinary study of African history, culture, and the arts, institutes and centers of African studies established in this decade at the universities of Ghana, Ife, Lagos, Nairobi, and Zambia provided avenues for musical research.

The research program developed in the Department of Sociology at the University of Ghana in the 1950s was transferred to the Institute of African Studies, which functioned, from the beginning, as a center for graduate studies. A course in African musicology designed for Ghanaians who had diplomas in Western music from British schools of music, and for those who had taken Amu's specialist music course for teachers, was established. The writing of a thesis formed part of the requirement of the diploma; hence, it enabled the institute to involve in its overall research program students who took this course. In addition to the diploma, provision was also made for graduate students taking the interdisciplinary M.A. (and later the Ph.D.) degree in African Studies to specialize in African music by taking the relevant course and writing a thesis or dissertation on a musical topic.

Another development, perhaps unique to Ghana, was the establishment and training of the National Dance Company of Ghana within the institute. This company consisted solely of young men and women who, having an aptitude for dance, could be trained to perform traditional dances from different parts of Ghana. A team of master drummers and other musicians representing different ethnic traditions in Ghana was recruited to perform for them, and to act as demonstrators, instructors, and resources. Though the objective of the training program was artistic and professional (rather than academic), it enabled the institute to stimulate general awareness of the traditional arts on the campus, which had been Western oriented in the arts.

Since the program in African musicology was primarily a graduate program, authorities decided to set up, in addition, a regular undergraduate school of music, dance, and drama. This school became another unit within the Institute of African Studies. Largely bicultural, courses in the school included both African and Western materials—an approach necessitated by the colonial legacy, part and parcel of contemporary Ghana.

A different approach was taken by the African Studies Institute at the University of Ife, for what seemed to be needed there was a creative arts center. The institute encouraged research, but had no teaching program in the arts. Musicians already established as composers (such as Akin Euba and Samuel Akpabot) were appointed as senior research fellows. Their task was to combine their research with creative work, so whatever original works they produced could be performed with other items at the performing arts center in town during an annual festival that became an important event in Ife.

Recognizing that the result of African musical research could have educational value, some African universities linked their music-research units to institutes or departments of education, or to some educational project. With the support of the Rockefeller Foundation, such a music-research unit was set up at Makerere University in October 1961. Solomon Mbabi-Katana, who had worked on African musical instruments while teaching in a secondary school in Uganda, ran it. The research concentrated on the vocal music of East Africa. By the end of the third year of the program, one hundred fifty songs had been collected and transcribed for use in schools; of these, one hundred were from ethnic groups in Uganda, twenty-five from Kenya, and twenty-five from Tanzania.

A similar music-research unit was established at the University of Ibadan in 1962. Fela Sowande, who had had experience in collecting and recording music for the program and archives of the Nigerian Broadcasting Corporation, was put in charge of it. He decided to concentrate on Yoruba religious music, particularly the music of Ifa divination. Intimate contact with Yoruba music changed his perspectives on musicology, and especially his attitude toward African music and approaches to be used in studying it. He became involved in problems of value and interpretation, in symbolism, philosophy, and psychology. This involvement led him to reject some of

What seemed important was a discipline that enabled scholars to approach the music of their society as Amu did, "with a trained mind."

the values on which he had based his work, and to deemphasize abstract musicological analysis in favor of approaches that dealt with meaning as a function of African world views.

Instead of setting up a small music research unit, the University of Nigeria (Nsukka) took a bolder course, establishing a full-fledged department of music for teaching degree-courses in music, which would offer specialization at the undergraduate level in music education, composition, and ethnomusicology. To assist the department in developing a bimusical program to include the traditional music of Nigeria, the university granted the faculty—consisting of expatriates and a couple of Nigerians, Echezona and Akpabot (before he joined the University of Ife)—money for fieldwork. The combination of teaching and funded research paid off, for Echezona, whose previous research had concentrated on the musical instruments of the Ibo (1963) studied music in parts of Iboland. He compiled his ethnography into eight mimeographed monographs—on the Afikpo, the Agukwu, the Egede, the Ibibio, the Nnewi, the Okpanam, the Owerri, and the Rivers area.

The faculty involved in their research some students majoring in ethnomusicology. The program required all third-year students to write a minor thesis on music in Nigeria, based on their fieldwork. Until the 1990s, the music department at Nsukka was the only institution in Nigeria that provided a degree course in music locally for Nigerians. Many of Nigeria's musicologists who emerged in the 1970s and after (Achinivu Kanu Achinivu, Lazarus Ekwueme, Meki Nzewi, Mosunmola Omibiyi, Tunji Vidal, and others) received their initial training in this institution.

The need for professional training in music and related arts along conservatory lines led also to the establishment of separate schools or institutions of fine arts in the Central African Republic, Côte d'Ivoire, Ethiopia (which established both the university's center for the creative arts and the Yared School), Senegal, Sudan, and Zaïre. Two related institutions were set up in Zaïre, one for training musicians and musicologists (Institut National des Arts) established in 1967 within the Department of Art and Culture and affiliated with the National University of Zaïre in 1971, and the other a research center for the Institute of Culture, which worked closely with the National Museum of Zaïre.

Kwanongoma College in Bulawayo, an offshoot of the Rhodesian Academy of Music, came into being in 1961. One of its founders' objectives was to provide "a focal point for a new African musical scholarship" (Williamson 1963:48). Christian missions also joined in the institutional search for African musical values. They encouraged their expatriate clergy and indigenous Africans to record, transcribe, and study traditional music in their areas (Mubangizi 1966:77–78).

Impact on scholarship

Though the institutional development of the period 1960–1970 was intended to meet the cultural development needs of African countries, it had repercussions on musicology in Africa. It affirmed the need for musicological studies that focus on African materials while responding to the challenge of the African environment in its formulation of theoretical concepts, its modes of interpretation, and its application of the results of research.

Though the foundations for this development had been laid by pioneers such as Ballanta and Amu and their successors, not enough progress seems to have been made everywhere in developing a balance between scholarly studies and practical activities. Cultural awakening and cultural revival create enthusiasm for music and dance, but not necessarily the scholarly orientation required for their study. It was the institutional arrangements for musical research that provided the stimulus for the latter, so African musicians would not only assert their consciousness of identity through their music, but would also be in a position to interpret it—to their own people, and to the wider world.

Study abroad for African scholars

The demand for Africans who could meet these objectives encouraged those who had first degrees or diplomas in music to pursue advanced studies in music, and to make musicology or music education a professional goal, since musicians with these specializations were needed for a variety of programs in institutions of higher education and ministries of education or culture, national museums, broadcasting, and mission-related institutions. In some countries, graduate training was incorporated into manpower development programs. Governmental or institutional sponsorship was provided in this and the following decades for African musicians to pursue such studies wherever they could gain admission. A few turned to the University of Ghana, while others went abroad. Some went to the United States, to study at the University of California at Berkeley and Los Angeles, the University of Chicago, Columbia University, the University of Illinois, Indiana University, the University of Michigan, Michigan State University, Northwestern University, the University of Pittsburgh, Stanford University, Wesleyan University, and Yale University. Some went to the United Kingdom (Belfast and London) or to Paris (the Sorbonne and the Musée de l'Homme). Some went elsewhere in Europe: Brussels, Cologne, Hamburg, Metz, Rome, Vienna.

While some Africans studied in institutions with programs in ethnomusicology, others studied in institutions with programs in historical musicology, theory, and composition, or in music education and other programs that permitted courses in ethnomusicology to be included in curricular requirements. African musicology of the 1960s and 1970s was thus enriched by the perspectives that African scholars exposed to a variety of Western approaches brought into their work. Irrespective of the program, their doctoral dissertations were invariably on an African topic—the music of a contemporary composer or performer, the musical instruments of an ethnic group, the music of a selected society, indigenous and syncretic choral music, drumming and other instrumental traditions, or selected musical genres. What seemed important was a discipline that enabled scholars to approach the music of their society as Amu did, "with a trained mind."

Themes of musical research

As a result of institutional developments of the 1960s, the number of scholarly contributions to African music increased. The topics examined include

1. Theoretical and technical issues in African music: (a) factors that shape and maintain music, the role of music in society, the problem of meaning in African music, historical evidence in music, sources of historical data on music, problems and areas of research in African music, and musicology in the context

In the 1970s, the formulation of national cultural policies and the planning of cultural development became central concerns of African governments.

of African culture (Aning 1968; Nketia 1962c, 1964a, 1970b; Sowande 1970); (b) technical issues, such as compositional techniques, hocketing, multipart structures, and other structures (Echezona 1966; Euba 1967; Mensah 1967b; Nketia 1962b); (c) new trends in music and problems of acculturation (Eno Belinga 1969; Euba 1970; Nketia 1964b; Sowande 1966); (d) traditional elements in Christian music in Africa (Mapoma 1970–1971; Mensah 1960).

2. Studies of musical genres, songs, and song texts, such as the Christian music of Ethiopia, the music of female choral groups, the epic literature of the *mvet* (a chordophone), and folk songs of Ghana (Aning 1965; Eno Belinga 1965, 1967; Kebede 1969; Nketia 1963b).

3. Musical instruments and ensembles, including (a) a general survey of resources; (b) instrumentation of African music, and trumpet ensembles; (c) classification of instruments; (d) studies of single instruments, such as the Ethiopian *krar* and xylophone traditions of Ghana; (e) terms for musical instruments; (f) drums and drumming (Akpabot 1966; Echezona 1963; Kebede 1968; Maraire 1967; Mensah 1966a, 1967a; Ndayizeye and Wymeersch 1965; Nketia 1963a, 1969; Turay 1966).

4. The musician (Anyumba 1970; Nayo 1969).

5. Overview of the music of single societies, countries, regions, and sub-Saharan Africa as a whole, including (a) ethnic traditions, such as those of the Ibo and the Yoruba of Nigeria (Adetoyese 1966; Echezona 1965), (b) countries and regions, such as the traditions of East Africa, Sudan, and Ghana (Ismail 1970; Kakoma 1970; Nketia 1962a), and (c) sub-Saharan African (Bebey 1969; Nketia 1961, 1966).

6. Bibliography and discography: (a) an annotated bibliography of music and dance in English-speaking Africa; (b) a catalogue of recorded sound (Aning 1967; Ojehomon 1969).

7. In addition to the writings of musicians and musicologists, African scholars made contributions in related fields. Because of the growth of interest in African folklore, oral literature, and drama, scholars in these fields made indirect but significant contributions to African musicology through their observation and analysis of events that incorporate music and dance, and more especially their collection, transcription, translation, and analysis of song texts as literature and sources of historical data (Alagoa 1968; Babalola 1966; Moore 1970; Munongo and Kimele 1967; Nguijol 1967; Towo-Atangana 1965). As musicians create and use song texts, musicians' studies of techniques of musical construction and verbal communication have an important place in African musicology, for they are an integral part of music making.

The intellectual stimulus that shaped the perspectives of African writers came to them not only from their disciplines, but also from the new African studies programs in Africa as they determined what their stances were going to be. As part of their self-reviews, they reconsidered Western assumptions about Africa as reflected in the scholarship of the colonial era and in scholarly achievements in the humanities and social sciences, particularly in anthropology, archaeology, history, and religion ("Tropical African Studies" 1964). Musicologists involved in such programs reviewed their stances in musicology or their approaches to particular problems.

The pan-Africanist view of African cultures as an aggregate characterized by unity and diversity also influenced the perspectives of African scholars, for this view allows one to see each musical culture in its own right and as part of a totality. African musicians and musicologists favored this approach to African cultures because eclecticism had taken root in Africa as a result of the pan-Africanist movement. In the postindependence period, it was not enough to be aware of the music of one's ethnic group, for Africa had come to mean more than a collection of disparate ethnic groups. One needed to be familiar with the music of one's immediate neighbors, and of others who belonged to the new nation-state, and with the meaning music and dance gave to the concepts of African personality and Negritude.

TRENDS IN AFRICAN SCHOLARSHIP: 1970–1980

The goals that inspired pioneers of musicology in Africa in the colonial and postcolonial periods continued to provide the basis for musicology in the 1970s, for decolonization and development—forces that confronted independent African states in the 1960s—continued to affect the arts. A new emphasis on cultural studies as an avenue for accelerating the process of decolonization gave further impetus to music and musicology. So did the formulation of national cultural policies and the planning of cultural development, which in the 1970s became one of the central concerns of African governments. In 1974, at the intergovernmental conference on cultural policies held in Accra under the auspices of UNESCO and the Organization of African Unity, the need for preserving, promoting, and presenting traditional music was confirmed in a resolution asking UNESCO to formulate and implement a ten-year plan to develop music and the performing arts in Africa.

As a result of all these trends, musicology continued to be recognized at the governmental level in some countries, both as an academic discipline, and as an enterprise that—through its primary activities (collecting, recording, archiving, analyzing, and building up a body of knowledge that could be applied constructively to nation-building, especially in training and educating future generations of musicians, educating the general public, and developing consciousness of identity and a sense of nationhood)—could contribute to cultural development. It was also believed that the results of musicological research could stimulate new directions in creativity and performance. These goals continued to inspire much of the research undertaken in the 1970s, and to shape current trends in African musicology.

The broad areas of research, and some of the topics dealt with, overlapped with those of the previous decade, while the primary focus of scholars continued to be music and musicology, for as Wachsmann observed, in African musicology music is the "primary subject," not "one of the secondary ones." This did not mean that considerations of the sociocultural context were ignored, for as Wachsmann pointed out later in the same article, "With music and musicology so strongly in the foreground, it seems as if these pressures leave little room for anthropology. But this is deceptive. It is simply that anthropology has come to serve musicology" (1966b).

Accordingly, the institutional arrangement for musicological studies almost everywhere in the 1970s made musicology an integral part of the programs of departments and schools of music and institutes of fine art, or multidisciplinary institutes

Composers grappled with problems of syncretism and philosophies of African personality and Negritude; performers trained in some area of Western music desired to retrain themselves in African music.

of African studies, rather than departments of anthropology. The idea that the study of African music or other forms of nonwestern music properly belongs to anthropology, not to departments of music, is a Western fiction, used only when convenient to provide temporary shelter for musical research in an underdeveloped, hostile, or conservative academic environment, in which music is erroneously believed to be "an art belonging almost exclusively to the European tradition" (Freedman 1978:59).

Even in the Western world, nurturing nonwestern musical studies in departments of anthropology, with a few notable exceptions, ceased to be the convention. Since about 1960, the trend

> has been reversed, and as the musicians and musicologists have begun to espouse ethnomusicology, the anthropologists, in the narrow sense of the term, have appeared largely to disengage themselves from its study. It is the one case in which the prefix 'ethno-' signals an advance in scholarship and an anthropological withdrawal. (Freedman 1958:59)

It seems likely that the emphasis on music and musicology will continue to be a major trend in Africa, for nearly all those who have turned to the scholarly study of music in Africa since the late 1960s have done so from some field of concentration in music—as musicians with training in Western musical theory, rediscovering and systematizing knowledge of music in their own societies (music that had hitherto seemed inconsequential to some of them); as composers, grappling with problems of syncretism and philosophies of African personality and Negritude; as performers, trained in some area of Western music, desiring to retrain themselves in African music; as teachers, needing to rethink their philosophy of education, methodology, and goals; or as educators, having to undertake the basic collection and analysis of traditional materials.

Though all these persons approached African music from a musicological point of view, they all tended to see problems in African music from both a general and a particular perspective relative to their interests and specializations. Thus, composers like Lazarus Ekwueme, Akin Euba, and Samuel Akpabot (all of Nigeria), Atta Annan Mensah, Zinzendorf Nayo, and Ato Turkson (all of Ghana), Joseph Kyagambiddwa (of Uganda), and Ashenafi Kebede (of Ethiopia) took particular interest in searching for definitions of African idioms, in categorizing creative output, in observing instrumentation, form, and structure in relation to creative process, or (in the case of Lazarus Ekwueme) in formulating or applying Western theory or analytical models, such as the Schenkerian model, to African materials (Ekwueme 1975-1976, 1972).

Similarly, those with backgrounds in performance, such as Nissio Fiagbedzi (of Ghana), Akin Euba and Tunji Vidal (both of Nigeria), and Kazadi wa Mukuna (of Zaïre), tended to concern themselves with the intrinsic values of African music, or with problems of musical communication and aesthetics, or of philosophy (Fiagbedzi

FIGURE 2   Percy James Mensah and his "Four-fold Amen" (1925), on a commemorative post-card—front and back. Photo courtesy Atta Annan Mensah.

1980b), while educators like Solomon Mbabi-Katana (of Uganda), William Amoaku, Atta Annan Mensah, and Gustav Twerefoo (all of Ghana), Christian Horton (of Sierra Leone), and Mosunmola Omibiyi (of Nigeria) were concerned with musicological research that facilitates the transfer of knowledge and skills formerly acquired through socialization to the classroom, and in the case of Twerefoo, its application in continuing education and therapy (Omibiyi 1979; Twerefoo 1975–1976).

Others—Mwesa Mapoma (of Zambia), Washington Omondi (of Kenya), Samuel Akpabot and Meki Nzewi (both of Nigeria), Francis Bebey and Pie-Claude Ngumu (both of Cameroon), Ben Aning and Atta Annan Mensah (both of Ghana)—also looked at problems of music, culture, and communication, or of music and related arts, sometimes both synchronically and diachronically (Nzewi 1979, 1984).

Programs in musical research in Africa showed
interest in the study of the interrelations between
music and dance, music and drama, music and
language, music and the visual arts, and music and
various aspects of behavior.

As a field of scholarly research, African musicology thus brought together
African composers, teachers, and others, to pursue advanced knowledge and understanding of music in Africa. Its theoretical stance and methods, and its practical aims,
were related to the challenges presented by the nature and scope of African musical
materials in their cultural, social, and political environments.

African musicologists of the 1970s were therefore concerned with the social and
cultural contexts of music—with the makers of music and the dynamics of music
making, in both traditional and contemporary contexts; with sound sources and the
values that guide their selection and use; with traditions (including myths and legends) associated with musical performance; with the art and technology of sound
media; with creative processes, performative techniques, repertories, modes of expression and presentation, and music as an object of aesthetic interest.

Programs in musical research in Africa showed interest in the study of the interrelations between music and dance, music and drama, music and language, music
and the visual arts, and music and various aspects of behavior; they are also concerned with political, religious, and social ideas, and with beliefs that inspired or
guided music making and values.

In addition to studies of the foregoing in different societies and regions, and in
the continent as a whole, studies of African musicians (both traditional and contemporary) also received particular attention, partly because of the need for a better
understanding of individual contributions to African musical cultures, and partly
because the anonymity of the past was no longer the rule. African radio stations did
not broadcast programs of traditional and contemporary music without mentioning
the names of individual artists, bandleaders, or composers, while record companies,
promoters, and managers often focused attention on artists and ensembles.

A subsidiary reason educators and others give for studying individual musicians
"who have produced and still produce the music written about, played, sung, danced
or realized through any agreeable combinations of these" was that "the lack of materials on African composers and their works has been one reason for the exclusion of
these from the curriculum of music colleges and departments of music of many
African countries" (Achiniyu 1979:11–12). Nigerian musicologists seemed taken
with this area of research, for their articles dealt with the problems of such composers, providing catalogues of them and their backgrounds. These included articles
on popular musicians (such as Sunny Ade, Bobby Benson, and Ebenezer Obey), and
full-length studies of composers (Achiniyu 1979; Alájá-Browne 1981, 1985; Omibiyi
1979, 1983; Sowande 1966, 1967; Uzoigbe 1978).

The study of oral traditions related to change and other historical processes (such
as differentiation and interdependency, patterns of transformation, and the mechanisms for controlling and diffusing innovation), and the study of the musical confluence of Europe, the Americas, the Caribbean, Asia, and Africa, engaged some scholars' attention, while educators focused on curricular materials, problems related to

tradition and continuity, processes of enculturation in informal and formal settings, and the institutionalization of musical instruction and training.

The pragmatic goals that in the 1970s inspired research or guided the ordering of priorities in research did not preclude interest in theoretical and methodological issues in ethnomusicology, or in African musicology in particular. Nor did African musicologists concern themselves merely with analysis and description. Reflection on such materials led some of them to look at specific problems, such as musicianship and bimusicality, determinants of style, and systematic problems in the tuning of chordophones (Aning 1982; Fiagbedzi 1980a, 1980b; Mapoma 1980; Mensah 1966b, 1971; Nketia 1981, 1982, 1984a, 1984b; Omondi 1984).

Some African writers were once preoccupied with demonstrating the integrity of African music, but it was the critical appraisal of scholarly statements about African music or particular approaches that seemed to interest others. Akpabot's writings often referred to Western writers' statements and ideas about African music, since he was concerned about the tendency to treat African music as "something peculiar." Juxtaposing his African and Western experience, he saw similarities or correspondences in procedure where others saw differences; hence, he decried the tendency to disregard the features that African music shares with other traditions, particularly those of the West, considering that some elements of twentieth-century musical practice appeared to him to be present in traditional African practices. For the same reason, he found the tendency toward overimaginative interpretation of cultural and musical phenomena reprehensible (1972, 1976, 1978).

Lazarus Ekwueme now and then took issue with statements made by scholars whose approach differed from his own or whose interpretation of Western praxis he could not accept. Commenting on the notation of African music, he pointed out that some researchers (like Arthur M. Jones), highlighting cross-rhythms among instrumental parts, had notated African music using noncoincident barlines. Their "misguided effort," he said, came from the idea that the barline implied "a metric accent on the note immediately following it (the first beat in the bar)—a notion that was probably given its greatest support by Hugo Riemann in his theories of meter and rhythm"; anyone who conceived African musical rhythm in this way, he added, confused musicians trying to read the notation (1972:249–250).

Outlook for the future

Though in the late 1990s the prospects for developing African musicology as an integral part of curricula in Africa are bright, two major problems need institutional and individual attention: the coordination of research, and the need for specialization within musicology. Inter-African cooperation in research has been minimal, while the choice of topics for research has been quasi-random. With few exceptions, it is unrelated to any kind of planning; hence, the picture that emerges when one looks at any single theme is rarely complete, not to speak of gaps in our information about single societies, countries, and regions.

Part of this problem is an imbalance in personnel. Some countries (such as Ghana and Nigeria) support trained African musicologists, but many countries lack such personnel, and have not yet seen their way clear to hire scholars from other African countries. But for the work of pioneer Western musicologists and their successors, contributions to musicological knowledge in countries without local musicologists would have been nil—a fact usually recognized by African scholars as they look at the positive contributions of the colonial era and the enrichment that comes from a synthesis of insiders' and outsiders' stances and methods.

The second problem, the need for specialization, has not received much consideration. Since specialization in problematic areas or branches of a discipline is neces-

The spirit of adventure and discovery played a significant part in the early history of Western exploration of African musical life.

sary for the advancement of knowledge, one hopes that this will develop in African musicology. The number of ethnic traditions and linguistic groups, the vastness of the territories, and the variety of problems, invite the enrichment of insights from cognate disciplines—aesthetics, anthropology, history, linguistics, psychology, and sociology.

It is this need that, despite doubts about its nomenclature and early definitions, has drawn many African musicians to ethnomusicology for an area of specialization; it has outgrown its exotic preoccupations to become a discipline that synthesizes formal and contextual techniques of analysis into holistic studies of music as a cultural phenomenon. Synchronic studies of the musical cultures of Africa, and investigations into musical problems of immediate relevance to cultural development and nation building in Africa, are greatly enhanced when they are approached from an ethnomusicological viewpoint—as integrated studies of music, society, and culture.

For the same reason, one hopes that a new generation of African musicologists will emerge and begin to specialize in other areas. We need scholars who will concentrate on historical approaches, making a point of keeping up with developments in methodology, sources, and interpretation in African history, archaeology, art history, and cognate studies; we need scholars who will develop lines of inquiry in historical studies of African music, studies that will embrace the history of all music in Africa—the history of traditional and contemporary African music, and the history of Western and Arabic music in sub-Saharan Africa. We need specialists to undertake intensive distributional and comparative stylistic analysis within the framework of historical studies. Similarly, systematic studies in aesthetics, psychology, and related fields should enrich the scope and quality of African musicology; they should enable scholars to contribute, in significant ways, on the basis of their own fieldwork, to all areas of scholarly studies in music.

It is important also that African musicology stay relevant, maintaining its commitment to the discipline, to the international world of musical scholarship, and to the society that cultivates the subject matter of its research. As the excitement of political independence wears off, and consciousness of national identity becomes less and less an issue, the inspiration that these qualities provided for initiating relevant research might also fade. Music, however, is such a practical and purposeful subject, one cannot lose sight of its role in society, and of pragmatic issues that surround it. Response to the environment, to the pressures exerted on it (internally and externally), and to the world of scholarship, will give African musicologists the versatility they need.

WESTERN SCHOLARS' CONTRIBUTION TO AFRICAN MUSICOLOGY

The growth of musicology in Africa was stimulated by African musicians' and writers' responses to social and political transformations on the continent, but Western contributions to African musicology seem to have been stimulated largely by Western writers' and scholars' responses to the existence of non-European cultures as sources of musical experiences and data.

The spirit of adventure and discovery, what Alan Merriam called the Western mania for collecting, played no less significant part in the early history of Western exploration of African musical life and resources, for African music is an art "forced upon the notice of the European as soon as he leaves the steamer and before he sets foot on African soil," a mode of expression "universally popular and universally practised" (Ward 1927:199).

The state of scholarship in 1965

Lionel John Palmer Gaskin's *Bibliography of Music in Africa* (1965), incorporating bibliographies by Varley (1936), Merriam (1951), and Thieme (1964), gives a good idea of the Western scholars and observers involved in exploring musical life and sources in Africa. It lists about 1,700 authors, including anonymous writers and authors of institutional articles and monographs. Less than 4 percent of these authors are African musicians and writers—a fact that shows both how much Western observers and scholars have contributed to African musicology, and the extent of Western interest in African musical life and sources. However, of the Western authors, slightly less than 2 percent are musicologists. This proportion includes comparative musicologists and ethnomusicologists who looked at African materials, or provided conceptual tools applied or tested in the field.

The bibliography lists not only books and articles on African music, instruments, and dance, but also references to these subjects in other books and 329 periodicals (in English and other European languages) that carried articles on Africa. Of 3,370 entries, 2,653 are references to music in different countries and regions of Africa; references to musical instruments and dancing are 768 and 321, respectively.

Since Gaskin believed "most musicologists would approach music and musical instruments primarily from a regional point of view," the entries in his work are listed geographically, beginning with those that deal with Africa in general (165 items), followed by those that deal with countries and regions or specific societies located in those countries. About sixteen countries have up to twelve entries on random topics, while ten others have twenty-one entries. Angola, Cameroon, Ghana, Nigeria, Sudan, Tanzania, and Uganda have forty to sixty entries, while South Africa and Zaïre have well over one hundred. As might be expected, it is difficult to get from these sources a comprehensive picture of music in any one country, since they often represent the casual observations of individuals who happened to be in those countries on missions unrelated to music.

Though the articles and monographs on subjects such as music and ritual, work and leisure, festivals, and so forth are not classified, two subjects are singled out for special listing: dancing and musical instruments. The entries for these are arranged geographically. In the case of musical instruments, a separate listing is provided for each major class of instrument. Drums attracted the greatest attention (213 entries), while chordophones and aerophones ranked second and third (ninety-six and sixty-one entries, respectively). Xylophones, mbira, and nonmelodic idiophones attracted about equal attention (thirty-six, thirty-five, and thirty-two entries); taken together, they come next after drums.

It was thus African percussive instruments (which had a wider distribution than other instruments) that attracted the greatest attention; however, organology was the subject least understood, not only because of the apparent strangeness of the sounds and textures, but also because of the assumption that the aesthetic principles or critical values of Western music provided a basis valid for approaching the music of other cultures.

As scholars questioned the traditional assumptions and approaches of comparative musicology, new approaches to the study of non-Western music were developing.

Complexities of understanding African music

Awareness of the difficulties that hampered understanding and the bibliographical gaps in knowledge seems to have determined, to a considerable extent, not only the orientation and scope of inquiry into African music by Western scholars since 1965, but also the way in which African materials are organized and presented, for Western ethnomusicologists tend to assume that most people outside the cultures they study are not only ill informed, but often biased and ethnocentric. Accordingly, Western ethnomusicologists' task is not unlike what Paul Bohannan spelled out for anthropologists, for ethnomusicologists are outsiders, who analyze a musical culture

> to classify it, understand it according to more or less scientific principles, and communicate it to colleagues, students and readers who have no experience in it and are, concomitantly, blocked to at least some degree by their own culture from understanding any other one. (Merriam 1964:31)

The concern for disseminating information about African music and enhancing understanding of it was shared to some extent by the pioneers of comparative musicology who contributed to African studies. Ethnographers' recordings enabled scholars like Erich M. von Hornbostel and his assistants at the Berlin Phonogramm-Archiv (George Herzog, Mieczyslaw Kolinski, Marius Schneider) to analyze and interpret samples of African music in terms familiar or understandable to the musicological world, and documentary source materials enabled others to include Africa in evolutionary studies of musical instruments, techniques, and history.

A growing accumulation of recordings, collections of instruments, and ethnographic data made it possible for the ethnology of African sound instruments and an overview of the music of sub-Saharan Africa as a whole to be attempted by Hornbostel (1928, 1933), an attempt emulated by other scholars, like Gilbert Rouget (1961), Herbert Pepper (195?), and Merriam (1958, 1959), all of whom provided overviews of African music or the music of a region. So established was the tradition of using secondary sources that Rose Brandel, a pupil of Curt Sachs, could write a whole book on the music of Central Africa (1961) without having set foot in the region, for she could rely on her ability to transcribe, describe, and interpret in her own terms what she heard on recordings, using familiar Western musicological categories and information on the societies and cultures in the region printed on record jackets and in ethnographic monographs.

Fieldwork

When the importance of fieldwork undertaken by musicologists became generally accepted, investigations into African music were undertaken, not only by musicologists who visited different African societies for short periods for this purpose, but also by permanent residents in South Africa, such as Arthur Morris Jones, Percival Kirby, Hugh Tracey, and Klaus Wachsmann.

Much of the groundwork in African musicology undertaken by these scholars was accomplished in the period 1920–1950, when information on African societies, cultures, languages, and physical environment encouraged international scholarship and the development of colonial institutes and research centers such as IFAN (Institut Français d'Afrique Noire). In emulation of the Berlin Phonogramm-Archiv, a comparative musicology section of the Musée de l'Homme was founded in 1929 by André Schaeffner, who between 1931 and 1958 organized six expeditions to West Africa—a practice followed by Gilbert Rouget, who became his successor in 1965.

European musicologists' interest in the on-site study of African music continued through the 1950s, the 1960s, and the 1970s, when new generations of British scholars (John Blacking, Anthony King, David Rycroft), French musicologists (Simha Arom, Hugo Zemp), and German and Austrian musicologists (Robert Gunther, Gerhard Kubik, Artur Simon), made important contributions to African musicology.

Parallel developments took place in the United States from 1950 onward, for academic interest in African music had been generated by the work of anthropologists of the earlier decades (like Melville Herskovits), of collectors of African music (like Laura Boulton), and of the results of expeditions to Africa, such as the University of Chicago expedition to Liberia, 1930–1931 (in which George Herzog, who had emigrated from Germany to the United States, participated), and the Marshall expedition to the Kalahari, in 1952–1953.

African roots of jazz became an issue, and as scholars questioned the traditional assumptions and approaches of comparative musicology, new approaches to the study of non-Western music were developing. In 1955, the Society for Ethnomusicology came into being—an event that in several institutions gave new impetus to the establishment of programs in ethnomusicology and to the initiation of fieldwork by American scholars and graduate students in different parts of Africa, notably in Central Africa, East Africa (Tanzania, Uganda), Southern Africa (South Africa, Zambia, Zimbabwe), and West Africa (Gambia, Ghana, Liberia, Nigeria).

American Africanists of 1950–1960 included two of the founding members of the Society for Ethnomusicology: Alan Merriam, who worked mainly in Central Africa; and Willard Rhodes, who did his initial research in Zambia and Zimbabwe, and later worked in West Africa (principally in northern Nigeria). Those who followed included Lois Anderson (Uganda); Fremont E. Besmer (Nigeria); Max Brandt (Nigeria); Roxane Connick Carlisle (Sudan); Nicholas England, who worked with the !Kung and other societies in Southern Africa (1958–1961), and later with the Anlo-Ewe of Ghana; Roderic Knight (Senegambia); Norma McLeod (Madagascar); and Darius Thieme (Nigeria). The number of active scholars increased considerably after about 1970.

Recording and documentation

The stimulus for fieldwork in the colonial period and the period of great transition also came from fields other than musicology. The goals of folk musical study and music education led several scholars from the periphery of musicology into the heart of musical fieldwork.

Hugh Tracey (1903–1977)

The chief of these, Hugh Tracey, viewed African music primarily as an artistic heritage to be shared, preserved, and promoted. These goals, which Merriam considered tangential to the purposes of ethnomusicology (1963:206–213) were central to

No single individual has collected as much African music over such a vast territory as did Hugh Tracey.

Tracey's research, since fascination with the African songs and tales of southern Africa impelled him into musical research.

The methods of Cecil Sharp and his assistant, Maud Karpeles, provided Tracey with an intellectual model. Two eminent composers—Ralph Vaughan Williams and Gustav Holst, who appreciated the contribution that systematically collecting African music could give to the world of music—offered encouragement and advice, reassuring Tracey that his objectives were worthwhile. With the support of the Carnegie Corporation and the Nuffield Foundation, he embarked on research with the Shona of Zimbabwe—an experience that gave him the practical tools he needed to plan and execute the music-research scheme with which his name is associated.

Writing about his fieldwork and the materials he first published as the core of his African Music Research Transcription Library (which he hoped would be acquired by overseas libraries, archives, and broadcasters), he wrote that most

> records in this library have been recorded out in the country, in the villages of the various tribes. Others have been found in municipal locations, mines and industrial compounds, missions and schools. They have been recorded on the latest types of high quality machinery by our field recording unit. High fidelity recording equipment is essential owing to the special difficulties associated with reproducing percussion sounds such as those of the drums and xylophones, of which so large a proportion of African music is composed. No effort has been spared to make these records of African music as effective as any studio recordings elsewhere.
>
> The standard of performance, though outstanding and vital in most cases, reflects the general run of performances by common people. In a country of such vast distances and poor communication, it is not always possible to trace down those individuals who have the highest reputation for performance in any one type of music, though we have done so wherever we were able.
>
> At this stage in our research into African music, it is more important to record a wide cross-section of the music of the people in the knowledge that the stimulus given to the artists of the various tribes should itself produce still better performances in future. Bearing this in mind, we have included in the library a number of records which were sung and played by artists of the second rank, by old people, or by children. The material which they offered was of far greater significance than their own ability to perform satisfactorily.
>
> Students of African music have thus been given a range of recordings, wider than that which, in the normal run of record publications, would have seen the light of day. A few re-recordings from our own library taken privately many years ago, having special musical virtue, have also been included in spite of occasional background noises and minor technical faults, as we considered that the interest of the music itself was worthy of permanent reproduction for reference and study. (1960:6)

Despite textual infelicities, I have quoted this statement extensively because it gives a good picture of the goals Hugh Tracey set himself, and the kinds of decisions and compromises he had to make at the initial stages of his fieldwork, when, because the aesthetics of the music he recorded had not been investigated, he could not afford to be choosy.

No single individual has collected as much African music over such a vast territory as did Hugh Tracey. Though he produced a few significant works, such as a study of Chopi musicians (1948a), collections of song texts (1948b), descriptions of dances (1952a), and reports on the state of music in Bantu Africa (1929, 1948c, 1949, 1950, 1952b, 1954b, 1957, 1961), he seemed to have been more concerned with what ethnomusicologists regard as primary research, involving activities such as recording, collecting information or background notes on recordings, identifying the music makers (so they could receive credit, especially on broadcasts), observing and cataloguing instruments and the process of their manufacture, assessing their tuning, taking note of what African musicians sang about, how they dressed and danced—in short, with information that could be documented, catalogued, and published with perceptive commentaries. For as he pointed out,

> African music without a reference library must necessarily remain the toy of any prejudice which stalks the countryside and at the mercy of those varieties of cant which so frequently bedevil African studies. The first essential towards a proper classification, and therefore, a fuller understanding of the humanities behind the special form of music, is the continual collection of a representative selection of African composition by the most practical means at our disposal, phonograph recording. . . . The second essential is the spread of information through the publication of the results of all work on African music. (1954a:7)

In addition to recording music, Tracey's experiences convinced him that contributions in the form of factual data to an "uncharted field" like African music could be made by a wide range of Westerners visiting or residing in Africa—educators, social workers, missionaries, administrative officers, choreographers, musicians, linguists, and other scholars specializing in African studies. As far as he was concerned, contributions to the knowledge of African music (from whatever perspective) and reports on musical activities should be welcome. Unlike some of his Western colleagues, he was not committed to any particular school, theory, or method. Nor did he, like Alan Merriam, feel the need to make a clear-cut distinction between the musician as artist and the musician as scholar, for musicologists must constantly integrate objectivity and experience.

The African Music Society

With Winifred Hoernle, in 1947, to bring all fieldworkers and interested people together in the hope that their support of African music would lead to widespread recognition of the integrity of African music, and that their collective contributions would similarly lead to pan-African recognition of distinctive African musicality in education (Tracey 1966–1967a:5), Tracey founded the African Music Society.

As Tracey saw it, the research of members of the society would be development oriented. It would be their task to work toward the discovery, analysis, and "appraisement of the virtues of African music," or as he put it earlier, the discovery of "the disciplines and foundations of African artistry for future generations to build on" (1963:5).

To ensure the existence of a forum for news and articles of all sorts on African music, he in 1948 founded and edited a newsletter, replaced in 1955 by the annual

In 1966, Alan P. Merriam listed seventy-one companies and organizations involved in processing and distributing long-playing records "designed primarily, but not exclusively, for the non-African market."

journal *African Music.* What started as the African Music Transcription Library of Gramophone Records eventually became the International Library of African Music, with John Blacking its first resident musicologist.

Paradoxically, the list of the members of the African Music Society published in 1954 shows that the society was a network of people of Western heritages—musicians, scholars, administrators, governors, and European settlers in Africa, plus musicians, musicologists, folklorists, and anthropologists in Canada, Cuba, Europe, Mexico, and the United States. Only five of 211 members were Africans; more than 40 percent were southern Africans who had no ethnic affinity with African music.

To compensate for the imbalance in the membership of the society, Tracey tried to arouse general African enthusiasm and support for indigenous music. He encouraged the formation of African music clubs. He lectured wherever he could. He urged his African assistants and others to contribute to the newsletter and journal, instituted awards for African musicians, and sponsored the publication of a monograph on Yoruba music (Phillips 1953).

Other researchers and recordings

It was not only Hugh Tracey who gave priority to systematically recording, cataloguing, and publishing phonograph records of African music, or even studying African music as an object of aesthetic and educational interest. Intensive research and better awareness of the nature and scope of relevant background information led increasingly to the publication of the recordings of other field workers as sources of new musical experiences or musicological documents. For records, the visual accompaniment of notes or illustrated booklets became a tradition that some commercial record companies—like Folkways Corporation, which provided outlets for publishing selections from the recordings—pursued vigorously. French companies and organizations—like SORAFOM (Société de Radiodiffusion de la France d'Outre-Mer, founded in 1956), and its successor OCORA (Office de Coopération Radiophonique, established in 1962), operated along similar lines.

In an annotated discography, *African Music on LP* (completed in 1966, published in 1970), Merriam listed seventy-one companies and organizations involved in processing and distributing long-playing records "designed primarily, but not exclusively, for the non-African market." In Merriam's estimation, more than 1,050 such records were available, in addition to the wealth of unpublished tape recordings in private collections and archives—a situation that led Alan Lomax to describe Africa as "the best recorded of continents" (Lomax 1968:xvi).

Another important area that has engaged the attention of Western scholars and writers is the cataloguing and documentation of musical instruments and art objects used in dancing. Many museum collections in the Western world, contributed by colonial governments and private collectors, often include older specimens and greater variety in geographical coverage. Such collections have encouraged measurements of tunings (however faulty) and systematic classification and distribution studies, such as the early series published by the Tervuren Museum (Boone 1936, 1951; Laurenty 1960, 1962, 1968, 1974).

Theoretical perspectives

Since classified and catalogued reference materials are important for advancing knowledge, particularly in a field maintained largely by oral tradition, scholars attached to museums and research institutes took these basic activities seriously. In addition to providing factual information and accounts, Western scholars have been interested in analyzing, describing, and interpreting such data and the implications of these and aspects of their fieldwork for theory and methodology.

In the work of scholars of the comparative musicology era, the value of such materials was seen in relation to general problems of history and the evolution of music, especially the possibility that lacunae in the ancient history of music in general, and Western music in particular, could be filled by appropriate methods of historical reconstruction with materials from the non-Western world.

However, as a result of the expansion in fieldwork and increased sensitivity to the relationship between music and culture, plus the need for intensive synchronic studies, Western perspectives on African musicology have broadened since the late 1960s. The evolutionary approach of comparative musicologists, for whom Africa represented a stage in the supposedly linear evolution of music, has been supplanted by interest in the history of music in Africa itself. New approaches to the problem of the historicity of music in African cultures are being explored, for developments in African historiography have demonstrated that limited application of distributional and other criteria and the use of historical evidence from documentary and oral sources, plus the findings of other disciplines (such as archaeology and linguistics), can provide a basis for reconstructing the history of music in precolonial Africa.

Much of Wachsmann's work was devoted to the study of "history in the making." Documentary sources, and musical instruments as repositories of stylistic and historical data, engaged his attention. In 1962, interest in developing a historical perspective in African music led him to organize a symposium on music and history in Africa at the Royal Anthropological Institute, London (Wachsmann 1971). Similar responses to developments in African historiography can be seen in the works of other scholars, such as Alan Merriam, who concerned himself with methodological issues involved in historical reconstruction (1967), and A. M. Jones, whose work on Indonesia and Africa (1964) raised controversy because of the seeming randomness of some of its supporting data.

In addition to historical studies concentrating on the precolonial era, the study of acculturation in music (begun at Northwestern University because of the stimulus provided by Herskovits's work) has received attention since the 1980s. Research into music in urban centers, plus the new types of popular music flourishing in Africa, begun on a small scale in the 1950s (Rycroft 1958), is being undertaken by the younger generation of Western scholars, for the idea (once prevalent among musicologists) that only "authentic" forms of traditional African music are worth studying because they are "outside of Western civilization" is no longer widely supported.

Interest in history and the study of music in culture has not diminished the traditional Western preoccupation with the technical aspects of music. Transcriptions and analytical descriptions of songs, drumming, and the music of instruments such as flutes, harps, harp-lutes, lutes, mbiras, musical bows, and xylophones have been attempted, for "to know what African music is really like," one must proceed by taking the step that "will lead to the heart of it"—producing a body of transcriptions

If from musicological methodology and theory Western scholars eradicate the vestiges of Eurocentrism, they can make greater strides toward developing perspectives on African musicology that are truly Africa-centered.

that "would enable a student to understand the principles and techniques of African music," producing "reliable scores" for musicians to "see what African music is like" (Jones 1959). Jones set himself the goal of reducing "the intangible, evanescent counterplay of rhythms in African dance" to objective, stable, and visible forms"—goals pursued by scholars.

Though scholars now recognize the importance of such goals, they are giving more attention to the cultural analysis of African music than Jones could do in his laboratory in London, where he worked with a master drummer, acting as principal respondent. The integration of transcription, structural analysis, and cultural data can be more readily done by scholars who have observed and recorded music in the field, for they can find correlations between music and context, including details of performative techniques, voice leading in polyphonic styles, and the interrelations of music with movement and ritual (Blacking 1965, 1969; Knight 1984; Koetting 1984). Aware of the advantage of the field, Jones expressed the hope that other scholars would continue from where he left off (1959:9).

Scholars are also interested in the terms and concepts used by African peoples to refer to their music, musical instruments, categories of musicians, and social contexts of performance. Some scholars have provided comprehensive glossaries of such terms, or have used them in historical studies (Ames and King 1971; Hause 1949); others have drawn on them in inquiries into aesthetics and the formulation of the theoretical principles of African music, or have used them as part of a framework for analyzing and interpreting musical occasions and events (Kauffman 1969; Knight 1984; Stone 1982). Because of the insight that indigenous terms provide, scholars are more cautious in their use of Western terms and descriptive categories than they were in the 1960s.

The integration of objectivity and experience has also concerned some Western scholars, for the idea that ethnomusicologists focus on music as an object of analysis, and not with music as an art and a creative experience, is not wholly accepted by scholars with backgrounds in composition and performance. Many scholars are continuing their studies of African music from where the scholars of the comparative musicology era left off; these include Lois Anderson, Roderic Knight, Gerhard Kubik, David Locke, and Andrew Tracey, who base their transcriptions and interpretations of African music on their practical knowledge of the performative techniques of the instruments they deal with. Other scholars are trying to refine theory and the interpretation of African music on the basis of their experiences as students of performance in some African traditions, such as Shona mbira or Dagomba and Ewe drumming (Berliner 1978; Chernoff 1979); some of them want to share in African musical experiences, and to make performance not only a tool of research (as Percival Kirby suggested in the 1930s), but also a source of aesthetic experience.

In the 1980s, interest in the technical and humanistic aspects of music began to broaden the scope of organology in African musical studies. Scholars did not limit themselves to the superficial description of materials, design, and construction, or to descriptions based on existing systems of classification. They also explored instrumental technologies, tuning systems, playing techniques, histories, and related issues (Tse and Kimberlin 1984; Woodson 1984).

Eurocentrism

What seemed to have been lacking among Western ethnomusicologists with field research interest in Africa was not sensitivity to theoretical and methodological issues, for several Africanists—Blacking, Merriam, Wachsmann—made a significant impact on the theoretical orientations of ethnomusicology (Nketia and DjeDje 1984).

What was lacking was a sense of the importance of Africa for its own sake. With the best of intentions, musical researchers labored under assumptions that had remained as Eurocentric survivals, vestiges of the colonial era, in which scholarship was the exclusive concern of the West, while other peoples and cultures merely provided laboratories for research. If from musicological methodology and theory Western scholars eradicate the vestiges of Eurocentrism, they can make greater strides toward developing perspectives on African musicology that are truly Africa-centered.

When we take the writings of Alan Merriam, a scholar who—through assiduous compilations of bibliographies, discographies, book and record reviews, and papers on theoretical and ethnographic issues—did much for the study of African music, we find that because he took his role as interpreter seriously, he seemed nearly always to address himself exclusively to Western audiences, for he was preoccupied not only with breaking down Western myths, prejudices, and false notions surrounding African music (Merriam 1957), but also with the need for examining or testing the cross-cultural validity of what he describes as "Western conceptual terms," such as "products which Westerners define as art," or "the conceptualization which Westerners call aesthetics." His essays contain statements or observations using Western frames of reference. The number of collocations with the descriptive term *Western* and *Westerners* reflects the Eurocentrism of his approach to the exploration of conceptual fields. Here are some examples from his posthumous collection of essays on African music (1982): "Western observer" (64), "Western listener" (84), "Western functions of music" (68), "Western rhythmic assumptions" (79), "Western concepts" (80, 85), "Western terms" (113), "Western influence" (82), "Western standpoint" (95), "music as it is known in the *Western world*" (126), "connotations to Westerners" (126, 136).

While it cannot be denied that because, as Bruno Nettl puts it, "one is perhaps unable to absorb new information about a musical culture except by making implicit comparison to something already known" (1974), cognitive ethnocentrism has some positive values, excessive dependence on this or the "validation method" of comparison leads to a lopsided view of African musical cultures. A cross-cultural comparison of concepts held by different African societies would be illuminating and even more valuable for establishing African typologies or consensus than a comparison of the concepts of individual African societies, like that of the Basongye, with those of the West.

Merriam was not alone in holding this stance, for in the 1970s, providing information of all types about African music and musicians for Western readers, demonstrating the subtleties of this music to Western musicians, or devising notation that helps Western readers approach African music with little or no interference from the cognitive systems of their own musical culture and performative habits remained common preoccupations of scholars eager to share the African experience with those who have little or no knowledge of it, or with those who have difficulty relating to it. There will always be a place for informing the public, a place for cognitive ethnocen-

It seemed natural that the stance of most Western scholars and collectors—even those who resided in Africa—should mostly favor institutions, readers, and the public in their home countries.

trism as an approach to knowledge, and the reactive approach, which responds to Western assumptions and biases.

It seems to me, however, that such approaches belong to the era in which the primary concern of musicologists was with Europe in the wider world, the era in which the search for historical, conceptual, and formal linkages and differentiations were primary goals, or the era of Western assertiveness in which scholars (like Jones) felt it necessary to present their observations and theories through a series of arguments and demonstrations intended to forestall all possible objections that ethnocentric or skeptical readers might raise. In the search for African values, African musicology can afford to be more positive and objective, for there is greater openness to what insights Africa itself can offer than was the case before. One goes to the field, no longer as a master and teacher (as in the period of colonial development), but as a student, eager to learn from master musicians and other carriers of musical traditions. Current trends in African musicology pursued by Western scholars who recognize the integrity of other cultures are therefore reassuring, not only in data and reference materials, but also in the search for a framework of analysis and interpretations that would reflect African aesthetic and cultural values in music and related arts.

THE CHALLENGE OF SOCIOPOLITICAL CHANGE

Though the colonial environment facilitated fieldwork and the accumulation of data on African music, it did not encourage the reciprocity that we expect of scholars, for there was no question about the legitimacy of Western researchers' fieldwork, since the principle and practice of studying other people's cultures had long been recognized and established. Institutional support for such research was available overseas, while avenues for scholars' interaction were provided through journals and membership in scholarly organizations or educational enterprises. These provisions, which strengthened African musicology in the West, were lacking in Africa during the colonial period.

A similar picture emerges when we turn to collecting. Most collectors did not have qualms about recording and publishing samples of traditional African music for Western markets. Copyright in folklore enjoyed no legal protections; and because colonial dependencies were not nations, but aggregates of "tribes," the notion that the music of traditional societies in a given territory could constitute a national heritage had not come into prominence. Africa itself seemed to have no need for such recordings, and in any case it lacked the resources to record and document its own music. Companies that published recorded materials for African markets paid more attention to new forms—popular music!—which had wide support in contemporary societies, for traditional music was not commercially viable.

It seemed natural, therefore, that in the colonial period, the stance of most Western scholars and collectors—even those who resided in Africa—should mostly favor institutions, readers, and the public in their home countries. Until the situation in Africa itself changed, or a substantial body of African scholars and a readership for publications on African music emerged there, scholars and collectors felt no need for changing their focus. Consequently, the enthusiasm with which they reported on the musical scene in Africa, or the eagerness with which they built up private collections of recordings, or deposited their materials in archives (or gave them to commercial publishers) was not matched by a similar concern for audiences and institutions in the places where they had worked.

This situation was not peculiar to colonial Africa, for, as Alan Lomax observed, most scholars of the 1960s were working to publish books and articles that, "like a good deal of research, have often been of more benefit to the researchers than to the people whose lives they closely concerned" (1968:9). Except among teachers, missionaries, and musicologists committed to education and development in Africa, and particularly attached to the countries where they worked, what we now regard as a moral or ethical issue was not then held to be so.

The political changes that took place in the 1960s introduced new factors into African musicology. These factors called for a new reciprocity between Africa and the West. Whereas in the colonial period outsiders saw Africa as a place from which to extract data, the new situation required them and their successors to see themselves not just in terms of what they might take back to Europe and America, but also in terms of the value that such data might have for Africa itself, then in the process of rediscovering, reinventing, and reasserting its own cultural values.

As a consequence of these changes, the open-door policy of colonial governments was curtailed—an action felt by field workers who had previously had unlimited (and often virtually free) access to music and musical life in African societies. In a footnote to an editorial in *African Music*, Hugh Tracey referred to experiencing "considerable difficulty" in getting adequate amounts of publishable data, owing to what he described as "the increasingly disturbed political situation throughout the continent," which, in many territories, had hindered or blocked his work (1963:5).

Since the primary challenge of political independence was national development in all spheres of life, African musicology and its basic activities were to be seen as areas of particular significance to cultural development, able to benefit from international collaboration. To ensure that copies of materials such as tape recordings would be deposited or sent back to the country with any relevant publications, theses, or dissertations, governments set up regulations to enable specified official bodies to identify visiting researchers, and to encourage them to collaborate or keep in touch with appropriate local institutions.

While some scholars interpreted this move as merely a requirement of their professional ethics, others welcomed the opportunity of making a contribution, however small, to the African awareness of the African heritage. In addition to depositing materials, some scholars (like Gerhard Kubik) tried to share the outcome of their researches through lecture tours, while others accepted African governments' invitations to record and document their national musical cultures; these included Herbert Pepper (who worked on the national aural archives of Senegal), Simha Arom (who over an extended period worked in the Central African Republic), and Jim Rosellini (who set up the visual and aural archive of Upper Volta, now Burkina Faso).

Discographies

In addition to individuals' contributions, some institutional responses to the new political situation emerged in the capitals of former colonial powers, which began to see cultural development as an area for technical assistance.

Within Radio France Internationale, departments and national institutions of the French government established an office of electronic cooperation (Office de

Hugh Tracey directed his editorials not only to musicologists but also to urban Africans "on the brink of cultural genocide" because of their neglect of their indigenous music.

Coopération Radiophonique) and later a center of African documentation (Centre de Documentation Africaine) for compiling distributional discographies of traditional African music. In view of the role taken by new African music and pop music in urban musical life, one of the aims of the project was to contribute to the preservation and dissemination of traditional music.

Conceived as country profiles of traditional music and dance, the discographies provided not only a catalogue of recordings, but also information on the state of musicological research and documentation in each country. Accordingly, the plan for the volumes included introductory essays on historical backgrounds, institutions concerned with music and music research, bibliographies of music and dance, relevant ethnographic works, catalogues of musical instruments, filmography, expositions on selected topics of musicological interest, lists of ethnic groups and performers, and the subject matter of the recordings. Profiles for all Francophone countries were projected. The first two, devoted to Mali and Upper Volta, came out in 1978. By 1982, nine of them had been compiled and published. The discographies incorporate those of Merriam, Tracey, and locally available sources.

Though in the 1960s the idea of preparing discographies of what had already been accumulated seemed all right as an immediate step, the pace of change suggested a different strategy to Hugh Tracey, whose field collecting made him more forward looking than backward looking, for he was more concerned with what had not been recorded (and might be lost forever) than with what had already been recorded and documented. In his view, what Africa needed was not reciprocity on the part of Western scholars and collectors, but their direct involvement in local research and education:

> One criterion which must certainly predominate, and not only in music, is that of relevance to Africa. Without this, non-African research in Africa will have to be seen as mere collecting, not giving.
>
> Of all the books and articles written about African music, one wonders how many are of use, or *in* use, in Africa. (1972:5)

Relevance, in Tracey's terms, thus meant writing texts designed for African audiences, texts that could be used in African schools and colleges, texts like his *Ngoma*, Graham Hyslop's *Since Singing Is So Good*, and Cootje van Oven's work on the music of Sierra Leone, designed as a sourcebook for teachers (Tracey 1948b; Hyslop 1964; Oven 1981). While music educators resident in Africa naturally respond to the needs of Africa, one cannot expect every scholar to be a textbook writer, or even to address pedagogic issues. The primary task of African musicology is to provide musical knowledge (Nketia 1970a).

Tracey believed, however, that for contributions to knowledge of African music to be relevant, a change of theoretical stance was required. He believed that what he and his collaborators were doing was what African musicology needed:

> The expounding of the theory of African musical techniques to non-Africans will continue to have an exotic and intellectual virtue, as well the teaching of non-African music to Africans. The heart and soul of the matter on this continent is more direct. It is to find a body of articulate men and women . . . who will undertake the discipline of actual performance and have the ability to convey their knowledge to Africans in terms related to African instruments, modality and circumstances. (1966–1967a:5)

The use of performance as a tool of research was nothing new in African musicology or ethnomusicology. Its rationale, long defended by Kirby, was accepted by Hood and explored by his students.

Tracey directed his editorials not only to musicologists (with whom he disagreed on goals and emphasis), and to scholars pursuing the study of African music "as a means of acquiring merit in the intellectual world of the universities" (as he put it), but also to urban Africans "on the brink of cultural genocide" because of their neglect of their indigenous music.

The Codification and Textbook Project

To remedy this situation, Tracey in the late 1960s proposed a plan, the Codification and Textbook Project. Covering all of sub-Saharan Africa, it would

- establish "accepted and local terms suited to African phenomena";
- confirm that "the many forms of African music scattered throughout the continent are integral parts of a distinctive culture of historic validity";
- bring "deep satisfaction to African musicians of the future in having their own poetry and musics culturally recognized for their intrinsic merit as never before";
- demonstrate that the study of African music is "far from being a study of obsolete phenomena," establishing "the virtue of continuity of their artistry—a prime consideration for all civilized persons"; and
- help Africans realize "their personality through their music, so that they may be a more fulfilled people." (Tracey, Kubik, and Tracey 1969; see also Tracey 1966, 1966–1967b)

To achieve these results, the goals of the project would be "to discover the practical basis of the music of this continent, and expound it in terms of its usefulness and comprehensibility in Africa." This Tracey planned to achieve by compiling a so-called tome, containing in several volumes "classified information on all aspects of African music," and then by producing a textbook, "of authoritative statements on the pattern of ideas behind indigenous styles of music" to bring "the subject naturally into the realm of African education" (Tracey, Kubik, and Tracey 1969:6).

The plan would cover a period of ten years. In the first five years, teams in each country would collect data, aiming to get one recorded item per 10,000 people; in the second five years, experts would analyze the collected materials, prepare samples for the tome, and write the textbook. The International Library of African Music, based in South Africa, directed by Tracey himself, would be the principal coordinating body, the central depository for all the recordings, responsible for publishing the tome and the textbook.

The period 1920–1950 was when African awareness of the need for studying and interpreting the African heritage of music began.

An extension of Tracey's mode of operation and his concept of fieldwork and musicological investigation, this plan raised conceptual and methodological problems for some ethnomusicologists, to whom the separation of fieldwork and writing, and the lack of a conceptual framework for the collection of data, seemed anachronistic. So was the idea, once popular in folk-musical research, that one could do satisfactory fieldwork by reading a pamphlet, "Practical Suggestions for Field Research."

Similarly, educators had problems with the idea of textbooks that would be written in a vacuum by experts browsing over data, while others were skeptical about resuscitating the colonial idea of books for Africa written by foreigners—for even though the stated intention was to involve qualified Africans in the project, many African countries clearly did not have scholars who could participate fully in it. To plan a textbook for independent Africa in the hope of enlisting the collaboration of graduate students from overseas universities did not seem like a progressive step to take at that time. The project was paternalistic and premature. It did not materialize.

An alternative to the project seemed to be

- to intensify the documentation of existing materials, in both public and private collections, and to make them accessible to all scholars;
- to train African musicians and scholars to undertake the writing of textbooks and other materials, taking into account their national needs, values, and aspirations; and
- to foster interaction and collaboration among African-oriented scholars.

Dialogue with African musicians and scholars

Another problem that surfaced in the 1960s was the gap (created by inadequate interaction and dialogue) that had developed from the colonial period between Western musicians and scholars and their African colleagues, and the failure of many Western scholars to recognize that Africans' roles in scholarly research and national development were changing.

The period 1920–1950 was also when African awareness of the need for studying and interpreting the African heritage of music began. Because of the politics of colonialism, no interaction occurred across the continent—between the pioneers in West Africa and the resident musicologists in South Africa, Uganda, and Zambia. Such was the state of affairs in 1953, that Tracey, reporting on folk music in Bantu Africa, could say to the conference of the International Folk Music Council at Biarritz that

it is only because we have found that the African is pathetically incapable of defending his own culture and indeed is largely indifferent to its fate that we, who subscribe wholeheartedly to the ideals of our International Council, are attempting to tide over the period during which irreparable damage can be done and until

Africans themselves will be capable of appearing at our conferences as well-informed representatives of their own people. (Tracey 1954b)

Yet twenty-seven years earlier, George Ballanta had represented Africa at the conference of the International Missionary Council in Belgium, where he had lectured on African music. The secretary of the conference acknowledged that Ballanta had made "a name for himself by his researches in African music" (Smith 1926:26).

The apparent lack of interaction continued in the 1950s, for the initial stimulus for academic research in music came from the academic environment of African universities, not from programs in ethnomusicology in the United States.

It was during the 1960s that African musicology in Africa and abroad began to converge—a process that continued in the 1970s, as more Africans received musical training, and as travel grants enabled the older generation of African scholars to keep in touch with international scholarship in music, and more especially with the work of Africanists—a development that Wachsmann welcomed because "the gap between Western musicology and music in Africa seemed about to be bridged in many places." He found it "fascinating to watch the change in the African role come about, to see history being made," for

> until not so long ago, African performers and listeners alike were cast into a passive role: they were "objects" on which Western attention and curiosity could focus. Now their role is active. One expects them to make clear and confident statements and to be thoughtful participants and initiators in everything that touches on the arts in their culture. (1966b:62)

The change of role described by Wachsmann was viewed with ambivalence by some Western ethnomusicologists, including leaders in the field. Writing in the mid-1960s, when African participation in musicology was becoming evident, Bruno Nettl observed that the consensus among ethnomusicologists was that

> ethnomusicology is, in fact as well as in theory, the field which pursues knowledge of the world's music with the emphasis on the music outside the researcher's own culture, from a descriptive and comparative viewpoint. (1966:11)

In other words, African musicology pursued by Africans could not properly be considered ethnomusicology, but the study of this music by an outsider (such as Merriam) would qualify as ethnomusicology because the field of research would be "outside the researcher's own culture." According to Nettl, the justification for this emphasis on "other" cultures was that "only in studying a culture foreign to himself can a scholar muster sufficient objectivity"—an assumption that invalidated not only the work of Western scholars who studied music in their own environment, but also the work of their colleagues who studied Western society and culture. Nettl believed, nevertheless, that "many would surely deny that studying one's own musical culture is ethnomusicology at all" (Nettl 1966:70).

Writing earlier, Merriam had similarly described the ethnomusicologist as

> the outsider who seeks to understand what he hears though analysis of structure and behavior, and to reduce understanding to terms which will allow him to compare and generalize his results for music as a universal phenomenon of man's existence. (1964:25)

This preoccupation with the outsider seemed to make what Nettl described as "the emergence of many scholars from the non-European societies whose main aim is the

What is significant about African scholarship is not what it obviously owes to the West, but what it is able to give back in knowledge and insight as it is shaped by the environments in which it operates.

study of their own cultures" something of a problem, for "this inevitably puts 'the field' into a different perspective." However, since studies of Japanese and African music had "become perfectly acceptable to Western musicologists," he referred to the study of one's own musical culture as "this newest branch of ethnomusicology," even though European scholars had long been studying the folk music of Europe.

Though insiders' participation in a scholarly field hitherto regarded as the preserve of outsiders seemed to have caused immediate concern, it did not take long for this to be resolved by legitimizing fieldwork undertaken in the Western environment by Western scholars, for as Nettl again pointed out, current ethnomusicology was not the study of non-Western music, but "the study of music in culture" (1982). What makes a study ethnomusicological was no longer the geographical location of the fieldwork, or who did it (insider or outsider), but the scholarly approaches used.

Scholarly competence

Another issue of concern to Western scholars was scholarly competence, for the works of non-Western scholars had to be "perfectly acceptable to Western musicologists." In the 1950s, when three monographs written by African musicians came out, Merriam observed that they were worthy of attention because "they are works by Africans speaking of African artistic traditions," and "such writing has indeed been rare in the past" (1956:290). However, unhappy with scholarly pitfalls in two of the books, he warned that "scholarly standards have been established in the Western world, and whether we like it or not, African writers are going to be judged by those standards when they venture into a scholarly field."

Speaking in a different context to an African audience, John Blacking reminded those present of the importance of scholarly standards and the need for acquiring the discipline of a field of study—requirements that one expects to find in both Western and African musicians who venture into the field of musicology. He observed that

> though by virtue of birth in a particular culture a person has certain essential qualifications to understand its music, it by no means follows that these qualifications are sufficient. For example, only a fraction of the thousands of Europeans who have disseminated European music in Africa are able to write down the sounds they hear without recourse to a piano, and still fewer have understood the first thing about the structure and cultural origins of the music that they have taught, though all of them have had the advantage of being reared in European cultures.
>
> Similarly, though Africans may best be able to appreciate the immediate social meaning of their music, it by no means follows that they are able to write about it with authority unless they adhere to certain standards of scholarship which apply to musicological research anywhere in the world. (1966:39)

In addition to the issue of scholarly competence, uncertainty lingered about how the contributions made by non-Western scholars might differ from those made by

Western scholars. At least two panel discussions on this issue were held at conferences of the Society for Ethnomusicology. Panelists tended to assume that some scholars invariably approached the music of their own cultures with the same assumptions as those held by their Western colleagues. While their Western colleagues could be original and imaginative, for example in their invention or use of notation, African scholars seemed to "have had a long conditioning to the usage of Western notation," to the point of not readily endorsing suggestions for other systems, like cipher notation (Hood 1971:100).

It was perhaps the thought of such conditioning that led Merriam to say Westerners and Western-trained Africans formed a single category (1982). I believe, however, there is some truth in Jean-Paul Sartre's assertion:

> A man can always make something of what is made of him. This is the limit I would today accord to freedom: the small movement which makes of a totally conditioned social being someone who does not render back completely what his conditioning has given him. (1970:22)

What is significant about African scholarship is not what it obviously owes to the West, but what it is able to give back in knowledge and insight as it is shaped by the environments in which it operates.

It was precisely this concern that drew those who were not part of Nettl's consensus to African writings so they could find out what Africans might have to offer when they became interested in knowledge about themselves and their cultures in response to their own consciousness of identity and awareness of their relationship to the wider world, for as Wachsmann pointed out,

> though one may not exchange one's own musical condition for that of an African colleague's simply by adopting his fashions, the dialogue with him adds new dimensions, new insight to one's own musical equipment, and this relationship works both ways. (1970:128–151)

Wachsmann's response to African scholarship encouraged Western initiatives in setting up a forum for positive dialogue.

Dialogue between African and Western scholars of African music

Of the events that resulted from this dialogue, two deserve mention. The first is the organization of summer sessions of lectures, seminars, and workshops in African music in an African university for American students, scholars, and educators who made a special trip to study with African professors, instrumental teachers, and dancers (Pantaleoni 1968:68). In the years that followed, the enrollment of Western students in the regular course of that university, or as associate students, became routine. African music could now be studied not only in Europe and America (as before), but also in Africa itself. In the spirit of scholarly interaction, the acceptance of visiting professorships or lecture engagements in Africa by Western scholars provided further opportunities for dialogue.

The second event was the hosting of the sixteenth annual conference of the International Folk Music Council in Ghana in 1966—an event that signified not only Africa's readiness to participate in international scholarship in music, but also the wider world's recognition of the need for changes in orientation that would broaden the international dimension of musicology and facilitate intercultural dialogue and communication. It was the first time the International Folk Music Council had met outside Europe and the United States.

Collaboration now extends beyond field situations and conferences to projects involving research, preparing texts, cataloguing materials (including instruments), and writing.

What these events (and others) suggested was that African musicology of the future would continue to draw its stimulus from ethnomusicology, folklore, and cognate disciplines, and that the primary activities of folk musical research would be an integral part of African musicology. The recording, documenting, classifying, cataloguing, preserving, and promoting of traditional music would receive as much attention as investigations into theoretical issues raised by the music and its sociocultural context. It is indeed this prospect that has encouraged African governments and cultural institutions to support African musicology as one of the fields of study that can contribute to cultural development in contemporary Africa.

Much more scholarly interaction between Africa and the West has taken place since the events of the 1960s. The participation of ethnomusicologists from the non-Western world is no longer a subject of debate, for the change in stance resulting from this has contributed to some extent to the search for "emic" values. As Maurice Freedman pointed out,

> there has been a tendency partly to disengage the study of non-European music from the framework established within Western musicology . . . [and] one stimulus for this development has been the emergence of a body of scholars within the "new" nations who, in studying their own music by the basic methods devised within the Western tradition, yet bring to their work a view from the inside. (1978:60)

As a result of this change in orientation, some scholars now plan their fieldwork in consultation with local institutions so they can participate in their overall research or teach while doing fieldwork. Many African institutions, being bimusical, benefit from the input of ethnomusicologically trained musicians sensitive to situational issues in the way some African musicians act as resources, or teach, or perform in the West while acquiring the conceptual tools and discipline they need for their own work.

Collaboration now extends beyond field situations and conferences to projects involving research, preparing texts, cataloguing materials (including instruments), and writing. To establish African musicology formally as an area of specialization and scholarly collaboration, much remains to be done, but these trends suggest that a basis for this development already exists.

CHALLENGES FOR THE FUTURE

The growth of a scholarly discipline depends not only on the quality and scope of the materials it deals with, but also on the extent to which its theories and methods are progressively refined in the light of new data, solutions to problems, and advances in knowledge contributed by cognate disciplines. These often go hand in hand with institutional support for research and related programs, an increase in the number and quality of scholars, and the conceptual cross-fertilization that results from scholars' interaction.

The history of African musicology outlined in this review is a history of growth that has taken place since the 1920s almost simultaneously within and outside Africa, and which needs to be consolidated and expanded and, in certain respects, reoriented to enhance its further development as a field of international scholarship and cooperation. Many aspects of this history are complementary, for on the African side it is largely a history of growth in the number of scholars, in institutional development, and response to the pressures and challenges of the African environment and Western praxis, while on the Western side it is largely a history of expansion in documentation, changing perspectives, and differentiation in fields of focus relative to individual interests and backgrounds.

In retrospect the decade 1960–1970 seems to have been the most exciting period of all for music and musicology in Africa, for the events of the decade established a bond between the study of music as an art (approached from the viewpoint of its theory and practice) and music as a scholarly discipline and a focus of research. Because of this, the history of musicology in Africa is bound up with the institutional development for the study of the theory and practice of music, while the history of music, and musicology are an integral part of the intellectual and cultural history of postcolonial Africa.

Because of the importance Africans attach to cultural studies and cultural development, African musicology will probably continue to receive support from future generations of African musicians. The music of many societies remains to be studied in depth, but from national and pan-African festivals, the work of African radio organizations, ministries of culture, and university institutions, accumulations of recorded data continue to grow. There will be room for both individual initiative and teamwork through which typologies of musical usages and features can be established, both for specific areas and subregions, and for the geocultural region as a whole.

A problem that musicology in Africa may have to face may not be just its lack of trained personnel, but also the lack of a reasonable balance between practical and scholarly goals, between the immediate requirements of cultural development programs and issues that may have no immediate application. More time and energy may be spent in recording music and collecting information for specific projects than in analyzing and writing up such materials, especially when the initial pressure of a dissertation or some other external pressure is out of the way. Alternatively, pressure from academic colleagues may lead an aspiring scholar away from the priorities of development to speculations on philosophy and aesthetics, or on theories of communication.

When scholars only look inward (and not outward), they run the risk of insularity inherent in regional specialization. Though African scholars have tried to minimize this risk by seeking formal links with international scholarship, it is important that this shows up also in the perspectives they bring, not only to African musicology, but also to musicology in general, for it is only when they deal with the implications of their findings for specific issues in musicology, or for the understanding of music as a cultural phenomenon and a worldwide art, that they can play an active role in the development of the discipline as a whole.

Narrowing the gap between communities

It is essential that what Wachsmann described as "the gap" between African scholars and their Western colleagues—a gap created by attitudes inherited from the colonial past, and by narrow definitions of ethnomusicology by scholars who still regard it as "a purely Western phenomenon" (Nettl 1983:9)—continue to be bridged though

The need for collaboration between African scholars and their Western colleagues cannot be overemphasized.

dialogue and collaboration, for the comparison of the topics covered by African writers and musicians since the late 1960s shows that concern for new approaches to history, acculturation, the study of new music, transcription, analysis, song texts, and terms used in African languages for musical instruments and performance, organology, and other areas of musicological investigation has become common in African musicology. The need for collaboration between African scholars and their Western colleagues cannot therefore be overemphasized, for African scholars and their Western colleagues may be studying the same musical cultures, observing the same events, and using the same teachers and respondents, though they may not always be asking the same questions or seeking solutions to the same problems.

For the same reason, African musicology of the future must take full cognizance of the outcome of the investigations of scholars (especially in the Caribbean and Latin America) who deal with African and Africa-related materials, and vice versa. A few scholars specializing in musicology in Africa, such as Kazadi wa Mukuna and Gerhard Kubik, have carried their investigations farther into Latin America, just as some Latin Americans interested in African rituals have extended their investigations to relevant parts of Africa.

As far as Western praxis goes, the issues in African musicology, being both theoretical and practical, call for contributions to both areas. The disciplinary affiliations of scholars and their musical sensitivity, plus the nature of the African musical materials and the changing African scene, will always raise theoretical issues or problems of methodology and interpretation. It is important that African musicology in the West continue to respond to these, though they may not always be of immediate relevance to the practical issues of cultural development, or to the problems of meaning encountered by Africans in the contexts of music making.

Always critical of its own methods, Western musicology persists in approaching, in the light of new ideas, the ever-widening vision of humanity and the proper place of the West in the postcolonial world community. This mechanism will continue to shape African musicology in the West, as scholars become aware of the international dimension of their discipline. Ideas emanating from responses to the Western environment of African musicology may not only provoke discussion by Africans, but also stimulate ideas that may enhance the quest for an African-centered approach to African musicology, "the search after wholeness of vision" that Wachsmann (1970) believed characterized African musicology after the 1960s.

The practicality of music demands that Western scholars not lose sight of the implication of their study for other musicians, and for those interested in the cultural dimensions of music, for as Richard Schlatter points out (1965), humanist scholars not only analyze and describe, but reassess, reintegrate, rediscover, and make available "the materials and the blueprints" with which their "contemporaries can build their own culture." Until the 1960s, "contemporaries" meant those in the Western world, but by the late twentieth century, Western musicians and scholars specializing in

African musicology had learned that they faced a dual obligation—to Africa, and to the West. A matching obligation equally guided African scholars, for their discipline requires that they also deal with Africa in the context of a wider world.

REFERENCES

Achiniyu, Achiniyu Kanu. 1979. *Ikoli Harcourt Whyte: The Man and His Music, A Case of Musical Acculturation in Nigeria.* Hamburg: Karl Dieter Wagner.

Adali-Mortty, Geormbeeye. 1958. "Ewe Poetry." *Black Orpheus* 4:36–45.

Adande, Alexandre. 1952. "L'evolution de la musique africaine." *Notes Africaines* (IFAN) 54:39–44.

Adande, Alexandre, and Pierre Verger. 1953. "Tam-tam avohu." *Notes Africaines* (IFAN) 59:72–76.

Addo, E. R. 1932, 1933, 1934. "Native Drumming." *Gold Coast Teachers' Journal* 4(2):49, 4(3):131, 5(1):39.

Adetoyese, Oba, *timi* of Ede. 1966. "Music of Western Nigeria: Origin and Use." *Composer* 19:34–41.

Akpabot, Samuel. 1966. "Organization of the African Orchestra." *Journal of the New African Literature* 1:74–76.

———. 1972. "Theories on African Rhythm." *African Arts* (Los Angeles) 6(1):59–62, 88.

———. 1976. "Fugitive Notes on Notation and Terminology in African Music." *The Black Perspective on Music* 4(1):39–45.

———. 1978. "Traditional African Music Elements in Twentieth-Century European Music." *Royal College of Music Magazine* (London) 74(1):33–38.

Alagoa, E. J. 1968. "Songs as Historical Data: Examples from the Niger Delta." *Research Review* (Legon) 1.

Alájá-Browne, Afọlábi. 1981. "Ayo Bankole." M.A. thesis, University of Pittsburgh.

———. 1985. "Jùjú Music: A Study of Its Style and Social History." Ph.D. dissertation, University of Pittsburgh.

Ames, David, and Anthony King. 1971. *Glossary of Hausa Music and its Social Context.* Evanston, Ill.: Northwestern University Press.

Amu, Ephraim. 1933. *Twenty-Five African Songs.* London: Sheldon Press.

Aning, Ben Akosa. 1965. "Adenkum: A Study of Akan Female Bands." Thesis for diploma in African music, University of Ghana.

———. 1967. *An Annotated Bibliography of Music and Dance in English-Speaking Africa.* Legon: Institute of African Studies.

———. 1968. "Factors That Shape and Maintain Folk Music in Ghana." *Journal of the International Folk Music Council* 20:13–17.

———. 1982. "Tuning the Kora: A Case Study of the Norms of a Gambian Musician." *Journal of African Studies* 9(3):164–175.

Anyumba, Henry Owuor. 1970. "The Making of a Lyre Musician." *MILA: Biannual Newsletter of Cultural Research* 1–2:28–30.

Arom, Simha. 1976. "Situation de la musique dans quelques pays d'Afrique Centrale et Occidentale." *Acta Musicologica* 48(1):2–4.

Azu, Enoch. 1949. *Adangme Historical and Proverbial Songs.* Accra: Government Printer.

Babalola, S. A. 1966. *The Content and Form of Yoruba Ijala.* Oxford: Clarendon Press.

Ballanta, Nicholas George Julius. 1926. "Gathering Folk Tunes in the African Country." *Musical America* 44(23): 3–11.

———. 1931–1932 [1930]. "Music of the African Races." *Negro Year Book* 1931–1932:441–444.

Bansisa, Y. 1936. "Music in Africa." *Uganda Journal* 4:108–114.

Bebey, Francis. 1969. *Musique de l'Afrique.* Paris: Horizon de France.

Berliner, Paul. 1978. *The Soul of Mbira.* Berkeley: University of California Press.

Blacking, John. 1963. "The Role of Music in the Culture of the Venda of the Northern Transvaal." In *Studies in Ethnomusicology*, ed. Mieczyslaw Kolinski, vol. 2, 20–53. New York: Oak Publications.

———. 1966. "Studying and Developing Music in East Africa." In *East Africa's Cultural Heritage*, 37–44. Nairobi: East African Institute of Social and Cultural Affairs.

———. 1969. "Songs, Dances, Mimes and Symbolism of Venda Girls Initiation School." *African Studies* 26(1):1–35, (3):149–199, (4):215–166.

Blyden, Edward Wylmot. 1882. *The Aims and Methods of a Liberal Education for Africans.* Inaugural address, 5 January 1881. Cambridge, Mass.: G. Young.

Boone, Olga. 1936. *Les Xylophones du Congo Belge.* Tervuren: Musée Royale de l'Afrique Centrale.

———. 1951. *Les Tambours du Congo Belge et Ruanda-Urundi.* Tervuren: Musée Royale du Congo Belge.

Brandel, Rose. 1961. *The Music of Central Africa.* The Hague: Martinus Nijhoff.

Caluza, Ruben Tolakele. 1931. "African Music." *Southern Workman* 60: 152–155.

Carrol, K. 1956. "Yoruba Religious Music." *African Music* 1(3):45–47.

Chernoff, John Miller. 1979. *African Rhythm and African Sensibility: Aesthetics and Social Action in African Musical Idioms.* Chicago: University of Chicago Press.

Cudjoe, Seth. 1953. "The Techniques of Ewe Drumming and the Social Importance of Music in Africa." *Phylon* 3:280–291.

———. 1958. "The Notation of Drum Music." *Music in Ghana* 1(1):70–80.

Cuney-Hare, Maud. 1936. *Negro Musicians and Their Music.* Washington, D.C.: Associated Publishers.

da Cruz, Clement. 1954. *Les Instruments de musique du Bas Dahomey: Populations Fon, Adja, Kotafon, Peda, Aizo.* Porto Noveo: Études Dahoméenes.

Djan, Oheneba Sakyi. 1942. "Drums and Victory: African Call to the Empire." *Journal of the Royal Asiatic Society* 41.

Echezona, William Wilberforce Chukudina. 1963. "Ibo Musical Instruments in Ibo Culture." Ph.D. dissertation, Michigan State University.

———. 1965. "Igbo Music." *Nigeria Magazine* 85:45–52.

———. 1966. "Compositional Technique of Nigerian Music." *Composer* 19:41–49.

Ekwueme, Lazarus. 1972. "Ibo Choral Music: Its Theory and Practice." Ph.D. dissertation, Yale University.

———. 1975–1976. "Structural Levels of Rhythm and Form in African Music with Particular Reference to the West Coast." *African Music* 5(4):105–129.

Eno Belinga, Samuel-Martin. 1965. *Literature et musique populaire en Afrique Noire.* Paris: Editions Cujas.

———. 1967. "'Oka' Angana', Un Genre musical et littéraire pratiqué par les femmes Bulu; Sud Cameroun." *La Musique dans la vie* 1:105–132.

———. 1969. "Musique traditionelle et musique moderne au Cameroun." *Bulletin of the International Committee on Urgent Anthropological and Ethnological Research* (Vienna) 11:83–90.

Etherton, Michael. 1982. *The Development of African Drama.* London: Hutchinson University Library for Africa.

Euba, Akin. 1960. "Nigerian Music." *Nigeria: A Special Independence Issue of Nigeria Magazine* 119–125.

———. 1967. "Multiple Pitch Lines in Yoruba Choral Music." *Journal of the International Folk Music Council* 19:66–71.

———. 1970. "New Idioms of Music Drama Among the Yoruba: An Introductory Study." *Yearbook of the International Folk Music Council* 11:92–110.

Fiagbedzi, Nissio. 1980a. "Observation on the Study of African Musical Cultures." *Journal of the Performing Arts* (Legon) 1(1):1-27.

———. 1980b. "On Signing and Symbolism in Music: The Evidence from among an African People." *Journal of the Performing Arts* (Legon) 1(1):54–65.

Firth, John R. *1951. Papers in Linguistics 1935–51.* London and New York: Oxford University Press.

Freedman, Maurice. 1978. *Main Trends in Social and Cultural Anthropology.* New York and London: Holmes and Meier.

Gadzekpo, Ben S. 1952. "Making Music in Eweland." *West African Review* 23(299):17– 19.

———. 1954. *Some Hints on the Production of Vernacular Broadcast Programmes.* Accra: Government Printer.

Gaskin, Lionel John Palmer. 1965. *Select Bibliography of African Music.* London: International African Institute.

Gbeho, Phillip. 1952. "The Indigenous Gold Coast Music." *African Music Society Newsletter* 1(5):30–33.

———. 1954. "Music of the Gold Coast." *African Music* 1(1):62–64.

Gold Coast Teachers' Journal. 1933. Advertisement, p. 320.

Hause, Helen. 1949. "Terms for Musical Instruments in the Sudanic Languages: A Lexicographical Enquiry." *Journal of the American Oriental Society,* supplement 7.

Hood, Mantle. 1971. *The Ethnomusicologist.* New York: McGraw-Hill.

Hornbostel, Erich M. von. 1928. "African Negro Music." *Africa* 1(1):30–62. Reprinted as *Memorandum IV.* Oxford: Oxford University Press for International African Institute.

———. 1933. "The Ethnology of African Sound Instruments." *Africa* 6:129–154, 277– 311.

Hyslop, Graham. 1964. *Since Singing Is So Good a Thing.* London: Oxford University Press.

Ismail, Mahi. 1970. "Musical Traditions of Sudan." In *African Music,* 17–25. Paris: La Revue Musicale.

Jones, Arthur M. 1959. *Studies in African Music.* London: Oxford University Press.

———. 1964. *Africa and Indonesia: The Evidence of the Xylophone and Other Musical and Cultural Factors.* Leiden: E. J. Brill.

———. 1976. *African Hymnody in Christian Worship.* Gwela, Rhodesia: Mambo Press.

Kagame, Alexis. 1951. *La Poésie dynastique au Rwanda.* Brussels: no publisher.

Kaggwa, Sir Apolo. 1934. *The Customs of the Baganda.* New York: Columbia University Press.

Kakoma, George. 1970. "Musical Traditions of East Africa." In *African Music,* 77–88. Paris: La Revue Musicale.

Kauffman, Robert. 1969. "Some Aspects of Aesthetics in Shona Music of Rhodesia." *Ethnomusicology* 13(3):507–511.

Kebede, Ashenafi. 1968. "The Krar." *Ethiopian Observer* (Addis Ababa). 11(3):154–161

———. 1969. "La Musique sacrée de l'Église orthodoxe de l'Ethiopie." In *Ethiopie: Musique de l'église Copte.* Berlin: International Institute for Comparative Music Studies and Documentation.

Keita, Foedeba. 1959. "The True Meaning of African Dances." *Courier* (UNESCO):18– 23.

Kintu, Y. Q. 1940. "Kisoga Music." *Uganda Teachers' Journal* 2(2). With notes by Klaus P. Wachsmann.

Knight, Roderic. 1984. "The Style of Mandinka Music: A Study in Extracting Theory from Practice." In S*elected Reports in Ethnomusicology V. Studies in African Music* (University of California at Los Angeles), 3–66.

Koetting, James. 1984. "Hocket Concept and Structure in Kasena Flute Ensemble Music." In *Selected Reports in Ethnomusicology V. Studies in African Music* (University of California at Los Angeles), 161– 172.

Kygambiddwa, Joseph. 1955. *African Music from the Source of the Nile.* London: Atlantik Press.

Laoye I, *timi* of Ede. 1954. "Yoruba Drums." *Nigeria Magazine* 45:4–13.

———. 1959. "Yoruba Drums." *Odu, Journal of Yoruba and Related Studies* 7:5–14.

Laurenty, Jean Sébastien. 1960. *Les Cordophones du Congo Belge et du Ruanda-Urundi.* Tervuren: Musée Royale de l'Afrique Centrale.

———. 1962. *Les Sanza du Congo Belge.* Tervuren: Musée Royale de l'Afrique Centrale.

———. 1968. *Les Tambours à fente de l'Afrique Centrale.* Tervuren: Musée Royale de l'Afrique Centrale.

———. 1974. *La Systematique des aerophones de l'Afrique Centrale.* Tervuren: Musée Royale de l'Afrique Centrale.

Lomax, Alan. 1968. *Folk Song Style and Culture.* Washington D.C.: American Association for the Advancement of Science. Publication 88.

Madumere, Adele. 1953. "Ibo Village Music." *Nigeria Magazine* Special Number:193– 210.

Mapoma, Isaiah Mwesa. 1970–1971. "The Use of Folk Music Among Some Bemba Church Congregations in Zambia." *Yearbook of the International Folk Music Council* 1:72– 88.

———. 1980. "The Determinants of Style in the Music of the Ingomba." Ph.D. dissertation, University of California at Los Angeles.

Maraire, Abraham. 1967. "Techniques of Drumming." *All-Africa Church Music Association Journal* 4:4–6.

Margai, Milton A. S. 1926. "Music in the Protectorate of Sierra Leone." *Magazine of the West African Student Union* 4.

Mensah, Atta Annan. 1958a. "Professionalism in the Musical Practice of Ghana." *Music in Ghana* 1(1): 28–35.

———. 1958b. "Some Problems Involved in the Arrangement of Folk Music for Radio Ghana." *Journal of the International Folk Music Council* 11:83–84.

———. 1960. "The Akan Church Lyric." *International Review of Missions* 49(194):183–188.

———. 1966a. "The Gomoa Otsew Trumpet Set." *Research Review* (Legon, Accra) 3:82– 85.

———. 1966b. "Musicality and Musicianship in Northwestern Ghana." *Research Review* (Legon, Accra) 2(1):42–56.

———. 1967a. "Further Notes on Ghana's Xylophone Tradition." *Research Review* (Legon, Accra) 3:62–65.

———. 1967b. "The Polyphony of Gyil-gu; Kudzo and Awutu Sakumo." *Journal of the International Folk Music Council* 19:79–88.

———. 1971. "Ndebele-Soli Bi-musicality in Zambia." *Yearbook of the International Folk Music Council,* 108–210.

"Mephisto's Musings." 1926. *Musical America* 84(26):6.

Merriam, Alan P. 1951. An Annotated Bibliography of African and African-derived Music Since 1936. *Africa* 21:319-29.

———. 1956. Review of Ekundayo Phillips, *Yoruba Music;* Joseph Kyagambiddwa, *African Music from the Source of the Nile;* J. H. Nketia, *Funeral Dirges of the Akan People. Notes* 13:290–291.

———. 1957. *Africa South of the Sahara.* Album notes. Folkways 4503 (formerly FF 503).

———. 1958. "African Music." In *Continuity and Change in African Cultures,* ed. William R. Bascom and Melville Herskovits, 49–86. Chicago: University of Chicago Press.

———. 1959. "Characteristics of African Music." *Journal of International Folk Music Council* 11:13–19.

———. 1963. "The Purposes of Ethnomusicology: An Anthropological View." *Ethnomusicology* 7:206–213.

———. 1964. *The Anthropology of Music.* Evanston, Ill.: Northwestern University Press.

———. 1967. "The Use of Music as a Technique of Reconstructing Culture History in Africa." In *Reconstructing African Culture History,* ed. Creighton Gabel and Norman Robert Bennett, 83–114. Boston: Boston University Press.

———. 1970. *African Music on LP* . Evanston, Ill.: Northwestern University Press.

———. 1982. *African Music in Perspective.* New York: Garland.

Moore, Bai T. 1970. "Categories of Traditional Liberian Songs." *Liberian Studies Journal* 9(2):117–137.

Mubangizi, Benedicto. 1966. "Preliminary Report of Two Months Research in Ankole." *African Music* 4(1):77–78.

Munongo, A. Mwenda, and J. Kimele. 1967. "Chants historiques des Bayeke recueillis à Bunkeya et ailleurs." *Problèmes Sociaux Congolaise* (Lumubashi) 77:35–139.

Nayo, Nicholas Zinzendorf. 1969. "Akpalu and His Songs." *Papers in African Studies* (Legon, Accra) 3:24–34.

Ndayizeye, Deogratias, and Patrick Wymeersch. 1965. "Ingoma: Essai sociologique et descriptif sur les tambours du Burundi." *Africa-Tervuren* 21(1–2):39–49.

Nettl, Bruno. 1966. *Theory and Method in Ethnomusicology.* New York: Schirmer Books.

———. 1974. "Comparison and Comparative Method in Ethnomusicology." *Yearbook for Interamerican Musical Research* 9:148–161.

———. 1982. "Alan P. Merriam: Scholar and Leader." *Ethnomusicology* 26(1):99–105.

———. 1983. *The Study of Ethnomusicology: Twenty-nine Issues and Concepts.* Urbana: University of Illinois Press.

Ngubane, Simon. 1948. "Music North of the Limpopo." *African Music Society Newsletter* 7:21–25.

Nguijol, Pierre. 1967. "Les chants d'hilum: Les Basia." *Abbia* 17–18:135–186.

Nketia, J. H. Kwabena. 1954. "The Role of the Drummer in Akan Society." *African Music* 1(1):34–43.

———. 1955. *Funeral Dirges of the Akan People.* Legon, Accra: University of Ghana.

———. 1956. "The Gramophone and Contemporary African Music in the Gold Coast."

In *West African Institute of Social and Economic Research: Fourth Annual Conference,* 191–201. Ibadan.

———. 1957a. "Modern Trends in Ghana Music." *African Music* 4:13–17.

———. 1957b. "Organization of Music in Adangme Society." *Universitas* (Legon and Accra) 1(4):9–11.

———. 1957c. "Possession Dances in African Societies." *Journal of the International Folk Music Council* 9:4–9.

———. 1958a. "Akan Poetry." *Black Orpheus* 3:1–27.

———. 1958b. "The Development of Instrumental African Music in Ghana." *Music in Ghana* (Legon, Accra) 1(1):5–27.

———. 1958c. "Festivals of Ghana." In *The Ghanian,* 2. Accra: Ministry of Information.

———. 1958d. "The Ideal in African Folk Music: A Note on Klama." *Universitas* (Legon, Accra) 4(2):40–42.

———. 1958e. "Organization of Music in Adangme Society." *African Music* 2(1):28–30.

———. 1958f. "The Poetry of Drums." In *Voices of Ghana),* 17–23. Accra: Ministry of Information.

———. 1958g. "Traditional Music of the Gã People." *African Music* 2(1):21–27.

———. 1958h. "Traditional Music of the Gã People." *Universitas* 4(3):76–80.

———. 1958i. "Yoruba Musicians in Accra." *Odu: Journal of Yoruba and Related Studies* 6:35–44.

———. 1959a. "African Gods and Music." *Universitas* (Legon, Accra) 4:3–7.

———. 1959b. "Drums, Dance, and Song." *Atlantic Monthly* 203(4):67–72.

———. 1961. "African Music: An Evaluation of Concepts and Processes." *Music in Ghana* 1(2):1–35.

———. 1962a. *African Music in Ghana.* London: Longmans Green.

———. 1962b. "The Hocket Technique in African Music." *Journal of the International Folk Music Council* 14:44–55.

———. 1962c. "The Problem of Meaning in African Music." *Ethnomusicology* 6(1):1–7.

———. 1963a. *Drumming in Akan Communities of Ghana.* Edinburgh: Thomas Nelson.

———. 1963b. *Folk Songs of Ghana.* London: Oxford University Press.

———. 1964a. "Historical Evidence in Gã Religious Music." In *The Historian in Tropical Africa,* ed. R. Mauney and Jan Vansina, 265–283. London: Oxford University Press.

———. 1964b. "Traditional and Contemporary Idioms of African Music." *Journal of the International Folk Music Council* 14:34–37.

———. 1966. *Music in African Cultures.* Legon: Institute of African Studies.

———. 1969. "The Instrumental Resources of African Music." In *Papers in African Studies,* Vol. 3, 1–23. Accra: Ghana Publishing.

———. 1970a. "Ethnomusicology in Ghana" Inaugural lecture. Accra: Ghana Universities Press.

———. 1970b. "Sources of Historical Data on African Music." *African Music,* 43–49. Paris: La Revue Musicale.

———. 1974. *Funeral Dirges of the Akan People.* Legon and Accra: University of Ghana.

———. 1981. "The Juncture of the Social and the Musical: The Methodology of Cultural Analysis." *The World of Music* 23(2):22–29.

———. 1982. "On the Historicity of Music in African Cultures." *Journal of African Studies* 9(3):1–9.

———. 1984a. "The Aesthetic Dimension in Ethnomusicology." *The World of Music* 26(1):3–28.

———. 1984b. "Universal Perspectives in Ethnomusicology." *The World of Music* 26(2): 3–24.

Nketia, J. H. Kwabena, and Jacqueline C. DjeDje. 1984. "Trends in African Musicology." In *Selected Reports in Ethnomusicology V: Studies in African Music* (University of California at Los Angeles), ix–xx.

Nkhata, Alick. 1952. "African Music Clubs." *African Music Society Newsletter* 1(5):17– 20.

Nzewi, Meki. 1979. "Dramatic Moments in Igbo Traditional Life Style." *Ugo* 1(3):32–41.

———. 1984. "Traditional Strategies for Mass Communication: Studies in Igbo Music." In *Selected Reports in Ethnomusicology V: Studies in African Music* (University of California at Los Angeles), 319– 338.

Ojehomon, Agnes A. 1969. *Catalogue of Recorded Sound.* Ibadan: Institute of African Studies.

Okeke, L. O. 1936. "The Ogwulugwu Dance of Awka." *Nigerian Teacher* 2(6).

Omibiyi, Mosunmola. 1973–1974. "A Model for the Study of African Music." *African Music* 5(3):6–11.

———. 1979. "Nigerian Musicians and Composers." *Nigeria Magazine* 128/29:75–88.

———. 1983. "Bobby Benson: The Entertainer Musician." *Nigeria Magazine* 147:18–27.

Omondi, Washington A. 1984. "The Tuning of the Thum, the Luo Lyre, a Systematic Analysis." In *Selected Reports in Ethnomusicology V. Studies in African Music* (University of California at Los Angeles), 263–281.

Onwona-Safo, F. 1957a. "An African Orchestra in Ghana." *African Music* 1(4):11–12.

———. 1957b. "Talking Drum in the Gold Coast." *Gold Coast Teachers' Journal* 2:9–12.

Onyido, Udemezuo. 1955. "The Nigerian Institute of Music." *African Music* 1(2):62.

Opoku, Albert Mawere. 1958. "The African Dance Drum." *Music in Ghana* 1(1):36–53.

Oven, Cootje van. 1981. *An Introduction to the Music of Sierra Leone.* Sierra Leone: Cootje van Oven.

Oware-Twerefoo, Gustav. 1975–1976. "Traditional Music in Life-long Education: The Situation in Ghana." *ISME Yearbook* (Mainz) 3:35–39.

Palisca, Claude V. 1965. "The Scope of American Musicology." In *Musicology*, ed. Frank L. Harrison, Mantle Hood, and Claude V. Palisca. Englewood Cliffs, N.J.: Prentice Hall.

Pantaleoni, Hewitt. 1968. "The First American Music Study Group in Ghana: An Unofficial Report." *African Music* 4(2):68.

Pepper, Herbert. 195?. "Afrique Equatoriale française." *L'Encyclopédie Coloniale Maritime.* Paris: Encyclopédie Coloniale Maritime.

Phillips, T. Ekundayo. 1953. *Yoruba Music.* Johannesburg: African Music Society.

Riverson, Isaac D. 1933. *Songs of the Akan People.* Cape Coast: Methodist Book Depot.

———. 1955. "The Growth of Music in the Gold Coast." *Transactions of the Gold Coast and Togoland Historical Society* 1:121–132.

Rouget, Gilbert. 1961. "La Musique d'Afrique Noire." In *Histoire de la musique, l'Encyclopédia de la Pléiade*, 215–237. Paris: Fasquelle.

Rycroft, David. 1958. "The New Town Music of South Africa." *Recorded Folk Music* 1:54–57.

Sartre, Jean-Paul. 1970. "An Interview with Sartre." *New York Review of Books* 26 March:22.

Schlatter, Richard. 1965. "Foreword." In *African Experience*, ed. John N. Paden and Edward W. Soja, Vol. 2, 128–151. Evanston, Ill.: Northwestern University Press.

Sempebbwa, E. K. R. 1948. "Baganda Folk-Songs." *Uganda Journal* 12:16–24.

Smith, Edwin W. 1926. *The Christian Mission in Africa.* New York: International Missionary Council.

Sowande, Fela. 1966. "Nigerian Music and Musicians: Then and Now." *Composer* 19:25–34.

———. 1967. *Six Papers on Aspects of Nigerian Music.* New York: Broadcasting Foundation of America.

———. 1970. "The Role of Music in Traditional African Society." In *African Music*, 59–69. Paris: La Revue Musical.

Stone, Ruth. 1982. *Let the Inside Be Sweet: The Interpretation of Music Event among the Kpelle of Liberia.* Bloomington: Indiana University Press.

Thieme, Darius L. 1964. *African Music: A Brief Annotated Bibliography.* Washington, D.C.: Library of Congress.

Tidjani, A. Serpos. 1954. "La Danse de Egougou." *Tropiques* (Paris) 368:29.

Towo-Atangana, Gaspard. 1965. "Le Mvet, genre majeur de la littérature orale des populations Pahouines." *Abbia* 9–10:163–179.

Tracey, Hugh [Travers]. 1929. "Some Observations on Native Music of Southern Rhodesia." *Nada* (Bulawayo) 7:96–103.

———. 1948a. *Chopi Musicians, Their Music, Poetry and Instruments.* London: Oxford University Press.

———. 1948b. *Ngoma, An Introduction to Music for Southern Africans.* Cape Town: Longmans.

———. 1948c. "Recording Journey from the Union into the Rhodesias." *African Music Society Newsletter* 1:12–14.

———. 1948d. *Zulu Paradox.* Johannesburg: Silver Leaf Books.

———. 1949. "A Study of Native Music in Rhodesia." *Nada* (Bulawayo) 26:27–28.

———. 1950. "Recording Tour 1949 (Mozambique, Belgian Congo, Rhodesia and Nyasaland)." *African Music Society Newsletter* 1(3):33–37.

———. 1952a. *African Dances of the Witwatersrand Gold Mine.* Johannesburg: African Music Society.

———. 1952b. "Recording Tour in Tanganyika by a Team of the African Music Society." *Tanganyika Notes and Records* 32:43–48.

———. 1954a. "Editorial." *African Music* 1(1):7.

———. 1954b. "The State of Folk Music in Bantu Africa." *African Music* 1(1):8–11.

———. 1957. "Recording in the Lost Valley (Zambesi)." *African Music* 1(4):45–47.

———. 1960. *African Music Research: Transcription Library of Gramophone Records: Handbook for Librarians.* Johannesburg: Gallo.

———. 1961. "Music of South Africa." *Music Journal* 19:76–77.

———. 1963. "Editorial." *African Music* 3(2):5.

———. 1966. "A Plan for African Music." *Composer* 19:7–12.

———. 1966–1967a. "Editorial." *African Music* 4(1):5.

———. 1966–1967b. "The Textbook Project for African Music." *African Music* 4(1):64–65.

———. 1972. "Editorial." *African Music* 5(2):5.

Tracey, Hugh Travers, Gerhard Kubik, and Andrew T. N. Tracey. 1969. *Codification of African Music and Textbook Project: A Primer of Practical Suggestions for Field Research.* Johannesburg: International Library of African Music.

Traore, Mamadu. 1942. "Une danse curieuse: le Moribayasa." *Notes Africaines* (IFAN) 15.

"Tropical African Studies in Africa." 1964. *Africa* 35(1).

Tsala, Theodore. 1955. "Nkui ou le tam-tam." *Presses Missionaires* 22:3.

Tse, Cynthia, and Jerome Kimberlin. 1984. "The Morphology of the Masinqo: Ethiopia's Bowed Spike Fiddle." In *Selected Reports in Ethnomusicology V. Studies in African Music* (University of California at Los Angeles), 249–262.

Tsibangu. 1953. "An Experiment in Congolese Dancing: Choreography by Tsibangu." *Belgian Congo of Today* 2(3):106–109.

Turay, A. K. 1966. "A Vocabulary of Temne Musical Instruments." *Sierra Leone Language Review* (Freetown) 5:27–33.

Twala, Regina. 1952. "Ublangu (Reed) Ceremony of the Swazi Maiden." *African Studies* 11:93–104.

Twerefoo, Gustav Oware. 1975–1976. "Traditional Music in Life-Long Education: The Situation in Ghana." *ISME Yearbook* (Mainz) 3:135–139.

Ukeje, L. O. 1953. "Urhore." *Nigeria Magazine* 76:29–44.

Uzoigbe, Joshua. 1978. "Akin Euba: An Introduction to the Life and Music of a Nigerian Composer." M.A. thesis, Queen's University of Belfast.

Varley, Douglas H. 1936. *African Native Music: An Annotated Bibliography.* London: The Royal Empire Society.

Wachsmann, Klaus P. 1956. Review of African Music from the Source of the Nile. *African Music* 1:80–81.

———. 1966a. "Negritude in Music." *Composer* 19:16.

———. 1966b. "The Trend of Musicology in Africa." In *Selected Reports in Ethnumusicology* (University of California at Los Angeles), 1(1):61–65.

———. 1970. "Ethnomusicology in Africa." In *African Experience*, ed. John N. Paden and Edward W. Soja, 128–151. Evanston, Ill.: Northwestern University Press.

———, ed. 1971. *Essays on Music and History in Africa.* Evanston, Ill.: Northwestern University Press.

Ward, William Ernest. 1927. "Music in the Gold Coast." *Gold Coast Review* 3(2):199–223.

Whyte, Harcourt. 1953. "Types of Ibo Music." *Nigerian Field* 18:182–186.

Williamson, Leslie. 1963. "Kwanongoma College, Bulawayo." *African Music* 3:48–49.

Woodson, Craig. 1984. "Appropriate Technology in the Construction of Traditional Musical Instruments in Ghana." *Selected Reports in Ethnomusicology V. Studies in African Music* (University of California at Los Angeles), 217–248.

The Representation of African Music in Early Documents

John McCall

African Music in Early Travelers' Accounts
Portuguese in the Congo
Representations of the Slave: The "Savage" as Commodity
Victorian Heroes, the "Law of Commerce"
Some Early Transcriptions
Evolutionary Theory and the Construction of the Primitive

The oldest extant written report of a European voyage of discovery is probably Hanno's *Periplus,* which survives in Greek records. The original, engraved in the Phoenician language on a tablet in a temple at Carthage, about 500 B.C., described a voyage through the "Pillars of Hercules" (the Straits of Gibraltar), and down the west coast of Africa (Hodges 1876:35). It told of an island in a bay, near what guides identified as the "Horn of the West":

> We could discover nothing in the day time except trees; but in the night we saw many fires burning, and heard the sound of pipes, cymbals, drums, and confused shouts. We were then afraid, and our diviners ordered us to abandon the island. (Palmer 1931:2)

This account mentions indigenous music, whose effect on Hanno and his diviners was to inspire fear. While the local populace may have directed their musical performance to that end, xenophobia informed other early representations of African music.

Because of the chronological and geographical range of this essay, I cannot claim to be presenting a comprehensive discussion of the pertinent literature. Most of the descriptions I cite are of the music of West and Central Africa; I cite material from other areas of Africa only when it is particularly illustrative. Many early accounts of Africa refer to music (and particularly to musical instruments), but I shall focus on works that joined the definitive body of reference literature, on which later writers felt obliged to base their accounts. I particularly want to examine the long-term historical construction of the "knowledge" and "facts" about African music—which became a body of reference for the study of "primitive music" for Richard Wallaschek, Erich M. von Hornbostel, and other founders of the discipline of ethnomusicology.

The depiction of the "primitive other" has always been the definitive endeavor of anthropology. The construction of "primitive Africa" as a meaningful analytical isolate informs the history of contact between Europe and Africa. It is the product, not of a linear development in European "thought," but of an amorphous field of forces, defined in the actions of political and religious leaders and zealots, slavers and abolitionists, merchants, scholars, slaves, pirates and adventurers, missionaries, and Africans.

In 1893, when Wallaschek published *Primitive Music,* he had little doubt "primitive music" was a meaningful category, and that African music belonged to it. Much history falls between Hanno's fearful retreat and Wallaschek's social-evolutionary embrace. In this examination of that history, I shall concern myself, not with the nature of African music as an "objective historical fact," but with African music as outsiders' texts have represented it, and with the cultural and historical context within which they have built their representations. This exercise takes a stroll through Wallaschek's bibliography, for a behind-the-scenes view of the raw material that attracted Victorian armchair scholars.

AFRICAN MUSIC IN EARLY TRAVELERS' ACCOUNTS

Many of the earliest accounts of voyages to Africa offer scant musicological information, because early traders had few cultural interactions with indigenous peoples. Less than a century after Hanno's voyage, Herodotus described the trade customs the Carthaginians established in West Africa:

> they unload their goods, arrange them tidily along the beach, and then, returning to their boats, raise a smoke. Seeing the smoke, the natives come down to the beach, place on the ground a certain quantity of gold in exchange for the goods, and go off again to a distance. The Carthaginians then come ashore and take a look at the gold; and if they think it represents a fair price for their wares, they collect it and go away; if, on the other hand, it seems too little, they go back aboard and wait, and the natives come and add to the gold until they are satisfied. (Davidson 1964:53)

This type of transaction did not lead to accounts with much descriptive substance. While Africans interacted with traders hailing from various Mediterranean and Middle Eastern ports, most of the records from the first millennium were ethnographically barren. After the 900s, several Arab travelers produced substantive records of cultural practices in Africa. Among these, that of Al Bekri (of Granada, Spain) briefly mentioned music in the royal court of Ghana in 1067:

> The beginning of a royal audience is announced by the beating of a kind of drum which they call *deba,* made of a long piece of hollowed wood. The people gather when they hear this sound. (Davidson 1964:72)

This account, though meager, tells of the function and context of performance, the construction of the instrument, and even the local name.

The accounts of Mohammed ibn Abdullah ibn Battuta are particularly valuable. In 1352, Battuta crossed the western Sahara into Mali. The record of his stay in the court of Mansa Sulayman includes a description of music performed in the pomp and circumstance of royal life:

> The sultan is preceded by his musicians, who carry gold and silver guimbris [two-stringed guitars], and behind him come three hundred armed slaves.

> He walks in a leisurely fashion, affecting a very slow movement, and even stops from time to time. On reaching the *pempi* he stops and looks round the assembly, then ascends it in the sedate manner of a preacher ascending a mosque pulpit. As he takes his seat the drums, trumpets, and bugles are sounded (Gibb 1929:326).

Involvement in the slave trade and Christian missionization finally brought Europeans into closer encounters with African lifeways; with those meetings came the first serious accounts of African music.

The early Arabic accounts, though lacking detail, were notably objective. Women's attire in Sulayman's court shocked Battuta—"women go naked into the sultan's presence, too, without even a veil" (Davidson 1964:83)—but in general, his report is not value laden, partly because, by the time of his visit, Mali was thoroughly Islamic. Further, Battuta was

> a wonderful teller of tales whose cast of character—whose quiddity—has sting and savor that bring him to life even after six hundred years. With its highly personal mixture of sophistication and simplicity, Ibn Battuta's narrative remains one of the best travel books ever made (Davidson 1964:80).

Battuta intended to observe, rather than exploit; like Herodotus, he was at heart an ethnographer.

In the 1500s, the excursions into Africa by Portuguese, Spanish, and English sea traders had more than a desire for "tales." Their routes offered a new and more immediate access to African commodities, bypassing Saharan trade routes and Arab middlemen. Seagoing traders wanted ivory and gold. Except when the manufacture of musical instruments (primarily ivory trumpets) required these substances, the earliest of the traders' accounts only briefly mention music. A note in Vasco da Gama's logbook described a reception by "the Sultan of Malindi" (a trading city on the Kenya coast):

> There were many players on *anafils*, and two trumpets of ivory, richly carved, and of the size of a man, which were blown from a hole in the side, and made sweet harmony with the *anafils*. (Davidson 1964:127)

Involvement in the slave trade and Christian missionization finally brought Europeans into closer encounters with African lifeways; with those meetings came the first serious accounts of African music.

PORTUGUESE IN THE CONGO

In the early 1500s, the Central African port at São Tomé was supporting a significant commerce with European slave traders. Two Portuguese missionaries, who had had little luck in their tries to convert the populace, decided to focus their efforts on an exiled Congolese royal heir named "Afonso." Their gamble paid off when he returned and, against strong opposition, succeeded to his father's throne (Duffy 1959:12). This period saw a significant Portuguese cultural presence in the Congo. Afonso brought to his court not only Christianity, but also a general affectation of European style. A sort of alliance between the crown of Portugal and that of the Congolese kingdom, based on a shared desire to spread Christianity in Central Africa, developed. Because of extensive contacts between the Portuguese and Africans, accounts from the region dating from this era are descriptively richer than those of earlier periods—and even, to a certain extent, those of later ones.

Duarte Lopes

The influence of the Portuguese in the Congo was to dwindle for the next two centuries, when some authors made engaging descriptions of music. Among these are the Portuguese explorer Duarte Lopes, who traveled to the Congo in 1591. His narrative is possibly one of the best reports from the early Portuguese penetration. He says (1969:111–112) the indigenous peoples celebrated feasts by singing love ballads

> and playing on lutes of curious fashion. These lutes in the hollow and upper part resemble those used by ourselves, but the flat side, which we make of wood, they cover with skin, as thin as a bladder. The strings are made of very strong and bright hairs, drawn from the elephant's tail, and also from palm-tree threads, which go from the bottom to the top of the handle, each being tied to a separate peg, either shorter or longer, and fixed along the neck of the instrument. From these pegs hang very thin iron and silver plates, fitted to suit the size of the instrument, which make various sounds, according as the strings are struck, and are capable of very loud tones. The players touch the strings of the lute in good time, and very cleverly with the fingers, having no key like the harp, but I do not know if I should call the sounds they call forth a melody, but merely such as pleases their senses. More than this (and very wonderful), by means of this instrument they indicate all that other people would express by words of what is passing in their minds, and by merely touching the strings signify their thoughts. They also dance and clap their hands together in time with the music. Pipes and flutes are also played with great skill at the king's court, whilst the people dance somewhat in Moorish fashion, with gravity and dignity. The common people use little rattles and pipes, and similar instruments, which are harsher and ruder in sound than those used by the nobles.

Lopes's account is significant. He devoted his journal to showing the degree to which "the Christian religion [had taken] rise in the Congo" (1969:108), and with it the customs and manners of Europe. He proudly recorded that the nobles of the court dressed in Portuguese fashions. Nevertheless, he recognized Congolese music and dance as a cultural entity. In addition to the detail of his description of the structure and performative technique of the lute, Lopes raised, possibly for the first time, theoretical questions that become central to later discussions of African music—in particular, the question of composition based on "such as pleases their senses" in opposition to "melody." Nearly three centuries later, this question resonated in arguments on the evolution of music. The comparison of music to speech was perspicacious, though to what extent Lopes understood the mechanisms of musical communication in African performance is unclear. His recognition of social-class distinctions as a dimension of musical genres encompasses a degree of analytical detail rare for observers of his time.

Michael Angelo and Denis de Carli

Portuguese missionaries to the Congo produced some of the earliest accounts of African music. Stationed for extended periods, they could gain access to events, and make observations that eluded earlier travelers and traders. The Capuchin missionaries Michael Angelo of Gattina and Denis de Carli of Piacenza went to the Congo in the year 1666. Michael Angelo died there, but de Carli survived to publish their writings, including this account of musical instruments and performance.

"The gentleman, or gentleman's sons, carry in their hands two iron bells, such as the cattle among us wear, and strike sometimes the one, sometimes the other, with a stick."

(1814)

They fell a playing upon several instruments, a dancing, and shouting so loud, that they might be heard half a league off. I will describe but one of their instruments, which is the most ingenious and agreeable among them all, and the chief of those in use among them. They take a piece of a stake, which they tie and bend like a bow, and bind to it fifteen long, dry, and empty gourds, or calabashes of several sizes, to sound several notes, with a hole at top, and a lesser hole four fingers lower, and stop it up half-way, covering also that at the top with a little thin bit of board, somewhat lifted above the hole. Then they take a cord made of the bark of a tree, and fastening it to both ends of the instrument, hang it about their neck. To play upon it they use two sticks, the ends whereof are covered with a bit of rag, with which they strike upon those little boards, and so make the gourds gather wind, which in some manner resembles the sound of an organ, and makes a pretty agreeable harmony, especially when three or four of them play together.

They beat their drums with an open hand, and they are made after this manner: they cut the trunk of a tree three quarters of an ell long or more; for when they hang them about their necks, they reach down almost to the ground: they hollow it within, and cover it top and bottom with the skin of a tyger or some other beast, which makes a hideous noise when they beat it after this manner.

The gentleman, or gentleman's sons, carry in their hands two iron bells, such as the cattle among us wear, and strike sometimes the one, sometimes the other, with a stick; which is seldom seen among them, this instrument being only carried by the sons of great men, who are not very numerous among them.

We preparing to be gone, our Macolonte made a sign for his Blacks to stand still, and be silent, which was done in a moment, and they had need enough of it, being all in a sweat. Having given them our blessing, we set out, and they began afresh to play, dance, and hollow, so that we could hear them two miles off, not without surprise and satisfaction, it being a consort of so many curious, and to us strange instruments. (Angelo and Carli 1814:160)

Once again, the detail is informative; but the full account covers the decline of the Congo missions, and portrays as "barbarous" the practices of the Africans. It thus stands in marked contrast to the appreciative assessment of Lopes.

Jerom Merolla da Sorrento

In Merolla's account (1682), the quality of alienation became profound. Merolla stood at the end of a failed missionary experiment. The unity of the kingdom of the Congo had deteriorated. São Salvador, once the seat of the Diocese of the Congo, was a deserted ruin (Duffy 1959:22). Merolla found solace in religious zealotry and cultural hubris. Incorporating in the same text description and mystical revelation, his narrative sometimes verges on the surreal:

This bird, not much unlike a sparrow, at first seems wholly black, but upon nearer view may be discovered to be a kind of blue. As soon as day breaks, he sets up his notes and sings; but the excellency of his song is, that it harmoniously, and almost articulately pronounces the name of Jesus Christ: which repeated by many of them in concert, is a heavenly music worthy of our special observation, seeing those heathen nations excited to own the true God by irrational creatures (Merolla 1814 [1682]:251).

Wherever Merolla looked, he found devil worship, and he punished with beatings the practitioners of indigenous beliefs. His perceptions of music had two contrastive domains: his descriptions of ceremonies in honor of nobles are valuatively neutral; but his discussions of the music of "unlawful feasts" bristle with projections of evil. The latter domain involved drumming, and the former involved other types of instruments. The following passage illustrates his descriptive detail, and the dichotomy of his values.

When the count [chief] comes to church, which is at least three times a week, he has a velvet chair and cushion, being brought himself in a net on the shoulders of two men, each with a commander's staff in his hand, one all silver, and the other only of ebony tipped. . . . Before him marches one musician above the rest, who has several little round bells fixed to and iron two spans long, wherewith he gingles, and chants to it the glory and grandeur of his lord: besides this there are several other sorts of musical instruments made use of at festivals, the principal whereof are those which in the country-language have the name of Embuchi, which I mention first because they belong only to kings, princes and others of the blood royal. These are a sort of trumpets made of the finest ivory, being hollowed throughout in divers pieces, and are in all about as long as a man's arm; the lower mouth is sufficient to receive one hand, which by contracting and dilating of the fingers forms the sound: there being no other holes in the body as in our flutes or hautboys. A concert of these is generally six or four to one pipe. The Longa (which is made of two iron bells joined by a piece of wire archwise) is sounded by striking it with a little stick: both these are carried also before princes, and that especially when they publish their pleasure to the people, being used as the trumpet is with us. The instrument most in request used by the Abundi, being the people of the kingdom of Angola, Matamba, and others, is the Marimba; it consists of sixteen calabashes orderly placed along the middle between two side boards joined together, or a long frame, hanging about a man's neck with a thong. Over the mouths of the calabashes there are thin sounding slips of red wood called Tanilla, a little above a span long, which being beaten with two little sticks, returns a sound from the calabashes of several sizes not unlike an organ. To make a concert, four other instruments are played upon by as many musicians, and if they will have six they add the Caffuto, which is a hollow piece of wood of a lofty tone about a yard long, covered with a board cut like a ladder, or with cross slits at small distances: and running a stick along, it makes a sound within, which passes for a tenor: the base to this concert is the Quilando, made of a very large calabash, two spans and a half or three in length, very large at one end, and ending sharp off at the other, like a taper bottle, and is beaten to answer the Caffuto, having cuts all along like it. This harmony is grateful at a distance, but harsh and ungrateful near at hand, the beating of so many sticks causing a great confusion.

Another instrument of this concert is that which the natives call Nfambi, and which is like a little guittar, but without a head, instead whereof there are five little bows of iron, which when the instrument is to be tuned, are to be let more or less

"All of them uniting their voices with the sound of the instruments, round the patient's bed, make a terrible uproar and din, which is often continued for several days and nights in succession."

(1776)

into the body of it. The strings of this instrument are made of the thread of palm-trees: it is played on with the thumbs of each hand, the instrument bearing directly upon the performer's breast. Though the music of this instrument be very low, it is nevertheless not ungrateful.

Over and above the great drums used in the army, there is another sort of a lesser size, called Ncamba; these are made either of the fruit of the tree Aliconda, or else of hollowed wood with a skin over one end only: they are commonly made use of at unlawful feasts and merry-makings, and are beaten upon with the hands, which nevertheless make a noise to be heard at a great distance. When the mission-ers hear any of these at night, they run to the place in order to disturb the wicked pastime. It fell often upon my lot to interrupt these hellish practices, but the people always ran away as soon as ever I came up to them, so that I could never lay hold on any to make an example of them. The Giaghi not only make use of these drums at feasts, but likewise at the infernal sacrifices of man's flesh to the memory of their relations and ancestors, as also at the time when they invoke the devil for their ora-cle. (1814:244–245)

Abbé Proyart

In 1776, the Abbé Proyart compiled missionary reports into an ethnographic overview of the region. He little respected African conduct, but was contemptuous of the Portuguese,

a set of men who have nothing of the Christian but the name, which they dishon-our, and whose worse than heathenish conduct makes the idolaters doubt whether the gods whom they worship be not preferable even to that of the Christian. (1814:563)

Perhaps it was for this reason that he was more open-minded about local cus-toms than many of his contemporaries. He criticized writers who considered it immodest that "the Negresses have . . . their arms and bosoms uncovered," pointing out that because "the custom is general; no one thinks of it. . . . It is less shocking to public decency in that country, than the half nakedness of our court ladies among us" (1814:563). Giving a detailed and enlightened account of marriage customs, he goes on to defend Africans' inherent morality.

Similarly, in his accounts of music, Proyart pays attention to the context of per-formance:

The physicians of the country know also a very salutary remedy, in their opinion, for all diseases; but this they only employ in favor of those who can afford the expense; when they are called in to a rich man they take with them all the perform-ers on musical instruments they can find in the country: they all enter in silence;

but at the first signal which they give, the musical troop begin their performance; some are furnished with stringed instruments; others beat on the trunks of hollow trees, covered with skin, a sort of tabor. All of them uniting their voices with the sound of the instruments, round the patient's bed, make a terrible uproar and din; which is often continued for several days and nights in succession. To an European the remedy would be worse than the disease; but this music, which charms the negroes when they are in good health, cannot make them feel, in sickness, a more disagreeable sensation than the most harmonious concert would be to one of us; and in this case the remedy must certainly not be so violent as might at first be imagined. Be that as it may, when the state of the patient begins to grow worse, they endeavour to draw from their instruments the most piercing sounds, and make the whole neighborhood resound with cries, as if they wanted to frighten Death and put him into flight. If they do not succeed in this as it often happens, they console themselves in the thought, that they have done their duty, and that the relations of the defunct have nothing to reproach them with. All the time the choir of musicians remain near the deceased, the physicians pay him frequent visits, and come at stated hours to administer different remedies to him, and to blow upon his pained part. (1814:572)

Proyart gives detailed descriptions of musical instruments, but his attention to the context of musical performance distinguishes his work from the earlier published accounts of the region. In addition to the passage on healing, he describes the use of music and dance in games and mourning.

From the beginning, the intrusion of slave trading undermined Portuguese aspirations for a relationship of alliance with the potentates of the Congo. A Portuguese account from 1680 estimates the slaves "dispatched" in the first century of the Portuguese presence "sum up to almost a million souls" (Davidson 1964:203). By 1700, the "Congo experiment" was over. Its history is critical to an understanding of the impact of the slave trade on the colonial endeavor in Africa. And such an understanding is vital, because commerce in slaves, which engaged Europeans in Africa for nearly four hundred years, had an institutional influence in shaping outsiders' ideas of "primitive Africa."

REPRESENTATIONS OF THE SLAVE: THE "SAVAGE" AS COMMODITY

The seventeenth- and eighteenth-century European literature on Africa is a vast body of texts, derived from a small core of primary materials. With minor editorial enhancement, authors often presented translations as original works—as with John Ogilby's *Africa* (1670), essentially an English-language edition of Olfert Dapper's *Description of Africa*, published in Dutch several years before. Many plagiarize outright. Thus, a few key individuals' representations echoed and reechoed in later texts, until offhand observations and judgments had become elevated to the status of facts, supported by a large consensus of writers. That authors generalized from isolated accounts, so one eyewitness's notice of a single incident might become the basis of a description of the "customs and manners" of a broad region (or of all Africa), compounded the problem.

Jean Barbot

Possibly one of the most influential of the early sources was Jean Barbot's *Description of Guinea* (1732). Agent-General of the French West India Company, Barbot made several trips to Guinea and the West Indies. His journals, written in French around 1683–1685, remained unpublished until 1732, when an English translation appeared. Some of his material, especially the section on Benin, looks borrowed

William Bosman   Dutch official in West Africa who stressed the importance of reporting actual observation

Archibald Dalzel   Supporter of the slave trade who described Dahomean ceremonies and the accompanying music

(without credit) from Dapper. The following is a passage from Barbot, on the funeral practices of "blacks" (opposed to "the Moors") in Senegal.

> Upon these occasions, they ask abundance of impertinent ridiculous questions, much in the same nature as the poor ignorant sort of *Irish* are reported to practice to this day; as for example, *Why he would leave them after that manner? whether he wanted millet, or oxen, or clothes, or wealth? whether he stood in need of any more than he had? or, whether he had not wives enough, what harm any body had done him?* and the like. All these queries are repeated by every one in the company successively, the *Guiriots* in the mean time acting their parts, continually singing the praises of the party deceased, and extolling his virtues, actions, and qualities. The dead person making no answer, those who have put their questions withdraw, to make room for others to succeed them, in repeating the same. (1732:52)

Barbot's work richly describes music, musical instruments, and dance; it usually contextualizes these subjects, albeit contemptuously.

William Bosman

With an increase of European commercial endeavors in West Africa in the 1600s, and the consequent increase in Europeans living on the coast, a new genre of descriptive texts began to emerge. At the age of 16, William Bosman left Holland for West Africa. His appointment as "chief factor" at the fort at Elmina made him "the second most important Dutch official on the coast of Guinea" (Bosman 1967:vii). To an uncle in Holland, he sent a series of lengthy letters, written with publication in mind. A compilation of these letters, published under the title *Description of Guinea*, became one of the most authoritative texts of its time. Vaguely alluding to the work of his fellow Dutchman, Dapper, Bosman criticized the "fabulous" [fabricated] accounts of earlier writers (1967:xiv). He presented his own work as one uniquely based on actual observation, and he was probably right. He was an apologist for the slave trade, in which he engaged:

> You would really wonder to see how these slaves live on board; for though their number sometimes amounts to six or seven hundred, yet by the careful management of our Masters of Ships, they are so regulated that it seems incredible. . . . I doubt not but this trade seems very barbarous to you, but since it is followed by meer [sic] necessity it must go on. (1967:xviii)

The supposed need for commerce in slaves—a key component of a body of extractive and exploitive relations between Europeans and Africans—led to a mode of representation compatible with the maintenance of slavery. At every opportunity, Bosman degrades Africans. The women, he states, "are a'most all Whores, tho' they indeed don't bear that Name" (Bosman 1967:214). He limits his musical observations to describing instruments, and expressing disgust at their sounds.

> Their Musical Instruments are various, and very numerous, but all of them yield a horrid and barbarous shocking Sound: The chief of them are the mentioned Horns, made, as I have already told you, of small Elephant's Teeth; though not so very small but some of them weigh betwixt twenty and thirty Pounds, and others more: To adorn these they cut in them several Images of Men and Beasts; and that so finely that it seems to be done Litterally in Obedience to the Second Commandment; for indeed 'tis difficult to discern whether they are most like Men or Beasts; at the lower end of these Horns is a piece of Rope coloured black with Hens or Sheeps Blood, and at the small end is a square Hole; at which by blowing they produce a sort of extravagant Noise; which they reduce to a sort of Tone and Measure, and vary as they please: Sometimes they blow upon these Horns so well, that though it is not agreeable, yet it is is [sic] not so horrid as to require a whole Bale of Cotton annually to stop ones Ears. . . .
>
> Their second sort of Instruments are their Drums; of which there are about ten several sorts, but most of them are excavated Trees covered at one end with a Sheeps-skin, and left open at the other; which they set on the Ground like a Kettle-Drum, and when they remove it they hang it by a String about their Necks: They beat on these Drums with two long Sticks made Hammer-Fashion, and sometimes with a streight [sic] Stick or their bare Hands; all which ways they produce a dismal and horrid Noise: The Drums being generally in consort with the blowing of the Horns; which afford the most charming Asses Musick that can be imagined: to help out this they always set a little Boy to strike upon a hollow piece of Iron with a piece of Wood; which alone makes a Noise more detestable than the Drums and Horns together.
>
> Of late they have invented a sort of small Drums, covered on both sides with a Skin, and extended to the shape of an Hour-Glass: The Noise they afford is very like that our Boys make with their Pots they play with on Holidays, with this difference only, that these have Iron-rings, which makes some alteration in the Sound. 'Twould be ridiculous to tire you with all the Instruments of the *Negroes*: I shall therefore take leave of this Subject, by describing the best they have; which is a hollow piece of Wood of two hands breadth long, and one broad; from the hinder part of this a Stick comes cross to the fore-part, and upon the Instrument are five or six extended Strings: So that it bears some sort of Similitude to a small Harp, or if you will, is not very unlike the Modern Greek Musical Instruments, and affords by much the most agreeable Sound of any they have here. (1967:138–140)

"Dismal," "horrid," "detestable," "Asses Musick," "Noise"—Bosman's judgment was certain. His likening African music to the noise "our Boys make with their Pots" made an intercultural conceptual clang that would sound for two centuries.

Archibald Dalzel

In European political circles in the late 1800s and early 1900s, the issue of the slave trade became a point of contention. In many works written on Africa during this period, opinions on this subject become a subtext. In the foreword to the 1967 edition of Dalzel's *History of Dahomy*, J. D. Fage calls the *History* as much a tract in support of slavery as a history.

> For such a defence, in view of the general belief in the superiority of western European society, and therefore of its history, a historical form was peculiarly apt:

Thomas Winterbottom   One of the most careful field ethnographers to visit West Africa before the mid-1800s

history could be used to show that Africans really were barbarians, and that they might actually benefit from being brought within the ambit of European society even as slaves. (1967:11)

Dalzel puts his musical comments in the context of royal Dahomean ceremony: swirling spectacles of the grotesque, complete with dancing dwarfs, severed heads on display, and extravagant dress, to which music added "confused noise" (1967:135).

Many writers defended slavery by calling Africans "barbarous," but critics of slavery did little to change or banish the image, which was not really at stake. People accepted it as a fact. By the mid-1800s, Europeans' moral position in relation to Africans was at issue, and a primary point of contention was whether Africans were descendants of Adam and Eve, or the products of a separate creation (the theories of monogenesis and polygenesis, respectively).

Believers in the essential unity of humankind took the position that Africans had degenerated to their present state:

The ordinary effect of misfortune upon mankind, when not under the influence of Christian feeling is to beget a selfishness, dead alike to the voice of nature and humanity. We accordingly find that the long series of miseries, which for ages pressed upon this unfortunate race, begat in them a brutish insensibility to human suffering. Occupied entirely with the care of their individual interests, and checked in their pursuit by no moral restraint, every imagination of the thoughts of the heart became their only rule of life, and the natural and inevitable consequence of this guidance was, of course, what unerring wisdom had declared it invariably to be, "Only evil continually." To such depths of degradation had man's natural depravity conducted the African, that the natives of more favoured lands, in the pride of superior acquirements, have sometimes scorned to admit them to an equality of origin. (1966:1–2)

Cruickshank's defense of this theory utilizes methods that were then the stock and trade of degenerationists, who, following the early work of Bowdich (1821), drew parallels between the customs of the Gold Coast and those of Egypt. Beginning with degeneration as a primary assumption, Cruickshank accounted for both "advanced" and "degenerate" qualities. His descriptions of music are mainly unsympathetic, though he goes beyond the simple description of instruments, and gives accounts of call and response, and of singing in praise or derision (1966:265–269).

Thomas Winterbottom

In 1803, Thomas Winterbottom published an important contribution to the debate on human genesis. Before the mid-1800s, he was "by far the most competent and careful field ethnographer to visit West Africa" (Curtin 1964: 209). In his work on

Sierra Leone, he included a chapter aimed at discrediting the polygenistic arguments of Charles White (1799). In 1806 (1865), J. F. Blumenbach, in his prolonged polemic with Georges Cuvier on the subject, cited him. Despite the generally progressive nature of his writing, his account of music is barely distinguishable from other accounts of the period.

He begins with a disclaimer: "Music, if we may apply the name to sound[s] distinguished rather by their obstreperousness than by their harmony, is never listened to alone" (Winterbottom 1803:111). With similar prejudice, he attributed the prevalence of dance in Africa to the human need for mental relief from indolence:

> The fatigue of dancing may appear incompatible with that state of indolence in which these people universally love to indulge: but even indolence, that fruitful source of ennui, requires some respite; and to avoid the languor and listlessness arising from sloth too far indulged, which is more unsupportable than continued bodily labour, the mind is gratified in being roused by an amusement in which it participates without fatigue to itself. This reason, perhaps, gave origin to so frivolous an amusement as that of dancing, one which modern times, probably from similar causes, find it convenient to retain. (Winterbottom 1803:111)

Such musings, from a writer whom the European public considered an antiracist, show how deeply the distortions that characterized the representation of African music infiltrated the European world view. The image of African music lay too far beneath the surface of consciousness to be affected by debates that argued the theories of genesis and their implications for race and slavery.

VICTORIAN HEROES, THE "LAW OF COMMERCE"

In the 1800s, the imagery central to the colonial enterprise was that of Africa as a wild continent. Images of wild men in a wild land were "the great artifacts: fetishized antiselves made by civilizing histories" (Taussig 1987:240). The "primitive other" was the ideological construction by which Europeans could realize the representation of the heroic justice of the colonial enterprise. The metaphoric opposition of the dark to the enlightened, the savage to the civilized, is beautifully illustrated in this passage from Henry D. Northrop's account.

> It must have occurred many times to the reader that no life on the globe is more rude, barbarous and uninviting than that found in Africa. What could tempt one to forsake the comforts of civilization, and remain in this dark land among hordes of savages and men more debased than savages, who, for gain, will trample upon every human instinct, rob helpless men and women of their liberty, and prove themselves to be brutes in human form? Yet Africa has had its heroes—brave souls who have done wonders towards enlightening and transforming that dark country. (Northrop 1889:832)

Sir Richard Francis Burton (1821–1890)

One of the most versatile writers of the 1800s was Richard Burton. A brilliant thinker, fluent in many languages, he made the world his home, and claimed, among other achievements, the credit for bringing *The Arabian Nights* to English readers. He was an outsider to the academy. Rusticated from Trinity College, Oxford, he joined the British army as an officer in the East India Company. Thus began a career that would traverse India, Arabia, America, and Africa.

Burton gave many accounts of African music (Wallaschek cites him frequently). His strong point was "thick description" of ritual context. He was an early practition-

Early European listeners mostly preferred choral music, which more often fulfilled their need for familiar melodic structures than did the complexly rhythmic productions characteristic of much of African music.

er of what Malinowski would call "participant-observation." Disguised as an Indian Pathan, he made a pilgrimage to Mecca. But despite his ethnographical studies, he was thoroughly steeped in his own culture's assumptions. The following excerpt, from his accounts of travels with Cruickshank, describes a visit with Gelele, King of Dahomey.

> Suddenly, as is his wont, Gelele rose, and came towards us. After snapping fingers, I thanked him for the spectacle. He showed me the rum for our hammock-men, and our share of provisions; after which we were all three told that we must dance, sing, and drum—the latter accomplishment, unfortunately, has not received from me the attention which it deserves. Dr. Cruikshank and I willingly consented to dance with the King, knowing it to be the custom, and that he greatly enjoyed it. We pleaded, however, successfully for Mr. Bernasko, who, being a Reverend, could only sing. . . . Whereupon we withdrew. The provisions which accompanied us caused a tumult till near dawn. *Pain et spectacles* are apparently the cardinal wants of these people; they sing, drum, and dance all the day, and they fight for their wretched provision half the night. When not engaged in these pleasures they are plundering the where-withal to procure them. Hence the melancholy state of the land. (1966:215)

Burton's early writings on Africa "are the true parents of the multitudinous literature of 'Darkest Africa'" (Lane-Poole 1911:4:865). Indeed, the metaphoric use of "darkness" in reference to Africa and Africans has a longer history. However, it was Sir Henry Morton Stanley's books, such as *Through the Dark Continent* (1878) and *In Darkest Africa* (1890), that established in the popular imagination an image of African darkness.

Sir Henry Morton Stanley (1841–1904)

Stanley's writings chronicle his quest to bring the "light" of Progress to this dark region. To many Victorians, Stanley's expeditions represented the front line of social evolution.

> The Dark Continent is dark no longer. To Stanley and his undaunted comrades the world owes a debt of gratitude which it will be difficult to repay. Africa has at last been opened up to the civilization of the future. Its vast tracts of wilderness will stimulate the enterprise of the pioneer, and the day is not far distant—within the lifetime of our children's children, perhaps—when the shrill echo of the engine's whistle will be heard on the rugged sides of snow-capped mountains which Stanley has explored; when those illimitable forests will resound with the woodsman's axe, and when the law of commerce will change the tawny native from a savage into a self-respecting citizen. Barbarism will retire from its last stronghold on the planet, as the darkness disappears when the sun rises over the hilltops. Long life seems a boon

when such a magnificent problem is in the process of solution (Northrop 1889:805–806).

For Northrop, Africa was a "magnificent problem" because it stood outside Europe's "law of commerce." His writing gave clear expression to the Victorian conflation of social evolution with capitalist expansion.

Stanley's journals can be seen as a study in the construction of the "primitive other." They repeatedly reaffirm Africans' savageness. He did not intend *Through the Dark Continent* (1878) to be ethnographic. Nevertheless, he often refers to war drums. If his accounts were complete and accurate, they would suggest that African music only occurred in preparation for battle. But his writing concerned, not so much the accurate description of African culture, as the mythography of the colonial mission—and with the construction of his own status as a hero. He did, however, give a positive report of Wanyamwezi choral singing in East Africa, which he compared favorably to the "dreadfully melancholic or stupidly barbarous" music of other African groups (Wallaschek 1893:11). Early European listeners mostly preferred choral music, which more often fulfilled their need for familiar melodic structures than did the complexly rhythmic productions characteristic of much of African music.

In Stanley's footsteps followed many lesser explorers. While a heightened representation of danger and adventure characterized all their writings, their expeditions were often less overtly military than Stanley's. Accounts of music in the work of Cameron (1969), Ward (1891), and Du Chaillu (1867, 1868), cited the performance of music and dance to support a representation "wildness" in African culture.

Paul Du Chaillu

Du Chaillu, an American, traveled widely in Africa. He produced the following description of a musical performance in what is now Gabon.

To-night there is a great dance in honor of the arrival of a spirit (myself) among them. This dance was the wildest scene I ever saw. Every body was there; and I, in whose honor the affair was, had to assist by my presence. The only music was that of a rude drum—an instrument made of a certain kind of wood, and of deer or goat skins. The cylinder was about four feet long, and ten inches in diameter at one end, but only seven at the other. The wood was hollowed out quite thin, and the skin stretched over tightly. To beat it the drummer held it slantingly between his legs, and with two sticks beat furiously upon the upper, which was the larger end of the cylinder.

This music was accompanied with singing, which was less melodious even than the drumming. As for the dancing, it was an indescribable mixture of wildness and indecency. (1868:110)

This account of the "wildness and indecency" of Africans served as confirmation of the evolutionary assumptions at the foundation of the colonial project: that Africans faced inevitable extinction in the face of European superiority. "The negro," Du Chaillu predicted, "will disappear in time from his land," and "will follow . . . the inferior races who have preceded him[.] So let us write his history." (1867:437)

Georg August Schweinfurth

Another important explorer of Africa in the late 1800s was Georg Schweinfurth, a botanist. To explore uncharted regions of the Congo in search of new species of plants, he obtained a grant from the Royal Academy of Science. His reports often

Thomas Bowdich deserves credit as the first
European to conduct genuine ethnomusicological
research in sub-Saharan Africa.

reach far beyond botany. He wrote extensively about music, and his work has served
as a resource for musicologists. His writing had a more scientific tone than that of
many other explorers of his time, but he tinted his representation of musical performance with imagery of untamed paganism, enhanced by a mystical allusion to the
thinness of the veil that separated Africans from the raw elements of nature.

For two nights and a day whilst I was in Geer, the natives were abandoning themselves to their wild orgies, which now for the first time I saw in their full unbridled
swing. The festival was held to celebrate the sowing of the crops; and confident in
the hope that the coming season would bring abundant rains, these light-hearted
Bongo anticipated their harvest. . . . In honour of the occasion there was produced
a large array of musical instruments . . . but the confusion of sound beggared the
raging of all the elements and made me marvel as to what music might come to.
(1873:183)

He goes on:

Often as I was present at these festivities I never could prevent my ideas from associating Bongo music with the instinct of imitation which belongs to men universally.
The orgies always gave me the impression of having no other object than to surpass
in violence the fury of the elements. Adequately to represent the rage of a hurricane
in the tropics any single instrument of course must be weak, poor, and powerless,
consequently they hammer at numbers of their gigantic drums with powerful blows
of their heavy clubs. (1873:289–290)

Confirming his civilization, he projected the image of wildness and savagery.
The full development of the opposition of the wild to the civilized as based in "natural law" was a tenet of the theory of social evolution.

SOME EARLY TRANSCRIPTIONS

Despite the tendency for pre-twentieth-century accounts of African music to consist
primarily of inventories of musical instruments and impressionistic portrayals of performances, some researchers made transcriptions of African music during the 1800s.

Thomas Edward Bowdich

An amateur naturalist and writer in the service of the British African Company,
Bowdich accompanied an expedition to negotiate with the Ashanti. The mission
traveled from Accra to Kumasi, and he eventually took command of it (Curtin
1964:169). His published account is much more than a narrative of the expedition: it
is a full-blown ethnography, which, with the writings of Joseph Dupuis (1824), readers throughout the 1800s accepted as an authoritative work on the Ashanti. Of par-

ticular interest is a chapter on Ashanti music. Bowdich approached the task with European assumptions, but was not so much prejudiced toward Ashanti music as simply confused by it. In playing the *sanko* (a chordophone), he says the Ashanti

> surpass all others. It consists of a narrow box, the open top of which is covered with alligator, or antelope skin; a bridge is raised on this, over which eight strings are conducted to the end of a long stick, fastened to the fore part of the box, and thickly notched, and they raise or depress the strings into these notches as occasion requires. The upper string assimilates with the tenor C of the piano, and the lower with the octave above: sometimes they are tuned in Diatonic succession, but too frequently the intermediate strings are drawn up at random, producing flats and sharps in every Chromatic variety, though they are not skilful enough to take advantage of it. I frequently urged this by trying to convince them they were not playing the same tune I had heard the day before, but the answer was invariably, "I pull the same string, it must be the same tune." (1966:361–362)

Bowdich prints transcriptions of 20 songs performed by the Ashanti, the Fanti, and other groups. To translations, he adds commentary and lyrics. Of one "Ashantee Air," he comments:

> A long tale accompanies No. 6. An Ashantee having been surprised in an intrigue with another man's wife becomes the slave of the King, and is obliged to follow the army in a campaign against the celebrated Attah, the Akim caboceer mentioned in the history. The Ashantee army having retired, this man either deserted or could not join his division, and after concealing himself some time in the forest, was taken by a party of Attah's. . . . The man's life, it was added, was preserved when he urged that he understood how to make sandals. The key appears to be E minor. (1966:366–367)

This degree of ethnographic sensibility was unrivaled by other writers in Bowdich's time. In his discussion of other songs, he elaborates details on dynamics and the interplay of various instruments. He knows his notations in some cases are "merely attempts to describe," and recognizes the limitations of Western notation to capture the distinctions in pitch and timbre of the ensembles of which he gives accounts. For these reasons, Bowdich deserves credit as the first European to conduct genuine ethnomusicological research in sub-Saharan Africa. It is therefore remarkable that in 1893, when Wallaschek compiled his treatise, he made no use of Bowdich's materials. He cited Bowdich's essay on Ashanti music only in a passing remark on the Ashanti flute, "through which the natives profess to be able to hold conversation with each other" (Wallaschek 1893:92). And even on this point, he cited Bowdich secondarily to Beecham (1841), a British armchairist, who derived most of his data from Bowdich's work.

Marie Armand Pascal D'Avezac-Macaya

Another study, important both to the history of African musicology and to the ethnology of Africa in general, is an account of life in Nigeria by Osifekunde, an Ijebu (a Yoruba group), seized by pirates in his youth and sold into slavery. After nearly twenty years in Brazil, he went with his master to France, where he met D'Avezac, then vice president of the Société Ethnologique of Paris. For weeks, D'Avezac interviewed "Joaquim" (as Osifekunde was known), and produced an ethnographic narrative, the first substantial account of the Yoruba (Lloyd 1968:217). It relies on memo-

FIGURE 1 Ijebu song for a royal procession. Transcribed by D'Avezac (Lloyd 1968:278).

A– wè e– rú Ob– bá.   A– wè e– rú Ob– bá.   O– bro– gó– lu– da.

ries of some thirty years past; but, nevertheless, its accounts of kinship, marital practices, trade, language, and ceremony made it unique for its time.

D'Avezac's ethnography includes a short section on Ijebu music. It includes transcriptions of songs sung by Osifekunde. D'Avezac's representation bespeaks a Eurocentric bias, and follows less than rigorous methods (he readily admits the accurate recording of music is not his primary intent), but his record of Yoruba music is unique. Of Ijebu music, he writes:

Negro instrumental music in general is, to European ears, nothing but a deafening noise, in which one tries in vain to discover something resembling melody or harmony. For the Negroes themselves, this music is nothing more than the accompaniment of their chants: the songs must take first place if we are to understand their musical abilities.

Among the Ijebu as among their neighbors, there are songs for every circumstance of life, for every daily event. By singing, they show joy; by singing they express sorrow; they sing to encourage work; and they even sing to make rest seem sweeter. Songs are mixed in religious ceremonies and in public celebrations. They are a continual expression of a lively and careless spirit, which dislikes silence and isolation.

I collected only a few Ijebu songs. They emerged during my conversations with Osifekunde only as a sidelight to a story or a description, and it was only thanks to their usual brevity that I was able to snatch them from the midst of other matter in which they were embedded. A Negro song, in fact, is hardly more than a phrase, being repeated again and again for hours on end.

I will relate, for example, how two of these songs are presented in their official character within the pattern of a solemn procession made by the king at certain times on the great square of his capital. On such occasions, as the king's *ofonkpwe*, or trumpeters, place their *oukpwe*, or great horns made of hollowed elephant tusks, to their mouths, his servants are busy covering the ground he is to walk on with tanned cowhides, and they all sound forth as from a powerful megaphone with this song, repeated a hundred times (figure 1).

The words mean: "We are all slaves of the king our sovereign." It is a call heard to the ends of the town. The nobles, the chiefs of every rank, the entire people, hasten toward the square to do homage to their prince and follow after him. . . . He walks with a slow and measured step, while the musicians (*oukbedou*, and one of the essential attributes of sovereignty) play a piece in which the *ofonkpwe* sing the words while the other musicians accompany them on a single great drum, each one drumming a special beat so as to perform a concert of indefinite duration repeating the same phrase without end. I have tried to write out the parts for the benefit of the readers (figure 2).

FIGURE 2 Accompanied Ijebu song for a royal procession. Transcribed by D'Avezac (Lloyd 1968:279).

The meaning of these words is: "Here is the bravest of the brave. Follow his example."

I must explain how the parts I have just written down are performed. The drum is in the form of a cylinder about three feet in diameter and two feet high and covered by a strong hide. It is hung from the neck of one of the musicians by a double sling so that without touching the ground the upper surface is not raised above the breast of the carrier, whose hands beat out near the rim of the drum head the part marked above by the word *aya*. A second musician armed with two short drumsticks is given the part marked *afere*. A third, with longer sticks, plays the part marked *agwako*. Two others with very long heavy drumsticks take the bass, called *ogwo*. Finally, the whole ensemble is controlled by a musical director, bearing the title of *omono*, who takes the *agwako* jointly with the musician who plays that alone. (Lloyd 1968:277–280)

D'Avezac transcribes two other songs, and gives attention to instruments and song texts, plus description of ceremonies. His work is exceptional for its detail. Again, remarkably, Wallaschek makes no real use of it. Aside from citing it to establish the Ijebu's use of ivory horns (1893:99), he reduces D'Avezac's findings to a single sentence: "Mr. Avezac states that a music corps is considered almost an attribute of a chief" (1893:131).

Captain William Allen

Other travelers, though not engaged in the kind of ethnographic reporting that distinguished the work of Bowdich and d'Avezac, transcribed songs they heard. In the narrative of Captain Trotter's 1841 expedition to the Niger, William Allen gives this account of the "Grébu of the Grain Coast."

The music of these people is very simple; the subjoined [figure 3] is a specimen.

They accompany all their songs with the tom-tom, or, if afloat, by striking the paddle against the gunwale of the canoe or boat. (Allen and Thompson 1848: 1:116)

In Nigeria, among the Igbo, he says musicians in the king's

retinue performed the royal air on the opé, a sort of wind instrument formed by hollowing out a young elephant's tusk: an oblong hole is bored at the upper third, into which the performer blows strongly, and by compressing the fingers over the

FIGURE 3   A song of the "Grébu of the Grain
Coast" (Allen and Thompson 1848:1:116).

lower aperture, several notes are produced of anything but a pleasing character; the
tone resembles more the discordant jar of a clarionet in the hands of a novice.
(Allen and Thompson 1848:1:206)

Robert Clarke

In 1843, Robert Clarke studied the physiognomy of Sierra Leoneans, and recorded
patterns of scarification and their tribal signification. He also noticed music:

> The Akoos, and indeed all the African Colonists here, are very partial to music and
> singing: some of them, as I have before stated, are tolerable musicians. I here sub-
> join a specimen of Akoo music.
>
> Their songs consist of short extempore verses, uttered in a recitative, as
> follows:

Sibi oti le shi.	You must do what you like.
Abalangku lu le.	Drums are beating.
Omma tu long shi.	Who have this child.
Moushi mah brimohdi.	He belongs to a great man.
Ju bie luju.	So you must dance.
Oh kuo imloh lu miloh.	Good by, go live for go.
Tabo mi sin ingya.	I show stranger the way.

> I am also informed, that they have occasionally regular dramatic entertainments,
> the management of the plot and denouement being well sustained. The performers
> on these occasions have their hair shaved, in curiously-shaped forms, some not
> unlike a parterre pattern, a custom which is also practiced by many of the Akoos in
> the Colony. (1969:161)

Captain Charles R. Day

In 1889, when the Royal Niger Company dispatched Captain Major Sir Claude
Maxwell MacDonald on an expedition to the Niger and Benu rivers, his mission was
primarily diplomatic: he was to meet with local emirs, kings, and chiefs

> over whom the Royal Niger Company claimed jurisdiction; to examine the admin-
> istration of the aforesaid company, and to visit the city of Ilorin, in Yorubaland,
> with the object of inducing the Ilorins to agree to a treaty of peace with the Ibadans.
> (Mockler-Ferryman 1892:vii)

As a secondary concern, the expedition collected scientific materials. Captain
Mockler-Ferryman compiled a report that includes a broad scope of materials, ranging from adequate (if prejudicial) ethnographic accounts of Nigerian peoples, to
ornithology, botany, and lepidopterology. Attached to his account is a chapter devoted to music and musical instruments, written by Captain Charles R. Day, who

worked with materials the members of the mission collected, using as guidelines a series of "notes and queries." Included are photographs of musical instruments, with detailed descriptions of construction and tunings. In addition, Day tried to classify types of music, and explored the relationship of music and folktales. He presented a collection of twenty-six songs, which he discusses in the following style:

> *Orgardiegbeni.* A traveller from Asaba land was lost in the forest. While there he heard the forest spirits singing and dancing. Concealing himself in a tree, he observed them closely, and upon his return home he taught others the songs and dances he had heard. The names of those who thus learnt were Oku Opa, Ubido, Ibuzo, Invanono, Ikpoazu, and Ekule. When this song is performed the dancers put on masks representing these people.
>
> *Ogbuka.* A young woman went into the forest for wood. She fell amongst the wood spirits, and her ears were cut off by them. Upon her return home, when the villagers heard that she had been with the wood spirits, she was told she must return to them again. She made, however, a last request, that she should be allowed to sing what she had heard in the forest. And so she sang—"Kiokogo, Kandi nogbuka, had a child, he was rich, he planted yams for himself and his family," &c. (Mockler-Ferryman 1892:280–281)

Alfred Burdon Ellis

Near the end of the 1800s, Alfred B. Ellis published a series of ethnographies of the southern Guinea Coast. These works included studies of the slave coast Yoruba (1894) and the Tshi-speaking peoples of the Gold Coast (1887). The latter, primarily examining practices sanctioned by the Tshi belief system, concluded with chapters on language, music, and folklore.

Ellis provides an insightful, if brief, discussion of drum language, with examples of texts. The chapter on music ends with six transcribed songs, prefaced by a disclaimer:

> The following are examples of native airs, but thus written they give but a poor idea of the effect produced by some thirty or forty voices, with reed flutes and drums, which all blend harmoniously. (1964:328)

Unfortunately, Ellis did not provide the texts associated with the songs he transcribed. Despite the value of his examination of drum language and his transcription of melodies, Wallaschek did not cite him.

The works of Bowdich, D'Avezac, and Day contained both notated songs and analysis of the material and its cultural context. Wallaschek cited them, but did not discuss their analysis. He used the material as earlier readers had used explorers' reports—as a source of facts. His method was that of a nineteenth-century encyclopedist: uncritically collecting a broad base of (supposed) facts reported in travel literature, and then calling these facts up in fragments and assembling them in strings of reasoned comparison. The exotica thus presented were an elaborate begging of the question that social evolutionists wanted to answer: how can we make sense of the differences we can show to exist between the manners and customs of Europeans and non-Europeans?

EVOLUTIONARY THEORY AND THE CONSTRUCTION OF THE PRIMITIVE

The works quoted above became primary references for nineteenth-century ethnology. In the 1800s, editors and translators reconstituted earlier texts in the light of the paradigm of social evolution. The ethical valuations that were a product of missionar-

Richard Wallaschek aimed his work at correcting prominent evolutionary theorists' dismissal of "primitive music." By trying to broaden our understanding of what constitutes music, Wallaschek was challenging Darwin's and Wallace's assessments.

ies' agendas became elements of a secular evaluation in relative progress—a temporalization of morality that could represent the ethics of racial inequality in a process unfolding through time by natural law.

The construction of the idea of the primitive in Victorian social science descended from evolutionary stage models of the Enlightenment. Nevertheless, the idea of primitivism differed in several ways from that of savagery. The primary distinction was in the racialism that pervaded the Victorian model.

George Stocking (1968:35) offers an excellent illustration of this transition as it took place in the mind of a single individual. Georges Cuvier, a leading exponent of polygenesis, became a leader in the development of racialist anthropology. Early in his career, he took a more Rousseauesque view of "savage" peoples. His career spanned the period of transition from romanticism to social evolutionism; he was a key player in its paradigm shift:

> In 1790 young Cuvier had chided his friend, C. M. Pfaff, for believing "some stupid voyagers" who alleged that the Negro and the orangutang were interfertile, and for attempting to explain "intellectual faculties" on the basis of differences in brain structure. On the contrary, Cuvier argued that the "stupidity" of Negroes resulted from their "lack of civilization," and (paradoxically) that their vices were the gifts of whites. In 1817, however, Cuvier maintained that Egyptian civilization had not been created by "any race of blacks," but by men of "the same race as ourselves," who had "an equally large cranium and brain," and who offered no exception "to that cruel law which seems to have condemned to an eternal inferiority the races of depressed and compressed skulls."

Stocking (1968:35–36) summarizes the paradigm shift:

> As it emerged in the later eighteenth century, the idea of "civilization" was seen as the destined goal of all mankind, and was in fact often used to account for apparent racial differences. But in the nineteenth century more and more men saw civilization as the peculiar achievement of certain "races."

The noble savage was remote, a mythic and symbolic character. As the colonial endeavor led to increasing cultural and economic articulation between Europeans and non-Europeans, it fortified the boundaries with the more impenetrable ideology of scientific racialism. The representation of "primitive man" reflected a theory of social evolution, but not the social evolution that had defined the "savages" of Enlightenment philosophers like Montesquieu and Adam Ferguson; it was the distinctly nineteenth-century variety of social evolution formulated by Herbert Spencer, who in his time was one of the most influential social theorists. He popularized the phrase "survival of the fittest" long before Darwin published on the theory of natural selection (Bohannan and Glazer 1973:3). On matters of human society, Darwin deferred to Spencer, whom he called "our great philosopher" (1871:119). However,

Spencer's evolutionary models were distinctly Lamarckian and racialist. He once wrote, "It needs only to contrast national characters to see that mental peculiarities caused by habit become hereditary" (Stocking 1982:240). Considering economic domination to be a natural outcome of racial supremacy, Spencer denounced many social programs—from public libraries to the administration of smallpox vaccination—as actions against natural law.

Wallaschek formulated an evolutionary theory of music when racialized models of social evolution were beginning to come into question. He aimed his work at correcting prominent evolutionary theorists' dismissal of "primitive music." In *The Descent of Man*, Charles Darwin writes:

> We see that the musical faculties, which are not wholly deficient in any race, are capable of prompt and high development, for Hottentots and Negroes have become excellent musicians, although in their native countries they rarely practise anything that we should consider music. (Darwin 1871:370)

Wallaschek quotes a similar passage from Alfred R. Wallace:

> Among the lower savages music, as we understand it, hardly exists, though they all delight in rude musical sounds, as of drums, tom-toms, or gongs; and they also sing in monotonous chants. Almost exactly as they advance in general intellect and in the arts of social life, their appreciation of music appears to rise in proportion. (1893:277)

Wallaschek considered his book "a contradiction" to these statements (1893:278)—not because he rejected the evolutionary model, but because he wished to embrace it fully, to prove that unlike civilized art music, music among "primitives" is adaptive behavior:

> With primitive man music, and painting and sculpture probably as well, are not purely aesthetic occupations in the modern sense, they are most intimately bound up with practical life-preserving and life-continuing activities, and receive only gradually their present more abstract form. And therefore a law like that of "natural selection" has original validity here as well, while it is less easily comprehensible in connection with the music of the present time whose conditions of existence have become too complicated. (1893:278–279)

By trying to broaden our understanding of what constitutes music, Wallaschek was challenging Darwin's and Wallace's assessments. He verged on the appreciation of the music and culture that Merriam (1964) advocated some eighty years later. Moving away from the assumptions that had traditionally cited the "wildness" of "primitive music" as evidence of a lack of social development, Wallaschek argued that among non-Western peoples, music was a basic source of social organization.

> Primitive music in its actual aspects, with the rhythmical element strongly pronounced, is an organising power which holds together the participants in the dance and makes a common action possible. This custom of the whole tribe to act in common as one body, and the skill evinced in doing this, cannot be without influence in the struggle for existence. (1893:275–276)

His defense of "primitive music" depended on its primitiveness. The subject matter of his work was the music of the non-European world, contrasted with "music of the present."

The representation of Africans as cultural time travelers has deep historical roots. The writings on Africa by the late-sixteenth-century encyclopedist Pigafetta included a description of Angolan musicians, accompanied by an illustration engraved by the

While professional vocabularies have purged themselves of the term *primitive*, this type of dichotomization still resides in much of our analysis.

printer De Bry, who had never seen the people he was depicting (Astley 1745–1747:3:281). What resulted was a print of three unmistakably Greek men in robes, playing drums (figure 4).Conscious or not, the engraver's decision to represent the unknown in the style of the known paradigmatically illustrates the method that has informed the representation of Africa throughout the history of contact with Europe. The construction of the primitive yielded a constellation of concepts to define the civilized.

Summarizing the "general character of African music," Wallaschek listed the following:

> the preference for rhythm over melody (when this is not the sole consideration); the union of song and dance; the simplicity, not to say the humbleness, of the subjects chosen; the great imitative talent in connection with the music and the physical exertion and psychical excitement from which it arises and to which it appears so appropriate. (1893:15)

He drew his representation of African music from a variety of sources, which he perceived—with ethnology in general—to be tokens, not so much of other cultures, but of what those cultures could say about the origins of our own, because their development had frozen at earlier stages of an ineluctably ordered evolutionary series. He therefore found the study of African music more profitable than the study of Asian music.

His appraisal of African music suggests the following oppositions:

European Music	African Music
modern	primitive
melodic	rhythmic
complex	simple
aesthetic	functional
mental	physical
intellectual	emotional
creative	expressive
product of culture	product of nature

I list these oppositions in full cognizance of the criticism of their anthropological use. Critics question the appropriateness of this type of classification to the myths and narratives to which scholars generally apply it, because it reduces to analytical diagrammatics the subtlety of mythic discourse (Fabian 1983:71–104; Goody 1977). The thrust of these critiques is that this type of structuralist dichotomization, being purely a product of synchronic and literalized discursive modes, reveals more about the cognitive system of "scientific" thought than the cognitive concerns behind the non-European ethnographic object.

FIGURE 4   *"Military dress* of Commanders & Common Soldiers in *Angola"* (Astley 1745–1747:3: facing 281).

These categories became the criteria on which twentieth-century comparative musicology based its judgments about African music. While professional vocabularies have purged themselves of the term *primitive*, this type of dichotomization still resides in much of our analysis. It is clear in the institutional isolation of ethnomusicology from musicology proper—which, commanding the generalized, unprefixed term, implies a specialization in European music only. The grounding of analysis in a dichotomy of "us" and "them" is a residue of the conceit of logical positivism (which placed the analyst in a superior position in relation to the object of study), and of the relations of colonialism (the background field of the historical development of the musicological representation).

The farther removed a representation is from our vantage point, the more easily we can see how it is a product of its time. We cannot view our own historical context objectively, but we can develop a sense of processes for constituting representations: "anthropology has been constructing its object—the Other—by employing various devices of temporal distancing, negating the coeval existence of the object and subject of its discourse." (Fabian 1983:34)

A similar danger lies in the artificial conceptual devices of spatial distancing. Scholars can no longer construe the non-Western world as a land apart. Its people participate in, and bear the consequences of, the decisions we make, the products we purchase, the foods we eat, the music we hear. When we try to transcend the limits of our vocabulary, we are at a loss for words; but we who study music have another medium at our disposal. If we are to represent African music with validity, we must treat it, not as data, but as music. We must play it, we must dance it, we must experience it. We can no longer accept the assumption that positivist analysis resolves all relational issues.

REFERENCES

Allen, William, and T. R. H. Thompson. 1848. *A Narrative of the Expedition . . . to the River Niger in 1841*. 2 vols. London: Bentley.

Angelo, [Michael,] and [Denis de] Carli. 1814 [1666–1667]. "A Voyage to Congo." In *A General Collection of the Best and Most Interesting Voyages and Travels in All Parts of the World*, ed. John Pinkerton, 16:148–194. London: Longman.

Astley, Thomas. 1745–1747. *A New General Collection of Voyages and Travels: Consisting of the Most Esteemed Relations, Which Have Been Hitherto Published in Any Language: Comprehending Everything Remarkable in its Kind, in Europe, Asia, Africa, and America*. 4 vols. London: T. Astley.

Barbot, Jean. 1732. *A Description of the Coasts of North and South-Guinea; and of Ethiopia Inferior, Vulgarly Angola: Being a New and Accurate Account of the Western Maritime Countries of Africa*. London: T. Astley.

Beecham, John. 1968 [1841]. *Ashantee and the Gold Coast*. London: Dawsons of Pall Mall.

Blumenbach, Johann Friedrich. 1865 [1806]. "Contributions to Natural History." In *Anthropological Treatises of Johann Friedrich Blumenbach*, ed. T. Bendyshe. London: Anthropological Society of London.

Bohannan, Paul, and Mark Glazer (eds.). 1993. *High Points in Anthropology*. New York: Knopf.

Bosman, William. 1967 [1705]. *A New and Accurate Description of the Coast of Guinea*. Facsimile of the 1705 (English) edition. London: Cass.

Bowdich, Edward T. 1821. *An Essay on the Superstitions, Customs and Art Common to the Ancient Egyptians, Abyssinians, and Ashantees*. Paris: J. Smith.

———. 1966 [1824]. *Mission from Cape Coast to Ashantee*. London: Cass.

Burton, Sir Richard Francis. 1966 [1893]. *A Mission to Gelele, King of Dahome*. London: Routledge and Kegan Paul.

———. 1967. *The Erotic Traveler*, ed. Edward Leigh. New York: Putnam.

Cameron, Verney Lovett. 1969 [1877]. *Across Africa*. New York: Negro Universities Press.

Clarke, Robert. 1969 [1843]. *Sierra Leone: A Description of the Manners and Customs of the Liberated Africans; with Observation upon the Natural History of the Colony, and a Notice of the Native Tribes*. London: James Ridgeway.

Cruickshank, Brodie. 1966 [1853]. *Eighteen Years on the Gold Coast of Africa*. 2 vols. London: Cass.

Curtin, Philip. 1964. *The Image of Africa: British Ideas and Action, 1780–1850*. Madison: University of Wisconsin Press.

Cuvier, Georges. 1827–1835. *The Animal Kingdom*. 16 vols. London: G. B. Whittaker.

Dalzel, Archibald. 1967 [1793]. *The History of Dahomy, an Inland Kingdom of Africa*, ed. J. D. Fage. London: Cass.

Dapper, Olfert. 1686 [1658]. *Description de l'Afrique, contenant les noms, la situation et les confins de toutes ses parties, leurs rivières, leurs villes et leurs habitations, leurs plantes et leurs animaux; les mœurs, les côtumes, la langue, les richesses, la religion et le gouvernement de ses peuples*. Amsterdam: Wolfgang, Waesberge, Boom & van Someren.

Darwin, Charles. 1871. *The Descent of Man*. New York: Rand McNally.

Davidson, Basil. 1964. *The African Past: Chronicles from Antiquity to Modern Times*. New York: Grosset & Dunlap.

Du Chaillu, Paul B. 1867. *A Journey to Ashangoland*. New York: D. Appleton.

———. 1868. *Explorations and Adventures in Equatorial Africa.* New York: Harper Brothers.

Duffy, James. 1959. *Portuguese Africa.* Cambridge, Mass.: Harvard University Press.

Dupuis, Joseph. 1824. *Journal of Residence in Ashantee.* London: Henry Colburn.

Ellis, Alfred Burdon. 1966 [1894]. *The Yoruba-Speaking Peoples of the Slave Coast of West Africa; Their Religion, Manners, Customs, Laws, Language, etc.* Chicago: Benin Press.

———. 1964 [1887]. *The Tshi-Speaking Peoples of the Gold Coast of West Africa.* Chicago: Benin Press.

Fabian, Johannes. 1983. *Time and the Other: How Anthropology Makes Its Object.* New York: Columbia University Press.

Goody, Jack. 1977. *The Domestication of the Savage Mind.* Cambridge: Cambridge University Press.

Gibb, H. A. R. 1929. *Ibn Battuta, Travels in Asia and Africa.* London: Darf.

Hodges, E. Richmond, ed. 1876. *Cory's Ancient Fragments of the Phœnician, Carthaginian, Babylonian, Egyptian and Other Authors.* London: Reeves & Turner.

Kuhn, Thomas. 1970 [1962]. *The Structure of Scientific Revolutions.* Chicago: University of Chicago Press.

Kup, A. P. 1961. *A History of Sierra Leone 1400–1787.* Cambridge: Cambridge University Press.

Lane-Poole, Stanley. 1911. "Burton, Sir Richard Francis." *Encyclopaedia Britannica,* 11th edition.

Lloyd P. C. 1968 [1845]. "Osifekunde of Ijebu." In *Africa Remembered: Narratives by West Africans from the Era of the Slave Trade,* ed. Philip Curtin, 217–288. Madison: University of Wisconsin Press.

Lopes, Duarte. 1969 [1591]. *A Report of the Kingdom of the Congo and of the Surrounding Countries; Drawn out of the Writings and Discourses of the Portuguese, Duarte Lopes, by Filippo Pigafetta in Rome 1591,* ed. and trans. Margarite Hutchenson. New York: Negro Universities Press.

Merriam, Alan P. 1964. *The Anthropology of Music.* Chicago: Northwestern University Press.

Merolla da Sorrento, Jerom. 1814 [1682]. "A Voyage to the Congo." Translated from Italian. In *A General Collection of the Best and Most Interesting Voyages and Travels in All Parts of the World,* ed. John Pinkerton, 16:195–316. London: Longman.

Mockler-Ferryman, A. F. 1892. *Up the Niger, with an Appendix on Music and Musical Instruments by Charles Russell Day.* London: G. Phillip and Son.

Northrop, Henry Davenport. 1889. *Wonders of the Tropics, or Explorations and Adventures of Henry M. Stanley and Other World-Renowned Travelers.* Philadelphia: Royal Publishing.

Ogilby, John. 1670. *Africa.* London: Thomas Johnson.

Palmer, H. R. 1931. *The Carthaginian Voyage to West Africa in 500 B. C.* Bathurst: J. M. Lawani.

Proyart, Abbé. 1814 [1716]. "History of Loango, Kakongo and Other Kingdoms of Africa." In *A General Collection of the Best and Most Interesting Voyages and Travels in All Parts of the World,* ed. John Pinkerton, 16:548–597. London: Longman.

Schoff, Wilfred H. 1912. *The Periplus of Hanno.* Philadelphia: The Commercial Museum.

Schweinfurth, Georg. 1873. *The Heart of Africa: Three Years' Travels and Adventures in the Unexplored Regions of Central Africa: From 1868 to 1871,* trans. Ellen E. Frewer. London: Sampson Low, Marston Low, and Searle.

Stanley, Henry M. 1890. *In Darkest Africa.* New York: C. Scribner.

———. 1899 [1878]. *Through the Dark Continent, or Sources of the Nile around the Great Lakes of Equatorial Africa and down the Livingstone River to the Atlantic Ocean.* London: Sampson Low, Marston.

Stocking, George. 1968. *Race, Culture, and Evolution.* New York: Free Press.

Taussig, Michael. 1987. *Shamanism, Colonialism, and the Wild Man: A Study in Terror and Healing.* Chicago: University of Chicago Press.

Wallaschek, Richard. 1893. *Primitive Music: An Inquiry into the Origin and Development of Music, Songs, Instruments, Dances, and Pantomimes of Savage Races.* London: Longmans, Green.

Ward, Herbert. 1891. *Five Years with the Congo Cannibals.* London: Chatto & Windus.

White, Charles. 1799. *An Account of the Regular Gradations in Man.* London.

Winterbottom, Thomas. 1969 [1803]. *An Account of Native Africans in the Neighborhood of Sierra Leone, to Which Is Added an Account of the Present State of Medicine among Them.* London: Cass.

Part 2
Issues and Processes in African Music

Music in Africa is part of a tightly connected bundle of arts that also include dance, drama, and folklore. A study of these performing traditions reveals the importance of such topics as sound, technology, time, religion, and the migration of populations both within and beyond the continent. By observing the ways in which these processes affect musical expression, we gain an understanding of how music in Africa is firmly embedded in its many societies.

The *kwela* embouchure demonstrated by
Donald Kachamba. Photo by Gerhard Kubik.

Identities: Music and Other African Arts

Barbara L. Hampton

Music and Content
Music and Poetics
Music and Speech Tones
Music and Narrative
Dance
Visual Art
Integration of the Arts

African performers weave dance, drama, language, and visual arts together with their music. To unravel this social fabric, ethnomusicologists have studied the content, the poetics, the relationships of speech and tones, and the narrative of texted African music.

MUSIC AND CONTENT

As used by ethnomusicologists, content analysis proceeds from a pretheoretical what-question, and (if required) translates the text into the language of the research report. Because the sense and the denotation of words are not independent of the language, the problem of translation is not simply one of finding a word in one language that is equivalent to or approximates a word in another.

Hence, content analysts must address four problems:

1. The rules or principles that make a language grammatically functional vary from one language to another—by tense, number, gender, case, person, proximity, shape, animation, and other criteria.
2. The ways in which languages structure their vocabularies vary.
3. One language world may not contain the same objects as another, and two languages may not have the same social institutions or abstract concepts.
4. The boundaries between the meanings of apparently semantically equivalent lexemes may not be coterminous.

Homonyms pose further problems, for meanings that attach to them in one language may not do so in another. For the meaning most germane to a context, translators must decode polysemes, lexical items with more than one meaning. Translators try to be faithful to both the language into which they are translating and to the original (Tedlock 1983). Finally, translators are mindful that reality has a structure independent of the lexical structure of particular languages.

In the first stage of content analysis, each African cultural or linguistic group—and they total more than eight hundred—presents a special challenge to ethnomusicologists. One example comes from the Gã of southeastern Ghana:

Kɛdzi oʃɔ la La-Kpa, naa dza obo agoo.
Commissioner Tete, kɛ e oʃɔ La-Kpa, naa dza ebo agoo.
Anyɛmimɛi fɛɛ, otele omusu, otele omanso.
Hewɔ akɛ eya dze yɛ ŋʃɔ ŋ, eya dze yɛ heko.

If you visit La nearby, you must beg to enter.
Commissioner Tete, if he visits La-Kpa, must beg to enter.
Siblings all, you carry own curse, you carry own trouble.
So they say it should happen in the ocean, it should happen somewhere.

Key words in the song are *agoo*, *omusu*, and *anyɛmimɛi*, none of which matches an English lexeme. Within this song, *agoo*, a term in everyday usage, becomes a concept imaged in an action. Gã architecture surrounds houses with courtyards bounded by walls whose entrances do not have hard surfaces. If there are outer doors, they stay open during the day. When visitors wish to enter a compound, they must pass through this entrance, before which they pause and call out "*Agoo*," a plea for permission to enter. When the principal celebrant calls for the attention of people gathered to open a ceremony, he or she utters the term. At the opening of a prayer, a supplicant seeking ancestral acceptance of an offering of words, food, and drink addresses it to the ancestors. A content analysis should explicate these ideas. The song's principal message is humility in social interaction, metaphorically expressed by the term *agoo*.

A *musu* is a spell or a curse. It stands within an elaborate classificatory scheme of curses invoked with words alone, or with words in combination with ritual acts. The curse in the song is the penalty for arrogance. Recognizing transformative and other powers in words, the Gã taxonomize curses. English, however, lacking such phenomena and concepts, collapses the scheme into one lexeme, conflating distinctions the Gã make.

To emphasize the universality of the admonition in the song, the composer introduces the word *anyɛmimɛi* 'siblings' (generalized to local, everyday people) and "Commissioner" (generalized to high-status, urban-industrial bureaucrats). *Anyɛmimɛi*, like the Gã third-person singular, is an ungendered term, marking both males and females ("brothers" and "sisters" in a classificatory kin system). The term fɛɛ 'all', emphasizing that those with financial privileges (like the Commissioner) and social power deriving from broad scale family support (as from one's *anyɛmimɛi*) are not exempt from the requirement of humility, reinforces this universality. English does not lexicalize a group that includes both and only siblings and first cousins, but does specify gender in the third person singular (Hampton 1983).

A song from the Niger Delta constructs an abstract concept, destiny (*oboratze*): "Destiny! O Death, Umubi now weeps, 'My daughter who is married at Aka two days ago, she ill yesterday, she is dying. Those who come from Aka bring the death news.'. . . Umubi weeps, 'My life is this?'" (Peek and Owheibor 1971:46). The woman deems her marriage a failure, since her only child has died. This was her destiny, what she, with the guidance of her spirit double, before entering the world, requested from the Creator (Oghene). Though one forgets the content of the request after entering the world, everyone makes a request. This and other Isoko songs remind people not to complain, because they receive only what they assumed they would need and requested. However, people of the Niger Delta believe they can change the course of their lives with hard work and good behavior, and they consult diviners to determine whether an occurrence is due to a decision or act committed in their everyday life, or to their *oboratze*.

Two songs can foreshadow but some of the issues involved in the first step of

musu   A spell or curse invoked with words alone or in combination with ritual acts among the Gã people

content analysis   Principles that make a language grammatically functional

poetics   Examination of the poetry of songs by studying aesthetic systems and compositional procedures

subaŋ   Character, reputation, social face as defined by the Gã people of Ghana and which is affected by song texts

content analysis. They suggest, however, that translations can lead to features of the nonlinguistic world, as in Africa they usually do. Ethnomusicologists (as Berliner 1978) have broadened content analysis to include the situational context, or the total nonlinguistic background—the immediate performance arena, the awareness by performers and audiences of previous events in the community, and pertinent shared beliefs. Following the lead of Malinowski (1930), ethnomusicologists also attend to the context of situations. Nketia (1955) analyzes utterances at the phonetic, grammatical, and semantic levels, and relates them to external-world features that may be pertinent. Researchers' reports may include contextual data appended to each translation of a song text, provide exegeses from consultants, insert a commentary on the text by the investigator, or all three, as in Kilson (1971) and Hampton (1983).

MUSIC AND POETICS

Shifting the plane of vision from the text as objectified entity to the text as energy and creative process, ethnomusicologists also examine poetics. Accompanying this shift are (1) a redefinition of tradition from the preserved to the renewed, the ever changing, the dynamic; (2) new methods and opportunities to bring investigators closer to the compositional process; and (3) the proliferation of studies of popular music. With poetics, the unit of analysis, the poetry of songs, is examined as the product of the aesthetic, creative use of musicolinguistic reservoirs within a culture. For ethnomusicologists, this has meant both understanding the aesthetic systems and compositional procedures to which African musicians refer, and following practitioners through to the sonic manifestation of these ideational structures in performances (Keil 1979; Hampton 1992; Stone 1982).

One approach to poetics begins with the ways in which a composer may acceptably craft one message or one kind of message, and why she or he might choose to do so. This approach requires the researcher to attend to both the aesthetics of compositional procedures and the socially shared concepts of song efficacy.

Another Gã example adumbrates the kind of understanding this approach might yield. In crafting a song text, Gã composers follow procedures that produce three distinct types of song. These procedures use conventions bearing terms that show the type of emotion constructed: (1) "good or happy," (2) "insinuating," and (3) "bad or insulting" songs. Aesthetic conventions require the composer to consider the form of reference, the manner of describing action, and whether (and how) the discussion embellishes the action.

The purpose of a song of the first type is to model desirable behavior, to present a standard against which one can measure social comportment. The second type usually reflects reports that an individual has violated social norms. Its purpose is to announce that the breach is widely known, and that the individual (whose anonymity it preserves) knows who she or he is; voicing the sentiment of the society, it urges the person to cease such behavior. People sing a song of the third type as a last resort, to expose bad behavior and a culprit.

The following examples, all of which have the same message ("People should not gossip"), illustrate these types.

> I am carrying thousands. My mouth.
> Because of this, I do not talk.
> I am carrying thousands (Hampton 1983:120).

> So and so *ee*! You dip with your legs *ee*!
> Myself, I have my own case.
> That is the reason you don't sleep at midnight.
> One who likes to meddle, with her legs dips.
> One who tells lies with legs deceiving me (Hampton 1983:120).

> Oblogo Laŋte's woman
> Oblogo Laŋte's woman,
> Don't give me out for hatred.

The efficacy of a song text is rooted in Gã concepts of the person, constituted, in part, by a *subaŋ* 'character, reputation, social face'—of special importance to the Gã because it eases, weakens, or negates successful interaction with others. Songs aim at the *subaŋ*. The first type enhances it; the second, by bringing the offense to public attention, damages it; and the third exposes a subaŋ already destroyed. The first type inspires its subjects to continue their good behavior; the second inspires its subjects to redeem their subaŋs by reforming their actions after being shamed; and the third type disgraces its subjects, though they may try to reform. The effect a song may have on the subaŋ moves people to change their ways to repair a damaged one. Improvisation is permitted—in the ecphonema (the outcry of woe, "my mouth") or the outcry of woe at the end of the first line of the first song, in the way the second song is elaborated, and in the name in the third. Thus, all three examples are durable over time and circumstance.

Since the Gã think speech lacks the necessary persuasive power, they believe messages of power should never be spoken. Speech identifies the message only with an individual speaker, severing the message from the realm of social imperative. This example particularizes for a single culture the generalization that African songs are mechanisms of social control. The kinds of questions put to music and language here have general applications, addressed by several investigations into the poetics of African song (including Coplan 1988).

This approach entails another problem of translation, for it shows how and why the stylization of a sung language might differ from that of a spoken one. It builds on content analysis, probing for aesthetics while considering situational and contextual factors. Finally, it adds to an understanding of culture-specific definitions of a compositional error in music.

MUSIC AND SPEECH TONES

African composers in many cultures work with languages in which pitch and duration have semantic value. Therefore, ethnomusicologists have studied relationships between language and music, involving matters of pitch, time, and timbre. African musicians perform in the speech mode by trying to reproduce the sounds, words, and phrases of spoken languages, usually on instruments. They do this directly, with

speech surrogate   Use of musical performance, often by instruments, to reproduce
relative pitch and rhythm of speech

atumpan   Single-headed barrel drum of the
Ashanti people that is played in pairs tuned
a perfect fourth apart

dùndún   Double-headed, hourglass-shaped
pressure drum of the Yoruba of Nigeria
that can produce glides of speech

attention to style. However, they employ special techniques if the text comes from
another language, if words are obsolescent in their indigenous language, if a word is
homophonous with another, or if it becomes so in the musical version. Not all
African languages are tonal languages, nor are all languages for which Africans create
musical surrogates African languages. The language of the Sangri is not tonal, and the
people of Gomera and Hierro, two of the Canary Islands, create musical vehicles for
Spanish texts.

Musicians usually select instruments to perform in the speech mode.
Instruments also perform in the dance mode and the signaling mode. The latter produces specific patterns of tones and timbres, which Africans understand to represent
specific messages: "There is a fire," "Come to search for a lost child," and so on. In
such instances, there is no attempt to create acoustic similarity between the message
and the sounds that convey it.

Common choices of instruments are drums, horns, iron bells, lutes, mbiras,
musical bows, slit drums, whistles, and xylophones (Carrington 1949; Kubik 1985;
Nketia 1971). Where more than one instrument acts as speech surrogate, performers
can usually make conversions. Investigators have found that factors influencing musicians' choices include ecology, technology, patterns of settlement, economic systems,
social organization, linguistic traits, the carrying power of instruments, and aesthetic
conventions.

Noninstrumental music performed in the speech mode includes whistling (used
by the Karangu and Shona of Zimbabwe, the Ibo of Nigeria, and the Venda of South
Africa), falsetto (used by the Jabo of Liberia), and syllabic substitution (used by the
Lokele, the Duala, and the Yaounde of Cameroon). Syllabic substitution can be
developed either directly by the voice (which will, like the instruments, intone the
patterns), or indirectly, when the voice imitates patterns performed first on a speech-
surrogate instrument, as do Nigerian Hausa musicians who use a technique like that
of African-American scat singers (Carrington 1949:74–76; Umiker 1974:497–500).

The verbal material patterned in music may be poetry, paraphrases of poetry,
proverbs, or brief, repetitive sentences. Ethnomusicological inquiry has been into
techniques used by musicians to produce the sounds, techniques for solving the special problems of individual languages, and the reception and responses of audiences.
Most percussive instruments can accommodate differences of pitch by assigning to
each instrument one speech tone level, or (if the instrument has a wide melodic
range) by assigning it a pitch for each speech tone level. Instruments with a large
vocabulary of pitches achieve timbral contrasts on linguistic surrogates by stepwise
progressions, and drummers achieve them by striking the drumheads in various
places. Timbral contrasts help distinguish the sounds of vowels or double consonants.
Time is conventionalized so that long or sustained tones are executed by repetition of
the note, or by silence. Music may not exactly maintain the rhythms and tempos of
speech, but it does not usually violate them. Intonational and temporal features mark

the boundaries of phrases at the same places where they would occur in speech. Changes in amplitude most often signify stress.

One problem arises when the number of tone levels available on instruments does not correspond to the number of tones in the language. Then, musicians may either make musical adjustments to replicate on the instruments the height, stress, and tempo of the speech tones (thus retaining the traits of speech), or alter the speech in some way. Like the Gā, whose language has three tones, the Ashanti perform the three tones on two *ntumpan* (sing. *atumpan*), single-headed barrel drums, tuned about a perfect fourth apart; a metal idiophone may be attached to the low-pitched drum. The Ashanti produce the third tone through timbral contrasts. However, the Ewe reduce to two tones the Twi patterns (borrowed through cultural contact): they play the middle one as a low tone in unaccented syllables, or they simply add another instrument and another performer to play it.

Glides in African languages pose a special problem. The Yoruba language has four tones and a glide. Musicians replicate it on a double-headed, hourglass-shaped, armpit-pressure drum (the *dùndún*), which, with the application or release of armpit pressure (before or while the membrane vibrates), can produce twelve tones per octave, plus glissandi. With two iron gongs, the Efik of Nigeria satisfy the same linguistic requirements. They play the upper three pitches on the high gong, and the lowest one on the low gong. They may play glides on either gong, depending on whether the glides fall (low) or rise (high). The special problem posed by glides resolves itself in other ways. The Luba simply avoid them; the Yaounde use two rapid tones in succession (Stern 1957:488–489).

Audiences use everyday linguistic competence to decode the messages. When performers borrow speech forms and their musical articulations from another language, or use obsolescent words in their own, another special problem arises. Audiences resolve it by translating the music into their indigenous or everyday language. Since there is no one-to-one correspondence between the musically sounded and spoken forms, meaning operates arbitrarily, in the manner of symbols. To maintain clarity for the audience, the musicians sharply and specifically define such messages. For the sake of clarity, they also abbreviate words.

To resolve the ambiguity homophonous terms pose, African musicians extend a message by replacing a word with a descriptive phrase. Performers may also shift the position of the word in the phrase, or omit it. Both techniques help the audience decode messages, and push music in the speech mode toward greater conventionality.

MUSIC AND NARRATIVE

African communities combine texts with music to create recitations of narrative songs, genealogies, and epics. Aside from a study on the Kpelle Woi epic (Stone 1988) and phonograph recordings documenting sung stories, genealogies, and histories of the Zulu, the Shona, the Karanga, the Duma, the Soga, the Wolof, and their West African neighbors, ethnomusicologists have given little attention to analyzing such music thoroughly. However, published accounts pinpoint certain issues associated with understanding it. These include concerns for plot and discourse in explorations of how Africans tell, understand, and use stories; the configurational and episodic dimensions of African narratives; time, not necessarily lineal or chronological in African storytelling; inaugural, transitional, and terminal strategies; rhetorical touches and flourishes; how stories give form to and convey experiential knowledge; how performers create and use the circumambient natural and social space; the multiplicity of sociomusical purposes; and audience anticipation, perception, and interpretation, including processes of projecting, imagining, construing, inferring, and hypothesizing.

More frequently, performers try to make audiences "see the music and hear the dance." Both are integral parts of public occasions in African societies.

Both within performances and without, African musicians employ additional textual elements and ideas, or combine music with text in distinctive, practical, and ideational ways. The Dogon believe the sound of the drum once revealed speech to humans (Dieterlen 1957). In a syllabic recitative, the Hutu sing biographies of cattle (Hiernaux L'hoest 1965). The Tutsi sing maps of their dogs' struggles with hunted game and roll calls of soldiers (Verwilghen 1952). The Nzakara imitate the sounds of a turtledove as a decoy for the animal while hunting it. The Maure set each poem in a meter or style that corresponds to set musical rhythms and modes (Dieterlen 1966).

Among the techniques ethnomusicologists study are verbal exchanges between audiences and performers, instruction in rhythm and rhythmic patterns using mnemonic phrases or syllables that show tone, time, and timbre (Knight 1974:28; Koetting 1970:120; Kubik 1972:169; Ottenberg 1973:32–33), the use of mnemonic phrases in dance instruction (Stone 1982:70), and syllables showing size, shadings, and luminescences (Lasebikan 1956:44; Samarin 1965:120). Composers of melody in urban industrial settings (Hampton 1983) have continued to manipulate language, stylize it, and follow its features: "It is scarcely an exaggeration to say that without African languages, African music would not exist" (Bebey 1975:122).

DANCE

Intertwined with African music is dance, which may accompany the music so a performance emphasizes an array of instruments and voices. Musical accompaniment to dance may foreground visual elements. More frequently, performers try to make audiences "see the music and hear the dance" (A. M. Opoku, personal communication, 1970). Either order of relationship may characterize an entire dance, or only a phase of it in combination with music. Both are integral parts of public occasions in African societies. This fact, with the dominance of functionalist paradigms, has led researchers to stress a definition of dance according to its uses, roles, and genres. Critiques by current researchers argue that the results blur social differentiation, and neglect how individuals partake of community aesthetics and use socially constructed emotions to dance their identities and experience them through dance. These critiques have given rise to reinterpretations of received data and newly formulated approaches to current investigations, beginning with danced-identity issues.

Meaning in African dance is bound up with societies' concepts of bodily movements and personhood (Blacking 1985:66). Researchers contend there is not one body, but many culture-specific bodies or notions of the body and movement. Through music and dance, societies may express interrelationships of different classes of being (supernatural and human), relationships among humans, and relationships between humans and the natural world. Idiographic studies prove these expressions configure in historically particular ways. The nomothetic view underscores music-dance elements and ideas that African societies share.

Investigators note indigenous concepts of style, stylistic variation, shape, and their manifestation through movement in musical arenas. They attend to the dynamics (or effort) of movement, including the range of movement, the use of body weight, quantitative time (rhythm, tempo), qualitative time (acceleration, sustained, deceleration, quick), and the flow of energy. They detail various uses of the body, in characteristic stances and shapes, and in kinds of action; the body parts emphasized in succession, simultaneously, and in overlapping ways; isolations; gestures and their patterns; basic posture and variations on it; and the relative importance of gestures and posture. They extend the analysis by considering the use of space, including pathways, levels, and group formations, the "kinesphere" or reach space around individuals, and the quality of movement through space (linear, sculpting, planal).

Elements of African movement may express ethnicity or cultural identities. Williams, Steemers, and Kumah begin their report on Ntwumuru dance by showing, by the exegesis of a song text, how the song's meaning forms the nucleus around which the *sokoade* unfolds Ntwumuru ethnic identity (1970:36–39, 80). The song says: "*Eee*, the weaverbird's child, the orphan comes to dance, dance, dance. This is the dance belonging to me. Dance. The child of the weaver bird, the orphan comes to dance." The exegesis says the dance ("orphan") is not restricted to those with special skills or statuses. However, like the weaverbird (whose nest is too complex for other birds to copy), the Ntwumuru are the sole owners of the *sokoade*. Its kinetic patterns include three segments: *kumumuwum* 'spinning'; *kikyen*, one short light step, followed by one long heavy step; and *kyenkyenbrika*, a step-step-turn-around pattern. The names of these patterns are kinaesthetic onomatopoeia and phanopoeia, pointing to linkages between movement, text, and music. Other patterns take their names from the accompanying drummed patterns (combined rhythm and sonority), one of which, *kedenkenkyew*, points up the verbal basis of the drumming. Seven drums, seven horns, and a gong accompany *sokoade*.

Early ethnographers of African dance recognized an "African orientation" of movements toward the earth; recent investigators have sought more detail and specificity (Blum 1973). Influenced by indigenous perceptions communicated through verbal discourse, researchers of ideography have recognized that a "tendency toward sameness in the dance is found in all performances at all times and in all sections of the tribe. . . . This uniformity . . . gives it some sort of ethnic identity" (Wembah-Rashid 1971:40). This would seem to call for a concept of movement signature, defined as an element of movement that consistently marks dances from a given culture, and distinguishes them from dances of other cultures. Ewe communities, and those of their Ghanaian neighbors, recognize the emphasis they place on sharp upper-torso movements, specifically rotation of the shoulders, upward-downward movements of the shoulders, and contraction-release of muscles over the shoulder blades. The neighboring Gā emphasize shuffling foot-movements, derived partially from the flow of the energy of hip movements. The Ashanti emphasize arm-and-hand gestures that succeed soft shoulder movements; the Dagbani emphasize rippled lower-torso movements, using stomach muscles. The Kasena-Nankani emphasize the raised knee. Maasai men punctuate their prancing with jumps, and Zulu dancers make leaps. The Nuer make high jumps in lines, their kinetic signature. Similar signatures are the Kikuyu's runs and leaps, and the Dogon's brief, repeated, motivic figures of little amplitude.

Dancing individual identities

Not only in the general ways of ethnicity, but also in specific intrasocietal ways, African people dance their identities. To celebrate the primordial experiences of individuals at the level of body cells and tissues, the Fang of Gabon perform *zen naombi* (Fernandez 1973). These song-dances, by recalling the mythological events of cre-

Most African cultures install and validate the initial
identities of individuals with dances at ceremonies of
naming.

ation and dispersion, emphasize satisfaction and depletion, and celebrate Fang culture. The Mbem of Cameroon have a special annual public dance informally to regulate conception and birth.

Most African cultures install and validate the initial identities of individuals with
dances at ceremonies of naming. In East Africa, a Maasai child of Tanzania will have
three such ceremonies. The first, after naming by the child's mother, features short,
stamping steps; music assumes the form of praise songs, and celebrants alternate
them with prayers for the child's health, success, and bravery. A festival featuring a
different genre of music follows a second naming, done by the child's father. After a
child learns to walk and receives its final and principal name for life, its family sponsors a third ceremony. Its dances mark a child's identity within the human community, the father's patrilineage, and the local society; its music refers to these aspects of its
identity.

Frequently, Africans welcome unusual births with special dances. After the birth
of twins, the Luo of Kenya let the infants derive their initial identities through a
month-long dance. Goatskin dress, ornamented by vine necklaces and belts, and finished with clay smeared on the body, set up the relationship between the twins and
locally important ecological features. Part of one's identity may derive from the circumstances of birth, so the dancing of a *miend kumu* helps identify Luo children
about whose conception the mother was ignorant for some time.

At ceremonies for puberty and weddings, the principal actors dance their identities. Dances of puberty refer to the initiates' future identities as spouses, parents, and
producers within the society. They embody a society's principal ideas about gendered
movement, for children must not enter adulthood without special instruction in the
conduct of their future personal and occupational roles. In African societies, the division of labor is itself usually gendered (Malos 1980:7; Boserup 1970; Tong
1989:183–186).

The central actor in Nyanga boys' ceremony of puberty is the circumciser, who
must sing and dance in three stages, the last for the collective of initiates sequestered
in the forest near a river, where they remain confined for at least three months. His
mask has a hornbill's beak (above the eyes) and feathers (on top), and he carries
implements symbolizing a honeybird. His dance employs rapid and abrupt steps and
gestures. His song texts are metacommunicative and aphoristic: "We shall do wonderful and astounding things in the valley near the river of white clay"; "He has bitter
pain"; "Oh! Mother-of-the-initiates, the astounding rain is sweeping; he is calling
imploringly for his mother" (Biebuyck 1973:89). Men tell the boys to be brave, calm,
and fearless. As with many peoples living in and near a forest, songs often use images
of birds: "a honeyeating bird," a hawk "who glides in the sky in the realm of the
eagle," and "carries off the chickens." For the Nyanga, dance has special powers: they
recount stories of heroes who use dance to escape danger, and of little people who
escape the dragon or forest specter using dance and song (Biebuyck 1973:89).

Shilluk boys encircle the drum, salute it, and dance, entering manhood with shambling and jumping movements, which conform to descriptions of maleness in the Shilluk ideology of gender. This is the first dance the boys perform, for dancing is an activity for adults. It is the first time boys use shields, ostrich-shell beads, and other ornaments appropriate for men. These provide percussive accompaniment for the dance. On the sidelines, other dancers mime the boys' future productive activity, lassoing a hyena or dragging the effigy of a goat. Bambara girls begin their puberty dance with steps measured like those of a child learning to walk; concluding with nine leaps, the girls pronounce their new identities as women.

The documentary record shows more elaborate puberty ceremonies for boys (in duration, number of arts, mode of artistic integration, community participation, and community focus). This view may stem more from past investigators' perspectives than from African artistic practices, and feminist researchers are questioning it. Daniel Biebuyck's report on Nyanga boys' puberty ceremony details women's involvement. He notes the proceedings exclude women, who must prepare and send their son's meals to them, and may not see the sacred instruments. Yet women sing their concern for their sons in dialogue with percussion sticks, played by the boys' tutors: "Ae, you initiate when you went to be circumcised. . . . I was sitting, thinking and agitated in my heart. . . . I was dead of tiredness. I was hanging around in the village. I was sitting thinking shall I sing about what I do not know" (Biebuyck 1973:88). Music and dance construct, and are constructed by, emotions associated with identities and identity changes.

Weddings, often ceremonial outgrowths of puberty ceremonies, emphasize the dominant ideologies of gender, the union of kin groups or lineages, and individual choice. An ensemble of flutes and drums, not uncommon in the West African Sudan, accompany Bambara brides' dances, though the focal point is the bride and her female friends, the dancers. They form a long line for her wedding dance, stretching their torsos and drawing them back slowly en route to the village gate. In Kenya, Samburu wedding dances occur in the afternoon. To the sounds of songs and dancers' ornamental costumes, women's shuffling dances and stepping dances invoke blessings on their fertility. Men perform their dance in two parts: display dances, the first, have thrusts, accompanied by low-pitched guttural sounds, portraying competitiveness among young men while young women look on; clan dances, the second, use springing movements, admit female participation, and emphasize unity.

Funeral dances may emphasize human relationships, interaction with the supernatural environment, and ideas about personhood. Many African societies view death as a force that transforms, rather than ends, life. It makes a mortal being an ancestral shade with supernatural abilities. In *molimo* 'death-ceremonies', the BaMbuti of Zaïre dance the identities marked by such views. They emphasize cooperation among the surviving mortals, who open the dance by singing to awaken the benevolent forces of the forest. Their song calls the attention of these forces to the dancers, who sway as they sing. An elder woman then dances, and the funeral ends with a dance to extinguish the ceremonial fire (Turnbull 1961). In some societies, funeral dances may take their organization from stages or microevents in preparation for interment. The Lus settlements of Cameroon have such dances, including a circular dance to shield the men who do the autopsy required for each adult corpse.

Music-dance associations perform at Igede funerals in Nigeria, led by a master dancer (*ayidewoh*), whose vocal sounds the people liken to those of a bird. Musicians—including performers of three drums, slit drums, a rattle, a bell, and a horn—play under large trees, over special objects buried in the ground. One performer, carrying a ceremonial shield, sacrifices a chicken to the slit drum. Two soloists perform a declamatory duet, overlapping the chorus in responsorial form.

asafu   A dance of the Fanti in Ghana that
may only be performed by men belonging
to the warrior company

gingiru   A four-stringed lute, which only
physicians among the Dogon may make;
provides rhythm for the spirit to heal

adowa   Dance of the Gã of Ghana performed
with bamboo stamping tubes and a bell or
rattle and that utilizes a timeline

When members of the audience hear their names drummed, each dances solo, while the others participate in a circle dance. Symbolizing death—fast, unexpected, invisible—is a special dancer, who arrives unexpectedly, salutes the musicians by jumping once in front of them, and then sprints to the cemetery. Robert W. Nicholls, who reports this performance, develops a discussion of issues around the problem of documenting this dancer, who, because his movements are rapid and abrupt, looks blurred in photographs. Nicholls wonders what this means—socially, artistically, and for field-research techniques and methods. He contrasts what one sees in the photographs with what one sees in performance: a dancer wearing a caramel or grey, crocheted body stocking, and a carved black or red head mask (1984:73). One Igede consultant asked, "How are you going to express it when someone you love dies? Are you going to kiss his dead lips and say goodbye? You will dance—that is the way to express your sorrow" (1984:74).

In addition to individuals' changes of identity, African dance may call attention to stable identities. For members of a social category, proscriptions on dancing may accomplish this, especially in stratified societies. Yet proscriptions and prescriptions mirror the same phenomenon. The Samburu believe mature men should distinguish themselves, not in dance, but in debate: dancing is for young men. Ganda society of Uganda permitted neither the kings nor their wives to dance, except among themselves. Passive participation at performance arenas in ways other than dancing signified Ganda royalty. In Mali (where masked dancing has saliency), the Dogon believe a duty to refrain from dancing marks superior status, so elder people should not mask. Dogon society prescribes special dances and music for priests, women, warriors, nobles, and people in other social categories. Shilluk begging dances are exclusively for parties of women who perform them to receive gifts of cattle from wealthy men in neighboring villages. In Fanti society in Ghana, only men who belong to the warrior's company may perform *asafu*, a genre of dancing and drumming. In Zambia, a Bemba man or woman may perform solo dances while singing for another out of respect. In this way, Bemba dancers fulfill social obligations to those of higher status. A Bemba commoner may dance for a chief, and a young man for an older person. A senior Bemba man may dance for a senior woman of his wife's family. The more energetic and joyful the dance, the more respect the dancer shows for the honored person.

Concepts of identity and person further involve notions of disease, disorder, disaffect in individuals, and (by extension to the collective) imbalance within the cosmic order. How dance operates medically or against disease is contingent on how societies define and diagnose disease, and on their philosophies of treatment. Dances in four societies illustrate this.

1. For the southern African !Kung, disease is a malevolent force that has entered a body; treatment centers on driving it out. !Kung women, singing and clapping

FIGURE 1   Labanotation of the basic movement of the *adowa*, a Gã dance.

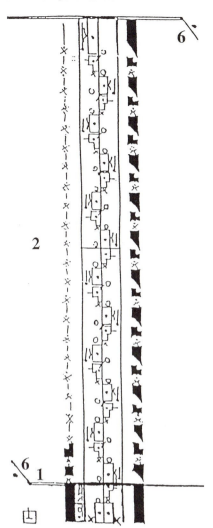

hands, inspire men to dance. Wearing rattles around their legs, the men (including the physician) stamp the ground, bending their waists. With controlled movements of their torsos, they lean forward. Once the physician is in trance, he can summon healing power (*n/um*), driving the disease out.

2. In West Africa, the Dogon, who believe disease is a loss of the forces of vitality in a personal soul, require patients to dance to the sounds of a *gingiru*, a four-stringed lute, which only physicians may manufacture. It puts rhythm into the descent of a spiritual being, who brings new life to earth, reinvigorating diseased souls.
3. In Egypt and Ethiopia, the Gurri have dances (*zār*) that entail convulsive movements with the power to mobilize the gods to possess tranced mediums and communicate through them. Prophetic and moralizing songs with hand clapping signal the gods' arrival and departure. The dances enable the mediums and gods to make a pact, restoring or maintaining balance in the cosmic order.
4. The divination of dreams helps the Lozi accomplish the same ends. Wearing special costumes, diviners make public through a dance the content of dreams.

African dances may serve purposes as diverse as military drills, taking censuses, testing weapons (as in Babungo, Cameroon), and fire-prevention demonstrations (as in Kom, Cameroon). At still another level, stock movements may frame a dance by recurring at predetermined points. The Kpelle open and close a dance with a side-and-forward step (*lokin*) and a jump (*kenema*). They also use intermittently occurring sequences, such as *sokopa* 'clockwise and counterclockwise movements' (Stone 1982). There may be dancing in place as a contrasting sequence in a larger pattern of movements, or to provide periods of rest.

African dances usually grow out of a defining set of kinetic elements. The rhythm of a basic movement, or a sequence of kinetic elements such as that of the Gã *adowa* (figure 1),is governed by a time line played on a bell, a rattle, or another musical instrument with strong carrying power. Dancers and musicians organize their performances according to this rhythmic pattern. In figure 1, the pattern is twelve beats at a tempo of about two beats per second. The basic movement of this dance consists of kinetic elements. Two other instruments also accompany it, but their rhythmic patterns are unvarying, repetitive, and circumscribed by the time line. Only one instrumentalist improvises rhythmic patterns, which should fill remaining silences and create shifting accents. They inspire, direct, or follow the dancer. Dancers must also improvise kinetic elements, thus elaborating the basic movement. These kinetic elements must also fit the time line.

The *adowa* uses bamboo stamping tubes. However, an array of drums, other percussion instruments, wind, and stringed instruments accompany other African dances according to similar principles. Some African societies with large repertories of dances often do not use or even have drums. For most Zulu dances, hand clapping and ornaments worn on the body provide the main accompanying sounds. In *igogo*, Igbo dancers of Nigeria prefer bells to drums as accompaniment. The !Kung and BaMbuti have no indigenous drums.

VISUAL ART

During a performance, dances develop in various ways. Performers embellish the basic movement with kinetic elements that reveal personal movement vocabularies (or idiolects) and individual styles of expression. Layering or texturing a performance may also involve a visual dimension. Forms and motifs within a dance space may expand the visual dimension of the performance.

Costumery

One of the ways African performers combine visual aspects of performance with music is through costumery, which may visually layer and sonically vary the dance. Costumery includes apparel, coiffure, scarification, cosmetics, jewelry, and held accessories.

Textiles

Researchers have focused on the relationship between movement and the design of textiles, noting the ways fabrics may mark the identities of participants in specific kinds of dances.

When dancers in societies of the West African Sudan perform, they set in motion the visual compositions on their indigo cloth. Yoruba, Fulбe, Malinke, Bambara, and other textile designers (most of them women), create resist-dye patterns diagonally from the selvage, the part of the cloth that stretches when moved. Dancers wear the cloth untailored (so as not to alter the design), and don it by wrapping themselves in it. Their movements animate the designs, which register social events and proclaim philosophical beliefs (Joseph 1978:36).

Ndebele women of South Africa extend the shape of a wedding dance with *nyoga* 'snakes', beaded dresses, hanging $1^1/2$ meters from their shoulders, and weighing $4^1/2$ kilograms. Covered by a blanket encrusted with intricately patterned beads, the dresses trail on the ground in a snakelike motion. The added effort required to dance in this apparel defines the character of the movement. The garment—of red, blue, and green, or of orange and white—lends a regal, legato, angular quality to the movement; without the extra length and weight, the same effort and shape applied to these movements would be staccato and sharper (Priebatsch and Knight 1978:24).

When the Gā king performs *adowa*, its overall shape changes. The costume he alone must wear affects his movements. Yellow, red, or bright blue, full-length, undulant garments, woven with gold threads, cause agitated movements to take on a visually soft quality. Heavily gold-studded sandals turn rotating foot movements into shuffling and jerking steps. Retainers accompany him into the arena, placing cloths on the earth in honor of his position. All other dancers must perform barefoot, in less elaborate attire, and solo. This variation, and the costume from which it derives, communicate the specialness of his identity.

African weavers produce cloth with verbal messages primarily for ceremonial occasions featuring dance and music. For durbars, enstoolments, coronations, and festivals, Ashanti dancers wear kente cloth. Ashanti kente weavers place weft designs perpendicular to the warp, the latter of which is one solid color or striped, containing the theme. These designs introduce another language-based channel into the performance, for they speak names, aphorisms, or proverbs. Some examples are: "Death has no fixed date"; "Work hard and constructively"; "One man cannot rule a nation";

"Don't kill my house and then mourn for me in public"; and "You pick a good tree to climb, and we will help push you up" (Smith 1975:38). Adinkra cloth, too, features stamped designs, carrying language-based messages.

Cloth designs worn in performances underscore the importance of music. The Bamana of Mali make mudcloth out of locally grown cotton and mud dyes. Against a dark brown background, white designs signify musical and other objects and ideas. *N'tamani* 'small drum' is the motif of an hourglass turned on its side; an upright hourglass inside a circle is a *wuowanyanko* 'Samory's griot standing in the stream'. Of this cloth, the Bamana make men's shirts, hats, trousers, and boubous (Imperato and Shamir 1970:32). Some women wear wrapped skirts made of it, but they prefer imported cloth.

Sound-producing accessories

Dancers use four types of accompaniment: (1) self-accompaniments, the main features of the dance; (2) those that are independent of the music; (3) those related to the music as a coordinated supplement; and (4) those serving as incidental or sporadic accompaniment, occurring at prescribed times (Kealiinohomoku 1965:293). With modifications, this scheme might apply to the analysis of African dancers' accessories, which include worn accessories such as those found in the nomadic Fulɓe ceremonial dance (*geerewal*). Dancers' anklets worn for the second suite of this dance provide a short-long rhythmic pattern with a weak-strong accentual scheme as accompaniment to rapid hops executed by fifty or more performers (*sukaabe*). Their sounds are principal features of this dance, performed in lineal formation (a long, single file) as they advance several meters, make a quarter turn, and repeat the sequence until they return to their original positions. For the first suite of ceremonial dances, performers stand erect, side by side, in one line with a kinesphere (the reach space on each side) of $2^{1}/_{2}$ centimeters or less, and rise to the tips of their toes. Then, while moving their heads alternately right and left, they bend their knees, and swing their arms forward in a long, legato turn. The songs for both suites are responsorial, with dancers singing the full response after the chorus performs it. Hence, the dancers perform both vocal and instrumental music.

African dancers also make music with strings of beads joined ladderlike (with small chains around their torsos), strings of metal and shells cross-gartering their legs, strings of small bells (wound across their torsos), corncob decoration, iron kneebells containing moving balls, heavy bracelets, iron and brass armlets, or ostrich eggshell girdles. The ostrich shell beads of Shilluk boys worn at their puberty ceremonies, the rattles worn by !Kung healers, and the ornamental costumes of Samburu wedding dancers, serve this purpose. Banana-shaped iron bells strapped above the knee joint, and bean-shaped ankle bells containing pellets, are common. Dancers also wear metal, bark, or cowrie shell anklets. Dancers' own stamps, runs, and jumps add to the rhythmic texture.

In addition to accessories worn especially for a performance, the sounds of quotidian accessories may identify participants at public performances. The data are uneven, but a few examples can clarify the potential of future investigations. To express parental pride, to amuse a child, and "to encourage rhythmic response" to sound patterns, Senufo children receive brass rings (with three bells) for their wrists and ankles, and they wear them until they reach eight years of age (Glaze 1978:63). Tuareg women give their daughters heavy brass rings (*jabo*), to be worn on their thighs until they have borne their first child. Royal and noble married women of Oyo-Ile, Ijebu-Ode, and Ile-Ife (Yoruba towns) wear Kangu bracelets, two on each wrist, which jangle when they dance (Awe 1975:71). Tuareg adults, male and female,

Miming and masking bring music, language, dance, and visual art together.

wear hollow rings filled with small pebbles, which rattle when the wearers' hands move (Mickelsen 1976:19). Depending on the structure of a dance, and how dancers use their limbs, these may provide incidental or sporadic sounds at prescribed times.

Other accessories

Worn accessories enable dancers to make music, as with the Ful6e (Woodabe); however, the accessories may not sound at all, but operate silently with other parts of the costume to enable the dance. To create variations within a timeline of twelve, Hausa-Dagomba *takai* stick or rod dancers do not improvise as individuals, but follow the dictates of the drum and the movements of the leader. They wear *dukusaru* trousers, which have gathers at the waist, much fullness in each leg, dropped or low horizontal (rather than rounded) crotch seams, and tapered ankle cuffs. Their turbans are designed to be full and pointed at the top, so the top hangs loosely to the right side of the head. Their shirts are loose-fitting and full, gored from a waistline seam. When they perform *takai*, the hems of their shirts swing out to form a circle, the tops of their hats flow outward, and their trousers expand to billowing cylinders. The sticks or rods they hold help shape the dance, but (they believe) the charms attached to their belts insure they will keep their balance (Harper 1970:52; Locke 1985:52).

Held and worn accessories may build the sonic dimension of a music-dance performance. Other African dancers carry millet stalks, swords, dancing sticks, and shields, as do the Shilluk boys cited above. Covered with brass, the dancing sticks resemble walking sticks; dancers clash or stamp them. Some held accessories, however, are silent, and visually embellish the dance. They may aesthetically and technically enable the dance, paralleling the worn *takai* charms. Paralleling the Luo vine necklaces and belts, goatskin dresses, and smeared clay worn at twins' naming dances, other held accessories may develop symbolism in the dance.

The *nky-gam* of Cameroon, danced by an association of diviners, features painted wooden stylizations of birds, which, as held accessories, "support the claim that every member can turn into a bird at will and thereby bring from distant lands the magic power that insures a plentiful harvest" of guinea corn (Gebauer 1971:11). With bent knees, while raising and lowering the birds, accompanied by pressure drums and xylophones, they move front and back. The birds have symbolic significance: as held accessories, they serve to expand and contract the range and color of the dance.

These examples hardly capture the richness and diversity of costumery in public African celebrations. They do, however, show that costumery can help define the motion and sonic contexts of African performances. Studies of costumery have largely focused on it as visual art, as a cultural artifact, and as economic goods with attached symbolism of status. Recently, researchers have tried to explain how its features operate systematically with those of music and dance, and to clarify how this operation relates to tastes and aesthetic priorities (Quarcoopome 1991).

Space

In Africa, spaces for performance tend to be temporarily, often spontaneously, devised, and sparsely furnished (Nketia 1974:1–15). Except in some urban instances, they are usually not enclosed, fixed, built spaces.

Musicians and dancers establish location in several ways. They may select a pre-existing site that is conceptually appropriate. Bali and Bata story-song performers of Cameroon set off a place in front of their clubhouse, where the doors are carved narratives of strong men and women, leopards slain, and victories in battle. Performers may simply use the only available site that will meet their physical requirements. In Mgbom, Nigeria, the Afikpo men's house (*obiogo*) is the only house in the village with a clearing around it. It has three oval platforms for seating, raised about three decimeters. Musicians and dancers perform in the clearing. To establish their location in space, they may manipulate and incorporate plant and animal materials into a conscious frame. The audience may so arrange itself in relationship to the performers, it creates a spatial design that helps the performance.

INTEGRATION OF THE ARTS

Miming and masking bring music, language, dance, and visual art together. In mime, performers improvise and integrate into a performance kinetic imitations of persons and natural phenomena. African audiences usually shift their spatial orientations to participate as dancers, and are (in most events) expected to do so. Therefore, they too, in addition to persons designated as performers, may mime. The flexibility in mimed performances and the fluidity of participation contribute to the muting of costumery. People usually wear everyday dress or dress considered standard and appropriate for the occasion, rather than the elaborate visual art found in masking. With masking, the dancer's donning a covering or disguise transforms him or her into whatever the mask represents or symbolizes. In a given society, only designated individuals perform masking.

Mime dances represent natural phenomena, sometimes symbolizing the relationship between people and their environment. Fang dancers outline the shape of a flower: with swaying hips, they bend backward to touch the ground; sweeping the ground right and left with the arms and head, they depict the blossoming, from bud to full flower. Bemba performers of Zambia move their feet to scratch the ground like a guinea fowl. Miming may take the form of hopping like a frog (as with the Matchappee, of Lesotho). Dancers imitate the gait, pace, and typical mannerisms of an antelope (as with the Gã), an elephant (as with the Fang), or a giraffe. Dancers representing animals may enact scenes of pursuit, capture, alliance, and assistance. After a successful hunt, the BaMbuti and the !Kung mime animal behavior or hunting activities.

Miming may point to the future responsibilities of the initiates at puberty celebrations (as with the Shilluk). It may represent the productive activities of adults: grinding maize, gathering potatoes, sowing seeds, making war, hunting game. It may honor the lifework of the deceased at a funeral ceremony (as with Gã variations on the *adowa*), or at other public celebrations. It may articulate the relationship between a political head and his principal symbol of office, thus expressing spiritual aspects of the polity. Underscoring the importance of understanding intent and meaning in African dance is the example of Zulu warriors who dance battle movements for training and practice.

One kind of setting that integrates music, language, mimed dance, and visual art is storytelling. The Ba-Benzele (Arom 1965) construct narratives around forest animals that are part of their everyday lives. Having observed animals closely, narrators frequently mime them in their comical aspect. Mimed movements, danced in place,

egungun   Masquerade dance of the Yoruba people of Nigeria in which bells are worn that mark the rhythm of the dance

gagalo   3-meter stilts used by dancers at a Yoruba harvest festival in Nigeria in honor of the town protector

balance their effects with solo passages performed parlando rubato. The narrator's solo part is the first half of a couplet completed polyphonically by other inhabitants of the camp, who form a choir. Ornamented pedal tones, melodic imitation, and improvised melismas around a cantus firmus create choral lines. These passages answer the soloist-narrator, who with a word, a few syllables, or onomatopoeic repetitions, shapes the story. Signals coordinate the solo and choral parts, some of which are mnemonics given by the soloist-narrator at critical points in the narrative. Overlapping parts, frequently found in African music, occur when the narrator improvises contrapuntal variations as the chorus sings. Rattles, hand clapping, and an inverted bowl struck with a stick may accompany the voices. Narratives develop by discussing episodes in detail and linking them conceptually, rather than chronologically. This is the aesthetic preference and commonest practice. Or the narrator repeats phrases or key words, and individuals in the audience (already familiar with the literature) use their knowledge and imaginations to reconstruct the narrative. Mime may depict posture, facial features and movements, gait, manner of eating, drinking, hunting, and other animal action.

Studies of masquerading or dancing masks attend to design, occasions of use, sponsorship, and purpose. African masks tend to be concentrated in the western and central regions of the continent, possibly reflecting the number of sedentary societies there. Ethnographers of art have taxonomized masks according to their structure and how people wear them. Covers worn over the face have holes for the eyes and mouth, occasionally the nose, and usually smooth backs. (Masks of other types need not provide for seeing or breathing.) Some, like masks that should eat, have no chins. Helmet masks are mounted on a smooth, firm, hemispherical surface, which rests on a snugly fitting base. Both the mask and the base are integral parts of a single object. Headdresses have masks attached to a separate object (as a cap) or resting in one (as a basket), which fits the head. Horizontal masks extend perpendicularly from the body, attached to a separate base, affixed to the head. Masks too small for an adult to enter are operated as puppets.

The remaining attire of the masked dancer may include raffia, cloth, plantain leaves, palm fronds, and other available materials. Many masks are painted with bright colors, or are finished with oil. Masked dancers may wear sonic accessories, like the metal ankle bells of Zahouli masked dancers, who through a series of leaps strike the ground with their feet, adding rhythmic patterns to that of a drum. *Egungun* (Yoruba maskers) wear atop their leather gaiters bells that mark the rhythm of their dance. There are many other examples of sonic costumery, including worn accessories that shape the dance. Such is the case of the 3-meter stilts (*gagalo*) used at a Yoruba harvest festival in honor of the town protector god, Orisa Oluwa. Ogede masks of the Edo, in Nigeria, carry clapperless bells, and play shields as rasps.

Masks help execute laws. They adjudicate and mete out punishment. They appear at funerals, festivals, religious ceremonies, and initiations. For the installation of religious or political officers, they may dance. They may appear simply to entertain audiences.

Masks identify the status of the dancers who wear them, as with the Tallensi of Ghana. They may identify the individuals who make and own them (as with the Dogon), or the principal artist-designer (as with *isinyago*, masks of the Makua of Tanzania), or the musicians who sponsor them. Elements of design, with the associated movements, may show the place of a particular dance mask within a symbolic hierarchy (as with the Igbo of Nigeria). This hierarchy, which may be elaborate, may include masks associated with secret or initiation societies (like the *guie'* and the *niangangon* of Côte d'Ivoire, and the *ekine*, a mask of Calabar, Nigeria), religious organizations and societies of religious practitioners (like the *zahouli*, a Yassua mask), and communal work groups (like the *tyi wara*, a Bamana mask). Masks may identify a village or a community as a whole (as does the stilt mask of the Makonde of Mozambique).

Masks represent a range of beings and concepts in African institutions. The *edjingi* represents spiritual beings, including gods (as with the BaNgombe of Zaïre), the *elerun* (a Yoruba mask) represents ancestors, and the *bundu* (a mask of eastern Sierra Leone) represents devils. Masks of this kind may appear in the imagined likeness of a spiritual being (as with the *nyau* of Marari, Malawi), or in such a likeness with human features added (as with the Kananga and Dogon). An assembly of masks may represent the world, and its dance the actions of the human community.

Masks may represent known and unknown animals (as the *nteepana*, a mask of the Yao in Tanzania). Among the Bobo of Burkina Faso, one such mask appears as a butterfly. The Bobo expect butterflies to swarm after the first rains of the season. To ensure the coming of the rainy season (essential for an abundant harvest), the Bobo use the masks for ceremonies at planting time and after harvesttime.

Masks may represent concepts pertaining to everyday life, including fertility (as with *amwalindembo*, a mask of the Makua of Tanzania), bad luck, gluttony, seniority, fidelity, honesty, and processes such as creation (as with *sirigue*, masks of the Dogon). Such masks may appear in the form of geometric shapes (as with the Dogon and the Tabwa).

Rarely are masks designed as individual humans or portrait masks, and these only for restricted occasions. The Bassa have a mask to depict a physically challenged person whose appearance might frighten others (Meneghini 1972:47). It dances with the crowd, tells jokes, and makes merry with a responsive audience, drawing attention to its body. The human portrayed may come out to greet the mask joyfully. It socializes the affliction, accustoms others to looking at it, and facilitates interaction with such a person, who might otherwise be avoided or cast out. The Marari of Malawi use a portrait mask, the *Dona* 'Lady' or *Maliya* 'Maria', to parody the Virgin Mary in a dance deriding undesirable behavior and teaching sexual mores (Blackmun and Schoffeleers 1972:41).

Some societies proscribe singing and speaking on the part of their masks, for fear of revealing the identity of the human who wears it. Other societies permit the masks to disguise their voices, and still others permit them to sing. Their songs may be metacommunicative, and may refer to themselves. One from Edo, Nigeria, sings the text "My glittering Igo mask." It thus describes the play of light on the palm fronds of its costume (Borgatti 1990:43). Some refer to the context of the performance, like the masks the Irigwe of Nigeria use at agricultural festivals: "You can harvest a thousand bundles of guinea-corn in a day. . . . A hundred people may spend a year farming, but they cannot harvest as you do" (Harper 1970:53). Masks may sing in reference to their age grade in initiation ceremonies. Masked dancers may exchange songs with onlookers, as do the *egungun*, for whom their audience sings praise songs and

In the basic posture, dancers bend from the ankles to the waist, highlighting the shoulder, a joint necessary for much of the work of farming.

incantations. Representing the ancestors, they respond with praise songs to the families of the town. Their songs incorporate concepts about the proper relationship between ancestors and their mortal kin, about cosmology, and about valued actions and concepts. Yoruba masks may criticize the political head in songs accompanied by *bata*-drumming.

Masks may dance improvisations to the accompaniment of set rhythmic patterns, identified with the deities they represent. They may also dance to rhythms a drummer creates. Masks not associated with deities may have their own choreography or prescribed pattern of movements, including special gestures and rhythms. Instead of dancing, masks may be danced for, depending on what they symbolize. As a physical object, a mask extends the possibilities for movement in some ways and limits it in others. Dance movements may match passages drummed in repeated alternation with a responsorial choral work (as a male duet, with a polyphonic choir, in *elewe* masking among the Yoruba). Maskers accompanying drums or other percussive instruments may dance simultaneously with vocal music; or they may dance to the accompaniment of drums or other percussive instruments, before or after a vocal work.

The structure of masked dancing is bound up with a given society's conception of space, and how ordering space becomes part of their experience. Masks are usually prepared in the bush or some other secluded or distant place; they usually perform within a village or town. Supervisors may guide the mask through a space where it must perform intricate steps. If the mask must dance at night, the space between the places of seclusion and performance receives special care; assistants will remove from the pathway the stumps of trees, smaller plants, and large stones. Some communities may even sweep the pathway clean. These actions appear to be primarily for negotiating the practical exigencies of masquerading, but others appear directed more at visual patterning and design. To accommodate the mask and the pathway of its dance, audiences may form undulating edges for an otherwise rectangular space.

The *tyi wara*

The *tyi wara* illustrates the integration of music, language, masked dancing, and the visual arts (Imperato 1975:8–13, 71–73). It comes from a narrative about a farmer, Tyi Wara, who taught people to cultivate the land. After they became lazy and wasteful, he in disappointment buried himself underground. The Bamana memorialize him by a mask, and appease and propitiate him at the shrine (*boli*) where his spirit resides. Patrons independently design the mask, and individual smiths carve it, so each differs from the others. However, they are stylistically unified by two principal designs:

1. They may have a horizontal, naturalistic design: the head and beak of a hornbill, with the body and horns of a roan antelope, or a mammalian head and snout with the body of an anteater.

2. They may have a vertical, abstract design: long horns, a series of triangular forms on neck and back, large ears, and a tapered face.

The *tyi wara* is a headdress of the wood of *Ficus graphalocarpus*, carried in a basket, blackened with ash, and adorned with red cloth fastened with metal. A veil of braided fibers, about 1¼ meters long, appliquéd with cowries and sewn to the basket, conceals the line where it meets the headdress. The same fibers, or cotton cloth strips, cover the masker's limbs. *Tyi wara* appears at agricultural work sites to inspire efficiency, and in the village to entertain with other masks representing forest animals. A collective of men and women sponsor the mask, but only men dance with it.

In the basic posture, dancers bend from the ankles to the waist, highlighting the shoulder, a joint necessary for much of the work of farming. After offerings and prayers at the shrine, the performance begins. *Tyi wara* moves slowly, with the end of a stick in each hand. Acrobatic movements, which include racing around the arena and jumping into the air, heighten the intensity of the dance. As it continues, movements accelerate. *Tyi wara* may invoke more blessings or mime an antelope. He ends the dance by jumping into a squatting position. Chosen for terpischorean abilities and short height (rather than for skill in farming), he does not rehearse. He dances between the farmers and an orchestra of drums and bells. While the ensemble claps rhythmic patterns in accompaniment, women sing a refrain as a choral ensemble to stanzas performed by a soloist. The mask emits interjections within the choral performances. Valorizing perseverance, hard work, and strength, and telling of excellent ancestor farmers, song texts say "Don't judge a man's looks, but his work," or "I would fearlessly call a lion because Tyi Wara is there" (Imperato 1975:8–13, 71–73).

In events surrounding *tyi wara*, Imperato explores how the auditory channel (the songs) amplifies the visual (the masked dance). He conjoins the three definitions of aesthetics as cited by McNaughton—aesthetics as canon of taste, canon of artistic skill, and system of critical contemplation (1991:52). He engages issues of spatial, temporal, and conceptual shifts in *tyi wara* (as the Bambara move *tyi wara* from farm to village square, from ritual to entertainment, and from "mythical personality" to "theoretical champion"), plus the Bambara concept of *dyo*, a state of stability and nonchange. He establishes that tradition is not static, but conventionally dynamic. This concept is not unlike those of Vogel (1991) and Munjeri (1991).

Imperato considers actors not by asking who and what roles they play, but rather by inquiring, albeit implicitly, who participates and what is the nature of their participation. These questions lead him to be inclusive of women and men (within the *tyi wara* society and without), children in the community, and individuals from different villages. Daniel Biebuyck (1973:88) posed similar questions, and recent explorations into African portrait masks place individual identities at the analytical center, teasing out both the "I" and "we" components of masking, and how they come to have meaning for individuals and their communities (Borgatti 1990). Margaret Drewal (1990), extending the concept of portrait masks beyond visual art, includes the various arts and their integration; she thus underscores the importance of understanding how African social life personalizes cultural forms, and conventionalizes personal experiences. Shifting from practice to meaning, Bradd Shore (1991:10) develops this point: the construction of meaning, he believes, "involves the perceptual encounter of a meaning-seeking subject and a culturally conventionalized object-world."

REFERENCES

Arom, Simha. 1965. *Ba-Benzele.* Bärenreiter Musicaphon BM 30 L 2303. UNESCO Collection. LP disk.

Awe, Bolanle. 1975. "The Asude: Yoruba Jewelsmiths." *African Arts* 9(1):60–70, 90.

Bebey, Francis. 1975. *African Music: A People's Art,* trans. Josephine Bennett. Westport, Conn.: Lawrence Hill.

Berliner, Paul. 1978. *The Soul of Mbira: Music and Traditions of the Shona People of Zimbabwe.* Berkeley: University of California Press.

Biebuyck, Daniel. 1973. "Nyanga Circumcision Masks and Costumes." *African Arts* 6(2):20–25, 86–92.

Blacking, John. 1985. "Movement, Dance, Music, and the Venda Girls' Initiation Cycle." In *Society and the Dance: The Social Anthropology of Process and Performance,* ed. Paul Spencer, 64–91. Cambridge: Cambridge University Press.

Blackmun, Barbara, and Matthew Schoffeleers. 1972. "Masks of Malawi." *African Arts* 5(4):36–41, 69, 88.

Blum, Odette. 1973. *Dance in Ghana.* New York: Dance Perspectives Foundation. Dance Perspectives, 56.

Borgatti, Jean M. 1990. *Likeness and Beyond: Portraiture in Africa and the World.* New York: Center for African Art.

Boserup, Esther. 1970. *Women's Role in Economic Development.* London: Allen and Unwin.

Carrington, John. 1949. *Talking Drums of Africa.* London: Carey Kingsgate.

Coplan, David. 1988. "Musical Understanding: The Ethnoaesthetics of Migrant Workers: Poetic Songs in Lesotho." *Ethnomusicology* 32(3):337–368.

Dieterlen, Germaine. 1957. *Musique Dogon Mali.* Ocora OCR 33. LP disk.

———. 1966. *Musique Maure Mauritania.* OCR 28. LP disk.

Drewal, Margaret Thompson. 1990. "Portraiture and the Construction of Reality in Yorubaland and Beyond." *African Arts* 23(3):40–49, 101–102.

Fernandez, James. 1973. *Music from an Equatorial Microcosm: The Fang of Gabon.* Folkways FE 4214. LP disk.

Gebauer, Paul. 1971. "Dances of Cameroon." *African Arts* 4(4):8–15.

Glaze, Anita. 1978. Senufo Ornament and Decorative Arts." *African Arts* 12(1):63–71, 107.

Hampton, Barbara L. 1983. "The Role of Song in a Gā Ritual." In *Sacred Song,* ed. Joyce Irwin, 111–126. Missoula, Montana: Scholars Press.

———. 1992. "Music and Gender in Gā Society: Adaawe Song Poetry." In *African Musicology: Current Trends,* ed. Jacqueline Cogdell DjeDje,

vol. 2, 135–149. Los Angeles: University of California.

Harper, Peggy. 1970. "A Festival of Nigerian Dances." *African Arts* 3(2):48–53.

Hiernaux L'hoest, Denyse 1965. *Rwanda-Burundi.* Bärenreiter Musicaphon BM 30 L 2302. Unesco Collection, recorded 1954–55. LP disk.

Imperato, Pascal James. 1975. "The Dance of Tyi Wara." *African Arts* 4(1):8–13, 71–73.

Imperato, Pascal James, and Marli Shamir. 1970. "Bokolanfini: Mud Cloth of the Bamana of Mali." *African Arts* 3(3):32–41.

Joseph, Marietta. 1978. "West African Indigo Cloth." *African Arts* 11(2):34–36, 95.

Kealiinohomoku, Joann Wheeler. 1965. "Dance and Self-Accompaniment." *Ethnomusicology* 9(3):292–295.

Keil, Charles. 1979. *Tiv Song: The Sociology of Art in a Classless Society.* Chicago: University of Chicago Press.

Kilson, Marian. 1971. *Kpele Lala: Gā Religious Songs and Symbols.* Cambridge, Mass.: Harvard University Press.

Knight, Roderic. 1974. "Mandinka Drumming." *African Arts* 7(4):25–35.

Koetting, James. 1970. "Analysis and Notation of West African Drum Ensemble Music." *Selected Reports in Ethnomusicology* (Los Angeles: Institute of Ethnomusicology, University of California at Los Angeles), 1(3):115–146.

Kubik, Gerhard. 1972. "Oral Notation of Some West and Central African Time-Line Patterns." *Review of Ethnology* 3(22):169–176.

———. 1985. "African Tone Systems—A Reassessment." *Yearbook for Traditional Music* 17:31–63.

Lasebikan, E. L. 1956. "The Tonal Structure of Yoruba Poetry." *Présence Africaine* N.S. 8(10).

Locke, David. 1985. "The Rhythm of Takai." *Percussion Notes* 23(4):51–54.

Malinowski, Bronislaw. 1930. "The Problem of Meaning in Primitive Languages." In *The Meaning of Meaning,* 2nd ed., ed. C. K. Ogden and I. A. Richards. London: Routledge and Kegan Paul.

Malos, Ellen. 1980. "Introduction." In *The Politics of Housework,* ed. Ellen Malos, 7–43. London: Allen and Busby.

McNaughton, Patrick R. 1991. "Is There History in Horizontal Masks? A Preliminary Response to the Dilemma of Form." *African Arts* 24(2):40–53, 88.

Meneghini, Mario. 1972. "The Bassa Mask." *African Arts* 6(1):44–48, 88.

Mickelsen, Nancy R. 1976. "Tuareg Jewelry." *African Arts* 9(2):16–19, 80.

Munjeri, Dawson. 1991. "Refocusing or Reorientation? The Exhibit or the Populace: Zimbabwe on the Threshold." In *Exhibiting Cultures: The Poetics and Politics of Museum Display,* ed. Ivan Karp and Steven D. Lavine, 444–456. Washington: Smithsonian Institution Press.

Nicholls, Robert W. 1984. "Igede Funeral Masquerades." *African Arts* 17(3):70–76, 92.

Nketia, J. H. Kwabena. 1955. *Funeral Dirges of the Akan People.* Achimota: University of Ghana.

———. 1971. "Surrogate Languages of Africa." *Current Trends in Linguistics* 7:699–732.

———. 1974. *The Music of Africa.* New York: Norton.

Ottenberg, Simon. 1973. "Afikpo Masquerades: Audience and Performers." *African Arts* 6(4):32–35, 94–95.

Peek, Phil, and N. E. Owheibor. 1971. "Isoko Songs of Ilue-Ologbo." *African Arts* 4(2):45–46.

Priebatsch, Suzanne, and Natalie Knight. 1978. "Traditional Ndebele Beadwork." *African Arts* 11(2):24–25.

Quarcoopome, A. 1991. "Adangme Arts." *African Arts* 24(3):56–65.

Samarin, W. J. 1965. "Perspective on African Idiophones." *African Studies* 24:117–121.

Shore, Bradd. 1991. "Twice-Born, Once-Conceived: Meaning Construction and Cultural Cognition." *American Anthropologist* 93(1):9–27.

Smith, Shea Clark. 1975. "Ashanti Kente Cloth Motifs." *African Arts* 9(1):37–39.

Stern, Theodore. 1957. "Drum and Whistle 'Languages': An Analysis of Speech Surrogates." *American Anthropologist* 59:487–506.

Stone, Ruth. 1982. *Let the Inside Be Sweet: The Interpretation of Music Event among the Kpelle of Liberia.* Bloomington: Indiana University Press.

———. 1988. *Dried Millet Breaking: Time, Words, and Song in the Woi Epic of the Kpelle.* Bloomington: Indiana University Press.

Tedlock, Dennis. 1983. *The Spoken Word and the Work of Interpretation.* Philadelphia: University of Pennsylvania Press.

Tong, Rosemarie. 1989. *Feminist Thought.* Boulder and San Francisco: Westview Press.

Turnbull, Colin. 1961. *The Forest People.* New York: Simon and Schuster.

Umiker, Donna Jean. 1974. "Speech Surrogates: Drum and Whistle Systems." In *Linguistics and Adjunct Arts and Sciences,* ed. Thomas A. Sebeok and Donna Jean Umiker-Sebeok, 497–536. The Hague: Mouton.

Verwilghen, Leo A. 1952. *Songs of the Watutsi.* Folkways FE4428. LP disk.

Vogel, Susan. 1991. "Always True to the Object, in our Fashion." In *Exhibiting Cultures: The Poetics and Politics of Museum Display,* ed. Ivan Karp and Steven D. Lavine, 191–204. Washington: Smithsonian Institution Press.

Wembah-Rashid, J. A. 1971. "Isinyago and Midimu: Masked Dancers of Tanzania and Mozambique." *African Arts* 4(2):38–44.

Williams, Drid, J. S. Steemers, and J. E. K. Kumah. 1970. "Sokoade Come and Dance!" *African Arts* 3(3):36–39, 80.

Time in African Performance
Ruth M. Stone

Themes of Temporal Organization
The Kpelle in Liberia
Epic and Time in Perspective

FIGURE I Kulung, epic performer of the Central Kpelle area in Bong County, Liberia.

TRACK 1

This study began with a puzzle. While working among the Kpelle people of central Liberia, I noted with some surprise texts that appeared disjointed, disconnected, and fragmented. What should I make of a verse like this?

> Sun falling, my friend Lanko Zoo-lang-kee.
> Was that Woi there?
> What is doing that?
> Let the song agree, let the song agree gently.
> Woi said, "That's fine." He said, "That's fine, then I'm ready for the fight."

At the moment I thought I was following a theme, a shift appeared, and another topic presented itself.

From that mystification, some fifteen years ago, I have been concerned with the problem of shifting themes in different areas of musical performance. I have studied how musicians cue one another; I have considered the drum patterns, horn hocketing, string ostinatos, and call and response of bush clearing (Stone 1982, 1985, 1986). In this article, I follow the facets of timing as found in *woi-meni-pele*, an epic that centers on the hero Woi. I am concerned not only with the rhythms of sound and the placement of text, but also with the larger flow of events, and ultimately with the movement of time for both the individual and the family.

The Woi epic combines singing, narration, dramatic performance, and instrumental accompaniment to tell the story of the superhuman hero and his adventures (figure 1). Its performance takes familiar elements and through magic makes them extraordinary. Woi is the epitome of brashness, bigness, boldness, and bravery, and his deeds encompass what the Kpelle say life is all about. His epic expresses in a microcosm the imagination of several generations of Kpelle artists.

THEMES OF TEMPORAL ORGANIZATION

Certain themes or patterns stand out in the foreground of what the Kpelle consider principles of timing. Built by the performers of the epic, time is experienced by both the characters and the audience. Performance time, in turn, is enveloped by the time of everyday life.

Kpelle time has several traits, which may be relevant to African musical performance generally.

Time emphasizes qualitative elements

Epic singers rely on onomatopoeic language to suggest timing. Similarly, recent research in music emphasizes African musicians' essential regard for timbre. Such attention stresses qualitative aspects, rather than quantitative and chronometric aspects (often mentioned in Western ordering of time in music). Drummers memorize mnemonic phrases that represent the subtleties of timbre that they wish to produce, rather than a numerical sequence of ordering pitches.

The lack of quantitative emphasis does not negate a complex level of synchronization. If African musicians do not stress counting, they are not thereby prevented from coordinating their movements. In fact, observers of African musical performance readily acknowledge that African rhythm is extremely intricate and complex. The result is achieved, for the most part, by synchronization that does not use a chronometrically based system of coordination. In other words, there is no clocklike basis for achieving split-second timing.

Western thought often equates quantitative time with precision. Thus, Thomas O. Beidelman comments that the Kaguru lack "precise" and "quantitative" ways of reckoning time (1963:19). When we look at time in songs and events in African music, we see precise timing evident with apparent absence of quantitative time reckoning. That Africans do not employ quantification in certain areas where Westerners do does not imply that they cannot or do not make use of quantification in other areas.

The absence of a clocklike mechanism for coordinating performance should not lead us to assume that Africans do not reckon time chronometrically. In Kpelle ritual performance, chronometric aspects assert an unusual importance not apparent in other types of performance. While the exact occurrence of some musical event is often difficult to predict, the timing of certain ritual events is quantitative and entirely predictable. A new mother and her baby emerge from the place of birth three days after the event if the baby is a girl, or four days after if the baby is a boy. Likewise, in Poro and Sande (secret societies, for men and women, respectively), young girls emerge three days after seclusion in a hut at the edge of the village, and boys emerge from seclusion after four days. Finally, the death feast occurs three days after death and burial if the deceased was a woman, and four days after if the deceased was a man. In Yoruba divination poetry (*ifá*), certain parts of the corpus repeat a specified number of times (Abimbola 1971:38). Elsewhere in Africa, similar examples occur.

These cases involve an inversion of the normal predominance of qualitative time to emphasize the quantitative on certain ritual occasions. In the Kpelle case, quantitative time is not associated with creative, progressive, or innovative elements; for the Kpelle, it denotes renewed creation and reproduction of the traditional aspects of life.

Some notable variations to the emphasis on the qualitative occur in Africa. Somali poetic performance is based on precise quantitative reckoning of moras (short syllables), chosen and grouped according to implicit rules (Johnson 1982, personal communication) [see MUSIC AND POETRY IN SOMALIA]. In other areas of life, Africans' skill with numbers is equally evident (Zaslavsky 1973).

Victor Turner's analysis of *mukanda* (initiation rituals in East Africa) provides further parallels. In those rituals, distinct from "rituals of rebellion," Turner notes a preference for relationships that stress "likeness rather than interdependence." These relationships represent, when ritualized, the unity and continuity of the widest soci-

Actions occur in three-dimensional space, and sounds occur "under," "above," "outside," and "inside." In epic events, heroes typically move in multiple planes and spaces, ranging from under the river to high in the sky.

ety, since they tend to represent the universal constants and differentials of human society—age, sex, and somatic features. By emphasizing these in the sacred context of a great public ritual, the divisions and oppositions between corporate groups and the total social system, viewed as a configuration of groups comprised of all or any of the component groups, are "played down" and forced out of the center of ritual attention (Turner 1967:265). The ritual context stresses unity and conformity, patterns of action different from those of everyday life [see HARMONY IN LUVALE MUSIC OF ZAMBIA].

Time delineates space

In many African societies, a musical performance is special and different from ordinary activity. It serves to create a marked-off sphere, within which people may relate to one another differently from how they do in daily life. The quality of time felt by participants in the event may correspondingly differ from that of ordinary life. The special status accorded to events in many African societies was noted as early as 1670 by John Ogilby, who describes a Sande girl's initiation-closing celebration:

> When they enter the Town, or Village, there the People gather together as if it were some Holiday, the sogwhilly [head of the initiation ceremony] leads to the Sporting-place, where one sits Drumming with two Sticks on a round hollow piece of wood. By the ill-tun'd Musick of which (if so we may call it) Instrument, . . . everyone understands his time; and they all seek to exceed one another in Dancing. (1670:451)

As we look at time through the epic, we sense new qualities. An event, here defined as a bounded sphere of interaction, frequently combines a complex of instrumental playing, singing, speaking, dancing, dramatization, and visual display, plus a variety of integrally associated arts. Music within an event demands a multifaceted analysis: viewing the event and its action requires a dynamic linking of multiple elements and features.

Kpelle performance places considerable stress on qualitatively distinguishing music by reference to space. Actions occur in three-dimensional space, and sounds occur "under," "above," "outside," and "inside." In epic events, heroes typically move in multiple planes and spaces, ranging from under the river to high in the sky. As an embodiment of time, music for the Kpelle has a character that contrasts to some Western notions of a flatter, more linear, progression.

The African emphasis on three-dimensional, spatial aspects of musical time should not be equated with timelessness. On the contrary, spatially delineated time is a special kind of time—a motion-filled percept.

Time emphasizes motion

According to the Kpelle, dancing, drumming, and singing all create aesthetic princi-

FIGURE 2   Kulung imitates Spider playing the slit drum.

ples of motion (figure 2). Even in the epic text, Woi's house moves to battle, the blacksmith's bellows pump, the woman's adze carves a bowl.

African accounts of performance in general provide ample evidence of emphasized movement and motion. Even in African-American contexts, the metaphor of motion is strong. It figures in artist Henry Dorsey's "placing of tractor wheels at certain corners of his house and along the edges of his property" to convey the image that the "earth itself was wheeled, could be mentally set in motion," and in black jazzmen's use of the sounds of railroad trains (Thompson 1983:156–158).

Time past informs time present

Stasis is by no means implied by the lack of linear progression: the past is dynamically manipulated in the present. Providing authority and sanction for the present, it constantly serves to create the present, in a most active and instrumental way. The present situation is a context for adjusting and reproducing the past to fit the exigencies of present action. Robin Horton's characterization of African thought as a "closed predicament" acknowledges the importance of the past, but it plays down the creative possibilities for manipulating that realm of experience (1967:177).

Performers incorporate departed ancestors and deceased great musicians in the music event to solicit actions favorable to the performance, particularly aid in improving their own playing or singing. Relationships of these departed are manipulated within the context of the present situation. Texts recall past utterances and knowledge, but are never simply repeated. As created anew in the present, they are viewed and experienced in the light of later sensibilities.

It would be a mistake to consider that in such acts the Kpelle are simply repeating what has already occurred. Change is inherent, even if not realized, in every reenacted social situation (Giddens 1979:210). The traditional is that which is authorized, rather than that which is never changing, for the authorized is subject to alteration within the context of performance.

The notion of historical past is particularly rich with implications. I will not argue, as Bonnie J. Barthold does, that pre-European Africa is characterized by a cyclic time, which later erodes into a period of temporal chaos, followed by a development of linear time (1981:6–7). Such an argument, with its undercurrents of cultural evolution, does not accurately accommodate the available evidence.

Barthold's characterization of African time as cyclic is a widely accepted generalization. This idea leads to the assumption that where there is cyclic time, there is no change. And going even one step further, one can reason that where there is no change, there is also no time (Giddens 1979:198). Thus, African music is performed, according to some writers, in a kind of timelessness. Such conclusions do little to illuminate the African and, particularly, the Kpelle perception of time.

Time is contingent

Elements that are part of the singer's repertory do not include the entire composition waiting to be reproduced like a score stored in the mind of the singer. Rather, the singer's stock of knowledge incorporates phrases, patterns, and proverbs to be woven and juxtaposed according to the needs of the moment. The knowledge of this process is crucial for ethnomusicologists. Unpredictable actions by participants may create an event that proceeds in any number of possible directions.

Time is multidimensional

From an analyst's perspective, we can use several of Alfred Schutz's ideas (1964) to study time as created in the Kpelle epic. As a phenomenological sociologist and amateur musician, Schutz explained that music—and he was referring to Western

quantitative time   Time based on clocks, metronomes, or other forms of chronometry

Poro   Men's secret society of West Africa that is a pervasive force in ritual and everyday life

Sande   Women's secret society of West Africa that is a pervasive force in ritual and everyday life

pele   Performance of the Kpelle of Liberia that features singing, dancing, playing instruments, and speaking

music—moves in a series of coordinated dimensions. Some of these dimensions are "outer time," serving primarily to coordinate the individuals making and experiencing music together. A conductor beating his baton is moving in this dimension, as is a metronome ticking the beats. Other temporal dimensions are "inner time"—subjectively experienced qualitative time. When two periods of time measured as equal by the clock seem quite different to us because of our experiential histories, we are referring to inner time. Though Schutz's conclusions derive from Western examples, the essential point is that musical time, because it coordinates simultaneously experienced dimensions, cannot be reduced to a single dimension. The nature of these dimensions in various African societies remains to be researched and described.

Kpelle musicians shift rapidly from the outer time of keeping together to various kinds of inner time. For them, however, outer time is not always quantitative. Furthermore, both outer and inner time can be qualitative time of different sorts.

Time exists only in the way a participant, a performer, or an observer experiences it. Time is lived by people. Their interpretation of it is central to the understanding of musical time. And since people live through time together, temporal flux is partially shared, and to the extent that it is shared, a mutually confirming synchrony among people results.

While we might easily accept this conclusion, we must consider how different it is from the commonsense notion of time as a unilinear entity. We have long thought of a musical composition as being created in a time that moves single-mindedly forward, measured, divided, and ordered by quantitative time. But upon reflection, we might accept that such a picture is not necessarily true.

For some years, ethnomusicologists interpreted African music from a limited view. Unlike many music theorists and musicologists, they may not have studied pitch more carefully than they did rhythm, but they still began their search from basic Western assumptions. Most fundamentally, they often assumed equally spaced underlying beats (Merriam 1977; Waterman 1985). While such studies usefully showed that rhythmic order and complexity are evident in African performance, Africans think about these concepts in subtly different ways.

More recent studies—by Gerhard Kubik, James Koetting, Paul Berliner, Roderic Knight, and others—have explored indigenous notions of timing and rhythm. Indeed, as Lewis Rowell has suggested (1985:5), our growing understanding of how Africans understand the temporal in music may lead us to ask whether there is not something new to learn about Western music when we apply African ideas to the practice of Western music—a practice little studied with ethnographic methods.

THE KPELLE IN LIBERIA

The Kpelle have been thoroughly studied by anthropologists and other social scientists. James Gibbs provides a good overall characterization in his essay "The Kpelle of

Liberia" (1965). Kpelle folklore has been examined by William Murphy (1976), Kpelle women's lives have been studied by Caroline Bledsoe (1980), and Kpelle cognitive patterns have been tested by John Gay and Michael Cole (1967).

My formal study of timing in epic performance began in 1970, when I spent the summer surveying musical performance genres throughout Bong County in central Liberia, but the background for my work had developed many years earlier. A great part of my impression and knowledge of the Kpelle stems from my childhood in Liberia, when I spent afternoons playing in the ricefields while Kpelle friends labored, or splashing in the local creeks where women fished. During that period I absorbed much of what I know about the Kpelle, including their language, without conscious effort.

After my initial musical survey (Stone and Stone 1972), I returned to Liberia in 1975, and for fourteen months studied two performing groups intensively (Stone 1982). During this time, while my husband and I lived in Totota, I recorded the epic performances to which I refer. At that time, however, I did not have a chance to study all the epic data. Only in 1982–1983 was I able to work through the earlier performances and conduct feedback interviews of the type that I had earlier conducted on cueing in music (Stone and Stone 1981). My epic text comes from a single area and a single storyteller, and though my interviews refer to neighboring traditions, I discuss it here as an example of a tradition that remains widespread, if sporadic, and as an illustration of patterns sometimes found in other kinds of performance. My aim is to pull apart one moment of performance (extended though it may be), using it to explain some salient temporal concepts of the Kpelle.

The Kpelle of Bong County participate in both an urban and a rural existence. To get cash for produce that is then whisked down the main highway to consumers in Monrovia, the rice farmers travel frequently to weekly markets like those at Totota, Sanoyea, or Yanekwele. For extended periods, some men live away from home to work in rubber and iron mining concessions. Others have moved their families to the concession towns, where houses with uniform exteriors stand in straight rows.

Living in villages reached by footpaths or auto roads, the Kpelle travel and move about a great deal. Some walk an hour or more each day to their outlying farms. Many frequent nearby or even distant towns, where relatives and friends reside. Some men work in the capital, Monrovia, some 145 kilometers away, and at month's end return to their families and homes, and to special musical performances.

A pervasive force in ritual and everyday life is Poro, the men's secret society, and the women's counterpart, Sande. Societies to which all adult Kpelle belong, Poro and Sande help socialize children and provide the enforcement of social hierarchy. They provide a source of authority not to be openly questioned. As the Qur'ān is considered to be at the core of Muslim life, Poro and Sande form the core of Kpelle life, shaping life through both ritual and ordinary action. The deep-seated temporal notions of these secret societies are continuous and changeless.

Aesthetic dimensions of performance

Kpelle aesthetic performances (pele) feature singing, dancing, playing of musical instruments, and speaking. They require people to listen, judge actively, and perform. Pele are vital to emotional life for the Kpelle. The temporal ideas of these events are characterized by segmentation and continual change, in contrast to those associated with Poro and Sande.

The Kpelle pattern differs fundamentally from more linear ways of organizing performance, which dominate Western culture. The Kpelle pattern influences how people think about performing and how they listen to and watch artistic performances. Pieces and patterns of sound vary not so much by sequence as by juxtaposi-

inside-outside   Distinction often made in describing social order or musical performance in West Africa

expandable moment   A segment of performance conceived as a unit and subject to layering of sound

wule   Term for song among the Kpelle of Liberia, which can be of various proportions

tion. The Kpelle might be better pictured as sculptors than as stringers of sound actions.

The textured moment in epic

For the Kpelle, *woi-meni-pele* constitutes a place and a time set apart from the ebb and flow of everyday life. To show that things happening within a *pele* are bounded from the rest of the world, participants comment, *Nga loi belei su* 'I'm entering the inside of the performance'. They emphasize that prior disagreements need not, and should not, be brought into the event. They often begin an event with the words *Zu e nee* 'Let the inside be sweet'. What happens during epic performance is inside, and the rest is outside.

The neighboring Kuranko of Sierra Leone emphasize the inside-outside distinction in balancing the social order (Jackson 1977:31), as do the Yoruba of Nigeria to distinguish the eyes gods use to see the heavens and those they use to see men and women (Thompson 1983:9), and as do the Tiv, also of Nigeria, to distinguish one's immediate surrounding from that with which one is unfamiliar (Abraham 1940:27).

The use of the concept of the moment implies time that is not perceived to be moving forward linearly. From the Kpelle point of view, this moment can expand like a bubble of soapy water, gradually blown fuller and fuller of air (Stone 1982:72). Furthermore, much as a large bubble can contain smaller bubbles, the large moment of epic can contain smaller moments.

FIGURE 3   A bottle-player provides rhythmic background to Kulung's performance.

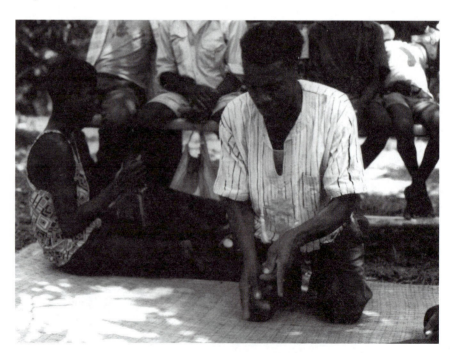

The Woi epic singer moves subtly and carefully to the inside of the performance. He does so by building the boundary that divides *woi-meni-pele* into stages. When he has the chorus and instrumentalists (figure 3) interweaving their patterns in endless repetition, he has made a beginning to the boundary. When the questioner asks his first question, "Whose voice is that?" the singer has his cue to begin building the narrative portion. Now there is not only epic being performed, but a distinctive story to be spun. The boundary adds up much like a crowd filling a Kpelle courtroom. First, people sit on the outer edges—in front, on the sides, at the back. Only with the border outlined do people begin to fill the middle, whether the room contains benches in straight rows or not. Once the narrator is moving within a particular part of the story, he begins his embellishment and weaving that will distinguish him as an individual singer.

Within the expandable moment

At a variety of structural levels, time is a "continuity of heterogeneous moments" (Gurvitch 1964:18). Moments are built at several levels of specificity. On the most general level, an entire performance can be viewed as a moment qualitatively different from other moments within the flow of life. Visually and kinesthetically, the Kpelle circumscribe and bound the spatial dimensions of the place where this moment is experienced. Before musicians enter a town to perform, they often process counterclockwise around its outer perimeter, employing sound as a spatial marker. As they circle it, they free the *pele* of malevolent spirits, and set it apart from everyday life.

On a more specific level, some moments exist coterminously with songs. Through creative improvisation, song (*wule*) is inflated to huge proportions. As one Kpelle performer explained, the longer one sings a song, the more one builds it. On its conclusion, however, moments of different sorts may be closely juxtaposed. At all times, the possibilities of expansion are contingent upon many elements, like audience response and performer synchronization.

On an even more specific level, within a song, observable moments can be distinguished from other moments. Such is the case when the event clicks in synchronous precision and a solo dancer emerges in the arena to display her skill in artistic motion. Before the beginning of the dance proper, she visibly defines the outer perimeter of her dance stage as she regally moves counterclockwise to circumscribe the area—and concomitantly the moment (Stone 1982:100–101).

Francis Bebey characterizes Gilbert Rouget's recording of Babinga dance as constructed of a series of short movements with interruptions (1975:128–130). In Hausa praise song performance, the singer figuratively inflates a patron as a blacksmith pumps bellows, and thus the audience member expands with the euphoria that the barrage of praises produces (Gidley 1975:98). Moments become "convergent and divergent movements which persist in discontinuous succession" (Gurvitch 1964:18).

Moments within the Woi epic

Key moments within the Woi epic use the ubiquitous Kpelle love for onomatopoeia. "Squirrel-Monkey has come out, *kili, kili, kili, kili.*" Contrast that with Yele-lawo moving to battle, "*va, va, va, va*"; or "Woi's wife was pregnant, *kpung-kung.*"

These moments build on proverbs and extracts. Such nuggets, by their particular positioning, embody much, lead to many associations, and raise the audience to new heights. The epic singer Kulung opens the first episode with the assertion that he was with Woi as he prepared to go to war. Kulung describes the people around Woi as a "sitting-on-the-neck crowd." The idea of sitting on a neck refers to a mother with so

But what is missing is both the description of the conflict of this episode and its embellishment with proverbs, the essence of the texturing. One person who heard a playback of it commented, "He isn't able to pick the inside of the voice."

many children that they hover around, clinging to her neck; to the Kpelle, this is a graphic and funny image.

In episode two, Kulung uses two proverbs to inspire the instrumentalists to work more precisely. After a direct comment, "Stop, you hitting it, hold it in your hand. Pass it on the direction of the mouth (opening)," he sings: "Iron doesn't like Left-behind. Cut it short, short, let's go. Hold it like rice and its tying rope." The proverbs and their link are masterfully joined. "Iron doesn't like Left-behind" refers to the bush-clearing crew, working collectively to remove underbrush and to fell small saplings: slow workers are unwelcome. The middle phrase is revealing, for in ordinary contexts one says "Cut it short, short, let's go" most often to encourage women hoeing the soil for rice planting to keep with one another. The third phrase is the second proverb, which recalls the manual dexterity of harvesting rice: while cutting the stalks with one hand, the harvester holds a rope to tie the bunch in the other.

The three phrases refer consecutively to the major rice farming seasons: clearing, planting, and harvesting. The first and the last are proverbs in common use, linked by a more straightforward cue to form an allusion for the instrumentalists. Kulung has used familiar language, joined in his own aesthetic pattern to sing to his cohort of performers. The care he wants in the music is the same cooperation people demand when they work together to clear land and make a farm.

In episode three, Kulung comments on the musicians' performance, requested in episode two. He sings the proverb "A dancer doesn't stand outside, / Then she has broken the law." Then he breaks into speech: "Initiated ones, thank you, thank you, thank you, thank you. That's the song, that's the song, that's the song, that's the song, that's the song." He has paid the players and singers a supreme compliment by comparing them to a dancer, for this proverb refers to a highly competent dancer. It means that when the music is playing properly, a really good performer must give in to it and dance. To resist the sound would deny the gift of her ability. These performers are being told they are skilled, and have moved the performance to a new level of competence. This cue is a sign that Kulung thinks the music is moving beyond the tuning-in stage, and is becoming focused on a kind of inner time.

This proverb also resonates with meaning for the plot. Spider has been brought to play the slit drum, but in his concern for eating would rather not perform (figure 4). He has no choice, as the food is circled around him. He needs to perform in exchange for the food, and will be in trouble if he does otherwise. His dilemma is even more poignantly explained through a proverb sung earlier in the episode:

FIGURE 4   Kulung imitates Spider eating a mound of rice.

The Poro is on a person, the matter angers him.
Night falls on him, the daylight bewitches him.

His plight is compared to the arbitrary and inarguable authority which the secret societies hold over people. Though he is upset about his required performance on the slit drum, he has no recourse in the matter. To say that night falls on him is another way to express that problems have come to him. The daylight itself bewitches him. He is a trapped person. This is a particularly tough spot for an individual in a society where most things are negotiable, subject to being argued.

The pathos of Spider is not without its comic element. For Spider cannot resist food, and the lengths he will go to obtain food are familiar in Kpelle folklore. With every bite he eats, he entraps himself further in the performance.

> NARRATOR. Ah, the food they are making! They are cooking rice again and packing it. And Woi is lying in the sky.
> AUDIENCE. What is he going to do?
> NARRATOR. When Spider is full, then Woi will get out of the sky and get down. Then the war is ready.
> QUESTIONER. Don't lie to me.
> NARRATOR. Very close. I can't do that. Woi has now done it, Spider's rice. They set out the rice, eddoes [a kind of starchy tuber], sweet potatoes, ripe bananas. All things they circle around him.

And thus we see Spider enclosed by his own undoing and weakness. Such a crisis endlessly amuses the Kpelle; perhaps it recalls the plight they often feel. The way his plight unfolds structurally resembles the way the episode unfolds. Circles move outward from the center of action. Whether Spider or the audience is in the center, the expanding circles are the way Kpelle life develops.

If each episode is a kind of moment to be built, episode six seems to be a moment whose expansion never properly happens. The textures of movements are placed with the sound of the house moving (*zi, zi, zi*), and the song of the frogs in the swamps, serenading the battle by singing Woi's name repeatedly. But what is missing is both the description of the conflict of this episode and its embellishment with proverbs, the essence of the texturing. One person who heard a playback of it commented, "He isn't able to pick the inside of the voice." It is this selection of essences that makes the performance aesthetically pleasing and fully expands the moment.

Moments in context

Ruth Finnegan mentions a range of events in Africa that feature musical performance—puppet shows of the Mande, masquerades, and epic enactment (1970:504). The performance of any event is determined by the intersection of temporal dimensions. Fundamentally, the activities of the agricultural cycle may impinge. During periods of heavy work, events are less frequent. Around harvesttime in many African communities, after the work is completed, events proliferate. In areas where people work primarily in concessions as wage laborers, a wealth of events may center around the monthly payday. The latter situation becomes more tied to the calendar and less to the social activities that serve to anchor life. Dale F. Eickelman comments on how the Bni Battu people of Morocco anchor the events of their lives.

> Events are sometimes remembered as occurring "before the sunset (prayer)," "at dawn," or "just before the market," but they are not ordered in a more abstract chronological sequence. Events like "Ahmed's death," "the famine," "the day the airplanes chased us," "before the Mahzen (government) came," "the sunup," "Hammu's wedding," and "when Sharef was small" are . . . largely unintelligible to outsiders since they can be translated only awkwardly into lineal concepts of time. (1977:44)

I eventually learned not to ask "What time will the performance begin?" but "How are the negotiations proceeding?"

The placement of events within the larger conception of time contains some fundamental differences from Western events, commonly anticipated to occur on a calendrical date, a point within a linearly conceived sequence of points.

Kinds of moments

Little research exists on African categorizations of musical events. J. C. Faris's work on the distinction between occasions and nonoccasions among Anglo-Americans in Cat Harbour, Newfoundland (1973:112–124), is particularly relevant because his research involved not only elicitation of terms, but observation of principles that produce the events, to better understand the distinction between levels. Faris concluded that the Cat Harbour inhabitants' categories did not necessarily coincide with outsiders' notions, for a concert or a supper was not an occasion, but a birthday was. He observed that an occasion was distinguished by its license for deviance, whereas events known as nonoccasions were not. With more research in Africa, we could better know what Africans conceive to be events and what they do not. From Charles R. Adams's research (1974), for example, we know that the Basotho performative domain puts music and games together within a single kind of event.

Alan Goldberg, writing about the performance of Haitian Vodun, comments that in looking at ritual events (and many musical events mark rituals), scholars who stress the qualities of emergence and indeterminacy in the unfolding of the event "indicate that while social contradictions may be mediated or expressed in ritual, one of the effects of such expression may be to induce social change. . . . The deeper a ritual becomes, the more it captures the energies and involvement of the participants, making it capable of inducing change as well as ratifying tradition" (1980:4).

Understanding the complexities of event time and learning to live in its flow are difficulties for most nonnatives conducting research in Africa. I vividly remember my own initiation to event timing in Kpelleland. Though I early developed a network of people who would inform me of musical events, I found it quite difficult, accustomed as I was to living by the clock, to determine when I should arrive at the scene of an upcoming performance. Kpelle acquaintances might tell me, "I hear they are going to play [perform] in Massaquoitaa for a death." If I pressed them for a time estimate, they would hesitate or offer some vague answer. My vivid memories, of early fieldwork especially, are of going to a location, only to arrive and find no evidence that a performance would occur, though people close to the deceased maintained that word had been sent calling the musicians. Hours passed as we waited, trying to keep busy by visiting with the local residents. The air was invariably relaxed and unhurried. When at last the musicians came walking into town, a protracted negotiation often ensued, as hosts and performers argued over the arrangements for the event. Characteristically, these talks threatened at several junctures to break down entirely, and sometimes the result was no music making at all.

Within limits, the clock time for the start of this performance was quite variable.

The hour the playing started depended to a great degree upon the quality of social interaction among the musicians and their hosts. As arrangements became more suitable to all, the performing time drew closer. Nevertheless, surprises were always possible, and last-minute demands often threatened to destroy the bonds of understanding. The host or sponsor of the event was the most crucial party to negotiations with the musicians. The entire population of the town, however, often played a part, since their opinion of the group was often important to their support of the negotiations. If the musicians had a fine reputation, residents would urge a quick end to deliberations, for they eagerly awaited the music. I eventually learned not to ask "What time will the performance begin?" but "How are the negotiations proceeding?"

Timbre in moments: action and tone color

In the Woi epic, the emphasis on aural texture is pronounced. A part of each episode is devoted to describing sounds. In the fifth episode, as the bowl is carved, the plot revolves around the play of sounds. Thus, what is introductory texturing in early episodes becomes the centerpiece of the moment.

Sounds and movements are textured with the voice, which, as the epic unfolds, shows that power. In episode five, the voice carves bowls and creates things of beauty. Later, in episode eight, the narrator explores the power of Woi's voice.

> Woi fixes everything with his voice. . . .
> Woi did things with just his mouth, with his voice.
> If he said a person should die, that one died.
> But, then, he doesn't do that because he is a chief.

Like transaction, timbre appears to be as much a focus for Kpelle as for some other African musicians. Sue Carole DeVale, analyzing harp and vocal music of Uganda, has developed a graphic notation to highlight tone colors rather than pitch (1984:285–318). She describes the harp as achieving a "rough, percussive timbre" with a buzzing that requires a separate line of notation.

Just as DeVale uses a metaphor of weaving to explain her notation, Jeanette Harries finds it an apt image for Berber song in North Africa. One Berber poet compares himself to a woman weaving motifs in song as yarn is made into fabric (1973:144). Robert Thompson makes a similar analogy as he describes the narrow-strip weaving of West Africa, where a garment is constructed of up to a hundred strips joined into a single cloth.

> As multiple strips are sewn together by their edges, the major accents (weft-blocks) of one strip may be staggered in relation to those of an adjoining strip, with careful alignment of further elements in the same cloth preempting any assumption of accident and indeed confirming a love of aesthetic intensity through this form of special contrast. (Thompson 1983:208–209)

Thompson compares the staggering of accents in cloth to offbeat phrasing in music. And indeed, the texture of musical performance is not limited to aural textures, or even to the visual textures that might result from a costume of such patterns as Thompson describes. Gerhard Kubik has long asserted that the visual kinesthetic component is equally critical. He notes that xylophonists in southeast Africa will often change the order of the keys on a loose log xylophone from one song to another; in doing so, they can transfer the same or similar motoric patterns to new key placement and get completely new combinations of sounds (1972b:30–31). Moses Serwadda and Hewitt Pantaleoni show how drumming and dancing are inextricably

lenjengo   Recreational dance from The Gambia

kutiridingo   Conical drum from The Gambia, played with one stick and one hand

TUBS   Time Unit Box System, a graphic notation with symbols indicating the kind of stroke to be played

ijala   Yoruba hunters' poetry that is sung and may also reproduce aspects of speech tone

mbira   Plucked lamellophone from Zimbabwe; keys may be designated as men's or women's voices

FIGURE 5   Comparison of mnemonic rhythmic syllables in 12/8 meter.

	x	.	x	.	x	x	.	x	.	x	x	
Nigeria: Yoruba	kon		kon		ko - lo			kon		ko - lo		(King 1960:52)
Nigeria: Yoruba	kon		kon		ko - lo			kon		ko - lo		(Kubik 1972a:169)
Cameroon: Bamenda	ko		ko		ko - yo			ko		ko - yo		(Kubik 1972a:174)
Ghana: Akan	kon		kon		ko - kon			kon		ko - kon		(Kubik 1972a:174)

linked: "A drummer will indicate the dance motions sometimes as a way of explaining and teaching a [drum] pattern" (1968:52).

Texts and tone colors

A recent direction in the analysis of rhythm has turned toward the timbre and verbal text of rhythmic patterns: "It is scarcely an exaggeration to say that without African languages, African music would not exist" (Bebey 1975:122). Many African musicians learn rhythms, including the timeline, through mnemonic phrases consisting of syllables that convey both timing and timbre: "The importance of sonority cannot be overemphasized" (Koetting 1970:120).

The standard 12/8 pattern has been identified by different phrases, rendered differently in local languages. A few are shown in figure 5. As Gerhard Kubik points out, syllables can distinguish timbral subtleties to an extent that Western staff notation cannot. In the first example in figure 5, Kubik points out that though *kon* and *lo* are notated exactly alike (as quarter notes in staff notation), the player of the hourglass drum (*kanango*) uses more energy to strike *kon* than *lo*, a legato stroke. The *n* denotes a silent pulse, providing a "complementary inaudible action unit" (Kubik 1972a:170, 176).

In a study of Mandinka drumming in The Gambia, Roderic Knight stresses the importance of timbre as opposed to duration when he points out that a drummer's skills are in part the ability to learn a rhythm as a "pattern of timbres" (1974:29). For *lenjengo*, a recreational dance, he goes on to explain the strokes used on the *kutiridingo*, a conical drum, played with one stick and one hand (figure 6). *Kum* is played with an open hand that bounces off the head; ba is a damped stroke produced when the fingers hit the head and press it to lessen the vibration; *din* is an open-stick stroke; *da* is a damped-stick stroke (Knight 1974:28). Thus, the syllables communicate a range of timbre much more complex than simple durational values.

Among the Kpelle of Liberia, mnemonic syllables for the drum timbre and rhythm indicate specific dance-movements, the syllables differentiating movement and sound. For example, the mnemonic phrase *kelen kelen* represents forward shuffling from side to side, and *se-ka-se-ke-kpa* represents a complex step-and-turn pattern (Stone 1982:70).

The conclusion that timbral elements, poorly communicated in staff notation,

FIGURE 6   *Kutiridingo* strokes in 6/8 meter in Mandingo drumming, The Gambia (after Knight 1974:28).

kum		ba	din		da
K	*	B	D	*	d

are essential to interpreting much of African music has resulted in several notational innovations. Serwadda and Pantaleoni have commented on the deficiency of Western notation symbols, "incapable of expressing the life blood of African drumming which is timbre" (1968:47). They propose a tablature-type approach, built from a prescriptive notation that indicates, in a kind of Labanotation, how the drum is to be struck. James Koetting has applied TUBS (Time Unit Box System) notation to West African drum-ensemble music: within the individual boxes of the graphlike structure, symbols characterize sonority by "representing the techniques used by performers to produce the pitch, loudness, tone quality, and carrying power of the sounds" (1970:127).

Vocables—syllables some observers call nonsense—can indicate rhythm. As Kubik points out, they are not properly termed nonsense at all, for they convey meaning about how a rhythm is to be realized in timbre and timing (1972a:169). That these mnemonic syllables derive from language should make us look more carefully at the use of language within songs. When an ethnomusicologist concludes that a great deal of repetition occurs, the text that accompanies a song may not have been taken into account; within the text, a great deal of variety may exist. The evidence often lies in the text as analyzed by folklorists, and not ethnomusicologists. Folklorists pay little attention to the music. That the texts of African performances are rich with clues about temporal organization is evident throughout Ruth Finnegan's volume *Oral Literature in Africa* (1970). The emphasis on timbre is evident in ideophones, employed not only in mnemonic devices, but also in song texts (Noss 1975:142–152). In Yoruba, a high-tone nasal vowel is often used to depict smallness, and a low-tone sound shows large size or slow movement (Lasebikan 1956:44). In Ewe and Gbaya, back rounded vowels are employed for ideophones indicating something dark or obscure (Samarin 1965:120).

Furthermore, phonemic tone, a feature of many African song texts, contributes to the overall temporal dimension. As Babalola points out in reference to Yoruba hunter's poetry (*ijala*), specific patterns of speech tones may repeat at irregular intervals, adding to the richness of songs (1964–1965:64–65). These speech tones may not be reflected in the melody, for a great many factors influence sung pitches.

In a related matter, in many areas of Africa instrumental or vocal parts are conceived not as inanimate sounds, but as voices (Berliner 1978:56; Stone 1979; Zemp 1971). Thus, timbral subtleties are essential to the understanding of how all these voices interweave through time. Among the Shona of Zimbabwe, "musicians often refer to the B manual, which contains the mbira's lowest register, as the 'old men's voices,' the L manual, the middle register, as the 'young men's voices,' and the R manual, or highest register, as the 'women's voices'" (Berliner 1978:56). Individual keys have names and individually named voices—a phenomenon recognized in many other African communities.

Visual textures

The Kpelle create in epic an aural type of texture augmented with dramatic gestures. Since the epic pourer is kneeling, the hands and upper torso are foci of movement. The body is still bent forward as in the posture of a standing dancer, but the normal concentration of movement in the feet is shifted to the hands and arms. The mat is the stage. Costume is not involved, nor is makeup, but the production involves diverse media. The epic is heard, seen, and felt.

In other parts of Africa, texturing may also involve visual displays. J. H. Kwabena Nketia describes the visual-display element at the durbar in Ghana, marking the climax of the forty-day ritual cycle honoring ancestor kings. On this occasion,

The song of the epic pourer is where, in allusive phrases and deep proverbs, the emotionally vivid life appears.

the paramount chief exhibits the regalia of his court in a splendid procession. Gold and silver ornaments abound, both on the king, and on members of the entourage. Of the music Nketia says,

> The drumming, singing and dancing during the procession keeps the procession alive. Different drum ensembles may be played simultaneously at different points within the procession. . . . As the music goes on, individuals may take turns at dancing in the open ring and the chief himself may grace the occasion by dancing to the music of the royal *fontomfrom* drums. (1973:82)

African visual displays have long been noted. Mohammed ibn Abdullah ibn Battuta, the great Arab traveler, set off in A.D. 1352 from Morocco, crossed the Sahara to Timbuktu, and traveled down the Niger (Jones 1957:8). Of the ruler of Mali, he notes,

> When the Sultan is seated, from the lattice of one of the casement windows is thrown down a silken cord to which is attached a striped kerchief of Egyptian make; when the people see this, the drums are beaten and the horns are sounded. Each commandant has in front of him his men, with their spears, their bows, their drums, their horns (the latter made of ivory, or elephant tusks), and lastly their musical instruments made of reeds and gourds, which are beaten with sticks and make a pleasant sound.

As the sultan processes to an open-air audience, before him

> go the singers holding gold and silver rattles; behind him are about three hundred armed slaves. The Sovereign walks leisurely. . . . Finally he slowly mounts the platform in the manner of a preacher mounting his pulpit; as soon as he is seated, they beat the drums, and sound the horn and trumpets. (Battuta 1858:403, 406, 411, in Jones 1957:8–9)

Whether aural, gestural, or regalia-derived, these elements of the texture serve to expand a moment of music making and give it the play that people delight in. Much more than just the proper rhythm or pitches, these textures make a contribution to what is thought to be beautiful, not only in the epic of Kpelle, but in many other musical performances in various African societies.

EPIC AND TIME IN PERSPECTIVE

Time exists only insofar as a participant—performer, audience member—experiences it. Temporal flux is partially shared by people who make music together, and to the extent that it is shared, a vital synchrony results. Their interpretation of that time must be regarded in seeking to understand it.

The coordination of temporal dimensions in Kpelle and, I think, other African music provides a kind of essential tension, which, in Kpelle performance, is represented concretely by the relationship of soloist and supporting singer (*tomo-son-nuu*), for here the soloist creates and weaves proverbs and allusory texts in a composition of split-second timing. As this artistry moves the performers and listeners to inner-time dimensions, they become aware, if only peripherally, of the supporting singer, who sings a never-varying ostinato, alternating with the soloist's fanciful variations. The supporting singer is moving in outer time, maintaining that dimension in an essential tension with the soloist's movements toward inner time.

The Woi epic is a microcosm of these dimensions. The speech and music that organize the performers and keep them on track move in a kind of outer time, where the nuts and bolts of keeping things together takes place. Discussions of raising a song in the small voice, rather than the large voice, and of placing a part properly, are all standard. Midway between outer and inner time, the narrative of the story is spoken, often in heightened speech, colorful and rhythmic language. The audience is moved to another world, much of it emphasizing the mechanics of action: the house moves, the squirrel climbs, the bird pumps the bellows. The song of the epic pourer is where, in allusive phrases and deep proverbs, the emotionally vivid life appears. Through music, as through the words of the music, a special kind of experience is possible, prepared by the movement through the background layers of outer time.

Another kind of essential tension exists between the qualities of ritual activity and those of nonritual activity. Nonritual music, with its constant change, segments, and layering, is quite different from the ritual, which continues endlessly, monolithic and unchanged. In the epic, these elements exist simultaneously. The continuity between episodes reflects the ritual aspect, while the creative segmentation of the mosaiclike bits and pieces reflects the nonritual aspect. An incredibly tight balance appears between the two themes, the eternal versus the segment, sometimes showing one in dominance, sometimes showing the other.

The uniqueness of Kpelle epic time, and, indeed, of time in Kpelle aesthetic expression, rests on the stress given the qualitative elements. While the elements in themselves are not unique, the way they are emphasized, particularly through movement and layering, is distinctive. The nuance of placement provides a subtle and yet striking approach to organizing music.

As we consider musical expression, viewed from several temporal perspectives, it becomes apparent that the Kpelle, and possibly other Africans, favor qualitative aspects, eschewing quantitative, and therefore linear, ones. Whether timbral nuances coordinate rhythm, or spatial differentiations communicate time, qualitative distinctions prevail, even in the outer dimension.

Kinds of time

The qualitative-quantitative aspects of time can be separated into distinct levels of analysis. First, we can begin with the most specific and fine-grained element—that of the song. Here we find the kind of time that can be called musical rhythm, a level where many of us settle our attention. Song time for the Kpelle is dominated by qualitative elements—timbre, segmentation, variation—juxtaposed against constancy.

A more encompassing level is that of event time, a musical concept incorporating an evening of songs, laughter, speech, and perhaps feasting. Like songs, events draw qualitative features to their time. Beginnings in both are drawn out, and endings are often abrupt. The quality of performance and collective interaction determines much about how long an event continues. As one kind of event, the epic shows the ritual overlay of continuity and seamlessness onto segmentation and variation.

We need to consider music equally as a process and as a product, applying the perspective of the African peoples to the motion, the dynamism, that, in many societies, is its essence.

Biographical time

Another time flow is that of biographical time. Each participant in epic has an individual trajectory from birth to death, and perhaps to ancestorhood. For the Kpelle, an individual's life proceeds not so much in quantitative terms, though the Kpelle do recognize the passing of time and the process of biological aging; rather, childhood can last an elastic number of years depending on the point of initiation into Poro or Sande, which marks the attainment of adulthood. Movement into old age confers high status on people, and particularly increases access to knowledge.

Interrelated to biographical time is the life cycle, which for the Kpelle consists of certain life-crisis rites or events. These are heavily regulated by ritual, and this time flow, more than any of the others, emphasizes the quantitative.

Social, calendric, and historical time

The temporal flow of everyday life, which we might call social time, moves as the interaction of people proceeds. For the Kpelle, this time is qualitative, built on continuing transaction to maintain its flux.

Calendric time, as the Kpelle conceive it, is not reckoned with precision in quantitative terms, except when the Kpelle have recourse to the Gregorian calendar. Yet the qualities of the days, and (more important) of the seasons, are noticed. The weekly rotating market days are a recent addition in most areas, brought by a network of roads and a demand for produce in urban areas.

Historical time, that flow of time that proceeds in the broadest perspective, is qualitatively important to the Kpelle because it provides authority for present action. But it is not of great depth, nor is it figured linearly or quantitatively; rather, it is continually adjusted to suit the needs of the moment.

Comparative temporal flows

The subtlety of these temporal flows may be the reason they are easy to miss. Perhaps this is why Western ethnomusicologists can apply other grids without great problems. The results can be viewed other ways, if one disregards the perspective of those musicians who create the music and of the audience who responds to it. To confuse things even further, with Western ideas being quickly infused into Kpelle (and, perhaps, other performance in Africa), one indeed finds examples of clocklike time, where such time has been adopted.

In my own research, however, I have found that concepts suggested by the Kpelle data are often corroborated with examples from other African peoples. Along the way, I have cited North African examples that underscore points made about Kpelle ideas, and my recent work in Arabia suggests even broader congruences. The sharp dividing line that has been implied in some of the literature between North Africa and sub-Saharan Africa is not nearly so clear as sometimes described. Isolated statements in the literature and some of my own fieldwork suggest parallels even with North Africa and Arabia.

If we accept that some peoples organize the outer time of their musics in a predominantly qualitative fashion, then the implications are pervasive, for we must accept some fundamentally different ways of approaching music.

Qualitative temporal coordination

The problem that must trouble us is how precision of coordination can exist in time reckoning that is not quantitative. With a clock as the symbol of Western temporal coordination, we question what coordination is possible in nonquantitative time. The careful timing in Kpelle and other African music, commonly acknowledged to require extreme precision, is surprising. If such precision of synchronization is possible, then is not coordination possible at a much higher level? Arguments against nonquantitative time-reckoning schemes have often centered on the fact that linear time is a prerequisite, but not the only one, for industrial, scientific development. Cyclical time, the characterization of African time, inhibits cooperation among large numbers of people, the kind of group effort necessary for that kind of development.

Since this study has concentrated on music, its conclusions can be based only on that part of human creativity. Nevertheless, the evidence from African music does not support the argument against large-scale cooperation. In the events studied, many people synchronize their activities in complex ways extending beyond what anyone who makes the generalization regarding the superiority of linear time should expect. If such precision is possible on a small scale, what makes it unexpected at a level where the precision required may not be so great? That linear time is predominant in most cultures should not lead us to conclude that it represents the only possible mode of time reckoning that can lead to technological development.

As I have elsewhere emphasized, African musical research has long looked at music at the level of song (Stone 1982). Thus music has been studied in Africa from an item perspective. Little information about historical styles of music in Africa is available, to say nothing about the lives of musicians, or even the social time reckoning. Furthermore, study has centered on the outer dimension of song; little is known or commented upon concerning inner time, a dynamic aspect of music.

The future study of time

The future study of time in African music embraces a large area. Ideally, researchers will consider the various kinds of musical time within a single study, even if they choose to focus on one particular kind. This will afford us data that integrate a variety of times rather than data that view time as unidimensional. Even more critical, we need to consider music equally as a process and as a product, applying the perspective of the African peoples to the motion, the dynamism, that, in many societies, is its essence. The results of such studies should provide us with a much richer and more detailed view of African performance. We presently see a mere part of a sketch.

Ethnomusicologists have good reasons to consider time more carefully. First, they have the professional training that qualifies them to consider rhythm at a microlevel. Rhythm at the level of songs has long been studied. Second, time provides important clues not only about the making of music, but no doubt, about the broader fabric of social life. While I would not maintain that the rhythms of music are determined by the rhythms of social life, they are certainly interrelated. Time in one domain of life links up with, and is related in some fashion to, time in another domain. As a consequence, rhythm in music and in overall temporal organization is of interest to social and cultural anthropologists, folklorists, and historians, crosscut-

Within a single musical performance, music, dance, and the plastic arts are parts of a conceptual whole, which the Kpelle find difficult to separate.

ting the disciplinary boundaries that artificially divide the whole of African social life.

The critic may still protest that the nature of time in Kpelle epic is not all that different from time in any other music. The answer must rest in the underlying shape and configuration of that time which, though composed of the same elements as any other time, becomes specially fashioned. Much like the writing of Gabriel Okara, an Ijaw of Nigeria, who ably renders in English the flavor of Ijaw expression, Kpelle ideas of time are carefully shaped.

> Outside he walked strongly with no fear in his feet and no fear in his inside. But as he passed, women moved away from his front, casting bad eyes at him and from dark interiors of houses people looked at him with Chief Izongo's eyes and behind him walked his friends, walking with Chief Izongo's feet. (1964:41)

In the end, the differences are profound, and they change one's perspective. They show how wispy the concepts we seek are, how fragile they seem, as we move through data looking for the overwhelming and the powerful. Those who understand this artistry may be the ones who have overlooked it in searching for more overwhelming answers.

Worldwide applications

The future of ethnomusicology in general, and of studies of African arts in particular, is affected by these findings in several ways. First, study in African arts draws on a multidisciplinary base. Time as discussed here would customarily be studied by at least three separate disciplines. Yet in the context of African music performance, these disciplines interlink closely. Within a single musical performance, music, dance, and the plastic arts are parts of a conceptual whole, which the Kpelle find difficult to separate. We need to avoid creating study objects that are artificial to Kpelle thinking.

Second, techniques and concepts for analysis of qualitative aspects need to be developed. The Western bias for quantitative analysis affords only crude techniques for understanding artworks constructed in qualitative terms. It is striking that timbre is possibly the least developed area of the Western analysis of musical style. Scholars have only a crude terminology for describing it, and little training in studying it. Yet the data reveal how important timbre becomes for understanding time, where the Kpelle and other Africans are concerned.

Third, models need to reflect a capacity to study several analytic levels. The nature of academic disciplines is partially reflected by the tendency to use models incapable of encompassing several levels. One model can focus specifically on song, but not broadly at such large temporal intervals as history embraces. The difficulty in working with models that focus at several levels is that they often project fundamentally different assumptions.

Kpelle time reckoning

The Kpelle case, many might argue, is not unique. Certainly other peoples, including Westerners, stress qualitative or three-dimensional spatial characteristics. If we seek to judge the case by any single criterion, a great many different points can be made with the same data. What gives time in the Kpelle experience its special quality is the configuration of all the temporal levels, seen as a coordinated set. If we consider music in time, looking at all the temporal levels included, we can begin to see what is involved.

For the most part, from a Kpelle perspective, time moves qualitatively. The fitting together of one part to another in outer song time is accomplished by resort to mnemonic devices based on verbal language. Musicians refer to how various parts fit and relate to one another, in many respects reflecting multiple points of organization. Though the struck idiophone provides an unvarying rhythmic pattern and can be one of the focal points, musicians do not single-mindedly relate to this one pattern. In the Kpelle case at least, it would be a mistake to think that a single beat or pattern serves as an essential musical glue.

The ways that intricate patterns are executed are stronger evidence that the dominant time patterning in music is qualitative. Kpelle musicians, from the present evidence, do not rely on counting or numbering to conceptualize and properly execute their patterns. Verbal sounds and vocal timbres indicate to them how a pattern will proceed.

The Kpelle epic singer is rewarded for his efforts through excitement and tokens of praise. An individual's biography affects what happens in the musical event. For a Kpelle singer, the past provides important and essential references for the present performance. The life span becomes a referential reservoir, though quantitative linear organization is not prominent. Linear progression appears crucial in the understanding of ideas about how a person is born, matures, and dies, though death is often viewed as simply a move to ancestral status, rather than as a final disappearing.

Social action impinges on musical performance through its larger patterns. The quality of this interaction affects what happens to enable events to take place. This social time becomes a fundamental mode for ordering musical activities. Within this, the unit of the day, as a kind of present, is the focus for life and the planning of activities. Within it, a great elaboration of activity is both possible and frequent. In Africa, this present can be embroidered to an extent that outsiders rarely experience.

History in Kpelle music making is most important, but not fundamentally quantitative. The past becomes essential authorization for activity in the present. The past is also considered dynamic and active, changing within the present situation as people regard it in new light and context. Singers invite ancestors' participation, and recount historical events to validate a present course of action. The past is vital to the creation of music, and it is a viable and dynamic element in that creation.

The Kpelle do recognize quantitative aspects of time, particularly as part of ritual activities, but these elements interest them less than do the qualitative and spatial dimensions. The qualitative elements are treated with the attention accorded to quantitative elements in Western conceptualizations of time. For this reason, the fabric of musical time exudes a different character.

In the past, the quantitative has been equated with precision and accuracy. Since Kpelle music shows that considerable precision is evident with predominantly qualitative reckoning, we now need to accept that the deemphasis of the quantitative does not mean the absence of precise time reckoning. Alternative modes of reckoning time

Alternative modes of reckoning time create exciting new vistas for study.

create exciting new vistas for study. Now we can broaden our approaches to time, enlarging our theoretical vocabulary as we study more systematically these data from more cosmopolitan perspectives. In the process, we may find a liberation from the linear quantitative straitjacket that has guided much ethnomusicological research.

Only through equal attention to theory and data will a clearer view of Kpelle musical time emerge. Only through concern for music as created and understood by the Kpelle and other Africans will we better grasp what is crudely sketched as time in *woi-meni-pele*.

REFERENCES

Abimbola, Wande. 1971. "Stylistic Repetition in Ifá Divination Poetry." *Lagos Notes and Records* 3(1):38–53.

Abraham, R. C. 1940. *The Tiv People*. 2nd ed. London: Crown Agents.

Adams, Charles R. 1974. "Ethnography of Basotho Evaluative Expression in the Cognitive Domain *Lipapali* (Games)." Ph.D. dissertation, Indiana University.

Babalola, S. A. 1964–1965. "The Characteristic Features of Outer Forms of Yoruba Ijala Chants." *Odu* 1(1):33–44, (2):47–77.

Barthold, Bonnie J. 1981. *Black Time: Fiction of Africa, the Caribbean, and the United States*. New Haven: Yale University Press.

Bateson, Gregory. 1972. *Steps to an Ecology of the Mind*. New York: Ballantine.

Battuta, Mohammed ibn Abdullah ibn. 1858. *Voyages d'Ibn Batoutah,* trans. C. Defrémery and B. R. Sanguinetti. Paris: Imprimerie Nationale.

Bauman, Richard. 1977. *Verbal Art as Performance*. Rowley, Mass.: Newbury House.

Bebey, Francis. 1975. *African Music: A People's Art,* trans. Josephine Bennett. Westport, Conn.: Lawrence Hill.

Beidelman, Thomas O. 1963. "Kaguru Time Reckoning: An Aspect of the Cosmology of an East African People." *Southwestern Journal of Anthropology* 19:9–20.

Berliner, Paul. 1978. *The Soul of Mbira.* Berkeley: University of California Press.

Bledsoe, Caroline. 1980. *Women and Marriage in Kpelle Society.* Stanford, Calif.: Stanford University Press.

DeVale, Sue Carole. 1984. "Prolegomena to a Study of Harp and Voice Sounds in Uganda: A Graphic System for the Notation of Texture." In *Selected Reports in Ethnomusicology: Volume V, Studies in African Music,* ed. J. H. Kwabena Nketia and Jacqueline Cogdell DjeDje (University of California at Los Angeles), 285–315.

Eickelman, Dale F. 1977. "Time in a Complex Society: A Moroccan Example." *Ethnology* 16:39–55.

Faris, J. C. 1973. "'Occasions' and 'Non-Occasions.'" In *Rules and Meanings,* ed. Mary Douglas, 45–59. Harmondsworth, England: Penguin.

Finnegan, Ruth. 1970. *Oral Literature in Africa.* London: Oxford University Press.

Gay, John H., and Michael Cole. 1967. *The New Mathematics in an Old Culture: A Study of Learning among the Kpelle of Liberia.* New York: Holt, Rinehart and Winston.

Gibbs, James L. 1965. "The Kpelle of Liberia." In *People of Africa,* ed. James L. Gibbs, 197–240. New York: Holt, Rinehart and Winston.

Giddens, Anthony. 1979. *Central Problems in Social Theory: Action, Structure and Contradiction in Social Analysis.* Berkeley: University of California Press.

Gidley, C. G. B. 1975. "*Roko*: A Hausa Praise Crier's Account of His Craft." *African Language Studies* 16:93–115.

Goldberg, Alan. 1980. "Art, Play, Ritual and Morality in Performance Events." Paper presented at the meeting of the Society for Ethnomusicology, Bloomington, Indiana, 21 November.

Gurvitch, Georges. 1964. *The Spectrum of Social Time*. Dordrecht: D. Riedel.

Harries, Jeanette. 1973. "Pattern and Choice in Berber Weaving and Poetry." *Research in African Literatures* 4(2):141–163.

Horton, Robin. 1967. "African Traditional Thought and Western Science." *Africa* 37:50–71, 155–187.

Jackson, Michael. 1977. *The Kuranko: Dimensions of Social Reality in a West African Society*. New York: St. Martin's Press.

Jones, Arthur M. 1957. "Drums Down the Centuries." *African Music* 1(4):4–10.

Knight, Roderic. 1974. "Mandinka Drumming." *African Arts* 7:25–35.

Koetting, James. 1970. "Analysis and Notation of West African Drum Ensemble Music." *Selected Reports, Institute of Ethnomusicology* (University of California at Los Angeles), 1(3):115–146.

Kubik, Gerhard. 1972a. "Oral Notation of Some West and Central African Time-Line Patterns." *Review of Ethnology* 3(22):169–176.

———. 1972b. "Transcription of African Music from Silent Film: Theory and Methods." *African Music* 3(4):28–39.

Lasebikan, E. L. 1956. "The Tonal Structure of Yoruba Poetry." *Présence Africaine* N.S. 8/10.

Merriam, Alan P. 1977. "Analysis of African Music Rhythm and Concepts of Time Reckoning." Paper presented at the meeting of the Society for Ethnomusicology, Austin, Texas, 4 November.

Murphy, William P. 1976. "A Semantic and Logical Analysis of Kpelle Proverb Metaphors of Secrecy." Ph.D. dissertation, Stanford University.

Nketia, J. H. Kwabena. 1973. "The Musician in Akan Society." In *The Traditional Artist in African Societies*, ed. Warren L. d'Azevedo, 79–100. Bloomington: Indiana University Press.

Noss, Philip A. 1975. "The Ideophone: A Linguistic and Literary Device in Gbaya and Sango with Reference to Zande." In *Directions in Sudanese Linguistics and Folklore*, ed. Sayyid H. Hurreiz and Herman Bell. Khartoum: University of Khartoum.

Ogilby, John. 1670. *Africa*. London: Thomas Johnson.

Okara, Gabriel. 1964. *The Voice*. London: Heinemann.

Rowell, Lewis. 1985. "Editorial: The Temporal Spectrum." *Music Theory Spectrum* 7:1–6.

Samarin, W. J. 1965. "Perspective on African Ideophones." *African Studies* 24:117–121.

Schutz, Alfred. 1964. *Collected Papers II: Studies in Social Theory*. The Hague: Nijhoff.

Serwadda, Moses, and Hewitt Pantaleoni. 1968. "A Possible Notation for African Dance Drumming." *African Music* 4(2):47–52.

Stone, Ruth M. 1979. "Communication and Interaction Processes in Music Events among the Kpelle of Liberia." Ph.D. dissertation, Indiana University.

———. 1982. *Let the Inside Be Sweet: The Interpretation of Music Event among the Kpelle of Liberia*. Bloomington: Indiana University Press.

———. 1985. "In Search of Time in African Music." *Music Theory Spectrum* 7:139–148.

———. 1986. "Commentary: The Value of Local Ideas in Understanding West African Rhythm." *Ethnomusicology* 30:54–57.

Stone, Ruth M., and Verlon L. Stone. 1972. *Music of the Kpelle of Liberia*. New York: Folkways FE4385. LP disk.

———. 1981. "Event, Feedback and Analysis: Research Media in the Study of Music Events." *Ethnomusicology* 25:215–225.

Thompson, Robert Ferris. 1983. *Flash of the Spirit*. New York: Random House.

Turner, Victor. 1967. *The Forest of Symbols: Aspects of Ndembu Ritual*. Ithaca: Cornell University Press.

Zaslavsky, Claudia. 1973. *Africa Counts*. Westport, Conn.: Lawrence Hill.

Zemp, Hugo. 1971. *Musique Dan*. Paris: Mouton.

Notation and Oral Tradition
Kay Kaufman Shelemay

Indigenous Musical Notations
Musical Transcripton in Africa
African Use of Western Notation

African music presents a notational paradox. Africans transmitted most of their musics orally, without indigenous forms of written representation, but their musical traditions stand among those most frequently sampled for transcription in foreign notational systems. Scholarly discussion of African musical styles has usually relied on systems of music writing to capture aural phenomena otherwise resistant to analysis, whether or not the discussion has explicitly acknowledged the centrality of the process of transcription. Any notational discussion of African musical traditions must therefore consider two distinct, yet related, subjects: the indigenous technologies Africans employed to transmit and convey their own musics, and the ways African musics have been transmitted and notated, primarily by outsiders, both within Africa, and to a broader world.

The word *notation*, derived from the Latin *notare* 'to mark', is conventionally defined as "the use of a system of signs or symbols," while a single unit of the same, the *note*, is defined as "a mark or token by which a thing may be known" (Webster 1978:1224). In practice, Western presumptions of literacy constrain these definitions, and locate considerations of representations primarily within written (or printed) technologies. As a study of the relationship between dance motion and artistic icon has proved (Thompson 1974), full consideration of indigenous African representations of music requires a broader framework, which may include other forms of the symbolic representation of music in, and as, performance. Additionally, through electronic notation of music on tape, video, and film, twentieth-century technologies of recording have provided new forms of representation within Africa, and have been integrated into the process of transcription as a source of, or model for, various written notations.

A second issue is the geographical boundaries of an inquiry into African notation. Any discussion of African music is incomplete, because of the size of the continent, the diversity of its musical traditions, and the massive body of scholarship these materials have generated. To limit its range and complexity, this discussion will exclude North Africa, which contrasts with most of the rest of the continent, in having generated an extensive corpus of indigenous written sources, some of which contain forms of musical representation. Developed largely within an Islamic cultural framework, and nourished by cultural trends from regions of West and Central Asia, North African musical sources have for decades received close attention from scholars, and are more properly treated elsewhere (Farmer 1957:453–454; Wright 1978:216–244).

INDIGENOUS MUSICAL NOTATIONS

Discussion is compounded by insufficient historical study of written African sources. Until the fifteenth century, such sources were evidently rare: except for indigenous Ethiopian manuscripts in Geʿez (the liturgical language of the Christian church in Ethiopia), writings of foreign travelers and geographers in classical languages and Arabic predominated (Djait 1981). After that century, autochthonous African literatures developed, first in Arabic and then in indigenous languages; scribes wrote the earliest contributions in Arabic script, but later contributions used the Latin alphabet.

The earliest West African texts in indigenous script were produced by the Vai in 1833. The beginning of the twentieth century saw the invention of a special script in Cameroon (Hrbek 1981:135–136). However, no forms of written musical representation emerged from these West African societies, nor has music writing been documented among other peoples of Central, Southern, or East Africa.

Music writing in Ethiopia

The most exceptional example of a written form of musical representation in Africa is an indigenous notational system in Ethiopia, a modern nation-state in the Eastern Horn, with historical roots of nearly two millenia in the Aksumite Empire. After the conversion of its emperor (A.D. 332), Ethiopia became a Christian country, and by the sixth century had its own literature and script in Geʿez. Though it maintained close ties with the Coptic Church of Egypt (which until 1950 appointed the Ethiopian patriarch), its church was otherwise independent, and developed a distinctive liturgy, associated with a complex musical system.

History

The writing of Ethiopian liturgical texts in parchment manuscripts dates back to the earliest periods of Geʿez literary activity, but the Ethiopian Christian musical tradition (*zēmā* 'chant') was for many centuries transmitted orally. A change occurred when a cataclysmic invasion by Muslim forces between 1529 and 1541 destroyed most churches and monasteries, and devastated much of Ethiopia's literary heritage. In what must have been a response to the near destruction of their musical and liturgical traditions, and an attempt to ensure transmission in the future, Ethiopian clerics in the mid-sixteenth century invented *melekket* 'signs', a system of musical notation. According to a manuscript of that period, "at the time of King Galawdewos [1549–1559], there appeared Azzaj Gera and Azzaj Raguʿel, priests trained in *zēmā*. And they began to make rules for the *melekket* of the *Deggwā* [hymnary] and taught the priests of Tadbaba Maryam, which this prince had built" (Basset 1881:336). Other sources mentioning Gera's and Raguʿel's contributions imply that the notation may have derived in part from earlier indigenous models, of which all evidence disappeared during the invasion. Whatever the precedents for the sixteenth-century innovations in music writing (and they do not seem to be widespread, or to predate the fifteenth century), the earliest surviving manuscript with musical notation dates from the sixteenth century.

The church has maintained the *melekket*: in handwriting on parchment, using medieval scribal techniques, Ethiopian students, as part of their training, still copy notated manuscripts. The continuity in the manuscript tradition, and its perpetua-

FIGURE 1   Ethiopian church notation for the
Day of Saint John (*Masehafa Deggwa* 1959:1).

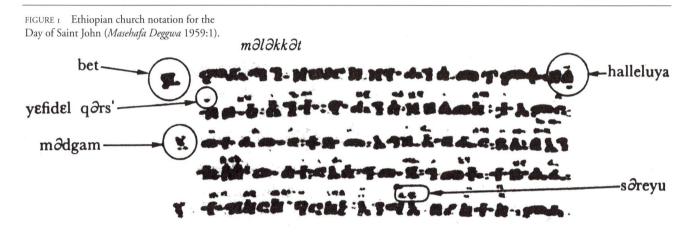

tion in performance, have made possible the combination of ethnographic research
with traditional source-and-text critical studies, permitting an understanding of this
African musical notation as transmitted and performed (Shelemay and Jeffery 1993).

Structure

The Ethiopian notational system primarily consists of some 650 signs, the *melekket*.
Each sign consists of one or more characters from the Geʿez syllabary. Deriving from,
and serving as an abbreviation for, a word or phrase from the text of a well-known
liturgical piece (known within the tradition as a portion), each sign cues the particular melody associated with that source text. Each sign cues a short melody, not an
individual pitch. When a *melekket* occurs above a word of another text from the liturgy, it indicates that the singer should chant that text to the melody associated with
the abbreviated word or phrase. Figure 1 is an example of Ethiopian church notation,
annotated to show the types of signs discussed below.

Slightly more than one hundred *melekket* make up a special class of signs, the bɛt
'house', abbreviations that identify the melodic group or family of which some liturgical portions are members. Unlike the interlinear *melekket*, a sign of a bɛt occurs in
the margin beside a text of a chant, signaling the text's relationship to other texts of
the same genre; each sign derives from the textual incipit of a particularly important
chant, which serves as the "model" for an entire "house."

In addition to the signs derived from the syllabary, the notation employs three
other types. The *yafidal qersʿ* 'shape of the signs' prescribe aspects of articulation, continuity, placement of melismas, motion, and vocal style (figure 2). Interlinear, often
modifying a particular *melekket*, these signs are *yezat* 'sustain', *chʿerat* 'accent', *darat*
'in the throat', *hedat* 'speed up', *rekrek* 'slide', *qenāt* 'melisma', *defāt* 'bend the voice',
ders 'cadence', *qertʿ* 'abrupt cutoff', *anber* 'cadence'.

In liturgical performance, many portions follow the word *halleluya*, sung from
one to ten times. Just before the beginning of each chant, the Geʿez word glossed

FIGURE 2   The *yafidal quers* in Ethiopian chant (Makonnen n.d.:7).

italicized term	definition	italicized term	definition
yezat	sustain	*ch'erat*	accent
darat	in the throat	*hedat*	speed up
rekrek	slide	*qenāt*	melisma
defāt	bend the voice	*ders*	cadence
qert'	abrupt cutoff	*anber*	cadence

"in," and a red numeral placed afterward, specify the number of repetitions: "in 1," "in 2," and so on. The halleluyas are sung to melodies derived from the bet.

A final type of sign is the *medgem*, a number placed in the margin alongside a portion, to specify how many times in liturgical performance it repeats.

Modal categories

The Ethiopian *melekket* divide into three categories, reflecting their correlation with one of the three classes of melody in the Ethiopian Christian musical system. Thus, knowledge of the notational signs both derives from and reinforces broader notions of musical organization. But while the notational system carries considerable information about the melodic and liturgical organization of the Ethiopian Christian liturgy, it does not provide a guide to specific pitches: it represents and cues phrases that have a substantially fixed textual and melodic identity; it leaves room for individual singers to reshape the basic musical materials according to contemporary, local, and personal norms.

Oral transmission

To read the notation, a singer must know all the notational signs, plus the melodies of the portions from which they derive. In practice, however, the *melekket* serve primarily as a mnemonic aid during training or study. During the day, musicians in training learn skills in reading and writing; at night, they practice the chants strictly from memory. During liturgical performances, most musicians sing from memory, without referring to notated manuscripts.

The Ethiopian Christian notational system does more than cue the melodic content of liturgical portions. It fuses word and melody, the smallest segments within the musical system, and revisits the learning process. In oral study, outside the context of a complete liturgical performance, the teacher often chants liturgical portions phrase by phrase; students repeat, in units that approximate the length of individual *melekket*. The notational system therefore emanates from, and refers to, the processes of oral acquisition.

Ethiopian musical notation is not a guide for the uninitiated: without prior knowledge of the oral tradition, it is indecipherable. It also does not provide a complete map for the Ethiopian musician, but encapsulates enough information to guide someone already immersed in the liturgical and musical materials. In contrast to the linearity of Western staff notation, the *melekket* symbolize a multidimensional, referential system. They intersect with the whole tradition at the microlevel of melodic segments, at a midlevel of portion type, and at a macrolevel of liturgical occasion. Notation implicitly encodes a broader world of practice. It draws on both the knowledge received from teachers, and the singer's personal experience. Furthermore, the notational system is in flux: each notated manuscript represents an open window on the processes of transmission: it merges tradition with individual innovation.

The notational system does not convey important aspects of the musical system and performance practice. Most strikingly, beyond subtle cues for tempo change associated with one of the *yafidal qers'*, the *melekket* give few hints about rhythmic

tusona   Graphic configuration of dots circumscribed by lines of the Luchazi culture of Angola and Zambia

beni ng'oma   A synthesis of dance and competitive modes, influenced by colonial brass-band music in East Africa

Orchestra Ethiopia   Ethiopian ensemble founded in 1963 for a modern presentation of traditional music

organization. The lack of notated rhythmic detail is a potentially important omission, for on holidays, the Ethiopian liturgy is accompanied by elaborate drumming, which demands years of special study. Yet other than occasional signs for choral entries, no written cues for the drumming exist. However, musicians name fixed rhythmic patterns, traced in the air during liturgical performance through motions of the prayer staff and sistrum, and danced during rituals (Shelemay 1989:184–190). Therefore, rhythmic aspects of the Ethiopian chant tradition may be notated kinesthetically, not tied to written guides, but traced in space by the musicians in the act of performing.

Other indigenous systems

To achieve a fuller understanding of what may be other indigenous representations of African music, scholars may need to move away from Western concepts of notation as music writing. Scholars have done little substantive research on this subject; yet the literature contains provocative references, such as the observation that Ewe call drumstrokes by "spoken syllables (vocables), which, in effect, constitute an oral notation" (Locke 1982:245). Because of the chance that scholars working within a framework shaped by literacy have overlooked alternative forms of musical representation in Africa, such suggestions merit discussion.

Angolan sand ideographs

In a study of space time concepts in Luchazi culture (of Eastern Angola and Northwestern Zambia), Gerhard Kubik discusses Angolan sand ideographs, *tusona* (sing. *kasona*), graphic configurations of dots circumscribed by lines, usually drawn with the fingers on a plane of white sand, on house walls, or more rarely, on objects (1987a:57). *Tusona* provide visual symbols of deep structures in the cultural heritage of the Ngangela-speaking cultures of Angola. Artists, who draw them to convey ideas about existing institutions, to stimulate fantasy, to abstract logical thinking, and to aid meditation, can give verbal explanations of the ideographs, some of which have long narratives and function as mnemonic aids.

While acknowledging that Angolan musicians do not derive musical connotations from the ideographs, and that he cannot find parallels between ideographic construction principles and music of the area of Angola where the ideographs occur, Kubik argues for relationships between the ideographs and music in more distant regions (notably among the Kiganda and in Cameroon). Space and time, he suggests, universally give rise to synesthetic experiences, because distance can be spatial or temporal; therefore, spatial distance can symbolize temporal distance. This hypothesis raises methodological problems in postulating a historical connection between Bantu traditions across different perceptual realms and remote geographical regions, but its exposition on the synesthetic experience of space and time challenges future scholarship. The documentation of "path images" of performances of tayil traced on the ground by Mapuche women in southwestern Argentina (Robertson 1979) confirms that such forms of musical notation exist elsewhere.

Composite systems

In urban Africa of the 1990s, multiple changes have led to several composite forms of expression, such as the *beni ng'oma*, a synthesis of indigenous dance and competitive modes, influenced by colonial brass-band music (Ranger 1975). A similar confluence of internal precedents and outside notational influences led to the invention of a system of music writing by Orchestra Ethiopia, an Ethiopian folklore ensemble. Founded in 1963 at the Creative Arts Centre of the then Haile Selassie (now Addis Ababa) University, it began as a forum for "modern presentation of orchestral songs through the traditional musical modes and instruments of Ethiopia" (Shelemay 1983:572). From disparate provinces, it recruited solo musicians, who together played a pan-Ethiopian repertory, performed in concert and on television. Its leaders quickly faced difficulties in getting the group to "play in symphony" and "adhere to set tunes and melodies" (p. 572). That the notational system they designed draws on concepts from both Ethiopian church notation and Western notation is not surprising: at the national music school (in Addis Ababa), all had seen both kinds of notation, and one had studied music in the United States.

Subsumed under the indigenous designation *melekket*, the orchestra's notational system uses four classes of signs (figure 3): alphabetic, diagrammatic, pictographic, numerical. Additional numerical signs specify strings or instrumental fingerings. If Ethiopian church notation is the clear inspiration for signs 1–15, many of the diagrammatic signs have precedents in Western rhythmic and percussive notation. In contrast, the pictographic signs are probably an innovation, independent of Ethiopian and Western models.

In Dakar, Senegal, at the École des Arts, *kora* player Mamadou Kouyaté developed a composite notational system (Knight 1972:29). To meet similar challenges of musical performance and pedagogy, additional composite systems may exist in other African urban centers.

MUSICAL TRANSCRIPTION IN AFRICA

From early dates, outsiders' systems of music writing have entered the discussion of African music. Long before 1885 (when musical scholarship formally emerged), travelers who encountered African music in live performance tried to notate it. Many of the earliest transcribers provided contextual information. They described or drew musical instruments, and related whatever details they could about musical content. Among the earliest such examples is a rendering by William Burchell (figure 4),which incorporates a drawing of a named musician playing the *goura* (musical bow), with a musical transcription in staff notation. After detailing the exertion necessary for the musician to produce the sound, Burchell describes his process:

> I was . . . obliged to exercise two faculties at the same time, one to listen to and learn the notes he was playing, so as to enable me to write them down correctly, the other to draw his figure and portrait. The accompanying plate presents a likeness of him and is a copy of the drawing made on the spot. Beneath are added the notes expressed in the manner in which they were played, or at least as they sounded to my ear. . . . The whole piece played once through occupied just seventy seconds,

NUMERICAL SIGNS

Krar

(ምልክት) of the Orchestra Ethiopia Notational System

Alphabetical Signs

#	Sign	Name	Meaning
1		ተዝታ ች	Tazzata mode
2		ባቲ	Bati mode
3		እንቺ ሆይ	Anči hoy mode
4		አምባሰል	Ambasel mode
5		ፈጠነ	Faster
6		በረ	Quiet
7		ጠንካራ	Pluck string hard
8		ጎጃም	Gojjam rhythm
9		ጎንደር	Gondar rhythm
10		ዶርዜ	Dorze rhythm
11		ወላሞ	Wollamo rhythm
12		ትግሬ	Tigre rhythm
13		ድርብ	Doubled rhythm
14		መሃል ጎንደር	Middle rhythm Gondar
15		መሃል ጎጃም	Middle rhythm Gojjam

Diagrammatic Signs

#	Sign	Name	Meaning
16		እረፍት	Whole rest
17		ሁለት	Half rest

#	Sign	Name	Meaning
18		እንደ	Quarter rest
19		ገማሽ	Eighth rest
20		እሩብ	Sixteenth rest
21		ጨማሪ	Add half t. rest
22		መቀጠል	Continuous playing
23		ተከታ	Repeat
24		አቁም	Stop
25		ኃይለኛ	Loud
26		ቀስታ	Soft
27		አጭር	Short cutoff
28		ጥርፍ	Staccato
29		ጉዞ	Walking pace
30		መከተል	Imitate

Pictographic Signs

#	Sign	Name	Meaning
31		ደስ	Pluck mildly (mäsänqo)
32		መፈር	Scrum string (mäsänqo)
33		ክራር	Krar
34		መሰንቆ	Mäsänqo

#	Sign	Name	Meaning
35		ወሸንት	Wašant
36		በገና	Bāqäna
37		እጅ	Clap
38		ጣት	Snap fingers
39		ማልሰ	Ullulate
40		ንካ	Pluck string (mäsänqo)
41		እስክስታ	Dance (əskəsta)
42		ወላ	Vibrato
43		መስፈሳ	Lengthen
44		ግባበስ	Close in time
45		ዝግ	Slower
46		ገጥ	Ornament
47		መዝጊያ	End of composition

Composite Signs

#	Sign	Name	Meaning
48		ጠርዝ	Hit drum frame
49		መሃል	Hit drum center
50		መሰንቆ ገበታ	Hit mäsänqo sound-board
51		ክራር ገበታ	Hit krar sound-board

FIGURE 4 "Bubi of Fernando Po Playing upon the Musical Bow" (Burchell 1810–1812, cited in Balfour, 1902).

FIGURE 3 (*opposite*) Four classes of notational signs used by Orchestra Ethiopia.

and was repeated without variations. (Burchell 1810–1812:458, cited in Balfour 1902:162)

Edward Bowdich, who sought to transcribe from memory in Western notation the West African musical styles he encountered, published another early transcription (figure 5). Bowdich comments on the problem of producing a descriptive transcription that does not distort the music of another culture: "To have attempted anything like arrangement, beyond what the annexed airs naturally possess, would have altered them, and destroyed the intention of making them known in their original character. I have not even dared to insert a flat or a sharp" (Bowdich 1824:197).

In addition to reflections on the processes and problems of representing in Western notation an unfamiliar music, some early transcriptions contain what has been verified to be extraordinarily accurate musical data. Visiting Zimbabwe, the German traveler and geologist Carl Mauch encountered the *mbira dzavadzimu*, and recorded in his journals of 1869–1872 the earliest sketch of that instrument, with a chart of its tuning, plus three transcriptions of instrumental patterns for three songs. Comparison of Mauch's tunings with those from transcriptions Andrew Tracey made some eighty-eight years later proved the two to be identical (Kubik 1971).

Other transcribers were less concerned with method and precise description than with the production of prescriptive notation. They harmonized African songs, and suggested that "some of these airs seem capable of ready adaptation to bugle or band marches"; this effort, they thought, extended "a nice compliment to the nations whose melodies have interested so many" (Moloney 1889:297).

As transcription became a standard part of the practice of comparative musicology, a few general theoretical discussions treated the subject cross-culturally (Abraham and von Hornbostel 1909–1910). In the study of African music, musical scholars came to use transcription almost universally; but during the first half of the twentieth century, with a few exceptions, explicit comments about the process of transcription are absent from their writings.

Only after 1950, with the emergence of technologies that both reshaped the conventional process of transcription and provided electronic aids, a new phase of theoretical discourse about transcription began (C. Seeger 1958). Ethnomusicological discussion tended to center on the reliability of conventional methods of transcription versus notations prepared with or by mechanical devices, but Africanists' interest in transcription focused more on other concerns: first, problems in notating multipart African music in a manner that made it amenable to analysis (Arom 1976:483); and second, a debate about whether such systems of representation, and

FIGURE 5 "The Oldest Ashantee and Warsaw Air," transcribed by T. Edward Bowdich (1824 [1819]:197).

prescriptive transcriptions   Notation that indicates to performers how to create particular musical sounds

direct transcription   Writing down music notations during live performances or from memory

inherent rhythms   Rhythms that may be heard by the listener, but are not played as such by any of the performers

the analyses stemming from them, could, or should, reflect indigenous perspectives on the music (Berliner 1978:53).

Concepts behind transcription

A recurrent issue in notating African music is the question of what percentage of a musical event or recording ought to be transcribed. Within discussions, many scholars incorporate brief transcriptions, which one source terms "specimens of tunes" (Kirby 1965:115). A. M. Jones argued forcefully against this practice. He recommended the transcription of full scores with "complete" performances of African music and dance (Jones 1959:7). Part of his argument was that these transcriptions were the necessary first step in achieving musical understanding, as well as the "accurate and definitive statement of facts" (Jones 1958:14). Virtually all transcriptions of African music have been thought by their preparers to be objective, and, at least in part, to serve purposes of description. Simha Arom, who intends his transcriptions to impart the germane aspects of pitch, duration, and form, thereby to provide "a satisfactory picture of . . . structural principles" (1991:170–171), endorses this argument. Some African musical studies have consisted entirely of descriptive transcriptions of recorded music, analyzed by the transcriber according to conventional (Western) notions such as melodic type, rhythm, and form (Brandel 1961; Günther 1964).

Whether or not transcriptions of African music were classed by their realizers as either descriptive or prescriptive (Seeger 1958), staff notation with metric markings and bar lines widely served both purposes; within the work of a single scholar, the same notation can serve both to describe, for analysis, one West African style of drumming (Locke 1982), and "to function like a score, guiding the instrumentalist toward adequate performance" (Locke 1987:4). The most important examples of prescriptive transcriptions (Jones 1957) are in Western notation, so they will be accessible to the audience for which they were produced.

The practice and discussion of musical transcription also provide a setting in which major theoretical assumptions about African music have resonated. The debate over the nature of time reckoning in African music, in particular the concepts of timeline and downbeat (Merriam 1981; Stone 1986) have provided a background for all attempts to notate African music. Yet how Western notation represents African rhythm is often markedly similar, whether the author's intent is to identify and notate aspects of African rhythm according to non-African notions such as "hemiola" (Brandel 1959), or to link concepts of African rhythm with indigenous ideas of the people who perform the music (Chernoff 1979). Through transcription, scholars have tested basic assumptions about aspects of African rhythm. They have explored musical-analytical issues (Agawu 1986), the relations between drum rhythm and language (Locke and Agbeli 1980; Agawu 1987), fixed improvisations (Rycroft 1958; Erlmann 1985; Agawu 1990), and connected motoric and acoustic images (Kubik 1962).

Sources for musical transcriptions

To evaluate systems of musical notation, one must scrutinize the transcription process. For transcriptions of African music, scholars have used varied sources: live performances, sound recordings, and films.

Live performances

Before the age of recordings, transcribers necessarily worked during live performances or from memory; but long after sound recording had become a standard tool, some Africanists continued to undertake "direct transcription." This undertaking became an explicit tenet of the philosophy of several leaders of musical research in Africa. For the researcher,

> nothing can take the place of the discipline entailed in the hard grind of direct transcription. . . . It brings us face to face with the fundamental problems involved and develops that detached critical attitude which takes nothing for granted and seeks for subtle checks within the score to prove whether the transcription is valid or not. (Jones 1958:12)

The need for observing different voices or instruments when transcribing multipart music likely contributed to the continuing emphasis on "direct transcription" in African ethnomusicology, long after new technologies had made it unnecessary.

Sound recordings

The recording industry entered southern Africa early in the first decade of the twentieth century (Coplan 1979:143), but regular recording on a large scale did not begin in sub-Saharan areas until the late 1940s (Gronow 1981:253). With the beginning of LP technology (just before 1950), scholars began to participate actively in recording for archival and commercial purposes. Hugh Tracey, viewing the LP as a tool to save endangered musical traditions on the continent, made sound recording his primary activity (Shelemay 1991:283). His recorded materials played an important role in the study of African music, and made possible historical perspectives of a substantial time depth on an array of African repertories from diverse geographical locales. Recordings also enabled scholars to transcribe and analyze African music without having undertaken fieldwork on the continent. An example of the latter phenomenon is Brandel's 1961 work, which contains fifty-two transcriptions, all prepared from field and commercial recordings made after 1930, some drawn from disks released by Hugh Tracey (Brandel 1961:107). Brandel fully transcribed the recordings, and measured pitch in cents. She usually included text underlay, but the roughly phonetic transliterations, made without knowledge of the languages involved, are problematic. For descriptive and comparative analysis, Sue Carole DeVale used field recordings made by Klaus Wachsmann and Hugh Tracey (DeVale 1985:286).

Africanists' resistance to transcription from recorded sources alone is manifest in a review of Brandel's book, which deplores the idea that the lack of firsthand "experience of the originals" is no bar to "an adequate method" of conducting research on them (Kubik 1962b:116). In Africanist scholarship, the strong censure of transcription solely from recorded sources emerges primarily from sensitivity to a perceptual quirk that occurs when listening to multipart music. Termed the "problem of inherent rhythms," it involves rhythms that "may appear to be heard by the listener but are not played as such by any of the performers" (Kubik 1962b:117). Thus, in African instrumental music, the "image as it is heard and the image as it is played are often different from each other" (Kubik 1962a:33).

While concern about perceptual issues has not prevented Africanists from using

> Musical transcription is a complex and multifaceted process, but it generates a visual product, which, to permit analytical examination, can be fixed in time.

sound recordings in the process of transcription (usually alongside careful observation of performance in the field), it has both informed their use of these technologies, and encouraged innovation. Recognizing the problems inherent in "composite recordings" of complex African rhythms, Jones proposed making "analytical records," on which each contributor would play separately (1958:11–12). Arom (1976) described a detailed methodology for preparing analytical recordings that could serve the purposes of transcription. Paul Berliner (1977:1) published an analytical recording of the sort Jones proposed.

Films

In addition to the problem of distinguishing between what the musician plays and what the ear perceives, Gerhard Kubik suggested (1962a:40) that African drumming sets up inaudible cross-rhythms between the movements of a musician's hands (the motoric image) and the pattern actually emerging in sound (the acoustic image). Kubik's proposal relates closely to the Africanist music scholars' long-standing concern with kinetic concepts of rhythm (Blacking 1955).

Seeking better to understand the interrelationships of motoric and acoustic images, Kubik proposed a methodology to transcribe multipart Mangwilo xylophone music from filmstrips (1965, 1971, 1987b). He also used sound recordings (1965:3). Though the aim of his method is primarily analysis, the method has a potentially prescriptive quality: "the final transcription is a kind of score"; from it, performers can reproduce the music (1971:32).

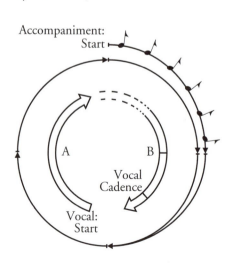

FIGURE 6   Notation for vocal and instrumental phrasing in a Zulu song for musical bow (after Rycroft 1975:63).

Visual representation

Musical transcription is a complex and multifaceted process, but it generates a visual product, which, to permit analytical examination, can be fixed in time. Scholars in African music have used many kinds of representations. The variables that shape the notational process in turn help determine the final form of a transcription. These include the nature of the musical tradition, the sources of the sounds, the problem under consideration, and (not infrequently) the intended audience.

Following the standard bias of staff notation, most transcriptions by non-Africans have sought to capture specific pitches and rhythms, even when using an alternative system of representation. However, some transcriptions incorporate elements beyond pitch and rhythm. Some individuals have sought to transcribe speech tones, often in relation to melodic contour, using diagrammatic notations or graphs (Carrington 1943; Blacking 1967:199; Simon 1989:198–199). Occasionally, novel diagrams have represented the structures and forms of phrases. Figure 6 reproduces a notation that diagrammatically shows how Zulu vocal and instrumental phrases interrelate.

Conventional staff notation

Nearly all published transcriptions of African music use conventional staff notation (Gray 1991). It often serves by default, and most frequently appears in sources where no rationale for the system of transcription occurs. Scholars often select it because of its ubiquity and easy readability. Occasionally, it "translates" another notational system. Kubik says, though "the graphic notation shows much more clearly than conventional notation what happens in this music, I have nevertheless transferred the graphic scores into staff to help the reader who might not be accustomed to the graphic notation" (Kubik 1965:37).

The drawbacks of using Western symbolic-linear notation for representing music outside the Western cultural orbit (Seeger 1958:169–171) apply to African music. There further exists the chance that the major theoretical issues in African musical studies, in particular the debate over aspects of rhythm, derive in part from the inability of staff notation to represent the complexities of multipart musics, and its tendency to force African music into a rigid, binary time continuum. Staff notation subtly embodies Western musical traits, and tends to transmit them to the music transcribed (Koetting 1970:125). For these reasons, African musical scholarship has seen an unusual amount of activity in designing new systems of musical representation.

Modified staff notation

The most straightforward manner by which scholars have tried to adjust staff notation to the exigencies of transcription followed widespread ethnomusicological precedent: scholars modified it with special signs. In the Africanist literature, many examples of modified staff notation exist; they serve both descriptive and prescriptive purposes. Rose Brandel's transcriptions (1961) employ it, modified by signs for raised or lowered pitch, glissando, and vocal register. To mark the occurrence of spoken interjections, she includes "clarifying phrases" (p. 120), which describe aspects of vocal style: "breathy-explosive" (p. 118), dancers' inhalations (p. 150), and the possible presence of harmonics (p. 169).

Jones (1959) uses conventional Western symbols, but tells readers to interpret them specially: at the right of the clef, he brackets sharps and flats, not to define a tonality, but to sharpen or flatten the notes "right through the piece unless accidentals occur"; they show "the special tuning of the drum for the particular dance." Though he used staff notation, he prepared his transcriptions from recordings enhanced with a mechanical aid: a drummer tapped on metal plates, which printed patterns on paper strips. He converted the patterns into staff notation.

Graphs

Primarily for transcribing the music of membranophones and idiophones, scholars of African music have developed graphic notations. The most widely discussed may be TUBS, the Time Unit Box System, developed at University of California at Los Angeles in 1962, for didactic purposes in West African drumming (Koetting 1970:125–126). TUBS uses boxes of equal length, put in horizontal sequence (figure 7). Within a piece of music, each box represents one instance of the fastest pulse. If no sound occurs in a time unit, its box remains empty. The box receives symbols for pitch, loudness, tone quality, and carrying power (p. 127).

For the xylophone, Gerhard Kubik designed a graphic notation that he characterized as a "kind of tablature" (Kubik 1972:31). Like a graph, the notation uses separate strips of five-line graph paper, but each line is equivalent to one of the five keys of the xylophone, with the respective hand identified by empty or black circles. The notation thus reads like a tablature. These transcriptions are of particular interest

FIGURE 7   Transcription of one of three ensemble pieces performed by Ashanti master drummer Kwasi Badu. The transcription shows the relationship of the *dawuro* 'gong pattern' and the *kete* 'master drum' (Koetting 1970:136).

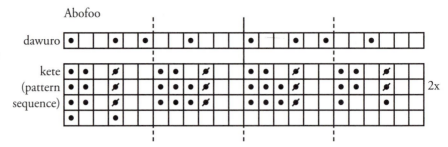

because Kubik made them from silent films, without reference to sound; marking off equal boxes, the vertical lines represent a single frame of film, not rhythmic values. The graphic notation of frames is rewritten to present basic rhythmic pulses; a third and final transcription is a "type of score," which shows the number of repetitions of each structure; from it, an instrumentalist can perform (p. 32).

Of particular concern to many Africanists has been the limited ability of conventional staff notation to convey aspects of musical sound such as texture. For the notation of texture in Ugandan music, Sue Carole DeVale developed a graphic system, applied to recorded sound of harp and voice. It employs a square time frame. Within each frame, the vertical placement of symbols shows the density of sounds, their intensity, and their volume (figure 8). Scholars have also used graphs to compare master drum rhythms with speech tone patterns, showing their close correspondence (Locke and Agbeli 1980:48–49).

Tablature

Tablature places numbers or letters on a diagram that resembles the strings or keys of an instrument; it specifies the location of the fingers on keys or strings (Read 1969:21). Like its historical use in Renaissance Europe, where it widely served for the lute, tablature has been employed in African music to notate music of chordophones, such as the *kora*. Because standard staff notation cannot adequately convey the playing technique of the *kora*, Roderic Knight designed a tablature (figure 9) that shows the interaction and coordination of the right and left hands (1972:30).

Other notational systems

Other scholars have innovated systems of visual representation idiosyncratic to a particular musical tradition or a specific analytic goal. For Ghanaian drumming, Moses Serwadda and Hewitt Pantaleoni designed a system of transcription, modeled after Labanotation (Serwadda and Pantaleoni 1968). For descriptive and analytical purposes, this notation represents the movements that produce sound, rather than the sound itself. Figure 10 reproduces one sign from the system. Reading from the bot-

FIGURE 8   Textural notation for harp and voice (DeVale 1985).

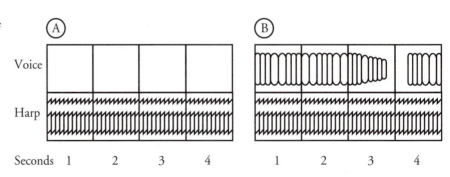

FIGURE 9   Four-column tablature for the strings
of the *kora* (Knight 1971:31).

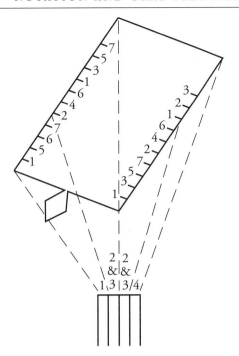

FIGURE 10   Notation for the slapstroke in
Ghanaian drumming (Pantaleoni 1972:6).

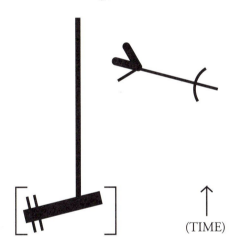

(TIME)

tom to the top, the action of the left hand occurs first; the vertical line drawn upward
from the left hand extends its pressing action through the moment when the right
hand contacts the skin of the drum (Pantaleoni 1972:6).

Scholars have developed notational systems for special purposes, including convenience of representation. Hugh Tracey's analytical system for Chopi orchestral
music conveys information in symbols that any typewriter can make (Tracey
1970:161). Knight has produced transcriptions of Mandinka *balafon* music in a
numeric notational system (Jessup n.d.:78).

Occasionally, scholars use multiple forms of representation. Alongside graph
notation, Artur Simon displays conventional staff notation and Western percussion
notation (1989:216–217). Figure 11 illustrates Kubik's use of staff notation to translate xylophone graph notation.

A study of Ethiopian Christian chant contains multiple representations, including reproductions of indigenous Ethiopian notation, transcriptions in conventional
staff notation, and electronically produced graphs (Shelemay and Jeffery 1993). The
650 indigenous Ethiopian notational signs (*melekket*) are further represented by
alphanumeric designations (like "G1" for the first *melekket* in the Ge'ez mode, cued
to a "dictionary of signs" in the publication). The alphanumeric symbols are subsequently used in charts comparing notation from a cross-section of dated manuscripts
and are superimposed on staff transcriptions to show the relationship between the
sign as notated in manuscripts and as actually sung.

AFRICAN USE OF WESTERN NOTATION

As a result of the European missionary and colonial presence on the continent, staff
notation was introduced to Africa and used by Africans. In an acknowledgment at
the end of a late nineteenth-century article on West African music, the author thanks
"two native gentlemen of considerable musical promise, Mr. A. C. Willoughby and
Mr. O. E. Macaulay, of Lagos, whose English education has enabled them to commit
to music the Yoruba, Dahomey, and Houssa melodies" (Moloney 1889:297). Some
of the transcriptions included in that article therefore may be among the first published by African musicians in Western notation. For transcription and analysis of
oral traditions, twentieth-century African scholars have preferred to use staff notation

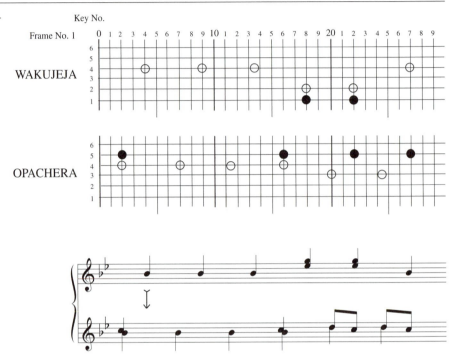

rather than alternative systems (Kyagambiddwa 1955; Nketia 1963; Ekwueme 1975–1976; Agawu 1987, 1990).

By the late twentieth century, Western musical notation, taught formally at schools of music in urban centers throughout the continent, had dispersed throughout Africa. Notated collections of African church music have circulated widely (Kaufman n.d.). In part a heritage from the colonial past, Western musical notation became domesticated and indigenized.

Tonic Sol-fa

Throughout Kenya and Tanzania, Tonic Sol-fa, introduced to East Africa by British music educator J. Curwen (1816–1888), widely serves in the transmission of Christian hymns (Gunderson 1991:44). It is placed above a staff: the vertical lines function as bars; the periods and dashes are rests (figure 12).

Transcription and the nature of scholarship

Attention to transcription in African musical studies has consistently characterized the work of scholars resident in Africa, and has often been published in the *Journal of the Society of African Music*, but there exists a broader international network of individuals engaged with transcription of oral tradition and an ongoing discourse about the subject of representation. Publications reflect much interaction between these

MANENO YOTE YA INJILI

1. Maneno yote ya Injili mitume,　}(x2)
   tangazeni pote duniani.

   Haya sasa fungueni masikio, (x2)　　　2. Yesu aliwaambia mitume:　}(x2)
   Maneno ya Injili yaenezwe.　　　　　　　　tangazeni pote duniani.

FIGURE 12　Tonic Sol-fa and staff notation in an East African hymnal (*Tumshangalie Bwana* 1988: 158–159).

scholars. Innovations in transcription have often entailed borrowing from a preexisting system. Knight's tablature for the kora draws on several different precedents: he borrows the rhythmic element of TUBS, while suggesting, "to maintain consistency with the examples of Labanotation and the Pantaleoni method, it should be read up" (Knight 1972:31).

In contrast to the decline of transcription in late-twentieth-century ethnomusicology, many scholars remain committed to musical transcription as an integral part of research in African music. Of particular interest is the response of Africanists to armchair ethnomusicologists, who transcribe music without studying it *in situ*. General ethnomusicology has criticized transcription based on sound recordings alone, because it separates music from the context of performance, and from broader fields of signification within the culture. In contrast, Africanist ethnomusicologists have largely rejected such efforts on perceptual grounds, believing that without the ability to see and hear music performed by live musicians, the scholar risks misinterpreting and misrepresenting the musical materials themselves. Scholarship on music in Africa has largely remained "music-centric," even as theoretical concerns of the discipline have elsewhere shifted to emphasize the humanistic and social aspects of music making.

REFERENCES

Abraham, Otto, and Erich M. von Hornbostel. 1909–1910. "Vorschläge für die Transkription exotischer Melodien." *Sammelbände der Internationalen Musikgesellschaft* 11:1–25.

Agawu, Kofi. 1986. "'Gi Dunu,' 'Nyekpadudo,' and the Study of West African Rhythm." *Ethnomusicology* 30(1):64–83.

———. 1987. "The Rhythmic Structure of West African Music." *Journal of Musicology* 5(3):400–418.

———. 1990. "Variation Procedures in Northern Ewe Song." *Ethnomusicology* 34(2):221–243.

Arom, Simha. 1976. "The Use of Play-Back Techniques in the Study of Oral Polyphonies." *Ethnomusicology* 20(3):483–519.

———. 1991. *African Polyphony and Polyrhythm*, trans. Martin Thom et al. Cambridge and Paris: Cambridge University Press and Editions de la Maison Des Sciences de L'Homme.

Balfour, Henry. 1902. "The *Goura*, A Stringed-Wind Musical Instrumental of the Bushmen and Hottentots." *Journal of the Anthropological Institute* 32:156–176, plus appendices.

Basset, M. René. 1881. "Etudes sur l'histoire d'Ethiopie." *Journal Asiatique,* 7th ser., 17:315–434.

Berliner, Paul F. 1977. *Africa: Shona Mbira Music.* New York: Nonesuch Records. LP disk.

———. 1978. *The Soul of Mbira.* Berkeley, Los Angeles, London: University of California Press.

Blacking, John. 1955. "Some Notes on a Theory of African Rhythm Advanced by Erich von Hornbostel." *African Music* 1(2):12–20.

———. 1967. *Venda Children's Songs.* Johannesburg: Witwatersrand University Press.

Bowdich, T. Edward. 1824 [1819]. "On the Music of the Ashantees," extracted in *The Harmonicon* 2:195–198.

Brandel, Rose. 1959. "The African Hemiola Style." *Ethnomusicology* 3(3):106–116.

———. 1961. *The Music of Central Africa: An Ethnomusicological Study.* The Hague: Martinus Nijhoff.

Carrington, John F. 1943. "The Tonal Structure of Kele (Lokele)." In *African Studies,* vol. 2, ed. J. D. Rheinallt Jones and C. M. Doke. Johannesburg: Witwatersrand University Press.

Chernoff, John Miller. 1979. *African Rhythm and African Sensibility.* Chicago: University of Chicago Press.

Coplan, David. 1979. "The African Musician and the Development of the Johannesburg Entertainment Industry, 1900-1960." *Journal of Southern African Studies* 5(2):135–164.

DeVale, Sue Carole. 1985. "Prolegomena to a Study of Harp and Voice Sounds in Uganda: A Graphic System for the Notation of Texture." *Selected Reports in Ethnomusicology,* vol. 5, ed. J. H. Kwabena Nketia and Jacqueline Cogdell DjeDje, 284–315. Los Angeles: University of California.

Djait, Hichem. 1981. "Written Sources before the Fifteenth Century." *General History of Africa,* 1, 87–113. Paris, London, Berkeley: Heinemann, California, UNESCO.

Ekwueme, Lazarun E. N. 1975–1976. "Structural Levels of Rhythm and Form in African Music." *African Music* 5(4):27–35.

Erlmann, Veit. 1985. "Model, Variation and Performance: Ful'be Praise-Song in Northern Cameroon." *Yearbook for Traditional Music* 17:88–112.

Farmer, Henry George. 1957. "The Music of Islam." In *The New Oxford History of Music,* vol. 1 (Ancient and Oriental Music), ed. Egon Wellesz, 421–477. Oxford: Oxford University Press.

Gray, John. 1991. *African Music: A Bibliographical Guide to the Traditional, Popular, Art, and Liturgical Musics of Sub-Saharan Africa.* Westport, Conn.: Greenwood Press.

Gronow, Pekka. 1981. "The Record Industry Comes to the Orient." *Ethnomusicology* 25(2):251–286.

Gunderson, Frank. 1991. "The History and Practice of Christian Gospel Hymnody in Swahili-Speaking East Africa." M.A. thesis, Wesleyan University.

Günther, Robert. 1964. *Musik in Rwanda. Ein Beitrag zur Musikethnologie Zentralafrikas.* Tervuren, Belgium: Musée Royal de L'Afrique Centrale.

Hrbek, Ivan. 1981. "Written Sources from the Fifteenth Century Onwards," *General History of Africa,* 1, 114–142. Paris, London, Berkeley: Heinemann, California, UNESCO.

Jessup, Lynne. N.d. *The Mandinka Balafon: An Introduction with Notation for Teaching.* N.p.: no publisher.

Jones, Arthur M. 1957. *Studies in African Music,* vol 2. London: Oxford University Press.

———. 1958. "On Transcribing African Music." *African Music* 2(1):11–14.

———. 1959. *Studies in African Music,* vol. 1. London: Oxford University Press.

Kaufman, Robert, ed. N.d. *African Church Music; Hymns from Many Countries.* Umtali, Rhodesia: All African Church Music Association.

Kirby, Percival R. 1965. *The Musical Instruments of the Native Races of South Africa.* Johannesburg: Witwatersrand University Press.

Knight, Roderic. 1972. "Towards a Notation and Tablature for the Kora." *African Music* 1(5):23–35.

Koetting, James. 1970. "Analysis and Notation of West African Drum Ensemble Music." *Selected Reports in Ethnomusicology,* vol. 1, no. 3. Los Angeles: University of California.

Kyagambiddwa, Joseph. 1955. *African Music from the Source of the Nile.* New York: Frederick Praeger.

Kubik, Gerhard. 1962a. "The Phenomenon of Inherent Rhythms in East and Central African Instrumental Music." *African Music* 1:33–42.

———. 1962b. Review of *The Music of Central Africa: An Ethnomusicological Study,* by Rose Brandel. *African Music* 1:116–118.

———. 1965. "Transcription of Mangwilo Xylophone Music from Film Strips." *African Music* 3(4):3–50.

———. 1971. "Carl Mauch's Mbira Musical Transcriptions of 1872." *Review of Ethnology* 3(10):73–80.

———. 1972. "Transcription of African Music from Silent Film: Theory and Methods." *African Music* 5(2):28–39.

———. 1987a. "Space/Time Concepts and Tusona Ideographs in Luchazi Culture." *Journal of International Library of African Music* 6(4):53–89.

———. 1987b. *Malawian Music: A Framework for Analysis.* Zomba: University of Malawi.

Locke, David. 1982. "Principles of Offbeat Timing and Cross-Rhythm in Southern Eυe Dance Drumming." *Ethnomusicology* 26(2):217–246.

———. 1987. *Drum Gahu.* Crown Point, Indiana: White-Cliffs Media.

Locke, David, and Godwin K. Agbeli. 1980. "A Study of the Drum Language in Adzogbo." *African Music* 6(1):32–51.

Makonnen, Berhanu, ed. N.d. "Selaqeddus Yared Tarik [Concerning the History of St. Yared]." Mimeographed typescript in Amharic.

Masehafa Deggwa. 1959. Addis Ababa: Berhananenna Selam.

McKechnie, Jean L., ed. 1978. *Webster's New Twentieth Century Dictionary.* Unabridged 2nd ed.

Merriam, Alan P. 1981. "African Musical Rhythm and Concepts of Time-Reckoning." In *Music East and West: Essays in Honor of Walter Kaufmann,* ed. Thomas Noblitt, 123–142. New York: Pendragon Press.

Moloney, C. A. 1889. "Of the Melodies of the Volof, Mandingo, Ewe, Yoruba, and Houssa Peoples of West Africa." *Journal of the Manchester Geographical Society* 5:7–9, 278–298.

Nketia, J. H. Kwabena. 1963. *Drumming in Akan Communites of Ghana.* Toronto: Thomas Nelson and Sons.

Pantaleoni, Hewitt. 1972. "Toward Understanding the Play of *SOGO* in *ATSIA.*" *Ethnomusicology* 16(1):1–27.

Ranger, T. O. 1975. *Dance and Society in Eastern Africa.* Berkeley and Los Angeles: University of California Press.

Read, Gardner. 1969. *Music Notation,* 2nd ed. Boston: Crescendo Publishers.

Robertson, Carol E. 1979. "'Pulling the Ancestors': Performance Practice and Praxis in Mapuche Ordering." *Ethnomusicology* 23(3):409–410.

Rycroft, David. 1958. "The Guitar Improvisations of Mwenda Jean Bosco." *African Music* 2(1):81–98.

———. 1975. "The Zulu Bow Songs of Princess Magogo." *African Music* 5(6):41–97.

Seeger, Charles. 1958. "Prescriptive and Descriptive Music Writing." *Musical Quarterly* 44(2):184–195.

Serwadda, Moses, and Hewitt Pantaleoni. 1968. "A Possible Notation for African Dance Drumming." *African Music* 4(2):47–52.

Shelemay, Kay Kaufman. 1983. "A New System of Musical Notation in Ethiopia." In *Ethiopian Studies Dedicated to Wolf Leslau,* ed. Stanislav Segert and Andras J. E. Bodrogligeti, 571–582. Wiesbaden: Otto Harrassowitz.

———. [1986] 1989. *Music, Ritual, and Falasha History.* East Lansing: Michigan State University Press.

———. 1991. "Recording Technology, the Record Industry, and Ethnomusicological Scholarship." In *Comparative Musicology and the Anthropology of Music,* ed. Bruno Nettl and Philip V. Bohlman, 277–292. Chicago: University of Chicago Press.

Shelemay, Kay Kaufman, and Peter Jeffery. 1993. *Ethiopian Christian Liturgical Chant: An Anthology,* 3 vols. Madison: A-R Editions.

Simon, Artur. 1989. "Trumpet and Flute Ensembles of the Berta People." In *African Musicology: Current Trends,* vol. 1, ed. Jacqueline Cogdell DjeDje and William G. Carter, 113–125. Los Angeles: University of California at Los Angeles.

Stone, Ruth M. 1986. "The Shape of Time in African Music." In *Time, Science, and Society in China and the West,* ed. J. T. Fraser et al., 113–125. Amherst: University of Massachusetts Press.

Thompson, Robert Farris. 1974. *African Art in Motion.* Berkeley and Los Angeles: University of California Press.

Tracey, Hugh. 1970. *Chopi Musicians.* London: Oxford University Press.

Tumshangalie Bwana; Kitabu cha Nyimbo. 1988. Nairobi: St. Benedict's Monastery.

Wright, Owen. 1978. *The Modal System of Arab and Persian Music: A.D. 1250– 1300.* London: Oxford University Press.

Issues of Timbre: The *Inanga Chuchotée*

Cornelia Fales

Generic Rules of *Inanga Chuchotée*
An Analysis of Two Songs

The domain of the artist and composer is one which challenges the predominant sensory patterns and evokes (among other things) the conscious transformation of perception by directing or beckoning one's attentional focus to different levels of form and structure in the work. What may at one moment be an "object" of focus for a listener may at another moment be an element collected into a composite image, wherein the object loses its identity but contributes to the quality of the more embracing image. (McAdams 1987:280)

In the front salon of the big house in Bujumbura, Torobeka sits wearily on a wicker stool. At least a dozen times, we have met together, the three of us—Torobeka, Rose (my assistant), and I—sometimes to make the journey east to Rusaka, to visit Torobeka's old teacher, Biranguza; sometimes, as tonight, simply to play and discuss music. Often, Rose and I will have just arrived, dusty and tired, burdened with equipment, from our little house in Muramvya, an hour into the interior. Muramvya is our base; many of our musicians live in the hills surrounding it. We always descend from the interior with a list of questions for Torobeka, provoked by our interviews with the *inanga* musicians of Muramvya and the surrounding areas.

Tonight, the session has been long but productive. We have finished the beer stage and are well into the tea stage, when, on an element of technique, Torobeka says not everyone can do it, not everyone can even hear it: the ability must be *mu maraso* 'in the blood'. We have heard that phrase often, and have tried with little success for details of description that will help us translate it into terms reflecting the technical requirements of the music. This is the first time Torobeka has used the phrase, and he winces when he realizes he has inadvertently ignited a new topic for discussion. What exactly does *mu maraso* mean? Can anyone have *inanga mu maraso*? How do you recognize someone with *inanga mu maraso*? More than any of the other musicians we work with, he seems to understand our questioning.

Behind all our questions lay the assumption that *inanga chuchotée*, like all genres of music, requires special acts of the listener. In this sense, each element of the genre and its performance must provide information about what the listener must do, and how to do it. If the musician is adequately following the generic rules of performance, the reaction of his audience will consist of their filling the requirements of the genre. From this point of view, music—perhaps any form of art—is provocation; its special characteristics, its rules for performance, require an intended reaction from the listener. This reaction can occur on many levels. At one extreme, if the provocation has been semantic or political (perhaps transmitted by a song text), the audience may be persuaded to belief, even to action. If the provocation occurs on a melodic or harmonic level, the audience may be moved to an emotional reaction. At the other extreme, provocation on an acoustic level will consist at least of the requirement that the listener process whatever acoustic elements the music offers.

That *inanga chuchotée* makes unusual demands of the listener is evident on first hearing. The genre takes its name from its accompanying instrument, the *inanga*, a trough zither of eight to twelve strings. With variations, the instrument exists in the countries surrounding Burundi, and eastward to the Indian Ocean. In Burundi, however, *inanga chuchotée* is unique: the performer whispers a text over an instrumental melody, hence the name *chuchotée* (French) or *bongerera* (Kirundi) 'whispered'. For a listener unaccustomed to the genre, the music is elusive; a listener who does not know the language of the text may have difficulty distinguishing one song from another. Even at first hearing, however, the quality of the whisper is striking, almost haunting. At second or third hearing, a careful listener begins to hear the central paradox of the genre: though by definition a whisper is pitchless, the musician, whispering his text, seems to be singing, following the pitch movement of the instrument.

The elusiveness of the phenomenon is not in itself surprising. Like all the senses, aural perception selectively allows into the conscious mind only the useful fraction of transmitted signals. At what level aural selective attention occurs is not clear, but subject response to a variety of psychoacoustic tests shows that such selectivity does occur. Further, aural perception efficiently combines into single perceptual unities what may be a multitude of acoustic elements. A single, familiar example: many people, until instructed, are unaware that when they hear a distinctly pitched tone from a single instrument, they are actually hearing multiple frequencies, harmonically related to the fundamental pitch; after instruction as to what to listen for, almost anyone can hear at least the second harmonic, an octave above the fundamental. Without a strategy, however, the perceptual mechanism forges together the harmonic frequencies of a single fundamental, to produce the sensation of timbre. This forging is a useful phenomenon, since timbre allows us to distinguish among sounds. At the same time, however, our synthesis of multiple frequencies into the sensation of timbre also deprives us of the ability to hear individually the frequencies of which timbre consists.

In terms of the provocative quality of genre, the *inanga* musician, by following specific rules of the genre, is provoking in his listeners an illusion of vocal melody, when in fact, there is no acoustic pitch movement. Characteristic of our discussions with Torobeka and the other *inanga* musicians was the effort to discover the provocative elements in the generic techniques of performance. The success of these techniques—or rules of performance—seemed to work a kind of magic, which produced in the listener a perceptual frame of mind, able to apprehend the genre's melody and text in an aural mode different from the modes used to perceive other music or speech.

GENERIC RULES OF *INANGA CHUCHOTÉE*

From a distance, and after much analysis of tapes, the rules of the genre seem hierarchical in power: some are inviolate, some follow an alternate rule under specific circumstances, and some are still more flexible. Whatever its place in the hierarchy, each rule falls into one of three classes: musical, linguistic, acoustic. Because of the hierar-

inanga   A trough zither with eight to twelve strings, found with variations in Burundi and surrounding areas

inanga chuchotée   A genre of "whispered song" employing the *inanga*

chy, we should consider competitive in nature the interaction of these classes. Each class insists on the preeminence of certain of its elements, and each is willing to bargain for the imposition of others. Like perception in general, the rules of *inanga chuchotée* frequently conflict, or are mutually exclusive. They operate on a trade-off system, which honors one rule and deposes another. As the sensation of timbre, for example, deprives the listener of awareness of multiple frequencies, so does one rule cancel the perceptual power of another.

Before beginning a discussion of individual rules, I will specify the use of three, otherwise misleading, terms. *Melody* will refer uniquely to the pitch-movement of the instrument. *Pitch* will refer to the elements of which the instrumental melody consists. *Tone* will refer to the linguistic tones of the Kirundi text.

Musical rules

The musical rules of the genre apply primarily to the role of the *inanga* and its production of melody.

The Rule of Melodic Downdrift

The first rule—inviolate, with no exceptions—is the Rule of Melodic Downdrift. Downdrift is a characteristic of much African music, and refers to a basic melodic movement from high to low. It is thought to mimic linguistic downdrift, a naturally occurring phenomenon, in which a vocal utterance gradually descends in pitch as the subglottal pressure in the speaker's vocal tract decreases—that is, as the speaker runs out of air before taking another breath. In *inanga chuchotée*, the contour of the pitches of the melody is consistently falling, often with primary pitches at the bottom of the descent.

The Rule of Melodic Integrity

The second musical rule, rarely violated, is the Rule of Melodic Integrity. The role of the melody line is fluid. We will see that it functions sometimes as the voice of the *inanga*, sometimes displaced to the voice of the singer. Whatever its role at a specific moment, the pitch movement of the *inanga* yields to the principle of melodic integrity, which specifies that the melodic structure—often established in a musical prelude before the performer begins to sing—must remain consistent. While this principle prohibits deviation from the basic melodic structure, it allows for variation or ornamentation within the structure, so the melody line can accommodate more than one role.

The Rule of Melodic A and B Themes

As part of melodic integrity, a third musical rule, also rarely violated, insists that each piece must consist of a melodic A and B theme, and that these themes must go with specific lines of text. Because of the ornamentation provision in the principle of melodic integrity, any melodic line can accommodate any number of text syllables. Assignment of a line of text to either theme has nothing to do with the metric rhythm of the line. Nor is there a consistent pattern of alternation for A and B themes; thus, assignment of a line of text to a theme has nothing to do with its position in the order of lines. A comparison of several renditions of the same song by different performers reveals that from one performance to another, occasional lexical variation occurs, some lines are omitted altogether, and many syntactic variations occur, both within and between lines. But there is little change in the assignment of a line of text—or its variation—to the A or B theme, no matter where in the song that line occurs. This consistency is remarkable, since *inanga* pieces may be hundreds of lines long, and the logic of assignment is neither rhythmic nor syntactic. Rather, as I presented in the section on acoustic rules, the division of text into alternate themes seems phonemically guided, according to the sound units contained in each line of text.

Linguistic rules

The linguistic rules of *inanga chuchotée* consist of any elemental constraint that is determined by, or has its origin in, the language of the text.

The Rule of Linguistic Tonality

The most important linguistic rule is the Rule of Linguistic Tonality. Kirundi is a tonal language, with pitch register constituting a distinctive feature, both lexically and grammatically. The rule of linguistic tonality requires that the pitch movement of the melody follow the tonal movement of the text. That an African melody parallels the tonal contour of its text is not unusual. The phenomenon becomes remarkable, however, when we remember that the musician is not actually singing, but whispering. Since a whisper is pitchless phonation, the text alone can give no sign of tonal difference; the performer must project his sense of linguistic tonality through his hands, onto the instrument, relying on the melodic movement of the instrument to provide tonal distinction.

The Rule of Linguistic Tonality is an exacting constraint. It provides a bit of flexibility, however, in the following way. In speech, Kirundi has two high, long vowels: anterior, for which the tone rises on the first mora and falls on the second; and posterior, for which the tone rises and falls on the second mora. *Inanga chuchotée*, however, is less precise: when a high, long vowel occurs in the text, the high tone may occur on either mora, regardless of where it would occur in speech. With this exception, a musician's performance rarely violates the Rule of Linguistic Tonality; but there are alternative ways of fulfilling the requirement.

The Rule of Moraic Rhythm

The second linguistic rule of *inanga chuchotée*, one that is as absolute as the downdrift principle among the music rules, is the Rule of Moraic Rhythm, distinguishing long from short vowels. Most frequently performers accomplish this distinction by assigning an indeterminate number of pitches to each long vowel, and only one pitch of short duration to a short vowel. Occasionally, they will give even a long vowel only one pitch, but there will be two strokes of the *inanga* with combined durations on the assigned pitch. In either case, they most often articulate long vowels as ornamentation within an otherwise unchanging melodic structure. A third alternative for indicating the long-short distinction is purely rhythmic—for example, by assigning a dotted value to a long vowel, in contrast to the eighth-note short vowels. The basic

The first and most obvious of the vocal acoustic rules is the Whisper Rule, which prohibits voiced singing of the text.

melodic structure may include regular alternation of long and short vowels, but this regularity does not preclude extra long or short vowels, whose moraic values ornamentation accommodates.

The Rule of Semantic Coherence

As the musical rules include the Rule of Melodic Integrity, so the linguistic rules include the Rule of Semantic Coherence. No matter how the performer arranges the text to meet metric requirements of long and short vowels, no matter how close the correspondence between tonal and melodic movement, the text must maintain coherence of plot or diction. Whatever textual manipulation is necessary to satisfy the various generic rules, this manipulation may not result in textual disunity. One cannot, for example, introduce an irrelevant character, simply because the character's name includes a convenient high or long vowel. However, the coherence requirement softens a bit in the allowance of certain formulaic, meaningless interjections, which serve to fill in several moras, or even whole lines, when the musician has had a lapse of memory or inventiveness.

Grammaticality

Functioning at a lower level of coherence is the Rule of Grammaticality. Like the rule of semantic coherence, the rule of grammaticality insists that the honoring of other rules must not interfere with the system of rules governing the grammar of Kirundi. Again, however, this rule softens a bit in the provision of tense flexibility created by the fact that the text rarely includes a rigorous sequence of events in time requiring precise tense markers. Thus, if the tonality of a far-past form will satisfy the Rule of Linguistic Tonality more efficiently than the tonality of the recent-past form of the same infinitive, this substitution can occur without violation of grammaticality.

Acoustic rules

Acoustic rules consist of those constraints that concern the quality of sound produced by the voice or the instrument.

Vocal acoustics

The Whisper Rule

The first and most obvious of the vocal acoustic rules is the Whisper Rule, which prohibits voiced singing of the text. To understand the significance of this rule, we must consider the acoustic qualities of a whisper. The difference between a whisper and ordinary voiced speech lies in the action of the vocal cords. In voiced speech, the pressure of air emitted from the lungs sets the cords into motion, emitting pulses of air. These pulses set up a periodic wave, consisting of a fundamental vibration and its harmonics. When the speaker tightens the vocal cords, the frequency of the pulses

FIGURE 1   Schematic of whispered source wave.

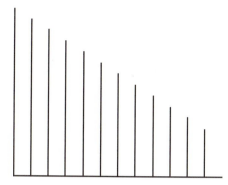

FIGURE 2   Schematic of voiced source wave.

increases, and the fundamental and all its harmonics rise in pitch. Above the vocal cords, the vocal tract is a constantly changing resonator, as the speaker alters the place and manner of articulation with each phoneme. Passing through the vocal tract, the source wave undergoes what is called the transfer function, during which the vocal tract acts as a selective filter, reinforcing the energy of some frequencies and dampening others. The result is that each vowel sound has characteristic harmonics of higher intensity, called formants.

Musical instruments operate on the same principle, except that in the vocal tract, the resonator changes with the articulation of each vowel and many of the consonants; in this sense, vowel quality is the same phenomenon as instrumental timbre. Thus, the voice is an immensely versatile instrument, made even more so by the looseness of the coupling between its source and resonator. This quality, present only in varying degrees in most instruments, is a necessary capability of the mechanism of speech, allowing a speaker to articulate the same vowel sound at different pitch levels. Tonal languages in particular depend greatly on the division of labor in the production of pitch and timbre.

In the production of a whisper, the vocal cords are loose. Rather than allowing air from the lungs to escape in the periodic waves of regular pulses, the vocal cords are caught in the blast, creating turbulent noise. The resulting sound is white noise, characterized by the presence of all frequencies at a constant amplitude within a certain range. Instead of a neat, harmonically organized source wave, voiceless speech begins with a noise block, containing a broad band of white noise, as shown schematically in figures 1 and 2.

Because the vocal tract, even in the production of a whisper, is configured according to the phoneme to be formed, the transfer function operates on the noise block in the same way it operates on a harmonically organized source wave. For this reason, a whisper is intelligible as speech. In voiced speech, the resonant frequencies of the tract modify the amplitudes of distinct harmonic frequencies; but in whispered speech, the transfer function operates on blocks of sound—frequency regions—as opposed to individual frequencies. The resulting whisper consists of bands of shaped noise. Figures 3 and 4 show the transfer function as it filters both a periodic wave (voiced speech) and a noise block (voiceless speech).

The perceptual difference between a whisper and voiced speech—one of the aspects that most interests us about whispered singing—is that both the noise block and the shaped noise resulting from the transfer function lack a fundamental

FIGURE 3   Transfer function of voiced speech.

FIGURE 4   Transfer function of whispered speech.

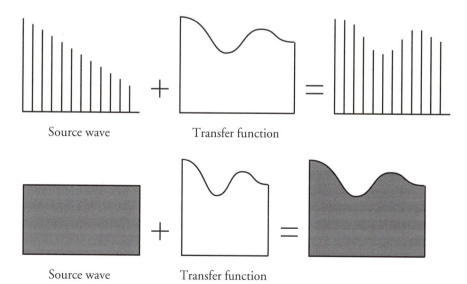

Source wave   Transfer function

Source wave   Transfer function

whisper   Soft speech in which the vocal cords are loose and caught in the blast of air, creating turbulent noise

spectrogram   Visual representation of aspects of sound including pitch, rhythm, and timbre over time

FIGURE 5   Narrow-band spectrogram of "To be, or not to be," voiced.

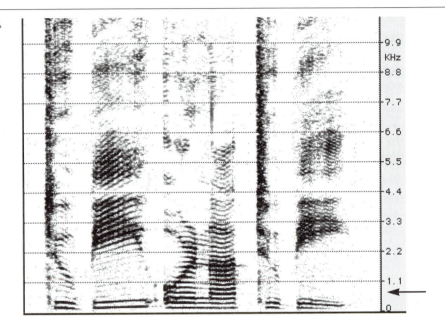

frequency, as indeed they lack all individual harmonics. Where a voiced vowel is composed of a distinct fundamental with all its harmonics (of which the arrangement of formants produces the characteristic vowel quality), a whisper consists of bands of shaped noise in the same region as the formants would be in voiced speech. Figures 5 and 6 are spectrograms of the author saying "To be, or not to be." The first spectro-

FIGURE 6   Wide-band spectrogram of "To be, or not to be," whispered.

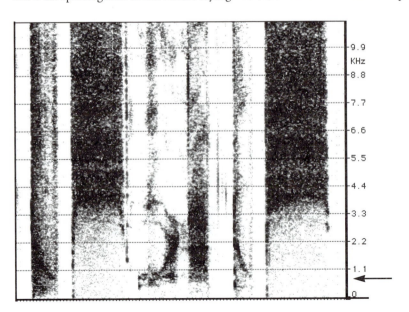

FIGURE 7   Spectrogram of Torobeka's voice as he whispers the words *"urya mwana."*

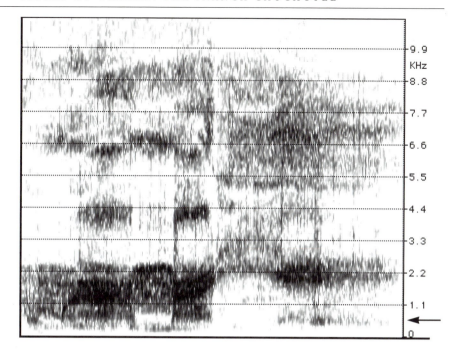

gram (of regular, voiced speech) shows individual harmonics, plus formant regions of higher amplitude, shown by darker shading. Notice the independence of the formants and harmonics—evidence of the labor divided between pitch and timbre—where the shaded area cuts across the downward movement of the harmonics. The second spectrogram shows the same sentence whispered. Most noticeable is that individual harmonics are no longer visible, and the first formant is weak or missing; clearly, there is no fundamental. A comparison of these spectrograms shows another striking difference: voiced speech consists of pitch and timbre; whispered speech is timbre only. In addition to a whisper's lack of fundamental, more important for our consideration of *inanga chuchotée* is the fact that perception of a whisper depends primarily on the second formant (F2), marked with an arrow in figures 5, 6, and 7.

Another way to visualize a whisper is evident in figure 7. As opposed to whispered (or spoken) speech, where phonemes are short and disconnected, whispered singing consists of sustained vowels with long continuous formants, broken by the noisy elements of consonants. Thus, in whispered singing, the second formant actually forms a band of shaped noise, whose lower and upper edges create a sense of shifting frequency as the formant rises and falls.

In addition to the shifts in F2, another source of the sensation of frequency is consonant noise, most often characterized, for fricatives, by short intervals of random and pronounced noise, with a band width determined by the place of consonant articulation; for stops, the interruption consists of more abrupt bursts of noise, whose frequencies are again determined by place of articulation. As turbulence interrupting the flow of a whisper's second and third formants, both fricatives and stops can be pronounced with various degrees of emphasis at strategic points in the text. In a whisper, especially as sung in *inanga chuchotée*, the primary perceptual elements are the shaped noise of shifting second formants, and the shapeless but band-controlled noise of certain consonants.

The Rule of Second-Formant and Consonant-Noise Substitution
The second acoustic rule counteracts the *inanga* melody's strict Rule of Melodic Downdrift. In tonal languages, down-drifted phonation often contains phrase-final

driven instrument   One whose vibrating system is driven by continuous stimulation; it produces a sustained tone

impulsive instrument   Plucked or struck instrument; between impulses the sound rings and dies out

high tones that are lower than phrase-initial low tones; in speech, therefore, tonality seems to depend on relative rather than absolute pitch levels. However, in the down-drifted melody of *inanga chuchotée*, which consists of short and repeated motifs, such relativity is perceptually difficult. Since the Rule of Melodic Downdrift is inviolate, the musician must find another method to show a high tone that occurs in the text at the down-drifted end of a melodic phrase. The Rule of Second-Formant and Consonant-Noise Substitution allows the use of high-frequency noise—either in the form of an ascending second formant, or in the form of a pronounced, high-frequency consonant phoneme—to substitute for the melodic ascension that ordinarily coincides with high tones.

The Rule of Predominant Phonemes

The third acoustic rule for the vocal part of *inanga chuchotée* is the Rule of Predominant Phonemes. It requires that the *inanga*'s A and B themes be defined by specific phonemes that occur predominantly in one or the other motif. These phonemes may be either vowels (a phenomenon linguists call vowel harmony) or consonant alliteration. In this rule, we see evidence of how generic rules constrain and limit the musician, but also provide the form that helps the musician's memory and creativity. Without the Rule of Predominant Phonemes, it is doubtful whether the *inanga* player could maintain the consistency of assignment of the text to the A and B themes.

Instrumental acoustics

Accompaniment

The first acoustic rule for the *inanga* corresponds to the Whisper Rule for the voice: the accompanying instrument must be an *inanga*. While this may seem self-evident, it is nearly the most important requirement of the genre. All performers insisted emphatically on the need for the *inanga*-whisper combination. Only once during my year in Burundi did a musician arrive with an *ikembe* (mbira), which he proceeded to perform to a whispered text, saying his *inanga* had broken. After a few lines, he put down his instrument and borrowed another musician's *inanga*, remarking in disgust the *ikembe* did not work.

The *inanga* has a shallow, concave, troughlike resonator, made of wood from a special tree, the *ikivumu*. At the ends of the resonator are slots called variously teeth (*amenyo*) and toes (*amano*), through which a single string winds from end to end, leaving seven or eight sections, each of whose pitches is regulated by the amount of tension strung into that section. The string traditionally consists of cow tendon.

In the simplest terms possible, musical instruments consist of two kinds of vibrating systems: driven and impulsive. In the first are instruments whose vibrating

FIGURE 8 Wave form of an *inanga* tone, 122 Hz.

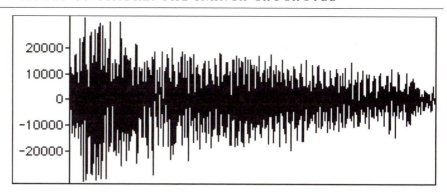

systems are driven by continuous stimulation, so that the instrument produces a sustained tone, characterized by a steady state, which endures as long as the system is driven. Many aerophones and all bowed chordophones are of this kind. In the second are instruments whose vibrating systems are excited by striking or plucking with repeating but discrete impulses, so that between each impulse, the sound rings and dies out, undergoing a complete cycle of attack and decay, with no harmonic steady state. Most idiophones and membranophones, and all plucked or struck chordophones (including the *inanga*), are of this kind.

The lack of a harmonic steady state in impulsively excited instruments means that at the moment of stimulation, the fundamental and all its harmonics begin to vibrate with an energy proportional to the degree of stimulus—in the *inanga*, the initial displacement of the string. Between the moment of stimulation and the next impulse, each frequency provoked by the initial stimulus begins to decay at varying rates of speed. The process of decay does not disturb the cycle repetition rate or the frequency of the harmonics: it disturbs the degree of wave displacement or amplitude. From millisecond to millisecond, the wave form of the resulting sound as determined by the relative amplitudes of the harmonics changes, because each harmonic of the fundamental excited by the impulse decays or dies out at a different rate of speed.

Figures 8 and 9 show two magnified wave forms. The first is of an *inanga* string of frequency 122 Hz; the second is of a sustained flute tone of frequency 292 Hz. Notice the consistent shape of the second wave's steady state, and the changing shape of the first wave's decaying state. If the wave form of the *inanga* (or any plucked stringed instrument) is changing from the moment of excitation, the sound can be said to exist entirely in a state of transience, and to consist of unstable timbre, which varies with each change of the wave form.

Figures 10 and 11 are narrow-band spectrograms of the wave forms of figures 8 and 9. Again, notice the uneven rate of decay of the *inanga*'s harmonics, as opposed

FIGURE 9 Wave form of a flute tone, 292 Hz.

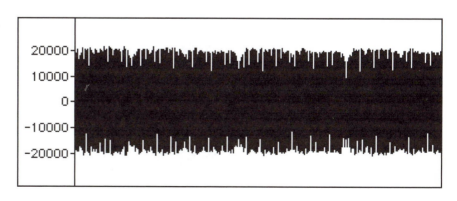

Two factors especially important to the *inanga* are the stiffness of the strings and the place and manner of the plucking. The stiffer the string, the greater the reduction of higher modes of harmonics.

FIGURE 10   Narrow-band spectrogram of an *inanga* tone, 122 Hz.

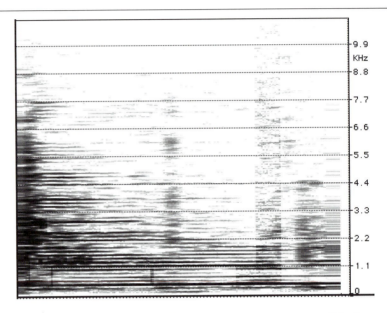

to the sustained harmonics of the flute. In consecutive tones of the instrument, only the lowest harmonics often last from one impulse to the next.

So far, what I have said of the acoustics of the *inanga* is true for all plucked stringed instruments. For any instrument, the specific conformation of harmonics at their relative amplitudes depends on many factors. Two factors especially important to the *inanga* are the stiffness of the strings and the place and manner of the pluck-

FIGURE 11   Narrow-band spectrogram of a flute tone, 292 Hz.

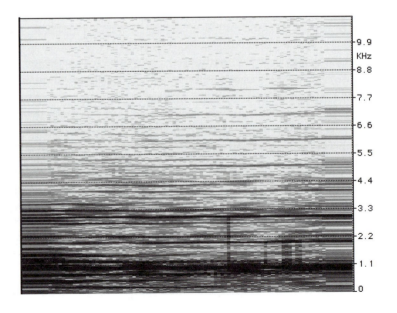

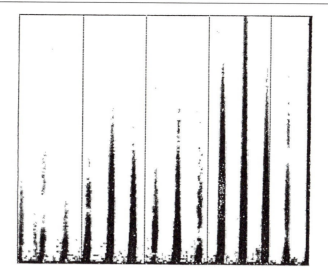

FIGURE 12   Narrow-band spectrogram of a guitar tone.

ing. The stiffer the string, the greater the reduction of higher modes of harmonics. Cowgut is stiffer than the strings on a twentieth-century acoustic guitar (figure 12). The higher partials of tones on a plucked *inanga* are weaker and decay more rapidly than those of tones on a plucked guitar. The width of the plectrum increases the effect of stiff strings. A method for varying timbre is therefore the use of the side of the thumb for plucking some strings, and of the fingertips for plucking others.

Another factor affecting the instrument's timbre is that plucking occurs at the fixed ends of each string section. Again, in a general and absolute sense, a string plucked at a point exactly $1/x$ of the length of that string will lose all partials that are multiples of x; more realistically, plucking near the same point will weaken all the same harmonics. Thus, another way to change the timbre of an *inanga*'s tone is simply to pluck it in another place: the closer to its middle a string is plucked, the more the harmonics of the resulting tone fade. Figure 13 is a spectrogram in which five notes, all of the same pitch, are plucked with the first three pitches struck at a different point from the second three. Because *inanga* players pluck with both sides of four

FIGURE 13   Narrow-band spectrogram of five *inanga* tones of 362 Hz, demonstrating the same pitch with two different timbres.

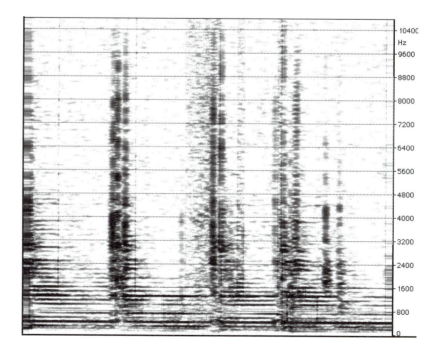

fingers, sometimes with their fingernails, sometimes with the fleshy part of their fingers, both the place and manner of plucking are easily—even automatically—altered.

Analogous difference of timbre and vowel quality

Timbre change is important because of another acoustic rule of *inanga chuchotée*. If two consecutive tones of the melody are the same pitch, but at the same time the sounds of different vowels are whispered in correspondence with them, either the timbre of one of the corresponding vowels must differ from that of the other, or the corresponding vowels must assimilate one to the other, so that formants are close in location. Conversely, if the same vowels are produced on consecutive tones of the same frequency, then the timbre of those tones must also be the same. In following this rule, the *inanga* disregards the independence of pitch and timbre characteristic of the voice, in allowing either to distinguish the sounds of the vowels.

If we take a spectrogram of a single *inanga* tone, like the one in figure 10, and trace as precisely as possible the component frequencies and their relative intensities (expressed in decibels), we discover three more acoustic properties of the instrument that will be important in understanding what the genre *inanga chuchotée* requires of its listeners. For the *inanga* tones and the guitar tones shown in figures 10 and 11, the spectra in figures 14 and 15 show component frequencies and their relative amplitudes.

A comparison of the spectra in figures 14 and 15 reveals one of the obvious differences between the *inanga* and the guitar to be the relative strengths of the fundamental and second harmonics of each. For most Western instruments, including the acoustic guitar, unless the fundamental is muted, it is often the most intense of the

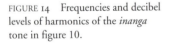

FIGURE 14   Frequencies and decibel levels of harmonics of the *inanga* tone in figure 10.

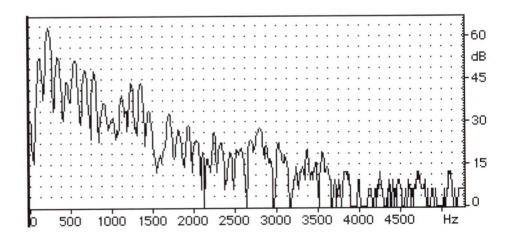

FIGURE 15 Frequencies and decibel levels of harmonics of the flute tone in figure 11.

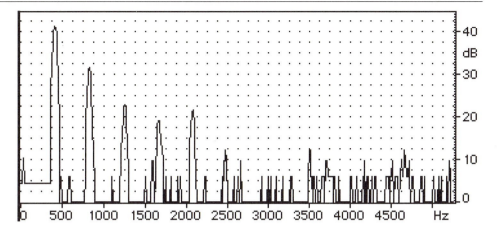

frequencies that constitute characteristic timbre. Clearly for the *inanga*, this is not the case; the second harmonic is stronger than the fundamental frequency.

Another fact visible from these spectra is the relative inharmonicity of *inanga* partials in comparison to guitar partials. In most Western, factory-manufactured instruments, the frequency relation between the harmonics of a single tone is that each higher partial is a multiple of the lowest or fundamental frequency. Thus, if the fundamental is 200 Hz, the second harmonic will be 400 Hz, the third 600 Hz, the fourth 800 Hz, and so on. In factory-manufactured guitars, where the vibrating column is smooth and even, the partials will deviate very little from this harmonic relation. However, with the *inanga*, whose strings are of animal tendon, twisted by hand, the surface edge is rough, and the string uneven. The resulting frequencies are markedly inharmonic. In discussing the perceptual organization of sound, we will see how the implications of both the instrument's weak fundamental frequency and the inharmonicity of its partials have consequences for the illusion provoked by the genre.

Two other acoustic facts visible in a comparison of the *inanga* and guitar are related, but individually important. If we look back at the narrow-band spectrograms of a single guitar tone and a single *inanga* tone, the first of these facts is immediately clear. The tone of the guitar looks neater; it shows stark harmonics, with clean nonharmonic frequency areas. The tone of the *inanga*, however, is dirtier, with less contrast between harmonics and the area between. While all instruments produce a certain amount of noise in addition to the periodic waves of their harmonic frequencies, the difference in contrast between the harmonic and noise frequencies of the guitar reveals its timbre to contain the nonharmonic frequencies at very low intensity, compared to true partials. The *inanga* timbre seems in comparison to contain a chaos of frequencies, with harmonics only mildly distinguished by intensity; in fact, we can find the partials only by tracing the intensity level as it rises and falls, with the peaks in intensity occurring at approximate multiples of the fundamental.

Notice that the peaks of the *inanga* tone are low, blunt, and wide; but those of the guitar are high, sharp, and narrow. The shapes of these spectra reveal something of the dampening function of each instrument, but the importance of this difference is that for an instrument like the *inanga*, there is little distinction between harmonic and nonharmonic tones; the *inanga*'s noisy frequencies are only slightly less intense than the harmonic ones. This quality will be important later, but for now we will observe that the more noisy frequencies an instrument possesses, the greater the noiselike quality of the tones it produces.

Visual evidence of an auditory phenomenon signifies little. The proof of the system is in the listening, not once or twice, but over and over, until the strangeness of the genre fades.

AN ANALYSIS OF TWO SONGS

For each of the areas of rules—musical, linguistic, acoustic—there exists a frequency contour, determined by the rules associated with it. Thus, the musical rules determine the melodic contour, the linguistic rules determine the tonal contour, and the acoustic rules determine the contour of the second formant. The first of these consists of the instrumental melody, which typically rises slightly and then descends, in accord with the Rule of Melodic Downdrift. The tonal contour, consisting of the rise and fall of linguistic tones, is in a literal sense nonexistent in the genre, because of the Whisper Rule. The second-formant contour consists of the sustained steady states of the whispered vowels and the transients that link them; in addition, consonant noise, and noise introduced in service to the tonal contour (according to the Rule of Second-Formant and Consonant-Noise Substitution), are part of the second-formant curve.

The curves of both the melody and the second formant belong in production to specific acoustic events—the former to the *inanga*, and the latter to the voice. As the generic rules may function in conflict with each other, so also do the melodic contour and the second-formant contour. Each has an integral role in its own acoustic system, to which such rules as the Rule of Melodic Integrity, the Rule of Semantic Coherence, and the Rule of Grammaticality, bind them. At the same time, both contours must, whenever possible, take on the role of the imaginary tonal contour: each must serve as a receptacle for the projected tonal curve. At an ideal moment, all three curves will find themselves moving in the same direction: a high tone will coincide with a natural melodic rise, and both will coincide with a vowel characterized by an ascending second formant. At other times, the contours of the melody and the second formant will trade off their responsibilities to the tonal contour. Both the melodic and the tonal curves have some leeway in the execution of their primary functions.

For the remainder of this section, I will explore the interaction of the three frequency contours. It must be remembered, however, that analytic evidence of an auditory phenomenon signifies very little. The real proof of the system is in the listening, not once or twice, but over and over, until the strangeness of the genre is lost.

The most efficient method to show the interaction of the three frequency contours would be to transcribe the Kirundi text of an *inanga* song according to orthographic conventions including vowel length and tone. Next, one would juxtapose each line with the tonal contour of the same line as spoken *in full voice* by a Kirundi-speaker. Finally, one would position together each transcribed line of text, the spoken line's tonal contour, and a music transcription of the *inanga* melody accompanying each line in *inanga chuchotée*.

The result of a juxtaposition of these lines would be to separate definitively three domains that are perceptually fused in the mind of a listener to *inanga chuchotée*. Each domain provides cues that inform the auditory expectations of the listener who looks for congruence between the domains in the music. Where disagreements between the three contours occur, auditory expectation provokes a listener to accept the operations of the Rule of Second Formant Substitution in compensation for the melody's failure to fill its role as a provider of pitch movement.

Interpreting the genre

What is the provocative power of music played on the *inanga*? If the musician has adequately followed the rules of performance, what does the result require of the listener? This is a subject we can examine on many levels. The scope of this paper requires that discussion be limited to the basic, acoustic, perceptual level; but we must remember that the theoretical implications of music as provocation become clear only with a more thorough examination of multiple levels. The usefulness of an acoustic or cognitive approach to music becomes clear only when we trace to higher levels the patterns we discover at the primary one.

The performance

Imagine a performance of *inanga chuchotée*, and observe what is happening. It is night. We are in the receiving room of a small house (*inzu*), high on the far side of Colline Busimba. The house stands in a clearing that has literally been cut level out of the hill in the middle of a banana forest whose trees cover the top half of the mountain. The door of the house and the wooden window covers are open, and we can hear the large banana leaves shifting with the wind. The room is crowded with people from all over the colline. A few of the oldest women and men sit on three-legged stools; the rest have spread cloths on the floor, where they are sitting.

On a small table in the middle, two candles do little to stop the night from entering the house: but inside, the darkness is warm, flickering, and intimate, with bodies close together. On the lowest stool sits an old man, bent over his *inanga*, which stands lengthwise, its longest edge perpendicular to the floor and facing the people. His head is as close to the "face" of the instrument as possible, not because he needs to see the strings, but in order to locate his own voice near the voice of the instrument. As he begins to play, the listeners fall silent, and their faces clear of all expression; even the smallest children stop rustling, staring at nothing in particular, with blurred eyes and open mouths. The setting is a muted one; there is little perceptual distraction from the music: the light is dim, and the night noises seem far away. Only the voice of the *inanga* murmurs through the room like a stream: *ijwi ry'inanga ririsuma*. The musician supplies the words, but it is the *inanga* that speaks.

For a long time, *inanga chuchotée* has probably been occurring in settings like the one described above. Indeed, musicians and audiences alike recognize the need for such a setting—one in which the auditory environment is undiluted with distractions from mundane life. *Inanga chuchotée* is understood by the Barundi as a subtle, intimate genre, not a spectacle for large crowds. Even the dance that sometimes accompanies the songs is subtle and graceful, flowing rather than sharply rhythmic. It is considered best danced by women, with winding, sinuous arm movements and arched neck, with little distinct leg-and-foot movement—a dance described as "feline" by one Murundi observer.

It is interesting, though not especially profitable, to speculate on the one hand as to whether the genre evolved because of the particular setting in which it is inevitably performed; or on the other, whether the setting was originally chosen because of the requirements of the genre. Whichever the case, it will become clear that the special provocation of the genre is probably most powerfully accomplished in a setting like that above. Earlier, we briefly characterized the provocative power of *inanga chuchoteé* as the ability to induce an aural illusion, contrary to the acoustic reality of the performance. Because this illusion involves a contrast between what appear to be primary and secondary points of focus in the music, it is important, as we will see, that no

Edgar Rubin, inventor of Rubin's goblet, developed one of the fullest descriptions of qualities that distinguish figure from ground. Another early student of the figure-ground illusion was Max Wertheimer, who formulated a series of principles for isolation of the figure.

FIGURE 16   Rubin's goblet.

FIGURE 17   Boot-sunflower.

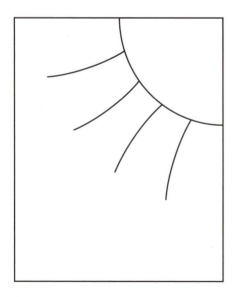

outside acoustic interference be present in the environment of performance to blunt the sharpness of this contrast.

The reversible figure-ground phenomenon

Researchers have done much work on contrasts between primary and secondary focal points in the visual domain, and in particular on illusions involving contrasts between focal point and background. Among these is a well-studied class of visual phenomena, figure-ground illusions. In the course of examining various studies of the figure-ground phenomenon, we will see that the illusion provoked by the genre *inanga chuchotée* is the *exact auditory analog* of the figure-ground illusion in vision.

One of the most common examples of the figure-ground phenomenon is "Rubin's goblet" (figure 16), reversible as either two profiles or a single vase or goblet, depending on which area the viewer perceives as figure. In this figure, though more so in more complex figures (such as the boot-sunflower picture, figure 17), several important features of the reversal phenomenon are clear.

If we concentrate with careful self-reflection on our experience of perceptual reversal in the drawings of figures 16 and 17, we see several aspects of the figure-ground illusion. The first is that, except with special training, we cannot reverse perception from one figure to another quickly or without effort. On first examination of a figure-ground conglomerate, we immediately grasp one of the possible figures. However, even if we know in advance the identity of the second possible figure, even if we have successfully switched from one figure to the other several times before, the process of reversal requires at least a short interval of time to achieve. During this interval, we feel almost as though we have left one perceptual position and are waiting to "click into" another. If the figure-ground conglomerate is not well drawn, we may find ourselves between perceptual positions for more than several seconds while we examine details of the drawing in the effort to perceive the new figure. In such a neither-nor position, we are uncomfortable: we know there exists a second figure to be perceived, and we cannot find it; arrival in the new position often accompanies a sense of "Ah, there it is," a release from the tension of being between two perceptual positions. In achieving reversal, it is not the case that we rest with our immediate perception of figure until the new figure becomes apparent: rather, we must almost consciously will ourselves to forsake the first perception before we are susceptible to the perception of a second figure drawn from the same conglomerate.

Edgar Rubin, inventor of Rubin's goblet, developed one of the fullest descriptions of qualities that distinguish figure from ground. Though many of his observations are reflective, rather than experimentally derived, his study has been cited and its details corroborated by researchers ever since its publication (1915). According to Rubin, in a figure-ground drawing, the figure is more impressive, more easily remembered, and dominates consciousness, while the ground appears to extend out into the environment; or we might say that in a figure-ground drawing, the area interpreted as ground imitates the more general background until it seems almost to blend into it. Rubin further points out that when experimenters ask about two figure-ground drawings, the answers always relate to the figures rather than to the grounds, even if the figure happens to be nonsense, such as an asymmetrical figure without referent in the real world. In reversible figure-ground drawings, like Rubin's goblet, a field perceived as figure looks richer, more highly structured, and more easily localized, than the same field when perceived as ground.

Throughout most of his discussion, Rubin cites the main distinction between figure and ground to be the "thing-like quality" of the figure, and the "substance-like quality" of the ground—terms he has difficulty defining. Despite his difficulty, the distinction is relevant to our concern with auditory illusion. We will sharpen the distinction by substituting the terms "definition" for "thingness," and "texture" for "substanceness."

Another early student of the figure-ground illusion was Max Wertheimer, who formulated a series of principles for isolation of the figure. Among these is the principle of similarity, which asserts that, between parts of a field, the greater the similarity in some visually perceived quality (size, shape, position), the greater the tendency to group these parts into a figure. A second principle is the principle of goodness of form: elements forming some "preferable class" of well-formedness will most likely group together as a figure. A last principle is the principle of common destination: elements "performing a joint translocation" (1923:44) will probably also group together.

Both Rubin and Wertheimer talk extensively of the role of contour in distinguishing figure from ground. Rubin says: "When two fields have a common border, and one is seen as figure and the other as ground, immediate perceptual experience is characterized by a shaping effect which emerges from the common border of the fields and which operates on only one field, or operates more strongly on one than on the other" (1915:85). In most figure-ground drawings, a line will run through the undifferentiated field that the viewer inevitably assigns to the figure as boundary after the figure is identified. In a reversible figure-ground drawing, such as Rubin's goblet, the line distinguishing figure and ground serves as contour, or outline, for either field, depending on which the viewer interprets as figure at a given moment. At any one time, the contour line belongs to only one of the fields; it is seen, not as a "common border" between them, but as the defining contour of just one field (that of the figure). This is the principle of mutually exclusive attributes: once a particular element has been perceptually organized within one field, it is eliminated as a possible contestant for the other; as soon as an attribute is assigned to one of several competing interpretations of an undifferentiated field, it cannot also serve to define an alternate interpretation. This principle usually expands beyond individual attributes to apply to entire image interpretation. In Rubin's goblet, the principle of mutually exclusive attributes describes the fact that we can see either two profiles facing each other, or a single goblet, but not both at the same time; we must stand in one perceptual position or the other, from each of which only one interpretation of the drawing is possible.

A more recent study of figure-ground phenomena is directly relevant to our discussion of successful and unsuccessful illusion, and particularly to the subject of *inanga chuchotée* as auditory analogue. Riani et al. (1986) define the ambiguity of a figure by the ease with which a viewer alternates between two or more alternative interpretations. The strength of each interpretation is measured by the probability that the viewer will choose it over the alternatives. The most successful interpretation will have the greatest possible chance of being chosen over the alternate image. The difficulty with which the listener can move to an alternative perceptual position, to

figure-ground   Perceptual grouping of elements in a visual or auditory field such that they form an image with background; in reversible figure-ground illusions, perceivers may reverse the figure and the ground

perceive an alternative percept, is a measure of the strength of that image. An ideally successful percept is one so heavily weighted in the competition between it and the competing percept, that it is chosen as the correct perceptual hypothesis with the greatest possible probability.

A final issue that Riani et al. (1986) discuss is the notion of figural complexity or simplicity. They define complexity of a figure, not by the number of details included in a given field, but by the number of details increasing the ambiguity of interpretation. The simplest figure may be one that has the highest number of details that empower one interpretation, and simultaneously the least number of details that empower the other. Thus, as they point out, either an increase or a decrease of details in a drawing may result in simplicity of interpretation. In a later section, we will see how each of the generic rules of *inanga chuchotée*, described earlier, functions to simplify the listener's choice of the illusory over the veridical (genuine) percept. Each rule serves to empower the illusion in the competition between it and the acoustic reality of the genre.

These studies concern visual phenomena. It is not unusual, however, for researchers to hypothesize correspondences between different modes of perception, and the heuristics governing the organization of visual and auditory data often show similarities. Researchers such as Helson (1925:32) and Gregory (1974:376) have suggested appropriate aural examples. One of the most pertinent attempts to find an auditory analog for the figure-ground phenomenon comes from *Gödel, Escher, Bach*, by Douglas R. Hofstadter:

> One may also look for figures and grounds in music. One analogue is the distinction between melody and accompaniment—for the melody is always in the forefront of our attention, and the accompaniment is subsidiary, in some sense. Therefore it is surprising when we find, in the lower lines of a piece of music, recognizable melodies. This does not happen too often in post-baroque music. Usually the harmonies are not thought of as foreground. (1979:70)

Hofstadter is talking primarily of Western art music, and one would like to question his distinction between melody and accompaniment. Furthermore, his "analogue" is less than precise, since at least in the visual modality, we have defined figure-ground configurations to be in some sense reversible. Hofstadter seems, rather, to be describing a conglomerate of sounds, of which—sometimes—more than one sequence may constitute a melody, and may thus claim priority of focus. This is not the same as the figure-ground contrast in which optical reality yields several conflicting interpretations.

Priority of focus: the Barundi

At the same time as we are criticizing Hofstadter, we would agree that most music has a priority of focus. To the extent that this priority is culture-specific, it may be a learned phenomenon. In Burundi, the distinction is broader than Hofstadter specifies. In all genres that include voice and other instruments, the primary focus lies with the voice. Few genres of Burundi music are not partly vocal. In most such genres, the voice carries the melody, and in this sense Hofstadter's distinction is consistent with mine. But for the Barundi, the voice is primary—not for the melody, but because in most cases it carries a text. The importance of discourse for the Barundi in an immense number of situations has been well established (Ntahombaye 1983). Thus, even in situations where the accompanying instrument mimics the melody of the voice, and more so when the instrument plays a different part, the voice is primary. It is significant that in a less commonly performed type of *inanga* music that includes *voiced* singing alternating with whispered verses, the instrumental part during the voiced sections dwindles from full melody to a repetition of one pitch, or at the most, several pitches.

The inanga *illusion*

Inanga chuchotée provokes an illusion. In what sense is this auditory illusion equivalent to the visual figure-ground phenomenon? The figure-ground illusion is a special case of normal differentiation of focus from background: both the focal point and the background are reversible. Depending on the type of figure-ground conglomeration, the fields may or may not be exactly reversible. In a figure-ground configuration, each element of visual data that stimulates the retina can have two or more interpretations—as part of the figure, or as part of the ground.

The same is true of *inanga chuchotée* as an aural version of the figure-ground phenomenon. However, in addition to the fact that the configuration exists here in a different sense-modality, the genre differs from the examples of figure-ground discussed earlier in one other important sense. Figures such as Rubin's goblet or the boot-sunflower are artificial, contrived to study object identification and other perceptual phenomena. Normal perception, or normal differentiation of affordance from background, assumes that only one hypothesis will have any chance of acceptance by the viewer. In normal perception, the correlation between what is in the real world and our perception of it is assumed to be one of identity; otherwise, our perceiving senses would be of little use to us. Generally speaking, we believe that the percepts resulting from the data we have received are always *veridical*.

A major difference between *inanga chuchotée* as a figure-ground and the visual examples cited earlier is that the experience of its audience includes both veridical and illusory percepts. By contrast, Rubin's goblet has no correct interpretation; both interpretations are there to be perceived.

The veridical percept

Until the onset of illusion, the veridical percept could well be considered the same as the normal perception of music—a percept resulting from the listener's choice of focal point, with the remainder of the sound constituting background. With the onset of the illusory percept, however, elements of what seemed to be the background become part of the focus, and both fields must then be reinterpreted. This is a type of figure-ground reversal, so that what might have been considered simple focal point and background must now be understood respectively as figure and ground.

If we recall the distinguishing qualities of figure and ground, we can determine which of the components of the genre *inanga chuchotée* is figure, and which is ground. One primary distinction exists between the contrasting qualities of definition and texture, belonging respectively to figure and ground. In the auditory domain, Albert S. Bregman has identified something of the same distinction between

We might almost conceive of the fundamental frequency of the *inanga* as the line dividing the fields of figure and ground, and specifically as the contour enclosing the tone of the instrument.

sounds characterized by regularly repeating amplitude modulation or frequency modulation (for example, a melody) and the quality he calls granularity.

> Think of the sound of a piece of metal being dragged across different surfaces. The amplitude changes rapidly over time in an irregular pattern. However, it is not entirely irregular. We can tell a lot about the roughness of the surface by listening to the sound. The best way to describe it is to say that the sound is granular, reflecting the granularity of the surface over which it is being dragged. . . . [In music,] though individual lines are not perceived, the granularity is, and the granularity of one piece can be quite unlike that of another, [as] the sound of a hand winnowing dry rice [differs from] the crunch of a footstep in low-temperature snow. (1990:116–118)

As explained above, one way to describe the formant regions of a whispered vowel is in terms of shaped noise, while in a voiced vowel, the same formant regions consist of groups of individual harmonics. I would propose that the difference between whispered and voiced phonation is exactly the difference between texture granularity and definition regularity of frequency modulation. Shaped noise is a particular bandwidth of all inclusive frequencies at irregular amplitudes. The result is the textured sound of noisy air. By contrast, the *inanga*, with individual harmonics and a rule-governed melody, is well defined and distinctive. We might almost conceive of the fundamental frequency of the *inanga* as the line dividing the fields of figure and ground, and specifically as the contour enclosing the tone of the instrument.

In the whisper-*inanga* conglomerate, other qualities of the figure-ground opposition mentioned by Rubin, Wertheimer, and others, are also clear. That the instrumental melody is repetitive, offering little new information to be assimilated with the passing of time, and that the whispered text offers, by contrast, new acoustic and linguistic elements with each line, means that it is the *inanga* that is "more impressive, more easily remembered"—a quality Rubin notes as characteristic of the figure. And during performances, when a member of the audience wishes to request or refer to a specific song, he or she will either hum the melody (rather than quote words from the text), or sing a bit of the text, voicing the instrumental melody. This tendency suggests either the person speaking is under the influence of the veridical percept, and remembers the melody better than the text, or was influenced by the text in a way that will become clear in the next section.

Both Wertheimer and Rubin point out in the visual domain, the ground appears to blend into the environment, while the figure is self-contained, bounded by real or illusory contours. Again, this distinction appears in the whisper-*inanga* conglomerate. The text, with its shaped-noise formants, and especially with its noisy features unattached by regular frequency modulation to the following prolonged formants, does seem to rise up and fade into the environment. Here, we see the reason for a performative setting like that described above. If a general background that surrounds the more circumscribed ground of the whisper includes too much noise, the noisy features of the text are augmented by those of the larger environment until they are distorted or, worse, drawn away from the melody of the *inanga*, thus weakening the strength of the illusion. This is especially true because, as noted above, the ground of a figure-ground conglomerate tends to imitate the larger background in regard to the figure. In that a whisper consists exclusively of noise, it is far more like the general background than the sound of the *inanga*, bound by specific, harmonically related frequencies that rarely occur in the natural world.

Relative to the ground, the figure is richer, more structured, and more easily localized. While richness may be considered a matter of taste, it is clear that the tone of the *inanga* is acoustically structured with more precision than a whisper. Further, to the extent that a whisper-ground blends into the general, soundful environment, it is more difficult to isolate, and thus more difficult to localize.

In the veridical percept, then, the *inanga* is figure, and the whisper is ground. If we grant that in Burundi, the focal point of most mixed genres is the voice, we begin to see the sort of features that act to weight the competition away from the veridical percept, toward some illusion more consistent with auditory expectation. The reality of *inanga chuchotée*, in a sense, is skewed. And to the extent a learned priority of focus acts to help in perceptual organization, the audience of *inanga chuchotée* has already been forced from a comfortable perceptual position by the unusual features of the veridical percept, even before the onset of the illusion.

As we discuss more features that act to simplify the ambiguity of percepts toward the illusion, we will see that some of these features are built into the genre—for instance, the A and B themes—and some rely on the skill of the performer. Furthermore, the cognitive flexibility to move from one perceptual position, the "readiness-to-respond in a certain direction" (Helson 1925:52), is not universal among audiences. And there are good musicians (those with *inanga* in the blood) and bad musicians (those whose attempts to provoke illusion fail for lack of skill). Similarly, there are listeners without *inanga* in the blood, who cannot make themselves susceptible to—cannot hear—the illusion, no matter how skilled the performance.

The illusory percept

I have alluded to the genre's illusory percept as consisting of a sensation of pitch movement in the vocal part, when in reality the whispered text is pitchless. How does this happen?

Under special acoustic and cognitive circumstances, the ordinary fusion of harmonically related frequencies into a single, timbered tone can be undone; that is, one or several of the component harmonics can separate from the conglomerate tone, changing the quality of both the isolated frequencies and the remaining, reduced, conglomerate.

Depending on the skill of the performer, a combination of the acoustic features of the *inanga*, the phonetic features of a whisper, and other aspects of *inanga chuchotée* as determined by the rules of the genre, two complementary processes will occur. At a single moment, the fundamental, or lowest frequency, of the instrumental tone will separate from the remaining harmonics producing the timbre of that tone, and will fuse perceptually onto the shaped noisy bands of the whisper, to act as the missing melody line of the voice. The result is that the vocal part is suddenly more appropriately defined, according to the priority of focus expected by a Barundi audience: suddenly, the voice seems not only to carry the melody, but also (and perhaps more important) to provide the high tones missing from the Kirundi text. Both the fission of the fundamental from the rest of the harmonic frequencies of the *inanga*,

fusion of the fundamental   Perceptual joining of the fundamental frequency to the rest of the harmonic frequencies into the universal percept of timbre

fission of the fundamental   Perceptual separation of the fundamental frequency from the rest of the harmonic frequencies so that it stands out as a separate pitch

and the fusion of the fundamental to the whisper, require a perceptual need for a definite frequency to complete the vocal part of the genre. There must be a perceptual sense that the fundamental frequency has a destination, once it separates from the rest of its harmonics. If the destination is lacking, the separation will not occur, and the illusion will fail.

In regard to the perceptual transfer of frequency from the instrument to the voice, two points remain to be made. First, if in the veridical percept, the *inanga* is figure and the voice ground, in the illusory percept, the parts have switched places. With the onset of illusion, the voice attains the definition it needs to take its place as primary focus, while the instrumental part has lost a large part of its definition, the foundation of its harmonic structure. In the veridical percept, the whispering voice consists of pure timbre, but in the illusory percept, the *inanga*, having lost its fundamental frequency, becomes acoustically (if not perceptually) pure timbre. Second, with the onset of illusion, *inanga chuchotée* becomes the auditory analog of a reversible figure-ground. In the Rubin's goblet reversal, the defining contour or outline of the figural profiles suddenly moves to delineate what was the ground, and becomes instead, the defining contour of the goblet. In the same way, the instrument's fundamental frequency, an essential ingredient of the *inanga* as figure, becomes the defining contour of the voice, which now becomes figure. In succumbing to the illusion of *inanga chuchotée*, the listener takes a portion of what was figure—the fundamental frequency of the *inanga*—and assigns it to a new figure, the voice, thus reversing auditory fields.

The organization of sound

If, like the figure-ground phenomena in the visual domain, the experience of *inanga chuchotée* consists of competition between percepts, then the acoustic reality of the *inanga*-whisper combination must contain elements interpretable in more than one way; and in the terms Riani et al. establish, reversal between percepts must occur when enough features exist at any one moment to simplify the ambiguity, to weight the competition in favor of one or the other of the percepts. The discussion that follows concerns the nature of those elements and the circumstances under which they occur.

What is it about the acoustic reality of *inanga chuchotée* that makes the audience susceptible to its violation? In any acoustic environment, what allows a distinction between reality and illusion? Answers to these questions come from disciplines that study the relationship between an acoustic stimulus and a listener, particularly the ability of the human listener to organize the multitude of acoustic signals reaching his or her ears in an ordinary, soundful environment.

Let us reconsider the scene in Colline Busimba. If a tape recorder were positioned somewhere in the midst of it, and if a segment of the resulting tape were submitted to spectroanalysis, the results would reveal that the sound waves from all the sound sources in the environment—the *inanga* and the musician's voice, the stirring of leaves, the sound of beer bottles settling on tables—combine to produce a single, complex wave form. This is because sound waves, like waves in water, are additive: they multiply in quality, rather than quantity.

The acoustic signal recorded by our tape recorder and analyzed as a conglomerate wave form reflects the motion of waves in the real world, and is the same as the signal entering the ears of any listener sitting in the same position. Unlike the spectrograph, the listener can resolve the signal, thus determining which sources have emitted sounds contributing to the conglomerate. This resolution will result in various source components, consisting of a multitude of frequencies at varying amplitudes.

The separation of a conglomerate or complex wave form into its components, and the recombination of these components into individual sound sensations, is a phenomenon described by Stephen McAdams as the formation of "auditory images" (1982), and by Bregman as "auditory scene analysis" (1984). Both phrases convey something of the interpretive quality of the organizational process as McAdams and Bregman conceive it. Part of this quality results from the fact that listeners must engage in a process that allows them to organize sound by grouping appropriate elements by source; and it is this grouping that, with reversible percepts like *inanga chuchotée*, determines which percept the perceiver will accept.

Because the possible combination of sounds that may simultaneously occur is virtually unlimited, our auditory processing system has developed what appear to be principles of organization to help in grouping. Research on auditory processing has uncovered an immense amount of information on organization of acoustic data; we will confine the discussion here to the principles directly related to the perceptual competition in *inanga chuchotée*. Unlike visual organization, auditory organization must occur in two directions at once. The grouping of frequencies occurs both simultaneously (as in the fusing of frequencies into timbre, or several timbres in the case of multiple tones at once), and sequentially (as in the case of a series of tones or noises occurring through time from the same source). One part of the auditory illusion in *inanga chuchotée* concerns the perceptual fission of the *inanga*'s fundamental frequency from the rest of its harmonics. To show the circumstances under which this process might fail to occur, we will concentrate, therefore, primarily on simultaneous grouping—particularly with the fusing of partials into the sensation of timbre.

Fission of the fundamental

Faced with a mass of undifferentiated sounds, the auditory system tries to determine, as much as possible, which sources have emitted which acoustic elements. It searches incoming elements for patterns or cues that might reveal their sources.

Onset synchronicity

One of the strongest cues is onset synchronicity. If a set of individual frequencies begin and end at the same time, the same source may have emitted them. Several studies (Rasch 1978; Bregman and Pinker 1978; Bregman 1981) show fusion of partials is most likely when partials exhibit asynchrony of no more than thirty to forty milliseconds. Kubovy and Jordan (1979) achieved onset asynchronicity by varying the phase relations of the harmonics. Asynchronous partials were "heard out" from the complex tone. Other studies have shown that offset asynchronicity has a segregating effect, though with less intensity (Handel 1989).

While McAdams (1987:288) seems to imply that the pulling out of a partial due to asynchronicity rarely occurs in natural instruments, Bregman claims that there may be an analog in the real world to his controlled-partial-segregation experiment.

Since the fundamental frequency of the instrumental tone is exceptionally weak, pitch determination, both perceptually and analytically, is often ambiguous.

Fusion may compete with sequential streaming in a natural environment, he says, or

> there may not be an ongoing stream at the frequency of the delayed partial to capture it, and it may remain in the stream of its own instrument. . . . Even if there is a capturing stream (perhaps a partial from some other instrument in a complex orchestral piece), the listener may simply group the asynchronous partial with the spectrum of the other instrument without noticing that it is gone from its own instrument. (1978b:26)

Whether or not natural instruments with individual partials so offset from their timbral complex as to be "heard out" exist, there is another issue. Vos and Rasch distinguish, in work on the onset of musical tones (1981), between perceptual and physical onset. Perceptual onset—"the moment in time at which the stimulus is first perceived"—generally occurs after the physical onset—"the moment at which the generation of the stimulus has started" (p. 299). The results of their experiments allow them to conclude that the threshold of perception of a tone's onset diminishes as the tone's intensity increases: the louder a tone, the earlier its perceptual onset.

Vos and Rasch are examining complex tones, whose perceptual envelopes, or the total energy of all partials minus masking effects, determine both the maximum and threshold levels of perception. The point that concerns us, however, is that tones of different amplitudes cross the perceptual threshold at different times, even if their physical onset is synchronous. While I am aware of no studies on the subject, we might hypothesize that the same discrepancies Vos and Rasch find between musical tones exist between the pure harmonics of a single complex tone.

Since the fundamental frequency of the instrumental tone is exceptionally weak, pitch determination, both perceptually and analytically, is often ambiguous. When the fundamental of a complex tone has only a portion of the intensity of the second harmonic, it may cross the perceptual threshold at a point later than that of other components of the tone. If this is true, the effect of the perceptual delay of its onset is the same as physical asynchronicity—leading to the likely fission-segregation of the fundamental from the rest of the tone.

Offset synchronicity
A final point remains in regard to *offset* asynchronicity, though this feature has been shown to have less potent segregating effects than onset asynchronicity. A primary feature of impulsive, including plucked, instruments is that partials begin to fade as soon as they are excited; the timbre of a plucked stringed instrument like the *inanga* is in a constant state of change, as partials die out after varying durations. What this means is that by definition, the offsets of the components of an impulsively excited tone are asynchronous. Thus, in the competition between fusion and fission of the

instrument's fundamental frequency, offset synchronicity—as evidence for a single source, and consequently for fusion—will be markedly weak, even nonexistent.

Harmonicity of components

The auditory system may discover a second pattern to link a set of concurrent acoustic elements to the same source if there are, among those elements, tones that are harmonically related—that is, which are all multiples of some common integer. The processing system assumes these tones are harmonics of the same fundamental, of frequency equal to the integer of which they are all multiples (Duifhuis and Slyte 1982; DeBoer 1976; Mathews and Pierce 1980).

What happens when the partials of a given fundamental are markedly inharmonic, that is, deviate widely from harmonic frequency variations, as with the *inanga*? Studies of truly nonharmonic complexes, as occur naturally in bells and gongs, show that pitch perception is ambiguous: listeners report two or more percepts (Mathews and Pierce 1980). In less drastically inharmonic complexes, McAdams (1984) and Cohen (1980) report "muddied" sensations of pitch. In other studies, researchers have tried to determine the percentage of deviation a harmonic can exhibit before it is completely segregated from the complex to which it belongs. Reports have varied from 7 percent (Bregman 1990), to 6 percent (Moore, Glassberg, and Peters 1985b), to 4 percent (Moore 1978). In most such studies, as harmonic deviation has approached the specified percentage, pitch perception of the complex has shifted up or down, according to the direction of deviation; beyond the specified percentage, it has stabilized, but the relevant harmonic has been segregated from the complex.

Figure 18 is a chart of the fundamental frequencies of the six most often used strings on a typical *inanga*, the ideal frequencies of their second harmonics, the deviations at 4 percent and 7 percent, and the actual values of the second harmonic of each string. The real values of this instrument's second harmonics are notably inharmonic: they approach the point—even if that point is 7 percent—where the partial risks being cast out of the complex. Thus, the fusion of partials appears to be loose, and the tone may at times forfeit harmonics to another grouping. Even the fundamental-tracking device that has been applied to tapes of the *inanga* (with and without voice) frequently indicates the second harmonic to be the fundamental, revealing the true weakness of this first partial. Furthermore, while transcribing the instrumental part of a song, one cannot always be sure in which octave a tone lies–especially with pitches at the bottom end of the tonal inventory. To a musically trained ear, accustomed to precise pitch designations, this is an uncomfortable feeling, and is an example of the phenomenon of moving from one perceptual position to another.

Proximity

In studies involving the "hearing out" of partials, Bregman (1978a) found several additional facts about harmonic segregation, or the fission of a partial from its timbral complex. First, he discovered the farther apart in frequency two partials are, the

FIGURE 18   The six most often used strings of the *inanga*: ideal frequencies of the second harmonic, deviations from the ideal at 4 percent and 7 percent, and actual values of the second harmonic.

Fundamental Frequency	Fn=2 (ideal)	4% deviation	7% deviation	Fn=2 (real)
78Hz	156Hz	+\– 6.24	+\–10.92	164Hz
88Hz	176Hz	+\– 7.04	+\–12.32	187Hz
103Hz	206Hz	+\– 8.24	+\–14.42	216Hz
118Hz	236Hz	+\– 9.44	+\–16.52	251Hz
134Hz	268Hz	+\– 10.72	+\–18.76	284Hz
154Hz	308Hz	+\– 12.32	+\–21.56	326Hz

During a performance of the *inanga chuchotée*, the *inanga* emits a series of tones moving stepwise, each a collection of harmonic frequencies bound vertically by principles of fusion.

less likely they are to fuse—and having fused, the more likely they are to split; thus, primarily in natural instruments, the lower partials are more likely to undergo fission.

For the *inanga*, the fundamental is most likely to segregate from the complex, not only because it is the lowest harmonic, but for another reason. The principle of proximity says a partial's nearest neighbors effect its fusion within a complex. The pitch sensation of a complex—what Terhardt has called tonalness, or the degree to which a complex can project an unambiguous sense of pitch—shows the intensity with which the fundamental fuses to the rest of the complex. Studies in the perception of pitch (Moore et al. 1985a; Stoll 1977; Terhardt 1978) disagree on which harmonics, other than the fundamental, contribute most toward the sense of pitch. Most researchers accept that the partials that most influentially determine pitch are among the first six harmonics.

On a string secured at both ends, the point where a performer plucks determines which harmonics are accented. The chart in figure 14 shows all harmonics that are multiples of three are attenuated: the musician is plucking the string near a third of its length. Whether or not the musician is aware of the implications of his playing technique, he has chosen exactly the point of stimulation along the length of the string to best facilitate the fission of the fundamental frequency of the string. If the pitch sense, and thus the degree of fundamental fusion, is determined by the first six harmonics, the more of these harmonics the musician is able to suppress, the looser the resulting fusion will be. To induce the attenuation of the greatest number of harmonics, the musician would have to excite the string as close to one-half its distance as possible, thus weakening all even harmonics; within the first six, this action would result in the attenuation of the second, fourth, and sixth partials. If the goal is to segregate the fundamental, however, the second harmonic, an octave above the fundamental, and *its* harmonics (the fourth, sixth, eighth, tenth, and so on) must be strong, in order to imitate a situation in which the second harmonic is the fundamental in the absence of the *true* fundamental. If the illusion is to succeed that the fundamental has segregated, leaving the second harmonic as "pitch carrier," then it is essential that as many of the even harmonics, especially the first two even harmonics, be strong. While the musician wants to weaken as many of the first six harmonics as possible, if he strikes the string at one-half its distance, he will also attenuate the second and fourth harmonics, which are necessary to the illusion. At a point a third of the length of the string, however, the musician is able to weaken the most harmonics with the first six—those determining the perceivable pitch—while also preserving the even harmonics.

Describing something of the same effect, Benade (1976) says that a flutist who has

a good instrument and well-developed embouchure can smoothly vary the strengths of the odd-numbered sinusoidal components of his sustained tone relative to the strengths of the even-numbered components. . . . He can produce the note A2 (just above piano middle C) whose fundamental component oscillates at 440/second, along with significant amounts of the first half dozen *exactly harmonic* components which lie at 880, 1320, and 1760/second (and so forth). The pitch of this tone is well defined. As the player alters his manner of blowing and progressively weakens the odd partials relative to the even ones, the pitch continues where it was, even when only the slightest traces of the odd-numbered 440 and 1320/second components are left in the tone. Beyond a certain point, however, the listener comes to realize that he is listening to a flute that is no longer playing A4, but rather the note A5 an octave higher, having therefore a fundamental at 880/second, with second and third harmonics located at 1760 and 2640/second. If the player is sufficiently skillful, the listener is unsure exactly when the transition takes place. (p. 71)

In regard to the *inanga*, in particular, a further application of the principle of proximity involves a competition between organizations. Studies have shown that various organizing heuristics may "compete" against each other in grouping acoustic elements. For example, the first two principles discussed above may find themselves in conflict if the processing system encounters a group of partials whose frequencies are in harmonic relation, but whose onsets are markedly asynchronous; such a collection of frequencies will offer evidence for both fusion and segregation.

A common competition of principles may occur among principles that encourage simultaneous grouping and principles governing sequential grouping (a stream of sounds emitted from a single source over time). This competition, occurring frequently in the natural world, is discussed at length by McAdams:

> With most of the sound sources encountered in everyday life, the simultaneous criteria at the lowest level of grouping assemble acoustic elements into source events and the sequential criteria connect events appropriately into meaningful source streams. In these cases, all grouping criteria mutually reinforce one another and what emerges may be considered as a stereotypical (or prototypical) grouping. . . . However, some work has shown that with certain stimulus configurations, even simultaneous and sequential grouping processes can conflict with one another creating situations with multiple perceptual interpretations. The resulting perceived qualities of the sources depend on the way the conflict is resolved. (1987:43)

The competition between horizontal and vertical organizing principles is one that operates as well in the experience of *inanga chuchotée*. In sequential grouping, the principle of proximity constitutes equally strong evidence of a single source as it does in simultaneous grouping. The closer together a time-bound series of elements are in frequency, the stronger the evidence that we should consider these elements a unified stream of tones emitted over time by a single source.

During a performance of the *inanga chuchotée*, the *inanga* emits a series of tones moving stepwise, each a collection of harmonic frequencies bound vertically by principles of fusion. Figure 19 shows this schematically: as the tones move, creating a melody, so do the harmonics. Once a fundamental has segregated from a single one of the instrumental tones, it becomes the first element in a potential horizontal stream of segregated fundamentals. With the segregation of each subsequent fundamental, the horizontal stream becomes stronger, until it is a competing configuration for the fundamentals of each of the following tones. In this sense, the process of fundamental fission from the instrumental tones is self-perpetuating. This quality is an example of what Bregman calls the *Old-Plus-New-Heuristic*.

FIGURE 19 Moving complex tones of an *inanga* melody with segregated first harmonics forming the stream.

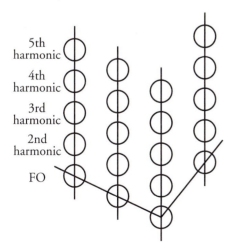

5th harmonic

4th harmonic

3rd harmonic

2nd harmonic

FO

The *inanga* seems almost a "whispering instrument";
it comes as close as an instrument with discrete partials can come to producing the shaped noise of a
whisper.

If you can plausibly interpret any part of a current group of acoustic components as
a continuation of a sound that just occurred, do so and remove it from the mixture.
Then take the difference between the current sound and the previous sound as the
new group to be analyzed. (1990:222)

Frequency modulation

One of the strongest cues to vertical fusion occurs when all the tones under examination show coordinated frequency modulation (Kubovy 1981; McAdams 1982, 1984;
McAdams and Bregman 1979; McNabb and Chowning, cited in McAdams 1982).
This cue is part of the principle of common fate: if all the elements in a collection
move in coordination, they are likely to belong to the same source.

Studies of the role of frequency modulation in the fusion of simultaneous pure
tones have examined modulations of all dimensions, and have reached several conclusions. For many collections of tones containing all elements (harmonicity, synchronicity) of naturally fused sounds except frequency modulation, fusion of partials
would not occur without the addition of at least a small amount of coordinated fluctuation. A possible reason for this result is that cues to fusion often reflect the nature
of sound in the real world, and most vocal sounds and many instrumental sounds in
that world undergo some degree of modulation. The voice, for example, even when
the speaker-singer intends to produce a straight, precise pitch, undergoes minute
fluctuations of frequency, due to the unsteadiness of the vocal folds. Modulation in
instruments originates in the same way: any periodic sound in which the driving
force can be perturbed or agitated will result in the same degree of perturbation in
the resulting frequencies.

A second conclusion of frequency modulation studies is that the larger the coordinated vibration of components, the better the resulting fusion: a slight, perhaps
unintentional, fluctuation will result in weaker fusion than a large and deliberate
vibrato. This result suggests another reason for the relative power of frequency modulation to invoke fusion. A spectrum shows the individual harmonics and their relative
amplitudes at a single moment; the peaks of a spectrum, its formants, show the frequency regions of greatest intensity, the harmonics of highest amplitude. The shape
of the spectrum, specifically the configuration of formants, is the spectral envelope.
For many instruments and for the voice, the spectral envelope characterizes timbre.
For the voice, and to a varying extent for instruments (depending on the range of
their pitches), the shape of the envelope remains constant, whatever the pitch; figures
20 and 21 show this schematically.

If harmonics are too widely spaced (as happens when the fundamental is
extremely high), the shape of the envelope may not be adequately delineated by the
available components. One of the results of any frequency modulation, but particularly of wide modulation like vibrato or portamento, is that as the harmonics move
up and down with the fundamental, the spectral envelope is more precisely traced

FIGURE 20   Schematic spectral envelope of a
low instrumental tone.

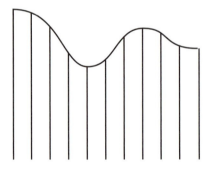

FIGURE 21   Schematic spectral envelope of a
high tone from the same instrument as in figure 20.

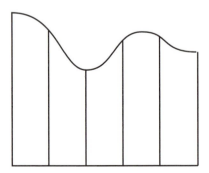

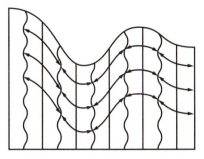

FIGURE 22   Frequency modulation "filling in" the spectral envelope.

out than it might be at a single, steady frequency. In figure 22, the harmonics (solid lines) determining the spectral envelope are shown with frequency modulations (wavy lines) that fill in more completely the envelope. If wider frequency fluctuations invoke fusion more easily, it may be because they cover a wider range, thus tracing out the spectral envelope more completely. To the extent the formant peaks are filled in, the characteristic envelope of a particular instrument or vocal enunciation is identifiable. As a cue to fusion, frequency modulation of any size may be more powerful than other cues, because it allows delineation of the spectral envelope into which the components are to be fused.

Important for this discussion is the fact that the *inanga*, unlike most other instruments, cannot support either deliberate or nondeliberate frequency modulation. As McAdams points out, nondeliberate frequency perturbations "are most likely to occur in physical forced-vibration systems" (1982:283). The *inanga* is neither forced nor driven, but rather, impulsively excited. Furthermore, unlike many Western plucked stringed instruments, it is neither stopped nor fretted. Once a player excites a string, it vibrates without interference until the next impulse. By contrast, one hand can pluck the string of a guitar, while the other vibrates it against the neck of the instrument, producing vibrato. Only a system in which the performer has sustained contact with either the driving source or the vibrating column itself will produce frequency modulation. Since contact with the *inanga* string involves only a single, narrow impulse, and since the player holds the longer edge of the instrument against the ground, there is little chance for unintentional or intentional modulation, either in the exciting of the string, or in the performer's contact with the resonating body.

The *inanga*, then, lacks what may be the strongest fusing cue available to a source of sounds. If it did not, if it could manage even a small modulation, several features that make it suitable for the auditory illusion its musicians provoke would disappear. First is the fact that any acoustic property leading to the tighter fusion of instrumental frequencies would lessen the likelihood of fission of the fundamental frequency.

Second, the instrument has an unusually high ratio of noisy to harmonic frequencies: the spectral peaks of formants are rounded, blunt, and not well discriminated from the almost-as-high intensity regions between peaks. This quality is essential to the reversibility of the auditory percepts. The whispered text basically consists of shaped noise bands, which replace the discrete harmonics of voiced singing. The spectrum of a whispered vowel also reveals blunt peaks with much noise in between. Thus, the instrument seems almost a "whispering instrument"; it comes as close as an instrument with discrete partials can come to producing the shaped noise of a whisper. From the standpoint of reversibility, the essential element distinguishing the *inanga* as figure from the voice as ground is primarily the fundamental frequency, since the *inanga*'s other frequencies are so poorly differentiated from the noise between them as to be almost textured or granulated, as we hear in the whisper. If the *inanga* could achieve the same degree of frequency modulation as other instruments, this effect would disappear, since in shifting frequencies up and down, the tracing of the spectral envelope would reinforce the distinction between harmonic and noisy frequencies. The textured quality of the timbre would diminish, with its ability to reverse into a ground percept from the loss of its fundamental.

Primitive and schema-based organization
That it is possible for the fundamental frequency of an *inanga* to segregate from the simultaneous frequencies it emits is not surprising; as mentioned above, even the computer is sometimes confused as to whether the lowest or the next lowest frequen-

Schema-based analysis of sound—top-down processing—is learned behavior.

cy of the tone is the indicator of pitch. To the perceiving ear, however, the fundamental of the instrument would be unlikely to segregate without the voice it accompanies. Why might this be? The answer lies in the distinction between levels of auditory processing, between bottom-up and top-down processing.

According to Bregman (1990), the auditory organization of sensory data uses both bottom-up and top-down processing. Primitive analysis—bottom-up processing—is instantaneous, probably innate; it consists of the sort of organizing heuristics discussed earlier in this section, principles based in part on the nature of the acoustic world. The role of primitive analysis

> is to employ heuristics that have been formed in the phylogenetic evolution of our sensory systems and to put together auditory features that have probably come from the same source. As clues to the correct grouping of features, it uses acoustic properties that tend to be valid in a wide variety of auditory environments. . . . They include such things as frequency proximity, spectral similarity, correlations of changes in acoustic properties. (1990:401)

Schema-based analysis of sound—top-down processing—is learned behavior. It consists of the identification of familiar acoustic patterns from which processing mechanisms construct a "hypothesis" about the stimulus. This hypothesis then guides the organization of relevant auditory details, which in turn confirm the hypothesis:

> The schema-driven (hypothesis-driven) process is presumed to involve the activation of stored knowledge of familiar patterns or schemas in the acoustic environment and of a search for confirming stimulation in the auditory input. (Bregman 1990:397)

Schema-based processing seems to operate over longer temporal intervals, to trace patterns over higher acoustic units such as words or melodies; it may require the playing out of several cycles of a pattern for recognition. In fact, says Bregman, by enlarging the temporal window of our pattern detection sample, "we are protected from damage to the quality of evidence at particular moments" (p. 404). Furthermore, once a schema is enacted in sound organization, it "enters a state in which it is primed to detect later elements" (p. 403).

The perceptual move from the veridical percept to the illusory percept in the experience of *inanga chuchotée* involves two complementary processes: the fission of the *inanga*'s fundamental frequency from its complex of harmonics, and its later fusion with the vocal frequencies that lack a fundamental. These processes clearly require both lower-level and higher-level systems of organization. I propose that the fission of the fundamental of the *inanga* is typical of primitive processes, and that the fusion of the fundamental with the voice involves processing on a schema-based level.

FIGURE 23   Old woman, young woman.

This distinction is consistent with Bregman's concept of the general interaction of primitive and schema-based organization: "It can be argued that the role of the primitive segregation processes is to *partition* the input, while the job of the schema-governed process is to *select* an array of data that meets certain criteria." (p. 408)

To understand the fusion of the instrument's fundamental to the vocal frequencies as schema based, let us return to the idea of reversible figures in the visual domain. In the discussion of visual ambiguity, I focused exclusively on reversible figure-ground drawings, since these were the closest in configuration to the illusion in *inanga chuchotée*. Reversible figure-grounds, however, are a special subclass of a broader class of configurations, reversible ambiguous figures (figure 23). The distinction between these classes is instructive in the mechanics of schema-governed perception.

The major difference between the reversal of old woman and young woman and the reversal of Rubin's goblet, for example, concerns the use of schema. Since both configurations involve a competition of percepts, the viewer faced with either a set of ambiguous figures or a reversible figure-ground must develop mutually exclusive schemas. For both ambiguous figures and reversible figure-grounds, the development of conflicting percepts requires three kinds of details. First, for each of the perceivable figures, there must be enough detail to provoke the formation of a schema. While researchers have done little work to show what sorts of features these might be, we know (at least according to Bregman and McAdams) that a schema consists partly of expectations derived from the context of the visual object. We might also guess that details necessary for schema development would include lines of broad contour, rather than smaller, discrete items.

The second kind of graphic details necessary for the formation of reversible percepts are those that will confirm the accuracy of each of the competing schemas. If the formation of a schema is best served by broad, contourlike features, the details most likely to confirm a schema may be the smaller, substantive items that fill in the schemic contours. Most visual illusions, whether simply ambiguous or reversible figure-grounds, are schematic (opposed to schemic) in form: they usually consist of only two contrasting colors; they are line drawings, lacking a sense of substance; and they often exclude details, leaving it to the viewer to imagine them. Thus, once the viewer has developed a schema, and begins searching for confirming features, the drawing must include enough details that not only confirm the schema, but also point to, or serve as index to, details that in the viewer's mind will fill it out. In figure 23, we see an example of the indexing function right below the young woman's eyelash, where a small section of the contour is missing; lines representing the nose would be located in this region, if they could also serve some function for the figure of the old woman. The artist of this configuration obviously decided such an item would be superfluous for the old-woman percept, and thus by omission indexed the nose of the young woman. We should not underestimate the importance of such features, since they are precisely the details that cannot be included because they apply to one figure, but not the other; and they are therefore precisely the details that distinguish ambiguous figures. In truly ambiguous figures, all the elements provided by the artist must fit somewhere into both schemas; only the imagined details can change.

What I have said so far applies to ambiguous figures and reversible figure-ground drawings alike. We shall see the difference between the two kinds of configurations if we consider a viewer at a stage of observation where he or she has already discovered both figures, has formulated schemas for both, and is comfortably able to switch perceptual positions at will. Such a viewer will require a short time to move from one percept to another, and will require the use of a schema to focus on each figure. For a set of ambiguous figures, the viewer will switch percepts by alternating

The imagination must not only supplement the
given details of each field, but also wipe clean the
details it has just created in one field.

schemas. We might almost picture these schemas as rotating perceptual grids, each
able to impress a different organization onto the same collection of features. With the
imposition of each schema, the viewer must organize confirming details, and invoke
the imaginary details to fill out the figure.

In reversible figure-ground configurations, however, the process differs. First, the
perceptual schemas the viewer uses to organize ambiguous figures always apply to the
same visual region (containing identical sets of features); but in reversible figure-
grounds, the viewer's alternation from one schema to another involves a literal shifting of the perceptual grid onto new territory, an entire redefinition of focal region.
Further, while schemas employed for ambiguous figures often have no direct relation
to each other, those defining reversible figure-grounds must be the obverse of each
other: where one schema dictates a contour with elements extending out into the
ground (in Rubin's goblet, the noses of the profiles), the obverse schema must dictate
a convex contour, allowing the ground to intrude into, or bend the shape of, the figure (as in the curvature of the goblet's stem, which obversely accommodates the
shape of the noses). A third and important difference between the perceptual operations required for ambiguous figures and figure-grounds involves the role of the
imagination. Whereas in ambiguous figures, the imagination functions to supplement the given details of the figure, in a figure-ground configuration, the imagination must follow the schema from field to field; the imagination must not only supplement the given details of each field, but also wipe clean the details it has just created in one field, as that field moves from figure to ground. As a region switches from
figure to ground, the viewer must not only find features in the newly figured field,
but simultaneously see the new ground as featureless or textured. The role of the
imagination as obliterator is clearer in figure-ground configurations (like the boot-
sunflower) that are more complex than Rubin's goblet.

The imagination is especially important, since, as auditory analog, *inanga chuchotée* differs from the figure-ground illusions I have been discussing: it is a real stimulus, not a configured artifact. In the reversible phenomena examined above, the
configurations are created so that either percept is accessible to the viewer: neither
percept is more legitimate or veridical than the other. In *inanga chuchotée*, however,
the stimulus occurs in the real world; the elements to be organized either as figure or
ground occur already organized, already grouped according to the sources that emit
them. Whereas an artifact consists of equally perceivable images, *inanga chuchotée*
consists of a veridical and an illusory image.

In the visual domain, an analogy to *inanga chuchotée* as real stimulus would be a
set of identical twins, facing each other in profile. With some imagination, we might
be able to use the symmetry of their features as the outline of a goblet. If we were to
position the twins in front of a black screen, and to cut from view all of their bodies
except what Rubin's goblet portrays (perhaps by surrounding their double profiles
with a rectangular frame, passing over the tops of their heads, descending along the

sides of their faces, with all outside the frame draped in black), the illusion of the goblet would be more easily accessible. If with chalk we were to whiten the twins' faces, the illusion would be even more accessible. To the extent we can make the real situation of the twins' profiles artifactual or schematic, its success as an illusion will increase. Because the perception of events in the world concerns organization of elements that already group according to source, the competition of percepts is naturally weighted toward the veridical percept. Even the real percept will have elements that pertain to the illusion (otherwise the illusion would be impossible); but unlike a true figure-ground artifact, the real phenomenon will have many features incongruous to the illusion. With the twins, any of their facial features beyond their actual profiles will weight the competition away from the percept of a goblet.

While artifactualization can help balance the competition between the veridical and illusory percept, more important, perhaps, is the role of the viewer's imagination. Even in true schematic figure-ground configurations, the imagination must function not only to fill in the contours of the viewer's schema for the figure, but also to obliterate the imagined features of the figure when that field becomes ground. In situations where the competition is between a veridical and an illusory percept, the imagination has even more importance, since it must operate to obliterate unimagined but real details. Thus, the viewer who is especially receptive to reversal may have no trouble seeing a goblet between the profiles of the twins, even without artifactualization. We might say, to the extent that a real situation is not artifactualized, that the viewer's imagination and attention or susceptibility to illusion become essential to the illusion's success. It is this quality that Torobeka, when he spoke of *inanga mu maraso*, probably envisioned. And it is the same quality McAdams describes:

> The necessary process can be more or less automatic or more or less subject to modification by the attention of the listener according to the degree of ambiguity or the level of structural complexity of the flow of events. (1987:92–93)

Susceptibility is a quality that

> requires a strong willingness to understand and requires relistening of the piece in order to appreciate it, but above all it almost forces the listeners to suspend their incredulity. (1987:93)

Fusion of the inanga's fundamental

I turn now to the schema-based process that results in the fusion of the fundamental of the *inanga* to the vocal component of the genre. The particular schema employed in the second part of the illusion functions to transform the voice into figure where before it had been ground—a phenomenon it accomplishes by organizing the fundamental frequency of the *inanga* as an element of the voice. The character of this schema is determined partly by the context of the genre, and partly by features inherent in the genre as specified by the generic rules. I will show how the performance of *inanga chuchotée* includes some artifactualization, requiring an active effort on the part of the audience toward susceptibility to the illusion.

Contextual confirmation

A thorough description of the aesthetic context into which *inanga chuchotée* fits would require discussion too lengthy for this paper. Researchers (perhaps too facilely) recognize that of all art forms in Burundi, the verbal arts are the "most developed." Among these are ritual forms, consisting of different kinds of formal speeches (with restricted substance and form), required at occasions ranging from *kuresha* (when a

The elements the illusory schema tries to find in *inanga chuchotée*, then, are contextual qualities of vocal music. Listeners are using what they know about their own musical environment to interpret the acoustic sample they are perceiving.

suitor's spokesman asks for his marriage to a chosen woman), to funerals and solicitation of one rich or powerful *murundi* by another, less fortunate, who begs a favor or goods (Ntahombaye 1983). Also traditional among the Barundi are diverse declamatory forms, consisting of praise poems or historical testaments, in metered poetry, with regular patterns of moras, and the deliberately downdrifted movement of pitches. Music, sometimes an *inanga*, occasionally accompanies these forms, though the Barundi consider declamation to be poetry, not singing; even by outsiders' standards, the difference between these forms and sung genres is clear. Finally, Burundi verbal art also includes a large body of vocal music. Excepting only the royal drummers, most Burundi genres include the human voice, no matter what the instrumental accompaniment; and there exist in addition many forms sung a cappella. Common to the sung genres is the mirroring of the tonality of the text in the melodic movement of the song to which the text is sung; depending on the genre, there may also be moraic regularity and melodic downdrifting.

Because of the character of this aesthetic context, even in an instrumentally accompanied genre, primary focus lies with the voice. Many of the qualities defining vocal music (even those whose expression the accompanying instrument shares) are equally present in the declamatory forms, and thus appear to be primarily vocal qualities, and only secondarily musical ones. For traits of a musical genre that are shared by the instrumental component of the genre, like tonal movement or melodic downdrifting, it is clear that it is the instrument that imitates the voice, not the voice that imitates the instrument; these are qualities that belong first to the voice.

If a perceptual schema generates expectations in the perceiver based on the context of the percept, what is the role of the context of *inanga chuchotée* as described above? As governed by the veridical schema, the genre must be perceived as a vocal anomaly, with elements out of place or starkly absent. Under the influence of the illusory schema, however, it becomes yet another instrumentally accompanied vocal genre, like most of the vocal genres that make up its musical context. Within this context, the voice is a familiar focus because of the importance of the text. Further, the voice carries the melody—which may or may not reflect the tonal movement of the text. Finally, the voice, as the vehicle for the text, is expected to follow the rules of language—in particular, the tonality of the language, without which the text is at best disorienting, at worst incomprehensible. The generic rules of melodic downdrift, melodic integrity, semantic coherence, and grammaticality are further attempts to fit *inanga chuchotée* into broader aesthetic and acoustic contexts.

The elements the illusory schema tries to find in *inanga chuchotée*, then, are contextual qualities of vocal music. In developing such a schema, listeners are using what they know about their own musical environment to interpret the acoustic sample they are perceiving. The objective of the illusory schema is to prove that this example emerging from the musical environment is not an anomaly, requiring a difficult revision of the schema's concept of the environment, but a legitimate member of the environment, contributing to its characterization. To this end, the schema searches for confirmation that *inanga chuchotée* is a typical example of accompanied song, with the voice as focus figure, singing a tonal text to a tonally inspired melody, as accompanied by the *inanga*.

Another source of confirmation of the illusory schema for *inanga chuchotée* is inspired by a more general acoustic context—in particular, the familiarity of most human speakers with the typical acoustic features of speech. The most important of these may be the spectral shape of the whispered vowels. The major difference in the production of voiced and whispered speech is that the resonant frequencies of the vocal tract operate on discrete harmonics (in voiced speech) and blocks of white noise (in a whisper). Because the resonant frequencies are the same, whether speech is voiced or whispered, the spectral envelope (the shape of the spectrum) will be the same—though for voiced speech the formants will consist of amplified harmonics, while for whispered speech, the formants will be amplified noise blocks. Confronted with spectra that resemble speech, the perceiver is likely to invoke a schema that will try to organize other acoustic features in terms of those required for the perception of speech. In regard to the spectral shape of speech sounds, McAdams has suggested that

> it would not be surprising, then, to find that the auditory nervous system can evaluate the shape of the spectral envelope of a source independently of its evaluation, at any given moment, of the presence of the frequency components whose amplitudes are shaped by that spectral envelope. (1982:285)

If this is true, then it is reasonable to conclude that the illusory schema for *inanga chuchotée* might ignore the absence of discrete frequencies in the spectrum, to use the spectral envelope of the whispered text as evidence of sung speech, just as it expects to find with all instrumentally accompanied genres of song within the Burundi musical context. This is especially true since the formants of the text, though whispered, are elongated with each connected to the sound following, just as voiced song would be. Having recognized the envelope of speech, the schema will then begin a search for confirming details within the envelope it has tentatively labeled "sung speech." It is logical that the confirming detail most sought after for evidence of sung speech is a discernible fundamental frequency to show the melodic movement of the voice; and as we have seen, the only fundamental frequency available is that of the *inanga*.

Another feature constituting evidence of the legitimacy of perceptually grouping the instrumental fundamental with the vocal frequencies lies in the acoustics of the whisper. All driven and many impulsive instruments inevitably undergo micromodulation. The voice in particular, because of the unsteadiness of the vocal cords, has strong characteristic modulation. The *inanga* is unusual, in that its strings produce little modulation. Since the absence of vocal-fold vibration, and thus of individual frequencies, defines a whisper, a major characteristic of speech—the micromodulation of frequencies—is also absent. In the illusory schema's search for justification for grouping the fundamental of the *inanga* with that of the voice, the fact that both the whispered noise blocks and the instrument's fundamental exhibit the unusual quality of steadiness of frequency might be taken as evidence that they both come from the same nonmodulating source.

Generic confirmation

In addition to contextual features that provoke and confirm the illusory schema, several confirming features are built into the genre by virtue of the generic rules discussed in the first section of this paper. The first of these results from the Rule of

The listener learns to be flexible in his or her search
for melodic or tonal melody: already the strict
division between figure and ground begins to blur,
in readiness for a more complete perceptual reversal.

Second-Formant and Consonant-Noise Substitution. This rule counteracts the Rule
of Melodic Downdrift, so if the instrumental melody is unable to show tonal movement, high-frequency consonant noise or upward movement of the second formant
can signify a rising tone. One of the results of this rule is that when it is in effect, the
listener learns to listen to the vocal component of the genre for the movement of frequencies, though this movement is symbolic and substitutive, rather than genuine. In
its search for a discrete fundamental to attach to whispered voice blocks, the perceptual schema may well take into account the listener's tendency to look to the voice for
melodic movement. At any rate, the listener learns to be flexible in his or her search
for melodic or tonal melody: already the strict division between figure and ground
begins to blur, in readiness for a more complete perceptual reversal.

The second rule-governed source of confirmation for the illusion schema is dictated by the Rule of Analogous Timbral Difference: for every vowel sound in the
voice, there must be a corresponding instrumental tone. If two vowel sounds fall on
the same pitch consecutively, the one-to-one correspondence of vowel to tone persists
only if the timbre of one of the identical pitches varies. By contrast, vocal distortion
can reduce the difference between the vowels, so the identical tones need not change.
In addition to perceptually linking the line and text of the *inanga*, this rule, sets up in
the minds of the listeners an equivalence between pitch and timbre by allowing either
to fill a single specific function. In effect, the rule says that if the pitch of an instrumental tone cannot distinguish between vowel sounds, the timbre can; in terms of
differentiation, pitch and timbre have equal weight. During a performance of two or
three hours, consisting of many long pieces, the equivalence of pitch and timbre may
become a perceptual habit for the listener. Such a habit will allow him or her to learn
a displacement of function: timbre for pitch, pitch for timbre, and either for vowel
quality. Thus, with rules such as these, the listener begins already to consider the
chance of multiple interpretations of a single acoustic element. Even in the veridical
percept, the listener must juggle interpretations, until he or she is ready for a reversal
of percepts.

The third feature confirming the illusory schema is the result of two complementary rules: the Rule of Melodic A and B Themes, and the Rule of Predominant
Phonemes. One objective of these rules is again to link the text and the melody by
including parallel changes in both components. As mentioned above, however, that
melody is exceedingly repetitive. In most pieces, the melodic A theme occurs with
much greater frequency than the B theme; the B theme occurs once, or at most
twice, before the A theme begins again. While the B theme serves to break the
monotony of the repeating melody, its occurrence primarily predicts the imminent
restatement of the A theme. The phonemic repetition, however, is irregular; to an
audience sensitive to alliteration and vowel harmony inherent in its very language,
the tendency to track the repeating phonemes must be irresistible; and given the other textual restraints of the Rule of Moraic Rhythm, the Rule of Semantic Coherence,

and the Rule of Grammaticality, the ability simultaneously to stick to one phoneme shows a poetic virtuosity that is equally difficult to ignore. Therefore, the Rule of Predominant Phonemes almost forces the listener's attention to the text. The more intense the listener's attention to the vocal component of the genre, the more this component gains the status of figure as predicted by the illusory schema, and the more the listener must search for the remaining elements that will give the voice the definition it needs to effect a reversal to figure. Primary among these is a distinct fundamental frequency.

Each of these factors strengthens the perceptual hypothesis embodied by the illusory schema. And each acts contrary to reality, to discredit the schema based on the veridical percept. The illusory schema posits the vocal component of the genre as primary, as figure, as filling all the functions required by instrumentally accompanied vocal genres. Because several of these functions require the movement of pitches, the schema-governed organizing mechanism looks for a sequence of frequencies that rise and fall, not only in a coherent melody, but also in the tones of the text. Meanwhile, the acoustic reality of the *inanga* is such that among the frequencies it produces is at least one, the fundamental, that is easily segregated. The primitive mechanisms of organization will, in its grouping, include the fundamental for lack of any alternative; but if a perceptual schema arises with a convincingly alternate organization (which provides another destination for the fundamental), more primitive inclinations will yield.

To describe an auditory figure-ground reversal in terms of which field will include the fundamental frequency is to make the situation too simple, as though *inanga chuchotée* were a true artifact. In fact, a live performance of the genre is more comparable to using human profiles to effect Rubin's goblet. In the same way that a true visual figure-ground drawing is artifactual, with the optic components it offers the viewer belonging naturally to no single source, a true auditory figure-ground might be comparable to synthesized music, where sources are imitated, where acoustic elements are produced in the absence of various sources, or from only one source, the computer.

To artifactualize a real-world situation, we would ideally disguise the roles of separate sources in producing the elements we must organize. And to a limited extent, players of the *inanga* would make the effort to disguise the sources by insisting performance take place at night, when visibility and extraneous sounds are minimal; for the same reason, musicians typically position their faces close to the face of the instrument, so that cues about localization will interfere with the illusion as little as possible. These practices are comparable to eliminating all features of identical twins except their profiles, so that elements weighting the competition toward the veridical percept and away from the goblet percept will be less intrusive. While it is doubtful that the first composer of *inanga chuchotée* ever sat down to develop a deliberate strategy of deception, we can hypothesize what that strategy might have been: given that real-world instruments are incapable of producing sourceless acoustic elements, the next-best plan would be to confuse the expected sources as much as possible. Thus, we have a voice without pitch singing, with the melody displaced onto an instrument; the text is sung in a tonal language, with the tonality displaced onto an instrument; a major change in the instrumental accompaniment is more markedly indicated by the phonemic change in the sung text; whenever frequency changes are indicated in the vocal component, these are expressed by elements, such as rising second formants and consonant noise, normally considered part of timbre, not pitch. Both natural instruments of the genre—the voice and the *inanga*—are ideally suited for such a strategy, since both are acoustically able to relinquish and attract elements to or from each other.

The listener must suspend disbelief, must be distanced from the real world—not simply by the stories the musician sings, but also by the inversion of acoustic reality the illusion creates.

Inanga mu maraso

Despite this strategy, however, for the illusion to succeed, listeners must be willing to surrender themselves, to put their concentration and imagination at the service of the illusion. As in artifactual figure-grounds, they must be able to imagine features that will augment the schema's interpretation, and to obliterate details of the figure when that field becomes ground. In a real-world figure-ground configuration, imagination must ignore or obliterate unbudgeably veridical features, thus detracting from the illusion.

For *inanga chuchotée*, the audience must be able to ignore such factors as localization cues, tempting listeners to recognize the distance between the sources of the voice and the *inanga*. They must be willing to disregard visual evidence, perhaps by averting their eyes, that the musician and his instrument are separate sources. If the illusory schema of a listener decides the vocal spectra are familiar as voiced speech (where is the fundamental?), the listener must be willing to forgo the fact that the instrument, with its full complement of harmonics, also produces familiar spectra (and that is where the fundamental is). Similarly, a whisper is familiar. It produces a familiar spectral shape, even without a fundamental, and the listener must resist the tendency to include in the perceptual schema that bit of knowledge. The listener with *inanga mu maraso*, then, must suspend disbelief, must be distanced from the real world—not simply by the stories the musician sings, but also by the inversion of acoustic reality the illusion creates.

The cult of Nangayivuza

It is said that in the north of Burundi there exist a very few survivors of a cult that arose in the 1950s. It was led by a man called Bashahu, who claimed to have special powers of healing, including an elixir of immortality. By the time of his suicide (1955), his adherents, the Abananga (People of the *Inanga*), had named him *Nangayivuza*. In 1962, the cult was outlawed and 30 of its members hanged, on the grounds that the cult practiced rituals involving cannibalism, sex, and elixirs containing obscene and noxious ingredients. These few facts are recorded in the proceedings of the court, and if their truth is suspect, even more suspect are currently popular beliefs about the Abananga.

Like everything else about the cult and Nangayivuza, the significance of his name is layered with mystery. Linguistically, the name *Nangayivuza*, a descriptive phrase, includes the noun *(i)nanga*, and the verb *-yivuza*. The Kirundi phrase that translates as 'play the *inanga*' is *kuvuza inanga*. *Kuvuza* is the causative form of the verb *kuvuga* 'speak', and *kuvuza inanga* can be glossed 'make the *inanga* speak'. In addition to the causative suffix, however, the verb portion of the name also includes a reflexive infix, *-yi*; the term *kuyivuza*, then, can be glossed 'make oneself speak'. Thus, literally, *Nangayivuza* translates as 'the *inanga* that makes itself speak'—or, less literally, 'the *inanga* that plays by itself'. This combination of reflexive and causative is itself mysterious.

Causative and reflexive forms

In most languages, the causative function involves an agent (the causer), a patient (the caused), and an action resulting from their interaction. Neither the agent nor the patient need be human, but the agent, even if inanimate, must be able to start some action, to transmit the energy to the patient; and the source of that energy must be understood or specified. Further, whether or not the agent is human, the patient cannot (without qualification) be made to perform an action of which it is incapable. Under ordinary circumstances, an agent's operation does not endow the patient with abilities it does not have: the agent contributes only motivation, energy, or reason. A test of the logicality of a causative statement lies in the phenomenon of predicate-raising, in which the patient becomes the subject of the action with the agent understood. "Bob made the vase fall" becomes "The vase fell"; this is satisfactory because, to know a vase can be made to fall, we do not need to know the agent's identity. But "The vase ran away" is not satisfactory, because unless specified, an ordinary agent cannot endow an ordinary patient with powers it does not have.

In a taxonomy of causative types, Talmy (1976:43–116), makes another point about the causative form. He distinguishes between degrees of causation as a function of the degree of "dynamic opposition" for the agent to overcome. Thus, in comparing sentences like "The satellite circled around the earth" and "The ball rolled along the green" with the sentence "The ball rolled along the green from the wind blowing on it," he comments,

> In the former [two sentences], the event seems one that unresistingly goes on of its own nature, whereas, in the latter, the same event seems one whose tendency would be not to take place but whose occurrence is forced from outside itself. (p. 61)

We can consider the subjects of the first two sentences to be raised predicates; however, both might easily find expression as real predicates in the causative form, without, in principle, changing the degree of causation necessary for the action described.

In view of these observations, the combination of the causative and the reflexive forms would seem logical only in certain circumstances: those in which the same person is both the agent who initiates action and the patient who, to act, needs the agency. Such a situation seems to require human actors for whom the "dynamic opposition" against acting is surmountable by the patient himself or herself (as in "John was nervous, but he made himself speak").

Kuvuza inanga

The phrase "*kuvuza inanga*" usually involves a human agent and an inanimate patient, *Torobeka avuza inanga*. A raised predicate often describes the action of playing: *inanga ivuga neza* 'the *inanga* speaks well'. The first point to notice about this usage is that the patient, either as subject or object, is made to perform an action of which it ought not to be capable—ordinary objects made of wood and cowgut do not speak. The second point is difficult to prove, since it is a matter of usage: the action "*kuvuza inanga*" appears to be 'one that unresistingly goes on of its own nature'—it requires, at least conceptually, a less intense degree of agency.

Kuyivuza

The combination of the reflexive and causative infixes is not improbable; in English, we saw an example of the verb in action. But it seems to require a human agent-

"Be careful, that you not invest too much energy or time in the *inanga*, lest it continue to speak and not let you die." It is the *inanga* that threatens, the *inanga* that may absorb energy, even against the musician's wishes.

patient, first because *kuvuza* implies human abilities, and second because the patient himself or herself must overcome the "dynamic opposition" to speaking. Thus, in *Nangayivuza*, not only is an inhuman object being made to perform a human action, but the object is being made to perform the action by the object. Assuming the "dynamic opposition" against which the *inanga* must struggle is the inertia of its own strings, plus its lack of (human) voice, the instrument described in the cult leader's name has received special qualities.

The musician and his instrument

The action *kuvuza inanga*, even without the reflexive infix, implies a relatively low degree of causation. What does that say about the relationship between the musician and his instrument? If the agency of the musician can inspire the *inanga* to perform an action of which it is not ordinarily capable, there must be something extraordinary about the musician, the instrument, or the combination of the two. Because of the frequency with which grammar expresses the action with the *inanga* as a raised predicate, if the instrument occupies a conceptual space where its need for an agent is minimal, we can justifiably consider the role of the musician to be peripheral to that of the instrument. In my year of talking to musicians, I began to see the interaction between the performer and his instrument as though the musician were an attendant or catalyst, as though the *inanga* were speaking through its player. The songs the musicians sing are compositions, rarely improvisations; and performers often claim the songs are so old, no one knows their origin. It would be foolish to imply that, for the Murundi musician, the instrument (which he himself may have made from materials he recognizes as ordinary) is an object of supernatural powers; but somewhere in the conceptual field of the genre, there may be the sense the performer is a tool of the instrument.

Nangayivuza

In addition to his reputation as a healer, Nangayivuza was famous as a virtuoso player of the *inanga*, which he used in his conferences with supplicants and in some of his rituals of healing. It is said that these rituals included his playing a melody while "speaking for" (*avugira*) his instrument, which said *uza gukira, uza gukira, uza gukira; imana ishimwe* 'be cured, be cured, be cured; god wills it'. Some sources say that toward the end of his ministry, he became sick with sores. Unable to cure himself, he hid behind a curtain during consultations, which continued to include advice given to the accompaniment of the *inanga*. The same sources say his followers gave him the name "Nangayivuza" as an honorific, a denial of the belief he was hiding his ailments. Another source claims it was Nangayivuza who said his instrument spoke without his intervention.

A third theory, advanced by Gervais Madagasha, an adult at the period of Nangayivuza's greatest popularity, is that the healer's instrument began to speak only at the moment of his death, because of a special custom concerning death. When an old person is about to die, the closest relatives must bring an object, something representative of the dying person's life, for him or her to hold. A carpenter may die holding his hammer; a seamstress, her needle; a shepherd, his staff. The person ready to die must wait patiently for this object, because it is a sign from the family that the person has permission to die: *bakamufasha kubandanya* 'they help him to continue'.

It is understood that when the old person has died, something of the lost life remains in the object, which they treat with reverence. So integral to his healing powers was Nangayivuza's *inanga* (at least in the minds of those in attendance at his death), that his followers brought him his instrument as the symbol of his life's work, and thus as a way to ease his passage into death. Unlike the instruments played by less gifted mortals, his instrument continued to play even after his death, as though the essence that passed from the musician to his instrument in the last moment of life was precisely the energy with which he had activated the instrument's voice.

Several additional insights into Madagasha's theory emerged in discussions in which I participated. While describing the need of bringing a special object to a dying person, the discussants described what seemed to them a typical deathbed situation, in which the person is uncomfortable, tired, and ready to die, but forbidden to do so until the arrival of the representative object. During an hour's discussion, they emphasized that without the object, *biramugora mu kirango abandanye ashika* 'it is difficult for him to continue on his way'—and what helps him or her on the way is the object. One musician described the teasing of neighbors who heard him playing for long periods of time:

> ati sha nyakuranduka wewe urasara. Ngw'imbere yo gupfa wewe kizokugora. . . . Nti kuki? . . . Ngo bazoguha iyo nanga uvuze uzocikana iyo nanga igume ivuga.

> and he says, my friend, don't be foolish. You are crazy. Before you die, it will be difficult. . . . I ask why? . . . Because they'll give you that *inanga*, you'll play it. You'll die and that *inanga* will keep speaking.

Context makes clear that these comments are meant as banter; yet there is something almost sinister in the neighbor's warning: "Be careful, that you not invest too much energy or time in the *inanga*, lest it continue to speak and not let you die." It is the *inanga* that threatens, the *inanga* that may absorb energy, even against the musician's wishes. If the symbolic object frees the dying person to go, by allowing him or her to deposit a legacy for the living, the instrument is dangerous, in actively taking what it needs from the musician.

The Barundi anthropomorphize the *inanga* more than any instrument but the royal drums. If there is the sense that the musician is an extension of, or catalyst to, the instrument, the name *Nangayivuza* and the beliefs surrounding its origin represent a greater degree of anthropomorphization—the incorporation into the object itself of the human agency required for the action *kuvuza inanga*. An even greater sense of the instrument's power occurs in musicians' comments cited above: in the conceptual vocabulary of the people, the *inanga* attracts, like a magnet, the human energy necessary to overcome the "dynamic opposition" of its own silence.

Artifactualization

If *Nangayivuza* constitutes the final anthropomorphization of the *inanga*, we can (in figure-ground terms) say the name is a kind of ultimate artifactualization. Since the ideally artifactualized figure-ground configuration is one that gives no evidence of sources, no natural grouping, the listener must overcome in the rearrangement of

The ultimate performance of *inanga chuchotée* involves an instrument that no longer needs its player.

acoustic elements, then *Nangayivuza* in absorbing the human agency of its musician, incorporating into itself both components of *inanga chuchotée*. It is like the synthesizer's generating an acoustic stimulus without regard for its source.

The man Nangayivuza occupies a place in the conceptual memories of the Barundi. In the mid-1990s, many people who lived during his highest popularity were still alive. Schoolchildren learn about him as part of the country's recent history; and for many young children, he is the local bogeyman, who eats naughty boys and girls. Among musicians, the name itself, besides its historic significance, represents the ideal *inanga*—an instrument so large and resonant that it practically speaks by itself. It is the unattainable instrument. In an abstract sense, the concept of *Nangayivuza* may express an eerie notion held by musicians and audiences: the ultimate performance of *inanga chuchotée* involves an instrument that no longer needs its player. As expressed by one of Nangayivuza's most renowned followers (Girwukwishaka 1969:67): "*Umwami yarikukiye, hasigaye ko Nanga yikukira nawe* 'The king is independent, it remains that Nanga be independent (depend on) himself'."

REFERENCES

Benade, Arthur B. 1976. *Fundamentals of Music Acoustics*. New York: Oxford University Press.

Bloothooft, Gerrit, and Reinier Plomp. 1988. "The Timbre of Sung Vowels." *Journal of the Acoustical Society of America* 84(3):847–860.

Bregman, Albert S. 1978a. "Auditory Streaming: Competition among Alternative Organizations." *Perception and Performance Psychophysics* 23:391–398.

———. 1978b. "The Formation of Auditory Streams." In *Attention and Performance* VII, ed. Jean Requin, 63–75. Hillsdale, N.J.: Erlbaum.

———. 1981. "Asking the 'What for' Question in Auditory Perception." In *Perceptual Organization*, ed. Michael Kubovy and James R. Pomerantz, 99–118. Hillsdale, N.J.: Lawrence Erlbaum.

———. 1984. "Auditory Scene Analysis." *Proceedings of the Seventh International Conference on Pattern Recognition*, vol. 1 (Silver Spring, Md.: IEEE Computer Society Press), 168–175.

———. 1990. *Auditory Scene Analysis*. Cambridge, Mass.: MIT Press.

Bregman, Albert S., and Steven Pinker. 1978. "Auditory Streaming and the Building of Timbre." *Canadian Journal of Psychology* 32:19–31.

Cohen, Elizabeth A. 1980. "Pitch Processing of Non-Harmonic Tones." *Journal of the Acoustical Society of America* 68, supplement l, p. S110.

DeBoer, E. 1976. "On the 'Residue' and Auditory Pitch Perception." In *Handbook of Sensory Physiology*, ed. Wolf D. Keidel and William D. Neff (Berlin, Heidelberg, New York: Springer-Verlag), 5(3):479–583.

Duifhuis, H., L. Willems, and R. Sluyte. 1982. "Measurement of Pitch in Speech." *Journal of the Acoustical Society of America* 71(6):1568–80.

Girwukwishaka, Ephrem. 1969. "Le néopaganisme au Burundi, Nangayivuza." *Que Vous Ensemble*, 1–20.

Gregory, Richard Langton. 1974. *Concepts and Mechanisms of Perception*. London: Duckworth.

Handel, Steven. 1989. *Listening*. Cambridge, Mass.: MIT Press.

Helson, Harry. 1925. "The Psychology of Gestalt." *Psychology Review* 36:25–62.

Hofstadter, Douglas R. 1979. *Gödel, Escher, Bach: An Eternal Golden Braid*. New York: Vintage Books.

Kubovy, Michael. 1981. "Concurrent-Pitch Segregation and the Theory of Indispensable Attributes." In *Perceptual Organization*, ed.

Michael Kubovy and James R. Pomerantz, 55–98. (Hillsdale, N.J.: Lawrence Erlbaum.

———. 1987. "Concurrent-Pitch Segregation." In *Auditory Processing of Complex Sounds,* ed. William A. Yost and Charles S. Watson, 299–314. Hillsdale, N. J.: Lawrence Erlbaum.

Kubovy, Michael, and R. Jordan. 1979. "Tone-Segregation by Phase." *Journal of the Acoustical Society of America* 66:100–106.

Lakoff, George. 1977. "Linguistic Gestalts." In *Papers from the Thirteenth Regional Meeting, Chicago Linguistic Society* (Chicago: Chicago Linguistic Society), 236– 287.

Lakeoff, George, and Mark Johnson. 1980. *Metaphors We Live By*. Chicago: University of Chicago Press.

Mathews, Max V., and John R. Pierce. 1980. "Harmony and Non-Harmonic Partials." *Journal of the Acoustical Society of America* 68:1252–57.

McAdams, Stephen. 1982. "Spectral Fusion and the Creation of Auditory Images." In *Music, Mind, and Brain*, ed. Manfred Clynes, 279–298. New York: Plenum.

———. 1984. "The Auditory Image: A Metaphor for Musical and Psychological Research on Auditory Organization." In *Cognitive Processes in the Perception of Art*, ed. W. Ray Crozier and

Anthony J. Chapman, 183–187. New York: Elsevier Science Publishing.

———. 1987. "Music: A Science of the Mind?" *Contemporary Music Review* 2:1–61.

———. 1989. "Segregation of Concurrent Sounds. I: Effects of Frequency Modulation Coherence." *Journal of the Acoustical Society of America* 86:2148–59.

McAdams, Stephen, and Albert Bregman. 1979. "Hearing Musical Streams." *Computer Music Journal* 3(4):26–43.

McNabb, Michael, and John Chowning. 1982. Demonstration performed at the Center for Computer Research in Music and Acoustics, as described in McAdams, Stephen, "Spectral Fusion and the Creation of Auditory Images." In *Music, Mind, and Brain*, ed. Manfred Clynes, 283. New York: Plenum.

Moore, Brian C. 1978. *An Introduction to the Psychology of Hearing*, 2nd ed. London: Academic Press.

Moore, Brian C., Brian R. Glassberg, and Robert W. Peters. 1985a. "Relative Dominance of Individual Partials in Determining the Pitch of Complex Tones." *Journal of the Acoustical Society of America* 77:1853–1860.

———. 1985b. "Thresholds for the Detection of Inharmonicity in Complex Tones." *Journal of the Acoustical Society of America* 77:1861–67.

———. 1986. "Thresholds for Hearing Mistuned Partials as Separate Tones in Harmonic Complexes." *Journal of the Acoustical Society of America* 80:479–483.

———. 1987. "The Perception of Inharmonic Complex Tones." In *Auditory Processing of Complex Sounds*, ed. William A. Yost and Charles S. Watson, 180–189. Hillsdale, N. J.: Lawrence Erlbaum.

Neisser, Ulric. 1976. *Cognitive Psychology*. New York: Appleton-Century-Crofts.

Ntahombaye, Philippe. 1983. *Des noms et des hommes: aspects psychologiques ascica et sociologiques du nom individuel au Burundi*. Paris: Éditions Karthala.

Peterson, Philip L. 1985. *Six Grammatical Hypotheses on Actions, Causes and 'Causes'*. Bloomington: Indiana University Linguistics Club.

Rasch, R. A. 1978. "The Perception of Simultaneous Notes Such as in Polyphonic Music." *Acustica* 40:1–72.

Riani, Massimo, Maria Teresa Tuccio, Antonio Borsellino, Jirina Radilová, and Tomas Radil. 1986. "Perceptual Ambiguity and Stability of Reversible Figures." *Perceptual and Motor Skills* 63:191–205.

Rodegem, F. M. 1970. *Dictionnaire Rundi-Français*. Tervuren: Annales du Musée Royale de l'Afrique Centrale.

Rubin, Edgar. 1915. "Figure and Ground." In *Readings in Perception*, ed. David C. Beardsley and Michael Wertheimer, 194–203. Princeton: Van Nostrand.

Stoll, Gerhard. 1977. "Spectral-Pitch Pattern." In *Music, Mind, and Brain*, ed. Manfred Clynes, 271–278. New York: Plenum.

Talmy, Leonard. 1976. "Semantic Causative Types." In *The Grammar of Causative Constructions*, ed. Masayoshi Shibatani, 43–116. New York: Academic Press.

Terhardt, Ernst. 1978. "Psychoacoustic Evaluation of Musical Sounds." *Perception and Psychophysics* 23(6):483–492.

———. 1979. "Calculating Virtual Pitch." *Hearing Research* 1:155–182.

———. 1987. "Gestalt Principles and Music Perception." In *Auditory Processing of Complex Sounds*, ed. William A. Yost and Charles S. Watson, 157–166. Hillsdale, N. J.: Lawrence Erlbaum.

Terhardt, Ernst, Gerhard Stoll, and Manfred Seewann. "Algorithm for Extraction of Pitch and Pitch Salience from Complex Tonal Signals." *Journal of the Acoustical Society of America* 71:679–688.

Thomas, I. B. 1969. "Perceived Pitch of Whispered Vowels." *Journal of the Acoustical Society of America* 46:468–470.

Treisman, Anne M., and Garry Gelade. 1980. "A Feature-Integration Theory of Attention." *Cognitive Psychology* 12:97–136.

Tsal, Yehoshua, and Lori Kolbet. 1985. "Disambiguating Ambiguous Figures by Selective Attention." *Quarterly Journal of Experimental Psychology* 37A:25–37.

Vos, Joos, and Rudolf Rasch. 1981. "The Perceptual Onset of Musical Tones." *Perception and Psychophysics* 29:323–335.

Wertheimer, Max. 1923. "Laws of Organization in Perceptual Forms." In *A Source Book of Gestalt Psychology*, ed. Willis David Ellis, 71–88. London: Routledge and Kegan Paul.

Yost, William A., and Charles S. Watson, eds. 1987. *Auditory Processing of Complex Sounds*. Hillsdale, N.J.: Lawrence Erlbaum.

Zee, Eric. 1980. "Tone and Vowel Quality." *Journal of Phonetics* 8:247–258.

Compositional Practices in African Music
Atta Annan Mensah

Local Composers
Continental Background
Types of Composers
Techniques of Musical Construction
Prospects

Academic knowledge of compositional practices in African music covers a large area thinly. A few vignettes and analytical summaries, identifying some of the ways in which local composers have crafted their works, will illuminate the scene.

LOCAL COMPOSERS

For Runyankore-Rukiga-Rwanda-speakers, living astride the southwestern boundary of Uganda, Benedikto K. Mubangizi (1968:42) composed "*Omwegyesa Ari Hanu*," a hymn (figure 1). After two lines comes a responsive phrase (*ekyakiiro*) at the end of each line of the stanza, and again a double-line refrain (*ekigarukwamu*). These make up one stanza, in the textual meter 10.10.10.10.9.9. (The numbers refer to textual syllables; the text of D starts with a pickup, effectively making D a ten-syllable poetical line.) The stanza has a melody of twenty-four measures; without phrasal repeats, the music runs for half that length. Mubangizi's arrangement, set out in the foreword to the hymnbook, puts each stanza into the form A–B–A′–B′–C–D. Group 1, the leading group, gives out phrases A and A′; the rest of the congregation sings B and its repeat, B′, as group 2 divides into sections 2_a and 2_b; the leading group sings C and D. At D, section 2_a repeats B while section 2_b and the leading group repeat C.

At the last four measures of each stanza, three parts ensue. This offers within twenty-four bars a contrast of massed-voiced strengths, plus a contrast of choral unison and harmony, bringing freshness to each recurring musical phrase, and facilitating the extension from twelve measures to twenty-four. Reading downward, we get the following: A, sung by leading group in unison; B, sung by rest of congregation in unison; A′, sung by leading group in unison; B′, sung by rest of congregation in unison; C, sung by leading group in unison; and D, B′, C′, all voices in three-part harmony.

The main points do not end there. The hymn has six stanzas, each with a different setting. Choir and congregation sing a through-composed piece, interspersed with harmonized refrains. The focus is clearly on melody. The piece, like many traditional melodies in the area, has a tonal resource of six notes within the octave. The seventh tone, which in Roman Catholic hymns (introduced by missionaries) tends to rise half a step, does not occur. The primacy of the eighth note is identifiable with the

FIGURE 1
"*Omwegyesa Ari Hanu*," Roman Catholic hymn by Benedikto K. Mubangizi (1968:42).

music of this area, though the regular division into four-foot lines is an influence from Christian hymnody.

In the closing four measures of the refrain (figure 2), the part singing violates Western rules of harmony: parallel fifths occur, the dominant has no leading tone, and the seventh of the dominant resolves wrongly (up, rather than down). However, in broad outline, the interplay of the combined lines follows these rules. Such combi-

FIGURE 2   The last four measures of "*Omwegyesa Ari Hanu*," showing the harmony that results from the simultaneous singing of three phrases of the hymn.

Lazarus Ekwueme, well schooled in Western harmony and counterpoint, works toward the preservation of the integrity of African traditions of tune making and pitch-line combination.

nations of melodies occur in the traditional music of the Bayankore, the Bakiga, and the Banyarwanda. In this piece, the admixture of tradition and innovation is clear.

Many school-educated Africans believe harmony is indispensable for achieving merit in composition. Joseph Kyagambiddwa's *Ten African Religious Hymns* (1963), settings for unaccompanied choir, dispels that myth. In the style of authentic Kiganda sacred music, it gives us solid lines of melody, disposed in pentatonic unison. Sung one after another in close succession, these hymns have cathartic power, which receives enthusiastic acknowledgment in Uganda, Kyagambiddwa's home. German audiences, which heard these songs during the early 1960s, the period of the composer's sojourn abroad, received the work favorably.

Kyagambiddwa believes the aptest hymns for any people take the style of their own music. With other theorists and practitioners, he believes the melodic and textual rhythms of the Baganda are interdependent. Accordingly, his hymn tunes derive from the tonal distribution and rhythmic patterns suggested by the texts, which the tunes in turn stress and clarify. Characteristically, "*Omununzi Azze*" features a rapid rate of utterance, with abrupt temporal contrasts.

Polyphonic patterns

Lazarus Ekwueme (Nigeria), well schooled in Western harmony and counterpoint, works toward the preservation of the integrity of African traditions of tune making and pitch-line combination. In the Christmas song "O Mary, Dear Mother" (figure 3), Ekwueme follows an Igbo-style melodic practice, with altos singing in parallel thirds almost throughout, and a quiet response by all parts at intervals of one measure on the vocables *za-mi-li-za* (the equivalent of "fa-la-la" in madrigals). The response is given out in stacked thirds in five voices. Tenors and basses take over the melody on four occasions, also singing thirds or in unison. In the last measure, given entirely to the vocables, we find stacked thirds and fourths for seven voices. Throughout, the composer maintains a modality of its own kind, confirmed at the final cadence, where an illusive surprise (interrupted) cadence on a fermata dissolves in a grand reiteration of a seven-voice chord raised on an Ionianlike final.

In "*Hombe*" (figure 4), however, Ekwueme gives freer rein to four mixed voices accompanying a frolicsome alto solo. To allow the alto to be heard clearly all the time, he keeps to a few plain chords in progressions of transparent harmony. In the middle section (not shown), the music passes through the dominant key. Right at the end, Ekwueme informs any doubting ear that he is up to an African game. The alto solo's closing phrase is an arch-shaped melody, whose penultimate note descends from G to D, not the other way round, as it might be in Western style. The four concluding measures bring back the nostalgic figure of two Bs kept apart by an auxiliary A; a feminine, plagal cadence in the last measure provides an unexpected resting place for the soloist's final note, the fifth of the scale.

FIGURE 3   Ending of "O Mary, Dear Mother," a Christmas carol by Lazarus Ekwueme (of Nigeria).

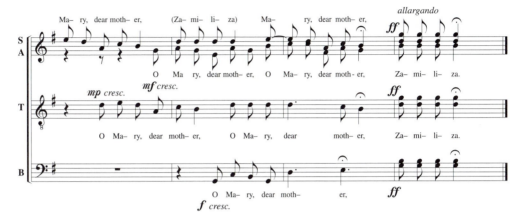

Incorporation of African elements

In Accra, the Pan-African Orchestra uses all-African instruments. About twenty-five virtuosos play in it. These performers are versatile: they use up to forty-five instruments in various combinations. At one performance in 1990, an observer counted ten notched flutes, twelve bamboo flutes (*atenteben*), two one-string violins (*gonje*), three xylophones (*gyile*), ten double bells (*nnawunta*), two enmeshed rattles, three hourglass drums, and one pair of Akan talking drums (*atumpan*).

With electrifying precision, this orchestra achieves unison passages; it produces a wide variety of concerted sounds, ranging from barely audible, eerie effects to an infernal din. For special effects, bell players change from hard, bare, wooden strikers to sheath-padded sticks. Bamboo flutes in leather drapery produce rounded tones. At phrase endings, they often melt into distant oily harmonics, heightening the effect of highly innovative cadences—atypical, but pleasantly surprising audiences of mixed backgrounds.

This orchestra most often plays music composed or arranged by its founder and director, Nana Danso Abiam. He gives his pieces evocative openings, followed by snatches of rhythmic motifs, which lengthen into full phrases, carried by melodic instruments. Frequent repetitions occur, with phrases and double phrases. Gapped melodies abound; within terminal sections of the music, diminuendos prevail.

To the delight of audiences, Abiam fully exploits the players' discipline: he sometimes assigns to three drummers or three xylophonists a part traditionally played by a soloist. The drum trio in the *kpanlogo* (a fast dance) is in perfect unison, breathless: it never fails to thrill. Abiam's forte lies in his creation of a new orchestral sound out of old traditional instruments. He works in an unconventional form of notation.

Yeo Kojo (alias Richard Graves), in a sudden musical break from the style of his father (Charles Graves Abayie), arranges six of his transcriptions of Fanti songs with piano accompaniments, which take turns with the songs in syncopations demanding extreme alertness on the part of the accompanists. Notes from audience research show that the harmonies of Western classical tradition, which the arranger uses, do not affect the integrity of these indigenous songs, which many local audiences know.

At the end, Ekwueme informs any doubting ear that he is up to an African game. The alto descends from G to D, not the other way round, as it might be in Western style.

FIGURE 4   Excerpt from "*Hombe*," a hymn by Lazarus Ekwueme (of Nigeria). The parts are alto solo, four-part chorus, and keyboard.

FIGURE 5 "Tribal Dancing Song" (*Six Negro Seculars*, no. 3) by Yeo Kojo, alias Richard Graves. The letters and marks above the soloist's line are Tonic Sol-fa notation, implying a key of E-flat major.

In "Tribal Dancing Song" published in 1951 (figure 5), Yeo Kojo begins with a major ninth chord, dismissing from the listener's mind any expectations of tonicism in Western terms. But prevailing tonal harmonies militate against this device, though the point is made again in measures 14–17 (not shown), where a D-flat major triad suggests a switch toward an A-flat tonal center; later, an E-natural confounds the mind thinking so, and the conflict resolves in an imitative rumbling, tossed between the accompanist's hands. By pushing at the edges of tonality, Yeo Kojo strives to maintain the modality of the original melody.

Western inspirations

For several decades, Samuel Coleridge-Taylor's *Song of Hiawatha*, a secular cantata for solo voices, chorus, and orchestra, enjoyed a long run of popularity in the United Kingdom. During the 1930s and 1940s, Achimota College and the Accra Choral Society between them staged many performances of *Hiawatha's Wedding Feast*, the first book of the *Hiawatha* trilogy. In Coleridge-Taylor's music and Longfellow's poem, three widely located peoples unite their love of good music. Coleridge-Taylor was a composer claimed by three nations: Great Britain, because of his mother and place of birth (Croydon); the United States, when referring to black composers of worth who visited and inspired; and Sierra Leone, his father's country.

Coleridge-Taylor's ethnic background also drew him toward the music of black peoples. In *Six Negro Melodies*, which he arranged for the piano, he expands short songs from ethnic groups of his choice into pieces of length and weight (Coleridge-

With music, it was in the Christian church that drift in the direction of Western inventive skills first manifested itself.

Taylor n.d.). In book 1, we find three pieces from Africa: two from the southeast, and one from South Africa. Book 2 contains one selection from South Africa.

The dance-song *Ringendge* is a thirteen-bar song of the Ba-Ronga. Coleridge-Taylor stretches this statement across 169 measures, now restating it astride breathless downward arpeggios, now breaking it into smaller units, passing them through chromatic harmony and unconventional transitions. He also staggers the rhythmic flow, setting up a meter of 2/4 (bars 49–53), but switching back to 6/8. On page 31, he gives the left hand eight counts to play, against the six of the right hand. In bars 77 and 89, a count of two leads to a count of three. The dynamics and variation of tempos are as active as the rhythmic gymnastics. Crescendos and diminuendos occur almost as often as *animatos*, *rallentandos*, and *a tempo*s. These underline the opening speed and dynamic marks: *allegro molto* and *molto leggiero*.

The extended works of Ato Turkson include two symphonies and a single-movement sonata, both employing the language of the twelve-tone system. The most readily available (in Ife Music Edition) is his *Three Pieces for Flute and Piano*, op. 14 (1975). This collection exhibits the essential features of the twelve-tone system. In contrasted tempos, each piece depicts the capabilities of wide contrasts of pitch and texture. Free use of chromatic scales brings the listener close to tonality, only to dissipate soon after the end of each scale, when atonality returns. By using quartal and quintal harmony, added seconds, and other devices of Schoenberg's compositional method, this piece proves the dispensability of the tonal center (figure 6).

CONTINENTAL BACKGROUND

A study of compositional practices over any continent can review only a selection of examples. In Africa, two factors limit the exercise to an uneven sample. The first of these is the lack of adequate communication—in the form of printing, recording, music journals, and radio and television programs—through which Africans may present to one another the entire musical output of the continent. The most established of these, the recording industry, decisively gives the bias to popular music, which lies outside the bounds of this coverage. The other hindrance lies in the lack of interest in the production of the original, worked-out, music compositions. This limitation stems from severe scarcity of facilities made available in the school system for introducing young persons to the excitement and challenge in this kind of music.

However, a little story of the way in which the art and craft of musical composition has developed in Africa over the century from the 1890s will show this to give a distorted picture. During the late 1800s and the first decades of the twentieth century, with the emergence of large numbers of school-educated men and women ready to serve the growing foreign business establishments and the colonial administration, there arose in some parts of Africa a new class of literate people, who had retained their love of the music they learned at school. Besides varied experiences with Christian religious music, it was in elementary school that the offerings of good read-

FIGURE 6   Beginning of the third of Ato Turkson's *Three Pieces for Flute and Piano*, op. 14 (1975), showing a twelve-tone system.

ing and good music from the Western world had reached them. Early experience led to later pursuit. Some of these people gained the skill to create original developments of models they had enjoyed reading and singing.

In anthologies of the successes in imaginative writing, D. Feuser and W. Feuser (1969), and Lomax and Abdul (1970), give good examples. With music, it was in the Christian church that drift in the direction of Western inventive skills first manifested itself. The churches raised choirs and bands, out of whose midst arose choirmasters and organists who wrote imaginatively.

These musicians discovered examination syndicates that offered instruction by correspondence. By the first decades of the 1900s, Victoria College of Music (founded in London, in 1890, by Dr. J. H. Lewis) was establishing centers in the Gold Coast (now Ghana). In its *Syllabus of Requirements* for 1933–1934, the London

The motivation for disciplining oneself in composition paralleled a fervent endeavor to retrieve the African identity, then submerging under the power of Western culture.

College of Music (instituted in 1887) lists Lagos, Nigeria, as one of its "Sundry Centers," among over five hundred centers across the world (including Australia, Burma, Canada, India, New Zealand, South Africa). The National Academy of Music (Liverpool) included on its list of the fourteen members of its Council and Board of Examiners of the early 1930s three Gold Coasters (all Ghanaians): Frank Aja Torto of Accra, J. deGraft Johnson of Cape Coast, and Jonathan S. Addo. Percy James Mensah, for nearly five decades a renowned Ghanaian music teacher, notes in his copy of the National Academy's *Regulations and Syllabus* that he joined the academy in 1923, having qualified by passing a diploma examination.

The writer of this article has personal knowledge of three of these pioneers of systematic music education in Africa. They were organists and teachers of music theory. The output of the products of these colleges consisted largely of hymns and other genres of sacred music for Christian worship. They were almost entirely in the style of Western music. Historically important examples are Percy Mensah's *Sixfold Amen*, and Charles E. Graves Abayie's *Threefold Amen* and *An Evening Calm*.

The motivation for disciplining oneself in the art and craft of composition paralleled a fervent endeavor to retrieve the African identity, then submerging under the power of Western culture. In music, this found its most ardent advocates in John Knox Bokwe of South Africa, Fela Sowande and T. K. E. Philips of Nigeria, and (later) Joseph Kyagambiddwa and Anthony Okelo of Uganda, and Ephraim Amu of Ghana. These sought, at least in some of their compositions, to reflect African traits. Facilities for doing so have been made possible by firsthand knowledge and skills that these advocates had picked up during their own lives, or by skills made available to them through the examples, documentation, and analyses of research material by others. Later, the work of music departments and academies, instituted in universities and colleges of higher education, provided these facilities, or extended them in various places. The following are among the outstanding ones, with their years of founding: Music Department, Achimota College (1949), later moved to Winneba, Ghana, to become National Academy of Music; Department of Music, University of Nigeria, Nsukka (1962); School of Music and Drama, University of Ghana (1962); Department of Music, University of Ife, Nigeria (1964); Department of Music, Dance, and Drama, Makerere University, Kampala (1971); Department of Music, Kenyatta University College, Nairobi (1973); Department of Music, University of Cape Coast, Ghana (1974); Department of Performing Arts, Ilorin, Nigeria (1981).

East and Central Africa

The central African states of Zambia, a large fraction of Zaïre, all of Zimbabwe, and Malawi, had access to compositional devices, right from grass-roots styles (as in *kuyabilo* of the Ila-Tonga) to urban pop and the music of schools and churches. But *phata-phata*, *tsaba-tsaba*, *manje-manje*, and *makwaya*, as urban popular dance-song types, which became popular in these regions during the 1940s and 1950s, were direct echoes from South African choral and pop music. Examples of this music were invariably original works by individuals whose identities were lost beyond their localities and times.

Sometimes, short melodies got lengthened through processing by extemporization. The harmonic overlay of improvised pieces grew thicker as they passed through successive hands. Sometimes, the original composer's identity did not fade through widespread usage, thanks to the *All-African Church Music Association Journal*, to which we owe a good deal of our knowledge of the process of musical development in this region. Robert A. Kauffman describes a method of composing songs for Christian worship: a small group elicits a new song from a model provided by traditional instrumentalists or another group; models so provided served as "a point of departure for something new" (1966:3). Though initially resemblances between the traditional and the new song were close, at an advanced stage of training, when the budding composers completed training to notate their own songs, they produced original compositions in traditional idioms they had known from childhood. Such gifted composers included Abraham Mairire and Patrick Matsikenyiri of Zimbabwe (then Rhodesia) and Cajetan Lunsonga of Zambia.

Pierre Kazadi (1973:271) draws attention to another method of composition from Zaïre. According to him, *Missa Luba*, a joint work by students of Father Guido Haazen at the Roman Catholic Mission in Kamina, blends the resources of Zaïrian music. In 1956, the Troubadours du Roi gave a stimulating performance of this Mass, drawing applause from many areas of sub-Saharan Africa. The work retains the liturgical Latin text but ingeniously fits it into traditional local melodic style. The Kyrie and the Credo are given out in the style of Luba mourning songs (*kasala*). The Sanctus and the Benedictus are identifiable with the style in which the Baluba (Luba people) present their traditional farewell songs. With rhythms taken from Kasai dance music, the drum and the rattle accompany the Hosanna. However, excepting the Agnus Dei, the choir provides, beneath the traditional melodies of this Mass, Western-style harmony, in a recurring I–IV–V–I pattern. The Agnus Dei keeps to traditional models of the vocal music of the Bena Luluwa, including cadential patterns. The singing in the entire work remains in Luba style.

Similar developments occur in East African countries: Kenya, Tanzania, Uganda. Above, I have illustrated Joseph Kyagambiddwa's contributions. His skill in manipulating Kiganda song style to high flights of emotion can also be heard in his *Uganda Martyrs Oratorio*. In their operas, Ugandan composers stress their commitment to development by extension of authentic Ugandan music and intensive exploitation of its instruments. The kingdoms (abolished in 1967 and restored some twenty years later) were highly musical institutions, which laid excellent foundations, hardly excelled anywhere on the continent. But in works for the theater, Ugandan dramatist-musicians proclaim their commitment to working out a national idiom, made up of the musical traditions of the major ethnic groups of the nation. The drama often provides cues for structuring extended forms that serialize the various musical styles under the most favorable conditions of receptivity: theater. Mbabi Katana's opera *The Marriage of Nyakato*, Robert Serumaga's musical *Renga Moi* (subtitled "A Muganda's Work Set in Acholiland"), and Cosma Warugaba's comic opera *The Hunt* (*Omuhiigo*), all feature large and small instrumental and vocal ensembles, which work out movements for stretches of various lengths of the dramas.

The musical play *Oluyimba Luwa Wankoko*, by Byron Kwadwa (playwright) and Wassanyi Serukenya (composer), first performed at the National Theater, Kampala, Uganda, on 6 November 1971, is a hilarious story. On behalf of a shy Ganda prince, Suuna, a palace worker named Wankoko goes on a mission to woo a beautiful Toro princess, Barungi. The plot plays out against continuous music, which, to make a

sefala   Musical poetry of the Sotho of
Lesotho in southern Africa

kwela   Popular music style of southern Africa

point, sometimes surges into the foreground. At one such moment, Wankoko returns to Suuna to sing back, in Kitoro style, Barungi's reply to Suuna's serenade song. He makes laughable false starts, ludicrous efforts to remember the Kitoro song style. The instrumental ensemble accompanying is a Ganda ensemble. However, Wassanyi Serukenya more freely incorporates Western ideas in his music to Byron Kwadwa's *Makula ga Kulabako,* first performed in June 1971; an actor even uses the microphone. But again, foreign elements fit congenially into unmistakably Kiganda music. The instrumental ensemble is all Kiganda: flute (*endere*), xylophone (*amadinda*), rattle (*ensasi*), drum (*engoma*), long drum (*engalabi*), lyre (*entongoli*).

East and Central Africa seem engaged in a reprocessing of heritage music in a search for twentieth-century patterns with wider subscription and stronger communicative power.

South Africa

Almost simultaneously with the active years of the All-African Church Music Association, South African musicians were composing music for weddings and other social occasions, largely by rote. In the Ndebele language, an example that reached Zambia through Zimbabwe is *Kudala Kwetu Sasi Valela.* Recreational activity in South Africa is replete with examples more embroidered and more heavy laden with tertian harmony, added sixths, passing notes, and incidental suspensions. An example is the little song "*Waya mulongolo.*"

David B. Coplan (1985) clears some of the mist covering the rest of that scene in Africa. In South Africa, as in some parts of West Africa, one may speak of clergymen-composers (Tiyo Soga, John Knox Bokwe), of schoolteacher-composers (Reuben T. Caluza)—composers in the modern sense of the word, after about 1875. There was also the traditional lyrics composing art of *sefala* (musical poetry) among the Sotho (compare Akan *kwadwom*, and Yoruba *oriki*). The tradition of composing is an old one, which late-nineteenth-century school-educated South Africans continued in new idiom. The most famous example, "*Nkosi Sikelel' iAfrika* 'God Bless Africa',"composed by Enoch Sontonga in 1897, is in the major mode and in four-part harmony. Soon after, as early as the days of the Zulu organist and pianist, Caluza, the influence of American ragtime appears in the music of South African composers of the first decade of the 1900s. Whether these influences also account for the rise of multipart singing among urban South Africans is moot: the artistry is uniquely South African.

A spate of songs with (sometimes heavy) instrumental support was largely generated through the activities of choirs in churches and schools, which also developed a tradition of staging musical plays. In time, theater became one of the main genres of new South African music. While music continued to thrive in streets, churches, and schools, South African popular theater became the mainspring of new music. This music turned back with conscious effort to recapture the polyphonic tradition of

South Africa's traditional singing. It was largely the music of the performer, after the composer had set the basic pattern. Around 1935, the composer spoke about a conscious practice: *Meloli le Litha Llere tsa Afrika* 'African Melody in Extemporary Harmonization' (Coplan 1985:119).

Playwrights Gibson Kente, Mthuli Sheze, Credo V. Mutwa, and other eminent men and women of South African theater, also seem to have preferred the macro approach to composition. Text generated, their music is shaped by the exigencies of the play, which, with dance, moves along, knits together, and fills up with fresh emotional currents.

Into the tide of musical creativity, in accordance with musical dialects, the AACMA catchment network roped in Zambians, Malawians, Zaïreans, East Africans, Zimbabweans, and South Africans. But other catalytic agents prepared composers for more elaborately worked-out pieces. Todd Matshikiza had a brief, but active and fruitful, career. He was a versatile, college-trained artist, an exquisite jazz pianist, a theater-conscious composer. In 1959, he teamed up with librettist Harry Bloom to produce a pace setter in jazz opera. When the cast went to London, however, the recordings they made there reflected drastic changes in the music, claimed to have been made for the sake of better orchestration to please Western ears. In the judgment of South Africans, these changes robbed Matshikiza's music of its power and meaning. Even so, much of Matshikiza remains. All the vernacular songs in this work remained in Xhosa—a feature that maintains African qualities in the music. The popular work song "*Tshotsholoza*" ("The Gumboot"), an original tune, which workers in the Reef (Witwatersrand Gold Mine) adopted from Natal Province, and the "Knife Dance," based on a Sotho war dance, retain, even in this new orchestration, the *kwela*-style vigor of South Africa, which Stanley Glasser, Sol Klaaste, and their associate orchestrators and arrangers did not destroy. Matshikiza, who also became an excellent journalist, did not live long enough to give the world an undiluted sample of South African musical excellence that his compatriot audiences recall in the original version of his *King Kong*, an opera. But the promise of his work and further evidence from his compatriots in music point to the formation of new fabrics in sound, which artistically blend the old and the new.

North Africa

Including North Africa, mainly an Arab region, in a survey of composition in Africa needs no justification. More than 60 percent of Arabs live in Africa, and many of those who address the arts in this region depict extra-Arab traits in their works identifiable with non-Arab Africans.

In North Africa, Islam became the dominant religious force. Its doctrine allows few opportunities for music, but to the ingenious, it leaves room for inventive musicianship. In 1932, by choosing Cairo to be the headquarters of Arab-culture studies, an all-Arab council provided for the continuance of a tradition of promoting studies in music theory and creativity.

In 1956, the Egyptian Ministry of National Guidance set up the Commission for the Survey and Improvement of Music. The commission said the music of Egypt largely consisted of Arab music bearing alien influences; composers and performers were neglecting purely Arab music. In response, the commission published a book (*The Stage, Music, the Cinema* 1956), in which it advocated the revival of Egyptian art music with folk music as its foundation.

The work of the succeeding generation of Egyptian composers reflects the heritage of Arab music, and suggests a systematic following of the trends set by the 1932 International Congress of Arab Music and the 1956 Commission, funded and hosted by Egypt.

microtones   Tones that compose intervals smaller than a minor second

santur   Hammered dulcimer or zither of North Africa and West Asia played with small mallets

oud   Plucked lute, with pear-shaped resonator, of North Africa

atonalism   Style of composition in which no single tonality is dominant; all of the pitches receive equal weight

Halim El-Dabh (b. 1921) incorporates African and Arab music idioms in his compositions, evolving a special notation to express some of the resultant concepts. These are identifiable in his use of rhythms and percussion. Gamel Abdel Rahim (b. 1924) makes use of Arab and Western ideas in his compositions. From Arab tradition, he features microtones, modal scales, and isorhythms (*iqamat*).

A six-minute piece, *Le jardin de les charmes* (*The Garden of Your Charms*), by Mohammed Abdel-Wahab (b. 1910), unites in a bold and engaging unison a chorus and an orchestra of Arab instruments. The melody features a combination of leaps and steps narrower than the semitone. In February 1990, at the ninth UNESCO-sponsored African Music Rostrum at Dakar (Senegal), the piece gained undisputed acceptance among an adjudicating panel of overwhelmingly black professional musicians. In another piece, "Cocktail," Wahab packs a stimulating variety of vocal quality: a chorus declaims, neatly featuring some part making and muezzin-style timbres; then, a female chorus sings a melismatic melody over a drone—all backed by a full orchestra, supported by tambourines. In *Le Fleuve immortal* (*The Immortal River*), Wahab uses a large Western string orchestra in a short dynamic movement, introduced by a slow opening.

Farid El Atrach (1915–1974) boldly calls his audience to a Western musical feast served in Arab melodic turns in unison and flavored with Near Eastern timbres. His *La melodie immortal* (*The Immortal Melody*) opens with trombones and trumpets. But the *santur* (a stringed instrument, played with small mallets) repeatedly makes biting sorties against the *ouds* (plucked lutes). *Les étoiles de la nuit* (*The Stars at Night*), also by Atrach, opens in contrapuntal style; a full orchestra features rapid flute melodies, bringing Tchaikovsky's orchestration to mind.

With masterly skill, these Egyptian composers domesticate Western orchestral technique; but with high artistic responsibility, they cling to their African musical heritage.

West Africa

A long list of references to music in West Africa can be drawn. These hardly address the craft of composition as understood here. Ato Turkson, of the University of Ghana, and Akin Euba (1988) do this. These authors, however, prove the fact of a growing population of composers with its headwaters dating from the late 1800s.

Pioneers in this field include F. C. Coker of Abeokuta, the Reverend J. B. Anaman of Ghana (a collector and composer of songs for the Fanti community in the Methodist Church of the Gold Coast), and—to include one who did not remain in West Africa, but never forgot his roots—Samuel Coleridge-Taylor, who studied violin and composition at the Royal College of Music, and became eminently renowned for his trilogy, *Song of Hiawatha*. After these come prominent composers: Charles Emmanuel Graves Abayie of Cape Coast, Gold Coast (Ghana), a church organist, educator, and music printer and publisher based in Cape Coast; Fela

Sowande of Nigeria, one-time organist at Holborn-Kingsway Methodist Church, London; Isaac Daniel Riverson of Cape Coast, Ghana, church organist and choir-master, educator, and composer; Ephraim Amu (1899–1995), of Ghana, educated at the Royal College of Music, and doyen of West African choral composers.

Next, in larger numbers, come other prominent composers, who explore deep into the newer world of atonalism: Akin Euba, a Nigerian composer of the finest order; Ayo Bankole, another prolific Nigerian composer, though short-lived; Joseph Hanson Kwabena Nketia of Ghana, internationally renowned as a scholar of African music, but also a prolific composer of good standing; Zinzendorf Nayo of Ghana, a symphonist who became one of the early directors of the Ghana National Symphony Orchestra; Gyimah Labi, another prolific composer of good substance.

These men and their contemporaries have committed their energies to the mastery of the grammar of Western art music, and have produced works of significant worth in its idioms. The early ones used the stylistic techniques of the "common practice" of composition. Some of these gained international recognition. Graves Abayie's *An Evening Calm,* a full-scale lament with Mendelssohnian flavoring, was published in 1913 by Pitman Hart and Company, London; during the early 1950s, African radio broadcasts featured Fela Sowande's *African Suite* for string orchestra (1947).

From the earliest days of compositional art in West Africa, some writers turned to the musical resources of their own peoples, out of an obligation to serve their interests and to advance their musical heritage. The little of Anaman's output known to those following him are songs in traditional Fanti idiom. Riverson, who in Western common-practice idiom composes hymns, choruses, and marches, also made collections of folk songs, especially, from the traditional Fanti lyric repertory, and arranged a few, keeping faith with their idiomatic integrity. He often set these to four-part harmony in modal style, lest he ruin their essence. In choral sections, this practice led to compromises with speech tones; in the lead cantor's lines, however, Riverson strictly matches the language-based tonal patterns with those of the tune.

Amu, chief advocate of the principle of matching the melody to the speech tone distribution, on the other hand, harmonized his songs all the way, according to the rules of the common practice. Even in deviant examples, the dominance of the tonal principle remains undisputed.

Fela Sowande's output includes plainchants for organ in Yoruba idiom. In these, modal harmony keeps the music out of the shackles of Westernism, in spite of the spacious organ sound. In his *African Suite,* he uses a West Coast highlife tune, showing solidarity with the best of urban music.

Nketia also incorporates elements that range in style from common practice (including chromaticism), through abrupt modulations, to atonal techniques. In this broad spectrum, he and Akin Euba share common ground, though the latter uniquely demonstrates new possibilities with the use of old traditional music instruments. Euba, again like Nketia, turns round now and again to reaffirm his faith in music as art, no matter on what instrument. Euba's return to the development of African pianism is in evidence here.

West Africa's march through the 1900s with music has not only been spontaneous as with the practice of old and new popular music; it has also been methodical and discipline oriented.

TYPES OF COMPOSERS

In the widest sense, any organization of musical elements into a music piece of any length is a composition, whether the original soundsmith is identifiable or not. The bulk of musical practice in most regions of the world does not stem exclusively from

By virtually ignoring African instrumentation, the mid- and late-twentieth-century African composer parts ways with indigenous traditions.

any particular originator. But in some African societies, as among the Ila-Tonga of Zambia, a composer may initially be an identifiable person, for he or she composes his or her own call sign, and makes some for others at request. His or her heirs may inherit the call sign; over time, the identity of authorship may cake into a legendary name.

Two celebrated examples are Kofi Tu of Northern Ghana, a man acclaimed as the founder of the music of the *gyilgo* 'lamellophone' among the Gonja of Ghana, and Vinɔkɔ Akpalu, founder of a school of musical creativity and performance among the Anlo of Southern Ghana and Togo. In both instances, as with Mwenda-Jean Bosco of Zaïre and Haruna-Ishola Bello of Nigeria (famed for *apala,* a major genre of popular music, which arose among the Yoruba in the 1940s and 1950s), individuals brought new life and originality to traditions inherited from the past, lived long enough to establish their contributions firmly among audiences, and left their stamp on the tradition and in the hearts of admirers who may not identify the specific contributions of their champions.

Now and again, debates arise over whether inventive musicians of this kind deserve recognition as composers. The debate continues, because it has not yet been proved whether imaginative musicians of this kind also, intuitively at least, juggle and reason with little units of musical ideas, address problems of structure and form, and use constructional devices, as the typical concert-oriented composer does. For the sake of discussion, I am not drawing a hard and fast distinction here, and am including as a composer anyone who creates a piece that has not existed before.

Going strictly all the way by this broad interpretation will make this article too long by having to survey countless instances of constructional techniques of old traditional African music and popular (or pop) musical types of Africa. A meaningful statement on musical invention in Africa must, of necessity, largely skirt this mountain. I have done this, while trying to cover significant styles of composition that may occur in a broader spectrum. I have examined works by a new breed of musicians, who have consciously set out to compose pieces that are identifiable with themselves as individuals.

These composers belong in three groups: (1) those who work strictly according to Western rules of composition, (2) those who seek to blend Western and African musical elements in original composition, and (3) those who seek to write new compositions for enjoyment as authentic African creations.

All three groups use crafts of composition derived from the West, many among them guided by the conviction that these crafts are logical achievements of universal benefit for all to use, no matter of what race. Without compromise, the first group uses in their works melodic styles, harmonies, and instrumental sonorities of non-African, mainly Western, origins. Composers of many of Africa's national anthems fall into this group (George Kakoma of Uganda, Enoch Sontonga of South Africa). The second group incorporates African musical elements, sometimes long melodic material and rhythm patterns; but they work within structures that are essentially Western. Some African patriotic national songs do this (Sowande, Amu). The third group also may consciously or unconsciously, use Western structural models; but they apply to their compositions heavier doses of African musical elements, especially rhythms, melodies, modal effects, and other elements derived from African music. These composers include Serukenya, Kyagambiddwa, Riverson at times, and Euba during his second period.

Among these groups, the tendency toward Western practice is evidence of a steady trend, unconsciously pulling together artistic thinking and expression reciprocated in the nineteenth and early twentieth century, through growing European appreciation of African and oriental arts. The accelerated flow of African sculpted pieces into the museums and folk art galleries of Europe, and the incorporation of African, Middle Eastern, and Southeast Asian musical elements into works by European composers, point toward a mutual attraction between Western and other cultures. A glance at the rise of symphony orchestras and Western-style opera houses in some nations of the Far East also reveals this compliment for the same Western achievement that has drawn in African composers.

TECHNIQUES OF MUSICAL CONSTRUCTION

A focus on techniques of musical construction found among composers across the African continent will be timely. Beyond the single musical note lies a variety of artistic possibilities in the organization of musical sound. The musical note manifests itself in a variety of sound types.

In old traditional African music, these sound types often reflect the choice of instruments. On the drum alone, the variety includes booming sounds, made when a stick passed through the head of a friction drum is moved up and down; dry, parched sounds, from the hand drum; fluffy notes, from the impact of a fanlike beater on the open mouth of a clay pot; liquid notes, coming from the impact of a cupped palm; clarity of pitch, when a stretched finger, or a stack of fingers, play on a drumhead. There are also the rap of the fingers in the manner of multiple acciaccaturas on the drumhead, and the elastic "dab" with dropped palm, which cuts off the sound, making a staccato. Though surprises in performance are endless, imagining the extent of the devices that also come from wind and stringed instruments should not be difficult.

Composers who consciously address themselves to written music do not usually exploit these timbral resources directly, though on Western instruments, a few of them (Euba, Nayo, Bankole, Kavyu, Kafui) occasionally do so. For specific sonorities, Euba returns to indigenous instruments.

The variety of timbres of stringed and wind instruments may match that of drumming. In the indigenous traditional music of Africa, the timbral spectrum includes diverse techniques of bowing, plucking, voicing, and resonating. Each area may specialize in a few varieties. By virtually ignoring African instrumentation, the mid- and late-twentieth-century African composer parts ways with indigenous traditions.

On the dimension of time, the moment one note joins to another, when a motive—the smallest recognizable unit of a composition—begins to emerge, the provenance of the style looms. As the notes accumulate, identification becomes clear, in the form of a timeline. The rhythmic pattern, which in many musical styles conventionally serves as a metrical foundation, begins at various points in any bar in different localities.

African composers frequently quote traditional phrase patterns. In newly composed pieces, phrases often incorporate traditional motives, and these provide the

Tonic Sol-fa   Vocal syllables that represent each of the relative pitches of a pitch inventory

dodecaphony   Twelve-tone system, or serial composition, in which the composer assigns equal significance to each note

FIGURE 7 (*opposite*) "*Mmɔbrɔ asɛm* 'God Bless Ghana'," Isaac D. Riverson's arrangement of a patriotic Fanti song.

tools for period-construction and working out an entire composition—what may be called a "well-made African musical piece." Identifiable in this type of musical piece are devices of simple one-unit form, extended form by accumulation of phrases, extended form by addition of introductory material, extension by interpolation of contrasting sections between statements of a recurring section, and extension by making a medley. These devices are widespread among old traditional musicians and modern popular bands. More common in the works of later African composers are the devices of extension by thematic development (Bankole, Euba, Nayo), extension by thematic variation (Amu and others), and extension by a sequence of movements (Sowande and others).

Modal practice

To speak of modal practice among African composers calls for clarification. Users of African melody in composition draw from a large stock of melodic styles that develop scales of various consistencies of notes and distribution of intervals. There are also varieties of phrases and tones. Most African melodies are practically (though not altogether) singable in Tonic Sol-fa, and now and again feature each of the identifiable tones at phrase ends. Even in the ears of those bred on Western tonal music, the effect of these melodies is distinct from that of Western classical examples or plainchant; an accompanying countermelody or sporadic harmony often stresses this distinction. To speak of modal practice among African composers therefore amounts to no more than distinguishing one style of composing from others within the African experience.

A striking example is an arrangement by Isaac D. Riverson (Ghana) of a Fanti song (figure 7). To serve practical needs, he sets it for soprano, alto, tenor, and bass. However, he consistently avoids chordal progressions as they reveal themselves in both Western classical and modal harmony, though his chords are tertian (in Akan fashion). He yields to the part-making habits of a new tradition of religious songs popularly known as "Fanti lyrics," smacking not a little of Palestrina. One can only describe this as "Riversonian-Akan harmonic style." In a different and equally convincing manner, we have an Nketia-Akan harmony in "*Mmɔbrɔ Asɛm*."

The Reverend Anthony Okelo of Uganda, on the other hand, rounds the corners of Acholi melodic style, to bring it in line with Western practice. He freely employs Western harmonies. In his *Missa Maleng*, however, he interpolates a few bars of rhythms played by ensembles of struck calabashes (*larakaraka*), favored by his people, the Acholi.

Dodecaphony

Many African composers have employed twelve-tone techniques. In dodecaphonic (serial) composition, the composer assigns equal significance to each of the chromatic tones within the octave. These tones may then be organized into a tone row, a musi-

Words written by:
J. C. Garbrah,
Methodist School, Anomabu.

Music composed by:
Isaac D. Riverson,
Komenda Training College, Komenda.

Key C Maestoso *f*

1. Glo- rious Gha - na.
2. God bless Gha - na.
3. God Al- migt- y

An - cient Gha - na, thou most be - lov - ed land!
Keep her home - steads make all her life se - rene,
Be our Lead - er Thy will in us ful-fil;

Treas - ured her - i - tage for which our fath - ers blest
With un- fail - ing stores fill ev - ery hearth and bower,
Thou who through the dark and troub- led cen - tur- ies

may thou for ev - er stand!
sweet and her wood-lands green;
and our De - fend- er still,

Toiled and fought and gave their dear - est and their best,
Gird her rul - ers all with heav - en's light and power,
Hast pro - tec ted, led and brought our race to peace

Be thou thro' all the years
And may His Spi- rit rest
Teach us to build still yet

the land of li - ber - ty,
up - on their gov-ern - ment;
a great - er Gha-na - land

The home of peace- ful men
And let good-will pre - vail
On Thee, E - ter - nal Rock;

who dwell in u - ni - ty,
As we with one in - tent
So shall she firm-ly stand;

With one God, one law, one aim, one Moth - er - land,
Live and la - bour, all for each, and each for all,
Help us, Lord, as we to high - er bliss a - spire

And who pledge the strength of head and heart and hand
And may Truth and Right still at our coun-try's call
That we, in our time, with might - ier flame and fire,

Crescendo poco accelerando   *f*

To thy ser - vice full and free Thus, dear land, we pledge to thee, We
Cham-pion and defend our cause And pre- serve our rights and laws, Both
May with nations link a - field, And a worth-ier world to build Whose

rallentiando   *ff*

will serve thee ev-er, God bless Gha - na!
now and for ev-er, God bless Gha - na!
peace nought can sev-er! So bless Gha - na!

Several avant-garde African composers have used
serial composition in a blend with other approaches.

cal unit, with no internal repeats, except by reiteration of a note. This melodic formula then serves as a matrix, consisting of forty-eight images of itself: in the original (positive) form, in inversion, in reverse, and in retrograde inversion. The row can occur at any pitch level. By intuitive criteria of judgment, the composer identifies aesthetically meaningful segments of these units, and uses them in various ways against the various manifestations of the row, sometimes by grouping notes into chords.

The possible manifestations of this device, like that of a fugal subject, are myriad, thus affording wide latitude in the expression of originality. Despite the tonal restrictions the method imposes, the composer remains free to adapt the system to other structural methods, as Alban Berg does, casting in sonata form Act I, Scene 2 of *Wozzeck*.

Several avant-garde African composers have used serial composition in a blend with other approaches, like the use of quartal, quintal, and secundal harmony, tone clusters, stacked notes, or pandiatonic harmony, which depict ingenuity at the expense of classical-style progression of chords. Akin Euba and Ayo Bankole of Nigeria, and Ato Turkson and Gyimah Labi of Ghana are the most prominent in the use of this style of composing. Though they mostly base their compositions on ideas derived from African music, the strongly atonal effect of these devices prevails, to give the music potential in traditional Western-derived theater, or in the film and video industries of Africa. This awaits a director of unaccustomed vision and sensibility.

Between atonal composers and a rapidly growing army of tonal composers lies a small group, highly innovative, but conservative, in keeping their musical adventures within the bounds of diatonicism, used in excess enough to threaten tonality, dissipating this pillar of reference within most listeners' receptive capabilities.

Africanization and domestication

Many examples of African composition illuminate two important developments. In the Uganda schools competition, the section on African musical instruments requires competitors to innovate new timbral palettes and other ideas, and they respond brilliantly. The Ghana National Symphony Orchestra often presents samples of modernization of African timbral concepts and Africanization of Western timbral concepts in a process of domestication, as illustrated by Nayo's *Volta Symphony*.

In the actual expressions of African compositions, timbral concepts reveal themselves in tonal organization, depicted in melodic and rhythmic units or sequences at appropriate tempi or dynamic levels, with or without pitch combination. In *Deux Nocturnes Nostalgiques*, Pierre Cary Kazadi (Zaïre) has applied harmonies and cadences common in music for the Luba xylophone. In this work he "unites Western and traditional musical fundamentals" (Kazadi 1973). Kazadi thus depicts in African terms the timbral sonorities of Western strings and woodwinds.

Gyimah Labi (Ghana) once said he composed for emotional and intellectual enjoyment, and to make a contribution to African music. His writing confirms this statement. The intellectual dimension looms large, and a benefit from listening to his music rests on an appraisal of this dimension, expressed in the concrete terms of quartal structures and added seconds, depicted both horizontally and vertically, and contrasted with intervening stretches of classical tertian sonorities.

Underlying Labi's compositions is what he describes as the "essence" of traditional (or indigenous) African music, which also inspires the tonal matrices he prepares for extended works. In composition, he follows the ways in which traditional musical instruments combine notes—an intellectual approach to creative construction in musical sound. Listeners can enjoy much of it directly, without overstraining the intellect.

Thus, folkloric material reenters twentieth-century creativity, but in distilled, symbolic form. Bars 171–192 of the first movement of Gyimah Labi's *Dialects* sport traditional African elements, with ubiquitous rhythmic drives (figure 8). The full breadth of musical expression sets out on a course of growth that, if left uninterrupted by political or ideological arrogance, will draw toward each other and yield new blossoms—as dignified as Akan *fontomfrom* music (royal resident drum orchestras in the courts of paramount chiefs and kings), as dynamic as the Chewa *gule wa mukulu* (large performances by chorus and drum orchestra, for propitiating spirits, commemorating the dead, and averting foreshadowed communal calamities), as magnificent as the Chopi *timbila* orchestra (a large ensemble of xylophones, known for its stratified style of delivery, with song cycles and dance cycles), as muscular as Azanian *makwaya* (powerful choirs, noted for multipart singing, chording devices, and other traits), or as spacious as the Acholi *bwola* orchestra (an ensemble of one hundred to two hundred fifty dancers, each playing a small drum in chorus, plus a core of three lead drummers, singing and dancing long cycles of medley). In this regard, such shining successes as West Coast highlife, South African *kwela*, East Coast *taarabu*, "Congolese" *soukous* will seem to have leveled off too soon before their zeniths.

PROSPECTS

For whom do African composers work? The most versatile and open-minded address widespread audiences and performers. Later composers also coalesced into groups, with the most versatile and open-minded of broad taste at the one extreme, and the most limited at the other end. The repertories of the former group illustrate the widest possibilities on a vertical axis. In the works of Ephraim Amu (Ghana), Akin Euba (Nigeria), and Farid El Atrach (Egypt), for instance, lie examples for popular choirs (*Festac 77*, an anthem by Euba; *Enne ye Anigye Da*, a choral song by Amu). These are straightforward, "see-through" pieces, with easy melodies and tertian harmonies, which bring joy to disparate ranks of performers and singers.

These composers also offer works in tertian harmony of a more complex nature, introducing some chromaticism and modulations beyond related keys, and featuring abrupt transitions at times. Advanced college choirs, instrumental ensembles, and a few church choirs attempt these works, and it is possible to hear them in Lagos, Accra, Nairobi, Lusaka, Kinshasa, other national capitals, and occasionally over the radio in Europe and North America. (The author first heard Fela Sowande's *African Suite*, a five-movement work for string orchestra, on a broadcast from Germany.) A few African provincial capitals promote this repertory of new African music. Nayo's *Hadzidzi* (SATB) and Nketia's *Volta Fantasy* are good examples. The audience for this kind of music is usually small, though a lot of people get captured at "command" performances, given to official audiences, or specially arranged to mark specific occa-

Except among a few professional musicians and highly accomplished amateurs, acceptance of avant-garde atonal or excessively chromatic music is nil in Africa.

FIGURE 8   Excerpt from the first movement of Gyimah Labi's *Dialects* (bars 171–192).

sions, such as national festivals, funeral ceremonies, and society weddings, where the inclusion of music items of this kind may be relevant.

Smaller still are audiences (and performers) for works in atonal or near-atonal idioms. Composers of such music evidently write for small, high-brow African audiences, with foreign patronage much in mind.

The audiences overlap broadly, though there are lovers of music in twentieth-century Africa who confine their patronage to one kind of music or another. Few African composers give special regard to night club audiences. By invitation, some assist with new ideas the popular bands that play at these places, thus reaching out to a slice of a largely captive audience. The main obstacles keeping down the growth of good-level compositions have been unfavorable conditions and adverse propaganda. The new sonorities being produced by avant-garde composers quickly antagonize opinion leaders, who set the minds of potential audiences against this kind of new music. A typical ideal is an unprejudiced audience that sets its mind ready to face any artist. It subconsciously looks forward to novelties and innovations that may stand out against familiar background. If this background is absent, this audience may turn away, but may not set itself permanently against the new piece. At the next opportunity, it may try again to understand the artist. With luck, this process may repeatedly recur, until artistry gets across from composer to audience.

The works of Ephraim Amu's second period went through this process. Opinion leaders in Ghanaian society raised the theory that after three years of training at the Royal College of Music (London), Amu's music took a turn for the worse. Over the years, as these works continued to be heard, the critical voices weakened, while the voices expressing positive appreciation grew. Eventually, Amu's students offered even more illuminating side views. The music described earlier as difficult and obscure was revealed to music lovers to consist of familiar elements, displayed first in classical compositions, but ingeniously applied in concepts derived and developed by Amu from the principles of basic time in African music, African speech tone distribution in rhythms, and free counterpoint based on tertian harmony.

This development has followed a trend that may be verifiable in other cultures of the world, certainly in Western musical culture. Innovations denounced by one generation come to be accepted as basic ground by another. Human beings, in all their musical variety, may follow a common trend, in which musical taste opens up to accommodate new constructions. African music illustrates this in steadily changing musical idioms, inspired and flavored with elements of Western music.

Anyone having doubts about the future of the African avant-garde in musical composition should reflect on statements made during J. S. Bach's lifetime. A critic frowned on Bach's "bombastic and intricate devices," and on his habit of "darkening beauty with overelaborate art"; but he called Bach a "great man," and said the composer should place these and other extravagances between his own work and the (German) nation's admiration of him (quoted in Serposs and Singleton 1962). Ralph Vaughan Williams (1987) bears witness that the mist and darkness that fell over the works of Bach did not emanate from the works: when the critical world gained more vision and insight, Bach's achievement no longer remained in dispute or obscurity.

This evidence should also provide hopes that this portion of contemporary African musical output will begin to gain recognition in the early years of the twenty-first century. But obstacles are real and vivid. Composers of this music use methods that produce unfamiliar musical sounds. Even those employing vocabularies and methods made familiar to African audiences through eighteenth- and nineteenth-century Christian religious music and current popular music often, in a typical bid to create something new, load their music with more chromaticisms, and more rapid transitions of harmony, than the audience can readily take. Except among a few pro-

Successful works with widely acceptable ethnic roots and with manageable technical challenges for performers stand the best chance of survival.

fessional musicians and highly accomplished amateurs, acceptance of avant-garde atonal or excessively chromatic music is nil in Africa, where many professionally trained musicians do not subscribe to the new compositional practices.

The next obstacle is the performer. To plod through and get up to performance standard a piece that not only jars the ear, but also requires new executive habits, irks many African performers; and most who have a free choice avoid these works. With choral pieces, the problem is more acute. In most places, amateur choirs are the only available performers. After a day's work elsewhere, nonprofessional singers look for familiar music—trouble-free recreation, to execute and enjoy without tears.

The problem of the performer may be a temporary hindrance. If a composer has been able to cultivate an audience, the composer's prestige may inspire a performer to go through the initial tedium of trying to learn music in a new idiom, and possibly to become able to communicate the artistry the work will eventually inspire. A more certain prospect is that some enlightened individual or agency will realize the work perfectly, through a synthesizer.

The best hope lies with the higher centers of learning. They have the obligation—professional, academic, moral—to seek the latest thinking, the most profound, the most direct and efficient methods of their fields, and then to pass these on. Someday, the universities and higher colleges in Africa will face and meet this obligation.

The fate of African avant-garde compositions hangs on a thin thread. There is little prospect of subsidization from audiences. In Africa, concert going is not an established tradition; even if auditoriums of the right size existed, audiences will continue to be small. Few persons patronize the propagation of this music—by disk, diskette, compact disc, cassette tape, and video. Composers of this music have not cared enough about cultivating audiences; even highly skilled performers find the mastery of difficulties in this music time-consuming beyond its worth. Composers ask for a faith they have not nurtured.

In the long run, successful works—addressed to national audiences, but with widely acceptable ethnic roots, and with manageable technical challenges for performers—stand the best chance of survival. This is especially likely with works that do not require elaborate infrastructure. Organ works by T. K. E. Philips, Fela Sowande, Riverson; solo and choral pieces by Nketia, Kyagambiddwa, Amu, Serukenya, and others; and easy-to-play-but-big-to-hear pieces for other keyboard instruments—these will pass down to future generations.

REFERENCES

Coleridge-Taylor, Samuel. n.d. *Six Negro Melodies,* transcribed for piano. London: Winthrop Rogers.

Coplan, David B. 1985. *In Township Tonight!* London and New York: Longman.

Euba, Akin. 1988. *Essays on Music In Africa*, vol.1. Bayreuth: Iwalewa.

Feuser, Dathore, and Wilfried Feuser. 1969. *African Prose*. Harmondsworth: Penguin.

Kauffman, Robert A. 1966. *All-African Church Music Association Journal* 4(3).

Kazadi, Pierre Cary. 1973. "Trends of Nineteenth and Twentieth Century Music in the Congo-Zaire." In *Musikkulturen Asiens: Afrikas und Ozeaniens im 19. Jahrhundert*, ed. Robert Gunter, 267–283. Regensberg: Gustav Bosse Verlag.

Kojo, Yeo [Richard Graves]. 1951. *Six Negro Seculars*. London: F. Pitman Hart.

Kyagambiddwa, Joseph. 1963. *Ten African Religious Hymns*. Munich: UNI Press.

Lomax, Alan, and Raoul Abdul, eds. 1970. *3000 Years of Black Poetry*. New York: Dodd, Mead.

Mubangizi, Benedikto K. 1968. *Mweshogorere Mukama*. Mbarara, Uganda: Mbarara Diocese, Roman Catholic Church.

Serposs, Emile H., and Ira C. Singleton. 1962. *Music in Our Heritage*. Morristown, N.J.: Silver Burdett.

The Stage, Music, the Cinema. 1956. Cairo: Ministry of National Guidance.

Turkson, Ato. 1975. *Three Pieces for Flute and Piano*, op. 14. Ile-Ife, Nigeria: University of Ife Press.

Vaughan Williams, Ralph. 1987. *National Music*. Oxford: Oxford University Press.

Art-Composed Music in Nigeria
Johnston Akuma-Kalu Njoku

Scholars of the arts in Africa have attended mostly to visual and verbal art forms—sculpture, pottery, masks, poetry, tales. They have neglected musical art forms, even when they know music is an integral part of people's artistic experience. Scholarly neglect has resulted in an incomplete historical record of the arts in Africa.

If uncorrected, this situation could hasten the demise of an important tradition. Correcting it will bring the study of African music into line with that of other musics of the world, ensuring its continued usefulness as a cultural and social art. By making this correction, we shall recognize African composers and musicians, especially in the area of art-composed music, whose compositions are seldom heard beyond the boundaries of their villages, towns, or countries (Tracey 1966:7). Their compositions—which, in Nigeria, total at least several thousand—will provide a chronicle of artistic activity, testifying to the vitality of the arts of musical composition and performance in Nigeria.

TYPES OF MUSIC IN NIGERIA

Nigeria has four identifiable types of music: traditional, folk, commercial, and art-composed music. These types of music draw their materials—themes, texts, melodies, rhythms—from a shared body of knowledge about art and artistic traditions, and from a shared stock of contemporary verbal, vocal, and artistic expressions. Each of them reflects a different facet of thought and consciousness; together, they make up a complementary system of musical genres, reflecting the artistic character of Nigeria as a multicultural nation.

Artistic creators produce art-composed music—often called classical music, and in Nigeria, school music and church music—by formulating or reproducing sonic and linguistic patterns to create formal musical beauty, usually written in staff notation or Tonic Sol-fa, and meant for performance in concert halls or on stages, with correlative practices such as conductors of ensembles and restraints on audiences.

Art-composed music in Nigeria embraces the traditions of various types of music, exhibiting a variety of styles, performative practices, and cultural expectations. Included in it are works by Nigerian composers: Ayo Bankole's *Piano Suite*, Lazarus Nyanyelu Ekwueme's *Nigerian Rhapsody* and "*Nwa N'eku Nwa*," Akin Euba's String

Quartet, Okechukwu Ndubuisi's *Igbo Rhapsody* and *"Ose Va,"* David Okongwu's *"Venite"* and *"Bianu Weta Ih'onyinye,"* and Fela Sowande's *African Suite* (which draws from a highlife tune popular in the late 1950s) and *Art Songs for Tenor and String Orchestra.*

LOCAL ORIGIN AND DEVELOPMENT

The history of the origin and development of the art music tradition in Nigeria divides into three periods: the Victorian era (1846–1914), the colonial period (1914–1960), and the late twentieth century.

The Victorian era began with missionaries' introduction of Christian music in the western part of Nigeria. Anglicans arrived in 1846, Wesleyans in 1847, and Baptists in 1850 (Sowande 1966:30). This era reached its climax in 1873, with the formation of the Lagos Philharmonic Society (Aig-Imoukhuede 1975:216). Standards of performance were understandably lower than in Europe, where musicians had fuller training. But importantly, performances in the Western art music tradition occurred in Lagos in the 1800s. That tradition received the support of the well educated and élite, made up of expatriate colonial civil servants and missionaries, the Brazilian community (which increased after emancipation there, in 1888), Sierra Leoneans (who worked as professionals and civil servants). Journalists' reports and reviews of operas, choral festivals, theatrical and other musical performances from as early as 1862 are available in archives and libraries. They contain information showing conflict between traditional chiefs and colonial masters over drumming and traditional music making in Lagos. Nigerian élites' passion for Western symphonic music, oratorios, and operas continued as part of a broader attraction to Victorian culture and European ideas in general.

The second period saw the emergence and increase of composers such as T. K. E. Philips, Fela Sowande, W. W. C. Echezona, Ayo Bankole, Lazarus Nyanyelu Ekwueme, and their students. Two types of musical compositions emerged from trained Nigerian musicians: in the first, compositions by Nigerians were hardly distinguishable from the compositions of their European models; in the second, recognizable Nigerian elements form the basis of the compositions (Sowande 1966). Examples of the fusion of Nigerian and European elements from this period are two compositions by Sam Akpabot and Ikoli Harcourt-Whyte. For Barclays Bank (now Union Bank), the former set a text in "broken" Nigerian-English to a melody with Western art musical melodic progressions (Aig-Imoukhuede 1975). Harcourt-Whyte composed *"Inwe Onwe,"* a piece about the independence of Nigeria. This was also a period that experienced a nationalist movement in Nigeria. Music in churches was becoming increasingly indigenous. Most compositional efforts in this area consisted of fitting Nigerian-language texts to Western tunes. However, from the 1920s on, traditional tunes began to serve for special religious events—harvests, Easter, and Christmas.

The third period continues. Technological innovations, most commonly tape recorders, are changing the way musicians make their compositions. Computer programs—such as the Deluxe Music Construction, Professional Composer, Custom Composer, and Finale—are fast revolutionizing the art of composition. It is possible to record sounds straight into computers such as the Apple Macintosh, and generate subsidiary patterns. As more Nigerian-trained musicians and composers get exposed to such programs, they will probably make extensive use of these potentials. Chinyere Ohia (who studied composition at the University of Pittsburgh) and I (who studied ethnomusicology at Indiana University) use computers in musical composition and research. Valuable bits and pieces of historical information on the current period appear in dissertations and theses.

Tonic Sol-fa   Verbal syllables used for an aural notation; very often used to teach choral music in Nigeria

onomatopoeic vocalization   Syllables for drumming or singing that represent the rhythm and timbre of the sounds depicted

A viable and desirable project could be to examine, compare, articulate, and combine into a standard text scholarly works done on art-composed music in various parts of Nigeria, from widely different cultural environments and historical circumstances. While we wait for such a work, it will be enough, based upon available evidence and upon my personal experience as part of its development, to postulate two points: (1) the origin of art-composed music in Nigeria can be traced to the missionaries and colonial masters who introduced Sunday school songs, singing (especially of English songs) in elementary and secondary schools of hymns, chants, canticles, cantatas, anthems, oratorios in churches, and secular madrigals, motets, anthems, and solo songs; and (2) the Nigerian version of art-composed music is the natural outgrowth of the efforts of Nigerians who, living in a multicultural musical and social environment, have devoted their creative time to the composition of music in certain standard forms.

TRAINING

Most composers and performers in the Nigerian tradition of art-composed music live in rural and suburban areas, where various types of music in the country surround them. Most of these persons—songwriters, soloists, organists, and other instrumentalists, especially those whom historians will overlook—write or perform mainly for churches and schools. Some grow up hearing indigenous instruments such as the *udu*, *oyo*, *ekwe*, and drums, accompany hymns in Sunday schools, and in churches and schools. Besides native airs, taught by rote, most people who become composers start their training at school, where they learn Tonic Sol-fa and play in marching bands.

By criteria the music teachers, music masters, choirmasters, and bandmasters determine, pupils gain entrance into school choirs, church choirs, and bands. Churches (especially those in the cities) and some secondary schools have organs, and some students begin their musical training by studying with the organists. Pastors and catechists usually learn to play the organ. Their sons and daughters then become organists in secondary schools, and pass on their skills to others.

Choral and orchestral societies, universities and colleges of education, military and police bands are other training grounds for potential musicians and town dwellers. Some schools offer lessons leading either to school-certificate examinations or different levels of skill for teachers of music. Private lessons are also offered to individuals who, as external candidates, seek to take the examinations of the Associated Board or the Trinity School of Music (London). Some of the more talented among these pursue degrees in music, and become composers and performers in the art music tradition.

Tonic Sol-fa in choral music

In Lagos, Abeokuta, and other major towns in the western part of Nigeria, organ, symphonic, and operatic types of music have existed since the arrival of the missionaries and colonial masters. There, staff notation is prevalent. But that is not the case in other parts of Nigeria, especially not in the eastern states, where art music forms are mainly introduced, and have continued to be taught to choirs largely by Tonic Sol-fa. Some musicians make a case for the use of staff notation, but the perceived basis of its development is instrumental. In practice, the realization of staff notation involves eye-hand coordination, but by far the largest number of art music compositions in Nigeria are vocal or choral, not instrumental.

Tonic Sol-fa is the readiest means to teach vocal or choral music in Africa. The ways musicians use it in choral rehearsals in many parts of Nigeria merit discussion. Reflecting upon my experience (as a singer and choirmaster, and one who has also studied and has a working knowledge of the keyboard, violoncello, and clarinet), I have come to recognize that the use of Sol-fa notation is more suitable for the teaching and learning of songs, anthems, and larger choral works. Using Tonic Sol-fa, I have taught and conducted Handel's *Messiah* and Haydn's *Creation*; from staff notation, I have taught and conducted Vivaldi's *Gloria*; and in Nigeria, the former notation is more efficient than the latter.

What is probably most important is that Tonic Sol-fa corresponds profoundly to African musical thought and practice. Africans think in words, and have difficulty drawing a line between text and tune, which conceptually merge in their minds. The closest vocal or verbal representation of a musical thought is singing, sometimes with syllables (such as *da de di do du*), or grouped vocables (such as *tu-ru-zan-zam tu-run-zam*), often called nonsense syllables. (To explain what some people call nonsensical syllables in African music, I sing "Here's a season to be happy, fa la la la la, la la, la, la.") Even for instrumental music, ask the African drummer what he or she is playing, and the most likely answer will be an onomatopoeic vocalization or verbalization of the sounds.

By representing musical ideas or thoughts with syllables—do, re, mi, fa, sol, la ti—in various pitch combinations, and by rhythmic configurations or patterns, composers create musical works. From the same, practical point of view, Sol-fa allows singers to verbalize, vocalize, and internalize sounds. Choristers in rehearsal, by repeating the Tonic Sol-fa many times over, internalize the "absolute" sounds of the actual pieces. The next step is to replace these internalized sound carriers, the Tonic Sol-fa, with actual song texts, which people then sing without much difficulty. Once they master the intended text, they abandon Tonic Sol-fa.

One of the advantages of the technique is that even when the song texts are forgotten, the Tonic Sol-fa remains. People can therefore carry their "music" (the absolute sound) with them. The possible ways this could lead to the emergence of new songs are easy to imagine. Sometimes, related phrases from known songs are grafted into works under construction. The composer-performer, drawing from patterns already stored in memory, matches one pattern with another. In performances that allow rapid composition and troping, this could be likened to the habit in narrative when stock phrases, even foreign ones, are freely grafted into discussions. In the same way, composers borrow from other types of music. The mutual interdependency or complementary relationship that exists among genres makes their borrowing possible.

VARIETIES OF ART-COMPOSED MUSIC IN NIGERIA
Bands

Nigeria does not have a national orchestra; neither does any state or city in the country. There are, however, several military, police, navy, and prison bands, some with

The choral life of Nigeria is vigorous. From the rural areas through the urban areas to capital cities, Nigeria vibrates with choral music.

well-trained conductors and bandmasters. They play mainly for major state occasions. Occasionally, they accompany performers, and play at university convocations or commencements. I have observed many such performances by the Anambara Police Band in Nigeria. I performed with them on several occasions: in Afikpo (during the funeral services of the late Lady Ibiam), at the University of Nigeria (during the performance of Haydn's *Creation*), and during convocations; in 1982, I conducted the band in performance with the University Choir during the convocation in the University of Nigeria Stadium at Nsukka. But the persistence of military government and the performances it commands allow band members little time for extra training. Members of the Anambra State Police Band whom I taught privately in preparation for the graded examinations of the Trinity College of Music sometimes expressed yearning and concerns for their musical advancement.

Chamber and orchestral music

Some churches—like the Cherubim and Seraphim, and the Salvation Army—own band and orchestral instruments, and give occasional concerts. Departments of Music in colleges of education and universities in Nigeria give faculty and student recitals. Some of these institutions provide forums for the performance of chamber and orchestral music. The University of Nigeria Choral and Orchestral Society performs operas, concertos, and the like. University campuses are favorite places for international or visiting performers—concert pianists, choirs, and string quartets—often sponsored by the embassies, consulates, hotels, and other organizations.

Choral societies and choirs

The choral life of Nigeria is vigorous. From the rural areas through the urban areas to capital cities, Nigeria vibrates with choral music. There are as many choirs as churches and seminaries; in fact, some churches have as many as four choirs. From these evolve vocal quartets and other groups. They sing various types of works: hymns, anthems, airs, canticles, chants, cantatas, oratorios, motets, masses. Circuits and parishes organize choral competitions. Individuals and corporations run choirs and chorales. Steve Rhodes, Ekwueme, and Achinivu are among the individuals running choirs and chorales in the country. Local, regional, state, and national councils of the arts run series of competitions and festivals. The Nigerian Broadcasting Corporation, and other major radio and television corporations, also have choirs run by Nigerian-trained musicians.

FACTORS MILITATING AGAINST MUSIC IN AFRICAN SCHOLARSHIP

Some historical and systematic musicologists, who naturally would have been intrigued by Nigerian art music composition, tend to look at African art-composed music with disapproval. Even contemporary Nigerian scholars and composers, who have been advocating the preservation of indigenous traits in their compositions do so, more for asserting national identity (in a bid to resist the supremacy of Western music), than as an artistic statement. For example, Akin Euba expresses concern that Western forms and techniques will come to overshadow African traits in compositions by Africans: "The influences at work here are so forceful that the music produced must be regarded as representing an almost total rejection of African norms" (1970:54). He discourages the wholesale importation of Western compositional techniques among African composers, and urges them to open themselves only to those foreign influences that are "so peripheral in nature" that they will not obliterate the African identity of their musical compositions.

Another reason musicologists have ignored art-composed music derives from the expense of publishing in Nigeria. Publishers of the Ife Music Editions have managed to publish selected works of famous educated and trained composers, whose compositions conform to standard forms of Western traditions. But the number of unpublished works in private holdings, in church libraries, and in music and music research departments of radio and television corporations in Nigeria show that a lot of musicological work remains to be done.

Ethnomusicologists, because of their preoccupation with traditional musics and ethnographic details, have largely ignored art-composed music. Indigenous art-composed music of Africa is one of the forms of music that has not received their attention. Part of the reason for the neglect of this genre as an art form is the lack of adequate knowledge about African perception of art as an organic phenomenon.

CHANGING ATTITUDES TOWARD MUSIC

Because art-composed music, compared with other types of music in Nigeria, is the least known to scholars, and because it provides tangible evidence for the investigation of artistic qualities of music of Nigeria, I shall concentrate on it here, highlighting its theoretical, research, and pedagogical possibilities. The music of one Nigerian composer, Okechukwu Ndubuisi, will serve as a case study in relating music (1) to Igbo perceptions of music as a systemic and organic phenomenon, (2) to the types of music and artistic traditions of music in Nigeria, and (3) to the arts in general.

Like their counterparts in other areas of the expressive and artistic culture of Nigeria, Nigerian composers have been producing musical works in various genres. When subjected to formal analysis, their compositions will pass for art-composed music by generally accepted standards, while maintaining immense affinity with other types of music and traditions of performance in contemporary Nigeria. As some contemporary verbal expressions, novels, and items of material culture of Nigeria are being studied as artistic and cultural phenomena by folklorists, art historians, literary critics, and anthropologists, so too can the art-composed music of Nigeria.

LATE-TWENTIETH-CENTURY DEVELOPMENTS

An encouraging development in Nigeria's musical tradition, and one that has importance for the history of composition in Nigeria, is the transformation of folk songs into art songs and other genres. Stemming from earlier tries at introducing indigenous tunes and instruments into the church came compositions by pioneers. Ikoli Harcourt-Whyte's choral compositions, Bankole's *Art Songs for Voice and Piano*, Felix Nwuba's "*O Nwa Mmuo Ka M Kara Gi,*" Ndubuisi's "*Sese Isantim,*" and Ekwueme's "*Nwa N'eku Nwa*" draw textual and melodic materials from Nigeria.

Contemporary scholarship on the emergence of new forms of music in Nigeria, indeed in Africa, recognizes two major influences: Christian and Islamic authority, and acculturation of Western norms. "Acculturation" is not only an African borrowing of Western culture traits, or a Western borrowing of African culture traits, but

melorhythmic codes   Sound elements of
music, as defined by Lazarus Ekwueme

also a result of interregional borrowings (Kauffman 1970:190). My first reaction
(Njoku 1987) to the acculturative approach to the study of musical change was that
changes and emergence in African music are not so much a result of Africans' coming
into contact with Western culture as they are an outgrowth of a way of life in multicultural societies. I argued that it is fundamentally the multicultural nature of Nigeria
that allows borrowings, adaptations, and blending of traditions that makes the transformation of folk songs into other forms or types of music acceptable in Nigeria. In
the countryside and urban areas, in village churches and cathedrals in major cities, in
the schools and universities, and in other institutions, radio and television companies, cultural centers, and art councils, the blending of cultures as a way of life is phenomenal. And in addition to the social and cultural basis of art-composed music in
Nigeria, there are some musical and artistic explanations for its emergence and development. Whatever their influences might have been, the works of many Nigerian
composers portray an artistic need that is always present in a multicultural society: to
fuse together musical traditions (including, in Nigeria, Western art-composed music)
and acquired techniques and resources.

Art-composed music embraces a complex network of expressive genres, especially songs, dances, and melorhythmic codes. (I borrow the term "melorhythmic code"
from Nzewi [1974]; I use it to cover the instrumental sound elements of music.) And
music in Nigerian life and thought is an integral part of culture, and maintains a
symbiotic relationship with the sociocultural environment and world view.

OKECHUKWU NDUBUISI, A REPRESENTATIVE COMPOSER

If there is a single twentieth-century composer whose works geographically and musically span the length and breadth of Nigeria, that person is Okechukwu Ndubuisi.
He is a brilliant and finished contemporary Nigerian performer, composer, arranger,
and educator. His compositions embrace what is uniquely Nigerian in content and
performance.

Ndubuisi's life

Okechukwu Ndubuisi (figure 1) was born on 6 July 1936 in Ozu-Item, in the Bende
local government area of Abia, Nigeria. He spent the most extended period of his
childhood in his village, Agboa, where he attended the Ozu-Item Methodist School,
and grew up surrounded by folk music. In this primary school (now renamed "Ozu-
Item Central School" and relocated at Akwampiti), Ndubuisi first came into contact
with Western music. As was usual in the 1940s, mission schools taught songs—usually English songs and hymns—for two goals: to promote enculturation, and to serve
as a preparatory ground for choristers for the village church. According to
Okechukwu Ndubuisi, his mother loved church music, and was a chorister in the village church and the treasurer of its choir.

The bimusical environment in which Ndubuisi grew up strongly influenced

FIGURE 1   Okechukwu Ndubuisi in his workshop at the University of Nigeria.

him. He still has nostalgic memories of one of his teachers, Mr. Nwafor, who was in charge of music and wrote songs and marches for the elementary school Ndubuisi attended. In July 1983 (during an interview with me), Okechukwu Ndubuisi said, "Mr. Nwafor helped to make my musical life what it is." Ndubuisi sang one of his favorite primary school songs, written by Mr. Nwafor; Ndubuisi has since arranged the piece for four voices (SATB).

In 1950, when Ndubuisi was in standard five (fifth grade), he left his village to join his uncle, Emenike Onuoha, who then taught at Ora in Bendel State, about two hundred miles from Ozu-Item. Ndubuisi completed his primary school education in 1951, and the following year he entered the Sabongari Ora Grammar School, where he joined the choir, and developed the admiration for choral works and organ music that determined his later career. With the help of the school organists, Ndubuisi learned how to play hymns such as "Stand up, stand up for Jesus" and "Once in royal David's city." In 1954, during Ndubuisi's third year at Sabongari Ora Grammar School, his uncle, who was putting him through school, died. Ndubuisi had to return to his hometown, only to discover that his father, too, had died.

Ndubuisi moved to Aba, a commercial city in Nigeria; with his knowledge of the keyboard, he became an apprentice, and later a journeyman, in a guild of organ makers in the service of Chief Otutubuike. Between 1955 and 1959, while Ndubuisi was working with Chief Otutubuike, he studied the theory of music privately, and took the graded examination of the Trinity School of Music (London). Soon, he passed Grade VIII as an external candidate.

During trips to Enugu for the graded examinations, Ndubuisi came to know about the musical life of the city, and he decided to settle there. Enugu, then the capital of the Eastern Region, was (and still is) the center for an annual festival of the arts (including Western music). There were also choral and other musical societies, including a jazz club and the Enugu Musical Society (a choral group). Among several church choirs, the Holy Ghost, the Christ Church, and All Saints' Cathedral choirs gave seasonal concerts. While at Enugu, the young Ndubuisi assumed the role of a performing musician. In addition to singing, he learned to play the clarinet and the trombone. His proficiency on these instruments, and at the keyboard also, gave him opportunities for performing. He performed with the Enugu Jazz Club, which met at the premises of the British embassy. He also performed with some highlife musicians.

His association with highlife influenced his compositional style. His scores con-

Enugu Jazz Club   Ensemble in which Okechukwu Ndubuisi performed and which met at the British Embassy

Enugu Operatic Society   Founded in 1960 to perform excerpts and occasionally full-scale operas and musicals

FIGURE 2   Measures 1–6 of "Ose Va," a choral piece, based on music in the midwestern part of Nigeria. Collected by J. Okoli, arranged by O. Ndubuisi.

tain instructions such as "Moderately with Humor in 'High-life' style," and "Moderately in Simple 'High-life' fashion" (as in figure 2). The Hausa song "Nyarinya," for voice and piano, is Ndubuisi's arrangement of a once-popular tune.

In addition to performing with the Enugu Jazz Club and the highlife bands, Ndubuisi performed with the Enugu Choral Society. His performance with this society brought to public attention the promise of his voice. One of the people who congratulated him after a performance was Mrs. Eliot, a singer who had received her training at the Royal Academy (London). She requested a private meeting with Ndubuisi.

The meeting with Mrs. Eliot "was a very fortunate incident," Ndubuisi says. Mrs. Eliot proposed the idea of helping Ndubuisi by giving him voice lessons. The young man could not ask for more. He took his lessons with determination, and made such quick progress that Mrs. Eliot suggested the formation of an operatic society. More voices were recruited, and in 1960 the Enugu Operatic Society came into being. The society started by performing excerpts, and in time, they embarked upon their first major project, *The King and I*, a musical by Oscar Hammerstein and Richard Rodgers.

Partially supported by the government, the production of *The King and I* in 1960 was a big event. The premier of the Eastern Region, Dr. Michael Iheonukara Okpara, attended. He was so impressed, he approved the awarding of scholarships to three members of the Operatic Society to study music in appropriate institutions in Europe. Ndubuisi was one of the lucky ones. The other two were Joy Nwosu-Lo Bamiloko and May Afi Usuah; the former eventually joined the faculty of the University of Lagos, and the latter became director of the Cross River State Cultural Center at Calabar, Nigeria.

In September 1961, Ndubuisi left for Britain, where he studied at the Guild Hall School of Music and Drama (London), as recommended by his mentor, Mrs. Eliot. He studied composition with Dr. Peter Wishart (later head of music at the University of Reading, London), voice (singing) with Arthur Fear, piano with Mr. Laffitte, and voice (speech) with Rex Walters. In three years, he obtained his diploma in music. He stayed another year for a teacher's course. He took part in operatic productions, in one of which (*The Song of the Goat*, by J. P. Clark) he was a principal. He also performed with jazz groups in Britain.

While in the Guild Hall, Ndubuisi did not abandon his technical interest in musical instruments. He took courses in musical instrument technology from the Northern Polytechnic Institute (London), later known as the London College of Furniture. (In 1977, he went back to take an advanced technology course.) He returned to Nigeria in 1966, and got caught up in the civil war. Until its end (in 1970), he performed with the Biafra Armed Forces Entertainment Band.

In 1970, Ndubuisi returned to Enugu, where he opened a workshop on Obiagu Road, particularly for repairing musical instruments and giving private lessons, by which he made his living. (In 1972, I was one of Ndubuisi's adult beginner piano students there.) The workshop soon became a meeting place for music lovers and performers. Pianists and other instrumentalists went there to practice, and singers went there to find accompanists. With these musicians, Ndubuisi revived the Enugu Operatic Society, which performed *The King and I* in 1971 and *The Vengeance of the Lizards* (by Ndubuisi) in 1972. It was getting ready to produce *Dr. Klujo* (another opera by Ndubuisi), when Ndubuisi moved to Nsukka to join the University of Nigeria.

Since the early 1970s, Ndubuisi's operas and choral works have received repeated performances, both in the Arts Theatre and in the Auditorium of the Music Department at the University of Nigeria in Nsukka (U.N.N.). Ndubuisi has served as the staff adviser of the Nsukka Jazz Club, the director of Mixed-Blood (a band formed by Ndubuisi and Jimmy Cutliff, an African American), and the organist of the Christ Church Chapel. As a teacher, Ndubuisi encourages the same seriousness and determination with which he composes, while he makes learning an enjoyable experience. Moreover, he awakens in his students a sense of historical thinking, and thereby supports their appreciation of style through knowledge of the past. He assigns appropriate materials from the music of various periods. He also teaches a course on folk music at the University of Nigeria. Since the U.N.N. is the biggest music-degree-awarding institution in Nigeria (upon which most of the Nigerian colleges of education, radio, and television corporations, and most other government agencies, depend for graduate musicians), the influence of Ndubuisi on art-composed music in Nigeria cannot be overestimated. But his works have not been adequately studied. Elsewhere (1987), I further examine the historical and sociocultural contexts of his compositions.

Ndubuisi's compositions

Ndubuisi's artistic works exhibit such a degree of overlapping of stylistic traits, it is

The Vengeance of the Lizards   Composed by
   Okechukwu Ndubuisi and performed by
   the Enugu Operatic Society in 1972

call and response   Structural response in
   which a solo phrase is followed by a choral
   or ensemble phrase

hard to see a chronological trend in his stylistic development. Simple works, such as "*Ozu- Item Obodo*" and "*Atuak Ukot Odo*," are interspersed among pieces more advanced in harmonic and rhythmic complexity and in chromaticism, such as "*Ife Di na Oba*," "*Erna Nne*," and *Igbo Rhapsody*. Some compositions, like "*Ose Va*," "*Akumampe*," and "*Ashiboko*," are written in highlife style, with simple, danceable rhythms. These appear to be intended for the public. By writing in this style using folk tunes, Ndubuisi widens the audience appeal of the music.

A remarkable feature of art-composed music in Nigeria, at least in Igboland, is how some of the compositions maintain musical links with other genres. Some of the compositions are appropriated from, and get reappropriated into, other genres, thereby producing new songs. The "*Ashiboko*" tune was popular in palm wine spots in Aba and Port Harcourt in the 1950s and 1960s. The melody of Ndubuisi's arrangement of the song, performed in Nsukka in 1980, is now sung to a new text, for a Mother's Day religious service. The following are the stanzas of Ndubuisi's arrangement, and the reproduced version as sung by the women of the Christ Church Chapel at Nsukka (where I served as assistant choirmaster to Achinivu K. Achinivu). First is the original; second, the Mother's Day version; third, an English translation of the second.

Ashiboko!
Ashiboko ni
Gbuela muo?
Oyogoyo.

Ewu nne muo!	O my mother!
Aga m eji gini	With just what
Wee kelee mam muo?	Will I thank my mama?
Ezigbo nne.	Good mother.

The frequent exchanges, substitution, and alternation of musical and textual materials among musical genres and their import on the development of art-composed music in Nigeria will make an important study.

Like other Nigerian composers, Ndubuisi has added new dimensions to the Nigerian tradition of composition. Nigerians no longer regard composition as an art based merely on spontaneous reproduction of music heard or one learned by participatory imitation and characterized by group participation. With the contributions of Nigerian composers, composition has become a formally learned skill, characterized by clearly defined conventions, the tangible outcome of which is attributable to an individual. The artistic position of some folk songs has risen: once an adjunct to bedtime stories, they now have an independent status on paper, on long-playing recordings, in concerts, and in theatrical pieces.

Another important characteristic of Ndubuisi's compositions, also a major contribution to compositional techniques, is the element of continuous lyricism. Most of the folk tunes from which Ndubuisi's compositions derive are, in their traditional settings or forms, short and simple; they usually have short motifs and conjunct melodic motion. "*Amigo Dudu*," "*Atuak Ukot Odo*," "*Mgbogho Delu Uli*," and "*Onye Naku na Onuzo Muo?*" are good examples of lyricism. Each of these tells a tale in song, and therefore has a more continuous melodic line than most folk songs. Ndubuisi turns the verbally narrated portions of the original chant fable into vocal parts. The overlappings that take place in the original versions disappear in the transformed or arranged versions.

In most solo songs, especially those based on songs in tales, Ndubuisi presents tunes and texts in their most familiar forms. In the transformed versions, one voice sings both of the original responsorial sections. Where the original version requires overlapping between the call and the response, the last note or sung text of Ndubuisi's call flows into the response. In "*Akwa Eke*," "*Onwuelo*," and "*Utu Chatoro N'elu*," the overlappings and alternated singing that take place in the original songs disappear in the transformed versions. In "*Akwa Eke*" (figure 3), the vowel of the text that ends the call resembles the one that begins the response. Ndubuisi achieves this through the technique of elision. Even the notes at this point (measure 6) show a similar correspondence, which makes the elision both textually and musically possible.

Other important techniques and innovations are (1) assigning specific keys to the songs; (2) casting them within specific Western musical forms; (3) using tempo,

FIGURE 3   Measures 1–8 of O. Ndubuisi's "*Akwa Eke*," an Igbo song in responsial form.

Preoccupying himself with sound, Ndubuisi
sometimes disregards the custom of making melodies
follow the tonal inflections of vernacular languages.

rhythm, and sound as expressive devices; and (4) adding piano accompaniments to
songs (most of which in their traditional contexts are not performed with instrumental accompaniments).

Scrutiny of the piano accompaniments for the solo songs and the choral works
reveals the right hand often doubles the vocal parts, and the left hand often has broken, arpeggiated, and block chords. The piano provides rhythmic contrasts and
impetus. One of the rhythmic accompaniments Ndubuisi often uses appears in the
left-hand part in figure 4. The pervasive use of this rhythm is so characteristic of
Ndubuisi's music, students of music may come to call it the "Ndubuisi bass," like the
Western pattern known as the "Alberti bass."

It is not possible to find in any single composition a blending of all the traits of
Ndubuisi's music. However, figure 5 can serve as an illustration. Its text comes from a
familiar tale, of the return of a missing child, who, as a result of her playmates' mis-
chievousness, gets lost in the bush, where she has gone to collect firewood. After a
chromatic four-bar introduction, the basses enter (measure 5) with what amounts to
a call, to which the altos immediately respond. The response to the call *onye n'aku
n'ọnuzọ mo?* 'who is it that knocks on my door?' is *ọbu nwa gi jere nku* 'it is your child
who went to get firewood'. Ndubuisi uses the piano not only as an accompaniment,
but as an integral part of the piece, part of the narrative. That the bass starts by asking "Who is it that knocks?" presupposes there was a knocking—and that knocking
actually takes place in the part played by the piano. The three staccato eighth notes in
the second half of beats 3 and 4 of bar 1, and in beats 1 and 2 of bar 4, suggest the
knocking. This rhythm could be underlayed *kpom kpom kpom*, the usual Igbo verbalization of the sound of knocking. As the narration continues, the staccato rhythm
remains in the accompanying vocal and piano parts.

Some specifically Western musical traits found in this piece include the chromaticism, the secondary dominants, and the augmented chords in measures 1–4;
clearly defined cadences at the start of 5 and 14; an abrupt modulation in 14; and
continuous melody achieved through various forms of melodic expansions and poly-
textuality later in the piece (in 41–44 and 49–54, not shown).

Fela Sowande has suggested that Nigerians "regard sound as evocative, or creative" (Sowande 1966:29). Preoccupying himself with sound, Ndubuisi sometimes
disregards the custom of making melodies follow the tonal inflections of vernacular
languages. The phrase *ndi agadi* 'elderly people' (mm. 20–21 in the song "*Enenebe
Ejeghi Olu*") is meaningless as it sounds in context. Another work, "*Onye Naku na
Onuzo Muo?*" (figure 5) contains instances of what seem to be wrong choices of
tones. This should not be mistaken to mean Ndubuisi does not write music that corresponds with the tonality of the Igbo language. The music of "*Enenebe Ejeghi Olu*,"
excepting the particular spot mentioned, is a perfect example of musical and textual
synapsis. The most difficult aspect of composition in Africa, with particular reference
to vocal or choral music, is the formulation of the text.

FIGURE 4 The Ndubuisi bass, in excerpts from three compositions: *a*, "*Atuak Ukot Odo*," measures 1–12; *b*, "*Oyili Onye Oma*"; *c*, "*Aru Eme* 'The Worst Has Happened'."

The works of Nigerian composers, like those of their Ghanaian and Zimbabwean counterparts, show ingenuity in the handling of sounds. Something about the sounds African composers produce makes the compositions feel African, especially to Africans. The works of Ndubuisi express what he knows about musical sound. He brings out the musical possibilities inherent in original tunes. One is tempted to liken his treatment of tunes to what happens when, if necessary, Igbo proverbs need explanation. Such explanations usually require more elaborate commentaries and longer sentences than the proverbs. With songs, however, it is easier to experiment with tunes than with text. Tunes are more malleable.

In pieces like "*Isantim*," "*Oji m Eme Onu*," "*Ose Va*," and others, Ndubuisi captures the moods of the original songs, and manipulates and extends them to art music without losing their native musical essence. A standard technique of his is to

FIGURE 4
(Continued)

use major keys to portray happy moods, and minor keys to portray sad ones. In depicting the joy and satisfaction in the dignity of labor in the songs entitled "*Oku*

FIGURE 4
(Continued)

Ngwo 'Palm Wine Tapper'" and "*Ogbu Nkwu* 'Palm Fruit-Harvester'," he uses C major; and for the showmanship and gaiety of "*Enenebe Ejeghi Olu,*" he uses C major. This is probably why these and some of his other works elicit physical and emotional reactions, such as dancing, ululating, and clapping. For the sad subjects of the songs "*Afufu Uwa* 'Suffering'" and "*Aru Eme* 'The Worst Has Happened'" (figure 4*c*), Ndubuisi employs the key of G minor. After performances of "*Aru Eme,*" members of the audience have offered the performers their sympathy.

The rhythmic pattern herein called the Ndubuisi bass (with a characteristic drone, produced by the repetitions of the dotted half note on the G in figure 4*c*, measures 1–3) sets the mood for the expression of grief that follows in the main thematic section (m. 5). Also noteworthy is how this rhythmic pattern pursues its path from measure 15 to measure 20 without hampering the lyrical and rhythmic freedom of the expressive melody in the voice. In measure 5, the abruptness of the agitation

Ethnic pluralism is so characteristic of Nigeria that it permeates every facet of cultural life and artistic productions.

FIGURE 4
(Continued)

excited by the repeated eighth notes in the accompaniment is in keeping with the intensity of the exclamation *Ewo!* in the vocal part. Dynamic expression changes from mezzoforte to forte, and the stressed offbeat entries by the soloist in measures 5,

FIGURE 5   Measures 1–8 of "*Onye Naku na Onuzo Muo?*" a song whose musical intervals sometimes clash with tonal motion implied by the language.

10, and 15, notably heighten the emotional effect of the song. See also the instances of wordpainting: the upward direction of the word *elu* 'up' (from the D of m. 9 to the B-flat of m. 10) is depicted by a leap of a minor sixth, the largest melodic interval in the piece; and the highest note of the piece sets the words that talk about death (mm. 15–16). This is a clear example of the use of a musical climax to highlight the most urgent part of the text.

WHAT IN NIGERIAN ART-COMPOSED MUSIC IS NIGERIAN?

Ethnic pluralism is so characteristic of Nigeria, it permeates every facet of cultural life and artistic productions. And that is what makes Nigerian art unique. Most musical compositions reflect their states of origin. The works of the late Bankole and those of

The compositions of Nigerian composers are
aesthetically beautiful, aurally interesting, and
ethnographically informative.

FIGURE 5   (Continued)

Euba represent the Yoruba musical tradition in the same way the works of Fiberesima and Akpabot depict the Ijaw and Ibibio musical traditions, respectively, and Echezona, Ekwueme, and Ndubuisi portray Igbo music. There is something decidedly Nigerian in Nigerian art-composed music, and that is because Nigerian composers go beyond the requirements of the standard forms of musical composition. Nigerian art-composed music can be seen as a means by which Nigerian composers manipulate their compositional skills in response to both aesthetic and social problems.

What exists in Nigeria is therefore an ethnic-bound music with considerable variety. By producing local versions of it, Nigerian composers relate their compositional techniques to indigenous concepts and traditions of performance. Herein lies the worth of Nigerian art musical composition for the academic study of music. Most Nigerian composers resort to creative exploration of music in expressing the political, social, historical, cultural, religious, and musical sentiments that most Nigerians share. The products of art-composed music in Nigeria are being ingeniously exploited by radio broadcasters, councils of the arts, and organizers of festivals of the arts.

PROSPECTS

By using the compositions of Ndubuisi as the study object, we can deal with certain persistent problems in ethnomusicology, such as musical change. The study of genre is possible by closely studying the sources of the compositions over time, and in a given area or place. By doing so in many different places in Africa, scholars can gain insight into what, how, and why performers process interchangeable musical variables and patterns. The emphasized features of performance could then point to aesthetic judgments of the people who sing, play, dance, listen, appreciate, reflect, and talk about music. The ways by which tunes have been adapted could then advance our discussion and deepen our understanding of several stylistic and artistic aspects of music in Africa.

The changing texts of selected songs will reflect what performers choose to talk about in their songs at different times and in various contexts, while the tunes and traits and practices will show how music reflects the changes. Then transformations that may have taken place will tell us what different cultural specialists—composers, singers, other performers—did. Beyond being a phase in the history of music, the compositions of Nigerian composers, as shown by the collected works of Ndubuisi, are aesthetically beautiful, aurally interesting, and ethnographically informative.

COLLECTED WORKS OF OKECHUKWU NDUBUISI

In approximate chronological order (the order in which they appear in the bound collections in my holding), the following table lists Ndubuisi's compositions finished before 1994. The letters "SATB" have their usual musical denotations (scored a cappella unless indicated otherwise); "V" denotes undifferentiated voice; "P" denotes piano. The instrument of no. 41 is an electronic organ; the duet of no. 64 is saxophone or other wind instrument plus piano. No. 59 is a war dance.

The dates of completion of some items are known: *12,* 27 Nov. 1978; *13,* 22 Dec. 1978; *14,* 4 April 1979; *16,* 14 June 1979; *17,* 30 June 1979; *18,* 14 July 1979; *19,* 29 Sept. 1979; *20,* 24 Jan. 1980; *21,* 29 Sept. 1980; *22,* 8 Nov. 1980; *36,* Feb. 1981.

Number and Title	Key	Meter	Language	Scoring	Status
1. Blue Nocturne	G minor	C	————	P	Composed
2. *Ife di na Oba*	G	12/8	Igbo	S + P	Arranged
3. *Anwie Ti, Mini Dze*	E♭	4/4	Igbo	S + P	Arranged

Number and Title	Key	Meter	Language	Scoring	Status
4. *Dim Oma*	F	2/4	Igbo	SATB	Arranged
5. *Ozuitem Obodo Mu*	B♭	4/4	Igbo	SATB	Arranged
6. *Erna Nne*	G	12/8	Igbo	SATB + P	Composed
7. *Kwi Saurare*	F	12/8	Hausa	SATB	Arranged
8. *Oba N'ikama Lo'oko*	F	12/8	Yoruba	SATB	Arranged
9. *Osumopi Kwikelo*	F	C	Benue	SATB	Arranged
10. *Isantim*	A♭	6/8	Efik	SATB	Arranged
11. *Azu Mbe Bu Ugwu Ya*	F	12/8	Igbo	SATB	Arranged
12. *Onina Manya Ogo*	F	12/8	Igbo	SATB	Composed
13. *Nwa Aramodu*	F	12/8	Igbo	SATB	Composed
14. *Mama G'abara Mu Mba*	F	4/4	Igbo	V + P	Composed
15. An Elegy for Cutliff (unfinished)	D	C	Igbo	SATB	Composed
16. *Oku Ngwo*	D	C	Igbo	V + P	Arranged
17. *Ogbu Nkwu*	C	4/4	Igbo	V + P	Arranged
18. *Nwa N'ebe Akwa*	B minor	4/4	Igbo	V + P	Arranged
19. *Ashiboko*	G	4/4	Igbo	SATB	Composed
20. *Ajama Akwara Ngwongwo*	F	12/8	Igbo	SATB + P	Composed
21. *Ogun Salewe*	F	4/4	Itshekiri	SATB	Arranged
22. *Nyarinya*	F	12/8	Hausa	V + P	Arranged
23. *Anoro Anokwuru*	E♭	12/8	Igbo	SATB	Composed
24. *Onye N'aku N'ọnuzọ M'o*	E♭	C	Igbo	SATB + P	Composed
25. *Amigo Dudu*	A♭	12/8	Igbo	SATB + P	Composed
26. *Ode Nji Nji*	A♭	12/8	Igbo	S + P	Arranged
27. *Enenebe Ejeghi Olu*	F	12/8	Igbo	S + P	Arranged
28. *Chukwuma*	C minor	12/8	Igbo	S + P	Arranged
29. *Mbogho Delu Uli*	E♭	12/8	Igbo	S + P	Arranged
30. *Agiligbo*	F	12/8	Igbo	S + P	Arranged
31. *Onye Di Nma N'azu?*	E♭	12/8	Igbo	SATB	Arranged
32. *Nwaruru*	C	12/8	Igbo	S + P	Arranged
33. *Olyili Onye Oma*	B♭	12/8	Igbo	V + P	Arranged
34. *Icheku Na Nwanneya*	B♭	6/8	Igbo	V + P	Arranged
35. *Oma Bu Nwunye M'o*	C	4/4	Igbo	V + P	Arranged
36. *Aru Eme*	G minor	12/8	Igbo	Baritone + P	Arranged
37. *Egwu Onwa*	F	12/8	Igbo	V + P	Arranged
38. *Nwa Enwe Nne*	C	4/4	Igbo	V + P	Arranged
39. *Okpanku*	B♭	12/8	Igbo	V + P	Arranged
40. *Utu Chatoro N'elu*	C	12/8	Igbo	V + P	Arranged
41. Igbo Folk Medley	C	12/8	———	Organ	Composed
42. *Nwannunu*	E♭	12/8	Igbo	V + P	Arranged
43. *Etuk Udo*	C minor	6/8	Ibibio	V + P	Arranged
44. *Onye Gagwazi Wa*	C minor	12/8	Ika-Igbo	V + P	Arranged
45. *Uwa Amaka*	B♭	4/4	———	P	Arranged
46. God Bless Africa	E♭	C	———	SATB + P	Arranged
47. *Den-dele K'urie*	D	12/8	Igbo	A + P	Arranged
48. *Atuak Ukot Odo*	G	12/8	Efik	S + P	Arranged
49. *Mgboye Nwoyi Diye*	C	12/8	Igbo	S + P	Arranged
50. *Onye Yabalu Di Nma?*	C	4/4	Igbo	S + P	Arranged
51. *Onwuelo*	G	4/4	Igbo	Baritone + P	Arranged
52. *Obogwu*	G	4/4	Igbo	V + P	Arranged
53. *Akpo Ughe*	D	12/8	Urhobo	V + P	Arranged
54. *Miri*	E♭	6/8	Igbo	V + P	Arranged
55. *Akw'Eke*	F	4/4	Igbo	V + P	Arranged
56. *Nwa Mgbogho Delu Uli*	E♭	12/8, 6/4	Igbo	S + P	Arranged
57. *Oji M'eme Onu*	F	4/4	Igbo	V + P	Arranged
58. *Afufu Uwa*	G minor	4/4	Igbo	V + P	Arranged
59. *Ikpirikpe Ogu*	E♭	4/4	———	P	Composed
60. *Ugani Egbue Umu Anu*	C	12/8	Igbo	V + P	Arranged

Number and Title	Key	Meter	Language	Scoring	Status
61. *Ose Va*	E♭	4/4	Edo	SATB	Arranged
62. *Eringa*	G	12/8	Igbo	SATB	Arranged
63. *Uma Wo*	C	12/8	Igbo	SATB	Composed
64. Igbo Rhapsody	C	12/8	———	Duet	Composed

REFERENCES

Aig-Imoukhuede, Frank. 1975. "Contemporary Culture." In *Lagos: The Development of an African City,* ed. A. B. Aderibigbe, 197–226. Lagos: Longman.

Euba, Akin. 1970. "Traditional Elements as the Basis of New African Art Music." *African Urban Notes* 5(4):52–56.

Kauffman, Robert. 1970. "Multi-Part Relationships in the Shona Music of Rhodesia." Ph.D. dissertation, University of California, Los Angeles.

Njoku, Johnston A.-K. 1987. "Okechukwu Ndubuisi's Contributions to the Development of Art Music in Nigeria." M.A. thesis, Michigan State University.

Nzewi, Meki. 1974. "Melo-Rhythmic Essence and Hot Rhythm in Nigerian Folk Music." *The Black Perspective in Music* 2(1):23–28.

Sowande, Fela. 1966. "Nigerian Music and Musicians: Then and Now." *Composer* 19 (Spring):25–34.

Tracey, Hugh. 1966. "A Plan for African Music." *Composer* 19 (Spring):7–12.

Theory and Technology in African Music

Simha Arom and Frédéric Voisin

Determining Musical Scales
An Innovative Methodology: The Case of Xylophones
Interactive Experimentation
Vocal Music: The Polyphony of the Aka
Perspectives

The scientific world began applying analytical technology to African music in 1905, when Parker F. Witte used a cylinder phonograph to record musical performances in Togo. Over the next decades, several important collections followed. European scholars, notably Erich M. von Hornbostel (1917), transcribed the cylinders and used the transcriptions to support hypotheses about African music (1928). But these cylinders, and the transcriptions they yielded, treated performance holistically, registering music only as it presented itself to the phonograph. They were less than fully adequate to the task, which required specific technical tools. The music was too complex, the machinery too simple. In particular, intricacies of rhythm and pitch invited the development of new technological devices.

In the 1930s, for studying African polyrhythms, A. M. Jones (1959) invented a drum recorder, capable of producing a real-time, schematic representation of rhythmic progressions. It consisted of two copper plates, which a musician could strike with electrified brass pencils. Marks on a moving strip of paper recorded contacts between the plates and the pencils; the distances between the marks corresponded to the rhythmic value of the strokes.

A few years later, Gerhard Kubik developed impact notation, a cinematographic technique, operating on much the same principle (1965). He began by filming a performance of Ugandan xylophone music, played by two musicians. He used a silent 8-mm camera, running at 24 frames per second. On a graph, he plotted each musician's actions: the *x*-axis showed time (in units representing the frames of the film), and the *y*-axis showed pitch (in units representing the slats of the xylophone). For each percussive action, the graph specified which player struck which slat.

Another method, intended particularly for the transcription of complex polyphonic or polyrhythmic music, is the field rerecording technique, developed by Simha Arom in the 1970s. The researcher makes a conventional recording of the piece under study (vocal or instrumental), and progressively reconstitutes it. The initial recording serves as a point of departure for a series of recordings. Through earphones, the first musician's recording is played back to the next musician, who sings or plays in coordination with it. Meanwhile, on separate tracks, another device records both parts simultaneously—the referential part and the second musician's part. With each consecutive musician in the ensemble, this procedure is repeated, until every part has been recorded. In this way, each recorded part is linked to the previous one—a condition essential to the transcription of the entire polyphonic construct (Arom 1976). The technique is interactive: each performer must choose which previously recorded part would best serve as a reference. Thus, for elaborating the analytical data, the experimental procedure depends on the musicians' participation.

Another area where technological development has been important is the study of musical scales, which requires precise measurement of pitch. Since the 1880s, researchers (Ellis 1885; Ellis and Hipkins 1884; Kunst 1949; Tracey 1958) have used devices such as the monochord and the tuning fork. With the development of electronic technology, new devices for measuring pitch came to the fore (Jones 1963, 1970; Kubik 1964, 1970; Wachsmann 1950, 1957). The Stroboconn was the most popular, but others—the oscillograph (Kubik 1961), the time pitch or melograph (Blacking 1959; Cooke 1970), the sonograph (Rouget 1969)—were among the tools researchers used for investigating scalar systems in African music.

The development of signal-processing stations in laboratories and (to a lesser extent) the availability of inexpensive electric tuners have contributed another dimension to the study of musical scales. Such technology, however, has inspired controversy about the accuracy of frequency measurements in determining pitch. So late as the 1950s, Hugh Tracey displayed a preference for the proven accuracy of the tuning fork: "Most electrical pitch indicators are not intended for such work and their calibration cannot be guaranteed" (Tracey 1958:15). Some researchers (Jones 1970; Kubik 1961) have observed that frequency is difficult to measure with precision, particularly when sounds are harmonically complex or of short duration, as is often the case with African xylophones.

A more important criticism of the use of electronic (and, later, of digital) technology is the claim that measurements and calculations derived from such equipment rarely correspond to perceived pitch. That the measured frequency of a sound can differ from the frequency of its perceived pitch stems from unpredictable aspects of the psychophysiological behavior of the human ear. When a sound is simple and stable (in music, it never is), predicting perceived pitch from measured pitch may be possible. For many musical instruments, however (especially percussive instruments, like the xylophone), the role of timbre in pitch perception is so important, researchers cannot assume a perceived musical pitch will correspond with its measured acoustic frequency.

Such measurements are usually geared to exhaustive acoustic analyses of sound, the results of which are not always relevant to perception. To the extent that acoustic measurements fail to account for the effect of timbre on pitch perception, they are useless for studying musical scales (Jairazbhoy 1977:266; Schneider 1990:288). Above all, the quantitative perspective obviously amounts to little, for it does not integrate the cognitive processes and their role in the perception and conception of musical scales. By observing indigenous procedures of tuning, with analysis reinforced by measurements made in the field, Klaus Wachsmann (1957:11) discovered that the tribal norm of the tuning of Ugandan xylophones was equipentatonic; unfortunately, researchers beyond Uganda have not pursued his procedure.

The use of sophisticated equipment is often troublesome, not only because the machinery poses problems of reliability, but also because it requires expensive logistical arrangements, involving electric generators, fuel, and electroacoustic devices. To produce devices that aid investigation in the field, science has had to wait for technological developments in distinct domains of musical research. By *synthetic analysis,* sophisticated devices would enable researchers to verify their measurements of pitch.

The lowest slat of the xylophone is usually the "mother," since it is from her that the tuning begins. Toward the high end are the "husband," and then the "children."

The ethnomusicological use of digital synthesizers began in 1985, when Pierre Sallée, to synthesize musical scales from a fragment of a polyphonic piece of the Bibayak of Gabon, used a Synclavier. But the comparison of the simulated fragment with its original failed to yield decisive results: too subjective, it produced an evaluation seemingly based on Western, rather than indigenous, perceptions. The essential question remained unanswered: what would be the judgment of the people themselves?

In 1989, in the ethnomusicology department of Langues et Civilisations à Tradition Orale, a laboratory of the Centre National de la Recherche Scientifique (Paris), Simha Arom assembled a group of researchers whose aim was to explore perspectives offered by the techniques of sound synthesis. These researchers included Vincent Dehoux, Susanne Fürniss-Yacoubi, Gilles Léothaud, and the authors. Their immediate aim was to investigate scales in the field. They wanted to invent a procedure that, methodologically and technologically, would respond to the imperatives of the cultural and musical characteristics of ethnic groups in the Central African Republic. With a view toward developing psychoacoustic experiments to investigate cognitive processes underlying the perception and conception of musical scales, they brought the technology of sound synthesis and digital sampling to that country (Arom and Fürniss 1992, 1993; Dehoux and Voisin 1992, 1993). Independently, the next year, using a digital-sampling technique, Peter Cooke (1990) undertook an experiment on Ugandan musicians' perception of pitch.

Ethnomusicological recourse to sound-synthesizer technology as the basis of experimental procedure in the field requires several remarks. If such a procedure tries to reconcile perceptual phenomena with a quantitative approach, researchers must be specific about the conditions in which the use of technology is applicable in the field.

> The use of technological media is valuable, but the assumption of media objectivity is untenable. The decisions made regarding their use and the use of the data they record need to be stated clearly, and the methodological and the theoretical assumptions implicit in media's use need to be considered carefully. (Stone and Stone 1981)

Indeed, when technology becomes a medium of communication between researchers and musicians, the researchers must identify the type of information sought, and stipulate the procedures to be used. It is essential to know *who transmits what type of information through what medium*: in societies that have no terminology to describe a pitch or an interval and lets everyone participate actively in musical events, the verbal response of a musician, placed by the researcher in the unfamiliar position of passive listener, is suspect. Researchers must adapt technological experimentation to the context of the musical practice of the culture being studied, and must corroborate musicians' verbal responses by analyzing other communicative reactions, especially the respondents' physiognomic and gestural displays.

DETERMINING MUSICAL SCALES

The perception of pitch operates in cognitive space: each pitch can be defined in terms of its distance from other pitches. For this reason, the perception of pitch is particularly amenable to objective quantification by simple devices, such as the monochord. There is a difference, however, between the precise determination of the structure of a musical scale and an explanation of the cognitive processes that beget the structure.

Since antiquity, theoreticians have understood that the intervals of Western musical scales are based on ratios of whole numbers, but only since the 1600s have analysts (most notably Marin Mersenne, Jean-Philippe Rameau, and Hermann von Helmholtz) scientifically explained the nature of these relationships. Though the systematic cataloguing of scales was begun before the late 1800s, the problem of cognitive representation remains unresolved. Researchers need to understand how the concept of scalar systems reflects associated mental representations. The members of a musical tradition recognize and evaluate scalar intervals as a function of what they know to be correct. A scientific observer needs to understand their *intention* as a reflection of an *internalized* representation of the system.

The limits of verbalization

Investigations we conducted in various African communities have revealed various types of metaphoric designation of the slats of the xylophone. In Central Africa, this vocabulary designates essential tonal functions: the "slat that commands," most often situated in the center of the instrument, is associated with the "slat that responds" or "gives the song." Another terminology designates each slat as a function of its relative pitch. It does so by referring to systems of kinship. The lowest slat is usually the "mother," since it is from her that the tuning begins. Toward the high end are the "husband," and then the "children." The "grandmother," when she is present, has a lower pitch than even the mother; but she is tuned last, either in relation to the "mother," or in relation to the "daughter" (figure 1). This kinship system is flexible: the Gbaya twelve-slat xylophone can contain from one to three "mothers" (of different pitches), and the other slats represent the "children" without distinction, while the father is absent.

Such terminology includes several indices of the hierarchy of scalar degrees, but lacks information about the nature and the size of intervals. Though a particular high sound may be labeled "little," and another low sound "larger," musicians may not verbalize the differences between interval sizes. In response to the question "Are these two sounds well tuned?" musicians have no difficulty responding "yes," "no," or "nearly." However, they are less successful at expressing the reason for which the relation is or is not correct. A verbal response often does not reflect faithfully the quantitative relations that a comparison of pitches produces. The expression "this sound is still a little too high," however, indicates the perception of a precise distance separating a sound from the one the tuner wants to attain. The difficulty is to know what sound must be attained. Well-tunedness, however, is a conceptual quality. The notion of distance between two pitches operates in a space of multiple dimensions, as does the space encompassing the notion of timbre: each space corresponds to the cognitive implications of the concept.

Several studies of verbal descriptions of pitch intervals in Central Africa show that musicians report the interval of a major second to be "the same" as that of a minor third; musicians also hear an identity between a minor sixth and a fifth, and

FIGURE I   Topology: names of slats and tuning order of the five-slat xylophone of the Manza, Central African Republic.

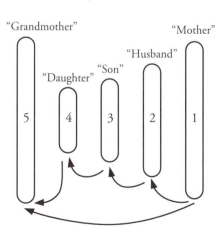

Widespread in Africa, the xylophone is of primary importance to the study of systems of pitch. It often serves as a reference for tuning melodic instruments.

between a fifth and a fourth. Can we conclude from these data, as Kubik has hastily done, that Central African scales are "elastic" (1983:352–360)?—or that such equivalences indicate an inability to discriminate among pitches (Leipp 1971)? It seems more plausible that those cultures merely have felt no need to develop a terminology specific to musical notions of scale, of pitch, and of interval—just as certain cultures have felt no need to develop a terminology for certain colors (Thomas 1989). Without understanding the musical concepts proper to each culture, the quantitative relations that define pitch structures cannot be adequately determined. Technology may therefore offer, not only a precise means of quantification, but also a method that can allow nonverbal knowledge to emerge.

Only within this perspective can musical technology begin to be relevant to studying scales nonverbally. By encoding musical events in the form of digital messages, synthesizers can furnish much of the data necessary for musical analysis: the act of pressing a key on the keyboard of a synthesizer can transmit to another digital instrument (or to a computer) a great deal of quantified data, usable then or later. If such a digital musical instrument can be made accessible to a traditional musician in a form compatible with indigenous styles of performance, each contact with a key will record the pitch of the note, the force with which the key is hit, its duration, its timbre, and other information. Thus, in the technological arena, researchers might encounter traditional musicians' intentions.

AN INNOVATIVE METHODOLOGY: THE CASE OF XYLOPHONES

Widespread in Africa, the xylophone is of primary importance to the study of systems of pitch. One of the few African instruments with fixed pitches, it often serves as a reference for tuning melodic instruments. However, even when a musician tunes and retunes pitches until the members of the same ethnic community consider them identical, the components of a scalar system may differ drastically from instrument to instrument. Where cultural outsiders perceive acoustic differences, insiders may consider the tunings to be "the same." This phenomenon occurs with other African instruments, such as harps, lamellophones, and horns.

On the xylophone, such deviations of pitch can be as great as a semitone, and it is virtually inconceivable that local musicians do not perceive such a difference. For indigenous musicians in Central Africa, "the same" seems to designate, not an "equality," but an "equivalence," a larger cultural notion. If we acknowledge that the members of a community are more qualified to evaluate their own scalar system than an outside observer (no matter how qualified), unanimity of response clearly rests on a *judgment of cultural equivalence*, which attributes a *field of variance* proper to each degree of the scale. Without knowledge of the size of the field of variance, or of the concepts that underlie it, researchers cannot determine the *mental template* of the scalar system the musicians carry within them.

FIGURE 2   Xylophones, a DX7 synthesizer, and a computer in the shade of mango trees.

The difficulties to be overcome in the analysis of musical scales of Central Africa are these:

indigenous concepts of scalar systems are nonverbal;
scalar systems provoke a sense of ambiguity in outsiders, who cannot determine with certainty the exact position of each scalar degree;
acoustic measurements alone are irrelevant to a comprehension of unfamiliar scalar systems.

In light of these difficulties, fully understanding how insiders conceive musical scales requires that research treat *conceptual behavior*—which, as the product of both physiological and cultural phenomena, appears to be mostly unconscious. Thus, researchers will uncover the faculties involved in auditory perception only by means of experimentation. Since such experimentation has most often been applied to Western music, current theories of scales seem doubtful in regard to African music.

Until the 1980s, the lack of information on the indigenous perception of scales was the result of the absence of technical devices suitable for experimentation in the field. But such experimentation is analytically insufficient: like ethnographic observation, ethnographic experimentation must handle nonobvious data. By participating in the elaboration of the material to be analyzed, traditional musicians can directly take part in the analysis. The experimental procedure must be truly interactive: it must enable musicians to respond to propositions hypothetically submitted to them, and (more important) to influence the experimental proceeding.

Interactive tools

Beginning in 1989, our team undertook successive missions to a dozen ethnic communities of the Central African Republic. To study musical scales, we developed a procedure of experimentation enabling musicians to interact with researchers (figure 2). While an appropriate tool met our needs, its adaptation for the field was problematic. The tool was an 8-bit, digital MIDI synthesizer (Yamaha DX7 II), capable of programming diverse timbres and musical scales with a procedure of microtuning to a precision of 1/85 of a semitone; at the time, it was the only portable apparatus available.

Tuning the synthesizer, musicians determine for themselves the pitches equivalent to those of their instruments.

To allow musicians to verify and tune the synthesized sounds as they do with their xylophones, we simulated a traditional xylophone: to the keys of the synthesizer, we attached appropriately sized slats of wood. Variety in the number of keys among the xylophones of different ethnic groups necessitated a variable configuration, easily realized by fixing self-sticking adhesive to the slats: in only a few seconds, researchers could configure the synthesizer so each musician would confront a simulated xylophone, of which the number and arrangement of keys corresponded to those of the musician's instrument.

As soon as musicians had become familiar with the experimental instrument, they could modify the simulated xylophone to realize a personal choice of sound: they could reconfigure different buttons of the synthesizer according to different possible scales or timbres. More important, since the synthesizer had an easily manipulable cursor, they could modify inappropriate pitches and timbres. The action of correcting an unsuitable scalar prospect indexed the distance between the researchers' hypotheses and the musicians' concepts: even when the correction was imperfect, it revealed the musician's intention.

Figure 3 schematizes this type of investigation. The linkage of loop 1 represents the musicians' actions (via the synthesizer) on the propositions submitted to them. The experimental verification of the researchers' hypotheses might conduce to a culturally recognized model, represented schematically by loop 2. The procedure is repeated as many times as necessary until, by verification or action, the results are no longer contradicted: the model then begins to match the mental templates of the participants of the musical tradition under study.

In the course of these investigations, the musicians were never alone with the researchers. Experimental trials took place in the presence, and with the participation, of other xylophonists belonging to the same ethnic group (sometimes to the same ensemble). Singers who regularly participated in the musical life of the group took an active part in the proceedings, as did certain prominent personalities, particularly from among the elderly, locally considered authorities on the subject. Rarely did the protagonists in the experimental situation disagree. The acceptance or refusal of a particular timbre or scale was never, therefore, based on the judgment of a single individual, isolated from the traditional environment; all choices were the product of consensus, proceeding from a culturally normative judgment, representing the collective musical heritage. In the rare cases where consensus was not unanimous, instrument makers—those who most frequently tuned instruments—made the judgment. In these cases, the reactions of specialists usually coincided.

FIGURE 3   Schematization of the interactive procedure.

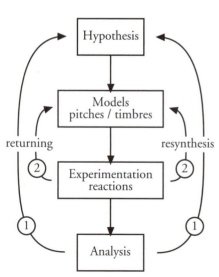

Perception and measurement

The principle of introducing "the phenomena of perception into the series of acoustical measurements" (Léothaud 1991), based on the pairing of measurable sounds with perceived pitches, is one that many psychoacousticians use for measuring pitches.

Paradoxically, acousticians and ethnomusicologists used this technique long before the appearance of specialized electrical devices. As early as the 1880s, Alexander Ellis (1885) determined instrumental pitches by matching carefully calibrated resonators to pitched sounds. When a resonator was tuned (often by ear) to the sound of an instrument, the vibrational frequency of the instrument's sound was considered equivalent to the resonant frequency of the resonator. Similarly, in the early 1900s, von Hornbostel and Kunst tuned monochords to the pitches of traditional instruments: by observing the vibrating length of the monochord, they deduced the frequency of the sound emitted by the instrument. Furthermore, according to Kunst (1974:11), the monochord was superior to other instruments because, being easily transportable, it was usable in the field. However, while the measurement of pitch by monochord or tuning fork may account for perception in one regard, results from these methods may suffer from the matching procedure that makes them more sensitive to perception: matching the tuning of the timbrally impoverished sounds of such instruments as a monochord or a tuning fork with the pitches of musically rich sounds can be a difficult task, whose results demand caution.

It is in the comparison of pitches that auditory discrimination is the greatest. A practical experiment in transcription showed "more agreement or concurrence among the transcribers in the notation of pitch than in the notation of duration" (List 1974:373). When matching pitches, the timbre of the referential sound, though simplified, should remain as close as possible to that of the sound to be matched. The referential timbre must be a model of the original, in retaining the traits pertinent to the musical culture in regard to the recognition of pitch. Under these circumstances, it becomes possible to deduce a reliable measure of pitch directly from the perception of the sound under examination. In permitting such modelization, sound synthesis thus represents a major development in the determination of pitch. Since the timbre to be synthesized and its effects on perception are completely controllable, researchers can make the pitches actually perceived correspond to the frequencies generated by the synthesizer. The primary objective in this technique is to tune in unison the sound to be measured with the referential sound (figure 4). The measured frequency can be considered the equivalent pitch, expressible in hertz. For sounds of the xylophone, this technique permits a level of discrimination on the order of 5 cents.

INTERACTIVE EXPERIMENTATION

To measure, study, and compare local musicians' pitch percept in tuning their instruments, the process of matching by equivalent pitch is an efficient experimental method. Tuning the synthesizer, musicians determine for themselves the pitches equivalent to those of their instruments. They soon become familiar with this technique, and often make a spontaneous association between the action of the cursor of the synthesizer and carving or scraping the slats of the xylophone. With this protocol, experimentation permits the precise determination of the musicians' margin of tolerance and field of pitch variance.

Extensive experiments carried out in the Central African Republic have shown that xylophonists tune the synthesizer to a unison with great deviation, whether or not they have a referential sound to use in this task. It would be a mistake, however, to consider these deviations as pitch tolerance on their part. If the unison as conceived by a given culture tolerates only a small deviation, musicians of that culture must know how to produce the unison independently of interval relations, independently of scalar context. So researchers must test whether these deviations are systemic as a field of variance due to the scalar system itself, or are due to a more general cultural or physiological feature, as both a pitch tolerance and a threshold of pitch.

During the process of tuning xylophones, traditional musicians do not compare

FIGURE 4   The synthesized referential sound is adjusted by ear to a unison with the sound whose pitch is to be measured.

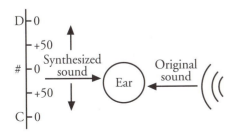

The study of musical scales must necessarily take into account the musicians' mental representation of timbre.

unisons. The importance of the unison is therefore doubtful within their scalar system. To test the variance allowed in a unison independently of the tuning, it appears necessary to tune the sounds of the original instrument one by one with the synthesized sounds, but using a procedure that does not resemble instrumental tuning. For investigating the variance of unisons, the synthesizer should not try to imitate the natural instrument, and all apparatus meant to resemble a xylophone must be removed; to avoid the notion of scalar degrees implied by adjacent keys, tuning must proceed on a single key of the synthesizer. Experiments with such revised synthesizers have revealed a margin of normal tolerance of less than ten cents among tuners of a unison; such a result is difficult to obtain when using the natural timbres of percussive instruments.

The strict unison therefore seems to have meaning in Central Africa, and if tuners rarely observe precise strictness, the cause may be that such a notion is unnecessary to the tuning system of xylophones. It therefore makes no sense to compare the xylophones of the same culture in terms of unison. The field of variance of pitches in the musical scales of Central Africa is not linked to a variable margin of tolerance on the musicians' part. The variance in observed pitches results, rather, from a principle of a cultural equivalence due to the scalar system. The exact terms and modalities of this equivalence remain to be studied.

Synthesis of sounds

The relevance of the results described above, notably those concerning the unison, intrinsically depends on the referential sound's timbral identity to the representation of the sound held by the bearers of the tradition. The study of musical scales must necessarily take into account the musicians' mental representation of timbre.

In 1989, during the initial investigation, Frédéric Voisin synthesized a first series of timbres with frequency modulation calibrated to the sound of each of the slats of the xylophones recorded in the field. Synthesis by frequency modulation is, indeed, guided by intuition. It seemed, however, to be the most efficient method of producing a predefined timbre. In effect, it permits the sharing of the modulation configuration in as many acoustic functions as the original instrument provides. The synthesis is not produced by a juxtaposition of independent acoustic variables (as in additive synthesis), or by the modification of the independent data (as in subtractive synthesis, or synthesis by waveform). On the contrary, the procedure of synthesis by frequency modulation maintains the strict interdependence of each of the frequency generators, and their configuration can thus relate directly to the organology of the original instrument. To synthesize the sound of the xylophone, three frequency generators in series simulated the spectrum and the temporal envelope of the slats; another three generators simulated the acoustic behavior of the resonator—and, via feedback, that of its mirliton (figure 5).

This synthesis is thus evolutive and operative:

FIGURE 5   For each xylophone, each chain of three frequency generators simulates the behavior of each slat and its resonator.

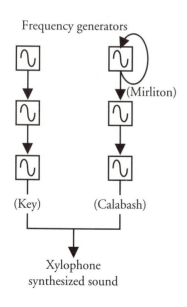

Frequency generators

(Mirliton)

(Key)   (Calabash)

Xylophone
synthesized sound

it can present a simple timbre, which may be rendered progressively more complex or more or less inharmonic, that is, with partials that deviate from harmonic relation;

it permits an association with the functions connected to the acoustic principles of the original instrument (thus, the musicians are familiar with the physical procedures involved in the synthesis);

it constitutes a basis of developments according to the musicians' actions or reactions.

Because the original sounds include inharmonic components (resulting in an ambiguous perception of pitch), the synthesized timbres must also contain inharmonicity. During the synthesis, we first created a purely harmonic timbre, of which we shifted each harmonic component, step by step. This shifting concerned essentially the position of the first harmonics, progressively displaced by a range of plus or minus 15 to 100 cents. With this displacement, the timbre became more and more inharmonic. The analytical difficulty lies in displacing the harmonics while simultaneously maintaining timbral fusion (Singh 1989), without changing parameters other than the harmonic ratios. The result of the synthesis was a collection of twelve more or less inharmonic timbres. At the first stage of the synthesis, we obtained the noise of the mirlitons (attached to the xylophone resonators) by adding white noise of several tenths of a millisecond, produced by strong overmodulation.

During experimentation, however, a Gbaya xylophone maker adjusted the intensity of individual harmonics, step by step, with the help of the synthesizer's cursor (figure 6). While the timbre created in this way showed little resemblance to the timbre of a real xylophone, the adjustments this musician made helped us understand more precisely the function of the mirliton. We had considered the device to be a simple noisemaker, but the xylophone maker's timbral manipulations revealed that the mirliton actually creates a harmonic vibration reinforcing that of the coupled slat resonator, insuring a quasi-harmonicity to the overall sound of the instrument. Since the mirlitons vibrate irregularly, we had not predicted this function.

In the course of research undertaken in 1991, the same xylophone maker helped

FIGURE 6   A Gbaya musician tunes up the DX7 synthesizer to his own instrument.

Contrary to what can be observed with the original instruments, musicians demanded that all slats of a single xylophone present a homogeneous timbre.

create a new sound synthesis. Frédéric Voisin incorporated his instructions and comments into the frequency-modulated synthesis. With successively finer adjustments to the timbre and tuning of each key, the musician finally achieved a result that satisfied him (figure 7).

The relevance of the acoustic properties created by these adjustments could be confirmed by other experimentations with musicians who rejected the alternation of two synthesized timbres intended to imitate the circumstance in which the mirliton is not vibrating consistently. Contrary to what can be observed with the original instruments, in fact, musicians demanded that all slats of a single xylophone present

FIGURE 7   A Banda-Gbambyia musician selects tone colors on the DX7 synthesizer.

a homogeneous timbre. Furthermore, their optimal judgment of the correctness of the tuning presented to them occurred when all the slats of the xylophone were close to the ideal timbre obtained by synthesis. Before the new timbre could serve as the basis of experiments with other Central African musicians, Voisin "touched it up," to render it more authentic. He thus avoided the risk that a synthesized timbre slightly different from the real sounds would make the procedure difficult for musicians unfamiliar with the experimental situation.

The importance of a temporal evolution of the spectral envelope in the recognition of the test timbres has been frequently demonstrated. The method of synthesis here under examination consisted in recovering the most clearly synthesized timbre, and in preserving its entire spectral structure, while attributing to this structure the temporal envelope of the sound of a real xylophone, correctly regulated. Digitally sampling the original sound effected this operation, from which we extracted the traits relevant to the envelope; we then imposed these traits on the spectral structure of the synthesized sound. The result was a sound comprised of few parameters (therefore easily modelable), perceptively indistinguishable from the original. The traits of this sound are

a quasi-harmonic spectral structure;

a large number of harmonics (more than twelve);

an almost constant intensity of harmonics (rather than the more usual configuration, with the intensity of harmonics inversely proportional to a harmonic's ranking);

stable fundamental frequencies;

an envelope that, following the attack transients of the initial vibration (20 ms), is similar to that of a sound of about 200 ms.

In light of these traits, Central African xylophones set up a paradox: though they are percussive, their timbre is sustained, much like that of wind instruments. Only the attack evidences the impulse that starts the vibrations.

Digital sampling

Another technology that can be applied to this type of experimental research is digital sound sampling, which allows the faithful restitution of the original sound of the instruments under study. In 1990, Peter Cooke used this technique to study the perception of pitch in Uganda; and in 1992, our team used it in the Central African Republic. Once the technique has been mastered, it is possible to sample traditional instruments, and then to resynthesize their sounds (on a keyboard, or on another device, usually a MIDI), enabling indigenous musicians to play the sampled and resynthesized sounds on the synthesizer's keyboard.

Unlike the process of synthetic analysis, digital sampling does not require a timbral modeling of the original instruments: the sound is reproduced exactly in the image of the original sound, so the parameters that are culturally pertinent to the perception of timbre and pitch are difficult to isolate. Because the exact pitch of the sampled sound remains unknown, however, it must be tested by an equivalent pitch—by synthesis.

Though the method gives little help in determining the pitch of the original sound, it can contribute to the study of scalar systems. Once sampled, an original sound can be submitted to analysis and modification on the computer. It can be filtered, mixed with other sounds, and transposed; it can be used as an element of further synthesis. For an experimental study of the culturally relevant features of timbre in various musical traditions, researchers can alter or elaborate a hybrid sound com-

cents Measurement of intervals based on the division of the octave into 1,200 equal parts

equipentatonic scale Pitch inventory with five equally spaced pitches to the octave

mɔbeke Whistle played by the Aka of the Central African Republic

posed of sampled and synthesized elements. One might create a sound in which the attack is obtained by synthesis, while the decay is sampled, and so on. By isolating different timbral parameters, researchers can measure the effect of timbre on perception. This kind of study is essential to understanding musicians' habits of listening. In African music, where percussive instruments predominate, it would be instructive to know whether musicians' perception of pitch privileges a sound's attack, its decay, or its whole duration.

Digital sampling also proves useful in verifying models created by synthesis. It eases an estimate of the distance separating a real timbre and its synthesized model, as in a task where musicians are to choose between a digitally sampled timbre and its synthesized equivalent. In 1992, we undertook such an experiment, with the help of a 16-bit digital sampler MIDI (Akaï S1000). After digitizing the sound of each slat of a xylophone, we proposed the sampled sounds to musicians in the same way as those synthesized earlier, and on the same prepared keyboard. To insure appropriateness between the sampled sounds and the musicians' expectations, the sampling took place in their presence and with their participation: their remarks helped us correct sampling errors that might have influenced their judgment. The next step was to elicit a comparison by exposing the musicians to the sampled sound of a xylophone under the same conditions as when they had heard the synthesized sound. Corroborating our synthesized timbres, they seemed to prefer the synthesized models to the sampled sounds, and they acknowledged that their own instruments often could be mistuned. This observation confirms the cultural relevance of the experimental context.

Scalar systems

Just as musicians preferred the timbres of modeled sounds to the original ones, so they preferred the models of tuning to the reproduction of the original tuning. They often reported that, when such-and-such a slat of their instrument was reproduced by synthesis or sampling, it "was not well tuned" (concerning pitch) or "sounded bad" (concerning timbre).

Beginning with less than ten hypothetical tunings (pentatonic, equipentatonic, harmonic series), subsequent missions by our team took samples of almost one hundred different tunings, submitted for judgment to the musicians of different communities. The consistency of response was reliable: even when the same series of tunings was proposed at intervals of several days, the contradiction rate of each musician did not exceed 6 percent.

Our experiments in the Central African Republic uncovered a scalar concept that relies on three sizes of constituent intervals—200, 240, and 280 cents, of which the variance does not exceed plus or minus 15 cents. Xylophone tuning rests on modalities combining these intervals, and differences of judgment among various ethnic groups seemed to occur with modalities of these combinations. Furthermore, all the queried musicians accepted equally a modal series containing a single interval of 240 cents, a perfect equipentatonic tuning (Voisin 1991, 1993, 1994; Dehoux and Voisin, 1992).

Equipentatonic tuning therefore appears to be a preferred system, common to the Central African ethnic groups visited: Ali, Azande, Banda, Banda Linda, Banda Mbiyi, Banda Ndokpa, Gbambiya, Gbaya, Manza, Ngbaka-Manza, Sabanga. The prevalence of the equipentatonic system would be difficult to establish if one were to use as evidence only xylophone tunings as they occur in Central Africa. Despite musicians' preference for synthetic equipentatonic tuning, they always tune their instruments using the three constituents mentioned above. Only by observing their tuning and retuning of the synthesized xylophones (precise within 10 cents) were we able to discover their tendency toward an equipentatonic pattern.

Given our observations in the field, we might say that an equipentatonic model transcends the reality of Central African xylophone tuning, and thus corresponds to a conceptual ideal.

The usefulness of video

The experimental procedure described above produces varied and complex data. For exhaustive analysis, we recommend that it be integrally filmed. From the initial development of hypotheses and presuppositions, to the musicians' forming of reactions and commentaries, visual documentation lets researchers retrace the heuristic phases of the research.

Similarly, the video recorder eases analysis of the musicians' cognitive processes. Musicians' reaction time to a particular tuning model is an invaluable indicator of the distance separating the scalar (or timbral) hypothesis from indigenous conceptions of the scalar system. From videotaped evidence, we determined that musicians' reaction time is directly proportional to the model's conformity to their conceptions.

VOCAL MUSIC: THE POLYPHONY OF THE AKA

In the music of the Aka, the determination of musical scales faces the same problems as those related above. These problems, however, take on a special interest in Aka polyphony because the music is essentially vocal. It has a percussive instrumental accompaniment (drums and machetes), whose function is purely rhythmic; melodic instruments participate in only a few circumstances, intimately associated with the voice. We tried to apply interactive experimental methodology to the study of the scales used in the vocal polyphony of these people, who reside in the southwest of the Central African Republic (Arom and Fürniss 1992; Fürniss 1991, 1992).

Viewed in the context of unaccompanied polyphony, the experimentation could not proceed as it had with xylophones. It was impossible to ask the Aka to reproduce on an electronic device the complexity of their vocal polyphony. We had no choice but to program on a sequencer (hardware or software that uses a digital device to record or play a musical score) polyphonies previously transcribed by Arom and Fürniss. To Aka musicians, we could then play these pieces back, in new versions, each corresponding to a theoretical model of a musical scale. Because of the difficulty of synthesizing the timbre of a sung voice, we decided to synthesize the transcribed polyphony with the timbre of little whistles (*mọbeke*), readily familiar to the Aka. Their recognition of this timbre, and the explanation of the experimental procedure in which the Aka were to participate, constituted a long initiation directed toward indigenous understanding of the purpose of the research. It was necessary, in essence, to make the Aka accept that a machine could sing, in several parts, with the sound of a whistle. Only when they had learned to recognize that the machine was executing their own songs, voice by voice, could the experiment begin.

pentatonic scale   Pitch inventory with five pitches to the octave

anhemitonic scale   Pitch inventory with no half steps or minor seconds within the octave

The experimental protocol consisted of asking the Aka to judge the rightness of two looped polyphonic fragments, realized according to ten musical scales (pentatonic, anhemitonic, equipentatonic, harmonic series). Contrary to our expectation, they judged all of the proposed scales to be good: to the extent they were in an unfamiliar position (passively listening to music they were accustomed to perform), the procedure was unable to determine the nature and size of the constituent intervals of the polyphony.

On a second try, we initiated another experimental protocol, which allowed the Aka musicians to be active—to sing with the synthesizer. This procedure combined the analytic technique of rerecording with synthetic simulation of the polyphony: the sequencer and the synthesizer produced a referential part, using diverse scales for each musician, who could sing while listening with earphones to the referential part. In this way, the referential part and the singer's part were separately realized as simultaneous recordings made on different tracks of a tape. The analysis of these recordings (which can be doubled on video), gives researchers access to the singers' reactions to the synthesized scales.

This type of experimentation is no more conducive to precise measurement of intervals than exposing the Aka to looped polyphonic fragments. Though rerecording allowed the Aka to participate actively, singers could not refer to other vocal parts—which (to determine intonations, voice placement, and the accurateness of vocal pitches) in a traditional performance they might do. Rather, they had to judge their intonation according to synthesized parts, whose timbre differed drastically from that of the voice: it is suitable, then, to disregard as irrelevant vocally produced variations of less than a semitone. Though at this stage of the research we had difficulty determining the nature of Aka musical scales, we observed that the equipentatonic system seemed the most comfortable fit for their intonation. Aka singers quickly recognized it, and consistently gave signs of approval (Fürniss 1992), which we took for indications of the relevance of the interval sizes in their scalar system.

We then revised our experimental method. For scales used earlier, we substituted polyphonic fragments of modes (five pentatonic, one equipentatonic). This revision led us to realize that the Aka conception of polyphony emphasizes melodic contours over individual intervals. Thus, a minor third and a major second can be substituted for their respective inversions, but only in certain positions of the song cycle. The positions that do not permit substitution become the harmonic pivot points of fifths, fourths, and octaves (Fürniss 1992).

PERSPECTIVES

Recourse to new musical technology in an experimental context lets traditional musicians materialize mental templates of their culture's scalar system, the ideally tuned scale. In tasks requiring comparative judgment, musicians demonstrate the same search for perfection. The best synthesized models of timbre and tuning are often judged better than the sounds of the instruments originally sampled—and in such a situation, musicians admit that their instruments "are not perfectly well tuned." It is therefore important to consider this: *the original instruments are not a faithful reflection of the concept (abstract and ideal) of the scale; they are only an actualization of this concept.* Musicians find themselves at the center of experimentation, necessarily with a perspective geared to model construction as much as researchers. Musicians can distinguish between their ideal concept and its musical realization. In this situation, the electronic device becomes not only an experimental tool, but also a privileged nexus, a place where musicians project a virtual and conceptual reality.

In this sense, then, technology aids theory. The carriers of diverse musical traditions can express and explicate their knowledge without having to rely solely on words. The task of researchers must be to adapt technology to the theoretical universe of societies under study, to choose (according to this universe) the medium most successful at transmitting the information, and to account for the consistency of this information through modeling. The interaction between musicians and researchers necessitates simulating traditional musical practice as fully as possible: slats of wood fixed to the keyboard of the synthesizer act to resemble those of the xylophone. Many musical instruments can be equipped with MIDI-captors, permitting a digitized treatment of traditional techniques of playing. Thus, each traditional instrument can potentially fill the same functions as the digital instruments.

The rapidity of the evolution of musical technology, especially its miniaturization, betokens the introduction of experimental research into most ethnomusicological domains, thus allowing the discipline to contribute a comparative dimension to the cognitive sciences. The learning of music, perceptual mechanisms, conceptual representation, and even relations between concept and realization, are implicit in a culture's musical activity. Experimental data on these subjects may advance the development of formalized systems of knowledge (such as artificial intelligence), and the study of psychophysiological phenomena.   —TRANSLATED BY CORNELIA FALES

REFERENCES

Arom, Simha. 1976. "The Use of Play-Back Techniques in the Study of Oral Polyphonies." *Ethnomusicology* 20(3):483–519.

Arom, Simha, and Susanne Fürniss. 1992. "The Pentatonic System of the Aka Pygmies of the Central African Republic." *European Studies in Ethnomusicology: Historical Developments and Recent Trends*, ed. Max Peter Baumann et al., 159–173. Wilhelmshaven: Florian Noetzel. Intercultural Music Studies, 4.

————. 1993. "An Interactive Experimental Method for the Determination of Musical Scales in Oral Cultures: Application to the Vocal Music of the Aka Pygmies of Central Africa." *Contemporary Music Review* 9:7–12.

Baumann, Max Peter, et al. 1992. *European Studies in Ethnomusicology: Historical Developments and Recent Trends.* Wilhelmshaven: Florian Noetzel. Intercultural Music Studies, 4.

Blacking, John. 1959. "Problems of Pitch, Pattern and Harmony in the Ocarina Music of the Venda." *African Music* 21(2):15–29.

Cooke, Peter. 1970. "Ganda Xylophone Music: Another Approach." *African Music* 4(4):62–80.

————. 1990. "Report on Pitch Perception Carried Out in Buganda and Busoga (Uganda) August 1990." *ICTM Study Group* 33:2–6.

Dehoux, Vincent, and Frédéric Voisin. 1992. "Analytic Procedures with Scales in Central African Xylophone Music." *European Studies in Ethnomusicology: Historical Developments and Recent Trends*, ed. Max Peter Baumann et al., 174–188. Wilhelmshaven: Florian Noetzel. Intercultural Music Studies, 4.

————. 1993. "An Interactive Experimental Method for the Determination of Musical Scales in Oral Cultures: Application to the Xylophone Music of Central Africa." *Contemporary Music Review* 9:13–19.

Ellis, Alexander. 1885. "On the Musical Scales of Various Nations." *Journal of the Royal Society of Arts* 33:485–527.

Ellis, Alexander, and Alfred Hipkins. 1884. "Tonometrical Observations on Some Existing Non-Harmonic Scales." *Proceedings of the Royal Society* 37:368–385.

Fürniss, Susanne. 1991. "Recherches scalaires chez les Pygmées Aka." *Analyse Musicale* 23:31–35.

————. 1992. "Le Système pentatonique de la musique des Pygmées Aka (Centrafrique)." Thèse de Doctorat, Université de Paris-III.

Hornbostel, Erich M. von. 1917. "Gesänge aus Ruanda." In *Wißenschaftliche Ergebnisse der deutschen Zentral-Afrika-Expedition 1907–1908*, 6, part 1, ed. Jan Czekanowski.

————. 1928. "African Negro Music." *Africa* 1(1):30–62.

Jairazbhoy, Nazir. 1977. "The 'Objective' and Subjective View in Music Transcription." *Ethnomusicology* 21(2):263–273.

Jones, Arthur M. 1959. *Studies in African Music.* Oxford: Oxford University Press.

————. 1963. "Experiment with a Xylophone Key." *African Music* 3(2):8–11.

————. 1970. "On Using the Stroboconn." *African Music* 4(4):122–124.

Kubik, Gerhard. 1961. "The Structure of Kiganda Xylophone Music." *African Music* 2(3):6–30.

————. 1964. "Recording and Study in North Moçambic." *African Music* 3(3):90–93.

————. 1965. "Transcription of Mangwilo Xylophone Music from Film Strips." *African Music* 3(4):36–41.

————. 1970. *Natureza e estrutura de escalas musicais africanas,* trans. João de Freitas Branco. Lisbon: Estudos de antropologia cultural, 3.3.

————. 1983. "Kognitive Grundlagen." *Musik in Africa,* ed. Artur Simon, 327–400. Berlin: Museum für Völkerkunde, Staatliche Museum Preussischer Kulturbesitz.

Kunst, Jaap. 1949. *Music in Java: Its History, Its Theory and Its Technique,* 2nd ed., trans. Emile van Loo. The Hague: Nijhoff.

————. 1974. *Ethnomusicology.* The Hague: Nijhoff.

List, George. 1974. "The Reliability of Transcription." *Ethnomusicology* 18(3):353–377.

————. 1969. "Sur les xylophones équihepta-toniques des Malinké." *Revue de Musicologie* 55(1):47–77.

Schneider, Albrecht. 1990. "Psychological Theory and Comparative Musicology." In *Comparative Musicology and Anthropology of Music,* ed. Bruno Nettl and Philip Bohlman, 293–317. Chicago: University of Chicago Press.

Schneider, Albrecht, and A. Beurmann. 1993. "Notes on the Acoustics and Tunings of Gamelan Instruments." In *Performance in Java and Bali: Studies of Narrative, Theatre, Music and Dance,* ed. B. Arps, 197–218. London: School of Oriental and African Studies, University of London.

Singh, Punita G. 1989. "Interaction of Timbre and Pitch in Spectral Discrimination Tasks Using Complex Tones." Paper presented to the annual meeting of the Acoustical Society of America.

Stone, Ruth, and Verlon Stone. 1981. "Event, Feedback, and Analysis: Research Media in the Study of Music Events." *Ethnomusicology* 25(2): 215–225.

Thomas, J. M. C. 1989. "Des noms et des couleurs." In *Graines de Paroles: Écrits pour G. Calame-Griaule.* Paris: Éditions du CNRS.

Tracey, Hugh. 1958. "Towards an Assessment of African Scales." *African Music* 2(1):15– 23.

Voisin, Frédéric. 1991. "La modélisation des systèmes d'accords des xylophones centrafricains." *Analyse Musicale* 23:42–47.

————. 1993. "L'accord des xylophones des Gbaya et Manza de Centrafrique: de l'expérimentation à la modélisation." Master's thesis, L'École des Hautes Études en Science Sociale, Paris.

————. 1994. "Musical Scales in Central Africa and Java: Modeling by Synthesis." *Leonardo Music Journal* 4:85–90.

Wachsmann, Klaus P. 1950. "An Equal-Stepped Tuning in a Ganda Harp." *Nature* 165.

————. 1957. "A Study of Norms in the Tribal Music of Uganda." *Ethnomusicology Newsletter,* p. 11.

Tumbuka Healing
Steven Friedson

Healing as Musical Experience
To Dance One's Disease
The Disease of the Prophets
Diagnostic Technology
Musical Experience of Clinical Reality
Making Music Together

FIGURE 1   To enact a divinatory trance, the Tumbuka healer Nchimi Ziloya "dances her disease."

For Tumbuka-speaking peoples of northern Malawi, musical experience is the structural nexus where healer, patient, and spirit meet. The din of the drum, the clapping of the choir, the responsorial singing, the noise of trance dancing, the jangle of tin belts and iron anklets—all contribute to the creation of an auditory field inside the diviner-healer's temple, the locus of a sacred clinical reality.

A "clinical practice (traditional and modern) occurs in and creates particular social worlds" (Kleinman 1980:38). These worlds, each a life world (*lebenswelt*), make up ethnomedical systems, but are not synonymous with them (Schutz 1973). Particular health-care systems may have many distinct clinical realities. Among the Tumbuka, the clinical reality met when a person consults a local herbalist (*sing'anga*) differs from that experienced inside a diviner-healer's temple (*thempli*). Specialization of healers in non-Western medical systems usually revolves around the distinction between diviners and herbalists (Foster and Anderson 1978:101–122). Both differ completely from the clinical reality experienced when one utilizes the services of Western-style hospitals and clinics, which also appear in northern Malawi.

In missionary and government hospitals and clinics, as for herbalists, music is not a part of diagnostic or therapeutic procedures. At the compound of a diviner-healer (*nchimi* 'prophet'), however, a musical context often frames the clinical reality. At all-night sessions, patients experience both diagnostics and therapeutics through singing, drumming, and dancing. It is within a phenomenal field of music that Tumbuka encounter the *vimbuza* 'spirits' in their full, existential reality; it is where both patient and healer "dance their disease" (*kuvina nthenda*) (figure 1).

Vimbuza—a multivocalic word, a complex of meanings and references—encompasses a class of spirits, the illness they cause, and the music and dance used to treat the illness. As spirit, *vimbuza* is the numinous energy of foreign peoples and wild animals; as illness, it is both a spirit affliction and an initiatory sickness; as musical experience, it is a source of musical heat. For patients afflicted by spirits, heating the spirits through music is, paradoxically, a cooling therapy; for adepts, it is the means of transforming a disease into a vocation; and for healers, it is an energizing heat, which fuels the trance of divination, the prime diagnostic procedure in the traditional sector of the Tumbuka health-care system.

Through music, with its resultant trance, Tumbuka
have the possibility of experiencing the present—and
hence, each other—in complete "fulfillness."

These aspects of Tumbuka healing—initiatory illness, diagnostic technology, dance therapy—are the ethnographic focus. My concern is with the phenomenology of these experiences. By using the term *musical experience*, I include under "musical" the full multimedia phenomena that are the reality of performed diagnoses and therapeutic dance; under the rubric of "experience," I follow Turner's (1982, 1986) sense of Dilthey's (1976, 1985) term *erlebnis* 'lived experience', which connotes a bounded or framed temporal process—in Tumbuka healing, musical experience that shapes clinical processes.

Turner distinguishes between general experience ("simply the passive endurance and acceptance of events") and particular experience, which "stands out from the evenness of passing hours and years" (1986:35). Lived experiences have determinate beginnings and endings—a "structure of experience" (Dilthey, quoted in Turner 1986:35.). *Vimbuza*, as an episode of illness, is such an experience. It has a definite beginning, which stands out from quotidian life: the onset of socially defined and recognized symptoms, in Turner's model of social drama (1974:38–42, 1982:215–221) the breach leading to the crisis. Continuing with Turner's model, this usually leads to redressive action, involving therapeutic intervention, which includes musical activity in the form of trance dancing. And finally, *vimbuza* affliction culminates in three possible outcomes: (1) reintegration, a cessation of dysfunctional symptoms; (2) irremediable schism, a failure of therapy, which may result in death; (3) transformation, which for those who are afflicted by the special form of *vimbuza* known as *nthenda ya uchimi* 'disease of the prophets', changes ordinary Tumbuka, both men and women, into diviner-healers.

The progression of events of the overall episode of illness from breach to outcome in *vimbuza* affliction is an experience in Turner's sense. However, as there are multiple clinical realities, there are also specific experiences, with their own beginnings and endings, discernible in each phase. Here, I am interested in the "musical construction of clinical reality" (Kleinman 1980:35), experienced in the redressive phase of healing.

In work on Ndembu rituals of affliction, Turner (1968) has dealt extensively with the symbolic import of this phase of social drama; however, he has not paid as close attention to surface phenomena, where the people foreground and experience the performative modes of music and dance. Though the Ndembu call their rituals of affliction drums (*ng'oma*), Turner never elaborates on musical material as he does with matrilineal kinship, the symbolic meaning of trees, or the sociological implications of witchcraft accusations. Yet for *vimbuza*, and probably for Ndembu healing, it is at this phenomenological level that the immediate structuring of clinical experience occurs. The basis for my description of the clinical reality of *vimbuza* is precisely the lived experience of foregrounded modes of performance.

Lived experience is "not given to me" (Dilthey 1985:223) as an object of reflection, something that points beyond itself. It is "there-for-me" in immediacy, before distinctions—between act and content, subject and object—that characterize representational consciousness (Dilthey 1989:26). Musical experience is reflexive, not reflective:

> There is no duality of lived experience and music, no double world, no carry-over from one into the other. Genius involves simply living in the tonal sphere as though this sphere alone existed. (Dilthey 1985:17)

Dilthey is discussing here the genius of a composer in the Western art music tradition, but he might as well be describing the experience of trance in *vimbuza*, for here the "genius" of Tumbuka music is most evident. This is the genius, not of an individual, but of a people. For Tumbuka gathered inside a temple, making music together is an intersubjective experience, which brings healer, patient, and spirit into an existential immediacy unparalleled in quotidian or ritual life. Through music, with its resultant trance, Tumbuka have the possibility of experiencing the present—and hence, each other—in complete "fulfillness."

Through lived experience, reflexive awareness gives a direct access to the world: "lived experience provides the basis for religion, art, anthropology, and metaphysics" (Dilthey 1985:223)—and to these, I add the healing arts, wherever they are found. I offer the following description as an example of musical experience in a clinical context—a phenomenon widespread in African ethnomedical systems.

HEALING AS MUSICAL EXPERIENCE

To state that music and healing are universal human experiences is to state the obvious; all cultures have some kind of music, and every society has developed ways of coping with sickness. The extent, depth, and complexity of interaction between these phenomena varies across cultures and ethnomedical systems. Musical experience in clinical settings can be as superficial as a Western surgeon listening to Mozart while performing surgery, or as intricate and complex as the musical interaction that takes place between a Tumbuka healer and his patient. One experience speaks to the almost total separation of music and healing in Western medical praxis. (The subdiscipline of music therapy is peripheral to mainstream Western medical practice; for Western medicine practiced in Africa, it is virtually nonexistent.) The other experience speaks to the near universality of music and healing in Africa.

In Western society, which reduces music to "the secondary realms of 'art,' 'entertainment,' and occasional 'religious music'" (Ellingson 1987:163), it is sometimes difficult for people to appreciate the significance of musical phenomena in a clinical context. Music is not part of the biomedically driven, clinical reality encountered in Western-style doctors' offices, clinics, and hospitals. Muzak may be piped into a doctor's waiting room, but its sounds have nothing to do with clinical practice, let alone an active musical experience.

In contrast, Africans approach healing through music and dance. Azande "witch doctors" eat special divinatory medicines, activated by drumming, singing, and dancing (Evans-Pritchard 1937:148–182). In northern Nigeria among the Hausa, the sounds of the *garaya* (two-stringed plucked lute) and *buta* (gourd rattle) call the divine horsemen of the sacred city of Jangare to descend into the heads of *bòorii* adepts, thus healing the people they have made sick (Besmer 1983). Similarly, the various *orisha* (Bascom 1944; Barber 1981) and *vodoun* (Herskovits 1938) spirits of the Guinea Coast, called by their particular drum motto, mount their horses (possess their devotees). The resultant spirit-possession dance, though religious in nature, is in the first instance often a therapy for those afflicted by the same spirits. Spirit affliction is healed through music and dance in Ethiopia and Sudan, wherever *zār* cults

Vimbuza are the spirits, not only of foreign peoples, but possibly also of animals.

occur (Boddy 1989; Lewis 1971). For the coastal Swahili-speaking peoples of East Africa, it is the *shetani* spirits who possess and afflict (Gray 1969); and for the Tonga of Zambia (Colson 1969) and the Shona of Zimbabwe (Gelfand 1964), it is the foreign *mashave*—a class that includes spirits as diverse as lion, European, guitar, airplane. Central, southern, and parts of equatorial Africa have examples of the *ng'oma* type of healing complex (Janzen 1991; Turner 1968), whose name (*ng'oma,* which can mean many things, including 'drum') points to the centrality of music in curative rites. In North Africa, members of the Hamadsha brotherhood obtain the healing power of *baraka* by a dance of self-mutilation, which itself is a meditation on Allah (Crapanzano 1973). At the other end of the continent, in perhaps one of the oldest forms of music and healing in Africa, !Kung bushmen dance to boil their *num,* the source of an energy that heals both individual and group (Katz 1982; Marshall 1969).

In each of these cases (and these are only a few of the documented ones), people experience sickness and healing through rituals of "consciousness-transformation" (Ellingson's term), whose experiential core is musical. And while ethnographers often interpret these types of experience as religious, the types, nonetheless, are part of long-standing indigenous health-care practices.

The phenomenal reality of music, trance, and healing in Africa, in fact, is hard to split into neatly defined classes of Western epistemological thought, such as religion and medicine. Trance that involves spirits is inherently religious, at least according to E. B. Tylor's minimal definition of the term (1920:424); yet in many instances, this kind of trance implies issues of sickness and health. In traditional African societies, religion and healing form an amalgam that is often functionally irreducible into constituent parts.

For the Tumbuka, though there is a substantial religious component, both traditional and Christian (most diviner-healers incorporate highly syncretic models in their healing), the pragmatic health-care aspect of music is continually foregrounded in *vimbuza.* Encountering spirits through music and dance is not so much a religious experience (as it possibly is for a Yoruba possessed by Shango), but a means of controlling spiritual energy for specific therapeutic and diagnostic purposes.

TO DANCE ONE'S DISEASE

The Tumbuka are a patrilineal people. Most of them, as farmers, depend on seasonal rains. Traditionally, they have had a decentralized society, based on the autonomy of heterogeneous clans. A system of village headmen, subchiefs, and chiefs (native authorities)—a vestige of British colonial rule—is in place; however, on a day-to-day basis, the clan group remains the functional sector of society. People live in extended family compounds, which usually consist of brothers and other patrikin. Each man owns a garden, from which he feeds his family, and in which he sometimes grows surplus produce, to raise funds for school fees, plus what people consider necessities: processed sugar, salt, soap.

These Bantu-speakers migrated to northern Malawi some three hundred to four hundred years ago (Vail 1972:153), and settled in "an ancient crossroads of Africa" (Wilson 1972:136). As a result, the Tumbuka have had a long history of contact with different cultures and societies. The spirits are, in many respects, a living history of these contacts.

The coming of ivory traders across Lake Malawi (in the eighteenth century), the migratory movement of Bemba-speaking peoples from Zambia, the invasion of the Ngoni (in the 1850s), and even the arrival of Europeans (in the late nineteenth century), have entered the pantheon of spirits. The spirits of the Ngoni "come out" in the *vimbuza* dance of *vyanusi*, and the spirit wind (*mphepo*) of the *ßalawoka* (the first group of traders from the east) manifests itself through the spirits of *ßaMwera*. The term *vyanusi* derives from Ngoni *izanusi* 'those who smell'; *izanusi* were Ngoni diviners and witch smellers (Read 1956:180–181). *Nchimi* appropriated many of the practices of the *izanusi*. One of the spirits not to actualize itself in dance is *mzungu* (European)—perhaps because dancing is not part of the Tumbuka's perception of Scottish missionaries and British government officials. *Vimbuza* are never the spirits of individuals, but are entire ethnic groups. What they have in common is their foreignness to the Tumbuka: they are the spiritual embodiment of "the other."

The translation of foreign groups into spiritual energy, with resultant affliction and therapy, can be seen as one mechanism by which the Tumbuka coped with cultural change. Events that were beyond the control of the Tumbuka became pacified, at least spiritually, through *vimbuza*. In a discussion of the "enlargement of scale," with which people in Central African societies had to deal, Terence O. Ranger and John Weller reach a similar conclusion:

> People had to deal with a wide variety of aliens—as raiders, or caravan porters, or trading partners. A first step to dealing with them seems often to have been the creation of a dramatic stereotype, expressing what were held to be the essential qualities of the alien group, and acted out through rituals of spirit possession. (1975:7)

The spirits are much more than a coping mechanism; but, for a full understanding of the phenomenon, scholars cannot ignore their historical implications. Virtually every people with which the Tumbuka have come in sustained contact have left their imprint on Tumbuka society through spirit possession, including the autochthonous population the Tumbuka first encountered in northern Malawi. These are possibly the original spirits, though no one is clear on this point.

Vimbuza are the spirits, not only of foreign peoples, but possibly also of animals. People attribute spirituality, not to domestic animals (such as goats or chickens), but to wild animals, which have the quality of foreignness. In comparison to the multitude of human spirits, animal spirits play a decidedly minor role. The lion, however, is considered one of the most powerful: *nkharamu*, as it is called, plays an important part in healing; during episodes of possession, it is one of the few spirits that can become seriously violent, wanting to kill people.

Vimbuza, whether the spirits of animals or of human beings, are the only spirits that can possess an individual. While the other major class of spirits, the ancestral *mizimu* (pl.), may come to people in dreams, and are an important element in healers' trance, only foreign spirits can enter a person's body. For the Tumbuka, the crossing of the boundaries of the physical body is not a symbolic gesture, but an existential reality. The belief that foreign spirits, not ancestral ones, possess individuals extends to other peoples of this part of Africa. Of the Bantu-speaking peoples of

The illness itself is caused by the fact that the spirits have not come out. It is in this sense that Tumbuka say the afflicted must "dance their disease."

South Africa, most "do not believe that the ancestors 'possess' a man. They say: *amathongo a hamba nomuntu*, 'the spirits accompany a man,' i.e. control him and sometimes speak through him, but the spirits are not thought to possess a man, as does the alien spirit among the Shangana-Tonga" (Hoernle 1937:231).

Vimbuza-caused illness emanates from this state of possession. The Tumbuka believe that health is, in part, a result of a balance in the body between hot and cold. When a spirit enters a person's body, it can upset this balance, causing an excess of heat, which results in illness. The Tumbuka give no explanation for why spirits possess someone; they consider spirits capricious, opportunistic, envious of the living.

Spiritual affliction may take virtually any form: headaches, infertility, malaise, death. As long as the spirits dwell in the physical body in a heated state and do not come out, they cause suffering. By intensifying the heat, music pushes the spirit up, past a critical threshold, causing a state of possession trance, in which the spirit expends energy, and thus cools off.

Most illnesses that result from spirit possession are not caused by the "radical discontinuity of the ego" (Bourguignon 1976:13). Possession trance, in this sense, usually occurs during treatment, when spirits take over the patient's personality, experiencing the world of the living through the *vimbuza* dance. The illness itself is caused by the fact that the spirits have not come out. It is in this sense that Tumbuka say the afflicted must "dance their disease."

For patients possessed by spirits, music is more than a structuring of clinical experience: it is clinical reality. Afflicted patients usually sit with their head almost touching the drum, when they begin to heat the spirits within them. The sound of the drums initially calls forth the spirits, and thus drumming permits a diagnosis of spirit affliction. While a diviner-healer may learn that spirits are the cause of illness, he cannot tell precisely which spirits are in play. Only through drumming can he make a diagnosis, and ultimately through drumming do these spirits come into a beneficial relationship to those who are afflicted. Spirits are not exorcised, but accommodated.

The Tumbuka have a theory of correspondence that relates spiritual energy to modes of drumming. Gilbert Rouget (1985:67) uses the term *motto* for roughly the same musical phenomenon, but I believe *mode* imparts more of the motivic improvisatory nature of the drumming, and hence its reality. If the drumming matches a spirit that is possessing the patient, the spirits will heat up and come out to "play with their children"—to dance. Only the rhythmic mode of *vyanusi* will heat the spirits of the Ngoni, and transform ordinarily shy young women into spearwielding Ngoni warriors. Similarly, only the rhythms of *nkharamu*, with a distinctive combination of open and stopped strokes, will call forth the lion's spirit wind, which brings both the threat of violence, and the blessing of divinatory power.

Multiple spirits are almost always involved in *vimbuza* possession, and through music and dance, each spirit must receive its due. In a typical session of trance dancing, four or five spirits will sequentially manifest themselves in the dancer's body. Patients will usually dance for an hour or two, while healers often dance throughout the night, seemingly gaining strength from the action.

Vimbuza dancing is directly tied to the rhythmic structure of drumming. The sound and the motion are not independent phenomenal streams, but are multilayered and intricately interrelated. Most of the dancing centers on a distinctive movement, which involves shaking the hips in rhythm with the lead drumming patterns. The patient usually does the hip shaking in a stationary position, with the ball of the foot in contact with the ground, and the heel being moved up and down in time to the drums. This movement is partly aimed at sounding iron jingles (*nyisi*), tied around the waist and ankles. Patients also wear a skin or cloth skirt (*mazamba*), cut into many thin strips. These paraphernalia enhance both the visual movement of the dance (the skirt sways to the movements of the hips), and transform movement into sound through the strategic placement of the idiophones. The jingles around the ankles give sound to the rhythmic movement of the feet, and a belt worn around the waist (*mang'wanda*) adds a loud and distinctive timbre. These idiophones transform the dancer's body into a musical instrument. The *vimbuza* modes are not music accompanying dance, or dance accompanying music, but a kinetic system (Kubik 1979:227).

In the initial stages of therapy, music often produces an uncontrolled state of possession, which results in an amnesic experience. People do not dance to become possessed by the spirits: they dance because they are possessed. These initial dance possessions can become wild, and handlers take precautions so dancers do not hurt themselves. Usually, within a short period (ranging from hours to weeks, depending on the patient), the possession trance settles into the culturally shaped movements of *vimbuza* dance. In Tumbuka terms, as the spirits become accustomed to experiencing the world through the dance, the disease matures (*kuvara*), as in the ripening of a fruit, and the dance begins to stabilize. The possession trance becomes socialized through spirit-specific music (Rouget 1985).

Once the disease becomes thoroughly stabilized, typically after a few months, preparations are then made for the most important ritual in the therapy, the *chilopa* 'blood sacrifice'. According to the Tumbuka, spirits want fresh blood, and if this desire is not satisfied through the drinking of blood from a sacrificial animal such as a goat or chicken, the spirits will start feasting on the blood of the afflicted, which could result in death. Similar ritual blood sacrifices occur throughout this part of Africa. The final ritual for a Zezuru medium of southern Zimbabwe is the drinking of fresh blood (Fry 1976:32); a similar ritual occurs for the Thonga of Mozambique afflicted by the "madness of the gods" (Junod 1962:479–493); for Zulu possessed by *indiki* spirits, sacrificing a goat is essential to therapy (Sibisi 1975:50–51); and blood sacrifice is part of therapy for the initiatory illness of Nguni *sangoma* healers (Hammond-Tooke 1955:18). In this kind of spirit possession, the drinking of fresh blood is basic to the healing process. Many of these rituals use the same terminology as the Tumbuka, and share other features that suggest either a common origin or previous contact. Though more research is needed before any definite conclusion can be reached, evidence points to a southeastern and southern Bantu-style affliction cult, differentiable from other spirit complexes, such as the divine horsemen of West Africa, or the *zār* cults of eastern and northern Africa.

THE DISEASE OF THE PROPHETS

For Tumbuka afflicted by spirits, the *chilopa* is the axial point of spirit possession; its outcome often determines whether afflicted persons will return to everyday life, or

chilopa   'Blood sacrifice'   *nchimi*   Diviner-healer among the Tumbuka

enter the world of prophet and healer. If after a *chilopa*, a patient's spirit cools to the point the patient becomes asymptomatic, treatment ends, at least for the foreseeable future, and the patient returns to normal life. This does not mean that the patient is cured; complete cures are nonexistent, for in the lives of the afflicted, *vimbuza* is an ongoing reality. Every other week, every other month, or every other year, the spirit may heat up, causing sickness. The califaction has no identifiable, set pattern; it varies with the individual: but when it occurs, to relieve the symptoms, the person will "dance the disease." In this way, *vimbuza* dancing takes on the form of maintenance therapy.

If, however, after the *chilopa*, the spirits (though cooler) stay sufficiently heated to produce symptoms, and the person begins to have the special dreams of the ancestors (*mizimu*), the patient has the disease of the prophets (*nthenda ya uchimi*), and is a new moon (*mutwasa*), with the potential to become an *nchimi*.

In northern Malawi, one does not choose to become a diviner-healer; one is chosen. The elect are called to their vocation—it is much more than a profession—through the special form of *vimbuza* affliction, the disease of the prophets. The illness takes on the basic form of an "initiatory sickness" (Eliade 1964:33); the person so afflicted will not get well until this calling is heeded. The transformation of sufferer into healer is a "remarkable characteristic in African drums of affliction" (Janzen 1992:210). One might question, however, how remarkable this trait is, since the concept of the wounded healer occurs in cultures throughout the world.

When spirit affliction takes this form, the person undergoes a long apprenticeship (usually from one to two years) with an established healer. This apprenticeship includes an extensive training in collecting and preparing herbal medicines, and, most importantly, learning how to access and control spiritual energy through the *vimbuza* dance.

During their initiatory sickness, most *nchimi* become possessed by the spirits, and, like ordinary Tumbuka afflicted by spirits, they dance, but do not remember. As their special illness matures, the dance changes, from a trance of spirit possession (with accompanying loss of memory), into the divinatory trance of seeing (*kuwona*), characterized by the conscious remembering of the dance experience. Healers state that when they dance, they recall the experience, and *must* remember, for if they did not, how would they know what was wrong with their patients, or how to heal them? During divination, the spirits are still activated ("heated," through drumming and singing), but their role in the trance changes from possessing spirit to a numinous source of energy.

This maturation of the disease, which in essence is the transformation from patient to healer, relates to the change in an adept's relationship to musical phenomena. When novices are brought before the drums, spirits fully absorb the psychic space; the experience is amnesic. But as adepts learn to focus their style of dancing, a "lucid form of possession" occurs, a kind of *verdoppelungerlebnis* 'consciousness doubling' (Oesterreich 1966), which involves the copresence of both person and spirit. Consciousness doubling is an essential part of divination, for without it a healer cannot "see."

The spirits, by themselves, however, are not sufficient to enact the divination trance. *Nchimi* need to incorporate the ancestral spirits to "see." The *mizimu* group into two subclasses: named ancestors (blood relatives who have died in the preceding few generations, usually grandparents and great-grandparents), and unnamed ancestors (who function as a kind of combined ancestral group). These are not rigidly defined classes, but logically blend into each other, as time elapses and named ancestors are forgotten. The *mizimu* do not possess a healer during the divination trance, but communicate within it. There is no consensus among healers about exactly how this occurs; however, the most common explanation is that a healer's ancestors contact the patient's *mizimu*. All agree that the *mizimu* do not possess people.

As long as the spirits fully possess the novice during the dance, people consider them to be too hot, and the *mizimu*, as it were, are shut out of the process. An important part of an adept's training to become a healer involves cooling the spirits enough to allow the *mizimu* to "go on top," so instead of possessing the dancer, the spirits act as a source of energy that pushes the *mizimu* up, to create the conditions necessary for "seeing." The *chilopa*, which sets the paradigm for the divination trance, achieves this configuration. For persons afflicted with the disease of the prophets, the drinking of blood cools the spirits just enough to let the *mizimu* "go on top."

In structuralist terms, the spirits are now in their correct alignment; the *mizimu* (read "culture") should be on top; the *vimbuza* (read "nature") should be on the bottom. The spirits represent foreign spiritual energy, and, as with nature, initially outside of cultural control; nature should serve culture, not the other way around. Before the drinking of blood, the spirits are, in a sense, overdetermined nature; in Tumbuka terms, they are overheated. Fulfilling the spirits' natural desire for blood within the culturally determined ritual of *chilopa* brings a helpful source of energy under the cultural control of the *nchimi*; it now fuels the divination trance. Significantly, in the final act of the *chilopa*, the *mizimu* are fed cooked meat from the sacrificial animal, further foregrounding nature-culture distinctions. The binary contrast of raw and cooked foods evokes comparisons with the ideas of Claude Lévi-Strauss (1969).

Nchimi do not have to drink blood (or eat cooked meat) every time they "see." Instead, the performance of music recreates the necessary conditions for divination. Music is a cultural artifact, yet, according to Tumbuka ideology, the music of *vimbuza* comes not from people (at least not from people in the flesh), but from spirits, through the dreams of those who are afflicted. Most diviner-healers report that in the first months of their initiatory illness, dreams are often filled with *vimbuza* songs, which usually form an important part of a diviner-healer's musical repertory. Through the spirits, music connects explicitly with nature. The seemingly incongruous position of music as flowing from both culture and nature is exactly what gives music such power in the *chilopa* and the divinatory trance. It is the prime mediator between nature and culture; it partakes of both man and spirit: it transforms the natural energy of the spirits into a culturally useful form.

In the musical time of *vimbuza*, the future, the past, and the present collapse, giving Tumbuka healers access to a wider and deeper world than that of their fellows. For *nchimi* who maintain a correct relationship to their spirits, divinatory trance reveals unparalleled knowledge. Through music and dance, they gain an opening to the world of the spirits. Within this opening, healers acquire the gift of "seeing."

Dancing is the public enactment of a healer's power and access to the spiritual realm. Much of what a healer achieves in his or her career is accomplished through the *vimbuza* dance, and much of what he or she becomes as a diviner-healer is a

Many *nchimi* relate the music to the batteries in radios: as batteries provide energy for radios to sound, so does music provide the energy for diviner-healers to "see."

result of being able to control the spiritual energy generated in the dance. In many respects, the gravitational center of the healing complex is the dance.

DIAGNOSTIC TECHNOLOGY

The Tumbuka world view embraces a theory of illness that postulates three etiologic agents: God, human beings, spirits. Illnesses said to be caused by God may be glossed as having a natural pathology; person-caused illnesses are disvalued states that occur as a result of witchcraft; and spirit-related illnesses are states that occur as a result of possession by spirits. According to Tumbuka theory, any of these agents may cause the same set of symptoms. Since different agents may produce identical symptoms, therapeutic intervention is initiated not according to the symptomatology that an illness presents, but according to which agent is responsible for the illness. Thus, treating someone for malarial symptoms is of little value when the real cause may be, not a mosquito bite, but the machinations of a witch, or the capriciousness of a spirit. Therefore, the divination trance, the diagnostic procedure nonpareil in Tumbuka society, is crucial to the efficacy of the entire indigenous health-care system. And since music and dance are the essential means to start and control the divination trance, they are part of an indigenous Tumbuka medical technology.

We do not usually associate such expressive aspects of culture as music and dance with technology, let alone a medical technology, but this is exactly how Tumbuka speak of *vimbuza* music. Many *nchimi* and lay Tumbuka relate the music to the batteries in radios: as batteries provide energy for radios to sound, so does music provide the energy for diviner-healers to "see." One produces electricity through chemical reactions, the other produces heat through music and dance. Both are technologies in the sense that they are cultural means—batteries with their characteristic chemical reactions are as much a cultural artifact as music and dance—of controlling energy for utilitarian purposes.

The first night I saw a diviner-healer dancing, I turned to the man next to me and asked what the dancer was doing. "He's X-raying the patients" was his reply. This brings up another metaphor, this time explicitly technological and medical in its associations. The divination trance is part of the health-care system of the Tumbuka, as X-rays are part of Western medical praxis: they both serve in diagnosis. They both "see," but in different ways, and sometimes for different purposes. The Westerner plugs in the machine; the Tumbuka play music. Metaphors are always abstractions; here, they are part of an indigenous theory about healing.

The status of music as part of an indigenous medical technology frames its phenomenological presence. This does not mean that healers and their patients do not experience an aesthetic dimension in the drumming and singing; but within this dimension of performance, the music becomes a numinously charged process, designed to summon and shape spiritual energy. In so doing, it becomes not merely a technology in terms of an instrumentality of means and ends, but a technology in

Heidegger's (1977) sense: a technology that reveals a world. The world that *vimbuza* music reveals, however, is of a different nature from the one revealed by battery-powered radios and other Western technology.

MUSICAL EXPERIENCE OF CLINICAL REALITY

When a patient enters a diviner-healer's temple, seeking answers to questions concerning illness and health, most of his or her time is structured directly through musical experience. People are not only patients, but also music makers, "musicants." Rouget (1985:103–107) distinguishes between "musicians" (professionals, whose sole purpose at ritual events is to make music), and "musicants" (usually adepts and spectators, whose "activity is to make music only episodically, or accessorily, or secondarily"). Though making music in the temple is much more than a "secondary phenomenon" (using Rouget's terminology for the performance of *vimbuza*), drummers are musicians and members of the choir (*kwaya*). Patients, considered members of the *kwaya*, are expected to sing and clap; in this way, they become active participants in their own therapy.

Universal participation is the ideal for *vimbuza* music—everyone inside the temple is expected to contribute to music making. This includes not only drumming (an activity open to any male who can correctly play the modes), but also the responsorial singing and clapping of patients and their relatives, who make up the *kwaya*. This ideal is never reached, but it does not negate the ethos of the experience. While drumming is the main musical means of heating the spirits, healers also need active musical participation from their patients. If the singing and clapping of the *kwaya* is not strong, *nchimi* will refuse to dance. Through music making, the healer, the patient, and the spirit, become true consociates, related specially to each other. By making music together, they bring their collective transactions into an intersubjective focus. Singer and dancer—patient and healer—are experiencing a common flow of musical time. The musical body of the dancer ties itself to the singing and clapping of the *kwaya*, and the rhythmic structure of the drumming relates directly to the dance.

This musical time has a specific rhythmic character, which directly affects lived experience; for those who gather in the temple, it has the power simultaneously to shape the flow of inner time and outer time. Art in general has "a particularly intense kind of contact" with that aspect of reality "where a unification of outer and inner experience takes place" (Dilthey 1985:21). In *vimbuza*, the rhythmic ratio of three to two, a hallmark of African music, connects patient-singer and healer-dancer (Brandel 1959; Jones 1959; Nketia 1974; Kauffman 1980). In the musical experience of *vimbuza*, rhythmic articulations of two pulses and three beats, and of three pulses and two beats, are always copresent in sound and motion. Shifting back and forth between movements based on these patterns, dancers create an intricate rhythmic gestalt of motion and sound. Some people in the *kwaya* confirm this gestalt by clapping in twos while others are clapping in threes. People freely shift between the beats; changing patterns of clapping is an individual decision. The drumming also reflects this rhythmic structure. A stream of steady pulses sounded on the *ng'oma* is articulated into phrases that, through timbral manipulation, shift between two- and three-beat configurations. Drummers continually shift between foreground-and-background relationships, based on this polymetrical structure. The free shifting of beats in dancing, clapping, and drumming suggests a fluid musical relationship. In turn, this fluidity affects the creation of a clinical reality that has sound and motion as its experiential parameters.

At this level of description, musical structure reveals itself as a kind of text, readable in terms of form. To create shifting rhythmical forms, twos and threes, even and

Within the acoustical and motional properties of singing, clapping, drumming, and dancing, people enter deep states of trance.

odd meters, are at all times copresent in the rhythmic structure of the music—sometimes overt, sometimes implicit, but always available to musicians and dancers. Music mediates the binary opposition of rhythms; in doing so, its structure becomes a paradigm. It artfully enhances human consciousness:

> There is a difference between music that is occasional and music that enhances human consciousness, music that is simply for having and music that is for being. I submit that the former may be good craftsmanship, but that the latter is art, no matter how simple or complex it sounds, and no matter under what circumstances it is produced. (Blacking 1973:50)

The art of *vimbuza* music can produce in the listener attuned to its rhythmic complexities a mode of being-in-the-world. Its musical time is fluid, yet stable; and its structure is conducive to the blurring of distinctions between subject and object—and between inner and outer time. The music can annihilate interpersonal distance, the distance between "I" (the people) and "thou" (the spirits), creating a concrete "we-relation" (Schutz 1973:63).

The visceral sensations of drumming felt in the chest, the social imperative to dance, the sheer intensity of singing—all contribute to a physical encounter with the aural reality of *vimbuza*. The music has a penetrating surroundability, which makes one feel pervaded by sound, both outside and inside. This phenomenon is not restricted to the present case:

> If I hear Beethoven's Ninth Symphony in an acoustically excellent auditorium, I suddenly find myself immersed in sound which surrounds me. The music is even so penetrating that my whole body reverberates and I may find myself absorbed to such a degree that [the] usual distinction between the senses of inner and outer is virtually obliterated. (Ihde 1976:75)

While this feature of music may not be present in every musical experience, it does raise the possibility that music has an inherent potential to produce this effect. For *vimbuza,* music is seductive. As the modes call out to the numinous, they simultaneously invite one in to give up one socially defined self for another, perhaps deeper, persona. In music, spirit and Tumbuka meet, and both are transformed.

MAKING MUSIC TOGETHER

The enactment of *vimbuza* is a special case of social interaction in Tumbuka culture—one that is transitory, repeatable, and affectively deep. In the community of healers, people regularly transform their consciousness, by their own account, through musical means. Within the acoustical and motional properties of singing, clapping, drumming, and dancing, people enter deep states of trance. The invisible spirits become visible in the bodily music of the trance dancer; and as visible presences, spirits and persons partake of the same experiential realm of sound and motion. The interior state of consciousness is not shared; it is not a group trance, as in Bali (Belo 1960). But those gathered inside a temple share, through an objective process, an intersubjective experience: making music together.

In Schutz's phenomenology of the *lebenswelt*, making music together is a particularly powerful example of prereflective social intercourse, involving "a mutual tuning-in process," a relationship that "originates in the possibility of living together simultaneously in specific dimensions of time" (1951:162). Following Bergson's concept of *durée* (the "form of existence of music"), Schutz conceives of musical experience as a pluridimensionality of inner time. This kind of musical passage cannot be quantified in clock time, nor is it merely the succession of abstract musical beats. It is a thick time, which allows consociates to share more than the inner *durée*, "in which the content of the music played actualizes itself; each, simultaneously, shares in vivid present the Other's stream of consciousness in immediacy" (1951:176). It both structures inner time, and is a "gearing into the outer world," which creates the possibility of an objective intersubjectivity between individuals.

Within musical intersubjectivity, the modes bring together the twos in the threes, and the threes in the twos; they mediate between the "I" and the "thou"; and through the *chilopa*, the modes bring into the correct relationship the energy of the *vimbuza* and the power of the *mizimu*. Music is the transformer of spiritual heat: it turns affliction by the spirits into the disease of the prophets; it is the means by which worlds reveal and construe themselves.

We are only beginning to understand the beneficial possibilities that an experience of this kind can have for clinical processes. These kinds of experience tend toward the liminal, between the numinous and the mundane, creating communitas, "a relational quality of all unmediated communication, even communion, between definite and determinate identities" (Turner and Turner 1978:25). In musically created liminality comes the possibility of a communitas that has the potential to release cultural forces of healing.

REFERENCES

Barber, Karin. 1981. "How Man Makes God in West Africa: Attitudes Towards the Orisa." *Africa* 51(3):724–745.

Bascom, William. 1944. "The Sociological Role of the Yoruba Cult Group." *American Anthropologist* 46:47–73.

Belo, Jane. 1960. *Trance in Bali.* New York: Columbia University Press.

Besmer, Fremont E. 1983. *Horses, Musicians, and Gods: The Hausa Cult of Possession-Trance.* Zaria, Nigeria: Ahmadu Bello University Press.

Blacking, John. 1973. *How Musical Is Man?* Seattle and London: University of Washington Press.

Boddy, Janice. 1989. *Wombs and Alien Spirits: Women, Men, and the Zar Cult in Northern Sudan.* Madison: University of Wisconsin Press.

Bourguignon, Erika. 1976. *Possession.* San Francisco: Chandler and Sharp.

Brandel, Rose. 1959. "The African Hemiola Style." *Ethnomusicology* 3:106–116.

Colson, Elisabeth. 1969. "Spirit Possession among the Tonga of Zambia." In *Spirit Mediumship and Society in Africa,* ed. John Beattie and John Middleton, 69–103. London: Routledge and Kegan Paul.

Crapanzano, Vincent. 1973. *The Hamadsha: A Study in Moroccan Ethnopsychiatry.* Berkeley: University of California Press.

Dilthey, Wilhelm. 1989. *Introduction to the Human Sciences.* Selected works, vol. I., ed. Rudolf A. Makkreel and Frithjof Rodi. Princeton, N.J.: Princeton University Press.

———. 1985. *Poetry and Experience.* Selected Works, vol V., ed. Rudolf A. Makkreel and Frithjof Rodi. Princeton, N.J.: Princeton University Press.

———. 1976. *Selected Writings,* ed. H. P. Rickman. Cambridge: Cambridge University Press.

Eliade, Mircea. 1964. *Shamanism: Archaic Techniques of Ecstasy,* trans. Willard R. Trask. Princeton, N.J.: Princeton University Press.

Ellingson, Ter. 1987. "Music and Religion." In *The Encyclopedia of Religion,* ed. Mircea Eliade. New York: Macmillan.

Evans-Pritchard, E. E. 1937. *Witchcraft, Oracles and Magic among the Azande.* Oxford: Oxford University Press.

Foster, George M., and Barbara G. Anderson. 1978. *Medical Anthropology.* New York: John Wiley & Sons.

Fry, Peter. 1976. *Spirits of Protest: Spirit-Mediums and the Articulation of Consensus among the Zezuru of Southern Rhodesia (Zimbabwe).* Cambridge and New York: Cambridge University Press.

Gelfand, Michael. 1964. *Witchdoctor: Traditional Medicine Man of Rhodesia.* London: Harrill Press.

Gray, Robert F. 1969. "The Shetani Cult among the Segeju of Tanzania." In *Spirit Mediumship and Society in Africa,* ed. John Beattie and John Middleton, 171–187. London: Routledge and Kegan Paul.

Hammond-Tooke, W. D. 1955. "The Initiation of a Baca Isangoma Diviner." *African Studies* 14(1):16–22.

Heidegger, Martin. 1977. *The Question Concerning Technology and Other Essays,* trans. William Lovitt. New York: Harper Colophon Books.

Herskovits, Melville J. 1938. *Dahomey: An Ancient West African Kingdom.* 2 vols. Evanston: Northwestern University Press.

Hoernle, Agnes Winifred. 1937 [1966]. "Magic and Medicine." In *The Bantu-Speaking Tribes of South Africa,* ed. Isaac Schapera, 67–94. London: Routledge and Kegan Paul.

Ihde, Don. 1976. *Listening and Voice: A Phenomenology of Sound.* Athens: Ohio University Press.

Janzen, John. 1992. "Ideologies and Institutions in Precolonial Western Equatorial African Therapeutics." In *The Social Basis of Health and Healing in Africa,* ed. Steven Feierman and John M. Janzen, 195–211. Berkeley: University of California Press.

———. 1991. "'Doing *Ngoma*': A Dominant Trope in African Religion and Healing." *Journal of Religion in Africa* 21(4):290–308.

Jones, Arthur M. 1959. *Studies in African Music.* 2 vols. London: Oxford University Press.

Junod, Henri A. 1962. *The Life of a South African Tribe.* 2 vols. New York: University Books.

Katz, Richard. 1982. *Boiling Energy: Community Healing among the Kalahari Kung.* Cambridge, Mass.: Harvard University Press.

Kauffman, Robert. 1980. "African Rhythm: A Reassessment." *Ethnomusicology* 24:393–415.

Kleinman, Arthur. 1980. *Patients and Healers in the Context of Culture: An Exploration of the Borderland between Anthropology, Medicine, and Psychiatry.* Berkeley: University of California Press.

Kubik, Gerhard. 1979. "Pattern Perception and Recognition in African Music." In *The Performing Arts: Music and Dance,* ed. John Blacking and Joann W. Kealinohomoku, 221–249. The Hague: Mouton.

Lévi-Strauss, Claude. 1969. *The Raw and the Cooked,* trans. John and Doreen Weightman. New York: Harper & Row.

Lewis, Ioan M. 1971. *Ecstatic Religion: An Anthropological Study of Spirit Possession and Shamanism.* Baltimore: Penguin Books.

Marshall, Lorna. 1969. "The Medicine Dance of the !Kung Bushmen." *Africa* 39:347–381.

Nketia, J. H. Kwabena. 1974. *The Music of Africa.* New York: Norton.

Oesterreich, T. K. 1966. *Possession: Demonical and Other.* Secaucus, N.J.: Citadel Press.

Ranger, Terence O., and John Weller. 1975. *Themes in the Christian History of Central Africa.* Berkeley: University of California Press.

Read, Margaret. 1956. *The Ngoni of Nyasaland.* London: Oxford University Press.

Rouget, Gilbert. 1985. *Music and Trance: A Theory of the Relations between Music and Possession,* trans. Brunhilde Biebuyck. Chicago: University of Chicago Press.

Schutz, Alfred. 1951. "Making Music Together: A Study in Social Relationship." *Social Research* 18(1):76–97.

———. 1973. *The Structures of the Life-World,* trans. Richard M. Zaner and H. Tristram Engelhardt, Jr. Evanston, Ill.: Northwestern University Press.

Sibisi, Harriet. 1975. "The Place of Spirit Possession in Zulu Cosmology." In *Religion and Social Change in Southern Africa,* ed. Michael Whisson and Martin West. Cape Town: David Phillip.

Turner, Victor W. 1986. "Dewey, Dilthey, and Drama: An Essay in the Anthropology of Experience." In *The Anthropology of Experience,* ed. Victor W. Turner and Edward M. Bruner, 33–44. Urbana and Chicago: University of Illinois Press.

———. 1982. *From Ritual to Theatre.* New York: Performing Arts Journal Press.

———. 1974. *Dramas, Fields, and Metaphors.* Ithaca, N.Y.: Cornell University Press.

———. 1968 [1981]. *The Drums of Affliction: A Study of Religious Processes among the Ndembu of Zambia.* Ithaca, N.Y.: Cornell University Press.

Turner, Victor W., and Edith Turner. 1978. *Image and Pilgrimage in Christian Culture.* New York: Columbia University Press.

Tylor, Edward Burnett. 1920. *Primitive Culture.* 2 vols. New York: Putnam.

Vail, Leroy. 1972. "Suggestions towards a Reinterpreted Tumbuka History." In *The Early History of Malawi,* ed. Bridglal Pachai, 148–167. London: Longman Group.

Wilson, Monica. 1972. "Reflections on the Early History of North Malawi." In *The Early History of Malawi,* ed. Bridglal Pachai, 136–147. London: Longman Group.

Dance in Communal Life

Patience A. Kwakwa

Functionality of Dancing
Dance as an Integrated Art
Dancers and Types of Dancing
Dancers' Training
Role of Drummers, Singers, and Praise Singers
Interdependence of Dancers and Musicians
Dancers and Musicians in Communal Life

Many people who watch African dancing enjoy the sight of the dance formations and body movements, and the sound of the music. Technically, however, other factors help give an event its aesthetic vigor and vitality. These factors are the unifying and sustaining dynamics of the interactions between dancers and musicians, and between dancers and local audiences.

Academic treatments of these concepts appear in scholarly publications by social anthropologists, students of African traditional religion, and writers on African art. The greater portion of the literature on African dance, however, is cursory. It consists of descriptions of specific dances and their contexts, and of captions to photographs of dancing. Such brief notices do not offer much insight into the tempers and complexities of African dances.

Of the literature in English, studies of African dances treat Zambia (Brelsford 1949), the *masabe* of the Tonga (Colson 1969), the *shetani* of the Segegu (Gray 1969), the Kalabari of Nigeria (Horton 1960, 1973), sub-Saharan Africa (Huet 1978), the medicinal dance of the !Kung (Marshall 1969), the Akan and the Gã (Nketia 1952), and vodoun of the Fon of the Republic of Benin (Herskovits 1967).

African Arts, a quarterly magazine published since 1960 by the University of California at Los Angeles, has featured studies of African dances (Rood 1969; Wemba-Rashid 1971; Monts 1984). These studies give detailed accounts of specific African dances—both as art forms and as social events.

At the University of Ghana, dance has been an academic subject since 1962, and the university has accepted several theses on indigenous dances of African countries (Sackeyfio 1968; Yamoah 1971; Serwaddah 1971; Awuku 1991; Affour 1992; Adu-Asare 1992). At the School of Performing Arts, final-year students in dance, each investigating a dance practiced by his or her own ethnic group, have uncovered deeper meanings (often symbolic or otherwise hidden) in the dances, and have provided information on how their respective communities maintain their traditional dances.

Traditional African dances do not occur in isolation. They often have a specific role within an event or a complex of events organized for a specific occasion. Many have value as entertainment, but entertainment is not their most important function: dancers perform for sociocultural, historical, political, and religious purposes. Thus,

chisungu   Nubility rite for a Bemba girl where scenes of maize grinding and potato collecting are enacted

fontomfrom   Slow dance that an Asante chief performs on installation. He portrays his predecessors to assert status

abofoo   Dance performed by Akan hunters that cleanses the hunter who killed the animal

sasa-ture   Dance for a chaotic social situation from the former Bauchi state, Nigeria

khomba   A turning dance to make Tsonga women fertile

the traditional dances of Africa differ from the artistic and contemporary dances of Africa, and from classical ballet and modern dance, performed in America and Europe for the entertainment of paying audiences.

FUNCTIONALITY OF DANCING

In many African communities, many occasions—the birth of a child, the initiation of boys and girls into adult status, the installation of chiefs, a marriage—present opportunities to express joy. In some instances, the rituals and ceremonies associated with them require elaborate preparations. These rituals and ceremonies take different forms. In general, there is feasting, drinking, and merrymaking. Within these contexts, dances serve as mediums for honoring, welcoming, and ushering individuals, and for incorporating them into the community at large as new members—as adults, chiefs, or married couples. In the *nsogwe*, danced by the Nsenga and the Southern Chewa, after the birth of a woman's first child,

> the women, entirely nude, assume a squatting posture, raising and lowering their bodies on the heels, accompanying the motion with quivering of their belly muscles. . . . The dance is a kind of lustration to cleanse the mother after a period of taboo. (Brelsford 1949)

Most of the dances performed during the *chisungu* (a nubility rite for a Bemba girl) enact scenes like maize grinding and potato collecting. The ceremony, called "dancing the girl," teaches nubile women the duties of womanhood.

On installation, an Asante chief performs the *fontomfrom*. To portray his predecessors (whose valor he has inherited), he employs symbolic gestures. His using these gestures asserts his status as a peerless leader, for others who take turns in the dance ring (a circular space, defined by the placement of audience and dancers) may not use a chief's gestures.

Dances performed at death ceremonies may be mediums for honoring the dead or placating ancestral spirits (Brelsford 1949), or, in Lugbara society, for signaling the destruction of the territory by the death of the elder (Middleton 1960). After killing a big animal, Akan hunters may perform the *abofoo,* a dance that cleanses the hunter who killed the animal, and protects him from its soul. Dances may also celebrate the long and prosperous life led by a deceased elder.

In worship and ritual healing, dances serve as mediums for characterizing and impersonating communal spirits, enabling them to converse with living persons. When the spirits come, they may cure illnesses they or others have caused, and may join in merrymaking as people give thanks for blessings the spirits have sent (Kwakwa 1974).

Specific occasions call for the performance of dances, and these serve clearly defined goals. In Ture communities (in former Bauchi State, Nigeria), what people consider a chaotic social situation might occasion the performance of *sasa-ture*, a dance that draws attention to interpersonal conflicts, and advises people to live peacefully. Approval for its performance can come only from elders of the community. The chief can command a performance, but must slaughter a fowl before it starts. Onlookers may not take part in it.

African dances may provide a socially sanctioned medium for behavior that under normal circumstances would be unacceptable. Performance of the *saransara* (a dance feast of the Maguzawa of Kaduna State, northern Nigeria) licenses people to express dissatisfaction with their chief. They put their sentiments into the texts of songs for dancing. During the *apoo* and the *aboakyere* (festivals of the Brong and Effutu of Ghana), any local resident may speak freely about the chief and get away with it. During festivals, the dance may serve as a background for other activities, or as a concluding event, in which, for blessings bestowed throughout the year, an entire community may express joy and thanks to God, lesser deities, and ancestors.

DANCE AS AN INTEGRATED ART

African dance is an integrated art, which can combine movement, music, mime, costume, ritual, ceremonial objects, official insignia and regalia, and makeup. In Zambia, *malaila* (from a Bantu word, *kulaila* 'to take leave of or say goodbye'), a dance performed amid praise singing by colleagues of a man slain in war, once used spears and sticks "to underline the prowess of the deceased" (Brelsford 1949).

Secret songs associated with Tsonga initiation for girls have connotations of fertility. The *khomba*—a turning dance, combining mime, dance, and music—"exhibits an extraordinary amount of functional complementarity, the purpose of which is to make women fertile" (Johnston 1974). In it, charms attached to leather belts strengthen the dancers, so they keep their balance. For guidance, masked dancers of the Bété of Côte d'Ivoire attach medicinal substances to their ankles and feet (Rood 1969).

DANCERS AND TYPES OF DANCING

As in music, African dances differ in importance and complexity, and in the extent of participation they offer. Some dances are open to everyone, but participation in others requires special knowledge and skills, and still others may be open only to members of particular social groups or associations. Those who interact in a dance event do so as both performers and members of a social group.

In a dance event, two groups of participants may be discernible: those who play specifically assigned roles (the dancers and the musicians), and those who have no specially marked status (the observers). These groups are often distinct, but in some informal and recreational situations, performers and observers may interact, at various levels of complexity. Temporarily, an onlooker may spontaneously step into a dance ring. Such a person may be a performer who lacks a role assigned for the occasion, a novice who wishes to test his or her skills, or a visitor from a neighboring community. A performer might step out of the ring to relax for a while—to instruct an inadequate performer, to appraise the event, or to make room for others to perform. Specific roles in the dance may be open only to a particular group of people within the community. Selection may depend on age, sex, occupation, sociopolitical status, affiliation with (or membership in) a religious group or cult, the context and function of the dance, and the distinctive feature, character, or nature of the dance. As a result, though people representing a cross-section of a community may perform many dances, some dances have exclusive associations with specific groups: youths,

dayirigaba   Dance of youths among the
Nyamalthu or Terawa of the former Bauchi
State in Nigeria

take   Praise-name performance among the
Nyamalthu of the former Bauchi State in
Nigeria

gagra   Dance that tests men's bravery among
the Higi of northern Nigeria

wasan maharba   Hunters reenact personal
experiences of going on hunts in this dance

adult males or females, girls, newly initiated men, newly married women, bachelors,
mothers, farmers, warriors, blacksmiths, hunters, royalty, cultists.

Among the Nyamalthu or Terawa of Akko and Gombe local government areas
in former Bauchi State of Nigeria, *dayirigaba* is a dance of youths. On the day of a
marriage, while people are taking the bride to the groom's or the groom's father's
house, young men and women perform it. It also serves purposes of courtship, for
some men choose their brides during a performance.

The same people consider *ngorda*—full of pomp and majesty—the dance of the
nobility. Only the *kuji* (chief of the Nyamalthu), the seven *basarake* (titled men), and
their wives, may dance it. Traditionally, people performed it on four occasions: when
the guinea corn flowers, during the harvest of millet and guinea corn, at the installation of a *kuji* or *basarake*, and at the funeral of a *kuji* or *basarake*. The Nyamalthu say
it is a gift from their supreme deity, whom it enables them to thank while entertaining themselves. Its movements consist of elegant walks and turns. Drummers help
the dancers move. To call each dancer, they play a special praise (*take*). A dancer
whom a drummer singles out must answer by kinetically interpreting the rhythms of
the drums.

The Nyamalthu consider the *dan* the dance of the brave. One person, usually a
man on whom the community has bestowed the title *jarumi* 'brave one', performs it,
on the occasion when he receives the honor. In the days of interethnic warfare, drummers incited warriors by playing music for the *dan*.

In some Higi communities, young men between the ages of seventeen and twenty who passed through the *zhita* (a boy's initiation ritual) performed the *zhita* dance.
Until quite recently, newly initiated youths had to dance at a ceremony organized to
mark the successful completion of their initiation. A youth who had not gone
through the *zhita* could not marry. One important social function of the *zhita* was
that youths who had gone through it together saw themselves as age mates. They
remained friends for life, and accorded each other certain privileges, such as not having to remove one's sandals in the house of another. *Zhita* was also the means by
which the youths showed the members of their communities, particularly their parents and young women, that they had come of age. *Zhita* occurred once a year, at
planting time. It involved an entire community. As the youths danced, members of
their clans gave them gifts. The organizers of the ceremony whipped any uninitiated
boys who tried to join in.

Gagra is a Higi dance that tests men's *mazakuta* 'bravery and magical power'. It
forms part of the activities organized by hunters' and warriors' guilds in honor of
renowned ones among them. Custom bars women and male weaklings from performances. The Higi also associate the dance *gula-gula* with bravery. Only married men
between the ages of twenty-five and thirty dance it. The occasion relates to ceremonies associated with the ripening and harvesting of a variety of guinea corn. The
Higi say a man who participates in *gula-gula* is mature and trustworthy. If a man's

first child dies, or his wife is barren, people attribute his misfortune to nonparticipation in the dance.

In courtship, Higi youths perform *garba* 'look for a wife', a dance organized when millet and other crops are ripe. The occasion, like that of the *dayirigaba*, creates a forum for young unmarried men to secure their wives. Hence, married men, who lead settled lives, do not show much interest in its performance. Youths believe if they do not perform *garba*, they will neither meet girls nor get married.

In northern Nigeria, many communities ascribe dance forms to specific groups of local residents. Similar observations are true for the Jarawa, the Bankalawa, the Galambawa, the Ham (Jaba), the Margi, and many other groups in northern Nigeria.

Sometimes the physical nature of a dance may be a factor in restricting a dance to one group of people. Team dances are dances of youths. These include *takkai*, performed by youths from Jamji; *gatzal* of the Bankalawa of Bajar; *kode* of the Kagoro; *sarewa* of the Jarawa; *saransara*, *rambada*, and *tabaje*, of the Maguzawa (in Malumfashi, Funtua, and Dustin-Ma); *ishedi-ishurwa* of the Piti; *woza* of the Kurama of Woba; *gaja* of the Chawai in Nigeria; *bawa* of the Dagari; and *agbekor* of the Anlo Ewe in Ghana. These dances employ energetic, intricate steps and movements, which require strength, versatility, and agility. To the Bankalawa, a vigorous display symbolizes youthfulness, while whipping proves courage and manliness. The physical demands of these dances make them difficult for elderly persons, who support performances only as onlookers.

Men actively participate in dances organized and performed in association with men's occupations. Women follow, singing or ululating; they execute simple steps or movements. Some men's dances are further restricted to men engaged in a specific occupation, or to those who belong to a specific association or guild. During public appearances, nonmembers (boys, and even adult males) may not perform with members. Dances of professional hunters, warriors, farmers, and blacksmiths, fall within this category. Nigerian examples include the *shappal*, the Jahunawa Fulani war dance; the *gagra*, the hunters' and warriors' dance of the Higi of Michika; the *ngangara*, the professional hunters' dance of the people of Guguba in Jega state; the *wasan maharba,* hunters' dance of the Ham (Jaba) of Kwoi; the *wasan noma,* farmers' dance; the *wasan garma* 'hoe play', and the *wasan makera* 'blacksmith play' of the Hausa in Kaduna state. The movements dancers execute in each of these dances resemble the movements the men employ in their respective occupations. The men may mime, or give stylized or exaggerated versions of the routine movements. War dances, while reenacting warriors' deeds through mime and movements, exhibit manly strength and power. To praise singing accompanied by the *molo* (a plucked lute), hunters in the *wasan maharba* reenact personal experiences of going on hunts. To fixed musical rhythms, farmers in the *wasan noma* stylize the movements of their labor in the fields. The goal of some performances is to impress onlookers into giving gifts.

Among the Bankalawa and the Galambawa, women do not usually take active roles in dances that involve the *dodo*, a masked dancer. (*Dodo* is a Hausa word that means 'anything frightful'; in this context, it refers to a masked dancer.) Some communities bar women from attending such performances, even as bystanders, for it is taboo for them to see a masked individual. Since communities punish culprits, women and children run and hide as the *dodo* approaches them. Galambawa women who see the *dodo* have to remove their head ties, and keep them off until the *dodo* has disappeared. But the *dodo* to the Bankalawa is also a medium for correcting social ills—a duty usually assigned to the men of a community.

Because of participation by one *dodo,* the *mijin dare* 'night male', Nomana women do not take part in the *wasan gora*, a dance performed in association with postharvest rituals. After dancing it in the bush, men return home at night, when

Interested individuals learn to execute the accepted steps and movements—by watching and imitating the experts in the dance ring, at home, and during recreational periods.

women will be out of sight. People consider any man who does not take part in the dance a weakling or a woman.

Dances organized and performed in association with what the people regard as female occupations are largely the prerogative of female members of a community. The *bala* (danced by married Kanuri women), the *dunu* (a suite of dances performed by women in the Kwayam and Bodiwe areas of former Borno state in Nigeria, and the *shila* (originally a Shuwa Arab dance) are examples. In Hausa communities, young girls dance the *kalangu* on moonlit nights during the dry season. In Ghana, to express values and ideals associated with female nubility, women and young girls dance the *otofo*, the *dipo*, the *nde*, or the *bragoro*.

Cult dances may be open only to members of the cult. Both male and female members may participate in them. The Maguzawa *wasan bòorii,* the spirit-possession dance that occurs in many Hausa communities, is an example. Male and female members perform it, mounted by their spiritual horses, so they become the media of the possessor spirits. Through the execution of dance movements and the use of costume, ritual paraphernalia, and speech, they exhibit the spirits' idiosyncrasies. They dance the *bòorii* to cure illnesses caused by malevolent spirits (*iskoki*). By contrast, at the early stage of performance, observers of the *akem* (a dance performed by the Akan in Ghana) may take turns in the dance ring; as soon as possessed priests and priestesses begin to enter the ring, they leave it.

DANCERS' TRAINING

Whatever the criteria for selecting dances are, dancers must go through some form of training to gain the technical skills necessary for executing the required movements and steps. Dancers must have a disciplined body, good musical sense, and a regard for decorum. They must have the intuitional tools for expressing feelings and ideas, the enactment of historical traditions, and the dramatization of beliefs and values. In some dances, a dancer takes a particular role because of an ability to follow precisely the rhythms of the drum and the nuances of the texts. In some dances, selection depends on the ability to shake the body well (Harper 1970).

The contexts provided for dances create informal opportunities for interested individuals to learn to execute the accepted steps and movements—by watching and imitating the experts in the dance ring, at home, and during recreational periods.

Some would-be dancers undertake formal and intensive training, which may occur in an initiation camp (as with *zhita* and *rawan dodo*), or in an occupational guild (as with *wasan makera*). The training inculcates technical skills and enables dancers to understand what they are doing, so they may do it well.

ROLES OF DRUMMERS, SINGERS, AND PRAISE SINGERS

The men of a community usually undertake its drumming. They are selected primarily on the basis of their ability to play the drum and other musical instruments.

Except within the context of a cult, considerations such as age and membership in a group may be unimportant.

Highly talented musicians receive training through a system of apprenticeship. Often, they learn their skills from a father or other man of the extended family, and some families have renown for the ability to drum and interpret rhythms. Hausa drummers are quick to say "*Mun gada* 'We inherited it'"; many claim descent from renowned drummers. Often, training begins at an early age. A few drummers claim they gained their skills by watching and imitating master drummers during performances, or in a recreational situation. Some musicians are excellent dancers. The Higi say the best dancers in the *shila* are horn players, for they can interpret the language of the drums.

During organized performances, drummers do not step into the dance ring. By playing rhythms that correspond to the dancers' steps and movements, they help dancers perform correctly. *Ngorda* dancers say the drummers help them move majestically.

In many Hausa dances, the role of the praise singer (*maroka*) is highly important. In young girls' dances and dances associated with royalty, hunting, farming, and marriages, he showers praises on individuals. In some dances, he is also the master drummer, or plays the only accompanying musical instrument. As he praises a married couple in the Kanuri *bala* or the Nyamalthu *dayirigaba*, he reminds them of their communal responsibilities. This is clear in a song for the *kuru*, the Maguzawa farmers' dance.

> Let us go back to the bush and farm, which is why we live.
> Whatever we get in this world, we get it from the farm.
> Young men, let us leave home to go to the farm.
> Those who do not make it in the educational system
> Will find their way back to school—their farms.

In the *turu* (the dance of Daura royalty), praise singers praise the dancer's parents and grandparents, in descending order, from the first chief to the present emir. Dancers say a praise singer makes them feel proud. They sense that their ancestors are watching them.

INTERDEPENDENCE OF DANCERS AND MUSICIANS

The reciprocal relationship between music and dance inevitably creates a similar type of interdependence between dancers and musicians. They ensure that their parts continue in the manner the community expects to see, and that through appropriate variations and signals (or the subtleties of expressions) they interact or respond spontaneously to each other during the performance.

Whether or not a performance reaches standards acceptable in a community may depend on the degree of seriousness with which local musicians and dancers regard their efforts. Music and dance go hand in hand. In various ways, dancers and musicians influence the animation of the performance.

DANCERS AND MUSICIANS IN COMMUNAL LIFE

Though dancers and musicians take important roles in communal life, they do not usually enjoy special treatment or privileges. Nevertheless, to suggest that other members of a community look down on dancers and drummers would be wrong. The degree of respect accorded them reflects the role dance itself plays within a community. If dance functions primarily as entertainment, and participants are people whom a

The Bankalawa equate dancing to going to school: it informs every aspect of their lives.

community considers inferior, dancers will get little or no recognition from the community.

The Kanuri believe musicians and dancers occupy a low position. Though much depends on how a performer comports himself, some praise singers have enjoyed patronage, and have even become wealthy, but are still not likely to move up the social ladder.

Higi, Bankalawa, Nyamalthu, and Longuda communities do not look down on dancers and musicians. The Higi may attribute certain types of ill fortune and weakness in men to lack of participation in a particular dance. In many communities like those of the Higi, dance provides a medium through which social relationships develop. Such communities, being more likely than others to appreciate the contributions made by dancers, praise singers, and drummers, accord them respect. The Bankalawa equate dancing to going to school: it informs every aspect of their lives. The Chawai say they like dancers and musicians because they make people proud of their group inheritance.

REFERENCES

Adu-Asare, Michael. 1992. "Extinct Akan Dance from the Akuapem Traditional Area." Diploma thesis, University of Ghana, Legon.

Affour, E. A. 1992. "The Role of Dance in the Daa Festival of the People of the Tongo." Diploma thesis, University of Ghana, Legon.

Awuku, Robert S. 1991. "Agbekor Dance of Anlo Afiadenyigba." Diploma thesis, University of Ghana, Legon.

Brelsford, W. V. 1949. *African Dances of Northern Rhodesia.* Livingstone, Zambia: The Livingstone Museum.

Colson, Elizabeth. 1969. "Spirit-Possession among the Tonga of Zambia." In *Spirit Mediumship in Society in Africa,* ed. John Beattie and John Middleton, 69–103. London: Routledge and Kegan Paul.

Gray, R. F. 1969. "The Shetani Cult among the Segeju of Tanzania." In *Spirit Mediumship in Society in Africa,* ed. John Beattie and John Middleton, 171–187. London: Routledge and Kegan Paul.

Harper, Peggy. 1970. "A Festival of Nigerian Dances." *African Arts* 3(2):48–53.

Herskovits, Melville J. 1967. *Dahomey: An Ancient West African Kingdom,* vol. 2. Evanston, Ill.: Northwestern University Press.

Horton, Robin. 1960. "The Gods as Guests." *Nigerian Magazine.* Special edition.

———. 1973. "The Kalabari Ekine Society: A Borderland of Religion and Art." In *Peoples and Cultures of Africa,* ed. Elliot P. Skinner. New York: Doubleday.

Huet, Michael. 1978. *The Dance, Art and Ritual of Africa.* New York: Pantheon Books.

Johnston, Thomas F. 1974. "A Tsonga Initiation." *African Arts* 7(4).

Kwakwa, Patience A. 1974. "Dance and Drama of the Gods." Master's thesis, Institute of African Studies, Legon.

Marshall, Lorna. 1969. "The Medicine Dance of the !Kung Bushmen." *Africa* 39(4):347– 381.

Middleton, John. 1960. *Lugbara Religion.* London: Oxford University Press.

Monts, Lester. 1984. "Dance in the Vai Sande Society." *African Arts* 7(4):53–59, 94.

Nketia, J. H. K. 1952. *African Music in Ghana.* Evanston, Ill.: Northwestern University Press.

Rood, Armistead P. 1969. "Bete Masked Dance." *African Arts* 2(3):36–43, 76.

Sackeyfio, Godfrey. 1968. "Music and Dance of Otu Gods of Gā Mashi." Diploma thesis, University of Ghana.

Serwaddah, Moses. 1971. "Ndongo, a Wedding-Dance of the Baganda of Uganda." Diploma thesis, University of Ghana.

Wemba-Rashid, J. A. R. 1971. "Isinyago and Midimu: Masked Dancers of Tanzania and Mozambique." *African Arts* 6(2):38–44.

Yamoah, Felix. 1971. "Installation Ceremony of An Ashanti Chief." Diploma thesis, University of Ghana, Legon.

Intra-African Streams of Influence
Gerhard Kubik

Research History
Methodological Considerations
Examples of Diffusion and Borrowing
Twentieth-Century Trends

Scholars have traditionally directed their attention to ways the external world has affected Africa. They have studied how European, Arabic, and southeast Asian cultures have influenced sub-Saharan African cultures. Because of a supposed lack of historical sources, they have given little attention to intra-African cultural exchanges. Only late in the twentieth century did they begin to feel a need to study cultural history internal to sub-Saharan Africa, including the history of music and dance.

For scrutiny, evaluation, and interpretation, a review of available sources—external and internal, pictorial and written, performative and artifactual, traditionary and observational—reveals a wealth of material. The earliest archaeological sources on African music and dance go back to the pre-Christian era, even if we exclude ancient Egypt. Later, sources become more and more coherent; in the 1600s, they become abundant.

RESEARCH HISTORY

In the 1800s, when cultural anthropology emerged as a science, researchers proceeded from an unverifiable premise: the idea of universal and unilinear cultural evolution. They thought all existing cultures had passed through the same stages along a programmed line: some reached the top earlier; some, later. Anthropologists assumed the societies they encountered—before the general "grayout" characteristic of the late 1900s (Lomax 1976:475)—had each occupied a somewhat fixed position within this hierarchy; they believed some of these societies had reached a stage of "high culture," while others had achieved lower degrees of "complexity."

From antiquity to the late 1800s (as in Morgan 1877), from the Kulturkreis school to neo-Marxism, evolutionary ideas have had a profound influence, not only on outsiders' perceptions of Africa, but also on many Africans' self-perceptions, which Western educational systems have helped shape (Mudimbe 1988). People still perceive Africa to be a repository of "traditional societies"—a concept that implies extreme social stability existed before the changes described as "urbanization," "industrialization," and "Westernization." Over the centuries, however, African societies have changed; in that respect, they resemble the other societies of the world.

As this volume was going to press, a new government in Zaïre had changed the name of the nation to "Democratic Republic of the Congo."

In African prehistory, there was always contact—
if not always by grand migrations, at least between
neighboring groups.

Thinking of precolonial Africa as a mosaic of rigidly traditional, tightly knit, autonomous, ethnic-linguistic units overlooked what might well have been the only stable trait in African cultural history, as it probably was elsewhere: continuous change. The processes of innovation sometimes went slowly and sometimes fast; abrupt leaps sometimes occurred: but no people, no cultural group, remained stagnant.

In African prehistory, there was always contact—if not always by grand migrations, at least between neighboring groups. In that manner, innovation spread from group to group, often as a trickle. In other instances, it spread by migrations through wide areas, even across the continent. And in the last millennium, innovations began to spread in a skipping manner: from king's court to king's court, with envoys exchanged between them; or from trading post to trading post, leaving large parts of the countryside untouched.

The knowledge of iron smelting, and of the technology of the manufacture of iron tools, spread from two centers: the Nile Valley, and northern Nigeria. In illustration of a consequential diffusionist process, this knowledge spread southward, throughout the subcontinent. The technology of iron working had important effects on the history of music in Africa, because it made possible the development of iron bells and lamellophones.

The concept of "traditional" music, and even of "ethnic" music, came from an ideology that saw Western influences as the major—and sometimes exclusive—agent for social and cultural change (Kubik 1982:6; Blacking 1989). Scholars of the mid-to-late-twentieth century often used the word *traditional* as a euphemistic surrogate for *primitive*, in much the same way their predecessors had used the word *primitive*.

Before about 1960, scientific paradigms assumed the existence of degrees of social complexity, and stages of cultural development (sometimes narrowed to "technological" development); but by 1960, the need for revision had become clear. In that year alone, a majority of African countries attained their formal independence.

One factor that helped researchers break away from relying on preconceived constructs was the discovery (or rediscovery) of many sources about Africa's precolonial past. In the 1950s, not only outsiders' reports, but also an abundance of internal documentation, became available; this evidence included archaeological material, such as rock paintings and petroglyphs. With the depreciation of a stance that had considered Africa a continent without a history, it was only a matter of time until African music history would suggest itself as a subject of study. Historical perspectives toward Africa control some of the literature of the first half of the twentieth century (Ankermann 1901; Hornbostel 1911), and even earlier. For systematic research, a new start was Klaus Wachsmann's *Essays on Music and History in Africa* (1971), which included contributions by J. H. Kwabena Nketia, Akin Euba, A. M. Jones, Gilbert Rouget, and others. The book made a profound impact. A few years before, Wachsmann had published a historically oriented article (1964a); and in 1969 appeared Walter Hirschberg's "Early Historical Illustrations of West and Central African Music" (1969), followed in 1974 by Veit Erlmann's account of written sources about music in western and central Sudan.

From the 1950s on, excavations in south-central Africa and Zaïre added another dimension to historically minded research. Particularly, the African history of single and double flange-welded iron bells became a subject of sharp discussion (Walton 1955; Vansina 1969; Hirschberg 1970; Schüller 1972). By the mid-1960s, an increasing consciousness of the value of oral tradition researched from a historical perspective rounded out the picture. Oral tradition rarely takes the observer farther back than 200 years, but its systematic study opened a new field of inquiry (Vansina 1965; Wachsmann 1971; Kubik 1982). A consensus emerged: by the strict application of historical methods, in combination with a suitable interpretive framework, scholars could reconstruct African music history, or at least large patches of it. Though the threshold between imaginative conclusion and pure speculation often runs thin, critics rejected speculation, wherever they thought they had found it. Jones hypothesized that about A.D. 700 the presence of Indonesian settlers in parts of Africa had led to the introduction of certain xylophones, tuning patterns, and musical structures (1964), but this hypothesis met with critical rejection. The rise in the new scholarship marked a new tendency in research: scholarly work proceeded increasingly from the notion African music history had its own dynamics. Scholars acknowledged they could no longer work by merely gauging the local repercussions of events outside the continent. They acknowledged they could not uncouple the history of music from the history of politics and culture, and they recognized they could use allied scholarly fields for mutual interpretation.

Finally, linguistic research began to affect cultural theory. Cultural anthropologists accepted that apparent formal identities in the cultural traits of different cultures (Gräbner 1911) made insufficient evidence for diffusion. Unless researchers, like linguists (Greenberg 1966), could diagnose identity in cross-culturally compared cultural forms and meanings, the argument for diffusion remained weak. A case in point is the distribution of certain penta-, hexa-, and heptatonic tonal systems, which occur across Africa. On the basis of form, some of the intervallic structures are the same across wide areas; on the basis of meaning, these structures reflect different, intraculturally defined, concepts.

The title of this article conforms with the spirit of that insight. After discussing methodology, I shall deal with selected regional themes chosen from sub-Saharan Africa. To derogate the importance of Africa's historical contact with the world beyond its continental contours would be unjustified; but I shall principally employ data drawn from autochthonous African cultures, to trace the historical processes of contact, diffusion, reinterpretation, and syncretism. I shall concentrate on reconstructing what happened in the music history of the African past within sub-Saharan Africa, including Ethiopia, the Sahara, and the lower Nile Valley.

A good part of Africa's music is internal to it; and many structural and technological inventions have made its music unique. Some of these inventions and devices began to spread, until, in large parts of the continent, they became general knowledge: but comparative studies also turn up cultural discontinuities, creative results that never attained general popularity, or quickly disappeared. African history is strewn with the musical carcasses of the inventive process. A closer look at allegedly aberrant forms of the lamellophone in Central Africa reveals dead ends in technological innovation. One specimen of a lamellophone from northeastern Angola, made of raffia material (figure 1), has metal-ring buzzers, slung around two deep-tuned lamellae (a trait apparently inspired by the *likembe* 'box-resonated lamellophone'); but in contrast to the *likembe*, these buzzers are attached near the playing ends of the lamel-

FIGURE 1   A raffia lamellophone (collected from a Kacokwe maker at village Citato, Lunda Province, Angola) shows unusual placement of metal ring buzzers (Lisbon, Museu de Etnologia, AL–351).

People transplant their culture into another geographical area, and often create a diaspora, the dispersion and continuity of a culture away from its original home.

lae, where the maker thins out the lamellae from both sides. This specimen was collected in Angola in 1967; and since no identical device has appeared in collections, or in the field, the makers must not have continued or elaborated that innovation.

Another example comes from the 1950s. Youngsters in South African townships, trying to imitate the swing jazz they heard on records and in films, developed a new type of oblique embouchure, which used the mouth's cavity as a resonator for a pennywhistle, a cheap metal toy they could buy in shops. Later, they developed a jazz genre that became known as *kwela* music: it used sets of these flutes to represent the brass or woodwind sections of U.S. bands. The new embouchure stayed popular for little more than fifteen years, until the *kwela* craze gave way to dance music performed with electrically amplified guitars. By the 1990s, few expert musicians in southern Africa continued this tradition; the most widely known was Donald Kachamba. Otherwise, practical knowledge of the *kwela* embouchure had become extinct.

METHODOLOGICAL CONSIDERATIONS

To reconstruct intra-African streams of musical influence, I am using a combination of methods inherited from history and cultural anthropology. These methods include (a) standard historical methods, whereby scholars test, comparatively and chronologically, contemporary sources of all kinds (artifactual, pictorial, written); (b) observations and analyses of the present states of musical cultures as the most recent manifestations on the time line of history, with the intention of extrapolating into the past; (c) the assessment of oral traditions, which often take the form of verbal accounts of the past. This methodology has included, more recently, aural reconstructions from the memory of a single individual, such as Donald Kachamba's playback recordings of music and musical groups he reconstructed by memory (Kubik 1980a).

Anthropologists have found the principal processes that generate cultural change to be innovation, borrowing, and reinterpretation. When receiving new cultural traits, a culture processes them, in one way or another. The processing follows certain behavioral regularities, particularly those of selection, retention, reinterpretation, and syncretism. Melville J. Herskovits (1938, 1944), who studied culture contact between culturally different groups in the Americas, conceptualized these regularities; but they turn up everywhere in the world, and for every period in history.

How diffusion happens

There are four possible ways by which diffusion of cultural traits happens. A trait, or a cluster of traits, can spread geographically, to take root elsewhere, by any of the following avenues (Kubik 1986).

Avenue 1: human migration

Included here are both voluntary and forced migration, such as slavery. People transplant their culture into another geographical area, and often create a diaspora, the dispersion and continuity of a culture away from its original home. The results of transplantation depend largely on the environmental circumstances of the new home, and on the kind of relationships with groups contacted (the people originally living there, or transplanted there, simultaneously or afterward). Various forms of transculturation are the result.

Human migration involves the movement of people, sometimes on a large scale, with people settling in other lands. However, it can also involve small groups that settle in neighboring locations. In Africa, some major causes of human migration have been (a) wars, sometimes unleashed by migrating groups; (b) family conflicts, with one group of relatives deciding to settle apart from the rest; (c) fears, as when a family experiences the deaths of its members at an accelerated rate without an apparent cause, attributes the deaths to witchcraft, and then goes to live elsewhere, though not normally distant from the prior home.

Avenue 2: contacts between neighboring groups

A difference between this avenue and the first is that no human migration occurs here. The cultural contacts involve neighbors, each party settled in its own area for a long time. If the terrain is difficult, these groups may have developed different cultures, because of long-term isolation from each other (as with certain populations in the Bauchi Plateau, northern Nigeria). When commercial exploitation opens the area up, neighborhood exchanges then compensate for such differences in culture. In this manner, innovations can spread rapidly between neighboring groups. In the 1900s, contacts between neighboring cultures have accelerated, because of easily accessible forms of transportation.

An important characteristic of this avenue of diffusion is that members of the groups in contact just visit each other; sedentary populations do not abandon their own areas of settlement, and hunter-gatherers or cattle-keeping nomads do not change the radius of their periodic movements. While the contacts lead to borrowing, stimulus diffusion, reinterpretation, and eventually cultural change, the people remain attached to their habitation. Many cultures of the Guinea Coast (West Africa) provide examples of this avenue.

Avenue 3: long-distance travel and migration

This avenue includes the dissemination of cultural traits by individuals or small groups that travel widely (for economic, religious, or other aims). It includes as agents of diffusion a range of travelers: traders, explorers, migrant laborers, royal envoys—plus traveling musicians and poets, such as the *griots* in Mali, and in parts of western Sudan. From their home countries, they bear cultural commodities, which they introduce into new locations. The difference between avenues 1 and 3 is that the human agents, though moving in different lands, stay abroad temporarily: they eventually return home.

Diffusion works both ways. The travelers assimilate some of the foreign traits they meet, and then take them home. An example is the eighteenth-to-nineteenth-century export of drums from northern Mozambique, through the Yao- and Swahili-controlled, southeast African slave trade, to places as far off as Iraq (Wegner 1982), and in return the same traders' introduction of Islamic types of music (like *sikiri*, from Arabic *dhikr*). Another example is Alur and Acooli domestic and railway workers' introducing the *likembe* from northern to southern Uganda, beginning about 1912; it was an instrument they had gotten from people of northeastern Zaïre.

In areas of the equatorial forest of Central Africa, a communicative network involved the loud, message-carrying slit drums.

Avenue 4: diffusion through media

The salient characteristic of this avenue of diffusion is the absence of visible human carriers. In contrast with the other avenues, the human agent who brings about diffusion rarely reaches the areas where the cultural contact occurs. While twentieth-century mass media, especially broadcasting and the recording industry, provide the outstanding examples, it would be erroneous to believe Africa before 1900 was medium-free. Various devices sent messages over large distances, and thereby disseminated cultural traits. At times, in areas of the equatorial forest of Central Africa, a communicative network involved the loud, message-carrying slit drums (Carrington 1969). In some areas of sub-Saharan Africa, from 1700 on, Western notation transmitted music—at first foreign, then increasingly local. Scholars have underestimated the importance of this fact. For a song to become known from a notated score, only one individual (a catechist, a teacher, a student) has to read the notation; this individual, by translating the notation for others, functions as a multiplicator. In this way, many church songs (written in Tonic Sol-fa more frequently than in staff notation) made their way throughout Africa, particularly between about 1850 and the early decades of the twentieth century. These songs had important effects on many local vocal styles, and on the harmonic patterns of several African musical cultures.

The merger of diffusionary avenues

Combinations of the avenues of diffusion have occurred in African cultural history, as they have elsewhere in the world. For methodological clarity, however, it proves useful to distinguish among them, because each avenue has its own potential and dynamics.

Sometimes an area was subject to changes in the ways diffusion took place. Human migration from the Bantu nucleus (in the area of eastern Nigeria and central Cameroon), to the Central African hylaea (rainforest), beginning in the period between 1000 and 200 B.C. (Phillipson 1977:227), brought speakers of Benue-Congo languages into contact with Pygmy aborigines, whose languages and musical cultures differed. The Bantu transplanted their modes of life to the new areas, and thereby affected the Pygmies, in a classical example of avenue 1; but once the Bantu had settled down (with the territory divided between the groups, and an economic symbiosis established between them), further contacts would fall under avenue 2.

Migration for labor can displace people temporarily, but "guest workers" have often married in their workplaces, eventually to settle there. During the 1900s, young men from countries like Mozambique and Malawi migrated to work in South African mines. The idea of taking root in foreign places finds expression in Cinyanja and Chicheŵa (languages of Malawi, Zambia, and parts of northern Mozambique), in the verb *kuchona* 'travel abroad but get stranded and eventually settle down'. Thus, what at first looks like avenue 3 sometimes ends up as avenue 1.

It is not always easy to identify diffusion, to the exclusion of other possible explanations for the occurrence of apparently identical traits in two or more societies. Cultural parallels can result from the independent, multiple invention of the same trait—in which case, the analogies do not result from cross-cultural contact. On the map, a broken, discontinuous picture of distribution (as for a type of tension-providing method in constructing drums) can, in theory, have a variety of alternative explanations: (a) the trait arose independently, in more than one place, or at different times (though the more technologically complex the trait, the more unlikely this possibility becomes); (b) the geographical distribution of the trait was originally continuous, but the trait has disappeared in certain areas, thus showing it is a long-established trait; (c) the present picture results from skipping diffusion, as from trading post to trading post, or king's court to king's court. There are other possible explanations.

The most direct method for identifying a case of diffusion is through observational testimony, such as an informant might give, in relating an eyewitness account as specific as this: "The *likembe* entered northeastern Angola from Zaïre, through cross-border contacts within the Kasai River region." For the reconstruction of twentieth-century music history in Africa, scholars could in the 1990s still obtain many such testimonies. For earlier centuries, we must depend to a large extent on the interpretation of other sources. Sometimes, with a fair chance for accuracy, we can confirm or discard a case of diffusion, merely by extrapolation from our knowledge of how the process works. Here, we can take advice from comparative linguists, as from Greenberg, who recommended linking form and meaning (1966).

We cannot explain as a case of diffusion the presence of apparently identical intervals of pitch in the tunings of lamellophones called *kembe* among the Mpyɛmɔ (Nola District, southwestern corner of the Central African Republic), and *budongo* among the Basoga (southern Uganda), because box-resonated lamellophones of this type share a common history. *Kembe* and *budongo* (sing., *kadongo*) both derive historically from the *likembe*, invented in the area of the lower Zaïre River, probably by the mid-1800s. The type then spread, first upriver, to the town of Kisangani, and then on to northeastern Zaïre, and beyond to Uganda. In the 1920s, homebound workers who had helped extend the railroad from Pointe Noire to Brazzaville carried it northward from Brazzaville, up the Sangha River, to the Mpyɛmɔ.

While many features of the parent *likembe*—like the characteristic layout (involving two deep lamellae: one in the middle, one at the right side), the ring buzzers, the vibrato hole—continued in the offspring, the tunings changed in response to local traditions. In eastern Angola, among the –Cokwe, –Luvale, and –Mbwela, *makembe* (pl.) typically display hexatonic or tempered heptatonic tunings; but the models found among the Azande, in northwestern Zaïre and the Central African Republic, have "harp tunings" (the harp is a prominent Zande instrument). The *budongo* of the Basoga are tuned equipentatonically, to the tonal system found on local log xylophones (*embaire*), and on local lyres (*endongo, entongoli*), which lent their name to the *budongo* (sing., *kadongo*). The dissemination of this lamellophone is one of the fastest known cases of diffusion (Kubik 1980b, 1982). All along its routes, tunings changed to suit the tonal systems of the localities into which the instrument advanced.

On its route from the lower Zaïre River to Uganda, the *likembe* shifted its tuning many times—from heptatonic to pentatonic, and again to heptatonic. The Alur and Acooli employ pentatonic tunings, but these differ from those of the Basoga. Thus, no direct and recent historical relationship can exist between the equipentatonic lamellophone tunings of the Mpyɛmɔ and those of the Basoga. In fact, Mpyɛmɔ tunings coincide with those of the people's immediate neighbors, notably the Gbaya and Bantu-speaking peoples in the northern parts of the Congo (Didier

The tuning and organological traits of a musical instrument do not always constitute an inseparable cluster of traits that travel together.

and Rouget 1946). Stroboconn measurements show the same patterns of pitch intervals in Mpyɛmɔ and Basoga lamellophones, but the concepts behind these tunings are probably different.

The preceding discussion shows the tuning and organological traits of a musical instrument do not always constitute an inseparable cluster of traits that travel together. Nevertheless, certain tunings, such as guitar tunings in central Africa, and banjo tunings in southern Africa (Kubik 1989a), have migrated with their physical instrument. With lamellophones, as Andrew Tracey has shown (1970), there is yet another consideration: the tuning layout (the arrangement of the tones in relation to each other) is often a more important and stable trait than the tonal intervals. It also follows that whatever may, from an external viewpoint, look identical need not, for the people who play the instrument, have the same meaning.

Cross-cultural understanding of meaning is difficult to investigate, because each meaning is by nature intrasystemic. Therefore, directly questioning musicians from two cultures cannot reveal more than what we already know: the tunings are part of an intracultural system of musical concepts. We cannot prove the extent to which these concepts are comparable in meaning. In the mind of Basoga musicians, the music for the *budongo* structurally relates to that of the *embaire*; sometimes pieces are transferred wholesale from one instrument to the other. Basoga musicians perceive the tunings of both instruments to be intervalically identical. The Mpyɛmɔ, it seems, make no such association.

Thus, while *budongo* tunings and *kembe* tunings belong to closed systems of meaning, whose carriers normally live about 750 miles apart, we can experiment by presenting musicians from one group with the lamellophone tunings of the other. Such an experiment, however, cannot crack the closed systems of meaning. The musicians of one culture reinterpret the alien material from the angle of their experience; they thereby perceive analogies, and even identities.

In 1983, during a visit to the Museum für Völkerkunde Berlin, Evaristo Muyinda, a musician of the Kabaka of Buganda, declared the tuning of one of the museum's Javanese gamelans was identical with *amadinda* tunings from his cultural area. To give weight to his statement, and to prove the identity, he played an *amadinda* tune cross-handed on the gamelan. Subjectively, the identity sensed by Muyinda was clear and convincing, but his statement cannot be taken as evidence for a case of diffusion: it confirms only that the gamelan tunings he heard fall within his margin of tolerance for the (equipentatonic) tunings of his cultural area.

This experiment shows local informants (though helpful in intracultural studies) cannot necessarily provide answers in the cross-cultural investigation of meaning. The identity one group diagnoses in the cultural commodities of another arises from intracultural bias, and not from a comparative standpoint. Identities so diagnosed can, by chance, coincide with factual identities in meaning between the cultures; but most often, they reflect reinterpretations.

EXAMPLES OF DIFFUSION AND BORROWING

The major known instances of intercultural musical exchange in Africa can conveniently be grouped in three periods: from about 4000 B.C. to the turn of the Christian era, during the first millennium, and during the second millennium.

Nilo-Saharan cultural belt southward, after 4000 B.C.

The harp

Reconstructions of languages and cultures in the (formerly green) Sahara Desert, in combination with a systematic evaluation of rock paintings in the Tassili n'Ajjer (Algeria) and elsewhere, have helped us write the history of the harp in Africa.

Looking at the late twentieth-century distribution of musical instruments, we see no harps appear south of a line that approximates the equator. The southernmost areas where harps prevail include Gabon in the west, and the area of Lake Victoria in the east. Excluding harp-lutes, such as the *kora* of Senegal and Gambia (because their history is probably unrelated to the harp proper), we find a concentration of harps in these countries: Chad, Central African Republic, northern Cameroon, northeastern Nigeria, Gabon, southern Sudan, Uganda, and border areas in northeastern Zaïre and northern Tanzania.

In antiquity, the areas in the south next to the Sahara Desert and the Nile cultures—from Chad to Darfur (Sudan)—were probably not isolated from contacts with the Nile Valley on the one hand, and the Saharan cultures on the other. The Sahel zone, and the cultures of the savannas north of the equatorial forest, were transformed by an important event in population history: the gradual southward shifting of Saharan populations, beginning about 4000 B.C. The people of these cultures probably spoke ancestral Nilo-Saharan languages, and they were carriers of the "aquatic lifestyle" of the Sahara (Murray 1981:46). With the desiccation of their homelands, they naturally moved toward areas where large bodies of water had remained: (a) to Lake Chad, one of the last Saharan bodies of water to survive; and (b) to the swamps of the Sudd region of the Upper Nile (Sudan). These areas were the closest available approximation to the "green Sahara." Other people also retreated into mountainous areas similar to the Tassili n'Ajjer, but still with plentiful vegetation: Tibesti and Ennedi in particular. These migrations, though they must have been slow, eventually put considerable population pressure on speakers of Niger-Congo languages to the south, especially speakers of the (developing) Adamawa-Eastern family. Simultaneously, the migrations disseminated southward the technological achievements of the aquatic cultures.

In music, the most important Saharan heritage that survives in areas farther south may be the use of harps, which appear throughout the Central African savanna—from northern Cameroon, across the Central African Republic. Harps were known in the ancient Sahara, and they have survived in some obvious Saharan retreats, such as Ennedi (see the *krding* of the Bäle-Bilia, in Födermayr 1969). A six-string harp appears in a rock painting a French team of researchers discovered in the Tassili n'Ajjer. This painting holds an important key to unlocking the remote music history of the northern parts of Central Africa. Tentatively dated within the "Period of the Horse," ca. 800–700 B.C. (Davidson 1967:187), it shows a harpist with a round head and an elaborate coiffure, sitting on a small stool, such as can still be seen in some areas of Chad. He holds a six-stringed harp, and directs the neck toward his body. He plays for a second person, who sits in front of him, as if listening. The second person is sitting on what could be a throne, and there is a lengthy object, perhaps a ceremonial stick, in front of him.

In 1973–1975, when I showed students (in west, central, and east Africa) a copy

harps:

spoon-in-the-cup type; the *ennanga* of the Baganda, found in the Great Lakes region

tanged type; the *kundi* of the Azande

shelved type; found in a small area of Gabon and in the southernmost Central African Republic

of this painting, it generated an immediate interpretive response. Many of the students believed the harpist was performing in front of a person in authority, and their belief implied the existence of social stratification in the Saharan cultures (Kubik 1988a:121–127). Besides the social implications of this painting, an examination of a drawing of the harp itself suggests it belongs to what Wachsmann (1964a), who researched the history of harps in Africa, and probed their links with ancient Egypt, called the tanged type. He distinguished three organological types: (a) the "spoon-in-the-cup," or arched, type (like the *ennanga* of the Baganda), found in the Great Lakes region in east Africa; (b) the "tanged type" (like the *kundi* of the Azande), found in the Central African Republic, in Chad, and in northernmost Cameroon; and (c) the "shelved type," found in a small area of Gabon, and in southernmost Central African Republic.

The diffusion of the harp from ancient Egypt—westward into the Sahara, and southward along the Nile Valley—is indisputable, though many details about each juncture in the evolution of sub-Saharan types remain unobserved, and the precise dating of this evolution is difficult to ascertain. We can assume, however, the late-twentieth-century Central African harps of the "tanged type" derive from Saharan ancestral models. The "spoon-in-the-cup" type, though, could have a different history. Apparent similarities in form with the Mauritanian *ardin* (Wegner 1984:162) are coincidental. Contacts among ancient Meroë, Napata, and the Great Lakes region, are difficult to prove; but on the history of the *ennanga*, and of many other cultural traits of Buganda, such contacts are a persuading possibility.

Local innovation can veil remote contacts, as we see in the buzzing rings of banana fiber sewn into swatches of lizardskin, attached to the neck of the *ennanga*, and moved close enough to each string that the string vibrates against it (figure 2). This trait does not characterize any of the harp types to the north and northwest of Uganda.

FIGURE 2   Tuning and closeup of the neck of an *ennanga* (arched harp) from Buganda, performed by Evaristo Muyinda, 69, in the Museum für Völkerkunde, Berlin, in June 1983. Photo Moya Aliya Malamusi (Private Archive Kubik-Malamusi).

The lyre

The present area of distribution of the lyre, though it overlaps with that of the harp, covers an area slightly to the east. In the late 1900s, lyres provided entertainment in Nubia (on both the Egyptian and the Sudanese sides of the border), along the Egyptian coast of the Red Sea, in Sudan, Ethiopia, Somalia, Kenya, Uganda, and border areas in northern Tanzania and northeastern Zaïre. The area of distribution of the lyre also extends beyond the Red Sea, past the Sinai and Arabian peninsula, into Iraq, and to the south into Yemen and Oman. Wegner (1982) found bowl lyres in Iraq played by the descendants of slaves, probably of Nilotic origin. Thus, there is a lyre diaspora.

The area of distribution of the lyre coincides with these linguistic zones: II.E.1, Eastern Sudanic (Nubians, Shilluk, Dinka, Nuer, Ingassana, and other Nilotes in the Sudan; the Luo in Kenya; the Kakwa in Uganda); III.A, Semitic (the Amhara in

FIGURE 3   Ideris, ca. 50, plays a *jaŋarr* (bowl lyre) at Boagilk Igamarr (area of Ingassana Mountains, southeast of Ed Damazin, Sudan), 20 January 1977.

Ethiopia); III.D.3, Eastern Cushitic (the Galla and Somali, plus many other Cushitic speakers). It also includes adjacent areas of II.E.2, Central Sudanic (only the Lugbara and Madi, in Uganda and northeastern Zaïre), and Bantu languages (the Abaluhya of Kenya; the Bagishu and Basamia in the border area of Kenya and Uganda; the Basoga and Baganda of Uganda).

We can partially reconstruct how the lyre spread to the peoples mentioned, and what modifications it underwent in organological structures, systems of tuning, and techniques of playing. Lyres with a resonator in the form of a chest or box, and with an asymmetrical (later symmetrical) yoke, existed in the Near East, by about 4000 B.C. A descendant of this form is the *begena* of the Amhara of Ethiopia. The second organological type, the bowl lyre (with a resonator in the form of a bowl) was popular in ancient Greece.

As made clear in Egyptian paintings of ca. 2000 B.C., lyres penetrated ancient Egypt, apparently taken by Semitic-speaking nomads (Kebede 1977:379–396). From the Meroitic Empire, the lyre is shown in frescoes (Mahi 1972:89). The bowl-resonated type could have spread from Meroë and Napata southward to the Ingassana Mountains (figure 3), and gradually to the entire Nilotic-speaking southern Sudan, where it survives. An alternative hypothesis, however, is that Axum (which flourished A.D. 100–350), rather than Meroë, was a center of dispersal for lyres into Ethiopia and the southern Sudan. Kebede collected an oral tradition (possibly based on earlier written testimonies) that the prototype of the *begena* went into Ethiopia with Israelites who migrated from Jerusalem to Axum, accompanying Menelik I, the supposed son of King Solomon and the Queen of Sheba. Unfortunately, the earliest germane pictorial testimonies from Amharic Ethiopia are manuscripts of the early 1400s (Leroy 1967; Kimberlin 1978).

From southern Sudan and Ethiopia, both organological varieties of the lyre spread farther south. While the bowl lyre eventually gained universal distribution in the region, the idea of the box resonator or chest resonator is also traceable in specimens found as far south as Kenya, in the *pagan*, the name of which obviously relates

The migration of the lyre seems to have taken place over a period of a few generations rather than one of centuries. (Wachsmann 1971:103–104)

to the Ethiopian *begena* or *bagana* (an alternative pronunciation). The various forms of the lyre have also influenced each other. The instrument Joshua Omwami, a Kenyan lyrist, used in 1976 belonged to the *litungu* type, as played by the Abaluhya of western Kenya (Kubik 1982:106–107), but it had a box-shaped resonator.

During the early 1800s, the lyre spread into southern Uganda. The Abaluhya of Kenya, a Bantu-speaking people, adopted it from the Nilotic Luo; then it spread farther west, by neighborhood contact (avenue 2), to the Bagishu, Bagwe, and Basamia. It eventually reached the Basoga, among whom were famous musicians who regularly performed at the royal court of Buganda. Thus, the instrument became known within the Kabaka's court music. Wachsmann (1971:103–104) collected oral traditions about the spread of the lyre in southern Uganda:

> Basoga musicians have definite views on the recent travels of the lyre. One of the Lusoga terms, *Namugwe*, indicates the Bagwe (the eastern neighbors of the Basoga) as a donor group. The migration of the lyre seems to have taken place over a period of a few generations rather than one of centuries.

In 1968, Maurice Djenda and I collected from the lyrist Aloni Kaja a Lusoga oral tradition on the origin of the lyre. It tells of Bámuta and Wani, two homeless travelers who lived by stealing food: when they tried to steal sweet potatoes, furious farmers killed Bámuta. At Bámuta's grave, Wani made a musical instrument with a bowl-shaped calabash as a resonator, and covered it with the skin of a monitor lizard. He called it *enkana*. His intention was to communicate with his dead friend, by playing the instrument at the grave (Kubik 1982:32). The term *enkana* (not a Lusoga word) may relate to *obokano*, the name of the lyre among the –Gusii in Kenya; it has remote etymological relationships with *pkan* or *pagan* among the Pokot (Huie 1979:13; Anyumba 1983:20), and finally with the Amahara term *begena* or *bagana*.

Over the course of six thousand years, the lyre has undergone many innovative changes, though it has maintained stability in its basic technological details, like the construction of the yoke. When the lyre arrived among the Basoga, the people made an important innovation, possibly to approximate its sound to that of the harp, which they already knew: they renounced the bridge. Using a monitor lizard skin to cover the bowl, they duplicated the buzzing their harps had. The technology is simple, but highly effective. The vibrating strings of the (bridgeless) lyre touch lightly the skin of the resonator's cover; the result is notes of a longer duration and a louder, pattering sound.

About three thousand years ago, harps and lyres in Africa were exclusively linked to the cultures of peoples speaking Nilo-Saharan and Afro-Asiatic languages, respectively; but the zone of contact between these peoples and the Adamawa-Eastern and emerging Bantu languages soon provided many other instances of intra-African streams of musical influence, going back at least two millennia.

After about 1000 B.C., the northern fringe of the equatorial forest from Cameroon to the Ruwenzori Mountains and Lake Albert became the setting for migrations from west to east. These migrations included speakers of Adamawa-Eastern (I.A.6) languages, and speakers of Benue-Congo (I.A.5) languages, who migrated from the Cameroon grasslands eastward to the Great Lakes, where, ca. 400–300 B.C., they established an Early Iron Age culture, archaeologically identified by Urewe ware, or "dimple-based" pottery (Phillipson 1977:228). In their push to take over new lands, these agriculturalists came into contact with autochthonous inhabitants, who had a hunter-gatherer economy. At the edges of the forest, which the Bantu eventually penetrated, the contact was with the Pygmies; and in East Africa, Bantu intrusions often challenged the rights of indigenous pastoral peoples, who spoke either Eastern Cushitic (II.D.3) or Eastern Sudanic (II.E.1) languages. These contacts resulted in repeated and profound processes of transculturation. Researchers have often noted the influence of Pygmy polyphony on the vocal music of their Bantu neighbors throughout Central Africa. Another case Wachsmann stressed (1964b, 1971) was the profound Nilotic and Cushitic influence on the Bantu musical cultures of East Africa, notably in the interlacustrine zone. Late in the 1900s, the analysis of musical contacts between Bantu and Khoisian speakers in southern Africa joined these investigations (Nurse 1972; Rycroft 1978; Westphal 1978).

Within Africa during the first millennium

San and Bantu interactions in music

Far back in prehistory, San hunter-gatherers discovered harmonic counterpoint. Their everyday experience probably led them to two musical discoveries: (a) a long, stretched string, as on some of their hunting bows, can emit variable sounds; and (b) the human mouth, as used to produce vowels, consonants, and click consonants in their languages, can serve as a variable resonator. The use of a bow as a musical instrument, dividing the string with a tuning noose, and employing the mouth as a resonator, led in turn to the discovery of the harmonic series, and selective reinforcement of lower partials over two fundamentals (Kirby 1932, 1961; Kubik 1988b).

When Bantu speakers began to migrate into areas in southern Africa (south of 14° latitude south), which the San had originally occupied, they met in the music of San speakers the use of a harmonic system that had no counterpart elsewhere in Africa. In contrast to later Bantu invaders, these early Bantu migrants, who had adopted certain traits appropriate to an East African, cattle-based economy, reacted positively to the music of the San: they took into their music several San traits, particularly in the realm of harmonic patterning.

A remote San musical heritage remains embedded within many Bantu musical cultures of southern Africa, notably South Africa, Namibia, Botswana, parts of southern Angola, and Zimbabwe (Kubik 1988b). San-Bantu interaction in that region began in the fourth century, when the first Bantu migrants pushed southward through the Zambian and Zimbabwean plateaus. About A.D. 1300, as rock engravings and rock paintings show, San-speakers were still living as far north as 14° latitude in Angola and Zambia.

In a broad belt across south-central Africa, San influence on the music of Bantu speakers affects various musical traditions. In Angola's southwestern province of Wila (Huíla), the (cattle-keeping and milk-producing) –Nkhumbi, –Handa, –Cipungu, and related peoples, have assimilated and adapted traits of San music. In that area, !Kung hunter-gatherers remain as a population segment, however small; and they have long lived in intensive economic cooperation with their Bantu neighbors.

onkhonji   Name in the Luhanda language of Angola for both hunting bow and musical bow

musakalunga   Shiver dance of the –Handa people of southwestern Angola

bavugu   Stamping tubes of the !Kung of southeastern Angola

FIGURE 4   Applications of a hunting bow (*onkhonji* in the Luhanda language). *a*, Pequenino demonstrates a mouth bow, passing the back of the bow stick past the lips, at Kalova, Provincia de Huſla, southwestern Angola, 15 July 1965. *b*, Lithundu Musumali, a !Kung (San) musician, demonstrates the insertion of the bowstick into the mouth, at the !Kung encampment at Vimphulu, southeastern Angola, in December 1965.

a

b

In Luhanda, one of the languages of this group of peoples, *onkhonji* is the name for both the hunting bow and the mouth-resonated musical bow (figure 4). The villagers themselves acknowledge it as a San heritage, as they do the *musakalunga* 'shiver dance'. According to oral traditions collected by the Angolan ethnologist Marcelina Gomes (personal communication, 1982), the idea of using a hunting bow as a mouth bow with alternate performative techniques—(a) inserting one end of the bow stick into the mouth, and (b) passing the center of the back of the bow stick past the lips—came from the !Kung, many generations back.

A comparable picture of transculturation appears at the southeastern end of the continent, in Transkei, among the Xhosa—with the difference, however, that in contrast to southwestern Angola, Khoisan-Bantu interaction also resulted in a partial physical merger. A separate Khoisan identity has not survived among the Xhosa; but physical anthropologists have traced the Khoisanid racial component, and culturally, a Khoisan heritage also appears in the Xhosa language, with click consonants shown in no less than 2,395 words (de Wolf 1983:270). In certain aspects of Xhosa music, Andrew Tracey's recordings near Lady Frere, Transkei, in 1990, preserved in the International Library of African Musics, Rhodes University (South Africa), the San heritage is unmistakable.

In the general history of San-Bantu interaction, it is probably significant that in Transkei, as in southwestern Angola, the Bantu-speaking migrants had strong pastoral proclivities. A comparable pattern, leading to a merger between invading pastoralists and local hunter-gatherers, however, in which the language remained within the Khoisian group, is visible among the Khoi-khoin of Namibia.

In Xhosa music of the northwestern parts of Transkei, the result is a mixture of traits that show remnants of San polyphony in some songs, and a hexatonic tonal system, based on the production of harmonics over two fundamentals. As in southwestern Angola, the Xhosa tonal system involves the manipulation of the range of harmonics up to the fifth or sixth partial, over two fundamentals a whole step apart. This tonal system represents an extension of San ideas, rather than direct borrowing, because the San exploit harmonics only up to the fourth partial.

Some Xhosa have settled in stony, barren, mountainous areas near Lady Frere; others live closer to the coast, near Umtata. The musical cultures of those groups differ. The northwestern group manifests the stronger San musical heritage. It also maintains the practice of overtone singing (Dargie 1988), a technique so far found only in one other part of Africa, among the Wagogo (central Tanzania)—a people who, like the Xhosa, exhibit a culture based on a pastoral lifestyle.

We do not yet completely understand why, in the remote history of southern Africa, Bantu-speaking peoples with some pastoral inclinations should have interacted easily with hunter-gatherers, in contrast to later, nonpastoral Bantu immigrants from Central Africa (such as the –Cokwe of eastern Angola), who have remained largely indifferent to San aesthetics (Kubik 1970). While the !Kung of southeastern Angola adopted from the –Cokwe and –Mbwela certain musical instruments (such as lamellophones and drums), their musical culture had no effect on that of the San, in contrast with the situation elsewhere in Angola.

San music, as the !Kung of southeastern Angola performed it in the late 1900s, exploited eight principal traits. (1) The use of vocal polyphony (in the Africanist definition of this term), and of yodel. (2) The presence of tetratonic tonal material, derived from the harmonic series up to the fourth partial, over two fundamentals produced by a musical bow tuned in (a) whole steps, (b) minor thirds, or (c) major thirds. (3) The potential fusion of the parts of this system, to form a combined and complex system, by linking tunings (a), (b), and (c). (4) The indigenous use of only two musical instruments: musical bows (four different applications of hunting bows), and stamping tubes (*bavugu*). (5) The adoption of exogenous musical instruments (multiple-bow lute, lamellophones, drums), and the modification of their tunings, to accommodate San harmonic and tonal concepts. (6) The presence of a bias for rhythmic patterns in cycles of 12 beats and multiples of 12, disposed in simple bimeter or polymeter (two-against-three patterns of clapping), but no asymmetric timeline. (7) The near absence of song texts; singers mostly use syllables and isolated words, but extensively employ the imitations of animal sounds, especially bird calls. (8) The presence of dance patterns that include the miming of animals; but there are also shiver dances, which sometimes induce trancelike states.

A remote San musical heritage also appears in parts of Zambia and Zimbabwe, notably in the musical cultures of the –Nsenga, the –Lala, the –Lamba, the –Swaka, the –Lozi, and the –Shona. Most of these peoples had no twentieth-century contact with the San, who had largely disappeared from Zambia and Zimbabwe by 1800. (Only small pockets of San remain in southwestern Zambia, overlapping into the Caprivi strip, Namibia.) It was not recent contacts (as between San and –Lozi) that were consequential, but earlier contacts, which involved sizable San populations. The resulting processes of musical transculturation led to one of the most inventive harmonic systems of Africa: fourth- or fifth-based sequences and cycles of chords, particularly in the music of the –Nsenga and the –Shona (Tracey 1970; Kubik 1988b). This system grounds itself in a certain progression of nuclear bichords that survives

FIGURE 5 Nuclear harmonies in San music and south-central African Bantu music, showing the San heritage.

Harmonics:

Fundamentals: Resultant bichords

I   II   II   I   II   I

in San musical-bow performances (figure 5). Tracey (1961, 1970) describes a –Shona chordal sequence that determines the structure of –Shona polyphonic singing, but I have suggested this sequence could be understood as a Bantu extension of an ancient San musical heritage (Kubik 1988b; discussion of this theory in Tracey 1989:47).

Clustered cultural complexes: masked performances, timelines, iron bells

A map of three ostensibly unrelated cultural complexes (figure 6), shows the areas these complexes characterize are roughly congruent, within a broad region of the subcontinent: Gabon, Congo, the western and southern half of Zaïre, eastern Angola, northwestern Zambia, eastern Zambia, central and southern Malawi, and the

FIGURE 6 The approximate African distribution of masked dancing, timelines, and iron bells, ca. 1965; compiled from the evidence of sound and cinematographic recordings, using major European collections and private sources.

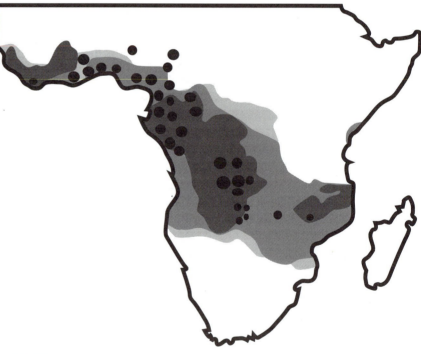

 Areas with frequent use of asymmetric timeline patterns (cycles: 8, 12, 16)

 Concentration areas of masked performances

 Areas in which flange-welded iron bells (single and/or double bells) were used by the mid-twentieth century (Archaeological evidence, e.g., from Zimbabwe or the Mozambique Coast is not included in this map)

Ruvuma Valley (Mozambique and southern Tanzania). They are equally characteristic of the Guinea Coast. The map considers the complexes in their broadest definition. A more detailed splitting of the content of each, distinguishing subtypes such as twelve-pulse-seven-stroke or sixteen-pulse-nine-stroke patterns, or by distinguishing various types of single and double bells, would result in a much larger and extremely detailed map, while not necessarily enhancing the understanding of the broad connections. For the same reason, a strictly statistical evaluation of the available sources and their cartographic representation would also exceed the present purposes.

Except for some border areas (for example, the use of iron bells in court music of the Hausa, who speak a III.E.4 language), it is also striking that the three mentioned complexes are virtually restricted to speakers of I.A. or Niger-Congo languages. Even within this language family, however, they give a patchy picture. The contours of distribution areas change throughout history, sometimes within decades (for example, the disappearance of iron bells in Zimbabwe and central Mozambique, where they are present in the archaeological record), but the mid-twentieth-century map still reveals far-reaching congruence in their distribution. By the mid-1960s, that congruence, was still strong enough to suggest a historical linkage in their spread. It is significant that all these complexes are absent in most of East Africa, excepting the southernmost areas of Tanzania, where the –Makua, the –Makonde, and other peoples, practice masked dancing (Wembah-Rashid 1975); they are also absent from South Africa and Namibia (unless imported into the Caprivi strip by Angolans). In West Africa, this cluster of traits is characteristic of cultures within the language subfamily I.A.4 (or Kwa), roughly all along the Guinea Coast. The picture emerging from a layout on a map also reveals that the distribution areas overlap with little skipping. Furthermore, the present distribution of masked dancing, timelines, and iron bells, largely coincides with those African song-style areas summarized by Lomax (1968:413) as 519 Guinea Coast, 517 Equatorial Bantu, and 513 Central Bantu.

Masked performances, and their meanings, link intimately with social structure. Invariably, excepting old traditions of masquerades for entertainment (often performed by children) and new folkloristic programs, masked dancing in West, Central, and Southeast Africa, occurs in tandem with the phenomenon of secret societies. These societies are usually unisexual. A typical men's society is the ɔmabe (leopard society) among the Igbo of eastern Nigeria (Aniakor 1978; Kubik 1989b:62–65); a typical women's, akulavye, a girls' secret society among the Mpyɛmɔ (Kubik 1992). Most secret societies are predominantly a men's domain.

FIGURE 7   *Ndenda* or *mupala*: mask used among the –Luvale, during the schools for boys' circumcision; inside the *mukanda* near the village of Sakatuta, Kazombo area, northeastern Angola, in December 1965.

In a broad belt of south-central Africa, masked men's societies go together with a matrilineal social organization, and often with uxorilocal marital residence. This social organization apparently fuels men's tendencies toward extrafamilial secret association, as we can see in the *makishi* masks of the –Luvale of eastern Angola (figure 7), in eastern Zambia, and in the *nyau* masked societies of the –Chewa and the –Mang'anja of Malawi (Kubik et al. 1987). In many areas, masked performances, as part of men's secret associations, accompany boys' initiation and circumcision. Settings for such performances include the *mukanda* schools of eastern Angola and northwestern Zambia, and the *likumbi* institution of the –Makonde of Mozambique (Dias and Dias 1970).

The ancestors of cultures that use masked performances, timelines, and iron bells, were mostly Late Iron Age agriculturalists. None of the pastoral peoples in Africa, and few among those under their influence, do so. However, among Central African hunters, the Pygmies of the Upper Sangha River (in Congo and Central African Republic), an instance of one mask in connection with men's secret societies has been reported (Djenda 1968). It is not known whether this mask represents an autochthonous heritage of the Pygmies' culture in that area. The same Pygmies use

FIGURE 8 A timeline of twelve pulses in seven strokes, used on the Guinea Coast and in West-Central Africa; mnemonic syllables in the Yoruba language.

FIGURE 9 A timeline of eight pulses, played on a bottle; used in traditions of Gabon and southern Cameroon (Kubik 1972:175).

FIGURE 10 A timeline of twelve pulses in five strokes, used in southern Malawi (Kubik et al. 1987:34, 78); mnemonic verbal pattern in the Chicheŵa language. Translation: "What has hurt him is the maize."

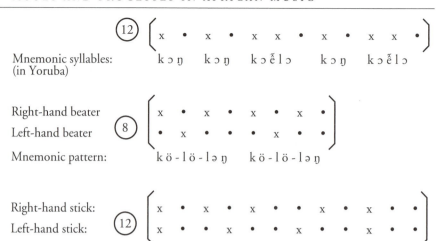

Mnemonic syllables: (in Yoruba)
Right-hand beater
Left-hand beater
Mnemonic pattern:
Right-hand stick:
Left-hand stick:
Mnemonic verbal pattern (in Chicheŵa):

the longest asymmetric timeline known in Africa; it has 24 pulse units. The people strike it on a percussion beam, to accompany *woyaya* and other indigenous dances.

J. H. Kwabena Nketia coined the term *timeline*, by which we understand mostly one-pitch rhythmic patterns, usually of asymmetric structure, used to steer and guide the performance of music and dance. Performers strike timelines on high-pitched objects, such as iron bells, glass bottles, concussion sticks, the bodies of drums, or high-pitched xylophone keys. People learn and remember them by mnemonic syllables or verbal phrases, as in figures 8, 9, and 10.

In the mentioned regions, such patterns are the backbone of many musical traditions. Over time, they must have been extremely stable, as we can infer from their mathematical structures, which allow no margin for variation: any structural change would destroy the pattern. Their accentuation and tempo, and even their relation to the dance steps, can vary from one musical culture to another, but the patterns remain the same, across a wide area, both in Africa, and in the African diaspora.

Performers can also play timelines on various objects used to accompany drums, lamellophones, xylophones, and vocal music; but in many cultures, they play the patterns predominantly on iron bells. The single flange-welded iron bell is inevitably associated with timelines, from West Africa to the –Pomo in northern Congo, to Katanga, and down to the –Ntumba on the Mozambique-Malawi border.

Several authors have tried to reconstruct the history of single and double clapperless bells in Africa, particularly on the subcontinent. Scholars have reached no consensus on details, but they agree that the knowledge of making bells spread by diffusion from West Africa, possibly from areas of eastern Nigeria and central Cameroon. It is likely that the processes of diffusion coincided with Late Iron Age technology. The spread of single and double bells southward can also be linked to the diffusion of several other traits not directly related to iron technology, such as central political organization in the form of strong chieftainship and royalty. Double bells "were a minor emblem of chieftainship, from Sokoto all the way to Barotseland. . . . Double bells present a broken distribution, with a bridge between them along the Ubangi and Congo valleys. Possibly the Sangha Valley may also provide a link" (Vansina 1969:190–191).

Archaeological evidence confirms the presence of "Guinea-type" double bells (figures 11 and 14)—a type common west of the Niger River, over to Ghana and the Côte d'Ivoire—in ancient Ife (Nigeria) during the Classical Period, roughly dated at the tenth to fourteenth centuries (Willet 1977:386). Single bells were excavated at Ingombe Ilede (Zambia), Sanga, and Katoto (Zaïre), and dated about A.D. 800.

FIGURE II   *Tatûm*: double bell kept by a –Pomo chief at Linjombo-Ng'benge, a village at the Sangha River on the border of Central African Republic and Congo; May 1966. This is a missing link in the "broken distribution" (Vansina 1969) of double bells in Central Africa.

Double bells with bow grip from Zimbabwe date from about 1450 to 1500 (Fagan 1965).

By 1992, the distribution of bells had receded in many areas where bells had been present a hundred years before. This change is probably due to the general decline that African iron technology suffered in the 1900s. From gaps in the history of the distribution, some scholars once inferred that bells had a broken distribution (Vansina 1969:191); later, however, new information closed some gaps. In the Sangha Valley in 1966, Djenda and I found double bells among the Mpyɛmnɔ and –Pomo (figure 11).

While bells are often associated with chieftainship or royalty, and timeline patterns are associated with single bells, the making of masks completes the picture of interrelationships, since, in most of the places mentioned, masks and secret societies support political authority. The people of eastern Angola consider a mask a *mukulu wa mwene* 'dead person associated with the ruler'; and in southern Malawi, local chiefs often control cells within the countrywide network of masked (*nyau*) secret societies.

Many details of the collected materials suggest a link among the selected cultural complexes, not only in the sociopolitical realm, but also in the historical. In many instances, these complexes spread jointly, in the form of clustered traits. Their absence in East Africa, and in southwestern Angola, implies their diffusion did not occur before the first migrations of Bantu speakers from the Bantu nucleus. From there, according to D. W. Phillipson (1977:227), two waves of migrations occurred: (a) about 1000 to 400 B.C., to the Great Lakes; and (b) 1000 to 200 B.C., southward into Angola. We cannot attribute to this period the spread of masked dancing, timelines, and iron bells. Most likely, that spread depended on the later diffusion of a large variety of traits from the Guinea Coast, adjacently into the equatorial forest zone (southern Cameroon, Gabon, Congo), and then to south-central Africa. This activity probably began toward the end of the Early Iron Age, during the last centuries of the first millennium. The spread of these traits did not necessarily follow the grand migrations, but could have come about gradually (at least in the western half of central Africa), until a more vigorous movement took place, from Central Africa to northern Mozambique and the Ruvuma Valley, transplanting these traditions to those areas, in parallel with the emerging ethnicity of the –Makonde, the –Makua, the –Lomwe, the –Ndonde, the –Yao, and related peoples.

Within Africa during the second millennium

Kings' courts: musical sponges

A factor that strongly influenced the course of African music history during the second millennium was the cohesive power centralized political organizations exerted. In many areas, from the interlacustrine kingdoms (in present Uganda, Rwanda, Burundi), to the "kingdoms of the savanna" (Vansina 1966), to Yoruba, Ashanti, Fõ, and other centralized states on the Guinea Coast, the royal courts functioned like sponges, absorbers of musical innovations from neighboring lands.

Conditions, however, varied; and the variance either promoted or inhibited such processes. Where the centralized organization was thoroughly indigenous—as in Buganda (most scholars reject the "Hima theory," which claims invading nomads created the kingdom)—an oligarchic establishment, driven by a need for entertainment, drew largely on local resources. Where state organization came from outside, as with the Fulɓe courts (in places like the towns of Toungo and Kontcha, on the northeastern Nigeria-Cameroon border), the invaders usually rejected local musical traditions; toward the peoples they had brought into subjection, they often practiced social and cultural apartheid.

entenga   Drum chime of the Buganda in Uganda

akadinda   Seventeen-to-twenty-two–note log xylophone of the Buganda in Uganda

amakondere   Horn ensemble of the Buganda in Uganda

kakaki   Long, end-blown trumpet of the Hausa of Zaria, Nigeria

ganga   Double-headed cylindrical drums, with snare string, of northern Nigeria

In fieldwork conducted in 1964, on the court music of the Lamido (Ful6e ruler) of Toungo and Kontcha (Kubik 1989b:82–85), no evidence that would point to the idea that, since the 1800s, the Ful6e oligarchy had absorbed traits from the musical cultures of the peoples they had subjugated (the Chamba, the Kutin, and others in the area) surfaced. On the contrary, in musical idiom and instrumental dimension, Ful6e court music perpetuated usages the rulers had adopted during centuries of contact with the old Hausa states.

An opposite example is Buganda, on the shores of Lake Victoria (East Africa), where no social stratification comparable to that in Nkore and Rwanda existed. Systematic study of the court music of the *kabaka* (king) began in the late 1930s, with Wachsmann's research. Several traditions—the *entenga* (drum chime), the *akadinda* (seventeen-to-twenty-two–note log xylophone), and the *amakondere* (horn ensemble)—did not extend beyond the confines of the court. A structural analysis of the court music (Anderson 1977; Kubik 1982, 1988a) revealed the music follows principles that do not differ from structural traits in the music of the villages that surround the court. These traits include tunings, and methods of contrapuntal interlocking. In part, the traditions at the king's court may have been esoteric; but stylistically they fit within the mold of southern Ugandan musical style. The interlocking technique used in *akadinda* music is probably ancient in Africa. Parallels have not been detected in other Ugandan xylophone styles (Anderson 1967:69; Kubik 1992), but three-part interlocking is common elsewhere in East and Central Africa: in *ngoma* drumming by Wagogo women (central Tanzania), in women's drumming during girls' initiation ceremonies (*cinamwali cha akazi*, in Malawi), and in the *ngwayi* drumming of the –Bemba of Zambia, where the principle of interlocking first came to outsiders' attention (Jones 1934:2).

Thus, the court music of Buganda retained certain ancient traits of Bantu musical construction, and shared many traits with neighboring cultures, especially that of Busoga. Oral traditions suggest Buganda, during its later history as a state, beginning with King Kintu (probably in the 1300s), often took musical inspiration from its vassal to the east, Busoga; Basoga musicians regularly visited the king's court (Wachsmann 1971:104). The structure of *embaire* (log xylophone) music in Busoga (figure 12) is comparable to that of the *amadinda* in Buganda. Though the themes played on the former instruments are usually less elaborate than themes played on the *amadinda*, there is evidence the court's musicians adopted from visiting Basoga musicians many *embaire* compositions, a well-known example of which is "*Mobuka ng'komera*," a composition the king's court knew under the title "*Alifuledi*" (Alfred). This song lampooned a man whose unsociability scared his neighbors.

In the period 1600–1900, other kings' courts also acted like cultural sponges. These included the famous kingdoms of Kongo and Luunda, and the state of the Kazembe at Lake Mweru, along important trade routes.

FIGURE 12   An *embaire* (log xylophone). The ensemble of George Mulabiza, ca. 18 (center), using an instrument of fourteen slats, with three players and other young men clapping hands. Two players, sitting obliquely opposite each other, combine their tone rows (played in parallel octaves) in duple-division interlocking technique. Nabigwali Village, near Bumanya, Busoga District, southern Uganda; January 1968.

Hausa and Ful6e: diffusion within a social stratum

Some instruments and musical traits that characterize Hausa and Ful6e court music ensembles—such as the groups that performed for the Emir of Zaria, in northern Nigeria (Kubik 1989b:96–97), or for the Lamido of Toungo and Kontcha (Kubik 1989b:82–87)—have a history that goes back to the 1200s and earlier. It suggests trans-Saharan contacts between North Africa and the western and central Sudan, and the development of a culture with a pinpointed geographical distribution existing for the benefit of oligarchic rulers. In the context of court music, the "imported" musical instruments, performative techniques, and stylistic traits became emblems of the ruling classes; the broader, often subdued, population of indigenous inhabitants did not share in these qualities. This situation exemplifies how the diffusion of a musical culture can remain within a social stratum, in this case the class that rules highly urbanized societies: former Hausa city-states, and (from the 1800s on) the Ful6e courts.

One of the instruments prominent in court music is the long trumpet (Gourlay 1982), an end-blown variety called *kakaki* among the Hausa of Zaria, and *gagashi* in the Ful6e dialect spoken in Toungo. In 1974, about fifteen court musicians in Zaria used three instruments, about 10 to 11½ feet long, with a mouthpiece. Artisans fashioned the trumpets of brass, reworked from industrial byproducts. In a recorded session, musicians performed with portable, double-skin, snared, cylindrical drums, which they struck with a bent stick. In the background were instruments the court musicians had adopted from the local culture: a side-blown animal horn, and double bells. The ensemble regularly performed on Fridays, and during ceremonial receptions, such as when the Sultan of Sokoto visited the Emir of Zaria (Ames 1964).

Scholars do not agree on when northern Nigeria acquired the long trumpet, the oboes, and the double-skin cylindrical drums of the *ganga* type. For sympathetic resonance, these drums have a snare string, and are struck with bent sticks. Interpreting the *Kano Chronicle* (a nineteenth-century manuscript), Veit Erlmann (1974) believed the long trumpet first saw service in the reign of Sarki Tsamia (1307–1343). The *Chronicle* specifies musicians played the instrument during the rule of Mohamma Rumfa (1463–1499) (Palmer 1908). Ken Gourlay (1982:50) theorized it reached Tunis by diffusion from the Islamic world in the mid-1300s, but in that period did not cross the Sahara; he supposed Mohammed ibn Abdullah ibn Battuta's mention of "horns and trumpets" in the court music of the Sultan of Mali (fourteenth century) did not refer to the long trumpet. Scholars agree, however, that the Songhai Empire (twelfth to sixteenth centuries) was a turntable of contact, which promoted the diffusion of North African musical traditions across the western and central Sudan. According to Kati and Ibn-al-Muḥtār, sixteenth- and seventeenth-century sources from the Songhai Empire (Gourlay 1982:51), the long trumpet came from the area of Aïr, farther north, after Askia Mohammed Tura had led an expedition against the Tildza people.

In the 1800s, an emerging Ful6e oligarchy adopted for its own court music the *kakaki-ganga-algeita* instrumental set, which the Ful6e have kept more segregated from local traditions than the Hausa have. In 1964, the court music of the Lamido of Toungo included dances (*nyawala, bonsuwe, chalawa*) that featured in turn several female praise singers, who cultivated an extremely narrow and raspy vocal quality. The accompanying instruments were one long trumpet, six *ganga* drums, and two *algeita* oboes.

The Ful6e were originally a pastoral people who adopted a I.A.1 (West Atlantic) language (Greenberg 1966). Their migration extended through the savanna and sahel zones of West Africa, from the Fouta Toro area (lower Senegal) to the Adamawa highlands (Cameroon). In the eleventh century, when the Islamization of the western

Cord-and-peg tension has a geographical
distribution that cardinally follows the Guinea
Coast, with not much extension inland.

Sudan began, and the Mali Empire arose, Islam first made converts in the ancient
Empire of Aukar (also known as "Ghana" in the literature, after the title of its ruler).
Fulɓe nomads made their first contact with an Islamic urban culture, and some of
them became urbanized. Islamic fervor, new military techniques, the development of
an efficient trading network, and the concentration of power in the hands of an oligarchy, combined to transform part of the Fulɓe from a pastoral population into an
urbanized one. (Those Fulɓe who have continued a nomadic lifestyle are known in
northern Nigeria as Bororo.) In the 1700s, a militant Islamic religious movement
emerged in the Futa Djallon Mountains (Guinea), with a *jihad* beginning in 1725.
"Holy wars" by the Fulɓe, such as the one Osman dan Fodio ("Uṭāmān ibn Fūdī")
waged in the land of the Hausa, beginning in 1804, led to the foundation of the
Islamic Sultanate of Sokoto. Throughout the 1800s, Fulɓe cavalry ravaged the western and central Sudan; but in many places, the Fulɓe migrants settled down, and
established their hegemony over local populations, modeled somewhat after Hausa
patterns.

The Fulɓe courts, with their musical traditions, survived Western colonialism;
after Nigeria and Cameroon achieved independence, the courts continued to exist in
the Adamawa region. The instrumental and stylistic resources of both Hausa and
Fulɓe court music shows how complex political forces interacted, to affect social and
cultural exchanges across the western and central Sudan, from the eleventh century to
the twentieth.

Cord-and-peg tension: diffusion within a neighborhood

In African musical cultures, a specific set of traits sometimes has a compact and
coherent distribution. If this picture combines with the presence of a complex technology, the historian can infer much about the history of local culture, to the exclusion of outside influences. A case in point is cord-and-peg tension, associated with
certain single-skin membrane drums of West Africa. The term translates the German
Schnurpflockspannung (Wieschhoff 1933). As it implies, the technology of drums
involves the use of pegs (sometimes of phallic shape), which describe a circular pattern around the drum's body. Strings wind elaborately around them, and a ring stabilizes the tension of the drumskin (figure 13).

When a technique is this elaborate and specific, it is unlikely to have been
invented more than once. Cord-and-peg tension makes a likely case for neighborhood diffusion. Moreover, if we correlate its present distribution with the ethnic and
linguistic map of West Africa, we discover that its incidence coincides with the area
of the I.A.4 (or Kwa) languages, only sporadically spilling over the linguistic border
to the west (as shown by its adoption in some Mande-speaking areas). East of the
Niger River, where (among the Igbo) wedge-and-ring tension is more common, its
incidence fades.

FIGURE 13   Cord-and-peg tension in Ewe drums kept by Hubert Kponton (1905–1981) in his private museum, Musée Historique et Artistique Kponton, in the Rue Kuassibruce, Lomé, Togo; January 1970. The museum no longer exists.

Thus, cord-and-peg tension has a geographical distribution that cardinally follows the Guinea Coast, with not much extension inland. Its distribution area is also roughly congruent with that of the Guinea-type double bell. By this term, I understand a type of iron bell that has, in the words of Danhin Amagbenyō Kofi, a Togolese researcher, "one large bell carrying a smaller one on its back like a mother carries her child" (figure 14). This distribution shows intensive cultural exchanges took place between the Guinea Coast peoples, roughly from the Niger River westward to the Republic of Benin (Dahomey), Togo, and Ghana; but it also shows their relative encapsulation, vis-à-vis non-I.A.4-speaking ethnic groups.

A small, well defined distribution area need not signify that the technology on which a trait depends is recent: it can alternatively imply a strong cultural and political coherence among the people who use it. Thus, non-I.A.4-speakers in West Africa

FIGURE 14   Technique of playing the Guinea type of double bells (*ogā*), among the Fō, Sada Gbonjenji, Togo, in January 1970. The left hand holds the double bell at the stem grip; the right hand strikes it with a wooden beater. Performers systematically modify the timbre by bringing the larger bell's orifice close to the plane of the ground.

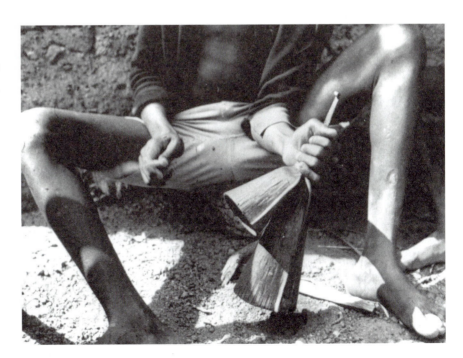

Lamellophones were even reintroduced to some parts
of West Africa from the New World (notably Cuba),
where knowledge of their use had spread with
slavery.

have shown a reluctance to adopt these drums, while speakers of Ewe, Fõ, and Akan
have taken the technology with them, wherever they have settled.

Outside West Africa, the only area to which cord-and-peg tension traveled was
the New World. In fact, wherever across the Atlantic this trait appears, its appearance
is a likely sign of an Ewe, Fõ, Akan, or (more rarely) Yoruba cultural heritage, resulting from the transportation of people from those cultural areas. Cord-and-peg tension turns up among the "Bush Negroes" of Surinam, in drums used in *candomblé*
cults in Bahia (Brazil), in Haiti, and in Cuba: there is even an instance of such a
drum from eighteenth-century Virginia (Epstein 1973).

In West Africa, cord-and-peg tension characterizes drums appropriate for specific contexts. These instruments prove to be "talking drums" par excellence. Texts and
pictures since the 1700s mention them. Their sounds were first recorded by J. von
Smend in 1905, in the vicinity of the Misahöhe, a mountainous area near the town
of Palime, Togo. The most famous "talking drums" are the *atumpan* of the Ashanti of
Ghana. Used in pairs, they often complete the ambience of funeral ceremonies
(Nketia 1963); during state ceremonies, they accompany the *fɔntɔmfrɔm* (dance of
warriors). As Nketia shows, they form part of the regalia of an Ashanti chief.

The Anyi, who inhabit a border area of Ghana and the Côte d'Ivoire, use similar
instruments (Yotamu 1979). The Anyi drums, called *chenepri*, are taller and slimmer
than *atumpan*; the drummers use L-shaped sticks. In 1978, at the funeral of the
mother of Chief Sakandiokro, the *chenepri* invoked the spirit of the deceased, begging her to reveal herself through a medium, to declare whether evil magic had
caused her death (Yotamu 1989:154–163).

The Ewe use similar cord-and-peg instruments, but prefer a more barrel-like
shape (figure 13) (Kubik 1989b:144–145). The Fõ use some tall, single-headed,
cord-and-peg-tensioned instruments, which they reserve for *vodu*-cult activities. An
example of the Fõ drums is the *oɣŋ* set: the *oɣŋvi* 'child drum', the *kpezi*, and the
jikpo; each is played with a curved stick (*aglakpovi*), in the form of a lazy "7" (Danhin
1989).

The case of cord-and-peg tension in drums of the Guinea Coast shows how an
ancient technology spread by contact between related neighbors, without any
involvement of long-distance migration (except the New World diaspora). In the late
1900s, the African distribution area was compact, and had a clearly regional character. In the previous century or two, the distribution area of cord-and-peg tension
shrank a little. Archaeological evidence points to a wider distribution area in the past.
A ceremonial pot excavated in Nigeria shows a cord-and-peg drum in a depiction
attributed to the Classical Period of Ife art, dating from the tenth to the fourteenth
centuries (Willet 1977; Kubik 1989b:107). The Edo (Bini) people knew the technology, as a Benin bronze plaque, dated from the mid-1500s to the end of the 1600s
(Kubik 1989b:98–99) proves. In Benin City, under Oba Oguola (ca. 1280–1295),
professional metal workers first made bronze plaques for ceremonial purposes. Both

Ife and Benin cultures were about 90 miles inland from the coast. In the early 1990s, they did not use cord-and-peg tension techniques, which had apparently disappeared from their area.

Lamellophones: diffusion without migration

Many cultures of the world know the principle of twanging a fixed tongue, or lamella. A common example is a one-note lamellophone. This principle developed elaborately in Africa, where multinote instruments of this type arose. Writers have discussed African lamellophones under various terms: *sansa*, *mbira*, *plucked idiophone*, *Zupfzungenspiel*, *thumb piano*, *hand piano*, even (disparagingly) *Kaffir piano*. These terms are incorrect—in spelling, or denotation, or application, or connotation. Eventually, the term *lamellophone* came into currency, first in French writings, and then in English.

By the late 1990s, it was impossible to identify the precise area in sub-Saharan Africa where lamellophones had originated. Around 1950, they were taking an abundance of forms; one of the most varied profusions occurred in Zaïre (Laurenty 1962). The development of so many variants implies that lamellophones had been present in sub-Saharan Africa for a long time; however, in four regions of the continent (discussed below), the instrument appeared only after the 1600s.

1. Most of East Africa.—In Uganda, and in southernmost Sudan, lamellophones of the Zaïrean, box-resonated *likembe* type appeared not earlier than 1900. Inspiration for the large lamellophones found among the Wagogo and Wanyamwezi (of central Tanzania) came from contacts with Zaïrean musicians; they derive from late-nineteenth-century Zaïrean models, which went to Tanzania with the caravan trade of the wapangaji (mostly Swahili-speaking Wanyamwezi porters). In Kenya, lamellophones are insignificantly present. The only area in East Africa where at least one type of lamellophone is probably indigenous is the Lower Ruvuma cultural area, divided between southeastern Tanzania and northeastern Mozambique. The Makonde/Mwera type, reported under the name *ulimba*, occurs there. This instrument has broad iron tongues, which hook into a box resonator. It is the only type of African lamellophone devoid of a bridge, a pressure bar, and a backrest; it has a permanent, unchangeable tuning; and it has other unusual traits, especially its shape.
2. South Africa and adjacent areas.—Lamellophones are not indigenous in South Africa. Only the BaVenda have adopted the instrument, which they base on Zimbabwean models. Migrant miners (from Angola, Mozambique, and other areas) sometimes play it.
3. Inland of the West African coast.—The lamellophone is foreign to the West and West-Central African sahel, and much of the savanna zone. It is sometimes seen in the hands of residents of the Guinea Coast.
4. The Guinea Coast.—Research implies that along the Guinea Coast, in areas west of the Niger River, lamellophones are a late introduction, linked to the maritime trade (Kubik 1989b:50–61, 70–77, 116–117, 138, 173). They may first have appeared along the coast in the 1700s, and in some places much later.

Lamellophones were even reintroduced to some parts of West Africa from the New World (notably Cuba), where knowledge of their use had spread with slavery. The *agidigbo*, a large box-resonated lamellophone among the Yoruba of western Nigeria, resembles the Cuban *marímbula*; it could be a case of a "return" of what was originally an African instrument.

It is no coincidence that the earliest written source to mention a lamellophone, João dos Santos's writings of 1609, comes from southeast Africa.

FIGURE 15   A lamellophone made of raffia; from near Chitambo Village (on the road from Milange to Molumbo), east of Lake Chilwa, Mozambique; 4 October 1962.

African lamellophones have lamellae made of iron or plant materials (usually raffia, occasionally bamboo). Whether metallic or vegetable instruments appeared first, is indeterminate. Evolutionists assume lamellophones using pre–Iron Age materials and technology came first. In some places, as in Mozambique, near Lake Chilwa (figure 15), children used to play a simple raffia lamellophone; when they reached adulthood, they proceeded to iron varieties: but this kind of evidence is also insufficient to set up an evolutionary line. In some regions, as among the –Cokwe of Angola, scholars supply counterevidence by noting that some raffia-made lamellophones are modeled after iron instruments. It is important to examine the tonal layout, because that attribute is crucial in defining types (Tracey 1972). A raffia lamellophone that clearly represents a *mucapata* type of –Cokwe lamellophone appears in the collection of the Museu de Etnologia (Lisbon, no. AH–622); the maker used raffia instead of iron, probably because iron was not readily available.

Lamellophones made of plant materials occur in many areas of sub-Saharan Africa where iron lamellophones abound; there, they often imply an inferior social position (used by children and learners). In other areas, raffia lamellophones occur exclusively. The largest of these areas stretches through the Cameroon grasslands to eastern Nigeria. In it, complex forms of the raffia lamellophone have developed: the

FIGURE 16   A twentieth-century southwestern Angolan lamellophone of a type identical with that drawn by Ferreira. The body is board-shaped, almost square; the soundboard and backrest for the lamellae are a single piece of wood; the bridge is U-shaped metal; the 16 iron lamellae are of spatula shape (broader at the playing ends); the layout of the lamellae is V-shaped; tuning wax and an iron bar with rattle rings rest at the front edge of the board (which in this specimen is lost). Museu de Etnologia, Lisbon, AP824; acquired in Namibe Province, Angola, in 1971.

timbrh of the Vute (central Cameroon), with ingenious raffia vibration needles; and the *mbɔŋgo* of the (neighboring) Tikar. In that area, where the raffia lamellophone is tuned in pairs and octaves, we find unusual performative techniques: (a) striking two adjacent tones at once with the thumb, and (b) using thumbs and index fingers of both hands for plucking, as with some Tikar *mbɔŋgo* (Kubik 1989b:56–57). Outside Cameroon, in one broad region, the Zimbabwe-Zambezi cultural area, players use an index finger to twang a lamella from below. In central Cameroon and eastern Nigeria, they also apply tuning wax to many raffia instruments. This custom bespeaks connections with Angola and southern Zaïre, where tuning wax is also an instrumentalist's accessory.

Were vegetable or metallic instruments the earlier norm? Two possibilities vie for attention; they are not mutually exclusive. If raffia lamellophones came first, the African lamellophone would have been a pre–Iron Age invention. The raffia instrument could have been invented in a zone of intensive raffia-palm cultivation, such as Cameroon and eastern Nigeria, certain parts of Zaïre, and ecologically similar places. If iron lamellophones came first, they could have taken inspiration from the knowledge of xylophones, in a desire to make "small portable versions of the larger instrument" (Jones 1964:34). The identity of many word stems used for both types of instrument supports this hypothesis. In this case, we should have to consider the African lamellophone an Iron Age development, and its invention could well have taken place in an intensively iron-mining and iron-working area. At the southern Zambian site of Kumadzulo, archaeologists have uncovered what could be iron lamellae, which they have radiocarbon-dated to between the fifth and seventh centuries. At Zimbabwean excavations, what might be lamellae of *mbira dza vadzimu* have turned up, with much later radiocarbon dates.

Where excavations document the extensive use of bells, such as in the artifacts from Ingombe Ilede on the Zambezi (Phillipson 1977:193–194), the technology for making lamellophones also existed. In view of this background, plus the fact that the Zimbabwe and Lower Zambezi cultural area displays a complex genealogy of different types (Andrew Tracey 1972), I believe, if iron lamellophones came first, southeast Africa was one likely location for the invention of the African lamellophone, and even if raffia instruments appeared earlier, southeast Africa was still the region where iron varieties could have originated. No other region in Africa demonstrates a greater diversity of types; this fact implies lamellophones had a long evolutionary history in this region. After Portuguese trading posts (Sena in 1531, Tete in 1532) arose on the Zambezi, this cultural area became an important secondary center of dispersion for lamellophones.

It is no coincidence that the earliest written source to mention a lamellophone, João dos Santos's writings of 1609, describing a nine-note "ambira" with iron lamellae, comes from southeast Africa; and that the next known source (although secondary), Filippo Bonanni's *Gabineto Armónico* (1723), also refers to what must be southeastern Africa, and shows a stylized drawing of a "Caffir" playing a nine-note lamellophone, with an expanse of water (the Indian Ocean?) in the background. The third known source, which describes and illustrates a lamellophone, does not come from Africa: it is Alexandre Rodrigues Ferreira's account of an instrument in the possession of an African slave the author encountered in northern Brazil, in the late 1700s. Instruments identical with Ferreira's appear in only a small area of Angola: the southwestern parts, Provincia de Wila and Namibe (figure 16). If an Angolan slave made a lamellophone of this type in Brazil in the last decades of the 1700s, it must have been present in southwestern Angola from roughly the mid-1700s on.

The *pombeiros* (African-Portuguese traders), who crossed Africa from Angola to Mozambique, along a trade route from Luanda via the Luunda Empire and the state

FIGURE 17   Two-part scheme of vocal combinations frequently heard in the area of Lake Malawi.

of the Mwata Kazembe (at Lake Mweru), down to Tete (on the Zambezi), spread various musical instruments and traditions from the Zambezi Valley to Malawi, northeastern Zambia, Shaba Province of Zaïre, and Angola. Some Angolan board lamellophones show organological connections with the small, fan-shaped *kalimba* lamellophones used north of the Zambezi, roughly along the ancient trade route. From eastern Angola (including adjacent areas in Zaïre) comes the only type of lamellophone with more than one rank of tongues observed outside the Zimbabwe-Zambezi cultural area: the *cisanji calungandu*; its remote connection with southeast Africa is likely.

Thus emerges a complex picture of intra-African streams of influence: lamellophone traditions from southeastern Africa connect with some of those of Central Africa and beyond—the Guinea Coast, and the New World. In the 1800s, the spread of lamellophones across Central Africa into East Africa added another dimension: porters and migrant workers carried box-resonated lamellophones called *likembe* from a dispersal center in southwestern Zaïre, up the Congo-Zaïre River, and then to Uganda, southern Sudan, the Central African Republic, and eastern Angola.

The Angoni: diffusion by migration

Among the most fully known consequential migrations of people within Africa is the Angoni migration of the 1800s. The Angoni were a South African people who invaded northern and central Malawi, southeastern Tanzania, and parts of northern Mozambique, where their descendants form cultural pockets, which keep musical traditions otherwise associated with Isizulu- and Siswati-speaking peoples in South Africa. The Nguni background is perceptible, particularly in the following characteristics of music around Lake Malawi.

1. The presence of a pentatonic, two-voice style of singing, characterized by certain harmonic stereotypes. There are unmistakable signs, affirmed by the music of people who were little affected by Ngoni culture, that, before the Angoni invasion, musical cultures in the area used hexatonic and heptatonic tonalities, and that the harmonic patterns shown in figure 17 have roots in the invaders' vocal music.
2. The presence of *izibongo*-style praise songs associated with chieftainship in groups of Ngoni descendants, as George T. Nurse documented (1967), at the installation of Chief Gomani III, at Mlangeni, Ncheu District. These songs derive from Zulu traditions.
3. The presence of the dances *ngoma* (among the southern Angoni), and *ingoma* (among the northern Angoni). These dances derive from South Africa, where they were originally warriors' dances, executed with spears and shields.
4. The presence of the women's mouthbow (*nkangala*) and men's gourd-resonated bow (*gubo*), musical instruments of Zulu origin.

FIGURE 18   Nasineya Zamunda, ca. 40, demonstrates the technique of playing the *nkangala* mouth bow; Njolomole Village, Ncheu District, Malawi, September 1967.

In the early 1800s, when South Africa was in a state of political turmoil, groups of Zulu and Swazi, swayed by charismatic personalities, migrated north. Along their routes, they assimilated recruits from other ethnic groups, without losing their ethnic identity. Oral traditions say they crossed the Zambezi during an eclipse of the sun, which astronomers fix at 19 November 1835. Migrating north, they plundered villages in Malawi, Mozambique, and southwestern Tanzania, where they caused further migrations, such as the flight of people into mountainous areas (Kubik 1982:42). After fighting as far north as Lake Tanganyika, they settled in several places, where they maintained their traditions. In John Hanning Speke's time (1863), they were known as the "Watuta," in areas south of Lake Victoria.

Among Zulu and Swazi traditions that survive in Malawi and Tanzania is the *nkangala* mouthbow (pl., *mikangala*), a classical instance of borrowing: name, instrument, and performative technique have remained identical. Pronounced /ŋkaŋgala/ in southern Malawi, and /mtyangala/ in northern Malawi and southwestern Tanzania, this term derives from Isizulu *umqangala*, a designation for an identical instrument among the Zulu of South Africa. (In Isizulu, "q" represents a palato-alveolar click sound; because speakers of Malawian and Tanzanian languages found it difficult to pronounce, they changed it into /ŋk/ and /mty/, respectively.) The *nkangala* is made from a straight stick of *bango*, a tall, noded reed (*Phragmites mauritanus*, of the grass family) with spine-tipped blades and large, plumelike panicles. It grows freely near rivers and lakes in southern Africa, where it serves in the manufacture of fences, mats, and other musical instruments, such as raft zithers. The string of the *nkangala* comes from the sisal agave (*khonje* in Chicheŵa). The instrument maker shaves off the outer fibers of the sisal, and then twists on a thigh the inner fibers. The resultant string passes through a notch carved into each end of the stick, where it is fastened.

Girls and women normally play the *nkangala* in times of solitude. For a girl to play it indicates the desire for company; for a married woman to do so, however, can invite social opprobrium. Nevertheless, many married women play it expertly. The instrument is mouth-resonated: one end of the stick is pressed on the right corner of the mouth. The player strikes the string with a small plectrum, held in the right hand, to produce two fundamentals a whole step apart. For sounding the lower one, she leaves the string open; for sounding the higher, she stops it with the middle finger of the left hand (figure 18). The range of harmonics reinforced by changing the size of the mouth's cavity goes up to the fifth partial for the lower fundamental, and the fourth partial for the higher one, thus producing the pentatonic scale and harmonic bichords characteristic of Nguni-influenced music around Lake Malawi (figure 19).

The calabash-resonated, unbraced musical bow called *gubo* by one informant in Malawi (Kubik 1982:170–171) is another instance of Ngoni introduction. The word is a corruption of the Zulu term *ughubu* (Rycroft 1976:50–60), which implies for this instrument a South African ancestry.

TWENTIETH-CENTURY TRENDS

The most important changes that occurred in twentieth-century intra-African music history depended on the catalytic effects of two developments in communication:

FIGURE 19   *Nkangala* harmonics and the resultant scale.

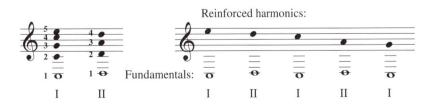

zeze   Flat-bar zither of East Africa

valimba (**or** *ulimba*)   Gourd-resonated large
    xylophone of southern Malawi

motor and air travel, and the rise of the mass media. Beginning in the 1800s, with new developments in transportation (steamers, trains, cars, trucks, airplanes), people could travel more easily. Areas that had had little contact with each other suddenly became neighbors. These developments eased the migration of laborers, and made possible the interethnic and interlanguage contacts characteristic of twentieth-century cultures. From the 1920s on, with the availability of radios and hand-cranked phonographs, musical pieces could spread quickly, even to remote villages, without human carriers. In the late 1800s, musical instruments such as the East African *zeze* or *sese* (flat-bar zither) could have spread to Zaïre and the Zambezi Valley, only because of the trade routes. In the early 1900s, migrant workers spread knowledge of the *likembe*. After the 1930s, the situation changed radically. Only in part did human carriers spread current styles of guitar music: individuals learned many songs from radio broadcasts.

These developments controlled the distribution of twentieth-century styles of popular music. In the 1950s, stylistic super-areas emerged: (a) a zone of highlife and jùjú music, along the West African coast; (b) a zone that featured the guitar styles of Central and East Africa, initially divided into a "western Congolese" guitar style and a "Katangan" one; and (c) a South African–inspired zone, based on *kwela* and *tsaba-tsaba*, extending to northern countries, such as Zimbabwe, Zambia, and Malawi. The last-named style also radiated to Katanga, as Mwenda-Jean Bosco's song "Mama na Mwana" proves (Rycroft 1962:95). These super-areas developed within a decade. Later, their contours became more and more blurred, because, from the late 1960s, the mass media began to reach for continentwide coverage; Zaïrean music, for example, was increasingly heard, not only in Central and East Africa, but also in some (notably Francophone) areas of West Africa, where it influenced local styles.

The background of African musical innovation in the 1900s, and the manner by which creative ideas began to influence each other across the continent, lay in the revolution in communications. Without that revolution, none of the factors usually cited—urbanization, industrialization, social change, ethnic transculturation—could have had the effects attributed to them.

After about 1950, African music also began to show the effect of changing values, sometimes merely by reflecting a colonial "holdover." What people widely considered "modern" or fashionable was dance music that exclusively employed factory-manufactured, imported instruments, such as electrically amplified guitars. Despite increases in the cost of these instruments, and the burden their purchase implied, popular opinion in Africa put them at the top of the musical hierarchy—an attitude comparable with that expressed toward the pianoforte in the 1800s and early 1900s in European concert hall music. There was little music educators could do about such sentiments. From the 1960s, the broad public wanted nothing short of the latest amplifiers; and, in the 1980s, popular evaluation in most areas not only contributed to the elimination of "acoustic" guitar styles, but forced any groups for whom "mod-

FIGURE 20 Kambazithe Makolekole and his *valimba* (xylophone) ensemble, a popular group of Sena musicians; Singano Village, Chileka, Malawi, September 1991. This ensemble uses a twenty-four-key gourd-resonated xylophone with equiheptatonic tuning, a small accompanying drum (*gaka*), and rattles (*nkhocho*). As is common with *valimba* groups, one deep-tuned slat—in this case, the second from below—is double (two slats on top of each other, bound together, not tuned). At a certain point in a song, instrumentalists use it to produce rhythmic patterns, imitating the machine-gun fire in Dube in 1980. Photo by Moya Aliya Malamusi.

ern" equipment was too costly either out of business, or into new strategies for survival. The all-pervasive model was the dance band with three electric guitars: lead, rhythm, bass. There was experimentation throughout Africa with homemade amplification: musicians themselves spun wires for electric guitars, but the model remained unchanged for nearly thirty years. That consistency left a small margin for an individual musician's dissident behavior: the market did not reward it. With the latest records continually dominating popular taste, and reinforcing the existing value system, musical groups (particularly those of lesser fame) had no choice but to change their style almost yearly, following the current fashions, or else go out of business. That consideration affected not only groups that played factory-manufactured dance band equipment (or its homemade imitations) but increasingly also groups that performed with what scholars call "traditional" instruments.

The trend began in the 1960s in West Africa, with groups such as the Richard Band de Zoétélé of Yaoundé (Cameroon), and the Miami Bar Xylophone Band; those groups performed songs current on records imported from Cuba, Zaïre, and the Congo. In eastern Nigeria in 1988, Artur Simon recorded a log-xylophone band that played music copied and adapted from that diffused by the mass media in the country (personal communication).

In southern Malawi, the *valimba* or *ulimba* (gourd-resonated large xylophone) probably survived into the 1990s, only because musicians learned to copy music from Kenyan guitar records (when those were popular), and later from Zimbabwean records, in a musical style much nearer to that of the Sena xylophone in the past, as recorded by Tracey, Kubik, Djenda, and others (Kubik and Malamusi 1989). Even the instrument began to change: in the early 1980s, it began to sport one double slat (figure 20), two xylophone keys placed on top of each other to make a concussive sound, perceived to represent the rattling of machine-gun fire. The idea came from a popular Zimbabwean song, "Take Cover," performed on an LP disk by the William Dube Jairos Jiri Sunrise Kwela Band (1980), which xylophone players in Mozambique and Malawi began to imitate on their instruments. Asena musicians still played *ulimba* music widely, in spite of the scarcity of gourds for resonators, due to the frequent closures of the border with Mozambique. There was a tendency toward changing the tunings of the xylophones toward major and minor scales.

Across Africa, among rural and semiurban populations, historical consciousness in music remained low. Youths—the cohort of the population whose tastes relied on the mass media, and whom in turn those media easily manipulated—often dismissed older styles as "out of date," and therefore worthless. The mass media turned out to be a double-edged sword. On the one hand, they opened the African continent, allowing intra-African streams of influence to flow faster, and thereby stimulating innovation in popular music; on the other hand, they set up a dictatorship of values. As a result, only a narrow margin for the development of nonconformist, personal styles remained, though individual artists were largely unaware of the new limitations on their creativity.

REFERENCES

Ames, David. 1964. *The Music of Nigeria, Hausa Music, I.* Bärenreiter- Musicaphon Records, BM 30L 2306. LP disk.

Anderson, Lois. 1967. "The African Xylophone." *African Arts / Arts d'Afrique* I:46–49.

———. 1977. "The Entenga Tuned-Drum Ensemble." In *Essays for a Humanist: An Offering to Klaus Wachsmann*, 1–57. New York: Town House Press.

Aniakor, Chike. 1978. "Omabe Festival." *Nigeria Magazine* 126/127:3–12.

Ankermann, Bernard. 1901. "Die afrikanischen Musikinstrumente." *Ethnologisches Notizblatt*, 3(1):I–X, 1–32.

Anyumba, Henry O. 1983. "Contemporary Lyres in Eastern Africa." *African Musicology* 1(1):18–33.

Blacking, John. 1989. "Challenging the Myth of Ethnic Music: First Performance of a New Song in an African Oral Tradition, 1961." *Yearbook for Traditional Music* 21:17–24.

Bonanni, Filippo. 1723. *Gabinetto Armónico*. Rome: Giorgio Placho.

Bosco, Mwenda Jean. 1951. *Mama na Mwana*. Gallotone, GB 1700 T. 78-rpm disk.

Carrington, J. F. 1969. *Talking Drums of Africa*. New York: Negro Universities Press.

Danhin, Amagbenyo Kofi. 1989. Untitled contribution. In Kubik 1989b:126–131, 134–141.

Dargie, David. 1988. *Xhosa Music: Its Techniques and Instruments, With a Collection of Songs*. Cape Town, Johannesburg: David Philip.

Davidson, Basil. 1967. *African Kingdoms*. Amsterdam: Time-Life International.

de Wolf, Paul P. 1983. "Xhosa." In *Lexikon der Afrikanistik: Afrikanische Sprachen und ihre Erforschung*, ed. Hermann Jungraithmayr and Wilhelm J. G. Möhlig, 270. Berlin: Dietrich Reimer Verlag.

Dias, Jorge, and Margot Dias. 1970. *Os Macondes de Moçambique*. Lisbon: Centro de Estudos de Antropologia Cultural.

Didier, André, and Gilbert Rouget. 1946. *Musique Bantou d'Afrique Equatoriale Française*. Editions de la Boîte à Musique, LD 324. LP disk.

Djenda, Maurice. 1968. "Les pygmées de la Haute Sangha." *Geographica* 14:26–43.

Dos Santos, João. 1609. *Ethiopia Oriental*. Evora.

Dube, William (William Dube Jairos Jiri Sunrise Kwela Band). 1980. *Take Cover*. Teal Record Company (Bulawayo), ZIM 32. LP disk.

Epstein, Dena. 1973. "African Music in British and French America." *Musical Quarterly* 59:61–91.

Erlmann, Veit. 1974. "Some Sources on Music in Western Sudan from 1300–1700." *African Music* 5(3):34–39.

Fagan, B. M. 1965. *Southern Africa during the Iron Age*. London: Thames & Hudson.

Ferreira, Alexandre Rodrigues. 1971–1974. *Viagem filosófica pelas Capitanias do Grão Pará, Rio Negro, Mato Grosso e Cuiabá, 1783–1792*. Rio de Janeiro.

Födermayr, Franz. 1969. "Lieder der Bäle-Bilia." *Mitteilungen der Anthropologischen Gesellschaft in Wien* 99:64–76, plates I–IX.

Gourlay, Ken. 1982. "Long Trumpets of Northern Nigeria in History and Today." *African Music* 6(2):48–72.

Gräbner, Fritz. 1911. *Methode der Ethnologie.* Heidelberg: Karl Winters Universitätsbuchhandlung.

Greenberg, Joseph H. 1966. *The Languages of Africa.* Bloomington, Ind.: Research Center for the Language Sciences.

Herskovits, Melville J. 1938. *Acculturation: The Study of Culture Contact.* New York: J. J. Augustin.

———. 1944. *The Myth of the Negro Past.* Boston: Beacon Press.

Hirschberg, Walter. 1969. "Early Historical Illustrations of West and Central African Music." *African Music* 4(3):6–18.

———. 1970. "Die Doppelglocke im Kongo/Angola-Raum." In *Musik als Gestalt und Erlebnis* [Festschrift Walter Graf zum 65. Geburtstag] (Vienna: Böhlau), 78–91.

Hornbostel, Erich Moritz von. 1911. "Über ein akustisches Kriterium für Kulturzusammen-hänge." *Zeitschrift für Ethnologie* 43:601–615.

Huie, Wade. 1979. "Tongong Returns to the City of Glass." *Nairobi Daily Nation*, 30 November: 13, 15.

Jones, Arthur M. 1934. "African Drumming—A Study in the Combination of Rhythms in African Music." *Bantu Studies* 8:1–16.

———. 1964. *Africa and Indonesia: The Evidence of the Xylophone and Other Musical and Cultural Factors.* Leiden: E. J. Brill. 2nd (enlarged) edn., 1971.

Kebede, Ashenafi. 1977. "The Bowl-Lyre of Northeast Africa. *Krar*: The Devil's Instrument." *Ethnomusicology* 21:379–395.

Kimberlin, Cynthia. 1978. "The Baganna of Ethiopia." *Ethiopianist Notes* 2(2).

Kirby, Percival. 1932. "The Recognition and Practical Use of the Harmonics of Stretched Strings by the Bantu of South Africa." *Bantu Studies* 6:31–46.

———. 1961. "Physical Phenomena Which Appear to Have Determined the Basis and Development of a Harmonic Sense among Bushmen, Hottentot and Bantu." *African Music* 2(4):6–9.

Kubik, Gerhard. 1970. *Música tradicional e acul-turada dos !Kung' de Angola.* Lisbon: Junta de Investigações Científicas do Ultramar.

———. 1972. "Oral Notation of Some West and Central African Time-Line Patterns." *Review of Ethnology* 3:169–176.

———. 1980a. "Donald Kachamba's Montage Recordings: Aspects of Urban Music History in Malaŵi." *African Urban Studies* 6 (winter):89–122.

———. 1980b. "Likembe Tunings of Kufuna Kandonga (Angola)." *African Music* 6(1):70- -88.

———. 1982. *Ostafrika: Musikgeschichte in Bildern.* Leipzig: Deutscher Verlag für Musik.

———. 1986. "Stability and Change in African Musical Traditions." *The World of Music* 27:44–69.

———. 1988a. *Zum Verstehen afrikanischer Music.* Leipzig: Verlag Philipp Reclam jun.

———. 1988b. "Nsenga/Shona Harmonic Patterns and the San Heritage in Southern Africa." *Ethnomusicology* 32(2):39–76 (211–248).

———. 1989a. "The Southern African Periphery: Banjo Traditions in Zambia and Malaŵi." *The World of Music* 31:3–29.

———. 1989b. *Westafrika: Musikgeschichte in Bildern.* Leipzig: Deutscher Verlag für Musik.

———. 1992. "*Embaire* Xylophone Music of Samusiri Babalanda (Uganda 1968)." *The World of Music.*

Kubik, Gerhard, and Moya Aliya Malamusi. 1986. "Nachdokumentation der Sammlung afrikanischer Musikinstrumente im Musikinstrumentenmuseum / Münchener Stadtmuseum: Entwurf eines Katalog-Textes." Munich: Münchener Stadtmuseum. Manuscript.

———. 1989. *Opeka nyimbo: Musician-Composers from Southern Malaŵi.* Museum für Völkerkunde, Musikethnologische Abteilung. Museum Collection Berlin, MC 15. Two LP disks and notes.

Kubik, Gerhard, Moya Aliya Malamusi, Lidiya Malamusi, and Donald Kachamba. 1987. *Malaŵian Music: A Framework for Analysis.* Zomba, Malaŵi: University of Malaŵi, Department of Fine and Performing Arts.

Laurenty, Jean-Sebastien. 1962. *Les sanza du Congo.* Tervuren, Belgium: Musée Royal de l'Afrique Centrale. Annales, 3.

Leroy, Jules. 1967. *Ethiopian Paintings: Late Middle Ages and during Gondar Dynasty.* New York.

Lomax, Alan. 1968. *Folk Song Style and Culture.* Washington, D.C.: American Association for the Advancement of Science.

———. 1976. *Cantometrics—An Approach to the Anthropology of Music.* Berkeley: University of California. Handbook and audio cassettes.

Mahi, Ismail. 1972. "Musical Traditions in the Sudan." *La Revue Musicale*, special number (African Music Meeting in Yaoundé, 23–27 February 1970, organized by UNESCO): 89–94.

Morgan, Lewis Henry. 1877. *Ancient Society, or Researches in the Lines of Human Progress from Savagery, through Barbarism, to Civilization.* Cambridge, Mass.: Harvard University Press.

Mudimbe, V. Y. 1988. *The Invention of Africa: Gnosis, Philosophy, and the Order of Knowledge.* Bloomington: Indiana University Press.

Murray, Jocelyn, ed. 1981. *Cultural Atlas of Africa.* Oxford: Elsevier Publishers.

Nketia, J. H. Kwabena. 1963. *Drumming in Akan Communities of Ghana*. Edinburgh: Thomas Nelson.

Nurse, George T. 1967. "The Installation of Inkosi ya Makosi Gomani III." *African Music* 4(1):56–63.

———. 1972. "Musical Instrumentation among the San (Bushmen) of the Central Kalahari." *African Music* 5(2):23–27.

Palmer, H. R. 1908. "The Kano Chronicle." *Journal of the Royal Anthropological Institute* 38:58–98.

Phillipson, David W. 1977. *The Later Prehistory of Eastern and Southern Africa*. London: Heinemann.

Rycroft, David. 1962. "The Guitar Improvisations of Mwenda Jean Bosco." *African Music* 2(4):81–98, 3(1):86–102.

———. 1976. "The Zulu Bow Songs of Princess Magogo." *African Music* 5(4):41–97.

———. 1978. "Comments on Bushman and Hottentot Music Recorded by E. O. J. Westphal." *Review of Ethnology* 5(2–3):16–23.

Schüller, Dietrich. 1972. "Beziehungen zwischen west- und west-zentralafrikanischen Staaten von 1482 bis 1700." Ph.D. dissertation, Universität Wien.

Speke, John Hanning. 1863. *Journal of the Discovery of the Source of the Nile*. Edinburgh: Blackwood.

Tracey, Andrew. 1961. "Mbira Music of Jege A Tapera." *African Music* 2(4): 44–63.

———. 1970. "The Matepe Mbira Music of Rhodesia." *African Music* 4(4): 37–61.

———. 1972. "The Original African Mbira?" *African Music* 5(2):85–104.

———. 1989. "The System of the Mbira." *Papers presented at the Seventh Symposium on Ethnomusicology, University of Venda, 2–5 September 1982*, 43–55. Grahamstown: International Library of African Music.

———. 1990. Lady Frere, Transkei: International Library of African Music, Rhodes University. LP disk and notes.

Vansina, Jan. 1965. *Oral Tradition: A Study of Historical Methodology*. London: Routledge and Kegan Paul.

———. 1966. *Kingdoms of the Savannah*. Madison: University of Wisconsin Press.

———. 1969. "The Bells of Kings." *Journal of African History* 9:187–197.

Wachsmann, Klaus P. 1964a. "Human Migration and African Harps." *Journal of the International Folk Music Council* 16:84–88.

———. 1964b. "Problems of Musical Stratigraphy in Africa." In *Colloques de Wégimont* 3:19–22.

———. 1971. "Musical Instruments in Kiganda Tradition and Their Place in the East African Scene." In *Essays on Music and History in Africa*, ed. Klaus P. Wachsmann, 93–134. Evanston, Ill.: Northwestern University Press.

Walton, James. 1955. "Iron Gongs from the Congo and Southern Rhodesia." *Man* 30:20–23.

Wegner, Ulrich. 1982. *Abūḏīya und Mawwāl: Untersuchungen zur sprachlich- musikalischen Gestaltung im südirakischen Volksgesang*. Hamburg: Karl Dieter Wagner. 2 vols.

———. 1984. *Afrikanische Saiteninstrumente*. Museum für Völkerkunde Berlin, Abteilung Musikethnologie, new series, 41. Berlin: Staatliche Museen Preussischer Kulturbesitz.

Wembah-Rashid, J. A. R. 1975. *The Ethnohistory of the Matrilineal Peoples of Southeast Tanzania*. Vienna: Verlag E. Stiglmayr.

Westphal, E. O. J. 1978. "Observations on Current Bushmen and Hottentot Musical Practices." *Review of Ethnology* 5(2–3):9–15.

Wieschhoff, Heinz. 1933. *Die afrikanischen Trommeln und ihre ausserafrikanischen Beziehungen*. Stuttgart: Strecker und Schröder. Studien zur Kulturkunde.

Willet, Frank. 1977. "A Contribution to the History of Musical Instruments among the Yoruba." In *Essays for a Humanist: An Offering to Klaus Wachsmann*, 350–389. New York: Town House Press.

Yotamu, Moses. 1979. "My Two Weeks' Field-work in Ivory Coast." *Review of Ethnology* 6(21–34): 161–192.

———. 1989. Untitled contribution. In *Westafrika: Musikgeschichte in Bildern*, by Gerhard Kubik, 154–163. Leipzig: Deutscher Verlag für Musik.

Islam in Liberia
Lester P. Monts

Since the 1750s, Islam has influenced the coastal forest region of present-day Liberia and Sierra Leone (Owen 1930:57). The assimilation of Islamic ideology into African life brought changes in the local world view. Muslim influence was variable and uneven: some ethnic groups staunchly resisted it; others blended it with traditional practice, after a syncretic model like that of other regions in West Africa. For the Vai ethnic group, however, it formed a unique relationship, and began a process that culminated in a move toward orthodoxy.

In northwest Liberia, over a twelve-year period (1977–1988), people in the town of Bulumi restructured the basic aspects of their lives, and conceptually reordered their musical system. Studying the impact of the new religious orientation on Vai artistic expression provides a tool for understanding Islamic development in West Africa, where changes in art reveal the profound effects a new ideology can have on aesthetic values.

ISLAMIZATION AND MUSIC IN VAI

West Africans, most of whom call themselves Muslims, know two general types of Islam: "normative" and "popular" (Levtzion 1979:215). The former type, the more orthodox and conservative, derives all social and moral codes from strict Islamic law, as perceived by local Muslims. The latter, the more marginal, tolerates variant practices: "For most people . . . acceptance of Islam meant no more than memorising a few Arabic formulae and using talismen sold by Muslim doctors. Of the five 'pillars' of Islam—confession of faith, ritual prayer, fasting, almsgiving, and (as an ideal goal) pilgrimage—it is unlikely that many people observed any of the last three" (Jones 1981:176). Echoing this notion, Lewis (1980:59) suggests that the requirements for a person to be considered a Muslim, especially during the early phases of Islamization, were to "acknowledge the fundamental doctrine—there is no god but Allah, and Muhammad is his Prophet—and a handful of related injunctions and prescriptions."

From the beginning, Islamic philosophy questioned Vai perceptions of social and religious order. Its entry into Vai life began a long-term dispute between two antagonists—tradition and modernity—and the contradiction between them was

Bulumi Vai town in northwest Liberia, Tombe chiefdom, on the Liberia–Sierra Leone highway

Poro Generic term for men's secret society in West Africa

ɓeli Vai term for the men's secret society, Poro

everywhere apparent, especially in the conflict between initiation societies and Islamic dogma. Until the late 1900s, the alternate factions were willing to compromise: "It is the compromising attitude—the symbiosis of Islam and the African traditional religion—which was typical of Islam in West Africa before the eighteenth century" (Levtzion 1979:208). By the 1970s, a stricter, more conservative Muslim religious order began to prevail. After 1977, several Vai towns experienced a striking shift from marginal Islam to a conservative orthodoxy, which affected the role of music in ritual, ceremony, and other celebratory occasions. Between the extremes arose a third type, transitional Islam. Changes during the period 1977–1988 document the dynamics affecting both musical and religious life.

The acceptance of a new ideology radically affects music, because music mirrors the cultural variables of traditional social and religious institutions. As a form of expressive culture, music is a pawn, an element over which conflict can develop. It is a battleground, where factions can test the strength of their cultural and spiritual values. A decline in the performance of a representative type of music can signal the demise of a religious ideology.

BULUMI IN 1977–1978

With a population of about three hundred fifty, Bulumi (often written "Bomi" or "Bumi") is the largest town in the Tombe chiefdom. It stands on a peninsula between the Atlantic Ocean and Lake Piso, along a road that connects the Liberia–Sierra Leone highway with Robertsport. Like most towns along this route, Bulumi lies within the sphere of influence of the urban areas of Monrovia and Robertsport. It receives radio broadcasts from Monrovia and from Freetown, Sierra Leone. Several townspeople have relatives in Robertsport and Monrovia, and many commute regularly to those areas. As the largest and most progressive town in the Tombe chiefdom, Bulumi takes the lead in social reform. Accordingly, Muslims seek to introduce their beliefs there (Levtzion 1979:1–20).

Secret societies and music

In the 1970s, two secret societies—Poro for men, Sande for women—dominated local life. (*Poro* is a generic term used throughout the region; the Vai refer to the institution as *ɓeli*.) They formed the crux of the crisis between Islam and traditional practice. People considered the societies at Bulumi among the best run in the region. The societies supported the practice of ancestor veneration. The sacred groves of the Poro conveniently grew near the graves of lineage leaders, where people frequently made sacrifices to ancestors.

For many Vai, participation in secret societies reinforced the search for metaphysical meaning. Basic to that search was the supposition of a reality beyond the realm of mortal perception, a powerful supernatural reality, which manifested itself in ancestral and nature spirits, and in a supreme being. To understand that reality, and to live in accord with it, the Vai relied on the powers of spiritual leaders or guardians. The secret society component first combined men and women as corporate units, and through the traditional belief system allied them with the forces in the spirit world. Unseen spirits, in their roles as guardians of values, represented the core of the Vai world view, which played itself out in ritual and ceremony.

Poro and Sande molded intermediary relationships with their authoritative entities of the spirit world. In Sande, a Zooba masked dancer impersonated a male ancestral water spirit; in the Poro, the *dadɛwɛ* (not impersonated by a mask) was a "bush spirit." Though a nature divinity, the *dadɛwɛ* was more powerful than the ancestral spirits impersonated by Zooba: Poro assumed a higher authoritative role than Sande.

The ancestors were intermediaries between the living and the supreme being, but their powers covered only the aspects of life they experienced. Human existence and well-being also depended on the environment, whose forces flowed from a pantheon of spirits—natural divinities, which, sometimes with ancestral spirits, lodged in cotton trees, in the depths of lakes and rivers, and on mountaintops (Johnson 1954:16). People regularly held sacrifices at those locations. The lore and mythology surrounding the secret societies tells of the powers of natural divinities and ancestor spirits.

Because of the multidimensionality of their roles, and the fine line that distinguished the sacred and the secular, the secret societies operated in alternate realms. On the sacred side, they instilled initiates with the basic elements of the belief system, including respect for the power of the supreme being, which manifests itself through the ancestors and the cultic spirits *dadɛwɛ* and Zooba. The basic belief was that an extraordinary force allowed people in the Poro and Sande to speak with "one voice," and to share in a set of behaviors and moral values that promote social continuity.

Socially, both Poro and Sande played central roles in the life cycle activities of its members. Membership established a lifelong fraternal or sororal bond, and initiates referred to one another as "brother" or "sister." The collective consciousness of the societies affected the funerary ceremonies of their members, especially chiefs and high-ranking officials. It was in part through the auspices of the societies that the doctors, morticians, musicians, gravediggers, and other specialists and ritual leaders, developed their skills.

Major occasions associated with the secret societies and other communal activities called for the services of music specialists. Bulumi was the home of several professional musicians, and of eight masqueraders. The male masqueraders included Bowu (figure 1), Nafali, Kɔlɔpɔɔ, Joobai, and Yavi. Male musicians performed on a conical drum (*saŋgba*); a wooden slit drum (*keleŋ*); a box-shaped lamellophone (*koŋgoma*); and a set of basket rattles (*jeke*). The Sande society sponsored two Zooba spirit impersonators, and female instrumentalists were the exclusive players of the *sasaa* (gourd rattle). Two of the chiefdom's most celebrated performers lived at Bulumi: Varni Tawe, a *saŋgba* player; and Kuna Kiatamba, the oldest and highest-ranking female musician in the coastal region (figure 2). Both of them played prominent roles in secret society activities. Several musicians of lesser skill stayed at Bulumi as students of Varni Tawe, and accompanied him at out-of-town performances. The local paramount chief and the county superintendent (based at Robertsport) frequently called for the services of drummers and masqueraders from Bulumi to entertain visiting dignitaries, or to accompany them to traditional and governmental occasions.

Because of the stature and skill of its musicians and dancers, Bulumi gained a reputation throughout the region as a dance town; it was the place to go for a good feast or holiday celebration. In 1977–1978, it hosted more feasts and holiday celebrations than any other town in the chiefdom. Such occasions were not the only reasons

imam   Islamic teacher, doctor, scribe, song leader, and interpreter of the Qur'ān

hadj   Pilgrimage to Mecca that devout Muslims are encouraged to make

d'aabo kulɛ   'Arabic voice', Vai stylistic designation for recitation of the Qur'ān

Ramadan   Month of fasting that faithful Muslims observe

FIGURE 1   The masked dancer Bowu. Bulumi, 1977.

FIGURE 2   Kuna Kiatamba, the celebrated *kengai* of Bulumi, performs on the gourd rattle (*sasaa*). Bulumi, 1977.

to celebrate. At the end of rice harvest season (October), communal dances occurred nightly there. When the rice harvest was bountiful, musicians and dancers from neighboring towns often joined in. On national and Christian holidays, Bulumi occasionally sponsored "cultural shows," which featured visiting masqueraders and musicians from as far away as Gola and Mende country.

Institutional Islam

Like all Vai towns, Bulumi had an imam (*aimaami*) and a mosque (*misii*), and though nearly everyone professed a commitment to Islam, a few men stood out as devout Muslims. Other than the imam (figure 3), no one in the town could read Arabic. Hence, the imam was the Islamic teacher, doctor, scribe, song leader, and interpreter of the Qur'ān. Several of the devout Muslims wanted to go on pilgrimage (*hadj*) to Mecca, but none had the money to do so; several, however, considered pilgrimage a lifelong goal.

During the day, people worked their farms, and did not regularly attend prayers in the mosque. Congregational prayer was not a common practice. The most devout Muslims kept prayer mats in huts on their farms, where they prayed daily. Even in the evening, attendance in the mosque was sparse. Many people, including most women, preferred to pray at home.

In 1978, the imam had seven boys in his school. Every night, they sat by an open fire near the imam's house, and recited the Qur'ān from inscriptions written on wooden boards (*wala*). In exchange for Qur'ānic training, three of the boys had come

to Bulumi to live with the imam, and to work on his farm. After successfully completing the first stage of training, the sons of clerics, with other boys who showed an interest in the religion, went away to regional Islamic centers for advanced studies. By the fire, the boys learned to chant the Qur'ān in a standard, rudimentary style. Further training would enable them to recite in a style called *ɗaabo kulɛ* 'Arabic voice'. While that is the Vai stylistic designation, the recitation of men who were said to have this technique was not stylistically similar to that of Arabic-speaking Qur'ān-reciters. The *ɗaabo kulɛ* was merely a more precise pronunciation of the Arabic text.

During the late 1970s, people seldom observed the major holidays of the Islamic calendar; and during Ramadan (*tɔŋ kalo*), only a few kept their fast. The Vai recognized and celebrated three major Islamic holidays: Milaji (Miraj), Mahodi (Mawlid), and Bɔtɔndɔ (Id al-Fitr). Excepting Bɔtɔndɔ, the town sponsored no major Islamic celebrations in 1977–1978. The other events, celebrated by a small group of people, were confined to the quarter where the imam lived. Bɔtɔndɔ was a celebratory occasion, and because drummers and masked dancers participated in the ceremonies, local and out-of-town guests participated freely. Though it was a sacred occasion, many less devout participants (which included most) drank alcoholic beverages, and engaged in other behavior Muslims considered unbecoming. Most people considered Bɔtɔndɔ a purely social occasion, and paid little attention to its underlying religious purpose.

During the 1970s, no local Friday prayer service took place at Bulumi, but the imam and a few men occasionally traveled to the town of Misila to pray. As a weekly obligation, Friday prayer was not a widespread practice among the rural Vai: only four towns in all of Vai country (Makbɔuma, Misila, Sinni, Zogboja) held it; immigrant Koniaka Muslims had founded all but one of these towns. Because of the conservatism of their religious principles, the Vai called them *Mɑli sanja* 'Muslim towns'. Only a few older people spoke the Koniaka language; and beyond allegiance to Islam, people in these towns considered themselves to be Vai, and accepted other aspects of Vai culture. In the late 1970s, influence from these towns, and from large Mandingo and Fula mosques in Monrovia, impressed on the rural communities that Friday prayer was an important part of their devotional commitment.

When people announced that the musicians had arrived and were about to begin a procession through the town, all other activities ceased.

Most of the people at Bulumi considered themselves Muslims. They measured their commitment, not by what they omitted from their lives, but by what they included. Compared with their immediate neighbors, the Vai had a clear commitment to Islam. Several elements of local culture were clues about the degree to which the people had appropriated Islamic elements. Funerary rites were one of the first traditional practices to absorb Muslim traits.

The fortieth-day death feast

The fortieth-day death feast (*ďaa*) is the most elaborate and frequent of Vai social occasions. By Islamic tradition, *ďaa* is the last of three celebratory feasts; the others occur on the third and seventh days after death. In the distant past, *ďaa* often lasted as long as one month; but in 1977–1978, because of employment, and the distances family and friends had to travel to attend, the feasts held at Bulumi lasted only three days, Friday through Sunday. The size of *ďaa* depended on two major factors: the social or political status of the deceased, and the fund-raising ability of the host family.

In 1978, a fortieth-day feast for a former paramount chief at Bulumi began on Friday, when out-of-town friends and relatives arrived and offered their condolences, with gifts of money and foodstuffs. At dusk, two micromusical events involving Islamic and traditional practices took place. To summon men to the mosque, the Muslim prayer caller (*wandai*) performed the call to prayer (*azan*). In a style adopted from Koniaka immigrants, his call was heightened speech (figure 4). The evening prayer consecrated the memory of the deceased, whom the imam eulogized.

In another part of town, women were pounding rice in a mortar to prepare their guests' evening meal; they accompanied their work with Islamic songs (figure 5). Throughout the night, small groups of people participated in processions, singing praise songs in honor of the deceased chief and his family; each group included a male representative, with singers and a rattle player. At the house of the deceased, a prominent male in the group made an oration to the family. (By custom, this person was one who had known the deceased and the history of his clan.) He recounted the deceased's exploits—as warrior, political leader, husband of many wives, and father of many children. Taking a section from the speech, singers accompanying the group extemporized a song of praise.

Woja nyi o o.
Woja nyi, woja bɛɛ bɛlɛ nyi, o mba o o.
O yaa. Woja nyi, woja bɛɛ bɛlɛ nyi.

To have a family is good.
To have a fine family is good, oh mother.
Oh yes. To have a fine family is good.

FIGURE 4 Excerpt from the call to prayer (*azan*), a kind of heightened speech. Bulumi, 1978.

By Saturday afternoon, most out-of-town participants had arrived, and the town was teeming with excitement. Everyone eagerly awaited the arrival of invited musicians and dancers: Seku Gbɔnda and his professional troupe. Without such participation, no major musical events could occur. When people announced that the musicians had arrived and were about to begin a procession through the town, all other activities ceased. To greet the musicians, crowds—including a senator, a member of the national legislature, and a county superintendent—lined the procession route. Afterward, to discuss accommodations and pay, the musicians met with the sponsors.

Just before sunset, the musicians began a procession to the center of town, where the masqueraders would perform. En route, for encouragement, persons in the crowd gave the musicians money. Six male masqueraders—Nafali, two Bowunu (the Vai suffix *-nu* marks the plural of nouns), Yavi, two Zooba—joined the musicians. On arrival at the dance arena, the musicians encouraged bystanders to participate in singing dance songs. As participants reacted to the competitive spirit and skill of the musicians and dancers, tension rose. After about two hours of masked dancing, the musicians began another procession through the town; throughout the night, it repeatedly visited the house of the deceased, to offer songs of praise and monetary gifts. Other processions also formed, and filled the town with music.

Early Sunday morning, men gathered in the mosque for the *fidao*, a ceremony of redemption held for the deceased. To perform the ceremony, men simultaneously read or recited from memory sections of the Qur'ān. After the *fidao*, in front of the mosque, local butchers slaughtered a cow and several sheep, and distributed the meat

FIGURE 5 A rice-pounding song as performed in Bulumi, 1978. Fragments of the text recall the original Arabic *La ilaha ila' Allah* 'There is no god but God'.

Vai text: ai lai lai hu lai lai hu lai la la hu lai ai
Text fragments of the original Arabic: La ilaha ila' Allah
                                    There is no god but God (Allah)

Traditional music and dance, and Islamic songs, recitations, and prayers, were cultural resources that supported a cohesive celebratory structure.

FIGURE 6   At the fortieth-day death feast (*d'aa*), the master musician Seku Gbɔnda performs on the basket rattles (*jeke*); instrumentalists accompany him on the box-shaped lamellophone *koŋgoma*. Bulumi, 1978.

to cook stations in each quarter of the town. Meanwhile, women began to prepare a special rice product called *dɛɛ*, for use in the final sacrifice. As they beat the rice with pestles in the mortar, they sang Islamic songs. After the midday meal, male relatives and participants met in the mosque for the final sacrifice. Male representatives from neighboring towns, or relatives living in Monrovia or Robertsport, individually offered the bereaved family condolences: words of praise, and money. People offered a sacrifice of money, kola nuts, and rice flour. The imam asked everyone to stand; with hands extended, he led them in a recitation of the *al fatiha*, the opening section of the Qur'ān. As the final formality, the *tɔmbɔjala-mæ* (the appointed event leader) proclaimed the feast a success, and acknowledged the donors of time and money. He made a special point of mentioning the musicians. The meeting adjourned with applause for Seku Gbɔnda and his troupe (figure 6).

This feast interwove Islamic and traditional practices. The participants did not consciously rate its traditional and Islamic contents. For them, those elements were alternative parts of a long, complex tradition. Traditional music and dance, and Islamic songs, recitations, and prayers, were cultural resources that supported a cohesive celebratory structure.

SACRIFICES AT ZÓNTORI

Remnants of another traditional religious practice continued surreptitiously in 1977–1978. Sacrifices to ancestors and natural divinities were essential in the practice of traditional Vai religion. To ensure peace and prosperity, people propitiated spirits by ritual sacrifice, which Muslim leaders considered blasphemous: they objected, not to the practice itself, but to the entities to whom the people directed it. They tried to impress on participants in those activities that a higher authority could grant benefits that far outweighed those of the ancestors, and that, with proper behavior and devotion, people could easily reap these benefits. Such proclamations had some effect, but did not stop the sacrifices.

One region where such rites continued was around Tombe: people thought mighty spirits inhabited the top of Cape Mount and the swamp areas near the coast. Legends extol the virtues of these spirits, and cite the benefits they have provided. Near the town of Latia,

> there is a piece of water "Zóntori," and the reason why it bears that name is as follows:—At the time of the conquest, when Zong, the king of the place, had lost his warriors in the battle, he fled into the forest with Tóri, his queen: there they met a benign being of the other world, who showed them a way down into the regions under the water, the happy abode of the departed. Thither all the warriors followed them, and the rest of their subjects. There they now enjoy an existence free from care and full of pleasure, and the sound of their songs, or the noise of their feasts and frolics, are sometimes heard by the living during the silence of the night. (Koelle 1854:iv–v)

Islam notwithstanding, people in the late 1970s made several sacrifices at these locations, under a dark veil of secrecy.

In traditional society, the success of these events depended on the participation of a strong specialist. During the late 1970s, two elderly women in the chiefdom reportedly had a special relationship with the spirits; each bore the title of *siekɛ-mɔɔ* 'offering bringer'. Authoritative figures in the local Zooba Sande, they resisted encouragement to pray as Muslims. For their traditional beliefs, people called them *kaffi* (from Arabic *kāfir* 'infidel'). Despite Muslim taunts, the women enjoyed an aura of fear and respect, because of the special relationship they had with the spirits that reigned supreme in Vai lore. People attributed to these women several miraculous acts, which caused some to fear and respect their power. During a sacrifice, when the spirits did not respond to the normal procedures, these women reportedly dived into the depths of the water, and conversed with the spirits for up to 45 minutes.

Unlike in the distant past, when the local *siekɛ-mɔɔ* (or *jakɛ-mɔɔ*) had considered ritual practices part of his or her contribution to society, the necessary special arrangements and extreme costs more recently associated with these practices made them unmanageable for most individuals. By 1978, a small group or an entire town would pool resources for single sacrifices. In addition to the $100 fee charged by the *siekɛ-mɔɔ*, patrons had to provide a 100-pound (45-kilogram) bag of rice, a white sheep, 3 gallons of palm oil, and several kola nuts. In 1977–1978, people reportedly sponsored three sacrifices: for a man seeking the office of paramount chief, for a Monrovia-based football team hoping to maintain a winning record, and for a person who simply wanted to be a "big man."

People traditionally held sacrifices to bring greater prosperity to the chiefdom, especially when they planned a new road, and when they believed rumors that construction of a port would occur at Robertsport. They consulted ancestors on actions to take to bring these prospects to fruition. They believed that despite Islam's fervor, only traditional means could resolve certain issues.

People considered ancestors music-loving spirits, and during the rituals, they

Music was an important element in these rituals; without it, the act would not have been valid.

sang old songs, dating from the ancestors' lifetimes. At the start of the sacrifice, the *siekε-mɔɔ* told the people the spirits wanted them to sing a particular song, while she was carrying out one of two procedures. One version required the *siekε-mɔɔ* to put a basin of sacrificial food on her head, and diving into the water, to serve it to the spirits; afterward, she would return, to report the spirits' advice. Another version says the *siekε-mɔɔ* cut the throat of the sheep, and allowed the blood to flow into the water: if it flowed in a straight line to the center of the pool, the ancestors had accepted the sacrifice, and would grant the people's request; much rejoicing and feasting would then occur, and the spirits sometimes participated. People believed they could hear singing from beneath the water, and thought several Zooba spirit impersonators had emerged from beneath the water to dance on the opposite bank. In still another version, the *siekε-mɔɔ* used a canoe to carry a metal basin containing sacrificial food to the center of the water: the basin floated on the surface; but after a few minutes, the water became turbulent, and the basin sank. People in the towns of Latia and Fali claim to have heard rejoicing from the waters throughout the night. The next day, if they found the basin on the shore and clean, they knew the ancestors had accepted the sacrifice.

Music was an important element in these rituals; without it, the act would not have been valid. Like the clandestine activities it accompanied, it was not performed openly. People were unwilling to sing out of context the songs associated with the sacrifices, and to allow their recording.

Unlike Vai funerary activities, these rituals did not include Muslim practices, ritual or musical. Some Vai viewed these activities as a serious challenge to Muslim teachings, while others justified them as a way to call upon powers that serve purposes outside the purview of Islam. This tension created turmoil between Muslim and traditional factions. The Muslim profession of faith—*Lai, lai, i lai, lai, lai, Muhammadu la sura lai* 'There is one god, and Muhammad is his prophet'—articulated the dispute. The practice of spirit veneration through sacrifice or idols (such as Zooba) conflicted with the central Muslim tenet.

In 1982, when the ideological crisis escalated in Bulumi, proponents of the secret societies emphasized the importance of coexistence. For more than one hundred fifty years in Vai country, Islam and the societies had operated side by side. Many people who in 1982 denounced the societies had formerly championed them. People at Bulumi began to discuss ritual sacrifices: discussion afforded catharsis for staunch Muslims who wished to allay the guilt surrounding their past participation. Eventually, the Muslim opponents of traditional ritual practices made a claim that impressed many townspeople: God could tolerate violations of Islamic doctrine only so long; for blasphemous acts associated with the societies, he had cursed Bulumi, and was holding back modern development and prosperity. The assertion persuaded many who had experienced hardship; others, however, kept the old ways. A wary tolerance between Islam and traditional religious practices continued.

THE END OF PORO, CHANGES IN SANDE

In 1984, two closely related events extensively remodeled religious life at Bulumi: the setting up of a Friday mosque, and the abolition of the traditional versions of the secret societies. In that year, the imams, with pressure from occasional itinerant Muslim missionaries, imposed a ban on all Poro activities in the Tombe chiefdom. Local Muslim leaders petitioned the regional Islamic Council to institute a Friday mosque (*jami*). The Council responded favorably, on condition that Bulumi ban all Poro activities. In a highly emotional sermon (*kabande*), the Makbɔuma Imam Momo Nyei, an outspoken opponent of the secret societies, brought the issue before the townspeople. Musa Deke, the head of Poro activities (*dazoo*) at Bulumi, was so moved, he stood up and repented, renouncing his past involvement in Poro, and calling for its end.

As the men moved to abolish Poro, pressure mounted to adopt the Muslim version of Sande. Without fanfare, Bulumi voluntarily transformed its Sande into an acceptable Muslim version called *mɔli* Sande; other towns followed suit. By the 1990s, most Vai towns in the coastal region had adopted the Muslim version of Sande, which does not have the Zooba. At Bulumi in 1977, a *zoo kɛŋ* 'ritual specialist's house', where people kept the Sande spirit impersonator costumes and other ritual paraphernalia, stood prominently in the center of town. The events of 1984 resulted in the razing of the *zoo* house, and its replacement with a civic meeting hall.

The decree to ban the traditional versions of Poro and Sande was a victory for the conservative Muslim faction, and a defeat for those who preferred coexistence between the secret societies and Islam. Many felt the town had relinquished to an alien force its ties to the past, and had succumbed to fanatical persecution. The secret societies had been arbiters of culture, patrons of the arts, preservers of tradition, and transmitters of social skills. Its carvers provided masks for dancers; its weavers and seamstresses designed and made costumes for initiate dancers and masqueraders in Sande and Poro; its master teachers had trained instrumentalists and dancers; and the events of the Poro-Sande cycles had afforded much communal entertainment, and had helped maintain the social order.

The abolition of Poro at Bulumi was not a fluke. By the late 1970s, Vai Poro was already on the decline. In the neighboring Gawula chiefdom, the Manobala clan had banned the institution about forty years before, and its men had ceased sending their sons for Poro training (Ofri 1972:6). Many men did not feel much impact, since they had other opportunities for employment, education, and camaraderie. The change, however, was particularly devastating to women, who had operated Sande lodges throughout the Tombe chiefdom. Women were left to ponder their social responsibilities, their mortality, and their musical roles in society. They no longer had a systematic way to develop their musical skills.

In traditional society, Sande songs had served a variety of purposes, ranging from instructional songs (to teach initiates personal hygiene) to highly esoteric ones. Sande songs—which included songs in the Mende, Gola, Dei, and Vai languages—represented the largest corpus of songs in the Vai music repertory. Outside of Sande, women used these songs as lullabies, to accompany work, or simply for pleasure. The banning of Sande halted the rituals and ceremonies that transmitted these songs from one generation to another. Many songs will live as part of Mende, Gola, and Dei Sande, since those ethnic groups shared the repertory; but for all practical purposes among the Vai, the songs will die with the last generation of women initiated into a traditional version of Sande. The Muslim version of Sande offers little hope of preserving traditional songs, since that repertory consists primarily of Islamic songs in Arabic.

The change to the Muslim version of Sande ended several feasts that contributed

Zooba   Masked dancer in the Sande society who impersonates a male ancestor water spirit

kengai   Vai women who supervise all Sande musical activities; expert dancers and singers

tɔmbɔ kɛ bɔɲiɛ-nu   Dance troupe for young initiates of the Sande society among the Vai people

to social life. Mɔli Sande retains many of the occasions, but the absence of the traditional music and dance components deprives them of fervor and excitement. A conservative Islamic approach to Mɔli Sande bans dancing and playing the gourd rattle (*sasaa*), though Bulumi does not subscribe to that outlook. Such is the case in the "Muslim towns," where Mɔli Sande started; Sande there provides the models from which other Mɔli Sande derive.

The fate of Zooba

The demise of once-important elements in Sande ritual and ceremony had a big impact on the traditional version of the Sande—and by extension, on most traditional music performed by women. Zooba, the central figure in this controversy, the Sande masked spirit impersonator, requires special discussion, since Muslims targeted it as one of the main violations of Islamic doctrine.

Tolerance for the male masqueraders was notably different from that accorded Zooba. Early in the 1900s, Yavi, Bɔwu, Nafali, Joobai, and Kɔlɔkpɔ, came from Mende and Gola areas. Among the Vai, they had no spiritual importance, and no connection with the Poro society. Little (1951:246–247) calls them Poro Spirits. Among the Vai, however, individual wealthy men or groups of men sponsored them in quasi-secret societies (*gbonji-nu*). Past observers' connecting them with Poro derives from the fact that formerly a man had to be a member of Poro in order to wear a mask. Masked dancing was like any manly endeavor: Poro membership was prerequisite to participation. Even in the late 1980s (well after the demise of Zooba at Bulumi), the male masqueraders continued to play an important role at celebratory occasions. But they were merely professional entertainers, members of an itinerant troupe who performed for pay. The Vai called them *tɔmbɔ kɛ feŋ-nu* 'playthings'. Since their activities did not challenge Muslim views on idolatry and spirit representation, their support was far different from that of Zooba.

In towns favoring marginal Islam, both Zooba and the male masqueraders continued, while the towns that adhered to a conservative Islam did not allow masked dancing. They may still have allowed dancing by the male masqueraders, but as Islam gained a greater hold, it too faced an unhappy fate. The continued presence of the male masked dancers, and the absence of Zooba, are key factors in characterizing Islam at Bulumi as transitional.

Zooba was more than an entertainer. Having been a part of the Vai Sande society for more than one hundred fifty years, it was part of a notable number of institutionalized ritual practices. Recognition of a masked spirit impersonator in Vai Sande first appears in Koelle (1854:203), under the designation "Nou"; later, Büttikofer (1890:255, 307–310), Johnston (1906:1032–56), and Ellis (1914:54, 71) mention the dancer, providing pictorial documentation.

Practically every Sande jurisdiction had one or more Zooba. As an important part of Sande, Zooba's participation had to occur at no less than five major esoteric Sande rituals, and possibly at others that took place in secret.

In traditional society, Zooba personified supernatural power. As the impersonator of a founding male ancestor, Zooba commanded the respect of its followers. Myth and lore register the origin of the Sande spirit guardian. Asked where the Zooba came from, Vai women say they found it near the river, or that it came from the water. The Mende and the Gola share that belief. For a fuller account of the Sande spirit impersonator among the Mende, see Phillips (1978) and Boone (1986); and among the Gola, see d'Azevedo (1973).

Muslims oppose the Zooba on legalistic grounds: as a spirit impersonator, it violates Islamic laws against idolatry. However, the psychological reasons go deeper. Zooba served as an agent of social control, and as the bearer of strong Sande medicines, for which men had no antidote. The mask bearer's identity was secret; and men were always curious as to whose wife was behind the mask. The Zooba mask may be the only mask women wear in Africa, though Vai women do not know that. Because of its controlling powers, Zooba was a major stabilizing force in conflicts between men and women. In the past, Sande women, bolstered by the power of Zooba, could levy heavy fines on men (or even uninitiated women) who violated laws protecting the Sande and women in general. In addition to fines, other Sande reprisals could result in a man's illness, including scrotal elephantiasis, a dreaded disease. Hence, it was in part men's fear of Zooba's underlying power that enforced traditional law. In the presence of Zooba, further restrictions limited men's freedom. Men could not lawfully approach within ten feet of the dancer. Without proper settlement, an accidental bump could result in a fine or a Zooba-induced sickness. Men often complained that their wives pledged greater allegiance to the Sande and Zooba than to them.

Musically, Zooba Sande provided opportunities for female musicians and dancers. Months or years of training preceded the artisans' taking part in public rituals. Women bearing the title *kengai* supervised all Sande musical activities. Well versed in Sande music, the *kengai* was the person most knowledgeable about the repertory. She was an expert dancer, singer, and *sasaa* player. Having received musical training in Sande herself, she had the responsibility of teaching to novice Zooba dancers, and to girls in the initiate dance troupe (*tɔmbɔ kɛ bɔɔniɛ-nu*), the intricate style of dance and its *sasaa* rhythms. Her musical responsibility extended to the general Sande membership. It was her job to teach the songs associated with all phases of Sande ritual and ceremony. For talented female dancers, instrumentalists, and singers, the traditional version of Sande was a pathway toward participation in local musical life.

Zooba Sande reaffirmed the solidarity of women, and served as a symbol of female values and beliefs. It was the mechanism women employed to identify themselves as a corporate unit, and to maintain boundaries between themselves and men. As a sign of both self-identity and group affiliation, Sande prescribed and asserted traditional social values.

Islamic Sande

In the mid 1980s, Zooba was no longer a subject for open debate, but some people at Bulumi still expressed opposing views on the new musical and social orientation for Sande. Many believed the advent of Mɔli Sande and its associative songs in Arabic deprived women of the intracultural communicative function of song. The songs of Mɔli Sande appeal to God and praise Muhammad, in affirmation of Islamic values. Unlike the songs of the traditional Sande, they are not the codified, denotative forms of expression that communicate direct and immediate meaning through a commonly

Zooba Sande reaffirmed the solidarity of women, and served as a symbol of female values and beliefs.

understood language. Traditional Sande provided women a power base from which to set up boundaries; each three-year session was a revalidation of women's aesthetic, sacred, and social values. Many people who otherwise opposed the new orientation believed it unlikely that Mɔli Sande would instill such a strong social consciousness among women. Because its sessions were short (three weeks), failure to provide substantive musical training, and inability to instill and strengthen a lifelong bond left many women unfulfilled, knowing their experience differed from that of their mothers and grandmothers.

The proponents of Mɔli Sande expressed different opinions about its role and purpose in contemporary society. Some said the training purportedly provided by Zooba Sande in the past was no longer needed. Girls' mothers could teach them about sexual behavior, childrearing, and other duties of wife and mother. By participating in the everyday life of women, girls could learn about fishing, rice farming, and their other occupational duties. Modern feminist philosophy was not foreign to this debate. Many women felt the longer session common to Zooba Sande deprived girls of opportunities to get a Western-style education, live in an urban area, and pursue a professional career.

Economic elements also entered the objection to Zooba Sande. Men, especially, decried the exorbitant amount of money needed to keep a girl in Sande for a three-year period. Beyond the religious challenge, many saw Sande as a moneymaking scheme. One man said it cost him five bags of rice and over one hundred dollars to keep an older daughter in Zooba Sande for three years; but his younger daughter spent only three weeks in Mɔli Sande, at a cost of only $25. Others said it cost less to send a girl through government school than to put her through Zooba Sande. They added that Mɔli Sande advanced the peace and prosperity of a community: it does not operate by secrecy and fear. Men could enter the secluded area, which formerly they never could have done. Muslim belief opposed fear-instilling elements, and there was no Zooba to scare people.

Mɔli Sande culled out the most offensive aspects of Zooba Sande, and retained those elements acceptable to his interpretation of Islam, including clitoridectomy. While the musical repertory was much smaller, the corpus of Mɔli Sande songs had a unique richness. The "Muslim towns" rejected traditional songs and *sasaa* playing; but from traditional versions, Bulumi retained instrumental performance, plus many of the song types in the Vai, Mende, and Gola languages. These included praise songs for new graduates, *ziawa* dance songs, and processional songs. Even songs that once served to praise the Zooba gained a new function, and often served to greet and praise the head of the Sande, known as *maazo*. Keeping in mind the religious intent of this version of Sande, the girls received the opportunity for formal religious training; and in the confines of secluded areas, male clerics gave them instruction. Most importantly, unlike Zooba Sande, Mɔli Sande had divine approval.

Overall, despite the absence of Zooba and the mysteries that formerly surround-

FIGURE 7   New graduates of the *Zooba Sande* society in traditional dress. Bulumi, 1977.

ed the institution of Zooba, and despite the singing of Islamic songs, the public face of Sande at Bulumi changed very little. The women did, in fact, try to maintain the female-bonding role and other essential attributes of Mɔli Sande. From the traditional version, they retained the sororal element, the aesthetic principles associated with femininity, the showering of gifts, and the special treatment and privileges accorded new graduates several weeks after graduation (figure 7). Islam's impact on the celebration affected only spirit impersonation and the rituals done in the bush—elements women would not discuss for the record.

BULUMI IN 1987–1988

By 1987, more changes had occurred. The scope of these developments provides an interesting contrast with the state of Muslim affairs in the period ten years earlier. At the individual level, changes had taken place in the occupational roles of religious leaders, musicians, and ordinary worshippers. On another level, changes in the secret societies and Muslim sectarian groups had occurred. Several classes of music had disappeared from the repertory, and Islamic classes had joined it. Social occasions that had required traditional musical resources now required Islamic interpretations. Bulumi had indeed changed, and much of the difference came from Islam. A look at some of the major developments can show the variety of the changes.

With the newfound commitment to Islam, Muslims sought to solidify their control over religious life. They had ended the secret societies, and people began to pursue the wider Islamic world. Local entrepreneurs sought to acquaint the citizenry with universal Islam. From Monrovia, they brought foreign-produced cassettes that contained recordings of prayers, call to prayer (*azan*), and koranic cantillation, educating local people on the eloquence of Islamic vocalizing. Books on Muslim formalities, ranging in scope from the role of women or bathing the dead to praise poetry for holiday ceremonies or picture posters of Muhammad, found their way into households. The new generation of young Muslims took a more conservative approach to the religion; the conflict that in previous years had erupted between Islamic and traditional factions did not distract them.

The musical life of the town also changed. Many of the younger schoolchildren

Some young men at Bulumi memorized the styles of
Qur'ānic chant on audio cassettes purchased from
sidewalk merchants.

were less familiar with the musical repertory of the secret societies than children of
the same age ten years earlier. Their knowledge of Islamic songs, however, far exceeded that of their older peers. The demise of the traditional versions of the secret societies, the importation of Islamic material items from urban centers, and changing
concepts of the role and performance of Islamic music, placed Bulumi on the path
toward a conservative Islamic environment.

Bulumi gained greater contact with the wider Islamic world when two young
townsmen returned from study in Guinea and Iran. In 1985, the town appointed
Varni Kamara an assistant imam, and in 1986 it hired Muhammad Manobala as the
Arabic teacher at the Mohammed Kamara English-Arabic School. In 1987–1988, in
addition to memorizing passages in the Qur'ān, several boys and girls were learning
to read and write Arabic. Music became an important part of the curriculum.
Students accompanied with song the morning flag-raising ceremony, and marched
between classes singing popular Muslim anthems.

Not all Vai people noticed the cultural achievements of Islamic societies. Young
scholars, through travel and education, in the Middle East and other parts of Africa,
were the main conduits for local people to learn about a world with a deeply intellectual, artistic, religious, and historical background. The influence of these young
scholars became a key impetus for further change in religious life at Bulumi. Among
the many innovations their influence spawned were fresh interpretations of the
Qur'ān and Muslim law, local libraries of contemporary books on the life and sayings
of Muhammad, and new approaches to the performance of music.

After four years of study in West Asia, Muhammad Manobala put his newly
acquired knowledge to use as the town's *suku-ba* (professional Qur'ānic reciter and
cantor). He had not received formal training in Arabic music theory or composition,
but his travels had exposed him to new concepts about the performance of music in
Islamic contexts. At prayer time, people often gathered around the mosque to hear
his call to prayer. His talent earned him a special distinction among townsfolk. He
was the one with the fine voice (*nyia kulɛ*). He was equally adept at reciting the
Qur'ān in genuine Arabic style. His talent earned him a reputation as the most professional music maker in town, and he often served as a celebrant for Muslim occasions in distant towns. In the past, before it replaced the call-to-prayer drum (*tabula*),
the *azan* resembled heightened speech; but with the new awareness of Islamic practices brought from Iran by Muhammad Manobala, it became routine to hear a call to
prayer containing melodic elements common to music in that region (figure 8).
Similar innovations occurred in ceremonies of prayer, and in Qur'ānic chant.

By 1988, young men at Bulumi began to strive to recite the Qur'ān in *d'aabo
kulɛ* 'Arabic voice'. Many of them traveled to study with expatriate Lebanese and
Syrian Muslims in Monrovia, while others memorized the styles of Qur'ānic chant on
audio cassettes purchased from sidewalk merchants. Many achieved exceptional
results, learning by rote the diction, timbre, embellishments, and melodic structures

FIGURE 8 Excerpt from a new *azan*. Bulumi, 1988.

common to Middle Eastern recitation. Most young scholars supported themselves as Arabic teachers; hence, they passed their musical tendencies on to their students.

Change was manifest everywhere. People integrated Muslim practices into their daily lives. Because they were away at work on their farms, few participated in day-time prayers at Bulumi, but they attended evening prayers in large numbers. In the 1970s, the town had no Friday service; but a decade later, it teemed with people from throughout the chiefdom, who made the weekly journey to pray. Theoretically, Islam recognizes no institutionalized clergy; yet local, regional, and national Muslim clerics functioned within a hierarchy. Musa Kamara, the town imam, became head Muslim celebrant in all of Tombe; for all practical purposes, he was the region's main spokesman on religious matters.

In the past, Musa Kamara and other imams had been hesitant to raise in public the issue of the secret societies and spirit worship. In 1977, many were openly apologetic to audiences about disparaging statements others had attributed to them. By 1988, the conservative faction asserted itself obtrusively. Imams publicized their opposition to secret societies, while spreading Islam's message of life, knowledge, and gratitude. People often accused the imams of practicing witchcraft, and of using the power of the Qur'ān in despicable ways, such as making poisonous potions, or empowering dangerous animals to attack opponents. People recognized, however, that the good works these men did in their communities (as doctors, advisers, clerics) offset such allegations. In addition to the power local clerics wielded in the religious arena, they also advised paramount and town chiefs on major political and social issues.

By the late 1980s, the people of Bulumi no longer participated in the activities at Zontori, or conducted sacrifices to local ancestors. Officials brought before the town court anyone accused of such acts. The songs associated with these practices were no longer a part of the repertory. People now frowned on activities involving secular forms of singing and dancing, and devout adherents were quick to point out blasphemous behavior, either directly to individuals, or through sermons in the mosque.

FIGURE 9 Portion of
dhikr. Bulumi, 1988.

ilai   ilai   i lai lai hu lai   ilai   i lai lai hu lai   ilai   i lai lai hu lai   ilai   i lai lai

SUFISM AT BULUMI

After the transformation of Sande and the abolition of Poro, the men of Bulumi were without a comparable sodality. There was an attempt to revive the age-old circumcision institution known as Bili; but like Poro, it did not meet Islamic standards. Men who desired a stronger relationship with the new religion, and who hoped to instill the sense of male camaraderie lost with the Poro, looked to the Islamic brotherhoods.

The two brotherhoods found among the Vai—Qaddiriyya and Tijaniyya—trace their roots to the Sufi sects of North Africa and West Asia. They do not, however, maintain the mysticism of the parent groups. Qaddiriyya, the first sect to enter Vai country, came with the Koniaka immigrants during the 1800s, and persisted in the region till the 1930s. In the early 1990s, it had only a few adherents, in Zogboja and Makbɔuma. Tijaniyya is widespread throughout Vai country, and is the only sect represented at Bulumi. It came first to Misila, introduced to Liberia in the mid 1930s, by the marabout Al-Hajj Mohammed Ahmad Tunis. After coming to Liberia (from southern Sierra Leone), he, through several miraculous acts, influenced the beginnings of the Tijaniyya in Vai country. (For an account of his influence, see Goody et al. 1977:289–304). His most influential student was Braimah Nyei, a resident of Misila, whose followers were instrumental in spreading Tijaniyya to Bulumi. People credit Tunis with bringing several new Islamic songs to Liberia, and his role as leader of the Tijaniyya sect inspired his followers to compose others.

Chief Elder Senesee Kroma and Imam Musa Kamara underwent training in Tijaniyya at Misila, and in turn became leaders of the sect at Bulumi. Musa Kamara became the local sect leader (*muqaddam*). Because of the required commitments and rigorous training, only six older men at Bulumi are Tijaniyya adherents. Only one of the young scholars mentioned earlier has attained the necessary status to begin the training for membership. Adherents to Tijaniyya represent the strongest of the faithful: they refrain from drinking alcohol, smoking tobacco, and other proscribed recreations, such as adultery and gambling. For them, becoming a member of the Tijaniyya means achieving a higher religious status, one that places them closer to the deity.

On Thursday nights, members of the Bulumi Tijaniyya gather in the mosque for the weekly *dhikr*. (A degree of secrecy surrounds the Tijaniyya; and while nonmembers are permitted to watch the *dhikr* and other activities, its adherents are reluctant to speak openly about its inner workings.) People discharge in private the other obligatory functions of the sect, or make them part of daily prayers. For *dhikr*, men dress in long gowns, spread a white cloth on the floor, sprinkle perfume about, and proceed to recite key Muslim phrases, only occasionally moving to a tonally elevated vocal production (figure 9). With the *tasabia*, a string of prayer beads, they tell the repetitions. During the ritual, they appear to move into a state of ecstasy, though the phenomenon of altered states of consciousness associated with some forms of Sufism is uncommon.

These men have no money for the pilgrimage to Mecca. Therefore, they forgo the external journey, and rely on the power of their faith as expressed in the *dhikr* for a purely inner voyage, a voyage to the birthplace of the faith. As Sufis, they seek within themselves the meaning behind the teachings of the Qur'ān. Through the ritual procedure of the *dhikr*, they hope to achieve the state of consciousness that made the advent of Muhammad possible. Meditation, reflection, and commitment to the faith, are the means of achieving the inner *hadj*. People reported that a Tijaniyya adherent in a nearby town had achieved such a close relationship with the deity, he miraculously traveled to Mecca each night to pray. Such reports, and the belief that such events actually occur, intensify faith in the power of the sect.

THE EVOLVED FORTIETH-DAY DEATH FEAST

Few traditional social occasions match the magnitude of the fortieth-day death feast (*d'aa*). These funerary celebrations now use music in novel ways. While crowds continue to attend such occasions, musical activities involving masquerades and itinerant professional musicians are less common. People disparage these activities, especially when a family that has accepted a more conservative approach to Islam sponsors the feast. People also understand that the Mahodi Kɔŋpiŋ will not contribute to the cost of hiring musicians or dancers. The Mahodi Kɔŋpiŋ is a voluntary association, originally set up to oversee the celebration of the prophet's birth, but it claims the added responsibility of financing the funerary activities of its members.

The main features of the fortieth-day death feasts in 1988 were the preparation of the rice powder (*dɛɛ*), which involved the singing of Islamic songs; the processions and speeches at the home of the deceased, which involved a mixture of Islamic and traditional praise songs; the collective reading of the Qur'ān (*fidao*); and the final sacrifice, involving Muslim prayers, songs, and eulogies. Thus, the Muslim elements that formerly mixed with traditional celebration of *d'aa* now stand alone, as the main features of contemporary Muslim feasts. People at Bulumi say there is no prohibition against the incorporation of traditional practices into *d'aa*. The consensus is that conservative Muslims reserve the right not to contribute to, or participate in, those portions that infringe on their religious principles.

CELEBRATION OF MUHAMMAD'S BIRTH

Large-scale celebrations of Islamic holidays are recent additions to Islamic life at Bulumi. Because of the cost associated with large social occasions, Bulumi and the nearby town of Tɛɛ jointly host the yearly celebrations of Milaji (Miraj, Muhammad's birth) and Mahodi (Mawlid). Besides Ramadan, people consider Mahodi the most important Muslim occasion. At Bulumi, the *Mahodi manja* 'Mahodi chief', leader of the Mahodi Kɔŋpiŋ, is responsible for inviting the celebrants, collecting contributions from townspeople, and coordinating with people of Tɛɛ the annual celebration. As with other holidays, the structure of Mahodi spread to Bulumi from the town of Misila, which celebrated its first Mahodi in 1937. Celebrations of Muhammad's birth had occurred (under the name *al nabi sota*) in previous years at Makbɔuma, another "Muslim town."

As in other parts of the Islamic world, Mahodi at Bulumi occurs on the twelfth day of the third month of the Islamic calendar (*rabi al-'awwal*). Its structure matches that elsewhere: retelling events from Muhammad's life, and offering praises of him (al Faruqi 1986:79). The Bulumi version lasts twelve hours. It occurs in the town's meeting hall, which has enough space and ventilation.

As an aesthetic form, Mahodi brings together many artistic elements the Vai rec-

The people of Bulumi think Muhammad, though physically absent, is in spiritual contact with them, and their celebrations provide the opportunity to exhibit commitment to his teachings.

ognize: the art of reading Islamic praise poetry, literature, and the Qur'ān; the elegant accoutrements of Islam, joyous singing, and dance. Celebrants come from the learned classes, those who have an exceptional knowledge of Islam and its teaching. They divide into three groups: readers (reciters), interpreters, and song leaders. Readers recite from the Arabic text in a style similar to that of Qur'ānic chant. In a normal voice, the interpreter speaks a phrase-by-phrase interpretation of the Arabic. Thus, both the readers and interpreters must be fluent in Arabic; during the event, they often exchange roles. The *suku-ba* is the song leader who interjects songs, which may derive from several sources, taking many forms—musical interpretation of a particularly profound statement in the text, a cantillation based on poetic verse that appears in the text, a set of improvised sections of the Qur'ān, or a famous Muslim anthem sung responsorially with the audience. The texts come from a variety of sources. At Bulumi, people call them simply Mahodi books. Publishers in the Sudan and Egypt ship them for sale in Islamic bookstores in Monrovia.

In 1987–1988, the *suku-ba* at the Bulumi celebration was also fluent in Arabic, and thus had the ability to improvise on the text. He cued the audience to provide a simple response, over which he improvised. When inspired, an audience member could begin a song, which all would join. In such musical interludes, people often sang commonly known panegyric anthems, in the basic responsorial style.

The people of Bulumi add a dramatic touch to the celebration of Mahodi. In general, the texts emphasize the moral state of the world before Muhammad's birth—the period leading up to the his birth; his mother's anguish in childbirth; discussions between God, Adam, and Gabriel about him; and his life on earth. During the episode leading to his birth (often the last segment of the event), three women dressed in white come forward and sit before the celebrants. One of the women takes the role of Muhammad's pregnant mother; the others take the role of midwives. The reading becomes impassioned, and the audience stands and joins in song with the celebrants. The celebrants hold a white sheet over the women's heads, and slowly lower it over them and the main celebrant. As the *suku-ba* leads the audience in song, people dance about, clapping and rejoicing. Underneath the sheet, moans and groans associated with childbirth sound. When members of the audience lift the sheet, the main celebrant appears, drinking milk from a glass. The climactic ending symbolizes the birth of Muhammad and the taking of his first nourishment from his mother. It inspires more intense singing and dancing, which spills outside the meeting hall. The celebrants and audience members conclude the event in an hour-long procession of singing and dancing around the town.

Like other major events, Mahodi is an auspicious, joyous occasion. The people of Bulumi experience a passion that moves them to dance, rejoice, and weep. They think Muhammad, though physically absent, is in spiritual contact with them, and their celebrations provide them the opportunity to exhibit commitment to his teachings.

CHANGING CONCEPTS ABOUT MUSIC

In addition to the changing role of music in solidly embedded traditions, or its role in newly introduced Muslim occasions, a deeply Islamic philosophical underpinning has changed Vai concepts about music. Islam's roots draw sustenance from a philosophy that challenges music itself. This philosophy commonly finds expression in the language used by the Vai to distinguish song for traditional purposes from song used for Islamic or Islam-sanctioned occasions.

The Vai language has no generic term for the Western concept of music, though there are words for 'dance' (*tɔmbɔ*), 'song' (*dɔŋ*), and 'instrumental performance' (*seŋ feŋ*). People do not use the term *dɔŋ* in association with Islamic music. They refer the form of sound perceived as 'song' to *suku*, from Arabic *shukran* 'give thanks'. This tendency has far-reaching implications for sung performances, in all their sacred and secular contexts.

Throughout the Islamic world, scholars make attempts to distinguish secular music from the systems of sound associated with Islam. They do not consider koranic chant, with its myriad melodic interpretations, song or music. Lois al-Faruqi makes an analogy that has widespread application in the Islamic world: in an Islamic context, *musiqa*, the Arabic term for music, does not apply. Hence, al Faruqi refers to "music" in Islam, not as *musiqa*, but as *handasah al sawt* 'the art of sound'. The implication is that Islam has no music, and people should avoid such a designation. The scholars at Bulumi recognized this concept: asked to translate the Arabic term *musiqa* into Vai, they overwhelmingly responded with the Vai word *dɔŋ*.

Al-Faruqi's distinction between *musiqa* and *handasah al sawt* is similar to the Vai's distinction between *dɔŋ* and *suku*, but still another factor is germane: that of textual language. Ideally, all *suku* should have an Arabic text; otherwise, the performer is not using the deity's words. The Vai believe Arabic to be sacred; the ability to read, write, and sing in it is a special gift. In a religious setting, this linguistic element transcends its customary use; and nowhere is the practice clearer than in the manufacture of amulets, medicines, and other magical items. The Vai tell countless stories of people with "special gifts" to influence malevolent and benevolent forces by reading sections from the Qur'ān. Muslims believe written Arabic words have power, which they can capture in inscribed talismans, or in holy-water medicine (made by washing Arabic texts from slates). The Vai believe power flows from the text of the Qur'ān. The musical extension of this belief is that the chanting of Arabic through Qur'ānic verses or prayers, and the singing of *suku*, are also assets of Islam. In any socioreligious context, the performance of *suku* is an act to invoke divine favor, and a step toward holiness.

The Vai believe *suku* has the power to enunciate a set of spiritual principles for all to espouse. Further research may record and illuminate the purposes *suku* serves, and the forms it takes. Its melodies and structures are nearly as variable as words in the texts; but beneath the apparent variety, it shares a common intent with ritual prayer and koranic chant—to communicate with unseen omnipotence.

THE ISLAMIC MUSICAL REPERTORY

Islam has no hierarchy of songs. The Vai do not consider koranic chant *suku*; and though they hold people in high esteem for reciting it in a sweet voice (*nyia kulɛ*) or an Arabic voice (*dʼaabo kulɛ*), they recognize no professional class or style of recitation. They believe everyone—regardless of status, gender, or ethnicity—is free to recite the Qur'ān, in direct communication with God.

Stylistically, Vai Islamic music has few similarities with that found in parts of the Islamic world outside of West Africa. Vai Islamic music is entirely vocal. The Arabic-inspired instruments and instrumental genres of Nigeria, Ghana, and regions of the

The profession of faith in song may serve aptly in a funeral, or at a chief's installation.

Western Sudan, have not penetrated the coastal plain. For an account of Arabic and Islamic musical influences in the Western Sudan, see Farmer (1924, 1939), Nketia (1971, 1974), and Hause (1948). Other than a few new approaches to the call to prayer or Qur'ānic chant, brought by people returning from lengthy visits to other Islamic regions (styles the people have not widely adopted), the traits of Vai Islamic music are similar to those commonly associated with West African music. Most of the repertory came with the Koniaka immigrants. It does not differ markedly from that found in other Islamized areas of Liberia, southern Sierra Leone, or southern Guinea, where Koniaka traders settled and spread the faith.

The structures of Vai Islamic music typically use responsorial patterns, choral unison, and sporadic harmony in organum at the fourth—features commonplace in traditional Vai music. The more sophisticated styles are two-part songs with repeated refrains and an improvised solo line, most commonly performed at holiday celebrations by a *suku-ba* with audience accompaniment.

The Vai do not recognize a hierarchy for pieces in the Islamic musical repertory; nor, though they designate some items as funeral songs, school songs, dance songs, and songs specifically for the Mɔli Sande, do they try to fit songs into neatly organized classes. Over several years, for the enactment of Mahodi, people at Misila composed a group of songs; but they also performed those songs as anthems at political meetings and funerals. Thus, many songs were transferable to different social and religious contexts. The profession of faith in song may serve aptly in a funeral, or at a chief's installation.

What role, if any, does original composition play in Vai Islamic music? The question is difficult, since the Vai do not approach composition formally. The Islamic repertory expands by incorporating precomposed songs, brought to Bulumi by itinerant clerics and learned from radio and commercially produced audiotapes. These songs serve as anthems and panegyric hymns.

From fragments of Qur'ānic verses or Muslim sayings or anecdotes, people compose other songs locally, and soon forget them; other songs last longer, to become permanent parts of the repertory. The texts of these songs are often mixtures of several languages (Vai, Koniaka, Arabic) and vocables. A textual analysis reveals little semantic coding. Texts have an implied meaning, however, which people cannot precisely explicate, because of their lack of command of the language; but as Nketia has noted, songs with unintelligible texts can have an "intensity value" outsiders may fail to appreciate:

> The obscurity of meaning resulting from the use of unintelligible texts and mixed languages or the use of a language foreign to worshippers does not detract from the intensity value of the songs as corporate utterances of worship. Worshippers may sing them with as much zest and religious emotion as they sing songs in familiar languages, for the intensity value of religious songs comes first and foremost from

awareness of their ritual value, that is, their value as avenues for establishing contact with the unseen. (1988:58–59)

The composition of Islamic song types follows constructive processes similar to those of the composition of traditional song types. In certain Islamic and traditional contexts, a successful occasion depends on the compositional inventiveness of the performers. Both Vai and Islamic traditions prize invention and creativity: the mutual ideal is to work with a standard set of conventions and formulas that townspeople learn as part of the normal enculturative process. What counts is the inventiveness and manipulation of these concepts—the ability to use them to exploit extemporaneously the excitement of an occasion.

REFERENCES

al Faruqi, Lois I. 1986. "Handashah al Sawt or the Art of Sound." In *The Cultural Atlas of Islam*, ed. Isma'il al Faruqi and Lois Lamya' al Faruqi, 441– 479. New York: Macmillan.

———. 1986. "The Mawlid." *The World of Music* 28(3):79–89.

Boone, Sylvia A. 1986. *Radiance from the Waters: Ideals of Feminine Beauty in Mende Art*. New Haven, Conn.: Yale University Press.

Büttikofer, Johann. 1890. *Reisebilder aus Liberia*. 2 vols. Leiden: Brill.

d'Azevedo, Warren L. 1962. "Some Historical Problems in the Delineation of a Central West Atlantic Region." *Annals of the New York Academy of Sciences* 96(2):512– 538.

———. 1973. "Mask Makers and Myth in Western Liberia." In *Primitive Art and Society*, ed. Anthony Forge, 126–150. London: Oxford University Press.

Ellis, George W. 1914. *Negro Culture in West Africa*. New York: Neale. Repr. New York: Johnson Reprint Corporation, 1970.

Farmer, Henry George. 1924. "The Arab Influence on Music of the Western Soudan." *Musical Standard* 24:158–159.

———. 1939. "Early References to Music in the Western Sūdān." *Journal of the Royal Asiatic Society of Great Britain and Ireland*, part IV (October):569–579.

Goody, Jack, et. al. 1977. "Writing and Formal Operations: A Case Study among the Vai." *Africa* 47(3):289–304.

Hause, Helen. 1948. "Terms for Musical Instruments in the Sudanic Languages." *Journal of the American Oriental Society* 68(1). Supplement 7.

Johnson, S. Jangaba. 1954. *Traditional History, Customary Laws, Mores, Folkways, and Legends of the Vai Tribe*. Monrovia: Department of the Interior.

Johnston, Harry. 1906. *Liberia*. 2 vols. London: Hutchinson.

Jones, Adam. 1981. "Who Were the Vai?" *Journal of African History* 22:159–78.

Koelle, S. W. 1854. *Outlines of a Grammar of the Vei Language*. London: Church Missionary House.

Levtzion, Nehemia, ed. 1979. *Conversion to Islam*. New York: Holmes and Meier.

Lewis, I. M., ed. 1980. *Islam in Tropical Africa*, 2nd ed. Bloomington: Indiana University Press.

Little, Kenneth. 1951. *The Mende of Sierra Leone: A West African People in Transition*. London: Routledge and Kegan Paul.

Nketia, J. H. Kwabena. 1971. "History and Organization of Music in West Africa." In *Essays on Music and History in Africa*, ed. Klaus P. Wachsmann, 3–25. Evanston, Ill.: Northwestern University Press.

———. 1974. *The Music of Africa*. New York: Norton.

———. 1988. "The Intensity Factor in African Music." In *Performance in Contemporary African Arts*, ed. Ruth M. Stone, 53-86. Bloomington, Ind.: Folklore Institute.

Ofri, Dorith. 1972. "Sowolo 1969: An Ethnomusicological Case Study of the Vai People in Liberia." Paper presented at the Conference on Manding Studies. School of Oriental and African Studies, University of London.

Owen, Nicholas. 1930. *Journal of a Slave-Dealer: "A View of Some Remarkable Axcedents in the Life of Nicholas Owen on the Coast of Africa and America from the Year 1746 to the Year 1757,"* ed. Eveline Martin. London: Routledge.

Phillips, Ruth B. 1978. "Masking in Mande Sande Society Initiation Rituals." *Africa* 48:265–277.

The Guitar in Africa
Andrew L. Kaye

Late Nineteenth and Early Twentieth Centuries
The 1920s and 1930s
The 1940s to 1960
The 1960s to the 1990s

In Africa as abroad, the guitar commonly has two types: acoustic and electric. These types accommodate many structural variations, which embrace distinctive sonic qualities, depending on the number and types of strings, the kinds of wood for the sound box, and—in electric guitars—the number and placement of pickups, the use of distortion, and other electrical or electroacoustic elements, such as solid body or hollow-body (semiacoustic) design. The Spanish or classical guitar, with a fretted neck and six strings (tuned E–a–d–g–b–e′), is a structural prototype for many varieties. There are several tablature notations for the guitar. Staff notation normally puts guitar music in the treble clef, to sound an octave lower than shown.

The system of von Hornbostel and Sachs (1961) classifies the guitar as a composite, lute-type chordophone. The earliest development of this group began in West Asian civilizations of the third and second millennia B.C. An Akkadian cylinder seal dated about the twenty-fourth century B.C. has the earliest known iconographic representation of the lute type, or more precisely, the "long-necked lute." Similar instruments appear in Egyptian iconographic sources of the New Kingdom, dated about the sixteenth to the thirteenth centuries B.C. (Anderson 1980:74).

The short or short-necked lute, the subtype to which Harvey Turnbull ascribes the guitar, probably developed in the first millennium B.C. (1984:89). From approximately the first century B.C., sculptures at Gandhara, in northwestern India, depict short-necked lutes. From the same period, a frieze at Airtam, Uzbekistan, shows an instrument with an in-curved waist, similar to the shape of a guitar (Turnbull 1984:89, fig. 2).

During Europe's Middle Ages, lutes evolved in a multiplicity of forms and directions. The term *guitar*, from Greek *kithara* (possibly via Arabic *qitara*), appears in European texts from about the thirteenth century (Marcuse 1975:218). Scholars, however, have difficulty sorting out the types and names of lutes that appear in iconographic and literary sources during the later medieval period, and confusion over medieval typologies—guitar, gittern, mandola, citole, viola—remains (Tyler 1980:xii, 15–17).

Despite persistent problems of overlapping terms and typologies, scholars agree that by the later 1400s, the guitar had appeared in Europe as a recognizably distinct instrument. It had at least two major subtypes, one with four courses, and one with five. Both subtypes usually had double courses of silk strings, wound with gut and wire. These instruments share the general outline of the modern guitar (which dates to the 1800s), but had smaller dimensions, though the specifics of size and structure varied notably (Evans and Evans 1977; Tyler 1980).

Possibly at that point, the guitar (as it was coming to be defined) entered into the African musical heritage. It may have been introduced into Africa by the Portuguese in the course of their exploration and trading along the West African coast, beginning in the early 1400s. Confirming evidence for this, however, is unavailable, and we cannot prove the European guitar was present in Africa until the end of the 1800s.

We find references to guitars or guitarlike instruments in missionaries' reports and travelers' accounts. Such references, however, must be understood to have been impositions of the European term onto a diversity of African stringed instruments, as a means of describing the instruments for European readers. One such reference, published in a late-seventeenth-century account of Guinea coast travels, cites "a sort of guitar" with six strings (Villault 1669 [1670]:208). This note, however, undoubtedly signifies the harp-lute, called by Bowdich (1819 [1966]) the *sanku*, and now known in the region as the *seperewa*, rather than the guitar.

There is also the curious case of the *ramkie*, a plucked lute with three or four strings, which southern Africans in the Cape Town area may have played as early as the 1730s, but whose origins are unclear (Kirby 1965:249–250; Rycroft 1977:241). The spread of this and other lutelike instruments along the East African coast and in Madagascar may well reflect Arab or Islamic influence and the Indian Ocean trade, as do certain other East African plucked lutes, such as the Swahili *udi* ('*ud*) and the Malagasy *kabosy* (in the Comoro Islands, *gabusi*). However, we know little about the process of diffusion of stringed instruments in Africa before 1800, whether via European or Islamic trade routes.

LATE NINETEENTH AND EARLY TWENTIETH CENTURIES

Toward the end of the 1800s, the development of the colonial system, and the encroachment of urban, commercial, and administrative centers, spreading inland from the coast, brought to Africa many European musical instruments; and surely the guitar was one of them. During the 1800s, the six-string guitar achieved its modern form, after the work of Antonio de Torres Jurado (1817–1892), a Spanish maker. The Spanish guitar may have entered Nigeria with Brazilian and Cuban immigrants in the late 1800s (Omibiyi 1981:162; Waterman 1990:31–32); it may have come to the west coast of Africa with Caribbean and black American immigrants to Liberia and Sierra Leone, and with sailors, soldiers, missionaries, and workers, coming from Europe or the Americas (Darkwa 1974:26).

Other possible sources for the nineteenth-century introduction of the guitar include black American minstrel troupes, which toured South Africa as early as 1887 (Coplan 1985:39). The guitar was well known in Cape Town by the late 1800s, and Cape musicians helped introduce a style of guitar playing like *tickey draai* to towns and mining compounds in the interior (1985:14).

An early twentieth-century photograph shows a racially mixed group of men posing with two guitars, a banjo, a flute, possibly a rattle, and a man holding a book. One of the men has draped over his knees what looks like an American flag. The guitars are of the six-string variety, comparable to flat-top acoustic guitars produced in Europe or America in the late 1800s and early 1900s, such as the American companies Martin, Bruno, and Washburn. The neck of the one on the left is capoed at the third fret. For acoustic guitar music, the use of a *capotasto* is common in Africa,

It is not surprising that the emergence of a circle of guitarists in and around Mombasa dates to the mid- to late 1920s.

FIGURE I   "Band on Primrose Mine" (Kallaway and Pearson 1986:22–23).

because it allows the musician to play in higher keys while using first-position finger- ings (Kubik 1965).

In 1918, a serialized short story mentions Africans' use of the guitar (Sekyi 1918). The account describes the festivities at Christmastide in Cape Coast.

> The town is gay, giddy, and unsafe for unhardened youths. Men are merry, and some roam the town in rowdy parties, singing songs and playing guitars, accor- dions, concertinas, tambourines, etc. Music and revelry and noise are abroad. (Sekyi 1918:378)

This account shows the guitar was a familiar instrument in Cape Coast, as it was in Lagos by the period of the Great War, 1914–1917 (Waterman 1990:45). Still, few authors cite the guitar in Africa up to that point, and we must assume the instrument was rare, even among Europeans—for whom brass bands, the organ, and the piano had greater cultural significance.

The passage of the guitar from a position as a limited instrument to one of cul- tural impact beyond the confines of European communities seems to have taken place in the mid-1920s and in the 1930s. This transition parallels a simultaneous change in interest in the guitar in the West (Danner 1986:296). The classical guitar revival largely associated with Andrés Segovia was one of several factors favoring the instrument in the 1920s. From that time, it had an increasingly prominent role in several American musical genres heard on records and radio, including the blues, country and cowboy music, Hawaiian guitar music, and jazz. Manufacturers developed and marketed diverse types or designs of guitars: the Hawaiian guitar, the Dobro resonator guitar, the twelve-string guitar, the arch-top and flat-top steel-strung guitars, the four-string tenor guitar. In the early 1920s, Lloyd Loar, working for the Gibson company (Kalamazoo, Michigan), experimented with electric pickups for guitars.

It is thus not surprising that the emergence of a circle of guitarists in and around Mombasa dates to the mid- to late 1920s (Kavyu 1978). Rao Rebman, a worker for the East African Railways and Harbours, was then supposedly one of the main guitar teachers. He may have learned to play from one "Jonathan Gitaa" (Kavyu 1978:113). He played with a band formed at the Nyika Club in Rabai in 1926; it included two guitars, banjo, violin, mandolin, double bass, saxophone, and clarinet (Kavyu 1978:117).

Afọlábí Alájá-Browne (1985) and Christopher Waterman (1990) similarly attribute to the 1920s and 1930s the emergence of Yoruba syncretic musical styles using guitars. Waterman suggests that by the 1920s, styles performed on the guitar in Lagos included Spanish, *maringa*, ragtime, European waltzes, and foxtrots (1990:46), plus "a two-fingered style of playing reputedly spread by Kru sailors from Liberia . . . and known by Lagos musicians as *Krusbass*" (1990:47). Several common guitar fingering patterns were associated with Kru styles: mainline, *dagomba*, and fireman (Collins 1989:222). Other patterns used in Nigeria were "Johnny Walker," *yaponsa* (from the Ghanaian song "*Yaa Amponsah*"), and "C-Natural" (Waterman 1990:46–48). These may have comprised the nascent coastal West African genre Collins calls palm wine guitar or palm wine highlife (1989:222); Waterman calls it "the urban West African palm wine guitar tradition" (1990:55). Collins further suggests that, while styles such as mainline should be associated with guitar-playing idioms in the larger towns and ports of the coastal regions, related styles, practiced in hinterland villages, resembled in many ways older traditional idioms. These were known under a host of other names: *ohugua, opim, odonso*, "native blues" (Collins 1987:180, 1989:222; Alájá-Browne 1985:14).

The contexts for guitar playing, as the multiplicity of prevalent styles implies, were variable. They included informal amateur playing and singing among friends, playing at palm wine drinking bars and urban nightclubs, playing for dancing, and performing at traditional or community occasions (weddings, "outdoorings," funerals). The use of Christian lyrics in some guitar songs from the 1920s suggests a possible church use for the guitar.

In the two-finger styles, scholars often assume influence from playing techniques of traditional African plucked stringed instruments. On the guitar, this technique involves the use of the thumb and index finger of the plucking hand (usually the right hand). The thumb picks out a bass figure on the lower three strings, while the index picks out an interlocking rhythmic pattern on the treble strings. Many variations occur, however: the thumb and index finger may work in strict alternation, play a variety of arpeggiated figures, or strike the strings simultaneously, with the index finger strumming a chordal figure over several strings (Kubik 1965; Low 1982b; Rycroft 1961, 1962).

A hint of this playing technique appears in a photo of an ensemble John Collins identifies as the Kumasi Trio (figure 2). He believes it was taken in London in 1928, on the group's recording tour for Zonophone (Collins, personal communication, 1988). The leader of this group, known as "Sam," was one of the pioneers of guitar

Early in 1932, [*The Gold Coast Spectator*] reported that Augustus Williams, "actor, tap dancer, guitarist and singer of comic songs," was the first stage entertainer "to accompany himself on the guitar."

FIGURE 2   Kumasi Trio, ca. 1928. Photo courtesy John Collins.

playing in Ghana (Collins 1985:13). Two of the musicians in the photo pose with guitars that resemble the guitar on the left in figure 1. As in that picture, the necks of the guitars are capoed at about the third fret, here with what looks like a pencil, held in place by a rubber band. The guitarist on the right holds the thumb and index finger of his right hand in playing position. The guitarist on the left appears to finger a C-major chord, or possibly C-dominant-seventh chord—two of the chordal configurations common in this music. This chord position is comparable to those in photos of American guitarists from the period (Oliver 1984:32, 50).

In figure 2, further signs are difficult to decipher. The strings were likely of steel, as they commonly were by the 1920s, though they may have been of gut. Judging by the fingering-position noted above, we may postulate the instrument uses the standard tuning for the six-string guitar. This, however, is by no means certain, since alternate guitar tunings abounded in Africa. Waterman reports that musicians in Lagos used tuning schemes such as Spanish (possibly influenced by American blues guitar tunings), and tunings similar to Hawaiian slack-key guitar tunings (for example, the open tuning consisting of the intervals fourth-fifth-fourth-major third-minor third) (1990:46–48).

It is not possible to determine the absolute tuning of the strings, but guitars in Africa do not usually vary much from the norm of tuning from E on the sixth string. They may be tuned slightly higher than E, but tend to be tuned slightly lower, to reduce tension on the strings, and thus to prolong their life (Kubik 1976:168).

THE 1920S AND 1930S

In the 1920s and 1930s, probably the strongest indicator of the coming importance of the guitar in Africa was the issuing of the first extended series of commercial recordings of African music that feature the guitar. Among more than four hundred gramophone records listed in a catalogue of West African records (*Catalogue of Zonophone West African Records* 1929), fifty-seven include the guitar. They include one instrumental trio featuring concertina, guitar, and drum; one guitar solo with vocal refrain; and sixty-two other songs with guitar accompaniment, or the accompaniment of a consort of instruments, including some combination of guitar, banjo, concertina, tambourine, castanets, and drum. The guitar is represented on performances by six of forty-three performers listed in the catalogue. Five of the performers—Daniel Acquaah, George Williams Aingo, Nicholas de Heer, Ben Simmons, and Harry Eben Quashie—were likely Ghanaians, since the catalog lists them as singing in Akan languages (Fanti, Ashanti, Twi). One, Domingo Justus, was evidently a Yoruba speaker from Nigeria. Though they may have made these recordings in Accra or Lagos, they may have made some of them in London (Collins 1985:13).

One of the Zonophone recordings available for analysis, held in the collection of the National Sound Archives (London), is George Williams Aingo's "*Na Mapa Nu Kyew*," called on the record label a "Song in Fanti with guitar and castanets" (Aingo n.d.:B). His commercial recordings of African songs with guitar accompaniment, dating to about 1925, are perhaps the first of their kind (Collins 1985:149–150). He may have recorded them in Accra, but more probably did so in London.

This song suggests an incipient form of the syncretic highlife idiom, which emerged during this period. If the tuning was standard, the guitar was likely capoed on the third fret, and played as if in the key of C in the first position (the actual key is about a minor third higher). Probably using the thumb and index finger, the guitarist picks out the bass line on the lower strings, arpeggiates and strums chords, and occasionally plays the vocal melody in parallel sixths. The song, which concerns a marital dispute (Kwabena N. Bame, personal communication, 1989), consists of a strophic repetition of a Western-type four-bar melody in 4/4 time, in these harmonies:

$$I--- \mid I^{\flat 7} - IV^6 - \mid IV - I^6_4 - \mid V^7 - I -$$

This pattern, which includes a dominant seventh on the tonic degree in transition to the subdominant chord with the added sixth, is common in guitar music of the Guinea Coast, and is familiar in the guitar music of some other African regions (Low 1982b:106).

Nineteen gramophone records by the Kumasi Trio appear in a later Zonophone catalogue, dating to about 1930. These include thirty-eight songs with guitars and castanets or guitars and drum. Four of them are "sacred songs," of which two have titles that name Jesus and David.

In addition to gramophone recordings, references to the guitar in *The Gold Coast Spectator*, a weekly journal published in Accra from the late 1920s, also suggest a growing presence for the guitar. Early in 1932, the paper reported that Augustus Williams, "actor, tap dancer, guitarist and singer of comic songs," was the first stage entertainer "to accompany himself on the guitar" ("Augustus Williams" 1932:207). Later, encouraging readers to study the instrument seriously, it singles out the guitar as "the most abused instrument," because players are "contented to manipulate one or two popular songs on the instrument without making any effort at improvement" (Danso 1932:432).

In 1934, Percival Kirby suggested the guitar was becoming more common in

FIGURE 3 A phrase from "*Na Mapa Nu Kyew*," a song by George Williams, ca. 1925 (Aingo n.d.:B).

South Africa, where it was available for purchase at cheap prices in trading stores. He noted that it and certain other European instruments "tend, in some cases, to supplant the natives' own" instruments (1965:257). He reported that popular guitar playing consisted of the "rhythmic strumming of two, or perhaps three, of the 'primary' chords" (1965:257).

In the mid-1930s, the British label His Master's Voice (after 1931, part of the EMI conglomerate) issued recordings in which the guitar figures even more prominently than in the Zonophone catalogue of 1929 (Collins 1985:150; Waterman 1986:201–202). This is especially so in the Twi and Fanti (Ghanaian) songs with guitar accompaniment. A later edition of the West Africa catalogue (ca. 1952) lists 118 such songs, by ten performers or groups, with guitar accompaniment. They were presumably recorded in Accra, between 1929 and 1939. Possibly excepting Sam, believed to have recorded with the Kumasi Trio, the performers probably differ from those who appear on the earlier Zonophone recordings. They include Kwamin, Kwesi Pepera, Mireku, Kwabena Mensa, Kwesi Menu, Kofi Mabireh, Piasah, Appianing, and Kamkam.

The typical ensemble for these Twi and Fanti guitar songs was a trio or a quartet. It included a lead vocal part provided by a solo male singer of the tenor range, supporting vocals provided by one or several other men's voices, one or two guitars, and simple percussion provided by a struck idiophone such as an iron bell, a bottle, a cigarette tin, or a wooden box (*adakem*), such as appears in figure 2. Occasionally a drum is indicated. A large lamellophone with three or four metal tongues, known under a variety of names in West Africa (*kongoma, prempresiwa, agidigbo*), sometimes appears.

Mainly by harmonic criteria, the songs group in two classes: (1) songs based on Western diatonic harmony, and (2) songs based on indigenous harmonies. Songs of the first type use cyclic harmonic patterns (sometimes called short forms), over which a human voice spins out a melody. The harmonic patterns are typically of a functional, tonic-subdominant-dominant-tonic nature. Songs of the second type use Western guitar chords, but in ways dictated by indigenous styles. (This distinction may match the stylistic division noted by Collins between coastal and hinterland styles, though these classes do not stand as real geographic divisions, since both styles occurred in both regions.) The use of the guitar in these styles also suggests the guitar was supplanting older, indigenous, stringed instruments (such as the *seperewa* harp-lute), which may previously have served for these idioms (Coplan 1978:101–102).

"*Ampa Afful*" (Sam n.d.), dated to about 1930, exemplifies the first type. It recalls the song of figure 3, but with much more complexity. The artist is again identified as Sam. The ensemble includes two guitars, a tapped idiophone, and a solo vocal part, sung in a high tenor register, with a forceful head voice. At the end of the song, the singers supply a cadential chorus. The song rhythmically develops an off-the-beat timeline pattern in common time (4/4), tapped out on the idiophone. This

FIGURE 4 "*Ampa Afful*," by Sam. Excerpt transcribed from the instrumental introduction (Sam n.d.). Original key is A-flat. Guitar 1 is capoed at the eighth fret.

Guitar 1 is capoed at the eight fret.
Actual key is A-flat.
Guitar 2 sounds major 10th lower than notated.

guitar 2 repeats last two measures
as a <u>basso ostinato</u> figure

pattern appears in highlife and related genres (figure 4). Its chord progression is similar to that of figure 3. It has a repetitive two-measure pattern, in a subdominant-dominant-tonic relationship.

By playing arpeggiated chords and dyads in sixths, the first-guitar part supports the singer during the verse. In the instrumental introduction, and between the verses, it fills in with a kind of *ritornello* figure, consisting of scalar runs and alternating thirds in a high register, played above the eighth fret. In a lower register, the second guitar provides an ostinatolike figure.

The vocal melody is structured over the eight-pulse cyclic rhythmic and harmonic pattern. It is sung in a recitativelike style, with rather short phrases that often follow a descending contour. The lyrics, sung in Fanti, are topical, with elements of praise song. The singer recounts how some Europeans with a recording machine got interested in recording their music (lyrics translated by Daniel Amponsah and James Osei, personal communication, 1989).

Figure 5 illustrates a song of the second type, "*Agyanka Odede*," by Kwesi Menu

FIGURE 5 "*Agyanka Odede*," by Kwesi Menu. Excerpt transcribed from the instrumental introduction (Menu n.d.). Original key is A minor. The guitar is capoed at the fifth fret.

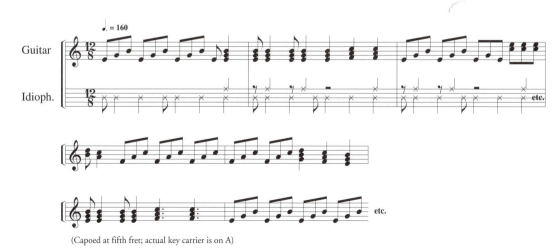

(Capoed at fifth fret; actual key carrier is on A)

In 1947, Bobby Benson, "the father of Nigerian highlife," introduced the first electric guitar in Lagos.

(n.d.), dating about 1939. In Twi, the title roughly translates as "The Orphan's Inquietude"; the lyrics express the complaints of a rejected soul (trans. Daniel Amponsah, personal communication, 1989). The timeline is a 12/8 pattern, common in traditional genres of the region, and widespread in African music.

The song uses a heptatonic scale, also common in traditional genres, and comparable to the mode beginning on the third degree of the diatonic scale (the Phrygian or E mode). The song is in verse-refrain form, with the verse sung by the leader, and a refrain sung by the supporting singers, with resultant tertial harmonies, also common in Akan vocal styles (Nketia 1974:161).

The guitar was likely capoed on the fifth fret, and played as if in the first position key of E minor (the original tonal center is a fourth above, on A). The guitar arpeggiates and strums two alternating chords, on the first and second scale degrees, and plays melodic passages of parallel thirds in the instrumental introduction and between the verses. In the middle part of the song, over a sustained, arpeggiated harmony (played on the guitar), the lead singer sings an extended passage in recitative style.

By the 1930s, the guitar was becoming a well-tuned addition to African ensembles, both for performance, and for original work. The Kumasi Trio and the groups represented in the His Master's Voice JZ series are prototypical for the guitar band (as it became known in Ghana), a commonly established ensemble type by the later 1930s and 1940s, at least along the Guinea Coast. The guitar band used several regional styles, including palm wine, native blues, and *jùjú* in Nigeria, *maringa* in Sierra Leone, and highlife in Ghana. In Ghana, guitar bands became associated with dramatic troupes, which toured towns and villages presenting "concerts" or "comic opera"; they thus reached a wide audience (Collins 1985:21–22).

As an ensemble typology, the guitar band contrasted with the dance band, another type of ensemble, which developed in the early decades of the twentieth century, contemporaneously with or slightly earlier than the guitar bands. Dance bands were distinguishable by instrumentation, repertory, and context. Instrumentation typically featured wind instruments (clarinet, trumpet, saxophones, trombone), stringed instruments (violins, double bass, guitar), and percussion. Repertories included European-international ballroom music (waltzes, tangos, foxtrots), American ragtime, and West African highlife. Urban contexts typically included formal ballrooms and dance halls (Collins 1986:3; Waterman 1990:42–44).

THE 1940S TO 1960

In the period after 1945, the story of the guitar in Africa grew more complex, as the acoustic guitar began to spread rapidly around the continent, while amplification and the electric guitar progressively entered the urban African musical scene. Other guitar varieties, such as the Hawaiian guitar, also found occasional usage in Africa. The Rhino Band, for example, formed by Joseph Sheila of Rabai (Kenya) in the early

1940s, featured one "Hawaii guitar," in addition to three guitars, mandolin, accordion, and drums (Kavyu 1978:117). African participation in the Allied armies, 1939–1945, was important for the expanding influence of Western music and its popular instrumentation in Africa (Kubik 1981:92).

No one knows when the first electric guitars arrived in Africa, but the instruments were probably not there before 1945. Several American companies (Rickenbacher, National, Gibson) first marketed them in the United States in the early 1930s. By the later 1940s, in both their semiacoustic and solid body varieties, they had secured increased importance in popular musical genres (jazz, country and western, rhythm and blues). In 1947, Bobby Benson, "the father of Nigerian highlife," introduced the first electric guitar in Lagos; and in 1949, amplified guitar was a standard part of the *jùjú* ensemble of Ayinde Bakare, a leading musician there (Waterman 1990:83–84). The Zaïrean guitarist Wendo first played an electric guitar in the Ngoma recording studio in Kinshasa in 1949 (Stapleton and May 1990:144).

The acoustic guitar, however, was still the predominant instrument; and by the late 1940s, we have references to its popular use in many corners of sub-Saharan Africa. Anglophone regions of Africa know the acoustic instrument as the box guitar and the dry guitar; Francophone regions, as the *guitare sèche*. In 1949, in Kissidougou (eastern Guinea), Arthur Alberts recorded a *jaliya*-type ensemble that featured singers identified as "Sudanese minstrels," accompanied by a *kora* and "two imported guitars" (Alberts 1950:18).

In field reports for 1948 and 1949, Hugh Tracey documented the use of guitars in South Africa, Zambia, Zimbabwe, and Malawi. In those countries, he found a mixture of influences on guitar-playing styles, including local zither-playing techniques (1950b:36) and music heard on Afrikaans recordings (possibly the guitar-accompanied style of the well-known South African folk singers Marais and Miranda). In "cowboy films" in Salisbury (Harare), he saw musicians, wearing four-gallon hats, "strum their guitars with monotonous loyalty to one key" (1948:11). In that period, American "singing cowboy guitarists" had influence in South Africa (Coplan 1985:187). Tracey also noted that guitar music influenced performances on African stringed instruments (1950b:37). Recalling the trend cited by Kirby in 1934, Richard Waterman observed that the guitar, at least in West Africa, had by 1950 "become in most respects a native instrument" (1950:10).

In 1952, the African Music Society awarded first prize of the Osborn Awards for "best African music of the year" to the guitar song "*Masanga*," by Mwenda-Jean Bosco, a guitarist from Zaïre, who would become widely known in Africa through his recordings and tours. In 1949 in Jadotville, Belgian Congo (now Likasi, Zaïre), Tracey had first recorded him (1953a:65–67; Rycroft 1961:81). Acknowledgment of Mwenda's song as "best African music" was a sign of the guitar's growing importance in African music.

Mwenda's songs have interested several ethnomusicologists. David Rycroft, who transcribed several of his guitar songs (1961, 1962), determined the music consisted of short cyclic sequences of "chords or broken chords," lasting from two to four measures in duple or compound meter, with 16-beat timeline patterns as rhythmic accompaniment, and often in modes similar to Western diatonic modes beginning on C or G (1962:87–100). Rycroft emphasized the complexities of Mwenda's accentuation and rhythmic play, and compared these traits to traditional African ones (1961:82–83, 1962:100–101). Collins proposed that "*Masanga*," as transcribed by Rycroft (1961:87–98), involved the "West African 'mainline' style played in the G position" (1987:192).

John Low, who, with Mwenda and others (particularly Losta Abelo and Edouard Masengo), did fieldwork in the Shaba region, southern Zaïre, has added detail to the

FIGURE 6   Cyclical pattern in *"Antoinette muKolwezi,"* by Ilunga Patrice and Misomba Victor (Tracey 1957a:B6). Original key is A. Guitar 1 is capoed at the fifth fret.

analysis of what he calls the Katanga guitar styles, which he dates to the 1940s and 1950s (1982b). He emphasizes the use of thumb and index-finger picking, including the alternating-bass style, where the thumb plays low notes on strong beats, and the index finger provides offbeat interest. This technique is allegedly similar to country blues and ragtime styles of the United States (1982b:19). He also identifies the use of the pull-off and hammer-on techniques (1982b:115), and the widespread use of certain common chords, notably the subdominant chord with added major sixth (F^6), which he suggests bears the influence of church music (1982b:106).

Low also identifies several common guitar tunings used by these musicians, and those in the neighboring region: Zambian guitarists call the tuning D–a–d–f♯–a–c♯′ *Espagnol*; Masengo guitarists call it *Hawaiienne* (1982b:95). Other common tunings include G–a–d–g–b–e′, F–a–d–g–b–e′, and F–a–d–g–c–e′ (1982b:107). He suggests that some of the tunings and nomenclature of tuning, with certain techniques of playing, show African-American influence (1982b:109–111). He finds the common alternation between high and low notes resembles techniques used for playing African lamellophones, but the musicians he worked with did not acknowledge "inspiration from a local traditional instrument" (1982b:103).

In the 1950s, Hugh Tracey issued several records, including one on the London label, with the title *The Guitars of Africa* (Tracey 1953b). These included guitar songs by Mwenda and several dozen others, recorded over a wide region in Central, Southern, and Eastern Africa, in field trips beginning in 1948 (Tracey 1973). A variety of guitar-playing styles appears in his recordings—from simple strumming to the thumb-and-index-finger technique. The general musical characteristics of these pieces resemble those of Mwenda's style; in many ways, they remind us of Twi and Fanti recordings of guitar-accompanied songs from the 1930s and 1940s.

Figure 6 transcribes an excerpt from the song *"Antoinette muKolwezi,"* performed by "Ilunga Patrice and Misomba Victor, and friends" (identified by Tracey as Luba-Hemba speakers), recorded in 1957, at the Kolwezi copper mine, Katanga (Shaba) Province, Zaïre (Tracey 1957a:B6). This song uses a diatonic major harmonic system, and a timeline in 12/8 meter. In the treble register, the first guitar plays a cyclic melody, which ornaments the vocal part. The second guitar plays an ostinato bass. Other songs in Tracey's collection, such as *"Iuwale-o-iuwale"* (Tracey 1957b:A3) from Zambia, show the guitar's usage in stylistically traditional idioms.

Between about 1956 and 1960, the electric guitar began to take on an increasingly dominant role in African music—not entirely displacing the acoustic guitar, but matching it, in its appeal to African youth and the radio-listening and record-buying public (Manuel 1988:98). We can note a particularly prominent role for electric guitars in the emerging Congolese urban pop of this period, centered in Kinshasa (then Léopoldville) and Brazzaville.

Between 1956 and 1959, O. K. Jazz, a Kinshasa-based band, which would soon become popular across sub-Saharan Africa, made recordings that featured two electric guitars (one playing "rhythm"; the other, "solo" or "lead"), two or three male vocalists, jazz and African-Latin percussion, muted trumpet, clarinet, tenor saxophone, and double bass. This group's instrumentation, urban setting, and repertory (songs based on Latin-American dance rhythms, but usually sung in local languages), suggest we should view it as a dance band, rather than a guitar band, though the distinction is fluid.

Judging from photographs of other urban African dance bands in the 1950s, we can probably assume the guitars used in these recordings are of the semiacoustic electric type, favored in American jazz and country of the period. A 1952 photograph of the Tempos Band, a prominent Ghanaian highlife group led by E. T. Mensah, shows two archtop semiacoustic guitars with f-holes—the type of electric guitars commonly used in this period in American jazz, and in country music (Collins 1986:25; similar photo in Coplan 1981:448). Dating to about 1956, a photograph of African Jazz, a leading Congolese dance band formed in Kinshasa in 1953, shows two similar instruments.

Latin American dance music strongly influences the recordings by O. K. Jazz. This influence comes in part from the popularity of a series of Cuban dance music issued by His Master's Voice, starting in the late 1920s or early 1930s, and circulating afterward in Africa (Low 1982a:23; Waterman 1986:131–132). During the 1930s and 1940s, Latin American dance music was likely heard over the radio in many African urban centers. Ngoma Records, one of the major record companies of Kinshasa in the 1950s, had a studio band, which from available records copied Latin styles of dancing, and reproduced them on disk. They sing in Spanish the lyrics of some of the songs (Kubik 1965:13). Jazz guitar styles performed in Kinshasa by resident European musicians influenced Congolese electric guitar technique; one of these musicians, Bill Alexander, a Belgian, bore the influence of Django Rheinhardt (Ewens 1986:13).

These early songs by O. K. Jazz follow basic Latin or African-Caribbean dance music structures, and it is also not surprising to hear elements of other styles of pop. Of the sixteen songs on the RetroAfric reedition of O. K. Jazz's early recordings, eleven are listed as rumba, two as "biguine," two as bolero, one as merengue, and one as "tcha tcha tcha." Most of the texts of these songs are in Lingala, a lingua franca of the western Congo region. The text of at least one, "*La Fiesta*," is in Spanish.

In this music, the rhythm guitar strums chords, while the lead guitar plays melodic lines, sometimes in parallel thirds, in single lines accompanying melodies played on the trumpet or clarinet at the third, and sometimes in counterpoint to the vocal and wind parts. The lead guitar often plays in a high register of the guitar, past the twelfth fret on the first two (highest) strings. The sound of the guitar is "open," with a touch of reverberation, for a ringing, bell-like quality.

In the eponymous song "*On Entre O. K., On Sort K. O.*," composed by Franco (Luambo Makiadi), guitarist and later leader and star of the group, the electric guitar harmonizes in thirds with a muted trumpet in the instrumental refrains, while the double bass provides a rumba rhythm. During the verses sung in Lingala, to punctuate the vocal phrases, the guitar interjects a figure in thirds. In "*Ejoni Banganga*," recorded between 1956 and 1959 (Franco 1987:B4), the guitar provides decorative counterpoint, complete with chromatic passages, scalar figures, and repeated notes high on the fretboard, which would become a staple in modern African electric guitar styles. In "*Passi Ya Boloko*," from the same period, also a rumba (Franco 1987:A3), an electric guitar solo recalls the blues-tinged guitar solos heard in bluegrass and rockabilly music of the 1950s, with its characteristic insistence on the opposition of the major-third and minor-third degrees of the scale (figure 7). In essential harmonic and melodic elements, "*Ejoni Banganga*" is almost identical to "*Pini Ochama*," a song

FIGURE 7   "*Passi Ya Boloko*," by O. K. Jazz. Excerpt of guitar solo (Franco 1987:A3).

THE 1960S TO THE 1990S

In 1959, A. M. Jones observed "the guitar bought from a European music shop" had been claimed by "the young African of today . . . as his own," and that "it is everywhere" (Jones 1959:257). The last statement was an exaggeration, but Jones's comments nonetheless suggest the guitar was coming to have a large impact in Africa, especially in the major towns and urban centers. In 1961, the Arts Council of Ghana sponsored a national guitar band competition, and bestowed on the winner, Kwabena Onyina, the title "King of Guitar." At about the same time, Franco gained fame in the Congo region (and later in many other parts of Africa), and became known by the sobriquet "*sorcier de la guitare*" (Ewens 1986:14). These trends reflect rising popularity in the guitar in the West during the period, and its prominent part in rock and roll, emulated by African bands in the early 1960s (Collins 1977:56).

In 1965, Kubik asserted the guitar was a "key instrument," located at the "middlepoint" of modern African musical developments (Kubik 1965:1–7). He argued that in urban Africa, the guitar, as a nontribal instrument, had become symbolic of modernity and opposition to rigid traditionalism (1965:16). An advertisement in *Drum* magazine (Ghana edition, February 1966) makes this kind of association explicit: above the caption "Progressive people bank with B·W·A" (Bank of West Africa) is a drawing of a television studio, showing a female worker taking notes, and a camera crew recording a male African musician performing on the electric guitar. A more potent and radical kind of symbolism, which the guitar has sometimes taken on in Africa, informs a political cartoon published in the same magazine a year later ("Guitar Boy" 1967). It depicts the "Guitar Boy," the nickname given to a young officer who led an abortive coup. The cartoon shows him firing a guitar as if were a rifle (figure 8).

The guitar's transition from a peripheral to a central position in African musical culture in the period between about 1920 and 1965, reflects broader, international trends in the instrument's history. In the United States, popular interest in the guitar, and guitar sales, increased dramatically between 1955 and 1965 (Fleming 1966:40–41; American Music Conference 1987:5). The extent of the guitar's musical usage in the urbanizing parts of Africa, and the fluidity of its symbolic usage, however, imply the processes of indigenization of the guitar in Africa seen by earlier writers were effectively completed by the mid-1960s.

A Zaïrean guitarist who had a wide influence on the playing of electric guitars in Africa during the 1960s was Nicolas Kasanda Wa Mikalayi, popularly known as "Docteur Nico." In 1953, he helped found the Congolese music ensemble African

FIGURE 8   Political cartoon depicting the "Guitar Boy" ("Guitar Boy" 1967).

Jazz. During the 1960s, as leader and lead guitarist of several groups (including African-Fiesta and African-Fiesta Sukisa) he was influential in expanding electric guitar sonorities and playing techniques for contemporary African popular music, and in the development of *soukous*, a Congolese style (Stewart 1989b:19).

A photograph published on the cover of a reedition of some of his material from the 1960s shows him playing a Fender-type solid-body electric guitar with three pickups and a "tremolo arm"; between his thumb and forefinger, he holds a plectrum. The Africa Fiesta recordings of the mid-1960s highlight his playing. His solos often combine contrasting timbres. He uses different pickup settings (as in "*Yaka Toya Mbana*," Nico 1985b:A3), echo, sustain, "choked" notes, and Hawaiian-guitar glissandos (as in "*Mambo Hawaïenne*," Nico 1985a:A7).

Alan Merriam singled out Francis Bebey as an exemplar of the "African art music guitarist" (1967:4). A performer on, and composer for, the classical guitar, Bebey added an extra dimension to the repertory of African guitar music. He was born in Douala, Cameroon, in 1929; at the age of 25, he moved to Paris, where he studied at the Sorbonne, and became influenced by Segovia's guitar playing. His first compositions for the guitar date to 1963, and he released his first album, *Pièces pour Guitare Seule*, in 1966. In the late 1960s and 1970s, he became known through his recordings and concert performances on the classical guitar. He played a mixed repertory, of arrangements of Western classical music, Brazilian and Latin American guitar music, and original compositions. In the use of folk material and dance rhythms, his pieces for guitar bear the influence of Spanish and Latin American styles; and his harmonic language sometimes reflects the influence of French Impressionist composers.

Bebey's compositions include "*Accra se mit à danser autour de Noël*" (Bebey 1978:B2), a fantasy, based on the Ghanaian folk song "*Yaa Amponsah*." His "*Ndesse*" (Bebey 1978:A2) provides guitar accompaniment to a recited poem by Léopold Senghor. To convey a sense of African rhythmic vitality on the guitar (Roberts 1979), he has applied special percussive playing techniques, including the tapping of the soundbox, as in "*Danse des Criquets Pèlerins*" (Bebey 1966:B6).

Most guitar playing in Africa since the 1960s has been associated with the popular urban bands (which play contemporary Western or African-American and African-Caribbean popular music), plus emergent African popular musical idioms. In Kenya, Roberts noted urban bands greatly indulged styles of pop: twist, *kwela*, "Congo-influenced" styles, and "urban electric-guitarred Kenyan pop song" (1968:53).

For other urban centers of Africa by the late 1960s, a similar picture emerges. Local rock bands modeled themselves after Western groups. They featured singers, electric guitars, electric bass, and trap drum set, and performed a mix of pop music styles. Naomi Hooker, who did fieldwork in Freetown, Sierra Leone, in 1969, reported (1970:12) that bands there performed "Congolese," soul, West Indian "rock steady" and "blue beat," and "mixed Latin" (meringue, cha-cha, pachanga, rumba). In Ghana, using the guitar, several bands arose in the 1960s and 1970s. They played pop music styles: reggae, soul, Afro-Beat. The Psychedelic Aliens, formed in 1968, "released records in 1971 combining the Jimmy Hendrix guitar technique with African drum rhythms" (Collins 1977:58).

Ethnomusicologists writing in the 1970s and 1980s continue to report on the growing importance of the guitar, and its tendency to replace older indigenous African instruments. Writing of Ghana, Esi Sylvia Kinney states, "the guitar has practically replaced the indigenous stringed instruments . . . and many guitars are made and redesigned locally" (1970:6–7). Robert Kauffman (1972) notes that in urban areas of Zimbabwe, the solo acoustic guitar mimicked the mbira, in both social function and musical relationship (1972:52). Similarly, Rycroft (1977) writes, "the most

soukous   Popular form of music from Kinshasa, featuring three guitar parts and solo singer

chimurenga   Liberation-movement music in Zimbabwe with dry, percussive guitar sound

mbaqanga   Popular music style of South Africa in which a clean lead-guitar sound is preferred

popular instrument among young Zulu men who come to town from the country, as temporary manual workers, is the common Western guitar. It has adopted almost exactly the functional role previously fulfilled by the *umakhweyana* gourd bow (1977:228–229). He also notes teenage boys commonly make their own instruments (1977:241). Writing of Zambia, Moya Aliya Malamusi notes, "the young generation is almost exclusively tuned to electric guitar based popular music" (1984:189).

In the 1980s, in the West, and to a certain degree in Japan and elsewhere, attention increasingly focused on African popular music and African styles of playing the guitar (Duncan 1989; Goodwin and Gore 1990). In 1982, Island, a British-American company, signed Nigerian *jùjú* star guitarist King Sunny Ade, who then began releasing records and going on international tours. In 1986 and 1987, Paul Simon released his *Graceland* album, and staged its world tour.

The role of the guitar in Ade's *jùjú* music was a central point of interest for his audiences. Nigerians knew him as *Alujonu Onigita* 'Wizard of the Guitar' (Waterman 1990:133). In February 1984, *Guitar Player* magazine devoted a feature article to him, with a separate article devoted to Demola Adepoju, the steel guitar player in his band (Kaiser 1984a, 1984b). Ade's nineteen-piece group, the African Beats, included four electric guitarists, a pedal-steel guitar, and an electric bass (Kaiser 1984a:32).

Describing the interrelationship of the guitar parts in contemporary *jùjú* ensembles, Waterman cites the use of ostinato "interlocking support patterns . . . frequently harmonized in thirds," played by the tenor guitars, which function in a similar way to "conga-type" drums (Waterman 1990:183–184). The guitar-playing of the "band captain" consists of "percussively struck triads" and "short distinctive motifs," often played in a high register; they signal new sections in the song. Solos may be played by a lead guitarist, who may employ a variety of effects, including echo, fuzz, and the sound of the wa-wa pedal. The Hawaiian or pedal steel guitar adds "sustained chords and swooping melodic figures," and sometimes extended solos (Waterman 1990:183).

In African popular music of the 1980s, produced for both African and Western audiences, the guitar prevailed, not only in sound, but in image. The symbolic placement of an African musician holding an electric guitar as the central figure on the cover of an issue of *West Africa* (17 December 1984) puts into visual form Kubik's suggestion that the guitar figured as the "middlepoint" of the new African music (Cover illustration 1984). In this drawing, the guitarist not only commands the center, but overshadows in scale the other musicians, including a *kora* player and a *balafon* player. For a much broader, indeed international audience, a similar symbolic conjoining of the electric guitar and African music came from the organizers of the Live Aid concerts, which took place in London and Philadelphia in 1985, and were televised internationally to a potential audience in the hundreds of millions. The logo for this event dramatically merged the shapes of the electric guitar and the continent of Africa (Gladwell 1986).

FIGURE 9   Excerpt from a Choc Stars *seben*. Transcription by Banning Eyre and Joe Gore (Eyre 1988:82).

Between 1985 and 1990, an increasing number of popular and scholarly books and articles, plus records and compact discs, highlighted the role of the guitar in African music. Congolese styles, Kenyan *benga*, and South African *mbaqanga*, prefer a "clean," "Fender-type" lead guitar sound, with few distortion effects (Mandelson 1985:10). "The major recording centre for modern Congolese music is now Paris," where a small pool of guitarists reproduces a "distinctive sound," which reappears in recordings by many different bands (Mandelson 1985:10; Stewart 1989a). In Zimbabwean *chimurenga* 'liberation' music, guitarists such as those in Thomas Mapfumo's band may "play double notes in fourths while deadening the strings at the bridge with the flesh of the palm" (Mandelson 1985:10). To imitate the sounds of traditional instruments (*balafon*, *kora*), groups from Mali, Senegal, Guinea, and Gambia, use special timbral effects: sustain, delays, fuzztone, chorus. These groups include Bembeya Jazz National of Guinea, led by guitarist Sékou Diabaté; Les Ambassadeurs of Mali, with guitarist Kante Manfila; and Youssou N'Dour's Super Étoile, a Senegalese group that specializes in *mbalax*, a dynamic popular musical style.

In a discussion of modern Afropop forms—mainly *soukous*, *chimurenga*, *mbaqanga*—Banning Eyre examines the role of the electric guitar (1988). *Soukous*, a popular form coming from Kinshasa but influential throughout central and eastern Africa, and in other parts of Africa, ideally has three guitar parts (solo, mi-solo, accompaniment or rhythm) and bass guitar. The solo guitarist plays a repeated figure in a high register, usually above the twelfth fret. In the densely textured *seben* section of the song, the mi-solo plays a contrastive rhythmic and melodic pattern (figure 9). The rhythm guitarist plays "an arpeggio figure or a steady bass line set off by a series of double stops on the middle strings" (Eyre 1988:82). Varying the use of plectra and finger picking achieves contrasting timbres. Despite the importance of the electric guitars in *soukous*, the singers take precedence as stars, and as musical centers of focus for the public in Zaïre, for whom lyrical and vocal qualities appear to provide primary values (Eyre 1988:82).

By combining two electric guitars and a bass, *chimurenga* replicates the structural relationships of mbira music (Eyre 1988:87). *Chimurenga* guitarists prefer a dry, percussive tone, which they achieve by using plectra and playing with repeated downstrokes, while damping the strings as described above. Figure 10 shows the interaction between the electric guitars and bass in such a passage. South African styles of playing include strumming, and, as in *soukous*, plectrum playing in a high register; to enable this "high-on-the-fretboard guitar work," Marks Mankwane uses a twenty-four-fret Ibanez Artist (Eyre 1988:85). The Zulu-guitar style featured in the playing of Johnny Clegg and others, emphasizes finger-picking styles, the use of open-string drones, a "regular pulse provided by the thumb," and "slides, hammer-ons, and pull-offs," executed in lower positions, below the fifth fret (Eyre 1988:86).

The period after about 1982 also saw a revival of interest in African acoustic guitar music, particularly among folk-musical audiences in the West. An increasing

FIGURE 10   Basic phrases from "*Gwindingwe Rine Shumba*," by Thomas Mapfumo. Transcription by Banning Eyre and Joe Gore (Eyre 1988:87).

Lead

Sub-lead

Bass

number of records issued on labels based in London, Paris, and New York, focused on this music (Richardson 1990). In 1982, the "comeback" of Mwenda-Jean Bosco was reported when he made a modest tour of Europe ("Mwenda Jean Bosco's Comeback" 1982). *Repercussions*, a British television documentary aired in 1984, included "Africa Come Back," a program on African popular music, directed by Dennis Marks. It featured the "palm wine guitar music" of the Ghanaian musician Koo Nimo. In 1988, in England, S. E. Rogie also made a comeback—as "the palm wine music man" (During 1988:670); he was a Sierra Leonean guitarist, singer, and songwriter, who in the 1960s had made some popular recordings, notably the song "My Lovely Elizabeth" (reissued on Rogie 1986:B1). The musical style of Koo Nimo and Rogie represents a development of the two-finger idioms of the Guinea Coast region, dating to the 1920s and 1930s, now called palm wine guitar (Fosu-Mensah 1990; Rogie 1989; Topouzis 1988).

A contrastive idiom of African acoustic guitar music finds expression in the music of Malian guitarists Ali Farka Toure and Boubacar Traoré, plus guitarists from the western Sudan region of Mali, Guinea, and Senegambia. The style of some of these musicians resembles that of American blues guitarists like John Lee Hooker; and Toure, for one, has acknowledged this influence (Richardson 1990:39).

On the album *Ali Farka Toure* (Toure 1987), Toure sings both original and traditional songs, in several regional languages (Malinke, Bambara, Songhai, Fula), to the accompaniment of a steel-strung acoustic guitar, calabash, and bongos. The guitar part in the song "Timbarma" (A1) features hammer-on trills, ornamental slides, and melodic runs on an anhemitonic pentatonic scale. These traits may recall the blues, but probably relate more closely to musical styles performed on the internal-spike lutes that may accompany the same repertory in the region. Traoré's style combines the musical idiom of Khassonke, his native region, with traits drawn from the blues and European folk song (Duran 1990).

The acoustic guitar finds other notable usage in western Sudan, where it entered several modern *jaliya*-type ensembles, either replacing the *kora* and *ngoni*- or *xalam*-type internal-spike lute, or, as in recordings issued in the 1980s by Amy Koita (1986), Tata Bambo Kouyate (1989), and others, playing side by side with the traditional stringed instruments. The guitar also finds at least occasional usage in village contexts. Pascal Diatta, a guitarist of the Casamance region of southern Senegal, performs the guitar at traditional events, like weddings and circumcisions (Anderson 1989:33).

Despite the diversity in the guitar's use, and its prominence as a pop music instrument, it remains limited in its distribution in Africa, because it is essentially an expensive import, beyond the purchasing power of most people (Eyre 1988:80). Even strings for guitars are often hard to find and buy. Professional musicians in Africa must sometimes rent their guitars, which may be in poor condition; to buy a satisfactory instrument, they often depend on finding work abroad. As musical centers outside Africa have become major centers for African guitarists, and for the recording and dissemination of African guitar music, this situation may have important repercussions for the future development of African styles of playing (Stewart 1989a).

In some regions in Africa, the guitar still has little use. As a performative and compositional instrument, it is a predominantly urban phenomenon (Kubik 1964:42). In parts of Ghana, "the guitar has practically replaced the indigenous stringed instruments" (Kinney 1970:14). In southern Ghana, it has replaced the *seperewa* 'harp-lute'; and at funerals and other traditional occasions, rural guitarists perform traditional idioms on it (Kwabena Nketia, personal communication, 1990). In rural northern Ghana, however, the indigenous *kologo* 'internal-spike lute' is far more common than the guitar.

In rural regions, even where the guitar does not enjoy local use, people know it as a cultural model almost exclusively through performances by groups touring from cities, plus through radio, cassette, and (less frequently) television, video, and cinema; and some local individual often plays it. In Madagascar, the *kabosy*, derived from West Asian pear-shaped lutes, and diffused along Islamic trade routes, commonly takes on the formal appearance of a miniature acoustic guitar. In towns in Cameroon, and undoubtedly elsewhere in Africa, children build nonfunctional copies of electric guitars and use them as "air guitars," playing imaginary roles as stars (Alec Leonhardt, personal communication, 1990).

By the 1990s, the guitar in Africa was thus a critical element in diverse musical styles, particularly popular ones, which dominate contemporary urban music, and are increasingly familiar in the countryside.

REFERENCES

Advertisement for the Bank of West Africa. 1966. *Drum* (Ghana edition), February.

Aingo, George Williams. n.d. *Na Mapa Nu Kyew.* Hayes, Middlesex: Zonophone EZ9, B. 78-rpm disk.

Alájá-Browne, Afọlábí. 1985. "Jùjú Music: A Study of Its Social History and Style." Ph.D. dissertation, University of Pittsburgh.

Alberts, Arthur. 1950. "Descriptive Notes." In *Tribal, Folk, and Cafe Music of West Africa,* 16–19. New York: Field Recordings.

American Music Conference. 1987. "Music USA 87." Chicago.

Anderson, Ian. 1989. "A Guitar Man." *Folk Roots* 70:28-33.

Anderson, Robert. 1980. "Egypt: Ancient Music." *The New Grove Dictionary of Music and Musicians,* ed. Stanley Sadie. London: Macmillan.

"Augustus Williams." 1932. *The Gold Coast Spectator,* 13 February, 207.

Bebey, Francis. 1966. *Pièces pour guitare seule.* Paris: OCORA. LP disk.

———. 1978. *Francis Bebey: ballades africaines: guitare.* Paris: Ozileka 3306. LP disk.

Bowdich, Thomas. 1819 [1966]. *Mission from Cape Coast Castle to Ashantee,* 3rd ed., ed. W. E. F. Ward. London: Frank Cass.

Catalogue of Zonophone West African Records by Native Artists. 1929. Hayes, Middlesex: British Zonophone Company.

Collins, E. John. 1977. "Post-War Popular Band Music in West Africa." *African Arts* 10(3):53–60.

———. 1985. *Musicmakers of West Africa.* Washington: Three Continents.

———. 1986. *E. T. Mensah, King of Highlife.* London: Off the Record Press.

———. 1987. "Jazz Feedback to Africa." *American Music* 5(2):176–193.

———. 1989. "The early history of West African Highlife Music." *Popular Music* 8:221– 230.

Coplan, David. 1978. "Go to my Town, Cape Coast! The Social History of Ghanaian Highlife." In *Eight Urban Musical Cultures,* ed. Bruno Nettl, 96–114. Urbana: University of Illinois Press.

———. 1981. "Popular Music." In *The Cambridge Encyclopedia of Africa,* ed. Roland Oliver and Michael Crowder. Cambridge: Cambridge University Press.

———. 1985. *In Township Tonight! South Africa's Black City Music and Theatre.* London: Longman.

Cover illustration. 1984. *West Africa,* 17 December.

Danner, Peter. 1986. "Guitar." *The New Grove Dictionary of Music and Musicians,* ed. Stanley Sadie. London: Macmillan.

Danso, Robert O. 1932. "Mistakes in Practical Music." *The Gold Coast Spectator,* 9 April, 432.

Darkwa, Asante. 1974. "The New Musical Traditions in Ghana." Ph.D. dissertation, Wesleyan University.

Duncan, Amy. 1989. "Ambassadors of Afropop." *World Monitor*, October, 74–77.

Duran, Lucy. 1990. Liner notes to *Boubacar Traoré: Mariama*. London: Stern's Africa 1032. LP disk.

During, Ola. 1988. "The Palm Wine Music Man." *West Africa*, 11 April: 670.

Evans, Tom, and Mary Anne Evans. 1977. *Guitars: From the Renaissance to Rock*. New York: Facts on File.

Ewens, Graeme. 1986. *Luambo Franco and Thirty Years of O. K. Jazz*. London: Off the Record Press.

Eyre, Banning. 1988. "Soukous, Chimurenga, Mbaqanga, and More: New Sounds from Africa." *Guitar Player* 22(10):80–88.

Fleming, Shirley. 1966. "The Guitar on the Go." *Hi-Fidelity*, July: 40–45.

Fosu-Mensah, Kwabena. 1990. *Koo Nimo: Osabarima*. Liner notes. Adasa Records, ADR 102.

Franco (Luambo Makiadi). 1987. *Franco et le T.P.O.K. Jazz: originalité—The original 1956 recordings of O.K. Jazz*. London: RetroAfric 2. LP disk.

Gladwell, Malcolm. 1986. "Fact, Fancy, and the Mystique of Africa." *Insight* (*The Washington Times*), 26 May: 8–11.

Goodwin, Andrew, and Joe Gore. 1990. "World Beat and the Cultural Imperialism Debate." *Socialist Review* 90(3):63–80.

Graham, Ronnie. 1988. *The Da Capo Guide to Contemporary African Music*. New York: Da Capo.

Grunfeld, Frederic. 1974. *The Art and Times of the Guitar: An Illustrated History*. New York: Da Capo.

"Guitar Boy" (cartoon). 1967. *Drum* (Ghana edition), August.

Hommage au Grand Kalle. 1984. African LP 360 142.

Hooker, Naomi. 1970. "Popular musicians in Freetown." *African Urban Notes* 5(4):11–18.

Hornbostel Erich Moritz von, and Curt Sachs. 1961. "Classification of Musical Instruments," trans. Anthony Baines and Klaus P. Wachsmann. *Galpin Society Journal* 14(March):3–29.

Jones, A. M. 1959. *Studies in African Music*. London: Oxford University Press, 1959.

Kaiser, Henry. 1984a. "King Sunny Ade: Nigeria's Jùjú Superstar." *Guitar Player* 18(2):32–42.

———. 1984b. "Demola Adepoju." *Guitar Player* 18(2):35–36.

Kallaway, Peter, and Patrick Pearson. 1986. *Johannesburg: Images and Continuities*. Braamfontein: Ravan Press.

Kauffman, Robert. 1972. "Shona Urban Music and the Problem of Acculturation." *IFMC Yearbook* 4:47–56.

———. 1979–1980. "Tradition and Innovation in the Urban Music of Zimbabwe." *African Urban Studies* 6:41–48.

Kavyu, Paul. 1978. "The Development of Guitar Music in Kenya." *Jazzforschung* 10:111–119.

Kinney, Esi Sylvia. 1970. "Urban West African Music and Dance." *African Urban Notes* 5(4):3–10.

Kirby, Percival. 1965. *The Musical Instruments of the Native Races of South Africa*, 2nd ed. Johannesburg: Witwatersrand University Press.

Koita, Amy. 1986. *Amy Koita*. Paris: Espérance ESP 7517. LP disk.

Kouyate, Tata Bambo. 1989. *Tata Bambo Kouyate*. London: Globestyle ORB 042. LP disk.

Kubik, Gerhard. 1964. "Harp Music of the Azande and Related Peoples in the Central African Republic." *African Music* 3(3):37–76.

———. 1965. "Neue Musikformen in Schwarzafrika." *Afrika Heute* 4:1–15.

———. 1976. "Daniel Kachamba's Solo Guitar Music." *Jazzforschung* 8:159–195.

———. 1981. "Popular Music in East Africa since 1945." *Popular Music* 1:83–104.

Low, John. 1982a. "A History of Kenyan Guitar Music: 1945–1980." *African Music* 6(2):17–36.

———. 1982b. *Shaba Diary: A Trip to Rediscover the 'Katanga' Guitar Styles and Songs of the 1950's and '60's*. Vienna: Fohrenau. Acta Ethnologica et Linguistica, 54.

Malamusi, Moya Aliya. 1984. "The Zambian Popular Music Scene." *Jazzforschung* 16:189–195.

Mandelson, Ben. 1985. "African Guitar Styles." In *Talking Book*, vol. 2, *An Introduction to Africa*, ed. Phoebe Beedell et al. (Bristol: WOMAD Foundation).

Manuel, Peter. 1988. *Popular Musics of the Non-Western World*. New York: Oxford University Press.

Marcuse, Sibyl. 1975. *Musical Instruments: A Comprehensive Dictionary*. New York: Norton.

McKinnon, James W., and Robert Anderson. 1984. "Lute, 2: Ancient Lutes." *The New Grove Dictionary of Musical Instruments*, ed. Stanley Sadie (London: Macmillan), 2:551–553.

Menu, Kwesi. n.d. *Agyanka odede*. Hayes, Middlesex: His Master's Voice JZ 5002. 78-rpm disk.

Merriam, Alan P. 1967. "Music." *Africa Report* 12(1):4.

"Mwenda Jean Bosco's Comeback." 1982. *African Music* 6(2):132–134.

Nico, Docteur (Nicolas Kasanda Wa Mikalayi). 1985a. *Merveilles du Passé: Éternel Docteur Nico, 1963–65: Orchestra African Fiesta*. Paris: African 360152. LP disk.

———. 1985b. *Merveilles du Passé: Éternel Docteur Nico, 1967: Orchestra African Fiesta*. Paris: African 360159. LP disk.

Nketia, J. H. Kwabena. 1974. *The Music of Africa*. New York: Norton.

Oliver, Paul. 1984. *Songsters and Saints*. Cambridge: Cambridge University Press.

Omibiyi, M. A. 1981. "Popular Music in Nigeria." *Jazzforschung* 13:151–168.

Richardson, Derk. 1990. "African Voices." *Acoustic Guitar* 1(2):38–41.

Roberts, J. S. 1968. "Popular Music in Kenya." *African Music* 4(2):53–55.

———. 1975. "Africa: the Guitar's Role." *Guitar Player* 9:22-23.

Rogie, Sooliman E. 1986. *The 60s' Sounds of S. E. Rogie,* vol. 1. Berkeley, California: Rogiphone R2. LP disk.

———. 1989. *The Palm Wine Sounds of S. E. Rogie: The King of Palm Wine Guitar Music.* Workers Playtime PLAYLP9. LP disk.

———. 1979. "Francis Bebey: African Third Stream," *Village Voice,* 19 Feb.

Rycroft, David. 1961. "The Guitar Improvisations of Mwenda Jean Bosco." *African Music* 2(4):81–98.

———. 1962. "The Guitar Improvisations of Mwenda Jean Bosco (Part II)." *African Music* 3(1):86–102.

———. 1977. "Evidence of Stylistic Continuity in Zulu 'Town' Music." In *Essays for a Humanist,* 216–260. New York: Town House Press.

Sam. n.d. *Ampa Afful.* His Master's Voice JZ 97. 78-rpm disk.

Sekyi, Kobina. 1918. "The Anglo-Fanti, Part I: Boyhood Festivals." *West Africa,* 6 July: 378.

Stapleton, Chris, and Chris May. 1990. *African Rock: The Pop Music of a Continent.* New York: Dutton.

Stewart, Gary. 1989a. "The Session Men." *The Beat* 8(6):28–29.

———. 1989b. "Soukous, Birth of the Beat." *The Beat* 8(6):18–21.

Topouzis, Daphne. 1988. "The Kings of Jùjú and Palm Wine Guitar." *Africa Report,* November-December:67–69.

Toure, Ali Farka. 1987. *Ali Farka Toure.* Mango MLPS 9826. LP disk.

Tracey, Hugh. 1948. "Recording Journey from the Union into the Rhodesias." *African Music Society Newsletter* 1(1):9–12.

———. 1950a. "Pini ochama." In *Sound of Africa,* B7. Roodeport, Transvaal: International Library of African Music, AMA TR-168. LP disk.

———. 1950b. "Recording Tour 1949." *African Music Society Newsletter* 1(3):33–37.

———. 1953a. "The Osborn Awards: The Best African Musicians of the Year." *African Music Society Newsletter* 1(6):65–67.

———. 1953b. *The Guitars of Africa.* London LB-829. Music of Africa, 5. LP disk.

———. 1957a. "Antoinette MuKolwezi." In *Sound of Africa,* B6. Roodeport, Transvaal: International Library of African Music, AMA TR-25. LP disk.

———. 1957b. "Iuwale-o-iuwale." In *Sound of Africa,* A3. Roodeport, Transvaal: International Library of African Music, AMA TR-19). LP disk.

———. 1973. *The Sound of Africa* Series. Catalogue. Roodepoort, Transvaal: International Library of African Music.

Turnbull, Harvey. 1984. "Guitar: Origins." In *The New Grove Dictionary of Musical Instruments,* ed. Stanley Sadie, 2:87–90. London: Macmillan.

Tyler, James. 1980. *The Early Guitar.* London: Oxford University Press.

Villault, Nicolas Le Sieur. 1669 [1670]. *Relation of the Coasts of Africk Called Guinee.* London: John Starkey.

Waterman, Christopher. 1986. "Jùjú: The Historical Development, Socioeconomic Organization, and Communicative Functions of a West African Popular Music." Ph.D. dissertation, University of Illinois, Urbana.

———. 1990. *Jùjú: A Social History and Ethnography of an African Popular Music.* Chicago: University of Chicago Press.

Waterman, Richard. 1950. "Laboratory Notes." In *Tribal, Folk, and Cafe Music of West Africa,* ed. Arthur Alberts, 5–11. New York: Field Recordings.

Kru Mariners and Migrants of the West African Coast
Cynthia Schmidt

Historical Background
Music of the Kru
Late Twentieth-Century Transitions

In the early twentieth century, the intermingling of cultures in African coastal towns and industrial centers led to the development of new musical genres. This process was most striking along the western seaboard, where the protagonists were mariners and migrant laborers.

At the forefront of these peoples was an ethnic group of workers, the Kru, originally from Liberia. Traditionally mobile and seagoing, the Kru have for several centuries traveled around the coast of Africa, and even to the Caribbean and England. They have spent much of their lives working away from home, often relocating permanently to ports, where they have interacted with people of other nations, regions, and ethnicities.

The Kru influenced many of the cultures they contacted. Scholars have credited Kru mariners as the disseminators of an important idiom of pidgin English (Tonkin 1971; Dalby 1970), but in contemporary musical expression their influence is more sweeping. Throughout West Africa, they diffused guitar-playing traditions, particularly in palm wine guitar style (Collins 1985, 1989).

Excepting random mentions of creative achievements and scanty information in scattered sources, the role of the Kru as composers and musicians has been inadequately described. This essay shows that they composed music and introduced instrumental styles that contributed to the emergence of popular music consciousness and repertory in the west and central African coastal region from the 1920s to the 1950s.

Music produced by members of an emergent African working class, and the cultural processes that surround migration, have been a focus of attention of several excellent studies (Coplan 1985; Erlmann 1991). The most effective mechanism of African cultural dynamics has been interethnic cultural contact through the migration of laborers (Erlmann 1991). An increase in the number of musicians, with other demographic, social, economic, and political factors of migration, precipitated important musical changes.

This essay draws on the notion of *musical confluence*, suggested by Barbara Hampton (1980) as a useful concept in studying the Kru experience. Various authors have pointed out the inadequacies of a more widely used term, *syncretism* (Collins and Richards 1982:37). Musical confluence refers to the merging of different streams of music, in which old and new elements combine to articulate an interethnic experience.

HISTORICAL BACKGROUND

Nearly every account of West African history since 1820 mentions the Kru; they were the African mariners most widely employed on land and sea in the nineteenth and twentieth centuries. Vessels engaged in legitimate trade on the Windward Coast sporadically hired Kru from the end of the 1600s, and hiring became regular during the 1780s. Kru involvement in European maritime activities was probably motivated by economics. Uneven economic development along the coast encouraged the migration of Kru labor. As a Kru seaman stated, "When times get hard, we travel."

Since Krumen had a long tradition of this type of work and were considered most adept, shipping companies preferred them. They were praised as "born sailors," as "industrious" and "robust" people, commanding special skills (such as swimming and language abilities), and having a reputation for "dependability" (Brooks 1972:3). Consequently, those attached to European traders enjoyed considerable personal freedom.

Some of the Kru were boiler cleaners, woodcutters, and stokers for wood-burning steamers. Some worked as deckhands on merchant and military ships plying the coast. Some were stewards, some loaded palm oil, and some relayed messages for the African Telegraph Company. Some moved between dock labor and stevedoring. The stevedores traveled down the coast, loading and unloading at various ports of call. American, German, and British shipping lines, knowing the advantages of working continuously with the same men, employed "shore headmen" and "ship headmen," who selected and controlled their gangs. Embarking at Freetown or Monrovia, they traveled down the coast to Douala or Congo-Matadi and back. Occasionally the headmen took on separate gangs at each port. The trips lasted a month or six weeks, or even longer. Between trips, the stevedores worked intermittently or "rested," finding time for leisure and music. Some stayed away from home for months or years, returning when they had gained property or money for their families.

Written nineteenth-century references and oral reports from older seamen tell how the work was "relieved by song." These men speak of "heavy-lift songs." When they did a difficult job, they sang "*Tobogee-o, Nyanwule* 'We will do this thing, Nyanwule [the name of a strong man]'." (As Ol' Man Thompson told me in 1987, Tobogee also referred to the older traditional war dances of the Kru.) The headman led the chorus:

> It is their custom to sing; and, as the music goes on, they seem to become invigorated, applying their strength cheerfully, and with limbs as unwearied as their voices. One of the number leads in recitative, and the whole company responds in chorus. The subject of the song is a recital of the exploits of the men, their employments, their intended movements, of the news of the coast and the character of their employers. (Bridge 1853:16–17)

An "Old Coaster" advocated being informed by their communications: "By singing extemporaneous songs, when at work, they communicate intelligence of any transaction on board, which is echoed from the nearest ship to the next, so that hardly a circumstance regarding trade, or any other matter, can transpire, but all become acquainted with it" (Smith 1851:105).

The mariners were given nicknames—such as "Shilling," "Bottle of Beer," "Flying Jib"—to which they answered through life. Their heroic deeds were sung and recited to crowds at parties in Kru country (Brooks 1972:28). Scholars have studied the contribution of the Kru to the spread of Kru pidgin English in West Africa in the

The Kru homeland is the southeastern Atlantic coastal area of Liberia.

late 1800s (Brooks 1970; Davis 1976; Tonkin 1971). The Kru were early known as interpreters, or talk men—sometimes called proper talk men by traders—and thus they became the chief agents for disseminating pidgin English along the West Coast and Indian assistants to the British for expediting commerce (Brooks 1972:19).

The Kru in Liberia

The Kru homeland is the southeastern Atlantic coastal area of Liberia. The Kru came from disparate communities there—small, dispersed settlements, often hostile to each other—whose autonomy may have prevented individuals from recognizing the common elements of the life they shared. These complexities are important because the Kru expounded varied attachments and localisms when working down the coast.

In the 1800s, there was some ambiguity in the term *Kru*. Mariners called Krumen (or Kroomen) and Kruboys (or Krooboys) represented different peoples of eastern Liberia—Kru, Grebo, later the Sabo and Gola—and of Ivory Coast. Wherever their homes, these men found security in identifying with other Liberians and feeling that they belonged to a wider community (Martin 1982:2). They were predominantly Liberian speakers of Kru or Krao, a language Joseph Greenberg tentatively classified as belonging to the Kwa group, though later linguists classified it as a separate branch within the Niger-Congo family.

Kru mariners were first recruited from five towns: Settra Kru, Nana Kru, Little Kru, Krobah, and King William's Town. Other types of migrant workers, however, seem to have come from other areas, such as Grand Cess and Sasstown. An individual's strongest affiliations were with the members of his or her *dako,* a communal unit, with a territorial and social identity and a specific dialect. The bulk of the Kru who manned ships sailing from Monrovia were from the Jloh and Gbeta *dako.* Certain *dako* came to be associated with particular Kru settlements in the diaspora. People originating from the five towns were associated with Freetown, and later with London and Liverpool; the Grand Cess people went to Accra and Lagos.

By 1900, nearly every town on the Liberian coast had sent laborers aboard ships. New Kru expatriate communities began to dot the coast, contributing to the expansion of the Kru-coast concept noted by historians: "The system of labor migration was patterned, continuous, integrated with life at home, and considered an important part of a mature man's development and the community's life" (Martin 1982:2). Kru who had never worked on ships were called bushboys, for the Kru believed that growing up required travel down the coast (Martin 1982:2).

The Kru have long lived in established communities in Monrovia, where they are one of the largest ethnic groups. Reports in 1879 described Monrovia as being made up of two sections, one being Krutown (at the northern base of the lagoon), which by 1900 had a population of about one thousand, with most of the men working on coastal ships (Büttikofer 1890). In 1945, for the building of a new port, the evacuation of Krutown led to a division of Monrovia along class lines. From the

1930s to the 1950s, Kru dock workers and stevedores were the largest locally concentrated work force in Monrovia (Fraenkel 1964:40). Most lived in newer Kru communities, formed on Bushrod Island, near the port; the largest are New Krutown, Claratown, and Westpoint. This series of communities and neighborhoods, isolated from some of the residential areas and from Monrovia's social and economic center of activities, remain ethnically the most homogeneous areas, excepting Bassa and Grebo seamen. The Kru population there increased during the 1950s, when immigrants from Freetown, Accra, and other West African ports arrived in Monrovia (Fraenkel 1964:74).

In 1959, the Kru governor in Monrovia organized a demonstration of Kru loyalty to President Tubman. In it, Kru representatives from settlements abroad—Ghana, Nigeria, Freetown—participated. The songs of solidarity sung during this celebration are still performed in Kru communities of Lagos and Freetown. Participation in the common occupation was the basis of strength of Kru urban organization. Since there was traditionally no mechanism for cooperation between the *dako,* the degree of implied ethnic solidarity was unusual (Fraenkel 1964:83).

The Kru in Freetown

The third-largest natural harbor in the world, Freetown was the first major objective of Kru traffic in the late 1700s. The first Kru laborers who traveled abroad reportedly arrived in Sierra Leone in 1793 as crewmen on British naval and trading vessels. They were attracted by the Sierra Leone Company, which, to reestablish the colony, had instituted standard wages for African laborers—an unprecedented practice for this part of West Africa. By 1800, the colony was employing fifty Krumen, and in the early 1800s the number increased. Recorded estimates of the number of Kru living in Freetown between 1800 and 1850 vary widely, and an estimated five hundred were living there in 1819 (Fyfe 1962:45).

In the following years, the number of Kru migrating to Sierra Leone, attracted by greater possibilities of employment aboard merchant vessels, continued to grow. By the 1850s, Freetown had the largest Krutown, exceeding that of Monrovia (Schuler 1986:185). Colonial authorities encouraged them to settle in Freetown, and in 1816 a special enactment allocated a section of Freetown as a Kru reservation. Kroo Town, overlooking the harbor and Kroo Bay, was the land set aside for exclusive use by the Kru for Kru migrant labor, the only separate neighborhood for a single ethnic group in Freetown. In the 1830s, five streets were cut through with names based on the Kru origins—Settra Kroo, Little Kroo, Nana Kroo, King Williams, and Grand Cess. The Kru migrants cohabited with liberated African and indigenous women until 1880, when Kru women began to settle in the area (Banton 1957).

Thomas Ludlam, governor of the colony for fourteen years (1797–1811), remarked on Kru adaptability to various tasks. Their chief diversion, he said, was dancing. Though he added few details on Kru dance and music, he mentioned shipboard dancing and a boat dance on an American man-of-war. He also noted how the Kru hoarded their earnings to invest in European goods to carry home: pursuing the "white man's fashion," they expected to take home clothes, hats, and other articles of the best attire, which, while they paraded through the streets at the end of their trip, they wore as symbols of their new life-style (Ludlam 1812:87).

The Kru constituted a single, oftentimes special, population; in some centers of the diaspora, local Africans preferred not to have contact with them. Their culturally distinctive unity—evident away from home, but not necessarily at home—resulted from intensified social interactions among them, and from competitive economic interaction with Africans of other ethnic origins who, like them, were seeking economic or political advantage in port city society (McEvoy 1977:68).

"down the coast"   The area south and east of Liberia, including Fernando Po and other West African countries

tuku   Single-headed, wooden goblet drum that accompanied music of the Kru living in Liberia

During the Great War (1914–1918), increased shipping and port activity offered more work for the laborers, whom it attracted in droves. Freetown became a port of assembly for merchant ships awaiting convoy. Because of Britain's special historic relationship with Sierra Leone, Freetown became the British base for Elder Dempster's line, and the Kru population increased from about 1,200 in 1891 to 4,744 in 1921 (Banton 1957:225).

The Freetown Kru community, as in other West African ports, divided into small groups with decentralized authority. The Freetown Kru remained isolated from the rest of the population—and were Christians, rather than Muslims. Cultural institutions that kept their vitality abroad were voluntary associations. While in Monrovia and Lagos these were primarily women's associations, which functioned as mutual aid groups; in Freetown, the Kru also organized "friendly societies," which were not gender specific. In the 1950s, forty-seven of these societies were registered, three of them Seamen's Clubs, modeled on officers' organizations on ships where the Kru worked (Banton 1957). Since the men were away from home for long periods, the women's societies were especially powerful. They pooled their resources to provide for their members' wakes and burials. They served both a cultural and an economic function, providing some basis for economic stability.

The Kru "down the coast"

By the 1830s, Kru migration had extended "down the coast" to cocoa plantations in "Nanny Po" (Fernando Po, formerly occupied by the Spanish); by 1848, some Kru were working as far south as Calabar, Nigeria. As their reputation grew, demands for their labor increased. In Lagos, both Nigerians and Europeans hired them. The bulk of their labor, concentrated in the Lagos and Oil rivers up to the time of the Great War, gradually shifted up the coast to Ghana, where they found employment in goldmines (Martin 1982:3). Later they worked in Accra, Sekondi, and Kumasi. They also worked in the Congo, present-day Angola, Namibia, and South Africa. They emigrated as migrant laborers to the Guianas, Jamaica, Trinidad, and Martinique (Schuler 1986:156). Some assisted in building the Suez and Panama canals. Many who in 1914 went to Liverpool, primarily from Freetown, never returned to live in Africa.

Most Kru remained versatile, working in many different jobs. The men always stressed that their work down the coast was temporary, even when they began to stay abroad for long periods of time. Englishmen frequently labeled Kru the Irishmen or Scotsmen of West Africa, because they sought their fortunes away from home. Though down the coast they took on a proletarian status, readily selling their labor, they worked to improve their lives back home.

Between 1900 and 1920, new types of work and patterns of living developed among the downcoast Kru. Both men and women traveled to Nigeria, and their links with the Nigerian communities increased, though they did not intend to take up permanent residence (Martin 1982:8). As they had done in Takoradi and Abidjan, they helped construct the port of Lagos and the railroad running north from Lagos.

The largest permanent downcoast Kru community emerged on Lagos Island behind Tinubu Square, where a majority of Krumen had gone since the 1870s (Martin 1982:9). By 1897, the acting governor estimated the "floating" Kru population to be 1,200, a number that by 1911 had more than doubled, surpassing the Kru population in Freetown. The census of 1921 shows that there were 13,000 Liberians in Ghana—most of them no doubt Kru, while in southern Nigeria 2,635 Liberians were counted.

MUSIC OF THE KRU

Kru music from the homeland in eastern Liberia is predominantly vocal music, accompanied by a single-headed, wooden goblet drum (*tuku*) and other percussive instruments. Aside from warrior songs, the oldest genre of Kru music is that sung by women's associations for wakes, funerals, and social gatherings (figure 1). These songs, called *si-o-lele,* are sung in a chorus-refrain style, with the chorus beginning with the nonlexical syllables that comprise the title. The export and exchange of these songs spread the repertory to Ghana and Sierra Leone. Two of them, recorded with contemporary orchestration in Freetown, have achieved wide popularity (Ajua and Victoria Dollah, personal communication, 1990).

The acquisition of new instruments

During their travels, the Kru acquired wealth and new ideas from other parts of Africa and the West. Among the new products from Europe on the African market were musical instruments. Consequently, the number of musicians increased rapidly, and these musicians began to link innovative musical developments with the introduction of novel instruments (Alájá-Browne 1989:234).

Of particular fascination to the Kru was the acoustic guitar. According to older seamen interviewed in the 1980s, guitars were sometimes available in shops in Ghana or Nigeria in the 1920s. The mandolin, also a popular instrument, could be purchased in Europe or places like Fernando Po. Stringed instruments were not unfamiliar to Kru musicians, who, back in their homeland, had played a plucked lute, a calabash with a carved stick for a neck, fastened with rattan and supporting five or six

FIGURE 1   A Kru women's group performs a *si-o-lele* song.

Kru musicians' trademark was a two-finger style of picking, in which all right-hand passages were played with the right thumb and index finger.

strings (personal communication, Jacob Musa, 1989). Accordions, banjos, concertinas, harmonicas, and tambourines were among the instruments available for those who could afford them.

The Kru along the coast in Liberia played a cane flute. Down the coast in urban areas, pennywhistles (and later, European flutes and piccolos) were among the instruments on which the Kru excelled. A famous pair, Sunday Davis and Friday Peters, developed a virtuosic style of flute playing that boosted Kru musicians' popularity and marketability in Nigeria.

In the late 1930s, brass bands became popular on the Kru Coast in Liberia. Though Grebo seamen were probably the first to bring them from Ghana, the Kru also participated for a while. Sibo, a man from Grand Kru County who had learned to play instruments in Ghana, established a band of brass instruments (*ba*), including trumpet, trombone, bass, sousaphone, and bass drum (personal communication Ol' Man Thompson, 1988, Monrovia). The bands played both European and African tunes, and for many years provided the music in Liberia for dances such as quadrilles, in which large numbers of people participated. To the accompaniment of palm wine guitar music or other Western instruments, one of the dancers called the figures, which the couples executed.

Palm wine guitar styles

Kru sailors had a reputation for being among the most innovative of African musicians. This reputation was partly based on their life-style, for leisure time in the ports gave them opportunities to relax, relate anecdotes of travel, and exchange musical ideas. But it was also based on their facility in playing palm wine guitar music, a style they introduced in ports from Freetown to Fernando Po.

According to Sylvester Thomas, a well-known musician in Monrovia, the sound of a ship's horn would bring local musicians down to the harbor to meet the seamen, hoping to find musicians on board. Thomas explained (personal communication, 1988):

When the ship came in, they always brought something new. We went aboard the ship carrying drinks and tobacco, and as we spoke and drank, we played music. Sometimes we sat under a large palmtree where we'd always meet. I watched their fingers [on the guitar], and that's where I got the training. For any unusual situation in town, we made lyrics to fit. Eventually there was a kind of social demand, particularly among the young people.

Palm wine guitar music swept the West African coast, and its popularity reached as far east as Zaïre. In the ports, a guitarist would join with local percussionists, who would tap out the rhythms on a bottle or kerosene can (*chegbe*), mesmerizing the audiences who gathered to dance and drink the local toddy.

Kru musicians' trademark was a two-finger style of picking, in which all right-hand passages were played with the right thumb and index finger. As seagoers, the Kru helped spread this style, which proliferated from the 1930s to the 1950s. Rather than imitating Western manners of playing, palm wine guitar musicians invented and developed a style of playing based on complex African patterns.

In Nigeria, the style based on the two-finger technique was called Krusbass (Alájá-Browne 1985:17). Kru gathered every weekend for merrymaking in the Elegbata (Olowogbowo) area of Lagos, where many resided (Alájá-Browne 1985:24). This style influenced early *jùjú* artists in Lagos, such as Tunde King, who also employed a Kru phrase to signal the end of his performances (Waterman 1990:72).

During the 1930s in Monrovia, from the name of a guitar-rhythm pattern in the song "*Dagomba Waye Tangebu* 'Dagomba [a ship] wired Tangebu [a seaman]'," Kru guitarists were called *dagomba* boys (Boy Davis, personal communication, 1990). Palm wine music in Monrovia was also called sea breeze music; it was played with a guitar and a bottle or a bamboo slit-drum (*kono*) (personal communication, Sylvester Thomas, 1988, Monrovia). A later variant of this style, developed by the descendants of African-American settlers, emphasized the strumming more than the picking.

Early highlife music in Ghana was rooted in palm wine guitar style. The Kru or Liberian style that most influenced early highlife in Ghana was also called *dagomba* style. However, *dagomba* was but one of three acoustic guitar styles that became popular in Ghana; the other two were "mainline" and "fireman" styles (Collins 1985:110). As early as 1928, Kwame Asare, a Ghanaian, recorded guitar music of this milieu. In the mid-1990s, Koo Nimo, a renowned Ghanaian guitarist, internationally performs palm wine guitar music and other styles. In the hinterlands of Ghana, where the *seperewa* (a harp-lute with six to twelve strings) is traditionally played, acoustic guitar continues to be a vital tradition in palm wine bars, perhaps because *seperewa* players have an affinity for interlocking African patterns, and for playing on unamplified stringed instruments.

In Sierra Leone, a popular meeting place during the 1930s and 1940s in Freetown was the club Prapade; located at Adelaide Street Junction, it drew a wide audience for palm wine guitar music. The Kru met there to play music with fellow seamen, most often with Krio musicians, who, despite antagonistic social relations based on Freetown class structure, enjoyed performing the same types of urban music. Kru guitarists of that era included Taiwo Toby, Ekun Daio, Anthony Forde—and Chris Walker, who wrote one of Freetown's favorite songs, "*Well, na de now* 'Well, the time has come'."

Another variant of palm wine guitar style was *maringa,* played by the Krios of Freetown. It made more use of strumming, and incorporated West Indian rhythms, predominantly a calypso beat, brought to the region by the West Indian Frontier Force, which in the mid-1800s came to stay in Freetown. *Maringa* was popularized by Ebenezer Calendar, a celebrity with his own program on radio (Bender 1991). In the mid-1990s, to audiences in London, S. E. Rogie, another accomplished guitarist from Freetown, regularly plays elegant and simple palm wine guitar songs from the 1940s and 1950s, such as "My Lovely Elizabeth."

Styles of guitar playing developed their distinctiveness in various parts of West Africa, depending on different musical influences. Superficial resemblances to West African music employing two-finger techniques could also be heard in Congo and Zaïre, where Zaïrian guitarist Wendo stated that sailors introduced the style in Matadi in the 1930s (Gerhard Kubik, personal communication).

Two-finger picking

The Kru adapted two-finger styles of picking to traditional melodies and patterns in complex and sophisticated ways. While repeating rhythms and varying them slightly,

A form of music that rivaled local musics in Freetown and Lagos was Liberian highlife.

the guitarist picked the strings with the thumb and index finger. Often a second guitar played the melodic phrases with an ostinatolike pattern continuing throughout. The style was strongly rhythmic, with interest added through cross-rhythms.

Figure 2 shows a typical Kru guitar song in *dagomba* style. Its text refers to Havana, Cuba, an active city at the time, particularly known to Kru musicians of the 1940s and 1950s, who were attracted to Latin rhythms and dances. It alludes to the reputed excesses of life in Havana—a life whose overindulgences can kill. A popular song, it was known from Freetown to Port Harcourt, Nigeria. It was sung in a form of pidgin English spoken in Nigeria similar to Sierra Leonean Krio. According to Packard Okie, who recorded this song in 1947 in Liberia, the guitarist and singer Mr. Freeman, as a ship's mechanic had learned it from a Kru seaman (personal communication, 1994).

The music of this song artfully mixes two basic patterns: L, patterns for solo guitar and instrumental variation between passages, which alternate with R, patterns in which the guitar supports the voice. Cross-rhythms can be heard in the larger four-beat phrase (R_1 or R_2). The second R-pattern seems to answer the first in a responsorial or conversational style. In an excerpt (figure 2), the R_1-pattern has the bass C–G–G–G, answered by the R_2-bass C–D–E–G. The guitar chords move from tonic

FIGURE 2   "*Abana kili mi, dai-o* 'Havana kills me, I die, oh','' a Kru song in *dagomba* style, transcribed by Steve Elster from a recording made in Bromley, Liberia (Okie 1955:B:4).

FIGURE 3 Two-finger picking patterns in "*Abana kili mi, dai-o*": *a,* R$_1$, a guitar rhythmic pattern, supporting the voice; *b,* R$_2$ a variant pattern, answering R$_1$ in responsorial style; *c,* L, a melodic pattern of the solo guitar.

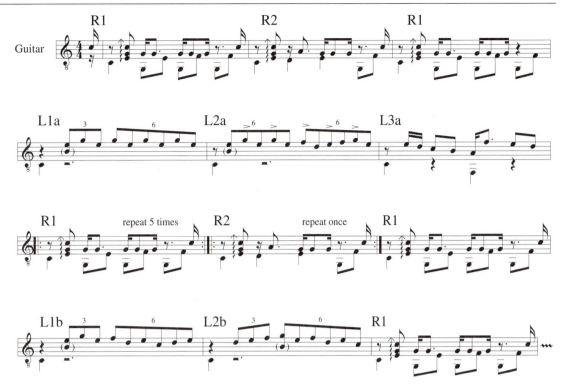

to dominant, shifting between the two repeated rhythmic patterns, and creating a contrast with the solo melodic passages (L$_1$ and L$_2$). A clear rhythmic pattern is presented, then varied, treating the guitar almost as if it were a drum. Each time the lead pattern returns, it receives subtle variation, displaying the artist's skill. The combination and sequence of patterns is variable.

Figure 3 shows the interplay of parts between the thumb and index fingers: the first two excerpts (R$_1$ and R$_2$) are guitar rhythmic patterns, and the third (L$_1$) is the melodic pattern. The transcriber, Steven Elster, an accomplished guitarist, notes that by using just thumb and index fingers, the player creates a close interlock between upper and lower voices, particularly in the dotted figures (R$_1$ and R$_2$), which, to be effective when played in two-finger picking style, require rhythmic precision. An additional feature of this example is an upstrum preceding the down-strum at the beginning of each phrase, adding a unique rhythmic feature that lends to the complexity and subtlety of the style.

Multiethnic mix: the 1940s and 1950s

The maritime industry declined in the early twentieth century, but Kru migrant laborers continued to travel to Sierra Leone, Nigeria, and Ghana, where they intermingled with other Africans, Caribbeans, and African-Americans. From the early 1940s to the late 1950s, multiethnic forms of musical expression emerged in the seaports and urban areas.

A form of music that rivaled local musics in Freetown and Lagos was Liberian highlife. Though guitar based, it employed a new type of orchestration, distinctively involving wind instruments such as pennywhistles and flutes. There was a craze for this type of music, particularly in Nigeria, where Kru musician Sunday Davis (also known as Sunday Harbour Giant) had introduced an improvisatory style of playing a penny whistle. He played a highly embellished melody or virtuosic phrases while interacting musically with other instruments. According to a Lagosian musician, other artists sought him out, wanting to imitate his style; he experimented with musical instruments such as the flute, the mandolin, and the organ (Alájá-Browne 1985:43).

Performing for radio broadcasting and recording became a means of generating income and fame.

Sunday Davis was a Kru seaman who went from Freetown to Lagos and became a truck driver. For nearly two decades, he remained well known in Lagosian musical life. He played with the Jolly Orchestra, comprised of Yoruba, Ashanti, and Kru musicians—such as BlueBlue, Motajo, Abiodun Oke, and Bobodi on guitar; Ambrose Adekoya Campbell on *jùjú* drum; and Sunday Harbour Giant on penny whistle. Their hit "*Àtàrí Àjànàkú*" was based on a Yoruba proverb: *Àtàrí Àjànàkú, kìí serú omodé* 'An elephant's head is not a load for a child'. This song, like others of the Jolly Orchestra, reflected the multiethnicity of performers in a blend of phrases sung in Yoruba, Kru, Pidgin English, and various Ghanaian languages heard along the marina in Lagos (Waterman 1990:49).

Music emphasizing flutes was played and recorded by the Kroo Young Stars Rhythm Group. Since this band consisted of Krio and Kru musicians, its music employed Krio and Kru lyrics. Its performances impacted Freetown and indigenous communities of Sierra Leone. Its rhythms closely resembled calypso rhythms and Cuban *charanga*, with long, flowing, improvisatory lines played on flutes. Its popularity paralleled the period of *tango ya ba Wendo* in Zaïre, when Latin American musical traits were introduced to Zaïre—a period when West African and Zaïrian musicians were intensively sharing ideas (Mukuna 1992:72–84).

The Kroo Young Stars transformed Kru music by adding new orchestration to older Kru songs. They expanded their audience by recording one of the *si-o-lele* songs sung by women's associations in Freetown. Though the song was never a big hit, the Kru appreciated the gesture because it opened up opportunities for Kru women to be recorded, and it introduced the *si-o-lele* repertory to the public. Subsequently, in the late 1950s, Ebenezer Calendar, a Krio musician in Freetown, also recorded a *si-o-lele* song in his trademark *maringa* style on a 78-rpm commercial record.

According to Kru musicians in Freetown and Monrovia, the tune of "*Àtàrí Àjànàkú*" (played by Sunday Davis's band) was based on "*O gio te bo* 'She has come for it again'," an older traditional Kru song, sung by the Freetown Kru. 'O.G.T.B.' as it was called in a version popularized by Kroo Young Stars, was a favorite among the Freetown Kru during the 1920s and 1930s, when it was sung at social gatherings and wakes. The Kru strongly identified with it, and it became a signature tune across West Africa among Kru musicians in various ports, and even in Liverpool. As one Kru guitarist in Liverpool said, "That song was grand. Everybody loved that tune, and a lot of songs came from it—different, different versions of 'O.G.T.B.' It was the main song for the Kru" (personal communication Danny Morris, Liverpool, 1990).

In many popular songs of the late 1940s and 1950s, renditions of "O.G.T.B." could be heard either in the melodic line, or in the improvisations of an accompanying instrument. The harmonic sequence and the interplay of phrases provided a musical formula or a model for many other songs which the Kru recognized as based on "O.G.T.B."

The advent of radio made syncretic adaptation possible on a new level, and regional styles became widely popular. Performing for radio broadcasting and recording became a means of generating income and fame. In the late 1940s, music could be heard on rediffusion boxes in homes in Lagos. According to one musician, the Nigerian Broadcasting Service brought musicians to its studio and paid them two pounds sterling, while paying singers 7 shillings each in 1953, to perform "O.G.T.B." for the music to be played on radio broadcasts.

European record companies sent representatives to scout West Africa for talent. In the early 1950s, British Decca Records of London even had a mobile studio unit in Freetown and other cities to record musicians such as the Kroo Young Stars. They drove this unit into the provinces, where they paid musicians a flat fee for full rights to their songs. The Kroo Young Stars, featuring Kun Peters on flute, recorded "O.G.T.B." on Decca Records in Freetown in 1953. Chris Walker, one of the most accomplished Kru seamen-guitarists, was lead singer and mandolinist for Kroo Young Stars. He had traveled frequently to Nigeria from the 1930s to the 1950s, and was recruited for the United African Company Band, where he learned to read music and play a variety of styles. Later, Ebenezer Calendar gained popularity in playing the guitar-based *maringa* music, with more of a vamping style; he recorded a rendition of "O.G.T.B." sung in Krio and Limba.

About the same time, another version of "O.G.T.B." was recorded in Ghana. It was frequently played at Sugar Baby, a Fanti club. Many Kru, stranded by the decline of the seafaring business, stayed on to live in Ghana.

LATE TWENTIETH-CENTURY TRANSITIONS

After the 1950s, the decline of the maritime industry was devastating to the Kru, and Kru music went into oblivion. With electronic amplification of instruments, the acoustic guitar played a reduced role in commercialized settings. Independence in African countries limited the musical, social, and economic role of Kru migrants.

The nationalistic tendencies of the period after African countries achieved independence brought changes in culture and the arts. Radio stations at the time were government subsidized. With liberation, West African governments revamped their cultural policies. Sources for musical material changed, often now linked to national issues.

Despite the potential to adapt and modernize, the Kru were linked to a minority group seen as marginal. Kru musicians talk of how Nigerians called for more indigenized music, and as one seaman states, "Before that, any nation could sing [in Lagos]." Kru musicians in the newly independent nations became, in a sense, marginalized. Their cultural and musical role did not transfer to a more political role that could easily survive the changing political climate in other parts of West Africa. Kru music was never promoted into the mainstream of African popular musics. Only several decades earlier could the Kru, in moving from place to place, create a broad audience and to some degree negotiate cultural differences through music.

The Kru experience represents an important stream of influence in the development of contemporary West African forms of expression. As the dissemination of the European-African lingua franca of pidgin English set patterns of communication in West Africa, so the propagation of African styles of guitar playing and the music of Kru mariners and migrant workers affected the development of music along the West African coast.

Relaxed social gatherings, palm wine bars, and music ensembles served as points of orientation for Kru migrant musicians, providing intersections between each worker and a network of musical interaction. The Kru were as adept at intermingling as they were at being musical adventurers and innovators.

Out of these settings, musical confluence emerged; the old and new forms combined with a multiethnic mix of expressive forms. The period was followed by an era of independence and nationalism, which created many difficult challenges for the Kru living away from their homeland. Their mobility ended, leaving few effects of a cosmopolitan life-style, but their musical legacy endures in ongoing forms of musical expression through Africa and the diaspora.

REFERENCES

Alájá-Browne, Afọlábi. 1985. *Jùjú Music: A Study of Its Social History and Style*. Ph.D. dissertation, University of Pittsburgh.

———. 1989. "A Diachronic Study of Change in Jùjú Music." *Popular Music* 8(3):231–242.

Banton, Michael. 1957. *West African City: A Study of Tribal Life in Freetown*. London: Oxford University Press, for International African Institute.

Bender, Wolfgang. 1991. *Sweet Mother*. Chicago: University of Chicago Press.

Bridge, Horatio. 1853. *Journal of an African Cruiser*, ed. Nathaniel Hawthorne. New York: George P. Putnam.

Büttikofer, Johann. 1890. *Reisebilder aus Liberia*. Leiden: E. J. Brill.

Brooks, George. 1970. *Yankee Traders, Old Coasters and African Middlemen: A History of American Legitimate Trade with West Africa in the Nineteenth Century*. Brookline, Mass.: Boston University Press.

———. 1972. *The Kru Mariner in the Nineteenth Century*. Newark, Del.: Liberian Studies Association Monograph.

Collins, John. 1985. *African Pop Roots*. London: W. Foulsham.

———. 1989. "The Early History of West African Highlife Music." *Popular Music* 8(3):221–230.

Collins, John, and Paul Richards. 1982. "Popular Music in West Africa." In *Popular Music Perspectives*, ed. David Horn and Philip Tagg, 111–141. Goteborg, Exeter: International Association for the Study of Popular Music.

Coplan, David. 1985. *In Township Tonight! South Africa's Black City Music and Theatre*. London and New York: Longman; Johannesburg: Ravan Press.

Dalby, David. 1970. "Black through White: Patterns of Communication." Bloomington: Indiana University African Studies Program.

Davis, Ronald. 1976. *Ethnohistorical Studies on the Kru Coast*. Liberian Studies Monograph Series No. 5. Newark: University of Delaware.

Erlmann, Veit. 1991. *African Stars*. Chicago: University of Chicago Press.

Fraenkel, Merran. 1964. *Tribe and Class in Monrovia*. London: Oxford University Press.

Fyfe, Christopher. 1962. *A Short History of Sierra Leone*. London: Oxford University Press.

Hampton, Barbara. 1980. "A Revised Analytical Approach to Musical Processes in Urban Africa." *African Urban Studies* 6:1–16.

Kroo Young Stars Rhythm Group. 1953. *O Gi Te Bi*. Decca DKWA 1335. LP disk.

Ludlam, Thomas. 1812. "The Account of a Tribe of People Called Kroomen on the Coast of Africa." *The African Repository and Colonial Journal* 1:43–55.

Martin, Jane. 1982. *Krumen 'Down the Coast': Liberian Migrants on the West African Coast in the 19th Century*. Boston: African Studies Center, Boston University. Working Papers, 64.

McEvoy, Frederick. 1977. "Understanding Ethnic Realities Among the Grebo and Kru Peoples of West Africa." *Africa* 47(1):62–80.

Mukuna, Kazadi wa. 1992. "The Genesis of Urban Music." *African Music* 7(2):72–74.

Okie, Packard, ed. 1955. *Folk Music of Liberia*. New York: Folkways Records, FE 4465.

Schuler, Monica. 1986. "Kru Emigration to British and French Guiana." In *Africans in Bondage: Studies in Slavery and the Slave Trade*, ed. Paul E. Lovejoy, 155–201. Madison: University of Wisconsin Press.

Smith, J. 1851. *Trade and Travels in the Gulph of Guinea*. London: Simkin, Marshall.

Tonkin, Elizabeth. 1971. "Some Coastal Pidgins of West Africa." In *Social Anthropology and Language*, ed. Edwin Ardener, 239–255. London: Tavistock.

Waterman, Christopher. 1990. *Jùjú: A Social History and Ethnography of an African Popular Music*. Chicago: University of Chicago Press.

Latin American Musical Influences in Zaïre

Kazadi wa Mukuna

The Role of Radio
The Role of Recordings
The Role of Concerts

As this volume was going to press, a new government in Zaïre had changed the name of the nation to "Democratic Republic of the Congo."

Until the late twentieth century, the scrutiny of cultural exchange between Africa and the Americas was a one-way concern. Scholars focused their attention only on the flow of African cultural elements into the New World. In addition to identifying those elements in the cultural fabrics of the Americas, scholars theorized on the processes by which those elements became transformed. Published studies of African influences on cultural expressions in the New World abound in anthropology, sociology, linguistics, religion, and history. In ethnomusicology, methodological guidelines like one proposed by the Grupo de Trabajo outline approaches that consider not only inferences drawn from the humanities and social sciences, but also the effects of cultural renewal, an effort by people to refresh their cultural knowledge.

In Africa in the 1970s, a new trend in scholarship, supported by studies in urban musicology, began. Scholars realized that urban musical expressions are legitimate sources of information about social change. African musical processes reflect the convergence of musical material from within and without the continent, summarize the world views of their societies, and record events that affect the lives of their makers and audiences. The rise of urban musical expressions in Africa warrants the analysis of their musical styles. The influence of Latin American music did not affect the parts of the continent equally, but the development of urban musical expressions in Africa may have resulted from the impact of a combination of similar phenomena and events, such as the installation of foreign companies, leading to the formation of detribalized centers, marked by the introduction of foreign musical instruments and musical forms.

The rise of Latin American societies and cultures has received attention from humanists and social scientists (Dealy 1992; Lang 1993; Zavala 1992). The convergence of three racial groups (African, European, Amerindian) in the New World tested several processes of acculturation and assimilation. These groups did not interact in similar ways or degrees. European masters had more opportunities to interact with their African slaves than with Indians, whose souls their church requested they save. The result was a new cultural expression, embodying elements from Europe and Africa.

Assimilation is an advanced stage in the process of cultural exchange. It follows

Of countless Latin tunes broadcast and sold on
records, none was more appealing and influential
than "*El Manisero* 'The Peanut Vendor'."

phases during which people accept or reject cultural elements as compatible or
incompatible with their needs. These phases include

- the listing of cultural materials, when people with different origins in an
  emerging society discover what they share, and define common denominators
  that might become features of their new culture;
- the evaluation of common denominators according to new sets of norms and
  values;
- the reinterpretation of compatible common denominators in the light of the
  new context, the stage at which, as they reach the point of assimilation, they
  change and receive new functions.

Cultural elements are either retained or rejected. Further examination of the process
of the emergence of a new cultural context brings to light three major levels of consideration that operate in concert, though not in a particular order: (a) the survival of
a context of which a cultural element is part; (b) the resilience of a cultural element
in the new society; and (c) the functionality of a cultural element for the needs of the
ruling class. Each of the racial groups that converged in the New World had a cultural background that people cherished and protected. To ensure survival in the emerging society, each group made itself receptive to a new set of norms and rules. The
continuity of a cultural element is an assertion of its persistence and assimilation.
Resilience of cultural elements to the new set of norms and rules made this process
possible.

African slaves brought to Latin America the knowledge of certain musical instruments and concepts of organizing certain musical elements. In the New World, these
elements survived within cultural manifestations that had surrounded them in Africa.
As a way of insuring their survival, African slaves began to recreate cultural details
that gave meaning to their lives. In certain areas, the European ruling class, by
encouraging the formation of social brotherhoods of slaves (such as those known in
Brazil as nations, and in Cuba as *cabildos*), fostered this process. Though Europeans'
primary intent was to control the slave population by keeping a firm hand on its
leaders (who had to answer for the misbehavior of their brothers), the brotherhoods
provided opportunities for slaves to recreate and perpetuate portions of their cultural
calendar. They were the basis for promoting observances of African social and religious festivals and rituals (Mason 1992:9).

The encounter of Spanish and African concepts of musical organization in the
New World resulted in the creation of new musical forms, including the *cumbia* in
Puerto Rico; the rumba, the *columbia*, the mambo, and the *guaguancó* in Cuba; the
samba in Brazil; the tango in Argentina; and the merengue in the Dominican
Republic. These styles displayed a distinct rhythmic tapestry, a product of the fusion
of rhythmic concepts from both worlds. Where there were not similarities (such as in

harmonic implication, melodic structure, style of vocal production, and melodic musical instrumentation), ruling-class adaptation to the new style was inevitable. By being compatible with existing local forms, most of these forms served as models for urban music and dances in African countries. In Zaïre, the impact of Latin music on urban musical expression was more momentous than elsewhere in Africa.

The date these forms initially became known in Africa is unknown, but musical contacts between Latin America and Africa began to flourish in the 1930s and 1940s, and continued until the 1960s. These contacts took three forms: radio broadcasts, recordings, and concerts (Rondón 1980:3–37; Mukuna 1993:65–71).

THE ROLE OF RADIO

The first two radio stations to operate in Kinshasa were the Jesuit-owned Radio-Léo, which began broadcasting in January 1937, and Radio Congolia (owned and operated by Joseph Hourdebise, assisted by his wife, Madeleine Demont), which began broadcasting on 4 September 1939. Radio-Léo's goals—bringing Roman Catholic culture to the European population in Zaïre and converting the local population—remained for the duration of its existence, which ended on 15 July 1967. Those of Radio Congolia, aimed primarily at bringing news and commercial advertisements to the black population, continued until 28 February 1948. Elsewhere in the country, five privately operated stations came into existence during that time, but Radio Congolia was "the first in Congo to broadcast programs for the black population" (Pauwels-Boon 1979:182).

The first government-controlled station, Radio Congo Belge (RCB), began operating in Kinshasa on 1 October 1940. Its primary goal was to inform the colonial population about developments of the war in Europe. In 1948, the central government took over the broadcasts of Radio Congolia, which it renamed Radio Congo Belge pour les Indigènes (RCBI). The new station operated for eleven years (1949–1960), and then became Radio Nationale Congolaise (RNC). Through programming, RCBI and Radio Congolia exposed the population of Kinshasa—and cities as far away as Accra, Dakar, and Lagos—to the musical styles of the Americas, and promoted Zaïrean urban music. Their broadcasts featured Congolese dance music with Latin American rhythms (Pauwels-Boon 1979:182). To diversify its programming, Radio Congolia aired live studio broadcasts of performances by bands that had achieved success in Léopoldville (Pauwels-Boon 1979:180). These broadcasts, coupled with the influence of traveling Latin bands, stimulated the creation of "jazz bands"—street ensembles that, despite their name, played music bearing little resemblance to American jazz.

THE ROLE OF RECORDINGS

Before 1948, when Ngoma (a Greek-owned studio in Kinshasa) began operations, 78-rpm recordings of Afro-Cuban music and American jazz were popular in Zaïre and other parts of the continent. These recordings became a source of musical materials that local bands learned by rote and performed in bars, which numbered about 100 in Kinshasa in 1945. The most successful recordings sold in Kinshasa that year were of dance music. To popular melodies, local composers sometimes added words in Lingala (a local language) or Spanish words (Comhaire-Sylvain 1968:36–39).

The proliferation of studios in Kinshasa, and the increase in air time of music from Latin America and the United States, reinforced this popularity. Of countless Latin tunes broadcast and sold on records (released on labels such as His Master's Voice, Vaya Records, and Fania Records), none was more appealing and influential than "*El Manisero* 'The Peanut Vendor'," in which the Cuban composer Moises Simon experimented with combining the rhythm of the *son* with that of the *pregón*.

musique Zaïroise moderne 'Modern Zaïrean music', a new style of guitar music in the 1960s

maringa Intertribal social dance, popular on the west coast of Africa from Sierra Leone to Zaïre

kwasa-kwasa Popular music in Zaïre from 1986, based on a variant of the rumba

zekete-zekete Popular music from 1977 to 1987 in Kinshasa, based on a variant of the rumba

madiaba Popular music in Kinshasa from 1988, based on a variant of the rumba

The popularity of this and other Latin tunes reached an apogee in the 1950s, and remained a fixed part of local bands' repertories until the late 1960s. By the mid-1960s, however, most Latin tunes had become obsolete. A new style of music for guitar, *musique Zaïroise moderne* 'modern Zaïrean music', taking traditional ethnic music as its inspiration, supplanted them. In the 1990s, Europeans were still miscalling this style by the name of its 1966 variation, *soukous.*

The studios played a role equally important in the dissemination, establishment, and promotion of Latin American music in Zaïre. A variety of profitable music-related activities—an increase in the number of musicians and musical ensembles in the country, and the adoption of the term *rumba* over *maringa* (an intertribal social dance, popular on the west coast of Africa, from Sierra Leone to Zaïre)—proves the strength of this role. For more than a decade (1948–1960), studios provided promising young Zaïrean musicians with European and Latin American musical instruments, of which congas, bongos, guitars, flutes, clarinets, saxophones, claves, and maracas were the most common. The studios hired European virtuosos to give lessons. The studios set up a pool of local musicians capable of accompanying traditional and Latin dance music on the new instrumentation. The result was an increase in the number of freelance studio musicians, who remained at the service of the studio that had trained them. Several important musicians started their career in this fashion, playing in occasional ensembles composed of musicians from one studio. Eventually, through recordings and performances in bars, some of the ensembles gained celebrity. Two of the most prominent of the 1950s were African Jazz and O.K. Jazz. The former, founded in 1953 by musicians from Opika studio, included Joseph "Le Grand Kalle" Kabasele, Charles "Dechaud" Mwamba, and André "Damoiseau" Kambite. The latter, founded in 1956 by musicians from Loningisa studio, included Luambo "Franco" Makiadi, Victor "Vicky" Longomba, Daniel "De-la-Lune" Lubelo, and Edward "Edo" Nbanga.

The marketing of Zaïrean popular music, both in the country and throughout Africa, was a deciding factor in the adoption of the name of the Cuban dance rumba in Zaïre. Examination of Cuban rumbas and Zaïrean variants reveals that what occurred in Zaïre was not the adaptation or assimilation of Cuban dance forms, but the reinterpretation of the name. The music returned to the style of the *maringa,* whose associated movements (comparable to those of the Cuban rumba) consist of shifting body weight from one leg to the other; but the studios maintained the name "rumba," since they found it had more commercial appeal. After the novelty of Latin influences had worn off, musicians looked back to *maringa,* which they could easily interpret on the new instrumentation, and fit to traditional musical patterns and dances. The new instruments added a dimension to *maringa* music that traditional musical instruments lacked. They brought new harmonic possibilities and new timbres, though their functions were at first limited to roles fulfilled by the traditional instruments they were replacing. (The guitar, for example, replaced melodic instruments such as the *mbira* and the *madimba*, a local xylophone.) With the new instrumentation, the Zaïrean rumba became adaptable to the structure of traditional music and dance. Traditional tunes could find their way into the rumba without modifying or giving up the principles of their rhythmic organization. Zaïrean rumba and its variants—*soukous* (1966), *zekete-zekete* (1977–1987), *kwasa-kwasa* (1986), *madiaba* (1988)— became a source of influences for rising urban musical expressions throughout Africa, including *makossa* in Cameroon, *jùjú* in Nigeria, *marabi* in South Africa, and *kwela* in Malawi.

THE ROLE OF CONCERTS

In 1912, foreign companies in Zaïre introduced a policy that allowed migrant workers to sign extended contracts, instead of the three-month contracts then in force. (The short-term contracts had forced workers to move repeatedly from one company to another.) The imposition of the new policy helped crystallize the foundation of detribalized centers, composed of people of different nationalities and ethnic backgrounds (Cornevin 1966:210; Alexandre-Pyre 1969:143). In Kinshasa, these companies mainly hired West Africans to work in offices (Comhaire-Sylvain 1968:49–55). The resulting concentration of West Africans brought changes to social and musical activities in the city. The brass tradition, introduced by West Africans with such bands as the Coastmen and Excelsior, provided a model that led to the creation of brass bands by Zaïrean musicians throughout Kinshasa, with such names as "L'Harmonie Kinoise" and "Odéon Kinois," both in 1940.

By the mid-1960s, the dissemination of Latin American musical sounds led to the local demise of the brass-band tradition. Surviving bands, such as L'Harmonie Kinoise, adapted their instrumentation to those of Latin *charangas* and *orquestas típicas*, which frequently toured the country. These musical formations had a profound impact, not only on the musical style of the country, but also on stage presentation, clothing, and even the artists' names—so an Edward became Edo, a François became Franco, a Nicolas became Nico, and a Baloji became Baroza. Latinized names served as musicians' stage names. The orchestration of rising new ensembles included stringed instruments (guitars: lead, rhythm, bass), woodwinds (clarinets, flutes, saxophones), and an array of percussive instruments (conga drums, maracas, güiros, claves, rhythm sticks).

Urban musical ensembles reached Kinshasa with the introduction of Latin American dance forms (cha-cha, *charanga*, bolero, mambo, merengue, rumba, *pachanga*), all of which had first gained popularity in New York, promoted there by Latin ensembles. (Some of the earliest preserved examples of *maringa* music were those recorded by Pepper 1942 and Tracey 1956.) One such ensemble was Machito and his Afrocubans, founded in New York in 1941 by Mario Bauza and Frank "Machito" Grillo. It included Latin American and Caribbean musicians, who performed regularly in such dance halls as the Palladium and the Blen Blen Club. Possibly the most influential of the traveling Latin bands was that led by the Dominican flutist Johnny Pacheco, whose name became associated in Kinshasa with the Latin sound. His influence was so strong, promoters invited him to perform at events associated with the championship fight between boxers Mohammed Ali and George Foreman (Kinshasa, 1974).

Latin musical genres provided expressions that served only for specific circumstances. Lyrics, imitating Latin ensembles, often took the form of broken Spanish (Comhaire-Sylvain 1968:36–37). For songs of humor and joy, audiences preferred the cha-cha, the merengue, and the *pachanga*; for lamentations and elegies, they preferred the slow tempo of the bolero.

By 1965, most forms of Latin music and dance had become obsolete in Zaïre.

However, the compatibility of the rumba and the *maringa* helped the adaptation and assimilation of the rumba into the musical expression of urban centers. Questions continue to arise about the African authenticity of the *maringa,* whose popularity had spread along the west coast of Africa from Sierra Leone to Zaïre well before 1970.

REFERENCES

Acosta, Léonardo. 1991. "The Rumba, the Guaguancó, and Tío Tom." In *Essays on Cuban Music: North American and Cuban Perspectives.* ed. Peter Manuel, 49–73. New York: University Press of America.

Alexandre-Pyre, S. 1969. "L'origine de la population du centre urbain de Lubumbashi." *Publications de l'Université Officielle du Congo à Lubumbashi* 19:141–150.

Bergman, Billy, et al. 1985. *Hot Sauces: Latin and Caribbean Pop.* New York: Quill.

Carpentier, Alejo. 1979. *La Música en Cuba.* Habana: Editorial Letras Cubanas.

Collins, John. 1985. *African Pop Roots: The Inside Rhythms of Africa.* London: W. Foulsham.

Comhaire-Sylvain, Suzanne. 1968. *Femmes de Kinshasa hier et aujourd'hui.* Paris: Mouton.

Cornevin, Robert. 1966. *Histoire du Congo Léopoldville-Kinshasa: dès origines préhistoriques à la République Démocratique du Congo.* Paris: Berger-Levrault.

Dealy, Glen Caudill. 1992. *The Latin Americans: Spirit and Ethos.* Boulder, Colo.: Westview Press.

Díaz Ayala, Cristobal. 1981. *Música Cubana del Areyto a la Nueva Trova.* San Juan: Editorial Cubanacan.

Lang, James. 1993. "Sociology and Development." *International Journal of Contemporary Sociology* 30(1):5–19.

Léon, Argeliers. 1991. "Notes toward a Panorama of Popular and Folk Music." In *Essays on Cuban Music: North American and Cuban Perspectives,* ed. Peter Manuel, 1–23. New York: University Press of America.

Mason, John. 1992. *Orin Orisa: Songs for Selected Heads.* New York: Yoruba Theological Archministry.

Mukuna, Kazadi wa. 1992. "The Genesis of Urban Music in Zaïre." *African Music* 7(2):72–84.

———. 1993. "L'évolution de la musique urbaine au Zaïre pendant les dix premières années de la Seconde République." *Aquarium* 11/12 (Printemps 1993):65–71.

———. 1990–1991. "The Study of African Musical Contributions to Latin America and the Caribbean: A Methodological Guideline." *Bulletin of the International Committee on Urgent Anthropological Research* 32–33:47–49.

Pauwels-Boon, Greta. 1979. *L'Origine, l'évolution et le functionnement de la radiodiffusion au Zaïre de 1937 à 1960.* Tervuren: Musée Royal de l'Afrique Centrale.

Pepper, Herbert. 1942. *Anthologie de la vie africaine.* AST 6001–03. 3 LP disks.

Rondón, César Miguel. 1980. *El Libro de la Salsa: Crónica de la Música del Caribe Urbano.* Caracas: Editorial Arte.

Roberts, John Storm. 1992. "The Roots." In *Salsiology: Afro-Cuban Music and the Evolution of Salsa in New York City,* ed. Vernon W. Boggs, 5–22. New York: Greenwood Press.

Schuler, Monica. 1986. "Kru Emigration to British and French Guiana, 1841–1857." In *Africans in Bondage: Studies in Slavery and the Slave Trade,* ed. Paul E. Lovejoy, 155–201. Madison: University of Wisconsin Press.

Tracey, Hugh. 1956. International Library of African Music. Roodepoort, Transvaal.

———. 1972. *The Music of Africa: Musical Instruments 6.* [The *maringa* music in Tracey 1956.] Kaleidophone KMA 6.

Zavala, Iris M. 1992. *Colonialism and Culture: Hispanic Modernisms and the Social Imaginary.* Bloomington: Indiana University Press.

Rural-Urban Interchange: The Anlo-Ewe

Daniel Avorgbedor

Background to Rural-Urban Interchange
Mechanisms and Facilitators of Rural-Urban Links
Formal and Informal Linkages
Urban Models of the Group as a Social Unit

The Anlo-Ewe, a subgroup of the Ewe-speaking people of the Volta region (Ghana), speak the Anlo dialect. They live in villages and towns along the southeastern coast, and near Keta Lagoon. In the early 1600s, after a series of migrations and wars, they settled in their present territory. Oral traditions follow their tracks from Nigeria and Dahomey (Benin), and trace their origin to uncertain locations farther beyond. In the 1800s, Europeans provided new avenues of cultural contact. These persons were mainly German, English, Portuguese, and Dutch merchants, missionaries, and colonial administrators. Formal education and mission programs—important aspects of the colonial agenda—became the most important source of influence on Anlo-Ewe personality, society, and culture.

Traditional Anlo-Ewe society (including government and politics) is centralized, with an official headquarters and a paramount chief; but in local affairs, villages and towns exercise much autonomy. Ceremonial contexts invoke the administrative and political powers of the paramount office. The Anlo state's subdivisions—*ɖusi* (or *We*), *Mia*, *Adontri* (or *Dome*), and *Lasibi* (or *Klobo*)—articulate political and social infrastructures. Each subdivision has a head, who owes allegiance to the paramount chief, Togbui Adeladza II, and his assistant (the *awoamefia* 'field marshal'). To engage in warfare, during the early days of migration and settlement, the subdivisions formed themselves into military units. Indigenous offices, roles, and functions, have lost many of their earliest known contexts and implications (Amenumey 1964).

A village or town divides into wards (pl. *towo*) each of which has its own heads (pl. *tokɔmegāwo*), male and female. Anlo society is patriarchal, patrilineal, and patrilocal (Nukunya 1969; Greene 1981:451–464). The privileges, responsibilities, and achievements of each ward find both musical and nonmusical expression. Musical participation becomes a social debt; and since music is an important medium for exhibiting group solidarity and social achievement, troupes from different wards are inherently in competition with each other. Well into the twentieth century, competition often escalated into an overtly disruptive form of music making, the *haló*, which insulted individuals and groups. Until 1960, when the Ghana government officially proscribed *haló*, performances provoked violent acts (Avorgbedor 1990–1991:61–80).

Despite contacts with foreign and neighboring civilizations and cultures, the Anlo-Ewe have consistently maintained a distinctive regional culture.

Forms of musical organization reflect and support the social hierarchy. The head of each ward oversees the activities of the ensembles. Each ensemble normally maintains the following hierarchies and procedures: *ʋumegãwo* 'big men or women of the drum'; *akametsiawo* 'key and reliable persons'; *hesinɔ* 'lead singer'; *hakpala* or *henɔ* 'composer'; *atsiawɔla* 'decorative dancer or stylizer'; *vunɔ* or *azagunɔ* 'master-drummer'; *kanɔ* 'whip man, disciplinarian'; *gbeåfaɖela* 'announcer'; *hatsovi* 'supporting female lead singer'. The persons who have these roles receive no pay, though the roles enhance their social images. Groups also form ensembles to reflect sex, age, occupation, and special interest (Fiagbedzi 1976).

The main form of Anlo-Ewe music making is *ʋufofo* 'drumming'—a concept that includes singing, dancing, playing of drums and other percussive instruments, costume, and related art forms. Each ward specializes in more than one musical ensemble, but throughout Anloland, certain classes of music commonly cross the boundaries of wards and villages (Fiagbedzi 1976).

Despite contacts with foreign and neighboring civilizations and cultures, the Anlo-Ewe have consistently maintained a distinctive regional culture, especially in the area of music, actively cultivated in both rural and urban areas of Ghana. Anlo social prescriptions and expectations stress communal participation; a variety of musical styles, and the zeal with which people cultivate them (at home and abroad), support the status of music. Though principles and basic functions of Anlo music invite innovation, music is one of the artistic mediums through which the people construct and reaffirm their cultural identity and group solidarity.

BACKGROUND TO RURAL-URBAN INTERCHANGE

In 1877, under British colonial administration, Accra assumed the status of a capital (Acquah 1958). An important import-export center, it drew people of all classes—from different parts of Ghana, and foreign countries. In 1959, to accommodate development (in trade, commerce, industry), an important harbor opened at Tema, eighteen miles away; but because Accra made available a diversity of jobs, it remained an attractive economic center. Like many capitals of developing countries, Accra is a central administrative center, the location of modern amenities, higher education, and a variety of opportunities (economic, cultural, social). After the early 1960s, immigration into the city accelerated. The capital, which originally had an indigenous population of a few thousand (members of the Gã ethnic group), now has one million, from diverse ethnic groups and foreign countries.

The Volta region of Ghana is a low-productivity area, unfavorable to economic returns, especially when compared with other regions of central and southern Ghana (Adarkwa 1981:39–62). Its main forms of economic activity are fishing, *kente*-cloth weaving, and agriculture. Women play an important role in processing and retailing. Because the weather is variable and economic opportunities are few, many Anlo-Ewe males migrate to other coastal areas of Ghana and abroad, where they seek profits in fishing (Lawson 1958:21–27; Willie 1969:396–410). Their wives and children often join them, undermining the human resources of villages. Sometimes villages cannot put on a satisfactory musical performance, because key musicians have joined the emigration—*kɔfeyiyi* 'going to village', including the shores of Accra (Avorgbedor 1992:45–57).

For the Anlo area from 1920 to 1960, censuses show the density of the population increased (Caldwell 1969). After 1960, emigration intensified, and the rural population's rate of growth decreased. Between 1970 and 1984, Volta's population grew 1.7 percent, the slowest of the nine regions. From 1960 to 1984, the population of Accra rose, from 337,800 to 859,600 (Ghana 1984). The reversal in the Volta region's population density from the early 1960s paralleled the development and increase of wages in Accra. The city became a major center, especially among the Anlo-Ewe.

Patterns of rural-urban migration among the Anlo-Ewe resemble those known for the rest of the country. Youths who have completed secondary school, mostly unmarried, actively migrate to Accra, where the use of the word *youth* in the name of voluntary associations (such as the Klikor Youth Association and the Seva Youth Association) underscores this pattern. Once youths land jobs, their relatives join them. These persons fall within two groups: parents, grandparents, in-laws (dependent on the host); and other recent secondary school graduates and members of extended families (who search for jobs).

Two popular songs reveal important aspects of the complexities of rural-urban migration among the Anlo-Ewe, especially about the unsuccessful few. This song, an *agbadza*, satirizes an unsuccessful trip to Accra (Gē). Senchi, a ferry port, bridges the main road leading into the city.

> Wobe yeayi Gē lo, ʋudoga hee.
> Wobe yeayi Gē lo, ʋudoga hee.
> ʋudoga meli o; sakabo tsi Senchi.

> She wants to go to Gē, but problem of the fare.
> She wants to go to Gē, but problem of the fare.
> There is no money for fare; prostitute is left at Senchi.

Another *agbadza,* popular in the 1960s, plays on the word *baya*, a style of dress then in vogue.

Afiawo loo, afiawo hee.	It serves you, it serves you good.
Oo, afiawo;	Oh, it serves you;
Oo, afiawo.	Oh, it serves you.
Dada gbloe ne wogbe,	Mother told her,
Fofoa gbloe ne wogbe.	But she refused.
Wobe yeayi Ge dume.	She wants to go to Accra.
Ge dume zu baya.	Accra came *baya*.
Oo afia wo.	Oh, it serves you right.

Censuses, though not precise, give enough evidence to confirm that the urban population of Ghana is growing fast, and that Ghana is one of the most urbanized countries in West Africa (Caldwell 1969; Zacharia and Nair 1981). In 1970, the Ewe dominated the urban population in these proportions: Northern Ghana, 4.6 percent; Ewe (including Anlo), 27.1; Akan, 15.0; Gā, 13.0; Hausa, 4.9; non-Ghanaian Africans, 34.6; non-Africans, 0.8 (Ghana 1984).

In many ways, the Anlo-Ewe reinforce their presence in Accra. Though they do

habɔbɔ   Voluntary associations of the Anlo-
          Ewe in urban centers

not maintain distinct ethnic enclaves, they dominate several sectors: Newtown (Lagos Town), Malata, Abeka, Kotobaabi, Nima. The self-employed engage in a trade, either newly learned or practiced before the migration. Most urban settlers are clerks or workers in factories, and some hold skilled jobs (in masonry, carpentry, tailoring). Many women continue in a former rural livelihood: the retailing of *akpeteshie* (local gin), rice, corn, fish, textiles, and other items.

The habɔbɔ

In sub-Saharan urban centers, the voluntary association is an important innovative form of social organization (Parkin 1969:90–95; Little 1965). Among urban Anlo, this form, the *habɔbɔ* (pl. *habɔbɔwo*), is the locus of social alignment. Its prototype, however, bears many distinctive social and musical marks. Urbanites find it convenient in building the symbiotic process between musical process and social formation, mainly because music is already a vital part of the sociocultural system. Voluntary associations therefore have two domains: musical and social (Avorgbedor 1986).

The system of voluntary association is formal and dynamic, though there are varying forms of informal face-to-face interactions, both on the job and at leisure. A hierarchical system assigns and confirms roles, and meetings proceed democratically. Persons hold such offices as chair, patron (*hamefofo* or *hamedada* 'group's father or mother'), secretary (*agbaledzinɔ* or *nuŋlɔla*), treasurer (*gadzikpɔla*), parliamentarian, financial secretary, sergeant-at-arms, and chaplain. Each new member receives a membership card and a copy of the constitution, sometimes an elaborate document of about forty printed pages. At general and executive meetings, discussions are usually in the Ewe language.

The most important sections of the constitution are those that specify the privileges of membership, such as the payment of a set amount toward funeral and hospital expenses, help for new arrivals in locating jobs and social partners, and rules of conduct. Participation in musical performance is a special area of attention, both according to the constitution and as interpreted in daily life, and members who cease to participate regularly in the music stand to forfeit their privileges and entitlements. One of the main requirements for joining an association is the demonstration of knowledge and skills in Anlo culture and music, through dancing before an executive committee. The central role of music among urban Anlo in reworking and reexperiencing original rural culture is, therefore, explicit.

Most *habɔbɔwo* formally register themselves with the Ghana government's Council for Youth and Culture. Registration legitimizes the association. The Council can call on members to participate in any voluntary program of work the Council wishes. During and after musical performances, the group identifies itself by wearing a uniform—often a T-shirt, featuring the association's motto. Because urban groups have village or home improvement as one of their principal aims, they usually maintain, in the village, a "home branch." This link enables them to communicate readily with the village.

MECHANISMS AND FACILITATORS OF RURAL-URBAN LINKS

Most urban Anlo have a way of experiencing situations in the rural area. Some of the mediums of maintaining the links include the exchange of letters, verbal messages, and visits.

Funerary events

Funeral contexts (to which music is indispensable) are among the collective and most significant mediums of musical interchange and social discourse (Anyidoho 1982). Death has important social and musical implications. Participation in funerary events is, therefore, one of the central responsibilities highlighted in the associations' constitutions. The conception, structure, and function of funerary events thus encourages active interaction between rural and urban Anlo. There is, however, a good reason for the assignment of constitutional status to such events: the lack of a supporting group ready in time and place, and the more fluid, artificial, and heterogeneous social contexts of Accra, are some of the important realities that prompt urban Anlo to attend to the situation of death in a structured, formalized fashion.

Both rural and urban groups emphasize and integrate musical performance with funerary events, but there are some significant differences in the variety, frequency, and quality of the music as people experience it in such contexts in both environments. Urban groups must perform for deceased members (or deceased next of kin), both in Accra and in the rural home, but a death in an urban area does not compel rural people to travel to Accra. When urban relatives and sympathizers of the deceased come from Accra to participate, they do so on the basis of individual initiative, not under any constitutional compulsion. Individuals are members of different voluntary associations. In addition, the visiting urban sympathizers do not usually plan to perform, but they may participate in the funeral music in the rural home.

In Accra, special laws and regulations govern entertainment and group behavior. Participants in funerals face conditions that limit workers' free time. From the police, they must get permits, which restrict performances to a certain number of hours in a specific place. Government curfews—due to tensions among rival political groups, or to clandestine activities of political insurgents—further complicate these restrictions. While music for rural funerals can continue for three days and three nights, urban conditions limit musical performances.

Urban groups perform in both the city and the rural area, especially when burial occurs in a rural area. The constitution entitles the family of the deceased to receive a sum of money, a coffin, emotional support, musical performance, and incidentals. After a death in the city, the rest of the members of the *habɔbɔ* schedule the first funeral music on the nearest weekend, preferred because of weekday constraints. Since urbanites can visit only on weekends, the scheduling of funerary events among the rural Anlo emphasizes weekends; however, after the major burial rites, the local rural group can have musical performances on any weekday. The routine and special temporal framing of monthly and weekend performances among urban Anlo thus provides additional evidence of how the rural and urban Anlo integrate their social and musical experiences.

When burial occurs in Accra, the geographic dimension of the musical performance is absent: only in rare instances might a group want to honor their deceased member by presenting a musical performance in the rural area. Opportunities of musical and social interaction among urban and rural groups are most conspicuous when urban groups transport a corpse home (to a rural area) for burial. Since the vis-

The framework of national politics and the new order and institution of the arts motivate both rural and urban troupes toward new musical standards.

iting group is musically adequate, members have the freedom to merge with the home music, perform in addition to the music, or restrain the rural group and assume full responsibility for performing. When the urban group performs, rural people join in spontaneously. Rural performers enjoy a chance to assess the competence of urbanites.

The musical performance by an urban group becomes the medium through which urbanites make important statements about themselves—and about their cultural, ethical, and musical proprieties. As they fulfill the constitutional requirements, they take on a dual identity. The funeral context in the rural area gives them a chance to exhibit how thoroughly they retain Anlo attitudes. Through their new form of urban affiliation, they can create for themselves a distinct environment.

By seeking to lift the burdens of the bereaved family, the association confirms its identity. The urban group cooks its own food, and ensures that its members can meet all practical needs. Though they pursue this consideration for practical and humanitarian reasons, it is also an unconscious recreation of rural practice: troupes on tour carry their food, instead of relying on the hosts to provide it.

Holidays

Besides funerals, Easter is an important event. It influences the level and quality of musical interaction between rural and urban groups. On Easter, rural families expect reunions and financial support from the *klakiwo* 'clerks' (scholars and white-collar workers). They see the holiday as a privileged occasion. Besides many spontaneous performances by different village groups, the town- or village-development committee assigns the responsibility of musical performance to one troupe, and participation is open to everyone. Social and musical reunions, though short-lived, play an important role in updating the knowledge and skills of urban groups.

National events

Urban people reexperience their rural background in other important ways. The Centre for National Culture (formerly the Arts Centre), promotes urban and rural art forms. During special political occasions and the yearly festival of the arts, it brings troupes into Accra to participate in the regional and national finals of the festival. On other occasions, as part of cultural-education programs, it brings rural Ewe troupes, but after the late 1970s, these programs became less frequent, because of lack of funds and housing. The presence of rural troupes in Accra constitutes a special moment for urban Anlo, who see an opportunity, not only to reaffirm their cultural and ethnic identity, but also to observe, critique, and derive useful musical ideas from musical presentations by rural Anlo troupes.

Organization and participation in the festival inspires musical creativity and innovation among the Anlo, because the festivals present contexts where urbanites can learn expressive elements of rural musical culture. In addition, the nature, prescriptions, and expectations of the festivals, have pushed the troupes toward new standards of staging: the festivals involve a podium, a stage, a panel of judges, and specification of the repertory (in type, length, and manner of presentation). The audience is a cross-section of the population, and the festival context presents the participating groups with new challenges, and the opportunity for critical reflection.

In Accra, Ewe troupes no longer have the privilege of a homogeneously rural audience, and they verbally express concern over the situation. The multiethnicity of Accra becomes a problem that troupes must solve. The amount of psychological stress visitors from rural areas must tolerate is, however, much less than the stress urbanites experience. The latter groups have become familiar with the problems of performing for non-Ewe audiences, but they are conscious of the competition endemic among urban ensembles. Sister groups sometimes become target audiences for one another, but the lack of a familiar audience remains.

The situation of the festival and the element of competition are, in addition, a different set of motivators that have important implications for innovative elements in rural music. In the early 1990s, the unmistakable examples of these tendencies extended only to choreographic and musical modifications of original dance and music tailored to suit the festival and political expectations.

National festival and political events influence the organization and performance standards of some urban Anlo troupes, better described as professional dance troupes. They follow the model set by the Ghana National Dance Ensemble, made up of professional musicians and dancers, versatile in local and pan-African art forms. These artists and their leaders have received training from the School of Performing Arts (formerly part of the Institute of African Studies), and most of them are Ewe. The nearness of the School, the Accra urban center, and the concentration of national programs in the city, help people set up troupes, drawing on the young urban Anlo population. A few of these troupes are panethnic, and their repertory similarly derives from the music and dance of Ghanaian ethnic groups. In their search for recognition and group identity, these troupes take special interest in the festival of the arts.

The cultural policies of Ghana encourage the festival participation of children and young people, whom the troupes include (UNESCO 1975). This policy is equally applicable to the rural parts of the country. The rural Anlo troupes who perform in Accra give a good representation of children's performance. This new form of musical participation thus bears many implications for social and musical interaction between rural and urban troupes.

The framework of national politics and the new order and institution of the arts motivate both rural and urban troupes toward new musical standards. Urban performers, however, enjoy several distinguishing factors: increased interaction with, and formation of, troupes of professional dancers; more frequent involvement with the festival of the arts and national events; contexts of relative autonomy; more opportunities for recording for broadcast on radio and television. Children's musical ensembles are part of the rural sociomusical experience, but it is the new national framework for the arts that has intensified music making among children. This emphasis has shifted the locus and responsibility from the traditional environment to the school compound. The school model is integrative: ensembles recruit children from all local wards, unlike the ward-based musical organizations typical of villages and towns.

FORMAL AND INFORMAL LINKAGES

Instances of rural-urban interchange also occur in such areas as formal social affiliation, and in the invention and promulgation of a new musical type.

In the quest for cultural continuity and authenticity, urban groups draw on rural musicians' talents.

In the homeland, when a troupe wants to add to the repertory, they invite, from other villages, musical experts (usually dancers and drummers), who attend rehearsals. Since conflicts and elements of competition exist among the wards within a village, a ward seeks musical help from an outside and neutral group, to avoid embarrassment and insults. This interaction sets up a formal social and musical linkage between the groups. Reciprocal performative visits reinforce it further: one group travels to perform for the other. Sometimes, the performance is purely recreational; sometimes, it is a display to arouse and satisfy mutual musical interests. When there is a death within the host group, other groups can perform music in sympathy and support. During this encounter, people exchange symbolic gifts (cash, drinks).

The urban Anlo have a growing tendency to realign their group structures and constitutional specifications along rural models. The funeral occasions and the musical performances in the rural area by the urban groups show how they define themselves dually—as both self-sufficient and rural. The visit to perform with rural groups is an effort toward preserving, at social and musical levels, rural models of affiliation and reciprocity.

More convincing examples of urban performance occur in Accra. The performers—invariably the voluntary associations—construct formal social partnerships with each other. Instances of this partnership are clearest during special or anniversary events. In 1986, when Kemelio Habɔbɔ celebrated its silver anniversary (for the period 1960–1985), other troupes with which they had formal affiliations attended events and made donations. In addition, Kemelio Habɔbɔ planned a trip to perform for a sister group in Tema.

In the quest for cultural continuity and authenticity, urban groups draw on rural musicians' talents. They most strongly feel the need for expert advice when they found new ensembles, dedicated to performing rural music. While founding ensembles, Miwɔnɔvi Kinka, Wheta Youth Association, and Kemelio (formerly Danger), have relied on musical expertise from the rural area. Without a formal linkage, an urban group consults any short-term visitor from the rural area who has musical skill. This visitor is often a composer, whose skills and ideas the urban group explores. Formal and informal contacts enable rural and urban groups to share and update their musical knowledge. Among the urban Anlo, this interchange is always a legitimate mode of exploring the benefits of collaborative action, in keeping with rural tradition.

URBAN MODELS OF THE GROUP AS A SOCIAL UNIT

During the early stages of the urban development of Accra (1940–1955), there were few Ewe voluntary associations. Each early association drew members from several villages. As the population of Accra (and that of urban Ewe) increased, the diversity in the new demographic structure led to the creation of many associations at the village-specific level. The new groups did not supersede the earlier ones; they complemented old roles and functions. A third stage involves the proliferation of associations at the village and ethnic levels—a process by which individuals assume plural membership.

The initial settlement of the Anlo in Accra shows a pattern that underscores the symbiotic relationship between musical and social processes. The initial population was conveniently a panethnic (Ewe or Anlo) association; a common musical type, *agbadza*, was the main form of musical recreation. The group had a formal head, the chief of all the members, or of all Anlo residents in Accra. He was the *Anlofia* 'chief of Anlo' (or the *Ewefia* 'chief of the Ewe'). His activities and responsibilities were both symbolic and real. He mediated between factions and interpersonal conflicts; by negotiating with the national government, he sought to improve the group's welfare. By the 1990s, however, the role of Anlo chief in Accra had yielded to the functions of patrons, chairpersons, reverend ministers, and secretaries of the voluntary associations, both village based and panethnic. The chief played a limited musical role, in contrast to the ascription of higher social status based on musical expertise among urban groups of the 1990s.

Agbadza, a recreational type of music commonly identified with the Anlo, and not restricted to one village, underscores the existence of ethnic-based associations. As an association expanded in membership and social-welfare services, so its musical repertory diversified, and *kinka* and *dunekpoe* became additional popular ensembles. The *habɔbɔ* is now the regular mode of social alignment, and urban Anlo actively perform both *agbadza* and other musical types. This is one important way by which forms of social and musical participation interrelate closely. Persons from one rural town or village (for example, Asadame, or Seva), may form their own village-based association, join that of another village, or seek a more inclusive group. In an Asadame Habɔbɔ, this group would not strictly follow a structure based on a rural model: Accra (or Senugɔme, one of the voluntary associations) is not Seva or Blamezado (Anlo villages). The urban *habɔbɔ* does not split into wards, and there is, therefore, no intragroup competition and rivalry at the social and musical levels, as one would expect in a rural village with two or more wards.

There are, however, some parallels in the area of musical organization. The associations, as they grow in human and musical resources (with up to five hundred members), form additional musical ensembles, drawn from the rural repertory, and thus build their repertory. In such large associations as Abeka Ewe Union, Miwɔnɔvi (Abor Kinka), Lɔlɔnyo, and Kemelio, members can participate in the additional ensemble; for example, Kemelio performs *gahu*, *atsiagbekɔ*, and *adzida*. The structural and organizational aspects of the additional ensemble are, however, more specific and restrictive: the leaders and key musicians are chosen according to new demands of music and group management. These persons thus differ from those appointed to another ensemble of the same association. A village-based association in Accra does not duplicate the structural traits of a village in the rural area, but the musical formation and organization draw from rural patterns.

One other important example that shows an innovative way of modeling social forms among the urban Anlo concerns the ascription, distribution, and articulation of roles. These roles bear a dual definition: musical and social. The group further acknowledges the urban musician (drummer, lead singer, composer) by assigning him or her a social responsibility. Musical status goes beyond the musical domain; it encompasses the social. While a composer or master drummer achieves respect for skill and achievement, he or she usually receives no additional status or responsibility. The top of the social hierarchy involves persons in these roles because of their moral and social integrity.

Examples from among the urban Anlo show new attitudes toward the concept

The conception and display of music as part of Anlo
personality and culture provide a rationale for the
continuing interaction between rural and urban
people.

TRACK 6
TRACK 7

and processes of selecting, ascribing, and distributing these roles. In the Noepe Youth
Association, songleader-composers and master drummers are not only members of
the "executive committee," but also take social responsibilities: public-relations officer, vice president, financial secretary, and so on. That their roles cross musical and
social domains confirms the duality of the definition of a voluntary association
among the urban Anlo. This dualism appears in the naming of the association:
Miwɔnɔvi Habɔbɔ is also known as "Avenor Kinka," *kinka* being the genre of the
music the group often performs; similarly, "Dunekpoe" is synonymous with
"Lɔlɔnyo," *dunekpoe* being the genre Lɔlɔnyo Habɔbɔ of Pig Farm (a sector of Accra)
often performs. In rural villages, wards have names that are abstract, connotative, or
geographical. The types of music performed do not usually take the name of a ward,
and the ward does not take the name of the music. While these examples reveal novel
approaches to musical and social organization, they also refer to the set patterns and
procedures of the rural area. The contexts of funerals, holidays, national events, or
festivals of the arts, and the construction of formal and informal linkages for musical
improvement, are an important and effective mechanism by which the Anlo-Ewe
exchange and update musical ideas. The examples show the common and specific
ways in which each environment integrates and interprets the sociocultural components of the music.

The urban examples show the interinfluences of industrial time, space, population dynamics, democratic and highly structured forms of sociation. By national policy, classrooms become a medium for the transmission of innovative ideas. Common
nonmusical mediums (letters, verbal messages, visits) that provide the necessary system of network between rural and urban Anlo affect this interchange.

The conception and display of music as part of Anlo personality and culture
provide a rationale for the continuing interaction between rural and urban people.
Since the rural environment is the reservoir of Anlo cultural and musical heritage,
urbanites try to maintain a connection with it, effectively to define themselves. The
rural area provides the cultural base for urban groups, especially when a large segment of the population consists of young secondary school graduates, many of whom
were not well informed in the musical and cultural practices of their village. Some
secondary schools encourage performance of, and participation in, "traditional drumming," but school settings often lack the resources of expert traditional instructors.

In a few musical areas, performers show increased collaboration. Rural people
encourage musical innovation, but only selectively; ensembles new after 1940 include
gahu, *kinka*, *akpalu*, and subforms of *adzida*. This instance and level of innovation
does not, however, include the borrowed and modified forms. The Ewe know a variety of genres of Western art music (especially Christian religious music). To give cues
and add minor embellishments, they use Dutch bugles, handbells, and whistles. In
their texts, they sporadically employ English phrases. To aid their memories, they
sometimes write down textual incipits.

Urban Anlo make an effort to appropriate and interpret these elements according to the tradition. They carefully monitor innovations. Increasingly, they are adopting the *zeʋu*, a pot drum, which relates to pot drums common in Nigeria. Though no person has yet been identified as the source of this novelty, the migration of the Anlo-Ewe into Nigeria may be the main link. This drum increases our evidence for rural-urban interchange among the Anlo. The *zeʋu*, though it is popular among urban groups, comes from the rural area (Akatsi), where people also make regular drums. Interest in the use of this drum is greater among urbanites, but one can speculate on the chance rural Anlo may adopt and integrate it in their ensembles, especially as urban groups continue to travel into rural areas.

The practice of *ʋuɔyɔ* is another example of an extension of a rural musical practice, and therefore not entirely new among the urban Anlo. In *ʋuɔyɔ*, the performance of several musical types introduces the main performance. In rural areas, this practice usually extends only to the performance of fast and slow *afãʋu* (music of the *afã* cult), performed as a prayer. Since urban groups do not have all the resources, convenience, and contexts for performing all pieces from the Anlo repertory, they take advantage of this introductory formula, momentarily to gain access to some of the pieces they want to experience. A performance of *kinka*, for example, would follow two or three short renderings: *takaɖa*, *kpɔmegbe*, *husãgo*.

REFERENCES

Acquah, Ione. 1958. *Accra Survey*. Accra: Bureau of Publications.

Adarkwa, Kwasi. 1981. "A Spatio-Temporal Study of Regional Inequalities in Ghana." *African Urban Studies* 11:39–62.

Addo, N. O. 1975. "Immigration and Sociodemographic Change." In *Population Growth and Socioeconomic Change in West Africa*, ed. John C. Caldwell, 367–382. New York and London: Columbia University Press.

Amenumey, D. E. K. 1964. "The Ewe People and the Coming of European Rule: 1850–1914." M.A. thesis, University of London.

Anyidoho, Kofi. 1982. "Death and Burial of the Dead: Ewe Funeral Folklore." M.A. thesis, Indiana University.

Avorgbedor, Daniel Kodzo. 1986. "Modes of Musical Continuity among the Anlo-Ewe of Accra: A Study in Urban Ethnomusicology." Ph.D. dissertation, Indiana University.

———. 1990–1991. "Some Contributions of *Halɔ* Music to Research Theory and Pragmatics in Ghana." *Bulletin of the International Committee on Urgent Anthropological and Ethnological Research* 32–33:61–79.

———. 1992. "The Impact of Rural-Urban Migration on a Village Music Culture: Some Implications for Applied Ethnomusicology." *African Music* 7(2):45–57.

Caldwell, John C. 1969. *African Rural-Urban Migration: The Movement to Ghana's Towns*. Canberra: Australian National University Press.

Fiagbedzi, Nissio. 1976. "The Music of the Anlo: Its Historical Background, Cultural Matrix, and Style." Ph.D. dissertation, University of California, Los Angeles.

Ghana. 1984. *Population Census of Ghana: Preliminary Report*. Accra: Central Bureau of Statistics.

Greene, Sandra E. 1981. "Land, Lineage and Clan in Early Anlo." *Africa* 51:451–464.

Hamilton, Ruth Simms. 1966. "Urban Social Differentiation and Membership Recruitment among Selected Voluntary Associations in Accra, Ghana." Ph.D. dissertation, Northwestern University.

Ladzekpo, Kobla. 1980. "Anlo Ewe Music in Anyako, Volta Region, Ghana." In *Music of Many Cultures*, ed. Elizabeth May, 216–231. Berkeley: University of California Press.

Lawson, R. M. 1958. "The Structure, Migration and Resettlement of Ewe Fishing Units." *African Studies* 17:21–27.

Little, Kenneth. 1965. *West African Urbanization: A Study of Voluntary Associations in Social Change*. Cambridge: Cambridge University Press.

Nukunya, G. K. 1969. *Kinship and Marriage among the Anlo Ewe*. London: Athlone Press.

Parkin, David. 1969. "Urban Voluntary Associations as Institutions of Adaptation." *Man* 1(1):90–95.

Peil, Margaret. 1972. *The Ghanaian Factory Worker: Industrial Man in Africa*. Cambridge: Cambridge University Press.

Robertson, Claire. 1984. *Sharing in the Same Bowl: A Socioeconomic History of Women and Class in Accra*. Bloomington: Indiana University Press.

UNESCO. 1975. *Cultural Policy of Ghana*. Paris: UNESCO. Studies and Documents on Cultural Policies.

Willie, R. 1969. "Migrant Anlo Fishing Companies and Socio-Political Change: A Comparative Study." *Africa* 39:396–410.

Wunsch, James. 1974. "Voluntary Associations: Determinants of Associational Structure and Activity in Two Ghanaian Cities." Ph.D. dissertation, Indiana University.

Zacharia, K. C., and N. K. Nair. 1981. "Demographic Aspects of Recent and International Migration in Ghana." In *Migration in West Africa: Demographic Aspects*, ed. K. C. Zacharia and Julien Conde. London: Oxford University Press.

Foreign-Indigenous Interchange: The Yoruba
Christopher Brooks

Rural Theater
Urban Theater
Cultural Nationalism and Religion
The *Aladura* Movement
Yoruba Music Drama
Music and Related Verbal Arts
Festivals
Islamic Musical Genres

Some 20 million Yoruba occupy the southwestern region of Nigeria, and part of Benin and Togo. They divide into several subgroups: Ife, Ketu, Awori, Egbado, Egba, Ijebu, Ijesa, Oyo, Ondo, Ekiti (Bascom 1969). Collectively, they are famous for the range of their musical traditions, including related verbal arts. In the early 1960s, their theatrical tradition, the most developed on the African continent, began to receive serious scholarly attention.

RURAL THEATER

Yoruba rural theater has its foundation in traditional beliefs. Traditional theogony recounts actions of a supreme being (*Olodumare* or *Olorun*), plus hundreds of intermediate deities (*orisa*), who deal with humans. Scholars have likened this system to Roman Catholicism, which recognizes a Supreme Being, plus hundreds of saints, who intercede for persons. But unlike that faith, traditional Yoruba belief posits no direct relationship between mortals and the Supreme Being; the *orisa* intervene on mortals' behalf.

Several festivals held throughout Yorubaland honor the *orisa*. Most celebrate a mythic or folkloric account of these deities' actions to resolve conflict, effect reconciliation, and make atonement. During these festivals, reenactments ritually retell myths or legends. Scholars like Joel A. Adedeji (1969), Oyinade Ogunba (1967), and Oludare Olajubu (1974, 1978) suggest that festivals were the earliest form of Yoruba theater.

Oral history has further obscured the beginnings of an established professional rural-theater tradition. From such accounts, Adedeji draws a picture of the *egungun* society as an early formal theatrical association, which emerged as early as the 1500s. He uses the term *egungun* to denote the reincarnation of the deceased ancestors, and a variety of masquerades. Kacke Gotricke (1984) and others, however, are more cautious about accepting mythic accounts as historically accurate because of their prodigious use of allegory. She says folklore and myth are good at explaining the presence, and in some cases, the origin, of a practice or tradition; but this tendency does not guarantee historical accuracy.

Most historians agree that by the 1600s, as several kingdoms emerged in

Yorubaland, a rural-theater tradition also developed. To royal courts in Ekiti, Ife, Ketu, Oyo, and elsewhere, theatrical entertainers and groups attached themselves; other professional parties toured from place to place. Some widely known troupes were the *alaarinjo* (one who dances as he walks), the *apidan* (one who performs magic), and the *onidan* (one who has tricks). These performers came out of the *egungun* tradition.

Throughout the 1700s, the Yoruba rural-theater tradition continued to thrive. At the beginning of the nineteenth century, many of the kingdoms within Yorubaland began to engage each other in warfare, which lasted much of that century and seriously interrupted the development of theatrical traditions. One of the famous conflicts involved Awole Arogangan, ruler of the Oyo kingdom. He ordered his general, Afonja, who was also his nephew, to attack a neighboring kingdom. Instead, Afonja overthrew his uncle and installed himself as ruler. Later, he fell in an attack by the northern Muslims, whose help he had sought in his own coup d'état. Later theatrical practitioners fashioned these events into music dramas: in *Yoruba Ronu* (1964), Hubert Ogunde created an allegorized version; and in *Beyiose* (1968), Duro Ladipo depicted the events more historically.

URBAN THEATER

For much of the 1800s, while many of the interior regional Yoruba subgroups embroiled themselves in civil war, the coastal areas, particularly Lagos, developed profoundly. Lagos, one of the major port cities along the West African coast, had exported slaves to Europe and the New World; much of that trade took place between 1600 and 1800. As the nineteenth century progressed, two groups aided in the emergence of an urban theatrical tradition. Members of both were repatriated Africans of Yoruba descent. The first group, the Saros (or Salos), were Yorubas who, as captives in the civil wars, had been sold into slavery. The British navy intercepted slave ships and released the captives in British enclaves along the West African coast, where they encountered British values, religion, and cultural practices. By the 1840s, many British-influenced Saros had returned to their native land, to resettle in Lagos and nearby coastal areas.

These people were eventually joined by another group, also of Yoruba descent: "Emancipados," emancipated Africans from Brazil and Cuba; the Yoruba language knows them as *agudu amaro* 'those who have been away'. Like the Saros, the Emancipados became Christians. Following British tradition, most Saros were Protestants; following Portuguese and Spanish practice, most Brazilians and Cubans were Roman Catholic. Cultural differences also manifested themselves in the surnames of the groups: the Sierra Leoneans commonly bore names like "Johnson," "Smith," and "Vincent"; the New World group bore names like "Andrade," "Pinheiro," and "Martínez."

By the mid 1860s, the Anglicized Sierra Leoneans and African-Brazilians had amassed enough social influence and power to form the nucleus of an economic élite within Lagos. The Sierra Leoneans imitated British models: they set up schools and academies, which produced, mostly under church sponsorship, dramatic performances and European-style concerts. The Brazilians and Cubans preferred social activities that recalled the dramatic presentations they had known in the New World: *bumba meu boi* 'bull celebration' and *senhor de bomfim* 'lord of good fire'. They also introduced a tradition of theatrical masking (*carreta*), a Brazilianized version of the Yoruba *egungun*, clearly mixing rural and urban traditions (Adedeji 1969).

By the 1880s, a Brazilian dramatic tradition had fully developed in Lagos. The Brazilian Dramatic Company, formed in 1880, staged several dramatic works and festival observances. It closed within a few years, but later Brazilian-controlled dra-

The members of the African church movement
sought to remold Christianity to meet the cultural
needs of the African.

matic companies took its place. In other events the companies mounted, they routinely honored the birthdays of famous Brazilian and Portuguese rulers. In 1888,
when Brazil formally abolished slavery, a series of performances marked the occasion.

Brazilianized Yorubas were among the élite in Lagos and other Yoruba-controlled
areas (Abeokuta, Badagary), but their performances and celebrations typically
allowed for the participation of indigenous people. Such was not the case in the Saro
community. In staging their celebrations, they did not include the indigenous population. They interested themselves more in developing a European music and theater
tradition.

In the 1880s, Robert Coker and Herbert Macaulay emerged as proponents of
this tradition. Both were of Yoruba ancestry, and each would become distinguished.
Coker studied music and theology in London and Germany; Nigerians regarded him
as the Mozart of West Africa. After returning from his studies, he annually promoted
Western-style musical performances, the Coker Grand Concerts. He became an
Anglican minister, and turned his talents to the production of cantatas. His first large
work on a biblical subject was *Joseph* (1886). As a choirmaster, he frequently performed major choral works of Handel and Mozart.

Herbert Macaulay was a protégé of Coker's. He first appeared at a Coker's Grand
Concert in the early 1880s, singing the Yoruba song "*Emi kole joke je* 'I cannot sit
quietly'." The practice of singing traditional Yoruba songs at such occasions was just
beginning, and it would gain wide acceptance. Macaulay, born in Lagos of Sierra
Leonean parents, and locally educated, represented the second generation of Saros. In
his teen years, he joined the Melodramatic Society. In 1888, he displayed his talent as
an impresario and producer by mounting a performance of Gilbert and Sullivan's
Trial by Jury. Two years later, he went to London, where he studied engineering and
music. He returned in the same musical mold as Coker, but the social climate of
Nigeria in the 1890s led him to a life of political activism, and he became the father
of Nigerian nationalism.

CULTURAL NATIONALISM AND RELIGION

Cultural nationalism, which would heighten the interaction of rural and urban traditions among the Yoruba, had its source in the emergence of the middle class and the
growth of the Christian church. In 1861, to quash the trade in slaves, British forces
annexed Lagos. Even before then, many Western-educated Yorubas had settled along
the Nigerian coast, eager to spread the message of Christianity, commerce, and civilization. As a buffer between Europeans and the indigenous population, they formed
the nucleus of a Westernized class, though many of them questioned Western ideology. In the period 1884–1886, by settlement, conquest, and treaty, the whole of
Nigeria came under the control of the Royal Niger Company, a commercial enterprise; on 1 January 1900, authority passed to the British Crown, and waves of civil
servants followed. When the government placed Europeans in civil service positions

above qualified Africans, the situation became tense. People ridiculed Anglicized Africans as "geographical and psychological monstrosities."

As the strain between educated Yorubas and their British counterparts grew, many of the Yoruba middle class began to abandon Western names, to adopt traditional Yoruba ones. David B. Vincent became Mojola Agbebi; Joseph Phythagoras Haarstrup became Ademuyiwa Haarstrup; George William Johnson became Osokale Tejumade Johnson. The movement to identify more closely with traditional Yoruba cultural practices and customs is visible in books that appeared in the 1890s, such as Samuel Johnson's *History of the Yorubas* (completed in 1897, published in 1921).

Yoruba religious leaders, often the ablest spokespersons of the Yoruba movement, were not indifferent to cultural-nationalist aims. Religious leaders, such as James Johnson and Mojola Agbebi, did not feel politically restrained by their clerical duties. With other clergy of the Yoruba cultural movement, they baptized children only under Yoruba names, encouraged the use of indigenous music in worship, supported the wearing of indigenous dress, and condoned customs they considered compatible with Christianity.

As the 1890s began, religious dissatisfaction among Yoruba Christians reached a new high. Between 1890 and 1920, the objections to Western-style Christianity became so strong that some educated Yorubas led a separatist movement. The Christian denominations broke away from their European and American missions, to set up African churches, more responsive to African (mostly Yoruba) traditional values and customs. The African denominations included the Native Baptist Church, the United Native African Church, Bethel African Church, and Jehovah Shalom.

The members of the African church movement sought to remold Christianity to meet the cultural needs of the African, instead of converting Africans' experience to Western-style practice. To accomplish these aims, they began to incorporate in religious services more and more indigenous cultural expressions, such as dance, poetry, art, and music. Though they Africanized the style of their worship, they kept their beliefs close to those of the parent church.

A dramatic tradition called native drama grew out of the African church movement. In the 1800s, blending European and traditional Yoruba theatrical elements was common; but by the early twentieth century, traditional Yoruba forms had resurfaced in the African churches. A dramatic organization, Egbe Ife (Ife Club), produced one of the earliest native dramas, under the joint sponsorship of several African churches. The work was *King Elejigbo*, a musical drama, composed by D. A. Oyele; it became the model that other native dramas copied (Leonard 1967). Eventually, the Egbe Ife evolved into the Bethel Dramatic Society and expanded its repertory to include several Western-style pieces.

By the outbreak of the Great War (1917), the nationalist movement had slowed down. More than fifteen separatist African churches had formed, but many had become as conservative as their parent churches. The degree to which Christian worship should accept traditional influences became a disputed issue. By the 1920s, this dispute split and polarized the African church movement. Mainstream European mission churches, proselytizing among the educated élite, competed for members. As the decade progressed, and factions became more doctrinaire, another religious movement gained momentum among the Yoruba; soon, it would move further toward blending traditional practices with Western-style Christianity.

THE *ALADURA* MOVEMENT

In the 1920s, an indigenous religious movement, *aladura* 'the owners of prayer', became popular among the Yoruba. It began with the formation of so-called praying bands. The *aladura* denominations sought to attract both the grassroot Yorubas of

aladura 'Owners of prayer'; an indigenous syncretic religious movement among the Yoruba

bembe Double-headed drum of the Yoruba incorporated into the *aladura* churches

samba Quadrangular, wooden frame drum introduced by Brazilian returnees to local churches

the interior and the coastal civil servants. By the early 1930s, several denominations had formed within the new tradition: the Cherubim and Seraphim, the Church of the Lord, the Celestial Church of Christ, and Christ Apostolic Church.

The *aladura* denominations went beyond the Africanizing steps the separatist churches had taken. They allowed polygamy, plus the practice of traditional Yoruba medicine, and maintained a basic belief in divine visions and prayer. They allowed certain traditional Yoruba instruments: the *bembe* (one of several double-headed drums) and the *samba* (a quadrangular, wooden frame drum, introduced by Brazilian returnees). They did not allow the use of the *dùndún* (hourglass talking drums) and the *bata* because of their association with traditional deities.

The *aladura* churches innovatively used hymns. Their hymnody developed from at least three sources. The first was Western musical practice. Hymns came directly from standard Western hymnals, with a Yoruba text substituted for an English one. Textual substitution was a widespread practice, not only among Yoruba Christians, but in other cultures of the African continent. The vernacular appeal to the indigenous population met with mixed results, because Western melodies did not always meet the linguistic demands of African languages.

The second source from which *aladura* hymns developed was original composition. Both indigenous and Western musical influences affect this repertory. Figure 1 shows a hymn that meets the linguistic demands of a Yoruba text, but follows a standard tonal formula: I–V–I–ii^6–I$^6_4$–V–I. In translation, the text reads:

> Jesus will reign, Jesus will reign,
> Whether the world wants it or not.
> Jesus will reign, Jesus will reign.
> There's power in Jesus' blood.

Another indigenous element found throughout the *aladura* repertory of hymns is the use of 'holy words.' These terms are a form of glossolalia which, within the *aladura* context, are words or phrases channeled to church leaders, or other members in divine visions. Though words such as *beraca, berad, korrabbannonm sajj, alloll, aybburra,* and *sahhojjallal,* appear phonetically well formed, and are intelligible to the individual who receives them, they do not always seem lucid to other indigenous Yoruba speakers.

The *aladura* denominations revolutionized Christianity for many Yorubas, but the African churches continued to develop their own hymnody. Several of them produced hymnals in the nationalistic spirit. These volumes included hymnals of the Native Baptist Church (1906), the West Africa Episcopal Church (1913), and the United Native African Church (1914). Outstanding among composers of hymns were A. K. Ajisafe and J. W. Vaughan.

By the late 1920s, the Protestant mission-church development of sacred music

FIGURE I First stanza of the hymn "*Jesu yio joba* 'Jesus will reign'."

among the Yoruba was clearly falling behind the *aladura* denominations and the African churches. Few works appeared during this period, but some talented musicians emerged from mainstream Protestantism. The most widely known hymnal was *Iwe Orin Mimo fun Ijo Enia Olorun ni ile Yoruba* 'Holy Songbook for Yoruba Churches' (Ransome-Kuti 1923). Most of its items, however, are European hymns, set to a Yoruba text. Because the tonal requirements of the Yoruba language were inconsistent with Western melodic style, the hymns did not fully communicate religious sentiments.

While the *aladura* hymns borrowed freely from traditional Yoruba folk song, and hence paid more attention to the tonal requirements of the language, the Protestant mission churches routinely avoided the practice. E. Ogumefu and the Yoruba musician and musicologist Ekundayo Phillips produced other works after the model of Ransome-Kuti. In a treatise on Yoruba music, Phillips states his position on the suitability of borrowing from traditional Yoruba folk songs for liturgical use:

> There is certainly something repulsive in hearing at a Sunday Service a common secular tune heard about the street during the previous week. . . . But there are folk-songs that have ceased to be popular or known at all by the majority of worshippers, whose tunes have been so long associated with sacred words that their original words are known only to antiquarians. There can be no harm in using this kind of tune. (Phillips 1953)

Phillips does not refer to the *aladura* or African hymn traditions. Finding relationships among folk songs, African-American spirituals, and other Protestant songs, he likens Yoruba folk songs to European Medieval and Protestant music. He believes

FIGURE 2 First stanza of the hymn "*Eniai ba* 'Mankind should give praise'" (Phillips 1953:15).

Ogunde introduced Western secular instruments and made prodigious use of African-Latin traits.

a pentatonic scale prominent in both traditions; many of his tunes (as in figure 2) use a pandiatonic pentatonic scale. In translation, the text reads:

> Elders, behold my reverence.
> Let the rat carry the ritual of death.
> Let the fish carry the ritual of death.
> May you never see death.

The text can be interpeted: "Mankind should give praise and thanks to God, who performs wonders all over the world. Let us express thanks together. Let us elevate him forever, and give him praise. Let us rejoice and worship together."

YORUBA MUSIC DRAMA

The Christian church played a big role in the development of Yoruba performance traditions, even those that borrowed heavily from traditional Yoruba musical expressions. The emergence of a secular professional theater tradition among the Yoruba has multiple roots in the Christian church. The Africanized hymns that came out of the separatist African churches were commonly called native airs. In the 1930s, the native-air repertory formed the basis of a dramatic tradition, the native-air operas. As these pieces came largely under church sponsorship, their topics were biblical. They incorporated secular and sacred songs, but implied little historical knowledge of the tradition. Their texts were in Yoruba. Throughout the 1930s, however, many important artists worked within the tradition: A. B. David, G. T. Onimole, A. Ajibola Layeni.

Hubert Ogunde's style

The movement toward a secularized theater tradition in the 1940s was the result of a cultural and political renaissance, which accompanied the push for political independence. It was evident in the theatrical style of Hubert Ogunde. His father was a Baptist missionary, but his mother came from a long line of practitioners of Yoruba beliefs. Yoruba religion provided his earliest exposure to a belief system. From that background, he learned a variety of Yoruba cultural expressions (singing, dancing, drumming), which would later influence his compositional style. Because of his father's Christianity, he attended Baptist mission schools, but chose to affiliate himself with the Church of the Lord (aladura). The aladura hymn tradition, with its free use of Yoruba folk song and adherence to the tonal inflections of the language, would influence Ogunde's style (figure 3). The text of figure 3 can be translated:

> Light on the earth, light in the heavens,
> Listen, listen, gatekeepers of heaven.
> Guard this gate.
> The people of the earth are coming again.
> They will soon come.

FIGURE 3   Melody of the opening chorus of Ogunde's music drama *Ayanmo.*

Many of Ogunde's early works, like *Africa and God* (1944a), *The Garden of Eden and the Throne of God* (1944b), and *Israel in Egypt* (1945a), developed the biblical native-air opera tradition, with Yoruba drumming and singing. Their performance often took place outside a church. His later musical stage works, such as *King Solomon* (1945b) and *Nebuchadnezzar's Reign* (1945c), though veiled in religious titles, were political in context. By allegory and allusion, they denounced the colonial administration.

Ogunde's lead also helped to shift Yoruba theater away from church sponsorship toward a professional and independent enterprise. He gradually introduced Western secular instruments, such as saxophones and trumpets. He also made prodigious use of African-Latin traits. Part of his style came from highlife musicians from Ghana, who frequently used similar instruments and styles in the "concert party," a musical genre developed in that country. By the early 1950s, other theater groups like Ogunde's began to emerge. As he had done, they began to travel around the country. Most of their performances were in Yoruba; but for audiences of many of Nigeria's ethnic groups, their singing and dancing transcended linguistic differences.

In the 1950s, throughout the era of Nigeria's independence movement, Ogunde continued to compose and perform. Because some of his works, in the government's view, incited public unrest, the colonial administration sometimes restricted him from performing in certain areas. His most severe ban, however, came in the mid 1960s, after Nigeria's independence. The work in question was *Yoruba Ronu* 'Yoruba Think' (figure 4), which appealed for Yoruba unity in the face of intra-Yoruba ethnic dissension:

I looked at the world; the world is thoroughly faded!
I looked up at the heavens; it was just as dark.
I said, "What is this!"
What has happened to the Yoruba, children of the Almighty?

FIGURE 4   Melody of "*Yoruba Ronu* 'Yoruba Think'."

FIGURE 5 European version of Duro Ladipo's "Easter Cantata."

It indirectly attacked the governing party, which responded by banning Ogunde from performing in the former Western Region, where Yorubas were dominant. In 1966, with the overthrow of the government, he resumed his public career.

Kola Ogunmola, another Yoruba composer, followed Ogunde's lead. Celebrated for consummate ability as an actor, Ogunmola was best known for his music drama *The Palm Wine Drunkard*, based on a Yoruba folktale. Musically, he employed many of the African-Latin conventions found in the style of Ogunde and highlife.

Duro Ladipo's style

Another Yoruba artist, Duro Ladipo, emerged at the beginning of the 1960s, and moved in another stylistic direction. Like Ogunde, he was from a family that subscribed to Yoruba religious beliefs; however, his father became a Christian, and raised his children in that faith. Though Ladipo remained a Christian, he knew well traditional Yoruba singing, drumming, and dancing, which throughout his life he witnessed at traditional festivals and ceremonies. He began his career as a church musician. To meet the tonal demands of the Yoruba language, he made structural changes in European hymns. Figure 5 shows one version of such a tune.

Ladipo began composing more complex sacred works: cantatas, which called for soloist, chorus, and instruments. One of the earliest of these works was his *Easter Cantata* (1960), for soloist, chorus, and drum accompaniment.

That the Anglican hierarchy received these works poorly caused Ladipo to leave the church. He then performed sacred works outside the artistic restrictions of that institution. In his early compositions, he displayed a range of procedures, such as recurring melodic motives and rhythmic patterns, metaphoric expressions, and a high sensitivity to the musical demands of the language. These features characterized his style in the works for which he is best known: *Oba Koso* (1964), *Oba Waja* (1963), *Moremi* (1973), *Beyiose* (1968). In them, he went in the opposite stylistic direction from Ogunde: he incorporated more traditional Yoruba songs, dances, and instrumentation, including stylized pieces and related verbal arts.

The 1960s and 1970s

In the mid 1960s, amid much intra-Yoruba ethnic rivalry and violence, Yoruba music dramas became politicized. The government called on—and sometimes forced—performers like Ogunde, Ogunmola, Ladipo, and others, to compose and stage artistic expressions that propagandized its aims. This situation characterized the musical stage during the Nigerian civil war, which lasted nearly three years.

By the 1970s, the Yoruba music drama had fully established itself as a flexible tradition, and shaken itself loose from its Christian origins. Major composers within the genre (Ogunde, Ladipo, Ogunmola) distinguished themselves outside Nigeria by

FIGURE 6 Example of *rara* from Duro Ladipo's *Moremi.*

participating in major performance events staged abroad, and through international tours. In 1984, Biodun Jeyifo (1984:200–203) found more than 100 professional theater groups active in Nigeria; more than half came from Yoruba areas of the country. The genre remains a highly developed form of theater.

MUSIC AND RELATED VERBAL ARTS

A largely unexplored area of Yoruba performance is the singing traditions. They are of particular interest because they appear in both rural settings (festivals, religious observances) and urban ones (Ogunde's and Ladipo's music dramas).

Among the widely known traditional arts are *oriki* and *orile*. *Oriki* is the most flexible of the Yoruba verbal arts. The performance praises or salutes an individual, deity, town, or even inanimate object. It highlights qualities or attributes (both positive and negative) associated with persons, places, or things. Most often, it is musically intoned. Unlike some of the stylized songs, there is no specific vocality associated with *oriki*, though because it salutes or praises, it occurs inside the stylized genres. A tradition related to it, and frequently confused with it, is *orile*, which also praises and salutes, but focuses more commonly on lineages, particularly of important or royal families, and of ancient kingdoms. Its performance also takes a freer style (without a regular meter or pulse).

Some singing styles have become associated with particular professions, such as hunter (*ijala*), honored in the vocal tradition *ijala are ode* 'hunter's entertainment music'. It has also become linked with Ogun, the Yoruba deity of iron, steel, and war. Because of that identification, worshippers of Ogun, as well as blacksmiths and warriors, use the genre. They perform it at festivals honoring Ogun, and at religious ceremonies or rituals where hunters gather.

Another singing style, *rara*, had its beginnings in a sacred context, but has since spread beyond that context. It was initially associated with Esu, the trickster deity, but was also practiced by wandering court musicians and minstrels. In the early 1990s, itinerant Yoruba musicians frequently performed it for money. Musically, it is closer to speech than are other styles of singing. Therefore, melodic contours and linguistic tonalities correlate highly (figure 6).

Among the stylized traditions of singing is *ohun*, which has several degrees, such as *sale ohun* (cracked) and *arin ohun* (muted); the most commonly heard is *aro ohun*. This latter tradition serves for weeping, lamenting, or funerary purposes. It employs vocal quavering, or a fast vocal tremolo and cracking, as in figure 7. *Aro ohun* is one of the most affecting styles within the Yoruba repertory.

Ohun orisa

There are at least three stylized Yoruba singing traditions, the *ohun orisa* 'voices of the deities', which, to some degree, have maintained their liturgical and traditional set-

FIGURE 7 Example of *aro ohun* from Duro Ladipo's *Moremi.*

FIGURE 8 Example of *ohun orisa* from Duro Ladipo's *Moremi.*

ting. They are distinguished by context and vocality. *Iwi* and a related form, *esa*, are vocal traditions associated with *egungun*, dead ancestors. It commonly occurs at *egungun* festivals throughout Yorubaland, and consists mainly of salutes or praises (*oriki*). Vocal delivery typically involves either of two manners. The first, and most vocally challenging, is what Olajubu (1974) describes as a "tight throat" and a "croaky voice." This vocal style, which takes years of training to master, is falsettolike, somewhat strained, raspy. Some singers can induce this style by swallowing herbal mixtures. The more common style of *iwi* is also falsettolike, but very nasalized in its delivery. This vocal quality, according to E. G. Parrinder (1969), comes from the Yoruba belief that the noses of the dead ancestors are broken, and their impersonators in reincarnated form sing in the manner of figure 8, translated as follows.

> Moremi Ajasoro!
> What is it you want me to do for you?
> Why are you so brave, brave,
> As to have sought for me here?
> Don't you know,
> When a child comes to a place of fear,
> He should be frightened?

Moremi, a beautiful mythic heroine, sacrificed her child to save the town of Ife from invaders. She is commonly hailed as a paradigm of Yoruba female strength and power.

Orisa pipe also belongs to this tradition. A generic term, it refers to sung or semi-sung praises, addressed to any deity; examples are *Ṣango pipe, Esu pipe, Obatala pipe.* The verb *pe* 'call, invoke, summon' suggests the singer is calling for help or aid. In the music drama *Moremi*, Duro Ladipo incorporated *Esinmirin pipe* in an invocational context: to petition the goddess, the heroine goes to the Esinmirin River. The *orisa pipe* may contain *oriki*, but it remains a singing style in which devotees express humility and devotion to a particular deity, as a translation of the text of figure 9 shows.

FIGURE 9 Example of *orisa pipe* from Duro Ladipo's *Moremi.*

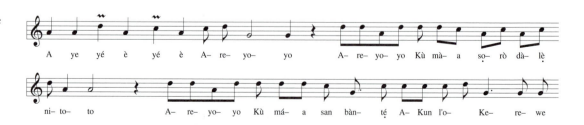

FIGURE 10 Song
from the Edi Festival.

E– ní K'e– bo má dà   a b'é– bo lo   A– sè– fi no   A Kì le b'o–ri–sa Ké– bo mó–dà   A– sè– fi– no

Look to the ground with eyes friendly as a melon.
Aye yeye o.

He said we should look at you with friendly eyes, yes.
In days of old! yes.

Another tradition of singing is *iyere ifa*. It does not appear outside sacred settings as frequently as the other singing styles, but composers like Duro Ladipo and others did include it in their musical stage works. It is more tonally oriented than some of the others. Frequently a responsorial pattern develops, with a soloist reciting the melodic line to a choral response such as *heen* 'yes, it is so'.

Other vocal forms that have developed among the Yoruba are the nuptial song, *ekun iyawo*, performed by intended brides the day before their weddings, and many vocal effects and techniques such as *fi fa gun*, vocal slides, which usually appear at the beginning or ending of phrases.

FESTIVALS

Festivals are a resilient and dynamic Yoruba institution. They serve as a major occasion of urban and rural performance. Through ancestor worship or memorialization, they express group identity and solidarity. Many occur at calendrically regulated intervals, but the timing of some rests with oracles. Researchers such as O. Eluyemi (1975) and Ogunba (1967) have chronicled festivals in myriad Yoruba towns, but the exact number of Yoruba festivals remains unknown.

The Edi Festival

Most Yoruba festivals are typically reenactments or observations of ancient events; and as Beverly Stoeltje (1989) points out, dramatic forms may resolve conflicts and other communal tensions. Such is the case with the Edi Festival, also called the festival of Moremi. It commemorates the heroine of Ife, who saves the town through ingenuity, symbolically renewing life by cleansing the town's sins. A frequently heard song associated with the festival—*A sefino, A ki le b'orisa kebo moda* 'Acceptable sacrifices must involve presentation of good offerings'—stresses the importance of sacrifice (figure 10). It sets the tone of the festival, and as in other examples, its melody conforms to the tonal requirements of the language.

Another component of this festival is the symbolic use of flames, by which, in ancient times, Moremi destroyed invaders. A song that accompanies the appearance of the flames, *A re sika, Ina ye ye jo ri reo, A re sika* 'The foreigner was wicked, but the mother's fire has burned brightly', is a reference to the heroine Moremi, hailed as mother *ye ye* (figure 11).

This festival incorporates female chiefs (figure 12), male chiefs (figure 13), and double-headed hourglass drums (*dùndún*, figure 14) as symbols of authority. It also

FIGURE 11   Song from the Edi Festival.

À– rè ṣì– ka I– ná yè yé jó ri– re o À– rè ṣì– ka

The sheer number of Yoruba festivals points up their role as cultural institutions. They are one of the enduring aspects of Yoruba life.

FIGURE 12   Female chiefs at Edi Festival, Ile-Ife, 1985.

FIGURE 13   Male chiefs at Edi Festival, Ile-Ife, 1985.

features the character Tele (figure 15), who symbolically carries away the sins of the town. People greet him and send him away with the song "*Telé níkau kù ú o lakaja* 'Tele alone dies'" (figure 16). This chant is performed partly sung and partly spoken in a call-and-response pattern: the first part, *Telé níkau kù ú o,* is sung, and the remaining word, *lakaja,* is spoken. Musically, the festival is unique because it allows no drumming.

Other festivals

Other Yoruba festivals are more liturgical in function. These include the Omoluaiye Festival, celebrated both on and off the African continent. Its purpose is to protect people from smallpox by invoking Sopona, the deity of the disease. Fearing his harshness and ruthlessness, people avoid his name. Figure 17 is a song from his festival (also known as the Babaluaiye Festival), celebrated at Oyotunji, a Yoruba village in South Carolina, made up of African-Americans who have adopted Yoruba traditions. Because such ceremonies in the New World have endured some form of transmutation, the melody would not be fully intelligible to an indigenous Yoruba speaker. Figuratively, it calls on the deity Babaluaiye (Sopona's praise name) to come into the presence of the assembled believers.

The sheer number of Yoruba festivals points up their role as cultural institutions. For social control and instruction, they are one of the enduring aspects of Yoruba life.

FIGURE 14 Double-headed hourglass drums at Edi Festival, Ile-Ife, 1985.

ISLAMIC MUSICAL GENRES

FIGURE 15 Tele the scapegoat, who symbolically carries away the sins of the town at the Edi Festival, Ile-Ife, 1985.

Islam began to spread among the Yoruba as early as the 1400s, long before Christianity made an impact on the group. By about 1800, a series of jihads waged by the northern Hausa-Fulani caused Islam to spread more rapidly among the Yoruba population. The spread was the result of Islam's tolerance of traditional Yoruba customs and practices—unlike Christianity, which rejected them.

By about 1970, there were more Muslim than Christian Yorubas in Nigeria. Scholars have explored Islamic musical traits less thoroughly than Christian ones. Islam's official position on music explains this situation. Except for Qur'ānic chanting and the call to worship, both of which require sustained intonation, Islam frowns on musical performance. Despite this position, many musical traditions have emerged among Islamicized Yorubas.

One of the basic Islamic influences appears in the vocal style, particularly in the use of vibrato, monosyllabic melismatic passages, and a tense vocal delivery. Akin Euba (1970, 1977, 1980) and Tunji Vidal (1977) have identified this in *waka*, a semireligious musical genre, frequently heard at weddings and other ceremonial occasions. Small bells initially accompanied it, but drums later did so. It is now common, not only on major religious holidays (like *Eid al-Fitr* and *Eid al-Kabir*), but in secular settings also.

Apala and *sakara* have developed among Yoruba Muslims as secular forms. *Apala* began within a religious context, but as professional musicians became involved as performers, they used for accompaniment a variety of Yoruba drums: the *dùndún*, the *bembe*, and others. In the early 1990s, *apala* and *sakara* were frequently secular enter-

FIGURE 16 Song from the Edi Festival.

Te- lé ní- kan Kù ú o la- Ka- ja   Te- lé ní- kan Kù ú o

FIGURE 17 *Baba e, baba soroso* from the Sopona Festival in South Carolina.

Ba- ba- e Ba- ba so- ro- so Ba- ba- e Ba- ba so- ro- so Ba- ba- lu-ai- ye i-yan- ko mo- de Ba- ba şi- re şi- re

tainment music. Later, another Islamic-inspired sung tradition, *fújì*, emerged among the Yoruba. It was similar to the other forms, but was more poetic in content, and more declamatory in vocal delivery. It relied heavily on the drumming, which shared musical importance equally with the singer. *Fújì* became one of the most popular musical genres in Nigeria. Other instrumental traditions that reflect Islamic influence are the *kàakàakii*, a long trumpet from northern Nigeria, and the *goje*, a single-stringed chordophone. Both accompany solo performances.

REFERENCES

Adedeji, Joel A. 1969. "The Alarinjo Theatre: The Study of a Yoruba Theatrical Art from Its Earliest Beginnings to the Present Time." Ph.D. dissertation, University of Ibadan.

———. 1971. "The Church and the Emergence of the Nigerian Theatre: 1866–1914." *Journal of the Historical Society of Nigeria* 6(1):25–45.

———, trans. 1972 *Moremi.* Ibadan: Institute of African Studies. Mimeograph.

——— 1973. "The Church and the Emergence of the Nigerian Theatre: 1915-1945." *Journal of the Historical Society of Nigeria* 6(4):387–396.

Bascom, William. 1969. *The Yoruba of Southwestern Nigeria.* New York: Holt, Rinehart and Winston.

Eluyemi, O. 1975. "The Role of Oral Tradition in the Archaeological Investigation of the History of Ife." In *Yoruba Oral Tradition,* ed. W. Abimbola, 115–156. Ibadan: Ibadan University Press.

Euba, Akin. 1970. "New Idioms of Music-Drama among the Yoruba: An Introductory Study." *Yearbook of the International Folk Music Council,* 92–107.

———. 1977. "An Introduction to Music in Nigeria." In *Nigerian Music Review,* no. 1, ed. Akin Euba (Ife: Department of Music, University of Ife), 1–38.

———. 1980. "Yoruba Music." *The New Grove Dictionary of Music and Musicians,* ed. Stanley Sadie. London: Macmillan.

Gotricke, Kacke. 1984. "Apidan Theatre and Modern Drama." Manuscript.

Jeyifo, Biodun. 1984. "Yoruba Popular Travelling Theatre." *Nigerian Magazine* (Lagos), 200–203.

Johnson, Samuel. 1921. *The History of the Yorubas.* London: Routledge & Kegan Paul.

Ladipo, Duro. 1963. "Oba Waja." Unpublished manuscript.

———. 1964. *Oba Koso.* Ibadan: Institute of African Studies.

———. 1968. "Beyiose. " Unpublished manuscript.

———. 1973. *Moremi.* Lagos: MacMillan Nigeria.

Leonard, Lynn. 1967. "The Growth of Entertainment of Non-African Origin in Lagos from 1866–1920." M.A. thesis, University of Ibadan.

Ogunba, Oyinade. 1967. "Ritual Drama of the Ijebu People: A Study of Indigenous Festivals." Ph.D. dissertation, University of Ibadan.

Ogunde, Hubert. 1944a. *Africa and God.* Lagos: Glover Hall.

———. 1944b. *The Garden of Eden and the Throne of God.* Lagos: Glover Hall.

———. 1945a. *Israel in Egypt.* Lagos: Glover Hall.

———. 1945b. *King Solomon.* Lagos: Glover Hall.

———. 1945c. *Nebuchadnezzar's Reign.* Lagos: Glover Hall.

———. 1964. *Yoruba Ronu.* Lagos: Glover Hall.

Olajubu, Oludare. 1974. "Iwi Egungun Chants—An Introduction." *Research in African Literature* 5(1):31–51.

———. 1978. "The Sources of Duro Ladipo's *Oba Koso.*" *Research in African Literature* 9(3):329–362.

Parrinder, E. G. 1956. "Music in West African Churches." *African Music* 1(3):37–38.

———. 1969. *West African Religion.* New York: Barnes & Noble.

Phillips, Ekundayo. 1953. *Yoruba Music.* Johannesburg: African Music Society.

Ransome-Kuti, J. J. 1923. *Iwe Orin Mimo ful Ijo Eni a Olorun ni ile Yoruba.* Lagos.

Stoeltje, Beverly. 1989. "Festivals." *International Encyclopedia of Communications.* New York: Oxford University Press.

Vidal, Tunji. 1977. "Traditions and History in Yoruba Music." In *Nigerian Music Review,* no. 1, ed. Akin Euba (IFE: Department of Music, University of Ife), 66–89.

Popular Music in Africa
Angela Impey

The Commercialization of African Music
African Popular Music and the International Market
Trends in the Major Regions of Africa
Intra-African Connections

Africa is an extraordinary and powerful continent. Almost three times the size of the continental United States, it consists of fifty-three countries, inhabited by some 700 million people. It has vast savannas, expanding deserts, tropical forests, lofty mountains, riverine valleys, palm-fringed coastlines, and spice-producing islands. Its people are differentiated from one another by ethnic identity and cultural practices, by religion, language, class, and urban and rural identification (Martin and O'Meara 1995:4).

Most African people still live in rural areas, but the continuous flow of people between town and country is a significant characteristic of the continent—a trait that remains basic to emerging expressive forms. The renowned Cameroonian saxophonist Manu Dibango has said that in Africa,

> you have a two-way traffic between town and village, village and town. You have a sound that arrives in the town and returns to the village, changed. The echo which comes back is not the original. When a note arrives in town from the village, the town returns it with electronic delay, with reverb, limiter and all the studio technology, but it is the same note that came from the village. (Ewens 1991:7)

Thus, modern-day national boundaries do not necessarily reflect differences between people, nor do they always carry meaning in relation to cultural and musical developments. The movement and interchange between artists from different countries who play similar kinds of music tend rather to reflect related languages, religions, and cultural practices. For instance, Manding *griot* music is played across West Africa, Congo-Zaïre rumba is prevalent throughout the Central and Eastern regions, *taarab* is performed by most coastal Swahili peoples, and elements of South African township music can be identified in the popular music of most southern African countries (Ewens 1991:24).

All the countries of Africa, with the exception of Ethiopia and Liberia, have undergone a period of foreign domination. Colonial governments, which occupied African territories between the 1880s and the second half of the twentieth century, brought with them trappings of a foreign culture, affecting, to varying degrees, the

Instruments such as guitars, violins, accordions, concertinas, and pedal organs were introduced into Africa by European traders, then reinvented to suit indigenous systems of tuning and styles of performance.

economic, political, and cultural infrastructures of the societies they controlled. These systems had a profound impact on the composition and distribution of popular cultures in Africa. For one, the adoption of European languages by colonized societies differentiated francophone West and Central Africa from the anglophone South and East and the lusophone states of Angola, Mozambique, and Guinea-Bissau. For another, colonial governments employed different strategies of cultural development, influencing the nature of the imaging, production, and distribution of popular music, both within their respective colonies and abroad.

The following survey of popular African music concentrates on the sub-Saharan region. On the basis of religion, North Africa is generally separated from countries south of the Sahara Desert, the north having been more influenced by Islam (Martin and O'Meara 1995:5). Though the discursive division of the continent is overemphasized (since much of sub-Saharan Africa is also Muslim), for the purpose of expediency I exclude the Maghrib [see NORTH AFRICA]. Further, I focus on musical genres that have circulated intracontinentally and internationally, and hence on the countries where those genres originated.

THE COMMERCIALIZATION OF AFRICAN MUSIC

This article discusses music mediated by a complex corporate network comprising companies that record, manage, advertise, publish, and broadcast mass-produced music. This network first reached into Africa around 1900, when entrepreneurs in the West began to recognize the potential for marketing musical instruments, gramophones, and records there. Since then, styles and peoples have circulated extensively between African centers and countries abroad. This circulation has included African influences on the music of the diaspora extending back through the slave trade, a circulation that is as much about commonalities of style as it is about ideologies of blackness. Influences also spread through the movement of artists between African countries and centers of production in Europe (mainly Paris and London), where technologically sophisticated studios and established performance circuits have long attracted professional African musicians.

Instruments such as guitars, violins, accordions, concertinas, and pedal organs were introduced into Africa by European traders. These instruments were reinvented to suit indigenous systems of tuning and styles of performance. The spread of acoustic guitars, and later electric guitars, was one of the most important developments in African popular music, both as topical acoustic music performed solo or in small groups, and as amplified music for dancing (figure 1).

The introduction of gramophone records (from 1907) presented African musicians with a new spectrum of imported styles. Among these were African-American jazz, Dominican merengue, Cuban salsa and *son*, Anglo-American rock and country, African-American soul, and Jamaican reggae. Radio was established in most parts of the continent by the 1920s, initially for a European listenership. During World War

FIGURE 1   In an informal setting in Chitungwiza, Zimbabwe, a youth plays a home-made guitar. Photo by Bror Karlsson.

II, the airwaves were used to broadcast to African audiences in the attempt to enlist material and moral support for the war effort. Shortly thereafter, in response to the demand for broadcast music, recording studios were established. These institutions became critical to the development of popular music, with competition between multinational companies and emerging local ones being a recurrent theme. By the 1930s, HMV, Odeon, Columbia, and Pathé-Marconi were distributing their products across Africa. Most foreign companies established subsidiaries in Africa, and the most advanced infrastructures were developed in Nigeria, Côte d'Ivoire, South Africa, Tanzania, Kenya, and Zimbabwe (Manuel 1988:89).

Most African music industries in the 1990s are extremely vulnerable to economic and political instability, and countries such as Nigeria and Tanzania, which once boasted thriving industries, are no longer significant producers of recorded music. Most industries are thwarted by the lack of vital resources, such as musical instruments, public-address systems, recording equipment, and capital to finance music production. Ineffective policing of copyright infringements and the rampant pirating of cassettes rob local industries of substantial income.

Local production of popular music formerly took the form of 45- and 78-RPM records. Albums were often released as compilations of national hits, and were produced in smaller numbers so as to be affordable to local buyers. The 1980s marked more or less the end of vinyl. Most local companies have invested in the high-speed C-60 cassette market, and cassettes now outsell records five to one. There is little evidence that the compact disc market will succeed in Africa apart from South Africa, since CD equipment is expensive, and CD technology is not yet considered hardy enough to withstand local conditions.

South Africa stands apart from the rest of the continent in that it boasts state-of-the-art recording technology with the potential to become the new center of production for African music. Started in 1914, when the Brothers MacKay, agents of His Master's Voice Company (based in London), began selling records from the back of ox-drawn wagons, the South African industry has developed into a multimillion-dol-

By the mid-1900s, gombay had gained mass appeal, and it had spread into other West African countries, where it became the basis for localized permutations, such as Ghanaian highlife.

lar industry, with transnational companies such as BMG and Sony operating out of Johannesburg alongside major local companies.

AFRICAN POPULAR MUSIC AND THE INTERNATIONAL MARKET

All African pop embodies creative interaction between foreign values and local styles. Popular music is therefore a site for adaptation, assimilation, eclecticism, appropriation, and experimentation. In light of the intensity of global communications (which have accelerated during the last century), stimulated by capital, conquest, migration, and technology, African pop has become a global phenomenon.

African pop is consumed internationally under the marketing tag of world music. World music is one of the largest growth areas in record stores in the UK and Europe. The term was coined about 1987 by small, independent, British labels (Hannibal, Sterns, World Circuit, and others) in response to growing interest in popular African and other non-European music and the lack of provision of dedicated space for such musics in record stores. The gap in the market was made more obvious with crossover ventures like Paul Simon's *Graceland* album, whose award-winning collaboration with South African musicians opened the way for major international labels to sign up groups such as Ladysmith Black Mambazo (Howard 1996:2).

The world-music movement has been fueled by an increasing interest in African music in the European, Asian, and American festival circuits. Perhaps the most important platform for launching popular African musicians has been the World of Music Arts and Dance (WOMAD) festival, conceived by the British rock musician Peter Gabriel in 1980. Now staged worldwide, these festivals aim to stimulate broad interest in the potential of global multiculturalism through concerts, workshops, and educational resources, and through the affiliated record label, Real World.

The term *world music* lacks definition. On the one hand, it may refer to musical diversity of the world, originating from all the world's regions and cultures. On the other hand, as a commercial label, it broadly refers to non-Western music, since mainstream rock and metal do not fall into its purview. In the context of world music, African pop is packaged as *traditional, authentic, roots* music, albeit a blend of local and international sources.

Images of tradition are partly created by the market to appeal to local tastes. For instance, some pop styles have been consciously traditionalized within African markets to reflect nationalist movements and symbolize cultural unity. Other African pop styles have deliberately maintained an indigenous sound through the use of traditional instruments (in an otherwise contemporary instrumental lineup) to appeal to Western audiences whose need for roots reflects their own sense of communal loss. The growing demand for "authentic" African music by the world-music market has profoundly affected the nature of the production of music, whose construction involves a complex trade in opportunity and exploitation, fantasy and imagination, style and recollection, appropriation, assimilation, and dispossession.

TRENDS IN THE MAJOR REGIONS OF AFRICA

The African popular-music market may be fraught with contradictions, but what remains uncontested is the energy and diversity of musical creativity in the continent. The following review is therefore only the tip of this iceberg, and further research remains to be done.

West Africa

West Africa hosts an immeasurable range of popular music. A comprehensive overview of the range of styles, with each one's own blend of local and external influences and fascinating social histories, regional permutations, and influences on diasporic musics, would require dedicated volumes. I feature those countries better known for their musical exports and therefore more likely to be accessible to foreign students. Since the major genres of certain countries (such as Nigeria) have been explored in detail in other articles in this volume, they are discussed only in passing.

Modern political boundaries in West Africa do not systematically reflect ethnic or linguistic groups. The *griot*, for instance, the itinerant poet-musician who remains the custodian of historical and cultural knowledge, dominates the making of music in Mali, Senegambia, Côte d'Ivoire, and Guinea Bissau. Today, the music, instrumentation, and vocal styles of the *griot* tradition provide the basis of much contemporary music from these countries, and are best illustrated in the music of Youssou N'Dour (Senegal), Salif Keita (Mali), Baaba Maal (Senegal), and Mory Kante (Guinea).

The fusion of musical influences occurred in West Africa long before the twentieth century. Coastal cultures experienced a long history of assimilation because of intercontinental trade. The prevalent pattern of West African popular styles is typically a blend of traditional sources with predominantly Cuban, African-American, and Congo-Zaïrean styles.

The first popular music of West Africa is believed to have developed in Freetown, Sierra Leone. Its style became known as *gome* or *gombay*, and is believed to have derived from the *gumbay*, a frame drum brought to Freetown by freed Jamaican slaves in the early 1900s. By the mid-1900s, this style had gained mass appeal, and it had spread into other West African countries, where it became the basis for localized permutations, such as Ghanaian highlife. Effectively, it represented the closing of a cycle of a musical idiom that emanated from Africa, developed in the New World, and returned to Africa (Collins 1989:221). Transatlantic feedback of this sort constitutes the substance of most African popular music, inspired by musical and political identification.

Côte d'Ivoire

Culturally, Côte d'Ivoire is a melting pot that has experienced significant domination by imported musics. Despite an attempt to establish an indigenous Ivorian popular style during the mid-1960s, the country has remained open to outside influences, such as Zaïrean *soukous*, Ghanaian highlife, and American soul. In addition, its music industry has attracted musicians from the entire west coast, establishing the city of Abidjan as a center for musical exchange (Wentz 1994:284).

Abidjan hosts an important biannual music industry trade fair, MASA (Marche des Arts et Spectacles Africains), and the sophistication of the city's industry is rivaled only by that of Johannesburg, in South Africa. Until 1995, MASA had been exclusively a marketplace and showcase for francophone African music, but its success has encouraged participation by other African countries. This fair has become an impor-

Salif Keita is undoubtedly one of the most talented and innovative musicians in the African pop world. Because he was a descendant of a noble family, his decision to become a professional musician was deeply scorned.

tant meeting ground for entertainment-oriented executives from all over the world, producing new possibilities for the growth of networks of performance and distribution, which until the mid-1990s reflected the colonial East-West continental divide.

Mali

Mali has a long regal history, associated with the ancient Mali kingdom of Mansa Musa. An ancient culture layered with influences of Islam and French colonialism, Mali boasts a rich cultural diversity. Though it has several ethnic groups marked by mutually unintelligible languages (Dogon, Peul, Manding, Songhai), the Mande-speaking peoples remain dominant. Manding culture retains the tradition of craft groups (castes) that have ritual responsibilities and professional obligations. Prominent among these is the caste of musicians, known locally as *jalolu* (sing. *jali*) and known abroad as *griots*.

When modern electric instruments were introduced in Mali, popular music developed in two directions: *jalis* provide the main source of inspiration to a cool, meditative genre of popular music, for which the gourd-resonated xylophone (*balafon*) remains the instrumental foundation. Second, guitar-based bands flourished in the capital, Bamako, and large groups such as the Rail Band and Les Ambassadeurs embraced a combination of modern urban pop with the harp-lute (*kora*), the gourd-resonated xylophone, and soaring Islamic vocals.

The women of Wassoulou

Mali stands apart from other West African countries in that a large proportion of Malian popular artists are women. Women play a particularly important role in the traditional making of music in the south, an area known as Wassoulou. Women of this area are nonhereditary musicians (unlike the *jalolu*), and their concerns focus on love, hunting, and the exploration of human goodness.

Wassoulou music is based on a pentatonic scale, and is characteristically accompanied by a six-stringed harp (*kamele ngoni*), a goblet-shaped drum (*djembe*), modern keyboards, and a double bass. Though some women of Wassoulou have been recording for more than a decade and have long been recognized in Mali (testimony to the vitality of the local cassette-recording industry), certain newcomers to the commercial scene, namely Oumou Sangare and Sali Sidibi, have become major attractions on the international performance circuit.

Salif Keita

Known as the golden voice of Africa, Salif Keita (b. 1949) is undoubtedly one of the most talented and innovative musicians in the African pop world (figure 2). His were not easy beginnings, however. He is a descendant of the most revered Malian ancestor, Soundiate Keita, founder of the Mandinka Empire in 1240. However, born an

albino, he was never fully accepted by his people. As a young adult, he sought solace in Islam and the soothing sounds of muezzins' calls to prayer, which awoke in him an intense interest in music. Because he was a descendant of a noble family, his decision to become a professional musician was deeply scorned. Though the traditional griot has an acquired status (albeit a low one), any band musician of the 1970s, despite the social importance of his or her function, was regarded as a vagabond and a drunkard. Undeterred, Keita moved to Bamako, the capital of Mali, where he joined the Rail Band, a state-sponsored big band, which performed a repertory that blended Cuban and Mandinka sounds.

Keita soon began to make a name for himself with his piercing, emotional vocals, which derived from a combination of muezzins' calls, Mandinka *griots'* vocals, and James Brown's style of singing. In 1973, Keita established his own group, Les Ambassadeurs, a twelve-piece band, with which he performed for five years before it moved to the capital of Côte d'Ivoire, where it became known as Les Ambassadeurs Internationaux. His move to Paris, in 1984, led him to a recording contract with Island Records' Mango label—-a deal that launched his international career on a monumental scale.

Senegal

Senegal is situated on the farthest point of West Africa, bordered by Mauritania to the north, Mali to the east, and Guinea and Guinea-Bissau to the south. Its capital, Dakar, has served as the center of francophone Africa for most of the twentieth century. The main languages spoken in Senegal are Wolof, Bambara, Tukulor, and Mandingo; most of them are also spoken in neighboring countries.

Precolonial music in Senegal, like that of Mali, was dominated by *griots*, whose mystical oratory and vocal styles provide the basis for contemporary Senegalese music known as *mbalax*, a Wolof word referring to percussion-based music. This genre highlights a combination of Cuban rhythms and *kora*-based traditional melodies, sung in high-pitched style. So influential was Cuban music in Senegal that only with independence from French colonial rule (in the 1970s) did local musicians begin to substitute traditional melodies and vernacular lyrics for Cuban covers sung in Spanish. To indigenize the music further, they reintroduced into the lineup the *kora*

The music of Congo-Zaïre has had the most widespread and lasting impact on commercial music in sub-Saharan Africa, and Kinshasa-Brazzaville, the twin capitals on the Congo River, have been the undisputed musical trendsetters.

and the gourd-resonated xylophone, and they added two drums, the *tama* (a small, "talking" drum) and the *sabar* (a congalike, upright drum).

It is undoubtedly the superstar Youssou N'Dour (b. 1959) who has placed *mbalax* on the international map. Though his initial performances were heavily influenced by Cuban styles and he began his career singing in Spanish, he was the first major Senegalese musician to draw on local styles, to sing in vernacular languages, and to reintroduce the *tama* into his rhythm section. His music is widely popular throughout West Africa, as shown in a review of a performance by N'Dour in Brikama, The Gambia:

> The place was packed. Couples danced the *pachanga*, the Cuban dance that Aragon and Johnny Pacheco made famous in Africa, and you could hear hundreds of feet shuffling across the cement floor as if one. Then, the *tama*, the little laced drum that 'talks', would play a short burst in counter rhythm, and something magical happened to the audience—-circles formed, people clapped to the rhythm, and dancers, abandoning their shoes and partners, stepped into the centre to do the Wolof dance the Gambians called *ndaga*; lots of swinging, suggestive hip, bottom, and leg movement. (Duran 1989:276)

Benin

Benin lies at a musical crossroads between West, Central, and North Africa, its soundscape colored by Cameroonian *makossa*, Congo-Zaïrean rumba, and North African Arabic *rai*. Formerly the Kingdom of Dahomey, and colonized by the French at the end of the 1800s, Benin is situated between Nigeria and Togo. Like most other African countries, it embraces a great many languages, cultures, and artistic traditions (Graham 1988:154). Dominated by the more commanding commercial musics of Ghana, Nigeria, and Senegal, it has not made much of an impact on the regional popular-music scene, but one Beninoise musician—Angelique Kidjo, the "queen of African crossover pop"—has won international acclaim.

Kidjo (b. 1960) grew up as an aficionado of the music of Earth, Wind, and Fire, Santana, *makossa*, rumba, and *rai*. It therefore comes as no surprise that the music she creates is highly eclectic. She made her musical debut as a jazz singer. Based in Paris since 1983, she has worked on many collaborations, such as Archie Shepp's 1988 *Mama Rosa* album. Her powerful voice and innovative compositions have moved through afrodisco to a style more closely linked to the sounds and sentiments of her home country. Her dynamism and vocal force often equate her with such divas as Grace Jones, Chaka Khan, and Tina Turner (Barlow and Eyre 1995:51).

Ghana

Ghana, the colonial "Gold Coast," is home to more than a hundred languages and countless musical styles. Rural music continues to play a central role in Ghanaians' lives, and it remains a rich source for urban electronic music. Ghana is best known for highlife, the British-derived entertainment style of dressing up and dancing—-living the "high life," to which the local elite aspired. The term was coined in Ghanaian coastal towns in the early 1920s. The genre, considered the national music, is regarded one of Africa's most popular, enduring, and potent forms of popular music (Graham 1994:288).

Highlife became popular primarily in anglophone West Africa (Sierra Leone, Liberia, Nigeria), and has evolved out of indigenous and Western influences. Over the decades, three distinct styles have emerged: dance-band highlife, developed by ballroom bands for the coastal Christian elite; *adaha* highlife, which grew out of colonial military-band music; and palm-wine highlife, a guitar-based style, associated with palm-wine bars frequented by "low-class" audiences. Highlife thrived from the 1930s through the 1960s, and records of it were distributed throughout the West African market. In Ghana in the 1970s, however, Nigerian Yoruba-based *jùjú* gained popularity [see YORUBA POPULAR MUSIC], as did the hundreds of disco bands in Ghana, and highlife experienced a decline in popularity. With the translocation of many of the prominent highlife artists to the recording centers of Europe and the subsequent development of the world-music market, the genre has experienced an international revival, regaining its position as one of West Africa's most influential popular styles.

Central and East Africa

While certain aspects of Congo-Zaïre rumba may be closely associated with West African highlife, the overwhelming influence of Zaïrean music on East African pop is irrefutable. The flow of ideas from Central Africa into the east was eased in Kenya by a thriving recording industry, which attracted artists from less fortunate countries and stimulated record sales throughout the region. In addition, a proliferation of Congo-Zaïre rumba bands in Kinshasa-Brazzaville forced artists to search for professional opportunities in neighboring states, particularly Kenya, Tanzania, and Uganda.

Central and East Africa are musically interconnected by the guitar, which Portuguese traders imported into Zaïre in the 1800s. During the early years of the twentieth century, the guitar made its way into Shaba, the southeastern mining district, where the Katanga style, best exemplified by Mwenda-Jean Bosco (b. 1930), was created. This style was characterized by a thumb-and-forefinger technique of plucking, to which was added a rhythmic timeline pattern struck by the blade of a knife on a bottle. For fuller effect, the mbira (*likembe, sanza*) and the accordion (*lindanda*) would occasionally be added. The style rapidly spread into Northern Rhodesia (Zambia), Southern Rhodesia (Zimbabwe), Nyasaland (Malawi), Tanganyika (Tanzania), Uganda, and Kenya, laying the foundation for much subsequent East African pop.

Congo-Zaïre and rumba

The music of Congo-Zaïre has had the most widespread and lasting impact on commercial music in sub-Saharan Africa, and Kinshasa-Brazzaville, the twin capitals on the Congo River, have been the undisputed musical trendsetters. Known variously as *soukous, kirikiri,* and *kwasakwasa,* the Zaïrean style is most widely known as rumba. It is lyrical and passionate, and comprises a simple musical formula that has inspired artists across the continent since the 1960s. It is slick, high-fashioned, and sophisticated, characterized by a flowing interplay of rhythm, guitar solo, and melodic structure, and accompanied by soft lyrics, sung in French and Lingala. Its most defining trait is its multilayered guitar riffs, which roll relentlessly above a strict bass-drum rhythm section. In essence, rumba is the quintessential mass-marketed music in Africa, aimed to appeal to the broadest public possible by transcending differences of language, class, gender, and age (Ewens 1991:126).

In the 1970s, a new generation of rumba musicians appeared on the scene with a bold and streamlined rendering known as *soukous.*

With the introduction of the gramophone in the 1920s, African-American and Caribbean music—-mainly the Dominican merengue and the Cuban salsa and *son*—found their way into local styles. Significant influences also came from Christian hymnody, with its characteristic harmonic constructions based on parallel thirds, and from military bands, which stimulated an interest in brass and winds (Ewens 1991:130). However, the real origins of rumba are disputed, and composers do not consider African rumba a derivative of Latin music. On the contrary, they believe that Cuban popular music was developed by African slaves sent to Cuba, and conclude that rumba is profoundly African:

> Many people think they hear a Latin sound in our music. Maybe they are thinking of the horns. Yet the horns are only playing vocal parts in our singing style. The melody follows the tonality of Lingala, the guitar parts are African and so is the rumba rhythm. (Luambo Mikiadi Franco, quoted in Ewens 1991:131)

During World War II, Radio Congo Belge was established, providing an important promotional outlet for local music. After the war, recording studios were established in Kinshasa by Greek settlers who recognized the commercial potential of local music. This period marked the *belle époque* of rumba. The first commercial bands to become publicly acclaimed (in the 1950s and 1960s) were brass-heavy big bands: OK Success, African Jazz, African Fiesta, Les Bantous, and Congo Success. OK Success later moved to Zimbabwe, where for years it remained a resident performing group.

The singer-composer Joseph "Le Grand Kalle" Kabasele (d. 1983) is considered the founding father of Congo-Zaïre rumba. He and his definitive band, African Jazz, attracted a following beyond the borders of Congo-Zaïre. He was succeeded by guitar genius Luambo Makiadi Franco (1938–1989) and his T. P. O. K. Jazz. Franco, one of the most widely known and loved postwar artists, was called the grand master of rumba, the Balzac of Zaïrean music, and the godfather of African music. He was such a prolific composer that at the time of his death, he claimed to have recorded more than a thousand songs, spanning a period of forty years and ranging in technology from 78-RPM recordings to digitally recorded compact discs (Ewens 1994:37).

In the 1970s, a new generation of rumba musicians appeared on the scene with a bold and streamlined rendering known as *soukous.* Led by the intrepid group, Zaiko Langa Langa, this music mingled indigenous sounds with the forceful pop attitudes of the 1960s. Perhaps the most favored among those who emerged on the new international scene was Papa Wemba. What distinguished him from many hundreds of other groups was his ability to merge slick Western production techniques with traditional expression. Wemba also became a high-profile leader of *sapeur* fashion, a scene that has become inextricably linked with Zaïrean music. *Sapeurs* (the Society of Ambienceurs and Persons of Elegance) characteristically dress in a style reminiscent of 1950s Paris fashion and eighteenth-century dandyism: pleated pants, slick jackets buttoned to the neck, pointed shoes, and carefully coiffed hair. Wemba established

FIGURE 3   Papa Wemba performs at MEGA Music, Johannesburg, 1996. Photo by Peter McKenzie.

his own fashion trend based on three-quarter-length trousers, colonial pith helmets, leather suits, and eight stylish ways of walking (Ewens 1991:148) (figure 3).

The women of rumba

Though the role of women in popular music in Congo-Zaïre has been limited, the establishment of recording studios in Kinshasa afforded women the opportunity to record from as early as the 1950s. More often than not, however, women were recruited simply to adorn male orchestras.

In the 1970s Abeti Masikini became the first female artist to lead her own band, Les Redoutables. One of her protégés, Mbilia Bel, began her career as a dancer with this band. She was subsequently recruited by Tabu Ley Rochereau (b. 1940), a popular rumba artist who had once featured in Franco's T. P. O. K. Success, and with whom she performed in the only male-female duo on the continent at the time. In the 1990s, she separated from Ley, and subsequently achieved the status of first female superstar of Zaïre. She was closely followed by the much admired M'pongo Love (1956–1990), who became known as *la voix la plus limpide du Zaïre* 'the clearest voice of Zaïre'. Love achieved international renown in the early 1980s, when she moved to Paris and recorded with some of the best West African musicians of the time. She was a role model for young female artists, most notably Tshala Mwana and the post-punk-styled Deyess Mukangi. While Mbilia Bel, M'pongo Love, Tshala Mwana, and Deyess Mukangi are somewhat out of the mainstream of Zaïrean rumba (which has always been dominated by male artists), their marginality has enabled them to experiment more freely with new ideas, and thus to contribute toward the development of the genre.

Though Lingala and French are the dominant languages of Congo-Zaïre, Kiswahili (spoken in eastern Zaïre) links the central region and Kenya, the Indian Ocean Islands, Tanzania, Uganda, Malawi, Zambia, southern Sudan, and northern Mozambique. Kiswahili is a lingua franca that identifies several different cultural groups and constitutes possibly the most widely established surviving culture in Africa (Ewens 1991:158). Swahili is an extremely old culture, which owes much to its

One of Tanzania's most enduring musicians is Remmy Ongala. With his newly formed group, Orchestra Super Matimila, he has become Tanzania's most important musical export.

roots in Arabic and Indian Ocean cultures. It is largely Islamic, though not all Kiswahili-speakers are Muslims. The historical capital of Swahili culture is the tiny island of Lamu, off the Kenyan coast, but Dar-es-Salaam and Zanzibar (in modern-day Tanzania) and Mombasa (in Kenya) have also served as historically important centers.

The manufacture and distribution of music

In East Africa, the manufacture and distribution of music has a long history. Nairobi has always been the hub of the East African music industry (Paterson 1994:337). The first recordings in Kenya were made in 1902, shortly after the establishment of British colonial rule. Much trade in East Africa was conducted by Asian merchants, and by the 1920s, 78-RPM recordings served to attract consumers into their shops. The market potential for African music was soon recognized, and by 1928, musicians were being sent to Bombay to record for the Indian Branch of the British HMV label. The first genre of music recorded was *taarab*, the music of Zanzibar, and records of performances of *taarab* were distributed throughout Kenya, Tanzania, Zaïre, and Uganda. By the 1940s, non-Islamic popular music began to flourish, and styles generically called *dansi* began to be performed in all dialects. One of the first interethnic styles to emerge was *beni*, associated with British marching bands from the Great War (1914–1918). Brass instruments were imitated on calabash kazoos, played to intricately designed processional choreographies. The genre spread to Tanzania (where it became known as *mganda*), Malawi (*malipenga*), and Zambia (*kalela*) (Ranger 1975:x). Today, beni continues to be performed in modified forms in Malawi, northern Mozambique, and Zimbabwe.

World War II was a definitive period in the evolution of popular music in East Africa. Many Africans were recruited into the British forces, serving in Ethiopia, India, and Burma. Some coastal musicians were drafted into the Entertainment Corps, where they collaborated with musicians from other East African countries. At the end of the war (1945), the Entertainment Corps continued to operate commercially as the Rhino Band. During the war, the establishment of the East African Broadcasting Corporation enhanced the subsequent distribution of Kenyan pop, and in response to the demand for radio music, recording studios proliferated in Nairobi in the 1950s.

Kenya

The ex-guitarist for the Rhino Band, Fundi Konde, emerged during the 1950s as a leader of a "new generation" of guitarists, further developing the style of plucking originated by guitarists from Katanga, Zaïre. Most Kenyan guitarists formed duos or small guitar-based bands. They sang in two-part harmonies to simple percussion accompaniment on maracas, woodblocks, a tambourine, and a struck bottle. In the 1960s, the simple acoustic-guitar style began to lose ground to more complex electric-guitar music, which incorporated newly introduced genres, like South African *kwela* and Congo-Zaïre rumba.

The 1970s were a period of transition in Kenyan music. While many dance bands preoccupied themselves with Congo-Zaïre covers, African-American soul, and international pop, a new style, called *benga*, began to emerge. Developed in the western regions among the Luo people, *benga* has come to be seen as the definitive Kenyan pop, played by most musicians regardless of language or regional identification. Probably the best exponent of the genre is D. O. Misiani (b. 1940) and his Shirati Jazz, whose style is characterized by soft, flowing two-part harmonies and a hard, pulsating rhythm section.

Tanzania

Much of Kenya's Swahili pop is rooted in the Tanzanian styles of the 1970s. Dar-es-Salaam has always been alive with music and competition between groups is fierce (Graebner 1989:247). The success of a band depends largely on the topicality of the lyrics of its songs and the force of its *mtindo*, the dance-and-fashion trademark it devises to attract a following.

One of Tanzania's most enduring musicians is Remmy Ongala. Born into a musical family in eastern Zaïre, he moved to Dar-es-Salaam in 1964 to join his uncle's band, Orchestra Makassy. In 1981, when Makassy disbanded, he joined Orchestra Matimila. His outgoing personality and challenging lyrics developed mass appeal, and with his newly formed group, Orchestra Super Matimila, he has become Tanzania's most important musical export.

Zanzibar and taarab

Off the Tanzanian coast, the "spice island" of Zanzibar has for millennia served as a focus of trade. In 1832, it came under the formal control of the Sultan of Oman; in 1890, it became a British protectorate; and in 1963, British rule was overthrown in a revolution conducted by socialists from the mainland. In 1964, Zanzibar joined Tanganyika to form the Republic of Tanzania. The island is a dynamic multicultural mix of African, Asian, and Arab influences, and the music that best expresses local people's identity is *taarab*.

Taarab originated on the island of Lamu, the ancient capital of Swahili culture. The genre is culturally linked to the Arabian Gulf and Asia, and is closely related to the Egyptian *firqah* orchestra, the precursor of modern Egyptian film music, prominent in the 1930s and 1940s. Latter-day *taarab* is strongly influenced by Indian film music. *Taarab* dances derive from Arabic styles and exhibit strong aspects of inland African dances and *ngoma* rhythms (see below).

Taarab (an Arabic word meaning 'joy, pleasure, delight') is an inextricable part of everyday life of the coastal Swahili peoples. *Taarab* is lyric poetry sung in Swahili and performed most notably at lavish weddings. The most famous of all Swahili musicians was the *taarab* singer Siti bint Saad, the first East African to be recorded in the Bombay HMV studios, in 1928.

In the 1950s, full-sized *taarab* orchestras were common in Stonetown, the capital of Zanzibar, and a typical orchestra would comprise ten singers, a short-necked plucked lute (*oud*), a tambourine (*rika*), an obliquely blown flute (*nai*), an Arabic goblet drum (*dumbah*, also called *dumbak*), an electric guitar, an organ (keyboard), an accordion, a cello, a double bass, and a variety of percussion instruments and drums. Today, violas, violins, and cellos occasionally join the lineup.

The emergence of women's *taarab* clubs is significant. Since it is women who organize weddings (the main context for *taarab*), women play an important part in determining the nature of musical performance. Poetry, music, and aesthetics from

Instruments were reinvented to suit new systems of tuning and arrangements of sound required by the emerging styles of South African popular music, which were rough and experimental and accompanied by vibrant dances.

other exclusively female African performative styles were incorporated into *taarab*, and women's groups became harshly competitive. While instrumental performance and musical composition remain the creative sphere of men, lyrics have become the expressive domain of women. Less concerned with issues of love and happiness (which dominated earlier *taarab* wedding songs), women's poetry today can be hard-hitting, addressing topical arguments and moral concerns. In a society governed by strict Islamic codes of gender separation, *taarab* has become a powerful medium of expression for women (Topp-Fargion 1993:133).

Southern Africa

Southern Africa comprises twelve countries, connected regionally by a cooperative forum known as the Southern African Development Community (SADC). Though historically interdependent, the region is characterized by vast economic disparities and cultural differences. The Republic of South Africa has the most advanced economy of the entire continent; Mozambique, however, is by some measures the poorest country in the world. SADC tries to formalize alliances between countries and to manage the regional distribution of resources. Regional cooperation has extended into the area of culture, and the first SADC Music Festival was held in October 1995:

> ZIMBABWEANS SOON TO RELISH IN REGIONAL RHYTHMS!
> Zimbabweans, prepare yourselves for a spectacular musical feast! The first-ever SADC Music Festival, which will be held between September 29–October 8, is an invitation to all those wishing to dance their way into summer, to do so to the sweet beats of the African sub-continent.
>
> *Marrabenta, taarab, kalindula, zamrap, maskanda, langarm, chimurenga, afroma* and *afrojazz* are but a sample of the musical smorgasbord which will be dished up by musicians from the 11 participating SADC states. From the Harare Sheraton Conference Centre, the Seven Arts auditorium, Rufaro stadium and three day-time stages at the Harare Gardens, there will permeate diverse musical flavours: some spicey and specific, some stirred, blended and remixed.
>
> The festival will be a musical voyage of discovery through the SADC region. Beginning at the southern-most tip of South Africa with the Malay and Khoisan-inspired Cape jazz sounds of master flute and saxman, Robbie Jansen, we then meander through South Africa to the sounds of Zulu guitars and concertinas and the pan-African melodies of the internationally acclaimed group, Bayete. We hear the gourd-bows, accordions and powerful vocal ensembles resounding from the mountain kingdoms of Swaziland and Lesotho. We travel northwest into Namibia to discover the Afrikaans-based *langarm* dance music of Peter Joseph !Augab and cross the desert into Angola to the beat of Brazilian-inspired tropical dance band, Os Zimbos. We move east into Botswana to the heavenly voices of the 60-strong Kgalemang Tumediso Motsete choir, and into Zambia to rave to *zamrap* with

Daddy Zemus, and rumba to *kalindula*, the urban guitar music of the northwestern provinces. In Malawi we discover, amongst others, the Makazi Band, a lakeside jazz band whose instruments are entirely made from tins, bottles and animal skins.

Violins, accordions and the sweet sounds of *dumbak, tabla* and *rika* percussion drift our way, *taarab*-style, from the Islamic Swahili spice island of Zanzibar. We hear the earthy call of gourd-heavy *timbila* xylophones emanating from the northern regions of Mozambique and pass through the vibrant *marrabenta* rhythms of Ghorwane in late-night Maputo. We finally arrive home to the ancestral call of *mbira dzavadzimu* performed by a mixed ensemble of master musicians, and settle into the *jit* and *jive* of Zimbabwe's very own Simon Chimbetu and Orchestra Dendera. (South African Development Community 1995)

This section reviews the popular music of South Africa, Zimbabwe, Angola, and Mozambique. Though a member of SADC, Tanzania is more closely affiliated with East Africa with regard to cultural, linguistic and religious practices, and is therefore featured under the Central and East African subsection.

The SADC region has a long history of interregional trade, which has inspired mass migration and has influenced linguistic and cultural interaction. Since the beginning of the twentieth century, however, the movement of people has been largely the result of domination by British, Dutch, Portuguese, and German interests, and of the development of a system of migrant labor in South Africa, Zimbabwe, and Zambia. The gathering of diverse people has resulted in new forms of cultural blending. Semiurban and urban styles of music have emerged out of a creative fusion of traditional musical structures and rhythms, and have fused with elements from Western trends.

South Africa

South Africa has the oldest and most sophisticated music industry in southern Africa [see POPULAR MUSIC IN SOUTH AFRICA]. Because of the magnitude of its infrastructure (which includes external networks for broadcasting, promotion, and distribution), South African music has had the farthest-reaching stylistic impact on regional pop. The economic backbone of South Africa rests on the mass migration of laborers to the mines, around which most of the present-day cities have sprung up. The music and culture that emerged from the ferment of colonial occupation, dispossession, and industrialization count among the most resilient examples of African urban expressive culture (Erlmann 1991:1).

One of the earliest urban settlements in Johannesburg was Sophiatown, which from the 1920s to the 1940s was inhabited by people of all racial, religious, and cultural backgrounds. It was overpopulated and squalid, known for its dangerous gangs, illegal bars (shebeens), and cultural energy. Shebeens were established in slum-dwellers' backyards. They were typically run by women, whose only source of income was the sale of home-brewed beer and prostitution. Enterprising "shebeen queens" would attract clients by providing live music. The entertainers who provided this music came from different musical backgrounds, reflecting the ethnic and regional diversity of the community. They came from various parts of South Africa, and from as far afield as Malawi, Zimbabwe, Mozambique, and Zambia.

Music was performed on an assortment of Western instruments: pedal organs, guitars, banjos, concertinas, pennywhistles, and violins (imported by German traders during the early 1900s). These instruments joined traditional African gourd-resonated bows, hand-held rattles, and drums homemade from paraffin tins, animal hide, and pieces of scrap metal. Instruments were reinvented to suit new systems of tuning and arrangements of sound required by the emerging styles, which were rough and experimental and accompanied by vibrant dances.

The album *Graceland* initially provoked international outrage. However, the record-breaking success of the album worked in favor of South African musicians, and helped to return them to the international limelight.

Fundamental to much of the musical mix was the influence of African-American jazz, introduced into South Africa by transnational record-distribution networks in the 1920s. Most South African jazz musicians could not read scores, so they developed their own jazz flavor, mixing American swing with African melodies. The dynamic blend of African-American structure and African style became the basis for early South African township jazz, known as *marabi*.

Most of the musical forms that emerged in the ghettos survived only through live performance, since it was not until the 1940s that the state-controlled radio and local white-owned record companies began to recognize their marketability. For instance, *kwela* (pennywhistle jive) was a genre performed in the 1950s by young boys on street corners. When local record companies recognized its commercial potential, recordings rapidly led performers such as Spokes Mashiyane off the streets and to the top of the charts. However, when Mashiyane transferred to saxophone, pennywhistle *kwela* was rapidly thereafter transformed into an urbane, brassy sound. This jive idiom became the most popular recorded black genre of its day, and was called by the newly coined term *mbaqanga* (Allingham 1994:378).

Mbaqanga thrived in the 1960s with the introduction of the electric guitar, and a new female vocal style, based on close five-part harmonies, was conceived. Occasionally, the women, called *simanjemanje*, would be fronted by a male "groaner," whose deep vocal style would contrast with that of a soft female chorus. Simon "Mahlathini" Nkabinde is an acclaimed groaner, and his accompanying *simanjemanje* group, the Mahotella Queens, have become one of the most internationally celebrated South African bands of the 1990s (Allingham 1994:380) (figure 4).

Bars and clubs became gathering places for black professionals in the 1950s. These were the spaces where jazz, and the culture of jazz, became linked with the struggle against apartheid. It was the era when many of the great South African jazz musicians—Miriam Makeba, Hugh Masekela, Abdullah Ibrahim—made their debuts. Increasingly repressive race laws of the 1950s and 1960s led many jazz musicians into exile with the political activists of the day, and the music, like the political movement with which it was associated, effectively went underground. It was not until the late 1980s that South African jazz began to experience a revival, which once again was associated with mass political action. Following the country's first fully democratic elections (in 1994), many exiled jazz musicians have returned to South Africa.

The mid-1980s witnessed two landmark musical collaborations that assisted in the relaunching of South African music on the international scene after long years of cultural isolation. Johnny Clegg (b. 1953), a white South African, joined forces with Sipho Mchunu, master of Zulu guitar-based music (*maskanda*), to form the innovative duo called Juluka. The traditional Zulu structure of their compositions, their inclusion of instruments associated with traditional and neotraditional Zulu music (including the mouth-resonated bow, *nqangala*, and the concertina), combined with

FIGURE 4   Mahlathini and the Mahotella Queens at the Johannesburg International Arts Alive Festival. Photo by Motlhalefi Mahlabe, 1993.

the integration of lyrics in English and Zulu, presented South African audiences with a dynamic new collaborative musical concept. In 1985, the duo disbanded, and Clegg formed a second group, Savuka, which has developed broad international appeal.

In 1986, Warner Brothers released the LP album *Graceland*, a musical collaboration between Paul Simon and various South African artists. This release initially provoked international outrage, and Simon was accused of appropriating South African music to serve his own musical and commercial ends; however, the record-breaking success of the album worked in favor of South African musicians, and helped to return them to the international limelight. After years of isolation, the recognition accorded to groups such as the male a cappella group Ladysmith Black Mambazo gave a major boost to South African music, which subsequently became valued worldwide (Meintjes 1990:40).

In the 1980s, a slick, highly produced, synthesized dance music known as bubblegum was popularized, principally by Yvonne Chaka Chaka and Brenda Fassie (b. 1964). Bubblegum has short melodic phrases sung in call-and-response patterns, programmed electronic drumming propelled by a disco beat, and mass youth appeal. While Chaka Chaka's popularity throughout the African continent is based on well-crafted melodies and socially responsible lyrics, Fassie's allure is her outrageously bad-girl image, not unlike that of Madonna. Brenda, dubbed South Africa's first lady of pop, has been grappling with excesses of her untamed spirit, and has recently turned to gospel, a genre that enjoys a major following throughout the country.

The South African cultural calendar is marked by several festivals involving music. The Standard Bank Grahamstown Arts Festival, held in July, is the largest and most securely established festival in the country. Vast and various, its program profiles the best performances and exhibitions selected from the previous year. Its offshoot, a fringe festival unfunded by the main festival, highlights more experimental, street-oriented, cutting-edge explorations from less mainstream creative quarters. The Johannesburg International Arts Alive Festival, established in 1992 and staged annually in September, encourages experimental interchanges between international and local artists, and nurtures an interest in the arts of the African continent and the diaspora. In the mid-1990s, the Karoo Festival, a cutting-edge Afrikaans-language festival, gained mass public appeal.

Thomas Mapfumo, the dreadlocked "Lion of
Zimbabwe" and Zimbabwe's most famous musician,
is credited with bringing the electric *mbira* to its
maturation.

Zimbabwe

Zimbabwe has a small, though tenacious, music industry. Its recording infrastructure
has long attracted musicians from Malawi, Zambia, Zaïre, Mozambique, Botswana,
and even Namibia, and many of them have settled in its capital, Harare, to perform
on the club circuit there.

As in South Africa, Zimbabwean music reflects its political past in dramatic
ways. Colonized by the British in 1890, Zimbabwe fell under the authoritarian
charge of British colonial rule with its program of Christian nationalism and separate
development. Christian choirs and traditional music were first recorded in the 1930s
by a one-track mobile recording facility of the government-controlled broadcasting
station. Commercial music production followed in the 1950s with the establishment
of white-owned record companies that operated as subsidiaries to South African
companies, and on whose marketing decisions they depended entirely. The record
companies were responsible for the distribution of recorded Anglo-American and
South African music in Zimbabwe and for establishing a touring circuit of South
African artists throughout the region.

Imported music inspired Zimbabwean musicians to form their own groups,
which, until the mid-1970s, were largely preoccupied with performing covers of
pieces in the repertories of jazz, soul, blues, rock, and *mbaqanga.* Zaïrean rumba also
made a notable impact on Zimbabwean music. A major transition in the popular
music of Zimbabwe took place during the war of liberation (1967–1980), when folk
songs were used to politicize rural people. These songs, known as *chimurenga* 'songs
of liberation' were based on ancient melodies and instrumental structures derived
from the music of the *mbira dzavadzimu* [see MUSIC OF THE SHONA OF ZIMBABWE].
In the mid-1970s to appeal to the tastes of urban nightclubs and bars, popular musicians began to adapt *mbira* melodies to a lineup of an electric bass, two guitars (lead
and rhythm), and drums. Electronic *chimurenga* rapidly became the most popular
musical genre of Zimbabwe, and it was equated with a new Zimbabwean cultural
identity.

Thomas Mapfumo (b. 1945), the dreadlocked "Lion of Zimbabwe" and
Zimbabwe's most famous musician, is credited with bringing the electric *mbira* to its
maturation. Initially venturing into a combination of traditional rhythms, characteristic Shona yodeling (*mahonyera*), and non- Zimbabwean features like reggae, he has
subsequently reincorporated *mbira* and hand-held rattles (*hosho*) into his lineup,
establishing a rootsier, more traditional, sound.

Mapfumo is by no means the only important *chimurenga* musician in
Zimbabwe. Oliver M'tukudzi (b. 1952) is well loved for his *chimurenga*-rumba-
mbaqanga music and for his morally charged lyrics. Comrade Chinx, one of the leading conductors of exiled *chimurenga* choirs during the war years, has subsequently
moved into synthesizer *chimurenga* with messages of love and reconciliation. In addition, Robson Banda, Simon Chimbetu, Leonard Dembo, Jonah Moyo, and Devera

Ngwenya combine elements of *chimurenga* with high-energy, rippling Zimbabwean rumba, as did the late James Chimombe (d. 1990).

Women set the ball of jazz rolling

Women have played a significant role in the Zimbabwean music industry; however, unlike South African women (whose careers in music have been inspired by role models such as Miriam Makeba), Zimbabwean women still battle to overcome prejudices regarding their place on the stage. Despite these prejudices, women have been actively engaged in Zimbabwean commercial music since the 1930s, either as backing singers or, as in the case of the Gay Gaieties and the Yellow Blues, as members of all-female groups. During the early years of the production of commercial music in Zimbabwe, women enjoyed public acclaim, as is expressed in this review of Lina Mattaka, reputed to be the first woman of the Zimbabwean stage:

> The era of Makwaya [choirs] came to an end and Lina was again to be seen pioneering in Tap-dance. For half a decade, tap-dance was chic, it really dominated the musical strata just to be replaced by Jazz in the late forties and who was to seen at the forefront? None other than Lina Mattaka and those other women who had followed in her footsteps. To this day, and more than any other woman alive, Lina tramped the thorny African musical Hi-Way. She toured and brought the message of stage emancipation of the African woman. (*African Daily News*, 1 February 1958, quoted in Impey 1992:82)

New trends

In the 1960s, a new trend, *simanjemanje,* emerged in South Africa. This was a term used to describe a style, something new. The music associated with *simanjemanje* was electric guitar-based *mbaqanga*, and was characterized by a male singer who fronted a troupe of women. Its rapid rhythms and synchronized styles of dancing stimulated the formation of similar female troupes throughout southern Africa. Many Zimbabwean women imitated these raunchy groups, such as the Mahotella Queens, provoking moral condemnation of women in popular music—a sentiment that continues.

Though *mbira dzavadzimu* is usually considered a men's instrument, some highly skilled women play it. Best known in Europe is Stella Chiweshe (b. 1946), the so-called queen of mbira, who combines sacred and commercial music while retaining the mystique of her instrument. Beauler Dyoko (b. 1945) of Zimbabwe (figure 5), originally from Mozambique, is another mbira player whose inspired compositions have come to be recognized in recent years. As she reveals in a brief autobiography, she received from the spirit of her father the metaphysical guarantee that enabled her to play the instrument:

> The time started about this mbira music, I started getting sick. I went to the doctors, to the hospital. They said, "I can't see anything wrong." But I was fainting, fainting for nothing! I went to the hospital and they say, "She is not sick." They said, "It is for the Africans. She must go to a herbalist."
>
> My mother, she was confused again. "I don't want to go to the *n'angas*!" She didn't want to hear about the herbalist or *n'angas*. She didn't want. She is a Catholic. Now she says that if you go to *n'angas*, they tell lies!
>
> Now it was sore, my body, my stomach, my legs, my head, my chest, all over, here. And then I said, "Mummy, well let me go then."
>
> I went with them [to the *n'angas*]. We were told, "Your child, she's got *mudzimu* [ancestral calling]."
>
> Now she [mother] says, "she's got *mudzimu*?" To her, these people [women], they don't possessed. "The brothers are here, why don't they go to the brothers? The *n'angas*, they just told me that she's sick about ancestors."

Like many African popular genres that have adopted strong Caribbean or African-American qualities, Angolan popular music has a strong Latin presence, largely because of a long history of transatlantic cultural exchange.

FIGURE 5   Beauler Dyoko in Chitungwiza, Zimbabwe. Photo by Bror Karlsson.

Now it started worrying me now, dreaming playing mbira, singing, dancing, dancing mbira. In the morning, I get up. "Mummy, I dream singing, playing mbira."

She says, "Playing mbira? Your father [who died when Beauler was an infant], he was playing mbira music. But how can it come to you?"

I say, "I don't know! But the music, it was so nice! I wasn't feeling sore in my body the time I was dreaming this thing."

She says, "Ah, I don't believe it, these things."

We stayed again. I was getting more sick, getting thin. The ancestors, they were punishing me! They were punishing me that I must agree. I mustn't refuse them. My mother says, "Okay, what must I do? I can do what the *n'anga* told me. They say that if you refuse, she'll die." That's the thing she didn't want to hear to the *n'angas.*

And then she brewed beer and had a *bira* [ceremony for the ancestors]. You feel funny, like a person whose getting mad, if you possessed [with the spirit of an ancestor]. My father, he says that time, "I'm here. I came for my job. She must play mbira, what I was doing. She must do what I was doing."

You know, when that spirit it will come to you, then you speak how he was speaking. Now he [father's spirit] was speaking Chichikunda from Mozambique. Now this mbira also in Mozambique, they play, but different made. They call it *njari*. Now from here they say, "I can't give those from Mozambique. People in Zimbabwe, the MaShonas, I must teach *dzavadzimu.*"

So my mother, she went, go and buy mbira. It was only five dollars. They were so cheap that time! I took that mbira. I put it under my bed, near to my head, that side. I started playing song, "*Nhemamusasa*." I get up in the morning. I told mummy that I dreamed playing this song. She says, "You joking! Playing these big wires? Do you think this is for you? It is for the man. They say if womens plays this, they don't cook good food!" You don't cook good food because you keep on thinking about playing mbira.

And I say, "It's not my fault, mummy. It's worrying me!"

I start again: "Let me try." I went, go and sit under the peach tree near the shed; put my mat there, sit down. Started just doing like that. Find it's same, the song I was singing in that dream. It was so nice! Even mummy, she wanted also that song. (Impey 1992)

Angola and Mozambique

Documentation of popular music from Angola and Mozambique is limited because of extreme poverty and widespread warfare, shortage of media facilities and recording infrastructures, and, under Portuguese rule, decades of political and cultural subversion and isolation.

Angola

The Angolan war of liberation from Portuguese rule occurred from 1960 to 1975. The achievement of national political independence soon led to an internecine civil war, which kept Angolans from forming a local recording industry; however, this is not to say that Angolan popular music has not developed and thrived.

Like many African popular genres that have adopted strong Caribbean or African-American qualities, Angolan popular music has a strong Latin presence, largely because of a long history of transatlantic cultural exchange. Angola provided a rich recruiting ground for the deportation of slaves to Brazil and Cuba in the 1600s and 1700s, and with the expatriation of substantial numbers of people, musical knowledge crossed the ocean. One particular Angolan instrument, a gourd-resonated bow (*mbulumbumba*) is recognized in Brazil today as the *berimbau* (Kubik 1975–1976:98).

Angolan music embraces a range of musical cultures. Before 1900, to quell internal rebellions, Portuguese colonizers used Brazilian soldiers, who brought to Angola the steamy percussive sounds that had originated in Africa. More recently, Angola hosted several thousand Cuban soldiers, whose tastes permeated modern Angolan music. Further, Angola shares a long-standing affinity with Zaïre, its neighbor to the east, exhibiting strong rumba roots.

Angola is too poor to support a competitive recording industry. Most local musicians cannot afford instruments, and few venues are adequately equipped to host major performers. Since 1975, the Ministry of Culture has monopolized most of the production of commercial music in the country. To revive the music industry, it has sponsored folklore-oriented groups and urban dance bands. It founded a national orchestra, Semba Tropical, to showcase some of the country's top artists, including the singer Kuenda Bonga. Likewise, Sensacional Maringa da Angola (a fifteen-piece merengue band) and Os Zimbos (who frequently join forces with a folklore-oriented group, Kituxe e os Acompanhantes) perform a powerful combination of merengue, rumba, and rural Angolan styles.

Mozambique

Like Angola, Mozambique is still suffering the devastation of war. Independent from Portuguese rule since 1975, Mozambique subsequently suffered a debilitating civil war, from which it has barely begun to recover. As in Angola, widespread poverty and trauma of the war did little to impede the quality, passion, and potency of Mozambican popular music (figure 6).

FIGURE 6   The lead dancer of the Mozambican national dance company addresses Mozambican refugees in Zimbabwe. Photo by Angela Impey, 1992.

Musicians, music companies, and governments in Africa are beginning to challenge the dominance of Europe and the United States in producing and promoting African pop.

Mozambique is a large, elongated country, which embraces many different languages. Each of several areas displays a unique tradition of music and dance. Possibly the best known Mozambican music is that of the BaChopi xylophone orchestra (*timbila*) [see SOUTHERN AFRICA]. Mozambican music is profoundly influenced by its history of coastal trade with Arabs from the Indian Ocean and the Portuguese—trade that dates back to the 1500s. In addition, its proximity to South Africa and the inclusion of many thousands of Mozambican men as migrant laborers in its mines and cities have resulted in the infiltration of South African urban styles into much Mozambican pop.

The popular style best known in Mozambique is *marrabenta*, best described as topical music. It developed in the 1950s in the suburban slums of Maputo (the city known as Lorenço Marques under Portuguese rule), where it communicated issues of the day and provided a revolutionary voice for oppressed people. It was performed on three guitars made from olive-oil tins or petrol canisters, and danced in a sexually suggestive style, modeled on rock of the 1950s and 1960s. Its basis is an indigenous rhythm known as *majika*, modified to incorporate new influences: ska, soul, rumba, reggae and Brazilian percussion.

Two Mozambican bands that became popular in the world-music market in the 1980s are Ghorwane, a large and highly impressive group (which uses a lineup of the usual three guitars, trumpet, sax, and percussion), and Eyuphoro, a spicy group from Ilha de Mozambique, a Swahili-speaking island off the northeast coast of Mozambique.

INTRA-AFRICAN CONNECTIONS

Much of this article has been concerned with the translocation of styles and influences, both intercontinentally and within Africa. The flow of styles between subregions has reflected trade, colonial commercial and broadcasting networks, and the migration of labor. Many of these exchanges have been determined by exogenous relationships of power, money, media, and ideology; however, since the late 1980s, a more concerted strategy to develop a viable internal live music and distributional circuit has begun to take root.

The existence of developed arts circuits and associated funding of the arts in the West has eased live performance of African music, and small recording labels and studios have stimulated the generation of musical products, but few benefits from the Western production and promotional infrastructure for African music extend to the continent itself. Though a market for cassettes thrives within Africa, most of these products do not appear in markets outside the continent. Music from Zambia, for instance, whose cassette culture produces a sizeable annual turnover of *zamrap*, *kalindula*, and *zamrock*, is little known outside of the country because of a severely under-resourced industrial infrastructure. A style such as *afroma*, pop music from Malawi, has emerged despite a severe shortage of resources, to the extent that much Malawian

FIGURE 7   South African musician Pops Mahommed plays a kora obtained from master Senegambian players during their tour in southern Africa. Photo by Peter McKenzie.

pop is performed on homemade instruments. However, musicians, music companies, and governments in Africa are beginning to challenge the dominance of Europe and the United States in producing and promoting African pop.

The importance of festivals

Music festivals in Africa have become important sites for the promotion and exchange of local musics. The SADC Music Festival (Zimbabwe) and MASA (Côte d'Ivoire) formalize more recent attempts to facilitate intra-African exchanges. In South Africa, Steve Gordon of Making Music Productions (Cape Town), through his Reconnection Project, is engaged in forging musical links within the continent by promoting performances by major West and Central African artists.

Highly acclaimed musicians such as Youssou N'Dour are testing the dominance of European production centers by building state-of-the-art recording studios in their home countries, thus assisting in the development of an infrastructure of local production and stimulating local talent. Similarly, musicians from various African regions are increasingly utilizing the sophisticated recording technology in South Africa, thus supporting emerging African centers of production over the established monopolies of Paris and London.

In the late 1990s, West African megastars such as Salif Keita have performed in South Africa, Botswana, Namibia, and Zimbabwe, forging links for the first time with the southern region of the continent. Their successes have encouraged southern African musicians to blend West African musical elements into new and experimental pan-African idioms. Important intra-African crossovers also include the intercultural exchange of musical instruments (figure 7).

REFERENCES

Allingham, Robert. 1994. *Township Jive: From Pennywhistle to Bubblegum: The Music of South Africa.* N.p.

Barlow, Sean, and Banning Eyre. 1995. *Afropop! An Illustrated Guide to Contemporary African Music.* Edison, N.J.: Chartwell Books.

Broughton, Simon, Mark Ellingham, David Muddyman, and Richard Trillo, eds. 1994. *World Music: The Rough Guide.* London: Rough Guides.

Collins, John. 1989. "The Early History of West African Highlife Music." *Popular Music* 8(3):221–230.

Duran, Lucy. 1989. "Key to N'Dour: Roots of the Senegalese Star." *Popular Music* 8(3):275–284.

Erlmann, Veit. 1991. *African Stars: Studies in Black South African Performance.* Chicago: University of Chicago Press.

Ewens, Graeme. 1991. *Africa Oye! A Celebration of African Music.* London: Sango Publications.

———. 1994. "Franco File." *Folk Roots* 136 (October):36–37.

Graebner, Werner. 1989. "Whose Music? The Songs of Remmy Ongala and Orchestra Super Matimila." *Popular Music* 8(3):243–258.

Graham, Ronnie. 1988. *The Da Capo Guide to Contemporary African Music.* New York: Da Capo Press.

———. 1994. "Gold Coast: Highlife and Roots Rhythms of Ghana." In *World Music: The Rough Guide*, ed. Simon Broughton, Mark Ellingham, David Muddyman, and Richard Trillo, 287–293. London: Rough Guides.

Howard, Keith. 1996. "Cultural Fusion." *Gramophone: World Music Supplement.* April:2.

Impey, Angela. 1992. "They Want Us with Salt and Onions: Women in the Zimbabwean Music Industry." Ph.D. dissertation, Indiana University.

Kubik, Gerhard. 1975–1976. "Musical Bows in South-Western Angola 1965." *African Music* 5(4):98–104.

Manuel, Peter. 1988. *Popular Musics in the Non-Western World.* London and New York: Oxford University Press.

Martin, Phyllis, and Patrick O'Meara, eds. 1995. *Africa*, 3rd ed. Bloomington: Indiana University Press.

Meintjes, Louise. 1990. "Paul Simon's Graceland, South Africa, and the Mediation of Musical Meaning." *Ethnomusicology* 34(1):37–73.

Paterson, Doug. 1994. "Until Morning: The Life and Times of Kenyan Pop." In *World Music: The Rough Guide*, ed. Simon Broughton, Mark Ellingham, David Muddyman, and Richard Trillo, 337–348. London: Rough Guides.

Ranger, Terence O. 1975. *Dance and Society in Eastern Africa 1890–1970: The Beni Ngoma.* Berkeley: University of California Press.

South African Development Community (SADC). 1995. Press release for first SADC Music Festival (October).

Topp-Fargion, Janet. 1993. "The Role of Women in Taarab in Zanzibar: An Historical Examination of a Process of 'Africanisation.'" *Proceedings from the Eleventh Symposium on Ethnomusicology, Durban, South Africa*, 130–134. Grahamston, South Africa: International Library of African Music.

Wentz, Brooke. 1994. "Ivory Towers: The Abidjan Recording Industry." In *World Music: The Rough Guide*, ed. Simon Broughton, Mark Ellingham, David Muddyman, and Richard Trillo, 284–286. London: Rough Guides.

WOMAD International Tour Book. 1991. Corsham, Wilts.: WOMAD Communications.

Part 3
Regional Case Studies

The regions of Africa—north, west, central, east, and south—reflect the great diversity that is a hallmark of the continent's cultural traditions. Representative studies of each region's musics give us insights into the factors that contribute to such variety. At the same time, we see those elements and processes that cross regional boundaries and create a distinctly "African" musical flavor.

Ngombi (eight-stringed harp) of the Faŋ played by André Mvome, priest of the Aŋgɔm-Ibɔʏa religious group at Oyem, Gabon, 1970. Photo by Gerhard Kubik.

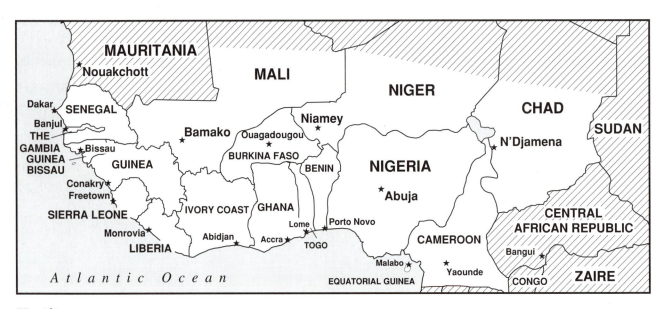

West Africa

West Africa

West Africa most clearly exhibits the polyrhythmic, multiple layered aspects of music in Africa. With a wide variety of musical instruments, performances here reflect the heritage of cultural interchange with North African traditions, especially in the savannas and deserts. It is in the west also that several of the early kingdoms and nation-states of Africa developed.

West Africa: An Introduction
Jacqueline Cogdell DjeDje

The Savanna
The Forest

The music of West Africa includes musical traditions from many different societies, but scholars regard this area as a homogeneous unit. To emphasize the point, they represent it with the music of a specific ethnic group, or a stylistic feature unique to one society. Their generalizations sometimes overshadow distinctions that may exist between different groups. Unity exists, particularly within certain regions, but there is much diversity.

Of the general studies of West African music, the most numerous are overviews and investigations of instruments and styles, primarily focusing on rhythm. Other studied topics are performers, the impact of African culture on the music of African Americans, the impact of Western music on African music, the development of contemporary genres, and relationships between Arab and African music (for sources on these subjects, see Gray 1991:61–67, 249–250). In the treatment of the material, overviews have used a similar approach. Themes or topics central to the musical culture of the area usually serve as the basis for discussion (as in Eno Belinga 1972 and Nketia 1971). Excepting a few publications (like Alberts 1950), scholarly works rarely include enough ethnographic and music material to give readers a thorough understanding of the area as a whole.

The geographical area of West Africa extends roughly from 5 degrees to 17 degrees north latitude, and from 17 degrees west to 15 degrees east longitude. It includes all or portions of Senegal, The Gambia, Guinea, Guinea Bissau, Mali, Burkina Faso, Niger, Nigeria, Benin, Togo, Ghana, Côte d'Ivoire (Ivory Coast), Liberia, and Sierra Leone.

The environment, which varies from forest in the south to grasslands and desert in the north, has dramatically affected history and culture in the area. The Sahel savanna (a region of low rainfall and short grasses, located directly south of the desert and north of the Guinea savanna) has been an area of significant population movement and political development. The invention of agriculture in Africa occurred among the Manding people, who live in the western part of the savanna belt of West Africa, around the headwaters of the Niger River (Murdock 1959:64–65). Much of the Guinea savanna (an area directly north of the forest) is sparsely populated, but some of the most densely settled areas are in the forest belt, which migrant groups settled from the north, displacing or absorbing indigenous peoples (Mabogunje 1976:5).

The languages of peoples that inhabit West Africa belong to three families: Niger-Congo, Songhai, and Chad (Greenberg 1970). As a result of differences in environment and culture, West Africa divides into two geographical regions: savanna and forest.

THE SAVANNA

Several groups in the savanna have played a large role in the history of West Africa, for some have established empires and nation-states. Most have felt influence from North Africa, and have to some degree adopted Islam. Many are agriculturalists, and several participate in cattle herding and trade. A few exploit industries in textiles and leatherworks. The social organization of many West African societies follows a stratified system, similar to that of the Wolof, which includes "a landed aristocracy, a hereditary military class, members of craft guilds, free peasants, hereditary house servants, and slaves" (Mabogunje 1976:19).

The musical culture of societies in the savanna displays much uniformity, particularly in social organization, role and status of musicians, types of instruments, and styles of performance. Despite the history of interaction, important differences among groups require a regional division into three clusters: the Western Sudanic, the Central Sudanic, and the Voltaic.

The Western Sudanic cluster

This region is the setting for many ethnic groups that have influenced the cultures of West Africa. Several of them (Soninke, Mandinka, Bambara) speak languages of the Mande subfamily of the Niger-Congo family. By the eleventh century, the Mandinka (Manding, Malinke, Mandingo, Maninka) had organized a small state, Mali. In the 1200s, the Mali Empire dominated most of West Africa—from the edge of the tropical forest in the south, to Senegal in the northwest and Aïr in the northeast. It went into decline in the 1400s, and by the late 1900s, Manding speakers had dispersed widely—into Mali, Guinea, Guinea Bissau, Senegal, The Gambia, and parts of Burkina Faso, Côte d'Ivoire, Sierra Leone, and Liberia.

To the west of the Mandinka are the Tukulor, the Ful6e (also Fulo, Fula, Foulah, Ful6é, Foulbe, Peul, Pullo, Pulo, Fulani, Fellani, Filani, Fellata), the Wolof, the Serer, and the Jola (Diola), collectively called Senegambians. Their language belongs to the West Atlantic subfamily of the Niger-Congo family. They live in Senegal, The Gambia, Guinea, Guinea Bissau, and Mali; and related peoples have migrated to Sierra Leone and Liberia.

Throughout the savanna region of West Africa from Senegal to Cameroon, the Ful6e are in the minority. They live among more populous groups, such as the Soninke, the Mandinka, the Bambara, the Hausa, and the Mossi. They came from the middle Senegal area, and are the product of an intermixture between the Tukulor and Berbers. Beginning in the 1100s and continuing into the 1800s, they spread eastward and southward across the savanna. Few accepted Islam, and most who were Muslims tolerated other religious beliefs. Their sedentary kinsmen—better educated, more sophisticated in political matters, less tolerant of non-Muslims—turned to military aggression in the form of a jihad to attain political dominance (Mabogunje 1976:26–27).

Because of migrations throughout West Africa, terms for the Ful6e are varied. Among groups in the Western Sudanic cluster, they are often called Ful6e (a Mande term); in the Central Sudanic and Voltaic clusters, they are called Ful6eni (a Hausa term). Other groups in West Africa call them as follows: Fellata, by the Karuri and

dyeli Also *griot*, in French; a professional musician among the Manding of Mali who usually belongs to a specific caste

kora Harp-lute of the Manding with nineteen or twenty-one strings; accompanies singing of praise or historical songs

xalam Also *halam* or *khalam*; five-stringed plucked lute of the Wolof

konting Mandinka five-stringed plucked lute found in The Gambia

bolon Large, arched harp, with three or four strings, of the Manding and Ful6e; has historical associations with war

nyanyuru One-stringed bowed lute of the Ful6e and Tukulor

diassare Five-stringed plucked lute in Senegal

others in the Chad Basin; Peul (a Wolof term), by the French; Ful6e, by the Germans; and Fellah by Arabs of the West Sudanic cluster. Many refer to themselves as Ful6e (sing. Pullo), and their language is Fulfulde (Stenning 1960:140, 1965:323).

The Wolof are a fusion of elements of diverse origins (Serer, Mande, Ful6e). Their ancestors occupied the southern area of current Mauritania, where they cohabited with the Ful6e. In the 1300s, the Wolof developed their Jolof states. By 1450, fiefs of their kingdom extended from the Senegal River to the Gambia River (Boulegue and Suret-Canale 1985:503–505).

The social organization of musicians within this cluster is similar. In each ethnic group, professional musicians or full-time specialists bear specific titles. Among the Manding of Mali, a professional musician is a *dyeli*, and among the Maninka of Guinea and the Mandinka of The Gambia, such a person is a *jali* (pl. *jalolu*). Originally, there was one Manding family (the Kuyate) of musicians; but over time, other families (such as Jobaté, Suso, Kanute, Sacko) have chosen the profession (Duran et al. 1987:235). The Wolof and Ful6e of The Gambia and Senegal call a musician *gewel* and *gawlo* (pl. *awlu'be*), respectively. Because members of the various cultures regard them as socially and ethnically distinct, they usually belong to a specific caste. Most craftsmen and artisans among the Ful6e are not pure Ful6e (*rim'be*, plural of *dimo*), but belong to one of the castes, generalized as *nyeeny(u)'be* (sing. *nyeenyo*). Three of these groups are musicians: *maabu'be* (sing. *maabo*), also weavers; *wammbaa'be* (sing. *bammbaa'do*); and *awlu'be*. The *wammbaa'be* have the longest and closest association with the Ful6e, and the others are of Sarakolle (Soninke), Mandinka, or Wolof origin. In the Ful6e context, the French term *griot* denotes singers in any of these categories (Arnott 1980:24).

Professional musicians' patterns of marriage vary, and this variance affects recruitment, training, function, and patronage. Those who belong to an endogamous family are born into the profession, and at a young age receive training from their kin. One generation teaches the repertory orally to the next. A musician's family adheres to a specific patron (a royal person, an important official, a particular occupational group). People expect musicians to know details about the history and genealogy of their patrons, sing praises in their honor, serve as custodians of the repertory, and act as advisers and confidants. Women are known primarily as singers, particularly among the Manding, where they excel as performers of historical songs and praise songs. Freelance musicians not attached to a patron or institution receive training through apprenticeship with an established musician. There is no specific age or time for a freelance musician's schooling; it begins when an individual expresses the desire to gain the skills necessary for that profession (DjeDje 1982).

In precolonial times, musicians relied on patrons for their livelihood, their housing, and their status. With the breakdown in the social structure of traditional society during the colonial period, both the role of the professional musician and the patronage system changed. No longer do musicians depend on the patronage of certain individuals. To some degree, political leaders provide subsistence because of the services that professional musicians can provide them, but most musicians must hunt for patrons. Begging is far more common. Since it interferes with listeners' appreciation for the music, people avoid musicians, and disdain their profession (Duran et al. 1987:235).

Nonprofessional musicians stand in the shadow of professionals, from whom their social role differs little. Manding drumming requires much training and skill. Musicians study with established artists before they feel capable of performing at activities. Those who perform for hunters enjoy similar patronage.

Musical instruments

Similarities in the Western Sudanic cluster are most apparent in material culture. Noteworthy is the variety of stringed instruments. Bowed and plucked lutes follow North African models, but harp-lutes and arched harps are indigenous to the region. The one-string bowed lute or fiddle (*nyanyuru, nyaanyooru, nyanyaur, gnagnour*) is associated primarily with Fulɓe and Tukulor cultures. As a result of Fulɓe interaction and migration throughout West Africa, other groups have adopted or referred to the instrument. Terms for the bowed lute usually derive from a word that describes the action of rubbing one string across another—in Senegal and The Gambia, Wolof *riti,* Fulɓe *nyanyuru,* and Mandinka *susaa*; in Sierra Leone, Temne *gbulu,* Limba *kuliktu,* and Mandingo *kalani.* The distinguishing feature of all fiddles within this cluster is the placement of the resonating hole on the gourd or body of the instrument, rather than on the membrane.

The plucked lute is common to most groups in the cluster. Excepting the *molo* of Senegal (constructed with one string), lutes have three to five strings. The shape (oval, circular, hourglass) and type of material (gourd or wood) used for the resonator vary. The Mandinka plucked lute—*konting* or *kontingo* (with five strings) in The Gambia, and *koni* (four strings) among the Maninka in Guinea—is similar to the Soninke *gambaré* (four strings), the Bambara *nkoni* (four strings), the Fulɓe *hoddu* (three to five strings), and the Wolof *xalam* or *halam* or *khalam* (five strings). Among the Fulɓe of Futa Djallon, the *kerona* (two to nine strings) is more common (Coolen 1984:124). In Senegal, the five-stringed plucked lute has a variety of names: *diassare, bappe, ndere*; most groups use it to accompany solo singing of praise songs. Some Manding use the *molo* for divination (Coolen 1984:123).

The harp-lute, *kora* (*soron* among the Maninka of Guinea), is distinctive to the Manding. An instrument at court, it has nineteen or twenty-one strings. Men play it to accompany women's and men's singing of historical songs and praise songs. Mandinka musicians for the hunter's society in Mali use another harp-lute, the *nkoni,* with six to nine strings.

Among the Manding, the large arched harp with three or four strings (*bolon* or *bolombato*) has historical associations with war. The Fulɓe use a similarly constructed instrument (also known as *bolon*). Smaller, the Manding six- or seven-stringed arched harp (*simbing* or *simbingo*) serves for the hunter's society. Occasionally, the Jola of The Gambia use it to accompany men's choral singing. The multiple bow-lute (pluriarc), mouthbow, and groundbow are other chordophones of this cluster.

The flute is the most characteristic wind instrument of the Fulɓe, particularly herdsmen (figure 1). It has a variety of names: *serndu* (transverse flute, The Gambia), *chorumbal* or *tiorumba* (Fulɓe, The Gambia), *tambing* (Fulɓe, Guinea). Flutes and horns serve without restrictions of caste in Manding culture in Mali; they appear particularly in chiefs' orchestras (Dalby 1980:575). Among the Maninka of Guinea, several wind instruments (bullroarers, mirlitons, whistles, horns, voice disguisers) served in the *komo* (a secret society) before Islam began suppressing it (Rouget 1980b:821).

FIGURE I   A Fulɓe musician in The Gambia plays a transverse flute (*serndu*).

Emphasis is on solo singing, with one or more instruments in accompaniment. A high-pitched, tense quality is common in both women's and men's voices.

A variety of membranophones occurs, but scholars have done little detailed research on drums in the Western Sudanic cluster. Since drumming rarely has associations with professional musicians, the drummer's musical role is less obvious. Historical accounts suggest the drum was a more common *jali*'s instrument in the past (Knight 1984:67). All groups in the cluster use the double-headed hourglass tension drum (*tama*), first noted in North Africa during the 1300s (King 1980a:309). Other types of membranophones include the cylindrical-shaped (double-headed), the conical-shaped, the bowl-shaped, the barrel-shaped, and the goblet-shaped. Drummers play them with their hands, or with sticks in sets of three, or in combination with other instrumental types in an ensemble. Drums serve a variety of functions: ritual, recreational, laudatory, and ceremonial.

Both melodic and rhythmic idiophones occur in this cluster. The *bala, balo,* or *balafon* (xylophone), an instrument also used by the *jali*, is distinctive among the Manding. In Sierra Leone, other Manding-speakers—Susu, Mandingo, Yalunka, Koranko—call the xylophone *balangi* (Oven 1980:302). The number of keys varies from fifteen to nineteen. The *lala, laala, laalawal,* or *laalagal* (a sistrum, with small pieces of round circular gourds threaded on a stick) and the *horde* (a hemispherical gourd calabash, held against the chest, and struck with finger rings) are common among the Ful6e. All groups use bells, metal scrapers, gourd rattles, slit drums, and water drums. Instruments associated with women include bells (*né* among the Mandinka of The Gambia), gourd rattles, and calabash water drums.

Musical styles

The stylistic features of music among different ethnic groups in the Western Sudanic cluster are similar. Emphasis is on solo singing, with one or more instruments in accompaniment. A high-pitched, tense quality is common in both women's and men's voices. Most songs consist of a soloist's long, rapid declamatory phrases. The melody is melismatic with much ornamentation, and when melodic instruments accompany singing, monophony or heterophony results. If solo singing has a vocal accompaniment, the response is dronelike: a short melodic or rhythmic phrase repeats variously.

The type of instrument used in performance determines the musical scale. The Maninka of Guinea tune xylophones to an equitonal heptatonic scale, but tune the *kora* to a nonequitonal heptatonic scale. Ful6e music, particularly that performed on the one-stringed fiddle, has a pentatonic scale. Wolof drumming is energetic, with complex polyrhythmic combinations of instruments.

People perform music for a variety of occasions. In precolonial times, a highly important context was for royalty. The traditional political structure has broken down, but musicians still perform for important officials and other patrons, singing historical and genealogy praise songs. Music also highlights festive occasions, work, seasonal events, religious rites, wrestling matches, and events of the life cycle—births,

weddings, and puberty rites. Exceptions occur with the use of music during Muslim holidays. Wolof drums accent a variety of occasions, but not funerals or Muslim holidays; only the *halam* serves the latter. For other groups, all types of music and instruments serve during the celebration of Muslim holidays, but not in the mosque.

The Central Sudanic cluster

Groups in this cluster include the Songhai, the Djerma, the Dendi, the Hausa, the Fulani, the Kanuri, the Jukun, and the Tiv. Most live in Nigeria, Niger, Mali, and Burkina Faso; some inhabit scattered locations in Benin, Togo, and Ghana.

The Songhai began to dominate large parts of Sudanic Africa during the 1200s, and the Songhai Empire reached its apogee in the early 1500s. It extended from close to the Atlantic in the west to include most of the Hausa states of northern Nigeria in the east. Like their neighbors to the west, the Songhai have felt influence from North Africa. Their language belongs to the Songhai family.

The Hausa were probably not a homogeneous ethnic group. The word *Hausa* had linguistic significance for betokening peoples for whom Hausa was a mother tongue. The Hausa language belongs to the Chad family. Many scholars believe Islam entered the area from Mali in the 1300s, but the religion may have arrived earlier, from the Kanuri of the Bornu Empire. For a while, the Hausa lived within the Songhai Empire, though they also paid tribute to the king of Bornu. Early in the 1800s, the Fulani conquered them and organized their territory into emirates (Mabogunje 1976:20–21).

Because of continuing contacts, much uniformity exists in the music of peoples of the Central Sudanic cluster. Influence from North Africa is most apparent in ceremonial music and types of instruments. Musical relationships between the Hausa and the Fulani are complex. The Hausa have adopted Fulani elements, and the Fulani have adopted Hausa elements, plus those of other local groups. Though the Songhai and Fulani conquered the Hausa (a conquest that resulted in the adoption of musical traditions from both), Hausa music dominates the Central Sudanic cluster with influences that extend to central and southwest Nigeria, the Guinea coast, and Voltaic peoples (King 1980a:309). Cultural contacts between the Hausa and the Kanuri suggest the Kanuri may have introduced North African musical prototypes into Hausa culture. Since no extensive investigation has been done on the music of Bornu, there is no way of knowing the extent the Kanuri may have influenced groups in the Central Sudanic cluster.

Similarities exist in the music of groups in the Western Sudanic and Central Sudanic clusters because of historical links, but several features distinguish the music of the two clusters. As in the Western Sudanic cluster, professionalism is central to the musical culture of Central Sudanic groups. Most musicians are full-time specialists and urbanites. Professional musicians belong to a distinct social class, but the distinctions between musicians and others may not be as rigid as in Western Sudanic areas. Musicians do not take the name of their family: they specialize in vocal or instrumental music, and use a specific term to identify that specialization. Any person who concentrates on acclaiming another is a *marok'i* (pl. *marok'a*), and a professional male singer and/or composer is known as a *mawak'i* (pl. *mawak'a*). *Maka'di* (pl. *maka'da*) is the generic term for players of membranophones, chordophones, and idiophones, but *mai busa* (pl. *masu busa*) denotes performers on aerophones (for other terms, see Ames and King 1971). Female performers bear names that differentiate them from men. A woman specializing in celebratory ululating is a *magu'da* (pl. *magu'diya*), but a professional female singer is a *zabiya* (pl. *zabiyoyi*). A female who acclaims is a *marok'iya* (pl. *marok'a*). Since groups in this cluster did not experience a major dismantling of their traditional social structure as a result of colonial policies,

goge   One-stringed bowed lute of the Hausa

kuntigi   One-stringed plucked lute among the Hausa

kalangu   Double-membrane hourglass tension drum of the Hausa; associated with butchers and recreation

horde   Hemispherical gourd calabash of the Fulani that is held against the chest and struck with finger rings

káakáakii   Long metal trumpet of the hausa used in ceremonial music

tambari   Large Hausa kettledrum with a resonator of wood; symbol of royalty

patronage in the Central Sudanic cluster has not felt such radical changes as in the Western Sudanic cluster.

Scholars have classified Hausa professional musicians in several ways. Ames (1973:257–268) uses five categories: musicians of occupational classes, musicians in political life, musicians of recreational music, musician-entertainers, and musicians for the *bori* spirit possession religion. King (1980a:311) uses four: ceremonial musicians, court musicians, freelance musicians, and classical praise singers. For most musicians, recruitment is hereditary; musicians permanently attach themselves to certain individuals and organizations, and their status depends on that of their patrons. Among such groups, there also exists a hierarchical structure with one person as the chief of musicians. Because of the ceremonial musicians' association with traditional power, their social status is high; other types of musicians in the society have lower status. Some performers become musicians through achievement, though they may serve a single patron. Praise singers compete intensely for the patronage of officeholders within the traditional government (King 1980a:311). Composers are valued for originality; only ceremonial musicians and musicians who play for spirit possession ceremonies are not judged on this basis. The training of professional musicians is formal, with either kinfolk or an established artist.

Musical instruments

Differences in the types of instruments are clear in the Western and Central Sudanic clusters, most obviously with prototypes based on North African models (like bowed and plucked lutes, and certain types of drums). Within the Central Sudanic cluster, similar terms serve for the one-stringed bowed lute (*goge*, *goje*, and *gogeru* among the Hausa, Songhai, and Fulani, respectively), and the resonating hole of the instrument is on the membrane, rather than on the resonator. The only exception in terminology appears among the Hausa, who call a smaller version a *kukuma* (DjeDje 1980). Fiddles in the Central Sudanic cluster have associations with spirit possession, entertainment, praise, and politics; but no evidence suggests a religious function for the bowed lute in the Western Sudanic cluster.

Plucked lutes in the Central Sudanic cluster have from one to three strings; lutes with more than three strings, used prominently in the Western Sudanic cluster, do not occur in the Central Sudanic cluster. There are terminological similarities between the clusters, but terms relate to different instruments. Both the Ful6e and the Wolof use the term *molo* for the one-stringed plucked lute; in Hausa and Songhai culture, the *molo* (Hausa) or *moolo* (Songhai) has two or three strings. The one-stringed plucked lute among the Hausa and Songhai is a *kuntigi* or a *kuntiji*, respectively. Ancestors of the two-stringed plucked lute, known as *gurmi* (hemispherical calabash) and *garaya* (oval wood) among the Hausa, date back to the 1300s in the Western Sudanic cluster (Coolen 1984:120; Gourlay 1976:327; Besmer

1983:53–54). That groups in the Central Sudanic cluster use no chordophones but plucked and bowed lutes suggests stringed instruments entered the area from outside.

Little detailed research has been done on membranophones in the Western Sudanic cluster, so it is difficult to be conclusive about similarities and differences between the two clusters. All groups in both clusters prominently use the double-membrane hourglass tension drum (Hausa *jauje, kalangu,* and *'dan kar'bi;* Songhai *doodo*). Constructed in a variety of sizes, the instrument has different functions. The Hausa reserve the *jauje* for royalty. They associate the *kalangu* and *'dan kar'bi* with butchers and recreation, though in some areas court musicians use them. Whether the single-membrane hourglass tension drum (Fulani *kootsoo,* Hausa *kotso*) has as wide a distribution as that of the double-membrane prototype is unknown. The Hausa associate the *kotso* with royalty, and regard it as a Fulani instrument (Arnott 1980:24).

Common to the Fulani and groups in the Central Sudanic cluster is the percussion vessel (Fulani *horde,* Hausa *kwarya,* Songhai *gaasay*), a hemispherical gourd, placed against the chest and beaten (with or without finger rings), or placed on the ground and beaten with sticks, hands, or fingers (with or without rings). In both clusters, this instrument usually serves in combination with others to accompany the one-string bowed lute.

Though differences exist in the construction and function of certain instruments, similarities in the types of instruments of the Western and Central Sudanic clusters suggest they entered the Central Sudanic cluster from outside, probably with the Fulani, whose movements had much to do with the spread of lutes (Coolen 1984:121). If the influence had come directly from the Manding, other instruments unique to the Manding—especially xylophones and harps—might have come too. Because instruments common to the Songhai and the Hausa do not occur in the Western Sudanic cluster, the influence cannot have come from the Songhai.

Other instruments based on North African models entered the area through interaction with the Songhai or the Kanuri. The long metal trumpet (*kàakàakii*), used in Hausa ceremonial music, is probably only one of several musical relics of Songhai dominance (Surugue 1980:523; Gourlay 1982:53). This trumpet and an oboe (*algaita*) were "most probably used first in the Bornu empire and subsequently spread to Hausaland" (Erlmann 1983:25). The Hausa *tambari* (large kettledrum), with resonator made of wood, may be a copy of the silver and copper drum the Songhai buried for safety during the Moorish invasions in the 1500s (Harris 1932:106). A symbol of royalty, the *tambari* relates in material form and ceremonial usage to the court at Fez around 1500 (King 1980a:309). Borrowings went both ways. The *shantu,* a percussion tube used by Hausa women, occurs in North Africa as a result of trade in female slaves. The Kanuri *ganga* (double-headed cylindrical drum), and the Hausa and Songhai instrument of the same name, are North African borrowings from West Africa (Hause 1948:23).

Membranophones and idiophones are the most numerous instruments in the cluster. In addition to those discussed above, other single-headed and double-headed drums are bowl-shaped, cylindrical-shaped, goblet-shaped, and circular frame drums. Idiophones include rattles, lamellophones, bells, tube vessels, sistra, clappers, and waterdrums. For personal enjoyment, Fulani cattle herders play end-blown flutes and lamellophones; the latter instruments (Songhai *bamboro,* Hausa *bambaro,* Fulani *bomboro*) are common to most groups in the area.

A variety of wind instruments occurs in Hausaland, including a flute (*sarewa*), a horn (*k'aho*), and several types of pipes (*bututu, damalgo, farai, til'boro*) constructed from guinea corn, wood, and reed. The Songhai use the *dilliara,* a clarinet.

Besides iron bells, rattles, flutes, and vertical drums, the only instrument indige-

In Hausa society, the emir (as traditional head and successor to the king) controls the occasions for the performance of state ceremonial music.

nous to people in central Nigeria is the idiochord raft zither (King 1980b:241–242); the use of the frame xylophone is a result of influence from forest belt groups.

Musical contexts

Professional specializations in Hausa culture involve ceremonial music, court praise song, general praise song, entertainment music, music associated with spirits, and vocal acclamation (King 1980a:309–312). State ceremonial music (*rok'on fada*), court praise (*yabon sarakai*), and rural folk music or popular music stem from nineteenth-century practice. Ceremonial music, probably the most esteemed form of music in Hausa society, is the symbol of traditional power. Two types of praise songs exist: urban classical and popular. Professional musicians who serve a single patron perform urban classical traditions of the past; the music has set stylistic and textual character-istics. Freelance musicians, who may have many patrons, perform popular music of a more recent origin. It rivals court praise song because it appeals to the same audience, and is similar to praise song in the artistry of its leading exponents. The instruments used in popular music—*kalangu, goge, kukuma, kuntigi*—distinguish it from court praise, as does musicians' freedom to praise and ridicule anyone, including rulers.

In Hausa society, the emir (as traditional head and successor to the king) con-trols the occasions for the performance of state ceremonial music. Ceremonial music thus occurs mostly during *sara*, a weekly statement of authority on every Thursday outside the emir's palace; Babbar Salla or K'aramar Salla, religious festivals at which the emir rides in procession to and from the mosque; *nad'in sarauta*, the installation of the emir and his officials; the emir's departure and return from a journey; visits from other emirs or important people; and weddings and births within the emir's family. The performance of court praise songs occurs at similar occasions, and when-ever there is a gathering.

Excepting *bori*, Hausa music and dance have no associations with religion. Music other than the call to prayer is rarely heard in the mosque or during Islamic ritual. *Bori*, a pre-Islamic religion, makes much use of music, which communicates with spirits during the possession ceremony. Freelance musicians perform popular music in all contexts: at work, for entertainment at beer bars and nightclubs, for events of the life cycle, or at any gathering.

Songhai music divides into two types: secular and religious. Secular music includes solo, choral, and instrumental music performed at wrestling matches and dances. While solo songs by men and women accompany work, songs by children and adolescents occur in games and riddles. Songs by adolescents occur during courtship. Choral songs (male, female, mixed voices) may have no accompaniment, or the accompaniment of the *kuntiji*. Texts treat historical events, politics, legends, fables, satire, or praise. Religious music known as *follay*, performed for a hierarchy of divinities, shows links with Hausa *bori*. Each spirit corresponds to a natural force (sky, rain, thunder, earth, river, rainbow), called by special melodies and rhythms.

Also like *bori*, the one-stringed fiddle (*goje*) and calabash gourds (*gaasay*) serve in performances of *follay*.

As court musicians, Fulani performers primarily sing the praises of chiefs and other wealthy patrons. They refer to genealogies, and cite the exploits of ancestors. Some musicians attach themselves to specific patrons, but others travel from one chief's court to another. Besides songs performed for the court, Muslim Fulani enjoy *gime* (sing. *yimre*), poems on religious themes and secular topics, composed in Fulfulde (language of the Fulfulde and the Fulani) since about 1800. The earliest came from Futa Djallon in Guinea and Sokoto in Nigeria. They are sung in private or in small gatherings for the pleasure and edification of the singer or his friends, and on special religious occasions; they have also become a specialty of blind beggars (Arnott 1980:24–25). Secular adaptations of religious poems have begun to appear in performances by nonprofessionals.

Fulani professional drummers have a specialized role in accompanying children's dance songs, and in performing at traditional castigation contests (*soro*, Hausa *sharo*). The latter are a test of manhood; drummers sing the praises of the young men taking part, and provide the instrumental music that helps build up morale and tension (Arnott 1980:24).

Song types performed by Fulani herdsmen resemble those of groups with whom they come in contact, including work songs (like women's pounding songs), lullabies, love songs, herdsmen's songs (in praise of cattle, sung while the cattle are grazing), children's dance songs, and songs associated with traditional dances (*ruume, yake, geerewol*) for young men and girls (Arnott 1980:24–25).

Musical style

In vocal style and melody, music of the Central Sudanic cluster does not differ much from that of the Western Sudanic cluster. Men and women use a tense vocal style, and the melody is usually melismatic with ornamentation. The structure of song forms depends on the text and language, and because Hausa is a tonal and quantitative language, the meaning of texts depends on syllabic pitch and length. Instruments imitate speech. Hausa vocal and instrumental music, melodically and sometimes rhythmically, depends on syllabic tones and quantities. The text is sung or vocally declaimed, or performed nonverbally by instruments. Instrumental music is predominantly for drums or strings with rhythmic accompaniment by an idiophone. In nonprofessional music, the text dominates in the reading and recitation of poems and incantations, and in the calling of praises. Songs are freer, though somewhat dependent on verbal patterns, chants, and acclamations.

The Voltaic cluster

Ethnic groups in the Voltaic cluster have not built empires comparable to those of their neighbors. As a result, the Voltaic cluster consists, not of a few homogeneous nations, but of many culturally distinct groups (Murdock 1959:78)—a fact reflected in the diversity of local music traditions. Throughout the cluster, the impact of Islam and Christianity is slight, though adoption of Islam is increasing among certain groups. Most Voltaic peoples are agriculturalists, and all their languages belong to the Voltaic-Gur subfamily of the Niger-Congo family.

Dispersed within Burkina Faso, Mali, and the northern regions of Côte d'Ivoire, Ghana, Togo, and Benin, the Voltaic cluster further divides into five linguistically, culturally, and musically similar groups: Mossi-Bariba, Senufo, Dogon, Kasena-Nankani, and LoDagaa. In some cases, the linguistic and musical subgroupings do not overlap, and societies fall together in one group solely because of musical considerations. For example, the language of the Birifor belongs to the Mossi group

In the context of performing for royalty and other patrons, specialists usually place emphasis on praise singing.

(Greenberg 1970), but because the Birifor use xylophones, they belong to the LoDagaa musical group (Godsey 1980).

The Mossi-Bariba

The Mossi-Bariba subcluster includes these ethnic groups: Mossi (a complex encompassing the Mamprussi, Dagbamba, and Nanumba), Konkomba, Gourmantché (also called Gurma), Bariba, Kusasi, Frafra, Namnam, some Gonja, and Yarse. Because of common origins, the existence of centralized political structures, and historical links with northern and southern neighbors, societies in the Mossi group are similar. During the 1400s and 1500s, when the Mossi kingdoms rose to power, the Mossi fought several times with the Songhai over control of the Niger Bend. In their campaign against groups in the south, they met the Gourmantché and the Kusasi. By the late 1600s and early 1700s, the growing acceptance of Islam opened communication between the Mossi kingdoms and those in the Western and Central Sudanic clusters, and the isolation that characterized the earlier phases of Islam in the area began to break down (Wilks 1985:476).

The Bariba are distinct because of their location. In the Benin Gap (an area covering roughly present-day Benin, Togo, and southeast Ghana), the savanna breaks through the tropical forest zone, and extends to the Atlantic seaboard. Navigable rivers and coastal lagoons facilitated human movement, and generated contacts and connections that stimulated cultural interchange between the forest and the savanna (Asiwaju and Law 1985:413). The Bariba occupied the land of Borgu (northwest of Yorubaland) during the 1500s, and their kingdom reached its height in the 1700s (Rouget 1980a:492). The Mande and Songhai exercised considerable influence on them, and the Hausa upon the Nupe; in turn, the Bariba and Nupe had a strong formative influence on northern Yoruba groups (Asiwaju and Law 1985:413).

Musical instruments

Influences from groups in the Western and Central Sudanic clusters are clear in the music of Mossi and Bariba groups. Professional musicians belonging to a distinct social class dominate musical life. Because of their attachment to royalty or important persons, most have high status. Instruments associated with North Africa (hourglass tension drum, bowed and plucked lutes, metal trumpets) occur in most cultures. Similar to the situation among the Hausa, these instruments symbolize power. The Bariba associate kettledrums, long metal trumpets, and hourglass tension drums with traditional power; but the Dagbamba associate both the hourglass tension drum (*lunga*, pl. *lunsi*) and the bowed lute (*gonje*; also *gondze* and *goondze*) with royalty (figure 2). There is no evidence that any Mossi group has adopted metal trumpets. The use of the harp-lute and xylophone is proof of Mande influence.

In addition to instruments adopted as a result of contact with outsiders, peoples of the Mossi-Bariba subcluster use a variety of other instruments. Among their

FIGURE 2   A Dagbamba bowed lute (*gondze*) ensemble in Ghana.

stringed instruments are the musical bow, various types of zithers, and various types of flutes. Their aerophones include an ocarina, a clarinet, a trumpet made from wood and animal horn, a bullroarer, a whirling disc, and a mirliton. Drums are made of a variety of materials (gourd, wood, clay), in several shapes: square frame, cylindrical, conical, and barrel. Idiophones include gourd rattles, sticks, lamellophones, and water drums. The Bariba use rock gongs and leg xylophones.

Musical style

The use of a high tessitura is widespread and closely related to the range of melodic instruments that accompany singing (Nketia 1980:329). The ambitus of Dagbamba vocal and instrumental music appears smaller in comparison to the music of groups in the Western and Central Sudanic clusters, where Islamic influence is heavier. Vocal quality is tense, similar to that in other Islamic areas. Most scales are pentatonic, and slight ornamentation occurs in vocal and instrumental styles.

Musical contexts

In the context of performing for royalty and other patrons, specialists usually place emphasis on praise singing. Praise songs in honor of royal persons reinforce the importance of history. Many include references to moral values important to the people. Similar to other groups in the Voltaic cluster, occasions for music making are various, including events of the life cycle (rarely is music used during puberty), work, harvest celebrations, religious rites, and festivals (figure 3). Among the Dagbamba, so much music and dramatic display occurs at funerals, they seem to be festive events. Unlike the Western and Central Sudanic clusters, societies within the Mossi-Bariba subcluster prominently integrate traditional African music at Islamic events. At Islamic occasions in Dagbon, drummers and fiddlers commonly perform historical or genealogy songs.

The Senufo

The Senufo are composed of several different ethnic groups, including the linguistically related Minianka, Tagba, Foro, Tagwana, Dyimini, Nafana, Karabora, and Komona, who live in Côte d'Ivoire, Mali, and Burkina Faso (Greenberg 1970:8; Swanson 1985:10; Zemp 1980:431).

The culture of the Senufo people is in many ways similar to that of their neigh-

ginguru Harp of the Dogon that is associated with soothsayers

wua Two- or three-hole flute of the Kasena-
Nankani of Ghana; most common
melody-producing instrument

FIGURE 3 At a Ramadan festival in Ghana, Dagbamba musicians play hourglass pressure drums (*lunsi,* sing. *lunga*).

bors, but several of their traditions are distinct. They have a caste system for some occupational groups, but do not have a caste of musicians. As with several peoples in Liberia and Sierra Leone, initiation societies for men and women are an important aspect of Senufo culture: music accompanies activities of the Poro, a secret society, especially "the coming-out of a group of initiates and the funeral of a member" (Zemp 1980:434).

The musical instruments of the women's initiation society include a water drum. Those of the men's include double-headed cylindrical drums, large anthropomorphic trumpets with built-in mirlitons, and small mirlitons held in front of the mouth. Ensembles of xylophones and kettledrums play at funerals. Other local instruments include iron scrapers, gourd rattles, trumpets, whistles, and the harp-lute. Senufo music has a pentatonic scale. Other traits include "instrumental polyphony (particularly in the music of the xylophone ensembles)" and "monodic vocal music" (Zemp 1980:434).

The Dogon

The musical culture of the Dogon, whose territory also includes parts of Burkina Faso, has barely felt outside influence: "of all the ethnic groups in Mali, they have probably best preserved their identity, customs," and religions (Schaeffner 1980:575). However, their musical instruments are common to all groups that live in the area.

The performance of drum music is an important aspect of Dogon society. Of the six indigenous types of drums (*boy*), two are single headed. The gourd drum (*barba*) is the only single-headed drum adults use. The double-headed drums are either cylindrical (*boy na, boy dagi*) or hourglass-shaped (*gomboy*); the latter is a tension drum considered foreign. A variety of idiophones includes a slit drum (*korro*), a sistrum (*kebele*), and a rattle. The Dogon associate the harp (*gingiru*) with soothsayers, and its role differs from that of others in Mali: the Dogon do not have a repertory of songs for it. Locally used aerophones are a transverse flute (played by children and youths) and a bullroarer. The latter, because of its association with masked dances and the belief that it is the mother, is central to Dogon culture. The hum of the bullroarer reproduces the voice or cry of *imina na,* the largest mask, and is also believed to imitate the groaning of old men. As a secret instrument, it is usually stashed in a cave with the masks; people play it only at the first and second funeral rites for adult males (Schaeffner 1980:576).

In addition to the performance of music at masked dances, music making occurs at festivals, funerals, initiations, religious observances (rainmaking, divining), and secular activities of children and youths. Collective dancing is important to all music occasions in Dogon society.

The Kasena-Nankani

This subcluster includes the Kasena-Nankani, the Awuna, the Builsa, the Nunuma, the Kurumba, and the Lyela. Only because of James Koetting's (1980) research on the Kasena do we have an idea of the organization of music among these people. Thus, the Kasena will serve as representatives for the area.

Before European contact, the highest office in Kasenaland was earth priest (*tegadu*). Each clan had its own earth priest, who distributed land for farming and settling, and offered sacrifices to spirits of the land. Hereditary political chiefs (*pios*) had authority in domestic and political matters not dealing with the land and shared power with the earth priest, but the clans did not organize themselves into a large union or hierarchy. During British rule, the colonial government appointed chiefs, both earth priests and political chiefs. As their positions became solidified, the chiefs' power grew to equal that of chiefs of centrally organized groups in Ghana.

Musicians in Kasenaland are semiprofessional: they have other jobs, and play music only as needed. Though musicians have high social status as respected and valued members of society, they play for personal enjoyment, rather than prestige (Koetting 1980:121).

The Kasena use several instruments. The *wua*, a two- or three-hole vertical flute, is the most common melody-producing instrument. It is widespread throughout the region, but only the Kasena and Builsa play it in ensembles (Koetting 1980:94). Other wind instruments include the *nabona* (a side-blown ivory trumpet, played in sets of six or seven), the *kaaku* (now used as a toy), and a notched flute. Membranophones or idiophones usually accompany wind instruments. The *gullu* (a cylindrical double-headed drum, played in sets of four), the *kori* (a gourd drum, played in a set of two), and the *gungonga* (hourglass pressure drum) are among the instruments that may combine with flutes. Available idiophones include the *kalenge* (metal pails or large tins) and a metal gong (struck with iron finger rings).

Music is not functional in the sense that an event cannot take place without the proper musical genres; rather, the social nature of the event comes first, and music is an outgrowth of it. The occasions for Kasena music making fall into four overlapping categories (Koetting 1980:57–62): entertainment associated with casual gatherings (children's game playing, gatherings at marketplaces or in private homes); entertainment associated with specific functions (funeral celebrations for elderly men and women, courting, weddings, and festivals); royal and state occasions (durbars, national and regional festivals of the arts, gatherings to honor visiting dignitaries or

Because the xylophone is associated with animism, the local rise of Islam in the late twentieth century has caused a decline in LoDagaa music making with xylophones.

the opening of a school); and ritual and other occasions where music plays a supporting role (agricultural ceremonies and work). Music for royal and state occasions is a tradition that people began to cultivate during colonial rule.

The types of music are not context specific. The same music and dance may mark a variety of social contexts. Some of the most popular genres are the *jongo* (a stomping dance, also called *juntulla*), the *nagila*, the *pe zara*, and the *linle*. Praise songs associated with royalty are the most valued form of Kasena music. Also, people commonly sing work songs.

Music performed by an ensemble of aerophones and membranophones is the distinctive feature among people in this subcluster. Three to six flutes or horns, or a mixed ensemble of both, accompanied by drums, play in a hocket style with polyphonic structures. The music is heptatonic, and polyphony derives from the third as a consonant interval. At final cadences, parts moving in parallel thirds resolve into unison (Nketia 1980:331).

The LoDagaa

This subcluster includes the Lobi (also called LoWilisi), the Birifor, the Lopiel, the Dagaba, the Sisaala, the Nuna, the Puguli, the Gan, the Gouin, and the Wara. Societies in this subcluster live in the northwest tip of Ghana, and in adjacent parts of Burkina Faso and Côte d'Ivoire. The little that is known about the music of peoples in this region comes from two studies of xylophone traditions: Godsey (1980) and Seavoy (1982).

The LoDagaa form a cultural and linguistic continuum that changes from west to east. People in the area acknowledge this situation by using forms of the directional terms *lo* 'west' and *dagaa* 'east' to point up differences between neighboring subgroups (Godsey 1980:xiii–xiv). Most ethnic groups share cultural traits with that of other peoples in the Voltaic region: a belief system based on a cosmic orientation to the land, ancestors, and nature; a social organization based on clans and kinship; and a complex funeral ceremony that involves communal dancing to the music of xylophones and drums (Godsey 1980:1; Seavoy 1982:12). A few participate in curative and protective religious groups such as *bɔɔre*, *dyoro*, and *bire* (Godsey 1980:1–2).

The history of peoples in the region is one of migration and warfare. Since the 1600s, clans migrating in and out of the area have made easy prey for slavers from surrounding states. Only after the British colonial government in Ghana implanted chieftainships did groups become centrally organized (Seavoy 1982:19). In exchange for salt, the Western Sudanic kingdoms of Ghana (to about 1200) and Mali (1200s to 1400s) got gold from unidentified peoples to the south, and Lobi goldfields may have played a role in this trade (Godsey 1980:16–17; Wilks 1971:354). Groups bear some cultural resemblance to the Mande of Senegal, Sierra Leone, The Gambia, and Guinea. The most important of these similarities is the use of xylophones, whose association with funerals, and with dancing at the compound of the deceased, parallel certain funeral practices among the Senufo and other Voltaic peoples (Godsey 1980:17).

Xylophones and drums are the principal instruments of peoples within this sub-cluster; but because the xylophone is associated with animism (a traditional LoDagaa religious practice), the local rise of Islam in the late twentieth century has caused a decline in LoDagaa music making with xylophones (Mary Hermaine Seavoy, personal communication, 1994). The type of xylophone is unique to the Voltaic and Mande areas. Its distribution extends from Senegambia eastward to northwest Ghana and southern Burkina Faso. The eastern limit of the use of xylophones among the Sisaala is also the eastern limit of its incidence in the Western Sudanic cluster. This distribution is discontinuous with the area of distribution for the next type of fixed-key xylophone found in Sudanic Africa, whose westernmost occurrence is in the Central Sudanic cluster in Nigeria (Seavoy 1982:47). Though a common xylophone is used within the Western Sudanic cluster, two major subtypes correlate with the Mande and Voltaic language groups.

> Xylophones in use by Voltaic-speakers are for the most part tuned pentatonically (in contrast to heptatonic tunings of Mande instruments), have fewer keys, lower register, narrower range, larger size, and greater weight. Their frames incorporate two interstitial poles, inserted between and parallel to the two trapezoidal elements that serve as anchor for the resonator cords. (Seavoy 1982:50)

Even within the Voltaic cluster, there are distinctions. The Sisaala *jengsi* and neighboring Dagaa *gyile* (to the west) are distinguished within the family of Voltaic xylophones by their greater length (about 1.75 meters), sharper keyboard slope (more than twice as high at one end as at the other), and higher number of keys. The *jengsi* has 17 tuned keys; the *gyile* has 17, plus one untuned key (Seavoy 1982:50). Xylophones found farther west, such as those among the Birifor and LoWilisi, have only 14 keys, and performances use only one xylophone. Those in the east (as the Sisaala) normally play xylophones in pairs.

Found throughout the area without any distinct pattern of distribution, drums have a variety of shapes and types: cylindrical drum, conical drum, kettledrum, hourglass tension drum, gourd drum. In addition to the hoe (whose blade commonly serves in accompaniment in xylophone and drum ensembles), people produce sounds from double bells, finger bells, and ankle bells. Among the string and wind instruments are a harp, a musical bow, a raft zither, a flute, and a horn.

The funeral ceremony is one of the most important contexts for the performance of LoDagaa music. As the only large-scale public ceremony, it can have an elaborate organization, with certain songs and dances performed at different points. Funerals for men elicit styles of performance that differ from those for women. Besides funerals, music making also occurs at ceremonies for different curative and protective religious groups. Work songs, games performed by children when they reach puberty, and dances used to commemorate events within the agricultural cycle are nonceremonial occasions for the performance of music. Musicians are semiprofessional (they also participate in farming), but people within the culture identify instrument makers and instrumentalists as specialists.

THE FOREST

Savanna dwellers have had contact with each other through the development of empires, the movement of populations, and the influence of North Africa. As a

The music of groups who live in the Eastern Forest most often serve as a model to represent the music of West Africa as a whole.

result, their cultures are similar. In contrast, the cultures of the forest and coast are diverse. The forest has provided refuge from peoples of the grasslands (Mabogunje 1976:5). Extreme ethnic fragmentation, among more than five hundred ethnic groups, results in differentiation in political and social organization. Several local societies evolved into complex nation-states, while others formed loosely organized confederacies. The linkages established covered small areas, and did not encompass the scope or size of empires in the Western and Central Sudanic cluster. Also, secret societies and agegrade associations have served as important institutions within many forest belt cultures. External influences apparently resulted from contacts with savanna dwellers and Europeans. Traditional African religions are prominent; however, some members of societies have adopted Islam or Christianity. For subsistence, most people participate in agriculture and hunting, but a few rely on fishing and livestock grazing.

Differentiation within the sociopolitical organization of societies is reflected in music making. Elaborate traditions of court music and masquerades are important. Features that characterize forest belt music include the use of percussive instruments and an emphasis on complex rhythms. Because similarities and differences exist (in how features are manifested and music is socially organized), forest belt music falls into two regions: eastern and western. The Bandama River, in Côte d'Ivoire, divides them.

Eastern Forest cluster

The languages of ethnic groups in the east belong to the Kwa and Benue-Congo divisions of the Niger-Congo family (Greenberg 1970). An extensive amount of musical research has been done on peoples of this region, but gaps remain. Studies exist on the music of societies in Nigeria, Ghana, and southern Benin, but few investigations have been done on peoples living in Togo, central Benin, and southeastern Côte d'Ivoire. The music of groups who live in the Eastern Forest most often serve as a model to represent the music of West Africa as a whole. Because of cultural diversity, the region subdivides into several subclusters: (1) the Igbo, (2) the Yoruba, (3) the Aja, (4) the Gã, and (5) the Akan.

The Igbo

Many ethnic groups whose people speak languages of the Kwa and Benue-Congo subfamilies live in southeastern Nigeria, but the Igbo will serve to characterize the area.

Igbo society favors decentralized and nonurban communities. Local rule is largely by councils of elders (Ottenberg 1965:24). No headmen or true chiefs exist. The agents of the Aro-Chuku Oracle, the final arbiter for intertribal strife, formerly provided a form of supracommunal religiopolitical organization. Age-grade organizations had importance as a framework for communal administration (Mabogunje 1976:23).

Music making displays the use of different practices in each local area. Proximity to the rural Edo and other communities in Nigeria makes it difficult to distinguish peripheral Igbo music from that of the rural Edo, the Ijo, the Ibibio, and others living to the south and east (King 1980b:239). Music making is not an Igbo class or profession, though individuals specialize according to their talents, and serve as interpreters of the music of the community. Training is informal, and consists of imitating others.

That the Igbo have been receptive to external influences from Central Africa is clear in several musical traits: the equal prominence of membranophones (*igba*) and slit-drums (*ekwe, ufie*); the presence of percussive rhythmic instruments (drums, bells, rattles, percussion vessels, wooden clappers) and melodic instruments (xylophones, lamellophones, flutes, trumpets, musical bows, pluriarcs); the use of a fast tempo with vigorous body movements in religious music and music for dancing; and the preponderance of simple vocal forms, based on the alternation of a solo with a rhythmic choral refrain (King 1980b:239–240; Echezona 1980:20–21).

The contexts for music making include the honoring of a ruler, public assemblies, funeral ceremonies, festivals, and storytelling (Echezona 1980:21–22). The Afikpo Igbo make topical songs by joining new words to old tunes. They sing these songs during performances of masked plays, when members of the local men's society satirize the behavior of persons who have defied tradition or broken customs (Ottenberg 1965:14, 34). Though Igbo is a tonal language, the relationship between music and speech contour is much freer than in Yoruba music.

The Yoruba-Edo-Nupe

Linguistically, groups in this subcluster relate to neighbors in the east; but musically, because of historical contacts, they have more in common with northerners. The Yoruba and the Edo will serve to represent the subcluster.

The Yoruba live mostly in southwest Nigeria, and in settlements scattered throughout the country of Benin toward the Togo border. They have more fully maintained their indigenous culture in Benin than in Nigeria, particularly in religion. With the religious center at Ile-Ife and belief in common descent from Oduduwa, the traditional culture of the Yoruba displays a high degree of homogeneity. Political organization depends on the existence of kingdoms, each under a divine king, ruling with the Ogboni secret society, an elaborate military system, and age-grade organizations. Religious beliefs include both an elaborate cult of ancestors and the worship of Olorun (a sky god), and of lesser gods, such as Ṣango (the thunder god). Islam has made inroads among the Yoruba; but since the 1840s, the activities of Christian missionaries have checked its advance.

The Yoruba kingdom of Oyo, the most powerful coastal state, rose to prominence before 1500. In the early 1800s, because of an outbreak of civil wars, it began to decline (Asiwaju and Law 1985:446). It had contacts with the Edo-speaking peoples (Benin kingdom) in the east, and by 1700 had involved itself in expansionist policies to the southwest. Its main trading interests were in the north with the Songhai Empire, and with Hausa and Nupe states.

As early as the 1100s, the Edo of Benin had established a nation-state. By the 1500s, it had subjugated most of its neighbors. The administrative organization was of a hierarchical type, with a king (*oba*) at the top. Nobles and groups of nonhereditary chiefs helped him govern. The ruling family, though not the people, claimed a consanguinary relationship with the Ife dynasty of Yorubaland. The Edo state was

As semiprofessionals, Yoruba musicians rely on farming or weaving for their living. Only performers of pop music maintain a livelihood as professionals.

one of the earliest African states to come into contact with Europeans. In the late 1400s, Christian missionaries began work in it, but they had slight success. Edo religious beliefs centered on a high god, and allowed for many lesser gods and quasi-mythological, deified heroes (Mabogunje 1976:23).

As semiprofessionals, Yoruba musicians rely on farming or weaving for their living. Only performers of pop music maintain a livelihood as professionals. The social status of musicians is not uniform. The status of pop musicians and priests is high, but that of some freelance performers is low. Recruitment, particularly of drummers, involves only the male line. Apprentices get their training formally, from kinfolk or established musicians. Most musicians specialize as instrumentalists, or within a specific type of vocal music.

Besides royal occasions, Yoruba music marks events of the life cycle, religious festivals, markets, and work, and serves for recreation and entertainment. The worship of deities (*orisa*), an important and complex context for music making, includes possession and dance with chanted text. Songs for *oro* (the secret society of night hunters, responsible for administering justice) are also central to the culture. People symbolize *oro* by playing a bullroarer—singly, or in combination with mirlitons and drums. The local repertory includes "light entertainment music for informal dancing, royal processional music, and many other types" (Thieme 1970:110).

People formerly made a distinction between urban music (in the royal capital of Benin) and rural Edo music. Though less elaborate, music for commoners no longer differs much from music for the *oba* and his court. Ceremonies celebrating calendrical and religious events (ancestral spirits, hero gods), plus events of the life cycle, occur at court and in rural areas.

In Yoruba society, drums are the dominant instrumental type. Musicians regard instruments within a drum ensemble as members of a family. The leader of the ensemble usually plays the principal instrument, the mother (*iya ilu*, or *iya'lu*). The name repeats as the name for the principal drum in more than one family or group: *iya'lu dundun*, *iya'lu bata*, *iya'lu bembe*. Because the system also includes common names for accompanimental or secondary drums within various ensembles, the names *kerikeri* and *isaju* occur in more than one family of drums, specifying instruments of different construction (Thieme 1969:3).

Contact with the north is clearest in the vocal style and the use of instruments. Those influenced by the north use nasalization and an ornamental, melismatic style of singing. Most singers in nonmelismatic areas seldom use ornaments and favor a clear, open, relaxed style. Yoruba instrumental borrowings from the north include the *kàakàakii*; the *famifami* (Hausa *famfami*, a short wooden trumpet); the *kanango*, the *gangan*, and the *dundun* (similar to the Hausa *kalangu*); the *koso* (Hausa *kotso*), the *bembe* (similar to the Hausa *ganga*), the *goje* (Hausa *goge*), and the *duru* (two-stringed plucked lute, similar to the Hausa *garaya* and *gurmi*). Musicians usually play wind instruments only for royalty, but drums have a wider usage; many are played at religious, ceremonial, social, and court events. The *goje* serves for entertainment as an accompanying instrument in *sakara* ensembles. The *duru* accompanies the singing of praise songs to Ogun (god of iron), and of hunting songs.

Besides instruments borrowed from the north, Yoruba families of drums include the *bata* (double-headed conical drum), used at ceremonies honoring Ṣango, and at *egungun* and *agbegijo* masquerades; the *omolu* (three pot drums and two pegged cylindrical wooden drums), used to worship Omolu, god of water and fertility; the *apesin* (single-membrane cylindrical drum), used at masquerades and *oro* festivals; the *kete* (globular cylindrical drum), used for entertainment at events of the life cycle; a variety of pegged cylindrical drums (*apinti, gbedu, igbin, agere*), used at masquerades, religious festivals, and ceremonies for royalty and hunters; and several single-membrane frame drums (*jùjú, samba, sakara, were*), commonly used by youth bands in the performance of urban popular music (Thieme 1969). Performances in Benin include a friction drum. Among the idiophones are the *sekere* or *aje oba* (set of gourd vessel rattles, covered with cowrie nets), *agogo* (externally struck bell, sometimes used in sets), *agidigbo* (box-resonated lamellophone), rhythm sticks, and percussion plaque.

Northern influence on the Edo is clear in the use of an hourglass tension drum, a metal trumpet, and kettledrums. Other Edo instruments include goatskin-covered drums made of hollowed bamboo, cylindrical-shaped drums, rattles, iron bells, wooden clappers, and lamellophones. Edo aerophones include notched flutes, ivory trumpets, and gourd trumpets.

Because Yoruba is a tonal language, Yoruba music depends for its melodic shape on textual tones and intonational patterns. In the reading and recitation of poems and incantations, and in the calling of praises, the text dominates. Though not as strict and sometimes performed more freely, the text is dominant in the performance of chants, praise acclamations, and songs. Instruments serve primarily for the accompaniment of vocal singing. Two vocal types (*orin* 'song', *oriki* 'praise chant'), plus several vocal styles, are available to singers. The Yoruba in the east often sing in unison, and those in the west often sing polyphonically. The use of fourths, which contrasts with polyphony in thirds (as used by the Ashanti and the Baoulé), allows Yoruba voices greater mobility (Rouget 1980a:492).

The Aja

The term *Aja* denotes a linguistic group including the Fon of the ancient Dahomey kingdom, the Gun (Egun) of the Porto Novo area, and the Ewe of Togo and modern Ghana. The Ewe use *Aja* as a general term for the Fon and the Gun, though not for themselves. The western Yoruba (such as those of Ketu) use the term *Ewe* as a general name for neighboring Fon and Gun (Asiwaju and Law 1985:414–415). This discussion applies the term *Aja* solely to the Fon and the Gun, and reserves *Ewe* for the Ewe people.

The Aja groups have traditions of a common origin—from Tado (in modern Togo), on the left bank of the river Mono (Asiwaju and Law 1985:429). Immigrants from Ketu to the east, possibly refugees displaced by Yoruba colonization, probably founded the city. In the 1500s, disputes within Tado led to the departure of sections of the community to found settlements of their own. One section, migrating westward, founded Nuatja (Notsie), which became the center for the Ewe's dispersal over the region between the Mono and the Volta rivers in Togo and Ghana. A second section, moving southeastward, settled in Allada, from where factions broke away to found the Fon kingdom of Dahomey at Abomey and the Gun kingdom of Porto Novo.

The Ewe who moved west evolved more than one hundred twenty microstates

axatsevu   Music of the Ewe; characterized by
rattles

akpewi   Music of the Ewe; dominated by
hand clapping or wooden clappers

that differed in dialect and other cultural traits, but their kin who went eastward created much larger and more centralized political units (Asiwaju and Law 1985:432). In the 1700s, the kingdom of Dahomey had an unusual degree of centralization of power. The king ruled the country through an administrative hierarchy of governors, chiefs, and local headmen, and maintained an elaborate court, with palatial ministers of both sexes (Asiwaju and Law 1985:436; Mabogunje 1976:24).

Bells and drums are the most frequently used instruments among the Fon, the Gun, and the Ewe. Most ensembles use bells, and a solo bell may provide rhythmic accompaniment for singing. Among the Fon and the Gun, other instruments include log xylophones, raft zithers, rattles, water drums, and percussion pots. Among the winds are the notched flute (believed to be ancient), whistles (used by hunters), and ivory horns (played by royal musicians in honor of kings and princes). Contexts for music making vary, and are not particularly different from those of other groups in the same region—events of the life cycle, seasonal rituals, work, and village festivals. Other contexts for the performance of music include ceremonies at court, elaborate ceremonies for *vodun* (in which possession occurs), and the secret society of night hunters (Rouget 1980a:491), all of which show similarities with Yoruba contexts.

Ewe religious practices resemble those of other Aja speakers and Yoruba speakers. The worship of Afã (the god of divination) and Yewe (the god of thunder and lightning) requires special drum music. Music for Afã occurs at public occasions in which nonmembers may participate; but music for Yewe, considered one of the most developed forms of Ewe sacred music, occurs only in festivities nonmembers may not join. In addition to music performed at religious ceremonies, much of Ewe life focuses on dance clubs—a context that functions as a form of entertainment, recreation, and ceremonial activity (Ladzekpo and Ladzekpo 1980:219).

Musicians are not professionals. They play music only when events arise: to welcome a government official or foreign visitor, to promote a political party, to inaugurate a new dance club, to install a new chief, or to perform at a funeral or a social gathering that might warrant dancing (Ladzekpo and Ladzekpo 1980:219). The clubs organize their members in age groups, and people expect all local adults (women and men) to belong to one in their community. Each club has composers who create music in any of three genres: *axatsevu* (music dominated by rattles), *akpewu* (music dominated by hand clapping or wooden clappers), and "specific style" (drumming and dancing that differs from that of the first two groups).

In addition to idiophones (bells, rattles, clappers), Ewe culture prominently uses membranophones (cylindrical- or barrel-shaped, played in sets of four or five). Among the aerophones are wooden flutes, plus trumpets made from elephants' tusks or bulls' horns. The latter are associated more with royal houses than with dance clubs (Ladzekpo and Ladzekpo 1980:228).

Important differences in the music of the northern and southern Ewe involve scales and harmonies. Northern Ewe music has a seven-tone diatonic scale, with polyphony based on the third as a harmonic interval. The northern Ewe borrowed these features from neighboring Akan groups. The Anlo-Ewe, who live in the south, use a five-tone scale, with harmony based on parallel fourths. They sing in a low tessitura, but the northern Ewe prefer a high one (Ladzekpo and Ladzekpo 1980:229).

The Gã

With the Adangme and the Krobo, the Gã live in southeast Ghana. They probably migrated from Benin in Nigeria and settled in modern Ghana during the 1500s (Hampton 1978a:35). Their music has felt strong influence from neighboring groups. They have adopted many traditions from the Akan (*adowa, asafo, otu, akom*), and share features with other groups in the area (like the Adangme). Song types include work songs, recreational songs for various age groups, music associated with political and military institutions, and songs for social occasions and ceremonies (Hampton 1978b:1; Nketia 1963). Contexts for music making include durbars, harvest festivals, events of the life cycle (but not marriage), celebrations or ceremonies associated with court, hunters, warriors, and cult groups (*otu, akon, me, kple*). People learn music by imitation—girls, from coresident matrikinswomen; boys, from coresident patrikinsmen. Musical ensembles are often unisexual (Hampton 1978b:2).

The Gã use drums prominently, but with limited variety. Excepting double-headed hourglass pressure drums and closed cylindrical drums, membranophones are single-headed open drums. Other instruments include bamboo tubes (*pamploi*), a clapperless iron bell (*nono*), and rattles strung with nets of beads (*fao*).

The Gã use both heptatonic and pentatonic scales. They have borrowed the heptatonic scale from the neighboring Akan. Gã songs are mainly anhemitonic pentatonic. Polyphony occurs in vocal refrains (Nketia 1980:331). Harmonic thirds occur in music using heptatonic scales, and singing in the pentatonic scale may be in unison or in harmony (Nketia 1958:26).

The Akan

Akan-speaking peoples (Ashanti, Brong, Akim, Kwahu, Akwapim, Akwamu, Wasa, Asen, Agona, Fante, Baoulé) inhabit widely dispersed areas in modern Ghana and Côte d'Ivoire (figure 4). The basis of their social organization is rule by matrilineal descent. Political organization, particularly among the Ashanti, is diffuse. The

FIGURE 4   Akan women perform at a deer-hunting festival in Winneba, Ghana.

Many groups in Ghana use the Ashanti talking drum (*atumpan*), and play it in the Akan language.

FIGURE 5   Ashanti women and men dance to the music of large cylindrical drums (*fontomfrom*).

Asantehene is paramount ruler of a confederation of provincial chiefs, and the chiefs in turn exercise authority over subchiefs and headmen of villages under their jurisdiction. The king is not an absolute ruler: a council—the queen mother, the chiefs of the most important provinces, the general of the army—controls him. The symbol of national solidarity is the Golden Stool, which came into being in the time of Osei Tutu (1700–1730), the fourth known king of the Ashanti, and the founder of the Empire. Ashanti religion acknowledges belief in an earth spirit and a supreme god, but lesser gods and ancestor spirits attract popular worship and propitiation (Mabogunje 1976:25).

Performances at the Ashanti royal court are a most important context for music making. Royal musicians permanently attach themselves to the Asantehene and other chiefs, and oral tradition attributes certain chiefs with the introduction of musical instruments, orchestras, musical types, and styles of singing. Such traditions appear in all Akan areas (Nketia 1971:14). The number of musicians, variety of instruments, and musical types are indicators of a king's greatness. Chiefs with a higher status may keep drums and other instruments that lesser chiefs may not.

Territorial expansion by conquest, and contact with peoples to the north and west of the Akan area, have led to the adoption of new traditions and musical instruments. Interaction with other peoples also pushed Akan influences into other areas. Many groups in Ghana use the Ashanti talking drum (*atumpan*), and play it in the Akan language. Interactions between Ashanti and the Dahomey kingdom have resulted in common musical types and instruments (Nketia 1971:19). Besides the use of music for royalty (*atumpan, kete, ntahera, kwadwom*), religious cults (*akom*), events of the life cycle (no music occurs at births or marriages), and recreation, there are occupational associations and an elaborate military structure with a highly organized repertory of traditional songs and drum music (Nketia 1963:18; 1980:331).

FIGURE 6   Ashanti men play trumpets (*ntahera*) at a royal funeral in Kumasi, Ghana.

Akan instrumental types most commonly include drums, as in ensembles of *fontomfrom, kete,* and *atumpan* (figure 5). Rattles and bells accompany drumming, either at court, at events of the life cycle, or during religious and recreational activities. Percussion logs accompany *asonko* recreational music, but percussion vessels occur only sporadically. Membranophones indigenous to the area are usually single-headed and open-ended, but as a result of interaction with neighbors, the Akan have adopted drums from the north: gourd drums (*bentere, pentre*) and the hourglass tension drum (*donno*). Two aerophones have associations with royalty: the *ntahera* (a set of five or seven ivory trumpets [figure 6], played at the court of paramount chiefs), and the *odurugya* (a notched flute, made of cane husk, played at the Asantehene's court). Other aerophones include the *atenteben* (played solo and in ensembles) and the *taletenga* (an idioglot reed pipe). There are few stringed instruments. Among them are the *seperewa* (a six-stringed harp-lute) and the *benta* (a mouth bow). The Baoulé, who live in Côte d'Ivoire, use a wider variety of melodic instruments: the lamellophone, xylophone (with keys laid over the trunks of two banana trees), the forked harp, and the harp-lute. Their use of these instruments may reflect their close contact with neighbors to the north and west.

Use of the heptatonic scale and singing in thirds is distinctive to the Akan. "Clearcut short phrases," phrases of a standard duration, and "longer fluid patterns" can occur within one composition (Nketia 1980:330). Phrasal variation is also apparent in Gã and Ewe drum ensembles.

Western Forest cluster

Of the indigenous groups that live to the west of the Bandama River in Liberia, Sierra Leone, and western Côte d'Ivoire, none evolved into kingdoms or states comparable to the political structures that arose among some forest dwellers in the east. Before about 1400, groups in this area, particularly those in Liberia and Côte d'Ivoire, felt little influence from the savanna empires of Ghana and Mali. This isolation permitted the development of small and widely scattered states, with enough contact to form confederations for defense and trade (Jones 1974:308). However, in the 1400s, with the disintegration of the Mali Empire, Malinke traders and warriors began to move from the savanna into the kola plantations of the forest, bringing merchandise and Islam. Migrations from the north, continuing until the 1800s, resulted in the invention of an indigenous alphabet among the Vai, and in secret societies (Poro for men, Sande for women) that were vehicles for the transmission of culture from one generation to the next (Jones 1974:309). The languages of peoples in this area belong to the Mande, West Atlantic, and Kwa subfamilies of the Niger-Congo family; only the Kwa are probably indigenous to the region.

As a result of migrations from the savanna, much unity is clear in the music of groups who inhabit the Western Forest cluster. This unity distinguishes local music making from that of the Eastern Forest. Unlike the eastern area, however, only a few societies in the western area have been the focus of intensive musical research. In a country like Sierra Leone, "musicians listen to each other and learn from each other. . . . There is considerable variety of music even within each group. . . . It would thus be futile to try and cut up Sierra Leone music into tribal sections" (Oven 1981:7). Though detailed information about all ethnic groups is lacking, enough is known for a discussion of the typical features of some societies. This subregion divides into three subclusters, based on linguistic families.

Mande-speakers

The musical traditions of Mande speakers (Susu, Lokko, Koranko, Kono, Krim, Yalunka, Kondi, Gallina, Mende, Kpelle, Vai, Belle, Loma, Mano, Gbandi, Gio,

The Dan attribute to animals or bush spirits the origins of musical instruments. Masks, the personifications of bush spirits, often express themselves in music.

Dan, Guere, Gouro) have had the most dramatic impact on this subregion. Being in the majority, they have heavily affected local social and political institutions. Much information is available on the music of the Dan, the Kpelle, the Mende, and the Vai.

The Dan straddle the borders of Côte d'Ivoire and Liberia. They share several musical characteristics with neighboring groups. Music making is a highly regarded profession, and musicians receive pay for their music. Anyone may become a musician, but usually the children of musicians choose to. Professional musicians formerly attached themselves to a person (like a chief) or an association (warriors, hunters, work groups, secret societies, recreational groups, wrestlers), or traveled from village to village. This type of social organization is moribund; few young professional drummers belong to a work association (Zemp 1980:432).

Musicians use a wide variety of instruments. Idiophones and membranophones are predominant. Among the former are gourd rattles, bells, and slit drums; the latter include mortar drums and cylindrical drums. Chordophones include the musical bow and harp-lute, the latter borrowed from northern neighbors. The most important aerophone is the sideblown ivory trumpet, played in sets of five to seven, and accompanied by drums. The Dan also use a mirliton, a bullroarer, a stone whistle, and a whirling whistle, but they regard these, not as instruments, but as masks, since they express the voice of masks (Zemp 1980:432).

The Dan attribute to animals or bush spirits the origins of musical instruments. Masks, the personifications of bush spirits, often express themselves in music (Zemp 1980:431). A highly important context for music making is puberty. Secluded youths receive musical training. To finish their initiation, they dance and perform music. The Dan have terms for three types of music: *tan* 'dance song' (also 'instrumental music' and 'dance'), *zlöö* 'praise song', and *gbo* 'funeral lament' (Zemp 1980:431). *Tan*, the most widely used, differentiates into the most subtypes, and involves the most instruments.

Most of the music has a pentatonic scale, but some songs (as the *zlöö*) are heptatonic. Polyphony occurs in *tan*; the solo singer usually has as a partner a second voice a fourth lower, and a chorus often joins the soloists responsorially. In larger vocal ensembles, two pairs of soloists (each pair singing in parallel fourths) alternate with the chorus. Singers usually perform *tan* with restraint, and most texts are fixed. A praise song singer uses a more effusive style, a kind of shouting. Improvisation plays an important part in performance (Zemp 1980:432–433).

Kpelle migrations into the area known as Liberia occurred between the 1400s and the 1800s. Most professional musicians work as subsistence farmers or laborers. Known as Kpelle singers, *ngulei-sîyge-nuu* 'the song-raising person', achieve renown for performing at festivals, funerals, and receptions: "Solo singers are often women, but male professional storytellers, and instrumentalists playing the pluriarc, the lamellophone, and the triangular frame zither, are also singers" (Stone 1980:716).

The Kpelle use two words to classify musical instruments: *fée* 'blown' and *ygále* 'struck'—a system similar to that of the Dan. Among blown instruments are a flute (*boo*) and a sideblown horn (*túru*) made of wood, ivory, or horn. Struck instruments include idiophones, membranophones, and chordophones. The Kpelle use a variety of melodic and rhythmic idiophones, including lamellophones (*gbèlee, kónkoma*); a xylophone (*bala*), which consists of free logs resting on banana stalks; slit drums (*kóno, kéleng*); rattles; and bells. Membranophones may be single-headed or double-headed, and are goblet- and hourglass-shaped. Some drums have feet (Stone 1980:717). Chordophones include a triangular frame zither (*konîng*), a multiple bow-lute (*gbegbetêle*), a single-stringed bow lute (*gbee-kee*), a musical bow (*kòn-kpàla*), and a harp-lute (*kerân-non-konîng*).

The organization of ensembles reflects the social structure of Kpelle culture. The largest and lowest pitched instrument in a slit drum ensemble is the 'mother' (*kóno-lee*), and the medium-sized and smallest slit drums are the 'middle' (*kóno-sama*) and the 'child' (*kóno-long*), respectively (Stone 1980:716–717).

The Kpelle play music on many different occasions. As with the Dan, activities associated with puberty—initiation into Poro and Sande—include more music making than other events of the life cycle. The Kpelle also have music associated with holidays, work, harvest, games, and masked dancing.

Kpelle melody is syllabic and percussive. Repetition is common, and in some traditions hocketing occurs. The scale is usually pentatonic. Ensembles include a combination of pitches with different timbres—voices, drums, rattles, and metal idiophones: "Entries are usually staggered, giving an accumulation of textures" (Stone 1980:718). Men sing in an upper vocal register, but women sing in a lower one. Vocal production, somewhat tight, is "pronounced in the men's voices when they sing bush-clearing songs" (Stone 1980:718).

As a result of common economic and political interests, the Mende (the largest group in the region), the Vai, the Gola, and the Dei, have close cultural interrelationships. Mende institutions of Poro and warfare may have been the main conveyors of musical influence, which passed through the Gola to the Vai and the Dei. The link between the Mende and the Gola is therefore stronger than that between the Mende and the Dei (Monts 1982:103–104). The strongest evidence of influence is in local musical instruments. Excepting the gourd rattle (Mende *segbura*), all of them—slit drums (*kele, kelewa*), lamellophone (*kongama*), drums (*sangboi, mbele*), horn (*bulu*)— are probably of Mende origin.

Though all groups perform the same types of songs, the origin of certain songs within the repertory does not yield such a clear picture of influence from the Mende. Many secret society songs are in Mende (particularly those associated with specific rituals and masked dancing), but "songs used for recreation and entertainment and others of less specific ritual importance" are in Mende, Gola, Vai, and Dei (Monts 1982:108). That initiates' dance troupes perform among the Mende and the Gola suggests "their origins may be with one of these ethnic groups" (Monts 1982:109), but no known evidence specifies which group. Rice songs are mostly in Vai and Mende because they came from the Mande eastern regions, where agricultural practices were more elaborate (Monts 1982:107). Hunting songs tend to be in Gola, for before the migrations of Mende and Vai into the region, the Gola had an economy based primarily on hunting and gathering. Topical songs are exclusively in the languages of the ethnic groups for which musicians perform them. They include "songs for transmitting tribal lore, for storytelling, and for calling attention to violations of social norms" (Monts 1982:112).

Percussive instruments usually accompany singing and dancing. Accompaniments "range in form from the accent of the cutlass striking the bush at regular intervals, as in agricultural labor songs, to the drumming of a professional musician" at masked dances (Monts 1982:106). One instrument usually provides the basic pulse, while another instrument supplies intricate rhythmic patterns. Most songs, particularly those associated with communal activities (social institutions, occupational groups, events of the life cycle) have one- and two-part structures. Songs performed in unison have the one-part structure. Songs based on a two-part structure may have a call-and-response pattern between a solo and a chorus, or between one chorus and another. Occupational groups that have a recognized leader normally make use of the solo-chorus format, but divisions based on sex, age, or no recognizable leader employ the chorus-chorus format.

West Atlantic–speakers

Most speakers of languages in the West Atlantic linguistic subfamily (Temne, Sherbro, Bulom, Limba, Gola, Kissi) live in Sierra Leone; a few live in northern Liberia. Many inhabit areas they have occupied since the 1400s. Though Greenberg associates them with the Senegalo-Guinean ethnic group (which includes the Tukulor, the Fulɓe, the Wolof, and the Serer), their Guinean type of civilization separates them from Senegambians (Boulegue and Suret-Canale 1985:504).

The Temne, who came from the mountainous region of Jallonkadu (an area that later became part of Futa Djallon) and settled on the coast north of the Bulom (Fyle 1981:7–8), are one of the most populous ethnic groups in Sierra Leone. Their music displays characteristics similar to that of other groups in the Western Forest cluster: prominent percussion, masked dancers, secret society music. It also includes features associated with groups in the Western Sudanic cluster: the occasional use of the fiddle (*angbulu, gbulu, rafon*), and the tendency of women to imitate a Sudanic singing style (Christian Horton, personal communication, 19 August 1991). The adoption of these elements may have resulted from interaction with the Fulɓe during Temne territorial expansion toward the east and northeast, and from the dispersal of the Fulɓe in Sierra Leone. Temne song types—dance songs, praise songs, festive songs, songs for chiefs, story songs, love songs, religious songs, work songs, war songs, topical songs—do not differ from those of other groups in the region (Oven 1980:5–6).

Kwa-speakers

Kwa speakers live in Liberia (Dei, Bassa, Gbi, Kran, Padebu [Padebo], Kru, Grebo, Jabo) and Côte d'Ivoire (Bete, Ubi [Oubi], Bakwé, Dida, Godie [Godye]). Data on the music of these groups are cursory and fragmentary, for scholars have not investigated them intensively. The Kwa in Liberia have felt heavy influence from migrants who have become dominant in the region (Monts 1982), and smaller groups (as the Jabo) have adopted elements from stronger Kwa neighbors, the Grebo and the Kru (Herzog 1945). Thus, elements from the indigenous Kwa ethnic groups have survived only minimally.

Kwa-speakers in Côte d'Ivoire have been more selective in their use of elements

FIGURE 7   A Bete masked dancer, Côte d'Ivoire.

from other groups. Masked dancing is an integral part of Bete culture (figure 7). Similar in function to that of the Dan, it serves to cleanse a village of alien forces, officiate at funerals, levy social criticism, greet dignitaries, preside over important trials, prepare men for the hunt, and lead people to war. The Bete, however, do not associate masks with the institution of Poro. Besides influences from the Mande, Bete religious and artistic traditions have close affinities with neighboring Kru and Akan groups. That old Bete songs use Akan-style drumming as accompaniment proves the Bete bridge the gap between the secret societies of Liberia and the Akan kingship traditions from Ghana (Rood 1969:40).

Instrumental types used by Kwa-speakers in the Western Forest cluster include membranophones, idiophones (slit drum, xylophone), chordophones (musical bow, triangular frame zither), and aerophones (wooden horn). Jabo slit drums belong to military organizations, whose members use the instruments during assemblies, social gatherings, and celebrations of war. At social gatherings, young men use a six-key xylophone to perform topical songs.

REFERENCES

Ajayi, J. F. A., and Michael Crowder, eds. 1971. *History of West Africa,* vol. 1. London: Longman

———. 1974. *History of West Africa,* vol. 2. London: Longman.

———. 1976. *History of West Africa,* vol. 1, 2nd ed. London: Longman.

———. 1985. *History of West Africa,* vol. 1, 3rd ed. London: Longman.

Alberts, Arthur S. 1950. *Tribal, Folk and Cafe Music of West Africa.* New York: Field Recordings. LP.

Ames, David. 1973. "A Sociocultural View of Hausa Musical Activity." In *The Traditional Artist in African Societies,* ed. Warren L. D'Azevedo, 128–161. Bloomington: Indiana University Press.

Ames, David, and Anthony V. King. 1971. *Glossary of Hausa Music and Its Social Contexts.* Evanston, Ill.: Northwestern University Press.

Arnott, D. W. 1980. "Fulani Music." *The New Grove Dictionary of Music and Musicians,* ed. Stanley Sadie. London: Macmillan.

Asiwaju, A.I., and Robin Law. 1985. "From the Volta to the Niger, c. 1600-1800." In *History of West Africa,* vol. 1, 3rd ed., ed. J. F. A. Ajayi and Michael Crowder, 412–464. London: Longman.

Besmer, Fremont E. 1983. *Horses, Musicians, and Gods: The Hausa Cult of Possession-Trance.* Zaria, Nigeria: Ahmadu Bello University Press.

Boulègue, Jean, and Jean Suret-Canale. 1985. "The Western Atlantic Coast." In *History of West Africa,* vol. 1, 3rd ed., ed. J. F. A. Ajayi and Michael Crowder, 503–530. London: Longman.

Coolen, Michael T. 1984. "Senegambian Archetypes for the American Folk Banjo." *Western Folklore* 43(2):117–132.

Dalby, Winifred. 1980. "Mali: Music and Society / Manding Music." *The New Grove Dictionary of Music and Musicians,* ed. Stanley Sadie. London: Macmillan.

DjeDje, Jacqueline Cogdell. 1980. *Distribution of the One String Fiddle in West Africa.* Los Angeles: UCLA Program in Ethnomusicology, Department of Music.

———. 1982. "The Concept of Patronage: An Examination of Hausa and Dagomba One-String Fiddle Traditions." *Journal of African Studies* 9(3):116–127.

Duran, Lucy, et al. 1987. "On Music in Contemporary West Africa: Jaliya and the Role of the Jali in Present Day Manding Society." *African Affairs: Journal of the Royal African Society* 86(343):233–236.

Echezona, W. W. C. 1980. "Igbo Music." *The New Grove Dictionary of Music and Musicians,* ed. Stanley Sadie. London: Macmillan.

Eno Belinga, Samuel-Martin. 1972. "The Traditional Music of West Africa: Types, Styles, and Influences." In *African Music: Meeting in Yaoundé (Cameroon) 23–27 February 1970,* 71–75. Paris: La Revue Musicale.

Erlmann, Veit. 1983. "Notes on Musical Instruments among the Fulani of Diamare (North Cameroon)." *African Music* 6(3):16–41.

Fyle, C. Magbaily. 1981. *The History of Sierra Leone: A Concise Introduction.* London: Evans Brothers.

Godsey, Larry Dennis. 1980. "The Use of the Xylophone in the Funeral Ceremony of the Birifor of Northwest Ghana." Ph.D. dissertation, University of California at Los Angeles.

Gourlay, Kenneth A. 1976. Letter to the Editor. *Ethnomusicology* 20(2):327–332.

———. 1982. "Long Trumpets of Northern Nigeria—In History and Today." *African Music* 6(2):48–72.

Gray, John. 1991. *African Music: A Bibliographical Guide to the Traditional, Popular, Art, and Liturgical Musics of Sub-Saharan Africa.* New York and Westport, Conn.: Greenwood Press.

Greenberg, Joseph. 1970. *The Languages of Africa,* 3rd ed. Bloomington and The Hague: Indiana University and Mouton.

Hampton, Barbara. 1978a. "The Contiguity Factor in Ga Music." *The Black Perspective in Music* 6(1):32–48.

———. 1978b. *Music of the Ga People of Ghana: Adowa,* vol. 1. Folkways FE 4291. LP disk and descriptive notes.

Harris, P. G. 1932. "Notes on Drums and Musical Instruments Seen in Sokoto Province, Nigeria." *Journal of the Royal Anthropological Institute* 62:105–125.

Hause, Helen E. 1948. "Terms for Musical Instruments in the Sudanic Languages: A Lexicographical Inquiry." *Journal of the American Oriental Society* 7:1–71.

Herzog, George. 1945. "Drum-Signaling in a West African Tribe." *Word: Journal of the Linguistic Circle of New York* 1(3):217–238.

Jones, Abeodu Bowen. 1974. "The Republic of Liberia." In *History of West Africa,* vol. 2, ed. J. F. A. Ajayi and Michael Crowder, 308–343. London: Longman.

King, Anthony. 1980a. "Hausa Music." *The New Grove Dictionary of Music and Musicians,* ed. Stanley Sadie. London: Macmillan.

———. 1980b. "Nigeria." *The New Grove Dictionary of Music and Musicians,* ed. Stanley Sadie. London: Macmillan.

Knight, Roderic C. 1984. "Music in Africa: The Manding Contexts." In *Performance Practice: Ethnomusicological Perspectives,* ed. Gerard Béhague, 53-90. Westport, Conn.: Greenwood Press.

Koetting, James Thomas. 1980. "Continuity and Change in Ghanaian Kasena Flute and Drum Ensemble Music: A Comparative Study of the Homeland and Nima/Accra." Ph.D. dissertation, University of California at Los Angeles.

Ladzekpo, Alfred Kwashie, and Kobla Ladzekpo. 1980. "Anlo Ewe Music in Anyako, Volta Region, Ghana." In *Musics of Many Cultures: An Introduction,* ed. Elizabeth May, 216–231. Berkeley: University of California Press.

Mabogunje, Akin L. 1976. "The Land and Peoples of West Africa." In *History of West Africa,* vol. 1, 2nd ed., ed. J. F. A. Ajayi and Michael Crowder, 1–32. London: Longman.

Monts, Lester P. 1982. "Music Clusteral Relationships in a Liberian–Sierra Leonean Region: A Preliminary Analysis." *Journal of African Studies* 9(3):101–115.

Murdock, George P. 1959. *Africa: Its Peoples and Their Culture History.* New York: McGraw-Hill.

Nketia, J. H. Kwabena. 1958. "Traditional Music of the Ga People." *African Music* 2(1):21–27.

———. 1963. *African Music in Ghana.* Evanston, Ill.: Northwestern University Press.

———. 1971. "History and the Organization of Music in West Africa." In *Essays on Music and History in Africa,* ed. Klaus P. Wachsmann, 3–25. Evanston, Ill.: Northwestern University Press.

———. 1980. "Ghana." *The New Grove Dictionary of Music and Musicians.,* ed. Stanley Sadie. London: Macmillan.

Ottenberg, Phoebe. 1965. "The Afikpo Ibo of Eastern Nigeria." In *Peoples of Africa,* ed. James L. Gibbs, Jr., 1–39. New York: Holt, Rinehart and Winston.

Oven, Cootje van. 1980. "Sierra Leone." *The New Grove Dictionary of Music and Musicians,* ed. Stanley Sadie. London: Macmillan.

———. 1981. *An Introduction to the Music of Sierra Leone.* Wassenaar, Netherlands: Cootje van Oven.

Rood, Armistead P. 1969. "Bété Masked Dance: A View from Within." *African Arts* 2(3):37–43, 76.

Rouget, Gilbert. 1980a. "Benin." *The New Grove Dictionary of Music and Musicians,* ed. Stanley Sadie. London: Macmillan.

———. 1980b. "Guinea." *The New Grove Dictionary of Music and Musicians,* ed. Stanley Sadie. London: Macmillan.

Schaeffner, André. 1980. "Mali: Dogon Music." *The New Grove Dictionary of Music and Musicians,* ed. Stanley Sadie. London: Macmillan.

Seavoy, Mary Hermaine. 1982. "The Sisaala Xylophone Tradition." Ph.D. dissertation. University of California at Los Angeles.

Stenning, Derrick J. 1960. "Transhumance, Migratory Drift, Migration: Patterns of Pastoral Fulani Nomadism." In *Cultures and Societies of Africa,* ed. Simon and Phoebe Ottenberg, 139–159. New York: Random House.

———. 1965. "The Pastoral Fulani of Northern Nigeria." In *Peoples of Africa,* ed. James L. Gibbs, Jr., 363–401. New York: Holt, Rinehart and Winston.

Stone, Ruth M. 1980. "Liberia." *The New Grove Dictionary of Music and Musicians,* ed. Stanley Sadie. London: Macmillan.

Surugue, B. 1980. "Songhay Music." *The New Grove Dictionary of Music and Musicians,* ed. Stanley Sadie. London: Macmillan.

Swanson, Richard Alan. 1985. *Gourmantche Ethnoanthropology: A Theory of Human Being.* Lanham, Md.: University Press of America.

Thieme, Darius. 1969. "A Descriptive Catalogue of Yoruba Musical Instruments." Ph.D. dissertation, Catholic University of America.

———. 1970. "Music in Yoruba Society." In *Development of Materials for a One Year Course in African Music for the General Undergraduate Student (Project in African Music),* ed. Vada E. Butcher, 107–111. Washington: Howard University Press.

Wilks, Ivor. 1971. "The Mossi and the Akan States, 1500 to 1800." In *History of West Africa,* vol. 1, ed. J. F. A. Ajayi and Michael Crowder, 344–386. London: Longman.

———. 1985. "The Mossi and the Akan States, 1400 to 1800." In *History of West Africa,* vol. 1, 3rd ed., ed. J. F. A. Ajayi and Michael Crowder, 465–502. London: Longman.

Zemp, Hugo. 1980. "Ivory Coast." *The New Grove Dictionary of Music and Musicians,* ed. Stanley Sadie. London: Macmillan.

Yoruba Popular Music

Christopher A. Waterman

General Features
Muslim Genres
Yoruba Highlife
Jùjú
Afro-Beat
Fùjí
"Traditional" and "Popular" Styles

About 30 million Yoruba live in southwestern Nigeria and parts of the Benin Republic and Togo. The term *Yariba* appears in written form in the early 1700s, in Hausa-Fulani clerics' accounts of the kingdom of Ọyọ, one of a series of some twenty independent polities (including Ile-Ifẹ, Ọyọ, Ibadan, Ilọrin, Ẹgba, Ẹgbado, Ijẹbu, Ilẹṣa, Ondo, Ekiti). Expansion of the Ọyọ Empire and its successor state, Ibadan, encouraged the application of this term to a larger population. The spread of certain musical instruments and genres—including the *dùndún,* an hourglass-shaped pressure drum ("talking drum"), now among the most potent symbols of pan-Yoruba identity, and the *bàtá,* an ensemble of conical, two-headed drums, associated with the thunder god Ṣango—played a role in Ọyọ's attempt to establish a cultural underpinning for imperial domination.

Inter-Yoruba wars of the 1700s and 1800s encouraged the dispersal of musicians, especially praise singers and talking drummers. We might regard such performers as predecessors of today's popular musicians, since their survival as craft specialists depended largely upon creating broadly comprehensible and appealing styles. Some performers, linked exclusively to particular communities, kin groups, or cults, were responsible for mastering secret knowledge, protected by supernatural sanctions; but other, more mobile musicians, exploiting regional economic networks, had to develop a broader and shallower corpus of musical techniques and verbal texts.

In the late 1800s and early 1900s, a pan-Yoruba popular culture emerged, but perceptions of cultural differences among regional subgroups survived. Dialect and musical style continued to play a role in maintaining local identities and allegiances, providing a framework for criticism of regional and national politics (Barber 1991; Apter 1992). Yoruba popular musicians have often drawn upon the traditions of their natal communities to create distinctive "sounds," intended to give them a competitive edge in the marketplace.

In the early 1900s, in and around Lagos (port and colonial capital), syncretic cultural forms—including religious movements, plus traditions of theater, dance, and music—reinforced Yoruba identity. By 1900, the heterogeneous population of Lagos included culturally diverse groups: a local Yoruba community, Sierra Leonean, Brazilian, and Cuban repatriates, Yoruba immigrants from the hinterland, and a

The practice of "spraying"—in which a satisfied praisee dances up to the bandleader or praise singer and pastes money to his forehead—provides the bulk of musicians' profits.

sprinkling of other migrants from Nigeria and farther afield. Interaction among these groups was a crucial factor in the development of Yoruba popular culture during the early 1900s. Lagos was also a locus for importing new musical technology, and, beginning in 1928, for commercial recording by European firms. Since the late 1800s, continual flows of people, techniques, and technologies between Lagos and hinterland communities have shaped Yoruba popular culture.

GENERAL FEATURES

Performances of most genres of Yoruba popular music occur at elaborate parties after rites of passage, such as namings, weddings, and funerals, and at urban nightspots ("hotels"). Recorded music of local and foreign origin is played, often at high volume, in patrilineal compounds, taxicabs, barbershops, and kiosks. Some genres of popular music are associated with popular Islam, and others with syncretic Christianity; some praise the powerful, and others critique social inequality; some have texts in Yoruba, and others in pidgin English; some are fast, vigorous, and youthful in spirit, and others are slow and solemn, "music for the elders."

Yoruba popular music fuses the role of song (a medium for praise, criticism, and moralizing) and the role of rhythmic coordination in sound and physical movement (an expression of sociability and sensory pleasure). As tradition is important to Yoruba musicians and listeners, so are the transnational forces that shape their lives. Yoruba popular culture—not only music, but also styles of dancing, televised comedies and dramas, tabloids, sports, gambling, slang, and fashion in clothing and hair—incorporates imported technologies and exotic styles, thus providing Yoruba listeners with an experiential bridge between local and global culture.

The organization of instruments in Yoruba popular music generally follows the pattern of traditional drumming (Euba 1990): an *iyá'lù* 'mother drum' leads the ensemble, and one or more *omele* 'supporting drums' play ostinatos, designed to interlock rhythmically. In *jùjú,* electric guitars are organized on this pattern. Another practice associated with deep Yoruba (*ìjinlẹ̀ẹ Yorùbá*) tradition is the use of musical instruments to "speak." Yoruba is a tonal language, in which distinctions of pitch and timbre play important roles in determining the meaning of words. *Jùjú, fújì,* and most other popular genres employ some variant of the *dùndún,* which articulates stereotyped contours of pitch, representing verbal formulas such as proverbs (*òwe*) and epithets of praise (*oríkì*). Imported instruments—such as congas, electric guitars, and drum synthesizers—also serve to articulate proverbs and epithets of praise, though musicians say such instruments are less "talkative" than pressure drums.

In most genres, the bandleader (often called a captain) is a praise singer who initiates solo vocal phrases (*dá orin* 'creates song alone'), segments of which a chorus doubles. He also sings responsorial sequences, in which his improvised phrases alternate with a fixed phrase, sung by the chorus. His calls are *elé,* the nominal form of the verb *lé* 'to drive something away from or into something else'. Both the responses and the vocalists who sing them are *ègbè* (from *gbè* 'to support, side with, or protect someone'). The social structure of popular music ensembles is closely linked to traditional ideals of social organization, which simultaneously stress the "naturalness" of hierarchy and the mutual dependency of leaders and supporters.

The practice of "spraying"—in which a satisfied praisee dances up to the bandleader or praise singer and pastes (*lẹ*) money to his forehead—provides the bulk of musicians' profits. Cash advances, guaranteed minimums, and record royalties are, except in the case of a handful of superstars, minor sources of income. The dynamics of remuneration are linked to the musical form, which is often modular or serial. Performances of *jùjú* and *fújì* typically consist of a series of expressive strategies—proverbs and praise names, slang, melodic quotations, and satisfying dance grooves—unreeled with an eye toward pulling in the maximum amount of cash from patrons.

Song texts

Some genres—and even segments of particular performances—are weighted more toward the text-song side of the spectrum, others more to the instrument-dance side. Colloquial aesthetic terminology suggests a developed appreciation of certain aural qualities—dense, buzzing textures, vibrant contrasts in tone color, and rhythmic energy and flow. Nevertheless, Yoruba listeners usually concentrate most carefully on the words of a performance. One of the most damning criticisms listeners can level against a singer or drummer is that he speaks incoherently, or does not choose his words to suit the occasion.

Yoruba song texts are centrally concerned with competition, fate (*orí* 'head'), and the limits of human knowledge in an uncertain universe. Invidious comparison—between the bandleader and competing musicians (who seek to trip him up), or between the patron whose praises are sung and his or her enemies—is the rhetorical linchpin of Yoruba popular music. Advertisements for business concerns are common in live performance and on commercial recordings. Musicians praise brands of beer and cigarettes, hotels, rug makers, football pools, and patent medicines.

Prayers for protection—offered to Jesus, or to Allah, or to the creator deity Eledumare—are another common rhetorical strategy. *Ayé* 'life, the world' is portrayed as a transitory and precarious condition, a conception evoked by phrases like *ayé fẹlẹ̀- fẹ̀ẹ̀* 'flimsy world' and *ayé gbègi* 'world that chips like wood or pottery'. Song texts continually evoke the conceptual dialectic of *ayínikẹ́* and *ayínipadà*—the reality that can be perceived and, if one is clever and lucky, manipulated; and the unseen, potentially menacing underside of things. Competition for access to patrons and touring overseas is fierce, sometimes involving the use of magical medicines and curses. Yoruba pop music stars have often carried out bitter rhetorical battles on a series of recordings. This practice harnesses the praise-abuse principle to the profit motive, because to keep up with the feud, audiences have to buy each record.

Another major theme of the lyrics of popular songs is sensual enjoyment (*igbádùn* 'sweetness perception'). Singers and talking drummers often switch from themes of religious piety and deep moral philosophy to flirtatious teasing, focused on references to dancers' bodily exertions. Many musicians have adopted good-timing honorifics, such as "minister of enjoyment," "father of good order," "ikebe [butt] king." The images of pleasure projected in *jùjú* and *fújì* are related to the themes of praise and the search for certainty. The subject of praise singing is rhetorically encased in a warm web of social relationships: surrounded by supporters and shielded from enemies, her head "swells" with pride (*iwúlórí*) as she sways to "rolling" (*yí*) rhythms.

wákà   Usually performed by women and originally intended for the spiritual inspiration of participants in Muslim ceremonies

sákárà   Music for social dancing and praising that is performed and patronized mostly by Muslims; also, a frame drum

gòjé   Single-stringed bowed lute made of a calabash and covered with skin

móló   Three-stringed plucked lute commonly used in sákárà ensembles in the 1920s and 1930s

àpàlà   Yoruba popular music that developed from music performed on *gángan* talking drums to entertain women

MUSLIM GENRES

Performing styles associated with Islam and Christianity have strongly influenced Yoruba popular music. One group of genres—*wákà, sákárà, àpàlà*—is associated with Muslim people and social contexts. Though Islamic authorities do not officially approve of indulgence in music, the success of Islam among the Yoruba (as elsewhere in West Africa) has depended on its ability to adapt to local cultural values. Many traditional drummers are Muslims, and some of the biggest patrons of popular music are wealthy Muslim entrepreneurs. Examples of the genres discussed in this section are included on the compact disc *Yoruba Street Percussion* (1992).

Wákà

The Yoruba adopted *wákà* music from the Hausa, probably in the early 1800s. Usually performed by women, these songs were originally intended for the spiritual inspiration of participants in Muslim ceremonies. They were performed unaccompanied, or with hand clapping. In the early 1920s, tin cymbals with jingles (*sèlí* or *pèrèsèkè*) became their preferred accompaniment. Soon after the mid-1940s, drums and other percussive instruments were introduced. By the 1970s, the typical ensemble included five or six singers, a pressure drum (*àdàmò*), one or more *àkúbà* or *ògìdo* (conga-type drums, based on Latin American prototypes), a bottle-gourd rattle (*sèkèrè*), and a bass lamellophone (*agídìgbo*). This development appears to have been centered in the Ijebu area. By the mid-1990s, *wákà* had come to be regarded as a specialty of the Ijebu, though Muslims in all the Yoruba subgroups performed and patronized them. The combination of instruments added to *wákà* groups after 1945—*dùndún, àkúbà, sèkèrè, agídìgbo*—and the rhythmic patterns they played on recordings suggest the influence of *àpàlà*, another popular genre associated with the Ijebu.

Though *wákà* songs were first recorded in Lagos in the late 1920s, only after 1945 did professional specialists perform them. Their lyrics increasingly dealt with secular matters, earning the approbation of orthodox Muslims. By the mid-1960s, the producer in charge of Muslim religious broadcasts for the Western State Service of the Nigerian Broadcasting Corporation had begun to refer *wákà* musicians to the corporation's music department (Euba 1971:178). *Wákà* bandleaders downplay the Islamic associations of the genre, claiming to have many Christian patrons. Though this stance is in part a matter of public relations, the most popular *wákà* singers have expanded their networks of patronage to include many non-Muslims. Popular *wákà* singers have included Majaro Acagba (popular in the 1920s and 1930s), Batile Alake (1950s–1960s), and the contemporary superstar Queen Salawa Abeni (b. 1965), who has brought aspects of *fújì* into her style.

Sákárà

A genre of music for social dancing and praising, *sákárà* is performed and patronized mostly by Muslims. Oral traditions attribute its origins to Yoruba migrants in Bida, a Nupe town (Ojo 1978:1–4), or to Ilorin, the northernmost major Yoruba town, a prominent center of Islamic proselytization in Yorubaland (Euba 1971:179; Delano 1973[1937]:153). Examples of the genre were being performed in Ibadan and Lagos during or soon after the Great War (1914–1918). Many influential *sákárà* musicians have come from the Egba Yoruba town of Abeokuta.

The term *sákárà* denotes an instrument, a musical genre, and a style of dancing. The instruments used in a typical *sákárà* ensemble include a single-membrane frame drum, with a body consisting of a circular ring of baked clay (*sákárà*); an idiophone made from a gourd cut in half (*ahá*), or a whole gourd held in both hands and struck with ringed fingers (*igbá*); and a single-stringed bowed lute, made of a calabash and covered with skin (*gòjé*). The ensemble is led by a praise singer, who often also plays the *gòjé*. The *gòjé* shares a melodic line with the lead *sákárà* drummer and the lead singer, and plays short variations on the melodic line in a highly ornamented style (Thieme 1969:393). The lead drummer cues changes in tempo and style, and plays praise names, proverbs, and slang phrases.

The *móló*, a plucked three-stringed lute, was commonly used in *sákárà* ensembles during the 1920s and 1930s (Delano 1937:153–157), but was eventually displaced by the *gòjé*. The *gòjé*'s greater volume and penetrating timbre made it the preferred instrument for live performance and recording. During the same period, the acoustic guitar displaced the *móló* in informal, small-group settings. The *móló* has virtually disappeared in Yorubaland (Thieme 1969:387–390).

Sákárà is regarded as a "solemn" style—a term denoting stateliness of tempo and demeanor, with a philosophical depth of lyrics. It has come to be regarded as a traditional genre, despite its association with Muslim contexts, performers, and patrons. This regard is partly due to singers' eloquence in using Yoruba poetic idioms, and partly to the fact that stylistic features of *sákárà* associated with Islamic cantillation—vocal tension and nasality, melodic ornamentation, melisma—have been reinterpreted as indigenous traits.

The first star of *sákárà* was Abibu Oluwa, popularly known as *Oniwáàsì* 'The Preacher'. In the late 1920s and 1930s, he was recorded by Odeon, His Master's Voice, and Parlophone Records. The biggest star on recordings of the 1940s was Ojo Olewale; in the 1950s and 1960s, S. Aka, Ojindo, and Yusufu Ọlatunji ("*Baba l'ẹgbà*") competed for supremacy, often engaging in thinly veiled character attacks, preserved on commercial recordings. In the 1960s, youths in towns throughout Yorubaland still performed *sákárà*, competing on the mass market with styles such as *jùjú* and *àpàlà*. However, by the 1970s, it was regarded primarily as a music for old people, and Yusufu Ọlatunji had been enshrined as the genre's founder.

Àpàlà

This genre originated in the Ijẹbu area, probably in the early 1940s. According to one practitioner, it developed from music performed on *gángan* talking drums to entertain women. It may have represented a conscious effort on the part of professional *gángan* drummers to counter growth in the popularity of *sákárà* and *ẹtikẹ,* a secular genre of *dùndún* drumming (Euba 1990:441). The effort was successful: during the 1960s and 1970s, as the popularity of *sákárà* faded, *àpàlà* became the dominant genre of popular music among Yoruba Muslims. Though the leaders of *àpàlà* groups were originally drummers, by the 1960s the most popular and influential bandleaders—Ligali Mukaiba, Kasumu Adio, Alhaji Haruna Iṣọla—were singers. By the 1970s, Iṣọla and Alhaji Ayinla Ọmọwura (an Ẹgba musician) were the brightest stars of *àpàlà* music.

The typical *àpàlà* group includes a lead singer (usually the bandleader) and

The tradition of highlife dance bands originated in the early 1900s in Accra, capital of Gold Coast (Ghana).

several choral singers, two or more drums from the *àdàmò* pressure-drum family (called *àpàlà* drums by some musicians), one or more *àkúbà* or *ògìdo,* an *agídìgbo,* and a *şèkèrè*. *Àpàlà* varies in tempo, and, as with other styles of social dance drumming, there are specialized styles for younger and older people. *Àpàlà* rhythms are organized along the basic principles of *gángan* drumming: one drummer takes the role of the lead drum *(iyá'lù)*, others act as the *omele,* and the *ògìdo* and the *agídìgbo* anchor the bass. A metal idiophone—an *agogo* 'iron bell', or a truck muffler or wheel—plays a repeated timeline. One of the rhythms commonly used in *àpàlà* is *wórò*, a social dance style of drumming that spread throughout Yorubaland during the political rallies of the 1950s.

The lyrics of *àpàlà* fit into the praise song mold. The recorded output of Haruna Işola, for example, includes hundreds of songs named after benefactors and important personalities (*gbajúmò* 'a thousand eyes know them'). Many of the human subjects of *àpàlà* lyrics are Muslims, but to attract a larger Yoruba-speaking audience, singers explore topics of broad interest. In 1959, Işola recorded a song on the Nigerian boxer Hogan Bassey's bout with David Moore:

L'ójó Sátidé l'Améríkà,
Máaşì ojó kejìdínlógún ni wón f'arésí,
Ni naintin-fiftinain-i nìjá'bósí.
Sé erójú ayé-o?
Hogan Bassey pèlú David Moore ni wón mà forí gbárí,
Níbi tí wón ti ńjà l'ójó yẹn.
Éjè lódí l'ójú kò rẹ̀nì kan.
Ọkan ò ri ojú inú ló ńlò.
David Moore bá fi èrú gba taitulù lọ tempoari.
Nwón tonra wọn jẹ l'ásán nii.
Kìnìún kò ní'jà k'ẹran wẹ́wẹ́ ta féle-fèle.
T'órí ẹ bá gbóná, t'o bá tọ gñrì alè,
Ẹran t'ó bá lọ débè ló mí a yámútù [Hausa word].

On a Saturday in America,
It was on the 18th of March that the contest was held.
The fight took place in 1959.
Do you see the eyes of the world? [Do you see what happened?]
Hogan Bassey and David Moore, they knocked their heads together,
Where they were fighting that day.
He had blood in his eyes, didn't see anybody.
Nobody saw him, it is his inner mind that he used.
David Moore used tricks to take the title away from him temporarily.
They [the Americans] are fooling themselves: it was vanity.

The lion will not fight; small animals start scattering (when the fight begins).
If he should get angry, if he should piss copiously,
Any small animals that go to that place must die.

To explain Bassey's loss, regarded as an international embarrassment for Nigeria, Iṣọla uses a tale about the power of the lion and popular beliefs concerning the efficacy of talismans. Vocalized in a nasal, melismatic style, and supported by interlocking rhythms, his song is at once Yoruba, Muslim, and cosmopolitan.

The golden age of *àpàlà* was the 1950s. By the 1990s, a few groups were still working in cities such as Ijẹbu-Ode and Ibadan, but *àpàlà*, like *sákárà*, was no longer a music for youths. The two charismatic stars of the genre, Iṣọla (of Ijẹbu-Igbo) and Ọmọwura (of Abẹokuta), died in the 1980s.

YORUBA HIGHLIFE

The tradition of highlife dance bands originated in the early 1900s in Accra, capital of Gold Coast (Ghana). Before the 1940s, Ghanaian bands (such as the Cape Coast Sugar Babies) had traveled to Lagos, where they left a lasting impression on local musicians. In the 1920s and 1930s, Lagos was home to the Calabar Brass Band, which recorded for Parlophone as the Lagos Mozart Orchestra. The core of the band was martial band instruments: clarinets, trumpets and cornets, baritones, trombones, tuba, and parade drums. The band played a proto-highlife style, a transitional phase between the colonial martial band and the African dance orchestra.

During the 1930s and 1940s, Lagos supported several African ballroom dance orchestras, including the Chocolate Dandies, the Lagos City Orchestra, the Rhythm Brothers, the Deluxe Swing Rascals, and the Harlem Dynamites. These bands played for the city's African élites, a social formation comprised largely of Sierra Leonean and Brazilian repatriates, whose grandparents had returned to Lagos in the 1800s. Their repertory included foxtrots, waltzes, Latin dances, and arrangements of popular Yoruba songs.

The 1950s are remembered as the Golden Age of Yoruba highlife. Scores of highlife bands played at hotels in Lagos and the major Yoruba towns. Bobby Benson's Jam Session Orchestra (founded in 1948) exerted a particularly strong influence on Yoruba highlife. A guitarist who had worked as a dance band musician in England, Benson brought the first electric guitar to Lagos (1948), opened his own nightclub (Caban Bamboo), and employed many of the best musicians in Nigeria. His 1960 recording of "Taxi Driver, I Don't Care" (Philips P 82019), was the biggest hit of the highlife era in Nigeria. During the 1950s and 1960s, many of his apprentices—Victor Ọlaiya ("the evil genius of highlife"), Roy Chicago, Edy Okonta, Fela Ransome-Kuti—went on to form their own bands.

The typical highlife band included from three to five winds, plus string bass, guitar, bongos, conga, and maracas. Though the sound of British and American dance bands influenced the African bands, the emphasis was on Latin American repertory, rather than on swing arrangements. Unlike *jùjú* bands, highlife bands often included non-Yoruba members, and typically performed songs in several languages, including Yoruba, English, and pidgin English.

By the mid-1960s, highlife was declining in Yorubaland, partly as a result of competition from *jùjú*. Some highlife bandleaders, including Roy Chicago, incorporated the *dùndún,* and in an attempt to compete with *jùjú* began to use more deep Yoruba verbal materials. Musicians such as Dele Ojo, who had apprenticed with Victor Ọlaiya, forged hybrid *jùjú*-highlife styles. Soul, popular among urban youth from around 1966, attacked highlife from another angle. The Nigerian civil war

jùjú Named for the tambourine, this popular music genre of the Yoruba emerged in
Lagos around 1932

aṣíkò Dance drumming style, performed
mainly by Yoruba Christian boys' clubs

sámbà Square frame drum that may have
been introduced to the Yoruba by the
Brazilians

ògìdo Bass conga drum of the Yoruba

(1967–1970), which caused many of the best Igbo musicians to leave Lagos, delivered the final blow. By the mid-1990s, highlife bands had become rare in
Yorubaland.

JÙJÚ

This genre, named for the tambourine (*jùjú*), emerged in Lagos around 1932. The
typical *jùjú* group in the 1930s was a trio: a leader (who sang and played banjo), a
ṣèkèrè, and a *jùjú*. Some groups operated as quartets, adding a second vocalist. The
basic framework was drawn from palm wine guitar music, played by a mobile population of African workers in Lagos (sailors, railway men, truck drivers).

The rhythms of early *jùjú* were strongly influenced by *aṣíkò*, a dance drumming
style, performed mainly by Christian boys' clubs. Many early *jùjú* bandleaders began
their careers as *aṣíkò* musicians. Played on square frame drums and a carpenter's saw,
aṣíkò drew upon the traditions of two communities of Yoruba-speaking repatriates
who had settled in Lagos during the 1800s: the Amaro were *emancipados* of Brazilian
or Cuban descent, and the Saro were Sierra Leonean repatriates (who formed a
majority of the educated black élite in Lagos). *Aṣíkò* rhythms came from the Brazilian
samba (many older Nigerians use the terms *aṣíkò* and *sámbà* interchangeably), and
the associated style of dancing was influenced by the *caretta* 'fancy dance', a Brazilian
version of the contredanse. The square *sámbà* drum may have been introduced by the
Brazilians (known for their carpentry), or from the British West Indies, perhaps via
Sierra Leone. Though identifying a single source for the introduction of the frame
drum is impossible, this drum was clearly associated with immigrant black Christian
identity.

Early styles

The first star of *jùjú* was Tunde King, born in 1910 into the Saro community.
Though a member of the Muslim minority, he learned Christian hymns while
attending primary school. He made the first recordings with the term *jùjú* on the
label, recorded by Parlophone in 1936. Ayinde Bakare, a Yoruba migrant who recorded for His Master's Voice beginning in 1937, began as an *aṣíkò* musician, and went
on to become one of the most influential figures in postwar *jùjú*. Musical style was an
important idiom for the expression of competitive relationships between neighborhoods. During the 1930s, each quarter in Lagos had its favorite *jùjú* band.

The melodies of early *jùjú*, modeled on *aṣíkò* and palm wine songs and
Christian hymns, were diatonic, often harmonized in parallel thirds. The vocal style
used the upper range of the male full-voice tessitura, and was nasalized and moderately tense, with no vibrato. The banjo—including a six-stringed guitar-banjo and a
mandolin-banjo—played a role similar to that of the fiddle in *sákárà* music, often
introducing or bridging between vocal segments, and providing heterophonic accompaniment for the vocal line. *Jùjú* banjoists used a technique of thumb and forefinger
plucking (*krusbass*) introduced to Lagos by Liberian sailors.

From the beginning, *jùjú* lyrics drew heavily upon deep Yoruba metaphors. In "Association" (recorded by Parlophone in 1936), Tunde King sings:

> Agbe ló l'áró; kìí ráhùn áró.
> Àlùkò ló l'ósùn; kìí ráhùn osùn.
> Lékéléké, kìí ráhùn ẹfun
> Ìyàwó àkọ́fé, kìí ráhùn ajé
> Òkèlẹ́ ẹ̀bà, kìí ráhùn ọbẹ́
>
> K'árìrà máà mà jẹ́ẹráhùn owó.
> K'árìrà máà mà jẹ́ẹ ráhùnọmọ.

> The blue touraco parrot is the owner of indigo dye; it doesn't usually complain
>   for want of indigo dye.
> The red aluko bird is the owner of rosewood; it doesn't usually complain for
>   want of rosewood.
> The white cattle egret doesn't usually complain for want of chalk.
> The first wife one marries doesn't usually complain for want of money.
> The first morsel of cassava porridge doesn't usually complain for want of soup.
>
> Good fortune, don't let us complain for want of money.
> Good fortune, don't let us complain for want of children.

Here, King draws on Yoruba oral tradition to forge a metaphoric correspondence between a natural relationship (birds, bright colors) and a cultural one (beginnings, abundance). Other examples of his style are on the compact disc *Juju Roots: 1930s–1950s* (1993).

After the mid-1940s, *jùjú* underwent a rapid transformation. The first major change was the introduction, in 1948, of the *gángan,* attributed to bandleader Akanbi Ege. Another change was the availability of electronic amplifiers, microphones, and pickups. Portable public-address systems had been introduced during the war, and were in regular use by Yoruba musicians by the late 1940s. The first *jùjú* musician to adopt the amplified guitar was Ayinde Bakare. He experimented with a contact microphone in 1949, switching from ukulele-banjo to "box guitar" (acoustic), because there was no place to attach the device to the body of the banjo. Electronic amplification of voices and guitar catalyzed an expansion of *jùjú* ensembles during the 1950s. In particular, it enabled musicians to incorporate more percussion instruments without upsetting the aural balance they wanted between singing and instrumental accompaniment.

In the postwar period, *jùjú* bands began to use the *agídìgbo* and various conga-type drums (*àkúbà, ògìdo*). This reflects the influence of a genre called *agídìgbo* and mambo music, a Yoruba version of *konkoma* music, brought to Lagos by Ewe and Fanti migrant workers (Alájá-Browne 1985:64). According to *jùjú* musicians active at the time, the *agídìgbo* and *ògìdo* (bass conga) provided a bass counterbalance for the electric guitar and *gángan*.

The instrumentation of Bakare's group shifted from one stringed instrument and two percussion instruments (before the war), to one stringed instrument and five percussion instruments (in 1954). By 1966, most *jùjú* bands had eight or nine musicians. Expansion and reorganization of the ensemble occurred simultaneously with a slowing of tempos. Slower tempos and expanded ensembles were in turn linked with changes in aural texture. Western technology was put into the service of indigenous aesthetics: the channeling of singing and guitar through cheap and infrequently serviced tube amplifiers and speakers augmented the density and buzzing of the music.

The birth of later jùjú can be traced to the innovations of Isiah Kehinde Dairo, an Ijesa Yoruba musician, who had a series of hit records around the time of Nigerian independence (1960).

The practice of singing in parallel thirds continued to dominate, but there were notable exceptions. Ekiti Yoruba bandleader C. A. Balogun utilized the distinctive polyphonic vocal style of his natal area, in which the overlap between soloist and chorus produces major seconds and minor sevenths. Many bandleaders produced records with a song in standard Yoruba dialect and mainstream *jùjú* style on the A side, and a local Yoruba dialect and style on the B side. Most *jùjú* singing shifted from the high-tessitura, nasalized style of the 1930s and 1940s to a lower, more relaxed sound closer to traditional secular vocal style and the imported model of the crooner. Tunde King's distinctive style of singing was continued by Tunde Western Nightingale, "the bird that sings at night," a popular Lagosian bandleader of the 1950s and 1960s.

Later styles

The birth of later *jùjú* can be traced to the innovations of Isiah Kehinde Dairo (1930–1996), an Ijeṣa Yoruba musician, who had a series of hit records around the time of Nigerian independence (1960). His recordings for the British company Decca were so successful, the British government in 1963 designated him a member of the Order of the British Empire. In 1967, he joined *àpàlà* star Haruna Iṣọla to found Star Records. His hits of the early 1960s, recorded on two-track tape at Decca Studios in Lagos, reveal his mastery of the three-minute recording. Most of his records from this period begin with an accordion or guitar introduction, plus the main lyric, sung once or twice. This leads into a middle section, in which the *dùndún* predominates, playing proverbs and slogans which in turn the chorus repeats. The final section usually reprises the main text.

The vocal style on Dairo's records was influenced by Christian singing of hymns. (Dairo was pastor of a syncretic church in Lagos.) It also reflects the polyphonic singing of eastern Yorubaland (Ileṣa, Ekiti). His lyrics—in Standard Yoruba, Ijeṣa dialect, and various other Nigerian and Ghanaian languages—were also carefully composed. By his own account, he made special efforts to research traditional poetic idioms. Many of his songs consist of philosophical advice and prayers for himself and his patrons, as in the song "*Elele Ture*" (1962):

> Òṣùpá roro, l'ójú òrun toòrò,
> Orí mi ọmọ j'áyé mi toòrò.
> Olú sọjí ọrun, ọmọ j'áyé mi toòrò.
> Ọba tí ómí pẹ́ṣẹ f'éku, ọmọ j'áyé mi toòrò.
> Ọba tí ómí pẹ́ṣẹ f'éyẹ, ọmọ j'áyé mi toòrò.
> T'ó ńpẹ́ṣẹ f'érà t'ù mí rìn l'álẹ́, ọmọ j'áyé mi toòrò.

> Moon shining in the peaceful sky,
> My destiny ["head"], let my life be peaceful.
> King who wakes in heaven, let my life be peaceful.

King that provides for rats, let my life be peaceful.
King that provides for birds, let my life be peaceful.
That provides for ants that walk on the ground, let my life be peaceful.

Jùjú continued to develop along lines established by Bakare and Dairo's experiments. The oil boom of the 1970s led to a rapid, though uneven, expansion of the Nigerian economy. Many individuals earned enough money from trade and entrepreneurial activity to hire musicians for neotraditional celebrations, and the number and size of *jùjú* bands increased concomitantly. By the mid-1970s, the ideal *jùjú* ensemble had expanded beyond the ten-piece bands of Bakare and Dairo to include fifteen or more musicians. Large bands helped boost the reputation of the patrons who hired them to perform at parties, and helped sustain an idealized image of Yoruba society as a flexible hierarchy (Waterman 1990).

Jùjú of the 1990s

Jùjú bands of the mid-1990s fall into three basic sections: singers, percussionists, guitarists. The singers stand in a line at the front of the band. The "band captain" stands in the middle, flanked on either side by choral singers. The percussion section includes from one to three talking drums (*àdàmò*), several conga-type drums, a set of bongos played with light sticks ("double toy"), *ṣèkèrè*, maracas, *agogo*, and in the larger and better-financed bands, a drum set ("jazz drums").

The leader's guitar is tuned to an open triad. He uses it to play simple motifs, which function as the leader's trademark, and cue changes in rhythm or texture. The guitar section also includes a lead guitar, which takes extended solos; two or three "tenor guitars," which serve as *omele* 'supporting instruments'; and a Hawaiian (pedal steel) guitar, which may play solo or add coloristic effects. Melodic patterns come from hymns, Yoruba songs, the old palm wine guitar tradition, and various other sources, including African-American popular music, country, and Indian film music.

Sunny Ade

One star of *jùjú* is King Sunny Adé. Born in Ondo in 1946, he started his musical career playing a *sámbà* drum with a *jùjú* band. He formed his own ensemble, the Green Spot Band, in 1966. He modeled his style on that of Tunde Nightingale, and his vocal sound represents an extension of the high-tessitura, slightly nasalized sound established by Tunde King in the 1930s. His first big hit was "Challenge Cup" (1968), a praise song for a football team, released on a local label, African Songs. In 1970, he added electric bass guitar (displacing the *agídìgbo*), and began to record with imported instruments, purchased for him by his patron, Chief Bọlarinwa Abioro. Adé quickly developed a reputation as a technically skilled musician, and his fans gave him the informal title *Àlùjànuń Onígítà* 'The Wizard of Guitar'. One of his earliest recordings, *"Bolarinwa Abioro"* (1967), is a praise song for Chief Abioro:

> Jẹ́ jẹ́ jẹ́ jẹ́ jẹ́ jẹ́,
> Bọ́lárìnwá mi, ọmọ Abíórò
> Ọkọ Múyìbátù mi, jẹ́jẹ́ ló l'ayé.
> Bọ́lá t'ó bí Bọ́láńlé ló b'Ádébáyọ̀ uṇ lẹ́ ló bí Ọláẹ̀ẹyẹ àti Ọláwùnmí pẹ́lú
>   Ọládọṣù.
> Ìpókíá n'ilé l'area Ẹ̀gbádò.
> Bọ́lárìnwá-o, l'àwá ńbá lọ-o; ibi amí rẹ́ l'àwá dé yìí-o.
> Má mà yún oko n'ígbà òjò;
> Má mà f'ẹsẹ́ kan nini.
> Abíórò, jọ̀-gbọ̀dọ́-e-e-e,
> Aláyé yẹ ẹ́-o.

Apart from Fela Anikulapo Kuti, King Sunny Adé—
"Golden Mercury of Africa, Minister of
Enjoyment"—is the only Nigerian popular musician
who has had significant success in the international
market.

Gently, gently, gently, gently, gently, gently,
My Bolarinwa, child of Abioro,
Husband of Muyibatu, softly, softly, so is the world.
Bola that fathered Adebayo has fathered Oláléye and Olawunmi with Oladosu.
Ipokia is your area, Egbado (region).
Oh Bolarinwa, we are following you; the place we're going to, that's where we've
    reached.
Don't go to the farm in the rainy season;
Don't step on the wet ground.
Abioro, important person,
The world is going to be good for you.

In 1972, splitting with Chief Abioro, Adé changed the name of his band to the
"African Beats." The LP *Synchro System Movement* (1976) artfully blended the vocal
style he had adopted from Tunde Nightingale with aspects of Afro-Beat, including
minor tonality, slower tempos, and a langorous bass. This LP was one of the first
long-play recordings to feature a continuous thirty-minute performance, a move
away from the three-minute limit of most previous recordings, and toward the typical
extended forms of live performances. By 1979, Adé had expanded his band to
include sixteen performers, including two tenor guitars, one rhythm guitar, Hawaiian
guitar, bass guitar, two talking drummers, *sèkèrè*, conga (*àkúbà*), drum set, synthesizer, and four choral vocalists.

Apart from Fela Anikulapo Kuti, King Sunny Adé—"Golden Mercury of Africa,
Minister of Enjoyment"—is the only Nigerian popular musician who has had significant success in the international market. For release by Island Records in 1982, he
recorded the album *Juju Music* in Togo, under the direction of French producer
Martin Meissonnier. The LP reportedly sold 200,000 copies, impressive for African
popular music. Later releases were less successful, and Island Records dropped Adé in
1985. In the mid-1990s, he continued to play to mass audiences in Nigeria, and to
make an occasional tour of the United States and Europe.

Ebenezer Obey

Born in the Egbado area of western Yorubaland in 1942, Chief Commander
Ebenezer Obey is the other star of *jùjú*. He formed his first band, the International
Brothers, in 1964. His early style, strongly influenced by I. K. Dairo, incorporated
elements of highlife, Congolese guitar style, soul, and country. His band expanded
during the years of the oil boom. In 1964, he started with seven players; by the early
1970s, he was employing thirteen; and by the early 1980s, he was touring with eighteen. He is praised for his voice, and for his philosophical depth and knowledge of
Yoruba proverbs. Like Dairo, he is a devout Christian, and many of his songs derive
from the melodies of hymns.

In the 1980s, decline in the economy, devaluation of the currency, and increased competition from *fújì* bands put many of the *jùjú* groups formed during the 1970s out of work. Adé and Obey's only serious competitor is Sir Shina Peters, whose album *Ace* was a big hit in 1990. Peters's style represents an attempt to bring dance rhythms from *fújì* music into *jùjú*. The history of *jùjú* provides many examples of strategic borrowing from competing genres.

AFRO-BEAT

Centered on the charismatic figure Fela Anikulapo Kuti (born in 1938 in Abeokuta), Afro-Beat began in the late 1960s as a confluence of dance band highlife, jazz, and soul. Though in style and content it stands somewhat apart from the mainstream of Yoruba popular music, it has influenced *jùjú* and *fújì*.

Fela is the grandson of the Reverend J. J. Ransome-Kuti (a prominent educator, who played a major role in indigenizing Christian hymns). His mother was Funmilayo Ransome-Kuti (a political activist, founder of the Nigerian Women's Union). It is said that Fela received his musicality from his father's family, and his temperament from his mother's. In the mid-1950s, he played with Bobby Benson's and Victor Olaiya's highlife orchestras. In 1958, he traveled to London to study trumpet at Trinity College of Music. While there, he joined with J. K. Braimah to form Koola Lobitos, a band that played a jazz-highlife hybrid. Fela returned to Lagos in 1963, and by 1966 had been voted the top jazz performer in a readers' poll, held by *Spear Magazine*. Though his reputation grew among musicians in Lagos, his music appealed primarily to an audience of collegians and professionals.

The popularity of soul among young people in Lagos during the late 1960s strongly influenced Fela. In particular, the success of Geraldo Pino, a Sierra Leonean imitator of James Brown, caused him to incorporate aspects of soul into his style. A 1969 trip to the United States, where he met black activists, changed his political orientation and his concept of the goals of music making. In 1970, on returning to Lagos, he formed a new group, Africa '70, and began to develop Afro-Beat, a mixture of highlife and soul, with infusions of deep Yoruba verbal materials.

In the early 1970s, Fela's style centered on Tony Allen's drumming, Maurice Ekpo's electric-bass playing, and Peter Animaṣaun's rhythm-guitar style (influenced by James Brown's playing). The band also included three congas, percussion sticks, *ṣèkèrè*, and a four-piece horn section (two trumpets, tenor sax, baritone sax). Jazz-influenced solos were provided by trumpeter Tunde Williams and the brilliant tenor saxophonist Igo Chico. Like many Lagos highlife bands of the 1950s, Fela's early bands included Ghanaians and non-Yoruba Nigerians. The original Africa '70 stayed together until the mid-1970s, when Fela's increasingly autocratic behavior led Allen and Chico to quit.

Over more than twenty years, the organizational principles of Afro-Beat have remained remarkably constant. The basic rhythm-section pattern divides into complementary strata: a bottom layer, made up of interlocking electric-bass and bass-drum patterns; a middle layer, with a rhythm guitar, congas, and a snare back beat; and a top layer, with percussion sticks and *ṣèkèrè* playing ostinatos. The horn section provides riffs in support of Fela's singing, and its members play extended solos.

Fela's early recordings included love songs ("Lover"), risqué songs in pidgin English ("*Na Poi*"), and Yoruba songs based on proverbs and tales ("*Alujọn jọn ki jọn*"). In the mid-1970s, Fela composed increasingly strident lyrics, attacking the excesses of foreign capitalism and Nigerian leaders. It was then that the textual content of Afro-Beat clearly separated from the mainstream of Yoruba popular music. Fela's political goals—shouted by his trademark slogan, "Music is a weapon"—led him to compose more in pidgin English, to reach a wider international audience.

fújì   Popular genre of Yoruba music in the
1990s; grew out of Muslim practices but
also gained a Christian audience

ajísáàrì   Music customarily performed before
dawn during Ramadan by young men
among the Yoruba

Records such as *Zombie* (ridiculing the Nigerian military), and *Expensive Shit* (recounting the efforts of police to recover drugs from Fela's feces) established his reputation as a fearless rebel, and consolidated his audience, composed largely of urban youth and members of the intelligentsia.

Fela was first arrested by the Nigerian secret police in 1974. Three years later, the military attacked his compound, the "Kalakuta Republic," and threw his mother from a window, causing internal injuries from which she died. Fela responded with the LP *Coffin for Head of State,* covered with a montage of newspaper clippings reporting his mother's death and funeral. Continued run-ins with the Nigerian government stiffened his resistance to authority.

In the early 1980s, Fela developed a mystical philosophy, based on reconstructed Yoruba religion, Afrocentrism, Egyptology, and the teachings of a Ghanaian prophet, Professor Hindu. He changed the name of his band to Egypt '80. In the mid-1980s, his band included nine horn players (three trumpets, one alto sax, three tenor saxes, two baritone saxes), two guitarists, two bassists, a drum set, three congas, two *ṣèkèrè*, and around a dozen singers and dancers. His typical composition became longer and more complex—"a song with five movements . . . a symphony but in the African sense" (Fela, quoted in Stewart 1992:117). The sound of the ensemble shifted toward a denser texture. In some subsequent recordings (like *Teacher Don't Teach Me Nonsense,* 1986), Fela experiments with polytonality: while the rhythm section stays near one tonal center, the horns explore another (a fourth or a fifth away).

Fela's music continues to exert influence on Yoruba musicians, though it achieves far fewer local record sales than *jùjú* or *fújì*. Fela's biographers have depicted him as a paradoxical figure: a revolutionary traditionalist, a materialist mystic, an egalitarian dictator, a progressive sexist. Yet for all his idiosyncracies, he is as much a product of Yoruba historical experience as King Sunny Adé.

FÚJÌ

This genre, the most popular one in the early 1990s, grew out of *ajísáàrì*, music customarily performed before dawn during Ramadan by young men associated with neighborhood mosques. *Ajísáàrì* groups, made up of a lead singer, a chorus, and drummers, walk through their neighborhood, stopping at patrilineal compounds to wake the faithful for their early morning meal (*sáàrì*). *Fújì* emerged as a genre and marketing label in the late 1960s, when former *ajísáàrì*-singers Sikiru Ayinde Barrister and Ayinla Kollington were discharged from the Nigerian Army, made their first recordings, and began a periodically bitter rivalry. In the early 1970s, *fújì* succeeded *àpàlà* as the most popular genre among Yoruba Muslims, and has since gained a substantial Christian audience.

The instrumentation of *fújì* bands features drums. Most important are various sizes of talking-drum (*dùndún, àdàmọ,* and sometimes a smaller hourglass-shaped drum, the *kànàngó*, two or three of which may be played by a single drummer). Bands often include *sákárà* drums (still associated with Muslim identity), plus the conga-type drums used in *àpàlà* and *jùjú*. Commonly, they also use *sèkèrè,* maracas, and a set of *agogo* attached to a metal rack. In the mid-1980s, *fújì* musicians borrowed the drum set from *jùjú*. The wealthiest bands use electronic drum pads connected to synthesizers.

Other experiments represent an attempt to forge symbolic links with deep Yoruba traditions. In the early 1980s, Alhaji Barrister introduced into his style the *bàtá* drum, associated with the Yoruba thunder god Ṣango. He named the drum "Fújì Bàtá Reggae." He dropped the *bàtá* after influential Muslim patrons complained about his using a quintessentially pagan instrument. On other recordings, he employed the *kàkàkí*, an indigenous trumpet, used for saluting the kings of northern Yoruba towns.

Later appropriations of Western instruments—the Hawaiian or pedal steel guitar, keyboard synthesizers, and drum machines—have largely been filtered through *jùjú*. Some *jùjú* musicians complain that *fújì* musicians, whom they regard as musical illiterates, have no idea what to do with such instruments. In fact, imported high-tech instruments are usually used in *fújì* recordings to play melodic sequences without harmonic accompaniment, to signal changes of rhythm or subject, and to add coloristic effects—techniques consistent with the norms of the genre.

Though *fújì* has to a large degree been secularized, it is still associated with Muslims, and record companies time the release of certain *fújì* recordings to coincide with holy days, such as Id-al-Fitr and Id-al-Kabir. Segments of Qur'ānic text are frequently deployed in performance, and many *fújì* recordings open with a prayer in Yoruba Arabic: "*La ilaha illa llahu; Mohamudu ya asuru lai* 'There is no god but Allah; Mohammed is his prophet'."

Fújì music is an intensively syncretic style, incorporating aspects of Muslim recitations, Christian hymns, highlife classics, *jùjú* songs, Indian film-music themes, and American pop, within a rhythmic framework based on Yoruba social-dance drumming. To demonstrate knowledge of Yoruba tradition, *fújì* musicians also make use of folkloric idioms, like proverbs and praise names. On his 1990 LP and music video *Music Extravaganza*, Barrister borrows from an animal fable to denigrate his rivals:

> Tí Àwòko bá ńṣeré, kéyẹ-kéyẹ má à fóhùn l'ẹyẹ oko.
> Àròyé n'iṣẹ́ ìbákà-o; igbe kíké ni ṣ'éyẹ.
> B'ólóògbùrọ́ ṣél'óhùn tó, ó yí foríbalẹ̀ f'Ọ́ba Orin.
> Ati àròyé ìbákà-o, at'igbe kíkẹ̀ ni ṣ'éyẹ̀,
> B'áwòko ò m'órin wá,
> Àròyé kín'ìbákà máa ríwí?
> Igbe kíl'ẹyẹ owulẹ́ kẹ́ lásọ́n-làsọ̀n?
> Kíni ol'óbúrò ó fi ohùn orin kọ?

> When *Awoko* is singing, all these lesser birds shouldn't make a sound.
> Incessant yammering is Canary's work; hoarse shouting is the birds' work.
> Even the speckled pigeon with a beautiful voice must prostrate before the King of Song.
> With Canary's babbling and the birds' chattering,
> If *Awoko* doesn't bring songs,
> What kind of babbling will the Canary do?
> What noise would the birds bother to make?
> What song would a speckled pigeon use her voice to sing?

If Yoruba popular music is a product of markets, it is also, in important ways, unlike other commodities. Yoruba musicians and audiences regard music as a potent force with material and spiritual effects.

Awoko, a local bird (known for the complexity and beauty of its call), is Barrister. Canary and Speckled Pigeon are his rivals. The melody to which these words are sung is modeled on that of "*Malaika,*" an East African song, composed by Fadhili Williams, copyrighted by Pete Seeger, and introduced to Nigeria in a cover version by Boney M. (a German-based Eurodisco band).

References to the overseas tours of successful bandleaders are also common. On the 1991 release *New Fuji Garbage Series III,* Barrister opens with a description of his success on a recent visit to London, narrated in the present tense:

> We dey for [are in] Great Britain, where we perform for people's enjoyment.
> We dey for Great Britain, where we perform for people's enjoyment.
>
> Òyìnbo [European] people dey dance Fújì Garbage for every corner.
> Naija [Nigerian] people dey dance Fújì Garbage for every corner.
> Jamọ̀ [German] people dey dance Fújì Garbage for every corner.
> Akátá [African-American] people dey dance Fújì Garbage for every pub house.
> DJs dem dey play [they are playing] Fújì Garbage for British-i radio.
>
> When I dey [dare] sing, people dey [they] dance-i-o.
> When I dey sing, people dey dance-i-o.

Later in the recording, Barrister sings the praises of Akeem Ọlajuwọn, center for the Houston Rockets (of the National Basketball Association), describing in pidgin English and Yoruba the art of dribbling:

> Baki-ball eré fẹ́lẹ̀ẹ́.
> Awa gbá sókè̀, a tún gbá sílẹ̀:
> Baki number 1, baki number 2, baki number 3, baki number 4.
> O yára jù bọ́ọ̀lù sínú ẹ̀wọ̀n,
> Bí t'Akim ọmọ Ọlajuwọn.
> Awa gbà basketball.
>
> Basketball is an energetically flapping [cool] game.
> You bounce it up, then you bounce it down:
> Basket number 1, basket number 2, basket number 3, basket number 4.
> You quickly throw the ball into the chains [net],
> Just like Akeem, son of Ọlajuwọn.
> We receive [dig] basketball.

On another album, Barrister transports the listener to Orlando, Florida, to visit a theme park he calls Destney World and describes the wonders of Western technology: "We all entered a big lift; suddenly the lights went out, and all the whites screamed, 'Oh, my mother!'" Verbal snapshots of adventures overseas allow listeners to share vicariously the superstar's transnational movements, and provide a medium for evaluating aspects of life in the West (*ìlú òyìnbo* 'land of the whites').

"TRADITIONAL" AND "POPULAR" STYLES

To draw a sharp boundary between "traditional" and "popular" music in Yoruba society is impossible. The criteria most commonly invoked in attempts to formulate a cross-cultural definition of popular music—openness to change, syncretism, intertexuality, urban provenience, commodification—are characteristic even of those genres Yoruba musicians and audiences identify as deep Yoruba. The penetration of indigenous economies by international capital and the creation of local markets for recorded music have shaped Yoruba conceptions of music as a commodity. Musical commodification did not, however, originate with colonialism and mass reproduction. Yoruba musicians have long conceived of performance as a form of labor, a marketable product. The notion of the market as a microcosm of life (captured in the aphorism *ayé l'ojà* 'the world is a market') and a competitive arena, fraught with danger and ripe with possibilities, guides the strategies of musicians, who struggle to make a living under unpredictable economic conditions.

If Yoruba popular music is a product of markets, it is also, in important ways, unlike other commodities. Yoruba musicians and audiences regard music as a potent force with material and spiritual effects.

Though the foregoing genres of music vary in instrumentation, style, and social context, each invokes deep Yoruba tradition while connecting listeners to the world of transnational commerce. Taken as a whole, Yoruba popular music provides a complex commentary on the relationship between local traditions and foreign influence in an epoch of profound change.

REFERENCES

Adé, Sunny. 1967. "*BGlarinwa Abioro.*" *African Songs* 21A. 45-rpm single.

———. 1976. *Synchro System Movement.* African Songs AS26. LP disk.

———. 1982. *Jùjú Music.* Island Records CID 9712. Compact disc.

———, and his Green Spots. 1967. *African Songs.* LP disk.

Alájá-Browne, Afọlábi. 1985. "Jùjú Music: A Study of its Social History and Style." Ph.D. dissertation, University of Pittsburgh.

Anikulapo Kuti, Fela. 1986. *Teacher Don't Teach Me Nonsense.* Polygram 833 525–2 Q-1. Compact disc.

Apter, Andrew. 1992. *Black Critics and Kings: The Hermeneutics of Power in Yoruba Society.* Chicago: University of Chicago Press.

Barber, Karin. 1991. *I Could Speak until Tomorrow: Oriki, Women and the Past in a Yoruba Town.* Washington, D.C.: Smithsonian Institution Press.

Dairo, Isiah Kehinde, and his Blue Spots. 1962. *Elele Ture.* Decca NWA 5079.

Delano, Isaac. 1973 [1937]. *The Soul of Nigeria.* Nendeln: Kraus Reprints.

Euba, Akin. 1971. "Islamic Musical Culture among the Yoruba: A Preliminary Survey." In *Essays on Music and History in Africa,* ed. Klaus P. Wachsmann, 171–184. Evanston, Ill.: Northwestern University Press.

Jùjú Roots: 1930s–1950s. 1993. Cambridge, Mass.: Rounder Records. CD 5017. Compact disc.

———. 1990. *Yoruba Drumming: The Dùndún Tradition.* Bayreuth: Bayreuth University. Bayreuth African Studies, 21–22.

Iṣọla, Haruna. 1959. "Hogan Bassey." 78-rpm 10-inch disk. Decca WA 3120.

Ojo, Ọlaṣebikan. 1978. "Sakara Music as a Literary Form." Senior honors thesis, University of Ibadan.

Stewart, Gary. 1992. *Breakout: Profiles in African Rhythm.* Chicago: University of Chicago Press.

Thieme, Darius. 1969. "A Descriptive Catalog of Yoruba Musical Instruments." Ph.D. dissertation, Catholic University of America.

Waterman, Christopher A. 1990. *Jùjú: A Social History and Ethnography of an African Popular Music.* Chicago: University of Chicago Press.

Yoruba Street Percussion. 1992. Original Music. OMCD016. Compact disc.

Praise Singing in Northern Sierra Leone
Laura Arntson

Terminology
The Concept of Genre
A Culture-Specific Concept of Genre

For the people who share the heritage of Manden, a political and economic center of the Mali Empire, praise singing holds special significance. Since the 1200s, individuals, families, and clans have emigrated from Manden. Several ethnic groups (Maninka, Koranko, Yalunka, Mandinka, Malinké, Bamana, Dyula) say their ancestors came from there. These groups share linguistic and cultural traits, and bear the collective name "Mande" (Dalby 1971; Bird 1971). People from these groups have dispersed throughout West Africa—into Burkina Faso, Côte d'Ivoire, Gambia, Guinea-Conakry, Liberia, Mali, Senegal, and Sierra Leone.

Manden represents a historical and mythic past, whose heritage endures in epics, extended narratives, and praise songs. In particular, performances of the *bolo gbili* repertory can recreate, through musical and verbal allusion, the history and myths surrounding the creation of, conflicts within, and migration from, Manden. These songs (singular, *bolo gbili*; plural, *bololu gbili*) are considered the oldest. In a praise singer's repertory, they are "heavier" or "weightier" than *tulon bololu* 'play songs'. Yet praise singing in West Africa has not received the attention epic performance has, because of a lack of scholarly interest in the interaction of instrumental patterns and texts, and a lack of scholarly appreciation of the significance of the music. An exception is Ruth Stone's analysis (1988) of a Kpelle epic tradition in Liberia. Two ethnomusicologists who have examined musical aspects of the praise song repertory are Roderic Knight (1971, 1973, 1984a, 1984b) and Hugo Zemp (1964, 1966); however, their analyses focus on performance, rather than on musical elements as they relate to a definition of the genre. Music plays an important role in defining the genre and practice of praise singing (Arntson 1992).

Both a verbal and a musical genre, praise singing involves instrumental performance, singing, and speech. Praise songs most often compliment an individual (or individuals) present at a performance; yet the vehicle for praise, and advice or challenges offered in the guise of praise, take the form of a song in praise of a historical or mythical person from the past. Praise singing offers more than mere praise: it invokes the heritage of Manden and its lineages; in addition, it publicly musters social roles and expectations related to this heritage, and to contemporary contexts.

Among the Maninka (Mandingo) and the Koranko of Sierra Leone, a verbal and musical specialist is known as a *jeli* or *yeli* (/j/ and /y/ are interchangeable). In a typical performance, a specialist (called a bard or griot by some scholars) begins by either singing text from a praise song or playing a recognizable pattern on a musical instrument, such as the *bala*, the instrument most often included in performances of the genre. Praise singing may be accompanied by other instruments: the guitar, often amplified through an altered tape deck or other apparatus; the *kora*, a twenty-one-stringed harp-lute, popular in Mali and Senegambia (Knight, 1971, 1973, 1984a, 1984b); or drums, the *jènbe* (which has a single stretched-skin drumhead, fastened with sinew or twine to a conical-bore log) and the *ban* (a small kettledrum, played with one stick).

The *bala* has wooden keys or bars, arranged in consecutive order of pitch, and fastened to a frame to which gourds are attached as resonators. Pieces of spider-egg casing or cigarette paper cover small holes in each gourd; they add a buzz to the sound, an aesthetic quality called *sèsè*. To add another texture, a *bala* player will tie rattles to the backs of his hands. The keys of most *bala*s are tuned so the octave divides into seven pitches, which approach equidistant tuning. The keys, which number from sixteen to twenty-one, lie in relation to one another in consecutive order of pitch, at a distance of about one and a half semitones, or an average of 145 to 180 cents. The latitude of a pitch area is greater than transcriptions in Western notation show; and variations in the tuning, whether intentional or the result of accidental chipping or splitting of the keys, do not invite correction. The sounding of pitches that deviate from absolute consonance (for example, an octave pair at a distance larger or smaller than 1200 cents) sets up a musical tension, an aesthetically desirable quality, which people do not consider aberrant. Also known as the *balafon* or *balanji*, the *bala* is played almost exclusively by *jelikèlu* 'male praise singers' (female praise singers are *jelimusolu*).

For a praise song, a *bala* player or *jeliba* plays, varies, and improvises on a basic pattern, the *balabolo*. While maintaining a recognizable kinesic and rhythmic contour, he may interject descending runs or sequences into it; he may vary the rhythms or selected pitches within it; and he may play a vocal song line, in more or less parallel octaves. When a performance includes several *jelilu*, most *bala* players will maintain the basic pattern for a song, while a recognized master in the group will improvise more. At a large gathering, such as a wedding or an initiation, all the *bala* players, *jelimusolu*, and drummers will play or sing simultaneously—which, with the crowd's singing, dancing, hand clapping, and talking, creates a dense texture. Throughout the variation and improvisation, however, a *jeli* maintains a single rhythmic impetus or drive, which helps shape the rhythms of the text. As he calls out praise words, a *bala* player may suspend his playing. The texts of praise words include proverbs or references to proverbs; a brief narration or description of the current situation; commentary, advice, or criticism; bits of text, drawn from a much longer narrative, to which the praise song alludes; or a praise name for a patron or the receiver of the praise at that moment. In performance, a *jeliba* will intersperse instrumental playing with praise words (*fola*), and a praise singer (of either sex) will guide a performance into singing (*donkilila la*) then back to praise words, and so on. When a female specialist is not speaking or singing, she may play rhythmic patterns on the *karinyan*, a cylindrical iron bell suspended by a string or cloth from a finger of one hand and struck with an iron beater held in the other hand. When women present know the choral response, a female specialist may lead a song; if no one is present to sing a choral response, she may do all the singing.

Most linguists and folklorists assign praise song performance to a people's oral literature. Like epic, to which it closely relates, praise singing draws on a body of customary, historical, and mythic knowledge, which in Western contexts usually appears

jeli   Verbal and musical specialist in praise singing, often employing the harp-lute for accompaniment

bala   Xylophone with wooden keys, arranged in consecutive pitch order and fastened to a frame of gourd resonators

bolo gbili   Praise song that recreates the past through allusion to history and myths

balabolo   Basic pattern of a Mandinka xylophone player

in literary forms. Yet these elements cooperate, and people who perform and listen to praise singing in Maninka society do not think them separate phenomena. It would be more accurate to call the genre and its performance "aural literature" (Yankah 1985). Even without the accompaniment of musical instruments, the delivery of text involves musical elements (rhythmic, melodic, stylistic).

For each song or piece in the repertory, the verbal text and the musical patterns performed on the *bala* are equally capable of calling to mind a larger text, a shared area of knowledge or story line—a text envelope, which includes bits of textual and musical information, with distinctive performative conventions. It is a fluid set of descriptive phrases, praise names, proverbs, songs, and instrumental patterns, which all feed into a story line or collection of deeds, actions, events, attributes, and social mores. It can be expanded, embellished, or condensed. Through verbal and musical reference or allusion, a praise singer can emphasize certain of its aspects, and augment or reshape listeners' notions of it.

The larger texts to which certain praise songs in the *bolo gbili* repertory refer are those text envelopes out of which heroic epics emerge. A *bolo gbili* relies on allusion to call to mind a larger text, and epic includes extended narration; but a text envelope is larger than either genre. It is more than a story line, and exists in its entirety only in the imaginations of the *jelilu* and, to varying degrees, other members of a culture. Because the text envelope is an area of knowledge to be drawn upon, instead of an actual text, it will not be realized in its entirety, even if a performance of an epic lasts for days. It is a fluid and dynamic area of knowledge, shared to varying degrees by different *jelilu*.

The praise song repertory consists of patterns of play (*tulon bololu*) and of *bolo gbili*. The latter are heavier, in the sense that they bear more historical resonance than the *tulon bololu*, which can deal with lighter topics. The designation *bolo* 'hand' refers specifically to the musical patterns on the *bala* that are the main elements in the identification of different songs in the repertory. Different *balabololu* or *bala* patterns and spoken or sung texts (including proverbs [*sanda*], truisms, praise names, and other phrases) both feed into the larger text of a song or pattern. The larger text or story is said to be "inside the song." Whether a praise song is told "inside the instrument" (*fo bala rò*) or with words "inside the mouth" (*da rò*), people will understand the reference to a larger text, and women will know which song to sing in response to phrases in the "text." Nimeh Kaleh explained (Arntson 1987–1988:133-A):

A b'a fo bala rò, ma' ye wo lamèn na. Ani fo da rò fanan tun, ma' tun na ye da rò si. Bala b'a donkili do la; hali yeliba ma kuma, mal' di donkili wulila.

He says it inside the *bala*; then we hear that. And when it is said inside the mouth also, we will have joined it inside the mouth then. The *bala* [plays] some song; even if the *yeliba* does not talk, we will raise up the song.

The musical patterns on the *bala* refer to words, but are not iconic: the sound of the *bala* is not a surrogate for speech; however, the patterns are recognizable enough to call to mind a larger text envelope.

As its name suggests, performance of this genre is a kind of praise. The way a *jeli* praises someone is, in the midst of performing a *balabolo*, to sing or play formulaic phrases, or other phrases from the text envelope, and to call out the name or praise names of the patron or recipient of the praise. A *jeli* "says the song and the proverb [inside the song] to a person, to praise him" (Arntson 1987–1988:133-B). When a *jeli* praises someone with a song from the *bolo gbili* repertory, he aligns that person with a past hero or leader, or with an idealized occupation: warrior (*kèlèkè*), hunter (*simbon*), farmer (*konkoba*).

By calling to mind the achievements and salient qualities of famous hunters of the past (real or mythical), a *jeli* likens to a larger-than-life character or an ideal the person receiving the praise. He attributes various qualities to a contemporary individual, and people expect the praised person to embody those ideals, or at least to respond with a gift to the praise singer. While alluding to a much larger vocabulary of references, praise singing steers public attention, praise, advice, and criticism. It calls attention not only to a contemporary individual, but to a historical or mythical character, his deeds and attributes, and the expectations or assigned attributes of members of the patrilineage to which both individuals belong or are aligned.

TERMINOLOGY

The terms *praise song* and *praise singing* display a musical bias. I have purposely chosen song and singing over poetry, to call attention to the importance of music in understanding the genre. The term *poetry* implies a literary understanding of prosody, and a certain enchantment with the text as a validation or record of an auditory form. Here, *song* is meant in its broadest sense, which includes verbal performance on a speech continuum—from speech or speaking, to singing, and then to instrumental music.

This genre by no means represents the only form of singing or performative speech among the Maninka and the Koranko of northern Sierra Leone. Some kinds of singing accompany tasks (agricultural labor, fishing). Some songs belong to initiation and women's societies; others, to folktales or storytelling performances. Such songs are performed primarily by nonspecialists. Praise singing is the domain of specialists. In societies originating in Manden, crafts such as praise singing, blacksmithing, leatherworking, and weaving are the privilege of specialists. For discussion of the social organization and specialization of ethnic groups that trace their ancestors to Manden, see Hopkins (1971) and Launay (1972). Nonspecialists join in to comment or react to a performance, to dance in recognition of praise, or to supply choral responses to the songs, but do not do the praising.

In societies with ties to Manden, artisans, including the *jelilu*, belong (ideally at least) to an endogamous occupational group: they marry within their occupation or specialty. Access to the learning and performance of epic and praise singing extends only to those who belong to or are aligned with certain lineages or families. Usually at the age of about seven or eight, a *jeli* begins learning to play *bala*, taught by his father, grandfather, or uncle. The surnames of most Maninka and Koranko *jelilu* are "Kuyateh," "Jibateh," and "Kamara."

This genre or expressive form has also been called panegyric (Finnegan 1970; Johnson 1980), panegyric ode (Finnegan 1977), praise poetry (Finnegan 1970), lyric poetry (Finnegan 1977), and royal song. The identification of "royal songs," which Charles Bird has also called literature of the courts (Bird 1970:155), includes both

Specialists must handle with care and respect the potential power in words and knowledge: *jelilu* do not praise indiscriminately.

epic and praise singing, and distinguishes this repertory and performance style from songs of praise directed at hunters, and songs and stories performed by nonspecialists. O. B. Hardison defines "panegyric" as "a speech or poem in praise of an individual, institution or group" (Preminger, Warnke, and Hardison 1974:597). Historically, "panegyric" was recognized as a poetic form that directed praise toward "present men and deeds" (Preminger et al. 1974:597) as opposed to past heroes or deeds. "Panegyric" comes close to describing an important portion of the *bolo gbili* repertory, especially with panegyric's "tendency to develop toward epic" (Preminger et al. 1974:597); but it does not adequately represent the practice or the form of praise singing in Maninka and Koranko contexts.

The *bolo gbili* and *tulon bolo* songs together make up the praise song repertory. Though *tulon bolo* songs address the present, *bolo gbili* songs refer to and update the past. *Tulon bolo* songs are more likely to praise contemporary individuals and social institutions or groups than past or present leaders. Panegyric, by definition, singles out, to the exclusion of music, speech and the poetic aspects of a form. Besides being on a footing equal with verbal aspects of the genre, music plays an important role in identifying the different songs in the praise song repertory. A repertory defines a genre in so far as it is the content of a performative type and practice. Repertory, essentially a genre performed, must be included in the definition and designation of a genre.

Among the groups whose ancestors allegedly came from Manden, the performance of epic and praise singing involves patronage, since a person must give something in return for offered praise. (For background on the patronage of *jaliya*, and on the art of praise singing, see Duran 1987). A *jeli* has a customary right and duty to praise others, and to receive something in return. The gift relays thanks to the *jeli*, reinforces his or her role as a praise singer, and places something between the recipient of praise and the inherent power in the *jeli*'s words. Watta Oumarou suggests a gift to a *jeli* is a kind of shield, since "it alone can avert the destructive power of name 'calling'"; if "the middle of a man is his name," which has "the power to collapse his center" (Oumarou 1986:24), then praise directed at a name is powerful indeed. Throughout much of West Africa, words and knowledge, and the ability to show acquisition of that knowledge (from general use and specialized repertories), imply power. By giving money, clothing, or other goods, one has made a sacrifice. A *jeli*'s words carry a certain "power of the occult" (Johnson 1986:23). After a performance in Mali, when a gift has been given to praise singers, they often say, "*Ka nyama bo* 'Let the occult power be taken away'" (Johnson 1986:23). According to praise singers, a person will be happy giving gifts to the praise singer because it is the custom; but patronage is more complicated than that, and a *jeli*'s role and access to power meet popular ambivalence. As one *jeli* pointed out, "All are afraid of praise singers; only the one who does not know the meaning of the praise singing, that is the only one who will not fear him" (Arnston 1987–1988:121-A). Specialists must handle with care and respect the potential power in words and knowledge: *jelilu* do not praise indiscriminately.

Praising is a central aspect of this genre as it is realized in northern Sierra Leone. It is not the only form of praise there. Yankah believes, instead of "praise poetry," oral literary scholars should employ the more neutral term "referential poetry" for application to cross-cultural and comparative research, "since scholars have yet to find a restricted genre in any African culture which is locally acknowledged to hold a monopoly over 'praise'" (1983:381). His point is apt; however, if the definition of a genre arises out of a culture-specific study, we may appropriately use terminology that adequately represents a practice in context. Genres are categories that may not have an equivalent designation within a given culture, but should nonetheless reflect a real practice, and avoid misconstruing or obscuring concepts of expressive forms of culture. Praise is central to this genre as I witnessed its practice in Maninka contexts. To obscure this aspect would misrepresent Maninka and Koranko praise song performance.

THE CONCEPT OF GENRE

We need to rethink the concept of genre as an analytical category, and its definition by performative context. Rather than begin with a general or reductive definition, I believe it more valuable to start from a culture- and context-specific one. When, to define a genre, we draw together selected elements from a variety of cultural practices, we necessarily take them out of context. Elements that may not be separable in the minds of those who perform certain genres are selected on the basis of how they fit into a preconceived category. Actual behavior and artistic practice are not so neat and tidy as such definitions imply. Definitions not rooted in specific cultural practices do not entirely represent a genre as it occurs in context.

In defining a genre, folklorists have most often sought out the shared characteristics of a practice among a variety of cultural groups. The result is a reductive definition, or a composite of selected elements. A problem with this approach is that diverse expressive forms are represented, not as they occur in a specific cultural context, but as they fit into a preconceived model. Praise singing as practiced by the Maninka has been represented as belonging to a form called panegyric (Finnegan 1970:116), but this designation excludes a portion of the repertory that defines praise singing for the Maninka and the Koranko, and does not recognize the role of music in the genre. The *tulon bolo* praise songs clearly belong to the same genre as the *bololu gbili*. Both the *tulon bololu* and the *bololu gbili* make up the performative repertories of music specialists—these specialists could be called quasiprofessionals, since, for a livelihood, they would rely solely on their special expertise and its patronage—and they share formal characteristics. Recognition of all the characteristics of this genre as it is performed in northern Sierra Leone may complicate a definition of the praise song genre, but it situates the definition in a real practice.

The construction of a genre does not have to represent an ideal form whose parts no other expression replicates. Within a culture and between disparate cultures, expressive forms share certain traits. That a genre has been defined should not exclude the chance that different cultural forms share imaginable genres that relate to one another to varying degrees. Such an admission does not lessen the impact or the value of generic designations: on the contrary, it allows for comparison of actual practice, to illustrate which traits are the same or different, how practices differ, and what such an analysis tells us about a more general practice or type of expression.

Other than *yeli la ka* 'a *jeli*'s domain or harvest', the Maninka and the Koranko have no single term to denote the practice of praise singing as a genre. They do recognize and appreciate a specialist's art, and a specialist's access to the knowledge and

Heightened speech, a primary characteristic of praise singing, involves rhythmic and dynamic elements that are not a part of everyday speech, whose primary function is communication.

performance of a repertory. The repertory, which includes both text and music (the *balabololu* or *bala* patterns in particular), with the performative style, modes of speech and performance by a specialists defines this practice as a unique form or genre in Maninka and Koranko culture. Praise singing, though the Maninka and the Koranko do not call it by any one name, belongs to a unitary realm of behavior and knowledge.

Richard Bauman (1992) suggests that genre is "a way of sorting out conventionalized discourse forms on the basis of form, function, content, or some other factor or set of factors." Form encompasses aspects of performance style and techniques such as prosody; modes of speech; aesthetic, rhythmical, and additional musical elements of performance; and structural or organizational characteristics. The function of a genre is equivalent to its role, place, and meaning in a culture and society; and an interest in the functions a genre holds for those who perform and those who see, hear, or otherwise experience its performance, comes out of a consideration of genre in context. That is, genre does not exist as a concept outside its realization or its notion as a performative repertory within a cultural context. The content (or subject matter) of a performative genre is especially significant to a culture-specific definition. For members of a society, the subjects portrayed, praised, criticized, or invoked in the repertory hold meaning, and reflect notions of history and culture.

Form

Textual aspects

Heightened speech, a primary characteristic of praise singing, involves rhythmic and dynamic elements that are not a part of everyday speech, whose primary function is communication. The poetic or musical qualities of speech that are out of the ordinary are self-conscious and performative in nature. The nonphonemic accentuation that occurs in such speech is a clue to its poetic character (Johnson 1986). In heightened speech, rhythm and accentuation serve an aesthetic value over communicative function, and the use that "rhythmic impulse makes of language for its own ends" (Preminger et al. 1974:669) is the subject of literary prosody. For "poetic" forms, then, the prosodic "structure" of speech becomes a subject of considerable interest. Bird suggests that, in a "Mande" epic-style praise song, "it is the rhythm of the background instruments that determines the prosodic structure of the line" (Bird 1976:92). The instrumental rhythms serve as "language-external constraints" (Bird 1976) on speech. In "Mande" epic performance, instrumental rhythms dictate rhythm and accentuation in speech, if we understand poetic speech to depend on "the rhythm generated by the accompaniment" (Johnson 1986:31).

What, then, in praise song performance, is the relationship between the rhythms of speech and the instrumental or underlying rhythms? Clearly, the prosodic patterns relate in some way to instrumental performance, but do the instrumental rhythms really serve as constraints, determinants, or generating forces? It may not be a pattern of scansion in the instrumental rhythm or a preconceived notion of measure and meter that generates the dynamic rhythms of speech in epic or praise song, but rather an interaction of different rhythmic motions and creations of rhythmic impetus. The rhythmic patterns, whether audible or not, set up a certain rhythmic impetus and expectation. Bird (1976) and others have noted that when a *jeli* delivers an epic text with no instrumental accompaniment, he may tap the instrumental rhythms to himself.

Musical aspects

When a *jeli* introduces into the rhythmic texture additional rhythmic ideas and impetuses, he creates aesthetic tension, "the device by which the master jostles the [expectations] of his audience" (Bird 1976:91); he thus displays his mastery of the form and its prosody. By introducing an additional rhythmic impetus drawn from rhythmic ideas available to and suggested by verbal performance, a *jeli* works "off" or with instrumental rhythms. In performance, the spoken rhythms deviate from the "natural" linguistic rhythms: they introduce nonphonemic accents, altered tempos, and nonlinguistic melodic contours. The languages spoken by the Bamana (Bambara), Dyula, and to a lesser extent the Maninka and the Koranko, are tonal languages; in praise singing, other melodic contours may alter or obscure linguistic tonal patterns. Performance heightens speech, thereby establishing a frame that says, "This is performance." Within the frame are either competing or aligned rhythmic impetuses. For more discussion of the framing involved in performance, see Goffman (1974) and Bauman (1977).

One technique a *jeli* uses to create a rhythmic tension is to deliver, in a fast stream (which pulls a listener away from an established pulse or rhythmic impetus), a verbal phrase such as a proverb, a praise name, or a bit of narration. A rush of words obscures expected accents, plus the sense of release or repose that comes with the end of a rhythmic pattern or phrase. Figure 1*a* illustrates this technique. In the *bala*'s lower register, the rhythmic impetus involves quarter-note pulses, outlined by the first and third eighth notes in each set of four. My assessment of where pulses are felt comes from observing how the performers or singers and dancers move to *bala* rhythms. The stream of words *jeliba* Pa Sanasi Kuyateh delivers creates a tension with the established rhythm.

Figure 1*b* illustrates aspects of Pa Kuyateh's delivery of praise words: his words are not aligned with notes on the *bala*. The rush of words occupies roughly the temporal space illustrated on the page in relation to the *bala* sound. The praise words answer, or explain more fully, the lower register's reference to the Sunjata text envelope. Therefore, in this transcription, I have transcribed the praise words in place of the *bala*'s middle register, said to "answer" or "explain" the notes of the lower register. I have also employed a *bala* tablature I have derived from a treble clef staff. Because of unavoidable discrepancies in the recorded frequencies of individual *bala* keys, I have opted for consistency in my representation of the sound. Rather than try to represent the unique tuning of each *bala* transcribed, I portray pitch relationships as *bala* key relationships. Each *bala* key can be represented on a particular line or space of a treble clef and its ledgers. Each note head on the staff and ledgers then represents a pitch area, or a particular key of a *bala*, rather than a pitch frequency. My transcriptions represent a balance of prescriptive and descriptive intent. To reflect the interplay of the mallets used in realizing a *bala* pattern, I have divided between two staves the keys (bars) of the *bala*. The notes on these staves roughly coincide with the keys struck by each mallet and the two registers as described by *bala* players.

Pa Kuyateh's praise words derive from the Sunjata text envelope. Sunjata, or

FIGURE 1   Excerpt from the Mansareh *bolo* (Arntson 1987–1988:110-B). The *balabolo*, a *bolo gbili*, is played in praise of those belonging to or aligned with the Mansareh patrilineage: *a*, in the lower register, the first and third eighth notes in each set of four outline quarter-note pulses; *b*, the words roughly occupy the illustrated temporal space.

Keita Manden Sumaworo Maramagan Jata, is known as the grandfather of the Mansareh clan, or the *Mansarehen bimba*. Oral traditions credit him with the founding of the Mali Empire, and credit the Keita clan (or Mansareh clan) with the development of the *jeli*'s art, and with *bala* playing in particular. *Keita* also serves as a praise name for the Mansareh clan. The surname Mansareh allegedly derives from

FIGURE 2 Excerpt from *Yan ka di* (Arntson 1987–1988: 120–A), showing the juxtaposition of the *dunya* rhythm with the rhythmic impetus established in the *bala* pattern: *a,* the mallets create a driving triplet pattern of eighths and sixteenths; *b,* a corresponding duple pattern.

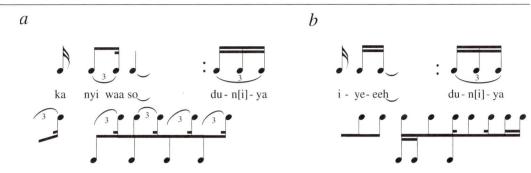

Mansa 'one who takes power', the word for 'leader'. Seni Darbo (1975) notes that, while *jelilu* were known once to have been in the patronage of certain families, it was probably Sunjata himself who firmly established the *jeli*'s role, after he had inherited his father's praise singers.

The Sunjata text envelope includes accounts and references to Sunjata's background (including various mythic origins), plus the battles that led to the formation of the Mali Empire. During the eleventh and twelfth centuries, the Keita clan unified several kingdoms of the Upper Niger (Niane 1984), but clans continued to struggle for power (Fage 1969). The unified clans of Manden eventually rose against Sumanguru, a Susu ruler, who had consolidated an area to the west of Manden; under Sunjata's leadership, they defeated Sumanguru in about the year 1235. Because of its ties to the origins of both the Mali Empire and praise singing, people consider the Mansareh *bolo* the oldest *bala* pattern and the first praise song.

Another technique that creates a certain aesthetic tension is the addition of a word or verbal rhythm at the end of a phrase—a technique that by complicating the rhythmic focus again deceives the listener's expectations of repose. On many occasions, *jelimuso* Hawa Kuyateh (Pa Kuyateh's daughter) added to the ends of phrases the word *dunya* 'world, universe'. The triplet created by the speech rhythm of *dunya* competes with an established rhythmic impetus, which causes an aesthetic tension at the end of a phrase. Figure 2 illustrates this juxtaposition of the *dunya* rhythm with the rhythmic impetus established in the *bala* pattern.

The driving triplet pattern of eighths and sixteenths created between the mallets, with an accent on the eighth note of the pattern in figure 2*a*, and the corresponding duple pattern in figure 2*b* (two eighths followed by a sixteenth, one eighth, one sixteenth, and so on) set up a rhythmic impetus. The introduction of a competing rhythmic idea complicates listeners' expectations of a forward rhythmic drive.

Figure 3 (from the same performance transcribed in figure 1) also illustrates the rhythmic juxtaposition of *dunya* at the end of a phrase. In addition, it illustrates the alignment of rhythmic impetuses in the singing or *donkilila la* portions of a performance, though the rhythmic sequences of the voices and *bala* differ. The singing develops a 3+3+2 rhythm. The *bala* pattern, however, represents a series of six "swung" sixteenth notes followed by an eighth note. The second of each pair of six-

FIGURE 3 Excerpt from the Mansareh *bolo* (Arntson 1987–1988:110-B).

Those who have access to power can unleash hidden energies or can control them; they are themselves handlers of *nyama*.

teenths (in this figure, sounded in the upper register of the instrument) is delayed slightly; the delay results in a long–short–long–short–long–short–long pattern. In this performance, a *jènbe* drum and *karinyan* reinforce the *bala* rhythm and contribute to the establishment of the rhythmic impetus. Neither the drum nor the *karinyan* rhythms appear in figures 1 and 3. The alignment of voices and *bala* occurs at those points represented here as the first pulse in a measure.

This approach to the rhythms in praise song performance calls for a different understanding of rhythm and perception of rhythmic textures. Instead of imagining rhythm as measures or sequences of accents that serve to segment time through vertical alignment of rhythmic lines or layers (as Western contexts most often depict it), we must picture a dynamic texture of rhythmic ideas. A transcription cannot fully represent the pull between two competing rhythmic impetuses, because it relies on an aligned segmentation of space (or distance across the page) equivalent to a passage of time. Representing the coordination of different rhythmic sequences, which together set up a single rhythmic impetus, is also difficult. The voices and *bala* in figure 3 are aligned only at those points where a pulse emerges in the rhythmic drive. They exist as two parallel, yet not always vertically aligned, rhythmic sequences. Because Western notions of rhythm inform transcriptions, we may have to put some distance between our notations and the rhythms perceived in performance, to focus on a concept of rhythmic motion and impetus. Thus, when we analyze the relationship between verbal and instrumental rhythms in praise singing (or in epic), we should not try to fit the rhythms into a meter (or an aligned segmentation of time), but should see the generation of rhythms as a way of negotiating and creating competing or complementary impetuses.

Interaction of verbal and musical elements

In epic-style performance, Bird identifies three modes of speech: narrative, praise proverb (Innes [1976] calls this the "recitation mode"), and song. The praise proverb and song modes appear in praise song performance. In his search for patterns of scansion and prosodic structure in epic performance, John W. Johnson discovers an increased melodic and rhythmic tension in the praise proverb mode, and a tendency toward zero tension in the song mode (Johnson 1986)—a lack that may result from the alignment of points within a rhythmic impetus (figure 3, excepting the *dunya* rhythm). The increased tension of the praise proverb mode is an intentional product of the juxtaposition of competing rhythmic impetuses (figure 1).

Praise proverb mode and song mode are etic distinctions or analytical groupings observers from outside a culture make. In Maninka and Koranko praise song performance, they are equivalent to the *fo* or *fola*, and the *donkilila la*. Among *kora* players in The Gambia, Knight (1973:61 and 64, 1984a) has found in use several Mandinka terms that distinguish between kinds and functions of modes of speech. These include *jamundiro* (patronymic praise that contains references to the past), *satandiro* (extemporized vocal lines), *mama jaliya* (recitation of genealogies), *jairo* (a more general praise), *jalikumolu* (miscellaneous commentary), and *mansalingo* (metaphorical proverb).

In praise singing, not only the rhythmic tension sets song apart from the praise words or the *fola*. Another formal characteristic of the singing is its occurrence through a call and a response, or the perception of *donkilila la* as answering. In singing, a *jeli* may begin a response or answer from a female chorus primarily of nonspecialists. The *jeli*'s words (or call) and the choral responses are all part of the song or singing. Praise words are not a song, but words. The women answer the song, not the words. They do not answer certain praise words, like "This man, he is a great man, he is a good man," and similar expressions. More directional than song, praise words can send praise directly to an individual, "as a gun sends a bullet" (Arntson 1987–1988:133-A), whereas singing rounds out a praise by adding to the text envelope customary knowledge, commentary, and references. The songs (*donkililu*) occur in a set form. In choral response, the text is not improvised like *bala* performance, praise words, praise word sequences, and some of the lines leading to a choral response. Because of the lack of improvisation, the *donkililu* do not specifically relate to a contemporary individual. Their potency is not in a directed, situational praise, but in a song's ability vividly to recreate past performances of a text envelope.

Specific *donkililu*, when sung in a praise song performance, and especially those in the older repertory (the *bololu gbili*), remain stable over time and distance. Like certain praise names, bits of narrative, and the *bala* patterns themselves, the *donkililu*, are associated with specific text envelopes. Since the epics concerning Manden and the *bolo gbili* praise songs draw from the same text envelopes, the *donkililu* sung within a performance of a particular epic will likely be included in the praise song of a particular epic hero. When various Manden groups over a large area of West Africa share a larger text, such as the conglomerate text envelope from which the Sunjata epic derives, the words in a *donkili* may differ slightly, but the sung melody will remain much the same. The song "*Nyin min nyama, nyama* 'That which is *nyama*'," or "*Nyama, nyama, nyama*" (Bird 1976:99), appears in many performances of the Sunjata epic. *Nyama* has been defined several ways. Literally, it denotes 'garbage', but it implies power, since items that are in a dangerous realm of society (as is garbage, at the outskirts of an inhabited area), unknown, hidden, or accessible only to a few, represent power. Those who have access to power can unleash hidden energies or can control them; they are themselves handlers of *nyama* (Bird 1976). For discussion of this subject, see Bird (1976), Bird and Kendall (1980), Johnson (1986), McNaughton (1988), and Meillassoux (1973). Bird suggests, in fact, that this is a "rather crucial song in the Sunjata epic" (Bird 1976:99).

Throughout West Africa, there are many variants of the Sunjata epic and other texts. Some songs may be more popular or well known in certain areas than in others, so this song does not necessarily appear in every performance of the Sunjata epic, or in the narratives and praise songs that refer to the same text envelope. It is also sung in performances of praise songs for Sunjata and in those belonging to or aligned with the Mansareh clan. When the Mansareh *bolo* is performed, whether *jelimusolu* and other singers are present or not, the *bala* part is likely to contain a version of the recognizable melody from "*Nyin min nyama, nyama*" (figures 4 and 5). In translation, the text of figure 4 is

> That which is Nyama,
> All things are hidden under Nyama,
> Nyama is not hidden under anything.

FIGURE 4 Excerpt from "*Nyin min nyama, nyama*," a famous song, appearing in many performances of the Sunjata epic.

Nyi min nya - ma, nya - ma,   Fen bèè ye dòn - do nya - ma le kò - ro,

Nya - ma tè dòn - do fen bèè kò - ro.

FIGURE 5 Excerpt from the Mansareh *bolo,* with a version of the melody of "*Nyin min nyama, nyama*" included in the *bala* improvisation; from a performance by Pa Sanasi Kuyateh (Arntson 1987–1988:112-B).

For interpretations of the meaning of this text as it occurs in performances in Mali, see Bird (1976:99).

The emergence of form

During a praise song performance, a *jeliba* varies or improvises on the basic *bala* pattern. When the performance moves into song, he may choose to parallel the *donkili* melody, continue with the *bala* pattern, or improvise further. By continually returning to or reinforcing important aspects of a pattern, he maintains throughout a performance the rhythmic impetus and a kernel of the basic pattern.

Bala patterns hold clues to the structure or musical organization of praise song performance. What, then, makes up a basic pattern? and how is it recognizable? *Bala* patterns exist as sets of rhythmic ideas or motifs with particular kinesic contours and, in some cases, an emergent melodic content. What Western audiences recognize as a melodic contour in a *bala* pattern, however, is more appropriately represented as a tonal-kinesic contour, since the Maninka do not perceive pitches as either high or low. Rather, they think of the different keys (or pitches) of the *bala* in a right-left relationship. Depending on which side of a *bala* a *jeli* sits, the notes we recognize as "lower" will be either to the right or to the left. The contour of a *bala* pattern, then, is a contour of the hand-and-mallet movement over the keys. Furthermore, some pitches within a pattern may vary, while the kinesic contour remains the same. The contours of the lower register (represented in the lower staff in the transcriptions) are tied to certain keys of the *bala* for each *bala* pattern, though particular intervals within a contour may vary. The kinesic contour is represented here at the point of the articulation, since the goal of hand-and-mallet movement is the articulation of sound.

From one performance to another, the Mansareh *bolo* (figure 5) is recognizable because of the contours maintained in both the upper and lower registers of the *bala*, an emergent melodic content, and the recognizable rhythmic motifs. The contour of the lower register is outlined primarily by the C-"half"-sharp (the lowest pitch and "oldest" key of the *bala*) and raised A. A recording of the individual pitches of Pa Kuyateh's *bala* reveals that three of the pitches match frequencies in a standard equally tempered scale, set at a=440. The pitch frequencies of the other keys can be calculated according to the deviation in cents from standard frequencies. The pitches of the keys of Pa Kuyateh's *bala* (from the lowest pitch, close to middle C, to the highest) are roughly equivalent to C-sharp (30 cents low in relation to a standard equal-tempered C#), D-natural, E-natural (20 cents low), F-sharp (25 cents low), G-natural (35 cents high), A-natural, B-natural (25 cents high), C-natural (35 cents high), D half-sharp, E-natural (20 cents low), F-sharp, G-sharp (15 cents low), A-natural (40 cents low), B-natural (35 cents high), C-sharp (20 cents low), D-sharp (35 cents low), and E-natural (25 cents high). A distinctive rhythmic motif of this pattern is the sixteenth (on an accented pulse in the pattern), followed in the upper register by three eighth notes, which alternate in a "swung" fashion with eighths in the lower register. By virtue of pitch and alignment on a pulse in the overriding rhythmic impetus, the first of the sixteenth-note pairs in a set is accentuated. Often, in performances of the Mansareh *balabolo,* an eighth-note triplet is introduced into the upper register, to create a rhythmic tension. Many performances of this pattern as played on the *bala* by different *jelibalu* also include a version or an adaptation of the melody of "*Nyin min nyama, nyama*" (figure 5). The rhythmic motifs, *donkili* melody, and kinesic contours, all come together in making the pattern recognizable as the *Keita Manden,* or the Mansareh *bolo.* Other praise songs involve combinations and realizations of different rhythmic motifs, *donkili* melodies, and kinesic contours. Rhythmic motifs may be realized primarily in one register, or as a result of the cooperation of two mallets. The elements that go into the making of a *balabolo* do not always occur in the same package, but are realized in different ways, according to performers' training, interests, and artistry.

The nature of the genre allows for extensive variation in text and thematic form. Motivic elements such as praise names, proverbs, and truisms, and thematic or narrative elements of the larger text envelope comprise the text of a praise song performance. Since a text envelope exists as a collection of ideas or an area of knowledge, rather than a sequence of details and events, various elements may be invoked outside a chronological order. In performance, the text displays a thematic area, rather than a "thematic form." In the definition of genres, Gregory M. Shreve and Ojo Arewa (1980) consider formal characteristics, including thematic form, to be primarily determinative. The bits of text both capture and contribute to qualities and perceptions of the larger text. For a reference to the text envelope to be successful, they do not have to appear in a set order; it is a thematic area, rather than a thematic form, that holds significance for our analysis.

The text of a Mansareh *bolo* praise song performance may successfully call forth many of the heroic qualities and myths surrounding Sunjata, though it may not be extensive, contain narration, or have a fixed form. Pa Kuyateh begins one perfor-

Because praise singing occurs during parties, celebrations, or other events that call for entertainment, a *jeli* carries a certain immunity from blame, and can therefore criticize and advise others, all in the guise of praise.

mance by playing the Mansareh *balabolo* or *bala* pattern and portions of the melody of "*Nyin min nyama, nyama*" (Arntson 1987–1988:110-B). He directs his praise words to Fanta's husband (*Fanta la kè*). The people of Sukurala named me "Fanta Kaleh." When my husband arrived in Sukurala, two months after I had begun my research, Pa Kuyateh praised him with the Mansareh *bolo.* After my husband acquired the name "Mohamadou Kondeh," he received praise with the Kondeh *bolo* that is the *bala* pattern used to praise those of the Kondeh lineage. The words *min di yaraden gbasi fo sanji* (or *min di yaraden gbasi fo kònkò*) 'the only thing that can beat a lion cub is rain' (or 'the only thing that can beat a lion cub is hunger') refer to Sunjata, known as the lion child (*yaraden*) and lion thief (Johnson 1986:132). People credit him with being able to turn himself into a lion, and believe the power (*nyama* or *fanga*) he has access to is subordinate to or hidden under (*dòndo . . . kòro*) nothing. Bird and Kendall (1980) present the "Mande" hero as having access to power or *nyama* and an ability to balance and use it. This pattern is Sunjata's own (*wo le balabolo kèla* 'his pattern is being played'). He is the grandfather of the Mansareh clan. The text challenges others to live up to his achievements, or otherwise not to draw a comparison between themselves and Sunjata, for not everything is sweet (good) to everyone (*ko ma di bèè la*). Power and achievement depend on both one's heritage and one's personal strength: after all, a rich man can produce a rich man (*bana le, bana wo l'la*), but a bastard child, whatever he tries, never gets to the end (*nyomòòden, bonya, bonya, a ti ko labanna*). An effective means to urge someone into action is to suggest that not only are there few men (or possibly none) as capable as Sunjata, but also the great men, the ones who could have taken up such a challenge and accepted such praise, exist no more (*kènu bara la* 'the great men have died'). And if one cannot accept the challenge and face adversity, then perhaps one is a coward (*kèlè ma di jito la* 'fighting will never fit a coward'). The words suggest it is difficult for a person to live up to the name Sunjata, his own grandfather (ancestor), made. Sunjata faced adversity and conquered it (*e bimba le ka kunban tè Kanban a ya rò, . . . ka Kanban kun fila kè nakelen ma di* 'your grandfather cut Kanban's head clean off, . . . making Kanban's shoulders one'). Kanban's identity here is unclear. I do not have the data to speculate about the relationship between this Kanban and the Kanban of the Koranko women's association, a Kanban its members are said to kill upon initiation into the society (Arntson 1987–1988:122-A). To be compared to such greatness is to imply that one too may accomplish what Sunjata himself achieved. The praise words and singing in the Mansareh praise song recreate, through allusion, the stories of Sunjata's prowess and the myths and attributes that surround him. A *jeli* places a contemporary individual in the midst of all this, thereby challenging him or her to live up to and be worthy of such praise.

Since a *jeli* improvises a praise song during performance and directs it toward an individual (or individuals), the form and length of the performance are shaped by context. If the praise singing moves a person, he (or she) will give something to the *jeli.* Praise singers will continue to praise someone until they feel they have received an appropriate gift for the praise, or until a point in the implied but tacit negotiation has been reached, so the praise singing will come to an end. As Nimeh Kaleh explained (Arntson 1987–1988:120-A): "To sing a song you enjoy and that others enjoy, it will help you [the *jeli*] get something from people. . . . When you keep on repeating it, it will bring more things to you and you won't leave the song quickly."

Function

The ability to obtain property through praise singing and patronage is only one aspect of a *jeli*'s praise. In Maninka and Koranko culture and society, the praise itself has many functions. In both the *tulon bolo* and *bolo gbili* repertories, praise singing has value as entertainment. Performance as entertainment can make people happy. Songs in the *tulon bolo* repertory "can make people forget about death and fighting"; when a *jeli* sings "adult songs, the ones adults enjoy, when they are together with their girlfriends," and sings of things they like, it will "make the young men's minds get up and move" (Arntson 1987–1988:120-A). Others will enjoy hearing the *bala* and the words because it reminds them of past times and of other occasions for praise singing.

Because, in part, praise singing occurs during parties, celebrations, or other events that call for entertainment, a *jeli* carries a certain immunity from blame, and can therefore criticize and advise others, all in the guise of praise. The *jelilu* I spoke with pointed out the value of advising others through praise singing. Nimeh Kaleh said, "a mature man will recognize the advice you are giving him and will give you something for that, because he will appreciate it" (Arntson 1987–1988:120-A). When people treat poorly their spouses, siblings, other family members, or friends, a *jeli* may offer advice about social behavior, as praise to someone else (and in so doing, draw a favorable or unfavorable comparison to others in a group). Through proverbs, truisms, and other references to social mores and shared stories or text envelopes, a *jeli* presents and reinforces shared ideals of behavior and personality. In praise songs, the portrayal of ideals and the references to behaviors serve to criticize and challenge others.

Another important aspect of praise singing is the receipt or acknowledgment of praise beyond simply giving something to a *jeli*. While a gift may deflect or mediate the power in a specialist's words or music, it does not do away with the fact that the *jeli* has directed praise toward an individual; and by accepting praise, a person takes on a debt. The *bolo gbili* praise songs are heavier with obligation than the *tulon bololu*, because they are older and therefore contain a greater number of historical references. Praise within the *bolo gbili* repertory is dense with layers of associations and references to mythic and historical personalities and events. By virtue of membership in or affiliation with a particular patrilineage, an individual can accept praise, and can dance (figuratively and literally) to certain *bololu gbili*. Each major patrilineage has its own pattern, employed when praising those with an identical or affiliated surname. Thus, the *bolo gbili* repertory contains not only the Mansareh *bolo*, but also the Kondeh *bolo*, the Koroman *bolo*, the Kamara *bolo*, and so on. This repertory also contains songs in praise of certain occupations, such as *Duwa* (for warriors), *Simba* (for hunters), and *Konkoba* (for farmers). By actively accepting the praise from one of the patterns (for instance, by dancing), a person takes on a mantle of attributes and expectations. In this way, he or she can gather strength and followers. Such praise may function to prepare and carry someone into battle or adversity; however, not everyone can accept the praise of certain *bololu gbili* or meet the power and obligation particular patterns carry with them. Pa Kuyateh explained:

"When this pattern is played, you will think about death, because it is played for those who are in battle."

The Mansareh pattern, not everyone can dance to it: only the Mansarehs can dance to the Mansareh pattern. Because it was the first pattern brought down from above, it is too heavy for anyone else; it is heavy. If you are not in a position to dance to that pattern, it will not be good for you. If you dance to it, you have to sacrifice something big, like a goat or a sheep, and give it to the praise singer. For instance, the hunters who dance to this pattern, they have to put blood [from the sacrificed animal] on the floor first, because this pattern also belongs to the Jinns. It is the first pattern Allah created. (Arntson 1987–1988:113-A)

In the Maninka and Koranko world, spirits are *jinns*. This reference, and the attribution of the performance tradition and repertory to Allah, reveal an Islamic cultural overlay.

Not only the acknowledgment and receipt of praise words, but also the ability to hear the sound of the *bala*, mean access to strength and power. According to the text of a performance of the *Kondeh bolo* praise song, the Kondeh are such strong soldiers, they can keep others from drawing strength and power from praise (Arntson 1987–1988:113-A):

Kondeh, Kondeh Buraima. . . . Ni Kondeh Buraima tunya, downu bòda le ban gbanna. Wo le ti bala kana mèn.

Kondeh, Kondeh Buraima. . . . [Because of] the true Kondeh Buraima, some would have their asses nailed to the ground. They would never hear the sound of the *bala*.

For the Maninka and the Koranko, the accession of power, strength, and cohorts, through the active receipt of certain *bala* patterns, is a part of preparation necessary for battle or adversity. A warrior or leader of Sunjata's stature (as was Almamy Samori, for instance) takes on the challenge of the mantle of attributes and expectations, and wears it as a protective cloak into battle. *Duwa* was played for Sunjata and Samori, among others. Especially heavy or weighty, *Duwa* implies a certain strength, stature, and an ability to take on the power and responsibilities of praise. Because of the significance and weight of its references, it is not appropriate for frequent playing. Pa Kuyateh explained that, when you hear *Duwa*,

your mind will tremble. The great man, this is the kind of pattern he dances to. When it is played, it makes everyone afraid and they think, "Oh, the fight will start!" When this pattern is played, you will think about death, because it is played for those who are in battle. The reason *Duwa* is a *bolo gbili* is because there is death behind it. (Arntson 1987–1988:113-A, 130-B).

Duwa will occasionally be played for those who are in a position of political or economic strength, though they may not be able to take on the mantle of power *Duwa* brings.

A challenge to amend behavior, to succeed when faced with adversity, or to carry through on intentions, may come in different forms. To push patrons into action, *jelilu* may actually insult them. Though what *jelilu* say may be "far from the truth, . . . [it can] cast doubts in the minds of people, thus forcing their patrons to prove the contrary by their actions" (Darbo 1975:10). Alternatively, a specialist may present a truism or an ideal as a challenge. The Mansareh *bolo* and *Duwa*, for example, both contain the phrase *kèlè ma di jito la* 'fighting is not good for (does not suit) a coward'. By pointing out that not all men are fit for battle, and that 'it is because you are not a coward that this praise can be directed at you,' a *jeli* can push someone into action. Other challenges may take more ambiguous forms. The text of another praise song says *Mòò ni mòò ma kelen* 'all people are not one' (or 'not everyone is the same') and "you cannot compare yourself with another person, especially if that person has many things and you have none. . . . You will never be able to defeat him, if you fight with him" (Arntson 1987–1988:133-B).

By praising someone with words that listeners can interpret several ways, thereby placing the responsibility of interpretation on others, a specialist may have even more power and influence. In a performance of a *tulon bolo* directed at me, for example, Hawa Kuyateh and Nimeh Kaleh captured something of the relationship between me and their role as *jelimusolu*. In so doing, they placed on me an expectation to continue offering them a certain patronage. By stating "if you give food to a hungry person, he will never leave you," and "if you give clothes to a person without clothes, he will never desert you" (Arntson 1987–1988:120-A). They pointed out certain obligations I had to them. To these words they added:

> Bi mòònu na mana mana kuma, kana bila wo fè. Bila sila kè ta, ti miiriya sa.

> The foolish talk of people today, do not follow it. The one who follows in your path will never spoil your thoughts.

These words added further emphasis to the trust between us.

Hawa Kuyateh and Nimeh Kaleh performed another *tulon bolo* (also directed at me), which they presented entirely as a *donkili*. The meaning and intended interpretations are obscure, possibly because, as a *donkili*, the words are less likely to vary from one performance to the next. It could be that, while the song directed praise toward me, it was meant as a criticism or challenge to someone else present who may have had occasion to brag to others about my patronage and attention. A portion of the text (Arntson 1987–1988:120-B) follows:

> Mari ba mòò min so, soli banda.
> A ti kun nabila, ti bila mòò la.
> Kòni, n'i n'a malo ma nyi.
> Ko n'bi sòòma.
> Ala ka da min tèè, a ti wo rakolònya.
> Aah, Fanta. . . .
> Saramo lamalo ma nyi, kana n'nèni. . . .

> A gift God [Mari] has given a person, it will not end.
> He never brags, never shows off.
> But, to involve you with another's shame is not good.
> Say, "Good morning."
> The mouth which God made, he will never leave it empty.
> Aah, Fanta. . . .
> To shame a popular person is not good, do not curse me.

In reference to *Duwa*, Nimeh Kaleh said, "Oh, my chest feels very cold when I sing this song."

TRACK 10

A challenge delivered through praise singing can do more than turn a person's thoughts to a subject and push him or her into action: it can actually change the person. Some people are credited with such access to power; they physically change as a result of hearing certain kinds of challenge or praise. On hearing the taunts of the praise singers sent from a rival, Sunjata allegedly turned himself into a lion (Johnson 1986:178–179). According to Pa Kuyateh, the words of certain *bololu gbili,* such as *Duwa,* have the power to make people change into leopards. The power such praise songs carry is perceptible. In reference to *Duwa,* Nimeh Kaleh said, "Oh, my chest feels very cold when I sing this song" (Arntson 1987–1988:120-B). In performance, the music and words in praise singing have a power and an agency to supply those who can accept the praise with a certain strength or cloak of invulnerability. Samori, for instance, when praised with the *Duwa* pattern, would "sit on top of his horse, and when [his enemies] would fire at him . . . with bows and arrows, all the arrows would fall down the front of his gown" without piercing him (Arntson 1987–1988:120-B). The power of praise singing lies in its capacity to challenge individuals to fulfill certain responsibilities, while providing an inner strength or source of power on which to draw. By calling up different voices of authority (authority of the past, of society, of customary knowledge and behavior), praise supplies individuals with strength, motivation, and personal pride.

The past has an authoritative voice. *Bolo gbili* praise song performances recreate past events and individual personalities and attributes, and bring them into the present in relation to individuals and patrilineages. That which has gone before, the way people remember it, and its representation in the present, receive attention and gain potency because of the reflexive frame (Turner 1977a). John J. MacAloon defines reflexivity as "that capacity of human beings to distance themselves from their own subjective experiences, to stand apart from and to comment on them" (1984:11). Within this frame, individuals test and redefine who they are and who others are; the past becomes a source for identity and pride (Bird 1970). A praise singer tells a person "who he is, where he came from, assures him that he is worthy and important, and thus gives him the courage to go ahead" (Darbo 1975:15). In addition, the use of the past within the present "affords a collective security and generates the illusion of cultural continuity" (Jackson 1977:19).

The past and the ideal or expected behaviors displayed in praise song performance serve as models and as challenges. According to a Gambian praise singer interviewed by Darbo, praise singers teach people the history of their ancestors, "to serve as an example for them" (1975:8). Praise singing is a model for, and a public representation of, a shared heritage of social expectations and lineal identities. If identity and behavior share a common frame of reference, and if identities are social products (Burke and Reitzes 1981), then the interaction between an individual's sense of self and a particular context, between a self and others' expectations and behaviors, and between a concept of self and self-revalidation through presentation, create an identity. The presentation of a heritage, and of an identity that occurs in praise song performance, are but one, albeit an important aspect of the creation and perception of identity. An individual's lineage and expectations of ethnic identity are exhibited primarily in *bolo gbili* praise songs; and a model of social identity, tied to perceived status and role in society (Cicourel 1970), takes shape through performance of both the *tulon bolo* and *bolo gbili* repertories. Not all members of a culture share the models and representations of lineal identity and of social roles or behavior; however, the assumptions that a *jeli*'s representation adequately reflects social and cultural expectations, and that a *jeli* plays the role of recreating and representing a shared heritage, are more important than the fact of inexact sharing. Musical and verbal performance is social interaction; and within that context, people interact on incomplete evidence (Cicourel 1974). To maintain a social situation, people need only a minimal degree of accuracy in their comprehension of other actors' intentions. A performance allows varying degrees of focus, concentration, evaluation, and comprehension. When different perceptions and expectations collide, an assumption of shared beliefs takes over, carries individuals through the process of negotiation, and results in the identification and representation of aspects of identity (McCall and Simmons 1966).

The texts in praise song performance are reflections and manipulations of a social institution (the *jeli*, his or her role and relationship to others) and a speech act (the text envelope and expectations of performance and previous performances). The past, as praise singing represents it, is a negotiated myth or reality. History is malleable; a *jeli* handles it and presents it to others. Since it is brought to life or "made" only in acts of speech (Sahlins 1981) or other performances, it exists only partially as a shared area of knowledge. A praise singer's art is more than an embellishment: like other arts, it is a way of knowing, coping with, and changing reality (Hawkes 1977:143). A *jeli* is entrusted with a memory and an access to a representation of past personages, their attributes and deeds, and a cultural heritage of myths, role expectations, and social behaviors and relationships. His memory and interests insert themselves into a mythicohistoric tradition, "carried forward by a continuing chain of transmissions and receptions" (Shils 1981:167). In this way, his memory and perceptions become the memory of a culture. (For further discussion of history as a shared or collective memory, see Vansina [1980] and Jackson [1977:20].)

As the *jeli*'s domains, text, music, and genre symbolize a cultural heritage and codify the relationship between it and contemporary individuals and society. Though the symbolism and meaning communicated through performative behavior may stand apart from the level of direct verbal communication, the participants in a performative event understand them. They do so because, within a cultural frame, symbolic behaviors accumulate assigned meanings with each renegotiation or representation of interpretations and references (Turner 1977b). Praise songs, because they put forth ideal lineage and social identities, can be understood, like epics, to be "collective mottoes" (Seydou 1983b). The transition from a symbol to that for which it stands is based on a concept promoted within a culture (Scheffler 1981). Since the Maninka and the Koranko empower praise singing with the capacity to maintain their cultural heritage and project into individuals its power and knowledge, it becomes a potent motto for Maninka and Koranko identity and behavior.

By acquiring "meaning beyond the bounds of its individual existence as a thing in and of itself" (Bogatyrev 1976:14), any item can become more than itself—as a word, object, or sound. "If signs are not that which is indicated, but rather serve to indicate (or to recall) that which is not there" (Eco 1975:11), then ideas can also be signs or symbols (Jakobson 1960). Mythic or historical reality as praise singing and epic represent it can be understood as a symbolic code (Seydou 1983a). Particular *bala* patterns and praise names also become symbols; however, part of what makes a

The tension is part of a shared aesthetic, and an aspect of a *jeli*'s power, role, and maintenance of that role.

symbol potent is the tension its ambiguity creates. Not everyone knows the full meaning of a given symbol; nor does everyone share a *jeli*'s interpretation and intention: but, because of the assumed complicity on the part of patron and singer, the singer's representation gains acceptance (momentarily, at least) as an "official" version. A *jeli* can act as a kind of mouthpiece for a group or a culture; however, the ambivalence and tension created by the representation of a heritage and social expectations are not lost. Performing within the constraints of culture, society, and performance, a *jeli* enjoys a certain interpretive latitude; yet the tension in the relationship between singer and patron, and between a singer's representation and another's interpretation, never quite resolves; nor do people intend it to. The tension is part of a shared aesthetic, and an aspect of a *jeli*'s power, role, and maintenance of that role. For artistry and power, a *jeli* plays on the ambiguity of the stock of symbols to which he or she has access, and in which certain aspects of Maninka heritage rest. If the symbols "a people develop, together with their meanings, concerning their experience as a people," are what make up a collective identity (Spicer 1980:347) or a collective heritage, then the text envelopes and the ideals of lineal identity and behavior represented in praise singing constitute an important aspect of a collective or an assumed notion of heritage and identity. The Maninka and the Koranko see themselves and their relationships with others, at least in part, in a singer's representation of this shared heritage.

Content

The *bolo gbili* repertory captures the past in characterizations of, or references to, historical characters. These songs allude to and, in a sense, reshape the personal attributes, deeds, exploits, and circumstances surrounding the origins and lives of heroes, leaders, and warriors of Manden. Individuals have inspired fear and admiration over the centuries (or, with Samori, decades) because their individuality and unique leadership, or other real or attributed qualities, have set them apart. A *jeli*'s portrayal of cultural heroes or of other significant characters makes them larger than life. In addition, mythical elements—drawn from both indigenous and Islamic beliefs—attach to them. Mythical and historical time collapses into a hero's own time. The hero is no longer a human being, but a larger-than-life representation of cultural beliefs and ideals. This character, his deeds, and the circumstances surrounding his existence, become a motto for his lineage and the lineages aligned with him.

A *jeli*'s repertory reflects the impact of certain cultural characters and occupations. A Gambian (Mandinka) *jali*'s repertory differs from that of a Sierra Leonean *jeli* (Knight 1973, 1982). Sunjata holds central importance in the world made by Manden because of his role in the founding of the Mali Empire, his promotion of artistic specialization (notably his patronage of *jelilu*), and the origins of clans or lineage names traced to the larger narrative or text envelope surrounding him. The

Maninka of Sierra Leone also place such personages as Kondeh Buraima, Fakoli, Jirikaranani, and Almamy Samori in roles that are important to their heritage.

In praise of warriors

The name "Kondeh Buraima" refers both to a man (also known as "Kanja Buraima"), who fought in battles against white people (Arntson 1987–1988:103-B), and to a composite character, who represents an ideal Kondeh warrior. Bird identifies an individual by the name of "Kanji" as one of Samori's generals (Bird, Koita, and Soumaoro 1974:xi). Mythic or historical individuals in the Kondeh lineage have added to the Kondehs' renown as warriors. Kondeh Buraima has come to epitomize the lineage's prowess in battle. This character also bears the inheritance of the praise names "Jimamin Kondeh" and "Dalamin Kondeh." In response to a challenge, a historical or mythic individual is said to have drained a lake (Arntson 1987–88:113-A), either before or during the "Mansareh's battles" (the conflicts between competing clans that eventually led to the founding of the Mali Empire). After drinking all the water, this patriarch received praise with the names "Jimamin (Water drinking) Kondeh" and "Dalamin (Lake drinking) Kondeh." In some versions of the Sunjata epic, it was the Buffalo Woman of Du who drank the lake (Johnson 1979; see also Bulman 1989). As a witch, this woman could change herself into a buffalo; she has been aligned with the Kondeh lineage (Johnson 1979, 1986), the Koroman lineage (Arntson 1987–1988:111-B), and the Tarawèlè clan (Jackson 1982:165). It was her demise that led to the selection of the wife who gave birth to Sunjata.

Fakoli, a patriarch of the Koroman lineage and subject of the Koroman *bolo,* also has ties to Sunjata and the Sunjata epic. Texts portray him as Sunjata's accomplice in the defeat of Sumanguru (Johnson 1979, 1986; Darbo 1975) and, under the influence of Jirikaranani, as a would-be traitor to Sunjata (Arntson 1987–1988:104-A, 111-B). Jirikaranani (of the Marah lineage) decided to fight Manden, though, as a Marah, he was a nephew of the Mansareh clan. Possibly in a try to gain the strength necessary to defeat Manden, he supposedly stole, from the Lake of Knowledge and Power, the powerful objects that the Mansareh clan owned (Arntson 1987–1988:104-A, 113-B, 131-A). These objects included a hat with horns of gold and silver. The Buffalo Woman of Du also had gold and silver horns, plus a tail of gold and silver threads (Johnson 1979, 1986). One of the Tarawèlè brothers, who had killed her, hacked off her horns, tail, ears, and hooves (Johnson 1986:120); they put these objects into a calabash (Johnson 1986:121) and most likely carried them to Manden, for they also brought to that place the woman who became Sunjata's mother. The Marah *bolo* contains references to Jirikaranani and his campaign against Sunjata. Jirikaranani (also known as "Yir'kar'nani" and "Yilkanani") takes on a variety of identities and origins. He has been identified as Dhul-Quarnein, a name that derives from the Arabic for "two-horned" (Jackson 1989:160), and as Djurukaranani, who from 1200 to 1218 was either a warrior from Kankan (Jackson 1989:159) or a chief of Ouagadou (Jackson 1989:159; Monteil 1929:80).

The narratives Pa Sanasi Kuyateh tells about Sunjata focus on Jirikaranani and his attempt to defeat Manden with the help of the Koroman clan. Pa Kuyateh's references to Sunjata's origins and founding of the Mali Empire appear in a narrative of the Buffalo Woman of Du known as *Danfèrèma Koroma* (Arntson 1987–1988:111-B), in the Mansareh *bolo,* and the *Duwa* and *Simbon* praise songs.

The song Duwa

Duwa praises warriors. It has accumulated layers of references to Sunjata—which may show it has been played a long time, as praise for Sunjata in his role of warrior. *Duwa* is a *bolo gbili,* specifically a *kèlèbolo* or "warrior pattern." It carries a mantle of

> *Duwa* was also sung in praise of the living Samori, a fearless leader and warrior, who, with professional soldiers (the *sofas*), tried to build an empire.

power. The praise name and praise song *Duwa* may have some relation to the most powerful of the men's secret associations in the area of West Africa under the influence of Manden. In performance, this song becomes an agent, because people credit it with the ability to prepare a warrior for battle and supply him with strength, power, and followers. It also carries a strong association with death, since it praises those who are such fierce warriors that the vultures (*duwa* or *duba*) will never go hungry in their path, and because the collected references to deadly conflicts are many. It contains the following *donkili* text (Arntson 1987–1988:120-B):

Jala ye ko san do,	A *jala* is up above,
Jala ye ko duu la.	A *jala* is on the ground.
Jala ka bon jala di.	[One] *jala* is larger than another *jala*.
Jala ma kunan ni jala ko.	[One] jala was more bitter than another *jala*.
Jala, jala, tun ka jala,	*Jala, jala,* there was a *jala*.
Jala ka duu ma.	It was on the ground.
Duwa ti fòla bèè ye.	*Duwa* cannot be played for everyone.
Duwa ti fòla kèbajito.	*Duwa* can never be played for a coward.
[Wo ye nabòri le], ka su rò sa.	He will run away, to go through the town.
Eeh Duwa, *eeh* Duwa.	*Eeh* Duwa, *eeh* Duwa.

Different warriors have different strengths: some are bigger and stronger than others; some have prepared for battle, while others have not. A warrior who has prepared properly for battle is one who has caused his "heart to come forth," thus making his flesh impenetrable to bullets or arrows. Such a warrior is said to have bitten the *jala* tree in his anger at having been fired upon; the bite caused the bark and flesh of the tree to become bitter (Arntson 1987–1988:120-B). The text of *Duwa* alludes to the differences between warriors, and to the tie between fierce warriors and the *jala*. A coward (*kèbajito*) can never accept the praise, or take on the weight of obligations and attributes a performance of *Duwa* carries, because he could not live up to cultural expectations about a true warrior.

Duwa was also sung in praise of the living Samori, a fearless leader and warrior, who, with professional soldiers (the *sofas*), tried to build an empire. In the 1860s and 1870s, he gained political and economic control over a large area of Guinea, including the Sankaran region. Sory Camara (1976) locates Sankaran across the headwaters of the Niger, Niandan, and Milo Rivers, in the area of Faranah and Kissidougou, just below Kankan. In 1874, Samori took the title of Almamy, and, in the guise of promoting Islam, promoted his own interests. In northern Sierra Leone, most of the Maninka (who call themselves Sankaran Maninka) are descendants of those who fled from Guinea as refugees from his battles. In the 1880s, he and his *sofas* captured areas in what is now the Northern Province of Sierra Leone; but by 1890, French campaigns against him weakened his hold. (For historical background on him, see Fage 1969; Fyle 1979; Hunwick 1965 [1970]; Ifemesia 1970; and Person 1967.)

As we can expect, Samori figures prominently in Sankaran Maninka references to former battles, to Guinea, and to the ambivalence that accompanies a fierce warrior or leader. Apparently Samori, fully aware of the power inherent in praise delivered via the *Duwa* praise song, requested that *Duwa* be played as he prepared for battle. As Pa Kuyateh explained (Arntson 1987–1988:120-B):

> when Samori sat on top of a horse, and when he was fired upon, then he would ask the praise singer to play Duwa. . . . When he took a gun and fired (kubun), a hundred people would die at once. This Duwa pattern was being played behind him. When he turned and pointed another way and [his gun] said, "Whuunn," another one hundred people would go down. By then people were saying, "He wants to 'convert' us."

Samori was allegedly captured because of hunger, rather than by means employed directly by the French and British. Though he is not praised with the Mansareh *bolo* (the praise song of Sunjata's lineage), the reference to hunger as the cause of his downfall calls in the authority of the praise associated with him: *min di yaraden gbasi fo kònkò* (that which can beat the lion cub is hunger alone), from the Mansareh *bolo*. Pa Kuyateh's portrayal of him displays an overlay of attributes associated with Sunjata, plus mythical motifs. Samori is said to have survived a lengthy voyage while sealed in a wooden crate, before being recaptured by the British (Arntson 1987–1988:121-A). Other sources point out that he died in exile, in Gabon, after fleeing to Liberia and elsewhere (Martin 1971). His battle, and the battle in Manden during Sunjata's time, belong to a past that includes not only a historical past, but also a remote and mythic past. Performative representation subjects history to manipulation. The historicity of events may become obscured, and individuals mythologized in performance. Samori and Sunjata belong to both a real and a mythical past, and they serve as symbols for various aspects of a Maninka heritage.

In praise of hunters

In addition to being a leader, a hero, and a warrior, Sunjata was a notable hunter. Possibly as a result of his stature, he has, over time, gained the ability to epitomize the role of hunter. *Simba* or *Simbon*, a praise song for hunters, bears many references to him, though it could have existed as praise for hunters before the development of the Sunjata epic. In narratives about Jirikaranani's campaign against Manden, Pa Kuyateh represents Sunjata as both Manden itself and as Mandenfabureh, the mythical grandfather of hunters (Arntson 1987–1988:104-A). Mandenfabureh is also the spirit of hunting and of hunters. An individual who had gone hunting with Maninka and Koranko hunters in the Koinadugu District told me that, after a successful hunt of a larger animal, hunters make a sacrifice to Mandenfabureh.

Many of the praise songs in the *bolo gbili* repertory invoke Sunjata as himself (the person), and Sunjata as Manden (the essence or symbol). Through performances of songs in the *bolo gbili* repertory, the representations of various individuals, attributes, occupations, and lineal identities rely on allusions to the past. Since the past is a conglomerate body of historical and mythical persons, events, and activities, some of the texts and their references overlap. It is the *balabololu* or the musical patterns themselves (contours, rhythmic motifs, *donkili* melodies) that clearly distinguish individual praise songs.

Patrons and *jelilu* alike employ praise singing dynamically, as a means to legitimate and negotiate social roles and expectations.

The repertory of tulon bolo

Because *tulon bolo* songs are much newer, and are not always tied to particular events or individuals, songs in this repertory do not accumulate references or weight the way a *bolo gbili* song does. Nor do *tulon bololu* rely so heavily on patterns of *bala* for their identification. *Tulon bololu* call on "cultural texts," and are perhaps as likely to be performed for enjoyment as for advising. Whether or not they are directed toward an individual or situation, however, their texts represent cultural values, attitudes, and expectations. *Baya*, for example, is a *tulon bolo* that advises against deception, or going behind another's back. One performance of it included the words *a na wulu, n'ko ma kumala; a na wulu, a fa wulu* 'his mother is a dog, who gossips behind me; his mother is a dog, his father is a dog' (Arntson 1987–1988:120-A). Pa Kuyateh also likened *Baya* to adultery. Referring to another performance of *Baya*, he explained: "This is the pattern called *Baya*; it advises people not to be dishonest with their friends; the example is just like politics [*a misali le ko polotiki*]." *Wodi tii* 'Moneyowner', another *tulon bolo*, points out the positive and negative aspects of having wealth: it is nice to have and can help a person gain friends and followers, plus the praise of a *jeli*; but it has no respect for anything. Money "molests gold, rice, horses, everything" (Arntson 1987–1988:115-A) because the love of money can make a person sell gold, rice, horses, or other items. Money can disappear quickly, and does not have the lasting power of other items.

The *tulon bolo* repertory depicts situations and valuable lessons that come out of contemporary experience. The changes in patronage of *jelilu*, different means of gaining economic and political power, and the social changes brought on by contemporary contexts, have had an effect on the functions and subjects of praise singing; however, the repertory maintains the form of the genre and the practice of praise singing. The tradition encompasses both the old (the *bololu gbili*) and the new (the *tulon bololu*).

A CULTURE-SPECIFIC DEFINITION OF GENRE

If, in fact, tradition is "a symbolic construction by which people in the present establish connections with a meaningful past and endow particular cultural forms with value and authority" (Bauman 1992:126), praise song performance must be understood as a strategy. A genre is thus, rather than simply a perceptual category, a resource for expression. Patrons and *jelilu* alike employ praise singing dynamically, as a means to legitimate and negotiate social roles and expectations.

To represent, legitimate, promote, or interpret social roles, interactions, and experiences, people call into the present the authority of their past. The symbolism and functions they attach to an expressive form are what make up a culture-specific definition of a genre. When we ask "how people use verbal art in the conduct of their social lives" (Bauman 1992:144), placing an expressive form within its cultural and situational context, "genre" becomes more than just an analytical construction. The term has been called an analytical creation (Derrida 1980). By focusing on actual occurrences of a form within a particular culture, we discover an idiom that may, in fact, display multigeneric or intergeneric qualities; but what is the purpose of defining a genre as multigeneric? Would it not be more valuable to let an expressive form define its own generic terms, thus freeing it from the constraints of a preconceived analytical model? Might not a context-specific definition of a performative genre allow for more productive cross-cultural comparative research than does a purely analytical category?

The concept of an area of performance or an expressive form, which I have identified as the genre of praise singing, exists in practice—and in the imagination of Maninka and Koranko musicians I interviewed. Praise singing, as I have defined it here, is a real and potent genre for the Maninka and the Koranko. It involves both verbal and musical elements, and the latter—rhythms, prosody, melodies of *donkili*, patterns of *bala*—are the main factors in the identification of its repertoire and practice.

REFERENCES

Arntson, Laura. 1987–1988. Field tapes recorded in Sukurala, Northern Sierra Leone. Deposited at the Archives of Traditional Music, Indiana University, Bloomington, Indiana.

———. 1992. "The Play of Ambiguity in Praise-Song Performance: A Definition of the Genre through an Examination of Its Practice in Northern Sierra Leone." Ph.D. dissertation, Indiana University.

Backus, John. 1969. *The Acoustical Foundations of Music*. New York: Norton.

Bauman, Richard. 1977. *Verbal Art as Performance*. Prospect Heights, Ill.: Waveland Press.

———. 1992. "Contextualization, Tradition, and the Dialogue of Genres: Icelandic Legends of the *Kraftaskáld*." In *Rethinking Context*, ed. Charles Goodwin and Alessandro Duranti, 125–145. Cambridge: Cambridge University Press.

Bird, Charles S. 1970. "The Development of Mandenkan: A Study of the Role of Extralinguistic Factors in Linguistic Change." In *Language and History of Africa*, ed. David Dalby, 146–159. London: Cass.

———. 1971. "Oral Art in the Mande." In *Papers on the Manding*, ed. Carleton Hodge, 15–25. Bloomington, Ind.: Research Center for the Language Sciences.

———. 1976. "Poetry in the Mande: Its Form and Meaning." *Poetics* 5:89–100.

Bird, Charles S., and Martha B. Kendall. 1980. "The Mande Hero." In *Explorations in African Systems of Thought*, ed. Ivan Karp and Charles S. Bird, 13–26. Bloomington: Indiana University Press.

Bird, Charles S., Mamadou Koita, and Bourama Soumaoro. 1974. *The Songs of Seydou Camara*, Vol. 1: *Kambili*. Bloomington: Indiana University African Studies Center.

Bogatyrev, Petr. 1936 [1976]. "Costume as a Sign." In *Semiotics of Art: Prague School Contributions*, ed. L. Matejka and I. R. Titunik, 13–19. Cambridge, Mass.: M.I.T. Press.

Bulman, Stephen. 1989. "The Buffalo-Woman Tale: Political Imperatives and Narrative Constraints in the Sunjata Epic." In *Discourse and its Disguises: The Interpretation of African Oral Texts*, ed. Karin Barber and P. F. de Moraes Farias, 171–188. Birmingham: Centre of West African Studies, Birmingham University African Studies Series 1.

Burke, Peter J., and Donald C. Reitzes. 1981. "The Link between Identity and Role Performance." *Social Psychology Quarterly* 44(2):83–92.

Camara, Sory. 1976. *Gens de la Parole*. Paris: Mouton.

Cicourel, Aaron V. 1970. "Basic and Normative Rules in the Negotiation of Status and Role." In *Recent Sociology, No. 2*, ed. Hans Peter Dreitzel, 4–45. New York: Macmillan.

———. 1974. *Cognitive Sociology: Language and Meaning in Social Interaction*. New York: Free Press.

Dalby, David. 1971. "Distribution and Nomenclature of the Manding People and Their Language." In *Papers on the Manding*, ed. Carleton Hodge, 1–13. Bloomington, Ind.: Research Center for the Language Sciences.

Darbo, Seni. 1975. *A Griot's Self-Portrait: The Origins and Role of the Griot in Mandinka Society as Seen from Stories Told by Gambian Griots*. Banjul: Gambia Cultural Archives. Occasional papers.

Derrida, Jacques. 1980. "The Law of Genre." *Critical Inquiry* 7(1):55–81.

Duran, Lucy. 1987. "Jaliya and the Role of the Jali in Present Day Manding Society." *African Affairs* 86(343):233–236.

Eco, Umberto. 1975. "Looking for a Logic of Culture." In *The Tell-Tale Sign: A Survey of Semiotics*, ed. Thomas A. Sebeok, 9–17. Lisse, Belgium: Peter de Ridder.

Fage, John D. 1969. *A History of West Africa: An Introductory Survey*, 4th ed. Cambridge: Cambridge University Press.

Finnegan, Ruth. 1970. *Oral Literature in Africa*. Nairobi: Oxford University Press.

———. 1977. *Oral Poetry: Its Nature, Significance and Social Context*. Cambridge: Cambridge University Press.

Fyle, C. Magbaily. 1979. *Almamy Suluku of Sierra Leone c.1820–1906*. London: Evans Brothers.

Goffman, Erving. 1974. *Frame Analysis*. New York: Harper & Row.

Hawkes, Terrence. 1977. *Structuralism and Semiotics*. Berkeley: University of California Press.

Hodge, Carleton, ed. 1971. *Papers on the Manding*. Bloomington, Ind.: Research Center for the Language Sciences.

Hopkins, Nicholas S. 1971. "Mandinka Social Organization." In *Papers on the Manding*, ed. Carleton Hodge, 99–128. Bloomington, Ind.: Research Center for the Language Sciences.

Hunwick, J. O. 1965 [1970]. "The Nineteenth Century Jihads." In *A Thousand Years of West African History*, ed. J. F. A. Ajayi and Ian Espie, 267–288. London: Redwood Press.

Ifemesia, C. C. 1970. "A Note on Samori Touré." In *A Thousand Years of West African History*, ed. J. F. A. Ajayi and Ian Espie, 283–288. London: Redwood Press.

Innes, Gordon. 1976. *Kaabu and Fuladu: Historical Narratives of the Gambian Mandinka*. London: School of Oriental and African Studies, University of London.

Jackson, Michael. 1977. *The Kuranko: Dimensions of Social Reality in a West African Society*. New York: St. Martin's Press.

———. 1982. "Meaning and Moral Imagery in Kuranko Myth," *Research in African Literatures* 13(2):153–180.

———. 1989. *Paths toward a Clearing: Radical Empiricism and Ethnographic Inquiry.* Bloomington: Indiana University Press.

Jakobson, Roman. 1960. "Closing Statement: Linguistics and Poetics." In *Style in Language,* ed. Thomas A. Sebeok, 350–377. Cambridge, Mass.: M. I. T. Press.

Johnson, John W. 1979. *The Epic of Sun-Jata according to Magan Sisòkò.* Bloomington: Folklore Publications Group, Indiana University. Folklore Publications Group, Monograph 5.

———. 1980. "Yes, Virginia, There Is an Epic in Africa." *Research in African Literatures* 11(3):308–326.

———. 1986. *The Epic of Son-Jara: A West African Tradition.* Bloomington: Indiana University Press.

Knight, Roderic. 1971. "Towards a Notation and Tablature for the Kora." *African Music* 5(1):23–36.

———. 1973. "Mandinka Jaliya: Professional Music of the Gambia." Ph.D. dissertation, University of California at Los Angeles.

———. 1982. "Manding/Fula Relations as Reflected in the Manding Song Repertoire." *African Music* 6(2):37–47.

———. 1984a. "Music in Africa: The Manding Contexts." In *Performance Practice: Ethnomusicological Perspectives,* ed. Gerard Béhague, 53–90. Westport, Conn.: Greenwood Press.

———. 1984b. "The Style of Mandinka Music: A Study in Extracting Theory from Practice." In *Studies in African Music,* ed. J. H. Kwabena Nketia and Jacqueline Cogdell DjeDje, 2–66. Los Angeles: Program in Ethnomusicology, University of California at Los Angeles.

Launay, Robert. 1972. "Les clans et les castes mandingues." Paper presented at the Conference of Manding Studies, London.

McCall, George J., and J. L. Simmons. 1966. *Identities and Interactions.* New York: Free Press.

MacAloon, John J. 1984. "Introduction: Cultural Performances, Culture Theory." In *Rite, Drama,*

Festival, Spectacle: Rehearsals Toward a Theory of Cultural Performance, ed. John J. MacAloon, 1–18. Philadelphia: Institute for the Study of Human Issues.

McNaughton, Patrick R. 1988. *The Mande Blacksmiths: Knowledge, Power and Art in West Africa.* Bloomington: Indiana University Press.

Martin, Bradford. 1971. "Al-Hajj 'Umar Tall, Samori Ture, and Their Forerunners." In *Papers on the Manding,* ed. Carleton Hodge, 159–165. Bloomington, Ind.: Research Center for the Language Sciences.

Meillassoux, Claude. 1973. "Note sure l'étymologie de *nyamakala.*" *Notes Africaines* 89:79.

Monteil, Charles. 1929. "Les Empires du Mali." *Bulletin du Comité d'Études Historiques et Scientifique de l'Afrique Occidentale Française* 12(3–4):291–447.

Niane, Djibril T. 1984. "Mali and the Second Mandingo Expansion." In *Africa from the Twelfth to the Sixteenth Century,* ed. D. T. Niane, 117–171. Berkeley: UNESCO.

Oumarou, Watta. 1986. "The Human Thesis: A Quest for Meaning in African Epic." Ph.D. dissertation, State University of New York at Buffalo.

Person, Yves. 1967. "Samori et la Sierra Leone." *Cahiers d'Études Africaines* 7(25):5–26.

Preminger, Alex, Frank J. Warnke, and O. B. Hardison, Jr., eds. 1974. *Princeton Encyclopedia of Poetry and Poetics,* rev. ed. Princeton, N.J.: Princeton University Press.

Sahlins, Marshall. 1981. *Historical Metaphors and Mythical Realities: Structure in the Early History of the Sandwich Islands Kingdom.* Ann Arbor: University of Michigan Press. Association for Social Anthropology in Oceania, special publication 1.

Scheffler, Israel. 1981. "Ritual and Reference." *Synthese* 46(3):421–437.

Seydou, Christiane. 1983a. "The African Epic: A Means for Defining the Genre." *Folklore Forum* 16(1):47–68.

———. 1983b. "A Few Reflections on Narrative Structures of Epic Texts: A Case Example of

Bambara and Fulani Epics." *Research in African Literatures* 14(3): 312–331.

Shils, Edward. 1981. *Tradition.* Chicago: University of Chicago Press.

Shreve, Gregory M., and Ojo Arewa. 1980. "Form and Genre in African Folklore Classification: A Semiotic Perspective." *Research in African Literatures* 11(3):286–294.

Spicer, Edward H. 1980. *The Yaquis: A Cultural History.* Tucson: University of Arizona Press.

Stone, Ruth M. 1988. *Dried Millet Breaking: Time, Words, and Songs in the Wòi Epic of the Kpelle.* Bloomington: Indiana University Press.

Turner, Victor. 1977a. "Frame, Flow and Reflection: Ritual and Drama as Public Liminality." In *Performance in Postmodern Culture,* ed. Michel Benamou and Charles Caramello, 33–55. Madison: Center for Twentieth Century Studies, University of Wisconsin at Milwaukee.

———. 1977b. "Process, System, and Symbol: A New Anthropological Synthesis." *Daedalus* 106(3):61–80.

Vansina, Jan. 1980. "Memory and Oral Tradition." In *The African Past Speaks: Essays on Oral Tradition and History,* ed. Joseph C. Miller, 262–279. Kent, England: William Dawson & Sons.

Yankah, Kwesi. 1983. "To Praise or Not to Praise the King: The Akan *Akpae* in the Context of Referential Poetry." *Research in African Literatures* 14(3):381–400.

———. 1985. "Voicing and Drumming the Poetry of Praise: The Case for *Aural Literature.*" In *Interdisciplinary Dimensions of African Literature,* ed. Kofi Anyidoho et al., 137–153. Washington, D.C.: Three Continents Press)

Zemp, Hugo. 1964. "Musiciens autochtones et griots malinké chez les Dan de Côte d'Ivoire." *Cahiers d'Études Africaines* 4(15):370–382.

———. 1966. "La Légende des griots malinké." *Cahiers d'Études Africaines* 6(24):611–642.

Hausa Performance
Fremont E. Besmer

Fieldwork
Studies of Hausa Music
Theoretical Considerations
Ethnographic Context
The Social Organization of Musicians' Groups
Possession Trance Performance
Court Musicians' Performance
Cultural Process and Meaning

For students of cultural process, performances by traditional Hausa musicians fill two paradigmatic contexts: possession trance cults and royal courts. In the first, during certain public performances, musicians receive gifts from hosts and guests; and gifts received are to be repaid (Mauss 1925 [1967]:10): but not only musicians appear to feel the need to reciprocate; other participants do also, and they reciprocate with further gifts.

Looking at the giver and the receiver of a gift only partly explains the exchange that involves the musicians, since, in the code of cultural process, something else is happening. What such exchanges illustrate is the role musicians play in what I call *griot*-model societies, societies with specific structural elements: a group of socially despised professional musicians, a highly stratified social fabric, and social events during which groups in this fabric (both musicians and nonmusicians) must interact.

The other case this essay examines involves the royal musicians of the Emir of Kano—musicians who, to escape somewhat the stigma of the *maròokaa* (masc. sing. *maròokii*, 'praise singer, musician, "beggar"'), draw on the prestige of their patron. Particularly during the last ten days of the Islamic month of fasting, Ramadan (*Ràmàdân*), royal musicians walk around the city after dark, waking up citizens so they may prepare food and eat before the first light of dawn. The targets of this practice are wealthy businessmen and aristocrats, who, while they can successfully ignore most roving musicians, appear unable to refuse to be generous to the royal musicians. What makes this activity notable for a student of cultural process is the way royal musicians create a stimulus for which gift giving is the only appropriate response. To solicit gifts, royal musicians use the definitions of the wake-up walk (*yaawàn tàashee*), which includes drumming and singing; but to transform the situation into one requiring gifts made on behalf of the emir, they add their professional positions and instruments. They manipulate cultural symbols, either to create and change reality, or to transform one context into another.

These cases provide two views of Hausa performance not seen by the casual observer, and occasionally missed by professional ones. Joseph Greenberg described in detail the non-Muslim content of the indigenous spirit cult, and how Islam had changed it (1946); but he characterized *bòorii*, the public possession trance

bòorii   Group organized around possession
         trance performance

component of this religion, as having cultural meaning only in its function as entertainment. Exchanges involving musicians and competing guests and hosts may not
have been obvious in the events he witnessed, but it is reasonable to suspect he directed his attention to other ethnographic details. Writing about interrelationships
involving professional musicians, M. G. Smith described ways high-status men's
obligations to be generous to those below them tie together the layers of the social
fabric (1957), but he did not explore why such men should be successful at resisting
these obligations with respect to ordinary musicians. The performances are similar,
and the statuses of the participants are alike: yet royal musicians have an unseen
advantage.

FIELDWORK

For the present essay, I collected data in Kano, northern Nigeria, between September
1968 and January 1970, and September 1972 and December 1973. I focused on
documenting traditional Hausa musical culture, and on understanding cultural
processes, particularly from the perspective of traditional musicians. Tapings of interviews and events in which royal musicians or *bòorii* musicians performed, photographs of people and the objects important to them, and notebooks full of observations, questions, and answers to questions (some of which were not asked) are all part
of these data.

Since most traditional musicians are not fluent in English, the language I used
was Hausa, which I had learned as a Peace Corps Volunteer in the early 1960s.
Throughout the fieldwork, I emphasized open-ended interview sessions to collect
qualitative data on life as musicians saw it: stories, conversations, lessons, explanations. While I had sets of ethnographic questions that required answers, I aimed at
gaining cultural literacy, an understanding of the cultural rules musicians used to create and participate in their society. Some of these rules were clear to them—concepts
they would discuss, and about which they had opinions. Others, implied in their
behavior, informed their cultural competence but were as hidden to them as a lin-
guist's written grammar of their language might have been.

The "ethnographic present" for this essay, 1968–1973, was the period during the
beginning of military rule in Nigeria and the end of the civil war. For some people,
mainly those associated with commerce in some northern cities, and with oil production in the southern part of the country, the standard of living was rapidly rising; but
life in rural areas was still stable. Nigerian deposits of petroleum, being low in sul-
phur, were valuable; and oil was quickly replacing other foreign-revenue sources
(groundnuts, cocoa).

Two decades after the time described here, traditional life has changed drastically. Some observers report that young people no longer know much of the richness of
their language—its poetry, its riddles, its proverbs—and the meaning of its music.
Increasing numbers of traditional musicians whose craft had supported them were

taking wage-labor jobs (messenger, cleaner, servant), and were managing to keep their old life-styles alive only in occasional performances and the memories of aging friends.

STUDIES OF HAUSA MUSIC

Readers who want a general description of Hausa musical activity may choose from a variety of sources. For two administrative and cultural areas (Katsina and Zaria), the systematic organization of Ames and King (1971) is especially useful: their work, alphabetically and topically arranged, bristles with details on instruments, performers, musicians' patrons, the occasions for which they play, and the types of performances in which they participate. On Hausa musical activity in Zaria, Ames (1973) has written a definitive statement, which follows analytical lines not unlike those suggested in Merriam (1964); he covers the range of Hausa musical activity and aesthetic expression, and addresses the paradox of important social role matched with low social rank.

For other discussions of Hausa musicians and their performances, the reader can consult two sources: a dissertation on court musicians in Kano (Besmer 1972), and a monograph on the two main Muslim festivals, *Kàràmar Sallàa* (Arabic *Id al-Fitr*) and *Bàbbar Sallàa* (Arabic *Id al-Kabir*), in which court musicians participate (Besmer 1974). Each of these includes a generative-structural analysis of the three musical styles used by Hausa musicians and presents detailed descriptions of performances. Primarily in response to the linear order implied by a liturgical form (King 1966, 1967), Besmer (1975) uses a transformational, generative, analytical model to try to explain the layered and conditional order of *bòorii* performances. Besmer (1983) gives a much more general account of the cult, its musicians, music, trancers, and traditions.

THEORETICAL CONSIDERATIONS

Social stratification

Seeking to understand the dynamics of social and cultural systems (rather than their origins), some anthropologists direct their attention to the structural-functional glue that holds stratified societies together. Smith describes how the performances of praise singers reaffirm the network of social strata; these levels are separate but linked (1957). In his discussion of patron-client relationships (in which men whose social statuses differ function together, to maintain the stability of the stratified system), he uses the same tactic (1959). In both cases, vertical ties hold horizontal layers together. A principal point he makes is that musicians' performances are social-structural events, as much as musical ones.

My approach to social stratification develops the ideas of alliance-and-exchange theorists. Stemming from the work of Claude Lévi-Strauss (1949 [1969]), alliance theory and the inductional method in structuralism concentrate on the relationships between social units, regardless of their specific forms. Exchange theory includes the basic elements of giving, receiving, and repaying (Mauss 1925 [1967]); and, as Rosman and Rubel (1971) point out, it overlays these with the concepts of separation (one cannot exchange anything with oneself), and bondedness (exchange links individuals and groups).

Trying to make sense of the fact that guests (or hosts) at a *bòorii* performance can prompt hosts (or guests) into giving gifts to musicians, the outsider must consider the ideas of exchange and alliance, and determine the type of stratified society in which Hausa musicians live. Groups and individuals who exchange gifts—goods or services, or both—stress both their separateness and their bondedness. When practice

Royal musicians are outwardly devout Muslims in a society in which a person's faith is frequently more important as a question for social placement than "race."

or ideology disjoins the main elements of the exchange (giving, receiving, repaying)—that is, when people do not expect musicians to give identically valued gifts back to those who have given gifts to them—the parties involved in the exchange are socially differentiated (stratified or ranked). Conversely, when giving, receiving, and repaying occur in an unbroken stream— when guests and hosts exchange demonstrations of generosity to musicians—reciprocal exchange between social equals results. Last, if the structures outlined by exchange have predictive value, they should survive when social structure is reordered or reaffirmed at events Rosman and Rubel call critical junctures: births, marriages, funerals (1971:179).

The type of stratified society that informs Hausa life resembles the *griot* model, which describes a structural relationship between musicians (who are nearly outside the social boundaries) and their patrons; this pattern occurs among the Wolof, among others (Merriam 1964:138–139). Alan Lomax's cantometric studies described *griot* societies as societies with "Oriental bards," part of a complex that also includes elaborate solo singing "within a system of rigid social stratification and . . . deferential etiquette" (1968:152). In the Muslim Hausa context, the *griot* model is painted with various ideological tints— generosity in giving, the persistence of the *bòorii* cult, and the cultural requirement that musicians not participate in funerals.

Symbolism, interpretation, social reality

Clifford Geertz believes anthropological analysis is at once the most accessible and allusive form of knowledge. For him, analysis is the process of sorting out the "structures of signification," and then determining, by searching for their meaning, how these structures inform their social context. He believes, "with Max Weber, that man is an animal suspended in webs of significance he himself has spun . . . [and] that culture [is] those webs" (1973:5). Hausa musicians spin such webs, interpreting and reinterpreting the strands as they go.

The position I take here comes from a concern in symbolic anthropology: how people formulate their reality (Dolgin, Kemnitzer, and Schneider 1977:34). Symbolic reality derives from tacit knowledge, which each individual must reconstruct (Sperber 1975:x); but since it is cultural, it is public. When participants in a cultural event agree on the definition of the event and the meanings of its components, the appearance of new parts changes the reality. I describe Hausa court musicians as manipulating the symbolic components of an event, both to create and change reality for their economic benefit.

ETHNOGRAPHIC CONTEXT

The Hausa, a predominantly Muslim people, live in northern Nigeria and neighboring areas. Their language, Chadic in origin, is spoken widely—in markets from western to central Africa. Alongside the Fulani, with whom they associated themselves after the Fulani Jihad of the early 1800s, they used to live in walled city-states ruled by an emir, a royal court, and a bureaucracy of ranked, titled officials. In the ethnographic present, the city walls in such places as Kano are a curious reminder of a glorious past—which people partly relive every time the emir and his mounted horsemen, musketeers, musicians, retainers, and vassal chiefs and headmen ride in parade, and when, in front of the palace, the emir accepts the charge of his horsemen and other loyal followers. Now, the emir and his royal kin hold mandated positions on a local government council, part of a federalized state government system enforced by the national army. Many minor functionaries have lost positions that depended on the largesse of a potentate authorized to collect taxes and administer a sizable budget; but such people as court musicians (instrumentalists, vocalists, panegyrists, praise shouters), whose activities were never a formal part of that budget, have managed to continue, dependent on institutionalized generosity and networks of obligations.

The Hausa social system is highly stratified, and the most important criterion for placing people in it is occupation. The hierarchical ranking of traditional political offices is part of this system, in which the emir holds the highest political and social position. No single hierarchy covers all the traditional occupations, and other considerations (ethnic membership, kinship, lineage, sex) often alter cases. All authorities agree that *maròokaa*—musicians and praise singers or praise shouters—stand at the same level as *griots* and Oriental bards in their societies, in the broadly lowest rank. Royal musicians, perhaps because of their association with the highest strata in the traditional social system, rank near the top of the *maròokii* class; and cult musicians, because of their association with widely recognized social deviants—gamblers, trancers, card players, drinkers, courtesans, transvestites—rank at the bottom. Islam is another factor in this ranking. Royal musicians are outwardly devout Muslims in a society in which a person's faith is frequently more important as a question for social placement than "race"; and while *bòorii*-cult musicians describe themselves as Muslims, their association with deviants and the *bòorii* pantheon makes their respectability difficult to defend. Other groups of professional musicians are not usually identified as non-Muslims, but their status is still in the lowest strata of Hausa society (Ames 1973; Smith 1959).

The Hausa do not have a single word for the Western concept of "music," nor do they use a single word for "musician." They speak of activities—drumming (*kiɗaa*), singing (*waaƙàa*), and blowing (*buusàa*)—and add to the list such "nonmusical" activities as begging (*ròoƙoo*), praise shouting, and celebratory ululating (Ames and King 1971). People commonly call the men who practice these crafts those who beg, thus placing emphasis on the social status of the craft, rather than its aural aspect. Terms are sex-specific, so a woman who "begs" is called *marooƙìyaa* or *zaabìyaa*.

Certain royal courtiers who practice this craft are classified as *maròokaa*, while others are described as "slaves" (*baayii*; masc. sing. *baawàa*). Royal beggar-minstrels have a status much lower than that of royal slaves, whose positions at court are hereditary, subject to the emir's confirmation; historically, they were one of the ways emirs protected from the treachery of their patrilineal relatives the integrity of their kingdoms, and their personal safety. As royal retainers, slaves do not usually depend on the payments of wealthy patrons (as musicians, even royal ones, do): they get regular allowances, and permanent access to farmland; some even go to the palace in chauffeur-driven automobiles.

THE SOCIAL ORGANIZATION OF MUSICIANS' GROUPS

Maròokaa, praise singers, and praise shouters—all of them professional musicians—divide into the following categories (Ames 1973): (a) the musicians of such craft groups as blacksmiths, hunters, farmers, and other musicians; (b) musicians in political life, who consist mainly of royal musicians and famous (recording-star) musicians

iskoki	Term for spirits	*buutàa*	Gourd rattle
bàndiirii	Set of two or more drums; a single membrane, circular frame drum, and a bowl-shaped drum	*gàraayàa*	Two-stringed, plucked lute

(Besmer 1970); (c) musicians of recreational music, who play for many different craft groups and social classes, in contexts not restricted by ceremony or religious ritual; (d) musician-entertainers and musician-comedians (Gidley 1967); and (e) musicians for the *bòorii* cult. Some praise shouters and panegyrists are not musicians in the English sense, but some royal slaves who play ceremonial drums are.

Royal musicians include those whose patrons are either the emir or other titular officials in traditional local government, especially district heads, department heads, and members of the aristocracy. Such musicians usually live in the same towns as their patrons, and people expect those who live in cities to perform at least once a week in the emir's court. The occasion for these performances is the regular Friday morning "greeting," when the emir receives visitors, holds court, and settles disputes people have brought to him. Other occasions when court musicians ordinarily perform are special events at court, signaled by word of mouth (or by two or three blasts from royal muskets), and religious festivals everyone understands.

Most of the instruments royal musicians use are highly restricted and context sensitive; people consider them symbols of status, and associate each instrument with a specific list of aristocratic titleholders. Culturally defined sensitivity is one of the symbolic factors royal musicians use in spinning their "webs of significance."

The emir's court, though stripped of powers it once enjoyed, has preserved in its system of ranked-title offices the outward structure of its former activities. Separate groups of court musicians, defined by the kinds of instruments they play, or by the specific "work" they do, model themselves on the pattern of the emir's court; and musicians whose activities are not directly connected with royal courts use the same pattern. With all musicians organized in such a system of ranked titles, the emir, during a turbaning ceremony in the court, customarily bestows a title on the leader of each group of musicians, who then turbans with subordinate titles selected members of his ensemble.

Bòorii-cult musicians do not regularly use courtly titles in Kano, possibly because such musicians' association with non-Muslim objects and practices makes it practically impossible for them to obtain titles with the emir's blessing. They insist that if they did not propitiate the spirits (*iskoki*) that live in and around the palace, the spirits would block access to the palace grounds, and no one could live there. They tell a story of a palace guard who refused to allow *bòorii* people to hold a series of performances that normally take place on the evenings of the two main Muslim festivals. Unsuccessful in their tries to persuade him of the need for holding the performances, they withdrew, knowing the spirits lurking in the palace would visit evil upon him. Later that night, people reported he had been seized by the neck, lifted into the air, and thrown to the ground, dead. The next night, his replacement, not being so foolish, allowed the children of the *bòorii* to enter the gate. *Bòorii* people believed the guilty ones were not mortals, but spirits (Besmer 1983:134).

Bòorii musicians, the most lowly ones in the *maròokii* class, are described as *maròokaa*, and not as "children of the spirits." Some have found their way into *bòorii* music by catching an illness diagnosed as the result of the malevolent actions of a spirit; and in this sense, they might be identified as former cult adepts. As musicians, however, those who have been "horses of the gods" are not recorded as falling into trance or participating in events in such ways that people might identify them as cult adepts. Cults enlist most other musicians through the usual process: the recruits are the sons of men who are *bòorii* musicians; and following this craft is more noble than freely choosing another (Smith 1959).

Bòorii musicians have little social prestige on which to draw, though some are accomplished musicians, recognized for their skill in singing songs to evoke spirits from their invisible city of Jangare ("somewhere to the east"), to control spirits' "horses" (mediums) during possession trance ceremonies, and to give exciting performances. The evaluation of their status may lie in the official position that music has no part in Islamic ritual (Ames 1973:140), even if the playing of the *bàndiirii* (a set of two or more drums: a single-membrane, circular frame drum, with or without circular metal jingles; and a single-membrane, bowl-shaped drum) is permitted in certain contexts. This evaluation may also lie partly in the bad company Muslim Hausa see *bòorii* musicians keeping.

All of this results in a paradox between who is most fluent in the grammar of *bòorii* performances (Besmer 1975), initiations, ceremonies, and esoterica, and who are *bòorii* people. *Maròokaa* (whose ascribed status is outside cult membership as such) control much of the cult's public possession trance activities, and are the repositories of its songs, cures, legends, and procedures; but they rarely undergo initiation as members of the cult, and carefully distance themselves from it.

POSSESSION TRANCE PERFORMANCE

Iliyasu Mai Buta (Iliyasu, Player of the *Buutàa* [gourd rattle])—a man who, besides speaking carefully and thoroughly, often brought up facts he thought I ought to know about the children of the *bòorii*—suggested we attend the upcoming *bòorii* ceremony at which Malam Shu'aibu Mai Garaya (Malam Shu'aibu, Player of the *gàraayàa,* a two-stringed, plucked lute) would be playing. My respondent was a member of Malam Shu'aibu's group, but his experience differed from that of other *bòorii* musicians: before becoming one of Malam Shu'aibu's apprentices and a *buutàa*-player, he had undergone initiation as a trancer. Malam Shu'aibu, then in his seventies, was widely recognized as the most proficient *bori garaya* musician in the emirate. He would have made sure that the best trancers accepted the kola nuts and hard candies that would compel them to be present, and everyone was looking forward to Thursday night. It would be exciting to see people dance during public *bòorii* performances, but nothing would be more exciting than being there when *bòorii* spirits attended, riding their favorite "horses."

Having seen many *bòorii* ceremonies before, and feeling confident I had learned most of the grammar of performances, I viewed this as a good opportunity to test the rules of process I thought participants used to organize them. What still mystified me was the patterns gift giving followed. It was not difficult to see that all the gifts went to the musicians, and that the musicians' shoes (which they removed as they sat down) served as collection baskets. What was yet unclear was whether there was any consistency, any pattern to the identities of the people giving and receiving gifts. From Iliyasu's point of view, the significance of the gifts was in their amount, and the amounts were seldom large enough for him to consider them generous.

Public *bòorii* performances occur at weddings and child namings, or for no apparent reason. They occur in nonsecluded portions of people's houses, or just outside their entryways.

A naming ceremony provides an occasion when the elements of social structure are reaffirmed. It bonds adjacent generations within a child's father's kin group; by the selection of proper names, it separates them.

To understand what gift giving had to do with social structure, I had to learn who gave gifts, why they gave, and to whom they gave. While the gods were riding their horses (that is, during active trancing), it was not always easy to remember to write down all the necessary facts about money gifts; but there eventually began to emerge patterns I recognized in Hausa social structure. Among giving, receiving, and repaying, the relationships are dual (Mauss 1925 [1967]). *Bòorii* musicians always received the gifts; and in exchange, they provided the service of witnessing the giver's generosity. Smith had seen that praise singing, by allowing givers to declare their loyalty to a system of social values, functioned to validate the social structure (1957:42). What I saw was sufficiently similar; there seemed little more to add. The trouble was, I had no way of knowing who was going to give musicians gifts, or what the actual amounts would mean.

Thursday evening came, and the *bòorii* ceremony got underway. I had managed to record everything I thought essential in the preparations. I felt confident I knew the reason for the event (the bringing of the bride to the groom's house), the identities of guests and hosts (they sat at opposite sides of the open area selected for the performance), and the way the trancers and musicians had been invited to participate (they had accepted a graduated series of gifts: kola nuts, hard candies, money). As the music began, I was annoyed at how frequently people interrupted the flow of the music and dancing. Every few minutes, one of the *maròokaa* walking about the area would accept someone's request to "make an announcement": he would stand next to the person with the message and shout for everyone's attention, elaborating on the message giver's identity ("father of so-and-so, giver of this or that, child or grandchild of so-and-so famous for this or that"). The announcement—a gift of money from the *maròokii*'s momentary patron to the performers—would follow, portrayed in the most elaborate of terms. The money would be brought forward and placed in a shoe in front of a musician. Not long after that, another message giver would repeat the process. I carefully wrote down who the giver had been, how much he had given, and whose shoe had received the money.

My first conclusions were that individual givers made a claim to the evaluation of their character as generous, and musicians reciprocated the gifts with their service, witnessing. The records of whose shoe received which monies was to be helpful in determining how the money would be distributed after the performance, and the distribution was to be a clue to the social structure of Malam Shu'aibu's ensemble. There seemed to be no special connection between anyone except givers and receivers, and this was a classically dual relationship. When I asked Iliyasu who, exactly, the givers were (whether hosts from the groom's family, or guests from the bride's family), I realized I had nearly missed the pattern in the identities of the givers.

Mauss writes about the way people feel the need to "make a return gift for a gift received" (1925 [1967]:5), but I never observed musicians being bothered by this feeling. Even Smith says the gifts were received "*on behalf of the society*" (1957:42, italics original), implying it would be impossible for musicians to reciprocate. However, the gifts I had seen presented to musicians made apparently disconnected people—nonreceivers—nervous, and a general outline of competitive generosity began to emerge. Iliyasu's explanations of which side givers represented (bride's or groom's) confirmed that gifts given by guests were matched and sometimes exceeded by gifts given by hosts: when a person rose to make a gift to the musicians, it was not musicians, but other potential presenters, who felt the need to reciprocate.

The rules of marriage for the Hausa do not follow "elementary structures of exchange," which include certain preferential unions between specified kin or cross-cousin marriage (compare Lévi-Strauss 1949 [1969]). Marriages do tend toward class endogamy, but even this tendency is modified by such factors as the traditional marriage alliances between widely different occupational groups, Qur'ānic scholars, and blacksmiths, for example (Smith 1959:249). When a marriage is "class endogamous," we might expect the two groups of in-laws to try to exchange items reciprocally, to preserve their social equality. The hosts and guests at this *bòorii* ceremony were from the same social rank. Iliyasu described the men in both families as traders, and that was why the ceremony took place at the groom's storefront in the Kano City market.

The meaning of the way people exchanged gifts at the ceremony thus became clear: two patterns were simultaneously present. One of them involved the outlines of a stratified social system, containing people of unequal status, who gave, received, and reciprocated different items. Money and other material gifts passed down the structure to musicians, who acted as professional receivers in exchange for a service, the witnessing of generosity. The other pattern followed the outlines of direct reciprocity—exchange between people of equal status, people whose acts of giving had to be reciprocated by equal acts of giving, but whom cultural rules prevented from exchanging directly with each other. This provided the meaning for hosts' discomfort when guests presented musicians with gifts, and vice versa. Taken together, the two patterns revealed people of approximately equal status competitively exchanging with each other by giving gifts to a separate, subordinate group.

This pattern occurs in *griot*-model societies, and further examples of it occur among the *griots* of the Wolof (Lomax 1968). People usually describe *griots'* activities as important; nevertheless, they ascribe to the *griots* themselves—including Hausa musicians—an extremely low status. Anthropologists usually think this anomalous, a paradox. The status of musicians is an example of one essential component in the *griot* model. The other two elements are a highly stratified social fabric, and situations during which members of socially disparate strata interact.

A naming ceremony (masc. sing. *suunaa*) provides an occasion when the elements of social structure are reaffirmed. It bonds adjacent generations within a child's father's kin group; by the selection of proper names, it separates them. Names normally pass on patrilaterally (from the father's side, though occasionally including, for example, the father's mother's relatives), but people avoid those from adjacent generations. The musicians call people to prayer, invoke blessings on the mother and child, and announce the child's name (Ames and King 1971:125); however, praise singers must wait to announce the child's name until a Qur'ānic scholar-teacher, a *maalàmii*, whispers it in the child's ear.

Both the musicians and the scholars are the principal recipients of gifts, given primarily by the child's father's relatives; but the child's mother's relatives may also give gifts. The musicians have the low status necessary to allow them to receive gifts; the Islamic practice of almsgiving permits the scholars to receive gifts. What the musicians and scholars share is social distance from the gift givers.

A final confirmation of the *griot* model of exchange structure exists at Hausa funerals. Muslims follow strict rules about how and when they must dispose of a

griot **model**   Socially despised professional musicians work within a highly stratified social fabric

kàakàakii   Long metal trumpet made from thin brass or metal from a kerosene tin

kòotsoo   Single-membrane, snared hourglass drum played with the hand

body; and for the Hausa, these rules include the nonparticipation of musicians, who may attend as friends or relatives of the deceased, but not as musicians. Both sides of the dead person's family—relatives by descent, and by marriage—attend the funeral. Musicians do not act as mediators between these affines, as the *griot* model might predict; but another group, that of the *malams*, does. The recipients of the alms (gifts) given to honor the deceased, *malams* occupy social positions that provide them with the social distance required for them to accept gifts. Their importance at funerals (in musicians' absence) shows that the structure of exchange outlined by the *griot* model persists, even when the identity of the gift receivers varies.

COURT MUSICIANS' PERFORMANCE

Royal musicians divide into groups on the basis of the instruments they play, or the kinds of "music" (including praise singing and shouting, panegyrizing, eulogizing) they perform. In recognition of their position, the emir gives the heads of groups of royal *maròokii* a title and a turban. Their instruments, the songs they perform, and the praises they shout, are all governed by a body of strict rules, which emphasize that their use belongs, not to individual musicians or titleholders, but to the offices they hold. The *kàakàakii* (long metal trumpet, made from the metal of a kerosene tin, or thin brass) may be played only for a first-class or paramount chief (for example, the emir), but the *kòotsoo* (single-membrane, snared, hourglass drum, played with the hand) may in addition be played for senior titleholders.

In Kano, people expect royal musicians to perform at the palace every Friday morning the emir is in town, and irregularly there when summoned for such events as turbanings and special visits. Musicians must also perform during the series of events associated with the two main Muslim festivals, including the "greetings" in the palace after dark, during the last ten days of Ramadan, the special celebration on *Daran Sallàa* (Sallah eve) (Besmer 1974), and the many Sallah parades.

Inside the most restricted parts of the palace, court musicians could go almost anywhere they pleased. As men, they could not enter the secluded areas restricted to women; but they could pass guard posts merely by showing themselves as musicians, or by flashing an instrument like a badge. I tagged along (with my camera, notebook, and tape recorder), explaining to the sentries, "I'm with *them*." Events in and about the palace happened only when the musicians were present: when the emir left on horseback, musicians led the processions; during the last ten evenings of Ramadan, they greeted the royal visitors to the palace; and they were frequent witnesses of the generosity and good character of all kinds of important people.

Sarkin Kid'àn Kòotsoo (Chief of the Kòotsoo Drummers) Musa Daɓalo was an old man who had contracted leprosy while serving in a Nigerian regiment of the British Army in World War II. Despite having deformed fingers and general poor health, he maintained high spirits and energy. Of the emir's musicians, he was one of the most charismatic and opinionated, though not the highest ranked (*Sarkim*

Buusàn ƙàhoo, the emir's Roan Antelope Horn Player, was); nor was he the most creative. In courtiers' opinions, Daɓalo stood near the center of social and cultural significance: wherever he was, and whatever he was doing were nearly always important.

However, unlike the players of the *kàakàakii*, classified as royal slaves, who could not play their instruments without an emir's authorization, or outside the context of a palace ceremony, *kòotsoo* players were royal beggar-minstrels, much less restricted in the audiences for whom they might play. These two dimensions became the key to understanding how *kòotsoo* and *kàakàakii* performances differed. The playing of the *kàakàakii* is part of the definition of royal ritual and ceremony, so the social reality in which it participates is fixed: it is describable and comprehensible only within the context of the palace. *Kòotsoo* performances are not prescribed like that, so Daɓalo and his group could combine their positions as royal musicians with their status as beggar-minstrels, sometimes to perform well outside the palace context.

To understand how Daɓalo and his *kòotsoo* players worked, we must determine the context in which the drum serves as a symbol. Daɓalo and other Kano musicians, while insistent that the emir is their primary patron (in contrast to the kind of support given by the emir to royal slaves, musicians depend on patron-client relationships), say the *kòotsoo* may also be played for the emir's district heads. This affinity with the prestige of the emir's title is important for *kòotsoo* players, because they use this aspect of the drum's attributes to create special obligations in those for whom they play. Daɓalo's audiences, however, contain a list that extends far beyond the roster of the emir's district heads, and includes senior police officials, wealthy traders, and other prominent people. He justifies his choice of audiences on the basis of a prospective patron's aristocratic kinship connection, and this can often be confirmed; but it is less important than the symbolic reasons for the rationale: people expect aristocrats to treat the emir's musicians specially. Daɓalo's technique is effective. He understands his performance must define a prospective patron as an aristocrat, so he can expect that person to be generous toward a kinsman's client.

In Kano, there are two *kòotsoo* groups: one (Daɓalo's group) has the officially titled position in the emir's court; the other has the more popular leader. *Kòotsoo* players are particularly active on Fridays, and on the last ten nights of Ramadan, going out to greet patrons after they have performed in the palace. It was obvious how *Gàlàadiimàn Kòotsoo* (the Galadima of the Kòotsoo) Abdurrahman could get paid for his performances; people recognized him widely as an excellent singer, inventive and original in his songs. What was not so clear was how Sarkin Kiɗàn Kòotsoo Musa Daɓalo could support himself in his craft, since people did not acknowledge him as a singer, and avoided him somewhat as a former leper. I guessed Daɓalo's technique to depend on cultural factors I did not understand, and so I accepted his invitation to "go walking" after each of the sessions in the palace.

The event, called wake-up walk, occurs during the last ten nights of Ramadan, when *kòotsoo* players join other musicians in waking people up to prepare food and eat before dawn. A common response from the citizenry thus provided with this service is to feign absence. This defense is rarely successful, because important people who are away from their houses leave watchmen, quick to explain to the musicians that no one is home. When no watchman appears, musicians know that the rules of social decorum and the observations of neighbors will require a patron to be "at home" and generous. Not to give an appropriate gift could result in an accusation of stinginess and prompt questions from the palace about relatives' obligations. Daɓalo's strategy was to use symbols to define the situation to his advantage.

As we approached the house along a darkened road in Yakasai Quarter, it was not hard to identify the compound of an important man. The master of the house

Deep within the emir's palace, in a dimly lit, open courtyard, I am sitting with Sarkin Kiɗàn Kòotsoo and other royal musicians; they complain about the chill of the night.

was a wealthy merchant; and while he may have had some aristocratic connection, he was not a titled official within the court. His house had a two-story entry building, a sheet-metal roof, washed-cement construction, and a garage; no lights were visible from the street. The foyer contained a night watchman, and some Qur'ānic students, who depended on the master of the house for both food and shelter. Daɓalo and his *maròokaa* had been walking silently, drums slung under left arms. We stood in front of the door, and the performance began with the only song used for such occasions, "*Launìi* 'Color'." The refrain began with Daɓalo and his chorus of two *kòotsoo* players and one praise shouter, who many times sang the song's refrain: *Allà Mài Gyarà tàbarà Sarkii, Allà tàbarà nà na ròokee ka, kà gyarà manà* 'Allah Repairer of All, Master of Emirs; as Allah is my master, I beg you to reward us'. After this introduction, Daɓalo sang improvised verses containing genealogical information about the master of the house, plus flowery descriptions of past accomplishments and "good deeds," each of which the refrain punctuated. While the chorus was singing the refrain, the praise shouter repeated the main content of each of Daɓalo verses. Occasionally, passersby or the people in the foyer would give him additional textual material, which he would pass on to Daɓalo, who would put them into the next verse. The musicians jokingly refer to this process as *zugàa* 'pumping up a fire with bellows'.

The prime symbols in this process are the *kòotsoo* and Daɓalo's status as Sarkin Kiɗàn Kòotsoo. These provide the connection between the royal court and the role of a beggar-minstrel. The appearance of the drum during the wake-up walk defines its audience as aristocratic (even when, as in this case, it is not), and its player as a royal client, someone to whom one must give gifts in the name of an aristocratic kinsman, the emir. Daɓalo can take advantage of the license he has to define the performance broadly as a part of the ceremony at court.

After a few minutes, we heard someone inside the foyer speaking quietly to the night watchman. Daɓalo kept playing; and as, from the house, people brought gifts of money and clothing, he included in the song an elaborate description of them.

Here I must record two additional observations. Kano citizens who do not have a connection with traditional government, or with the value system on which the legitimacy of the emir stands, are poor candidates for the drummers' attention. They do not accept the definitions of the basic symbols in the process, and so are immune to the drummers' efforts to manipulate them. Second, drummers must use skill in tapping the (somewhat artificial) obligations of those for whom the symbols are meaningful. The Beggar Control Act of 1960 legislatively tried to control musicians' activities: it requires musicians to avoid abusive language in their songs. Etiquette dictates that musicians not appear excessively greedy. When they ask for gifts, it also dictates that patrons not complain.

What such royal musicians as Sarkin Kiɗàn Kòotsoo do is transform or recreate events by manipulating symbols for audiences selected because they accept and

understand them. They do not simply emulate other strolling musicians, taking what they can get. That they use symbols to create a situation in which gift giving is the only proper behavior for a prospective patron is best seen when they are the prospective patrons and must give gifts. This confirmation of the essential elements of cultural process came on an evening when, at a palace session during the end of Ramadan, a minstrel-comedian attended with the other royal musicians.

Maalàm Àshaanaa ("Mister Match") is a musician, but he is narrowly known as a *d'an Kaamàa* 'Son of Catching'. He claims a title given by the emir, but few other musicians confirm the claim. In performance, he is typically as unpredictable as he is entertaining, but his songs usually fall into various types. When the occasion demands, he can be serious; but his specialty is humor, which he achieves through either original songs on popular topics, or the satirical treatment of other musicians' performances. The way he defines and redefines situations and events is an outstanding aspect of his performances.

Deep within the emir's palace, in a dimly lit, open courtyard, I am sitting with Sarkin Kid'an Kòotsoo and other royal musicians. These men are subordinate to the emir and his councilors. They anticipate receiving the gifts to which their social position entitles them. Nearing the end of Ramadan, bored with the length of the councilors' visit with the emir, they complain about the chill of the night. Malam Ashana enters the courtyard with his group. Their music is curiously out of place; their instruments are caricatures of musical instruments. After a short praise song for the emir, he launches into a song on the civil war, which describes it as following the course of a meal the Federalists eat (win). After he has satirized Sarkin Kid'an Kòotsoo's singing style and those of many of the musicians present, he ends his performance with an intoned prayer (Besmer 1972:247–248). Some Arabic prayer words have a form similar to his first phrase: between the terms *wa* and *kum*, he inserts the names of foodstuffs; his chorus translates.

Wà-gùraasà-kum! — And-wheaten food-you!
    CHORUS: Dà "gùraasà." — CHORUS: That means "wheatcakes."
Wà-nàañiiyà-kum! — And-flour confection-you!
    CHORUS: Dà nàañiiyà. . . . — CHORUS: That means it is sweet . . .
Jàma'à, za nì àddu'à ko mu taashì. — Citizens, let's have a prayer before we leave.
    CHORUS: Gaafàrtà, maalàm! — CHORUS: Attention, please!
Ya àllaahù gwaazaa àllaahù ruusgà faaràa, — Allah-koko yam-Allah crunched [a kola] first,
Wà dakà namù, ùban gijìn gàyyaa. — And pounded our corn, the Lord of all people.

    EVERYONE: Àmin! . . . — EVERYONE: Amen! . . .
Yinì dà yunwà, dai Allà sauwaakii manà. — Daylight and hunger, may Allah preserve us from them.
    EVERYONE: Àmin! — EVERYONE: Amen!
Ìdan mu kà jee neemaa wandà ba yà dà shi, — If we search for something somebody does not have,
Ya kàr'baa à gurin d'anuuwan sà ya ba mù. — He receives it from his relatives and gives it to us.
Im mu tàfi warwàree jàma'à na ànnabì — If we go away untangled [from him], people of the Prophet.
Koowaa ya cêe "àmin" — Everyone say "amen."
    EVERYONE: Àmin! — EVERYONE: Amen!

Tôo!—bâa sadakà, jàma'à? — What!—no gifts, citizens?
sai àmin, àmin, àmin? — just amen, amen, amen?

> Like other *griots*, Hausa musicians perform to earn a living; they do everything they can to increase their rewards.

At this point, some of the court musicians uneagerly reached into their pockets to give Malam Ashana a shilling or two. Sarkin Kiɗàn Kòotsoo was one of those who gave, and the smile on his face suggested he was aware of what Malam Ashana had done.

We had all witnessed Malam Ashana sing to singers and beg from beggars. He had used their shared craft to (re)define his audience: he had transformed court musicians from a group of performers into an audience. His status as a minstrel-comedian and his satirical song texts were symbols necessary to draw into unexpected roles and behavior the people in the courtyard. The royal musicians had been singing their songs to the invisible aristocratic audience inside the palace, and Malam Ashana's performance started exactly that way. By the time his "prayer" was over, however, he had transformed and redefined the event into an entertainment for royal musicians. Gift giving by the audience of royal musicians was the only correct response, and some of them recognized their obligation.

CULTURAL PROCESS AND MEANING

Earlier studies have concentrated on musical data or the analysis of song texts, but this study selects two types of Hausa musical performance out of a long list of performances by both professional and nonprofessional musicians to illustrate the search for process and meaning. Performances contain pieces of this meaning, but they do not summarize or somehow typify it: "The culture of a people is an ensemble of texts, themselves ensembles, which the anthropologist strains to read over the shoulders of those to whom they properly belong" (Geertz 1973:452). Hausa performances are examples of such texts.

The ensemble that contains *bòorii* performances also contains Islam, a highly stratified social structure with musicians in a bottommost layer, cultural explanations for illness and misfortune, and entertainment. Illnesses caused by spirits are also subject to their cure, and this recalls Turner's cult of affliction among the Ndembu of Zambia (1968). Groups of people formerly afflicted by spirits but now able to domesticate them treat people currently afflicted. The most commonly identified aspect of *bòorii* is its value as entertainment.

Court musicians' performances are also a text, much of it about traditional life in an elegant and glorious past. Royal musicians witness the institutions and aristocrats they serve, but they have their own interests. They appear in the ethnographic literature on the Hausa as greedy but clever, irritating but necessary. The wake-up walk is only one of many performances that feature royal musicians, but all performances contain a special meaning—the system of values underlying Hausa society.

Broadly interpreting the rules for performance, royal *kòotsoo* players use their instruments to define their prospective patrons as recipients of their music. Using recognized symbols of the royal court to create a situation in which people must take specific roles involves the same process other players (such as Hausa comedians) use to place the mantle of expected generosity on royal musicians. Everyone understands the required behavior, which does not extend to royal slaves. *Griots* use many techniques to inspire potential donors to give; but with people outside the social system (strangers or Europeans, people who use different texts), these techniques are unreliable.

Like other *griots*, Hausa musicians perform to earn a living; they do everything they can to increase their rewards. They sense the potential in situations where people motivated by prestige must give gifts and have their generosity witnessed. They also understand that where the degree of generosity is a measure of social standing, musicians can reap rewards. These actions may mean nothing more than the ways musicians earn their living and thank those who are instrumental in giving them gifts; or they may be the thread that keeps a highly differentiated social fabric together.

REFERENCES

Ames, David W. 1973. "A Sociocultural View of Hausa Musical Activity." In *The Traditional Artist in African Societies*, ed. Warren d'Azevedo, 128–161. Bloomington: Indiana University Press.

Ames, David, and Anthony V. King. 1971. *Glossary of Hausa Music in Its Social Contexts.* Evanston, Illinois: Northwestern University Press.

Besmer, Fremont E. 1970. "An Hausa Song from Katsina." *Ethnomusicology* 14:418–438.

———. 1972. *Hausa Court Music in Kano, Nigeria.* Ann Arbor, Mich.: University Microfilms.

———. 1974. *Kídàn Dárán Sállà: Music for the Muslim Festivals of Id al-Fitr and Id al-Kabir in Kano, Nigeria.* Bloomington: African Studies Program, Indiana University Monographs.

———. 1975. "Bòorii: Structure and Process in Performance." *Folia Orientalia* 16:101-30.

———. 1983. *Horses, Musicians, and Gods: The Hausa Cult of Possession-Trance.* South Hadley, Mass.: Bergin and Garvey.

Dolgin, Janet L., David S. Kemnitzer, and David M. Schneider, eds. 1977. *Symbolic Anthropology: A Reader in the Study of Symbols and Meanings.* New York: Columbia University Press.

Geertz, Clifford. 1972 [1973]. *The Interpretation of Cultures.* New York: Basic Books.

Gidley, C. G. B. 1967. "'Yankamanci—The Craft of the Hausa Comedians." *African Language Studies* 8:52–81.

Greenberg, Joseph H. 1946. *The Influence of Islam on a Sudanese Religion.* New York: J. J. Augustin.

King, Anthony V. 1966. "A Bòorii Liturgy from Katsina: Introduction and Kírárìi Texts." *African Language Studies* 7:105–125.

———. 1967. "A Bòorii Liturgy from Katsina." *African Language Studies,* supplement 7.

Lévi-Strauss, Claude. 1949 [1969]. *The Elementary Structures of Kinship,* ed. J. H. Bell, J. R. von Sturmer, and R. Needham. Boston: Beacon Press.

Lomax, Alan. 1968. *Folk Song Style and Culture.* Washington, D.C.: American Association for the Advancement of Science, publication 68.

Mauss, Marcel. 1925 [1967]. *The Gift: Forms and Functions of Exchange in Archaic Societies,* trans. Ian Cunnison. New York: W. W. Norton.

Mead, Margaret. 1978. *Culture and Commitment: The New Relationships between Generations in the 1970s,* rev. ed. Garden City, N.Y.: Anchor / Doubleday.

Merriam, Alan P. 1964. *The Anthropology of Music.* Evanston, Ill.: Northwestern University Press.

———. 1972. *The Arts and Humanities in African Studies.* Bloomington: African Studies Program, Indiana University.

Rosman, Abraham, and Paula Rubel. 1971. *Feasting with Mine Enemy: Rank and Exchange among Northwest Coast Societies.* New York: Columbia University Press.

Smith, M. G. 1957. "The Social Functions and Meaning of Hausa Praise Singing." *Africa* 27:26–45.

———. 1959. "The Hausa System of Social Status." *Africa* 29:239–252.

Sperber, Dan. 1975. *Rethinking Symbolism,* trans. Alice L. Morton. Cambridge: Cambridge University Press.

Turner, Victor. 1968. *The Drums of Affliction: A Study of Religious Processes among the Ndembu of Zambia.* Oxford: International African Institute.

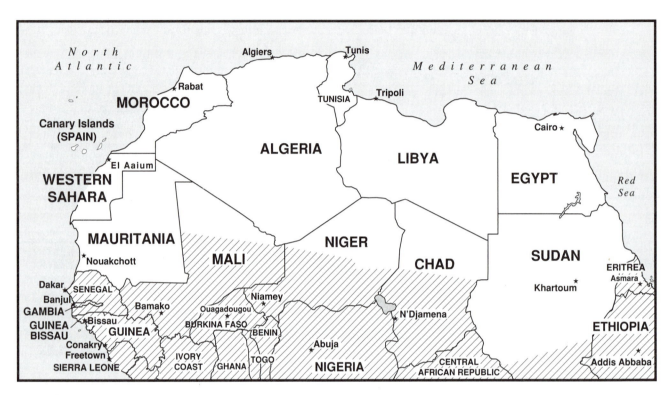

North Africa

North Africa

The music of North Africa—played by Arabs, Berbers, and black Africans—combines elements from the Middle East with those from sub-Saharan cultures. Blends of northern and southern musical practice are common throughout this region.

North Africa: An Introduction
Caroline Card Wendt

The People
Culture History
The Arab-Andalusian Tradition
Music and Islam
Music in Folk Life
Popular Music

As a culture area, North Africa extends eastward from the Atlantic coast to encompass the Mediterranean nations of Morocco, Algeria, Tunisia, and Libya, known as the Maghrib, to the western desert of Egypt. The area reaches southward into the Sahara to include Mauritania and northern sections of Mali and Niger. The Atlas Mountains, which extend from Morocco to Tunisia, divide a narrow stretch of fertile and densely populated agricultural land along the Mediterranean coast from the sparsely populated, arid expanses of the Sahara. Major elements unifying the peoples of this area are the religion of Islam and the Arabic language—the official language of each country except Mali and Niger. All the countries were formerly subject to one or another of the European powers, which in varying degrees influenced their present economies, educational systems, and development. Because the political boundaries are often inconsistent with ethnic distributions, some groups (such as the Tuareg) divide into several different nationalities.

THE PEOPLE

The population consists principally of Caucasoid Arabs and Berbers, and of negroid Africans known in the Maghrib as Gnawa. The Arabs are descendants both of early Muslim invaders from the Arabian Peninsula and of native Berber inhabitants long assimilated into their society and culture. The Berbers, whose ancestors may be the earliest inhabitants of Mediterranean North Africa (Murdock 1959), comprise numerous groups who speak related dialects of a Hamito-Semitic language (Greenberg 1966) and exhibit similar traits. The largest Berber populations are located in Morocco and Algeria. The black Africans are descendents of indigenous Saharans and immigrants from the broad intermediate zone at the southern edge of the Sahara known as the sahel or Sudan. Though black Africans are a minority in the Maghrib, they form a noticeable portion of the population of Mauritania and the Saharan regions of the other countries. The musical traditions of the Arabs, Berbers, and negroid Africans, though not untouched by acculturation, stem from different cultural heritages, which merit separate consideration. Of relevance, also, are patterns of nomadic, village, and urban ways of living that often cut across ethnic and regional categories.

CULTURE HISTORY

The early Berber tribes dwelled on the coast until the arrival of Phoenician traders, about 1200 B.C. Together, the Phoenicians and Berbers built Carthage and a civilization that spread across western North Africa and the Mediterranean, from Sicily to Spain. In 202 B.C., the Romans took Carthage. By A.D. 40, they controlled an area from the Atlantic coast to present-day eastern Libya. About six hundred years of Roman rule ended with the invasion of Vandals from Scandinavia, soon followed by Christian Byzantines. In 688, at the time of the first Muslim Arab invasion, North Africa was widely, if superficially, Christian. Within a century, the Arabs were masters of all Mediterranean North Africa and Spain, and though their empire eventually receded, most of the lands and peoples they subjugated were irreversibly changed, in language, religion, and culture. Subsequent European conquests hardly affected Arabic cultural patterns.

The character that distinguishes North Africa from the Arabic-speaking Muslim Near East arises in large measure from its Berber subculture. While urban Berbers were receptive to the culture of their conquerors, rural and nomadic Berbers were much less so. Withdrawing into mountain villages or retreating deep into the desert, they remained resistant and even hostile to foreign intrusion. As a result, Berber language, culture, and tribal patterns have persisted in the Moroccan Atlas, in the Algerian high plateaus, in desert towns in Mauritania and Libya, and in oasis communities and nomadic encampments across the Sahara. In remote areas, Islam and the accompanying Arab traditions penetrated slowly, forming a veneer of Muslim culture over pre-Islamic customs and beliefs. In the Ahaggar region of the Algerian Sahara, long an impenetrable mountain stronghold of warrior Berber Tuareg tribes, Muslim religion and culture had little effect until the latter part of the 1800s.

Gradually, the Arab culture of the Maghrib filtered southward to permeate the Sahara with Islamic character. Over centuries the trans-Saharan trade routes, mainly under control of the Berber Tuareg, carried Mediterranean arts and technology southward. The northern Berbers introduced methods of irrigation, fertilization, and animal husbandry that enabled sahelian cultivators to grow crops farther north into the arid zone (Murdock 1959:125–126). In varying degrees, many Sahelian cultivators were incorporated into Tuareg society and culture, and elements of sub-Saharan music became part of Tuareg traditions.

Sahelian arts and music have also moved northward. In cultivation centers throughout the Sahara, rhythms, vocal styles, and dances of sub-Saharan origin predominate. In the Maghrib, black Muslim brotherhoods perform Sahelian-style music for exorcisms, rituals of curing, and Muslim celebrations and festivals. Blends of northern and southern musical practices are clear, also, in the Mauritanian bardic tradition, which, combining modal structures akin to Arab tradition with rhythmic patterns related to those of West Africa, forms styles the musicians term white and black ways (Guignard 1975a, 1975b; Balandier and Mercier 1952; Nikiprowetzky 1961, 1964; Duvelle 1966). Since the 1960s, recurring drought, increasing population, and political strife have prompted migrations in many directions: herders drive their animals farther in search of water and pasture, and pastoralists and cultivators abandon rural areas for employment in towns and cities. The musical result of these migrations is the rapid evolution of new genres from older and borrowed sources. For source material and inspiration, composers of urban music have turned increasingly to rural repertories and foreign music. Radio broadcasts and cassette recordings convey to the most remote areas a wide range of musical styles.

The musics of the region, therefore, do not form ready categories. As modern composers and arrangers adapt old traditions to new performance situations, the distinctions among classical, folk, and popular genres are often blurred. Due to the per-

nuba   A suite of songs, in five movements in
         Morocco, each in one of five rhythmic
         modes performed in fixed order
rabab Two-stringed fiddle in North Africa
'ud   Plucked lute with pear-shaped resonator

tar   Hand-held frame drum with attached
           cymbals
derbuka Single-headed, goblet-shaped drum
           of North Africa

vasiveness of the media, some repertories once specific to particular villages or regions are now more widespread. Conversely, urban styles and instrumentation, with their special appeal to youth, increasingly influence the performance of traditional musics in rural communities. The distinctions between religious and secular genres are equally unclear, for the texts of many songs sung for secular purposes have religious content or sentiment, and some religious music collectively performed exhibits folk genre traits. Furthermore, some genres performed exclusively by traditional specialists at folk-life celebrations straddle the categories of folk and professional, and of religious and secular. Musical styles, subject matter, and performance practices continually interplay with the social contexts and histories that underlie and inform the musical cultures.

THE ARAB-ANDALUSIAN TRADITION

In A.D. 711, Arabs crossed the Mediterranean to conquer Spain (el-Andalus), beginning a period of Muslim rule on the Iberian Peninsula that endured for nearly eight hundred years. Arab music flourished at Córdoba, Seville, Granada, and other Andalusian cities. Though modeled on the seventh- to ninth-century music of the court of the Umayyad dynasty in Damascus and that of the early Abbasid dynasty in Baghdad, it soon developed a distinctly Andalusian character. The reconquest of Spain by the Christians, beginning in the 900s, resulted in the retreat of the Muslims to North Africa in three large migrations: Seville to Tunis (Tunisia) in the tenth to twelfth centuries, Córdoba to Tlemcen (Algeria) and Valencia to Fez (Morocco) in the twelfth, and Granada to Fez and Tetuan (Morocco) in the fifteenth. Andalusian music, stemming from diverse locations and periods, further evolved into regional Moroccan, Algerian, and Tunisian schools, each differing slightly in terminology, modal practice, theory, and repertory. The environment proved less favorable than the Andalusian to the cultivation of the arts, and much of the old music was subsequently lost; less than half the original repertory is presently known. Nevertheless, musicians regard the music they perform as a continuation of the Andalusian tradition.

Since independence (in the 1960s), Algerians and Tunisians have made efforts to revive old music, and to move it from an esoteric sphere into that of public education. Their movement has succeeded in stimulating interest among the younger generation. In 1972, a professional four-year program in Arab-Andalusian music, employing traditional oral methods of instruction, was established at the School of Music at Fez (Loopuyt 1988). Other schools throughout the Arab world offer programs directed toward the preservation and continuing development of the tradition.

The original Andalusian repertory consisted of twenty-four *nubat* (sing. *nuba*), each based on one of twenty-four melodic modes. A *nuba* in Moroccan tradition is a suite of songs (*sana'i*; sing. *san'a*) in five movements (*miyazen*; sing. *mizan*), each in one of five rhythmic modes performed in a fixed order. Each vocal movement follows an instrumental prelude. An Algerian *nuba* consists of nine alternating instrumental and vocal movements; the Tunisian counterpart, ten (Pacholczyk 1980:265–266). The meters and sequences differ in each of the schools. Essentially monophonic, the music contains no harmony other than an occasional drone accompaniment.

Though the music stems from oral tradition, the poetic texts come from literate sources. The principal poetic forms are the *qasida*, the *muwashshah*, and the *zajal*. The *qasida* is a solo improvisation of earlier Near Eastern tradition. The *muwashshah*, a court poetry, and *zajal*, a popular form, developed in Spain concurrently with the Andalusian *nuba*. Strophic texts with instrumental refrains are characteristic of *muwashshah* and *zajal*. The subject matter is romantic in its praise of human love, beauty, nature, and earthly pleasures. The texts of some *nubat*, notably "*Ramal al-Maya*," praise Muhammad and divine love. As many as forty poems may occur within a single movement of a *nuba*, which can last for more than an hour. A complete *nuba* is rarely heard; more common are abbreviated versions, or selected movements from several *nubat*.

The modal structure, vocal style, and phrasing characteristic of the Arab-Andalusian *nuba* are attributed to the legendary ninth-century musician and theorist Ziryab. Educated in Baghdad, and trained in Persian and Arab traditions, Ziryab brought to el-Andalus not only expertise in performing and teaching, but also a musicotherapeutic system, known as the "tree of modes," or the "tree of temperaments." The system was based on concepts then prevalent in Arab medicine: relationships between parts of the body and elements of earth and Heaven believed to underlie human physical and psychological states and behaviors. Ziryab's system, which he presented as a revelation rather than a theory, associated specific modes (*tubu*ʿ; sing. *tab*ʿ), with body organs (heart, liver, brain, spleen) and human temperaments (anger, calm, joy, sadness). The musical modes were further linked with natural elements (air, fire, water, earth), colors (red, yellow, white, black), and conditions (heat, cold, humidity, dryness). Ziryab's system contained twenty-four modes, one for each hour of the day; particular modes were performed at set hours. From this elaborate scheme evolved the rules on which the twenty-four *nubat* were constructed and performed.

Ziryab and his followers' concern with the cosmic and ethical qualities of music outlasted that of their Near Eastern counterparts, who, influenced by Greek theorists, became more occupied with modal analysis, an area of less concern in Andalusia and North Africa. Also, cultivation of the musical arts in Andalusia depended more on urban support, as the less powerful Andalusian courts were unable to provide the degree of patronage afforded artists and performers in the East. The Arab-Andalusian tradition thus evolved in more popular directions, with greater emphasis on composed orchestral and choral forms, and less on the solo improvisation favored in the Eastern courts (Pacholczyk 1976:3). Later performance practices in North Africa reinforced the divergence of the idiom from its Eastern source.

Male professionals perform Arab-Andalusian music, mainly for state functions and private celebrations for those who can afford the orchestra. The size of the ensemble varies according to the occasion, the patron's wishes, and regional custom. Normally included are a two-stringed fiddle (*rabab*), several violins or violas (sing. *kamanja*) held vertically on the knee, one or two four-stringed plucked lutes (sing. ʿ*ud*), a hand-held frame drum with attached cymbals (*tar*), and a single-headed, goblet-shaped drum (*derbuka*). If the instrumentalists do not double as vocalists, the ensemble may also include one or two solo singers. The *rabab* is traditionally played by the leader, though its use has declined since the introduction of the violin (in the 1700s). In modern practice, it is often replaced by a violin, viola, or other melodic instrument. Since the 1930s, orchestras have grown in size to include as many as thirty or forty musicians (Saada n.d.:2). Doublings and additions of new instruments

Music occupies an ambiguous position in Muslim life. Since the beginning of Islam, Muslim authorities have disputed the question of whether music should be permitted in worship.

(such as mandolin, guitar, piano, and saxophone), with increased use of metal strings, equal temperament, and higher tunings, now produce qualities of sound unlike those of earlier ensembles (Saada n.d.:2; Schuyler 1984:17).

MUSIC AND ISLAM

The Muslim call to prayer (*adhan*), intoned five times daily, is a familiar sound in local towns and cities. Its style varies according to regional tradition and the personal style of the muezzin (*muʾadhdhin*), or caller. The calls range from stylized recitation on one or two tones to highly melismatic renditions based on specific melodic formulas (*maqamat*) of the Middle Eastern Arab tradition. Familiar, also, are the sounds of children intoning memorized verses from the Koran at neighborhood mosques and religious schools. Children are rewarded for precise and artful recitation, which may follow, depending on local custom, one of several established methods of Qurʾānic chant (Anderson 1971:154–155). The calls to prayer and the scriptural recitations are performed in Arabic, the language of the Qurʾān. Whether simply spoken or elaborately sung, they emphasize clarity of pronunciation and strict adherance to the rules of Arabic.

Music occupies an ambiguous position in Muslim life. Since the beginning of Islam, Muslim authorities have disputed the question of whether music should be permitted in worship. Because music, especially instrumental music, was associated with pagan practices and sensual entertainments, early authorities declared the act of listening to music "unworthy" of a Muslim. The debate continues. To avoid secular associations, references to music are usually avoided in mention of calls to prayer, Koranic recitations, and other forms of religious expression (Anderson:146–147). In some communities, music making of any kind—religious or secular—is discouraged in the name of Islam. A few forbid music altogether, as do members of the puritanical Mozabite sect of Algeria (Alport 1970:228, 234–235). Nevertheless, the sung praise of the Islamic deity is standard practice in most of the region.

The annual departure and return of pilgrims to Mecca (*hajj*), the beginning and ending of a journey every Muslim tries to make at least once, are occasions for singing religious songs. In the holy month of Ramadan, during which the faithful fast in the daylight hours, families sing religious songs as they gather for the evening or predawn meal. Special Ramadan songs also occur in street processions. Muhammad's birthday (*mawlid*) is celebrated with hymns of praise and epic songs depicting events in his life. The best known of these is *el-burda* 'the Prophet's mantle'. The religious music is mainly vocal, but instruments are used in certain contexts, as in the ceremonial Thursday evening proclamations of the holy day in Morocco, with trumpet (*nfir*) or oboe (*ghaita*) accompaniment. Pairs of oboes or trumpets, in ensemble with drums, such as the double-headed cylindrical types (*gangatan*; sing. *ganga*) played in Niger, herald the beginning and end of Ramadan.

Pre-Islamic beliefs and unorthodox practices of Sufi mystics have mingled with canonic precepts to produce a unique form of Islam, in which the veneration of saints (*marabutin*; sing. *marabut*) is a feature. The concept of saints as mediators between divinity and humanity, and as sources of good health and fortune, became a feature of Islamic worship in western North Africa after A.D. 1200. Religious brotherhoods (sing. *zawiya*) arose around legendary holy figures, often revered as patron saints or village founders. The activities of the brotherhoods center on small cupolaed mosques, which enclose the tombs of the saints. Some of these structures also contain facilities for lodging and teaching. Each year, thousands of worshipers make pilgrimages to the tombs of locally revered saints.

Hymns are regularly sung at the tombs. In Tunisia, canticles of praise are performed to the accompaniment of *mizwid* (bagpipe) and *bendir* (single-headed frame drum) (Erlanger 1937:9). In the Atlas Mountains of Morocco, Friday, the holy day, is celebrated weekly at the tomb with a procession of oboes and drums. The musicians, by virtue of their close identification with the saint, are believed to possess some of the holy man's spiritual power (*baraka*), enabling them to aid the sick and offer protection to the community (Schuyler 1983:60–64).

Featured in the rituals of the religious brotherhoods are songs and recitations of Sufi origin, known collectively as *zikr* (or *dhikr*), meaning "in recollection" of Allah. Though the *zikr* is usually sung in Arabic, vernaculars are occasionally used, as is the custom among the Berber Tuareg. Some practices include the repetition of raspy, gutteral utterances on the syllable *he*. These increase in intensity, and lead the participants into states of trance (Rouget 1985:271–273).

On Muhammad's birthday or other occasions deemed appropriate, the *zikr* may be part of a larger ceremony known as *hadra*, a term meaning "in the presence of," with allusion to the supernatural. Though the *hadra* takes many forms, it typically includes special songs and rhythms, rigorous dancing, and altered states of consciousness. In trance, a participant may become possessed or may express emotional fervor with acts demonstrating extraordinary strength or oblivion to pain. In other instances, participants seek exorcism of unwanted spirits believed to be the cause of illness or misfortune (Rouget 1985:273–279; Saada 1986:46–48, 80–82). In Libya, where the *hadra* is a curing ceremony, a ritual specialist performs exorcisms to an accompaniment of songs and drums—a procedure that, if the illness is severe, may be repeated for seven days or more (El Miladi 1975:3–4). In Morocco, the music for the *hadra* is played on the *ghaita* and *tbel* (kettledrum) by professional musicians (Schuyler n.d.:2). In Algeria, use of melody instruments is rare (Saada n.d.:8–9). In the *hadra*, Islamic concepts of spirits (*jinn*), as described in the Qur'ān, merge with pre-Islamic beliefs and practices.

The Gnawa brotherhoods specialize in the manipulation of spirits, and are much in demand for exorcisms, curing rites, circumcision ceremonies, and purification rituals after funerals. Their ceremonies appear to consist mainly of a blend of Islamic and pre-Islamic black African beliefs and practices. Prominent is their use of the *qarqabu* (or *qarqaba*), an instrument, likely of Sudanic origin, found in Hausa communities in many parts of North Africa. It consists of two pairs of iron castanets, joined by a connecting bar; the player uses two of these instruments, one in each hand. The Gnawa also play a *gumbri*, a three-stringed plucked lute, known by different names to black musicians throughout North and West Africa. The possession and curing ceremonies of the Gnawa, in particular, resemble those of Sudanic practice, though cultural elements from other sources may also be present. At annual celebrations of the Tunisian Gnawa in honor of their patron saint, Sidi Marzuk, the ritual texts are sung in a language, *ajmi*, apparently neither of Arabic nor Berber derivation and unknown to the present participants (Laade 1962:4).

The Tuareg of Niger conduct curing ceremonies, known as *tende n-guma*, in

The pastoral Tuareg of Niger customarily hold weddings after summer rains, when they assemble their herds of camels on the plains near In-Gall—an event known as the *cure salée*.

which men's raspy, gutteral sounds, uttered on the syllable *he*, mingle with women's songs and the rhythms of a mortar drum (*tende*) and hand clapping. The men's vocal sounds are similar to those heard in performances of the *zikr*, to which they may be related. Sudanese Sufi orders practice an African form of *zikr*, in which repetitions of certain syllables, including the breathy *he*, appear to have replaced most of the original texts (Trimingham 1965:213–217). The Tuareg deny, however, that the curing ceremonies are religious. Secular songs are sung, though always in duple meter and in slower than normal tempo (about M.M. 75–96) to accommodate the swaying movements of entranced patients (a behavioral feature also of Sudanese *zikr*). Though local Muslim leaders denounce the rituals as pagan and contrary to the teachings of Islam, the Tuareg view them as psychotherapeutic, and exhibit no conflict between their concepts of a spirit-filled world and their Islamic faith. If these rituals once had religious associations, they are unknown.

MUSIC IN FOLK LIFE

Religious festivals, national holidays, and life cycle celebrations are major occasions for music making in folk life. The Muslim holidays, local saints' festivals, and political or national holidays are the most important annual events; weddings and circumcisions are the most celebrated moments of the life cycle.

Annual events

Muslim festivals follow a lunar calendar, containing about 354 days. Because of the shorter annual cycle, the religious holidays rotate through the seasons, arriving about eleven days earlier each year in contrast with the solar cycle. The religious observances normally contain no music, but the accompanying festivities are occasions for music and dance. On 'Aid el-Fitr (Id al-Fitr), the festival marking the end of Ramadan, the townspeople of Agadez, Niger, gather in the courtyard of the Sultan's palace to hear the ceremonial oboes and kettledrums (sing. *ettebel*) played by the court musicians. When this ceremony is completed, the musicians, mounted on horseback, lead the Sultan's parade through the streets of the city, playing the oboes and large cylindrical drums suspended from their shoulders. On the tenth day of the twelfth month occurs the feast of 'Aid el-Adha (also known as 'Aid-el-Kbir and Tafaski), which commemorates Abraham's sacrifice of a sheep in place of his son, at God's command. This holiday provides an occasion for Algerian Tuareg women to gather around a mortar drum to sing from a repertory of festival songs. The community crowds around them, emitting shouts and shrill cries of approval while clapping rhythms in synchrony or in hemiolic contrast with those of the drum. On Mawlid (the twelfth day of the third month), townspeople in Libya have musical gatherings and fireworks after the religious observances (El Miladi 1975:3–4).

Saints' festivals (*moussem* or *ziara*, sing.) are often linked to dates in the Muslim lunar calendar. The annual pilgrimage to the tomb of Mouley Abdallah in Tazruk, Algeria, occurs fifteen days after 'Aid el-Fitr (Saada 1986:50–51). In the Moroccan

Rif, the Aith Waryaghar make an annual pilgrimage to the tomb of Sidi Bu Khiyar on the day before 'Aid-el Adha (Hart 1970:4). Such events, which often draw thousands of people, typically last two days. In the hope of obtaining personal good health and fortune through exposure to the spiritual power of the saint and the holy area surrounding his tomb, people say prayers and perform rituals. Social reunions, feasting, and music follow the ritual observances.

Many of the saints' festivals follow a seasonal schedule, occurring regularly during the summer months. Some of them have an economic role and religious and social functions. The *moussem* of Imilchil in central Morocco, held annually at the autumnal equinox, attracts thousands of pilgrims to the tomb of Sidi Mohamed el-Merheni. After devotions, the participants turn to bartering goods and animals, performing music, dancing, and carrying on courtships (Bertrand 1977:115–127). *Tazz'unt*, a Berber festival in the Moroccan High Atlas, occurs on 31 July, in accordance with the Julian calendar (12 August by the Gregorian). Though the functions of the festival resemble those of a *moussem*, the event is limited to the inhabitants of neighboring villages who share bonds of lineage. The rituals performed are for the collective well-being of the community, rather than for individuals (Jouad and Lortat-Jacob 1978:50–60).

Political or patriotic celebrations follow a solar calendar. Each country in the region commemorates its independence and important historical moments with annual holidays featuring military parades and the singing of patriotic songs. Public presentations of regional music and dance that highlight the nation's ethnic heritage often have a part.

Life cycle celebrations

Weddings normally occur during favorable periods in agricultural or pastoral cycles, which govern the lives of the people. In the Moroccan Atlas, Berber weddings usually occur during the festival season in late summer, after the first harvest (Lortat-Jacob 1980:23). The pastoral Tuareg of Niger customarily hold weddings after summer rains, when they assemble their herds of camels on the plains near In-Gall—an event known as the *cure salée*.

The sequence of rituals constituting a traditional Muslim wedding gives rise to several kinds of music, some of it performed or led by professionals. Special wedding songs are sung by women to the bride and by men to the groom, seeking blessings on the union and instructing each in the duties of marriage. Ritual verses are sung, also, during the ceremonial application of henna to the bride's and groom's hands and feet. Professional praise singers extol the virtues of the couple and comment on the generosity of the guests. Musicians with tambourines, oboes or flutes, and drums—the sizes and shapes varying with local custom—lead the bride and groom in processions. Separate musical entertainments are provided for male and female guests. A professional bard may sing traditional poetry to the men on religious, heroic, or romantic themes, while female specialists lead the women in lively songs and dances to their accompaniment of hand-held drums or tambourines (Westermarck 1914, chapters 3–8; Jamous 1981:268–276).

Circumcision is regarded as a young boy's first step toward manhood. As a rite of passage, it is both a sacred and a festive occasion. Though the preferred age is four or five or younger, the event is often postponed because of the cost of the ceremony and attendant feast. To minimize expenses, several families with boys of an appropriate age may collaborate in a collective ceremony, or a family may choose to perform the rituals as part of a larger, annual festival. In Algerian tradition, the event consists of several stages: a ceremonial haircutting (*tahfifa*), attended by men only; a ritual application of henna and the bestowal of gifts, attended by women only; a ceremonial

The professional singer-poets, ritual specialists, praise singers, and instrumentalists are commonly members of hereditary musician clans or artisan castes who specialize in particular traditions.

feast for relatives and guests; and finally, the actual surgical operation. During the henna ritual, the women sing the child's praises, and exhort the nervous mother to be joyous and proud. Their songs and activities are interspersed with shrill ululations of approval. The henna ceremony concludes with singing, which may last for hours, of songs dedicated to Muhammad (Toualbi 1975:91–95). Moroccan village custom contains similar elements, but in a different order. The surgery, which precedes the feast, is announced with intermittent volleys of gunfire. During the operation, men recite prayers and women sing special ritual songs (*urar*), similar to those sung for marriage, but with other texts (Lortat-Jacob 1980:83–84). Ceremonies for circumcision may also include the services of Gnawa musicians, who perform special ritual songs and dances of mystical or magical significance.

Musical specialists

The professional singer-poets, ritual specialists, praise singers, and instrumentalists who perform at festivals and family celebrations are commonly members of hereditary musician clans or artisan castes who specialize in particular traditions. Gifted singer-poets were formerly attached to the courts of tribal chiefs or other persons of power and wealth. Their heroic ballads and songs of praise enhanced their patrons' status and imbued the surrounding community with a sense of shared history and identity. Though the patronage system has almost disappeared, the traditions and functions of praise and epic singing are perpetuated by musicians who perform at weddings, religious festivals, and private parties.

In Mauritania, professional, hereditary poet-musicians (*griots*) sing panegyric poetry to the accompaniment of an elongated four-stringed lute (*tidinit*), played by men, and a harp-lute (*ardin*), played by women. In addition, a large, hand-struck kettledrum (*tbel*), played by women, is occasionally used. The tradition is sometimes termed *classical*, as it demands not only instrumental virtuosity and a command of classical Arabic and Moorish poetry, but also mastery of an elaborate and complex body of theory. In Mali, Niger, and southern Algeria, Tuareg *griots* of the artisanal caste practice a related tradition. Known to the Tuareg as *aggutan*, they typically entertain at weddings, celebrations for births, and small, private parties. Their repertory similarly consists of heroic legends and praise poetry, sung to the accompaniment of the *tahardent*, a lute similar to the Mauritanian *tidinit*. Their tradition embraces a system of rhythms and modes, serving as the material for improvisation, and a set of rules (though less explicit than the Mauritanian) that govern composition and performance. In the late 1960s, the *tahardent* tradition of the Tuareg of Mali began spreading to urban centers throughout the Sahara.

Many musical specialists are itinerant. During the festival months of late summer, the *imdyazn*, professional musicians native to the eastern regions of Morocco, travel in small bands through the villages of the High Atlas. A typical group consists of a singer-poet and several accompanists, whose instruments include a double clarinet (*zammar*) or a flute (*talawat*), one or two frame drums (sing. *daf*), and an alto fiddle (*lkmnza*), similar to a European viola (Lortat-Jacob 1980:41–42). The *rways*, itinerant musicians from southern Morocco, wander throughout the country performing an acculturated music derived from Arab-Andalusian, European, Arab-popular, and West African styles. These musicians often perform at Djemma el Fna, the grand square in the heart of Marrakesh, which for centuries has been a center for traditional musical entertainments (Grame 1970:74).

For the sedentary performer, music is more often a part-time activity, supplemented by some other line of work, and payment for services is frequently in gifts, rather than in money. In this category are the women who as ritual specialists perform at weddings, births, and circumcisions. Some of them are also professional mourners and singers of funeral laments. In Morocco, female entertainers (*haddarat*) accompany their songs with *bendir*, *tbel*, and the clay cylindrical drum *ta'riya* (Chottin 1938:9–10). In Algeria, urban female professionals (*msam'at*) accompany their songs and dances with *derbuka* and *tar* (Saada n.d.:5). Tuareg singers, traditionally members of artisanal clans, employ small, double-headed, hand-held drums (*gangatan*; sing. *ganga*) or a kettledrum (in Algeria, *tegennewt*; in Niger, *tazawat*).

Poetry and song

Vocal music, except when used for dancing, functions primarily as a vehicle for poetry, a highly developed and esteemed art in North Africa. Frequent topics are love (always in allusive or idealized form) and current or historical events. The texts are interspersed with praises and evocations of Allah, or exclamations such as "O my soul!" or "O my mother!"; the singing of poetry is largely improvisatory. Singers much in demand are those who can set to a familiar melody a spontaneously composed, rhyming text, concerning persons and events of immediate interest. Equally in demand are singer-poets who draw their material from traditional lore, embellishing and adapting well-known themes to suit each occasion. From one performance to the next, however, songs for ritual purposes vary little in melody or text. In this category are the Berber *urar* (also *ural*) verses, sung usually by women at weddings and ceremonies for circumcisions (Lortat-Jacob 1980:51).

Topics pertaining to valor in battle, actual or allegorical, form an important part of the *tesîwit*, a repertory sung solo by pastoral Tuareg men. *Tisiwit* consists of strophic poems sung to formulaic melodies or motifs of corresponding rhythm. Though some texts are customarily sung to particular melodies, the poetry and music are essentially independent and do not form fixed units. The songs may be sung unaccompanied or with *imzad*, a bowed lute, played by Tuareg women. Without imitating the singer's style or synchronizing with the singer's melody, the instrumentalist reinforces the vocal line with a rendering of the same melody. Interludes between strophes provide instrumentalist opportunities for improvisation on the melodic material. Performances of *tesîwit* poetry with *imzad* by legendary artists of the past reached high levels of artistic achievement.

Songs for dancing belong to a separate category. Instruments, infrequently used with other vocal genres, hold an important role in dance music. They typically include the *bendir*, the *tabl*, and the *ghaita*. The texts, of secondary importance, usually consist of formulaic verses, often with ostinato or vocable responses.

The characteristics of song vary by territory, ethnic group, genre, and occasion. Melodies range from little-ornamented, repetitive forms, to complex and highly melismatic structures. Much of the regional character derives from the rhythms, which adhere closely to the meters of regional poetry. The repertories of village and nomadic Berbers are possibly the least acculturated of local traditions. Pentatonicism of various types is common, and melodic use of an augmented fourth above the tonic

The dance begins slowly, with barely perceptible steps, and builds to a climax, when a high-pitched ascending glide on the flute coincides with a sharp cry by the solo singer and a formulaic ostinato by the chorus.

is often prominent. Microtonicism in melodic structure and ornamentation occurs in Berber song, but is more characteristic of Arab styles. Though Arab song is similarly linked with poetry, it is less closely associated with dance. In Tunisia, Andalusian songs and customs have been preserved in the traditions of particular occupational groups, such as the fruit and vegetable merchants of Tunis (Erlanger 1937:10). The songs of the Gnawa, like those of black cultivators in the Sahara, make occasional use of thirds and fourths, intervals rarely heard in Arab or Berber music. Furthermore, the vocal styles and repertories characteristic of sedentary and nomadic groups often cut across regional and ethnic divisions. Agricultural and other types of work songs are prominent among sedentarists, while songs for caravans and ballads about warriors are characteristic of nomads. Within the same group, the vocal styles of men often differ from those of women (see Nikiprowetzky 1964:81–83).

Instrumental music

Instrumental music, played for the primary purpose of listening, is uncommon in the folk life of towns and villages. Instruments serve mainly for dances and ceremonial purposes, such as wedding processions and the proclamation of a holy day or the onset of Ramadan. Instrumental improvisations serve as interludes between verses sung by professional bards, but they are rarely performed apart from vocal contexts. It is principally in the traditions of pastoral groups that purely instrumental music has a prominent place.

Music for solo flute is common among herdsmen and others in lonely occupations. An end-blown flute, held in oblique position, with finger holes arranged in two groups, is played by Arab shepherds in the Maghrib and Mauritania, and by Tuareg herders in Algeria and Niger. The Arab *gasba* (or *qasaba*), made of a hollow reed, has five or more finger holes; the four-hole *zaowzaya* of Mauritania is made from an acacia root or bark; the four-hole Tuareg *tazammart* (also *tasensigh* and *sarewa*) is made from a reed or a metal tube (Card 1982:63–65; Guignard 1975a:172; Nikiprowetzky 1961:6; Saada 1986:92–95). *Tazammart* players in the Algerian Sahara sometimes accompany their melodies with a vocal drone produced in the throat while blowing into and fingering the instrument; the drone functions as a pedal point to the melody. Flute music, though traditionally played for solitary pleasure or the entertainment of a few companions, is now heard by a wider audience through recordings and radio broadcasts of accomplished performers.

Another instrumental genre is the music for *imzad* played by Tuareg women (figure 1). The melodies for solo *imzad* belong to a genre apart from the vocal music accompanied by it. The chief purpose of this music was formerly to inspire men before combat and to honor heroes on their return. Played mainly by women of the dominant or "noble" caste, the *imzad* symbolized the values of the traditional society. The music also embodied Tuareg concepts of gallantry toward women; thus, the

FIGURE 1   Jima (Ajo) wult Emini plays an *imzad*. Agadez, Niger.

music of the *imzad* was a featured part of courtship. Though the *imzad* was less often heard after the 1980s, it retains an esteemed position in Tuareg musical culture. Its repertories are regional, closely associated with local persons and events. Its styles of playing differ by region: those of the Algerian Sahara are believed to be older than those of the southern and western areas. Instruments similar to it are found among neighboring peoples, but played by men, often to accompany the player's own singing.

The regional traditions often bear the imprint of a celebrated local performer, whose personal style has been much emulated. During the late 1900s, the scope of such influence increased, in town and country, with the availability of cassette recordings (Card 1982:102–109). The result is a reduction in local musical activity. The trend toward homogeneity is constrained, however, by the strength of tradition.

Dance

The most widely known Berber dances of Morocco are the *ahidus* (also *haidous*) of the middle and eastern High Atlas, and the *ahwash* of the western High Atlas. The dancers stand shoulder to shoulder in a circle, or in two incurved, facing lines. The musicians, who both accompany and direct the dances, stand in the center. Musicians for the *ahidus* include a singer-poet (*ammessad*), one or more assisting singers, and drummers with instruments of diverse sizes and pitches. The rhythms, which include solo improvisations, are frequently in quintuple meter. The songs (*izlan*, sing. *izli*) contain short verses with choral responses, sung to melodies composed of small intervals within a narrow range (Chottin 1938:5–6; Jouad and Lortat-Jacob 1978:86; Lortat-Jacob 1980:68–69). The structure of the *ahwash* is more complex. The drumming begins slowly, in duple or quadruple meter, but is transformed at midpoint into a rapid, asymmetric rhythm. The songs, sung to pentatonic melodies, consist of two-line verses, exchanged between the men and women. The *ahwash*, involving an entire village, is a highlight of festivals. Care is lavished on a performance, for its quality is said to determine the success or failure of the festival (Lortat-Jacob 1980:65–70, 120–124). Another Moroccan Berber dance is the *tamghra*, specific to weddings. To a men's accompaniment of *bendir*, it is performed for or by the bride and her attendants. The rhythms are similar to those of *ahidus*, but include no solo improvisations (Jouad and Lortat-Jacob 1978:86; Lortat-Jacob 1980:124–125).

Some dances are specific to particular villages or areas. An example is the *ahelli*, a nocturnal festival dance unique to Gourara, Algeria. It features the use of a six-hole wooden flute (*temja*). Standing in close formation, the dancers encircle the flutist, a solo singer, and several dance leaders. An introductory flute prelude sets the pitch for a drone, hummed by the dancers. An additional prelude precedes each of a series of songs with choral responses, sung in a high vocal register. The dance begins slowly, with barely perceptible steps, and builds to a climax, when a high-pitched ascending glide on the flute coincides with a sharp cry by the solo singer and a formulaic ostinato by the chorus (Augier 1972:307–309; Saada n.d.:8). Another example is the *guedra*, performed at Goulimine and certain oases in the Bani area of southern Morocco. The principal solo dancer begins on her knees, and as the encircling musicians gradually quicken the tempo, rises to her feet. The dance takes its name from a pottery drum used in accompaniment (Sheridan 1967:45).

Dances of the same name often assume different regional forms. The *saʿdawi* of Tunisia is a scarf dance, usually performed by women, featuring rhythmic movements of the hips and undulating gestures with a hand-held scarf. The dance is accompanied by a large kettledrum, *tbel*, and a mouth-blown bagpipe, *zukra*

The Arab *fantaziya* (or fantasy) of the Maghrib is a choreographed spectacle involving horses and men. To an accompaniment of drums, mounted riders armed with swords maneuver and race their horses.

(Erlanger 1937:9). Among the Ouled Naïl of Algeria, this dance involves both men and women. The men, armed with rifles, fire intermittent salvos above the heads of the women, who with small steps leap and turn (Saada n.d.:5).

Movements emulating the gestures of battle are a part of many local dances. Some dances incorporate religious elements. Popular is the gun dance (*baroud*, also *berzana*), of which variants occur throughout the region. In the Algerian form, male dancers armed with loaded muskets arrange themselves in a circle or in facing lines. The dancers turn shoulder against shoulder, taking small steps as they respond to the melody of the *ghaita* and rhythms of the *qallal* or *dendun*. Alternating vocal soloists chant invocations of Muhammad in the form of brief couplets with choral responses. On cue, the participants point their muskets to the earth and fire in synchrony, bringing the dance to a noisy, smoky climax. The gun dance is performed at any time (Augier 1972:305–306; Pottier 1950:120, 122; Saada n.d.:7).

Similar dances are performed with swords and sticks. In the *zagara*, a Tunisian saber dance, men perform in pairs. Each brandishes a sword in the right hand, while making shielding motions with the left. The dance has the accompaniment of *zukra* and *tbel* (Erlanger 1937:9). Stick dances in imitation of swordplay, said to be of ancient origin, are often a part of saints' festivals and other large celebrations. In the Algerian Sahara, men perform the ʿ*lawi* dance with large sticks or batons. As they weave past one another in response to the orders of a leader, they strike their batons in intricate patterns. Musicians accompany the dance with kettledrums, tambourines, vase-shaped pottery drums, and double-headed cylindrical drums, which impart variety of pitch and timbre to intricate hemiolic interchanges of duple and ternary rhythms.

The *sebiba*, unique to the oasis of Djanet in southeastern Algeria, is a choreographed spectacle that once a year or more involves the entire town. The origins of the event are obscured in conflicting legends. Costumed inhabitants of opposite sectors of the town, representing rival lineages, engage in stylized battle. The musicians and dance leaders are women, who play small drums (sing. *tobol*) struck with curved beaters (sing. *takurbat*). Any woman who can play a drum may participate. Two columns of women in close formation, each with its leader and followed by dancers, follow a circular path, which defines the arena. The participants, their number limited only by the availability of costumes, form two circles. Armed with mock lances and mock swords, they begin the gyrations of the dance. Incited by the leaders and encouraged by the songs, claps, shouts, and shrill cries of the spectators, the dancers continue for hours. The ensuing revelry continues throughout the night (Gay 1935:61–66; Pottier 1950:161–165).

Dance in North Africa is not limited to human beings (figure 2). The Arab *fantaziya* (or fantasy) of the Maghrib is a choreographed spectacle involving horses and men. To an accompaniment of drums, mounted riders armed with swords maneuver and race their horses. The maneuvers culminate in elaborate displays of horseman-

FIGURE 2   Tuareg camel parade at a festival. Ahaggar region of Algeria.

ship and swordplay. The *fantaziya* symbolically reenacts battles waged by the warriors who carried the "sword of Islam" to establish the Muslim Empire in North Africa (Saada n.d.:5). A similar spectacle, involving camels, is the Tuareg *ilugan* (or *ilujan*), sometimes termed a "camel fantasy." To an accompaniment of women's *tende* singing and drumming, the camels, under the direction of their riders, perform a series of stylized movements. The rhythms of the women's songs, usually in duple meter with ternary subdivisions, are said to imitate the gait of the camels. The warrior elements, infused with Tuareg concepts of gallantry, often lead to flirtatious exchanges between the men and the women. Though *ilugan* is an important part of Tuareg weddings, it is occasionally performed also at saints' festivals and other large gatherings (Blanguernon 1955:115; Nicolaisen 1963:104–105; Saada 1986:55–56, 59).

POPULAR MUSIC

The rapid growth of the media in the early 1900s spurred development of new genres and hybrid styles. The recording industry, present in North Africa as early as 1910, promoted widespread dissemination of regional and foreign styles (Danielson 1988:160). Young urban composers and singers, infused with nationalist spirit, began to turn to regional repertories for material and inspiration. The attraction of modern styles from the Middle East and Europe led them to experiment with foreign tonalities, instruments, and methods of arranging.

The Arab-Andalusian repertories provided further material. Popularized versions of the classic repertory were in evidence early in the century. In 1913 on a visit to Biskra, Algeria, Béla Bartók documented simplified renditions of *nubat* (1920: 489–501). Continuing popularization of this music produced genres that adhere in varying degrees to the classical models. Citing Algerian examples, Saada identifies several levels of transformation from Arab-Andalusian music to popular urban versions. *Arabi*, a music consisting of poems sung in local dialects to well-known classical melodies, resembles traditional sources, but adheres less strictly to the rules of classical composition. Departing further from the tradition is *hawzi*, a genre popular in the Tell region, consisting of love poems sung in the regional dialect to highly simplified versions of Arab-Andalusian melodies; its singers are usually men. Representing a third step is *sha'bi*, a music widely popular throughout the Maghrib, containing a blend of Arab-Andalusian formal elements and nonclassical rhythms, accents, ornaments, and harmony. Foreign instruments (such as guitar, organ, accordion) are commonly used. The texts, which contain topical, down-to-earth subject

In the 1980s, a cabaret music, *rai*, derived from bedouin Arab recitations, emerged in northern Algeria.

matter, are often sung in common street dialect. Finally, a music of more remote derivation is *zendani*, played and sung by urban female professionals who entertain in small groups at family festivals. The songs, consisting of strophic love poems sung to melodies accompanied by *derbuka* and *tar*, are performed for dancing (Saada n.d.:4–5).

A modern Moroccan music, *azri*, rooted in Middle Eastern traditions but influenced by others, first gained popularity in the early days of radio, when broadcasts of urban music from the Middle East began to reach the Maghrib. Composers of *azri* draw from many sources, including Moroccan, European, and American traditions. Western influence is evident mainly in the instrumentation, and in the occasional use of diatonic intervals imposed by such instruments as piano and organ (Schuyler 1977:n.p.).

In the late 1960s, *tahardent* music of the Malian Tuareg began to move eastward with the migration of drought refugees into Niger (figure 3). Among the migrants were artisanal specialists, *aggutan*, whose former patrons could no longer support them. Finding little success in singing Tuareg legends of Mali to mixed urban audiences in Niger, they quickly turned their talents to more marketable material. Most successful was the setting of new strophic texts with romantic and risqué themes to

FIGURE 3   Hattaye ag Muhammed Ahmed plays a *tahardent* left-handed. Agadez, Niger.

takumba, an existing rhythmic-modal formula of Malian origin. Many *aggutan* further augmented their opportunities by learning to sing in several local languages. The instrumental interludes between strophes, a traditional practice, provided attractive displays of virtuosity with appeal to urban audiences. Astute performers emphasized particular stylistic elements common to several related traditions, thus making their music more accessible to audiences of diverse ethnic backgrounds. Itinerant musicians gradually carried the music across Niger into southern Algeria. Though verses of heroism and praise continue to be sung for those who request them, *takumba* and its stylistic successors are the mainstay of modern Tuareg professionals (Card 1982:161–182).

In the 1970s, a hybrid music emerged in Morocco, derived from Arab, Berber, and Gnawa sources, mingled with Western elements. The music was begun by urban youths concerned both with the preservation and modernization of Morocco's traditional musics (Danielson 1988:160). Spurred by the Moroccans, youths in western Algeria initiated a similar movement. Simultaneously, a modern music rooted in the traditions of the Kabyle region spread throughout Algeria. In the 1980s, a cabaret music, *rai*, derived from bedouin Arab recitations, emerged in northern Algeria. At first denounced because of its sensual texts, *rai* became accepted as an expression of the yearnings and sufferings of modern youth (Saada n.d.:10). In the 1990s, recordings included trumpet, accordion, guitar, keyboards, and rhythm instruments.

REFERENCES

Alport, E. A. 1970. "The Mzab (Algeria)." In *Peoples and Cultures of the Middle East*, ed. Louise E. Sweet. New York: Natural History Press.

Anderson, Lois Ann. 1971. "The Interrelation of African and Arab Musics: Some Preliminary Considerations." In *Essays in Music and History in Africa*, ed. Klaus P. Wachsmann, 143–169. Evanston, Ill.: Northwestern University Press.

Augier, Pierre. 1972. "Ethnomusicologie saharienne: les documents sonores recueillis récemment en Ahaggar et au Gourara." *Libyca* 20:291–311.

Balandier, G., and P. Mercier. 1952. "Notes sur les théories musicales maures à propos de chants enregistrés." *Reports of International Conference of West Africanists*, II, Bissau, 1947 (Lisbon: Ministério das Colónias, Junta de Investigações Coloniais), V, pp. 137–191.

Bartók, Béla. 1920. "Die Volksmusik der Araber von Biskra und Umgebung." *Zeitschrift für Musikwissenschaft* 2:489–501.

Bertrand, A. 1977. *Tribus Berberes du Haut Atlas*. N.p.: Vilo.

Blanguernon, Claude. 1955. *Le Hoggar*. Paris: Arthaud.

Card, Caroline. 1982. "Tuareg Music and Social Identity." Ph.D. dissertation, Indiana University.

Chottin, Alexis. 1938. *Tableau de la musique marocaine*. Paris: Geuthner.

———. 1948. "Les visages de la musique marocaine." In *Maroc: Encyclopédie coloniale et maritime,* ed. E. Guernier, 543–560. Paris: Editions de l'Empire français.

Danielson, Virginia. 1988. "The Arab Middle East." In *Popular Musics of the Non-Western World*, ed. Peter Manuel, 141–160. New York: Oxford University Press.

Duvelle, Charles. 1966. *Musique maure*. OCORA, OCR 28. LP disk.

El Miladi, Salem. 1975. "Music and Magic in Year Cycle Rites in Libya." Unpublished manuscript.

Erlanger, Rodolphe de. 1937. *Mélodies tunisiennes*. Paris: Librairie orientaliste Paul Geuthner.

Gay, Le Capitaine. 1935. "Sur la Sébiba." *Journal de la Société des Africanistes* 5:61–66.

Grame, Theodore. 1970. "Music in the Jma al-Fna of Marrakesh, Morocco." *Music Quarterly* 56: 74–87.

Greenberg, Joseph. 1966. *The Languages of Africa*. Bloomington: Indiana University Press.

Guignard, Michel. 1975a. *Musique, honneur, et plaisir au Sahara*. Paris: Geuthner.

———. 1975b. *Mauritanie: Musique traditionnelle des griots maures*. SELAF/ORSTOM Collection Tradition Orale. ORSTOM CETO 752–3. 2 LP disks.

Hart, David Montgomery. 1970. "Clan, Lineage, Local Community and the Feud in a Rifian Tribe [Aith Waryaghar, Morocco]." In *Peoples and Cultures of the Middle East*, vol. 2, ed. Louise E. Sweet, 3– 75. Garden City, N.Y.: Natural History Press.

———. 1976. *The Aith Waryaghar of the Moroccan Rif: An Ethnography and History*. Tucson: University of Arizona Press.

Jamous, Raymond. 1981. *Honneur et baraka: Les structures sociales traditionnelles dans le Rif*. London: Cambridge University Press.

Jouad, Hassan, and Bernard Lortat-Jacob. 1978. *La saison des fêtes dans une vallée du Haut-Atlas*. Paris: Seuil.

Laade, Wolfgang. 1962. *Tunisia*, vol. 2, "Religious Songs and Cantillations." Folkways FW 8862. LP disk.

Loopuyt, Marc. 1988. "L'enseignement de la musique arabo-andalouse à Fes." *Cahiers de musiques traditionnelles* 1:39–45.

Lortat-Jacob, Bernard. 1980. *Musique et fêtes au Haut-Atlas*. Paris: Ecole des Hautes Etudes en Sciences Sociales.

Murdock, George Peter. 1959. *Africa: Its People and Their Culture History*. New York: McGraw-Hill.

Nicolaisen, Johannes. 1963. *Ecology and Culture of the Pastoral Tuareg*. Copenhagen: National Museum.

Nikiprowetzky, Tolia. 1961. *La musique de la Mauritanie*. Paris: Radiodiffusion Outre- Mer Sorafom.

———. 1964. "L'ornémentation dans la musique des Touareg de l'Aïr." *Journal of the International Folk Music Council* 16:81–83.

Pacholczyk, Jozef M. 1976. *Andalusian Music of Morocco*. Ethnodisc ER 45154. LP disk.

———. 1980. "Secular Classical Music in the Arabic Near East." In *Music of Many Cultures*, ed. Elizabeth May, 253–268. Berkeley: University of California Press.

Pottier, René. 1950. *Le Sahara*. Paris: Arthaud.

Rouget, Gilbert. 1985. *Music and Trance: A Theory of the Relations between Music and Possession*. Chicago: University of Chicago Press.

Saada, Nadia Mécheri. 1986. "La musique de l'Ahaggar." Ph.D. dissertation, University of Paris.

———. N.d. "La musique d'Algérie." Unpublished manuscript.

Schuyler, Philip. 1983. "The Master Musicians of Jahjouka." *Natural History*, October, 60–69.

———. 1984. "Moroccan Andalusian Music." In *Maqam: Music of the Islamic World and its Influences*, ed. Robert H. Browning, 14–17. New York: Alternative Museum.

———. 1977. *Morocco: The Arabic Tradition in Moroccan Music*. EMI Odeon 3C 064-18264. LP disk.

———. N.d. *The Music of Islam and Sufism in Morocco*. Bärenreiter-Musicaphon BM 30 SL 2027. LP disk.

Sheridan, Noel. 1967. *Morocco in Pictures*. New York: Sterling Publishing.

Toualdi, Noureddine. 1975. *La circoncision: blessure narcissique ou promotion sociale*. Alger: Sociétée Nationale D'Edition et de Diffusion.

Trimingham, John Spencer. 1965. *Islam in the Sudan*. London: Frank Cass.

Wendt, Caroline Card. 1994. "Regional Style in Tuareg *Anzad* Music." In *To the Four Corners*, ed. Ellen Leichtman. Warren, Michigan: Harmonie Park Press.

Westermarck, Edward. 1914. *Marriage Ceremonies in Morocco*. London: Macmillan.

Music in Sudan
Artur Simon

Music and Islam
Zār **and** ***Tambura***
Traditional Cultures of Music
City Music

The largest country in Africa, Sudan covers an area of about 2,500,000 square kilometers. To the north, it borders on Egypt; to the west, Libya and Chad; to the south, the Central African Republic, Zaïre, Uganda, and Kenya; to the east, Ethiopia. Eastward, across the Red Sea, lies Saudi Arabia, an important neighbor since before the 600s. Except in the south, large tracts of desert are almost devoid of habitation. In 1992, the country had a population of 26.6 million.

Without the green belt of the Nile, which penetrates the desert, the whole north of the country—from the Egyptian border to the capital (Khartoum)—would support almost no inhabitants. About 60 percent of the Sudanese live along the Nile Valley; 23 percent inhabit the cities. Nearly 70 percent of the people are peasants; 10 percent are nomads, or breeders of cattle or camels. About 40 percent to 50 percent are Sudanese Arabs; 10 percent are Nubians; 30 percent are southerners, belonging to several ethnic groups (Dinka, Shilluk or Colo, Nuer, Azande).

Except in southern Sudan, Islam prevails over cultural and ethnic identity. The relation between Islam and music, varying from ambivalence to repression, is always open to interpretation by different parties. National Islamization has always been an aim of north Sudanese cultural politics (Mohamed Abdel Hai 1982:12). However, besides the language, the traditional practice of music is an important aspect of local identity. Therefore, not surprisingly, each ethnic group in Sudan has a distinctive music.

Since ancient times, the land strip along the Nile has linked the old civilizations in West Asia and North Africa (Mesopotamia and pharaonic Egypt) and inner parts of Africa in southern Sudan, Ethiopia, Uganda, Central Africa, and the Western Sudan. A second route led directly across the Red Sea from South Arabia (Yemen, Hadramaut) to Sudan and Ethiopia. From long before the penetration of Islam, we know about cultural interrelations, which date back to pharaonic Egypt, where dancers and drummers from inner Africa performed before nobles. The earliest evidence of a wooden cylindric drum of the African type comes from one of the Beni Hassan tombs (about 2000 B.C.). About the same time, musical instruments like the long-necked lute and the lyre reached the Nile Valley with people from West Asia. These chordophones and an indigenous Egyptian bow harp found their way into

Sudanese religious ceremonies and songs developed
in Sufism, the mystical religious movement in Islam.

other African cultures of music. The lyre became prominent in many areas of the
Sudan. The harp, though no longer played in Egyptian and Sudanese parts of the
Nile Valley, is present in parts of southern Sudan, and Darfur in the west. An important link of interrelations between white and black Africa might have been the kingdoms of Napata (or Kush) and Meroë (725 B.C.–A.D. 350) in northern Sudan (Dixon
1971). Some rare sources, like a Hellenistic *auloi* found in a Meroitic tomb or depicted on a sandstone statue (Dixon and Wachsmann 1964), seemed to play only a marginal role within the broader Sudan.

MUSIC AND ISLAM

To praise the deity, orthodox Islam theoretically tolerates only elevated speech (or
recitation), and bans music. Daily practice, however, shows otherwise: not only popular customs in various regions, but also many Islamic orders, include song and
music in religious expression. In popular parlance, those who praise Allah and his
prophet in this manner are not "singers," but "speakers," "readers," "reciters." This
tendency, which strives to veil the psychological facts, cannot add much to the analysis of musical procedure. It illustrates the paradox of Muslim attitudes toward music.
Old men, set in their ways, are hostile toward popular music making and dancing;
they participate, however, in religious events richly adorned with singing. They listen
with as much interest to solo singers performing the vocal forms *madīḥ* or *qaṣīda*, as
they join in choral singing with religious fervor, whereby the linear melodic construction differs little from that in the secular forms. This attitude seems based on certain
social aspects rooted in the interpretation of the Qur'ān, and in the problem of
retaining authority while growing old.

Sudanese religious ceremonies and songs developed in Sufism, the mystical religious movement in Islam. Everything known about Sufism elsewhere—the organization of its fraternities, their ceremonies, and especially their music—applies to
Sudan. Coming to Sudan chiefly from the Hijaz (in Arabia), the representatives of
these religious movements proclaimed a new religious way of life and brought its ceremonial performances. This then blended with characteristic Sudanese elements.

In the self-representation of Sufism, *ḏikr* 'remembrance, recollection of the deity,
invocation' is the main liturgical element. Among the Sufis, it shows the incessant
repetition of the deity's name in praise, referring to Qur'ānic instruction: "Remember
God in frequent remembrance!" (Qur'ān XXXIII, 42).

Karāma

A convocation with *ḏikr* consists of several sections, mostly an alternation of songs
and recitals from the *Mūlid an-Nabbi* 'the prophet's birthday, the prophet's life and
works', a book written by the founder of the order. The ceremony usually begins with
the formula *lā ilāha illa'llāh* 'there is no God but God', and closes with a *ḏikr*, includ-

ing exclamations of *Allah!*, plus terms like *al-ḥayy* and *ḥayyo* 'the living being' and *al-qayyūm* 'the eternal being'. This invocation can be faint, mental, or even loud, heightening to the verge of trance.

In comparing the liturgies of the brotherhoods, one finds many variants, determined by ethnocultural factors. J. Spencer Trimingham (1949:213) mentions that in the Sudan especially, the older orders took over African elements in singing and in the *ḏikr*. I found Arabic-Islamic elements in the ceremonies of a brotherhood in Nubia: as in many other places in Nubia, the people of Abri joined a fraternity called Khatmīya or Mirġanīya, after its founder, Mohammed ʿUṯmān al-Mirġani (1793–1853), whom Sayyed Ibn Idrīs (his teacher) sent from the Hijaz to the Sudan.

The *ḏikr*, elsewhere in Sudan also called *nōba*, is part of a larger ceremony: *lailiya* 'evening session' (the meeting on Thursday evening), *mūlid* 'the prophet's birth', or *karāma* (honoring a person, a pilgrim, a deceased person).

In Nubia, a *karāma* begins after evening prayer, around 6:30 to 7:00 p.m.; it normally ends around 11:00 p.m. If possible, organizers invite a well-known soloist to perform solo songs, *qaṣāʿid* (sing. *qaṣīda*). The formal structure of a complete ceremony, as I documented it, consisted of thirty-five sections in a sequence of songs, readings, and *ḏikr*—of which only the readings, the *ḏikr*, and certain choral songs were obligatory. The solo songs have no fixed number. The structure divided into two large parts, interrupted for a meal. The first part consisted of readings from the founder's book, *Mūlid an-Nabbi*, which consisted of fourteen chapters (*alwāḥ*; sing. *lōḥ* 'tablet, board', also 'writing tablet'), on which a chapter had been written; today, there are books, usually printed in Cairo. Each chapter was recited by a different participant, for which a book was passed around. The participants sat on the floor.

The second part evoked movement. This part stood under the sign of the *ḏikr*, preparing the climax with strict rhythmical singing, alternating between one to three soloists and the group, who stood in a rectangle or in two rows. For the dynamic phase, rhythmic movement and increased tempo are characteristic. At the end, participants should reach a state of mystical ecstasy or rapture, according to the aptitude and disposition of the individual participant. In the ceremony under discussion, participants performed two *ḏikr*. With the word "Allah," the *khalīfa* began the closing *ḏikr*. The group answered with "*Ḥayyo!*" The tempo was at 103 quarter notes per minute. At the twenty-third "Allah," the lead singer entered with the melody from the introduction (figure 1). The tempo increased further. In contrast to the first *ḏikr*, the choral declamation was a kind of rhythmical shouting, not on a specific pitch. After people had declaimed "Allah" 144 times, the closing phase of the *ḏikr* began. One group proceeded from the syllables "*ḥay hu*" to "*ḥay qayyūm*," where all participants joined in. At that point, many of the participants stood mentally apart from their surroundings. In the closing phase, which lasted slightly more than two minutes, participants hopped up and down in place, their arms stretched out in front of them. The tempo increased even more, from 200 to 240 quarter notes per minute. About 30 seconds before the end, the ecstatic climax occurred, and the inner tension abated in a long, drawn-out cry. From beginning to end, the increase of tempo was 133 percent.

Nōba

Nōba (or *nawba*), the ceremonial of the Qādirīya brotherhood, held every Friday afternoon in Omdurman, is different. Since the 1500s, the order has spread in the Sudan. About the *ḏikr* of the Sudanese Qādirīya, Trimingham aptly remarks: "Their performances are more distinctively African than any other order" (1949:222). Maybe because of this, the order has many followers among other ethnic groups of the country. I found performances of the Qādirīya *nōba* among Islamized Berta (also

tār Frame drum	*madīḥ* Praise, praise poem, glorification; may be in honor of Allah and the prophet Muhammad
riqq Two-stringed fiddle in North Africa	
naqqāra Small kettledrums	

FIGURE I Part of a *ḏikr*.

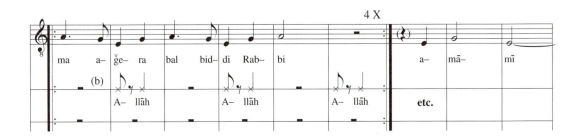

Bertha, Bartha, Bεrta), who live south of Ed Damazin, in the southernmost part of Blue Nile Province, near the Ethiopian border (Simon 1983b:304).

The African elements are percussive and rhythmic. Several percussion instruments accompany the event: at Omdurman, usually two frame drums (*tār*); one tambourine (*riqq*); two small kettledrums (*naqqāra*), with one player each; and a pair of hand cymbals (*kās*), of about 25 centimeters in diameter. There were also two large cylindrical drums (*nōba*), on which drummers beat rhythmical figures, similar to the manner in West African music, while the other drums, playing the role of timekeepers, provided a constant rhythmical background (figure 2).

Madīḥ

Madīḥ (pl. *madā'iḥ*) denotes 'praise, praise poem, glorification'—and, in this connotation, 'praise hymn in honor of Allah and the prophet Muhammad' (figure 3). One of the most famous *madīḥ* traditions in northern Sudan goes back to Hajj El-Mahi, who lived in Kassinger (near Kareima), from about 1780 to 1870. People say he composed about 330 religious poems, performed since his day by singing with an accompaniment of two *tār*. More than 130 handwritten works remain in the keeping of his family, whose members still cultivate the tradition. Belonging to the northern Sudanese people of the Shaiqiya, the Mahis are well known, far from their ethnic borders. The pressed voice quality and the prolonged singing on consonants (which point to the influence of Arab singing) distinguish this song style from those other-

FIGURE 2   Part of a *nōba*.

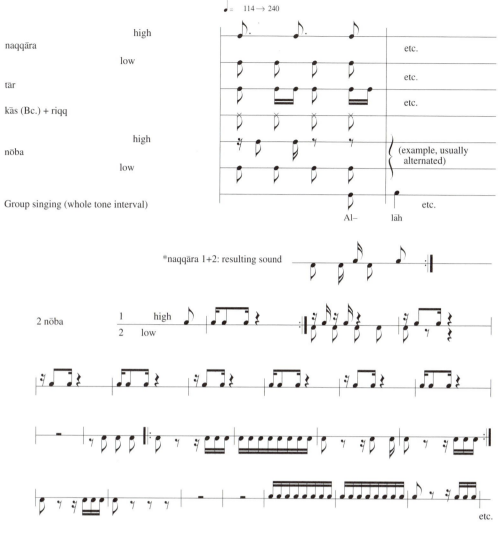

1   naqqāra   high
2   low

3   tār

4   kās (Bc.) + riqq

5   nōba   high
6   low

7

Group singing (whole tone interval)

Al–   lāh

♩ = 114 → 240

etc.
etc.
etc.
(example, usually alternated)
etc.

*naqqāra 1+2: resulting sound

2 nōba   1   high
         2   low

etc.

frequent rhythmical figures:

FIGURE 3   The *madīḥ*-singers Maidub M. Hajj El-Mahi and Ali A. El-Hajj playing frame drums, from Kassinger (Kareima), 1974.

wise present in northern Sudan. The content of these songs often proves an enthusiastic religiosity, or a moralizing intention. The language, mostly symbolic, attracted a peasant audience, which usually could not read.

Since many *madīḥ*-singers have adopted pieces from Hajj El-Mahi's repertory, one can hear them everywhere *madīḥ* is performed: at the farewell or welcome of a pilgrim, at the festivity for a naming or a circumcision, at a commemoration or a

zār   Spirit-possession healing ceremony orga-
    nized by women

tambura   Spirit-possession healing ceremony,
    with men as musicians, that occurs at the
    sacred residence of the lyre

dalūka   Clay drum from North Africa

memorial, in the streets at the markets, or in front of a mosque. These pieces have
become part of Sudan's oral literature. Allusions or pictorial comparisons—derived
primarily from the world of desert caravans, the Nile landscape, the Qur'ān—allow
for ambiguity in translation.

ZĀR AND *TAMBURA*

Besides the Sufi ceremonies (strictly reserved for men), other choral ceremonies of
supraregional distribution, such as *zār* and *tambura*, belong to the women's domain.
With some exceptions, men may take part in the ceremonial procedure, as in *tambura*, where the musicians are mostly men. The apparent reason for these ceremonies is
spirit possession. It stands as a vehicle for a complex system of beliefs, social restrictions, sociopsychological and mental disturbances, the curing of organic diseases, and
group therapy and collective amusement for participating women.

A *zār* may take place anywhere, but it usually occurs at the home of the patient
undergoing initiation, or in the house of the *sheikha,* the master of ceremonies and
head of the communion (association) of worship. A *tambura* occurs only at the sacred
residence of a lyre. A special room in a house or hut holds the accessories for the performance. The object of these cultic requisites is the *tambura* or *rababa*, a large lyre,
usually with six strings. The skin that covers the soundbox has two round holes,
"eyes" through which the spirit of the *tambura* sees the participants. Only a man may
play the lyre. Other musical instruments are two or three drums (*noggaara*); calabash
rattles, shaken by the women; and a rattle belt (*mangūr*), worn by a dancer on the
hips, so rhythmical twisting produces a sharp rattling sound (Hickmann and
Mecklembourg 1958:49).

Scholars believe the *zār* originated in Ethiopia, in or near the town of Gondar.
Between 1850 and 1900, it spread in the Islamized Sudan and Egypt.

> The Zar ceremony is not merely a curative means but it acts as a theatre for singing
> and dancing, and as a club and restaurant for women, who are excluded and are not
> permitted to join their husbands in such places and on such occasions. This social
> status, discrimination and isolation reflect themselves in some psychological distur-
> bances, depression, frustration and even temporary, partial paralysis. The function
> of the Zar is to cure or to relieve the psychosomatic ailments and psychological dis-
> turbances, and it has proven effective in many cases. (Ibrahim 1979:170)

For case studies and details of the ceremonial procedure, see Ibrahim (1979:171),
Kennedy (1967), Simon (1983a:290–292), and Zenkovsky (1950).

Singing, dancing, and drumming form an essential part of *zār*, as does physiology:

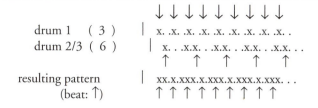

FIGURE 4   Cross-rhythm at a *tambura*
ceremony.

The patient does not lie on a couch, but is emotionally stimulated by rhythm, music, and physical action to the point of emotional exhaustion. But the catharctic release is preceded by a tremendous increase of tension and anxiety. This seems to be as important for the inducement of trance as for catharsis (Kennedy 1967:193).

The pantheon of *zār*-spirits consists of Muslim, Christian, and Ethiopian spirits. Each responds to a special tune. These are simple antiphonal songs, started by a special female lead singer, and answered by the other participants, who accompany themselves by hand clapping. The lead singer beats a clay drum (*dalūka*), or a drum substitute, such as a segment of a fuel drum or a kerosene tin. The noise of the latter nearly drowns out the singing. The monotonous hammering of percussive rhythm (sometimes intensified by increasing tempo) and the ostinato type of singing are the musical tools for inducing trance.

Omdurman is a center of the *tambura* cult, which people practice elsewhere in Sudan. In 1982, I found it among the Berta, south of Ed Damazin. Songs and dances of possession were accompanied by a large lyre, the *tambura*, three cylindric drums (*noggaara*), and hand rattles (*asoso*), the only instruments named by their original Berta names. The other names point to a Sudan-Arabic origin: the smallest drum was the *tabla*, and the larger ones were also *tambura*. The shape of the drums, however, matched the African type. The same is true of the musical structure, dominated by typical cross-rhythms played on the drums. The smallest drum and the rattles provided a steady beat, which coincided with the fast movements of the female dancers, who jumped up and down. The two beats played on the larger drums fell exactly between the other beat in a typical interlocking technique (figure 4). The sound of the lyre, the only instrument played by a man, was barely audible (Simon 1983a:291–292, 1983b: example 45).

TRADITIONAL CULTURES OF MUSIC

Many cultures of music in Sudan remain unknown to the world outside. With few exceptions, ethnomusicologists have worked and published only sporadically on the country. One reason for their absence is that political problems within Sudan have made continuous fieldwork difficult.

Music of the Nubians, northern Sudan

The ruins of temples, churches, castles, fortresses, and houses testify to a history reaching far back to eras dominated by pharaonic Egyptian, Meroitic, Christian, and Islamic cultures, and even by Turkish rule. The Nubians continually absorbed alien influences into their language and customs, but maintained their cultural identity in many aspects of life. Their musical traits are distinguishable from those of neighboring Egyptians and Sudanese Arabs.

Nubia flourished at the time of the kingdoms of Nobatia, Makuria, and Alwa. From the sixth to fourteenth centuries, Christianity, adopted by most Nubians, was the official religion. Both Christian and Muslim travelers' accounts from that period, plus archaeological findings since the 1960s, tell of a blooming country: thanks to adept and intensive irrigation, its residences, monastaries, and farms (orchards, vine-

Women organize and perform ceremonial acts and songs. In a few exceptions, such as the groom's procession, men participate; such songs usually praise the bride or the groom.

yards, grainfields) stretched far into the desert. A century after Christianity had sunk roots in Nubia, Islam began expanding over western Asia and North Africa. In 641, its defeat of Egypt cut Nubia off from the Christian West. A period of Arabic (and parallel Islamic) infiltration began, and in the 1300s, culminated in the fall of Christian Nubia. In the ethnic and possibly cultural sense, the designation "Nubian" is broader than in the linguistic. In northern Sudan, a few peoples considered Sudanese Arabs are probably Arabized Nubians; these include the Jaʿaliyīn and the Shaiqiya (Ibrahim 1979:15), who speak Arabic, but have much in common with other Nubians.

Musical instruments

In comparison to Egypt, which boasts a multitude of musical instruments, northern Sudan—especially Nubia—has few instruments: the lyre (Nubian *kisir,* Sudan-Arabic *ṭanbūr* or *ṭanbūra*); the frame drum (*taar*); and the single-headed clay drum (*dalūka*). Other instruments, such as the Arab tambourine (*riqq*) or the Arab lute (*al-ʿūd*) have come in recent times from Egypt or Khartoum. The *dalūka* is a cup-shaped drum, made from air-dried clay or mud, open on the bottom; the skin, which has the average diameter of 30 centimeters, is glued to the body. Played at weddings (and especially at *zār*), it is the only instrument women play. Another, smaller type of a clay drum is the *shatam*, which can stand in for the *dalūka*.

Music in culture and society

Two forces affect Nubian social life. The first is Islam. The second is the peasant way of life, which, since ancient times, has formed the economic basis of the Nile Valley. World view, manner of conduct, and traditional customs largely keep within this frame. Nubians usually celebrate only a wedding (*balee*) on a large scale, with music and dance; only a few songs accompany other ceremonies in the life cycle. At weddings (which last up to seven days) and in nuptial songs and dances, one can differentiate between two spheres: strictly ceremonial acts, and evening dances (taking place partly parallel to, and partly supplementary to, the ceremonies). These dances entertain guests and villagers.

Women organize and perform ceremonial acts and songs. In a few exceptions, such as the groom's procession (*seera*), men participate; such songs usually praise the bride or the groom (Simon 1980b:D2–D5). Alongside these official acts, a program entertains those not belonging to the family circle. At a wedding, nonparticipating spectators see these songs and dances first. Aside from such modern appearances at youth clubs or school, dance evenings offer the only opportunity for villagers to have public amusement. For premieres at such occasions, talented poets and musicians in Nubia compose songs about love and songs for dancing; also, families engage professional musicians for them.

Songs for boys' circumcision and girls' clitoridectomy belong to the female realm, and are usually the same as the praise songs sung at weddings.

Here is an outline of traditional musical life in Nubia.

A. Male sphere.
1. Dance songs with instrumental accompaniment (*kisir* or *taar*), especially at weddings.
2. Dance songs, or dances without instrumental accompaniment, especially at weddings.
3. Dance music without song, with *kisir* or *taar*, hand clapping and foot stamping, especially at weddings.
4. Songs with instrumental accompaniment for entertainment at weddings and other festivities or social occasions.
5. Songs for entertainment in a small group of men: (a) *kalakiya* while drinking date wine, (b) at other occasions or of personal enjoyment.
6. Work songs, for example at the bucket waterwheel (*eskalee*) and during fieldwork.
7. Religious songs.
8. School songs, partly using repertory from no. 1, partly of modern character.

B. Female sphere.
1. Songs during domestic work, with religious or narrative content.
2. Songs for weddings and circumcisions.
3. Lullabies.
4. Dirges, songs at death.
5. Songs for farewelling and welcoming pilgrims.
6. School songs for schoolgirls.
7. Songs for *zār*, with Arabic texts.

In 1973 and 1974, at Sukkot and Mahas (the central part of Nubia), there were four professional singers and at least five semiprofessional ones. Others, mainly teachers, presented new songs at weddings and other festivities. In this manner, the repertory continually renewed itself. Two of the professional singers were blind: Dahab Khalil (born 1920; died June 1977, in Khartoum), from Dibasha on Saï Island; and Hussein Muhammed Wagiya Allah (born 1933), from Abud by Abri. The other two were Nasr Tawfiq (born 1953), from Ashkan by Abu Fatima (Mahas); and Muhammed Awad (born 1949), from Badin by Kerma, an island in the Nile. Of these, Dahab held the central position (Simon 1975a).

The music

Just as there are different language districts in Nubia, one can also detect several regional musical styles, which, however, do not correspond with the language districts. Taking into account the male sphere's dance and entertainment songs with instrumental accompaniment, we find the following current distribution.

Wadi Halfa and New Halfa

Typical for this region is the alternation between one or two solo singers and a choir, accompanied by two, differently sized frame drums (*taar*). One only rarely finds the lyre (*kisir*). A special feature of Halfa style is *ollin aragiid* 'hand clapping and dancing'. In it, the dancers accompany themselves with complicated patterns of clapping—a style that also appears among the Kenuzi Nubians in Egypt (Hickmann and Mecklembourg 1958:8–11; Simon 1980b: example 6).

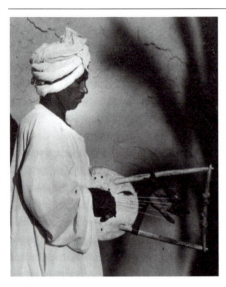

FIGURE 5   The Nubian singer and *kisir* player Hassan Fagir, from Abri, 1973.

Sukkot and Mahas

Here, the *kisir* is the dominant instrument, while the frame drums are unknown. The *kisir* serves as accompaniment to dances and songs for entertainment (figure 5). In contrast to the Halfa style, with an alternating soloist and choir, the solo singer, accompanying himself on the *kisir*, has greater salience. An important element is the rhythmical accompaniment of songs and lyre playing with hand clapping and foot stamping, performed by four or more young men, who can also function as an ensemble in alternation with the soloist. The rhythm is duple, with a few exceptions.

Dongola region

Here, too, the lyre is the predominant instrument. The musical style is less uniform than in the other regions. An independent Dongolowi style is barely discernible, because of alternating singing with short melodic phrases, which point to influences from the Shaiqiya region and the adoption of Sudan-Arabic melodies. As among the Shaiqiya, some groups accompany singing and lyre playing with a goblet-shaped clay drum of the *darabukka* type (*dalūka*), named like a somewhat differently shaped drum, used by the women.

The tuning of the Nubian *kisir*, always five stringed, is anhemitonic pentatonic. A standard tuning is e_1–g–a–c_1–d_1, though many deviations appear (figure 6). Men play the lyre with a plectrum. Striking all the strings at once produces a pentatonic sound cluster. Melodic playing results when the performer allows the strings to vibrate freely, one after another, as he lifts a finger from a string. A finger-plucked technique serves especially for melodic fillers, small motifs inserted between the main beats of a rhythm.

One could conclude that Nubian singing is always pentatonic. However, the remaining song forms—*kalakiya*, narrative songs, work songs, lullabies, nuptial songs, circumcision songs, dirges—also use anhemitonic tetratonic, pentatonic, and hexatonic structures. Unlike Arabs' pressed-voice singing with elongated consonants, Nubian singing is less emphatic, with only a few ornaments.

Music of the Hadendowa, eastern Sudan

The Hadendowa belong to the Beja group (Ababda, Bisharin, Amarar, Hadendowa, Beni Amer). They breed animals (camels, cattle, sheep), farm the land, and labor at farms and the harbor of Port Sudan. In 1980, Ernst Emsheimer and Albrecht Schneider carried out the only ethnomusicological fieldwork known to have resulted in musical recordings among them (Emsheimer and Schneider 1986).

Their most important musical instrument is the five-stringed lyre (*bāsān-kōb*, *basamkub*). For its tuning, see figure 6. The technique of playing is the same as in northern Sudan. It seems to be the only traditional instrument still played. As a symbol of power, the chiefs of the Beja formerly owned large kettledrums (*naqqāra*,

FIGURE 6   Tunings of Sudanese lyres.

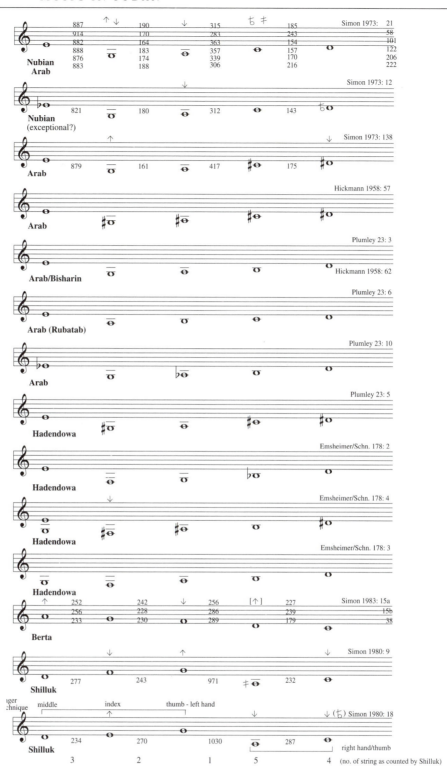

nahās), which men played at important ceremonial occasions, such as the installation or death of a chief, or in wartime.

In 1980, the musical repertory of the Hadendowa consisted of love songs, songs in praise of women, camel songs, tribal songs (about historical events, places, areas, seasons, caravan trade), songs played at festivities (like weddings), and improvised songs (*daw beit*, *dobet*, found in other parts of north, west, and central Sudan).

The Baggāra have a strong tradition of female poets and bards (*hakamma*), the most respected personalities in the society, bearers of tradition.

Songs may be performed by a singer/player alone, but most of the *bāan-kōb* players we met prefer to have a group of hand clappers (they also may add foot stamping) to practice antiphonic singing and for marking the rhythm which sometimes differs from that of the *bāan-kōb* or changes within one piece. Rhythm patterns which could be interpreted and notated as 4/4 or as a 7/8 do occur, but the real problem is that they obviously consist of units not having always the same duration. (Emsheimer and Schneider 1986:11)

Music of Kordofan and Darfur

Desert in the north and savanna in the south, with two mountainous areas (the Jebel Marra in South Darfur, and the Nuba Mountains in South Kordofan), form the landscape of central and western Sudan. Several Sudan-Arabic tribes inhabit the plains. These are *Abbāla* 'Camel breeders' (in the north), and *Baggāra* 'Cattle breeders' (in the savanna). The Zaghawa, another ethnic group of probably Saharan origin, came from Borno to Darfur in the 1200s. Many centuries ago, the autochthonous African population retreated to the Nuba Mountains and Jebel Marra. "Nuba" is the general Arabic name for some fifty different ethnic groups, living as peasants on the inselbergs of Kordofan.

The Arab tribes have a rich oral tradition of genealogies, memorized in special songs. The Baggāra have a special type of praise or satirical songs or songs of censure (*gardagi*). Performed in small gatherings, they require the accompaniment of a one-stringed fiddle (*umkiki*).

The neck is made of wood while the resonator is a bowl-shaped gourd covered with leather. The string is tuned to give one tone, but the player who is at the same time the singer, called locally (*al-hadday*) produces extra notes by stopping the string in different positions and hence creating a hemitonic pentatonic pattern of scale. (Daw 1985:50–51)

Instead of the *umkiki*, the Baggāra of Darfur have a five-stringed harp (*kurbi*, Daw and Muhammad 1985:63; *al-bakurbo*, Ismail 1970:92).

The Baggāra have a strong tradition of female poets and bards (*hakamma*), the most respected personalities in the society, bearers of tradition. People appreciate them for their wit, and fear them for the sharpness of their tongues.

Besides her general bardic duties, like the songs of praise and encouragement, a *hakamma* might be called upon to ride into battle with the men and sing during the fighting to encourage them. She leads the dances both of men and women and may accept, though not demand, payment for social singing. Materially the tribal council sees to it that she needs nothing to live comfortably. One of the most important roles of the *hakamma* may be found in the system of tribal justice where she may be called upon at the sentencing of a convicted man or woman to sing of the crime and the punishment, but she can refuse to do that if she disagrees with the judgment. (Carlisle 1975:266)

As in other parts of the Arabized Sudan, the ruling families of the Baggāra own copper kettledrums (*nihas*, from Arabic *nahās* 'copper'), a symbol of power and tribal sovereignty, played only at exceptional occasions. The kettledrums may have come from Hadramaut or Yemen.

Roxane Carlisle provides information about the music of the Zaghawa, the camel-breeding (and formerly camel-raiding) people of Darfur.

> A typical example of an older woman's song of praise, an *abi*, addresses the Zaghawi camelmen who have just returned from a difficult desert search for natron. Such a song may be performed during a *tirtir*, that is, an old Chadian dance in a slow tempo reminiscent of the dignified walking gait of camels. In the centre of a ring of men and women dancers stands one drummer who strikes his *ehti* drum with a stick held in his left hand, while his extended right hand beats the other skin head. The men and women who were assembled for the *tirtir* performed a kind of solemn hopping and circular dance around the drummer, and only the women replied to their song leader in a symmetrical form of litany with variations, while the men brandished their staves and swords in rhythm to the drum. The song unfolds the whole story of a particular desert journey and begins usually with praises to the leader, a Zaghawi man "strong as stone," and to his fine camel as both man and beast prepare for the long desert trek to the alkaline springs. . . . There exists today a single overall woman's approach to song performance, and there are no sharply distinct melodic types for different textual subjects. Free vocal rhythm and simple meter throughout, undulating and generally descending solo melodies ranging within an octave, great importance given to meaningful text, a syllabic setting of text to tone level, and a generally relaxed and thoughtful performance of songs— these are the traits present in the repertories of Zaghawi female bards and nonspecialist singers. (Carlisle 1975:255–259)

Most Kordofan and Darfur songs link with dances, and their names usually apply to both song and dance. This is also the case among the Fur and Nuba, though their music and life-styles differ much from those of their neighbors. Too little ethnomusicological research has been done in these areas, and detailed information on their music is scarce (Beaton 1940; Carlisle 1975).

According to Carlisle, the Fur have a small instrumental ensemble, *kolokua*, which plays at harvesting and circumcision festivities. It consists of two drums, an end-blown flute, and two side-blown antelope horns. Some names of the instruments (*gangan* 'cylindric drum', *tumble* 'bowl-shaped drum') point to relations with Chad and northern Nigeria. The West African Fellata, mainly Hausa, served as transmitters.

> The melodic range of Fur women's song is rather wider, beyond an octave, by contrast with the songs of the Zaghawi women, which hover under an octave. Whereas Zaghawi melodies favoured small intervals like a halftone, the Fur songs tended towards a greater use of whole tones. Vocal accents were forceful in Fur women's songs in contrast to the more relaxed singing style of the Zaghawi women. (Carlisle 1975:261)

Many groups of Nuban mountaineers (like the Miri, near Kadugli) are strongly Islamized, though they still practice traditional music and dances as an important ele-

At the nights of full moon during the dry season, unmarried youngsters meet at dance places for so-called moonlight dances, the principal occasions for entertainment, flirtation, and courtship.

ment of their ethnic identity. Each of the fifty groups of languages has its own songs and dances. The favorite instrument, played by young men for musical accompaniment, is the five-stringed lyre. Males play it nearly everywhere: herding cattle, walking around, sitting under a tree. In the Nuba languages, it has different names, including *fedefede* (Tumtum Nuba), *benebene* or *beriberi* (Masakin), and *kazandik* (Miri). As in northern and eastern Sudan, players use a plectrum. The resonator consists of a piece of cowskin-covered calabash. The wire strings are knotted to strips of cloth, strung around the yoke, a wooden crossbar.

The women of some areas (like the Masakin) play a frame zither or a musical bow with a calabash resonator. Within a rounded bough, they tie a string four times to get four sections, each with a different pitch (Wegner 1984:51).

Two kinds of drums are played: a cylindrical dance drum with two skins (Miri *umva*, Masakin *bamba*, Tumtum *bajé*), and a ceremonial drum, played only at special festivals and death ceremonies. Among the Miri, it is an earthen-pot drum (*kola*), played at the rainmaking *kola* festival (Baumann 1987:87). When played with a lyre, a gourd pot (*bukhsa*), struck with a thin piece of wood, replaces the dance drum. A set of small gourd trumpets is called *bukhsa* or *kanga:* "The Dajo ethnic group of the Nuba mountains have trumpets of four to six different sizes and lengths. This kind of trumpet is called '*kanga*'" (Daw and Muhammad 1985:78).

At the nights of full moon during the dry season, unmarried youngsters meet at dance places for so-called moonlight dances, the principal occasions for entertainment, flirtation, and courtship.

> The Miri stamping dance *Serkalla*, until twenty years ago the customary opening of almost any 'moonlight dance', has been replaced by another stamping dance known as *kirang*. *Kirang* originates among the Nuba of Heiban, but has spread throughout Kadugli and its environs. Though its musical idiom is thought very similar to that of the Miri stamping dance *Serkalla*, its texts are without exception in colloquial Arabic and often concerned with events in Kadugli and its suburbs. (Baumann 1987:52)

In some places, the *kirang* dance is accompanied by the *kirang*, "a cone-shaped drum with only one wide opening covered with goat skin, tightened by skin strips across the bottom of the drum and other horizontal strips to increase the tension" (Daw and Muhammad 1985:11). More and more, traditional dancing is yielding to *dalūka* songs, commercially produced popular songs from northern Sudan, which Radio Omdurman features in broadcasts. Girls sing them, accompanied by one or more earthen *dalūka*. The texts are in Arabic. Married women do not take part in moonlight dances; they use another musical genre, that of grindstone songs, whose texts are locally topical (Baumann 1987:96). It can be considered the sung poetry of the Miri.

In the Nuba mountains, the major musical and dancing events are three to four seasonal festivals, which take place mostly in the dry season. Initiations of young men into adult society were once prominent, but during the 1970s and 1980s, various groups abandoned them. In the western hills, an outstanding dance of initiation was the *kambala* (Corkill 1939). During the rainy season, the Miri continue to perform it (Baumann 1987:84).

At harvest festivals (October to December), ensembles of gourd trumpets, which provide one pitch, accompany special dances.

Each oracle night is concluded by the performance of the dance *Sorek.* . . . Like many Miri dances, it is performed by women and men forming concentric circles around the musicians, women taking the inside circle and moving in anti-clockwise direction, men forming the outside one and moving in clockwise direction. The movements of the dancers consist in a slow, seemingly syncopated shuffle that, however, receives its momentum from spinal contraction and relaxation, rather than hips or legs.

The music for *sorek* is played by adult men forming an ensemble of at least five, and up to twelve, slim tubular gourd trumpets, called *lela ma sorek* ('children of the gourd'). Each of them is tuned to a different pitch. Their joint musical performance creates an instrumental transformation of the men's bawdy songs *tazu ma sorek* ('songs of the gourd') by using the hocket technique: each player contributes one pitch or one short pattern of a continuous musical phrase which results from the well-timed and most subtle interlocking of single phrases. The *tazu ma sorek* songs, short couplets of a content considered bawdy or often obscene, are the most popular songs of married men, and their performance, as well as ideally knowledge of their words, are reserved for males in informal company. Their transformation into instrumental music at *tanyara ma rogak* and *tanyara ma siga* [harvesting festivals] marks their only appearance on a public occasion and one involving the presence of women. (Baumann 1987:85–86)

Blue Nile: Ingassana, Gumuz, Berta

This region has some pervasive musical features: the five-stringed lyre and ensembles of one-pitched wind instruments combine to form a resultant melody.

"Ingassana" is a name Arabs give to several ethnic groups living in the Tabi Hills, about 50 kilometers southwest of Ed Damazin. Protected by the hills, the people have for centuries maintained a defensive position: against the Sultanate Funj (at Sennar, ca. 1500–1821), Turco-Egyptian invaders (1823–1885), slave hunters, and the Mahdi's armed forces (1884–1885).

The most characteristic music of the Ingessana is *bal* music, played at weddings and harvest festivals, in accompaniment to the *bal* dance. An ensemble for the *bal* consists of five *bal*, vertical stopped bamboo flutes without finger holes, one gourd trumpet (*siŋar*), and one gourd rattle, played by one of the flutists. Additional flutes may cover the lower octave. All players are boys or men; women, with other men, sing and dance. The patterns played on the one-pitched flutes interlock cross-rhythmically, to produce a melody sung by the dancers, or to outline its melodic contour by playing the main tones. The pitches of a set of flutes and the *siŋar*, as recorded and measured by Gerhard Kubik (1982:98), may serve as an example: *wɔn*, 544 Hz; *diaɣ*, 624; *yezə*, 488; *təltya*, 404; *aswān*, 440; *siŋar*, 288. From the lowest to the highest pitch, we get distances of 586—148—179— 188—237 cents; according to the disposition as listed above: 237—425—327—148—734 cents. It remains a mystery how Gottlieb (n.d.:II) interprets these and other pitch relations of the Blue Nile region as equipentatonic scales (Simon 1989b). The pitch of the gourd trumpet

waza   Trumpet of the Berta of Sudan

(*siŋar*) seems unimportant for the musical structure; it provides a rhythmical counterpattern to the melodic process.

The Ingassana people call the lyre *jangar* or *jaŋar*. For a resonator, they cover with cowhide half a hollowed log. The Shilluk, along the White Nile, use the same construction. This is not the only evidence for historical relations between these areas. The playing technique of the *jaŋar*, however, belongs to the northern style, which uses a plectrum; the instrument of solo singers, it accompanies also certain dance songs.

The Sudanese Gumuz live east of the Blue Nile, around Roseires. Their traditional homeland lies in Ethiopia, west of Lake Tana and Gondar. They have two classes of music: "songs of an intimate nature," sung by "small groups without drum accompaniment," and "larger community ensembles, . . . accompanied by drums" (Gottlieb n.d.:I).

Their five-stringed lyre (*sangwe*) has a more bowl-shaped resonator than the Ingassana lyre. Gottlieb mentions three tunings: d_2–e_1–g_1–$b\flat_1$; d_1–e_1–g_1–$b_1\downarrow$–D_2; D_1–$F_1\downarrow$–g_1–a_1–d_2. Three or four gourds (*pina* or *penah*) accompany the songs with lyre. Each gourd has a hole at each end; the player blows or hums into the one at the bottom. Such an ensemble accompanies the exorcism dance (*moshembe da*), "performed to free a sick person or a house from evil spirits" (Ismail 1980:328). Another ensemble is the women's *ba tum-tum*; while singing to it, some women beat on kitchen utensils made of gourds, and others clap their hands.

The *kome-m'dinga* ensemble provides music for light recreation with singing and dancing. It consists of ten end-blown vertical flutes (*kome*) and a large barrel drum (*m'dinga*), played on both sides with the hands. The *kome-m'dinga* is one of the one-pitch wind ensembles typical of the region:

> The shapes of the kome and the timbres produced are unusual. Each instrument is tapered. Its width gradually diminishes towards the lower end. The inner-bore is also tapered this same way. In addition, a very tiny hole is pierced through the bottom end of each instrument. This is important as it produces the shrill timbre which is considered to be aesthetically pleasing. (Gottlieb n.d.:I:5–6)

A trumpet (*trumba*), made of animal horn or aluminum, serves for signaling. One ensemble of *kome* had this scale (from the highest to the lowest pitch): 267–151–376– 322–240–231–360–358–198 cents (Gottlieb n.d.:I).

At special occasions (death, epidemics, war), Gumuz villagers perform examples of another important genre (*gaya* 'song'), in call-and-response technique between a lead singer and a group. Two clay kettledrums (*nagara: duma*, a small one; *sarma*, a large one), each beaten by one player with a wooden stick, accompany the singing. The barrel drum (*m'dinga*) joins this ensemble.

The Berta (also Bertha, Bartha, Bęrta) live south of Ed Damazin in the southernmost part of the Blue Nile Province. A part of the Berta lives beyond the border, within the Ethiopian Governorate-General of Wallāga, which calls them "Bela Shangul." Doing research among the Sudanese Berta in 1982 and 1983, I could not miss the superimposition of the Arab language and Islam. The main classes of their traditional music are songs with the lyre (*abangarang, abaŋgaraŋ*); *waza*, the music of the *waza* trumpet ensemble; *bɔlo shuru*, the music of the *bɔlo* flute ensemble; *bal naggaro* (Arabic *naqqāra*, Amharic *nagārit*), the music of *bal* flutes and the drum *naggaro*; and dance songs for the harvest festival, *hokke* (Simon 1989b).

The *waza* trumpet ensemble is the most distinguished instrumental music of the Berta (figure 7). The ensembles I recorded consisted of ten to twelve trumpets. One person owns and keeps in his house the whole set, with percussion sticks (*bali, baali*). *Waza* music and the *bal naggaro* must have related to former rulership or *mek*-chieftainship, and later to the class of the *waṭāwīṭ*, and maybe also to the *jellāba* here and there. The strong symbolism of the *waza*, however, has disappeared from the areas I visited. A whole village enjoys every performance, which usually takes place after sunset. A crowd of villagers joins the musicians as a company of singers and dancers, who perform *waza* at public or communal events, and at family festivities celebrated on a larger scope. They do not perform it during the rainy season.

The *waza* are conical trumpets, which vary from about 50 to 180 centimeters long. Each trumpet consists of conical segments of calabashes, telescoped together, and held in place by pieces of bamboo and ropes. A complete set consists of ten trumpets, divided into two sets (trumpets 1 to 5, and 6 to 10). The leading instrument of the set is the first trumpet, *wazalu* 'head of the *waza*'. One or two higher-pitched instruments, the *mušāhir* 'announcer, proclaimer', can join the ensemble. These trumpets are the only ones with an Arabic name. The additions they play are not important for building up the typical structure of *waza* music.

Several percussive instruments accompany the trumpets. The most important are the *bali*, played by trumpeters 1 to 5. The *bali* is a wooden crotch, carried over the right shoulder, and beaten with a cow horn (*buluŋ*). The player holds the trumpet with the left hand, and the horn with the right. Another instrument is a calabash rattle (*asɛzaghu, asɔso*), played by trumpeter 7. Some women, who participate as singers and dancers, wear leg rattles made of dried fruits (*atitish*). Sticks and rattles provide the basic beats or pulses.

FIGURE 7   A *waza* trumpet group of the Berta, playing at a circumcision feast, near Gessan (Blue Nile Province), 1983.

At a performance I recorded, the flutists and the singers (both women and men) formed a circle, and then moved counterclockwise.

A performance of a *waza* begins with a woman's singing once or twice the tune the ensemble is going to play. Then the trumpeters try to find their starting points. If this is to produce a single melody, nearly every player must have another starting point or pattern of impact. The *wazalu* player opens by starting to beat the elementary pulses on his *bali*, and begins to play his part, usually starting at the beginning of the timeline pattern. Next, trumpeter 2 starts playing a cross-rhythm against the *wazalu*, and so on.

The composition "*Aba Musa ladoya* 'Greetings by Aba Musa'" has a complex structure. Both groups, high and low, nearly coincide. Additional trumpeters, 01 and 02, reinforce the *wazalu* and the second trumpet. The singers have offbeat phrasing. For trumpets numbered 01, 02, and from 1 to 10, the following patterns develop; the asterisked starting points yield patterns in cross-rhythm.

Trumpet	Pattern	Starting Point
01	6+3+3 (4+2+3+3)	1
02	3+6+3	12 *
1	6+6	1
2	3+3+3+3	12 *
3	3+3+6	1
4	12 (9+3)	10
5	3+3+3+3	12 *
6	6+6	1
7	3+3+3+3	12 *
8	3+3+6	1
9	8+4	2 *
10	3+3+3+3	12 *

The transcription (figure 8) notates in horizontal lines the impacts of each instrument. The vertical lines mark the elementary pulses, and the number 12 gives the duration of the timeline pattern. It is principally a nondurational notation, because it notates only the impacts or starting points of the tones; it circles the main notes of the melody the instruments play.

The *bal naggaro* 'flute drum' is an ensemble of ten to twenty-one end-blown flutes. The *bal* are stopped, and have no finger holes; their material is a special kind of bamboo. Each plays one pitch. The kettledrums come from the Ethiopian area. In the Funj Sultanate and in Ethiopia, they have been a symbol of status and rulership; the *bal naggaro* ensemble has also had the same function. The instruments could be played only with their owner's consent. The music, however, in honor of the *mek* or his guests, served as entertainment for all participants. At a performance I recorded, the flutists and the singers (both women and men) formed a circle, and then moved

FIGURE 8   Transcription of "*Aba Musa ladoya*
'Greetings by Aba Musa'," a *waza* composition
of the Berta.

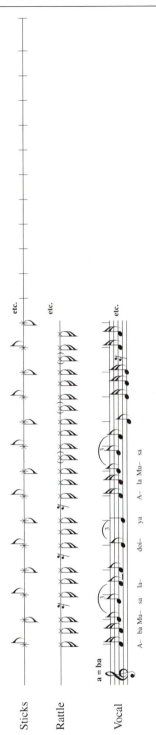

Nyikaya, the mother of Nyikang, is the spirit of a crocodile in the Nile. Because she serves as patron saint of newborns, barren women appeal to her for help.

counterclockwise. Sometimes they changed direction by dancing a figure eight. The flutists arranged themselves in tonal sequence. The drummer stood in the middle of the circle, beating the drum with two sticks. Some women shook a rattle.

The tuning is pentatonic, but not equipentatonic. Intervals are either small (in a range from 189 to 272 cents), or large (in a range from 286 to 409 cents). The technique of ensemble playing and the strucure of the resulting music are the same as in *waza* music. The impacts of the one-pitched flutes link together, to build up melodic progressions, which usually coincide with choral singing, but countermelodies also occur.

Another flute ensemble with stopped one-pitched flutes without fingerholes is the *bɔlo shuru*, which consists of two main groups of 2×4 flutes with several optional lower flutes.

White Nile: Shilluk, Dinka

Nilotic peoples (Shilluk or Colo, Dinka, Nuer) inhabit the area of the White Nile. Their rich music cultures are nearly nondocumented. The missionary Wilhelm Hofmayr published a chapter on songs, music, and dance of the Colo (1925), and I made an unpublished collection of recordings (Museum für Völkerkunde Berlin, Phonogrammarchiv, Abteilung Musikethnologie: Simon Sudan 1980:M 25.233–372). Useful information appears in publications of A. N. Tucker (1932, 1933a, 1933b), in three records of traditional Dinka music (Deng 1976a, 1976b, 1976c), and in a book of Dinka song texts (Deng 1973).

The Shilluk (or Colo, as they call themselves) live mainly on the western bank of the White Nile, approximately between Kaka and Tonga. The head of the Colo is a king (*reth*). The thirty-third king, Ayang, traces his genealogy back to Nyikang, the first king, who led the Colo into the present region of settlement, and whom the people worship. Many songs praise his deeds and those of historical kings. Such songs use the lyre (*tom*) as an accompanying instrument. As in the north, it has five strings. In contrast to the northern plectrum techniques, the Shilluk pluck the strings one by one, with the fingers, in the African style.

The Colo have a strong ceremonial life, accompanied by songs and dances—dances of warriors, of the king's women, and of women at death ceremonies. The Colo distinguish three kinds of dance ceremonies: pleading or raindances (*tom*); festival dances (*bul*); and funeral or memorial dances (*ywok*), performed at *koje*-feasts. *Tom*, ordinarily the name for the lyre, is here the name for the holy drum, which accompanies only religious and royal dances. One highlight of such dances is the point when priests (*baret*) become possessed by Nyikang's spirit (Hofmayr 1925:497).

The *bul,* named for the accompanying drum, are mainly for the entertainment of younger people. Young men dance with wooden dance clubs. Singers include young female lead singers and a chorus. The *bul* is a long conical drum, played on

FIGURE 9   Colo women dancing the *ywok*, a memorial dance for a deceased man, at a *koje* feast; the widow beats the *bul*.

both ends; a smaller cylindrical or conical drum has the same name. Among the royal drums are two small kettledrums (*leleng, lelɛŋ*).

At a *koje* I witnessed, the widow beat a *bul* while female relatives danced with the belongings and spears of her late husband (figure 9). The next day, many activities happened simultaneously. In the afternoon, as warring units from other villages approached, marching and singing toward the dance ground, female relatives danced around the village. Men blew signals on the traditional *adalo* (horn of a kudu or a waterbuck, with a lateral mouthhole and a calabash for a bell) and on a *kang* (a small, metal trumpet, originating in Omdurman). While the *adalo* produced a long, deep, muffled sound, a military signal was blown on the *kang*, and female wailers were moaning at the grave. To the warriors' songs (in call-and-response structure), volleys of rifle fire added noise.

Another Colo religious ceremony accompanied by songs is the Nyikaya ceremony. Nyikaya, the mother of Nyikang, is the spirit of a crocodile in the Nile. Because she serves as patron saint of newborns, barren women appeal to her for help. In accompanying songs addressed to her, people put into the water the halves of a calabash, and beat them with their hands.

An important institution of Colo society is the bard, a poet-composer-singer-lyrist (*ček, wau*). The most esteemed bards are those who praise the king and his predecessors (figure 10).

The Dinka distinguish several classes of song: ox songs; "cathartic songs" (complaints); age set insult songs; initiation songs; war songs, owned by the warring unit; women's songs; songs in tales; children's play songs; religious hymns addressed to a deity, spirits, or ancestors; and school songs (Deng 1973). Among these, the praise songs for an ox have special importance for individual Dinka: young men praise their oxen, and young women praise their husbands' or boyfriends' animals (Deng 1976a:2). In certain war dances, the ox serves as a symbol of wealth: a dancing man forms with his arms the horns of a bull. A large drum (*loor*) and a small one (*leng*) accompany war dances.

FIGURE 10   A Colo bard plays the *tom*.

Singing and dancing for the Dinka are skills of splendor in which a person finds profound gratification and elation. The vigor and the rhythm with which they stamp the ground, the grace with which they run in war dances, the height to which they jump, the manner of pride and self-esteem with which they bear themselves,

One of the best of the early popular singers was Abdallah Al-Mahi, who in 1929 traveled to Cairo, where he made the first gramophone recording of Sudanese music.

and the way in which the high-pitched solo receives the loud unified response of the chorus combine to give the Dinka a euphoria that is hard to describe. As the singing stops, the drums beat even louder, the dance reaches its climax, and every individual, gorged with a feeling of self-fulfillment, begins to chant words of self-exaltation. (Deng 1976a:2)

Musical instruments of the south
Bongo, Azande, Ndogo

Georg Schweinfurth, who traversed the southwestern region of the Sudan between 1868 and 1871, gave a description of musical instruments. He said (1873:314) the Bongo, living north of the Azande, in an area east and south of Rumbek, were passionate musicians. A later monograph on the Bongo (Kronenberg and Kronenberg 1981) lists and depicts most of the instruments he mentioned.

An extraordinary Bongo instrument is the large wooden trumpet *mandjindji*, mostly anthropomorphic, with a carved head on its top (Kronenberg and Kronenberg 1981: figures 82–84, 100–101); its origin seems to be connected with satirical songs (*ngoyo*) and clan feuds, because they represent an enemy (1981:80). When people play it in public, the mockery against a person increases. However, the Kronenbergs (1981: figure 102) say three drums and two of these trumpets usually accompany Bongo dances.

The Bongo probably adopted from the Azande the *kundi* 'harp'. Also anthropomorphic, this is the most exceptional Zande instrument. In the international art trade, older pieces fetch high prices. Zande harp music was first analyzed by Kubik (1964, 1983); Giorgetti (1965) commented on it. The tuning of the *kundi* as published by Kubik is approximately anhemitonic pentatonic: e_1–d_1–c_1–a–g. Giorgetti published other tunings (1965).

The log xylophone (*kpáníngbá, kpaningbo, kpäningbä*) with usually twelve to fourteen keys, has the same tuning. Different from this type of xylophone is the Ndogo *rongo*, with long gourds as resonators. Other Azande instruments are a lamellophone (*kondi*), also played by the Moro, and a slit drum (*gugu*).

CITY MUSIC

Between 1900 and 1950, a new urban music developed in Khartoum and Omdurman (Simon 1991). It was an amalgamation of traditional Sudanese, Egyptian-Arabic, and European elements. In the 1980s, it felt the influence of international pop genres (such as reggae). The basic musical structure, melodic conception, rhythm, phrasing, and vocal intonation, form the basis of Sudanese style. Styles of ensemble playing, and certain musical instruments (Arabian lute, drums, violin), are an Egyptian contribution; other instruments (accordion, guitar, electric guitar, electric bass, transverse flute, saxophones, electric keyboards, synthesizers) came from Europe and other industrial countries.

Around 1900, new social and economic institutions (plantations, trading companies, European administration, post, military, schools) brought together people of different ethnic traditions. Arabic was their lingua franca. The bookshop Al-Bazar as-Sudani, the newspaper *Khadarat as-Sudan*, and Gordon's College (founded in 1902, the first college Sudanese could attend) provided the basis for urban culture.

The first musicians propagating an urban popular style were singers who accompanied themselves with wooden sticks, soon replaced by the Egyptian *riqq*. One of the best of them was Abdallah Al-Mahi, who in 1929 traveled to Cairo, where he made the first gramophone recording of Sudanese music. There, the musicians became familiar with other instruments, such as *al-ʿūd*, violin, accordion, and *tabla* (*darabukka*).

In the 1920s, another setting for urban music was the private circles of poets and music lovers. The *ramyah*, a vocal introduction in free rhythm, was fashionable. The most popular singer of this tradition was Serror, who worked with the poet Ibrahim al-Abadi. Serror accompanied himself on the *tanbūr*; at the end of the 1920s, he also used newly introduced instruments.

A central personality of the new music was Khalil Farah. After listening to records of Egyptian singers (including Abdu al-Khamouli and Sayyed Darwish), he decided to buy a lute and learn how to play it. An engineer at the telegraph office in Khartoum, he never performed in public. His friends, including Al-Amin Burhan, popularized his compositions.

At that time, Cairo was already a center of the recording industry in the Middle East. After 1925, stores in Khartoum also sold records, record players, and the new instruments. In 1931, Serror and Khalil Farah made recordings in Cairo, the latter accompanied by lute, piano, and violin. Soon after, coffee shops in Khartoum played their records. Businessmen began to produce more records, with Sudanese singers (including the men Ibrahim Abdul Jalil, An-Naim Muhammed Nur, Karoma, Al-Amin Burhan, and Ali Shaigui, and the women Mary Sharif, Asha Falatiya, and Mahla al-Abadiya). They were accompanied by lute, accordion, piano, violin, flute, *riqq, tabla*, and (later) bongos. Other famous artists of that period were Zingar, Ismail Abdel Muʿain, Hassan Atya, and Awonda. The first concert of city music took place in 1938.

On 9 April 1940, Radio Omdurman began broadcasting. It produced a weekly program of city music produced on records. After 1945, technological developments led to changes in the instrumental ensemble, which added electric guitars, basses, and organs. The lute, however, remained the most prominent instrument.

There is a characteristic Sudanese style of lute playing, which individuals adapt to their tastes. The style of Muhammed El Amin has influenced many young musicians. With subtlety and intuition, he ranks among the famous artists of late twentieth-century Sudanese music. He is the prominent representative of *al-aġānī al-kabīra* 'the great songs'. Long introductions, played by the instrumental ensemble, postpone and prepare the star's entrance; they increase tension, which, as soon the soloist starts singing, applause releases.

In 1969, the Institute for Music and Drama opened, under the direction of Mahi Ismail. At this institute most professional musicians—Abdel Aziz El Mubarak, Abdel Gadir Salim, and above all, the musicians of the accompanying ensembles—studied. The size of these ensembles varies according to economic conditions. The orchestra of Radio Omdurman consists of one lute, ten to fifteen violins, an electric bass or double bass, two violoncelli, electric guitars, keyboards, saxophones, flute, and drums.

Ensemble playing follows a melodic and heterophonic conception, with chordal interspersings here and there. Typical for these arrangements is a bass that practically

"One song was about a waterwheel which went round and round the whole time. The singer used this as a symbol for the government, which just like a poor blindfolded camel or bull keeps on going round in circles."

follows the melody. Most of the texts are about love, though many of them bear an undercurrent of criticism.

Sometimes, though, you could get away with doing songs that were so subtly written that it took a while for them [the censors] to tumble to their meaning. When the authorities finally realised what they were about, of course, they'd take them off the air. One song, which was broadcast many times, was about a waterwheel which went round and round the whole time. The singer used this as a symbol for the government, which just like a poor blindfolded camel or bull keeps on going round in circles. It was played on radio and television for a while before it was banned. (Mahi Ismail in Kilby 1986:68)

"*Nura,*" one of the famous songs of Mohamed Gubara, is a political song on a text by Mohamed Al Hassan Salim. It names a girl, but on another level betokens the country.

The song talks of how beautiful she is, in her soul; how she is always helping other people and will feed others before she feeds herself. She became ill and the traditional medicine men treated her with such cruelty, by burning her with fire, but she survived that. Once she had a dream and in this dream she saw a bird eating its baby; she saw a thief who had become worshipped as a god. And when she told people about her dream, they said she has lost her mind. What the song is trying to say is that people who are running the country are misusing it—they think that they help but they always do the wrong thing like the traditional medicine people, they just apply more suffering and pain. (Yassin and Benhassine 1986)

City music is a twentieth-century creation of Sudanese musicians. It is difficult to say something about its future development, and, above all, if it can resist other pop music influences coming from outside of the Sudan.

REFERENCES

Baumann, Gerd. 1987. *National Integration and Local Integrity: The Miri of the Nuba Mountains in the Sudan.* Oxford: Oxford University Press.

Beaton, A. C. 1940. "Fur Dance Songs." *Sudan Notes and Records* 23:302–329.

Carlisle, Roxane. 1975. "Women Singers in Darfur, Sudan Republic." *The Black Perspective in Music* 3(3):253–268.

Corkill, N. L. 1939. "The Kambala and Other Seasonal Festivals of the Kadugli and Miri Nuba." *Sudan Notes and Records* 22:205–219.

Daw, Ali al-, and Abd-Alla Muhammad. 1985. *Traditional Musical Instruments in Sudan.* Khartoum: Institute of African and Asian Studies, University of Khartoum.

———. 1988. *Al-mūsīqa al-taqlīdīya fi maǧtamaʿa al-Berta* [*Traditional Music in al-Berta Society*]. Khartoum: Institute of African and Asian Studies, University of Khartoum.

Deng, Francis Mading. 1973. *The Dinka and Their Songs.* Oxford: Oxford University Press.

———. 1976a. *Music of the Sudan: The Role of Songs and Dance in Dinka Society: 1. War Songs and Hymns.* New York: Ethnic Folkways Records FE 4301.

———. 1976b. *Music of the Sudan: The Role of Songs and Dance in Dinka Society: 2. Women's Dance Songs.* New York: Ethnic Folkways Records FE 4302.

————. 1976c. *Music of the Sudan: The Role of Songs and Dance in Dinka Society: 3. Burial Hymns and War Songs*. New York: Ethnic Folkways Records FE 4303.

Dixon, David M. 1971. "A Note on Kushite Contact with the South." In *Music and History in Africa*, ed. Klaus Wachsmann, 135–139. Evanston, Ill.: Northwestern University Press.

Dixon, David, and Klaus Wachsmann. 1964. "A Sandstone Statue of an Auletes from Meroë." *Kush* 12:119–125.

Emsheimer, Ernst, and Albrecht Schneider. 1986. "Field Work among the Hadendowa of the Sudan." *Anuario Musical* 39/40:173–188.

Giorgetti, Filiberto. 1951. *Note di Musica Zande*. Verona: Museum Combonianum N.5. Missioni Africane.

————. 1965. "Zande Harp Music." *African Music* 3(4):74–76.

Gottlieb, Robert. N.d. *Sudan I: Music of the Blue Nile Province: The Gumuz Tribe*. Cassel: Bärenreiter Musicaphon BM 30L 2312).

————. N.d. *Sudan II: The Ingessana and Berta Tribes*. Cassel: Bärenreiter Musicaphon BM 30L 2313.

Hai, Mohamed Abdel. 1982. *Cultural Policy in the Sudan*. Paris: UNESCO Press. Studies and Documents on Cultural Policies.

Hickmann, Hans, and Charles Grégoire Duc de Mecklembourg. 1958. *Catalogue d'Enregistrements de Musique Folklorique Égyptienne*. Strassburg and Baden-Baden: Ed. Heitz.

Hofmayr, Wilhelm. 1925. *Die Schilluk*. Mödling and Wien: Anthropos.

Ibrahim, Hayder. 1979. *The Shaiqiya: The Cultural and Social Change of a Northern Sudanese Riverain People*. Wiesbaden: Steiner Verlag.

Ismail, Mahi. 1970. "Musical Traditions in the Sudan." *La Revue Musicale* 288/289:87–93.

————. 1980. "Sudan." *The New Grove Dictionary of Music and Musicians*, ed. Stanley Sadie. London: Macmillan.

Kennedy, John G. 1967. "Nubian Zar Ceremonies as Psychotherapy." *Human Organization* 26(4):185–194.

Kilby, Jak. 1986. "Sounds of the Nile (Interview with Mahi Ismail)." *Africa Events* March:67–69.

Kronenberg, Waltraut, and Andreas Kronenberg. 1981. *Die Bongo*. Wiesbaden: Steiner Verlag.

Kubik, Gerhard. 1964. "Harp Music of the Azande and Related Peoples in the Central African Republic." *African Music* 3(3):37–76.

————. 1982. *Ostafrika*. Leipzig: VEB Deutscher Verlag für Musik. Musikgeschichte in Bildern I, 10.

————. 1983. "Kognitive Grundlagen afrikanischer Musik." In *Musik in Afrika*, ed. Artur Simon, 327–400. Berlin: Museum für Völkerkunde.

Schweinfurth, Georg A. 1873. *In the Heart of Africa: Three Years' Travels and Adventures in the Unexplored Regions of Central Africa from 1868–1871*. London: S. Low, Marsten, Low, and Searle.

Simon, Artur. 1975a. Dahab—ein blinder Sänger Nubiens. Musik und Gesellschaft im Nordsudan. In Baessler-Archiv N. F. 23. Berlin (1975):159–194. Reprinted in *Musik in Afrika*, ed. Artur Simon, 260–283. Berlin: Museum für Völkerkunde.

————. 1975b. "Islamische und afrikanische Elemente in der Musik des Nordsudan am Beispiel des ḏikr." *Hamburger Jahrbuch für Musikwissenschaft* 1:249–278.

————. 1980a. "Musikstile und Musikleben im Nordsudan." *Bericht über den musikwissenschaftlichen Kongress Berlin 1974* Cassel:Bärenreiter Verlag, 618–622.

————. 1980b. Musik der Nubier / Nordsudan (Music of the Nubians / Northern Sudan). Beiheft zu 2 Schallplatten, Text-und Musikübertragungen. Museum Collection Berlin MC 9. Berlin.

————. 1980c. *Ḏikr und Madih. Gesänge und Zeremonien. Islamisches Brauchtum im Sudan*. Berlin: Museum Collection Berlin MC 10.

————, ed. 1983a. *Musik in Afrika*. Berlin: Museum für Völkerkunde.

————. 1983b. "Musik in afrikanischen Besessenheitsriten." In *Musik in Afrika*, ed. Artur Simon, 284–296. Berlin: Museum für Völkerkunde.

————. 1989a. "Musical Traditions, Islam and Cultural Identity in the Sudan." In *Perspectives on African Music*, ed. W. Bender, 25–41. Bayreuth: Bayreuth African Studies, Series 9.

————. 1989b. "Trumpet and Flute Ensembles of the Berta People in the Sudan." In *African Musicology: Current Trends*, ed. Jacqueline C. Djedje and William G. Carter, 1:183–217. Los Angeles: Crossroad Press (Festschrift J. H. K. Nketia).

————. 1991. "Sudan City Music." In *Populäre Musik in Afrika*, ed. Veit Erlmann, 165–180. Berlin: Museum für Völkerkunde.

Trimingham, J. Spencer. 1949. *Islam in the Sudan*. London: Oxford University Press.

Tucker, A. N. 1932. "Music in South Sudan." *Man* 32:18–19.

————. 1933a. "Children's Games and Songs in the Southern Sudan." *Journal of the Royal Anthropological Institute of Great Britain and Ireland* 63:165–187.

————. 1933b. *Tribal Music and Dancing in the Southern Sudan (Africa) at Social and Ceremonial Gatherings*. London: W. Reeves.

Wegner, Ulrich. 1984. *Afrikanische Saiteninstrumente*. Berlin: Museum für Völkerkunde.

Yassin, H. M., and Amel Benhassine. 1986. *Sounds of Sudan, Vol.3: Mohamed Gubara*. London: Record World Circuit, WCB 005.

Zenkovsky, S. 1950. "Zar and Tambura as Practiced by the Women of Omdurman." *Sudan Notes and Records* 31:65–85.

Tuareg Music
Caroline Card Wendt

The Musical Culture
The *Anzad*
The *Tende*
Musical Curing Ceremonies
The *Tahardent*
Other Instruments
Other Vocal Genres
Dance Traditions

For more than a thousand years, Saharan travelers have reported encounters with the Tuareg people. From the pens of Arab and European explorers come tales of tall, veiled, camel-riding warriors who once commanded the trade routes from the Mediterranean to sub-Saharan Africa. Most of the reports dwell on the appearance and ferocity of the warriors, but those who looked more closely noted distinctive cultural traits, such as matrilineal kinship and high status among unveiled women, rarities in the Muslim world. As Saharan travel became easier, observers from many backgrounds—missionaries, militaries, colonial administrators, traders, scholars, tourists—ventured among the Tuareg and reported their findings. The result is a large, varied, and often contradictory, body of literature.

The name *Tuareg*, a term outsiders conferred on the people, suggests a sociopolitical unity that has probably never existed. The people constitute eight large units or confederations, each composed of peoples and tribal groups with varying degrees of autonomy. These groups and their locations are: Kel Ahaggar (Ahaggar mountains and surrounding area in southern Algeria, southward to the plains of Tamesna in northern Niger); Kel Ajjer (Tassili n-Ajjer region of southeastern Algeria, eastward into southwestern Libya); Kel Aïr (Aïr mountains of northern Niger, and plains to the west and south); Kel Geres (southern Niger, south of Aïr); Kel Adrar (Adrar n-Foras mountains of Mali, southwest of Ahaggar); Iwllimmedan Kel Dennek, or "eastern Iwllimmedan" (plains between Tawa and In-Gal in western Niger); Iwllimmedan Kel Ataram, or "western Iwllimmedan" (along the Niger River, southwestern Niger); Kel Tademaket (along the bend of the Niger River, between Timbuktu and Gao, Mali). The word *Kel* denotes sovereign status.

Censuses, like much other information on the Tuareg, show little agreement. In addition to the difficulties of conducting a census in the Sahara is the question of Tuareg identity. Lloyd Cabot Briggs dealt with the problem by limiting his work to an estimated ten to twelve thousand Tuareg in the "Sahara proper," excluding large numbers in the south, whom he regarded as assimilated in varying degrees with sub-Saharan peoples and thus not "true Tuareg" (Briggs 1960:124). Most surveys, however, have included the southern Tuareg: Francis Nicolas estimated the population at 500,000 (1950:foreword, n.p.), Henri Lhote at 300,000 (1955:157), and George

Peter Murdock at 286,000 (1959:405–406). The differences in these and other estimates arise in part from divergent opinions on whom to count. Some observers regarded as "true" Tuareg only the camel-herding warrior-nomads (*imuhagh, imajaghan, imushagh*), often called nobles, who formerly held the dominant position within the social hierarchy. More commonly, scholars have included the subordinate goatherds (*imghad*, or Kel Ulli), sometimes called vassals, who physically and culturally resemble the dominant Caucasoid Tuareg. Only occasionally have observers paid attention to the artisans (*inadan*), including those specializing in music, whose origins are uncertain and whose social position is often ambiguous. Not until late in the 1900s did the designation *Tuareg* extend to Negroid agricultural and domestic workers, descendants of formerly subjugated peoples, who live among or in association with the pastoral Tuareg, sharing their language, identity, and many aspects of culture. Late-twentieth-century governmental estimates of the population, reflecting an official emphasis on national unity, usually ignore ethnic divisions, and therefore offer few specific data on the Tuareg and other minorities.

The question of identity is further compounded by regional differences in self-designated terms. The regional cognates *imuhagh, imajaran,* and *imushagh,* for example, vary as to whom they include (Card 1982:30–34). Tuareg musical traditions and other cultural traits vary by region. The dialects of the Berber language spoken by the Tuareg—*tamahaq* (north), *tamajag* (south), *tamashaq* (west)—are sufficiently different as to be mutually unintelligible to many speakers.

Countering the cultural diversity is the cohesion generated by a set of ancient ideals and values flowing from the nomadic traditions that form the society's cultural core. The heroic images reach outward from their source, endowing on all within their sphere a shared identity and the legacy of a glorious past. The perseverance of the Tuareg as a people has been due less, perhaps, to the prowess of its warriors than to the ability of the dominant group to impose its culture on others. Thus, Tuareg identity endures, only slightly diminished by the cessation of warfare and raiding, economic hardship, and loss of sovereignty. Ancient values, expressed in modified forms, continue to give Tuareg culture its character.

THE MUSICAL CULTURE

Music occupies a prominent position in the social, political, and ceremonial life of the Tuareg. It plays an important role in celebrations of birth, adulthood, and marriage, and in religious festivals, customs of courtship, and rituals of curing. It is the focus of many informal social gatherings. Tuareg music and poetry are well developed arts: some traditions reach far into the cultural past. The Tuareg highly esteem the verbal arts, of which they consider music an extension; and they recognize and respect outstanding composers and performers. They look down on professionalism, in the sense of a livelihood earned from musical performance; it is limited to specialized members within the artisanal caste. Musical ability, however, wherever it emerges, does not go unrecognized, and the people much admire skillful musicians of all social ranks.

Most Tuareg music is vocal; but much includes instruments, primarily a one-stringed fiddle (*anzad*), a mortar drum (*tende*), and a three-stringed plucked lute (*tahardent*). Though few in kind and number, these instruments have greater cultural significance than their quantity might suggest, for each has an association with specific poetic genres and styles of performance, and each serves as the focal point of particular social events.

THE *ANZAD*

The one-stringed fiddle (*imzad* in northern dialect, *anzad* in southern, *anzhad* in western), played only by women, is basic to the traditional culture. Its use has

anzad   One-stringed fiddle of the Tuareg,
         played by women

ahal   A courtship gathering that features love
        songs, poetical recitations, jokes, and
        games of wit

declined markedly since about 1900, but it continues to enjoy a symbolic place in the culture. The Tuareg have long believed it a mighty force for good, a power capable of giving strength to men and of inspiring them to heroic deeds. Its playing formerly encouraged men in battle and ensured their safe return; in the late 1900s, women play it, though much less often, for the benefit of men working or studying in distant places. For all Tuareg listeners, its music evokes images of love and beauty. Charles de Foucauld, foremost among early Tuareg scholars and field workers, eloquently summarizes Tuareg feelings about it:

> The *imzad* is the favored musical instrument, preeminently noble and elegant; it is preferred above all others, sung of in verse, and yearned for by those absent from the land it symbolizes and the sweetness it recalls. (Foucauld 1951–1952, trans.)

Much of its power was in reality the power of the women who played it. Tuareg society required repeated recognition of heroic acts, and constant revalidation of the behavioral ideals that motivated them; its melodies and accompanying songs of praise were a potent force toward that end. In 1864, warriors in combat strove always to act courageously, lest their women deprive them of music: the prospect of silent fiddles on their return renewed their courage in the face of defeat (Duvéyrier 1864:450; see also Lhote 1955:329).

To play the *anzad* well requires years of practice. The Tuareg say a woman cannot acquire the necessary skill under the age of about thirty. Formerly, a mature woman of talent and imagination could command respect, and if she combined these endowments with noble lineage, she would enjoy high status. Tuareg women of all social levels have been known to play the instrument, but it was mainly those of the camel-herding warrior aristocracy with slaves to attend them who had the leisure to learn to play the instrument well. In the early 1900s, during the economic decline that followed a defeat by the French and the abolition of slavery, most women of noble lineage lost this advantage over their lower-born sisters; and consequently, the number of highly accomplished fiddlers diminished. The end of warfare as a noble occupation probably reduced some of the incentive to play, for the Tuareg look upon most types of modern work as degrading and little worthy of celebration in music and poetry.

In addition to its significance in the ethos of warfare, the *anzad* symbolizes youthfulness and romantic love. Musical evenings with it usually continue to function as occasions for unattached young people's courting. An *ahal* 'courtship gathering' features love songs, poetical recitations, jokes, and games of wit. Presiding over the event is an *anzad* player, whose renown may attract visitors from far away. So closely associated is the *anzad* with the *ahal* that "the name of one brings to mind the other." Attendance at an *ahal* carries no shame, but discretion requires that young people not mention the word *ahal* in the presence of their elders. For similar reasons, they must speak the word *anzad* discreetly (Foucauld 1951–1952:1270–71).

For religious leaders among the Tuareg, who are mostly Muslim, the *anzad* distracts the mind from thoughts of Allah and the teachings of Muhammad. They claim it aggrandizes the position of women and encourages licentious behavior. Worse, the mystical powers they believe the instrument and its music contain do not derive from their scriptures, but hark back to animistic beliefs. They therefore discourage fiddling; in some communities, they forbid it. Responding to the demands of fundamentalist movements, some elders who played the fiddle in their youth have voluntarily put it aside. Instead of claiming the celebrated role of musical and social leader that might once have been theirs, they have chosen a more submissive and pious role. For centuries, the preservation of Tuareg culture has rested with women, whose undisputed authority on cultural matters was enough to counteract most outside influences. The undermining of that authority thus threatens, not only the *anzad* tradition, but the continuity of all Tuareg traditions.

According to context and point of view, the *anzad* has diverse meanings. It symbolizes intellectual and spiritual purity and traditional behavioral ideals. It connotes gallantry, love, sensuousness, and youth. It evokes images of a distant, pre-Islamic past. The traditions surrounding it reflect the high status of Tuareg women, unusual in the Muslim world. Yet within this diversity there is no contradiction: the *anzad* is a multifaceted symbol of Tuareg culture and identity.

Techniques of construction and playing

The *anzad* is a one-stringed bowed lute, commonly found among West African peoples (DjeDje 1980:1–8). The name, glossable as 'hair', refers to the substance of the string. The body of the instrument is a hollow gourd 25 to 40 centimeters in diameter, cut to form a bowl. Tightly stretched leather, usually goatskin, covers the opening; lacings usually attach it to the gourd. A slender stick, inserted under the leather top at opposite edges, extends 30 to 36 centimeters beyond the body on one side, and serves as a neck. One or two large sound holes—the number varying with local tradition—are cut into the leather near the perimeter of the gourd. The string, formed of about forty strands of horsehair, is attached at each end of the inserted stick. Short twigs, crossed and bound with leather, positioned beneath the string near the center of the skin surface, form a bridge. As the string tightens, the neck arches forward. The bow consists of a slender stick, held in an arc by the tension of the attached hair. To improve contact, people rub resin on both bow hair and string. In the northern regions, people often finger-paint the fiddle and the bow with colorful geometric designs; such decoration is rare in the south, though some instruments sport ornamental leather fringes. Players tune the instrument by moving a leather strip that binds the string to the neck near the tip, thereby adjusting the length of the vibrating portion of the string. Players vary in choosing a pitch for tuning the string; but from one performance to another, a player's pitches are consistent.

The player sits, holding the fiddle in her lap with the neck in her left hand. Rarely during the performance of a single piece does she change the position of her hand, though she may do so in preparation for another piece, using her thumb as a stop to effect a new tuning without changing the tension of the string. She fingers the string with a light touch. (Women do not try to press the string to the neck, which does not function as a fingerboard.) By extension of the little finger, the performer can readily gain access to the secondary harmonic, which sounds an octave above the open string. A few performers employ additional harmonics. By exerting light pressure on the string, they produce brilliant tones, and can increase the pitch

Many Tuareg think the *anzad* originated in Ahaggar, the northernmost Tuareg region, now a part of Algeria; and it undoubtedly has deep roots in the region's warrior traditions.

range beyond an octave. The result is a rich musical texture, a kaleidoscope of tone colors.

To exploit the instrument's imitative possibilities, a skillful fiddler may vary the speed and length of the bow strokes. Slow strokes combined with rapidly fingered notes can suggest a melismatic singing style, and short strokes paired with single notes can produce a syllabic effect. Short, light strokes coupled with harmonics may simulate the tones of a flute; rapid use of the bow in tremolo style may depict animals in flight; halting, interrupted strokes may portray a limping straggler. Storytellers use these techniques, which can support a singer's text or vocal style.

Music for solo *anzad*

The *anzad* is both a solo instrument and an accompaniment for voice. Though performers occasionally play vocal melodies as instrumental pieces, the melodies they most often perform as solos are airs (*azel*; pl. *izlan*), composed specifically for the instrument.

The styles of playing and composing for the *anzad* exhibit distinctive regional characteristics. Many Tuareg think the instrument originated in Ahaggar, the northernmost Tuareg region, now a part of Algeria; and it undoubtedly has deep roots in the region's warrior traditions. The music, often called old style, exhibits distinctive traits from an earlier period, traceable at least to the 1920s. During much of the twentieth century, to a degree not found among other groups, the Ahaggar Tuareg guarded their musical traditions against change. Domination by the French, which began about 1900, evoked a highly conservative response from the Ahaggar Tuareg—a response later intensified by opposition from the colonial government. In 1962, after Algeria attained independence, exposure to different political ideologies, educational policies, and national media intensified cultural differences between the Ahaggar Tuareg and their southern kinfolk. The division of the Tuareg into separate nationalities thus reinforced the cultural isolation of the Ahaggar Tuareg and encouraged the conservation of older musical traits and repertory (Card 1982:85–97).

Characteristic of the Ahaggar style of composition for the fiddle is a formulaic structure. Short melodic formulas, or motifs, are linked together in phrases of varying lengths. A typical unit consists of a rapid cluster of tones centered on one or more pitches. The basic unit may be further elaborated with acciaccaturas, mordents, turns, and other ornaments. Many of the melodies structured in this manner, such as "*Tihadanaran*" (figure 1), have become fixed in the repertory, with minimal variation. In Ahaggar style, rhythm is usually subordinate to melody; in many compositions, the pulse is difficult to discern.

In tribute to an old tradition that has continued to grow and change, the Tuareg describe *anzad* music in the Aïr region of Niger as "a still-flowering plant." Though French domination brought an end to traditional fighting there (as it had in Ahaggar), it did not evoke the same reactionary response. The features that distinguish the Aïr style from that of Ahaggar are due largely to individual variation, a vital part of the old *anzad* tradition that has continued to thrive in Aïr. As in Ahaggar style, rhythm is subordinate to melody, and is based on formulaic motifs; however, the units join more smoothly, to the extent that it is often more difficult to determine where one ends and another begins. The phrases tend to have simpler structures, with less profuse ornamentation. Notable, too, are long phrases of original or developed material, particularly in recent compositions. Newer pieces are often through composed, in contrast to older compositions. In general, people more readily accept musical innovations in Aïr than in Ahaggar.

In marked contrast is the rhythmic style of Azawagh, a region of Niger west of Aïr. There, *anzad* music has strongly accented rhythms, metric melody, short phrases, and regularly recurring pulses. Though the music is constructed of formulaic material, the melodic elements, unlike those of Aïr and Ahaggar, are subordinate to rhythm. Performance often has an accompaniment of hand clapping, and sometimes of dancing; both rarely occur in connection with *anzad* music elsewhere. The distinctive style and performance practices of the *anzad* tradition in Azawagh suggest an unusual degree of acculturation has occurred between the pastoral Tuareg and the region's Sudanese peoples, of whom many are former Tuareg captives or clients. In the music of other Tuareg regions, evidence of acculturation turns up, but it is more pronounced in Azawagh.

The styles discussed are but three of many regional traditions. Traits characteristic of one area often appear in another. Interregional borrowing of repertories and genres has long been a part of the *anzad* tradition.

Anzad n-asak: music for fiddle and voice

A large portion of the *anzad* repertory is designed for performance with voice. When accompanying a vocalist, the fiddler reinforces the vocal line with a heterophonic rendering of the melody. Each performer expresses it in a personal style, emphasizing different aspects of the melody or rhythm, and each makes little effort to synchronize the lines. Interludes between the strophes of the texts provide opportunities for instrumental display and for improvisation on the thematic material (figure 2). If accompanying herself, a woman may play but a single drone, reserving for the instrumental interludes a display of her musicianship. Men, however, are the preferred vocalists, and if male singers are available at a gathering, women seldom sing. It is possible that women once sang more in mixed company, for there are many references in the older literature to women's songs of praise and encouragement for warriors.

The texts constitute a genre known as *tesîwit*, which represents the highest achievement in Tuareg poetic arts. The principal subjects are love and heroism. In diction rich in imagery, the poems extol the virtues of courage in battle and gallantry in love, ever confirming the ideals of the warrior aristocracy. People may sing *tesîwit* alone, or to the accompaniment of the *anzad*; but they never sing it with any other instrument. The *anzad*, in turn, is rarely heard with other poetic genres. A *tesîwit* may take one of several meters traditional to a region; composers then set it to a new or existing melody that corresponds with the meter (Foucauld 1925:I:iii–x; Nicolas 1944:9–18). The subject matter, also regional, refers frequently to local persons and events. New texts and melodies continually come into being; the repertory retains many older ones, with the names of the composers.

The male vocal style in singing *tesîwit* is typically high pitched, tense, and much ornamented with mordents, shakes, and other graces, unlike the usual male singing of other genres. The nomadic Tuareg admire high-pitched singing, produced with high tension of the throat muscles, and singers often strain to attain the ideal. A

When accompanying a vocalist, the fiddler reinforces the vocal line with a heterophonic rendering of the melody. Each performer expresses it in a personal style, emphasizing different aspects of the melody or rhythm.

FIGURE 1 *"Tihadanaren,"* an *anzad* melody in Ahaggar style. Soloist: Bouchit bint Loki ag Amilan. Tamanrasset, Algeria, 1976.

range extending to an octave above middle C is common. When women sing *tesîwit,* they do so at a more relaxed midrange, thereby exhibiting none of the piercing quality that characterizes the style of male singers.

FIGURE 1 (continued)

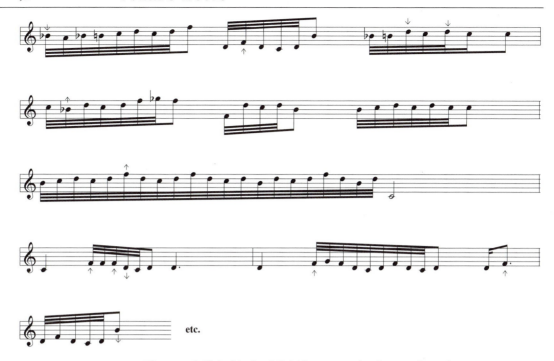

The song "*Chikeshkeshen* 'Girls'," an example of *tesîwit* from the Aïr region, conveys the anguish of a young man who feels unjustly ignored by the women of his community, for in their recognition of him as a valiant warrior lies his sense of self-worth. The text also conveys his need to reconcile the ancient values with the principles of Islam (Nikiprowetzky 1963:B1; trans. Dominique Casajus, Mahmoudan Hawad, Caroline Card).

Girls, today I am ill.
My illness is not the fever,
Nor even a pain in the stomach or a chill;
These days I do not hear my name.
Even though a great blow of the sword could not penetrate my shield,
This eats into my legs up to the calves.

When it occurs, women are indifferent to me, and
I am no longer a cause for jealousy among my age-brothers.
Unloved, my camel's spirit [my prowess] will be broken.
It will destroy my saddle [riding ability] and cut my arms,
Like breaking off the branches of an acacia tree.
I, myself, am greater than a great tree trunk, or at least equal to it.
My proud bearing is like that of the trunk of the largest acacia.

These are the words of a young man filled with pride,
Carrying at his side his gun and his threatening sword.
By day, when our enemies swept down upon our tents,
I fired the gun from behind the saplings that support the tent.
With it I put to flight hundreds of horsemen.
I with my sword, that dog of combat,
Remained standing, sword in hand, refusing to mount my steed.
By the mosques of Takreza and Aglal, and by the marabout of Rayan,
And by the one who dwells at Tin-Wasaran,
Allah, don't make me love my enemies!

tende   Mortar drum, the music performed to
         its accompaniment, and the social event
         that accompanies it

May those who hate me with a vengeance never pass my way!
They have no desire but to cut my throat.
If they cut my throat, they would be jubilant.
Let them not look to Allah to vilify me!
Let them not look to Satan to pursue me!
It is an evil spell that they have spread over the earth for me,
But I have avoided it. I have the help of the marabouts.
By heaven and earth, we are in the hands of Allah!

THE *TENDE*

The word *tende* (in northern dialect, *tindi*) refers to a mortar drum, the music performed to its accompaniment, and the social event that features it. Though the
Tuareg hold *anzad* music in higher esteem, *tende* is the music they more often perform. It is central to Tuareg camel festivals and curing ceremonies, and is also a part
of certain dance traditions. In addition to drumming, both men and women take
part—by singing, dancing, clapping, and shouting. Unlike the *anzad*, the mortar
drum does not require years to learn acceptable skills, and the person who plays it,
unless unusually gifted, receives little special attention. A singer of *tende* occasionally
gains recognition, but most performers are nonspecialist members of the community.
Tende is a music of ordinary people; its appeal is immediate and communal.
Residents of urban areas increasingly employ its various forms, but it remains a music
of the bush, a symbol of earthy values.

Construction

The *tende* is a single-headed mortar drum, named for the wooden vessel from which
people make it. Because it is constructed of a mortar and pestles—items used daily in
the preparation of food—the drum appears only on festive occasions, when people
assemble it for a few hours of use. Its construction requires a footed wooden mortar,
two heavy wooden pestles about $1^1/_4$ meters long, a piece of moistened goatskin, and
a length of rope. The ends of dampened goatskin wrap around the pestles, which
serve as grips for stretching the skin over the opening of the mortar. In some traditions, people discard the pestles as soon as they have secured the skin with rope.
Commonly, however, they attach the pestles to the drumhead as part of the instrument, providing for later tuning and adjustment. To hold the ends of the pestles parallel, and to form seats (on which women, stones, or bricks may sit), people tie rope
between the ends of the pestles. (For photos of the construction of *tende*, see Borel
1981:112–114.) The weight on the pestles increases the tension on the attached
drumhead, thus tuning it: the heavier the weight, the higher the pitch and the
brighter the timbre. This form of mortar drum is unique to the Tuareg.

Periodically during performance, to keep the goatskin moist and pliable, people
sprinkle water onto the drumhead. In some traditions, they fill the mortar with water

FIGURE 2   "*Ezzel n oufada aoua etteb ales ou n abaradh* 'Young man's song about a man leading a camel'." Performers unidentified. Holiday and Holiday 1960:A3.

Songs of love and praise form a large portion of the traditional repertory, and criticism and scorn have their place too. Nearly any topic of interest is fitting subject matter.

before stretching the skin over it; by tipping the mortar, they can then moisten the head from the inside. This use of water in the drum has led some to identify it mistakenly as a water drum.

The rise of *tende*

The use of the mortar as a drum may be a recent development. The earliest report of such an instrument is that of Francis Rodd, who in Aïr in 1926 described and sketched a *tende* with attached pestles weighted with stones (1926:272). In Timbuktu in 1934, Laura Boulton made a recording of a Tuareg drum that, though she said it was a water drum, appears to have been a *tende* of the type without attached pestles (Boulton 1957:A:86b). In Ahaggar, a *tende* first appears in a text collected by Ludwig Zöhrer in 1935. His collection from that period includes several recordings of what may have been *tende*. In his later writing, based on this material, he speaks of *tende* as the only "truly Tuareg drum" other than the ceremonial *attebel* of the chief (1935, item 11; 1940:141). Despite the earlier southern references, some believe that the instrument originated among vassal tribes in the Adrar n-Foras region of northeastern Mali, and that it spread from there into Ahaggar and Niger (Mounier 1942:155; Blanguernon 1955:154). Others believe its use to have been introduced or strongly influenced by sub-Saharan slaves (Holiday and Holiday 1960:4; Lhote 1955:184). Whatever its origin, the *tende* did not become prominent in Tuareg musical life until after 1930.

If *tende* was indeed originally a vassal tradition, its emergence may have accompanied the shifts of wealth and power that in the late nineteenth and early twentieth centuries favored the vassal tribes of the north. During that period, the vassals of Ahaggar gained greater control over the camels (Keenan 1977:56–61), and were consequently able to take a more prominent role in camel festivals. Mounier states that about 1930 the vassal drum began to replace a small hand-held drum formerly used by noblewomen at the Ahaggar festivals (1942:155). In the southern regions, the *tende* as a Tuareg festival instrument appears to have merged with Hausa dance traditions. In a 1944 publication on the Tuareg of Azawagh, Francis Nicolas mentions *tende* as a Tuareg alternative to a Hausa drum, *ganga*, used to accompany the dance songs of Tuareg slaves (Nicolas 1944:3, 7). In Niger by the 1950s, the mortar drum had become an established part of musical culture (Holiday and Holiday 1960:4). The diversity of the *tende* traditions that have developed may best be understood in the light of these cultural fusions. For further discussion, see Card (1983:155–171).

Camel-festival *tende*

The mortar-drum music most often mentioned in the literature is *tende n-əmnas* 'mortar drum of the camels'. These events celebrate weddings, births, honored visits, and other joyous occasions. Featured are camel races and dances. In its classic form, women sing and play the drum, while men parade or race their camels around them, in a fashion sometimes described as a "fantasy," and known in Tuareg dialects as *ilugan*, *ilujan*, and *ilaguan*. The races and displays of precision riding, combined with the men's flirtatious behavior toward the women, perpetuate the traditional virtues of male prowess and gallantry. In the late 1900s, as the nomadic herders become urbanized, the music of *tende n-əmnas* is increasingly performed out of context; and in some areas, male artisan-specialists play the drum.

The texts of *tende n-əmnas* burgeon with personalized references to camels, extolling with esteem and affection their beauty and merits. Mere ownership of a superb riding camel is often sufficient for a man's commemoration in song, and texts praise good riders for their skill and rapport with their animals. But though the references to camels are numerous, the real subjects are people. Songs of love and praise form a large portion of the traditional repertory, and criticism and scorn have their place too. Nearly any topic of interest is fitting subject matter. Some texts, set to familiar tunes, develop extemporaneously, and include the singer's commentary on local persons and current events. Such songs function in a journalistic capacity, and performers skilled in this kind of improvisation attract an appreciative following.

Characteristic of the style of northern *tende n-əmnas* is the women's choral drone, which functions as a pedal point to the solo line (figure 3). People rarely use the drone south of Tamesna, except in the rainy season during the period known as the Cure Salée, when cameleers from many regions assemble their herds on the salty plains of Niger near In-Gal. This is a time for weddings and social gatherings with much celebrating and music making, especially *tende*. In the southern regions, a choral ostinato in responsorial style replaces the uninterrupted drone. The rhythms, said to imitate the gaits of the camels, are of two types: those based on equal beats in duple meter with syncopated duple or ternary subdivisions, and those based on unequal beats of 3+4+3 in several variations (Saada 1986:186–194). The drummed rhythms may actually direct the movements of the camels, for the riders take their cues from the women at the drum (Borel 1981:120–123). Characteristic, also, are pentatonic structure and quick tempos (typically about M.M. 132–146), usually faster than those of other types of *tende* (figure 3).

Dance *tende*

In Niger, people perform *tende n-tagbast* 'dance *tende*', at many birth and marriage celebrations, and at other special events. Only artisans, sedentary blacks, and (to a lesser extent) vassals dance it. Traditionally, noble Tuareg do not dance (Lhote 1951: 98–103). The word *tagbast* is the nominal form of the verb *egbas* 'circle the waist with a belt'. By extension, it bears the sense of "elegant attire" or "stylish dress," and with *tende*, denotes a musical occasion celebrated with fine clothes and dancing. Dancers perform within a circle of spectators. Dancers, alone or in groups, enter the circle and perform a few steps, then retreat, to be followed by others. Men's shouts and women's flutter-tongued cries of approval reward expert exhibitions.

Women sing the texts, but the *tende* is usually played by men of the artisanal caste, whom women accompany on an *assakalabu* (a gourd upturned in a basin of water). The instrumental ensemble may also include a frame drum, *əkänzam*, which men or women play. The use of instruments with the dance may be a recent addition to a formerly unaccompanied dance tradition; and if instruments are not readily available, the dances take an accompaniment of singing and hand clapping only. Dance music without instruments is known as *ezele n-tagbast*. Artisan-musicians familiar with the tradition of *tende n-əmnas* may have introduced the mortar drum into the dance. The texts praise and commemorate good dancers, much as texts of *tende n-əmnas* praise good riders; and many of the texts similarly speak of love.

Duple meter with duple subdivisions, occasionally syncopated, are characteristic

assakalabu   Instrument created by upturning a gourd in a basin of water that is struck with a stick

tende n-əmnas   Events where the mortar drum is played and that feature personalized references to camels

FIGURE 3 *Tende n-əmnas* song for the Tuareg celebration of the annual Muslim festival of sacrificial sheep. Vocal soloist: Lalla bint Salem. Tamanrasset, Algeria, 1976.

of the genre. Ternary subdivisions are rare, except for brief hemiolic exchanges within the melody, or between parts. The pulse, strongly marked and accompanied by hand clapping, receives further reinforcement from steady, equal beats struck on the *assakalabu*. Though slower than *tende n-əmnas*, the tempos of *tende n-tagbast* vary according to the dance. The formal structure can be either antiphonal or responsorial. In the former, a melodic line alternates between two choruses, or between a soloist and a chorus; in the latter, a solo line follows or overlaps a choral ostinato, as is characteristic of the southern *tende n-əmnas* tradition.

MUSICAL CURING CEREMONIES

The use of music to cure certain types of illnesses is widespread throughout the Sahara. Musical curing practices have an origin in ancient beliefs in good and evil spirits, known to the Tuareg as *Kel Asuf* 'People of the Solitude'. The spirits, believed to inhabit fire, water, wind, caves, darkness, and empty places, are responsible for most Tuareg mental illnesses, and for other sufferings from unseen causes. The pre-Islamic animism of the Tuareg has merged with Muslim concepts of the spirit world, and in some regions the curing ceremony is known by the Arabic name *el janun* (in Ahaggar, *alhinen*) 'possession, madness'. The term derives from the Arabic word *jinn*, denoting earth-dwelling spirits (described in the Qur'ān), which aid or hinder the lives of mortals. In the Tuareg traditions of Niger, the ceremony is known as *tende n-gumatan*. The word *guma* (pl. *gumatan*) refers to the patient—more often a woman—for whom people hold the ceremony (Rasmussen 1985). The origin of the term is uncertain, but Tuareg from the Aïr to Niamey recognize its sense as "*tende* of the possessed" or "*tende* of the emotionally ill."

Because the Tuareg believe music—especially strong rhythms—attracts spirits, curing ceremonies feature singing, clapping, and drumming. In some cases, music entices unwanted spirits from the body; in others, it restores harmony between the patient and his or her personal spirit. The ceremonies, always held late at night, include a chorus of women, a *tende* player (male or female), and often an *assakalabu* player (always a woman). Necessary, also, are male participants, who utter raspy, rhythmic grunts (*tahəmahəmt*). At the center sits or stands the *guma*, who sways to the rhythms of the drum. Members of the family and community, who contribute with hand clapping and cries of encouragement, surround the immediate group. The spirited songs, rhythms, and raspy grunts of the men lead the patient and some participants into altered states of consciousness. People may repeat the ceremony for as many consecutive nights as necessary. The Tuareg say that because the spirits' natures are well known to the community, they can usually project at the outset how many nightly rituals they will need to effect a cure.

In the past, the rituals of curing probably had specific texts, and possibly special music, but current practices permit the use of any songs the patients or their families desire. The tempos of the songs conform to a *tende n-gumatan* standard (about M.M. 73–96), slower than usual for either *tende n-əmnas* or *tende n-tagbast* (Borel 1981:124; Card 1982:150). The slower tempos and the guttural utterances of the men, who force their breath rhythmically through constricted throats, are the major features that distinguish the music of the curing ceremonies from other types of *tende*.

THE *TAHARDENT*

A popular music and dance associated with the three-stringed lute *tahardent*, is performed in urban centers across the Sahara from Mali to Algeria. Men of the artisanal caste, many of whom earn their living as professional musicians (*aggu*; pl. *aggutan*),

tahardent   Three-stringed lute played in
urban centers across the Sahara from Mali
to Algeria

takəmba   New Tuareg genre where seated listeners respond to rhythms with undulating
movements of the torso

perform the music. Such men once performed as bards in the courts of chiefs, singing
the praises of their noble patrons and reciting tales of battles and heroes of local
Tuareg legend to the accompaniment of the plucked lute. But the *tahardent* repertory
that is now popular among urban Tuareg is not the heroic music of the past; it is
music for entertainment, which friends and acquaintances of diverse ethnic backgrounds can share.

The *tahardent* has long been a part of Tuareg traditions in Mali, but not until
the late 1960s did the instrument begin to spread into other Tuareg areas. The movement of *tahardent* music from its source (between Timbuktu and Gao) began about
1968, when Malian Tuareg suffering from drought began to seek relief across the border, in Niger. Among the refugees were many artisan-musicians whose traditional
patrons could no longer support them. To increase their opportunities, the itinerants
quickly altered their repertories to appeal to a more diverse, multiethnic audience.
Crowded conditions in the refugee centers forced many to continue their migration
northeastward. By 1971, *tahardent* music began to be heard in Agadez, and in 1974
it reached Tamanrasset, Algeria. Since 1976, Malian *tahardent* players have been
active in most urban centers across the Sahara and Sahelian borderlands, and recordings of *tahardent* music are in wide circulation throughout West Africa.

The *tahardent* is not unique to the Tuareg, and it almost certainly did not originate among them. The Hausa and Djerma of Niger call the same instrument *molo*;
throughout West Africa, it goes by other names; in Mauritania, professionals play the
tidinit, a similar instrument with four strings. In all the traditions, the music is performed exclusively by musicians whose professions are normally hereditary, and
whose social roles and statuses are similar. The close resemblance of the Tuareg tradition to its neighboring counterparts accounts for much of its present popularity in
the multicultural urban areas. Hausa, Djerma, Fulani, Songhay, Tuareg, and other
West Africans can find shared enjoyment in the music, for the similarities of the
styles, repertories, and performance practices, particularly in their modern forms, are
greater than the differences.

The new genre, popularly known as *takəmba*, consists of accompanied songs and
instrumental solos. To provocative rhythms, seated listeners (both men and women)
respond with undulating movements of the upper torso and outstretched arms.
People exchange prized recordings of star performers and hit songs, and copy them
from one tape to another. The texts are sensuous. At vital moments, people express
approval in rhapsodic exclamations of "*ush-sh-sh!*"—as in the following translation
(Card 1977: tape XVII, track 1, item 3).

TRACK 12

> My soul loves what it will,
> O my Khadisia!
> The best woman is one who is fat,
> Not one who is thin!

Or else a woman who has a low stomach
  Which is soft, nice to touch,
Or one who has fleshy arms and calves,
  Ush-sh-sh-sh!

Songs of this type appeal most to Tuareg who have accepted urban life and contemporary values. Those who adhere to traditional ways are often vehement in their disdain for the instrument, the music, and its devotees: they denounce *tahardent* music as a corrupt, urban product, and not a true Tuareg art. To them, it matters little that the *tahardent* represents an old and respected Tuareg tradition in Mali. Their attitudes toward it highlight an emerging division between conservatives and progressives.

Construction and playing

The instrument has an oblong body covered with cowhide or goatskin. Artisans carve the body from a single block of wood, and cover it with cowhide or goatskin, which they attach with tacks or lacings. A length of bamboo, inserted under the skin, and extending beyond the body, serves as a neck. A large sound hole is cut into the skin just below the bridge. The instrument comes in two sizes. The larger (and more commonly used) has a body length of about 51 to 53 centimeters, a width of about 18 to 20, and a neck of about 30. Three strings, of differing lengths and thicknesses, are attached to a mounting just above the sound hole. They stretch over the bridge, where they are fastened to the end of the neck with leather bindings that are adjustable for tuning. The strings, nowadays made of nylon, are collectively called hairs. Individual strings bear animal names: the lowest is *ahar* 'lion'; the middle, *tazori* 'hyena'; and the highest, *ebag* 'jackal', or *awokkoz* 'young animal'. The two lower strings are tuned to a perfect fourth or perfect fifth, depending on the music. The upper string—occasionally plucked, but not fingered—sounds an octave above the lowest; its principal function is sympathetic vibration. A metal resonator (*tefararaq*) dangles from the end of the neck, where it buzzes.

The player sits cross-legged, and normally holds the neck in his left hand. On his right index finger he wears a plectrum (*esker*), made of bone and leather. He plucks the middle string with the index finger, the lower with his thumb. With the other fingers he taps accompanying rhythms on the instrument's surface. With his left-hand fingers he stops the strings against the (unfretted) neck. As the melodic range rarely exceeds an octave, hand shifts during the course of a composition are unnecessary. A player may occasionally slide a finger along the string in a glissando, but normally the fingering is crisp, and the pitches clearly articulated. Esteemed performers exhibit virtuosity in their improvisations on the basic rhythmic patterns, particularly in the instrumental interludes between vocal strophes. People do not perform separately or with other instruments the poetry they sing or recite to the accompaniment of the *tahardent*, whether of the old tradition or the new.

Musical styles

Many Tuareg, unaware of historical and stylistic distinctions, refer to all *tahardent* music as *takɔmba*. To the performers, however, *takɔmba* is but one of several compositional formulas, which they call rhythms. Each rhythm has a name, is suitable for a specific context, and may bear distinctive modal and rhythmic characteristics. The rhythms *n-geru* and *yalli* (figure 4) serve only in the performance of heroic ballads, a tradition that may be several hundred years old; both have five-pulse rhythms, but

FIGURE 4   Rhythmic structure of *n-geru* and *yalli*.

FIGURE 5   Twelve-pulse patterns in several configurations as they appear in *abakkabuk, ser-i, jaba*, and *takɔmba*.

different tonal (or modal) structures. *Yalli* was first recorded by Laura Boulton in Timbuktu in 1934 (African Music item 86A). In her documentation, the term *yalli* (given as *Yali*) became confused with subject matter; musical analysis, however, confirms the identity of the rhythm. The rhythms *abakkabuk, ser-i, jabâ*, and *takɔmba* (figure 5) serve for light entertainment and dancing. All rely on twelve-pulse patterns in various configurations. *Abakkabuk* is an old rhythm unique to the Tuareg. *Ser-i* 'toward me' is a traditional pattern played for the enjoyment of members of the artisanal caste, to which the musicians belong. *Jabâ* and *takɔmba*, of more recent origin, are rhythms that praise youth and youthful pleasures; according to performers, *jabâ* is the product of a commission in 1960 by wealthy patrons of the Kel Tamoulayt; similarly, *takɔmba* is a rhythm composed for the chief of the Malian village of that name near Bourem.

Few outsiders have studied *tahardent* music, and recordings are scarce. Comparison of the limited data with that of similar neighboring traditions points to relationships between the heroic forms (*yalli, n-geru*) and Arabic music of North Africa and the Middle East, particularly in tonal structures and sociomusical meanings. The dance music, with its twelve-pulse horizontal hemiolas, shows greater affinity with sub-Saharan Africa (Duvelle 1966; Anderson 1971:143–169; Card 1982:166–174). The *tahardent* tradition of the Tuareg thus reflects the intercultural status of its artisan-creators, who, more than other musicians, have drawn freely upon both Middle Eastern and sub-Saharan sources.

OTHER INSTRUMENTS

Tuareg musical culture also includes a variety of drums and a herdsman's flute. Some of these instruments are limited to particular regions, others to particular persons or events.

Drums

The *assakalabu*, or *aghalabo*, consists of a hemispherical calabash floating in a basin of water. The earliest written reference to the instrument is that of Francis Rodd, who observed a basin filled with milk, rather than water (1926:272, plate 22). The player, always a woman, strikes the calabash with a stick. Slight variation in timbre is possible by regulating the depth of the gourd in the liquid; the more forceful the stroke, the deeper the tone. The instrument, used only with *tende* and *tazâwat*, appears at camel festivals and other celebrations, dances, and curing ceremonies. Because it serves only to reinforce basic beats (women play no rhythmic subdivisions on it), it offers opportunities for young women to take part in ensembles, and to become acquainted with the drumming traditions.

The *tazâwat* is a medium-sized kettledrum, played by women in the Azawagh region of Niger. Accompanied by *assakalabu*, hand clapping, and occasionally *anzad*, the drum frequently serves in the curing ceremonies of this region, where people deem it especially effective in treating illnesses attributed to *jinn*. The (seated) player rests the drum on the ground before her, and strikes it with her hands. Some *tazâwat* players exhibit rhythmic versatility and virtuosity. People construct the drum from a half calabash, covered with cowhide or goatskin. Lacings threaded through eyelets in the leather, and knotted at the bottom of the bowl, hold the drumhead taut. A northern variant, *tegennewt*, occasionally seen in Ahaggar, is made from a wooden or enameled metal bowl (Saada 1986:99–100). One of the few recorded collections of *tazâwat* is in the archives of the Musée d'Ethnographie, Neuchatel, Switzerland (Borel 1981:116).

The *ɔttebel*, a large ceremonial kettledrum, is the traditional symbol of Tuareg chieftainship—and formerly, of tribal sovereignty. Selected people play it on important ceremonial occasions, such as the installation of a chief or the celebration of an annual Muslim festival, and formerly played it to summon men to battle (Nicolas 1939:585). The *ɔttebel* is similar in construction to the *tazâwat*, but it is wider and deeper, and is played differently. Two men suspend the drum by ropes above the ground, and strike it alternately. Because the Tuareg believe the drum has mystic powers, its handling, playing, storage, and repair, are traditionally subject to rituals and taboos (Nicolaisen 1963:396). Since the end of tribal sovereignty, however, the ceremonial drums, though still played occasionally, have lost much of their former significance, and people less rigorously observe the traditions concerning them.

The *ɔkänzam* (pl. *iɔkänzaman*) is a single-headed, shallow frame drum, similar in appearance to the European tambourine, but without jingles. Hand held and played by either a man or woman, it typically measures 25 to 30 centimeters in diameter. Southern *tende* ensembles, especially those in which artisan-musicians are the principal performers, may include one or more.

In Hausa, the term *ganga* (pl. *gangatan*) is a generic 'drum'. For the Tuareg, it has assumed regional meanings: in Ahaggar, it refers to a hand-held, shallow, double-headed drum, played by women to accompany the singing of songs for weddings; in Aïr, it refers to a suspended, double-headed cylindrical drum, played by musicians attendant on the Sultan of Agadez, who serves as chief of certain Tuareg groups in the Aïr and southern Niger.

When a mortar drum is unavailable or too much trouble to prepare, a plastic or metal container popularly known as a "jerry can" often substitutes for it. Some Tuareg actually prefer a jerry can to the traditional mortar drum. In Ahaggar, as a result of an inscription ("made in Germany") that appeared on the first cans imported into the region, people began to call the container *jermani* (Saada 1986:103). Though not properly a musical instrument, the wide use of the jerry can in this manner justifies its inclusion among Tuareg musical instruments. Jerry cans are readily available, and have the advantage of needing no preparation. When used as a drum, the jerry can is often called a *tende*.

The flute

For private pleasure or as an aid in controlling animals, herdsmen traditionally play an obliquely held flute, termed *tazammart* in the north and *tasansagh* or *sarewa* (Hausa) in the south. The instrument, about 1 meter long and 2 to 5 centimeters in diameter, contains four holes. Formerly made from a hollow stalk or from the root of the acacia tree, it is now more commonly constructed of metal or plastic tubing. The flutes sometimes sport a traditional decoration: a dyed-leather fringe.

Flute repertories vary regionally, and have no accompanying vocal texts. In the Algerian Sahara, the music of the flute is often accompanied by a vocal drone produced in the throat of the player as he blows into and fingers the instrument. The

The Tuareg regard any type of rhythmic movement as dance, whether they perform it standing or sitting. The stylized movements of camels under the control of their riders are also called dance.

---

drone, like that accompanying *tende* songs in this region, serves as a pedal point to the melody.

People play the flute in small groups, but rarely at large social gatherings. The urbanization of herders, and increasing media exposure of outstanding performers, are gradually giving new status to the flute as a solo instrument. Some performers, recorded and broadcast by Radio Niger (which regularly includes flute music in its programming) have become well known for musicianship and virtuosity.

OTHER VOCAL GENRES

Aliwen

A large body of wedding songs (*aliwen*), sung by women, constitutes a major musical genre in the Ahaggar and Tassili-n-Ajjer regions of Algeria. The poetic texts are one of the finest and most elaborate of the region's traditions, second only to the *tesîwit* poetry associated with the *anzad*. The wedding songs, which frequently take the accompaniment of *gangatan*, may represent a tradition dating from the mid-1600s or earlier. Many of the older texts, having retained their ceremonial character, appear little changed over time. People occasionally add new songs, but the songs conform to the older metric, rhythmic, and semantic traditions: they continue to emphasize the communal and social aspects of marriage (Saada 1986:71–74, 212–234). That little new composition of *aliwen* has occurred in the late 1900s reflects the conservatism characteristic of this Tuareg area.

Specific *aliwen* mark the ceremonial stages of the wedding. The singing begins in the bride's quarters on the first morning of the festivities, which usually last for a week. Special songs further celebrate the grooming of the bride, the erection of the nuptial tent, the parade of camels (*ilugan*), and the processions of the bride and bridegroom to the tent. Two groups of women sing verses antiphonally, or a soloist and chorus sing responsorially. In Tassili n-Ajjer, believed to be the source of the tradition, the songs are always accompanied by the *ganga*, and vocal and drum rhythms synchronize rigorously. The rhythms consist of complex combinations of beats of unequal length. In Ahaggar, where people use the drum less regularly, the rhythms are less complex. When the drum is used, the rhythms are usually independent of the melodic line (Augier 1972:298; Saada 1986:115–127, 181–182).

Religious music

Orthodox Muslims frown on music for worship. Religious vocal music, unaccompanied by instruments, is an accepted practice in much of the Sahara and the southern borderlands. Religious performance was not a part of ancient Tuareg culture, and though it is increasing in importance with the growth of urban populations and the spread of fundamentalist Muslim movements, the entire population does not perform it. The men participate in all types of Muslim observances more than the women, who, as traditional guardians of culture, are more supportive of pre-Islamic beliefs and practices.

The religious music takes two forms: *ɔzziker* and *amadikh*. The former, a term derived from Arabic *dhikr*, is a ritual music sung in recollection of Allah in the less orthodox mosques and improvised places of worship along the desert routes. Though the *dhikr* is common to all Muslim peoples, the Tuareg form is unique in musical style, which resembles that of the dance traditions and curing ceremonies, its use of Tuareg dialects (rather than Arabic), and its perspective (said to express the special manner in which the Tuareg envision Allah). *Amadikh* is panegyric poetry sung in praise of Muhammad. Both men and women sing this music anywhere, away from places of worship. The texts, like those of *ɔzziker*, are in the vernacular; and the music, though strongly regional in style, exhibits distinctive traits, such as triple meter, uncommon in most Tuareg music. Commercial recordings of *ɔzziker* and *amadikh* are rare. For programming, however, Radio Niger has made a sizable collection.

Children's songs

The unaccompanied songs that mothers sing to their children include a wide variety of styles and subjects. Some lie partway between speech and song; some consist of vocables sung to simple, repetitive melodies of two or three pitches; and others have elaborate structures and contain many verses. Lullabies seem to differ from other women's songs in their more supple style, the use of semitones, and a dissymmetric structure subordinate to the demands of improvised texts (Augier 1972:298–299). Zöhrer says the texts consist of a mixture of endearments and religious matter (1940:145–146). Many women, however, amuse their children with any music that comes to mind. The song may be taken from a repertory of dances, or it may describe a men's hunt. In Ahaggar, women sing a song to children about an ostrich, a bird that has not been seen in that area for a century. As they sing and clap, they prompt the children to imitate the imagined movements of the bird. At an early age, however, parents encourage children to participate in their elders' music making.

DANCE TRADITIONS

The Tuareg regard any type of rhythmic movement as dance, whether they perform it standing (as in *tende n-tagbast*, *tehemmet*, *tehigelt*, *tazengherit*, and *arokas*), or sitting (as in *takamba* and often *tende n-gumatan*). The stylized movements of camels under the control of their riders (*ilugan*) are also called dance. Standing dances, once performed exclusively by slaves for the entertainment of the nomads, are now more widely performed, though usually by men of lower-than-noble rank. Women, especially those of noble lineage, rarely participate in such dances. Seated men and women of all social ranks respond to the rhythms of *tahardent* music with undulating movements of the arms and shoulders, and patients being treated in *tende n-gumatan* may respond vigorously, standing or sitting, with swaying movements described as head dancing.

Tehigelt and *tehemmet*

The dance called *tehigelt* in Ahaggar and *tehemmet* in Tassili n-Ajjer (where people say it began) is accompanied by songs, hand clapping, and one or more drums. The event always occurs at night, in celebration of a joyous occasion. The dance, formerly performed only by slaves, is now joined by men of all ranks, and occasionally by women, who participate with modest movements. The dancers form a large circle. As performed by men, the movements consist of hopping steps, with knees lifted high and arms outstretched. Sometimes the men engage in mock-battle gestures. The

tazengherit   Ecstatic form of music and
dance performed in Ahaggar, particularly
at the oases of Tazruk and Hirafok

arokas   A dance performed in the Agadez
area of Niger with a women's chorus,
soloist, and spirited hand clapping

musical accompaniment, similar to *tende n-əmnas*, includes a chorus of women, a
vocal soloist, and drummers. The rhythms of *tehigelt* and *tehemmet* are distinct, but
the antiphonal and responsorial styles of singing differ little from those of *tende*
(Augier 1972:295; Saada 1986:79–80). In Tassili n-Ajjer, the ensemble may include
several *gangatan* and jerrycans; in Ahaggar, the use of a single drum (traditionally a
tegennewt, but now more commonly a *tende* or jerry can) is more common.
Increasingly, the dances are performed to recorded music taped at previous events
and replayed on portable players, or over loudspeakers.

Tazengherit

Tazengherit is an ecstatic form of music and dance performed in Ahaggar, particularly
at the oases of Tazruk and Hirafok, where certain groups specialize in it. Men dance
exclusively to the accompaniment of a women's chorus, one or two female soloists,
hand clapping, and their own gutteral utterances (similar to those of *tende n-
gumatan*). No instruments are used. People sing *tazengherit* songs in sets of three to
five, following an established pattern, each more intense and structurally elaborate
than the preceding. For many of the participants, the event culminates in frenzied
dancing and altered states of consciousness (Augier 1972:295–296).

Arokas

Arokas, a dance performed in the Agadez area of Niger, involves the accompaniment
of a women's chorus, a female soloist, and spirited hand clapping. The songs and
movements are nearly identical to those of *tende n-tagbast*, but no instruments are
used. The word derives from *erked* 'to dance'.

REFERENCES

Anderson, Lois. 1971. "The Interrelation of
African and Arab Musics: Some Preliminary
Considerations." In *Music and History in Africa,*
ed. Klaus P. Wachsmann, 143–169. Evanston, Ill.:
Northwestern University Press.

Augier, Pierre. 1972. "Ethnomusicologie saharienne: les documents sonores recueillis récemment
en Ahaggar et au Gourara." *Libyca* 20:291–311.

Blanguernon, Claude. 1955. *Le Hoggar.* Paris:
Arthaud.

Borel, François. 1981. "Tambours et rythmes de
tambours Touaregs au Niger." *Annales Suisses de
Musicologie* 1:107–129.

Boulton, Laura. 1957. *African Music.* Folkways
Records, FW 8852. LP disk.

Briggs, Lloyd Cabot. 1960. *Tribes of the Sahara.*
Cambridge, Mass.: Harvard University Press.

Card, Caroline. 1977. Field collection. Archives
of Traditional Music, Indiana University.

———. 1982. "Tuareg Music and Social
Identity." Ph.D. dissertation, Indiana University.

———. 1983. "*Tende* Music among the Tuareg:
The History of a Tradition." In *Cross Rhythms,
Occasional Papers in African Folklore,* ed. Kofi
Anyidoho et al., 155–171. Bloomington, Ind.:
Trickster Press.

DjeDje, Jacqueline Cogdell. 1980. *Distribution of
the One String Fiddle in West Africa.* Los Angeles:
Program in Ethnomusicology, Department of
Music, University of California. Monograph in
Ethnomusicology 2.

Duvelle, Charles. 1966. *Musique Maure.* OCORA
Records, OCR 28. LP disk and notes.

Duvéyrier, Henri. 1864 [1973]. *Les Touareg du nord.* Liechtenstein: Nendeln [New York: Krauss].

Foucauld, Charles de. 1925. *Poésies touarègues: dialecte de l'Ahaggar.* 2 vols. Paris: Editions Ernest Leroux.

———. 1951–1952. *Dictionnaire touareg-français: dialect de l'Ahaggar.* 4 vols. Paris: Imprimerie national de France.

Holiday, Geoffrey, and Finola Holiday. 1960. *Tuareg Music of the Southern Sahara.* Folkways Records, FE 4470. LP disk.

Keenan, Jeremy H. 1977. *The Tuareg: People of Ahaggar.* London: Allen Lane.

Lhote, Henri. 1951. "Un peuple qui ne danse pas." *Tropiques* 337(December):99–103.

———. 1955. *Touaregs du Hoggar.* Paris: Payot.

Mounier, G. 1942. "Le travail des peaux chez les Touareg Hoggar." *Travaux de l'Institut des recherches sahariennes* 1:133–169.

Murdock, George Peter. 1959. *Africa: Its Peoples and Their Culture History.* New York: McGraw-Hill.

Nicolaisen, Johannes. 1961. "Essai sur la religion et la magie touarègues." *Folk* 3:113–162.

———. 1963. *Ecology and Culture of the Pastoral Tuareg.* Copenhagen: National Museum.

Nicolas, Francis. 1939. "Notes sur la société et l'état chez les Twareg du Dinnik." *Bulletin de l'Institut français d'Afrique noire* 1:579–586.

———. 1944. "Folklore Twareg: poésies et chansons de l'Azawarh." *Bulletin de l'Institut français d'Afrique noire* 6(1–4).

———. 1950. *Tamesna: les Iullemmeden de l'Est, ou Touareg "Kel Dinnik."* Paris: Imprimerie nationale.

Nikiprowetzky, Tolia. 1963. *Nomades du Niger.* OCORA Records, OCR 29. LP disk.

Rasmussen, Susan. 1985. "Gender and Curing in Ritual and Symbol: Women, Spirit Possession, and Aging among the Kel Ewey Tuareg." Ph.D. dissertation, Indiana University.

Rodd, Francis Rennel (Lord Rennel of Rodd). 1926 [1966]. *People of the Veil.* Oosterhut, Netherlands: Anthropological Publications.

Saada, Nadia Mécheri. 1986. "La musique de l'Ahaggar." Ph.D. dissertation. University of Paris.

Wendt, Caroline Card. 1994. "Regional Style in Tuareg *Anzad* Music." In *To the Four Corners,* ed. Ellen Leichtman. Warren, Mich.: Harmonie Park Press.

Zöhrer, Ludwig. 1935. "Protokoll zu den Phonogrammen Ludwig Zöhrers von den Tuareg der Sahara."

———. 1940. "Studien über die Tuareg (Imohag) der Sahara." *Zeitschrift für Ethnologie* 72:124–152.

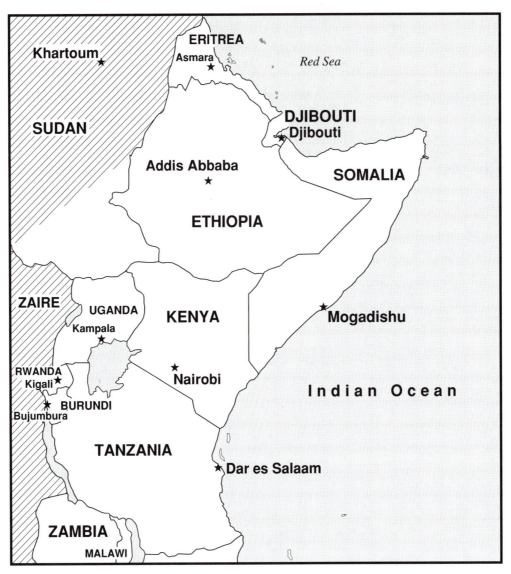

East Africa

East Africa

East African musical performances reveal practices from the Arab world to the north as well as South and Southeast Asian musical elements from the east. Royal ensembles of drums, flutes, trumpets, and xylophones—historically connected to the courts of rulers from Ethiopia to Kenya—persist in a variety of contemporary settings.

East Africa: An Introduction
Peter Cooke

The Settled Peoples
Nomadic and Seminomadic Peoples
Indonesian, Arabic, Islamic, and European Influences
Late-Twentieth-Century Developments and Urban Music

East Africa ranges from the dry scrubland of northern Mozambique to the empty deserts of northern Sudan and Eritrea, and from the seasonally dry savanna bordering the Indian Ocean inland to the mountain–rain-forest mosaic of Rwanda and Burundi.

More than 100 million people live in this area, and their life-styles and origins vary as much as anywhere else in Africa, though they exclude large areas of Sudan, Ethiopia, and Somalia. About 118 different languages have been identified in the Sudan alone, and almost as many in Ethiopia; and since language and musical style are often closely related, it is not surprising to find that musical traditions vary as much as languages and dialects.

In contrast with anthropological research, musical research in this area has been patchy, often nonexistent, and the task of attempting an overview is complicated, as elsewhere in Africa, by a past that has known considerable population movement but has produced little or no historical documentation. Theories about the origins and movements of whole societies remain speculative; myths are often the only available evidence.

From time to time, debate on the extent to which Indonesian peoples penetrated and colonized East Africa (bringing their cultural practices, including music, with them) still surfaces (Jones 1964). Archaeologists and historians are uncertain about the origins of the Cwezi, powerful cattle folk, who probably in the 1300s appeared in the area around the northwestern shores of Lake Victoria, where they established dynasties that ruled until 1966.

Changes in religious practices have affected traditional music and dance. Islam continues to gain converts throughout East Africa—a spread that in earlier centuries was associated with trade with the Arab world, rather than conquest, but which need not always have been connected with the introduction of the Arabic language. Islamic prohibitions on musical practices, though important in some countries, have little effect in many parts of Africa. Western missionaries, initially antipathetic to almost all aspects of traditional culture, have had a greater impact on musical practices by introducing harmonized hymns to cultures that had nurtured primarily monophonic styles of singing. This process has been intensified since the 1970s through partnership with the tools of the Western media, which floods Africa with Western popular music. In the twentieth century too, students and urban migrant workers who maintain links with their home villages are ensuring the spread of modern town-music styles into the most distant villages.

Leaving aside questions of Western musical influence, it is possible to comment generally on the similarities and differences of traditional musical style and function among three principal groups of peoples. The first are the traditionally nomadic and pastoral peoples, many of whom are said to have moved southward and westward out of the region of the Horn of Africa during the past several centuries. They include groups such as the Baggāra (wandering the deserts and scrubland of the Sudan); the Karamojong, the Jie, the Pokot, and the Turkana of eastern Uganda and neighboring parts of Kenya; and the Maasai of the rift-valley plains farther south in Kenya and Tanzania. The second group are sedentary agriculturalists, such as the Nilotes of Sudan and the Bantu-speaking peoples who many centuries ago moved southward and then eastward and northward, it is thought from a Bantu heartland on the west side of the continent. Third are the Cushitic-speaking Amhara and Tigre, and other peoples of present-day Ethiopia and Somalia.

Within these cultural divisions there is considerable musical diversity, often linked to contacts between peoples. The Bantu-speaking Meru and Gogo of Tanzania have absorbed elements of musical style from their pastoralist Maasai neighbors who came from northern Kenya; and the Kuria, a small, Bantu-speaking group of pastoralists in northwestern Kenya, only late in the twentieth century have turned to agriculture.

But all these peoples tend to have the same uses for music as do Africans elsewhere in the continent: providing an essential ingredient in most rituals and ceremonies, and accompanying the daily tasks of men and women.

THE SETTLED PEOPLES

In East Africa, the so-called Bantu line, marking the northern limit of the northward and eastward movement of Bantu-speaking agriculturalists from the forests of the southern Congo, runs irregularly from east to west across central Uganda; it then dips south around the dry, central plains of Kenya and northern Tanzania. Farther east, pockets of Bantu-speaking peoples inhabit east-central Kenya, parts of the coast, and inland river valleys as far north as southern Somalia.

In a detailed historical survey of East African music, Gerhard Kubik (1982) divides the area south of the Bantu line into four smaller areas: first, the interlacustrine region, formerly comprised of kingdom-states in southern and western Uganda, Rwanda, Burundi, and northwestern Tanzania; then a Tanzanian area, divided into eight smaller music-style areas because of the variety of peoples living there; third, the Swahili-speaking coastal area, where Swahili and other coastal groups have absorbed Arabic and Islamic influence; and last, the Nyasa-Ruvuma area, stretching from Lake Nyasa down to the coast on either side of the Tanzania-Mozambique border, whose peoples (which include the Makonde) Kubik considers, in the light of historical, linguistic, and other evidence, are related to the Shaba of southern Zaïre, and so have more in common with other central African peoples.

North of the Bantu line in southeastern Sudan and southern Ethiopia live many groups of Nilotic- and para-Nilotic-speaking peoples who, though settled in small villages, practice a good deal of pastoralism. In the Sudan in particular, there is increasing Islamization, with varying effects on older musical practices.

Klaus Wachsmann and Kathleen Trowell's survey of the sound-producing instruments of Uganda (1953) illustrates the variety of musical instruments in use in

begana Box lyre that was an instrument of
the Amharic aristocracy in Ethiopia

omulanga Harpist for the rule of Buganda
in the area of Lake Victoria

akadinda Xylophone associated with the
Uganda court and played by several players

entenga Drum chime associated with the
Uganda court

southern and western parts of East Africa. It lists stringed instruments, such as musical bows, zithers, arched harps, lyres, and tube fiddles; end-blown flutes (mostly of the notched type), cone flutes (of clay, bamboo, wood, or horn), vessel flutes (often made from spherical seed shells and small gourds), end-blown and side-blown trumpets (often played in sets); idiophones of many kinds, including several types of xylophone; and lamellophones (known generically as *sanza* or *mbira* in southern and central Africa, but by neither of these names in the area under discussion, where names using the roots *-embe* or *-dongo* are more common). Last, there is a variety of drums, including tall single-headed ones, usually hand beaten, and the cylindroconical "Uganda drum," which, though it has two skins, is beaten by hand, or with sticks or clubs, usually on one head only.

Many of these instrumental types are also found among the settled Nilotic peoples of the southern Sudan, some of whom (the Luo) migrated south through northern and eastern Uganda as far as the Kavirondo gulf on the eastern side of Lake Victoria. The lyre is such an example. Its distribution in Africa is limited to the northeast of our area. The presence of lyres in the Arabian peninsula, as far north as Iraq—and even on the western coast of India—are a reminder of the extent of the movement of African sailors and slaves to the Arab ports of the Near East and India. Many musicians active in professional and semiprofessional ensembles in the coastal areas of the Arabian peninsula have African origins.

The box lyre known as *begana* was formerly an instrument of the Amharic aristocracy in Ethiopia. Box lyres are also used in northern Kenya and in the region around Mount Elgon on the Kenya-Uganda border, but bowl lyres are more widespread, not only throughout Ethiopia, but also in the Sudan and around the northern shore of Lake Victoria. Lyres are popular instruments among young men in large areas of the Sudan and Ethiopia, and the Bantu-speaking Ganda and Soga of Uganda apparently adopted their bowl lyre after the mid-1800s from their Nilotic (Luo) neighbors to the east.

Styles of playing vary greatly: in much of the Sudan, the popular technique is to strum across all strings with a plectrum held in one hand, while using the fingers of the other hand to mute all but one string at a time. The result is that the unmuted pitches, usually comprising the basic pattern of the song (lyres usually accompany singing), ring out through the dry rhythmic texture of sound created by the muted strings. Ganda and Soga musicians prefer rapid plucking by fingers and thumbs, and the notes of the scale, as in the case of many lamellophones, are divided out on both sides of the instrument so each hand can pluck patterns that interlock.

Political institutions greatly affect the music of both the settled peoples of highland Ethiopia and those of the interlacustrine highland region, which extends south like a spine from the headwaters of the Nile. In both areas, the "Sudanic" concept of kingship took root: powerful kingdom-states evolved, and music flourished within their courts. Specially named drums symbolizing chiefly power were carefully guarded as part of the royal regalia, to be sounded only at coronations and other important state occasions.

This is true among certain Sudanese pastoralist peoples also. Among the Murle, four sacred drums represent the four separate "drumships" of the tribe, the instruments being sounded only in two circumstances: to invoke divine assistance in time of feud, and to announce the outlawing of a wrongdoer.

The former emperor of Ethiopia included in his processions forty-four pairs of kettledrums (*nagarit*), and allowed his princes only twenty-two pairs each. More important, perhaps, than the symbolic nature of such music is the fact that rulers through their patronage made possible the growth of professional classes of musicians.

The former kabaka of Buganda, like other rulers in the area of Lake Victoria, maintained several ensembles at court. He had a private harpist (*omulanga*), and his palatial ensembles included a flute consort (requiring flutes of six sizes, accompanied by four drums), two xylophones (the larger instrument, an *akadinda,* requiring a team of six players), a drum-chime (*entenga*), a bowl lyre ensemble, and a band of trumpeters—in addition to large numbers of royal drums.

Trumpet ensembles were formerly part of the music at the courts of other East African kings and rulers. These trumpets are usually side blown, made from wood, bamboo, or sections of calabash. Each instrument sounds one or two pitches; the performer produces the second by opening a small tip in the narrow end near the mouth hole. The trumpeters combine their pitches in hocket to produce multipart pieces usually derived from well-known songs, whose texts convey chiefly praise and recall royal histories. In many cases, royal musicians were accorded special privileges, such as grants of land, and they usually kept their skills within their own family or their own clan. In Uganda, royal patronage ended in 1966, when the autonomy of the kingdom-states was overthrown.

Trumpets played in hocket style are common in other parts of Africa, and in East Africa many smaller societies (such as the Waza of southern Sudan and the Alur of northwestern Uganda) perform in similar ensembles for dances they regard as having central importance in reinforcing social cohesion. Gerd Baumann has detailed the importance of the *sorek,* a dance performed during the ritual harvest festivals of the Miri of the Nuba Mountains (Sudan), when the entire community participates, dancing in concentric circles around the trumpeters, who play instrumental transformations of songs which in other contexts are for the ears of men only. At such times, virtually all "are carried away by the intricate beauty of the gourds' interlocking sounds, the supple rhythm of tension and relaxation in the dancing, and the physical experience of being 'in tune' with others" (Baumann 1987:85, 182). He sees the "moral power" of such music and dancing as "essential to the reintegration of Miri communities" struggling to preserve their ethnicity in the face of growing political and economic integration into the Islamic state of Sudan.

There is a good case for regarding other hocketing ensembles as performing essentially similar roles. Sets of end-blown flutes played in hocket also appear in many parts of East Africa. They consist of sets of single-note flutes of graded length, made from reeds or bamboo, most of which are closed at the lower end by a natural node or a movable plug. They are reported to accompany the communal circle dances of various peoples in the central highlands and valleys of Ethiopia, among the Ingessana of Sudan (Kubik 1982) and along the western rift valley as far south as the Transvaal in southern Africa and the desert areas of Botswana and Namibia.

A sample shows the basic structure of a song recorded from a group of young adolescents in Madi, in the West Nile district of northern Uganda. The whole group sang the text first, indulging in improvisation that produced occasional harmonies in

The use of music to entertain and enhance the
dignity and status of rulers in East Africa must have
contributed to the richness of musical traditions.
Not all the ensembles have ceased to function; some
were recruited to serve new political leaders.

fourths and fifths. The men then began blowing their one-note flutes to outline the
melody in more than one octave. Almost before the melody was established among
the flutes, a good deal of variation making in individual parts had appeared, as players inserted single notes at extra points in the basic pattern, elaborating their own
one-note rhythms. The result was a lively harmonic and polyrhythmic ostinato,
absorbing and surrounding the vocal line, with the texture further enriched by drumming and hand clapping. More research needs to be done before one could confi-
dently say this style is essentially representative of other stopped-flute– and trumpet-
playing traditions in East Africa.

Given the social and ritual importance of such ensembles, it was perhaps not
surprising that powerful chiefs frequently took control of them. In addition to royal
trumpet ensembles, powerful chiefs in Rwanda, Burundi, and western Uganda maintained smaller ensembles—of cone-shaped flutes, made of clay, wood, or short
lengths of bamboo. These ensembles were known as *esheegu* among the Banyankore
of Uganda, and *isengo* among the musicians of the former king of Rwanda. Though
the institution of kingship no longer exists in these regions, the clans responsible for
these ensembles maintain the tradition.

Interlocking techniques are further exemplified in traditions of playing xylophones and drums in Uganda. In the Ganda *amadinda* style, two players, seated one
on each side of a twelve-key log xylophone, beat out, each in octaves, two isochro-
nous pentatonic patterns, derived from the melody of a song. By listening to the pattern the first two players sound on the two bottom notes of the instrument, and by
reduplicating it two octaves higher on the top two keys of the instrument, a third
player extracts another part. Ganda musicians have expressed wonder at the
unknown inventors of such a simple and beautifully logical means of realizing their
songs on this instrument.

The use of music to entertain and enhance the dignity and status of rulers in
East Africa must have contributed to the richness of musical traditions; and though
the political upheavals of the 1960s and 1970s saw the demise of royal power and its
associated music in East African countries, not all the ensembles have ceased to function. Some were recruited to serve new political leaders. Musicians from others teach
their art in schools and colleges, or have joined "national" music and dance ensembles. Hence it was possible to record the *amakondeere* trumpet band of the former
omukama of Bunyoro performing at a trade fair in Hoima (Bunyoro, western
Uganda) in 1968, two years after the disbanding of the kingdoms in Uganda, and
several key members of Heartbeat of Africa, a national troupe, were formerly musicians in the palace of the kabaka of Buganda.

Indigenous political institutions did not always monopolize music and dance
traditions. During the colonial period, the formal parades and military bands of the
ruling colonial powers inspired the rise of competitive associations known as *beni*
(from the English word "band"), *kingi* (from the English word "king"), or *scotchi*

(imitating Scottish kilts and bagpipes). Originating on the East African coast in imitation of the regimentation of the Royal Navy (and later the regiments of the King's African Rifles), *beni ngoma* 'dance, feast, drum' and its derivatives eventually spread throughout East Africa. Wherever they were performed, precision of movement seems to have been an ever-present concept, combined with the use of European instruments (wherever possible) and formal European dress. *Beni* was an expression of competitiveness within nontribal society (Ranger 1975).

In British East Africa, native recruits readily learned skills on European band instruments: the kabaka of Uganda established a military band for his private army, and several police regiments also formed similar bands, playing European tunes from sheet music. Immediately after independence, the same bandsmen began composing their own music and arranging traditional melodies for their bands.

In contrast to the official institutions, these associations were small independent organizations. They originally appeared in the ports of the East African coast, among the Swahili. Where their musicians were unable to obtain European trumpets and bugles (or, in the case of *scotchi,* sets of bagpipes), locally made kazoos or gourd trumpets and drums sufficed. A Ugandan poet and writer, Okot p'Bitek, reported how the concept of "armyness" was introduced to the Acooli Jok cult, and its possessed participants behaved in a characteristically military way.

Ex-members of the King's African Rifles took the idea of *beni* and its music, dress, and choreography back to their home villages in many parts of British East Africa, and though the original *beni, kingi,* and *scotchi* have been superseded among the urban coastal communities where they originated, stylistic features of *beni* survive in the *goma,* a men's dance with slow, precise movements, using walking sticks, dark glasses, and other "European" accoutrements (Campbell and Eastman 1984). Furthermore, one can find stylistic features of *beni* in the choreography of village dances in many inland areas of East Africa, where quite often the dances are regarded as "traditional." Examples are the *mganda* in Tanzania, the *malipenga* of northern Malawi (Kubik 1985:194–195), the *beni* of the Yao, and the *dingidingi* (a girls' dance) of Acooli, Uganda—the last no doubt a product of the parallel development of women's associations.

Summarizing a survey of *beni* and related associations Ranger considered these "societies were not pantomimes of white power, nor protest movements set against it . . . but concerned with survival, success and reputation of their members, acting as welfare societies, as sources of prestige, as suppliers of skill (1975:75). Though *beni* seem to have stood for features of twentieth-century music in Eastern Africa normally explained as the result of Europeanization, "the brass band itself had extra-European origins, and apparent exoticisms, like danced drill and mimed combat, were in fact derived from the long-standing competitive dance traditions of the Swahili coast" (Ranger 1975:164).

Religious institutions

Evidence suggests that the repertory and style of music at court paralleled, as one might expect, the high conservatism of the royal institutions. Royal music itself was often perceived as having a quasi-religious function, associated with the notion of the king's divinity.

Such conservatism is even truer of the music of the Monophysite Christian church of highland Ethiopia, founded in Axum in the fourth century. Its liturgy (*zema*) and religious poetry (*qene*) is chanted in the classical Sabean language known as Geʿez, and in the shaking of the sistrum to mark the ends of lines, it has parallels with religious performances in Jewish synagogues. Ecstatic liturgical dance (*aquaquam*) is another feature of this worship.

enswezi   Cult in southern Uganda whose
music is marked by the use of four drums
interlocking in fast triple rhythms

emibala   'Drum texts' that accompany
special songs addressed in turn to specific
spirits

A similar complex liturgy (also in Geʿez) was the subject of recent research among the Falasha of northern Ethiopia, where Kay Shelemay (1986) has established with convincing musical evidence that the religious tradition of the so-called Black Jews was strongly influenced by contact with Christian monasticism in the four-teenth and fifteenth centuries—and, indeed, that its very Jewishness may have stemmed from such contacts. In 1984, Operation Moses took most of the Falasha community to Israel, where the Falasha ritual will probably not survive.

Many traditional religious cults are based, as in many other parts of sub-Saharan Africa, on ancestor worship and a belief that ancestral spirits and other spirits have the power to intervene in the affairs of mortals. Examples are the *zār* cults of Sudan and parts of Ethiopia and Somalia, and the *bacwezi* cults of western Uganda. In southeastern Uganda, traditional healers of the *enswezi* cult use songs invoking indi-vidual spirits (*lubaale* 'gods' or *mayembe*), and these songs combine with dancing, drumming, and the use of loud rattles to help induce a variety of states of possession. Those who become possessed may be the sick persons, professional mediums, or even the officiating priest-healer.

Such religious music is usually distinguishable from secular music. In Busoga, southern Uganda, music of the *enswezi* cult is marked by the use of four drums inter-locking in fast triple rhythm, and with the lead drummer (who beats the three lower-pitched drums) inserting appropriate *emibala* 'drum texts' while accompanying spe-cial songs addressed in turn to specific spirits. Another ingredient in the musical tex-ture is provided by women cult members known as "daughters of Kintu." (Kintu was the chief ancestor of the cult, the legendary first king of the Ganda.) They join in the wordless refrains with voices disguised by singing into their kazoos (*engwara*), made from narrow conical sections of dried gourds.

Most systems of musical tuning in East Africa are pentatonic, and among the people of southern Sudan and Uganda there is a strong tendency toward equipenta-tonicism (Wachsmann 1950, 1967). The Wagogo of central Tanzania sing, often in parallel harmony, melodies that are basically tetratonic, and which Kubik (1985) considers are based on selective use of the sequence of natural harmonics from par-tials four to nine.

Kubik's own most recent research, however, suggests that interval size differences in such pentatonic scales are probably not emically significant. When presented with a wide range of pentatonic tunings of sample xylophone scales and melodies, even the most skilled traditional musicians (Ganda, Soga, Teso) judged them acceptable. The implications of such tests of perception require further investigation.

NOMADIC AND SEMINOMADIC PEOPLES

Vast areas of the Sudan, nearly all of Somalia, and parts of Ethiopia and the plains of inland Kenya, Tanzania, and northeastern Uganda, consist of desert or dry scrubland, thinly inhabited by pastoral peoples. They include the Cushitic-speaking Somali and

Oromo (sometimes known as "Galla") of southern Ethiopia, para-Nilotic peoples such as the Karamojong, Turkana, and Pokot to the southwest of Lake Rudolph, and the Samburu and Maasai of the rift-valley plains of Kenya and Tanzania. For many of these peoples, musical instruments would be an encumbrance. Their music is purely vocal, save for the occasional rhythmic accompaniment of hand clapping, or the sounds of stamping feet, sometimes enhanced by the jingling of ankle bells or other items of personal adornment. In Arab-influenced areas, frame drums or kettledrums may accompany such singing.

Historical traditions, war, and—above all—cattle are common subjects in nomads' repertory of songs. The melodies, like those of most Bantu- and Nilotic-speaking peoples, are mostly pentatonic; but unlike the melodies of these peoples, the phrase tends to be longer and more undulating, with frequent use of long-held tones. An example shows the refrain of a song performed by men of the Jie tribe in Karamoja, northeastern Uganda. Different soloists took turns to sing out brief utterances in a rapid speech rhythm between refrains. A wide range of nonlexical vocal utterances, some using explosive sounds from the diaphragm, typify the refrains.

Though call-and-response form is ubiquitous in Africa, among pastoralists the choral response tends to be longer than the call, and sometimes overlaps the soloists' parts to produce simple part singing, or includes ostinati, creating harmonies of fourths and fifths. However, such generalizations can be faulted. Kenneth Gourlay (1972) has shown the relative proportions of soloists' parts among the singing of Karimojong men's songs can vary greatly, depending on the genre. He has distinguished two categories of men's song, personal "ox songs" and choral songs, and has demonstrated how in the former the soloist's part can dominate the structure, while in the latter the choral refrains make up the major part of the pattern. Part singing in long choral refrains is a feature of the Nandi and Kipsigis peoples of western Kenya.

INDONESIAN, ARABIC, ISLAMIC, AND EUROPEAN INFLUENCES

The coastal peoples of East Africa have long had contact with the Arabic world, and with other cultures around the shores of the Indian Ocean. However, in a critical survey of the evidence (presented by Leo Frobenius, Erich M. von Hornbostel, Arthur M. Jones, and Jaap Kunst), R. Blench plays down the degree to which Indonesian influence penetrated the African continent. He concludes that while there is ample reason to suppose there was an influx of a people from some part of Indonesia to the Malagasy Republic (Madagascar) and the neighboring African coast, the evidence for Indonesian colonization and influence on parts of the interior (as suggested by Jones, who cites a good deal of musical and organological evidence) is "thoroughly insubstantial." Nevertheless, the *valiha,* the tube zither with wire strings fitted around a large tube of bamboo and played in Malagasy and in other parts of Tanzania, is a striking example of Indonesian importation. The *marimba,* a box-resonated xylophone, played in the islands of Zanzibar and Pemba and on the mainland nearby, is possibly additional evidence of cultural contact with Indonesia.

Myths sometimes provide tantalizing glimpses into the past. The "national" dance of the Baganda, most commonly performed for feasts, and said to have long been associated with the court of the former kabaka, is the *baakisimba*—a term derived from the verb *okusimba* 'to plant', and the steps are said to symbolize pressing the offshoots of plantains into the ground, and this action in turn is associated with the ancestor-god-king Kintu, who supposedly brought the plantain to Buganda. Plantains became not only the staple diet of the area, but also the chief ingredient of the beer and spirits necessary for celebrations and feasts (personal communication A. Ssempeke, 1988).

Most of the Sudan is Arabic-speaking, and Islam is the official religion of that

Quite apart from Arab contacts, the East African coast has long had a history of contact with the outside world.

country. The practice of Qur'ānic chanting in schools has accompanied the spread of Islam south into all the other countries of East Africa. Arabic poetry is enjoyed by the Arabic-speaking communities of the north and along the East African coast, and men of the Sudanese Sufi order perform the ecstatic ritual known locally and elsewhere in the Islamic world as *zikr* or *dhikr* 'remembrance'. The participants use a special, rhythmic, deep-breathing technique, combined with rhythmic movement and utterances of the name of Allah, to help them achieve communally their aim of communicating directly with their deity.

In many areas, however, musical practices associated with pre-Islamic cults, such as *zār* often flourish alongside Islamic practices. Young Miri women living in the Nuba mountains of Sudan enjoy singing commercially produced Arabic *dalūka* songs, which for them stand for, celebrate, and allow access to and indulgence in, "much of what they think best in the urban Sudan," while relishing the performance of their traditional rituals (Baumann 1987).

Early in the first millennium, Arab traders set up stations along the East African coast. Arabic influence is particularly noticeable on the islands of Zanzibar and Pemba, and to a lesser extent in the music of the coastal Swahili peoples, where epic songs (*utenzi*) and lyrical poems (*shairi*) use meters and strophic structures similar to those of Arabic poetry. Swahili heptatonic melodies, delivered with a certain amount of melisma, differ distinctly from the songs of most other Bantu-speaking peoples (Jones 1975–1976).

Descriptions of the types of *ngoma* performed in and around the port of Lamu (Campbell and Eastman 1984) show that Swahili culture has a mixed nature. Excepting the *goma*, these *ngoma*s, while using the *nzumari* (an Arabic shawm) or the *tarompet* (a Western cornet) and Arab-derived tambourines, feature styles of dancing that, with an emphasis on circular hip movements, are similar to the styles of dancing of other Bantu-speakers of inland East Africa. Farther inland, the Nyamwezi, a Bantu-speaking people of central Tanzania, who for centuries controlled the ivory trade routes to the interior, also sing in "Arabic" style—with diatonic melodies that have a certain amount of melisma. In the extreme southwest of East Africa, the Yao appear to have absorbed considerable Islamic influence.

Without other evidence of culture contact, it would be a mistake to assume Arab influence wherever diatonic or melismatic structures appear. For example, it would be difficult to show Arab musical contacts with the Konzo, who inhabit the Ruwenzori mountains along the Uganda-Zaïre border, despite their use of heptatonic songs and instruments, such as harps, flutes, zithers, and xylophones (Cooke and Doornbos 1982). The same is true for the Makonde of northern Mozambique and southern Tanzania, whose music is primarily hexatonic, based on roughly equal steps of 160–180 cents, and who in ensembles sing parallel thirds. The Makonde and their neighbors may be related more to the peoples of the Shaba province of southern Zaïre than to their Tanzanian neighbors farther north (Kubik 1982).

A highly melismatic and tense-voiced style, used by Hima pastoralists in western Uganda and their Tutsi counterparts of Rwanda and Burundi, is more problematic. These peoples have absorbed the language, but neither the musical style nor the diet and life-style, of the Bantu peoples they live among, and over whom they established ruling hegemonies.

Instruments have traveled more easily than musical styles. In the past century, the tube fiddle (a bowed lute, probably derived from the Arabic rebab) has migrated across Kenya, through southern Uganda, and as far west as Rwanda and Burundi. In the mid-to-late-twentieth century, townsfolk adopted Western instruments in considerable numbers, but rural people less frequently used them.

LATE-TWENTIETH-CENTURY DEVELOPMENTS AND URBAN MUSIC

Quite apart from Arab contacts, the East African coast has long had a history of contact with the outside world. Madagascar was extensively colonized by Indonesians. In the 1500s, Portuguese traders came to the coast of East Africa, but in the 1600s, they were ejected from Fort Jesus at Mombasa: their musical legacy may perhaps be the violin, still used alongside lutes and frame drums in small Arab orchestras playing the hybrid music known as *taarabu*.

Taarabu is found along the whole of the east coast of Tanzania and Kenya, particularly in the larger towns—Dar es Salaam, Malindi, Mombasa—where large instrumental ensembles perform music obviously based on that of Arabic orchestras. Indeed, in Dar es Salaam one of the first groups to be formed called itself "The Egyptian Music Club." Indian influences, mostly derived from Hindi film sound tracks, are also heard in the music of these groups. Indian harmoniums and Arabic instruments (notably the ʿudi, an unfretted lute derived from the Arabic ʿud) appear in the ensembles and in Lamu Island songs, sung in either of three languages—Swahili, Arabic, Hindi.

The harmonized hymns that Christian missionaries introduced to British and German East Africa after the 1850s are tending to be replaced. Christian Africans, sometimes called "Sunday composers," are experimenting in composing, for educational and religious choirs, traditional African-style melodies, not all of them harmonized in four parts in hymnbook style. Some are performed to accompaniments of drums and rattles, but in many newer churches in towns like Kampala, electric organs, bass guitars, and synthesizers are coming into use, and sects such as the Baptist and Free Presbyterian churches are popularizing the gospel-hymn repertory.

In the 1960s, the Roman Catholic Church in western Uganda adopted Benedicto Mubangizi's hymnbook, *Mweshongorere Mukama* (1968), which contains ninety-five hymns, many of them composed in call-and-response form. Its preface enjoins users not to introduce harmonies other than those produced by overlapping refrains in some of the hymns. Like other composers—such as Joseph Kyagambiddwa, a Muganda, whose *Uganda Martyrs' Oratorio* has been published, performed, and recorded in Europe and East Africa—Mubangizi takes care to compose in a way that does not disregard the traditional rules controlling the relationship between speech tones and melodies. During the 1980s, however, more and more of his hymns were being performed in four-part harmony.

In Kenya, Uganda, and Tanzania, school-music festivals have stimulated the production of innumerable secular and religious compositions in quasi-traditional style, staged alongside the performance of traditional tribal songs and dances, European scholastic songs, madrigals, and Christian spirituals. Arrangements of traditional songs are now part of the repertory of village cultural societies, which meet to rehearse and perform traditional songs and dances of the community in new contexts, grouped and sometimes acted out as miniature dramas.

In the 1960s, Zaïrean bands mingled with bands performing a new wave of *kwela* music, Congolese jazz, and popular European and American styles in the nightclubs of Kenya.

One would expect Western influence to be found in the popular urban music of East Africa. The guitar is ubiquitous. Even in rural districts it often vies for popularity with traditional stringed instruments, such as lyres and zithers. African radio networks are accountable for much of this development, though the first guitar music recordings appeared around 1945. J. Low (1982) identified the successive adoption of a variety of styles of playing in Kenya—from the simple vamping of Swahili-language town music to the complex finger styles of Congolese musicians like Mwenda-Jean Bosco and Musango. This variety gave some indication of the degree to which popular musicians circulated around East Africa.

The appearance of electric guitar bands in the 1960s allowed other Western instruments to join the ensembles, and at that time Zaïrean bands (whose musicians had migrated from their hometowns during the civil wars there) mingled with bands performing a new wave of *kwela* music, Congolese jazz, and popular European and American styles in the nightclubs of Kampala, Nairobi, and Mombasa. In the 1970s, singers tended to become more important in such bands, with much part singing and call-and-response patterns using local languages, while guitar parts were tending to become more rhythmic than melodic. Though Western popular music is continually making inroads, much of this music includes African-American, Caribbean, and Latin American styles—all of which owe much to an African heritage.

In rural areas most distant from towns (though such music is readily available on transistor radios), any imitations of Western popular music have tended to be dominated by essentially African features. Intervillage competitions held in Acooli (northern Uganda) during the late 1960s featured groups of youths playing three sizes of *likembe,* lamellophones, in ensembles of up to fifteen. Though the *likembe* itself was a newcomer to Acooli (having traveled northeast from the Congo during the previous thirty years), and though the youths' repertory included pieces entitled "Rumba" and "Vals" and "Foxtrot," plus tunes said to have been inspired by the white American country singer Jim Reeves, the way each instrumental part was composed, and the way it interlocked with the other parts, were purely Acooli in style, closely related to the style of music played on the Acooli trough zither (*nanga*).

REFERENCES

Baumann, Gerd. 1987. *National Integration and Local Integrity.* Oxford: Oxford University Press.

Blench, Roger. 1982. "Evidence for the Indonesian Origins of Certain Elements of African Culture: A Review with Special Reference to the Arguments of A. M. Jones." *African Music: Journal of the International Library of African Music* 6(2):81–93.

Campbell, C. A., and C. M. Eastman. 1984.

"Ngoma: Swahili Adult Song Performance in Context." *Ethnomusicology* 27(3):467–494.

Cooke, Peter, and Martin Doornbos. 1982. "Rwenzururu Protest Songs." *Africa* 52(1):37–60.

Gourlay, Kenneth A. 1972. "The Making of Karimojong Cattle Songs." Nairobi: Institute of African Studies, University of Nairobi. Discussion paper 18.

Jones, Arthur M. 1964. *Africa and Indonesia: The Evidence of the Xylophone and Other Musical and Cultural Factors.* Leiden: E. J. Brill.

———. 1975–1976. "Swahili Epic Poetry: A Musical Study." *African Music: Journal of the African Music Society* 5(4):105–129.

Kubik, Gerhard. 1982. *Ostafrika: Musikgeschichte in Bildern,* vol. 1: *Musikethnologie,* part 10. Leipzig: VEB Deutscher Verlag für Musik.

———. 1985. "African Tone Systems: A Reassessment." *Yearbook for Traditional Music* 17:31–63.

Low, John. 1982. "A History of Kenyan Guitar Music: 1945–1980." *African Music: Journal of the International Library of African Music* 6(2):17–36.

Mubangizi, Benedicto. 1968. *Mweshongorere Mukama* [*Sing to the Lord*], 2nd edition. Kisubi, Uganda.

Ranger, Terence O. 1975. *Dance and Society in Eastern Africa 1890–1970: The Beni Ngoma.* Berkeley: University of California Press.

Shelemay, Kay Kaufman. 1986. *Music, Ritual and Falasha History.* East Lansing: Michigan State University Press.

Wachsmann, Klaus P. 1950. "An Equal-Stepped Tuning in a Ganda Harp." *Nature* 165:40–41.

———. 1967. "Pan-Equidistance and Accurate Pitch: A Problem from the Source of the Nile." *Festschrift für Walter Wiora,* ed. Ludwig Finscher and Christopher-Hellmut Mahling, 583–592. Cassel: Bärenreiter.

Wachsmann, Klaus P., and Kathleen Margaret Trowell. 1953. *Tribal Crafts of Uganda.* New York: Oxford University Press.

Music and Poetry in Somalia
John William Johnson

Musical Instruments
Innovation of Musical Forms
Linguistic Traits of Somali Prosody
Musical Traits of Somali Prosody
The Classes of Genres
Somali Professional Music

Uniquely in Africa, the people of Somalia constitute a single ethnic group. In the early 1990s, the national population was about five million, only one percent of which were non-Somalis. During the colonial period (late 1800s, early 1900s), political decisions severed from the main body another one and a half to two million Somalis, who live in frontier regions of Djibouti, Ethiopia, and Kenya. Though unified in religion (Islam), language, and ethnic identity, Somalis divide into clan families, with lineages and subgroupings based on agnatic patriliny. Until 1991, one central administration governed the country.

The Somali language is in the Eastern Cushitic branch of the Afroasiatic family (Greenberg 1970:49). The spelling of Somali words here follows the alphabet devised for the language and put into general use in 1972 (Andrzejewski 1974). Because non-Somalis do not commonly recognize indigenous orthographical conventions, alternate spellings of certain words in this article parenthetically follow their first occurrence.

Several socioeconomic traditions distinguish the country. The main ones are nomadic herding (camel, sheep, goats, cattle), settled farming, and urban dwellers' mercantile pursuits. At independence (1960), 75 to 80 percent of the people participated in nomadic animal husbandry; by 1987, however, only an estimated 44 percent were still nomads. Since 1900, Somalia has seen an increase in urbanization, though the mercantile cities of Berbera in the north, and Muqdishow (Mogadishu), Marka (Merka), and Barawa (Brava) in the south, have had permanent settlements for centuries. Also since 1900, a portion of the populace has shifted from nomadism to agriculture.

Until the Italian scholar Francesco Giannattasio began studying Somali music, ethnomusicological research in Somali verbal and musical arts was virtually nonexistent. Academic knowledge about Somali music included only one primary article (Johnson 1980), plus casual observations in publications dealing with disciplines other than music, or in accounts published by travelers (Barblan 1941; Battista 1969; Carboni 1983; Duchenet 1938; Heinitz 1920; Omar Au Nuh 1972; Pesenti 1910; Vianney 1957; Wachsmann 1965).

Most scholarship on Somali oral performance has focused on the oral poetry of northern, pastoral Somalis (Ahmed Ali Abokor 1990; Andrzejewski 1982; Andrzejewski and Lewis 1964; Johnson 1988, 1993). In discussing poetic texts, a few articles mention Somali music; some describe word-music relationships (Johnson 1974), and include musical scores (Berghold, 1899; Johnson 1972). By systematically applying scholarly methods, Giannattasio's most important articles (1983, 1988a, 1988b) have changed the academic understanding of Somali music.

MUSICAL INSTRUMENTS

Socioeconomic diversity leads to regional differences in Somali cultural expression, including music. Important regional differences exist in the use of instrumental musical accompaniment with the songs and poems of northern nomads, southern farmers, and urban populations (of both ancient and recent origin). Until the late 1940s, northern nomads used no musical instrument except a drum, beaten by women. Hand clapping and foot stamping as rhythmic accompaniment, however, are common throughout Somalia.

In the performance of oral genres, people in agricultural and older mercantile cities employ a variety of musical instruments. In southern regions, they use three drums (*durbaan, yoome, nasar*) and hand-held clappers. Some clappers are of carved wood (*shanbaal*). Some, with resonating chambers whittled from their centers, have little decoration, unlike their West African counterparts; though not so large (about a third of a meter in length), they resemble eighteenth-century European military officers' cocked hats. Other clappers (*sharaq, biro*), with a flat, triangular shape, are of metal. They resemble metal hoe heads and axheads, and hoeing may actually be their primary function; in fact, one Somali lineage calls the clapper and the hoe by the same term (*yaambo*).

For musical accompaniment and signaling, coastal Somalis use *Bursa, Turbinella,* and other gastropod seashells (*buun, caroog*). By buzzing their lips into a hole drilled in the apex, or on the side of the spire of the shell, skilled users can produce a loud sound. For the same purpose, southern Somalis use the horns of antelopes (*gees, gees-goodir*), plus a variety of horns carved from wood and cane (*siimbaar, malakata, sumari, parapanda*). They also play a six-stringed lyre (*shareero*).

Some Somali instruments occur over a wide geographical range, and appear among other groups in eastern Africa. Between 1950 and 1960, musicians in Somalia also began to play the principal instruments of Western orchestras and bands.

INNOVATION OF MUSICAL FORMS

The history of music in Somalia from the early 1940s reflects artistic innovation, which brought about important changes in Somali musical expression. Scholars often call older forms of Somali music and poetry traditional, and newer forms modern; but it may be more useful to view the process of Somali musical and poetic traditions as continuous, with a multiplicity of aspects. Some pieces are older, and some newer; some indigenous, and some of foreign origin; some conservative, and some more open to change. Perceiving older forms as "traditional" gives a false sense of their cultural stagnation, and tends to deny that they too were once innovative. Some of them show the influence of foreign modes of expression, as some newer Somali forms do.

Certain aspects of Somali musical behavior have widespread representation among other Cushitic nations in East Africa. An alternative view is to call the older forms nonprofessional and the newer ones professional. Nonprofessional Somali genres are still composed and performed by men and women who, though skilled musicians and poets, do not make a living from musical performance. People who receive government support (through bureaucratic agencies such as the National Theater)

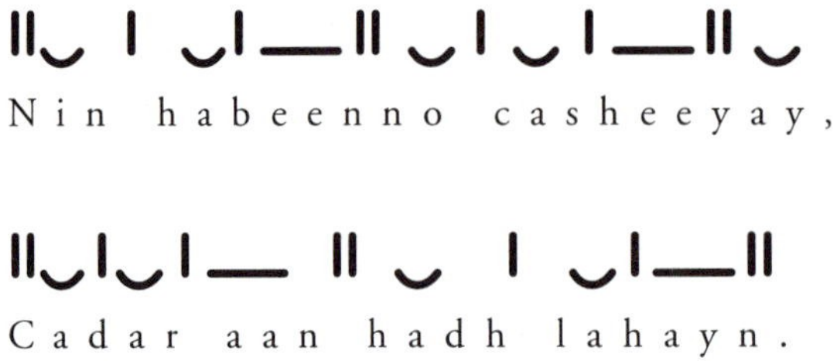
Nin habeenno casheeyay,
Cadar aan hadh lahayn.

FIGURE 1 Closed-set morosyllabic relationship in *geeraar.* Translation: "He who sups plentifully every night, / [Whom pride shrouds like] a shadeless cloud."

and public support (through the sale of tickets to privately produced performances and mass-produced cassettes) create professional forms.

Until the 1990s, Somalis in their oral expression made no dynamic distinction between music and poetry. All forms of poetry can be sung, and some are always sung. The domestic classification of the forms of Somali oral performance rests on a combination of structures, only one of which relates to music. To differentiate one genre from another, four criteria—scansion, melody, topic, function—act in concert. If any criterion changes, the genre may change. Two forms may have the same scansion, the same melody, and the same subject matter, but be different in function. Most of the time, more than one criterion actually differentiates genres. Moreover, Somalis group genres into larger classes, according to function and social context.

LINGUISTIC TRAITS OF SOMALI PROSODY

The prosody of Somali poetry takes a patterned configuration of long and short vowels (Johnson 1988). The temporal duration of a short vowel, a mora, occupies an amount of time analysts call a seme. In a given poem, a monoseme contains a short vowel of one mora, but a diseme contains two moras.

Three principles characterize the relationship between moras and syllables. First, a closed-set morosyllabic relationship allows only long vowels to fill disemes, resulting in an identical number of syllables and vowels (long or short) in each line, with a fixed number of moras. Second, an open-set morosyllabic relationship allows either one long or two short vowels to fill disemes. Since there are two moras in a diseme, the number of syllables may vary randomly, depending on how many vowels occur. Finally, in a semiopen-set morosyllabic relationship, with a specified number of disemes and a specified number of syllables, there are always more disemes than long-vowel requirements, so some disemes must contain two short vowels, while others must contain long vowels. Poetic license lets composers choose which disemes to fill with long vowels, and which to fill with short vowels. All Somali genres have specific rules about the arrangement of disemic and monosemic patterns in a line of poetry. Such arrangements sometimes result in units comparable to feet in English prosody. In some cases, the line is the smallest recurrent pattern of semes. Terms like *foot, line, mora,* and *seme,* used here for convenience, do not represent indigenous Somali lexemes. Much of the local understanding of these rules is implicit, and critical terminology, when it occurs, tends to be metaphoric, not systematic.

The key to understanding how Somali poetry scans is an uncompromising rule: long vowels may not cross semic boundaries. A description of the semic configuration in the genre Somalis call *geeraar* illustrates a closed-set morosyllabic relationship. In figure 1, a micron symbolizes short vowels, and a macron symbolizes long vowels; vertical lines separate semes, and double vertical lines separate feet.

An additional symbol illustrates an open-set morosyllabic relationship, which may be symbolized by a dotted vertical line between the halves of the diseme. The

FIGURE 2   Open-set morosyllabic relationship in *jiifto*. Translation: "And have you not openly admitted this, / In the full light of day?"

Sow duhur dharaareed,

Dibnahaaga ka ma qiran?

following lines come from a poem of the genre called *jiifto*, always recited in couplets (figure 2).

The only instance of a semiopen-set morosyllabic relationship so far discovered appears in the second hemistich of the *gabay*, where three possibilities may occur (figure 3). There are always six syllables, and always eight moras. Three lines from a *gabay* composed by the Sayyid Maxamed Cabdille Xasan (Mohamed Abdulla Hassan), the famed "mad mullah of Somaliland," illustrate these possibilities (figure 4).

Somali rhyme always involves alliteration. The *geeraar* of figure 1 alliterates in 'C', Somali orthography for the phoneme *cayn* (IPA /ʕ/). The *jiifto* above alliterates in 'D' (IPA /d/), and the *gabay* alliterates in 'J' (IPA /č/).

MUSICAL TRAITS OF SOMALI PROSODY

Somali music—both the older, nonprofessional, and the newer, post-1945 professional—uses a pentatonic scale, the tones of which are not standardized by pitch. There is a window of frequencies in which notes are acceptably "on pitch." The resulting intervals are also unstandardized; but relative to the pitches on either side of them, they are more predictable.

Melody helps differentiate Somali genres. Subservient to language-internal

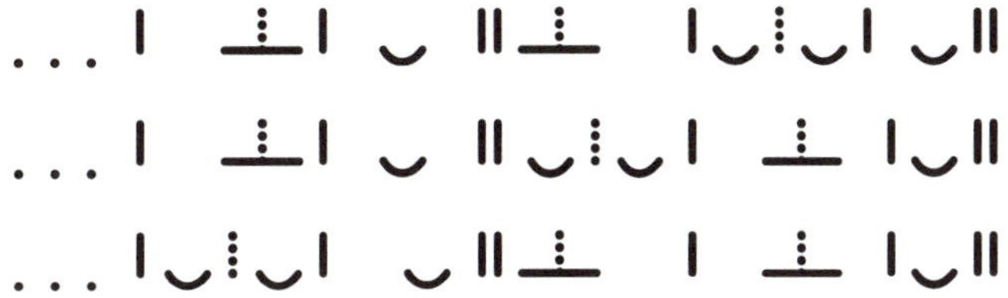

FIGURE 3   Semiopen-set morosyllabic relationship in *gabay*.

FIGURE 4   Excerpt from a *gabay* composed by Sayyid Maxamed Cabdille Xasan, with various morosyllabic relationships. Translation: "You did not abandon me when the ignorant ones fled in fear. / You did not go to the [Abyssinian] emperor when your relatives did. / Any man who does not kill infidels is a kinsman of hell."

Adaan iga jadeer wacin markuu,

jaahilkii diday e,

Jaanhooy adaan qaban markuu,

jiitay gacalkaa ye,

Raggaan gaalo jeefaafin waa,

ehel iaxiimaad e.

FIGURE 5 The first line of a *heello*, by Caweys Geedow, composed in 1965. Translation: "Let me give you some advice, O youths, / For water has been found."

A— ni— laa— bal— la mee— bar–baar — eey — bi– yo waa— la hel– ee, —

constraints (Bird 1976), indigenous Somali musical traits are predictable from the scansion of the poetry. A small number of melodies belong to each genre, and a musician can utilize any one of them to sing any poem in the genre; but each of these melodies is subservient to the prosody of the genre. Hearing a Somali whistling, one might guess the genre, but not the poem. Conversely, Somali professional poetry reflects language-external constraints. Each poem within a genre has its own melody, which sets up a rhythm that supersedes linguistic prosody: "the movement of speech through poetry to song is in fact a continuum" of ever-increasing constraints (Bird 1976:95).

The interaction between music and words represents a polyrhythmic relationship in Somali scansion. Because linguistic scansion is quantitative, its perception—through short and long durations of vowels (annotated by scholars with macrons and microns)—is rhythmic. Duration in music is also quantitative, and its perception—through short and long sung vowels (annotated by scholars with musical notes)—is the element that gives music its rhythm. Simultaneously, audiences and poets alike can perceive the poetic and musical rhythms, and can follow their interrelationships. At the same time, in the same stream of speech, a performer recites two parallel systems of rhythm. This kind of polyrhythm is unique in Africa.

In closed-set moromusical relationships, long notes occur in music when long vowels occur in the scansion; similarly, short notes occur with short vowels, whether in monosemes, or when two short vowels occur in disemes. An excerpt from a *heello*, represents long vowels with quarter notes or their equivalent (two eighth notes), or with notes of longer duration, and represents short vowels with eighth notes (figure 5). Microns and macrons annotate scansion. Apart from the rhythm generated by the music (a recurrent pulse of short–short–long), there is no regular scansion in the poem, which exemplifies language-external constraints. In the second and fourth measures, where long vowels last longer than the duration of a quarter note, the accompaniment (not shown) continues to carry the rhythm of short–short–long.

In open-set moromusical relationships, there is no relationship between note duration and vowel length. No matter what scansion occurs in the poem, short notes occur in the music. This lack of relationship might be characterized as free verse. Like all Somali nonprofessional poetry, it exemplifies language-internal constraints.

Figure 6 illustrates this relationship. In the scansion, long musical notes set long vowels; likewise, short musical notes set short vowels. (This pattern sometimes reverses.) The resulting polyrhythmic juxtapositions produce rhythmic syncopations.

The excerpts of figure 7 illustrate rhythmic syncopation. Triangular note heads show short vowels sung to long notes; square note heads show long vowels sung to short notes; regular, elliptical note heads show the use of short notes with short vowels and long notes with long vowels. The first line of the poem sets the scansion with a nonsense formula of varying vowel lengths; after the second line, the figure skips to the fifteenth. A silence of one diseme's length completes the second foot in the line.

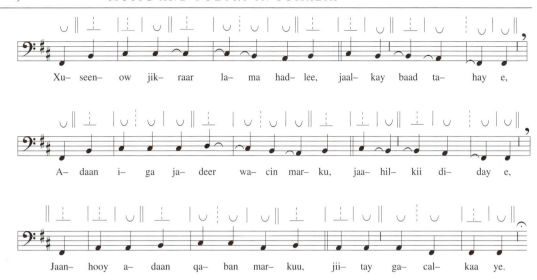

FIGURE 6   Excerpt from a *gabay* by Sayyid Maxamed Cabdille Xasan, composed about 1910. Translation: "O Hussein, do not speak obstinately; you are my friend. / You did not abandon me when the ignorant ones fled in fear. / You did not go to the [Abyssinian] emperor when your relatives did."

In the last line, Somali grammar requires that the morpheme *ma* (question marker) be short, but Somalis say it sounds long to them. Against an argument the vowel has to be short or it would be misspelled, they insist it is long, though they do not understand why. That the note duration of this prosodic slot is also short would make a short-voweled morpheme appropriate, but what listeners expect to hear in this prosodic slot is the syncopated reversal of vowel length and note duration, conditioned from previous lines. Investigation with a computer program that digitizes speech and prints it in wide-band spectrograms shows the duration of this slot is short. Somali listeners perceive the vowel to be prosodically long, though it is grammatically and phonologically short.

THE CLASSES OF GENRES

Somalis combine groups of genres into classes, determined mainly by function and context, reflected topically. Three of these classes are most prominent, and scholars have labeled them from two points of view: students of literature call them classical poetry, work poetry, and recreational poetry; students of music call them poetry, song, and dance. Somalis call them *gabay*, *hees*, and *cayaar* (or *ciyaar*). These terms are easy to gloss ('poetry', 'song', 'play'), but researchers have difficulty understanding how Somalis view the concepts the terms convey. To Somalis, each class is both poet-

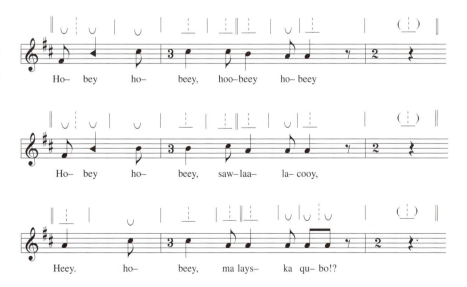

FIGURE 7   Excerpt from a *hees maqasha* 'lamb- or kid-watering song', by Cibaado Jaamac Faarax (Ibado Jama Farah), composed in 1987. Translation: "*Hobey hobeey, hoobeey hobeey, / Hobey hobeey*, O you who scamper about, . . . / *Heey hobeey*, why are they [not] cast out?"

The *hees* class includes many work songs, differentiated mainly by function and performer's sex. People sing when driving camels to watering points, watering them, rewatering them, driving them to grazing areas, driving them to corrals, and loading goods onto their backs.

ic and musical. However, the newer, professional form is not; and the duality of names Somalis give to it bears witness to their problem of integrating it into their poetic-musical tradition. By naming it *heello*, they emphasize its poetic origins. *Heello, heellooy,* and *heelleellooy,* are words used in an introductory formula, the main function of which is to set the scansion of a poem. Other linked vocables (such as *hobaale, hobeeye,* and *balwooy*) serve the same purpose. Sometimes, however, the same genre is a *hees* 'song', a term that emphasizes its musical characteristics. Each *heello-hees* has a unique melody, and does not employ a generic one—which may account for the duality of nomenclature and the confusion.

Classical poetry

The *gabay* class includes the genres *gabay, geeraar, jiifto,* and *buraambur*. The most prestigious genre in this class is also called *gabay*. (For naming a category, Somalis often use one term in a list of related terms.) The *gabay* is known as *guurow* in the south, where a variant name, *masafo,* also exists for the *jiifto*, especially when it covers religious topics. Except for the *buraambur* (reserved for women), these poems are composed and recited by men. Topics these genres deal with include politics, war, peace, social debate, interclan negotiations, and philosophy. Their performance, which occurs only in serious contexts, functions similarly to newspaper editorials, political speeches, and philosophical exegeses.

For each genre, the scansion is tight and unified. A poem of poor scansion elicits severe criticism, and its composer often fails to persuade. Except for the *buraambur*, alliteration involves only one consonant per poem, which may have as many as seventy or eighty lines—a mental feat few can manage. Alternately, all the vowels alliterate together, so a poem may alliterate with words that begin with any vowel. The rules tax memory so strenuously, some poets limit their repertories to a few consonants for alliteration.

Poets compose classical poems in private, and memorize them verbatim for public performance. Some people have skill in composing classical poetry, but others specialize in memorizing and reciting in public. People often remember composers by name, as creators of specific poems. Though some variation occurs between the recitations of the same poem by different people, evidence gathered in fieldwork suggests that, from one performance to another, individuals do not vary much in their own recitation of a given poem. In 1987, I collected about 6,000 lines of poetry from a memorizer, with about nine months between performances; in the second performance, he changed only three words. In versions of the same poem recited by different people, more (and often significant) differences occur.

Work songs

The *hees* class includes many work songs, differentiated mainly by function and performer's sex. Each socially defined form of work is represented by a genre. The various forms of work associated with camels, for example, result in separate genres. People sing *heesaha aroorka* when driving camels to watering points; *heesaha shubaaha*, for watering them; *heesaha rakaadda*, for rewatering them; *heesaha fulinta*, for driving them to grazing areas; *heesaha carraabada*, for driving them to corrals; and *heesaha raridda*, for loading goods onto their backs. Similarly, poems exist for watering cattle (*heesaha lo'da*), watering sheep and goats (*heesaha waarabinta adhiga*), herding sheep and goats (*heesaha kaxaynta adhiga*), herding lambs and kids (*heesaha maqasha*), weaving the mats used as outer walls of the portable nomadic house (*heesaha kebedda, heesaha aloolka, heesaha harraka*), churning milk (*heesaha lulidda*), pounding grain (*heesaha mooyaha*), and comforting and rocking children (*heesaha carruurta*). This list is only a partial one.

The scansion of some of the genres in this class is so complex, they may have been memorized verbatim for public performance, as matweaving *heeso* are. But other genres, like the *heeso* for pounding and milk churning, are simpler in structure and rhythm. So much repetition occurs, composition is formulaic (Lord 1960); but different singers repeat so many words exactly, memory obviously plays a role.

Dance songs

The third class (*cayaar*) is musically the most complex. It contains many generic forms, whose musical performance researchers have little explored. The names of these genres may not always indicate a set pattern of scansion, and much regional variation complicates their analysis. A *dhaanto* in one part of the country, for example, is not the same as a poem with that name in another part. Moreover, a term that represents a genre to one singer sometimes represents a larger generic class to another, even to a person from the same region. One poet used the word *dhaanto* synonymously with the larger class of *cayaar*. Some of the most common dance genres from different regions of Somalia are *gaaleysi, saar-lugeed, saddexley, saar-mooye, wale-saqo, ceerigaabo, bariyo, jaan-dheer, guuxo, dawladamiin, shaba-shabaay, gabley-shimbir, balwo, hirwo, dhaanto, wiglo, shirib, balaqley, tur,* and *jiib*.

Unlike the other two classes of Somali genres, dance poems are not composed once and memorized. Their topics often deal specifically with activities surrounding the performance. There is so little refrain in their lines, however, they may not be formulaically composed, though composition is simultaneous with performance.

The description of one session will shed light on composition in performance. On 29 May 1987, dancers from all over Somalia attended a street festival in Muqdishow, the capital. As usual at national festivals, groups competed for public attention, starting about four o'clock in the afternoon, and continuing until sundown. In one group, Cabdillaahi Xirsi "Baarleex" (Abdillahi Hirsi Barleh), a singer from the Ogaadeeniya (Ogaden) region of Ethiopia—the far western area, where Somalis live—performed a poem he called a *dhaanto*. The rest of his company surrounded him in a circle. In his verses, he maintained a consistent scansion, and sang eight to fifteen lines of solo at a time; but enjambment obscured where one line ended and another began—a phenomenon unknown in *gabay* and *hees*. He did not maintain a consistent rhythm.

The lines of figure 8 illustrate the style of the solo part. The scansion is the same as for the classical *geeraar*: two feet to the line, in a closed-set morosyllabic relationship. After the second foot, an optional monoseme may be truncated, though it is always a monoseme, even if its vowel is long.

At a certain point, the soloist began singing a rhythmic refrain of two lines. During this performance, he taught this refrain to two choirs (one male and one female), which quickly learned their parts and sang it antiphonally. After several solo performances (all followed by choral refrains), the soloist changed the refrain, which

After about 1943, more and more musical innovations came into being, in both style and instrumentation (electric guitars, electric organs, Western drum sets). Radio stations in Muqdishow and Hargeysa became the principal medium of diffusion for the new genre.

FIGURE 8 Excerpt from a *dhaanto* by Cabdillaahi Xirsi "Baarleex" (Abdillahi Hirsi Barley), from the Ogaden region, 29 May 1987. Translation: "The nation knows me: / How often have I, in my country, / Great literature and song / Performed in my language! / God created it in me."

TRACK 15

did not scan identically with the previous one. After he started each refrain, the second choir began singing with the first choir at the caesura of the second line, and would then sing both lines, joined by the first choir during the second hemistich of the second line. So it proceeded, until a cue from the soloist allowed him to begin another burst of solo. Figure 9 illustrates one of the choral refrains.

The solo-choral refrain repeated about a dozen times; and then suddenly, untaught by the soloist, the choirs began singing a different chorus, in a different rhythm. This time, the lines were twice as long as before, but again each choir antiphonally sang two lines of refrain. This rhythm cued dancers to enter the center circle. When they finished dancing, the entire process would repeat. Each performance (soloist, choral refrain, dance) lasted from twenty to thirty minutes, and the singers and dancers would then rest for a while.

SOMALI PROFESSIONAL MUSIC

The *heello-hees* originated in the period just after 1945, when foreign influence caused Somali musical behavior to change. During World War II, the introduction of radio had exposed Somalis to English, Italian, Arabic, and Indian musics. Somali men in Hargeysa, capital of the then British Somaliland Protectorate, formed a theatrical company, the Brothers of Hargeysa (*Walaalo Hargeysa*), whose innovations included use of the newly emerging *heello-hees*, with the introduction of a small orchestra (flute, violin, tambourine, drum). Because this company's productions sounded political themes (topics earlier reserved for classical *gabayo*), the new form rapidly gained popularity in the drive toward independence.

FIGURE 9 The choral refrain in a *dhaanto*; Parliament Square, Muqdishow, 29 May 1987. Translation: "I have fallen for you. Do you feel the same?"

Change from the older forms included the accelerating introduction of foreign musical instruments. In distinction to nonprofessional genres (which drew from a common stock of melodies), the *heello-hees* had melodies unique to each newly composed poem. The new distinctions of composer of poetry, composer of music, professional singer, and professional musician, joined the composer-reciter distinction of nonprofessional poetry. Like its foreign models, the earliest of which was Indian, the new form made extensive use of patterned refrains, sometimes sung by male and female choirs. Much of this innovation stems from the British practice of paying royalties to Somali composers of poems broadcast on radio. Because the British paid more for longer poems, refrains became popular among Somali *heello-hees* composers and musicians.

After about 1943, more and more musical innovations came into being, in both style and instrumentation (electric guitars, electric organs, Western drum sets). Radio stations in Muqdishow and Hargeysa became the principal medium of diffusion for the new genre, but stations abroad began to play Somali music and poetry too: by the 1970s, radio stations in Addis Ababa, Djibouti, Cairo, London, Moscow, and Peking, featured Somali music and poetry. With radio, the burgeoning Somali theater continued its use of the new poetry and music. In Muqdishow, an Italian military conductor formed an orchestra, which performed on radio, at military parades, and at special public events. During this period, private ensembles playing both Somali music and foreign music began to emerge. In both these spheres of support (government and private), the new genre began to gain in prestige alongside the classical genres, because it began to include political topics.

Another innovation in the public use of this poetry helps clarify the relationship of music and poetry to social structures on the Horn of Africa. Nonprofessional poetry represents a more gerontocractic hierarchy of control in the composition, performance, and use of serious poetry; but the *heello-hees* allows much younger men—and even more radically, women—to have a voice in politics. To be taken seriously, the classical genres of *gabay, jiifto,* and *geeraar,* which hold the highest prestige in nomadic life, have to be composed by old men. A description of the Somali tradition of *silsilaad* 'poetic chain combat' illustrates this fact. Somali poets challenge each other to poetic duels in the classical genres. The most admired poem composed in answer to another is not only in the same genre, but also in the same alliteration. The D-alliteration in one such poem of the 1980s dominated some sixty-seven *jiiftos* before it changed. Moreover, only poets of equal reputation may contribute to the chain. Violations of this rule, and debates on the abilities of specific poets and on political issues, result in lively arguments and disagreements about the levels of pres-

In the early 1960s, high government officials suppressed the use of poetry and song in political debate. To slip past the censors, Somali poets returned to forms of traditional speech—veiled for airing on radio.

tige surrounding poems in the same chain; but Somali youths may not participate in this tradition.

Unlike veiled political and social commentary in work songs and recreational poetry (where younger men and women of all ages have found an outlet for expressing their views in the context of Somali nomadic life), the *heello-hees* class of professional poetry has always been a medium under the control of youths. Participation of younger Somalis in the political life of the country is an innovation in Somalia. That the first major political party in the southern regions of the country bore the name Somali Youth League is no accident. Beginning in the 1950s, many *heello-hees* treated political themes; hence, Somali nomadic elders held professional poetry in contempt. Including political topics in this genre placed it in an ambiguous position.

Another turn of events resulted from the rise of power among youths. In the early 1960s, high government officials suppressed the use of poetry and song in political debate. Censorship grew highly effective; and to slip past the censors, Somali poets returned to forms of traditional speech—veiled for airing on radio. Early in 1967, Axmed Suleebaan Bidde (Ahmed Suleman Bidde) composed the poem "*Leexo* 'Swaying To and Fro'." It may initially have contained a veiled message, but its later use proved more sensational. Its overt topic was unrequited love, but its textual imagery invited varied interpretations. In those days, the parliament, not the public, elected the national president, who would appoint a prime minister to form a government. The incumbent president, Aadan Cabdulla Cismaan (Adan Abdulla Osman) was running for reelection, challenged by Cabdi-rashiid Cali Shar-Ma-Arke (Abdi Rashid Ali Shirmarke) and others. On the first two ballots, no one gained a majority. Radio Muqdishow was carrying the process live. During the caucus after the second ballot, it aired—and through loudspeakers, broadcast to the parliamentary floor—the poem *Leexo*. On the third ballot, the assembly elected Shar-Ma-Arke president. On charges of subverting the parliamentary system, the police then arrested the radioman responsible for airing the poem. However, because of the veiled speech in the poem, and because he was neither the composer nor the performer, the court acquitted him. *Leexo* has since become known as "the poem that overthrew a government."

It would not be surprising if *Leexo* became known as "the poem that overthrew *two* governments." In late 1990 and early 1991, civil war raged in Muqdishow. The forces of the president, General Maxamed Siyad Barre (Mohamed Siyad Barré), were weakening daily. Though staffers at the British Broadcasting Corporation in London thought the airing of *Leexo* tantamount to taking sides in the conflict, the Somali section of the corporation received permission to air it, and on 26 January 1991, at about 5:30 p.m. (Somali time), broadcast the poem. About an hour later, the president fled the capital, and his government fell. Though the broadcast had little to do with toppling the régime, its timing will likely add to the aura that surrounds the poem.

Study of the performance of Somali music and poetry in everyday social interaction—old or new, professional or nonprofessional, accompanied by musical instruments or merely by hand clapping—adds to the academic understanding of Somali social systems. Future study of Somali verbal art may help unravel some of the knottiest issues of human artistic behavior. Somalia is an ideal site for studying how memory and formula relate to the composition and diffusion of oral poetry, and how music relates to poetic scansion.

Somali classical poetry (*gabay*) consists of texts composed in private, and memorized verbatim for public performance. Work songs (*hees*) seem highly formulaic, though some of them are probably composed in performance, as the rhythms of work and poetry join. Finally, poetry in dance songs (*cayaar*) is composed and recited simultaneously, but not within the formulaic method.

A skillful Somali may participate in all three traditions. A young man growing up around people who sing formulaic work songs may learn to compose work songs while laboring among his livestock. As a youth, he may learn to compose dance songs during their performance at festivals. When he becomes an elder, he may refuse to compose dance songs because of the lowliness of their social prestige, and may then compose classical poems.

REFERENCES

Ahmed Ali Abokor. 1990. "Somali Pastoral Work Songs: The Poetic Voice of the Politically Powerless." M.A. thesis, Indiana University.

Andrzejewski, Bogumił Witalis. 1974. "The Introduction of a National Orthography for Somali." *African Language Studies* 15:199–203.

———. 1982. "Alliteration and Scansion in Somali Oral Poetry and their Cultural Correlates." In *Genres, Forms, Meanings: Essays in African Oral Literature,* ed. Veronika Görög-Karady, 68–83. Oxford: Journal of the Anthropological Society of Oxford.

Andrzejewski, Bogumił Witalis, and I. M. Lewis. 1964. *Somali Poetry: An Introduction.* Oxford: Oxford University Press.

Barblan, G. 1941. *Musiche e Strumenti Musicali dell'Africa Orientale Italiana.* Naples: Triennale d'Oltremare.

Battista, P. 1969. *Somalia—Storia, Folklore, Tradizioni, Poemi, Poesie, Canti.* Naples: Il Galo.

Berghold, Kurt. 1899. "Somali-Studien." *Wiener Zeitschrift für die Kunde des Morgenlandes* 13:123–198.

Bird, Charles S. 1976. "Poetry in the Mande: Its Form and Meaning." *Poetics* 5:89–100.

Carboni, Fabio. 1983. "780 Musica." In *Bibliografia Somala—Primo Contributo,* ed. Fabio Carboni, 155–156. Rome: Ministero degli Affari Esteri.

Duchenet, Edouard. 1938. "Le Chant dans le Folklore Somali." *Revue de Folklore Français* 9:72–87.

Giannattasio, Francesco. 1983. "Somalia: La Terapia Coreutico-Musicali del Mingis." *Culture Musicali* 2(3):93–119.

———. 1988a. "Strumenti Musicali." In *Aspetti dell' Espressione Artistica in Somalia,* ed. Annarita Puglielli, 73–89. Rome: University of Rome.

———. 1988b. "The Study of Somali Music: Present State." In *Proceedings of the Third International Congress of Somali Studies,* ed. Annarita Puglielli, 158–167. Rome: Il Pensiero Scientifico Editore.

Greenberg, Joseph H. 1970. *The Languages of Africa,* 3rd ed. Bloomington and The Hague: Indiana University Press and Mouton.

Heinitz, W. 1920. "Über die Musik der Somali." *Zeitschrift für Musikwissenschaft* 2:257.

Johnson, John William. 1972. "The Family of Miniature Genres in Somali Oral Poetry." *Folklore Forum,* 5(3):79–99.

———. 1974. *Heellooy Heelleellooy: The Development of the Genre Heello in Modern Somali Poetry.* Bloomington, Ind.: Research Center for the Language Sciences.

———. 1980. "Somalia." *The New Grove Dictionary of Music and Musicians,* ed. Stanley Sadie. London: Macmillan.

———. 1988. "Set Theory in Somali Poetics: Structures and Implications." *Proceedings of the Third International Congress of Somali Studies,* ed. Annarita Puglielli, 123–132. Rome: Il Pensiero Scientifico Editore.

———. 1993. "Somali Poetry." *The New Princeton Encyclopedia of Poetry and Poetics,* ed. Alex Preminger and T. V. F. Brogan, 1164–65. Princeton, N. J.: Princeton University Press.

Lord, Albert Bates. 1960. *The Singer of Tales.* Cambridge, Mass.: Harvard University Press. Studies in Comparative Literature, 24.

Omar Au Nuh. 1972. "Songs That Derive from Folk Dance." *New Era* (Mogadishu) 7:19–21.

Pesenti, G. 1910. "Canti e Ritmi Arabici, Somalici e Suahili." *Bollettino della Reale Società Geografica Italiana* 47:1409–32.

Vianney, J. J. 1957. "La Musica Somala." *Somalia d'Oggi* (Mogadishu) 37.

Wachsmann, Klaus P. 1965. "Somali." In *Die Musik in Geschichte und Gegenwart,* ed. Friedrich Blume. Cassel: Bärenreiter.

Music in Kenya
Paul N. Kavyu

Musical Zones
Intra-Kenyan Influences

The Republic of Kenya, independent since 1963, lies along the East African coast. It shares boundaries with Tanzania to the south, Uganda and Sudan to the west and northwest, and Ethiopia and Somalia to the north and northeast. Its land lies within the rift-valley region. Important lakes—Victoria to the west, Turkana to the north—partly define its boundaries. Its rift-valley areas and coastal regions receive abundant rainfall, but the rest of the country is dry. The coastal plains rise to the Nyika plateau, and then gradually to highlands. The peak of Mount Kenya stands more than 3,000 meters above sea level.

Kenya's climate is largely tropical, with two rainy seasons: short rains from November to December, and long rains between March and June. Agriculture is the chief foreign-exchange earner. The warmth of the climate, the sandy beaches, and the wild game attract the most tourists of any African country.

Kenya is multilingual. Its languages belong to four major groups: Bantu, Paranilotic, Nilotic, and Kushitic. Typical examples of these are the Kamba, the Nandi, the Luo, and the Somali, respectively (Whiteley 1970:13). Kiswahili, a Bantu language, is the national language; English is the official language.

A rapidly changing country, Kenya has not experienced serious political problems since independence. It is the regional base for many nongovernmental organizations that operate in Africa. Similarly, regional representatives of multinational organizations have made it their continental headquarters.

MUSICAL ZONES

Kenya has three main musical zones: semiarid, savanna-grassland, and rainy. The semiarid and savanna-grassland zones support pastoral communities of Paranilotic and Kushitic peoples. The savanna-grassland and rainy zones support Bantus (such as Akamba, Taita, Kikuyu) and Nilotics. Local music reflects native vegetation, environmental factors, and subsistence practices. It also records popular responses to two political periods: colonial and postcolonial.

Regions of vocal music prominence

Vocal music—solo and choral response performance without instrumental accompa-

niment—is a feature of the Nilotic and other pastoral communities. From the eastern slopes of Mount Kenya in the Akamba and Ameru communities, unaccompanied singing stretches north and westward (Kavyu 1977). In the north, vocal music reaches the Somali border, and is popular with the Boran, the Orma, and other people of Kushitic origin. To the west, it extends down the rift valley, and covers the northwestern region bordering Ethiopia and Sudan.

Semiarid regions display specific vocal styles. In the rift valley, large groups of men (as among the Pokot, the Maasai [figure 1], and their neighbors the Samburu) typically perform together. Long melodies develop, mostly in free rhythm. Maasai men sing an underlying ostinato against a solo line. Commonly, the responding group repeats the syllables *ho-la-le-i-yo* in unison. From that pattern, they form an interlude to the performance: *laleiyo laleiyo, laleiyo*. As the soloist approaches the end of his phrase, he prepares the choral group, either by transposing an octave above, or by giving a certain word as a cue. In the central highland regions, the chorus follows the soloist, who sets the end of the performance; alternatively, especially in songs that lack improvisation, the group sings a predetermined number of verses.

Musician-composers who practice the art of solo singing comment on the social, political, and economic dimensions of life. In the 1950s, many songs composed during the "emergency days"—seven years of armed resistance against British colonial rule—were major sources of information. During the earlier colonial period, some songs provided a kind of eyewitness that disputed the written colonial documents (Kavyu 1977).

Singing revolves around daily occupation. The popular music of agricultural people accompanies cultivating, threshing, and grinding cereals. In the pastoral communities, animal themes dominate the vocal music. Performers cite the importance of cattle as a store of wealth, or praise the finest bulls in the herd.

Regions of instrumental music prominence

Instrumental music spreads from the coastal region westward to the hinterland. Bantu communities have a greater variety of instruments than Nilotic and Kushitic

FIGURE 1   Maasai Moran warriors, 1987.

The vegetation of the three regions affects the variety and distribution of musical instruments. In semiarid regions, there are few instruments, and they are light. In wet, fertile regions, there are both big and small instruments.

ones. The distribution of instruments moves in two lines. The main one starts from the Mijikenda people at the east coast (along the Tanzanian boundary), and moves through the Wataita, Kisii, and Kura people up to the Lake Victoria region. Around the lake, the Luo and their northern neighbors (the Luhya, of Bantu stock) have a wide variety of instruments. The second line, starting at the same point, moves north and northwestward, up to the Mount Kenya region, ending in the Akamba area.

The Nilotic communities are famous for their lyres. The Luo and the Kalenjin, plus their Bantu neighbors (the Abaluhya, the Kisii, the Abakuria), practice two styles of playing: plucking the strings (Luo and Abaluhya) and strumming with the right thumb and index finger (Kalenjin). In the latter style, the left hand mutes strings to change their pitches. Singing and performance on rhythmic idiophonic instruments also accompany performance on the lyre.

Bantu communities in Kenya favor drums. Bantus of the western highlands (Luhya and Abakuria) play sets of three drums. Coastal Bantus also play sets of five: the Digo and Duruma people use a tuned set, accompanied by a flute (*chivoti*), a double-reed aerophone (*nzumari*), and several percussive instruments; the Giriama, the Chonyi, and other communities of the northern coast of Kenya use an untuned set.

The coastal Bantus are the only communities in Kenya that play two instruments popular elsewhere in Africa: the xylophone (*rimba*) and the mbira (*karimba*). Musicians may play these instruments solo, but they also play the xylophone as part of the instrumental ensemble of the *kiringoringo* (a boys' and girls' dance, accompanied by vocal and instrumental music), or in an ensemble of light idiophones (instruments that do not weigh much, and are easy to carry).

The vegetation of the three regions affects the variety and distribution of musical instruments. In semiarid regions, there are few instruments, and they are light. In wet, fertile regions, there are both big and small instruments—instruments for solos, and instruments for groups. Adults exclusively play some, and children play others. Such variety in instruments offers nearly limitless forms of accompaniment for vocal music.

Some dances have constant instrumental motifs, which repeat many times throughout a performance. The *kilumi* (a dance of the Akamba people) and the *kishavi* (a dance of the Taita people) are good examples. In other dances (like the *mwinjiro* of the Mbeere people, and the *mwanzele* of the Rabai people), short rhythms form phrases and regulate performances. Certain instruments duplicate the rhythmic grouping of syllables. Among the most commonly used instruments in duplicating vocal rhythm are the drum and the *kayamba*, a rectangular reed box, filled with stones or seeds, played by all coastal communities. In dances like *nguchu*, the Mbeere people of Mount Kenya use leg bells (*igamba*) and a horn (*coro*). In the central highlands, the *muchungwa* (a dance of the Kikuyu people) also uses idiophones attached to dancers' legs.

Stringed instruments

Stringed instruments, like lyres and fiddles, double the melody of songs. These include the one-stringed lute-fiddle (Luhya *shiriri*, Luo *orutu*, Aembu *wandidi*). Among the chordophones, innovation has appeared in two instances: the seven-stringed *litungu* (of the Abaluhya people) has become an eight-stringed instrument with a heptatonic inventory of tones; and the single-stringed *wandindi* (of the Kikuyu) has received an extra string, which usually sounds a fourth below the original string, and functions as a drone.

Drums

Drumming in Kenya involves three styles: the hand technique, the stick technique, and the stick-and-hand technique with the armpit controlling the pitch. The style of hitting varies with the drum, the mode of drumming, and the purpose of the performance. No drummer uses two sticks. The right hand serves for hitting the drumhead; the left hand mutes the sound and produces various tones.

Musicians in Christian churches commonly use the stick-and-hand technique (figure 2), a transformation of Luhya traditional drumming, which involves mainly hand technique. The sizes and shapes of drums used for sacred performance differ from the sizes and shapes of those used for secular performances. In outdoor performances, musicians prefer the stick technique for its amplitude.

INTRA-KENYAN INFLUENCES

Some local instruments have crossed ethnic boundaries to enrich other instrumental accompaniments. Two instruments from the coast have spread fast. One is the small, cylindrical, military-shaped drum (closed on both ends), played in most churches during Sunday services. The other is the *kayamba*. Played for the articulation of rhythm, these instruments have spread in the country through festivals sponsored by churches and schools. Two instruments used in festivals and other forms of competition are the one-stringed fiddle (found throughout Kenya) and the xylophone (formerly used only along the coast).

Several imported instruments have joined traditional ensembles. Waswahili, Kikuyu, and Luo communities play the accordion. Each group has developed a new way of using it. The Waswahili use it for melodic accompaniment; the Luo employ it for harmonic purposes; and without melodic or harmonic emphasis, but with a frequent polyrhythmic effect between the instrument and voice, the Kikuyu create a rhythmic dialogue between it and the voice (Zake 1986:19).

FIGURE 2   Church drums, 1984.

With the arrival of European music, styles unrelated to local traditional music in content and form came into local existence. Christianity introduced congregational hymn singing, four-part harmony, and Western instruments like the piano and brass instruments.

The colonial period

The colonial contribution to late-nineteenth-century musical taste in Kenya in some cases started with suppression of certain sociocultural institutions: traditional initiations, religious activities, military institutions, and others. In some areas, these institutions died out because they could not compete with those supported by the colonial system. Some musicians, however, fulfilled a traditional duty by singing praise songs to indigenous politicians, whom they made into heroes of the struggle against colonialism.

With the arrival of European music, styles unrelated to local traditional music in content and form came into local existence. Christianity introduced congregational hymn singing, four-part harmony, and Western instruments like the piano and brass instruments (Kavyu 1990:4).

New venues started replacing older ones. Popular band music developed through the support of mass media. The beginning of popular music, however, goes back to the settlement of freed slaves around Mombasa in Freetown and Rabai (Kavyu 1978). From this seaport, popular music spread in towns along the railway routes up to Nyanza and Western Kenya. People employed on railways and in post offices along the line were among the first to have gramophones, and their children heard the popular music of the day. Henry Awuor Anyumba, Kenyan literary critic and musicologist, during a discussion informed me that his father as a post office worker was, in the 1930s, among the first Kenyans to own a gramophone.

New forms of music spread fast between the urban centers and the countryside, often carried by migrant workers. Urbanization then married the tonal organization of traditional music with that of churches and schools. Foreign musical instruments became popular for accompanying newly created dance forms. Compositional themes came from issues such as landholding, reduction of livestock, and freedom of movement to urban centers.

Servicemen returning from the world wars increased the pace of musical change. Some of them had learned to play Western musical instruments. On their return home, they simply continued playing. Where the precise instruments like trumpets were lacking, Kenyans manufactured imitations. For playing in the *beni* (a newly invented dance), they devised a wooden version of the trumpet.

In the early 1960s, just before independence, many songs praised local political leaders, encouraged political movements, and voiced disdain for the colonial system. Some songs spread over wide areas. One such song, "*Nkosi Sikelel' iAfrica*," became popular in eastern and southern Africa. It later became the anthem of the African National Congress, the national anthem of Tanzania and Zambia, and the second national anthem of South Africa.

Troupes and venues

In Kenya, many troupes of musicians have spread from large urban areas to small rural ones. They have acquired a national dimension. At any soccer stadium whenever the Abaluhya-dominated team is playing, hired dancers and club supporters perform "*Mwana wa mberi*," a song for the *sikuti*, a dance from Western Kenya. In urban areas, the *hukabe humze* (a dance from the coast), the acrobatic *mukanda* or *beni* (an Akamba dance), the *sengenya* (a dance of the Digo), and the *muchungwa* (a dance of the Kikuyu) are popular.

The Ministry of Education and the Ministry of Culture organize performances of national music festivals in the countryside. During national days, provincial administration of the Office of the President coordinates and supervises performances of music and dance. Public and private organizations and individuals support musical groups of three sorts: (1) private choral groups, composed of people with other common interests such as fellow businessmen or old schoolmates; (2) institutional groups, supported by churches, states, local communities, and private firms; and (3) professional groups with private management, including popular bands and dance groups.

Groups of the first category practice and usually perform in members' homes. Singing hymns and anthems, married couples perform the vocal parts they performed during their school days. Occasionally, by invitation, groups perform in a church that has invited one of their members to give a sermon.

Groups of the second sort practice and perform at work, during office hours, even if they have additional obligations in the evening. As musicians, they have access to the benefits enjoyed by other workers in the organization.

The third sort of performers includes the self-employed. Bandleaders, unemployed youths, and owners of bars organize some groups, which perform for fees in restaurants, nightclubs, and big hotels. When they play in small, rural bars, the patrons of the bar or the owner pays them.

A growing number of musicians in Kenya earn a living from playing music. Particularly in Nyanza and the Western provinces, some play in their home villages, where they entertain gatherings of guests. They accompany their performances with the lyre, single-stringed lute, and more rarely a drum. They may perform for hire at a wedding, where they play various dances, as in the Digo and Giriama communities; at a funeral, where they perform both ritual and secular dances (including dances of war) in Luo and Abaluhya communities; and at beer parties in Luo, Kikuyu, and other areas, where they praise generous individuals. At weddings and funerals, musicians attend by invitation, and play for a fixed fee. For the beer party, they simply appear, and individuals pay a small fee if they want a song played for them, or if they want an improvised song to praise them. Alcoholic beverages are also a reward for playing.

Musicians travel from one market to another in Nyanza, the western, central, and coastal regions. Musicians in Nyanza and western Kenya usually play the lyre and fiddle. Those in the central highlands usually play the accordion (*kinanda*), accompanied by a motor-engine flywheel (*karing'aringa*). Their counterparts on the coast play either drums, xylophones, or an ensemble of drums, *kayambas*, and other instruments found in the region.

In the cities, low-cost residential areas and slums become another venue of performances by semiprofessional musicians, who are either invited by the proprietor or visit the premises on their own initiative. Residential areas with a majority of people from the same ethnic origin will be frequented by musicians of that particular ethnic group, though groups with broad ethnic composition and repertory can reach wider audiences. Kaloleni Estate in Nairobi, predominantly the home of Luo people, is the main venue for Luo musicians. In the same way, at Bahati Estate, which has a high concentration of Kikuyu people, Kikuyu musicians often entertain bar patrons.

Street performances are another form of entertainment. In large towns (Nairobi,

If popular musicians use texts considered subversive, governmental authorities, questioning their motives, will work against them. But musicians who play to small audiences and stay out of the spotlight can echo in song what people say privately.

Mombasa, Nakuru, and others), musicians stage spontaneous performances in places like bus stops, and at the entrances of busy shops. In Nairobi, these musicians often sit near the main supermarkets, or within 50 meters of the Hilton Hotel. In Mombasa, they play along Kenyatta Avenue, Digo Road, and Moi Avenue. After attracting an audience, they ask people to put a small fee in a hat or a container. Some musicians shyly let listeners decide the amount the performance is worth.

Since the late 1980s, secondary schools have invited musicians who play indigenous instruments to train students preparing for national music examinations. The schools invite the musicians to teach students the instrument prescribed for examination. The musicians receive a fee to enable them to maintain themselves during the period of residence. Those who manage to visit several schools a week can make a comfortable living. If the instruments the musicians play are not among those prescribed for examination, their income from the schools may be low.

Some musicians work in the Department of Music at Kenyatta University, where they give practical tuition to the students of African instruments. Not regular employees of the University, they must often scrounge for other means of subsidizing their income. During scholastic vacations, they earn money by playing music in the tourist hotels of Nairobi.

Once in a while, broadcasters invite musicians to perform on radio or television. They do so mainly during music festivals, when prominent musicians are in Nairobi. After recording a program, musicians receive a royalty, but get no further compensation when the station airs the performance.

Local and international mass media aggressively market local and international musical hits. After the achievement of rural electrification (from the mid-1970s), jukebox and disco music became part of rural entertainment. Since developmental aid is mainly technological, the population is gradually changing from traditionally based to technologically based entertainment.

Commentary through music

Commercially recorded praise songs exist, but there are few recorded songs of antigovernmental protest, which recording and marketing companies may not accept. Through mass media, popular urban musicians use Kiswahili, the Kenyan lingua franca, to capture a large market. However, if they use texts considered subversive, governmental authorities, questioning their motives, will work against them. Musicians who play to small audiences and stay out of the spotlight can echo in song what people say privately.

Every musical group has a stock of current-event songs, which include praise songs for national leaders. They perform such songs for politicians' official visits to their region. To give people time to compose praise songs, the government always announces in advance a visit by prominent leaders. The refrain of such songs is often a known tune with a new text. The soloist improvises, using key words of reference to the visitor.

In eastern Africa, Christian choirs frequently conduct interstate visits. Visiting groups always bring newly composed songs in praise of the political leaders of the host country. These songs often cite the strength of the relationship between the two states. During state visits, the most highly valued choirs are among musical groups invited to welcome the state guests.

Musical organizations

There are several musical organizations in Kenya, and each one has specific goals. The Permanent Presidential Music Commission (established in 1988) is responsible for promoting, developing, and protecting all forms of music and of musicians in the country. The Nairobi Music Society (founded in 1938) and the Kenya Music Trust (established in 1977) involve themselves exclusively in promoting Western symphonic and vocal music. The Kenya Music Festival for Education Institutions (begun in 1927) encourages the study and creation of music. The Kenya Music Festival for Non-Educational Institutions and Clubs (begun in 1988) promotes local talent in folk music and other styles.

Music in schools

Kenyan schoolchildren know a mixed repertory of songs—from ethnic groups other than their own, and even from areas outside the country. In lessons and activities, they have opportunities for performing. Classroom music includes songs used as aids by teachers, songs performed during games and physical-education activities, songs mastered for festivals of drama and music, and songs absorbed as part of religious worship.

Throughout Kenya, choirs of children from neighboring primary schools form massed choirs, of up to a thousand voices. These choirs sing mainly on public holidays and national days. Musicians compose some songs specifically for such groups, and borrow other songs from other choirs. In sound and movement, children show their determination to participate in national issues.

Religious schools, which most Kenyan school-age children attend, consist of Christian Sunday schools and Islamic religious classes (*madrasa*). At home, children sing songs learned in these contexts, like this Sunday school song, in Kiswahili:

> Shetani akija, sote tuko tayari.
> Shetani akija, sote tuko tayari.
> Akija mbele zote,
> Kanyanga, kanyanga, kanyanga, kanyanga; sote tuko tayari.
>
> Mwokozi akija sote tuko tayari.
> Mwokozi akija sote tuko tayari.
> Akija mbele zote,
> Pokea, pokea, pokea, pokea; sote tuko tayari.
>
> When the devil comes, all are ready.
> When the devil comes, all are ready.
> When he comes from the front,
> Crush him, crush him, crush him, crush him; all are ready.
>
> When the savior knocks, all are ready
> When the savior knocks, all are ready.
> When he comes from the front,
> Receive him, receive him, receive him, receive him; all are ready.

tumbuizo Genre of songs performed by
women in Kenya, singing in Swahili

kutahiri Circumcision celebrations in the
rural, coastal areas of Kenya

For *akija mbele zote* 'when he comes from the front', additional stanzas substitute *akija nyuma zote* 'when he comes from the back' and *akija pande zote* 'when he comes from all directions'.

Music in churches

Christian churches in Kenya prominently affect the development and performance of music. Most churches use instrumental accompaniment. Drumming maintains the tempo of performance and stimulates movement, which makes the service lively and interesting; it also attracts people to services. Large churches sponsor music festivals, and maintain groups for the improvement of congregational singing.

As required by law, religious denominations and sects—more than 200 of them —have registered in the offices of the Registrar of Societies. Each has its own songbooks. Some of the songs are arrangements or adaptations of local songs, many with poorly applied Western harmonization.

Continuity and change distinguish performances in these churches. In the Akikuyu, Luo, Abaluhya, and other communities, traditional singing combines with congregational hymn singing to create new musical styles. Drums, several indigenous idiophones, and Western instruments have become features of late-twentieth-century worship.

In some independent churches, garments and associated objects are defining parts of worship services. In the Israelite group of churches, the members of the congregation wear white, pink, or blue robes. Some congregations processionally carry flags, which they plant in the place of worship. Some meet for worship under a tree, in a social hall, or at a school compound. Processions (accompanied by singing, drumming, stamping, and clapping) are essential to the worship. Four elders start a procession. Behind them follow drummers, leading two lines: one for men, and the other for women. Energetic music and dance progressively intensify all stages of worship: people sing loudly and dance vigorously, starting slowly and building to a climax.

Music in public transport

Kenya has several forms of public transport. Airplanes, trains, and buses carry passengers over long routes (about 150 kilometers to 500 kilometers); vans are the usual means of transport within cities and over short distances (up to 150 kilometers). Music in public transport occurs only in vans and long-distance buses. In Nairobi, Mombasa, Nakuru, Kisumuu, and other cities, to provide enjoyment and attract business, managers of commuter traffic have installed expensive music systems.

Urban transport firms play local and international hits. The repertory includes religious choral music, secular songs, and local songs from the destination of the vehicle. In Nairobi by the 1980s, highly traveled routes to Eastleigh, Kibera, and Eastlands featured traveling disco, music played at high volume in crowded commuter vans, with youths swaying to the rhythm of the beat. Compact cassettes, high-speed dubbing, and the black-market availability of expensive systems helped this music spread fast to other parts of the country. In the 1990s, commuter vehicles in Nairobi began to use videos to entertain travelers.

Music in nightclubs

Nightclubs cater to tourists, local Asian businesspeople, and Africans who can afford the expense. The musicians play well-known international and local hits, including their own compositions, drawn from different ethnic communities. One dance rhythm underlies all the songs.

Music in Swahili communities

In Swahili communities (heavily influenced by Islam), certain musical occasions are for women or men exclusively. Showing affinities with Arabian and Islamic practices, Swahili women perform *tumbuizo*, *nyimbo*, and other types of sung poetry. Many songs fall into the genre known as *tumbuizo*, deriving from a word glossable as 'soothe by singing'. Women perform this genre by creating texts to suit the occasion, like this work song (collected in 1992 by Geoffrey K. King'ei):

> Banat ndugu wa kike, mwatupa shauri gani?
> Yafaa tuzitundike, nguo za usichanani,
> Tena majembe tuyashikem twendeni tukalime.

> Women, our sisters, what advice do you give us?
> We should hang up our maiden robes,
> Then get hold of hoes and go dig the land.

The singing of work songs (*tumbuizo za kazi*) lightens tedious jobs like cultivating, pounding, and grinding grain into flour. For women in labor, women sing such songs "to comfort pain," as they say; they also sing songs that pray for the safety of fishermen at sea.

Weddings are among the most prominent events of Swahili communities. In large towns, participants commonly dance *lelemama*, *chakacha*, and *vugo*. In rural areas along the coast, songs of the latter two genres accompany circumcision celebrations (*kutahiri*).

Swahili taarabu

Taarabu, Arab-influenced music, has been popular since the 1970s. It employs electric and electronic instruments, like guitars and organs. Actors prominent in India frequently visit and entertain the Indian communities of East Africa. In a vocal form in the 1980s, *taarabu* introduced techniques of Indian movie music.

Taarabu increasingly voices political views. It has thus become an important vehicle for disseminating national cultural values and aspirations. This political song, collected in 1992 by G. K. King'ei, reproaches dishonest politicians:

Mwalikitumia khila,	You used tricks,
Na urongo mkiapa.	And swore any lies.
Sasa hamba lahaula,	Now you curse your luck,
Na mmekuwa lutanda.	And have become desperate.
Pesa zenu tumekula,	We have eaten your money,
Na voti hatuku wapa.	But we did not vote for you.

Taarabu plays an important role in the life of both Kenya and other East African coastal communities.

REFERENCES

Kavyu, Paul N. 1977. *An Introduction to Akamba Music.* Nairobi: Kenya Literature Bureau.

———. 1978. "The Development of Guitar Music in Kenya." *Jazzforschung* 10:111–120.

———. 1990. "The Development of New Intercultural Music in East Africa: A Preliminary Survey." *Proceedings of the Intercultural Music International Symposium and Festival, London.*

King'ei, Geoffrey K. 1992. "Language, Culture and Communication: The Role of Swahili Taarab Songs in Kenya, 1963–1990." Ph.D. dissertation, Howard University.

Whiteley, W. H. 1970. "The Classification and Distribution of Kenya's African Languages." In *Language in Kenya,* ed. W. H. Whiteley, 13–69. Oxford: Oxford University Press.

Zake, W. G. S. 1986. *Folk Music of Kenya.* Nairobi: Uzima Press.

Music in Tanzania
Stephen H. Martin

People and Language
History
Areas of Musical Style
Musical Instruments
Neotraditional Music Forms

After a succession of colonial occupations (Arab, German, British), Tanganyika achieved independence in 1961. Zanzibar, consisting of the islands of Zanzibar and Pemba, achieved independence from Great Britain in 1963. For several centuries, these states had had close cultural ties. In 1964, their political union established the United Republic of Tanzania.

With a land area of nearly a million square kilometers, Tanzania is the largest country in East Africa. It is one of the least urbanized African countries: only 15 percent of its people live in urban areas. Its largest cities include the coastal capital of Dar es Salaam, Zanzibar (on Zanzibar Island), Mbeya (in the eastern highlands), Mwanza (on the southern shore of Lake Victoria), Dodoma (the new capital, in the center of the country), and Tanga (a port, north of Dar es Salaam). In 1990, the national population was about 26.3 million.

Geographical regions

Tanzania has three major geographical regions: narrow coastal lowlands and islands, central plateaus, and highlands. The first lies along an 800-kilometer coastline on the Indian Ocean. It is Tanzania's most densely populated region, and its hottest and wettest. Included in it, several kilometers northeast of Dar es Salaam, are Zanzibar (the largest coral island off the coast of East Africa) and Pemba.

A gradual rise from the coastal region to the central plateaus causes the climate to become drier and cooler. The character of the central plateaus ranges from grasslands (of the Maasai Steppe, in the north), to a grassy plateau (which covers about a third of the country's area). Drought is common, and the poverty of the soil limits agriculture.

The northern highlands contain the country's highest mountains, among them Kilimanjaro, the highest peak in Africa. The Rufiji, Tanzania's principal river, flows out of the southern highlands; scrub woodlands characterize the eastern highlands. In the central highlands, mild temperatures and abundant rainfall encourage high population density.

PEOPLE AND LANGUAGE

About one hundred twenty diverse, mainly Bantu-speaking, ethnic groups populate

In music making, traditional sex roles persist most strongly in rural areas. An increased involvement of women in music making is visible in such urban musical forms as *taarab* and jazz.

Tanzania. A unique feature of the country's demography is that no single group makes up a majority. The largest is the Sukuma, about 13 percent of the national population. Most of the remaining groups make up no more than 3 percent to 4 percent each; several groups, among them the Maasai, equal less than that.

Other language groups include some derived from the Khoisan family (like the Sandawe), some Nilotic groups in the north, and various nonindigenous groups (Arabs, Indians, Pakistanis, Europeans), mostly in urban areas. Though some ethnic groups (Sukuma, Nyamwezi, Makonde, Haya, Gogo, Chaga, Nyakyusa, Ha) have exerted influence politically, the general ethnic balance of the country has aided governmental efforts to build a national character, thus avoiding major ethnic upheavals and political rivalries.

Another important unifying factor in Tanzanian culture is the national language, Swahili. Though people speak it alongside English, Tanzania is one of a handful of African nations that use an indigenous African language for official communication. Swahili is a lingua franca; it developed through active commercial interchange among Arabs, Portuguese, and Bantu-speaking inhabitants of the Tanganyikan interior. That the language does not come from a specific ethnic group has helped lessen tribal rivalries.

Despite the impact colonial governments made on urban growth and national rule, Tanzania has principally an agrarian economy. Its only large city, Dar es Salaam, is a legacy of the colonial presence. Nevertheless, several forces have wrought changes in people's life-styles. The introduction of Western education, the spread of Islam and Christianity, the establishment of *ujamaa* villages (relocation habitats, established under President Nyerere's régime), and the building of roads and railways, have been agents of social and cultural change. To deal with intertribal marriages, the temporary absence of males from villages (while seeking employment in urban areas), and rapid urban growth, traditional tribal customs have had to change. The music of urban Tanzania reflects many of these issues.

Though Tanzanian law treats women the same as men, traditional values of male dominance still have social effects, especially in villages. In music making, traditional sex roles persist most strongly in rural areas. An increased involvement of women in music making is visible in such urban musical forms as *taarab* and jazz.

The religious culture of Tanzania consists of three strata, each of which represents about one-third of the population: indigenous practices centering on ancestor worship, Islam, and Christianity. Indigenous religions predate the arrival of colonialism. Islam came by way of Zanzibar through Arab traders, documented from the tenth century at the latest. Its impact is visible mostly in the coastal region and on the islands, and to a lesser extent in some of the interior regions, into which it penetrated during the 1800s. Christianity arrived in the 1840s. It brought an emphasis on Western education and health. It also exerted some political influence: most of the country's leaders got their education in mission schools.

HISTORY

The East African coast has a long and well-documented history. The earliest document in print, the *Periplus of the Erythrean Sea*, is a guidebook to the Indian Ocean, written by a Greek merchant in the first century (Blankaart 1683). It describes the interaction between the Arab traders and the coastal inhabitants. In the first century, many of the Bantu-speaking peoples of Tanzania arrived; by the twelfth, the intermarriage of Arab traders and African women created an Arab-African culture, and produced the beginnings of Swahili culture and language.

The arrival of the ancestors of the Bantu- and Nilotic-speakers of the interior may have begun in the first millennium. The migrations of the Bantu were probably from the south, southwest, and west; the Nilotes came from the north or northwest, southern Sudan, and possibly western Ethiopia. Before these migrations and the beginning of the Iron Age, Bushman hunters and gatherers inhabited most of Tanzania. Evidence of their presence is visible the rock paintings of central Tanzania, near the territory of the Sandawe, Khoisan (click language) descendants of the Bushman population. Eric Tenraa's studies (1963, 1964) of the music of the Sandawe give further evidence of this connection. Kubik (1967, 1968) has posited that musical scales based on portions of the natural harmonic series also show relationships between living cultures and those of early inhabitants. He points out that elements such as polyphonic vocal music, yodeling, and the use of tetratonic and pentatonic scales (derived from partials of the harmonic series) are features of Bushman music. According to his analysis, these features appear in the music of the Gogo. Though the Gogo are linguistically unrelated to Bushmen, he says they may have absorbed these musical elements from earlier occupants of the land.

From this point, the development of Tanzanian history is visible in several stages, beginning with the development of Zanzibar as a center of trade and the seat of the East African Arab sultanate, the arrival of the Portuguese explorers, and the colonial occupations of the German and British regimes, followed by independence and unification.

The development of Zanzibar followed the success of Kilwa, a community on the Tanganyikan coast. By the early 1300s, it was a prominent Arab center of trade; its contacts reached as far eastward as India and Persia. With the Kenyan coastal town of Mombasa, Zanzibar soon overtook Kilwa as a major commercial center.

At the end of the 1400s, the arrival of Portuguese traders boosted Zanzibar's commercial status. Though the impact of the foreign presence in Zanzibar and Mombasa was important, the Portuguese exerted little influence on the Tanganyikan mainland. Their primary interest was in India.

By the mid-1800s, Omani sultans had seized power in Zanzibar, and were controlling a lucrative trade in slaves and ivory. Meanwhile, the incursion of Arab slavers created unrest in the interior, and led to political realignments and the reshuffling of power. From the north, invasions by the Maasai, and the resistance of the Hehe, took place; from South Africa, the Ngoni began migrating.

Europeans were also present on the mainland in the 1800s. Richard Francis Burton, John Hanning Speke, David Livingstone, and Henry Morton Stanley—all explored or lived in Tanganyika in the mid-to-late 1800s. By the 1870s, British representatives were pressuring the Omani sultanate to end its trade in slaves, but until well into the 1880s, they had little effect on independent traders, like Tippu Tib, who created a virtual Arab empire west of Lake Tanganyika, an area rich in ivory; he also completed the first known coast-bound caravan from central Africa to Dar es Salaam.

German influence began in 1890, with the establishment of the German East Africa Protectorate. Treaties worked out by Karl Peters with the interior inhabitants

Drums reveal, or hold the key to, historical information about earlier Tanzanian societies. In Iramba, where prehistoric rock shelters and caves exist, archaeologists have found seventy-eight drums, which predate by two hundred years or more the current inhabitants of the area.

laid the groundwork. Nonetheless, such groups as the Hehe and the Chagga vigorously resisted further German incursion into the mainland.

The Great War had major effects on East Africa. More than two hundred fifty thousand Africans died in Tanganyika alone. The Treaty of Versailles placed Tanganyika under mandate to the League of Nations, which assigned it to British administration. The biggest impact of World War II was the movement toward independence. In 1954, the Tanganyikan African National Union (TANU), led by Julius Nyerere and others, brought Tanganyika closer to independence.

Musical scholarship

Little is known of the music history of Tanzania. Terence O. Ranger's study (1975) of dance clubs, and Hartwig's study (1969) of the Kerebe of northwestern Tanzania, are important examples of musical scholarship. Ranger takes a comprehensive look at a single musical style as it occurs throughout East Africa. Hartwig examines the music of a single area: he tries to reconstruct Kerebe culture history. He focuses on a zither, the only chordophone the Kerebe used before 1900. It originally accompanied a beer-drinking ceremony. Over time, it and the social context of its performance evolved. Instead of accompanying elders with songs having historical texts, it began to serve purely for entertainment, in association with hand clapping and dancing. On the arrival of colonialism, young men and women became the principal performers.

AREAS OF MUSICAL STYLE

Tanzania has eight areas of musical style, some of which spill over into other nations (Kubik 1982:38). These areas include (1) the coastal regions along the Indian Ocean, and the islands of Zanzibar and Pemba; (2) the areas of the WaNyamwezi and WaSukuma, north-central Tanzania; (3) the area of the WaGogo, central Tanzania; (4) the area of the WaChagga, Kilimanjaro; (5) the area of the Karagwe and Buhaya, northwestern Tanzania (with cultural ties to the royal traditions of southern Uganda, Burundi, and Rwanda); (6) the western area, including the Wafipa and others; (7) the area around the Ruvuma river valley, extending into the northern part of Mozambique; (8) the area of the Ubena and the Upangwa (southwestern highlands), and the area around Lake Nyasa.

MUSICAL INSTRUMENTS

Unlike other parts of Africa, especially West Africa, the documentation of music and musical activity in Tanzania is sparse. Perhaps the largest body of available knowledge pertains to musical instruments and their geographical distribution throughout the country. Such studies, many based on collections of instruments in the National Museum in Dar es Salaam, have been undertaken by both Tanzanian and non-Tanzanian researchers. Some remain unpublished. The following organological overview summarizes this information.

Membranophones

Membranophones occur throughout Tanzania in a variety of forms and sizes. Certain drums have an association with specific regions. For drums, the most important shapes include kettle, cylindrical, barrel, conical, hourglass, footed, and goblet-shaped versions. How the heads are attached varies from region to region. Larger drums usually have heads made of cow skin, goat skin, or zebra skin; smaller drums have heads made from the skin of reptiles.

In the West Lake area, a typical type of drum is the braced conical drum, the "Uganda drum." Like most Tanzanian drums, it is made of wood, though some examples have copper bodies. The tops are open; the bottoms, closed. Cowhide, braced with narrow leather strips, covers both. The top half of the drum is cylindrical, and the bottom tapers like a cone with the point sliced off. The tops are open; the bottoms, closed. Cowhide, braced with narrow leather strips, covers both. The Haya drum (*ng'oma*) comes in several sizes. The same drum occurs in Uganda, Rwanda, and Burundi. Among the Kerebe (on Lake Victoria), a similar instrument occurs in royal sets, believed to have been made by Haya and Ganda slaves. Another drum is the *iduffu,* a large, circular, frame drum, used by the Haya in the *kuzikiri,* a Moslem ritual dance. With Islam, this drum penetrated the interior.

In the central plateaus of the country, drumming conforms with Islamic principles. In the Tabora area, for the installation of new chiefs, the Nyamwezi formerly used a set of royal drums. These drums—large, round, bowl shaped, footed—were traditionally played only on special occasions. For royal ceremonies, the Nyamwezi also used other, nonfooted, and smaller drums. In rituals connected with secret societies, the Sukuma still use large, double-headed, cylindrical drums. Near Dodoma, among the Gogo, drumming occurs only in women's ceremonials, and only women play the instruments. The drums, used to accompany *ng'oma* dances, are large, hourglass types, with only one end covered with skin; the other end is open. Pegs fix the skins to the drums, whose body sometimes has a carved handle at the waist. To play, women hold the drums between their legs, and hit the heads with their hands. The largest of the set, played by the master drummer, is the *ng'oma fumbwa;* the smaller ones are *nyanyulua.*

In the coastal region, in areas like Mtwara, Lindi, and Dar es Salaam, cylindrical drums in a variety of sizes are characteristic. Also found are differently sized goblet drums, with pegged membranes. To accompany the *mbeta* dance, the Zaramo (of the Dar es Salaam area) use drums and other percussive instruments with flutes. A variety of *msondo* (cylindrically shaped drums), with pegged or tacked-on heads, also occur along the coast, and in Morogoro and the south. In dances such as the *gombesugu* and the *sindimba,* the Makonde (southern region) and Zaramo use a large hourglass drum. In the coastal areas, and to the north from Morogoro to Tanga, braced cylindrical drums accompany the *selo* dance.

Among the Fipa (Rukwa, southern highlands), a low, goblet-shaped instrument has a pegged drumhead of snakeskin. On the head, several lumps of beeswax act as a paste for tuning. The drum specially accompanies marimba music.

In addition to being musical instruments, Tanzanian drums have symbolized power and authority, as the variety of royal drum sets shows. Also, drums reveal, or hold the key to, historical information about earlier Tanzanian societies. In Iramba, where prehistoric rock shelters and caves exist, archaeologists have found seventy-eight drums, which predate by two hundred years or more the current inhabitants of the area (Hunter 1953:28). Hidden in sixteen caves, these drums were concealed with rocks, possibly to protect them from an imminent invasion. Nothing is known of the original tribes to which they belonged, but these caves are a place of wonder to the Nyampala, a subgroup of the Nyisanzu, who inhabit the area.

Idiophones

Among the major classes of instruments in Tanzania, idiophones are the oldest and most numerous. This class divides into two groups: untuned and tuned idiophones.

Untuned idiophones

Untuned idiophones group as bells, rattles, scrapers, and shakers. These instrument-types are found widely throughout the country. In general, they serve as part of percussive batteries, or are used alone to provide rhythm for otherwise unaccompanied singing (as with the bells used in the *msunyunho* choral singing of the Gogo). Additionally, dancers wear some idiophones.

The Swahili term *njuga* denotes a string of small bells, which dancers wear around the ankles. Bean shaped, the bells are iron, with one or several metal balls inside. Dancers string together about fifteen bells; shaken, each bell chimes at a unique pitch. The Gogo stitch these bells onto strips of leather about 20 centimeters long. The Maasai Moran have a larger set of bells, the *ol-tnalan*. Worn on elaborate leather bands, sometimes decorated with cowrie shells, these bells are iron, and have several iron balls inside. Among the Chagga, male dancers wear on their backs *shimo-lo*, sets of bells.

In southern Tanzania, the Mawia and the Mwera wear ankle rattles, made of small, hard fruit shells, strung together in rows. With the dancers' foot stomping in performance, these musical adornments provide a distinct cross-rhythmic pattern against the patterns of the accompanying battery of drums.

In southern Tanzania, scraped idiophones, like the *tatarizo,* are often used. The *tatarizo* is made of a bamboo stem, with twenty or more serrations carved around it. In several musical contexts, people play it by scraping a small wooden stick across the serrations.

The Swahili term *manyanga* is the generic name of an array of shaken, seed-filled rattles, mostly made of dried calabashes or coconuts, and spread widely around the country. Their shells often have perforations, which serve the functions of decoration and sound amplification. They are often played in pairs, but they may be played singly. The Sukuma and the Haya use them in trance-inducing rites.

Another kind of shaken idiophone is the *kayamba*, a reed rattle, two layers of reeds stitched together, with small seeds in the space between the layers. Used in a variety of contexts, it is found in southern Tanzania—among the Burungi, the Luguru, the Ngoni, the Sukuma, and others. It is shaken with both hands, whose thumbs provide additional rhythms by slapping against it.

Tuned idiophones

Tuned idiophones are of two types: mbiras and xylophones. In Tanzania, the term *marimba* often specifies either of these groups, and the Swahili phrase *marimba madogo* 'small marimba' refers to the mbira.

Mbira

A range of mbiras occurs throughout the country: some are boards, mounted in gourd resonators; others are box resonated. The number of lamellae may vary from as few as six to several dozen. The keys are usually metal, bamboo, or rattan, and their vibrations resonate in a box resonator (among the Gogo, the Makonde, and the Mwera); or the keys, attached to a board, resonate in a calabash (among the Makua). Often, to add a buzz, each key has a loosely attached metal ring, or the resonating cavity contains idiophonic modifiers, like a small hole covered with the membrane of a spider's nest.

Among the Tanzanian mbiras are the Makonde *ulimba,* possibly the oldest mbira in Tanzania (Kubik 1985:5); the Makua *rumpa,* a flatboard mbira with eight iron keys and a calabash as a resonator; and the Gogo *marimba,* a box-resonated form, which has versions with nine to forty-five keys (Nketia 1968:80). Young men play the nine-key version for personal enjoyment; the larger versions have thirty-four to forty-five keys; one uses fifty-six (Hyslop 1976:2).

The instruments with thirty-four to forty-five keys are played in an ensemble of six musicians, three of whom play the *marimba* in a responsorial relationship: one player acts as leader, and each player also sings. Each performer plays slightly different ostinato patterns, which utilize tones about a third apart. The part of the lead singer-player overlaps constantly with the part of the responsorial chorus of player-singers.

The tuning of the instruments is pentatonic, with tones that roughly equate the sequence D–F–G–A–B. For the simultaneous sounding of any of these tones to be consonant in Gogo terms, they must be a third or a fourth apart. The typical sound of the ensemble gives the impression of a constantly sounding dominant-seventh chord (figure 1). The other three performers include two who play hand-held rattles, and a dancer who wears ankle bells.

The significance of the Gogo *marimba* in Tanzanian musical culture is shown by the fact that in 1970 it was chosen to represent the nation in a special issue of four postage stamps, illustrating musical instruments of East Africa.

Xylophones

Among the xylophones in Tanzania are log xylophones and box-resonated xylophones. The Makua play the *mangolongondo,* a log xylophone that has nine keys that vibrate freely on two logs, on which they rest. Along the coast, the Zaramo play a box-resonated xylophone, which they simply call *marimba.* It has eight or nine keys, and in performance is usually paired with a similar instrument. In such instances, one instrument, the *marimba ya kuanza,* starts the piece; the other, *marimba ya kugenkizia* 'marimba that turns the tune around', elaborates on the basic pattern. Three drums of different pitches—*boi, msondo, seberea*—complete the ensemble, which normally accompanies songs. Box xylophones also occur among the Sambaa and Bondei, and on Zanzibar and Pemba. Frame xylophones (such as the Mandinka *balofon* or the Chopi *timbila*) are not traditional in Tanzania, though in the mid-1970s, after a tour of West Africa, members of the national troupe brought them into the country.

FIGURE 1   Vocal harmony of the Wagogo people: *a,* basic vocal harmonies; *b,* extended vocal harmonies.

Only women play mouth bows, often for lullabies.
The women's bow is a small, straight piece of split
bamboo, with a copper wire or fiber string.

Chordophones

A large assortment of chordophones occurs throughout Tanzania. They range from simple musical bows to unusual and sophisticated lutes, one of which is simultaneously bowed and plucked. Typical also are lyres and bow harps, chordophones common throughout all of East Africa.

Musical bows

Only women play mouth bows, often for lullabies. One example is the *nganga* of the Fipa, who live southeast of Lake Tanganyika. This bow, and many others used only by women, show little resemblance to the hunting bow: the women's bow is a small, straight piece of split bamboo, with a copper wire or fiber string.

Braced bows—with gourd resonators attached to the center of the stick, and a wire noose attached to the same spot on the stick, subdividing the string—are found in western and central Tanzania. In Tabora, the Nyamwezi use the *igubu,* a large example, to accompany songs. To accompany dances, young Sukuma men and women play a musical bow, the *yazoli.* Another example is the *donondo,* found among the Nyaturu. Unbraced musical bows also occur in the southern areas of Tanzania, among the Pangwa and Sangu.

Zithers

Bar zithers are generically known as *zeze* (as are bows and lutes), while board zithers are called *bango.* The latter, which occur mainly in coastal and southern areas, use calabash resonators. One Gogo musician, Lubeleje Mkasa Chiute, has developed a unique version of the board zither, the *chipango* (Gogo for *bango*). He invented it while a student at the College of Art, Bagamoyo.

In Iranga District (south central highlands), where the population is mostly Wahehe, a board zither, the *kipango,* has six strings, with a gourd resonator at one end. It occurs throughout this area, and in Malawi and Mozambique. Traditionally, a musician sits, and sets it between his thighs. However, guitar music has affected its playing: many of its musical patterns resemble those of guitar music. Young performers actually play the instrument like a guitar.

The Hehe zither is the *ligombo,* a narrow, three-stringed, trough zither. Its most famous performer, Pancras Mkwawa, played for recordings made by Hugh Tracey in 1951. For a resonator, the *ligombo* has at its base an open gourd.

Two other types of trough zither also occur: the Sandawe *tloto* has six strings, derived from wrapping a single strand through holes on the high ends of the trough. The trough ends in a handle on one side of the instrument. The other type is the *inanga.* It is larger and proportionately much wider, with a rim around the entire trough, and carved notches for the wrappings of the single stand at each end. This version occurs in the West Lake area, and in Tabora.

Lutes

The term *zeze* also covers lutes. Of the ethnic groups that play lutes, the Gogo have probably the richest musical heritage—a fact most Tanzanians readily acknowledge. Known as the *izeze* among the Gogo, these instruments come in a variety of sizes, with different numbers of strings (from one to twelve). Musicians pluck or bow them, and sometimes perform both ways at once. Gogo musicians are also famous for virtuosity in performance.

In the 1970s and 1980s, Tanzanian fiddles began to undergo innovation, especially at the hands of Hukwe Zawosi, one of the nation's most celebrated musicians. The largest *izeze* is more than a meter long. Attached to tuning pegs, the strings extend rearward from the neck; the skin of a dik-dik covers the body, a calabash shell. The lengths of the pegs vary, and the strings keep clear of each other. The body bears burned etchings and ornamental tacks. The tuning of this instrument (as with other pitched Gogo instruments) uses "the 4th to the 10th partials of the harmonic series, with a diminished 5th occurring between the 5th and 7th partials" (Kubik 1980:567–571) (figure 2).

Harps

Bow harps are seven-stringed, boat-shaped instruments. Cowhide covers their resonators, intricately decorated with burned-in parallel and diagonal lines. The Ha traditionally use bow harps; people of the Morogoro and Iringa areas call them *kinubi*.

In Tanzania, the bowl lyre, typical in East African cultures, occurs only among the Kuria (Mara area), who know the instrument as the *litungu*, an eight-stringed version. People formerly made the bodies of bowl lyres from a carved wooden bowl; by the late 1900s, a metal bowl, of a kind common in households, served the same purpose. Sections of zebra skin, lashed together, cover both sides of the resonator. The use of gut for its strings has given way to the use of nylon, which permits greater stability in tuning. Werema Masiaga Chacha, a Kurian musician, is Tanzania's leading performer on the *litungu*.

Aerophones

Many kinds of aerophones occur in Tanzanian traditional music (Gnielinski 1985). They range from simple flutes to composite trumpets. In traditional contexts, aerophones are often associated with magical practices and beliefs, as in the land around Lake Victoria, where they serve as rainmakers or storm deterrents (Wachsmann 1961:48), or as symbols of authority in connection with war, hunting, or convening communal gatherings.

FIGURE 2   Comparison of Wagogo tuning and harmonic partials of the overtone series: *a,* basic four-tone scale with the number of the harmonic overtone series (top number) and the number of cents between overtones (bottom number); *b,* extended scale, with same numerical indicators as above.

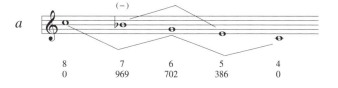

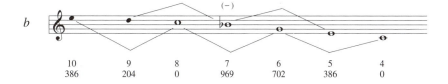

imbutus   Horn used by the Kumbu as the emblem of the chief and considered the most sacred possession of chiefdom

beni ng'oma   Social dance clubs of East Africa with dance steps that reinterpreted military drills of European models

Trumpets

The most striking indigenous aerophones are trumpets (Swahili *baragumu*). In some societies, they serve both musical and nonmusical functions. Fishermen in Bukoba and Zanzibar use them to call customers. The Butu and Maasai used them as a part of military campaigns. The Kimbu used a horn called *imbutu* as the emblem of the chief, and considered it the most sacred possession of every Kimbu chiefdom.

Other trumpets include the *ntandara* (also *ntanduka*), end-blown wooden trumpets of the Ukerewe. About 1.8 meters long, these were played in sets. They resemble the Ugandan *amakondere*. Side-blown trumpets, made of kudu horns (*nzamba*), occur in the West Lake area. The *lilandi*, a deep-sounding trumpet, is a composite, made of seven to fourteen gourds, attached by stitches and special gum; the largest gourd serves as the bell. The Kabwa (Mara area) use this trumpet in wedding rituals, and play it all night before circumcisions (Hyslop 1976:54). They also use it to accompany singing, and they play it in ensembles with membrane drums and stringed instruments. In central Tanzania, bamboo trumpets (*mputa*) occur. These are side-blown instruments, with a round gourd attached as a bell.

Flutes and reeds

Flutes in Tanzania tend to be side blown—like the Hehe *kilanzi*, the Makua *npeta*, and the Makonde *mwanzi* (Swahili for 'bamboo')—and occur throughout the country. These instruments are mostly bamboo, but are occasionally stalks of millet. Those made of the latter are often played by children. Many traditional flutes have begun to be displaced by modern versions, even those imported from China. Traditional flutes, however, continue to play an important role in more traditional songs and contexts, where musicians are still reluctant to use nontraditional flutes. Flutes are apparently used to express personal feelings, and in traditional settings often add rather individual touches to the musical fabric. They are also used by shepherds herding cattle, and by children playing in fields.

Reed instruments, though found in parts of the country, are not indigenous to Tanzania. Along the coast, and on Zanzibar and Pembe, an Arabic reed import—the *zumari*, a single-reed clarinet—is found. In the area of Dar es Salaam, the Zaramo people use the *zumari* in some religious musical activities, but elsewhere in Tanzania, it is rare or not seen at all.

NEOTRADITIONAL MUSICAL FORMS

After 1945, music in Tanzania, as in other parts of East Africa, began to undergo a series of changes that pointed toward the development of a new cultural consciousness. This change was roughly parallel to the political changes that began to surface in the country: the mutual recognition, by both Africans and Europeans, of the inevitability of political independence (Kubik 1981:83). Africans who had participated in World War II returned from Europe, having seen and heard unfamiliar musical forms. By the 1950s, recordings of Cuban rumbas and other Latin American styles began to become popular in Zaïre, where local bands adapted and imitated these rhythms, and eventually developed them into Congolese jazz, which became highly influential in Tanzania.

Beni ng'oma

The impact of Western influence on Tanzanian music took many forms. One of the most revealing absorptions of this influence into the African cultural framework involved the European brass band. In the early 1900s, East Africans became familiar with the music of German and British brass bands. As early as 1906 in Dar es Salaam, German bands recruited Africans. In 1919, when the British entered the city after the war, they found among Africans an abundant supply of trained brass-band performers. The impact of British brass bands had already been felt elsewhere in East Africa, with the formation of the King's African Rifles (KAR) in Kenya and Uganda in 1906.

The degree to which Tanzanians admired the regalia of European military ensembles and metaphorically reinterpreted this phenomenon in their own terms is visible in the array of musical and social adaptations their own traditional culture made, in the form of social dance clubs, *beni ng'oma*. These clubs, originating along the Kenyan coast as competitive dance associations, have a deep-rooted history, and actually date from the 1890s. Some of the features of this tradition were European military titles for officers and dance steps that imitated military drills. Despite these traits, *beni ng'oma* is essentially African in character, and the meanings of its dance steps and titles are quite different from those of its European models (Ranger 1975). The language used was Swahili. The popularity of *beni ng'oma* penetrated well into the interior, but by the 1930s it began to wane. By 1945, interest was beginning to shift toward dance bands. The decline of *beni ng'oma*, coinciding with the end of the colonial era, became a sociomusical token of the decline of colonialism. The demise of the dance clubs revealed the acculturative forces that were exerting themselves on Tanzanian music.

Christian music

From the earliest presence of Christian missionaries until the 1930s, the music of the Christian Church in Tanzania was merely Western music performed on Tanzanian soil. To European and American hymns, missionaries added texts in indigenous languages, without regard for tonal inflection and other linguistic subtleties. Despite missionaries' early resistance to change, the efforts of young missionaries and enterprising African Christians eventually Africanized the church. Within rituals, they included African musical elements, and they encouraged the composition of liturgical pieces that incorporated African elements.

The first use of African music in Christian worship was among the Ngoni people of Malawi in the late 1800s (Jones 1976:39). But this situation was exceptional. In Tanzania, African music began to appear in Christian churches in the early 1950s. Various articles discussing this development began to appear in the *Journal of the African Music Society* in 1956. Tanzanian composer and clergyman Stephen Mbunga published a list of records of music composed by Africans, including music for Christian worship (1963:125–164, 209–211).

An example of ecclesiastical Africanization is Mbunga's *Missa Baba Yetu* 'Mass of Our Father' (1959), a work whose vocal parts have typically African harmonic and rhythmic relationships, especially in the Gloria. In addition to composing, Mbunga acted as a spokesman for Africanizing the music of Tanzanian churches. In an article on musical reform (1968), he called for educational reorientation, like the kind out-

Tanzanian jazz bands emerged most prominently in Dar es Salaam. Their development was fostered not only by the Africanization of European musical instruments and musical concepts, but also by the impact of African-American music and culture.

lined by Nyerere, Tanzania's first president. In his 1967 speech "Education for Self-Reliance," Nyerere had called on the nation to move, educationally and culturally, toward an African mentality. Mbunga claimed the same reorientation was necessary in music. He cited the need for a "cultural self-adjustment," and made suggestions for future directions in the nation's policy on music. He also wrote a book on music in the Christian churches of Africa (1963).

Training centers

In the 1960s, to spark a sense of musical nationalism, the Tanzanian government set up official agencies. One such agency was the Music Conservatoire of Tanzania, Limited, founded in 1967 in Dar es Salaam. This conservatory helped Tanzanians rediscover their musical heritage, and provided musical training in Western musical performance and composition. However, it emphasized the European classical tradition, and thus did not reach the goal of creating a nationalistic framework.

In the 1970s, other training centers began to appear around the country. At Bukoba, the Ruhija Music Centre, under the direction of Mr. W. Both and the Lutheran Church, primarily trained local musicians. On the coast, the Bagamoyo College of Arts also began a program in musical training. At the University of Dar es Salaam, such scholars as Graham Hyslop, a British musician and musicologist who specialized in East African music, began teaching courses in music and working with African choirs. In 1974, to oversee the development of a nationalized cultural pride, President Nyerere reestablished the Ministry of National Culture and Youth.

Jazz

Tanzanian jazz bands emerged most prominently in Dar es Salaam. Their development was fostered not only by the Africanization of European musical instruments and musical concepts, but also by the impact of African-American music and culture, which, by the 1960s, was being felt in many parts of the continent. Another important musical influence was the new music coming out of Zaïre. This style, derived from the Latin American rumba, entered Tanzania by way of 78-rpm records, and later by an influx of Congolese bands, which dominated popular music in East Africa for more than a decade. Eventually, Tanzanian bands, aided by the government, began to borrow some of the stylistic features of the Zaïrian bands, and developed a Tanzanian style of jazz.

Tanzania's lack of facilities for commercial recording and manufacturing limited the commercial production of jazz. Nevertheless, people elsewhere in Africa managed to hear this music on records and tape dubs pirated from Radio Tanzania broadcasts. During the 1970s and 1980s, this station recorded local bands, and thereby generated dynamic musical activity. In 1979, the station recorded more than 6,000 traditional-music ensembles, 120 jazz bands, 60 *taarab* groups, 50 choirs, and 30 brass bands (Wallis and Malm 1984). Using its library, more than 1,500 tapes (as of 1980), which featured more than 60 bands, Radio Tanzania's national radio broadcasts helped preserve the uniqueness of Tanzanian jazz as it aided its development.

Three socioeconomic factors affected the development and proliferation of the new popular musical forms: the availability of European instruments, the rise of panethnic communities in urban areas, and European discovery of the commercial viability of African popular music (Kubik 1981). Companies like Odeon, Victor (His Master's Voice), and Columbia were the first to record popular music in East Africa. Even the packaging of the recordings appealed to a specific African market—the emerging, but sparse, African middle class.

In the mid-1970s, the jazz bands of Dar es Salaam reflected the variety of cultural and musical influences that for two decades had affected popular music. Three bands performing in Dar es Salaam in the mid-1970s prove this point: the Orchestre Maquis du Zaïre, a Zaïrian band, included Tanzanian female dancers (figure 3); NUTA Jazz Band represented the National Union of Tanganyika Workers; Sunburst consisted of native Tanzanians, African-Americans, and a Jamaican. Each of these bands performed music that reflected different spheres of musical influence: the first played Congolese style, the second favored a style more closely related to Tanzanian traditional music, and the third displayed influences from African-American culture and the West Indies.

Taarab

A musical style popular throughout coastal East Africa, *taarab* centers principally in Zanzibar. Related more closely to Egyptian café music than to music of the Tanzanian mainland, this style finds its roots in the same soil as Swahili. In addition to serving as social entertainment, *taarab* reinforces, preserves, and elevates, the position of Swahili. Its music, a heterophonic orchestral style, traditionally accompanies Swahili love poetry known as *mashaira*. The typical *taarab* orchestra consists of a trapezoidal zither (*kanuni*), violins, cellos, string basses, accordion, lute (*udi*), end-blown flute (*ney*), a battery of percussion, and sometimes an electric guitar and electric keyboard or organ. A chorus and vocal soloists join the instrumentalists, so a typical Zanzibari ensemble consists of twenty-five to thirty-five performers.

Taarab developed about 1950. It grew out of Egyptian *firqah* orchestras, which, during the 1940s, provided sound tracks for Egyptian films. By the mid-1950s, *taarab* music clubs had sprung up in every district of urban Zanzibar. They played mainly for local weddings and other festive activities. After the revolution of 1964,

FIGURE 3 Orchestre Maquis du Zaïre, a Congolese-style band with Tanzanian female dancers.

the song texts became politicized to reflect the ideology of the Afro-Shirazi Party, and several ensembles received governmental sponsorship. On the Tanzanian mainland, song texts often reflected the ideology of President Nyerere. In the 1980s, some *taarab* groups went back to performing Swahili love poems.

In Zanzibar, *taarab* clubs were not exclusively a male domain. Women's clubs, though not initially so prominent, existed as a network of smaller ensembles. Unlike the male groups, the female clubs had loose structures, and were small. The most famous *taarab* singer was a woman, Siti binti Saad.

Nationalization

Utamaduni, the Tanzanian National Dance Troupe (founded in 1964), is possibly the clearest embodiment of the notion of neotraditional music in Tanzania. Authorized by the Ministry of National Culture and Youth, it was the means by which the ministry tried to develop a nationalized form of music—one that amalgamated musical styles from the nation's ethnic groups. This ensemble assembled a corps of some of the nation's finest musicians from a variety of ethnic backgrounds.

In 1974, to accelerate the process of musical nationalization, the government set up Baraza la Muziki la Taifa, the National Music Council. Other institutions involved in nationalization are the Tanzanian Film Company (to which the government granted sole rights to release recordings of Tanzanian music), and Radio Tanzania.

REFERENCES

Blankaart, Stephen. 1683. *Periplus Maris Erythræi*. Amstelodami: Apud Jansonnio-Waesbergios.

Gnielinski, Anneliese von. 1985. *Traditional Music Instruments of Tanzania in the National Museum.* Dar es Salaam: National Museums. Occasional paper 6.

Hartwig, Gerald W. 1969. "The Historical and Social Role of Kerebe Music." *Tanzania Notes and Records* 70:41–56.

Hunter, G. 1953. "Hidden Drums in Singida District." *Tanganyika Notes and Records* 70:41–56.

Hyslop, Graham. 1976. "Musical Instruments of Tanzania." Manuscript.

Jones, Arthur Morris. 1976. *African Hymnody in Christian Worship: A Contribution to the History of Its Development.* Gwelo, Zimbabwe: Mambo Press.

Kubik, Gerhard. 1967. "The Traditional Music of Tanzania." *Afrika* 8(2):29–32.

———. 1968. *Mehrstimmigkeit and Tonsysteme in Zentral- und Ostafrika.* Vienna: Österreichischen Akademie der Wissenschaft.

———. 1980. "Tanzania." *The New Grove Dictionary of Music and Musicians*, ed. Stanley Sadie. London: Macmillan.

———. 1981. "Neo-Traditional Popular Music in East Africa since 1945." *Popular Music* 1:83–104.

———. 1982. *Musikgeschichte in Bildern: Ostafrika.* Leipzig: VEB Deutscher Verlag für Musik.

———. 1985. "Tanzania Music Areas." Manuscript.

Martin, Stephen H. 1991a. "Brass Bands and the Beni Phenomenon in Urban East Africa." *African Music* 8(1):72–81.

———. 1991b. "Popular Music in Urban East Africa." *Black Music Research Journal* 11(1):39–53.

Mbunga, Stephen B. G. 1963. *Church Law and Bantu Music.* Schoeneck-Beckenried, Switzerland: Nouvelle Revue de Science Missionaire. Supplement 13.

——. 1968. "Music Reform in Tanzania." *African Ecclesiastical Review* 10:47–54.

Nketia, J. H. Kwabena. 1968. "Multi-Part Organization in the Music of the Gogo of Tanzania." *Journal of the International Folk Music Council* 19:79–88.

Ranger, Terence O. 1975. *Dance and Society in Eastern Africa 1890–1970.* Berkeley: University of California Press.

Simon, Artur, ed. 1983. *Musik in Afrika.* Berlin: Staatliche Museen Preussischer Kulturbesitz, Museum für Völkerkunde.

Tenraa, W. F. E. R. 1963. "Sandawe Musical and Other Sound Producing Instruments." *Tanganyika Notes and Records* 60:23–48.

——. 1964. "Sandawe Music and Other Sound Producing Instruments: Supplementary Notes." *Tanganyika Notes and Records* 62:91–95.

Wallis, Roger, and Krister Malm. 1984. *Big Sounds from Small Peoples.* New York: Pendragon Press.

Central Africa

As this volume was going to press, a new government in Zaïre had changed the name of the
nation to "Democratic Republic of the Congo."

Central Africa

In Central Africa, music reflects interchanges with styles from such distant sources as Portugal and Latin America. Within the region, the polyphonic singing of the Pygmies has influenced—and been influenced by—the music of their neighbors. Royal chiefdoms, secret societies, migrant laborers, and European Christian evangelization have all added to the richness of the musical palette.

Central Africa: An Introduction
Gerhard Kubik

Musical Cultures in the Adamawa-Eastern Subregion
Musical Cultures in the Bantu Subregion

Since the mid-1800s, perceptions about the identity and location of the central part of the African continent have changed repeatedly. For David Livingstone (1857), the center lay near the Zambezi River; for Georg Schweinfurth (1875), it occupied Mangbetu country, in the northeast of what in the late 1900s was the Republic of Zaïre. In 1960, Ubangi-Shari, one of the four territories of French Equatorial Africa, proclaimed independence under the name "Central African Republic"; in 1966, it became an empire; and in 1979, after a coup d'état, it became a republic again.

Thus, "Central Africa" is not an observational fact, but a geographical concept, with social and cultural implications. Such concepts change over time. They vary from culture to culture, and from author to author; compare the notion of "West-Central Africa" (Murray 1981:154).

For descriptive purposes here, Central Africa is the portion of Africa where people speak languages belonging to either of two divisions:

(1) Adamawa-Eastern languages, or family I.A.6 (Greenberg 1970), spoken mainly in Cameroon, the Central African Republic, and northeastern Zaïre.
(2) Bantu languages of zones A, B, C, H, L, K, and (in part) D and M (Guthrie 1948).

The Bantu languages fall together with the Semi-Bantu and Bantoid languages of the Cameroon grassland, in family I.A.5, or Benue-Congo languages (Greenberg 1970).

There are good reasons for correlating cultural-geographical boundaries with languages, rather than with other aspects of culture. First, as J. H. Kwabena Nketia and others have noted, language joins intimately with music. In Central Africa, people do not merely conceptualize sounds, but often verbalize them. Instrumental patterns produced on the Azande harp and box-resonated lamellophone evoke verbal associations, which inspire musician-composers to find new text lines (Kubik 1964:51–52). By repeating mnemonic syllables (which may or may not constitute lexically meaningful words), performers learn timbral sequences and rhythmic patterns; and in the rain forest from Cameroon to Congo and Zaïre, large slit drums

As this volume was going to press, a new government in Zaïre had changed the name of the nation to "Democratic Republic of the Congo."

Central African linguistic zones

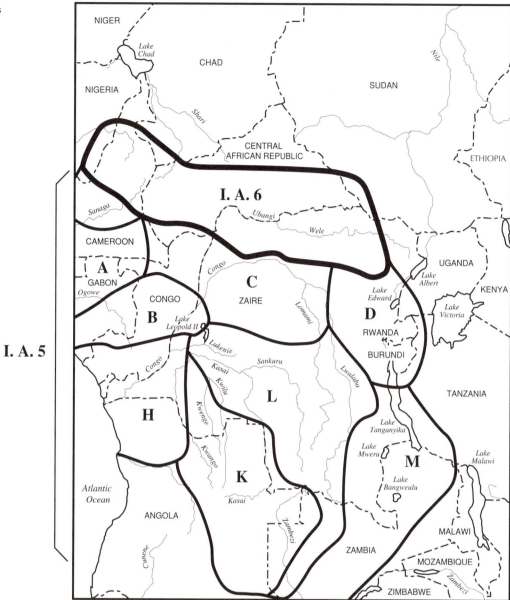

have served as "talking drums," to send messages in speech tones (Carrington 1949, 1956, 1975). Second, the languages of the African continent have been much better and more systematically researched than the musics; linguistic relationships unlock important chapters in African history, and throw indirect light on music history.

On a map of Central Africa, the line between the I.A.6 and I.A.5 languages marks a stylistic divide between Central African musical subregions. Most of Zaïre, all of Gabon, Equatorial Guinea, the islands of São Tome and Principe, Congo, most of the Central African Republic, and large parts of Cameroon, Angola, and the northern parts of Zambia, make up what I call Central Africa. This grouping acknowledges a combination of linguistic and cultural affinities, patterns of migration, and musical styles. Because of a historical migration of pastoral peoples from the East African Horn, and the presence of specific patterns of political organization in the interlacustrine area, Rwanda and Burundi are properly perceived as belonging to East Africa, rather than to Central Africa. On similar grounds, I exclude the southwestern part of Angola (particularly the Province of Huila), which, as Guthrie's zone R (1948), includes the cultures of the Nkhumbi, the Handa, and others.

Three women, pestles in hand, stand around a mortar. They strike alternately into the mortar, to produce an interlocking beat. Sometimes, between the main working strokes, each woman lightly taps her pestle on the rim of the mortar, to create accents and rhythmic patterns within a twelve-pulse cycle.

So defined, Central Africa is a vast region, diverse in musical cultures. In large expanses of the rain forest, the musical cultures of Bantu-speakers have supplanted an ancient culture, which survives in pockets, dispersed from southern Cameroon across the Congo to the Ituri Forest: that of the Pygmy hunter-gatherers. Though the Pygmies adopted Bantu languages long ago, their musical culture retained distinctive traits, which influenced the later arrivals. Wherever contact occurred among the three ethnic-linguistic entities (I.A.6-speakers, Bantu I.A.5-speakers, Pygmy I.A.5-speakers), cultural exchange and adaptation followed. In addition, cultures from outside Central Africa repeatedly made inroads into the region.

MUSICAL CULTURES IN THE ADAMAWA-EASTERN SUBREGION

This area lies north of the equator. It extends from the border of northeastern Nigeria, across Cameroon and the Central African Republic, into parts of the southern Sudan, including northern parts of Zaïre (see map).

The people who settled in this subregion can be classed in the following cultural clusters, proceeding from west to east (Murdock 1967).

(a) Chamba-Yungur (cluster 66), in the west; with individual peoples such as the Chamba, the Kutin, the Longuda, the Yungur, the Ndongo, the Vere.
(b) Adamawa (cluster 68), also in the west; including the Mundanga, the Fali, the Mumuye, the Mbum, the Lakka, the Namshi.
(c) Banda-Gbaya (cluster 71); including the Gbaya, the Banda, the Manja, the Ngbandi.
(d) Azande (cluster 72); including the Azande, with all their subdivisions, plus the (related) Nzakara.

The ecology of this broad area draws on a uniform savanna landscape, which supports a small population. Intermittently mountainous areas (especially the Adamawa massif) have often served as a retreat for invaded autochthonous peoples.

Certain stylistic and structural traits in music occur saliently throughout this subregion, as an extensive sample of recordings, obtained during the mid-1960s, shows (Kubik 1963–1964). These traits encompass tonal systems, singing in parts, patterns of movement, and instrumental resources. Some of them occur in the whole subregion, and some in parts of it.

Possibly all these peoples use pentatonic tonal systems. In western areas, the typical scale is often a plain anhemitonic pentatonic one, with seconds and minor thirds. In the more eastern areas, narrower intervals occur, as in some forms of Zande music (Kubik 1964). In several cultures, this scale combines with a homophonic two-part style of singing, with a predilection for simultaneous fourths and fifths. Despite differences in the intervals actually preferred in different areas—even within a homogeneous musical culture, like that of the Azande—simultaneous fourths and fifths are

Elementary pulsation: ca 430 M.M.

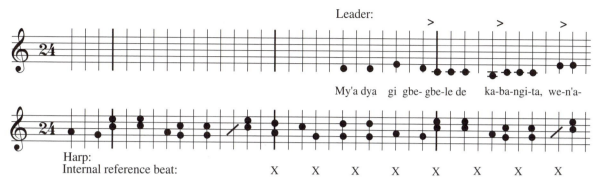

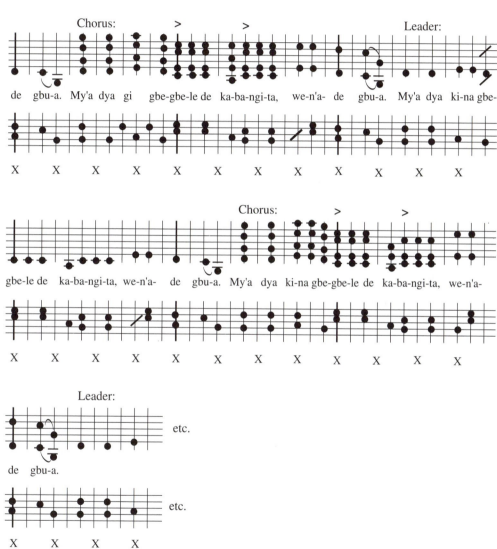

FIGURE 1   *Wen'ade gbua:*
Zande song, performed by
Antoine Gbalagume (about
thirty years old) on the
harp, with a leader and a
chorus of men and women,
at Djema, Central African
Republic, May 1964 (Kubik
1963–1964:R47/B). In this
notational system, a note
head on the staff marks the
impact point of a note to be
sung or played; in singing,
the note is held until it is
revoked by the sign for a
stop (/). Thus, duration is
expressed indirectly, by
marking the moment on
the timeline when sound
production stops.

perfect (that is, aimed at 498 and 702 cents, respectively). In this subregion, no evidence for the use of a tempered tonal system has turned up. Figure 1 shows typical Zande style: a leader and a chorus homophonically perform a multipart song, accompanied by a five-stringed harp.

In the western part of this subregion, some cultural anthropologists have considered the peoples who inhabit highland or mountainous areas an old Sudanic or pale-

kundi   Term for the tanged type of harp in
the Central African Republic

FIGURE 2   Kutin performers on double bells.
Kontcha, northern Cameroon, 1963.

FIGURE 3   Three Chamba women rhythmically
organize their work. Northeastern Nigeria, 1963.

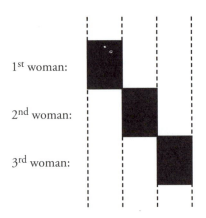

1st woman:

2nd woman:

3rd woman:

FIGURE 4   Interlocking patterns of beats produced by millet-pounding strokes.

onigritic stratum: these peoples are the descendants of long-established agriculturalists of the savanna. Music may retain survivals from the remote past. Therefore, it is
significant that here we find evidence of the presence of kinetic patterns combined in
interlocking style. In figure 2, Gonga Sarki Birgui and Hamadjan, who live at
Kontcha (a Ful6e-dominated area), play together on *toŋ ito*, two double iron bells of
the Central African flange-welded type, with bow grip (Kubik 1963–1964:B8910,
B8920). The bells are individually called *toŋ senwa* 'the higher' (1=B_M+40 cents,
2=F_H+5), and *toŋ deni* 'the lower' (1=F_M–5, 2=A_M+30, Korg Tuner readings).
Subscripts in these readings indicate the octave range: M, middle; H, high. The bells,
positioned with their openings toward the chest, are played in a two-tone pattern
with a softwood beater held in the right hand. The patterns interlock. By varying the
distance between the opening and the chest, the musicians modify the timbre of the
bells. Both these techniques of structuring are probably ancient in African music;
they also occur in the instrumental music of other regions, as in the *mvet* of zone A.

Among the Chamba, who are related to the Kutin, evidence of tripartite interlocking has turned up in the organization of women's millet-pounding strokes (figure
3). Three women, pestles in hand, stand around a mortar. They strike alternately into
the mortar, to produce an interlocking beat (figure 4). The photograph shows the
technique: one woman has just struck, the second one has lifted her pestle to the ver-
tex, and the third is halfway down her stroke. But the total action is more complex:
sometimes, between the main working strokes, each woman lightly taps her pestle on

FIGURE 5   Watched by children, Lazaro Tourgba of Zemio, Central African Republic, plays a Zande harp, 1964.

the rim of the mortar, to create accents and rhythmic patterns within a twelve-pulse cycle. From time to time, with lips, palate, and tongue, the women also produce sucking and clicking sounds; they thereby add to the percussion another timbre-melodic line (Kubik 1963–1964: B 8609). Figures 3 and 4 show an approach to patterning that is basic to much African music: they suggest, in tandem with the known history of these populations, the antiquity of the concept.

From northernmost Cameroon (which falls partly into Greenberg's family of III.E, or Chadic languages), across the Central African Republic, into southern Sudan, stretches what can be called Africa's most cohesive harp territory. The harp, an ancient Egyptian-Saharan heritage, found widespread footholds in the savannas at the northern fringes of the rain forest. From the specimens played among the Ngbaka, south of Bangui (Arom 1967), to those of the Nzakara and Azande (Dampierre 1963; Kubik 1964), most of the peoples mentioned under (c) and (d) above, except for the Gbaya in the west, play harps (figure 5).

In the Central African Republic, the harps belong to what Wachsmann (1964) called the tanged type of African harp. Ancient connections are still visible in stylistic analogies in harp music across this subregion, including nomenclature, with the frequently heard term *kundi* (Zande, Nzakara) and its variants, like *kundeŋ* (the Karre at Bozoum). In the northwesternmost areas of the Adamawa-Eastern division of languages, harps accompany iron smelting, and are played by associates—often close family members or junior apprentices—of a blacksmith working at the furnace (Gardi 1974). In the southeast of this subregion, harps have spread into the land of the Mangbetu, speakers of a Central Sudanic language, whom outsiders have often erroneously associated with the Azande. In the early 1900s, Mangbetu carvers, exploiting what were the beginnings of a lucrative colonial trade in touristic art, produced thousands of ivory harps with carved motifs and body coverings made of reptile skin. (A large collection reposes at the Musikinstrumentenmuseum, Munich.)

> *kponingbo*   A twelve- or thirteen-key log
> xylophone, accompanied by a slit drum
> (*guru*) and a double-skin membrane drum

FIGURE 6   A sequence of bichords in Zande music.

I   II   III   IV

European tourists bought these specimens of Mangbetu harps, which ended up in the international trade of African art, or in public collections.

Harp music of the Azande, Nzakara, and Banda has been studied by several authors (Giorgetti 1957; Dampierre 1963; Kubik 1964 and 1967). In the older styles of the Azande, one often finds asymmetric patterns within a regularly cyclical number, such as twelve or twenty-four pulses (figure 1). Harmony in Zande music for the harp includes sequences of four bichords (figure 6), which also appear in vocal harmony. The tonal-harmonic system of Zande music strictly regulates the occurrence of each of these bichords; the relationship to the referential beat usually follows the same scheme as in figure 1. The scale is a descending pentatonic one, which musicians memorize with the aid of a text they often play to check the tuning at the beginning of a piece (figure 7); here is its translation.

> Little by little, that's work.
> One must play the harp, and sing its song.
> The ancient things implicate work.

Zande tunings, however, vary; two notes in particular, identified in figure 7 by a parenthesized macron, may be lowered by almost a semitone.

The harp is not the only prominent Zande instrument; the Azande have a wide range of instrumental resources. Three types of xylophone appear in this area: the *manza*, the *longo*, and the *kponingbo*. The first of these, associated with Zande royalty, has a pentatonic tuning, in two large, one medium, and two small intervals. A specimen documented by Kremser (1982) in Zaïre had gourd resonators; another, found at Chief Zekpio's place in Dembia, Central African Republic, had five logs placed over banana stems. A chief's relative played it, to accompany the chief's harp music (figure 5). The term *manza* may connect with other xylophone terminology in the northern part of Central Africa. Though no evidence on Indonesian origins has presented itself (compare Jones 1964:151–52), relationships with xylophone names farther west from the Azande are likely: *mɛndzāŋ* in Ewondo (southern Cameroon), and *mɛntʃaŋa* in Mpyɛmɔ (southwestern Central African Republic). These cognates imply historical relationships in the distribution of xylophones in this subregion. The *longo* (also pronounced /rongo/) is a portable, gourd-resonated xylophone. The specimen documented among the Azande at Dembia (figure 8) resembles types found in Chad, and falls clearly within the northernmost area of gourd-resonated xylophones in Africa.

FIGURE 7   A Zande phrase for checking the tuning of the harp (*kundi*). It is performed in free speech rhythm.

Wili pai sa su– nge   Mu ta ku– ndi ki bi bya– le– u ki– ndi, ku– luo pai sa su– nge

FIGURE 8   For a recording, a Zande musician plays a gourd-resonated xylophone (*longo*). Djema, Central African Republic, 1964.

FIGURE 9   The military-inspired notched flute and drum ensemble of Rafai, Central African Republic, 1964.

The *kponingbo*, a twelve- or thirteen-key log xylophone, accompanied by a slit drum (*guru*) and a double-skin membrane drum in the *kponingbo* circle dance, is likely an Azande import from farther south, possibly as far as language zone L. In pieces for *kponingbo*, this origin is suggested by a rhythmic pattern that seems to be a remolding of a timeline associated with music in Katanga and eastern Angola (zones L and K). Characteristically, the Zande xylophones are not played in interlocking style, though those of Uganda and northern Mozambique are.

The instrumental resources of the Azande also include one flute ensemble, which consists of a set of notched flutes, with four finger holes each, and accompanied by marching-style drums. Based in Rafai (Central African Republic), it was first reported by Mecklenburg (1912); it still existed in 1964 (figure 9). All the evidence available suggests it was a late-nineteenth-century adaptation of military music that bands had performed on expeditions in the southern Sudan during the Mahdi rebellion.

MUSICAL CULTURES IN THE BANTU SUBREGION

Pygmy cultures

The linguistic and cultural map of the tropical–rain-forest areas of Central Africa in 3000 B.C. differed distinctly from that of the late 1900s (Murray 1981:26). Before about 1000 to 500 B.C., when speakers of early Bantu languages migrated from the Bantu Nucleus (a zone embracing parts of western Cameroon and eastern Nigeria) to western parts of Central Africa, the equatorial forest was inhabited by bands of hunter-gatherers, who differed racially from other speakers of Niger-Congo languages, namely the Pygmies. Despite some authors' repeated claims to have discovered an original Pygmy tongue, no such claim has survived scrutiny. All the sylvan hunter-gatherers that remain speak Bantu languages believed to be adaptations of the ancient Bantu tongues spoken by the first migrants with whom the Pygmies had con-

luma   Reed pipes that are popular among the
         Ituri Forest Pygmies of central Africa

jenge   Men's society, featuring masking, of
         the Bangombe Pygmies along the Sangha
         River

tact. In music, however, a pre-Bantu Pygmy musical culture may have survived. Pygmy music distinctively combines a polyphonic style of singing with an extremely developed technique of yodeling. These traits appear in the music of Pygmy groups in widely separated areas, as shown by a comparison of recordings: in the Ituri Forest, Zaïre (Tracey 1973); among the Bangombe and Bambenjele of the Upper Sangha, Central African Republic (Djenda and Kubik 1964, 1966 Phonogrammarchiv Vienna); and among the Bambenjele (Ba-Bénzélé) and the Aka, south of Bangui (Arom 1967). Even outposts of Pygmy culture prove the persistence of a Pygmy musical style, as witness recordings by barely a dozen individuals staying at Ngambe (in the Cameroon grasslands), and associating with the Tikar chief of that town (Kubik 1963–1964: B 8650).

The strength of Pygmy musical culture also shows in the fact that the Pygmies' neighbors have almost invariably borrowed, however imperfectly, the Pygmies' vocal polyphony. In one musical genre or another, these neighbors adopt a Pygmy style of singing, which quite often associates with hunting songs. Bantu-speakers such as the Mpyɛmɔ and Mpompo, in the southwestern Central African Republic and southeastern Cameroon, have adopted Pygmy musical traits; but so have semi-Bantu-speakers, such as the Tikar, notably in a dance called *ngbānya* and in hunting songs called *nswē*. The Mangbetu, speakers of a Central Sudanic language in northeastern Zaïre, have also adopted some elements of Pygmy polyphony. Therefore, on finding Pygmy-style vocal polyphony among any sedentary population in Central Africa, a listener can conclude there has been Pygmy contact in the past, even if none occurs at present.

Similarly, Pygmies have adopted musical traits from their neighbors, with whom they have economically associated themselves since the early contact era. These traits include playing reed pipes, such as the *luma*, popular among the Ituri Forest Pygmies (Tracey 1973); playing various types of drums, and even the polyidiochord stick zither, used by the Pygmies of the Upper Sangha (and borrowed from Bantu speakers of zones A and B); and performing pieces drawn from the expressive repertory of secret societies, such as the *jenge* (Djenda 1968). Practiced in the area of the Ogowe River, Congo, *jenge* was first documented and recorded by André Didier and Gilbert Rouget (1946); it was later studied extensively by Maurice Djenda. Among the Bangombe Pygmies (along the Sangha River), *jenge* is a men's society, which centers on a "masked monster" (also *jenge*). The mask boasts strips of raffia leaves; it resembles a moving bell or robe. In public performance, accompanied by drums, the monster performs rapid twisting movements in front of women and children. Noninitiates believe the monster lives in the forest, where it controls hunters' luck. Totemistic ideas also play a role in the perception of *jenge*, since the people considered the monster the ancestor of one of the oldest members of the group in the camp (Djenda 1968:40). While the songs sung at public *jenge* performances correspond in style with general Upper Sangha Pygmy traits (as in dances like *wunga* or *moyaya*), an unusual song for rituals in homophonic harmony uses simultaneous fifths: members of the secret society sing it, while they carry raffia leaves back from the river, to build the mask. The members run through the village, where they end the song with shouts.

Some scholars, in particular Grimaud (1956) and Rouget, have claimed to have found similarities between Pygmy and San polyphony. They have taken inspiration from evolutionary perspectives on African music history, rather than from systematic comparisons of data. Independent inquiry has not confirmed the existence of a musical culture shared by African hunters, despite the findings of the Cantometrics Project (Lomax 1968). Most likely, the musical styles of Pygmies in Central Africa, and of San in southwestern Africa, have in common only two general traits: yodeling and vocal polyphony (in the African definition of the term). But Pygmy polyphony clearly derives from different principles and a different tonal system from that of the San; it possibly makes use of extracts of the harmonic series over a single fundamental, while !Kung' and other San tonal resources makes use of two fundamentals, at varying intervals, with their harmonics up to the fourth partial. San tonal material clearly derives from experience with the harmonics of braced musical bows, but no instrumental inspiration for Pygmy polyphony has been traced, and Pygmy tonal sequences differ from those of the San.

Bantu musical cultures in zones A, B, C, H, L, K

These musical cultures are diverse. This diversity is partly explained by the complex patterns of successive migrations, cultural divergence, and cultural convergence, during the past two thousand years. The tentative division of the Bantu languages into zones (Guthrie 1948) is still a useful yardstick, because it reflects, if only imperfectly, cultural dividing lines.

Zones A and B

These zones cover southern Cameroon, Equatorial Guinea (mainly a Faŋ-speaking area, with a certain absorption of Spanish culture), Gabon, and parts of the Congo. Zone A is situated in the northwesternmost Bantu area, where evidence proves contact with (a) the Semi-Bantu and other (non-Bantu) cultures of the Cameroon grasslands, and (b) West Africa, notably eastern Nigeria. Included in zone A on the Cameroon coast are the Duala (group 20), who had early contact with the Germans; the Basa (group 40); and the Yaounde (Ewondo-speaking), Bulu, Beti, and Faŋ (group 60), a large group, which extends far south into Gabon.

Musical documentation of this area began in colonial times, with the arrival of German administrators and missionaries: after July 1884, the diplomat Gustav Nachtigal established the Deutsch-Kamerun Schutzgebiet (German-Cameroon Protectorate). Early collections of musical instruments date back to the late 1800s (Ankermann 1901), including notes on the music of ethnic groups, particularly the Faŋ, or "Pangwe" (Hornbostel 1913). Establishing Christian missions in this area had, from the beginning of the 1900s, a notable influence on musical traditions. By the 1950s, this influence had given rise to an indigenous Christian music, such as Pie-Claude Ngumu's *Maîtrise des Chanteurs à la Croix d'Ébène* in the Cathedral of Yaoundé (1971). Ngumu later turned musicologist, and wrote (1976b) on the structure of *mendzaŋ* xylophone music, which he had also used in his ecclesiastical compositions. Another Cameroonian specialist, Albert Noah Messomo (1980), concentrated on the social and literary side of *mendzaŋ*.

Stick zithers

A prominent musical instrument that particularly characterizes language zone A, and overlaps slightly into zones B and C, is the "Cameroonian" or "Gabonese" polyidio-

With the impact of Latin American phonograph records and highlife from West Africa, music for xylophones in southern Cameroon changed considerably. Starting in the 1960s, xylophone bands played increasingly for young people's parties in dance halls. Their tuning became uniformly diatonic.

chord stick zither, called *mvet* in more northerly areas. Probably an autochthonous instrument of the Bulu-Beti-Faŋ group, it gives this culture area an unmistakable identity, since *mvet* is not only an instrument, but also a genre of oral literature. We do not know how far back in history it was invented, but it is one of those Central African instrumental traditions that has a small and compact geographical distribution: the instrument is not known in any other part of Africa.

The *mvet* is made from a stick of a raffia frond, from which idiochord strings are lifted and hooked into a notched bridge placed in the middle of the stick. From one to five gourd resonators are attached to the stick. By adjusting rings made of raffia, a musician can accurately tune the instrument. A *bom-mvet* 'stick zither poet' uses the zither for accompanying epic poetry, and sometimes for the narration of tales. In the area east of Nanga-Eboko (Cameroon), this zither is known under the name *ebenza*. A full performance in public often includes mime and dance.

In cultures outside the Bulu-Beti-Faŋ cluster, the stick zither is often known as *ngombi*, which among the Faŋ is the term for another stringed instrument, the harp. Surprisingly, Pygmy hunter-gatherers have adopted these zithers in the northern Congo and in the southwestern Central African Republic, where in the mid-1960s they appeared in Pygmy camps that were otherwise nearly devoid of nonutilitarian material wealth (Djenda and Kubik 1964; Djenda 1968).

Xylophones

Another instrument widely found in zones A and B is the gourd-resonated portable xylophone, whose presence is perhaps explained by diffusion from areas of southwestern Zaïre and northwestern Angola (zone H), during the sixteenth to eighteenth centuries. Until the late 1900s, such instruments, often called *mēnjyāŋ* or *m‑endzaŋ* in southern Cameroon, were associated with chieftainship, and served as chiefly representatives; they were sometimes played during processions, as was usual, for instance, in the ancient kingdom of Congo. Among peoples such as the Ewondo-speaking groups (Ngumu 1976a, 1976b), four such xylophones usually constituted an ensemble, accompanied by drum and rattle. The names for the individual xylophones vary from language to language. Among the Mvele (at Minkolong, near Andom, between Nanga-Eboko and Bertoua, southern Cameroon), the following names were used in Daniel Mbeng's group, from the highest to the lowest pitched: *ololoŋ* (with ten keys), *ombek* (with six keys), *gboŋgboŋ* (with six keys), *eduma* (with three keys). Some of these names are onomatopoeic; all of them relate to musical functions in the ensemble.

The tunings of southern Cameroon xylophones have sparked controversy. Ngumu (1976a:14–18) gives intracultural evidence about the conceptualization of the process of tuning. According to him, tuning begins with a note in the center of the (middle-range) *omvək*, transcribed as note 1 in figure 10. Musicians consider this note analogous to the head of a family. Tuning then proceeds in descending tonal

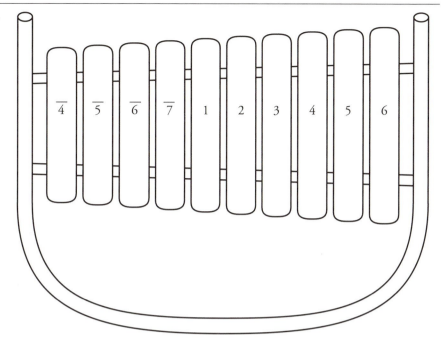

order: 1–2–3–4–5–6. Next, the octaves (sometimes called the wives) are found for
notes 6, 5, and 4; in figure 10, these are notes #6, #5, and #4, in ascending order.
Ngumu states that, in Ewondo-speaking areas, *omvɔk*-type xylophones originally had
nine notes and hexatonic tuning. His main informant, however, told him some musicians had begun to introduce an additional note (#7 in figure 10), from an area called
the Etenga country. Local musicians accept this note, called spoilsport (*esandi*), with
reluctance (Ngumu 1976a:15). Thus, while the original tuning of the southern
Cameroonian xylophone was probably hexatonic, after some time—perhaps at the
beginning of the twentieth century, and possibly under the influence of German
scholastic music—it gained a seventh note. Though Ngumu thinks *mendzaŋ* tunings
were locally variable in their exact intervals, the cents figures of some old tunings may
point to a predilection for neutral thirds between notes spaced one key apart (1 and
3, 2 and 4, and so on). In this style, thirds and octaves are the harmonic sounds of
the xylophone parts and the vocal parts. In contrast to Ngumu, Jones believed, on
the basis of Stroboconn measurements, that the hexatonic tunings were gapped equiheptatonic scales (1971, 1978).

   After the 1940s, with the impact of Latin American phonograph records and
highlife from West Africa, music for xylophones in southern Cameroon changed
considerably. Starting in the 1960s, xylophone bands played increasingly for young
people's parties in dance halls. Their tunings, as in the case of the Richard Band de
Zoetele (which traveled overseas, and achieved fame in the Cameroonian mass
media) became uniformly diatonic. From the 1970s on, the repertory of many southern Cameroon xylophone dance bands consisted of popular rumba, cha-cha, and
pachanga tunes, taken from Zaïrean, Congolese, and Cuban records. A case in point
was the xylophone band at the Miami Bar (figure 11), performing in what was the
red-light district near the port of Douala; sailors from many nations frequented the
bar.

Harps and pluriarcs
Little material remains to elucidate the remote history of the musical cultures of
zones A and B. The most remarkable evidence, however, is in a seventeenth-century
European source (Praetorius 1620), which depicts two musical instruments that

Harps with carved heads are used for religious instruments by Faŋ priests. The people consider the harp the deity's "house." In Faŋ cosmogony, it symbolizes the female principle.

FIGURE 11   The xylophone band at Miami Bar. Douala, Cameroon, 1969.

could have been collected only on the coast of Gabon: a seven-stringed harp and a pluriarc, described as *Indianische Instrumenta am clang [sic] den Harffen [sic] gleich* 'Amerindian instruments, in sound like the harp'. The illustrator drew them from life, and his grouping of instruments implies he had access to a collection of specimens, probably in a German nobleman's house.

Comparison with late-twentieth-century instruments suggests the pluriarc is likely to have come from the Gabon-Congo border (language zone B)—perhaps from the population cluster that later fanned into the Nzabi (group 10), Fumu (group 30), Mbede (group 20), or even Mfinu, Yanzi, and Mbunu (all in group 40). Alternatively, it could have come from the ancestors of the present Bateke, who in the late 1800s still used pluriarcs similar to the one Praetorius depicted (Wegner 1984:82).

The harp depicted by Praetorius provides more important evidence for the music history of western Central Africa. It falls organologically within Wachsmann's type III, or "shelved type" of African harp (1964). Most probably, a sixteenth-century Kele maker produced it. The Bakele group are considered long-established on the coast of Gabon. By 1470, European sailors had landed on the Gabon coast, where they gradually built up trading contacts. In the nineteenth and twentieth centuries, Kele harps sported a hook or extension, which in some specimens looks like a "7," and in others like the high heel of a shoe. Normally, Gabonese harps have eight strings. Praetorius's specimen may not even be an exception, since an enlargement of the drawing reveals what looks like a loose string with a peg on its end.

Praetorius's illustration, compared with late nineteenth- and early twentieth-century Gabon harps in museum collections, reveals an organological stability over more than 370 years. Gabon is the southernmost distribution area of harps in Africa. Some authors associate Gabonese harps with the origin of the Faŋ people, who are said to have come from the northeast, that is, somewhere in non-Bantu-speaking areas of the Central African Republic. The Faŋ migrants, probably limited in number, are supposed to have mixed with the local population in northern Gabon, and to have adopted a Bantu language. While there is no doubt Gabonese harps originated in the northeast, their presence in Gabon by the early 1600s (as suggested by Praetorius's illustration) predates the supposed Faŋ migration. Moreover, this illustration proves Wachsmann's type III was already developed four hundred years ago, and probably much earlier; it may have originated in type II ("tanged type"), by the absorption of organological ideas from local stringed instruments in Gabon and the Congo, notably the pluriarc.

The "shelved type" of African harp has a strictly defined distribution, concentrated in the territory of the Republic of Gabon. The northern subtype, called *ngombi* in Faŋ, has a carved head instead of the shoe heel; the head represents an important female deity, *Nyiŋgɔn Möböγɔ*, often translated by Faŋ informants as *Esprit Consolateur* (Consoling Spirit). Harps with carved heads are used for religious instruments by Faŋ priests, such as André Mvome in Oyem. The people consider the harp the deity's "house." In Faŋ cosmogony, it symbolizes the female principle; it contrasts with the male principle, betokened by the color white (to the Faŋ, the color of sperm), and by the *beŋ* 'mouth bow'.

Zone C

This is a large, diversified ethnic-linguistic zone, which covers mainly the northern parts of Zaïre and the Congo. It extends through much of the rain forest, from the borders of southeastern Cameroon and Gabon, across the northern Congo into Zaïre, down to Lake Léopold II, and to the Lwalaba River. It includes speakers of languages such as Buŋgili and Kota (group 10), Ŋgombe (group 30), Moŋgo-Ŋkundu (group 60), Tetela (group 70), and many others. In this zone, there are no less than thirty-eight distinguishable languages (Guthrie 1948).

This zone has supported the fieldwork of many cultural anthropologists, historians, and ethnomusicologists, including Alan P. Merriam (1959); Erika Sulzmann, among the Ekonda (1959); Jan Vansina, among the Kuba (1969); and J. F. Carrington (1949, 1956, 1975), who studied the relationship between tone and tune in message drumming, particularly on slit drums. For the northern Congo and adjacent areas, there are recordings by Didier and Rouget (1946), and by Djenda and Kubik (1964, 1966), and scattered recordings of later dates.

Typical harmonies

One of the characteristics of this zone is the presence of rich harmonic styles of singing, which, among the Bakota and Buŋgili in the northern Congo, result in three-part homophonic chord clusters. Buŋgili harmonic patterns derive from triads that shift along three steps of a diatonic heptatonic scale, as recordings Kubik made in the northern Congo in 1964 prove.

The basic chords, written over F and G in the notation of figure 12, could be mouthbow-derived. From Gabon across the northern Congo into Zaïre, Western Central African tunings for mouth bow usually have two fundamentals a whole tone apart, and the performer almost always makes use of the sound spectrum up to partials 5 or 6 of both fundamentals. This combination creates a basically hexatonic system, consisting of the clusters F–A–C and G–B–D.

For reasons not yet fully understood, this system extends, in Buŋgili and neigh-

FIGURE 12   Melodic and harmonic mouth bow progressions.

Melodic split of cluster I with an extension resulting in step III

Progressions suggesting a basis in mouth-bow harmonics

boring peoples' vocal music, to include one more third on top of the deeper chord, in the cluster F–A–C–E. Hence in Buŋgili and Bakota vocal performances, one finds melodic and harmonic patterns like the scheme of figure 12, abstracted from recordings made near Liouesso, northern Congo, in 1964. The background in these harmonic patterns is also revealed by the fact that the tonal center is F.

Farther north, among the Mpyɛmɔ ethnic group, living in the southwestern corner of the Central African Republic, songs show comparable harmonic clusters. The Mpyɛmɔ have oral traditions that claim the people migrated from northern parts of the Republic of the Congo, up the Sangha River, to their present habitat, about the beginning of the 1800s (Djenda 1967). Mpyɛmɔ harmonic patterns often employ two roots a semitone apart. The result is simultaneous vocal sounds, as in the story-song "Atɛndɛ" (figure 13).

This harmonic progression, however, is only one aspect of the conglomerate of styles and techniques that make up Mpyɛmɔ music. The Mpyɛmɔ had various contacts with other musical cultures, both during their migration north, and in their present homeland (Djenda and Kubik 1964, 1966), as four traits show:

1. *Harmonic patterns exclusively use major triads, and shift between two basic notes a semitone apart.* This type of organization, which occurs only in *sya* 'chantefables', is probably an ancient heritage from the Congo. The tonal system associated with these harmonic patterns is hexa- or heptatonic, with the melodic compass of individual voices never reaching an octave.
2. *Parallel fourths, in a pentatonic system,* whose origin is unknown; the trait was possibly introduced by contact with nearby non-Bantu peoples, such as the Gbaya and the Karre.
3. *Pygmy-style polyphony,* showing the close contacts this group has had with the Pygmies of the Upper Sangha.
4. *Unison singing,* to the accompaniment of gourd-resonated xylophones (mɛntʃaŋa) and the box-resonated lamellophone (*kembe*), introduced in the 1920s by migrant workers returning from employment in railway construction between Point Noire and Brazzaville.

Among the Mpɛmɔ, the *kembe* is tuned to a tempered (possibly equidistant) pentatonic system, and is accompanied by a well-known five-stroke twelve-pulse timeline.

Musical instruments

Musical instruments in zone C illustrate the full use of the natural resources of the rain forest. The slit drum (*kuli* or other names) plays an important musical role; it also serves to send standardized messages (Carrington 1975). There is a variety of membrane drums, with two prevailing kinds of tension (Wieschhoff 1933): (a) in the

FIGURE 13 *"Atɛndɛ"*: Mpyɛmɔ story-song, with leader and chorus. Performed by Nyaŋgɔ-Bɛbɛnisaŋgɔ, a woman about fifty years old, at Bigene, Nola District, Central African Republic, June 1964.

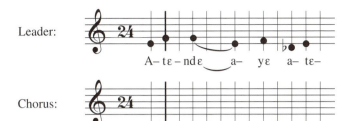

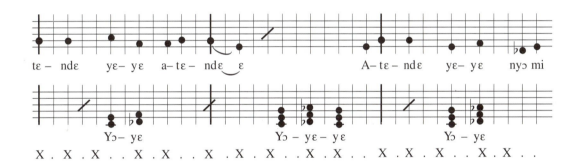

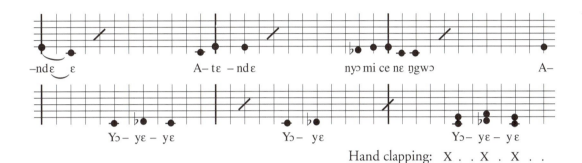

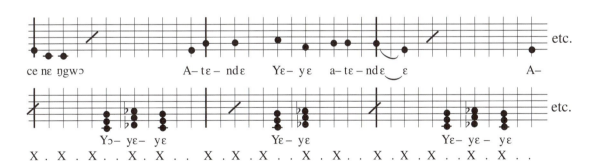

west of zone C, the predominant form is wedge-and-ring tension (*Keilringspannung*), characterized by a wedge-tensioned girdle attached to leather lacings around the body of the drum (figure 14); (b) in the southern parts of zone C, "Kasai tension" (*Kassai-Spannung*) seems restricted to a single area in Zaïre, and is especially common in drums of the Bakuba.

In museum collections, the tall drums from the "Kingdoms of the Savannah" (Vansina 1966) are famous for elaborate relief carvings with abstract, often ideo-

"When all the instruments are played together, a truly harmonic effect is produced from a distance; nearby one can hear the sticks rattling, which causes a great noise."—from seventeenth-century account of music in Congo

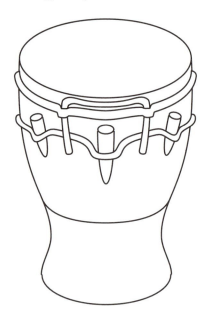

FIGURE 14   A membrane drum of zone C, tuned by wedge-and-ring tension (*Keilringspannung*).

graphic, motifs, and sometimes with the depiction of a hand on the side of the drum. Catalogues often record such instruments as "Kuba king's drums," though the number of kings must have been small, compared with the number of extant drums. As elsewhere, a lucrative trade in ethnographica developed by about 1910; and the fame of Kuba royalty made a market for these drums, so long as they bore appropriate labels.

Zone C also favors a single-note, asymmetric, rhythmic pattern, which accompanies many musical performances. The area where this timeline occurs in Central Africa may indicate migratory patterns, because timelines are diachronically stable. For structural reasons (which can be expressed mathematically), they cannot change the relationship of their beats without instantly losing their identity. Secondary traits, like accentuation and speed, can change more easily.

A five-stroke, twelve-pulse pattern, x . x . x . . x . x . . (with x meaning a stroke, and a period meaning an empty pulse), is found in much of zone C; it extends eastward into zone D, where it appears in music of the Lega, group 20 in zone D (Kishilo w'Itunga 1976). But farther south, in zones L and K, it is mostly replaced by its inverted mirror image, the seven-stroke, twelve-pulse pattern. Wherever in Central Africa one of these timelines occurs, the other is excluded, hidden, or reduced to a complementary pattern, struck simultaneously with the first.

The five-stroke, twelve-pulse pattern links Central Africa to West African cultures of the Kwa (I.A.4) linguistic family (Greenberg 1970), where timelines are also prominent; the pattern separates Central Africa from most of East Africa, except the Nyasa-Ruvuma cultures and the Zambezi valley.

Zone H

Thanks to early contacts established between Portugal and the kingdoms of Congo, Ndongo, and Matamba, zone H is unique on the map of Central African musical cultures: a large amount of written and pictorial sources date from the 1500s on. If nowhere else, music history can be at least partially reconstructed there for the last four hundred years.

The major language of the zone is Kikoongo (group 10), including related languages such as Yombe and Sundi, spoken in southwestern Zaïre; other languages of the zone include Ndoŋo (group 20), and Taka and Mbaŋgala (group 30). Kimbundu is the most important language spoken in Luanda (Angola), and in the hinterland into the Province of Malanji. The zone includes southwestern Zaïre, southern Congo, Cabinda (with the Loango coast), and northwestern Angola.

European influences and research

The kingdom of Congo was an area of early Christian evangelization. Whether by the 1600s missionaries had affected the music of Kikoongo-speaking peoples is difficult to assess; but there were probably considerable influences, not only from

Christian religious music, but also from military and ceremonial music. European wind instruments came into use at that time (Schüller 1972), and their knowledge spread far into the interior of Angola, where wooden trumpets figure among the paraphernalia of secret societies. The smaller types have a separate mouthpiece, similar in size and bore to sixteenth-century European trombones (Kubik 1981). The introduction of church bells into the kingdom of Congo spawned an industry that produced small clapper bells with local metallurgical techniques.

During the late 1600s, detailed accounts of music, musical instruments, organology, and musical sociology, came from the research of two Capuchin missionaries: António Giovanni Cavazzi and Girolamo Merolla. Cavazzi went to what is now northern Angola in 1654; for thirteen years, he lived and traveled in the kingdom of Congo and adjoining areas. Many of the illustrations in his book (1687) depict musical scenes. One shows warriors playing a bell and a "double bell" (Hirschberg 1969:15). Since the discovery of his original paintings, new sources on the music of the Congo and neighboring kingdoms have opened up. Merolla traveled to Luanda from Naples in 1682; he worked for five years in the town of Sonyo, traveled up the Zaïre River, and visited Cabinda. Some historians have considered his information on musical instruments (1692) secondary and largely based on Cavazzi, but it is probably more independent. Similarities or identities with Cavazzi's account are likely explained by the fact that these missionaries were near contemporaries, and had contact with the same cultures, albeit at a distance of more than a decade.

Merolla's testimony, written with obvious love for African music, equals that of Cavazzi. One famous etching shows several musical instruments: a gourd-resonated xylophone (*marimba*), a pluriarc (*nsambi*), two types of scraper (*kasuto, kilondo*), a double bell (*longa*), a goblet-shaped single-skin drum (*ngamba*), and an end-blown horn (*epungu*).

Referring to the kingdom of Congo and neighboring areas, Merolla describes some of these instruments:

> One of the most common instruments is the *marimba.* Sixteen calabashes act as resonators and are supported lengthwise by two bars. Above the calabashes little boards of red wood, somewhat longer than a span, are placed, called *taculla.* The instrument is hung round the neck and the boards (keys) are beaten with small sticks. Mostly four *marimbas* play together; if six want to play, the *cassuto* is added—a hollowed piece of wood four spans long, with ridges in it. The bass of this orchestra is the *quilondo,* a roomy, big-bellied instrument two and a half to three spans in height which looks like a bottle towards the end and is rubbed in the same way as the *cassuto.* When all the instruments are played together, a truly harmonic effect is produced from a distance; nearby one can hear the sticks rattling, which causes a great noise. The *nsambi* is a stringed instrument consisting of a resonator and five small bows strung with strings of bark fiber, which are made to vibrate with the index finger. The instrument is supported on the chest for playing. The notes sound weak but not unpleasant. (Hirschberg 1969:16, 18)

The four-piece xylophone ensemble described by Merolla does not survive in the territory of the former kingdom of Congo; in fact, xylophones seem to have disappeared from there. Some people have thought, therefore, that Cavazzi and Merolla were describing xylophones from one of the neighboring kingdoms, possibly Matamba, in the present Malanji Province of Angola, where large, gourd-resonated xylophones appear in association with chiefs. However, present-day Malanji xylophones, played on the ground and not carried on a strap around the musicians' shoulders, are probably not related historically to the depicted seventeenth-century specimens.

kakoxa   Two-stringed bowed lute that was inspired by seventeenth- or eighteenth-century Iberian stringed instruments

madimba   Gourd-resonated xylophones from central African area that probably derive from southeast African models

musique moderne zaïreoise   Guitar-based music that emerged after the 1940s in the Brazzaville and Kinshasa area

Survivals

The xylophone tradition seen by Cavazzi and Merolla does survive, however—though not in the kingdom of Congo, but farther north, where, in organology, attitude of playing, and other traits, including the fact that four xylophones play together, the xylophones of southern Cameroon provide the closest parallel to what Merolla described. This situation exemplifies a pattern frequently met in cultural history: a tradition migrates away from its original center of distribution, but survives in lands on the periphery, while it disappears from its original home.

The same consideration applies to the other instruments depicted by Merolla. The "quilondo" (*kilondo*) survives in some Latin American music, as in the type of *reco- reco* used during the Festa de Santa Cruz in Carapicuiba village, State of São Paulo, Brazil, though it is smaller than the specimen Merolla depicts (*Folclore de São Paulo*, n.d.:2). The slave trade exported the *nsambi*—and its name—to Brazil, where several nineteenth-century painter-authors reported its use.

In zone H, scrapers (*cassuto*) survive, particularly among Kimbundu-speakers in Angola. In Luanda, these scrapers (*dikanza*) have served particularly in novel twentieth-century ballroom dance traditions, such as the *rebita* and *semba*, dances characterized by the belly bounce, a light abdominal touch or shock. In Angola, scrapers also accompany military-music-inspired dances, such as *kalukuta*.

Not much of the sixteenth-to-seventeenth-century tradition has probably survived in zone H. Extensive contact with the outside world—via sea links to West Africa, Europe, and Brazil; via trade links to the interior of Africa, from the 1700s on, especially by the *pombeiros* (Portuguese-African traders who crossed Africa from Luanda to Mozambique)—has many times remodeled the musical cultures of the zone.

Bell-resonator lamellophones

Among the traditions of the Loango coast (Cabinda and adjacent areas), one tradition that has aroused considerable interest is the "Loango-sanza" (Laurenty 1962). It is a type of lamellophone belonging to the broad category classed by Tracey as having a bell-type resonator: the resonator, made of wood, is hollowed out from below. In Loango lamellophones, the cavity is usually in the shape of a half moon; the number of notes is small (usually only seven); in contrast to many other lamellophones in Africa, the notes lie in ascending scalar order from left to right.

Loango-type lamellophones have a narrow distribution area in Central Africa; they appear mainly along the Loango coast. By chance, however, the oldest specimen preserved in collections is of the Loango type; it was collected, not on the Loango coast, but in Brazil, where it was undoubtedly made by a slave from the Loango coast, not later than 1820. Together with a collection of ethnographic objects belonging to a North American furrier who was (1827–1848) American consul to the Habsburg Empire, it was acquired by the Museum für Völkerkunde, Vienna, where it remains (Janata 1975; Kubik 1977). It has a carved head—a trait that must have been common in the 1800s, because Stephen Chauvet (1929) prints a photograph of another specimen with a carved figure on top, in contrast to many later-collected specimens, which have only a somewhat extended top. Compare the instruments in the collections of the Musée Royal de l'Afrique Central (Laurenty 1962). The symbolic presence of a carved head, and the half-moon shape of the cavity of the resonator, are elements that imply strong cultural contacts with zones A and B.

There could be a historical sequence from the Loango-type lamellophones to what is a later (and possibly mid-nineteenth-century) development in the lower Congo-Zaïre area: the *likembe* (with a box resonator), though this type has a V-shaped or N-shaped arrangement of the lamellae. The *likembe* is a development that originated in zone H. With Belgian colonial penetration up the Zaïre River, it spread rapidly: by the 1920s, it had reached all of Zaïre and Congo, most of Uganda and northeastern Angola, and a few areas beyond.

Instrumental innovations

Widespread innovations in instrumental technology and musical style have their origins in zone H, which has absorbed and modified many exogenous traditions. The *kakoxa* 'two-stringed bowed lute' took inspiration from seventeenth- or eighteenth-century Iberian stringed instruments. The *madimba* 'gourd-resonated xylophones', found in Malanji Province, probably derive from southeast African models, whose techniques of playing and manufacture were carried to northern Angola by personnel who regularly traveled with the *pombeiros*. These traders followed the route from Luanda to Malanji, to the Lunda Empire, to Kazembe near Lake Mweru, and down south, through the Maravi Empire, to the Portuguese trading posts Tete and Sena, on the Zambezi in Mozambique.

Musical innovations that emerged from zone H also include developments in urban music, in the area of the twin cities of Brazzaville (Congo) and Kinshasa (Zaïre). After the 1940s, these municipalities, separated only by the Zaïre River, witnessed the rise of a new guitar-based music, generally called *musique moderne zaïreoise* and *musique moderne congolèse* (Kazadi wa Mukuna 1973), or Western-Congolese guitar style (Kubik 1965a). According to verbal accounts by Wendo, a guitarist of the 1950s, guitars first came to Matadi and Kinshasa (then Léopoldville) in the 1930s, brought by Kru sailors from West Africa.

Local music for solo guitar, with performers such as Wendo and Polo Kamba singing in Lingala (the Congolese trade language), developed; it was recorded on the Ngoma label by the Firme Jeronimidis, based in Kinshasa. An ensemble style of music for guitar also developed; it was heavily influenced by Latin American records, which brought to Central Africa African-American music from Latin America and the Caribbean.

This infusion culminated in the development of electric-guitar styles in the 1960s, advanced by bands that achieved international renown: O.K. Jazz, Rochereau Tabu Ley and his African Fiesta, and others. Some bands, such as that of Jean Bokilo, with his celebrated "Mwambe" series of recordings of many versions of one song, tried to integrate into the new styles "traditional" patterns—in Bokilo's case, harmonic patterns. Though these styles originated in zone H, they cannot be considered extensions of Kikoongo "traditional" music, because they include elements from many regions of Zaïre and the Congo, in reflection of the ethnic mix in cities like Kinshasa and Brazzaville.

Zone L and (in part) zone M

This area extends from central parts of Zaïre, across Katanga, into northwestern

FIGURE 15   A *mukupela* 'double-skin hourglass drum' (Zambia, 1971).

Zambia; it includes languages of the Pende (group 10), Luba (group 30), Kaonde (group 40), Lunda (group 50), and Mbwera-ŋkoya (group 60). It has been well researched, particularly by musicologists associated with the Musée Royal de l'Afrique Centrale, Tervuren (Belgium), including Gansemans (1978, 1980), Gansemans and Schmidt-Wrenger (1986), and Laurenty (1971, 1972). It is also one of the rare areas in Central Africa where archaeological evidence of musical practices is available. South of the equatorial forest, several Iron Age cultures developed; they produced a surplus population, which, beginning about A.D. 1000 to 1100, began the Third Bantu Dispersal, from a wide area in northern Katanga, with migration taking effect to the southwest (Angola), south (Zambia), and southeast (Malawi, Mozambique). From graves at Sanga and Katoto (in Katanga), single iron bells and other iron objects have been dated to about A.D. 800, and coincide in time with findings farther south, especially at the site of Ingombe Ilede.

Iron bells in this area, as elsewhere in Central Africa, figure among the regalia of chiefs and other officials of centralized states. Their study therefore has relevance to the broader history of the "Kingdoms of the Savannah." Other musical instruments associated with chieftainship or kingship in this area include the *mukupela* 'double-skin hourglass drums' (figure 15), of the Luba-Lunda population; because of their materials (wood, skin), there is little chance any can be recovered from archaeological deposits.

Merriam's study of a Songye village in the Lwalaba River area (in 1959–1960) became a classic example of an approach that linked music with the broader cultural and social panorama, and focused on the status and the creativity of individuals. Later, research on the music and dance ethnography of the Hemba by Pamela Blakely (1993) garnered a large amount of data on one of the lesser-known peoples of group 30 in zone L. In precolonial times, trade routes going through Katanga from both west and southeast left their mark on the music of zones L and M. Small, board-shaped lamellophones known in Shiluba as *cisanji* (Tracey 1973) probably developed from southeast African models that had been reduced in size for use by long-distance porters coming up the Zambezi. The Maravi Empire (1600s and 1700s), through which the trade route passed, was the source of single-note xylophones called *limba*, used in religious contexts that similarly became known farther north. East African trade routes ending in Katanga led, not only to the rise of a sizable Kiswahili-speaking population there (speaking Kingwana, a Swahili dialect), but also to the introduction of instruments such as the flatbar zither (Shiluba *luzenze*) and the board zither (*ngyela*), played in "vamping style" with a pendular motion of the right index finger (Laurenty 1960, 1971). The friction drum (*ng'oma wa bimrunku* or *tambwe ng'oma* in Shiluba) points to contacts with the Lunda cluster of peoples and eastern Angola; for description of this instrument, see Laurenty (1972:44–45).

The presence of centralized political structures among the peoples of zones L and M found expression in the royal music associated with traditional rulers, such as the drums called *cinkumbi* by the peoples of Mwata Kazembe, in the Lwapula Valley near Lake Mweru. Mwesa I. Mapoma (1974) studied royal musicians among the Bemba in Luapula and Northern Provinces of Zambia. The importance of music for initiations in this zone, particularly for the initiations of girls—such as the *cisungu* rites among the Lenje, the Soli, and others in Zambia—stresses the continuation of a social structure with a matrilineal system of descent.

Christian evangelization

In the twentieth century, both southern Zaïre and northeastern Zambia proved to be fertile areas for establishing Christian missions. The result was two byproducts that have affected the musical cultures of those areas: scientific research by Christian missionaries, and indigenous acquaintance with Christian hymnody.

Many missionaries interested themselves in the local musical cultures; their efforts led to the study and development of the music. A. M. Jones worked from 1929 to 1950 as a missionary and principal of St. Mark's College (Mapanza, Zambia); he studied the musical cultures of the Bemba, the Nsenga, and other groups. Also in Zambia, Father Corbeille collected musical instruments, which remain in the University of Zambia.

Introducing Christian hymns and school music had many effects, and eventually stimulated the emergence of a new ecclesiastical music, both in the established churches (for example, the work of Joseph Kiwele, who in the 1950s composed *Messe Katangaise*; see Kishilo w'Itunga 1987), and in the separatist ones.

For Zambia, Mwesa I. Mapoma (1980:20:630) says

music among Christian denominations has consisted mostly of Western hymns set to local languages, usually taking little account of the tonal inflection or the rhythmic structure of the text, provided the religious text fits the meter. Earlier some denominations introduced religious texts set to traditional Zambian music, but Western hymns were substituted as soon as more people had been attracted to the church. In the early 1950s African-led Christian churches such as the Emilio and Lumpa appeared. The worship of the Emilio sect, led by a former Roman Catholic seminarian, resembled Catholic church practice but used African music and vernacular languages. The Lumpa sect led by Alice Lenshina, a self-styled prophet, also used traditional music in worship, but because of the increasing fascination of the Lumpa followers the sect was banned in 1964. The example set by these two churches has since been followed by the Roman Catholic and other churches. . . . In some churches even dancing has been introduced and the interior of the church adapted accordingly.

Zones L and M have also seen the emergence of a new, guitar-based, popular music for dancing, in response to multiple factors, including urbanization and migrant labor. This process started in the 1930s, particularly along the copper belt on both sides of the Zaïre-Zambia border, an area that attracted miners from many parts

In the dark of night, men of the secret society bring the tubes up to the village, and emit into the mouthpiece fearful vocal sounds, which the tubes seemingly amplify.

FIGURE 16   The Katanga guitarist Mwenda-Jean Bosco, 1982.

of Central Africa. A township culture soon developed around the emerging major centers (Kolwezi, Likasi, Lubumbashi, Ndola), where a Katanga "guitar style" arose (Kubik 1965b, 1966; Kazadi wa Mukuna 1980; Low 1982). Hugh Tracey (1973) first recorded pieces in this style; he also discovered Mwenda-Jean Bosco, alias Mwenda wa Bayeke (figure 16), a Luba-Sanga guitar composer, who in the 1950s and 1960s rose to be one of Africa's foremost guitarists (Rycroft 1961, 1962).

Zone K

This zone covers all of eastern Angola, northwestern Zambia, and adjacent areas in Zaïre. Musicologically, it is one of the most thoroughly studied parts of Central Africa, and it has also been one of the most attractive to researchers in art, because of the intimate interrelationships among music, masked dancing, and visual art. It is a zone of highly institutionalized musical practice connected with initiation schools and secret societies. Included in zone K are the following languages: Cokwe, Lwena, Luchazi, Mbwela, Nkhangala (group 10); Lozi (group 20); Luyana (group 30); and Totela (group 40). The latter two groups have perhaps more links with southern Africa than to Central Africa.

Within zone K, the cultures of group 10 show clearly ancient affinities with the Luba-Lunda cultural cluster (zone L). The Lunda-related cultural history of the Cokwe, the Lwena, and the so-called Ngangela peoples (including the Lucazi, the Mbwela, the Nkhangala, the Nyemba, and others) is obvious; their history explains it, as do the patterns of migration from the ancient Lunda Empire after the 1500s. Migration of the Cokwe to new lands continued until late in the twentieth century. In the 1800s, Cokwe families penetrated farther and farther south from their original homes (in northeastern Angola); they settled on river grasslands in the Kwandu-Kuvangu Province of Angola. They have had much cultural influence on the Ngangela-speaking peoples, with whom they developed close affinal relationships. Cokwe masks, such as *Cikūza* or *Kalelwa* (figure 17)—the latter depicting a nineteenth-century Cokwe king, Mwene Ndumba wa Tembo—appear all over eastern Angola and in northwestern Zambia. In musical performances, these masks proceed to the public dance place (*cilende*) in a village, stop in front of the set of long, goblet-shaped drums (*vipwali* or *zing'oma*), and speak a recitation (*kutangesa*), which drum strokes guide, cue, and interrupt (Kubik 1965b, 1971, 1981).

In zone K, most music is performed within the traditional institutions of education for the young, the secret societies, and the context of royalty. Among the Lozi or "Barotse" on the Zambezi (southwestern Zambia), the paramount chief presides over the *kuomboka* ceremony, a picturesque festival, marked yearly by a procession with boats. Every year, when the Zambezi inundates the plains up to the highlands, the Lozi people migrate ceremonially to the dry places, to the accompaniment of instrumental music and dancing (Kalakula 1979). Their music stands stylistically apart from most of the music in zone K, because of the historical links of the Lozi people

FIGURE 17   Two prominent Cokwe masked characters: above, *Kalelwa;* above right, *Cikūza.*

with the south, and because of their proximity to Ndebele culture in Zimbabwe. In contrast to the multipart singing style of the group 10 peoples in zone K, their style emphasizes fourths and fifths as simultaneous intervals, structured in a manner comparable to Shona-Nsenga harmonic patterns (Jones 1959; Kubik 1988). The tunings and chords of Lozi gourd-resonated xylophones called *silimba* reflect the nature of this tonal system.

Among the peoples of group 10 in zone K, the performance of certain musical works marks royal events, especially the death or installation of a chief. Luchazi, Cokwe, and Lwena chiefs keep in their assortment of regalia the *mukupele* or *mukupela* drum, and sometimes a double bell. The *mukupele* is played only at a royal death or installation. The sound owes its loudness to an ingenious device, a small piece of calabash neck covered with a mirliton (a spider's nest covering), and inserted into a hole on the side of the drum.

Megaphones

Another ritual for dead kings or chiefs that involves sound is in the Ngangela languages called *vandumbu,* a term that also refers to the principal musical instrument of the occasion, a megaphone; its sound is not considered *mwaso* 'song, music' (pl. *myaso*): it represents the voices of the dead kings. Its production is a secret, whose knowledge is reserved to those who have passed an initiation ceremony; those persons keep the *vandumbu* under water all year long, in a shallow place in the riverine marshlands. Individual megaphones, up to 4 meters long, consist of wooden tubes with a round mouthpiece, cut from tall trees; the orifice often takes the shape of a crocodile's mouth, or that of some other ferocious riverine animal. The body of each tube is wrapped with plant fiber.

In the dark of night, men of the secret society bring the tubes up to the village, and emit into the mouthpiece fearful vocal sounds, which the tubes seemingly amplify (Kubik 1981). Three megaphones are normally used during the ceremony. In front of them, as in a procession, walk the players of three smaller instruments, real trumpets (*nyavikali*), about 1.5 meters long; by overblowing, the players can produce the harmonic series. During the event, people make a sacrifice of millet beer: while they dip one of the horns into a mortar, they pour the beer onto its teeth. The ceremony tries to guarantee the fertility of the village, by gaining the dead kings' goodwill. The

The characteristic vocal tendency is to proceed by step, as in a song that expresses the secluded initiates' yearning for their return home, at the beginning of the rainy season.

FIGURE 18 (below and opposite)   "*Tangwa ilombela mity'e* 'The day the trees will sprout'": song in Luchazi, as performed in the lodge of a circumcision school (*mukanda*). Mikula village, Kabompo District, Zambia; 29 July 1971. Mingonge I & II and Tutanga I are concussion sticks.

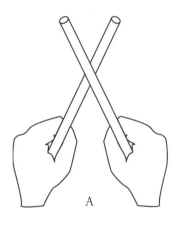

A

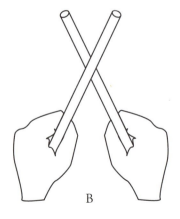

B

salient aspects of this procession resemble those of royal receptions in the kingdom of Congo in the 1600s, as described by seventeenth-century authors.

Initiations

Other musical performances in group 10 of zone K highlight the public aspects of age grade rites of initiation. Every year during the dry season, from about May to October, *mikanda* 'circumcision schools' for young boys, aged six to twelve, are established outside the villages. In that season, one can probably find a *mukanda* (sing.) every six to twelve miles through the more densely populated areas across eastern Angola, northwestern Zambia, and adjacent border areas in Zaïre.

The circumcising surgery marks the beginning of a *mukanda*, and precedes the building of the lodge in which the recuperant boys will stay in seclusion for several months. In the *mukanda*, besides other subjects, music and dance instruction play an important role (Kubik 1981). In a Luchazi *mukanda*, three kinds of musical instruction occur.

1. *myaso yatundanda* 'songs of the initiates', performed with the *kuhunga* and *kawali* dance-actions, accompanied by *vipwali* drums. There are also songs for the initiates to perform on specific occasions—when receiving food, at sunrise, and at sunset ("greeting the sun").
2. *kutangesa* 'recitations by the initiates'. The music teacher, sitting astride a *cipwali* drum, cues the group of initiates, who recite long texts, sometimes with historical content.
3. *myaso yakukuwa* 'songs performed at night by initiates' (and their teachers and guardians), accompanied with concussion sticks.

The songs performed at night display three- or four-part harmony. Vocal music among the Cokwe, Lwena, Luchazi, and related peoples in group 10 of zone K, exemplifies a homophonic multipart style, in a hexa- or heptatonic system, which emphasizes simultaneous sounds in triads, either in thirds plus fifths, or in fourths plus thirds.

A song for circumcision

The movement of individual voices can be parallel, oblique, or contrary; the characteristic tendency is to proceed by step, as in a song that expresses the secluded initiates' yearning for their return home, at the beginning of the rainy season (figure 18).

The singers of figure 18 accompany themselves on concussion sticks in two groups: *mingonge* 1 and *mingonge* 2. Each person holds two sticks, one in each hand. The letter "A" indicates that the right-hand stick strikes the left-hand stick from above; the letter "B" indicates that the left-hand stick strikes the right-hand stick from above. This motion is achieved, not by the individual action of one hand alone, but by an even and absolutely regular left-right, up-down alternation of the movement of both hands. The sticks then hit each other at a point in the middle of the path described by the hands.

The performance of figure 18 includes a third rhythmic part: two or three *tutanga* players hold in the left hand a wooden slat (*katanga*) about 6 decimeters long, and strike it with a stick (*mungonge*) held in the right.

The text of the song of figure 18 expresses yearning for the village. A *mukanda* is normally closed at the end of the dry season, when the trees begin to sprout. So the boys in seclusion, and their guardians and teachers, are looking forward to that day:

FIGURE 18 (continued)   Elementary pulsation: 430 M.M.

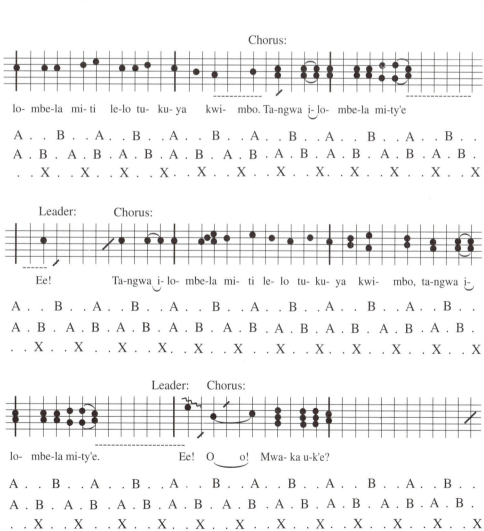

All masks are made in a *mukanda* by the guardians of the secluded initiates. It is the guardians who appear disguised as masks in front of the women of the village, to reassure them of their children's well-being.

LEADER	Tangwa ilombela mity'e—	LEADER	The day the trees will sprout—
	Tangwa ilombela miti,		The day the trees will sprout,
	lelo tukuya kwimbo.		that day we return to the village.
CHORUS	Tangwa ilombela mity'e.	CHORUS	The day the trees will sprout.
LEADER	Ee!	LEADER	*Ee!*
CHORUS	Tangwa ilombela miti,	CHORUS	The day the trees will sprout,
	lelo tukuya kwimbo.		that day we return to the village.
	Tangwa ilombela mity'e.		The day the trees will sprout.
LEADER	Ee!	LEADER	*Ee!*
CHORUS	Oo! Mwaka uk'e?	CHORUS	*Oo!* Which year?

As in this song, each singer can form his own voice by choosing any of the notes shown in the transcribed chord cluster, and he can vary it from one repetition to another. Each singer must follow a basic rule, however: the melody of any voice line must move strictly stepwise.

Neutral thirds
The older harmonic singing style of the Cokwe- and Ngangela-speaking peoples incorporates the use of thirds that can be described as neutral, while fifths and fourths tend to be sung as perfect intervals. The neutral thirds seem to fluctuate between the values of 330 and 380 cents, according to measurements of instrumental tunings (Kubik 1980). Whether they derive from the idea of equidistance or not is difficult to ascertain. They probably result from continual adjustments in intonation, whereby singers try to maintain throughout a song a uniformly euphonic consonance—a consonance that creates consistent "major" triads on adjoining steps of the scale (figure 18).

Adjusting intonation to conform with the euphonic expectation of the Cokwe and Ngangela ear has also been noted in songs of the women's secret *tuwema* society. The term *tuwema* (sing. *kawema*) 'flames' refers to a show staged by women at night. In the darkness, while the women sing and dance, they wave glowing bark cloth strips attached to their arms. This action creates an impressive display: sparks fly in vivid patterns. How the women effect the show is their secret. For this area, it illustrates the intimate relationship of aural, visual, and kinetic arts.

This interrelationship also informs masked dancing, both by the *makisi a vampwevo* 'masks of the women', in which body paint is used, and by the *makisi a vamala* 'masks of the men'. Every year, the men construct individual masked characters. Most of the masks are anthropomorphic; some are zoomorphic. All are made in a *mukanda* by the guardians of the secluded initiates, and it is the guardians who appear disguised as masks in front of the women of the village, to reassure them of their children's well-being. During the *mukanda* season, many public mask fests take place. A performance late in the evening, after supper, may feature the individual appearances

FIGURE 19   The young woman (*mwanaphwo*), a famous carved mask of the Cokwe.

of the *cileya* 'court fool', or of the *mwanaphwo* 'young woman', one of the famous carved masks of the Cokwe (figure 19).

Recent innovations, such as the wig (*ciwiki*), with its Afro hairstyle, can also appear. These masks appear singly; but in contrast, a dramatic masquerade takes place in the daytime, at the *cilende*, or village danceplace. It features a dozen masked characters in succession, until the feast closes with the appearance of the madman, a spectacular mask, taking the highest rank; it is variously called *mpumpu* (in Mbwela), *lipumpu* (in Lucazi), and *cizaluke* (in Lwena-Luvale). In southeastern Angola, the person wearing this mask sports a simulated penis, which he wags during the performance. The madman represents an ancient king, Mwene Nyumbu, who after his sister insulted him is said to have instituted circumcision by circumcising himself.

All masked performances are accompanied by the standard *vipwali* or *zing'oma* drums, sometimes three of them played by one person. In the latter case, this set of instruments is called *tumboi* among the Mbwela and Nkhangala of southeastern Angola.

Musical instruments

In instrumental resources, zone K is characterized by the predominance of percussion—strangely reminiscent of the situation on the Guinea coast (West Africa)—from the families of idiophones and membranophones.

Stringed instruments include only the friction bow (*kawayawaya*), imports such as the *kalyalya* (two- or three-stringed bowed lute, based on the *kakoxa* of zone H), and, beginning in the mid-1900s, homemade banjos and guitars.

Mnemonic patterns

Rhythmic patterns are taught by syllabic or verbal mnemonic structures, such as *macakili, macakili, kuvamba kuli masika* 'in the circumcision lodge there is coldness', and *mu cana ca Kapekula* 'in the river grasslands of Kapekula'. These mnemonics are almost notations of the accentual, rhythmic, and conceptual characteristics associated with the patterns they represent. Plosive sounds, such as /p/, /t/, and /k/, represent accented strokes, the affricate sound /tʃ/ (orthographically spelled "*c*," and pronounced as in English "church") usually shows the position of the referential beat, while nasal sounds tend to represent silent or unaccented pulse-units. The mnemonics transcribed in figures 20 and 21 come from the Ngangela repertory of eastern Angola, where these patterns serve as accompaniment and timeline in several genres of music and dance.

FIGURE 20   A Ngangela mnemonic pattern (*macakili macakili*, for rattles).

$$\circled{8}\ \left[\ \uparrow\ \ \circ\ \ \blacktriangle\ \ \downarrow\ \ \uparrow\ \ \circ\ \ \blacktriangle\ \ \downarrow\ \right]$$

Mnemonics: m a – c a – k i – l i   m a – c a – k i – l i

Reference beat: 1   2   3   4

FIGURE 21   A Ngangela mnemonic pattern (*mu cana ca Kapekula*, struck on any object with two sticks). For the symbols, see figure 20.

$$\circled{8}\ \left[\begin{array}{cccccccc}\cdot & X & \cdot & \cdot & X & \cdot & X & \cdot \\ \cdot & X & \cdot & X & \cdot & X & \cdot & X\end{array}\right]$$

Mnemonics: mu–ca–na   ca–Ka–pe–ku–la

Reference beat: 1   2   3   4

FIGURE 22   The *kachacha* timeline. The referential beat starts on the stroke over the numeral 1, but the pattern begins on the first stroke of the mnemonics as written. This notation captures both concepts: top line, in mnemonics; bottom line, in the pattern's relationship with the referential beat.

either

Mnemonics: (16)
x • x • x • x x • x • x • x x •
ŋ b ɔ   ŋ b ɔ   ŋ b ɔ   ŋ b ɔ lɔ   ŋ b ɔ   ŋ b ɔ   ŋ b ɔ lɔ

Reference beat: 2   3   4   1

or

Right-hand stick:
x • x • x • x x • x • x • x x •
Left-hand stick:
• x • x • x • • x • x • x • • x

(16)   2   3   4   1

FIGURE 23   The *muselemeka* timeline, transcribed in mnemonics with a referential beat.

Mnemonics: (12)
x • x • x x • x • x x •
ŋ b ɔ   ŋ b ɔ   ŋ b ɔ lɔ   ŋ b ɔ   ŋ b ɔ lɔ

Reference beat: 2   3   4   1

Timelines

Two standard asymmetric timelines (figures 22 and 23) are most prominent for steering performances with drums, lamellophones, or other instruments. In Luvale, they are called *kachacha* or *muselemeka,* respectively, because of their association with the kinetic pattern of dances of the same name. Among the Lwena-Luvale, *kachacha* is a dance genre that involves a set of single-skin goblet-shaped drums (*jing'oma*), and sometimes a two-note xylophone (*jinjimba*). It also accompanies masked dancing.

In contrast to the Guinea coast, where this pattern also plays a dominant role in many musical genres (Jones 1959), its relationship to the dance beat, or musicians' referential beat, is different in southern Central Africa. Beat 1 coincides here with the second *lɔ* in the mnemonics.

By contrast, in Yoruba usage of the same pattern, beat 1 coincides with the first *lɔ*, which falls off the beat in *muselemeka*. Both timelines in zone K are usually struck with two sticks on the body of a drum. When accompanying a *likembe*, a second performer strikes the sticks against the body of the *likembe*; when accompanying some other types of lamellophones, the second performer strikes the resonator. When a friction drum (*pwita*)—always characterized by internal friction (as in figure 24)— plays with other drums, the timeline is struck on the body of the *pwita*. The friction stick is rubbed with wet hands; performers keep a water vessel beside them, to wet their hands intermittently.

Among the instrumental resources within zone K, lamellophones have also played an important role; among the Cokwe, five different types are distinguishable.

1. *cisaji cakele* often refers to lamellophones with a board-shaped composite body, made of material from the raffia palm, from which the lamellae also derive.
2. *cisaji cakakolondondo* has a board-shaped body, with ten iron lamellae arranged in a V-shape. Tuning is often achieved by attaching differently sized lumps of black wax to the underside of the playing-ends of each lamella.
3. *cisaji calungandu* has a board-shaped body, with two interspersed ranks of lamellae, six in each, in ascending order from left to right. Tuning is with wax, as above.
4. *mucapata* has 17, 19, or more, iron lamellae, arranged in sections according to tonality. The body is hollowed out from the end facing the player (the "bell-shaped" resonator in Tracey 1948). Tuning is carried out exclusively by adjusting the length of the lamellae that extend over the bridge.

FIGURE 24   Friction drum (*pwita*) of the Luvale and Lwena (northeastern Angola), showing internal friction; a *lihongo*, a kind of reed, is the friction stick.

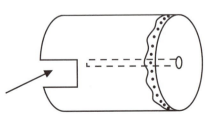

5. *likembe* has a box resonator, normally (in this area) with eight notes, arranged in an N shape—that is, with two deep notes, one in the middle, one on the right (as seen from the player's viewpoint). A trait of the playing technique of this type of lamellophone is the extensive use of the sound hole at the back of the box; opening and closing it gives a "wow" effect.

The history of these lamellophones, like the history of Central African music in general, involves the forces of diffusion, adaptation, and innovation. The *likembe* is a twentieth-century introduction to zone K, for which its history has been reconstructed (Kubik 1980). The raffia lamellophones are either ancient, and linked with cultures across Central Africa (such as Central Cameroon, where they play a prominent role), or imitative of lamellophone types with iron lamellae, now found among the Cokwe. One of the raffia lamellophones in the collections of the Museu de Etnologia, Lisbon (no. AH–622), is clearly modeled after the *mucapata*. The *cisaji cakakolondondo* and the *cisaji calungandu* may have remote connections with the Lower Zambezi Valley; and from the 1700s, the ideas leading to their invention may have spread from there to Angola, with the trading of the *pombeiros*. Alternatively, *mucapata*—undoubtedly an original Cokwe or Cokwe-Mbangala invention—may have some historical connection with the Loango-type lamellophones. This possibility is suggested by the shape of the top part (where the backrest is often missing), the presence of a bell-type resonator, and certain patterns in the arrangement of the notes.

REFERENCES

Ankermann, Bernhard. 1901. "Die afrikanischen Musikinstrumente." *Ethnologisches Notizblatt* 3:I–X, 1–32.

Arom, Simha. 1967. "Instruments de musique particuliers à certaines ethnies de la Republique Centrafricaine." *Journal of the International Folk Music Council,* 19:104–108.

Blakely, Pamela A. 1993. "Performing Dangerous Thoughts: Women's Song-Dance Performance Events in a Hemba Funeral Ritual (Republic of Zaïre)." Ph.D. dissertation, Indiana University.

Carrington, John F. 1949. *A Comparative Study of Some Central African Gong-Languages.* Brussels: Institut Royal Colonial Belge.

———. 1956. "Individual Names Given to Talking Gongs in the Yalemba Area of Belgian Congo." *African Music* 1(3):10–17.

———. 1975. *Talking Drums of Africa.* New York: Negro Universities Press.

Cavazzi, Giovanni António. 1687. *Istorica Descrizione de 'tre' Regni Congo, Matamba et Angola.* Bologna: Giacomo Monti.

Chauvet, Stephen. 1929. *Musique Nègre.* Paris: Société d'éditions géographiques, maritimes et coloniales.

Dampierre, Eric de. 1963. *Poètes Nzakara.* Paris: Institut d'Ethnologie, Université de Paris. Classiques Africains.

Didier, André, and Gilbert Rouget. 1946. *Musique pygmée de la haute-Sangha.* Paris: Boîte à Musique, BAM LD 325. LP disk.

Djenda, Maurice. 1967. "Les anciennes danses des Mpyèmo." *African Music* 4(1):40–46.

———. 1968. "Les Pygmées de la Haute Sangha." *Geographica* 14:26-43.

Djenda, Maurice, and Gerhard Kubik. 1964. Field-Research Notes: Central African Republic. Vienna: Phonogrammarchiv.

———, and Gerhard Kubik. 1966. Field-Research Notes: Central African Republic. Vienna: Phonogrammarchiv.

Erlmann, Veit. 1981. *Populäre Musik in Afrika.* Berlin: Staatliche Museen Preußischer Kulturbesitz. Veröffentlichungen des Museums für Völkerkunde Berlin, Neue Folge 53, Abteilung Musikethnologie 8.

Folclore de São Paulo. n.d. Brochure. São Paulo: Secretaria de Cultura, Esportes e Turismo.

Gansemans, Jos. 1978. *La musique et son rôle dans la vie sociale et rituelle Luba.* Tervuren, Belgium: Musée Royal de l'Afrique Centrale. Sciences Humaines, 95.

———. 1980. *Les instruments de musique Luba.* Tervuren, Belgium: Musée Royal de l'Afrique Centrale. Sciences Humaines, 103.

Gansemans, Jos, and Barbara Schmidt-Wrenger. 1986. *Zentralafrika.* Leipzig: Deutscher Verlag für Musik. Musikgeschichte in Bildern, 1, part 12.

Gardi, René. 1974. *Unter afrikanischen Handwerkern.* Graz: Akademische Druck- und Verlagsanstalt.

Giorgetti, Filiberto. 1957. *Musica Africana.* Bologna: Editrice Nigrizia.

Greenberg, Joseph H. 1970. *The Languages of Africa.* Bloomington, Ind.: Research Center for the Language Sciences.

Grimaud, Yvette. 1956. "Note sur la musique vocale des Bochiman !Kung' et des pygmées Babinga." *Colloques de Wégimont* 3:105–126.

Guthrie, Malcolm. 1948. *The Classification of Bantu Languages.* London: International African Institute.

Hirschberg, Walter. 1969. "Early Illustrations of West and Central African Music." *African Music* 4(3):6–18.

Hornbostel, Erich Moritz von. 1913. "Musik." In *Die Pangwe,* ed. G. Tessman, 320–357. Berlin: E. Wasmuth.

Janata, Alfred. 1975. *Musikinstrumente der Völker.* Vienna: Museum für Völkerkunde.

Jones, Arthur M. 1959. *Studies in African Music.* 2 vols. London: Oxford University Press.

———. 1964. *Africa and Indonesia: The Evidence of the Xylophone and Other Cultural and Musical Factors.* Leiden: E. J. Brill.

———. 1971. *Africa and Indonesia: The Evidence of the Xylophone and Other Cultural and Musical Factors,* 2nd ed. Leiden: E. J. Brill.

———. 1978. "Review of 'Les mendzaŋ des chanteurs de Yaoundé' by Pied-Claude Ngumu." *Review of Ethnology* 5(2–3):23–24.

Kalakula, Likando. 1979. *Kuomboka: A Living Traditional Culture among the Malozi People of Zambia.* Lusaka: National Educational Company of Zambia (Neczam).

Kazadi wa Mukuna. 1973. "Trends of Nineteenth and Twentieth Century Music in the Congo-Zaïre." In *Musikkulturen Asiens, Afrikas und Ozeaniens im 19. Jahrhundert*, ed. Robert Günther, 267–284. Regensburg: Gustav Bosse.

———. 1980. "The Origin of Zaïrean Modern Music: A Socio-economic Aspect." *African Urban Studies* 6:77–78.

Kishilo w'Itunga. 1976. "Structure des chansons des Lega de Mwenga." *Revue Zaïroise des Arts* no. 1 (Sept.), 7–22.

———. 1987. "Une analyse de la 'Messe Katangese' de Joseph Kiwele." *African Music* 6(4):108–125.

Kremser, Manfred. 1982. "Die Musikinstrumente der Azande: Ein Beitrag zur Musikgeschichte Zentralafrikas." In *Bericht über den 15. Österreichischen Historikertag in Salzburg, 14. bis 18. September 1981*, Referate und Protokolle der Sektion 7, 295–300.

Kubik, Gerhard. 1963–1964. Field-Research Notes: Nigeria, Cameroon, Central African Republic, Congo, Gabon. Vienna: Phonogrammarchiv.

———. 1964. "Harp Music of the Azande and Related Peoples in the Central African Republic." *African Music* 3(3): 37–76.

———. 1965a. "Neue Musikformen in Schwarzafrika: Psychologische und musikethnologische Grundlagen." *Afrika heute* (Bonn), Sonderbeilag 4, 1 March, 1–16.

———. 1965b. Field-Research Notes: Angola. Vienna: Phonogrammarchiv.

———. 1966. "Die Popularität von Musikarten im Afrika südliche der Sahara." *Afrika heute* (Bonn), 15 December, 370–375.

———. 1967. "La musique en République Centrafricaine." *Afrika* (Bonn) 8(1):43–47.

———. 1971. Field-Research Notes: Zambia. Vienna: Phonogrammarchiv.

———. 1977. "Die 'brasilianische Sanza' im Museum für Völkerkunde, Wien." *Archiv für Völkerkunde* 31:1–5, plates 1–2.

———. 1980. "Likembe Tunings of Kufuna Kandonga (Angola)." *African Music* 6(1):70–88.

———. 1981. *Mukanda na makisi—Circumcision school and masks.* Berlin: Museum für Völkerkunde, MC 11. LP disk and notes.

———. 1988. "Nsenga / Shona Harmonic Patterns and the San Heritage in Southern Africa." *Ethnomusicology* 32:39–76.

Laurenty, Jean-Sebastien. 1960. *Les cordophones du Congo Belge et du Ruanda-Urundi.* Tervuren: Musée Royal du Congo Belge.

———. 1962. *Les Sanza du Congo.* Tervuren: Musée Royal de l'Afrique Centrale.

———. 1971. "Les cordophones des Luba-Shankadi." *African Music* 5(2):40–45.

———. 1972. "Les membranophones Luba-Shankadi." *African Music* 5(2):40–45.

Livingstone, David. 1857. *A Narrative of Dr. Livingstone's Discoveries in South-Central Africa.* London: Routledge.

Lomax, Alan. 1968. *Folk Song Style and Culture.* Washington, D.C.: American Association for the Advancement of Science.

Low, John. 1982. *Shaba Diary: A Trip to Rediscover the 'Katanga' Guitar Styles and Songs of the 1950's and 60's.* Vienna: Föhrenau. Acta Ethnologica et Linguistica, 54.

Mapoma, Mwesa I. 1974. "Ingomba: The Royal Musicians of the Bembe People of the Luapula and Northern Provinces of Zambia." Ph.D. dissertation, University of California, Los Angeles.

———. 1980. "Zambia." *The New Grove Dictionary of Music and Musicians*, ed. Stanley Sadie. London: Macmillan.

Mecklenburg, Adolf Friedrich, Herzog zu. 1912. *Vom Kongo zum Niger und Nil.* Leipzig. Berichte zur Deutschen Zentralafrika-Expedition 1910–11.

Merolla, Girolamo. 1692. *Breve, e Succinta Relazione del Viaggio nel Regno di Congo Nell' Africa Meridionale*, ed. Angelo Piccardo. Naples.

Merriam, Alan P. 1959. "The Concept of Culture Clusters Applied to the Belgian Congo." *Southwestern Journal of Anthropology* 15:373–395.

Messomo, Albert Noah. 1980. *Mendzan: Etude ethno-littéraire du xylophone des Beti Yaounde.* University of Yaoundé.

Murdock, George Peter. 1967. *Ethnographic Atlas.* Pittsburgh: University of Pittsburgh Press.

Murray, Jocelyn, ed. 1981. *Cultural Atlas of Africa.* Oxford: Elsevier.

Ngumu, Pie-Claude. 1971. *Maîtrise des Chanteurs à la Croix d'Ébène.* Victoria, Cameroon: Presbook.

———. 1976a. "*Les mendzaŋ des Ewondo du Cameroun.*" *African Music* 5(4):6–26.

———. 1976b. *Les mendzaŋ des chanteurs de Yaoundé.* Vienna: Föhrenau.

Pinto, Tiago de Oliveira, ed. 1986. *Brasilien.* Mainz: Schott.

Praetorius, Michael. 1620. *De organographia.* Wolfenbüttel: Praetorius. *Syntagma Musicum*, 2.

Rycroft, David. 1961. "The Guitar Improvisations of Mwenda Jean Bosco [I]." *African Music* 2(4):81–98.

———. 1962. "The Guitar Improvisations of Mwenda Jean Bosco [II]." *African Music* 3(1):86–102.

Schüller, Dietrich. 1972. "Beziehungen zwischen west- und westenzentralafrikanischen Staaten von 1482 bis 1700." Ph.D. dissertation, University of Vienna.

Schweinfurth, Georg. 1875. *Im Herzen von Afrika: Reisen und Entdeckungen im Centralen Aequatorial-Afrika während der Jahre 1868 bis 1871.* Leipzig: F. A. Brockhaus.

Sulzmann, Erika. 1959. "Les danseurs ekonda à 'Changwe yetu'." *Zaïre* 13:57–71.

Tracey, Hugh. 1948. *Handbook for Librarians.* Roodepoort: African Music Society.

———. 1973. *Catalogue of the Sound of Africa Recordings.* Roodepoort: International Library of African Music.

Vansina, Jan. 1966. *Kingdoms of the Savannah.* Madison: University of Wisconsin Press.

———. 1969. "The Bells of Kings." *Journal of African History* 10(2):187–197.

Wachsmann, Klaus Peter. 1964. "Human Migration and African Harps." *Journal of the International Folk Music Council* 16:84–88.

Wegner, Ulrich. 1984. *Afrikanische Saiteninstrumente.* Berlin: Museum für Völkerkunde. N.S., 41.

Wieschhoff, Heinz. 1933. *Die afrikanischen Trommeln und ihre außerafrikanischen Beziehungen.* Stuttgart: Strecker und Schröder. Studien zur Kulturkunde, 2.

Musical Life in the Central African Republic
Michelle Kisliuk

Sounds of the City: *Zokela*
Sounds of the Forest: BaAka Pygmies
Conclusion

This essay laces together two musical narratives set in Centrafrique (Central African Republic) in the early 1990s. The introductory narrative focuses on an urban dance music based in the capital, Bangui. The second description, by contrast, addresses the performative, political, and social circumstances within which BaAka pygmies—who live mostly in the rain forest area in the southwest of the country—are negotiating their daily lives.

A link between these two musical domains might at first seem unlikely, but the urban music is in fact stylistically rooted in the Lobaye River region, which overlaps with the home area of BaAka (Aka) and other pygmies (see map). These domains also connect as performances of modernity—how people situate themselves within a changing world. As I shall describe, the BaAka among whom I lived include within their repertory a form that mixes together hymns from various Christian sects, pop-song snippets from the radio, and rhythms and melodies from neighboring Bolemba pygmies (whose lives and culture, unlike BaAka, are relatively integrated with those of their nonpygmy counterparts). BaAka meld all these aspects into a dance form that is about being modern. Concurrently, urban musicians in a collection of bands called *zokela* draw on local song styles—including Bolemba and Mbati pygmy styles—situating their electric sound in regional culture.

I write in the first person here because I want to emphasize that ideas and information about musical performance are by nature embedded within personal experience, bound and defined by moment and circumstance. This viewpoint is particularly appropriate for addressing African performance, intimately tied in most cases to the socioaesthetic moment (Chernoff 1979; Stone 1982). My descriptions are based on several years of research among BaAka pygmies, spanning eight years (1986–1994) and including a two-year stay. The material on urban music in Bangui is culled from the same period.

SOUNDS OF THE CITY: *ZOKELA*

It is a weeknight in Fatima, a section of Bangui. Fatima is the neighborhood where people originally from the Lobaye region tend to gather (the Lobaye river area is in the southwest of the country). In an open-air dance bar, the disk jockey switches

zokela   An urban dance music based in the Central African Republic city of Bangui

soukous   Urban music style from Zaïre

makossa   Urban music style from Cameroon

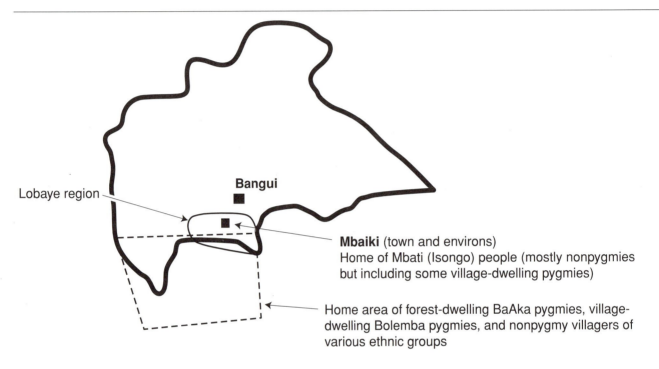

Lobaye region

Bangui

Mbaiki (town and environs)
Home of Mbati (Isongo) people (mostly nonpygmies but including some village-dwelling pygmies)

Home area of forest-dwelling BaAka pygmies, village-dwelling Bolemba pygmies, and nonpygmy villagers of various ethnic groups

Central African Republic (Centrafique). This map highlights only areas mentioned in this article. The Central African Republic is bordered to the south by the Republic of Congo, to the north by Chad, to the east by Cameroon, and to the west by Zaïre.

from a current *soukous* hit from Zaïre to a tune by *zokela*—musicians who play and sing in a vigorous style based on multiethnic rhythms, harmonies, melodies, and topical themes from the Lobaye. Though the dance floor had been far from empty before, suddenly just about everybody seated at the little wooden tables leaves beers and sodas behind, grabbing friends to get up and dance *motengene,* the loose, ribcage-rotating, regional dance.

Originally the name of a band, *zokela* has burgeoned into a full-fledged style. On a weekend, those in search of an evening of energetic dancing, social commentary, and proverbs set to the rhythms of the Lobaye might find one of the *zokela* bands playing at a club (only one band would be playing at a time, since three or more bands must share instruments). Inside an open-roofed club, after paying a fee of 500 francs (about $1.50 in 1996), one would find the musicians and patrons warmed up by about 9:00 P.M. Four singers standing in a row, each behind a stationary microphone, would be trading lead lines and overlapping choral responses with tight harmonies. Occasionally a singer might withdraw, replaced by one who had been waiting casually at the sidelines.

Though overshadowed internationally by neighboring urban musical styles from Zaïre and Cameroon (like *soukous* and *makossa*), musicians from Centrafrique, and the Lobaye region in particular, have been developing their own style of electrified band music since the late 1970s, and their popularity with the Centrafrican people is high.

This story of the genesis of the *zokela* sound is based on my conversations with members of the original band, and on discussions with Lobayans who form the core of the listening and dancing community for *zokela*.

The origins of *zokela*

Several people I spoke with began the story of *zokela* by recounting an incident from 1981. Musiki, an established rumba-style band from Bangui, was touring the country. For a few days, Musiki stayed in the town of Mbaïki, where they discovered aspiring boy-musicians calling themselves *zokela* (Mbati) 'noise'—a noise like water gurgling down a stream, or like women ululating at a funeral dance, or, less literally, like the sound of the life-force.

Kaïda Monganga, the leader of the original *zokela*, later narrated his recollections of how *zokela* began (my translation):

> I learned music from my mother. When she would take me to the fields, she would sing, so she taught me how to sing. In Mbaïki, at the age of eight I got together with some friends to sing Mbati songs from traditional legends, funerals, and ceremonies—songs that were part of our upbringing—and we also began to interpret music from Zaïre on homemade guitars. This was at the age of about 10, between 1970 and 1974. We were actually imitating the Centrafrican bands who were themselves imitating the rumba style from Zaïre; but as kids, we could not enter the local nightclubs. Then Piros, a composer among us, arranged an interpretation of a traditional song, and each time we would sing it, lots of people would gather on the path to listen, and they would encourage us. We formed two little groups, and after several more years of encouragement we got together as one and decided to choose the name Zokela, meaning in the Mbati language 'acclamation, joy, heat, ambience, noise.'
>
> One night in Mbaïki, an *orchestre* came to play at a dance bar. They played from 8 p.m. until 2 a.m. And we youngsters, with our little group, we came there to ask them to let us play, but they made us stay outside. . . . We really suffered out there until 2 a.m. But when the evening was over, and the people began to leave, they said "there's a little group here, you should let them come in and play." And we went and played only one song, and it was that traditional song. When we played it there was pandemonium, and even though we'd only been allowed to play one song, we were very happy because it was the first time we had ever picked up an electric guitar and mic. Oh! That was the end! Oo-la-la, we were overjoyed.

Everyone who heard the young members of Zokela that night in Mbaïki was stunned that they had captured on modern instruments the insistent and vital sound of ceremonies and funeral dances. Accented by a trap set, the bass guitar and glass bottle (tapped with a stick) caught the texture of village drums. The bass emphasized high-low contrasts (like the open and muted strokes of a low-pitched drum), while the bottle added the syncopated triplets of a matching high-pitched drum. Two lead guitars built on that rhythmic base, playing interlocking, repeating riffs—brighter sounding than in *soukous*—jumping octaves and rolling in cycles like a tumultuous brook.

TRACK 17 Though this was not the first time a band had tried to integrate musical elements from the Lobaye into an urban sound, it was the first time a group had succeeded in getting the melodies, harmonies, vocal quality, and especially the *motengene* dance rhythms and energy into the music. After the leader of Musiki heard Zokela for the first time (in 1981), he and a financially successful music lover from the

While *zokela* musicians continue to compose their own tunes and lyrics, they are delving progressively deeper into local traditions and creatively elaborating on urban culture

Lobaye invited the young men to Bangui to perform several club concerts there. This exposed the band to the Bangui public, and they exploded onto the cultural scene, soon beginning to play regularly at Club Anabelle, in the Fatima neighborhood. Over the following months, the band struggled to remain in Bangui, all of the musicians living in one house—at least four singers, two lead guitarists, drum set player, and bassist.

Kaïda continues:

> In 1982, we were invited to make our first recording, and when we introduced that rhythm, Zokela took Bangui by storm. We wanted to stay in Bangui because that way we'd at least have access to instruments and to repairs. So since 1983, we have been in Bangui.
>
> At that time, we began to expand our repertory, to compose, to create, based on traditional music. But we also began to compose some songs in the national language [Sango], instead of only in our regional languages from the Lobaye, so the people who did not understand would no longer feel excluded, and we were very successful. To attract attention, we costumed ourselves in animal skins, traditional dress—that is, panther skins—and when I came out on stage: boom! the people were very interested.

Since then, the band has remained popular.

Zokela began singing not only about their experience as Lobayains, but also about urban life in Bangui, to which people from all regions of the country could relate. In rhythm, vocal style, and lyric, Zokela voiced the contemporary and complex experience of urban Centrafricans, melded with ethnic roots. Nevertheless, the band was at a disadvantage because the government would not aid a group from the Lobaye (birthplace of the deposed Emperor Bokassa), and because their songs, like the traditional forms that inspired them, contained social commentary unlike the beautiful but unthreatening love songs of most of the other rumba-style bands in Bangui.

According to several of the members of Zokela, there was a problem of tribal jealousy. Kaïda recalls, "Some people wanted Zokela to disappear. Even our songs on the radio were censored because we were very successful. They were afraid we would develop our region, and then come again to dominate. We went along for 10 or 11 years with that tribalistic regime [of President André Kolingba], but it seems that now there will be a change. [The new president, Ange] Patassé promised to support Centrafrican artists."

While Zokela were staying in Bangui during their initial entrance onto the scene in the early 1980s, several of the more established Bangui bands (including Musiki, Makembe, Cannon Stars, Cool Stars) began tempting the singers to join them—and they succeeded to some extent because they had instruments and some money. A growing core group of singers and players was so large, there were still many musicians left to fill the places of those who had moved on. As a result, rather than seeing their sound and energy become diffused and destroyed by recruitment from other bands, Zokela not only continued on their own, but infiltrated to varying degrees the sound of most of the other bands in Bangui.

Kaïda continues the story:

> We did not have our own instruments, we were renting instruments, and to put up a concert was very expensive. But for us it wasn't just the money, but our future. We needed to make ourselves known on a national level so we could develop as artists. We didn't concern ourselves with earning money; women loved us, and life was beautiful. The important thing was to produce, to perform.
>
> In 1985, a local producer who wanted to work with us approached us. He provided instruments, a makeshift studio, but then he began to want to dominate us. We were the creators of the music, but he wanted everything to pass his approval first. . . . But how could he do that? This was our group; we were the ones who formed it.
>
> So the rest of us, those of us who had brought the music from Mbaïki in the first place, we decided to look for other people to help us. And so those who stayed with that producer for the sake of the instruments formed the subgroup Zokela Motike ['Orphans'], and we became Zokela Original. We were the four founders of Zokela: Mabele, Ilonga, Degoumousse, and Kaïda. The rest went with that producer.
>
> So I took other new singers, and we mounted a coup again, in 1986, and we put out an album [homemade cassette] . . . that was very, very successful. We recorded and toured a lot throughout 1988–89, . . . but we were still renting instruments. Then there was another disagreement within Zokela Motike. Luanza, the head of Motike, decided to break and form yet another Zokela. . . . So I accepted that there be many Zokelas because I wasn't afraid: I know my position; I know the secret of this music. I'm not afraid to share it with the youngsters. . . . So Luanza made "*Zokela National*" in late 1992, and it was very successful, even more so than Motike. And it gave me a lot of pleasure to see the youngsters that we trained.

The members of all the *zokela* groups, despite their conflicts, continue to cooperate, covering each other's songs without hesitation, and by necessity sharing instruments. One of the musicians explained that the reason Zokela keeps splitting off into new bands is that they are all like brothers, having grown up together in the same town, and therefore nobody can really boss anybody else around. Instead of following a leader when conflicts arise, they just split off. This situation accommodates the younger musicians from Mbaïki and elsewhere in the Lobaye who want to be connected with the *zokela,* and has strengthened the style and its influence, moving *zokela* further toward becoming a national style.

In January 1993, a French-owned beer company sponsored an event that the announcers on Radio Bangui called a concert of *la musique traditionelle moderne* 'modern traditional music' (figures 1 and 2). All three *zokela* bands, plus a potential fourth band, played at this concert, held at the upscale nightclub Punch Coco. The Banguisois audience, of mixed ethnic background, crowded in to hear and see the latest *zokela* compositions and *motengene* dancing, and responded enthusiastically to songs that captured the collective experience of economic and political crisis in the country.

FIGURE 1   Mixed *zokela* bands perform at club Punch Coco in Bangui, 1993. The singers break for an interlude of dancing, while bassist Maurice Kpamanda stands behind them. Photo by Justin Mongosso.

"... We go to work in the fields, a long walk away, to survive. I talk to my dead relatives, who can no longer help me; I cry."—from a *zokela* song

FIGURE 2   Lead *zokela* guitarists and percussionists, with the bottle player seated behind the drum set. The beer company slogan, *la blonde qui fait courire l'Afrique* 'the blonde that makes Africa chase after her', is displayed behind the musicians. Photo by Justin Mongosso.

While *zokela* musicians continue to compose their own tunes and lyrics, they are delving progressively deeper into local traditions and creatively elaborating on urban culture (weaving in references to Christian religious music or advertising jingles), much in the way that the Mbati songs elaborate and comment on social surroundings. For example, in 1995, a hit by Zokela National—"*Essa Messa* 'I Call You'"—used several regional languages, plus Sango, to express a proverb whose theme is reciprocal assistance: "During tough times, you can call on a real friend to help you, but I called you and you did not answer." (This may covertly criticize the government—something *zokela* is known for.) "But what befalls me now will befall you later. If you need my help, I must help you." The song goes on to name all the musicians in the band, who will be there to help each other.

Another song, "*Exode Rurale* 'Rural Exodus'," warns villagers not to leave their fertile earth behind and move to the city. It describes the difficulties of survival in Bangui. But many *zokela* songs—like that first one they played as boys—are modern arrangements of the exact melodies and words of traditional songs. In Mbaïki and in villages throughout the Lobaye, one can hear *zokela* tunes playing regularly on family tape players, while next door at a funeral or a ceremony people may be singing the songs that form the basis of that style. One important difference in the urban musical setting is that musical performance there is dominated by men, while in the village, women have an equal or greater role.

Another *zokela* song, a hit by Zokela Original, is "*Motike* 'Orphans'" (on CD track 17). The text, in the Mbati language, laments the difficulty of being musicians:

Zokela nzonga mawa.
Ngo si mbi ko Bangui ngo ke sio na Isongo.
Ngo simba tene ngo kpoua na lele.
Nya kolo eti.

Zokela is unhappy, pitiable.
We go to work in the fields, a long walk away, to survive.
I talk to my dead relatives, who can no longer help me; I cry.
And I have crippled feet [a reference to a guitarist (figure 2)].

As you listen to the audio example, try isolating the bass, played by Maurice Kpamanda of Zokela Original, said to be the only bassist who truly captures village rhythms. The lead singer at the opening of the song is Kaïda Monganga.

Partly as an effort to escape the paralysis of ever-deepening poverty, *zokela*'s latest move has been toward what Kaïda calls spectacle—an international pop-show style that emulates *soukous* bands touring from Zaïre. Holding a movable microphone, the lead singer, or "star" (Kaïda himself, in this case), is separated from the "chorus." And whereas in a club setting the singers dance *motengene* informally, occasionally adding a small choreographed bit to an instrumental interlude (figure 1), the spectacle introduces highly choreographed dance numbers with female dancers.

In the Bangui soccer stadium in 1994, during a spectacle showcasing Centrafrican superstar singers, Kaïda tried to add a folkloric-show aspect to the spectacle. As one of several singers who performed that evening, he brought pygmies from the Mbaïki area to come on stage with him and imitate their forest-dwelling BaAka cousins, whose styles of music and dance differ widely from those of the Mbati pygmies. Mbati pygmies normally dance a version of *motengene* as their traditional dance, while BaAka generally do not (the hip swiveling and rib rotating of *motengene* contrasts with the square-hipped chugging and buttock-bobbing steps of most BaAka dancing). During this spectacle, however, the Mbati pygmies were asked to provide an introduction, wearing BaAka leaves and loincloths, and singing in BaAka style (which they could only approximate). Kaïda himself could then explode onto the stage with his modern sound, spurring the "pygmies" to drop everything and dance *motengene* instead. These Mbati pygmies were at first so reticent to perform in front of the crowd that the organizers had to get them drunk before they were willing. Their dancing was nonetheless impressive, if unsteady, and the crowd, of mostly urban Lobayans (many of whom do not distinguish between BaAka and Mbati pygmies), cheered wildly.

This incident highlights both the creative tension and the possible pitfalls when a visceral identification with local roots meets an enticing modernity. Extending that tension, *zokela*'s struggle to find footing as a regional, urban, then national style was almost eclipsed here by a simultaneous wish for dramatic impact and international appeal. Kaïda, who had at first refused to give up his autonomy to a producer in exchange for some measure of security, now, even while making explicit the roots of his style, blurred the realities of those roots for the sake of spectacle.

The story of *zokela* resembles that of many urban musics developing throughout Africa. In their very sound, they have been reclaiming and redefining experience in the postcolonial era, first by experimenting with electric instruments and a "modern" sound, then expanding to a national public with a regionally or ethnically based style; then, some of them have leaped toward an international market. But the consequences of an international leap for a music like *zokela*—potent mainly for its localness—are uncertain in the climate of worldbeat.

The music of African pygmies has held a special place in ethnomusicological imagination. The yodeling and hocketing of pygmy singing has served as an icon of social and musical utopia.

SOUNDS OF THE FOREST: BAAKA PYGMIES

The music of African pygmies has held a special place in ethnomusicological imagination. In the writings of Colin Turnbull (1962), Alan Lomax (1976), Robert Farris Thompson (1989), and Simha Arom (1978, 1985), the yodeling and hocketing of pygmy singing has served as an icon of social and musical utopia. Pygmies who call themselves BaAka (sometimes Bayaka, depending on the regional accent) live between the Sangha and Oubangui rivers in the southwestern Central African Republic, and extend as far south as Imfondo in the Republic of the Congo. They live mostly in densely forested areas, and their culture is based largely on hunting and gathering. Since the 1960s and 1970s, however, these pygmies (like most other pygmies of equatorial Africa) have become more involved in farming—either as seasonal laborers for village-based farmers of other ethnic groups, or, increasingly, on their own plots cut in the forest.

I use the term *pygmy* (French *pygmée*) with reluctance. It derives via Middle English *pigmei* and Latin *Pygmæi* from Greek *Pygmaîoi* 'people pertaining to the *pygmé* (the distance from the elbow to the knuckles)', denoting a mythical dwarfish people, who repeatedly warred with and were defeated by cranes. H. M. Stanley had applied the term to them in 1887, but Paul Schebesta (1933) introduced the term formally, replacing an older term, *Negrillo*. An alternative term, such as *forest people*, while at first preferable to pygmy, inadvisedly attaches to a people an essentialized place. (What happens when pygmies move out of the forest? or when the forest recedes?) While awaiting a more neutral alternative, or at least a time when *pygmy* will be free of pejorative connotations, it is preferable to use the term each group uses for itself (Efe, Mbuti, Twa, Baka, BaAka, and others), reserving pygmy for general use.

The BaAka whom I came to know best in Centrafrique live near Bagandou, a rural community in the Lobaye region south of Mbaïki, crossing the border with the Republic of the Congo. The Bagandou have a long-standing, hereditary exchange relationship with the BaAka of the region. Various terms have been used to characterize this relationship—*clientship, symbiosis, parasitism, servitude* (Bahuchet 1985:554–555). These conceptions betray the complexity and variability of relationships between pygmies and their neighbors across equatorial Africa. The BaAka term for Bagandou villagers and other Africans is *milo* (pl. *bilo*). By itself, the term simply designates nonpygmy dark-skinned Africans, whom BaAka see as separate and distinct from themselves. When I refer generally to non-BaAka Africans, I use either *milo* (*bilo*), or Turnbull's term *villagers*.

BaAka dances: *mabo* and *dingboku*

During my initial research (1987–1989), I became familiar with, and participated in, the current repertory of BaAka hunting dances and women's dances in the Bagandou area (Kisliuk in preparation). I spent most of my time living with one particular

FIGURE 3 The
theme of *"Makala,"*
the basic melody,
from which spring
variations, elabora-
tions, and counter-
melodies.

Ee yn ee yn Ma — ka la eh (ah) ee yn na le le oh — ho ho

extended family, but I also traveled as far as the northern Congo to gain a sense of the flow and exchange of new *beboka* 'singing, dancing, drumming' (sing. *eboka*) coming in and out of the area. Below, I describe two of the BaAka dance forms (*beboka*) that I came to know well during that period.

A popular hunting dance

One of the most popular BaAka dances of the late 1980s is *mabo,* a hunting dance. Because it was new (new dances emerge every few years, some survive for generations, and others fade away), I was able to learn the songs. Whereas songs for older dances have been elaborated over the years to the point where the underlying melodic themes often completely drop away (though people still hear the themes in their minds), with new songs, people sing basic melodic themes from time to time, and therefore improvisations and elaborations are easier for newly initiated ears to recognize.

One of the most frequently performed songs at the time is one I call *"Makala,"* the name of an unknown person, probably a deceased BaAka child from the Congo. (BaAka do not actually name their songs, as they have no occasion to objectify them in that way.) I learned to recognize a basic "theme" of *"Makala"* by chance. I was walking along a path with some BaAka teenagers, who suddenly sang out the theme in isolation. I then recognized that theme and others during dances, when I would hear a whole chorus of singers elaborating.

During a dance in my home camp, several young women gathered by the recorder to play with the level-indicator lights by singing into the microphone. This playful moment makes their various improvisations easier to hear. The basic theme of *"Makala,"* as transcribed into conventional Western notation (figure 3), shows interlocked and yodeled sections. You will be able to pick out this theme on the recording.

Each BaAka dance form has particular rhythms, played on at least two (often three) drums, made from hollowed tree trunks. On each end, each drum has a head made from antelope skin—a type of drum borrowed from Isongo villagers. One drummer will sit straddling a drum, while another man behind him might play a cross-rhythm with a stick on the side of the drum. The basic rhythm for *mabo,* played on the smaller of two drums, is a triplet pattern played steadily with alternating hands, thus implying a three-against-two feeling.

In the following excerpt, adapted from an ethnography of BaAka performance (Kisliuk 1991 and in preparation), I describe a particular instance of how it feels to dance and sing *mabo:*

TRACK 18

My senses tingled; I was finally inside the singing and dancing circle. The song was *"Makala,"* and singing it came more easily to me while I danced. As I moved around the circle, the voices of different people stood out at moments, affecting my own singing and my choices of variations. Ndami sang a yodeled variation (*mayenge*) I had not heard before. I could feel fully the intermeshing of sound and motion, and move with it as it transformed, folding in upon itself. This was different from listening or singing on the sidelines because, while moving with the circle, I became an active part of the aural kaleidoscope. I was part of the changing design inside the scope, instead of looking at it and projecting in.

The physical task of executing the dance step melded with the social interac-

dingboku   A dance performed by a line of women related by residential camp or clan

mabo   A hunting dance that was one of the most popular BaAka dances of the late 1980s

mokondi   General name for dances involving BaAka spirits

beboka   Singing, dancing, and drumming of the BaAka

tions of looking, listening, smiling, reacting, that kept us all dancing. Since our camp was built on a hill, it took extra effort to dance the full-soled steps while going up or down hill. Running the bottom of my foot inchwormlike across the ground required the sturdy support of all the muscles in my leg. All this while trying to stay loose enough to follow through with my whole body and keep up with the beat. As I continued to dance, trying to refine my step, I noticed more fully the inward and delicately grounded concentration of the movements, like the blue duiker (*mboloko*, a small antelope). Someone cried out "*Sukele!*" (an interpretation of the French *sucré* 'sweet').

Suddenly, a few people shouted rhythmic exclamations that suggested a shift to the *esime* (the intensified rhythmic section), and the singing stopped. Tina stepped into the center of the circle and walked in the opposite direction to the one in which we were dancing. He shouted "*Pipi!*" (imitating a carhorn), and the group answered "*Hoya!*" (an exclamation). He continued, "*O lembi ti?* 'Are we tired?'," and we answered "*O lembi (o)te!* 'We aren't tired!'" As the *esime* continued, people "got down" in their dancing, crying "heeya, heeya" repeatedly on the beat, and sometimes jumping forward with a scoot instead of stepping to the beat.

At one point, the women grabbed the shoulders of those in front of them in line, and began chugging ahead on the beat. I joined in, finding it hard to jump all the way up the hill while staying as close as possible to Ndoko, whose shoulders I held onto in front of me. Someone was behind me, I don't recall who, but she had to grab my waist because she could not reach my shoulders comfortably. It was unavoidably clear at this moment that I was bigger than everybody else.

A women's dance

Ongoing, informal negotiation and disputed expectations, as part of BaAka social dynamics, are highlighted in performance. An egalitarian sensibility, coupled with individual autonomy, make for a cultural climate of constant negotiation (Dumont 1986; Turnbull 1962; Moise 1992). In the context of BaAka women's dances, gendered wills intensify the social fray. *Dingboku* is a dance performed by women in a line (often several lines—of women related by residential camp or clan). They stand linked at the shoulder, and then step forward and back together (figure 4). The subject of *dingboku* is a celebration of women's sexuality, and some of the songs mock men. But only male BaAka play drums, and therefore drumming sometimes becomes a focus of tension during the women's dances—even in *dingboku,* which has no drum accompaniment.

In a performance I witnessed, Sandimba and Djongi (two women from my home camp), who knew the dance best, gestured cues to the other women, indicating how they should link up in line and how to proceed. For fifteen minutes within the hullabaloo of chatting, milling around, and extemporaneous drumming, they tried to establish two lines. Finally, throngs of men, and some women, stood aside to watch.

FIGURE 4   BaAka women dancing *dingboku*. Sandimba is at the end of the line, on the left.

When the second line of dancers was ready to begin, someone started a song, "*Ooh Leh.*" Short and syncopated, the phrases in this song established a driving beat, to which the women, in two lines, hopped percussively from foot to foot. The lines repeatedly approached each other and then separated. The line of less experienced dancers got tangled, and Sandimba called out, "*Hoya!*" a signal to end the song, and the group responded unanimously, "*Ho!*"

Then Sambala, a man, stepped in to try to reorganize the women, but they managed to get themselves in line and ready to continue. Sandimba introduced a slower, less syncopated song, emphasizing the dance beat; this intervention helped unify the company. The lines faced each other, an arm's length apart, and moved together as a unit across the space and back.

Several minutes later, after dancing energetically, the women were tired, and Sandimba called up a final, slower song. The lines faced each other and moved as a group across the space at close range, one line stepping forward, the other backward. This song had no words, only vocables (*eeya oh eeye*), with a lush interlock and harmonious overlap. The central melody, based on three descending phrases that form an asymmetrical repeating pattern, produced a gentle tension and cyclic drive. The performance coalesced now to a solid groove, the slowed stepping and lush harmonies making some of the women seem to fall into a dreamy, trancelike state.

Amid this euphoria, some drummers began to play *mabo* triplets in the background, but actually fell into time with *dingboku*. Maybe the drumming men wanted to participate in this mood, or else they hoped to move the event along into *mabo*. The effect, intentional or not, was to articulate a cross-rhythm that heightened the intensity of the moment.

BaAka responses to missionization

In 1989, some BaAka encountered Christian evangelism for the first time. The most concentrated episode began in late 1988, when American missionaries from the Grace Brethren Church, a fundamentalist sect based in Wonona Lake, Indiana, started a campaign to plant churches among the BaAka of the Bagandou region. This was my first significant encounter with missionaries too, and I was not sure how to react. I tried my best to keep an open mind, believing that most missionaries have good intentions, and often give in positive ways. Besides, I knew of many instances where missionized peoples reinterpret the lore of the missionaries, resulting in a spirited resistance to the "colonization of consciousness" (Comaroff and Comaroff 1989).

Komba   Creator god of the BaAka

gano   Traditional legends in which Komba,
the creator god, is a friend and caretaker

nzapa   The term for the Christian God in
the Sango language of Central Africa

BaAka in this region (with the Baka pygmies of Cameroon) recognize the creator god Komba, but they cite him mostly as a character in *gano*—traditional legends, in which Komba is a friend (*beka*) and caretaker (*kondja*). Otherwise, I did not hear people refer to Komba except in an occasional exclamation like "Komba's mother!" or, when someone's luck was down, "Komba is a bad person." But once I asked my friend Sandimba if Komba and *nzapa* (the Sango word used for the Christian God) were the same entity. She hesitated slightly, then answered they were. Linking Komba and *nzapa* had likely circulated to Sandimba from BaAka who had been exposed to an evangelist strategy of paralleling Christian beliefs as much as possible with indigenous ones, then "explaining" where indigenous beliefs go wrong.

The god dance

An earlier wave of Christian influence among local BaAka had started about a year before. Cousins from one family had migrated to the west, toward the town of Nola, where they were "converted" by Baptist missionaries. When these cousins came back to Bagandou to visit, they began convincing their relatives to take up *nzapa*. The idea slowly spread through the forest. In the camp where I was living, one evening after a *mabo* had ended, I saw Tina lead some men in a brief burst of preaching and hymn singing. They mixed songs and practices from various Christian sects observable in the village, calling all of it the god dance (*eboka ya nzapa*), and made up their own form of preaching; anyone could decide to play the role of preacher on the spur of the moment.

A common expression I heard while BaAka prayed was *ame* 'amen'. Diaka *ame* can be glossed as English 'me', and repeating "me" at the ends of phrases became part of their version of praying. BaAka children started singing songs about *nzapa* during their play, and a parent sometimes absentmindedly sang along *alleluia ame* 'alleluia, me'. Early one morning, Sandimba's boy Mbaka was distractedly singing in falsetto a song with the words *eeya, Malia, oh, na nzapa,* from a local Roman Catholic hymn. When I asked Sandimba what the song was about, she said it did not refer to anything, but was just a song heard around lately.

Nevertheless, during the following coffee harvest season (when many BaAka converged in temporary camps near Bagandou to help with the harvest), little by little rumors began to circulate that some BaAka thought dances like *mabo* were satanic (*ba sata*). Then suddenly some of the most ardent followers of *nzapa* refused to dance and started accusing other BaAka of being satanic. A split developed between those who had been mildly interested before, but were now becoming suspicious of the *nzapa* craze, and those who were following what an increasing number of *nzapa* fanatics were saying.

One weekend early in this heated controversy, I missed a big dance in a neighboring camp because I had to go to Bangui. When I returned, Sandimba told me that during that dance she had challenged the *nzapa* fanatics in front of everybody. She had told them:

> We BaAka have dances, like *elio* [a curing dance], like *monjoli, djoboko* [both older dances, associated with spearhunting], *mabo, monina* [another women's dance], all belonging to us, to BaAka. But *nzapa* is a *bilo* thing, it comes from far away. It's for the *bilo* because they can read and write, but a Moaka has never written the name of his friend [Komba]. . . . I yelled at them, "You are liars, big liars." I yelled, "Liars, liars!" and the others applauded. We haven't changed our decision.

Sandimba said that after her speech they danced both *mabo* and *dingboku,* but the *nzapa* followers refused to participate. In our camp that evening, we could hear the *nzapa* people having a "god dance" in the distance. From inside a hut, Sandimba grumbled: "That's the *nzapa* of monkeys." Always ready with witty insults, she continued, "They wear clothes like monkeys with tails. They're dirty and always wear the same dirty outfits that smell of urine"—instead of the white robes that some "real" Christians wear.

BaAka traditionally believe in ancestral spirit entities, *bedjo,* some of which are personalized and belong to families, and others of which are more general and nameless (Hewlett 1986:92). As proprietors (*bakondja*) of the forest, *bedjo* play a role in the success of the hunt. Many of the rituals and protocols around the hunt focus on securing their help (Bahuchet 1985:451). Related to the *bedjo* are *mokondi.* Most BaAka understand *mokondi* to be a grouping of ancestral *bedjo* connected to a dance form efficacious for the hunt, or for the purpose of redressing social conflicts within the hunting group. *Mokondi* is also a general name for dances involving any of these spirits, including *edjengi,* a category of spirits. (Elanga, my friend and a respected elder, explained to me that for the dance *edjengi,* each family has its personalized *bedjo*). One day, my youthful friend Ndanga was sitting next to me looking at a religious pamphlet and casually praying in Sango, reproducing actions he had seen among village Christians and thinking, perhaps, that I might approve of his efforts. To his mumbled monologue, he added the word *Christo.* When I asked him what *Christo* is, he said it is a spirit (*edjo*).

The firstfruits of Balabala's work

The most focused evangelical activity of this period was sponsored by the Grace Brethren Church. I had heard that this project was led by an American woman known locally as Balabala. Balabala devoted much of her energy—in the form of brief but intense appearances—at Dzanga, a permanent BaAka settlement west of the area where I was spending most of my time. As yet unaware of any details, I set out to visit Dzanga—to compare *beboka* repertories, and to get a sense for the choices BaAka in different areas were making in response to missionization.

At Dzanga, I was shocked by what I saw. The BaAka there had stopped performing their traditional repertory of music and dance (such as *mabo* and *dingboku*). Whereas in neighboring areas BaAka had been hotly debating the value of what the Christians were saying, at Dzanga all of the BaAka had been convinced by Balabala and her Centrafrican evangelists that their own music, dance, and traditional medicine were satanic. BaAka at Dzanga told me proudly—assuming I would approve, since I am white, like Balabala—that they now performed only one kind of *eboka.* Now they would only sing hymns to the Christian god in church. These hymns were not in their own language, but in Sango, which many BaAka, especially women, do not understand.

The church at Dzanga was not quite finished. It consisted of support poles and the beginnings of a thatch roof, but rows of log seats were in place (figure 5). On

I saw the god dance as a means of addressing modernity. These BaAka were claiming any "otherness" that surrounded them and usually excluded them, and mixing it into a form they could define and control.

Sunday morning, the BaAka of Dzanga gathered in churchlike clothing, wearing it as close to the style of villagers as they could manage. One woman had a matching blouse, cloth, and head wrap in a bright green and white pattern. Other women were not so fancy, but covered their heads with an old cloth. Several men sat at the front of the enclosure: one wore a long, white Muslim gown (*bubu*) and huge sunglasses; another man, the choral director, wore jeans and a corduroy vest, and no shoes. The choir consisted of women and girls, who in enthusiastic harmony sang hymns in Sango.

A Moaka stood in front of the congregation. In Diaka, he told the story of Adam and Eve from Genesis, using the word "Komba" for "God," as he had likely been instructed to do. Another Moaka, sitting at the front of the church with a copy of the Bible, read a few words haltingly in Sango. A third man, the one wearing the sunglasses, sat next to the preacher with a second copy of the Bible, which he held upside down. The man who had been reading then proceeded to catechize the congregation, asking repeatedly "Who created us?" and they answered halfheartedly "Komba created us." He continued, "Where did we come from?" There was no answer, just confused murmuring. He repeated, "Where did we come from?" and a voice piped up, unsure, "From earth" (*sopo* 'ground, earth'). Then the choral director struck up another hymn, to the accompaniment of a homemade guitar—perhaps emulating Balabala, who plays guitar.

I had been traveling (by foot) with my longtime friend and assistant, Justin Mongosso of Bagandou. When the service was over, Justin asked if he could comment. Everyone stayed to listen, expecting, perhaps, that he would constructively critique their praying technique, as the evangelists do. But instead, he began by saying that he wondered what would happen now that they had stopped using their traditional medicine. Many of the listeners, especially the elders, nodded with concern. Where would they get treatment? There was no clinic anywhere nearby, Balabala was not providing care (we found at Dzanga an especially large clientele for our first aid), and praying was not going to cure them. Why were they abandoning their medicine? They answered that they worried that if they continued, they would die among bad spirits (*sata* and *goundou*). Gone were the vacant smiles of moments earlier. Brows were furrowed, and for the moment, people leaned forward in their seats, listening intently.

Three years later

In 1992, when I next returned to Centrafrique, I saw a somewhat different picture. At the Dzanga settlement, though BaAka were still rejecting BaAka song forms and dance forms, people had begun to significantly recontextualize the Grace Brethren Church material. The BaAka church was no longer standing. Apparently the *nzapa* leaders among them had traveled to Balabala's field school at another BaAka settlement, Moali, and those remaining at Dzanga had not bothered to maintain the church.

The evening of my arrival at Dzanga, the BaAka held a god dance similar to what I had seen years earlier at my home camp, but this one was more elaborate. The dancers, mostly children and teenagers, moved in a circle, using *motengene*-type steps with the singing style and drum rhythms of Bolemba pygmies. Bolemba recreational dances are also emulated by nonpygmy Bagandou teenagers in nearby villages (and by *zokela* in Bangui)—which is probably how these BaAka, in turn, became familiar with the style. Many adults stood by, some joining in the dancing, others watching enthusiastically and singing along. Grace Brethren songs were preceded and followed by Bolemba-style interpretations of hymns from various Christian sects represented in Bagandou village, including Baptist, Apostolic, and even Roman Catholic hymns. They not only blended all that into the same dance, but mixed in Afro-pop snippets in Lingala (from radio tunes from Zaïre and the Congo).

TRACK 19 Audio example 19 is an excerpt from this event. The man calling out the solo line sings an alleluia, and adds a few disconnected words in Sango; the chorus responds in Bolemba-style harmonies with an initial alleluia, followed by pygmy singing sounds, which jump large intervals on the syllables *oh* and *eh.*

Confused about this transition from hymns in church to dancing, I asked a man whether, as some claimed, Balabala had taught them this dance. He said yes, and when I asked if she actually dances, he answered in the affirmative, demonstrating by imitating her bouncing movements as she played the guitar to accompany hymns. Balabala and the Grace Brethren do not allow dancing in their religious practice, but since no one was present to enforce a European-style distinction between music and dance, the hymns had become the basis for a new dance form.

As I witnessed this performance, I saw the god dance as a means of addressing modernity. In an effort to reinvent themselves as competent in a changing world, these BaAka were claiming any "otherness" that surrounded them and usually excluded them, and mixing it into a form they could define and control. Three years earlier, the BaAka I had come to know best, unlike those at Dzanga, had been heatedly arguing the validity of the Christian material. But by 1992, the controversy had subsided. My old friend Djolo explained to me then that the god dance is just one among many *beboka*; they could dance their own dances and still pray to god. They had placed the god dance within a BaAka system of value, poised uneasily within a wider, dynamic repertory vying to define an emerging identity.

Though those BaAka most directly affected by the missionaries could be left without the tools to renew a solid sense of identity with which to construct a future, many BaAka have the resilience to use the missionaries' presence to their advantage. Vast distances, difficult terrain, widely varying reactions, and dynamic cultural trends help subvert the missionary influence. In the most positive possible scenario, the missionary effort will have given some BaAka the foreknowledge to face other challenges ahead—including the depletion of the forest by loggers and farmers, the diminishment of the supply of game, and state pressure to make pygmies conform to an official image of modernity.

CONCLUSION

Scholars, artists, journalists, missionaries, politicians, and profiteers have repeatedly placed African pygmies in a timeless cultural box. Each to a different purpose, and even in dialogue with each other, they have marked the forest people as utopian or backward, savage or sublime. At the same time, urban African bands like Zokela, hurtling into a realm of marketable worldbeat, have faced the prospect of being stripped of regional potency to survive.

The overlapping musical spheres described in this essay illustrate that categories like "traditional," "popular," and "modern" are metaphors for ways of seeing, defined by local politics and creative circumstances. This view of cultural processes can challenge categories that become oppressive if left unquestioned. In a flourishing and ever-changing expressive world, teenagers in Bagandou village enjoy performing the dances of their Bolemba pygmy neighbors, and those village children in turn inspire BaAka pygmies in the forest and *zokela* musicians in the city to interpret similar styles—all to different, though thoroughly modern, rooted, and relevant ends.

REFERENCES

Arom, Simha. 1978. *Anthologie de la Musique des Pygmées Aka.* 3 OCORA 558.526.27.28. LP disks and notes.

———. 1985. *Polyphonies et Polyrhythmies Instrumentales d'Afrique Centrale.* 2 vols. Paris: SELAF.

Bahuchet, Serge. 1979. "Notes Pour L'Histoire de la Region de Bagandou." In *Pygmées de Centrafrique: Etude Ethnologique, Historique, et Linguistique sur les Pygmées "Ba-binga" (Aka, Baka) du Nord-Ouest du Bassin Congolais,* ed. S. Bahuchet. Paris: SELAF.

———. 1985. *Les Pygmées Aka et la Forêt Centrafricaine.* Paris: SELAF.

Chernoff, John Miller. 1979. *African Rhythm and African Sensibility.* Chicago: University of Chicago Press.

Comaroff, Jean, and John L. Comaroff. 1989. "The Colonization of Consciousness in South Africa." *Economy and Society* 18(3):267–296.

Dumont, Louis. 1986. *Essays on Individualism.* Chicago: University of Chicago Press.

Hewlett, Barry. 1986. "The Father-Infant Relationship among Aka Pygmies." Ph.D. dissertation, University of California, Santa Barbara.

Kisliuk, Michelle. 1991. "Confronting the Quintessential: Singing, Dancing, and Everyday Life among Biaka Pygmies (Central African Republic)." Ph.D. dissertation, New York University.

———. In preparation. *"Seize the Dance!" Performance and Modernity among BaAka Pygmies.*

Lomax, Alan. 1976. *Cantometrics: An Approach to*

the Anthropology of Music. Berkeley: University of California Extension Media Center.

Moise, Robert. 1992. "'A Mo Kila!' (I Refuse!): Living Autonomously in a Biaka Community." M.A. thesis, New York University.

Mouquet, Eric, and Michel Sanchez. 1992. *Deep Forest*. Celine Music and Synsound (Dance Pool). Sony Music Entertainment (France) / Columbia Records DAN 4719762. Compact disk.

Schebesta, Paul. 1933. *Among Congo Pygmies*. London: Hutchinson.

Stone, Ruth M. 1982. *Let the Inside Be Sweet: The Interpretation of Music Event among the Kpelle of Liberia*. Bloomington: Indiana University Press.

Thompson, Robert Farris. 1989. "The Song That Named the Land: The Visionary Presence of African-American Art." In *Black Art: Ancestral Legacy: The African Impulse in African American Art*, 97–138. Dallas: Dallas Museum of Art.

Turnbull, Colin M. 1962. *The Forest People: A Study of the Pygmies of the Congo*. New York: Simon and Schuster.

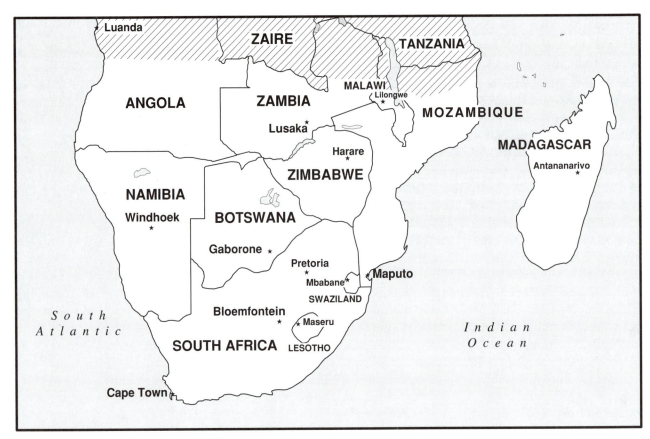

Southern Africa

Southern Africa

Music in southern Africa, as elsewhere on the continent, has long been associated with political power and royal musicians. During the colonial and apartheid eras, music provided a crucial means of communication for people with limited means of social expression. Today, popular music here still has important social and political implications.

Southern Africa: An Introduction
John E. Kaemmer

Indigenous Music of Southern Africa
Issues Concerning Indigeous Music in Southern Africa
Impact of the Wider World

Studies of southern Africa usually define their subject as the southern tip of the continent. However, to focus on the music requires special consideration of the northern boundary of the area, often considered the Zambezi River. This boundary does not include the area west of the Zambezi, nor does it help clarify matters by dividing Mozambique. The people of northern Mozambique are culturally related to central African peoples, and unlike other peoples of southern Africa, most of them have been influenced by the Arabic cultures of East Africa. Madagascar is geologically a part of southern Africa, but its culture, including its music, derived from cultures of Southeast Asia, whence came its languages and the ancestors of most of its inhabitants.

Modern political and economic divisions are also relevant to the definition of southern Africa. The Southern Africa Development Council consists of Angola, Botswana, Lesotho, Malawi, Mozambique, Namibia, Swaziland, Tanzania, Zambia, and Zimbabwe. Many of these countries include areas with cultural and linguistic characteristics of central or eastern Africa. A common feature of the countries of southern Africa is involvement with the mines of South Africa, where miners from all of them have migrated to work. The cooler climates in southern Africa enable people to raise cattle; but because of problems with tsetse fly and sleeping sickness in central Africa, cattle are not common there. The presence or absence of cattle relates historically to wealth and social stratification, which in turn affect musical activities.

Languages are another important criterion in delineating this area. All speakers of the Khoisan languages in the southwestern part of the continent are in southern Africa. All of the non-Khoisan languages are classed as belonging to the Niger-Congo branch of the Congo-Kordofanian family of languages (Greenberg 1970:30–38), more commonly referred to as Bantu. Following Guthrie's classification of Bantu languages (1948), southern Africa includes those ethnic groups in language zones R (southern Angola and Namibia), S (Venda, Sotho, and Nguni of South Africa), and T (Zimbabwe and southern Mozambique), plus those in parts of Zones M (southern Zambia) and N (southern Malawi). The Ovimbundu of Angola speak a southern Bantu language, even though they are not oriented to cattle raising, as are most speakers of southern African Bantu languages.

Musical criteria also play an important part in defining southern Africa. All groups south of the Zambezi sing with harmonies in octaves and/or fifths, but groups that sing in thirds are farther north (Jones 1959:222). Included in southern Africa for this article are the areas of the "south-central African tonal-harmonic belt," including southern Zambia, much of Zimbabwe, and central Mozambique (Kubik 1988:46). Harmonic patterns in these areas are distinct from the music farther north, and from the styles of most of the peoples of South Africa.

Since music is a part of human culture, the cultural traits of southern Africa are relevant to the study of music there. George Peter Murdock (1959) has not used the term "southern Bantu" to label any of the groups he describes, but he notes several features that distinguish southern Africans from his Central African Bantu group. Central African societies have traditionally been matrilineal in social organization, but most of the societies in southern Africa have been patrilineal. The societies included in southern Africa in this article are basically those listed in Murdock's chapters "Bushmen and their kin" (9), "Middle Zambezi Bantu" (47), "Southwestern Bantu" (48), "Shona and Thonga" (49), "Nguni" (50) and "Sotho" (51). A good working definition for general consideration of southern Africa is to include those areas south of the fifteenth parallel of southern latitude.

INDIGENOUS MUSIC OF SOUTHERN AFRICA

The peoples of southern Africa share many musical traits with other African peoples, particularly the Bantu. These include the ubiquity of polyrhythms, various degrees of influence of linguistic tones upon melody, and numerous instruments, particularly drums, plucked lamellophones, and xylophones. The prevalence of some sort of rattling or buzzing arrangement on instruments is another common feature. Also widespread is the use of cyclic form, with variations and extensive improvisation, both in music and in text.

Southern Africa shares with much of central Africa a history of hierarchical societies with similar traits. In southern Africa, as elsewhere in the continent, music has been important as a symbol of political power. The symbols by which kings maintained power included ritual fires, an important female secondary ruler, and the sponsorship of royal musicians. The history of these kingdoms is in part the history of colonialism. Many of these kingdoms were destroyed during interethnic fighting and the impact of Europeans in the last two hundred years, but many headmen of small groups maintain symbolic drums or xylophones. Music has played an important part in areas with puberty-initiation rites, particularly where control of the rituals is a mark of political strength.

Many peoples in southern Africa define music in terms of the presence of metered rhythm. This means that drumming alone is considered music, and chanting or speaking words is singing, so long as it is metrical. When the singing voice is used without rhythm, the resulting vocalization is not usually considered singing. Many of the groups have no word which would accurately be glossed as 'music'; most of them have distinct words for singing, for playing an instrument, and for dancing.

Languages are an important and fascinating part of the story of southern African music, but they will be dealt with here only as they affect music. Like other African languages, those of southern Africa are tonal, so the nature of the language tones restricts to some degree the freedom to move melodically. The languages of southern Africa are not so highly dependent upon tones as are the languages of West Africa, so the match of speech tone with melody is more a matter of aesthetics than comprehension. Among the Venda, singing adheres to the linguistic tones most closely at the beginning of phrases, and with rising more than falling melodic intervals; adherence to linguistic tones is stronger in the beginning line of a song than in later ones

One feature distinguishing southern Africa is that the musical bow is the major chordophone.

FIGURE I   A boy plays a gourd-resonated bow in southern Mozambique, Johannesburg, 1953.

(Blacking 1967:166–70). Studies of the musical effects of linguistic tones have been done by Jones (1959:230–251) and Rycroft (1971:223–224).

One feature distinguishing southern Africa is that the musical bow is the major chordophone. A few general comments on musical bows will enable the reader to follow more easily the discussions of bows found in the subareas. Musical bows commonly have one string, fastened with tension at each end of a curved stick, so the string makes a sound when put into motion. One of the basic differences between bows is how the string is caused to vibrate. It can be struck by something, usually a small stick, or it can be plucked by one finger, or by the thumb and index finger together. Indirect action on the string also puts it into vibration, including scraping a stick across notches carved into the bow (friction bow) or blowing onto a feather attached to a bow (*gora* or *lesiba*). Scraping the string, as in bowing any chordophone, has also been practiced in the area.

The sound of a bow is resonated in different ways. With a mouth bow, part of the bow is inserted in the player's mouth, and movements of the player's mouth and throat emphasize different overtones. With a gourd bow, the resonator is a gourd fastened to or held against the bow; the player can produce tunes by moving the gourd against his or her body, emphasizing different overtones by varying the volume of air resonating in the gourd.

Musical bows are made so that they can produce more than one fundamental tone. Sometimes, as with a braced bow, a thread links the string to the bow somewhere along the length of the string, making the string vibrate in two sections. Other bows produce different fundamentals as the player stops the string with a finger or an object (figure 1).

Southern African societies exchanged cultural and musical features far back in the past (Johnston 1970:95). The most accurate term for referring to this music is *indigenous*—a term applicable, for example, to the Khoisan adoption of Bantu lamellophones, but not to their use of the guitar. Though the following treatment of different groups gives the impression of distinct differences, the actual situation consists of ethnic boundaries that are frequently indistinct. The same is true of differences between musical traditions.

A survey is heavily dependent on the literature, and a problem in gaining an accurate view of the area is the extreme variability of sources. Some ethnic groups have been thoroughly studied by people whose principal interest and skill lies in music and anthropology; many other groups have not been adequately described at all, or available descriptions focus on nonmusical matters. The varying ages of studies are also important, since the musical traits of societies studied fifty years ago may differ profoundly from the practices of those societies today.

Khoisan peoples

At the end of the 1400s, when Europeans first found the southern tip of Africa, that area was already inhabited by several diverse peoples. The pastoral groups in the area around the Cape of Good Hope were called Hottentots by the Europeans; the hunter-gatherers farther north were called Bushmen. Both of these peoples differ physically from the rest of the people in Africa. Their languages, which exploit several clicking sounds, have been classified as either click languages or Khoisan languages. The latter term comes from the names these people use for themselves: Khoi or Khoikhoi for the Hottentots, and San for the Bushmen.

In the late 1400s, the people who spoke Bantu languages were living farther to the north and east of the Cape, and were interacting with the Khoisan peoples. Archæological and linguistic evidence indicates that the Bantu-speaking peoples of southern Africa arrived there from the north within the last thousand years, and either overran or pushed aside the indigenous peoples (Phillipson 1985:208). Many of the Khoikhoi were enslaved by the European settlers, and eventually mixed with Europeans and workers brought from Asia to form what are now called the colored people of South Africa. Though the San were traditionally hunters and gatherers, they are increasingly becoming cattle herders and farmers.

The Khoikhoi

The Khoikhoi included four major groups: the Cape Hottentots, the Eastern Hottentots, the Nama (or Namaqua), and the Korana. These groups no longer exist; most of these people either disappeared or became assimilated into the colored population of South Africa. A few groups speaking dialects of Khoi languages are still found in Namibia. The musical practices of the Khoikhoi as recorded in early documents are important because of their influence on later developments. Many of their songs were reportedly based on a descending four-note scale, equivalent to D–C–A–G (Rycroft 1980a:730–731).

Among the major instruments of the Khoikhoi were musical bows, of which they played several types. Men played a braced mouth bow. Women played a longer bow, *kha:s.* Seated, a woman secured the instrument by one foot, resting its center on a hollow object serving as a resonator; she held the upper part of the bow near her face, touching it with her chin to obtain a different fundamental tone. She could also modify that tone by touching the center of the string (Kirby 1934:211–212).

The most notable Khoikhoi bow was the *gora,* used to accompany cattle herding. It consisted of a string that the player put into motion by forcefully inhaling and exhaling over a feather connecting the string to one end of the bow. Variations in the way it was blown would make the instrument bring out different tones of the harmonic series. The *gora* was borrowed by neighboring Bantu speakers (Kirby 1934:171–192).

Single-tone flutes were important to the Khoikhoi, especially the Nama and the Korana. These flutes were about 40 centimeters long, made from reeds with all the nodes removed, or from the bark of a particular root (Kirby 1934:139, 145). In either case, a plug was inserted in the bottom, which could be raised or lowered to modify the pitch. The flutes were played in ensembles for dancing, with each man sounding his note as needed to create a melody in hocket. Seventeenth-century descriptions indicate that men and women danced in separate, concentric circles; which sex danced on the inside varied from one group to another.

The Khoikhoi made drums by placing skins over their cook pots. The Europeans called this instrument a *rommelpot,* though the *rommelpot* in Europe is a type of friction drum (Kirby 1934:16).

The San

The San live in scattered places in Botswana, Namibia, and southern Angola. As

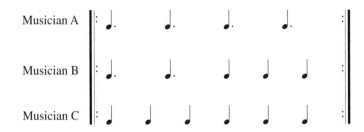

FIGURE 2   Rhythms played on the San group
bow (after Kubik 1970:29).

hunter-gatherers, they did not have complex musical institutions. Much of their music was for self-expression, dealing with everyday topics, such as the success of the hunt. Songs also accompanied curative dances, in which men would go into a quivering trance representing internal heat, which could cure the sick (Katz 1982).

In the 1960s, the San in the Cuito-Cuanavale area of southeastern Angola and nearby areas of Namibia were the only ones who could give a clear idea of their indigenous musical styles (Kubik 1970:12). Their most widely used indigenous instrument was the bow; classifiable in four musical-bow complexes, of which three used the common hunting bow. The player resonated the bow by putting one end in his or her mouth, resting the other on the ground. By changing the shape of the mouth, the player emphasized certain overtones, creating melodic interest. By stopping the string, the player obtained different fundamental tones. Because the bows were long, they were stopped near the end, thus producing two fundamental tones, separated by intervals of a second, a minor third, or a major third (Kubik 1970:22, 26). The bows were also used with a gourd resonator, not fastened to the bow, but held against it; the gourd was moved in contact with the bare chest, causing a variety of overtones to resonate.

A third tradition, the group bow, involved three individuals who played on one bow (Kubik 1970:27–33). The bow was laid with one end on the ground and the center resting on an upended pan or gourd, serving as a resonator. The first player (A) secured the bow with his foot, and held a piece of gourd with which he stopped the string at either of two places, depending on the song; with a short stick, he beat the string in steady triplets. The second performer (B), at the upper end of the bow, played an irregular rhythm with his stick, with duplets on one part of the string and triplets on another. The third player (C), sitting between the other two, beat the stick in duple rhythms (figure 2). The name of the instrument when used this way was *kambulumbumba*. The same technique was used by children among surrounding Bantu-speakers. For a variety of reasons, including the name of the instrument, it is probable that this bow was originally a Bantu instrument. The San also have a tradition of mouth-resonated friction bows made especially for musical purposes with a palm leaf ribbon, rather than with a string (Kubik 1970:33–35).

The musical bow produces multipart music in the interplay between the fundamental tone and overtones. San vocal multipart music becomes a type of counterpoint as singers are encouraged to sing individual variants on a basic line. Singers also employ techniques of canon and imitation, singing with few words (England 1967:59–61).

In San multipart music, tones that can be used interchangeably or occur simultaneously are always in the same harmonic series (Kubik 1970:66). Many San songs have a tetrachordal structure, in which two tones at the interval of a fifth are used with another fifth, placed a second or a third above the first pair. The most common occurrence of this involves the use of the first, second, fifth, and sixth scalar tones (*do, sol, re, la*). This structure would naturally result from playing two bows together if they were tuned a second or a third apart.

A prehistoric use of hunting bows for music making is indicated by a San rock painting whose location is now unknown (Kirby 1934:193). The painting shows one person playing seven bows lined up on the ground.

The San also use raft zithers (*kuma*) and a form of stamping tube (*bavugu*) (Kubik 1970:35–44). The latter instruments were made with three gourds or mock oranges assembled one above the other and held with wax. A hole was cut through all three, which were then beaten against the upper thigh with the top of the instrument struck with the hand. This instrument was played only by women, who were reticent about showing it to the researchers. It probably had something to do with female initiation or fertility (Kubik 1970:42).

The San are using more and more of the musical resources of the people surrounding them. In addition to the group bow, they have adopted the plucked lamellophone (*likembe* or *mbira*).

The San sing with multipart and hocket techniques. San singing differs from responsorial singing elsewhere in Africa because San soloists in a group interweave their singing without necessarily responding to each other (Kubik 1970:53). When players of a mouth-resonated bow begin to sing, they must temporarily stop bringing out melodic overtones with the mouth, so the alternation of vocal and instrumental sections results in a kind of two-part form. Both Khoikhoi and San yodeled as they sang. Yodeling is not commonly found in Africa, other than among the Shona of Zimbabwe.

Nguni peoples

Nguni is a term scholars use to denote the southernmost Bantu-speaking people in Africa. That they interacted extensively with earlier non-Bantu inhabitants of southern Africa is shown by the fact that unlike Bantu farther north, they have clicks in their languages.

Two Nguni groups, the Xhosa and Zulu, constitute a major part of the indigenous population of South Africa. The Xhosa were closest to the Cape of Good Hope, and at least some of them settled among Khoisan peoples and mixed with them (Dargie 1991:33). They were also the first Bantu-speakers to come into conflict with Europeans as the latter spread beyond the cape. These conflicts weakened them, so they did not form strong kingdoms as did the Zulu and Swazi, their neighbors to the northeast. The Zulu are descendants of clans united into a nation by Chaka, who ruled from 1816 to 1828 (Joseph 1983:54). They fought against the Boers and the British, finally being defeated in 1879. The Swazi were also organized as a kingdom, eventually becoming a British protectorate, and later the independent nation of Swaziland.

During the early 1800s, the Boers emigrated north to escape the English, and the indigenous peoples became involved in wars with the whites and with each other. Various groups separated themselves from the Zulu kingdom and fled, conquering others as they went. A branch of the Nguni went north, to become the Ndebele of northern Transvaal and Zimbabwe. People now called Ngoni invaded what is now Malawi, mixing with other peoples there. The Shangaan (or Shangana) in Mozambique, and along its border with Zimbabwe and South Africa, are also descendants of the Zulu dispersion. Thus, the ethnic configuration in these countries is complex, with traits of Nguni culture often appearing in non-Nguni contexts.

General traits of Nguni music

Several features typify Nguni musical culture. In communal musical events, choral

Among Xhosa women and girls, a form of overtone singing occurs. This technique involves singing a low fundamental tone while shaping the mouth to emphasize different overtones.

singing is the most important form of music. Singing is considered best when done with an open voice, "like the lowing of cattle" (Tracey 1948b:46). Singing is polyphonic and responsorial, with the divergence of parts occurring as phrases begin and end at different points. The Zulu language causes sung tones to be lowered in pitch when the vowels follow voiced spirants and stops except the phoneme /b/ (Rycroft 1975–1976:44).

Another typical feature is the traditional prominence of the musical bow. Scales are based on the natural tones of the musical bow, often omitting the seventh. Nguni musical cultures have diverse scalar systems; the seventh is often missing, and perfect fourths and fifths are often important (Rycroft 1971:230). The use of semitones may be due to the traits of the bow (Rycroft 1971:218–219). Among the Nguni people, a "tonality shift" or "tonality contrast" is important (Rycroft 1971:235). This feature is noteworthy farther north, and would seem consistent with the practice of using the overtone series from nonidentical fundamentals, as is often done with the musical bow.

Though drums are not commonly used in many Nguni traditions, they are known. The friction drum and double-headed drum are used in some rituals (Joseph 1983:67).

Among the Zulu, the major form of communal music consists of choral dance songs (Rycroft 1975–1976:63; Joseph 1983:60). This form of communal music occurs in many rituals, including puberty ceremonies, weddings, and divinations (Joseph 1983:64–77). Drinking songs and work songs are also in this style. Men's praise poetry is performed without meter; therefore it is not considered music, though the clearly pitched singing voice is used (Rycroft 1980b:201).

Individualistic forms of song, such as lullabies and songs for personal enjoyment, were traditionally accompanied on the musical bow—a practice that has long been declining. One of the musical bows used by the Zulu was the *ugubhu,* an unbraced gourd-resonated bow more than a meter long. Another bow, the *umakhweyana,* was braced near the center and gourd resonated; it is thought to have been borrowed from the Tsonga, to the north (Rycroft 1975–1976:58). Braced bows have the main string divided in different ways, so the differences in the fundamental tones range from a whole tone to a minor third.

Among Xhosa women and girls, a form of overtone singing, *umngqokolo,* occurs (Dargie 1991). This technique involves singing a low fundamental tone while shaping the mouth to emphasize different overtones. This kind of singing is said to sound somewhat like a performance on the *umrhubhe,* a bow, played by scraping a string with a stick. The style may have developed from a practice of small boys: they impale a beetle on a thorn, put it in their mouths, and isolate various overtones produced by the insect's buzzing (Dargie 1991:40–41).

The Xhosa have a quivering dance (Rycroft 1971:215), which calls to mind the curative dances of the San.

Single-tone flutes are found among the Zulu and Swazi. The latter use them during their first-fruit rituals. These flutes are long, tuned by means of plugs—as was the practice among the Khoikhoi (Kirby 1934:112–117).

Sotho peoples

Murdock included many ethnic groups in the Sotho cluster (1959:386–387), but in the ethnomusicological literature, only three major groups regularly appear: those living in Lesotho (the southern Sotho), those living in Botswana (the Tswana or Chwana, or western Sotho), and those living in South Africa (the Pedi, or eastern Sotho). The Sotho of Lesotho are a mixture of refugees who in the mid-1800s were united into a state. Their leader, Moshoeshoe I, asked for missionaries in 1833, and sought status for his kingdom as a British protectorate in 1868. This action led to strong European influences and to Lesotho's becoming politically, but not economically, separate from South Africa. This branch of Sotho is the only one whose language incorporates clicks from the Khoisan languages (Adams 1974:387).

The Sotho peoples share many musical features with the Nguni, such as the importance of choral singing (*mahobelo*) and the use of one-stringed chordophones and reed flutes. The Tswana, who originally lived on open plains with few trees, have a strong tradition of choral singing. Their vocal music is primarily pentatonic (Mundell 1980:89). Unlike Nguni musical textures, the Sotho responsorial parts do not often overlap.

Dancing to instrumental sounds may be a twentieth-century development in Lesotho (Adams 1974:142), but not with other Sotho peoples. The Sotho outside Lesotho have customarily performed flute dances. Perhaps the people of Lesotho lacked such dances because they were drawn from many ethnic backgrounds. Reed-flute dances occurred among the Tswana, possibly adopted from the Khoikhoi (Kirby 1934:146). Reed-flute ensembles are among the prerogatives of a chief. Though the Sotho in Basutoland do not have the flute dances, they do have flutes, which resemble those of the Nguni. Pedi boys also use a one-tone flute, but when they play it, they whistle with their lips while they inhale (Kirby 1934:90).

The southern Sotho have adapted an instrument from the Khoi *gora*. They call it *lisiba,* from their word *siba* 'feather'; it may well be called an air-activated stick zither (Adams 1974:89, 109). Both inhaling and exhaling, players cause air to move past the feather; they produce most overtones while inhaling. Exhaling often produces laryngeal sounds, except during an expert's performance. Changes of pitch can be caused by changes in breath pressure and changes in the shape of the oral cavity (Kirby 1934:188–191).

The songs the southern Sotho sing with the *lesiba* have a special name, *linon'.* The instrument is connected with cattle herding, as it was among the Khoikhoi, and the Sotho use its sounds to control their cattle (Adams 1974:111). The feather from the instrument ideally comes from the cape vulture, the bird the instrument represents.

Sotho peoples use rattles made from cocoons and animal skins, but not from gourds (as used by people farther north). Pedi cocoon rattles are worn by women only; their dance skirts, made of reeds, rattle during dancing (Kirby 1934:10).

Southeastern African peoples

Several groups in southeastern Africa appear to have lived in the same area for several hundred years. These include the Venda in the eastern Transvaal, the Chopi in southern Mozambique, and the Shona between the Limpopo and Zambezi rivers. The Thonga include several groups formed when the Zulu wars of the early 1800s sent

makhololo   Rulers of the Venda who are distinguished from common people

tshikona   National music of the Venda produced by an ensemble of one-pitch pipes
played in hocket

bepha   Among the Venda and the Tsonga,
collective visits by youthful performers sent
by one chief to another

conquerors and refugees eastward into the coastal lowlands; these groups include the
Tswa, the Ronga, the Tsonga, and the Shangaan (Tracey 1980:662).

Because the Zulu dispersion brought many Zulu-speakers into southeastern
Africa, the area is now characterized by a mixture of languages. Many of these languages (and Shona) pronounce sibilant fricatives, /z/ or /s/, with something of a
whistle. The Venda have been influenced by the Sotho, but they share many aspects
of language and culture with the Shona.

The musical cultures of southeastern Africa emphasize instruments, rather than
choral singing. The separation between the two parts of responsorial forms is more
distinct, and polyrhythms occur both in the accompaniment and in its relation to the
singing. Musical bows among the San and the Nguni are usually played with fundamentals a second or a third apart, but Shona and Tsonga bows usually have fundamentals a fourth or fifth apart. Southeast African single-toned flutes are played in
hocket, but they are constructed differently from those of the San and Nguni.
Instead of having plugs for tuning, the nodes are retained in the bamboo or the reeds,
and the instruments are tuned by being shortened or by receiving extra sections.

The musical cultures of southeast Africa have several instruments in common,
including a variety of drums, mbiras (lamellophones), and xylophones. Since the
Shona are the topic of another article in this volume, the treatment given here will
focus on other southeastern Bantu, and will include comparisons with the Shona.

The Venda

The Venda, living in a mountainous area of northeastern South Africa, submitted to
European rule in 1899. When John Blacking did research among them (in the
1950s), they were still performing many of their traditional musical events. They distinguish sharply between commoners and rulers (*makhololo,* a term used in western
Zambia for the Sotho conquerors of the Lozi).

The Venda are believed to have crossed the Limpopo river from the north several
hundred years ago; their language and culture closely resemble those of the Karanga
branch of Shona. Though Venda musical skills are widespread, public performances
require some form of payment. The Venda assume that any normal person is capable
of performing music well (Blacking 1973:34).

The national music of the Venda is the *tshikona,* an ensemble of one-pitch pipes
played in hocket. Traditionally, men played pipes, and women played drums. Each
chief had his *tshikona,* which would perform on important occasions, such as first-
fruit ceremonies. The chiefs vied with each other to create the best ensemble, sometimes using it to further their own political ends. Venda men working in the mines of
South Africa perform the dance there, doing their own drumming. The tonalities of
tshikona music are the most important feature of Venda tonal organization (Blacking
1965:182).

Tshikona is not the only music sponsored by chiefs. The Venda share with the

Tsonga the practice whereby each chief sends youthful performers on collective visits (*bepha*) to other chiefs to perform and bring back gifts. Thus, each chief succeeds in building up a corps of devoted followers (Blacking 1965:35). Among the Tsonga, such performing groups are competitive (Johnston 1987:127).

The nature of musical sponsorship means that little social commentary is expressed through song. However, in individual musical performances, people may express their feelings and frustrations, including criticism of other people, without fear of negative consequences (Blacking 1965:28).

The Venda have a wide variety of instruments. Differential tuning—some instruments using heptatonic scales, and others using pentatonic scales—indicates different origins for different instruments. The pipes used in *tshikona* are ideally made from bamboo from a secret grove in eastern Venda country, and are heptatonic within a range of three octaves; metal and plastic pipes are also used. The Venda also play reed pipes, pentatonically covering two octaves.

Venda instruments include a twenty-one-key xylophone, the *mbila mutondo* (nearly obsolete), plus a twenty-seven-key lamellophone, the *mbila dzamadeza*. They also have a friction bow (*tshizambi*), obtained from the Tsonga, and the *dende*, a braced gourd-resonated bow. The *ng'oma* is a huge pegged drum with four handles, played with *tshikona* and in rainmaking rituals (Kirby 1934:34, 38).

The Venda have borrowed some of their musical practices from neighboring peoples. Circumcision schools with their related music have come from the Sotho. These schools are sponsored by individuals, who from them gain financial and political advantages. Venda possession cults have come from the Karanga, one of the Shona groups to the north.

An important feature of Venda music is the "principle of harmonic equivalence" (Blacking 1967:168). Though the rise and fall of tones in various verses may differ objectively, the Venda consider them the same, so long as the notes involved are within the same harmonic series. By substituting pitches in this way, the Venda can allow for variations in the rise and fall of linguistic tones in different parts of the text.

The Chopi

One of the most important musical traditions in southern Africa is that of the Chopi. They seem to have inhabited their lands, just east of the mouth of the Limpopo, since the early 1500s (Tracey 1948a:122), and they were not subjugated by the Zulu invasions of the 1800s. To accompany dance cycles (*ngodo*), they use large ensembles of xylophones.

The ideal Chopi ensemble consists of xylophones (*timbila*) in five sizes, covering a range of four octaves. The slats are fixed to the framework, each with a resonator attached below it (figure 3). Originally the resonators were gourds, each being

FIGURE 3   Traditional mime dance performance with Chopi xylophones, Johannesburg, 1953.

The Tsonga believe that individuals can become possessed of evil spirits of people from outside ethnic groups, usually people thought to have died outside their home territory.

matched to resonate best with the slat to which it was attached. Carefully checking the tuning of these xylophones by using a set of tuning forks and asking the players which fork most closely matched each slat resulted in a scale that approximated an equidistant heptatonic scale (Tracey 1948a:124).

Each chief formerly sponsored a xylophone ensemble. The lyrics often related to popular social concerns, and could criticize wrongdoing. To keep the messages up to date, new compositions were created every few years, with the lyrics created before the music. A complete dance cycle, lasting about forty-five minutes, had nine to eleven movements.

The Tsonga

The Tsonga formerly inhabited the coastal lowlands of southern Mozambique. Pressed by the Zulu wars, they moved to the eastern Transvaal. They now live south of the Venda, or interspersed with them.

The Tsonga share many musical practices with their neighbors, particularly the Shona and the Venda. They have a mouth-resonated braced bow (*chipendana*), which resembles the Shona *chipendani* in having a thick handle carved onto the center of the bow. Both groups use a friction bow (Tsonga *xizambe,* Shona *chizambi*). Instead of a string, these bows employ a palm leaf ribbon; it can be stopped in as many as four places by one player's fingers, and the player's mouth brings out a variety of overtones. When two bows are played in duet, they are tuned a fifth apart (Johnston 1970:86). In playing this bow, melodic notes are sometimes displaced an octave higher, so they will not be in the range of feebly heard low notes—a form of harmonic equivalence. Mnemonic syllables help teach *xizambe* rhythms, and indicate the rhythmic complexity found in other Tsonga music (Johnston 1970:83).

With the Shona, the Tsonga believe that individuals can become possessed of evil spirits of people from outside ethnic groups, usually people thought to have died outside their home territory. The Tsonga become possessed of spirits of Zulu or Ndau origin. Rituals are designed to rid these individuals of the spirits, using music bearing a resemblance to the musical styles of the Zulu or the Ndau people. The quasi-Zulu songs are pentatonic with the *mandhlozi* rhythm, in rather straightforward duple time; the quasi-Ndau songs are heptatonic with a triplet drumming the *xidzimba* rhythm (Johnston 1972:10). The Shona become possessed with spirits of the Ndebele, or of the light-skinned traders who formerly connected them with the Zambezi valley. The Shona traditionally value possession by ancestral spirits, and rituals for these other spirits tend to emphasize dealing with the spirit properly, rather than exorcising it.

The national dance of the Tsonga, the *muchongolo,* is known in the eastern part of Zimbabwe as the *muchongoyo.* It represents the actions of warriors in battle, and features asymmetrical rhythms.

Like all southeastern Bantu peoples, the Tsonga have a variety of drums: the *xigubu,* a double-headed drum, made of metal containers; the *ndzumba,* used for puberty school; and the *ng'oma,* for beer drinks. *Ncomane,* a type of tambourine, are used for rituals of exorcism. Drumming is also taught by the use of mnemonic syllables. Drums are used in communal music associated with specific events.

The Tsonga have instruments that they do not share with the Shona. They use a three-hole transverse flute (*xitiringo*), a mouth-resonated cane bow (*mqangala*), a large gourd-resonated braced bow (*xitende*), and a ten-slat xylophone (*mohambi*) (Johnston 1971:62).

The Sena and the Nyungwe

In the Shire and Zambezi river valleys of southern Malawi and central Mozambique live several groups whose culture is seldom classed as southern African, but whose music is closely related to that of the southeastern area as a part of Kubik's "southcentral African tonal-harmonic belt." The most prominent traditions in this area are Sena xylophones (*valimba*) and zithers (*bangwe*), and Nyungwe reed-pipe dances. As a result of many peoples' flights from civil war during the 1980s in Mozambique, some of these traditions have been studied in southern Malawi.

The xylophones of the Sena use the musical structure characteristic of Shona mbiras, but some features indicate that the tuning of the instrument is intended to be equiheptatonic. Andrew Tracey found a wide discrepancy in the tuning of an instrument he was studying, but he also noted that the musicians cared little what tone they started their songs on—an indication of equidistant tuning (1991:88). The tuning of the *bangwe* was closer to equiheptatonic, as are the tunings of Sena lamellophones (*malimba*) (van Zanten 1980:109).

Nyungwe reed-pipe dances are of two types: *nyanga* have only one instrumental tune, with which singers improvise their parts; *ngororombe* have many different tunes played on the pipes. These dances differ from Sotho flute dances in that each performer has two to five pipes. These dances are performed for enjoyment, including when performers are hired for weddings, funerals, or parties. The music follows the chordal sequence typical of mbira music of the Shona. The rhythmic structure is similar also, with twenty-four-pulse or forty-eight-pulse segments. Male players alternate a sung note, a blown note, and an inhalation. They also dance, and are accompanied by a lead singer and a women's chorus (Tracey 1971).

Middle Zambezi peoples

To the north of the Zambezi River in Zambia are several ethnic groups culturally considered a part of southern Africa: the Tonga live in the area bordering the river to the east of Victoria Falls; the Ila live farther to the northwest, along the Kafue River; still farther west are the Lozi and the Nkoya, groups that have consistently maintained stratified societies, with kings and royal musical ensembles.

The Ila and the Tonga

In the 1800s, both the Ila and the Tonga, particularly the latter, suffered from raids by the Lozi and the Ndebele. As a consequence, they no longer have symbolic African kingdoms within the modern state. Their musical practices relate more to communal events and individual enjoyment.

In the 1930s, Arthur M. Jones found many types of songs among the Ila and the Tonga. It is important to these people that individuals, both young men and young women, compose songs that are distinctively theirs. Some songs sung on informal occasions are specific to each sex: *impango* for females, and *ziyabilo* for males.

Three kinds of songs were sung for dancing, specific ones for the *cin'ande* (a dance for young people) and the *mucinko* (a dance for young women), and others for

ngongi Double bells, which can be used only by royal ensembles of the Lazi and Nkoya

kuomboka A ceremony the Lozi perform to mark the retreat from the floodplain as the river rises seasonally

dances involving all ages. Other kinds of song include the *mapobolo* for slow, gentle singing; the *mapobaulo,* formerly used for fighting; and the *zitengulo,* for mourning (Jones 1949:14–19).

Among the Ila, who were less susceptible to raids, chiefs controlled the performance of the double-flange-welded clapperless bells resembling those of West Africa. In seclusion during puberty, girls used to play horns. Flutes were used to call cattle.

The Ila have two types of lamellophones: the larger (*ndandi*), with fourteen keys, and the smaller (*kankobela*), with about eight (Jones 1949:28). The *ndandi* resembles the instruments of Lozi commoners and the Nkoya (Brown 1984:378). Ila xylophones are tuned to the same notes as the *ndandi* (Jones 1949:30). The keys of the *kankobela* and the lower eight keys of the Lozi xylophone (*silimba*) contain the same tones as the *kalimba* that Andrew Tracey considers the "original African *mbira*" (Kubik 1988:64–65).

The Lozi and the Nkoya

The Lozi (also called Barotse, formerly Luya) and the Nkoya are neighbors along the Zambezi near the Zambian border with Angola. Both have a strong monarchy, whose leaders are thought to have come from the Lunda kingdoms in Zaïre. The Lozi inhabit the floodplain, where annual runoff from the rainy season brings silt that enriches the soil; the Nkoya inhabit the hills, depending less on agriculture and more on livestock and hunting. The richness of the soil has led to differences in the wealth of the two groups—differences that influence the relationship of their royal families and their musical practices (Brown 1984).

In 1840, the Lozi were conquered by the Kololo, a Sotho group; they freed themselves in 1868. In the late 1800s, their king negotiated for his kingdom status as a British protectorate. This status helped keep the kingdom intact; in fact, both the king and the royal musicians received salaries from the colonial government (Brown 1984:63). The Lozi language is a mixture, basically Southern Bantu Luyana with heavy borrowing from Sotho. The Nkoya have a Central Bantu language.

In both groups, royal music is distinct from commoners' music. Royal ensembles, consisting of a xylophone and three drums, always accompany the king and symbolize his status. Only the chiefs can use double bells (*ngongi*)—a usage common in West Africa, but usually found farther south only in archaeological excavations. Unlike most xylophones, Lozi and Nkoya xylophones are played by only one person each. To facilitate being carried in processions, each instrument is secured by straps around its performer's neck, held away from his body by a bowed piece of wood. The drums used in royal ensembles include the *ng'oma* (the most important one), which has tuning paste added to the head to deepen its sound. The other two drums are double-headed pegged drums; they have higher pitches than the *ng'oma,* with a buzzer arrangement; the *ng'oma* player does the major improvisations (Brown 1984: 126–128).

Instruments are not the only feature that distinguishes royal music from commoners' music. Linguistic distinctions are important: Lozi royal musicians sing in Luyana, the archaic language, but commoners sing in Lozi (Brown 1984:393). Nkoya beliefs concerning sources of music help strengthen the differences of status between royalty and commonalty. The Nkoya believe that spirits taught royal music to the people, but nonroyal music is not of divine origin; royal dances are more restrained than those of commoners (Brown 1984:141–142, 472).

Music also highlights the differences between the Lozi and the Nkoya: Nkoya instruments are pitched higher (Brown 1984:358). The Lozi have a special kind of music, *lishoma,* which they consider their national music (Brown 1984:329). Lozi songs concern cattle, including raids and conquest; Nkoya royal songs emphasize death and dying (Brown 1984:44, 170). Lozi texts are the more detailed and organized (Brown 1984:221).

Lozi xylophones usually have eleven keys, with the lower three separated by thirds. The other keys approximate the diatonic scale, but with a flat third and no seventh. The vocal range is a fourth or less, but that may be simply the nature of certain songs. The songs are polyrhythmic, with certain types of songs having sixteen-pulse units and others having twelve-pulse units; the latter type facilitates duple and triple rhythmic mixes (Brown 1984:407–427, 434).

Music plays a big part in an important Lozi ritual, the *kuomboka,* a ceremony that occurs as the people retreat from the floodplain to higher ground when the river rises. An important feature of this ceremony is the royal barge, which carries the king to his palace on higher ground. In his entourage is the *maoma,* the national drum. It is unusually large, about a meter in diameter. Its head is painted with dots, and its side bears carvings of human and animal figures. Only royal men play it. During the *kuomboka,* the ancient Luyana language is used. After it come two days of dances: the *liwale* for women and the *ng'omalume* for men (Brown 1984:326). The latter includes dancing to drumming without singing (Brown 1984:30–41). Because the Nkoya do not live on a floodplain, their major ritual is a first-fruits ceremony, the *mukanda* (Brown 1984:271).

Lozi music is not limited to royal ensembles. Music called *makwasha* is sung by everyone. It deals with various subjects, including hunting, and also serves for paddling canoes. It is played on fifteen-key lamellophones (*kahanzi*), with lower keys tuned like royal xylophones (Brown 1984:159).

Southwestern Bantu peoples

The Bantu-speakers living in southern Angola and northern Namibia are classed as Southwestern Bantu (Murdock 1959:369–374). The major groups in this area are the Ovimbundu in central Angola, and the Ovambo and Herero in Namibia. Information on the music of these groups is sketchy, largely because the political climate has not been conducive to research by outsiders. Smaller, related groups in southern Angola include the Humbi. Gerhard Kubik made a short visit there in 1965, from which he produced recordings and an article (1975–1976).

The Ovimbundu

The Ovimbundu appear to be Central Bantu, since they do not raise cattle, and they lack the almost mystical focus on cattle that typifies most of the people of southern Africa; however, they are the northernmost people who speak a Southern Bantu language. The railway passing through their area connects them economically and culturally with the copper belt of Zaïre and Zambia, and with South Africa. They may be transitional between the cultures to the north and those in the southwestern part of Angola (Kubik 1980:432).

The Ovambo share with other groups in this area a pluriarc (multiple bow lute), consisting of a board with five to eight curved sticks fastened to one end, and strings fastened from the ends of the sticks to the opposite end of the board.

The Ovimbundu once maintained a distinction between aristocrats and commoners, but it has weakened, reducing its effect on musical activities. A signal feature of the society is that for recreation, rituals, and court cases, each village has a central area, the *ocila,* from the word *okucila* 'to dance' (Childs 1949:26). The Ovimbundu danced most often during the full moon, and also at funerals. They had work songs and road songs, presumably for walking on their trading expeditions.

The Ovambo

The Ovambo live along the border between Namibia and Angola. They share with other groups in this area a pluriarc (multiple bow lute), consisting of a board with five to eight curved sticks fastened to one end, and strings fastened from the ends of the sticks to the opposite end of the board; South Africans called this instrument an Ovambo guitar. The Ovambo call an eight-stringed form of it *chihumba.* Kubik attributes the instrument to sources in northern Angola; Kirby suggested a possible historic relationship with a row of hunting bows depicted in a prehistoric cave painting (1934:243–244).

The Nkhumbi

The music of the Nkhumbi differs distinctively from the music of west-central Africa, especially regarding "vocal style and motional patterns" (Kubik 1975–1976:98). However, though most of the groups in southern Africa sing in octaves and fifths, the Nkhumbi sing and play the pluriarc in parallel thirds—a trait that tends to indicate a northern origin of the instrument.

It is not surprising that musical bows would be important among these people. They have a gourd-resonated bow (*mbulumbumba*), whose two fundamental tones are produced by increasing tension on the string, and by stopping it with the thumb (Kubik 1975–1976:103–104). Unlike the San *kambulumbumba,* this bow is played by one individual.

Two mouth-resonated bows differ in the way the bow is placed at the mouth. The *sagaya* is braced with a short thread, dividing the main string into two parts, giving fundamentals about a whole tone apart; it is loosely held across the mouth. The *ohonji* is a hunting bow, braced in the center to form "two not quite equal parts" (Kubik 1975–1976:102). Its end is pressed against the inside of the player's right cheek. Performers do not sing with it, but associate bow tunes with language. They play the bows so the paired fundamentals are a whole step apart.

Other musical instruments found by Kubik among the Nkhumbi were drums (including a friction drum), a pluriarc, gourd rattles, lamellophones, percussion sticks, and bullroarers. Performers in this area often accompany their instrumental music with various vocalizations.

The Herero

The Herero are a primarily pastoral people in northeastern Namibia, with some groups in Botswana. While women sing and clap, men dance. The Herero customarily sing dirges at funerals. New songs are composed by professional singers, often dealing with cattle or horses. During colonial wars with Germany (1903–1908), the Herero suffered a disastrous military defeat; crossing the desert as refugees, many perished. People still remember this experience, which they commemorate in their songs, especially those that concern death and mortuary rituals (Alnaes 1989).

ISSUES CONCERNING INDIGENOUS MUSIC IN SOUTHERN AFRICA

Several important theoretical questions about African music are raised by musical practices in southern Africa. One of the most complex issues is the tuning of musical instruments. Indications are that in southeast Africa, some xylophones and lamellophones are tuned with equiheptatonic scales. The widespread use of musical bows, however, has led in many places to tunings based on the harmonic series. The pitches of the tones of the equiheptatonic scale do not match the pitches defined by the harmonic series. Several reasons for the use of equiheptatonic tunings have been suggested, including origin in Southeast Asian musical practices (Jones 1964), and development from singing in thirds (Kubik 1985:35). Another possibility is that, like the tempered scale (whose pitches are also equidistant), it provides a way of being able to sing at any convenient pitch level without having to retune an instrument.

The nature of the influence of the San and their music upon the music of southern Africa is also an important question. Dealing with it in detail, Kubik has argued for a relationship between San musical bows and the nature of harmonic progressions in the musical traditions of the southcentral African tonal-harmonic belt. This belt represents practices distinct from those of other parts of Africa. These practices, however, are not so distinct from those of many groups in southern Africa. The music of the tonal-harmonic belt shares many features with that of the Nguni-Sotho peoples, who use two- or three-bow fundamentals and their overtones, resulting in a "tonality shift" or "tonality contrast" (Rycroft 1971:235). All these traditions share an overriding intonational trait, Blacking's principle of harmonic equivalence: tones that can be sounded simultaneously, or that can be substituted for each other, must belong to the same harmonic series. All these practices exemplify harmony in the sense of progressions of prescribed aural combinations (Kaemmer 1993:105). Perhaps the tonal-harmonic belt represents the result of interplay between the chorus-bow traditions of South Africa and the xylophone-mbira traditions of the southeast.

There is also the possibility that certain African musical traits originated in Indonesia. If people from Indonesia could discover and settle the island of Madagascar, it is highly possible that they could have landed on the mainland of Africa. Whether they actually did or not is the issue. The nature of Chopi xylophones raises this question, especially the equidistant tuning. Moreover, the nature of the Chopi ensembles differs from that of xylophone ensembles elsewhere in Africa. The theory of Indonesian origins includes cultural and musical features all over Africa (Jones 1964). Compelling evidence to settle this issue may never be found.

Another issue concerns the origin of the lamellophones, used all over Africa for entertainment. Only among the southeastern Bantu are lamellophones regularly used for ritual. In that area, they are also larger and more complex. These lamellophones (mbira) may have originated from xylophones (Jones 1964). This possibility is argued from the fact that one xylophone is commonly played by two players, one on each side—which means that for one player, the low notes are on the left, and for the other, they are on the right. Many *mbira* have low notes in the center, meaning they

mbila   Chopi word for a xylophone key;
         closely related to the term *mbira*, which
         designates a lamellophone

are on the left for one hand, and on the right for the other hand. However, if Andrew Tracey's theory about the original *mbira* is valid, the layout of tones may more closely relate to the notes of the harmonic series than to any of the equitonic xylophones. It is possible that the low notes are often in the center because of the way the instrument lies under the hands.

Africans talk about xylophones and lamellophones with closely related words. Many of the languages of the area use a type of retroflex /r/, which if moved somewhat farther back in the mouth sounds something like /l/. For example, the term Maravi is used by Murdock (1959:294) to denote a cluster of people in Malawi, but the two terms differ only in the orthography of the /r/ and the /l/ (and of the bilabial fricative). The term for lamellophone in southeastern Africa is *mbira,* a word closely related to the Chopi word for a xylophone key (*mbila*), but with the same phonetic difference. It is also possible that the words *mbila* and *mbira* are related to *limba* and *rimba,* as in *ulimba* and *marimba*—all of which in some places denote both xylophones and lamellophones. These various noun stems can receive prefixes—like *ma-* and *ti-* for plural, and *ka-* for diminution—that add to their meaning. In many Bantu languages, the verb-stem for the concept 'to sing' is *-imba,* and the relational suffix that relates the verb to something else is *-ila* or *-ira.* Thus, *-imbira* or *-imbila* would mean 'to sing for'. Recognizing such closely related sounds is important in determining possible historical relationships.

The issue of the origins of the mbira is complicated by the fact that the lamellophone is played in West Africa with the free ends of the lamellae away from the player. This has been considered a case where the instrument diffused from one area to another without the related playing skills. Since the origins of the mbira lie in antiquity (lamellae having been found in archaeological sites), the details of its prehistoric development may never be known.

IMPACT OF THE WIDER WORLD

Though interethnic borrowing of cultural features has occurred in southern Africa as far back in time as we can determine, it is only in the last three hundred fifty years that the impact of non-African societies is clear and overwhelming. The impact of non-African societies comes partly from the musical practices themselves, but the impact of social and cultural changes brought about by European conquest has been paramount.

The musical practices of all of southern Africa have been heavily influenced by unique factors emanating from the Republic of South Africa, which has the largest proportion of Europeans of any country in Africa, largely because of the temperateness of its climate and the wealth of its minerals. Settlers sent by the Dutch East India Company landed in Cape Town in 1652. Before long, they had brought in Asians to help work their farms. English settlers arrived after armed forces had defeated the Dutch. All these immigrants brought musical traditions with them.

Mining

In the 1800s, with the discovery of diamonds in Kimberly and gold in the Transvaal, the European influence in southern Africa intensified. Conflict developed between the English and the descendants of the Dutch, who had precipitated devastating wars by moving into areas occupied by Africans. The impact of the British spread with the colonization of Southern Rhodesia (now Zimbabwe) and the discovery of copper in Northern Rhodesia (now Zambia). The explorations of David Livingstone brought Malawi into the British orbit, leaving Angola and Mozambique to the Portuguese and Southwest Africa (now Namibia) to the Germans.

The wealth in the mines lured many African men from their communities. Most had no choice but to leave their wives and families behind. Their absence from home meant that village rituals, with their associated music, had to be adapted to weekends or holidays, or else they died out. The communities that grew up around the mines provided meeting places where people of many ethnic groups heard each other's music, including that of Africans of European descent.

The companies that ran the mines often sponsored indigenous African dances as entertainment on Sundays, the miners' day off. These dances helped maintain differences of ethnic identity among the men, and gave them an outlet for entertainment and self-expression. These dances also catered to tourists, providing outsiders with convenient views of exotic music and dance.

In nonmining areas, Africans who worked for Europeans were either people educated in Western knowledge (who became clerks and household help), or people uneducated in Western forms (who worked on plantations). Many Africans who worked in the big mining centers were not Western educated, but became permanently urban. They sought to become recognized as city dwellers, rather than "tribesmen," and used skills in European music to demonstrate their claims (Coplan 1985:12).

Apartheid

South Africa was unique in having such strong European influence so early. In most of southern Africa, intensive European domination did not occur until after the Treaty of Berlin (1885). Major wars of colonial conquest occurred in Namibia, Zimbabwe, and South Africa. Africans were subject not only to military activity, but also to the presence of military bands, with instruments that seemed new and exciting to them. Since African tradition viewed musical spectacles as an important symbol of political power, military bands were seen as a new type of power, and were often imitated as a new kind of dance (Ranger 1975).

The policy of apartheid, strict racial separation, heavily influenced music in both South Africa and Namibia, which from 1915 to 1990 was under South African control. Racial separation was a continentwide practice; but in South Africa in 1948, after the Afrikaner party had taken electoral power, it became official policy. Until then, musical events mixed Africans and Europeans, with Africans often providing the music.

Under apartheid, Africans were eventually forbidden to perform at European nightclubs, thus losing economic opportunity and a means of interracial communication. The lack of resources devoted to African education meant that African schoolchildren had less formal training in music than European schoolchildren. Songs in African theatrical performances became a major form of social commentary in South Africa, where theater was seen as a form of communication, rather than an aesthetic activity (Coplan 1985:225).

Missions and education

An important feature of musical change in southern Africa was the activity of

The stigma attached to Africans and their culture by European racism and ethnocentrism directly influenced musical practices in a variety of ways.

Christian missionaries, both as proponents of new religious doctrines, and as purveyors of European education. Most missionaries had difficulty distinguishing between Christian doctrine and European culture. They tended to disparage African customs and African music, which they believed not only inferior, but also sinful.

Many Africans viewed religion as a form of power that equaled spears and guns. Consequently, they viewed Christianity as an important reason for European domination and thus a more effective religion. New converts who accepted the rituals also adopted the music that accompanied them. They turned away from indigenous forms of music, accepting the notion that they were sinful and inferior. Missionaries often translated their hymns into African languages, unaware of the importance of linguistic tones to the understandability and aesthetic quality of the music.

Some missionary agencies, recognizing the importance of indigenous forms of expression to their converts, created hymns and songs in indigenous styles. The Livingstonia mission in northern Malawi did so from the beginning. In the 1960s, the Methodist mission in Zimbabwe began a program of fostering the use of indigenous musical idioms in the church, but older people had already formed negative opinions about them. Workshops on indigenization of the arts have been held regularly since then, with many churches cooperating. After the second Vatican Council (1962–1965), the Roman Catholic church began using vernacular languages in services—a change that afforded an opportunity to adopt indigenous musical styles to accommodate the new languages of worship.

Education, fostered by the missions until the various countries became independent, was oriented to European culture. Its aim was preparing workers for government and business; training in music played only a small part in it. The curriculum used in the schools of the colonial power was also taught in Africa, including the songs. Being related to the missions, schools usually promoted choral singing.

One type of music became popular all over southern Africa: the *makwaya,* from the word "choir." It involved singing, complex marching routines, and special costumes. Adaptations of jazz in responsorial form, accompanied by drumming and dancing, have become popular with young people.

In the Anglophone areas of southern Africa, schools commonly sponsored musical contests. The judges were usually Europeans, who formed their judgments on the basis of European musical criteria. Having African judges was avoided in South Africa, for fear that African judges would be biased in favor of their kinsmen (Coplan 1985:154).

Sociopolitical factors

In the twentieth century, during struggles for political liberation, songs served to politicize people and motivate fighters. In Zimbabwe's struggle, composers and performers emphasized the indigenous aspects of culture; during the 1960s and 1970s, the mbira became more popular than the guitar among young people, but since independence, the situation seems to have reversed.

The stigma attached to Africans and their culture by European racism and ethnocentrism directly influenced musical practices in a variety of ways. In most of southern Africa, the mastery of European music was seen as prestigious—resulting in considerable decline of indigenous traditions. The Venda of South Africa, however, refused to use European music because they resented foreign control over their lives (Blacking 1973:38). In most parts of the country, the performance of indigenous music was often seen as implying support of "separate development" (that is, apartheid), and was thus avoided.

That socioeconomic factors play an important role in musical change does not mean that musical interest is irrelevant in itself. From the earliest days of European settlement, the Khoikhoi at the cape were utilizing Malay and Dutch musical idioms (Coplan 1985:9–11). Black vaudeville entertainers from the United States not only helped improve Africans' self-respect, but also served as musical models for African musical entertainers (Coplan 1985:70). As early as 1890, African-American choirs were traveling to South Africa to perform (Erlmann 1991:21–53). That the Nguni peoples valued choral singing helped them relate to African-American singing. The improvisational nature of African-American music also struck a responsive chord with them (Coplan 1985:146).

Musical instruments

The adoption or imitation of European instruments has been significant in southern African music. Simply adopting the instruments has not necessarily meant that Africans have played European music on them (Kirby 1934:257; Rycroft 1977; Kauffman 1973.) Double-headed drums are common in southern Africa, especially in separatist religious groups. Both the use of round metal tins in the manufacture of these drums and their style of playing indicate that they were copied from the European bass drums used in military bands. In the early days of the Cape Colony, the Khoikhoi were copying violins and guitars, creating the *ramkie,* a homemade lute (Kirby 1934:246–256).

Commercially produced European instruments were found to be not only louder than indigenous instruments, but also more versatile. The most important of these was the guitar, which became a major instrument all over southern Africa. Though the acoustic guitar was popular for many years, the electric guitar is taking its place. Guitars have often supplanted musical bows because the latter are soft in sound, and much of their appeal is only to the performer. Among Xhosa girls, imported lamellophones took the place of bows (Rycroft 1994:132). Pennywhistles experienced a surge of popularity in the 1950s in South Africa because they were not only versatile, but cheap (Coplan 1985:62, 155–156).

Independence and international relations

Independence has changed the situation in many southern African countries. A major development has been in the amount of readily available modern education. While pedagogy has not usually covered music in depth, the increasing consciousness brought about by Western education has carried over into music. Many traditional African musicians can perform superbly on their instruments, but cannot explain, in Western terms, what they are doing and how they are doing it; younger musicians who have been to school, however, have become aware of what is happening in their musical traditions—such as young Shona mbira players, able to explain the four sections of a cycle of their music.

Political changes have affected the organization of indigenous music. In

Mozambique, chiefly power was curtailed, so chiefs no longer sponsor xylophone ensembles. Though to many people these ensembles represent Mozambican music, other governmental agencies now sponsor them. They are also being integrated with European instruments (Celso Paco, personal communication, 1993)—a process that will doubtlessly modify the tradition.

Increased contacts with the outside world have led young people to see the possibility of producing records as a way of building a successful career. With some exceptions, young musicians tend to imitate the popular music stars they hear, apparently shunning the music of their elders. Both South Africa and Zimbabwe have active recording industries, serving local and international markets; however, the control of production is in the hands of international corporations, who seek to market worldbeat on the basis of technical simplicity and exotic appeal. European producers and technicians in South Africa tend to impose their own values and criteria on African performers, whom they have often considered merely laborers (Meintjes 1994). Some studios are beginning to pay the performers royalties instead of a onetime fee.

REFERENCES

Adams, Charles R. 1974. "Ethnography of Basotho: Evaluative Expression in the Cognitive Domain Lipapali (Games)." Ph.D. dissertation, Indiana University.

Alnaes, Kirsten. 1989. "Living with the Past: The Songs of the Herero in Botswana." *Africa* 59(3):267–299.

Blacking, John. 1965. "The Role of Music in the Culture of the Venda of the Northern Transvaal." In *Studies in Ethnomusicology*, ed. Mieczeslaw Kolinski, 2:20–53. New York: Oak Publications.

———. 1967. *Venda Children's Songs: A Study in Ethnomusicological Analysis.* Johannesburg: Witwatersrand University Press.

———. 1973. *How Musical Is Man?* Seattle: University of Washington Press.

Brown, Ernest Douglas. 1984. "Drums of Life: Royal Music and Social Life in Western Zambia." Ph.D. dissertation, University of Washington.

Childs, Gladwyn Murray. 1949. *Umbundu Kinship and Character.* London: Oxford University Press.

Coplan, David B. 1985. *In Township Tonight! South Africa's Black City Music and Theatre.* London: Longman.

Dargie, David. 1991. "Umngqokolo: Xhosa Overtone Singing and the Song Nondel'ekhaya." *African Music* 7(1):32–47.

England, Nicholas. 1967. "Bushman Counterpoint." *Journal of the International Folk Music Council* 19:58–66.

Erlmann, Veit. 1991. *African Stars: Studies in Black South African Performance.* Chicago: University of Chicago Press.

Greenberg, Joseph H. 1970. *The Languages of Africa,* 3rd ed. Bloomington: Indiana University Press.

Guthrie, Malcolm. 1948. *The Classification of the Bantu Languages.* London: International African Institute.

Johnston, Thomas. 1970. "Xizambi Friction-Bow Music of the Shangana-Tsonga." *African Music* 4(4):81–95.

———. 1971. "Shangana-Tsonga Drum and Bow Rhythms." *African Music* 5(1):59–72.

———. 1972. "Possession Music of the Shangana-Tsonga." *African Music* 5(2):10–22.

———. 1987. "Children's Music of the Shangana-Tsonga." *African Music* 6(4):126–143.

Jones, Arthur M. 1949. *African Music in Northern Rhodesia and Some Other Places.* Livingstone, Zambia: Rhodes-Livingstone Museum.

———. 1959. *Studies in African Music.* London: Oxford University Press.

———. 1964. *Africa and Indonesia.* Leiden: E. J. Brill.

Joseph, Rosemary. 1983. "Zulu Women's Music." *African Music* 6(3):53–89.

Kaemmer, John E. 1993. *Music in Human Life: Anthropological Perspectives on Music.* Austin: University of Texas Press.

Katz, Richard. 1982. *Boiling Energy: Community Healing among the Kalahari !Kung.* Cambridge, Mass.: Harvard University Press.

Kauffman, Robert. 1973. "Shona Urban Music and the Problem of Acculturation." *Yearbook of the International Folk Music Council* 4:47–56.

Kirby, Percival R. 1934. *The Musical Instruments of the Native Races of South Africa.* London: Oxford University Press.

Kubik, Gerhard. 1970. *Musica tradicional e aculturada dos !Kung de Angola,* trans. João de Freitas Branco. Lisbon: Junta de Investigações do Ultramar, Centro de Estudos de Antropologia Cultural. Estudos de Antropologia Cultural, 4.

———. 1975–1976. "Musical Bows in South-Western Angola, 1965." *African Music* 5(4):98–104.

———. 1980. "Angola." *The New Grove Dictionary of Music and Musicians,* ed. Stanley Sadie. London: Macmillan.

———. 1985. "African Tone Systems—A Reassessment." *Yearbook of Traditional Music* 19:31–63.

———. 1988. "Nsenga / Shona Harmonic Patterns and the San Heritage." *Ethnomusicology* 32(2):39–76.

Meintjes, Louise. 1994. "Mediating Difference: Liveness in the Production of Mbaqanga Music in Johannesburg." Seminar paper presented to the Institute for Advanced Study and Research in the African Humanities, Northwestern University, 9 November 1994.

Mundell, Felicia H. 1980. "Botswana." *The New Grove Dictionary of Music and Musicians,* ed. Stanley Sadie. London: Macmillan.

Murdock, George Peter. 1959. *Africa: Its Peoples and Their Culture History.* New York: McGraw-Hill.

Phillipson, David W. 1985. *African Archaeology.* Cambridge: Cambridge University Press.

Ranger, Terence O. 1975. *Dance and Society in Eastern Africa: 1890–1970.* London: Heinemann.

Rycroft, David K. 1971. "Stylistic Evidence in Nguni Song." In *Essays on Music and History in Africa,* ed. Klaus P. Wachsmann (Evanston, Ill.: Northwestern University Press), 213–241.

———. 1975–1976. "The Zulu Bow Songs of Princess Magogo." *African Music* 5(4):41–97.

———. 1977. "Evidence of Stylistic Continuity in Zulu 'Town' Music." In *Essays for a Humanist: An Offering to Klaus Wachsmann,* 216–260. New York: Town House Press.

———. 1980a. "Hottentot Music." *The New Grove Dictionary of Music and Musicians,* ed. Stanley Sadie. London: Macmillan.

———. 1980b. "Nguni Music." *The New Grove Dictionary of Music and Musicians,* ed. Stanley Sadie. London Macmillan.

———. 1994. "African Arts, Music: Musical Instruments." *Encyclopaedia Britannica,* 15th ed. 13:132–135.

Tracey, Andrew. 1971. "The Nyanga Panpipe Dance." *African Music* 5(1):73–89.

———. 1972. "The Original African Mbira?" *African Music* (2):85–104.

———. 1980. "Mozambique." *The New Grove Dictionary of Music and Musicians,* ed. Stanley Sadie. London: Macmillan.

———. 1991. "Kambazithe Makolekole and his Valimba Group: A Glimpse of the Technique of the Sena Xylophone." *African Music* 7(1):82–104.

Tracey, Hugh. 1948a. *Chopi Musicians: Their Music, Poetry, and Instruments.* London: International African Institute.

———. 1948b. *Ngoma: An Introduction to Music for Southern Africans.* New York: Longmans, Green.

van Zanten, Wim. 1980. "The Equidistant Heptatonic Scale of the Asena in Malawi." *African Music* 6(1):107–125.

Harmony in Luvale Music of Zambia

Tsukada Kenichi

Mukanda among the Luvale
Investigating Luvale Musical Perception
Culturally Different Perceptions

Formulating "a humanizing ethnomusicology," Kenneth A. Gourlay has stressed the importance of the active aspects of "an ethnomusicological dialectic" (Gourlay 1982:412). His notion of dialectic develops from a series of arguments over the stance of researchers in the ethnomusicological enterprise (Gourlay 1978:13–23). Many scholars (Berreman 1972; Blacking 1981; Blum 1975; Crick 1976; Gourlay 1978; Herndon 1974; Seeger 1971; Stone 1979; Wachsmann 1971), while questioning that stance, have decried researchers' self-exclusion from the process of research. Concepts such as Gourlay's "constraints," Seeger's "bank of ideation," and Wachsmann's "mind programmed by previous experience" suggest a concern with researcher's conceptual and perceptual frameworks.

Their methodologies, however, do not imply the uncritical inclusion of researchers' cultural perspectives in the interpretive process—a process that would be ethnocentric. What research shows to be desirable is an analysis of what I call a "confrontation"—of the ethnomusicologist's and culture bearers' modes of conception and perception, and of systems of meaning. An ethnomusicologist can achieve this confrontation only by adopting a stance that allows an "active intrusion" (Herndon 1974:248). The elevation of stance to an active role is essential for creating a situation that highlights the contrast between cultural systems.

Scholars of culture sometimes intervene actively. Studying colors as perceived by the Hanunóo, Conklin (1955) "intruded" into his respondents' conceptual world: he asked about color specimens in terms of his own perception. This procedure ended in confusion, and proved no consistency in the Hanunóo system. Conklin then changed his approach. He asked his respondents to relate and contrast specimens in their own terms. Their responses revealed a coherent classification, whose existence brought to light a disparity between the Hanunóo and European systems.

John Blacking (1967) tried a similar method. When he sang stanzas of a Venda song to the melody of only the first, the Venda reacted negatively. Their reaction led him to perceive that the melody should vary with the text. Surprisingly, however, the Venda accepted as genuinely Venda his next try—to sing deliberately "out of tune." By repeating such processes, he found principles of Venda melodic formation.

Each of these cases exemplifies a researcher's active intervention. The researcher

Areas of Luvale population in Zambia.

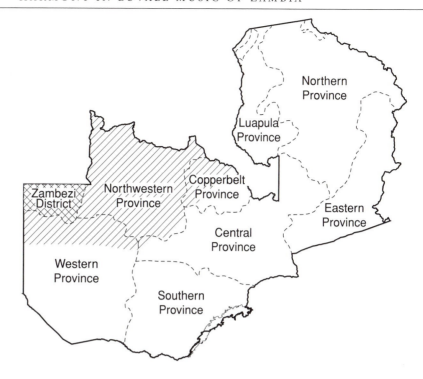

brings his or her perspective into the interactional context, and then shifts that perspective to that of the culture bearers. The shift reveals discrepancies in the researcher's and the culture bearers' systems of meaning, and allows the researcher to discover underlying cultural principles.

The issue of harmony in Central Africa provides ground for further study. Some scholars (Merriam 1959; Kauffman 1984) have questioned the application of the term *harmony* to African music, but others use it extensively (Kubik 1985, 1988). I use it in reference to what Nketia calls "homophonic polyphony" (1974:164). That some features of harmonic organization in Central Africa are comparable to those of Western music allows investigators trained in Western music to "intervene." As the search for the organizing principles of Central African harmony advances, discrepancies in conception and perception between investigators and culture bearers become obvious. I shall illustrate this by exploring the principles of harmonic organization in the music of the Luvale of Zambia, with reference to rites of boys' initiation, which I studied in the Zambezi District of Zambia in 1982–1984.

MUKANDA AMONG THE LUVALE

The Luvale people, numbering about one hundred thousand in Zambia, belong to an ethnic group that inhabits eastern Angola, northwestern Zambia, and southern Zaïre, and has a homogeneous culture, derived from the ancient Lunda-Luba empire. In Zambia, most Luvale live in Northwestern Province, particularly in the Zambezi District. They are a matrilineal and virilocal people, engaged largely in cultivation, with sporadic fishing in the rainy season. Despite twentieth-century changes in their culture, some of their traditions survive.

Among the Luvale and allied groups, the word *mukanda* denotes the traditional educational institution for boys (figure 1). It usually begins in August or September (the cold, dry season). The age of novices usually ranges from six to twelve. After a large, festive ceremony (*kuputuka*) of singing, dancing, and drinking throughout a night, candidates undergo circumcision in the bush to become novices (*tundanji*). With poles, branches, and leafy twigs, the participants and chance observers then construct a rectangular enclosure, which serves as a lodge for novices and guardians.

The *mukanda* fulfills the functions of a rite of passage (to achieve the transition from boy into man), and of a school (to enculturate children into society).

FIGURE 1   The newly built lodge of Luvale *mukanda.* On the day after the operation, an enclosure is constructed in the bush.

During an intensive period of seclusion there, a *nganga mukanda* 'mukanda doctor' protects the novices from supernatural danger. Guardians (*vilombola*) make the novices follow special rules and taboos. The period of seclusion lasts until the wound has healed (three to four weeks). After a riverine ceremony of purification (*kulyachisa*), the novices enjoy more liberty: they return to life in the village, free of many taboos (figure 2). A few months to about two years later, they graduate from *mukanda* with a ceremony (*kulovola*) that grants them full entry into village life, with a new social status (figure 3).

The *mukanda* fulfills the functions of a rite of passage (to achieve the transition from boy into man), and of a school (to enculturate children into society). In its daily routine, singing is central. By performing in groups, novices learn the importance of discipline and cooperation. The texts of their songs reinforce this lesson. One of them, in its most common version, goes:

Twalala kuchihongo.	We sleep in the reedy marsh.
E, lelo twalala,	Yes, today we sleep,
Twalala mbimbe.	We sleep like locusts.
Mbimbe katete	Like locusts we get up early
Kusongo yawande.	At the edge of the field.
Twalala, twalala mbimbe.	We sleep, we sleep like locusts.
E, lelo twalala.	Yes, today we sleep.

The text compares the novices to locusts, which during the cold of night stay in the reedy marsh, but with the warmth of day take to the air. Thus, the song teaches the novices to rise early in the morning. For detailed information about Luvale

FIGURE 3 (*above*) *Kulovola* ceremony in the village. A masked dancer (*likishi*) is carried on the shoulders by the young.

mukanda, see Delille (1930), Gluckman (1949), White (1953, 1961), Mwondela (1972), and Tsukada (1982, 1988, 1990, 1991a, 1991b).

INVESTIGATING LUVALE MUSICAL PERCEPTION

In *mukanda*, singing occurs on diverse occasions. Playing instruments is forbidden, except for the use of a pair of sticks for rhythmic accompaniment. There are thirteen categories of songs sung at the lodge. Four of them—songs of sunrise and sunset, food-ritual songs, nocturnal songs—are the main categories of routine songs for novices (Tsukada 1988). In particular, the nocturnal songs (*myaso yakukuwa hamukanda* 'songs of joy at the lodge') are important for the special secrecy of the category. At night, around the ritual fire in front of the enclosure, the novices, their guardians, and ordinary men from the neighboring villages, sing the songs of this category (here called *kukuwa* songs). They do so every two or three nights. To produce rhythmic accompaniment while singing, they strike pairs of wooden sticks, *mingwengwe* 'human bones'. Especially on the night before the ceremony of purification, they hold a feast at the lodge, where to express joy for the novices' recovery, they sing *kukuwa* songs all night. The repertory of these songs is rich, with a diversity of styles and tonal organizations.

In the field, I made several observations concerning *mukanda* songs, of which the most important was that the Luvale identified as "the same" (*chochimwe* 'it is one', implying interchangeability) some versions of songs that sounded different to me. How could they regard variant versions as "the same"? and what were the identifying parameters of the songs? These questions have long interested folklorists and ethnomusicologists, but my interest and aims differ from those of previous work. The scholarly tradition handles musical variants in two ways. The first focuses on the concept of "wandering melodies," the migration of texts and tunes over large geographical areas (Bronson 1959–1972; Danckert 1939; Sharp 1965). The second uses comparative methods to abstract archetypes from related versions (Bronson 1951; Mersmann 1921). Both approaches have historical or diachronic perspectives, and both concentrate primarily on the form and structure of a song. My approach, how-

FIGURE 4 Three types of tonal patterns. The whole notes represent the last note of each pattern.

ever, has nothing to do with a historical perspective. My main concern is how performers and listeners perceive a song, and how they accept its variant versions under the same title.

Luvale music favors parallel singing in thirds, except for a few categories of songs that employ parallel fourths. Songs are in responsorial form. Choral responses are usually in parallel thirds, formed by a pair of tonal patterns derived from a heptatonic system. (I use the term "tonal pattern" to denote a series of tones employed in each voice part of a choral section.) Earlier (Tsukada 1982), I suggested, though the Luvale employ many types of tonal patterns in parallel thirds, the most frequent types were those shown in figures 4a and 4b. The intervals are inexactly equal to the intervals implied by tempered tuning. These tonal patterns allow variations through the omission or addition of thirds. In *kukuwa* songs, the latter set of tonal patterns (figure 4b) is more common; it often extends, as shown in figure 4c. In this type of parallelism, cadences usually fall on a minor third, A–C, with occasional emphasis on the harmonic intervals B–D or G–B.

Now let us consider the problem of Luvale identification of songs. Figure 5 shows three versions of the sunrise song "*Kumbie! Neha Musana!* 'Sun! Bring light!'" I set up some tests in which I sang several possible melodies of the song with one musically knowledgeable Luvale, who took part in the response section. I intended to investigate which versions were acceptable for the Luvale. Despite harmonic differences in the choral section, the Luvale regard all three versions as performances of the same song, and make no particular distinctions among them. This is more surprising, if one considers that the choral section of figure 5c, in Western terms, looks and sounds like a transposition to the relative minor of the choral section of figure 5a.

FIGURE 5 The sunrise song "*Kumbie! Neha Musana!* 'Sun! Bring Light!'"

The variance in sonority between these versions exerts no influence on the process of their identification of the song.

My primary concerns are whether a coherent system underlies the Luvale perception of music, and what principles operate within their music. By analyzing *kukuwa* songs, I shall try to discover the basic principle of their musical perception and organization. I use Western staff notation, but because African rhythmic organization and concepts of time differ from Western ones, I do not use time signatures. For the same reason, I employ short lines for bars. For a translation of the texts, see Tsukada (1988).

The melodic and harmonic principle

The first difficulty I faced was in transcribing and notating the songs, which I tried to do without using a key signature. I gradually understood, however, that the pitch of certain tones sometimes moved about a semitone lower or higher, and later settled at that new pitch. After confirming (from various examples) that the change was not haphazard, I had to be careful about whether to notate a song with a key signature or not, and in what notational layout to transcribe the tonal patterns. Otherwise, my transcriptions would collectively have shown disorder and inconsistency. (Analysis started with the assumption that every culture should reveal itself with a certain degree of consistency and order.) While I was struggling to transcribe the music, the presence of a principle gradually became clear.

Some performances bewildered me. One of them was of "*Ali Nalengo* 'He Has a Girlfriend'." I first transcribed it as in figure 6a. Because the notes A, C, and E appeared so frequently in both solo and choral sections, I regarded the tonal patterns employed there as extensions of those of figure 4c. If that were the case, two problems would remain. First, what was the significance of the frequent appearance of B flat throughout the piece? Was it the result of pitch alteration of the tone B? The pitch alteration of certain tones is a trait of the Luvale tonal system. (For describing it, I use the terms "sharp" and "flat" as rough indications of pitch. I shall show that B is one of the tones liable to alteration.) Second, the notation shows that this performance begins with F in the solo section and D–F in the choral section. An inquiry into various types of *kukuwa* songs, however, shows that such a beginning is rare and unusual.

Viewed from another perspective, however, these problems resolve themselves. I learned this song by hearing and singing it. I have an idea of how it sounds and should sound. If I recall it, and write it down in staff notation, it resembles figure 6b, which covers the choral section, leaving out some details. A solo section simply follows the upper part of the chorus. This is only one of the possible forms of tonal patterns for singing this song, and it strikingly exhibits the typical tonal patterns of figure 4c.

A comparison between figures 4 and 5 may at first puzzle us—again, because in spite of the overall similarity, a precise transposition of figure 6a to figure 6b down a minor second is impossible because of the intervallic difference. When one considers that the solo melody and the upper part of the chorus in figure 3a correspond roughly to the lower part of the chorus in 6b (particularly for the first few measures), the relationship between the two becomes comprehensible. That is, 6a is in effect notated a perfect fourth higher than 6b. Accordingly, it can be transposed down a perfect fourth, as in figure 6c. We are now in a better position to compare the performances.

The result of this comparison is that, though these examples may look different in notation, a consistent musical logic dominates the performances. Except for four notes, each step of the melodic line maintains a relationship in a vertical series of thirds to the other line. This principle is indispensable for understanding the music:

Melodically and harmonically, the notes that belong to a vertical series of thirds are equivalent to each other. This is a paramount principle of Luvale musical identification, and of the melodic and harmonic formation of *mukanda* songs in general.

FIGURE 6a   One performance of the *kukuwa* song "*Ali Nalengo* 'He Has a Girlfriend'."

melodically and harmonically, the notes that belong to a vertical series of thirds are equivalent to each other. This is a paramount principle of Luvale musical identification, and of the melodic and harmonic formation of *mukanda* songs in general. I have not yet fully investigated the other genres of Luvale music; it likely holds for them, excepting genres with parallel fourths. Examination of individual cases will show how this principle works in practice.

Melodic variation and unity

My interest in the melodic formation of Luvale songs arose when I was listening to the recording of one *kukuwa* song. The piece sounded unfamiliar. I had difficulty

FIGURE *6b and c*
Two other perfor-
mances of the *kukuwa*
song "*Ali Nalengo* 'He
Has a Girlfriend'."

identifying it from the words, because sundry voices obscured their enunciation. Suddenly, with surprise, I realized it was a piece I knew well: "*Twalala Kuchihongo* 'We Sleep in the Reedy Marsh'." The performance was so different, I had not noticed it was the same piece. Careful listening gradually made me aware of rhythmic and

Such freedom in the melodic lines seems to derive chiefly from independence of melodic movement from the speech tones of the text.

minor harmonic similarities. In melody, however, both solo and choral sections sounded different from what I remembered. This experience led me to question how the Luvale could classify such "different" melodies as the same.

The main difficulty in recognizing the song came from the lead singers' melodic variation, one of the distinctive traits of the performance of *kukuwa* songs. I therefore aimed my analysis at identifying the common traits of the melodies of solo sections. Despite an apparent lack of similarity, two "different" melodies prove to follow rules that enable the Luvale to relate them to each other, and to recognize them as the same.

The song "*Twalala Kuchihongo*" illustrates this point. Figure 7*a* shows the lead melody of this piece as sung by Sanele Kafwale, my teacher of Luvale music. (This version has long been the basis of my memory of this song.) Figure 7*b* shows one melody extracted from the chorus in a performance that at first eluded me. This melody was sung, among others, in a loud voice, starting a perfect fifth lower than the uppermost melody. As a result, the tune changed. To me, it sounded different from the piece I knew as "*Twalala Kuchihongo*." However, a close comparison reveals that each note of figure 7*b* (excepting two points) enters into intervallic relations of a unison, a third, or a fifth with its counterpart in figure 7*a*. For all the seeming disparities in sound, a solid principle operates in the melodic formation of figure 7*b*, which regulates melodic lines to keep a constant relationship of a unison, a third, or its multiple, with other potential melodies. Since a third (whether major or minor) acts as the basic interval, I call this "the principle of third relations."

Figures 7*c* and 7*d* further illustrate this point. These are melodies sung by two individuals. Despite freedom in melodic improvisation, they follow closely the principle of third relations. Exceptions occur in the twelfth, fourteenth, and fifteenth measures.

Another noticeable feature, notwithstanding the restrictive influence of the principle of third relations, is the comparative freedom in formation of melodic lines. Such freedom seems to derive chiefly from independence of the melodic movement from the speech tones of the text. Many cases prove this. At least seven melodic patterns serve for the phrase *twalala* 'we sleep' (figure 8). Contrary motion inevitably involves the disagreement between melodic pattern and speech tone pattern—a phenomenon rare in the music of peoples who speak tonal languages.

Paying attention to this phenomenon among some Angolan-Congolese groups, Kubik (1968:50) suggested the possible connection between the frequency of contrary motion and the degree of tonality of a language. Nketia (1974:187), however, attributed such disagreement partly to a performer's creativity. In either case, figure 8 shows that the speech tones of the phrase *twalala* exert little influence on the formation of melodic patterns. Similar observations can be made in the melodic patterns for other words, such as *e lelo* 'yes, today', *njimba* 'whydah', *mbimba* 'locust', *songo* 'edge', and *yawande* 'of field'. It can be argued that the comparative independence of

FIGURE 7 *"Twalala Kuchihongo* 'We Sleep in the Reedy Marsh'."

melody from speech tone helps generate a diversity of melodic lines, whereas the strict observance of the principle of third relations might facilitate musical identification. To other examples, Tsukada (1988) applies a similar analysis.

Though the principle of third relations dominates melodic formation, it does not lessen the chance of generating a variety of melodic patterns. There are three rea-

FIGURE 8   Melodic patterns for "*Twalala Kuchihongo.*"

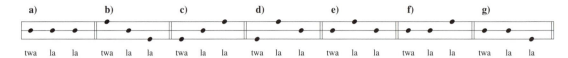

twa la la   twa la la   twa la la   twa la la   twa la la   twa la la   twa la la

sons for this. *First,* diverse melodic lines are built up fairly independently of speech tone patterns. *Second,* "a shift of center" is a device commonly used to enrich melodic variation. ("A shift of center" here refers to the melodic movement that in performance changes the tonal pattern from one to the other; see Hornbostel 1928; Herzog 1934; Schneider 1944; Jones 1959; and Blacking 1967.) In Luvale music, the tonal pattern usually shifts to a third above or below the original. The alteration of a voice from one range to the other seems indispensable for creating the richness and diversity of variants. *Third,* the principle of third relations does not always require parallel motion in the chorus. This is obvious from the examples, particularly figure 7*b,* since the illustrated melodies may potentially be sung at any time. A combination of these factors thus achieves melodic variation, and the result might be the cause of perplexity for an outsider's ears. However, for the Luvale, the principle of third relations is the major clue to structural coherence.

Harmonic variation and unity

Our next task is to examine how the principle of third relations operates in the harmonic structure of choral sections. An overall analysis of performances of *kukuwa* songs (of which I have collected more than one hundred forty) demonstrates that two vertical series of thirds form the foundations of Luvale harmony (figure 9). In choral sections, usually, a third or double thirds (a triad) are chosen alternately from these two series. A chorus ordinarily starts with the first series of thirds. An inquiry into various choral sections shows that in starting position and principal tonal range, the tonal patterns fall roughly into three classes: I, II, and III (figure 10). However, since this is a simplified model, devised for analytical convenience, some songs have tonal patterns that do not suit this scheme. For improvisatory factors, the patterns are subject to alteration. The patterns in figures 3*a* and 3*b* are included in classes II and III.

Performances of the song "*Kangongwe* 'A Small Mouse'" (figure 11) give a simple and powerful illustration of the scheme. A comparison of the choral sections proves the successive performances represent classes I, II, and III, respectively. At each melodic and harmonic progression, these performances maintain with each other the relationship of thirds. This fact establishes four points: the principle of third rela-

FIGURE 9   Two series of thirds.

FIGURE 10   Three classes of tonal patterns.

FIGURE 11
"*Kangongwe* 'A Small Mouse'."

tions; the alternation of two series of thirds; the scheme of classes I, II, and III; and the interchangeability of these classes in performance.

Relationships between thirds

As the analysis progressed, however, it became obvious that the distinction between these classes was not always clear, for certain tones in the Luvale tonal system could

FIGURE 11
(continued)

undergo pitch alteration about a semitone lower or higher. This alteration sometimes made distinguishing between two classes difficult. The first difficulty was in the distinction between classes I and III.

Two performances of the song "*Kanga Nakanga* 'Two Guinea Fowls'" (figure 12) serve as an illustration of this. The choral section of 12*a* is transcribed as two-part singing, except for a few additional notes, since two voices are especially prominent against the background voices in the recording. This section can be in either class I or class II, depending on whether another voice part is above or below the thirds. The appearance of E and D in the uppermost part implies this section more likely belongs to class II.

Figure 12*b*, however, caused me trouble in notation and analysis. It is among the examples that are most perplexing for "Western" ears. The primary problem is the pitch written as F in the choral section. Since it is nearly fixed between F-sharp and F-natural, the choral section can be heard as either class I or class III, depending on the time of listening and the psychological state of the listener. Whereas by "performance" I mean a series of repetitions of an entire song, I apply the term *execution* to each presentation of a song in a performance. In this performance, all four executions regularly produce a pitch between F-sharp and F-natural in the choral section and F-

FIGURE 12 *"Kanga Nakanga* 'Two Guinea Fowls'": *a,* choral section transcribed as two-part singing; *b,* the third execution, with sharpening of the F.

natural in the solo section. In the last execution, however, the pitch is closer to F-sharp in both sections. Figure 12*b* shows the third execution.

I usually hear the choral section more often as class III, rather than class I. The question of the tone F suggests how closely these classes are akin to each other in structure of tonal patterns. The only difference is in the pitch of the fifth degree of the second triad in each class. Therefore, I carefully examined whether this music should be notated down a perfect fifth, to lie in the same tonal range as figure 12*a.* In that case, the pitch in question would lie between B-natural and B-flat. This would result in frequent formation of perfect fifths and a drastic decrease in unisons between the solo melodies, though the relation of thirds would mostly be sustained.

"Kanga Nakanga" caused me trouble in notation and analysis. It is among the examples that are most perplexing for "Western" ears. The primary problem is the pitch written as F in the choral section.

FIGURE 12
(continued)

Variations in the same tonal range usually involve the formation of unisons and thirds, but not perfect fifths. However, as written in figure 12*b*, the two solo melodies maintain relationships of unisons and thirds with each other. Thus, despite the complications of the tone F, the notation of figure 12*b* seems adequate and consistent with other data. The example in question, therefore, suggests the legitimacy of class III, with the qualification that the pitch of the tone F may lie somewhere between F-sharp and F-natural.

Reexamination of other examples of class III suggests there can be two pitches of F in class III: F-natural, and an F between sharp and natural (which I shall call "neutral F" and mark as "F+"). For convenience, I shall call class III with the neutral F "class III′." It is likely produced to avoid the tritone B–F.

B-flat and class I

The distinction between classes I and III raised another question, illustrated by two more performances of "*Twalala Kuchihongo*" (figure 13). Performance 13*a* could be regarded as belonging to class I because the two-part singing seems to represent the upper parts of parallel triads, judging from the context of the chordal sequence. In the uppermost voice part, one individual sings E and D only temporarily.

Figure 13*b* presents the problem of interpretation of the note B-flat. During the repetition of this performance, the pitch B varies between B-natural and a B between natural and flat, and finally establishes consistent use of B-flat. There are two executions of this song in this performance. In the first, the solo melody constantly uses

FIGURE 13(*a* and *b*) Two more performances of "*Twalala Kuchihongo*."

FIGURE 13
(continued)

B-natural, but the chorus sometimes uses B-natural and sometimes a B between natural and flat. The second execution (figure 13*b*) features consistent use of B-flat in both sections, excepting one short B-natural in the solo section. This example may appear to represent class I, modified with B-flat. But if the pitch B in class I is flatted in performance, why not notate it in the position of class III? B-natural can be represented as F-sharp in class III, since this class also has an unstable pitch for its counterpart in class I. The major ground for notating this performance as class I lies in the extreme resemblance in melodic movement of solo and choral sections between figures 13*a* and 13*b*. If we accept this notation, B-natural can be interchanged with B-flat in class I. I shall call class I modified with B-flat "class I′."

When I noticed the structural identity of class I′ and class III, I tried to reclassify

FIGURE 14 *"Kweza Ngonde* 'Where the Moon Rises'."

all the examples of class III as class I′, and to renotate them in that tonal range. However, that procedure was inadequate. Class III existed as tonal patterns that could replace class II. Further, some performances show an unambiguous relationship between classes II and III. Class I′ and class III must therefore be distinct, and their differentiation is theoretically important.

From a Luvale viewpoint, however, these two classes may make no practical difference. Both begin with a major triad, and the pitch of the fourth degree from the root of this triad can be natural, sharp, flat, or neutral. If the pitch F in class III rises close to F-sharp, class III sounds like class I. If the pitch B in class I falls a semitone, class I in turn becomes identical to class III. From a practical point of view, the Luvale are likely to perceive classes I and III as the same.

Neutral C and class II

The third difficulty came from the alteration of the tone C in class II. Two executions in a performance of the song *"Kweza Ngonde* 'Where the Moon Rises'"* (figure 14) illustrate this. When the repetition continues, the tone C gradually rises and later stabilizes between natural and sharp. Depending on a slight fluctuation upward or downward in pitch, and on the psychological state of the listener, the triad A–C–E can be heard as either major or minor. In figure 14*b*, the tone C is close to the tempered relative pitch C-sharp.

Figure 15, a performance of the song *"Sawono"* (a personal name), provides a further illustration. The pitch of C fluctuates between natural and sharp. The musical notation shows one instance of this: in the latter half of the choral section, a pitch close to C-sharp replaces C-natural. Two other traits are also distinctive of this performance. First, there is a tendency to raise the tone C at the end of each phrase in the choral section. At the end of the chorus in many performances of other songs, this tendency is also observed. Second, when C goes sharp, the tone G is also apt to vary; in some cases, it is fully sharpened. This is also characteristic of other performances with pitch alteration of C in class II. I shall call class II with the neutral or sharpened C "class II′."

Some readers may argue that the tonal patterns of class II′ could fall into either class I′ or class III, but I doubt it. In these performances, the positional relationship between classes II and II′ is clear, and there is no question about the range in which the tonal patterns should be notated. The salient feature of class II′ is the pitch instability of the third scalar degree (C-sharp). (However, this degree in classes I′ and III is usually stable; this is an important difference between class II′ and the others.) In class II′, the fourth degree is usually stable, as opposed to classes I′ and III. Thus, class II′ is essential for the classification of the tonal patterns.

Unstable tones and classification

The discussions above refer to the pitch alteration of four notes: B, C, G, and F; they may change into approximately B-flat, C-sharp, G-sharp, and F+. The altered pitch-

neutral third   The interval of a third that is larger than a minor third but smaller than a major third

skipping process   A uniquely African way of producing harmony by singing a note and the next one after skipping one

FIGURE 15   *"Sawono"* (a personal name).

es, however, are not fixed as such, but are often unstable. Their pitch alteration is strictly conditioned by the structure of tonal patterns. The alteration of B to B-flat most frequently occurs in class I, but the alteration of C to C-sharp and G to G-sharp occurs only in class II. The neutral F occurs only in class III.

Figure 16 shows the harmonic structures of the classes: I, I′ (modified with B-flat), II, II′ (modified with C-sharp), III, and III′ (modified with F+). Among these, class II may occur most frequently. Though simplified, this could represent a possible systematization of the harmonic structure of *kukuwa* songs. Luvale musical thought regards all six classes as equivalent. The principle of third relations underlies Luvale harmonic perception.

FIGURE 16   Classification of Luvale harmonic structures.

Kubik's theory and its implications

Nearly a quarter century before me, but from a different perspective, Gerhard Kubik (1968) dealt with the same problem in his study of the music of the Mbwela and the Nkhangala, Angolan ethnic groups that have a close cultural relationship with the Luvale. He sought to set up a unitary theory that makes Mbwela and Nkhangala musical complexity intelligible. In many respects, the results of his analysis coincide with those of mine. This coincidence confirms the affinity of the musical cultures of the Luvale and the peoples he studied.

Kubik focused on the principles of multipart singing and the origin of neutral thirds. One of his important concepts is that of a "skipping process" (1968:27–31), a uniquely African way of producing harmony—"by singing a given note together with the next note but one in the scale, skipping one step" (1986:28). According to Kubik, the application of this principle to a heptatonic system leads to parallelism in thirds, and its double application leads to "a chain of triads," which expands the range of possible choices of notes for harmonic formation, and increases the chances of melodic variation. My concept of the principle of third relations rephrases his notion of the skipping process as applied to heptatonic scales.

Kubik's description of multipart singing of the Mbwela and related groups is fully applicable to Luvale songs. Harmonies, he says, derive from the "loose combination of individual voices, fluctuating in their omnibus appearance between triads, bichords," and other accumulations of notes. Chordal outlines "may change with every repetition of the choral phrase," and vocal motion can be parallel, oblique, and contrary (1986:47). Another concept underlying his theory is the notion of the indigenous "ideal of euphony," represented by the major third, the perfect fifth, and the major triad (1968:45–46). He considers the use of neutral thirds a measure necessary to attain a sequence of euphony in a heptatonic system. Because of the interruption of minor triads, a diatonic scale cannot produce a continuous series of major triads. To avoid minor triads (which do not fit the ideal), singers raise the thirds a little. Through this procedure, these notes can both sustain their identity as scalar notes, and can fulfill the harmonic requirement of euphony, thus effecting a practical compromise.

According to Kubik, three tones require such change: F/F+, G/G+, and C/C+. Kubik illustrates this tonal system by marking with "(+)" the changeable tones (figure 17). These tones appear at the three places in the scale where minor triads would otherwise form. In addition, the neutral thirds occur only in specific musical contexts. For example, the tone C-natural is raised to C+ with A below and E above; but it remains natural with F-natural, forming a perfect fifth.

FIGURE 17   The tonal system of the Mbwela and the Nkhangala (after Kubik 1968:47).

At many points, our observations are similar. Particularly notable are Kubik's identification of three unstable tones (F, G, C), and his description of the circumstances in which the alteration of pitch occurs. He presents the tonal system beginning on A. This coincides with the tonal system of the most frequent basic pattern in Luvale music. My only modification to this is the addition of B/B-flat as a changeable note.

A theoretical discrepancy highlights our views on minor triads. Kubik contends that, since minor triads are not regarded as consonant (according to the ideal), they are avoided by the use of neutral thirds. In Luvale vocal music, however, minor triads occur as frequently as major triads. In a more recent work (1981), Kubik is less clear on this point. He says singers regard fifths (fourths), octaves, and thirds as consonant; but it is unclear whether he includes minor triads. Repeated listening to his records (1981) gives me the impression that Mbwela and Nkhangala *mukanda* songs exhibit no striking difference from Luvale songs, and that minor triads often occur in them. Kubik mentions in a footnote that "in many places, minor thirds are simply tolerated" (1968:47). Kubik's theory is perspicacious and inspiring, but the problems of how to define another people's aesthetic ideal of sound, and whether that ideal embraces minor thirds and triads, remain.

CULTURALLY DIFFERENT PERCEPTIONS

One of the crucial results of my study is awareness of the discrepancy between Luvale and Western perceptions of unstable tones. In my analysis, I have discussed the pitch alteration of several tones because such fluctuation and instability are the most conspicuous phenomena from a Western point of view. This is the reason neutral thirds have attracted so much attention in scholarly literature.

I have also taken pains to identify whether an unstable tone is natural, sharp, or neutral, each time it appears. Through this process, I have come to the conclusion that such distinctions have little significance for the Luvale, who neither conceptually nor perceptually differentiate major and minor intervals, as analysts of Western tonal music do.

Kubik points out such a discrepancy between the investigator and the culture bearers. To Westerners, the thirds, "the crux of the system," sound unstable; but to culture bearers, notions of stability "are irrelevant and alien" (1981:28). Blacking, too, showed concern for this issue. He analyzed two melodies that sounded different to Western ears, and showed how the "principle of 'harmonic' equivalence" underlay the identity of these melodies to the Venda (1967:168–169).

Investigator as part of research

The gap between the investigator and the people investigated comes to light only when the investigator plays an active role in research. With my own musical perception, based on previous professional training in Western music, I intruded into the domain of Luvale music. My analysis thus started from the surprises and perplexities that came from this intrusion. I sought the source of such cultural experiences. This method allowed me to discover elements of the Luvale musical system, and revealed discrepancies in Luvale and Western musical conceptions and perceptions.

When the researcher becomes an essential factor in research, the evaluation of his or her perceptions, and the problem of incorporating them in the analytical process, are important issues. The confrontation of culturally different perceptions reveals the qualities of each culture. Such research can be conducted only by investigators who, though foreign to the culture they study, are sensitive to its perceptions.

REFERENCES

Berreman, Gerald D. 1972. "Is Ethnoscience Relevant?" In *Culture and Cognition,* ed. James P. Spradley, 223–232. San Francisco: Chandler.

Blacking, John. 1967. *Venda Children's Songs.* Johannesburg: Witwatersrand University Press.

———. 1981. "The Problem of 'Ethnic' Perceptions in the Semiotics of Music." In *The Sign in Music and Literature,* ed. Wendy Steiner, 184– 194. Austin: University of Texas Press)

Blum, Stephen. 1975. "Towards a Social History of Musicological Technique." *Ethnomusicology* 19(2):207–231.

Bronson, Bertrand H. 1951. "Melodic Stability in Oral Transmission." *Journal of the International Folk Music Council* 3:50–55.

———. 1959–1972. *The Traditional Tunes of the Child Ballads.* 4 vols. Princeton, N.J.: Princeton University Press.

Conklin, Harold C. 1955. "Hanunóo Color Categories." *Southwestern Journal of Anthropology* 11:339–344.

Crick, Malcolm. 1976. *Explorations in Language and Meaning.* London: Malaby Press.

Danckert, Werner. 1939. *Das europäische Volkslied.* Berlin: B. Hahnefeld.

Delille, A. 1930. "Besnijdnis bij de Alundas en Aluenas in de strakten Zuiden van Belgisch Kongo." *Anthropos* 25:851–858.

Gluckman, Max. 1949. "The Role of the Sexes in Wiko Circumcision Ceremonies." In *Social Structure: Studies Presented to A. R. Radcliffe-Brown,* ed. Meyer Fortes, 145–167. Oxford: Oxford University Press.

Gourlay, Kenneth A. 1978. "Towards a Reassessment of the Ethnomusicologist's Role in Research." *Ethnomusicology* 22(1):1–35.

———. 1982. "Towards a Humanizing Ethnomusicology." *Ethnomusicology* 26(3):411–420.

Herndon, Marcia. 1974. "Analysis: The Herding of Sacred Cows?" *Ethnomusicology* 18(2):219–262.

Herzog, George. 1934. "Speech-Melody and Primitive Music." *Musical Quarterly* 20(4):452–466.

Hornbostel, Erich Moritz von. 1928. "African Negro Music." *Africa* 1(1):30–62.

Jones, Arthur M. 1959. *Studies in African Music.* 2 vols. London: Oxford University Press.

Kauffman, Robert. 1984. "Multipart Relationships in Shona Vocal Music." In *Studies in African Music,* ed. J. H. Kwabena Nketia and Jacqueline C. Djedje, 145–159. Los Angeles: Program in Ethnomusicology, University of California.

Kubik, Gerhard. 1968. *Mehrstimmigkeit und Tonsysteme in Zentral- und Ostafrika.* Vienna: Österreichische Akademie der Wissenschaften.

———. 1981. *Mukanda na Makisi.* Berlin: Museum für Völkerkunde, Musikethnologische Abteilung. Museum Collection Berlin MC.11. 2 LP disks and notes.

———. 1985. "African Tone Systems: A Reassessment." *Yearbook for Traditional Music* 17:31–63.

———. 1986. "A Structural Examination of Homophonic Multi-Part Singing in East and Central Africa." *Anuario Musical* 39–40:27–58.

———. 1988. "Nsenga/Shona Harmonic Patterns and the San Heritage in Southern Africa." *Ethnomusicology* 32(2):211–248.

Merriam, Alan P. 1959. "African Music." In *Continuity and Change in African Cultures,* ed. William R. Bascom and Melville J. Herskovits, 49–86. Chicago: University of Chicago Press.

Mersmann, Hans. 1921. *Grundlagen einer musikalischen Volksliedforschung.* Berlin: Berlin Technische Hochschule.

Mwondela, William R. 1972. *Mukanda and Makishi: Traditional Education in North- Western Zambia.* Lusaka: Neczam.

Nketia, J. H. Kwabena. 1974. *The Music of Africa.* New York: Norton.

Schmidt-Wrenger, Barbara. 1979. *Rituelle Frauengesänge der Tshokwe: Untersuchungen zu einem Sakularisierungsprozess in Angola und Zaïre.* 3 vols. Tervuren: Musée Royal de l'Afrique Centrale.

Schneider, Marius. 1944. "Phonetische und Metrische Korrelationen bei Gesprochenen und Gesungenen Ewe-Texten." *Archiv für Vergleichende Phonetik* 7(1/2):1–6.

Seeger, Charles. 1971. "Reflections upon a Given Topic: Music in Universal Perspective." *Ethnomusicology* 15(3):385–398.

Sharp, Cecil J. 1965. *English Folk Song: Some Conclusions,* 4th ed. London: Mercury Books.

Stone, Ruth. 1979. "Communication and Interaction Processes in Music Event among the Kpelle of Liberia." Ph.D. dissertation, Indiana University.

Tsukada, Kenichi. 1982. "Musical Culture and Mukanda amongst the Luvale of Zambia." Typescript. Report submitted to the Institute for African Studies, University of Zambia, Lusaka.

———. 1988. "Luvale Perceptions of Mukanda in Discourse and Music." Ph.D. dissertation, Queen's University of Belfast.

———. 1990. "*Kukuwa* and *Kachacha*: Classification and Rhythm in the Music of the Luvale of Central Africa." In *People and Rhythm,* ed. Tetsuo Sakurai, 229–276. Tokyo: Tokyo Shoseki. In Japanese.

———. 1991a. "*Mukanda* Rites and Music: A Study of Initiation Rites in Central Africa." In *Ritual and Music II,* ed. Tomoaki Fujii, 177–228. Tokyo: Tokyo Shoseki. In Japanese.

———. 1991b. "*Kalindula* in *Mukanda*: The Incorporation of Westernized Music into the Boys' Initiation Rites of the Luvale of Zambia." In *Tradition and its Future in Music,* ed. Yoshihiko Tokumaru et al., 547–551. Tokyo: Mita Press.

Wachsmann, Klaus P. 1971. "Universal Perspectives in Music." *Ethnomusicology* 15(3):381–384.

White, Charles M. N. 1953. "Notes on the Circumcision Rites of the Balovale tribes." *African Studies* 12:40–56.

———. 1961. *Elements in Luvale Beliefs and Rituals.* Manchester: Manchester University Press. Rhodes-Livingstone Papers, 32.

Music of the Shona of Zimbabwe
John E. Kaemmer

Musical Performance
Shona Concepts of Music
Uses and Functions of Shona Music
Change in Shona Music
The Music Industry
Music and the "Uprising"

The Shona, a population of about 9 million Bantu-speakers, live mostly in Zimbabwe and partly in Mozambique. They speak five major dialects—Zezuru, Korekore, Manyika, Kalanga, Karanga. The source of the term *Shona* is unknown, but it has long referred to these groups, whose dialects follow a single orthography. The Shona people still recognize the areas of linguistic difference, which partly coincide with variation in traditional music.

Until the 1400s, the culture of these groups centered in what are now stone ruins near the town of Masvingo, ruins that gave their name to Zimbabwe. Possibly because of ecological collapse, the kingdom moved its headquarters south to Dhlodhlo, near Bulawayo; and in the north, another kingdom, Monomotapa, developed. Both kingdoms carried on maritime trade. In the early 1800s, as European influence expanded in southern Africa, the Ngoni people passed through the Zimbabwe Plateau and destroyed the Shona kingdoms. Independent chieftainships then became the major units of social integration. In 1890, European settlers set up a colonial regime that lasted ninety years.

Little of the early development of Shona music is known. The Shona practice of yodeling suggests influences from Pygmies, who probably inhabited the area before the arrival of Bantu-speakers. Scattered among archaeological excavations in Zimbabwe, lamellae (prongs) attest the early importance of the mbira. Tonal harmony among the Shona and neighboring peoples possibly relates to the musical system of the San, who presumably inhabited the area originally; the Shona may stand within a "southcentral African tonal-harmonic belt" (Kubik 1988:46), characterized by heptatonic or hexatonic scales, with patterned movements of bichords in fourths and fifths. Since the San share several cultural features with the Bantu of the area, they may also share musical features with them. The Shona, however, have not adopted the clicks of San languages, as have some Bantu-speaking populations in South Africa. The musical system of the San may reflect the harmonic series created by the two fundamental tones a musical bow produces as the string is stopped in two segments. Gerhard Kubik found that a group of San in Angola tuned their musical bows in three ways, with the two segments of string producing tones 400 cents apart (a major third), 300 cents apart (a minor third), or 200 cents apart (a whole step).

Using no more than the fourth harmonic, a player on each bow could produce a four-tone scale, with characteristic progressions of fourths and fifths. Kubik explains the presence of pentatonic songs by suggesting the San conceptualize as a unit the tones produced by two differently tuned bows. If all three tunings were played or conceptualized together, as in hocket, they would produce a range of tones typical of the hexatonic or heptatonic scales characteristic of the Shona mbira (Kubik 1988:47–71). We may never know whether Shona music actually arose from playing musical bows, but the affinities between the harmonics of a musical bow and the structure of Shona mbira are unmistakable.

With the arrival of European settlers, Shona music underwent profound changes. In military units, schools, and churches, settlers exposed the Shona people to European music. The impact of European musical values varied with the intensity of European occupation and the proximity of mission churches and schools. The central part of the country experienced stronger European influence than hotter, less desirable fringes.

The history of music in Shona life divides roughly into three periods. The first displayed only indigenous or traditional musical practices, which, before the arrival of Europeans, were common everywhere. (In some areas in the early 1990s, people were still practicing music in indigenous styles.) The second period reflects the impact of European colonization on musical activity, including the introduction of European music, and the exploitation of Shona music to influence political struggles. The third period includes the struggle for independence, and the years immediately after.

MUSICAL PERFORMANCE

Mbira

The most distinctive feature of Shona music is the use of the mbira, a lamellophone plucked by thumbs and forefingers (figure 1). The instrument is widespread in Africa, but the Shona have developed the largest instruments, and use them the most frequently in rituals. The mbira may have arisen as a portable version of a xylophone (Jones 1971:34 and passim), but evidence to prove this origin will probably never appear. In the late 1900s, the principal mbira was the *mbira dzavadzimu* 'mbira of the ancestral spirits', an instrument with twenty-two or more wide keys, which the Shona recognize as the mbira of the Zezuru people (Tracey 1970a; Berliner 1978). Players use the forefinger of the right hand and both thumbs. The Korekore people have traditionally used a type of mbira variously termed *hera*, *munyonga*, *matepe*, and *madhebhe* (Tracey 1970b). This form has about twenty-nine narrow keys, played with both thumbs and both forefingers. In comparison with other forms of mbira, its music is much faster, it has lower bass notes but a lighter sound, and its rhythms are more complex. The *njari* form came from the Zambezi River Valley in the 1700s (Tracey 1969:87–91). It has served in rituals involving tutelary spirits (*mashave*); but in the late 1900s, old men played it, mostly to accompany nonritual singing (Tracey 1961). The *karimba* (in many areas, *kalimba*) type is usually smaller than the other kinds, and does not have ritual uses. Andrew Tracey suggests (1972) it was the prototype of all forms of mbira in the region. It often serves as a novice's instrument.

All mbira consist primarily of a sounding board and an assortment of lamellae, hammered from metal. The board is hollow in the *hera*, but not in the other kinds; it is usually about 19 centimeters wide, and slightly larger from front to back. In pre-European times, blacksmiths made lamellae from smelted iron; in the late twentieth century, people pounded them from nails, or from the wire found in the springs of

FIGURE I   Tuning a newly made mbira by playing it with an older instrument, eastern Zimbabwe, 1971.

mbira   Plucked lamellophone of the Shona that is played singly or in ensembles

mbira dzavadzimu   'Mbira of the ancestral spirits', a lamellophone with twenty-two or more wide keys

chuning   Borrowed from the English *tuning*, but includes pitch as well as timbre, loudness, and other factors

standard harmonic pattern   Harmonic cycle for playing the mbira that involves a succession of fifths with prescribed motion

seats of bicycles and cars. Longer (lower-pitched) lamellae stand near the center of the instrument; shorter ones, on the outside edges. One end of each lamellae rests on wood at the upper edge of the board, and a metal piece passes under all the lamellae about 5 centimeters from the same end. Above the lamellae, between the wood and the metal piece, a clamp holds the lamellae tightly in place; the other end is free for plucking. For tuning, a player can move a lamella back and forth. Like the English word *sheep*, the Shona word *mbira* is both singular and plural: in the singular, it denotes one of the metal prongs; and when referring to the instrument, the Shona use the plural forms of verbs and modifiers.

The mbira has a subdued sound, often increased by a resonator and a typically African buzzing sound. For personal entertainment or practice, players often omit the resonator. To produce the desired volume of sound in rituals and public performances, the player puts the instrument inside a gourd resonator. The gourds, which have to be uncommonly large, require for sufficient growth either virgin soil or fertilizer; they often serve as containers for water or beer, before musicians make them into resonators by cutting off their tops. The buzzing comes from a series of rattles, strung along the rim; formerly pieces of land snail shell, the rattles are now usually bottle caps. The *hera* and related types also have metal rattles, placed in the hollow part of the board, but the *mbira dzavadzimu* has them attached to the outside of the board. For the buzzing, the *njari* type of mbira relies only on the rattles on the resonator.

Early researchers assumed tuning was as important in Africa as it is in European music. This assumption led to differences in understanding the tuning of mbira. In 1932, Hugh Tracey found, "In my experience there is always this absolute tuning which will be recognized by the local people as being 'perfect,' but it does not necessarily mean that every tuner of an African instrument has the skill to attain it" (1969:81). However, Tracey's findings show flexibility in tuning exists. He noted the keys of the mbira sometimes sounded, not the fundamental, but an overtone (if the latter happened to be louder); sometimes the overtone was an octave higher than the intended note, but people still considered that placement acceptable (1969:81). He also noted different districts preferred different tunings (1969:83). From factors related to the study of instrumental tunings (inadequate accuracy of the observer, limitations of apparatus, lack of skill, temperature, loud overtones and harmonics), Tracey omits the possibility of greater flexibility in the acceptable norms of pitch.

More recently, Berliner says Shona mbirists, talking about tuning, use a term borrowed from English: *chuning*. Unlike the English *tuning*, the idea of *chuning* includes not only relative pitch, but also timbre, loudness, the nature of octaves and unisons, and the relationship of overtones to fundamental tones. Berliner finds players of the *mbira dzavadzimu* sometimes use a change of tuning to get variety in the sounds they produce (1978:60–62). This idea contradicts the findings of Andrew Tracey, who maintains the Shona tune the *matepe* to a heptatonic equitonal scale

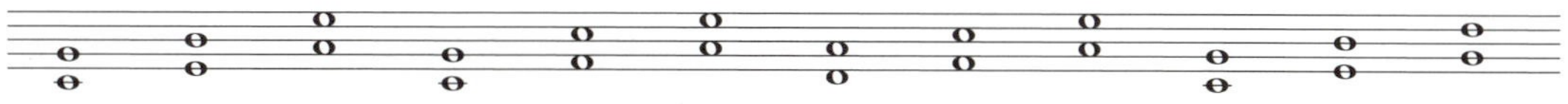

FIGURE 2 The standard harmonic pattern on the mbira.

FIGURE 2 The standard harmonic pattern on the mbira.

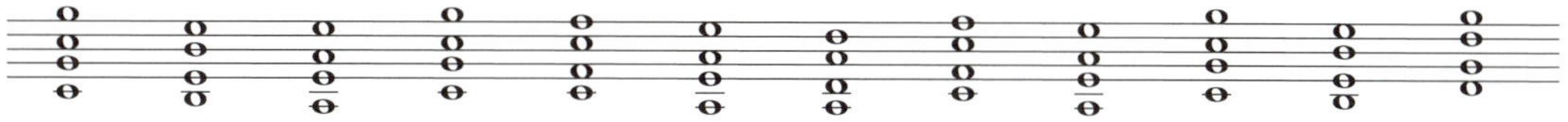

FIGURE 3 Potential tones for the standard harmonic progression.

(1970b:46); he adds that a mbira purchased in 1932 was still acceptably in tune with other mbira when taken to Zimbabwe in 1969. It is possible the *matepe* or *hera* shows a more standardized form of tuning because it persists in the areas of Zimbabwe where European influence has been weaker. In the early 1930s, Hugh Tracey noted very few *mbira dzavadzimu* were in existence (1969:83), so the tradition researched in the 1970s by Berliner may be more flexible because it has passed through the hands of few players.

As the piano provides a conceptual basis for the Western musical system, so the mbira provides a conceptual basis for the Shona, which is primarily an improvisational tradition, with both vocal and instrumental performances based on recurring harmonic and rhythmic cycles. The harmonic cycles involve a succession of fifths (bichords) whose lower notes move in prescribed ways. The most common pattern consists of the movement of fifths in groups of three, with each group only slightly different from the group preceding it. These patterns can be most easily explained by reference to what Andrew Tracey has called the standard pattern (1970b:39). Many mbira songs follow this pattern, but other patterns of harmonic progression are common. They are best presented in a modified musical notation. In the musical examples, the five-line staff should facilitate visualizing the outline of the music. In figures 2, 3, and 11, the staff represents a treble clef, but the absence of a clef serves as a reminder the tuning is different. The clefs in figures 4, 6, 9, and 10 are also omitted, with the understanding that the right hand indicates treble clef, and the left hand indicates bass clef. To show the fingers' movements, the notes produced by the index finger have rising stems; those produced by the thumb have descending stems. In writing about southern African music, the placement of notes on pulse lines without rhythmic indications has become standard practice. In these examples, an eighth note indicates a pulse. The note values will focus the reader's attention on the variety of patterns inherent in the tonal and rhythmic relationships.

The standard harmonic pattern mentioned above appears in figure 11. The patterns are not limited to the two notes of the fifth, since the Shona consider notes an octave apart to be equivalent. Consequently, any note from the fifth can sound, as in figure 3. Among the combinations of notes in figure 3, all the stepwise movement is descending. The principle of ascending in thirds and fourths and descending in seconds is the basis of Shona harmony. To maintain important kinetic and rhythmic patterns, musicians sometimes insert extraneous notes into the basic harmonic pattern, despite an incomplete keyboard. These notes often include a third, which gives the outside observer the impression the Shona are using triads. Figure 4*a* shows how this pattern appears in the lowest notes of a basic pattern in a well-known Shona song. These principles of harmony are important, because they relate closely to Shona rhythm. In the literature on Shona rhythms, as on African rhythms in general, different usages of the words *pulse* and *beat* have led to confusion. Sometimes, authors use them interchangeably, but carefully distinguishing them explains Shona music more clearly. In Shona music, the term *pulse* is best reserved for the rapid and equal rhythmic units often heard in fast drumming. The term *beat* more effectively refers to the somewhat slower rhythmic units that are combinations of pulses and are not always even; the beat often coincides with dance steps.

The *kushaura* (leading) part plays the melodic and higher notes, while the *kutsinhira* (following) part emphasizes the root movements of the harmonic patterns.

FIGURE 4   The song "*Nhemamusasa* 'Cut [materials for] a shelter in the bush'": (*a*) *kushaura*, the part that leads; (*b*) *kutsinhira*, the part that follows.

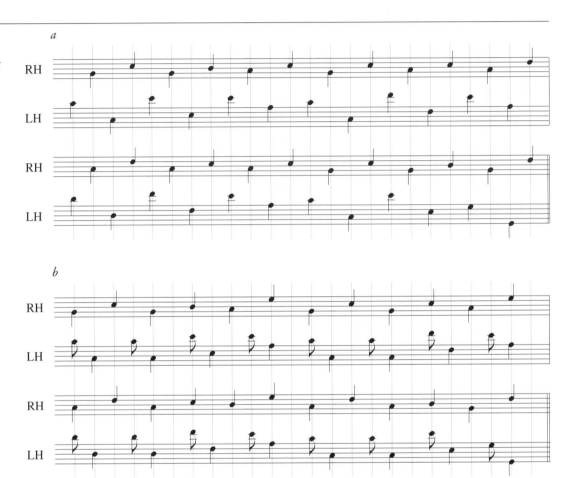

In the performance of a classic mbira song, the four harmonic segments repeat constantly, with variations. In most songs, each of the harmonic segments becomes a twelve-pulse rhythmic segment, to produce forty-eight pulses in each cycle of the song. In each segment, the progression from one bichord to the next produces a distinctive harmonic rhythm. Using an eighth note to signal each pulse, the harmonic rhythm is often even, with each segment containing three beats (figure 5*a*). Four-beat segments are common, forming an uneven harmonic rhythm (figures 5*b* and 5*c*). The four-beat patterns usually form the basis for dance steps. Sometimes the change from one chord to another is ambiguous, because the third tone in one chord anticipates the jump of a third in the root tones. This ambiguity permits two forms of harmonic rhythm to combine to produce rhythmic complexity.

The rhythms within each twelve-pulse group are subject to extensive variation. When two mbirists play together, one may follow a triple meter, while the other fol-

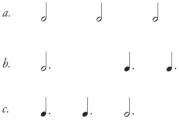

FIGURE 5   Harmonic rhythms.

lows a duple or quadruple one, thus creating polyrhythm, as in figures 4a and 4b, played together. Duple pulse patterns on the mbira result from interlocking the actions of the right and left hands (figures 4a and 6); this interlocking results in an even harmonic rhythm, or in patterns of triple beats. The triplet pulse patterns often vary, as in figure 7, and in the left hand in figure 4b. Various asymmetrical pulse patterns can contrast with the basic beats, particularly with the *hera*. In the twelve-pulse segments of ritual songs, the basic asymmetrical or additive rhythms are seen in figures 8a and 8b; as performers substitute 8c or 8d for the dotted quarter note, these rhythms vary extensively. Often depending on the relationship with the text, the perceived beginning of a pattern may occur on any of these notes. Since many nonritual songs have fewer than twelve pulses in a harmonic segment, the two patterns of 8e often sound together, as do those of 8f. Hemiolas are also used, as in the left hand of figure 6.

FIGURE 6   *Dambatimbu,* a novice's version of a *munyonga* song.

TRACK 20

All the major mbira songs have two parts, in contrasting and complementary rhythms. In figures 4a and 4b, the right-hand parts are similar, though one is a pulse behind the other. The *kushaura* (leading) part plays the melodic and higher notes, while the *kutsinhira* (following) part emphasizes the root movements of the harmonic patterns (figure 4b). Ideally, one person is available to play each of the parts; people expect a soloist to play something of each part, and they judge his competence accordingly. In improvisation, the player of the *kushaura* starts the changes from one mode of playing to another, and the *kutsinhira* follows. Not every cycle of forty-eight pulses varies, but people play several cycles one way before making a change to another. The *munyonga* tradition of northeastern Zimbabwe reserves simplified versions of the songs (*dambatimbu*) for use in learning. Figure 6 is one of these versions.

FIGURE 7   Variable triplet pulse patterns.

FIGURE 8   Variations in rhythmic patterns.

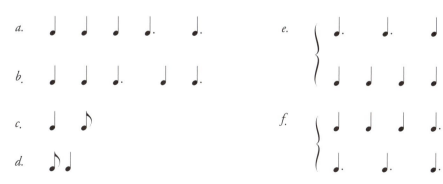

FIGURE 9 Variations on figure 4a.

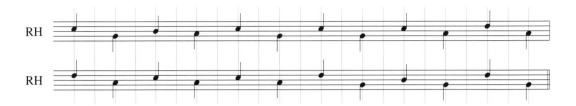

FIGURE 10 Variations on figure 4b.

Mbirists often change the harmonic and rhythmic relationships by playing certain patterns of notes louder, then changing to emphasize other notes. The right-hand notes (figure 4a) can be played as in figure 9. Figure 10 shows how the playing of the lower notes of figure 4b can vary. By changing the loudness of the thumb notes or the index-finger notes, performers emphasize different rhythmic features. Perceived differences also come randomly from the shapes of the resonators, and from the positions of the instruments in the resonators.

Other instrumental and vocal genres

The mbira is a harmonic and rhythmic instrument; melody comes from the human voice. Indeed, the popular evaluation of mbirists rests largely on their skill in singing. Shona singing includes yodeling, responsorial form, and improvisation. When people are singing without the mbira, vocal sounds still follow the instrumental harmonies. The bass type of singing (*mahon'ra*) consists primarily of the roots of the bichords, with ornamentation such as yodeling. This type of singing, frequently hummed, can accompany mbira music or stand alone. Also frequently sung are four-tone melodic patterns typical of the upper voices of the tonal progression in figure 11. This pattern, an important feature of the *dambatimbu*, appears in figure 6 as the first, fifth, and ninth pulses of each left-hand pattern. Within each harmonic segment, the pattern skips when ascending, and moves stepwise when descending; such patterns provide the basis for improvising melodies.

In songs with responsorial form, the group-response parts are usually fixed, but the lead part (also called *kushaura*) has considerable leeway in improvising both text and tune. Certain fragments of text are appropriate only for specific songs, which they serve to identify. In many songs, other fragments of text serve interchangeably. The singer is also free to invent new words to fit the occasion. A sung phrase often starts on a high note and descends, with the sound of the high notes affecting the configuration of the rhythms. Phonemic linguistic tones affect the melodic structure, but no detailed study has determined how.

FIGURE 11 The four-tone melodic pattern.

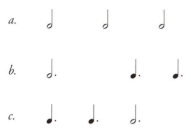

FIGURE 5   Harmonic rhythms.

lows a duple or quadruple one, thus creating polyrhythm, as in figures 4a and 4b, played together. Duple pulse patterns on the mbira result from interlocking the actions of the right and left hands (figures 4a and 6); this interlocking results in an even harmonic rhythm, or in patterns of triple beats. The triplet pulse patterns often vary, as in figure 7, and in the left hand in figure 4b. Various asymmetrical pulse patterns can contrast with the basic beats, particularly with the *hera*. In the twelve-pulse segments of ritual songs, the basic asymmetrical or additive rhythms are seen in figures 8a and 8b; as performers substitute 8c or 8d for the dotted quarter note, these rhythms vary extensively. Often depending on the relationship with the text, the perceived beginning of a pattern may occur on any of these notes. Since many nonritual songs have fewer than twelve pulses in a harmonic segment, the two patterns of 8e often sound together, as do those of 8f. Hemiolas are also used, as in the left hand of figure 6.

FIGURE 6   *Dambatimbu,* a novice's version of a *munyonga* song.

TRACK 20

All the major mbira songs have two parts, in contrasting and complementary rhythms. In figures 4a and 4b, the right-hand parts are similar, though one is a pulse behind the other. The *kushaura* (leading) part plays the melodic and higher notes, while the *kutsinhira* (following) part emphasizes the root movements of the harmonic patterns (figure 4b). Ideally, one person is available to play each of the parts; people expect a soloist to play something of each part, and they judge his competence accordingly. In improvisation, the player of the *kushaura* starts the changes from one mode of playing to another, and the *kutsinhira* follows. Not every cycle of forty-eight pulses varies, but people play several cycles one way before making a change to another. The *munyonga* tradition of northeastern Zimbabwe reserves simplified versions of the songs (*dambatimbu*) for use in learning. Figure 6 is one of these versions.

FIGURE 7   Variable triplet pulse patterns.

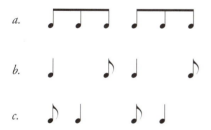

FIGURE 8   Variations in rhythmic patterns.

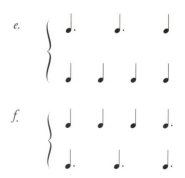

FIGURE 9   Variations on figure 4a.

FIGURE 10   Variations on figure 4b.

Mbirists often change the harmonic and rhythmic relationships by playing certain patterns of notes louder, then changing to emphasize other notes. The right-hand notes (figure 4a) can be played as in figure 9. Figure 10 shows how the playing of the lower notes of figure 4b can vary. By changing the loudness of the thumb notes or the index-finger notes, performers emphasize different rhythmic features. Perceived differences also come randomly from the shapes of the resonators, and from the positions of the instruments in the resonators.

Other instrumental and vocal genres

The mbira is a harmonic and rhythmic instrument; melody comes from the human voice. Indeed, the popular evaluation of mbirists rests largely on their skill in singing. Shona singing includes yodeling, responsorial form, and improvisation. When people are singing without the mbira, vocal sounds still follow the instrumental harmonies. The bass type of singing (*mahon'ra*) consists primarily of the roots of the bichords, with ornamentation such as yodeling. This type of singing, frequently hummed, can accompany mbira music or stand alone. Also frequently sung are four-tone melodic patterns typical of the upper voices of the tonal progression in figure 11. This pattern, an important feature of the *dambatimbu*, appears in figure 6 as the first, fifth, and ninth pulses of each left-hand pattern. Within each harmonic segment, the pattern skips when ascending, and moves stepwise when descending; such patterns provide the basis for improvising melodies.

In songs with responsorial form, the group-response parts are usually fixed, but the lead part (also called *kushaura*) has considerable leeway in improvising both text and tune. Certain fragments of text are appropriate only for specific songs, which they serve to identify. In many songs, other fragments of text serve interchangeably. The singer is also free to invent new words to fit the occasion. A sung phrase often starts on a high note and descends, with the sound of the high notes affecting the configuration of the rhythms. Phonemic linguistic tones affect the melodic structure, but no detailed study has determined how.

FIGURE 11   The four-tone melodic pattern.

FIGURE 12 Dance performance in north-eastern Zimbabwe, 1972. *Left to right,* three common types of Shona drums: *mutumba, mhito,* and *danda*

In addition to the mbira, the Shona use many instruments, of which drums are the most important (figure 12). Though people often play the mbira solo, in some areas they accompany it (particularly the *hera*) with drums. Drums alone often accompany singing. In their major drum ensemble, the Shona have three types of traditional drums, all of which are open ended, with pegs to fasten the head to the body. The smallest, the *mhito,* is about 30 centimeters tall and 18 to 20 centimeters in diameter; often beaten with sticks, it maintains the basic rhythm. The *dandi* is larger (30 to 36 centimeters high), with a diameter as large as 30 centimeters. The *dandi* player performs with hands, sticks, or a combination of both; he is the principal player of improvised variations. The performer on the *mutumba* (a low-pitched, waist-high drum) plays a limited amount of variation; he straddles the drum as it lies on the ground, leans the drum against his knees when sitting, or stands beside the upright drum. The names of drums vary notably among the districts.

In the northeastern part of Zimbabwe, Shona sometimes use panpipes (*ngororombe*) for entertainment (figure 13). They play the pipes in groups, with each per-

FIGURE 13 Panpipe (*ngororombe*) ensemble, northeastern Zimbabwe, 1972.

The Shona describe particularly good musical performances as causing people to run off and allow their cooking pots to boil over.

FIGURE 14   Hand rattles, panpipes, and leg rattles being prepared for a performance, northeastern Zimbabwe, 1972.

former blowing two or three pipes in hocket with the others, while playing a rattle, and sometimes even breaking into song. At Bindura in 1972, pipers played regularly for entertainment, and sometimes took engagements to play for special events.

Formerly, while herding, boys played a type of musical bow resonated in the mouth (*chipendani*). About 3 feet long, the bow produces highly complex music. The string is connected near the center of the bow, to produce segments about a fourth apart; the player plucks one segment of the string with the thumb and forefinger, while he creates rhythmic patterns on the other segment with the index finger. Because cattle no longer range so far and most boys now attend school, these instruments are declining in use.

Rattles (*hosho*) are extremely important, because they accompany singing, the *mbira dzavadzimu* ensembles, and the panpipe ensembles. Their most popular type is a knobby gourd, cleaned out and filled with seeds. People also use loud rattles made from tin cans and stones, because they are easy to prepare. When played with the *mbira dzavadzimu*, two rattles are shaken, one in each hand. Shona want each to have a distinct sound, which readily comes from instruments of different sizes. They play in contrasting rhythms, often two against three. The panpipers shake a rattle in their left hand, and handle the pipes in their right. The irregular pattern in the rattle helps them keep track of the rhythm. In some districts, leg rattles (also called *hosho*) accompany dancing: large rattles (*magavhu*) employ three 9-centimeter-diameter gourds on each leg; smaller ones (*tswawo*), groups of eight 4-centimeter-diameter gourds. The two sets of leg rattles have different timbres (figure 14).

SHONA CONCEPTS OF MUSIC

In the Shona language, no word precisely translates the Western concept of "music." The Shona have separate words for singing (*kuimba*) and for playing an instrument (*kuridza* 'cause to cry out'). Since dancing includes both instruments and songs, the word for dancing (*kutamba* 'play') implies the combination of these three elements.

The Shona value music highly, and ascribe power to it. Many folktales include songs that so charm or distract the characters, they follow someone's wishes. The Shona describe particularly good musical performances as causing people to run off and allow their cooking pots to boil over.

Traditionally, the Shona believed music implied supernatural power. They thought the ability to play the mbira came to a young male in a dream, from the spirit of an ancestor, often a grandfather. They believed special ability in drumming or dancing was a sign of the favor of ancestral spirits, and they perceived such talents to be a sign of mediumistic potential.

They assumed their ritual songs, including those of the mbira, took forms the ancestors set. Creative activity in singing and playing the mbira consisted of inventing new ways of playing an existing song, rather than creating new songs. Mbira songs enjoy many ways of playing (*miridziro*), which pass in and out of fashion, while the songs themselves retain popularity. The differences in forms of mbira correlate with views of repertory. Some songs belong to certain kinds of mbira, and not to others. This distinction relates to the common expression that songs are "in the mbira," and the player simply brings them out.

A song's identity is not always clear, even to many Shona, who classify together songs that follow the same harmonic progression. Because the location of the basic pitch of a harmonic pattern can be on two different keys of the mbira, listeners can confuse songs. To listeners, particularly those unfamiliar with the mbira, the difference in pitch is sometimes vague. Many times, a line of text will provide a clue to the identity of a song, but the mbira itself does not provide such guidance. The place in the harmonic progression where the singing begins is another clue to the song. Mbira songs are often differentiated by characteristic patterns of melody or rhythm played on the mbira.

The Shona classify songs as being modern (*chimanjemanje*) and traditional (*nziyo dzepasi* 'songs of the earth'). The former stand apart from songs of church and school. The latter are classified primarily by use: play songs, hunting songs, death songs, children's songs, songs of ancestral spirits (*mudzimu*) and tutelary spirits (*mashave*).

The Shona do not have rigid practices concerning the musical roles of the sexes. One of the dances used in rainmaking, the *mapfuwe*, was traditionally done by women, but men now take part, at least when it is danced for entertainment. Traditionally, men played the mbira, but women are occasionally taking it up without losing esteem. In public performances, men normally play the drums, but women know how to play. Sometimes women even show the men how to "do it right."

USES AND FUNCTIONS OF SHONA MUSIC

In pre-European Shona society, music served purposes beyond mere entertainment. One of the most important of these was the enhancement of rituals related to the chieftainship. Traditionally, a chief had at his headquarters a set of drums reserved for official purposes. At the home of an old Korekore chief, I saw such a set: though all but one of the instruments resembled ordinary drums, each had a special name, and all served to announce a chief's installation or death, or events the chief was sponsoring. Elderly informants in the area in the 1970s remembered praise songs for chiefs, sung in token of respect.

In the past, work songs were particularly important. The most popular types accompanied threshing and grain grinding. The songs also served to express social criticism, improvised through their texts. On occasions of exchange labor, people sang threshing songs; the texts, often ribald, held wrongdoers up to public criticism and ridicule. Grinding songs were usually sung by women individually, and served to air domestic grievances without fear of reprisal.

Songs are an integral part of many rituals. Shona rituals are structurally simple, but they often follow a night of dancing and singing. Many of them concern death, burial, and the activities of the spirit of the deceased. Burials usually follow a wake, when the relatives and friends of the deceased maintain a nocturnal watch over the body, as they participate in music and dancing. Older people sometimes sing traditional songs inside the hut where the body rests, and young people sing modern dance songs outdoors. Carrying the body to the grave is accompanied by a special class of songs (*ngondo* or *dendende*). Traditional Shona belief holds that the deceased will hover about the grave site for several months, and will then be ready to wander

The ordinary spirit-possession ceremony (*bira*) provides an opportunity for members of the community to beg guidance and assistance from their deceased ancestors.

about, to find a medium through whom to speak. The ceremony *kurova guva* serves to show the descendants have not forgotten the deceased, and to free the spirit from the grave. This ceremony also involves a night of singing, dancing, and beer drinking, often accompanied by spirit possession on the part of several mediums. At dawn, the mourners sing burial songs as they proceed to the grave, where they clean the area; they then offer a sacrifice to show that the spirit is free to seek a medium.

TRACK 21

The ordinary spirit-possession ceremony (*bira*) provides an opportunity for members of the community to beg guidance and assistance from their deceased ancestors. Various members of the community are known as spirit mediums, meaning that a particular spirit permanently inhabits their bodies. Because of ritual restrictions, life as a medium is onerous, but the traditional community highly respects persons having this status. There is no idea of exorcising a spirit from the individual, but the Shona intend the rituals to cause the spirit to come out (*kubuda*), appearing to the community. When it does, the medium goes into a trance, and the Shona consider whatever he or she says the voice of the spirit. In most cases, music is essential for bringing on the trance or state of possession. In theory, each spirit has its favorite song; and when people sing that song, the medium goes into trance: at a *bira*, mediums often begin a song they know will put them into trance.

A problem occurs when new mediums and new spirits are being discovered. People consider a person who shows skill in music or dancing a potential medium; other signs are unusual behavior, and a tendency to express undue emotion. Sometimes, when a family has been suffering misfortune or problems, its members organize a *bira*: by bringing about possession in suspected mediums, they seek to determine if a neglected spirit has been causing the difficulties. This search involves discovering, by trial and error, which songs will cause a spirit to appear in a potential medium; it also involves some expense, since the organizer of the event must provide beer for the participants, and hire drummers and mbirists. Since the latter cost more, people try to bring about possession without them; and only if a potential medium fails to go into trance do people hire them.

The course of a *bira* follows a standard format. As the crowd assembles, singing and dancing spontaneously take place, but the proceedings officially begin with a song begun by the drummers or mbirist(s). Then, the principal medium sits on a mat and receives a pot of water and several cloths. To the spirit within the medium, the organizer tells the purpose of the event, after which the music resumes. During this period, people expect the principal medium and others in attendance to go into trance. As the mediums show signs of possession, they put on special black and white cloths, and the music eventually stops, so the participants can greet and converse with the spirits. The remainder of the night, the mediums and the participants dance and sing together.

In the 1970s, the spirit-medium cult and the *bira* served to politicize rural people. Instead of taking part in rituals in their home area, some mediums would go from area to area. The occasion of a *bira* brought many people together, and provided an opportunity for discussing political matters. Many of the songs sung had subtle political connotations.

CHANGE IN SHONA MUSIC

During the twentieth century, Shona musical practices changed markedly, mainly because of the impact of European colonization. In the central plateau, where most of the European immigrants established themselves, many features of traditional Shona music fell away, and the traditional style survived only through the knowledge and continued practice of a few mbirists. Where the European population was not abundant, traditional practices continued.

A major factor that caused changes in Shona musical life was the teaching in churches and schools. Schools taught European music, and enabled young people to find work in the towns and cities, where contacts with Europeans led to changes in the musical idiom and value system. A few Shona people learned to appreciate various types of European music, but by far the most popular types of music in the towns were the syncretistic or hybrid musical styles. Before the 1950s, a style that frequently appeared in school activities was the *makwaya* (from English "choir"), with choral singing in the South African style, frequently accompanied by displays of marching. Dance songs for youth passed regularly through cycles of popularity. In the 1970s, middle-aged people enjoyed dancing to *jocho*, a type of song that showed little European influence. Youths, however, preferred a style called *jiti* or *jez* (jazz), which combined African drumming and simple European harmonies in songs with responsorial form.

The missions affected Shona music in several ways. In their enthusiasm to gain converts, they expressed a disdain for indigenous culture. They also prepared Shona translations of European hymns, ignoring the phonemic tones and the unavailability of European instruments. Consequently, it became usual to sing the hymns a cappella, with one singer beginning a hymn in a manner reminiscent of responsorial form; this texture was at odds with the nature of the European strophic form.

In the colonial period, many separatist African churches broke away from the missions, partly because of the latters' restrictions on plural marriages. These churches established their own behavioral codes, ritual forms, and music. The degree of westernization in music paralleled westernization in other aspects of church life. The Vapostori, for example, were less westernized than the mission churches, because they permitted polygamy but not the use of beer or African drums. The Zionists, on the other hand, remained farther from Western values, since they both permitted polygamy and used African beer and drums in their rituals. The songs of both churches were responsorial.

In preindependent Zimbabwe, several European-led organizations affected the development of musical style. In Bulawayo, the Kwanongoma College of Music undertook the training of music teachers for the African schools, and taught an appreciation of traditional African music. They taught skills in mbira and introduced xylophones. The Church Music Service, organized by Methodist missionaries, sought to encourage the use of traditional-style music in the churches and conducted workshops encouraging African composers.

THE MUSIC INDUSTRY

A major impact on Shona music has been the development of electronic media and the music industry, which developed in tandem with the spread of radio, since the latter disseminated new types of songs that became extremely popular. The radio originally broadcast foreign music, including European and American popular music,

The term *chimurenga* became a common term for any song related to the uprising, or to modern Shona political processes.

and songs from Zaïre and South Africa. In the early 1950s, the Rhodesia Broadcasting Corporation began recording traditional music in the rural areas, to broadcast for Shona people who had gone to the cities to find jobs.

> The early recordings were done by a mobile van from the Rhodesia Broadcasting Corporation which used a simple one-track tape recorder with a microphone. This music was stored on tapes and was used mainly for the African Service Radio broadcasts to entertain the Blacks. The van went round the country to tap talented musicians who were paid 1′ [one shilling] per song, if the song was broadcast on the radio. (Zindi 1985:3)

Urban Shona people heard much foreign music and began to copy it, using inexpensive or handmade instruments. The locally produced music in foreign styles first served for radio commercials; and later, people engaged local troupes to play dance music for nightclubs, beer halls, and hotels in the urban areas.

Many of these troupes sprang up because people saw producing live music as a means of making money when jobs were neither plentiful nor gratifying. By the 1970s, popular bands required not only expensive foreign instruments, but also amplifiers. Therefore, many of the bands sought the sponsorship of wealthy businessmen, who provided the instruments and equipment in exchange for a share of the profits from the performances. Such arrangements frequently involved blatant exploitation. In one case, the municipality paid an agent £100 per week for arranging a band, and the agent paid the band only £8 per week (Zindi 1985:26–27). Many such bands found it more profitable to tour the countryside, where they built up a following. In the 1970s, companies began recording popular Shona bands and selling their records. One reason for this trend was that the Shona people preferred records with Shona texts, rather than unknown languages. Since independence (1980), these Shona bands have become popular in the countryside, while urban people have developed a preference for music from England, America, and Jamaica (Zindi 1985:8).

MUSIC AND THE "UPRISING"

Near the end of the colonial period, indigenous music, particularly that of the mbira, became an important symbol of Shona identity. The mbira and related ancestral-spirit rites helped politicize rural people, who resented the conditions of their lives, but were not so politically aware as urban people. People called the war the *chimurenga* (uprising), the same term that in the mid 1890s had referred to a rebellion against white settlers. The term *chimurenga* became a common term for any song related to the uprising, or to modern Shona political processes. Educated urban Africans, who preferred hybrid musical styles, organized the struggle for independence; but in rural areas, the indigenous styles still appealed to many people. *Chimurenga* were eclectic in style. They included *makwaya, jocho, jiti,* Ndebele songs, modern rock, mbira, and hymns: all received words related to the war.

In the 1970s, the "freedom fighters" used a radio station in Mozambique to broadcast opposition to the propaganda given by the Rhodesia Broadcasting Corporation. In Zimbabwe, the popularity of bands that broadcast and sold records of Shona songs provided an additional opportunity for African nationalists to use music for politicizing the African population. At first, the studios concerned themselves with limiting their production to songs with nonpolitical topics, but Shona words were often extremely subtle, so many political songs seemed to be innocent.

Thomas Mapfumo (b. 1945), a popular singer and songwriter, created many of the *chimurenga.* The Teal Record Company put many of his songs on disk and changed some of the lyrics so the songs would be acceptable to the government. Thus, it became possible to disseminate Mapfumo's songs by selling his records, though the government banned the songs from radio. Mapfumo was once taken into custody, but a public outcry effected his release. He said:

> I recorded all my war experiences on an album called 'Hokoyo' and it became quite popular. As I was frightened of the law, I sang most of the songs on the L.P. using innuendoes and ambiguous language, but it was all there. The message was loud and clear to all Shona speakers, "We must topple the government". As I had half expected, the authorities banned my music from the radio. (Zindi 1985:34)

Songs decrying the problems of poverty became indirect attacks on the colonial system: these included "*Itayi cent cent vakomana, ini ndachona* 'Please boys, chip in a cent each so I can survive too'" and "*Butsu yangu yapera hiro* 'The heel of my shoe is worn out'" (Zindi 1985:5–6). Messages were not limited to lyrics. The song "*Tumira Vana Kuhondo* 'We are sending our children to war'" used an old tune from the RAR (Rhodesian African Rifles), so it could be taken to mean that the children were fighting on the Rhodesian side. The African population knew it referred to fighting on the side of liberation (Frederikse 1982:108).

Mapfumo's songs were not the only ones sending political messages. Some songs used traditional imagery of fighting or hunting, such as "*Baya wabaya* 'Spear those who spear'." Some songs, related to the 1896 uprising against the settlers, included references to tribal and ancestral spirits, which, people believed, provided help in the struggle; one was "*Gwindingwi rine shumba* 'There is a lion in the forest'."

After 1980, the position of Shona music was changing. The class of *chimurenga* expanded to include songs praising the leaders of Zimbabwe. As a matter of policy, Radio Zimbabwe gave Shona music a position similar to those of Ndebele music, hybrid kinds of music, and European music. Rather than presenting Shona music on programs designed for specific audiences, it programmed all types on all the broadcasts, though in differing degrees. In Harare, the College of Music, which first fostered serious European music, undertook the teaching and development of music in the Shona idiom.

REFERENCES

Berliner, Paul. 1978. *The Soul of Mbira: Music and Traditions of the Shona People of Zimbabwe.* Berkeley: University of California Press.

Frederikse, Julie. 1982. *None but Ourselves: Masses vs. Media in the Making of Zimbabwe.* New York: Penguin Books.

Jones, Arthur Morris. 1971. *Africa and Indonesia.* Leiden: E. J. Brill.

Kubik, Gerhard. 1988. "Nsenga/Shona Harmonic Patterns and the San Heritage in Southern Africa." *Ethnomusicology* 32:39–76 [211–248].

Tracey, Andrew. 1961. "The Mbira Music of Jege Tapera." *African Music* 4(2):44–63.

———. 1970a. *How to Play the Mbira.* Roodepoort, Transvaal: International Library of African Music.

———. 1970b. "The Matepe Mbira Music of Rhodesia." *African Music* 4(4):37–61.

———. 1972. "The Original African Mbira?" *African Music* 5(2):85–104.

Tracey, Hugh. 1969. "The Mbira Class of African Instruments in Rhodesia (1932)." *African Music* 4(3):78–95.

Zindi, Fred. 1985. *Roots Rocking in Zimbabwe.* Gweru: Mambo Press.

Popular Music in South Africa
David B. Coplan

Cape Town
Kimberley
Christian Religious Music
Influences from the United States
Johannesburg
Jazz, *Marabi*
Jazz: The "Respectable Response"
"Our Kind of Jazz": *Mbaqanga*
Black Show Business under Apartheid

The study of popular musical traditions in South Africa stretches over three centuries of cultural turbulence, across linguistic and political boundaries, to the far reaches of the subcontinent, and to the capitals and colleges of Europe and America. It encompasses the contributions made by South Africans of European and African origin, and by Americans of African descent.

From the late 1600s, increasingly dominant European colonists overwhelmed the cultures of the majority population. Popular musical forms emerged and spread within a colonial context: European settlers, mainly from the Netherlands and Britain, developed an industrialized economy, based on the exploitation of an indigenous, slave-labor force. Since the 1860s, the growth of urban centers accompanied that development and produced environments where intensive interethnic and interracial contacts took place, amid institutionalized racial segregation and the processes of class formation.

In the late 1800s and early 1900s, South African mining and manufacturing grew prodigiously and created a demand for labor that, reaching nearly to the equator, transformed the face of southern Africa. The African communities most affected by Christian missionization responded readily to the prospect of better employment in Kimberley or Johannesburg; yet colonial taxes and seductive labor recruiters also drew to the mines thousands of cattle keepers and farmers. So it was that black people arriving with circumscribed provincial patterns of African and Afro-Western (African Christian) culture found themselves at once enmeshed, not only in what people described as "a welter of the tribes," but in a welter of races, values, customs, languages, nationalities, social conditions, levels of education, and world views.

In those circumstances, performances and styles played a crucial role in black people's social self-definition and cultural reintegration. Traditionalist or Christian, rural rooted or urbanized, Africans moved continuously between town and country. Their movements assured that urban and rural performance cultures would continue to influence each other. By the mid-1800s, white townspeople were beginning to fear the increase of Africans and people of mixed race, who crowded into ghettos or "locations" (as people termed black residential areas attached to every town). In the late 1800s, after the discovery of the world's largest known deposits of diamonds and gold

Founded in 1652 as a refreshment and refitting station for the Asia-bound ships of the Dutch East India Company, Cape Town is aptly called South Africa's "Mother City."

in South Africa, the government institutionalized in a migrant labor system the permanent oscillation of tens of thousands of black workers between country homes and urban workplaces. In the decade after the Great War, despite the increasing severity of influx-control regulations (designed to slow the movement of black people to the cities), black urban communities swelled.

Those conditions provided the context for the development of a stylistically diverse, but strongly interactive, popular-performance culture. The forms that appeared were tied to the expressive and recreational preferences of a given ethnic, regional, or class-based audience, yet coexisted with newly incorporative styles and performance venues, designed by their performers to attract an unrestricted clientele (figure 1). Both the audiences and the influences involved in developing a particular music-and-dance form usually varied more than popular stereotypes supposed. While in rural areas new forms often evolved in the context of changing realities, urban spaces—"locations," mine compounds, factory hostels, schools, churches, welfare centers, union halls—became the crucibles of creativity and dissemination. The cities, in particular Johannesburg, also became the centers of local recording and broadcasting industries, the largest in Africa after the 1940s. So the cultural history of South Africa's cities and towns frames the description of the country's indigenous popular music.

CAPE TOWN

Founded in 1652 as a refreshment and refitting station for the Asia-bound ships of the Dutch East India Company, Cape Town is aptly called South Africa's "Mother

FIGURE 1   Gabriel Thobejane of the group Malombo, 1977.

City." Race relations there, under a system of chattel slavery (which accommodated communities of free blacks), set the pattern for the development of South African society. Cape Town, too, gave birth to South African popular music, the styles that arose among the people of the colony's farms and thoroughfares. There, the resident population—Dutch burghers; displaced Khoikhoi and San ("Hottentot" and "Bushman"); slaves from Madagascar, Mozambique, the Dutch East Indies, the Malabar coast of India—grew with new arrivals, transient merchant-sailors, and adventurers. The interbreeding of that population, in particular the mating of Dutch males with Khoi-San, south Asian ("Malay"), and Malagasy slave females, gave rise to South Africa's "coloured" (mixed-race) people. Earning a place in Cape society as skilled artisans and craftsmen, coloured performers (both slave and free) became South Africa's first professional popular musicians.

In seaport taverns, at white colonial balls and banquets, and on country plantations, slave musicians learned to play European instruments for the delectation of their masters' families, guests, and customers. As early as 1676, the Dutch governor had an orchestra of slaves. Music became a marketable trade, and musical ability enhanced a slave's value. Formal instruction was minimal, but slave musicians displayed a talent for playing by ear. Performing European dance music led coloured musicians to create musical blends, accommodating black and white musical cultures. Surviving examples are the Cape white "picnic song" and the Cape Malay "drum song," with texts in Afrikaans (South African creole Dutch): except for the race of the performers, these songs are stylistically indistinguishable.

Coloured musicians also played for their own communities. In the 1700s, British influence at the Cape grew; and in 1806, the British took the colony over. Among both whites and their servants, English country dances then became fashionable. From the 1730s, servants held "rainbow balls," whose grace, glamour, and spectrum of skin color bore comparison with antebellum New Orleans.

Less formal entertainments that flourished among coloureds took place in city backyards, on beachfronts, and on country farms, where Afrikaans trade-store instruments—violin, guitar, concertina—formed the basis of coloured folk musical culture. Eventually, coloureds, Bantu-speaking blacks, and white tenant farmers (*bywoners*), would introduce these instruments into all the folk-musical cultures of South Africa. The ubiquity of these instruments led not only to the blending of indigenous and European dance musics, but to new developments within indigenous musical traditions. These developments included neotraditional styles: elaborations and reinterpretations of African traditional music, made possible by the enhanced technical capacities of the imported instruments. Africans referred to this process by coining terms for its products, such as the Zulu *maskanda* (from Afrikaans *musikant*), showing the new instruments' local culture of origin. Neotraditional music also involved the invention of new instruments based on European models. These included a four-stringed plucked guitar (the Khoi *ramkie*), and two homemade violins (*t'guthe* and *velviool*). Black Africans later developed their own versions, including the *igqonqwe* (a Zulu *ramkie*), and the *mamokhorong* or *sekhankure* (a one-stringed Basotho violin). By about 1900, people had reconceptualized the trade-store instruments as "traditional African instruments"; in the late twentieth century, musicians referred freely to the music of the "Zulu traditional guitar" and of the "Basotho traditional concertina" (later, accordion).

KIMBERLEY

The late 1800s saw striking developments in urban popular music. In the 1870s, in the remote north of the Cape Colony, a diamond rush led to the rise of Kimberley, an "instant city." To its opportunities flocked fortune hunters, whites and blacks

sefela　Long, musical poetic narratives developed by the Bosotho veteran migrants on their travels to the mines

tickey draai　Dance that was accompanied by the guitar and popular until the 1940s

oorlams　Popular working-class musicians who were coloured or black Africans and served as cultural brokers

abaphakathi　South African popular performers whose competence and versatility secured a free existence for them

alike: workers and professionals came from all over southern Africa. Many rural Africans were target workers, people who intended to stay only until they had earned enough to buy a rifle and other sought-after European goods, and to pay the taxes that would permit them to keep their lands. The innovations they made in their musical culture went far beyond instruments and dances. Thoroughly transforming their forms of expression, they created new genres of dance, song, and oral poetry. In those genres, they assimilated to familiar cultural categories and social values new experiences and conditions. Among the familiar genres was the traditional praise poetry of the Xhosa, which served to flatter and satirize overseers in the mines (both black and white), and to apostrophize rural chiefs. Another such genre was the Zulu men's walking-and-courting song (backed now by the guitar, the concertina, and the violin), which pilloried the moral shallowness of friendship and romantic love. Among the richest examples were the Basotho's veteran migrants' songs (*sefela sa lit-samaea-naha*), long musical poetic narratives, developed on "long walks" from Basutoland to Kimberley (Coplan 1988).

In the migrants' texts, Kimberley became a symbol of immorality. In 1984, more than a century after the Basotho first ventured there, Majara Majara of Lesotho could sing, in his *sefela*:

Ke buoa ka Kemele;	I speak of Kimberley;
Ke buoa ka Sotoma.	I speak of Sodom.

It was not only the male migrants who found themselves singing new songs: women, their lives disrupted by the prolonged absence of their men, also migrated. In the canteens of Kimberley, some of them became famed singers and dancers.

Except for the privileged colonial élite and entrepreneurial class, life in early Kimberley was so rough and disorganized, the government could not enforce South Africa's usual pattern of racial segregation. In time, whites built closed compounds, which imprisoned African male migrant workers. Other black people crowded into "locations." At first, however, the poorer classes of all races and nationalities lived jumbled together in shantytowns, which resounded with the music of canteens, concerts, dance halls, honkytonks, and house parties. Black and white "diggers" caroused together to the music of banjos, guitars, pianos, concertinas, and violins; the men enjoyed the companionship of camp followers, mostly black women, drawn from the countryside. Among the prospectors were Americans (both white and black), who brought to the canteens their own instrumental styles.

Among the most popular performers were coloured musicians. Some were itinerant professionals; others, artisans with profitable musical avocations. On the violin and guitar, these players obligingly created blends of Khoi, Cape-Malay-Afrikaans, British, and American popular melodies. One genre that emerged from this musical mix was the dance *tickey draai* (Afrikaans) 'turn on a tickey [threepence]'; played on the guitar, it was popular until the 1940s.

The social identity of Kimberley's popular working-class musicians was significant, because it set the pattern for artistic leadership in black popular music elsewhere in the country. The musicians were mainly proletarian coloureds or black Africans who spoke Afrikaans or English, which they learned in workplaces, rather than in mission schools. Called *oorlams* in Afrikaans, or *abaphakathi* 'those in-between' in Xhosa, they served as cultural brokers, or middlemen between black and white. In the process, they earned a reputation for being too clever by half. Many discovered that musical (in addition to linguistic and cultural) competence and versatility could secure a free and independent, if itinerant, existence. From their ranks came more than one generation of innovative black popular musicians. It may have been among such musicians in nineteenth-century Kimberley that the tonic–dominant–subdominant harmonic progression became established as the signature of South African black popular music.

CHRISTIAN RELIGIOUS MUSIC

European Christian hymnody first became a factor in the development of black South African music in the early 1800s. Strife between white settlers and Xhosa pastoralists led to the uprooting of many African communities in the eastern Cape. As early as 1816, Ntsikana, a Xhosa prophet and visionary, prescribed for the cultural reformulation of Xhosa society a blend of African and Christian religious beliefs, values, and practices. For his congregation, he composed several Afro-Christian hymns, which choirs performed and transmitted orally. In 1876, a mission newspaper published in Tonic Sol-fa notation his hymn "*Ulo Tixo Mkulu* 'Thou, Great God'." In 1884, John Knox Bokwe, renowned Xhosa composer and Presbyterian choirmaster, republished it, with three of Ntsikana's other hymns. Ntsikana's style strikingly infuses Protestant hymnody with the stateliness of Xhosa melody, harmony, and rhythm.

On mission stations, refugees from successive frontier wars in the eastern Cape and from the rapid expansion of the Zulu kingdom to the north found shelter, farms, work, and access to the religious and educational requirements of life in colonial society. There, the choral part singing that became the foundation of all indigenous southern Bantu music making achieved a fit with Christian hymnody.

Blacks thought congregational singing one of the most attractive aspects of Christian ritual. African choirs made harmonies, not on the basis of a dominant melodic line, but by polyphonically embellishing a bass ostinato. Though Western concepts of tonality were foreign, blacks enshrined as a choral set piece Handel's "Hallelujah Chorus" (*Messiah*, 1742). More importantly, the melodic direction of southern Bantu part songs tends to follow the tonal patterns of the words. To Bantu-speakers' ears, the violation of traditional tone-tune relationships and patterns of syllabic stress made many of the early translations of European hymns unlovely, but converts eventually got used to it. In the mid-1800s, Tiyo Soga, the first ordained black minister in South Africa (Free Church of Scotland), adapted several Scottish melodies to Xhosa texts.

By the 1880s, a movement toward cultural revitalization and nationalism was growing among mission blacks disappointed with their lack of social advancement. John Bokwe, a leader in the movement, preserved semantic tones while achieving a high musical and literary quality—a happy marriage of African and European compositional principles. His efforts pioneered a new black South African choral style, widely known as *makwaya* (choir), which he used in Scotland to support his studies for the ministry, and to gain for black South African Christians a sympathetic hearing. Since then, many illustrious figures in black South African choral music—

In Cape Town, the Virginia Jubilee Singers'
appearances led to the emergence of the minstrel
parades of the "Cape Coon Carnival," which became
a permanent institution of coloured performances.

Benjamin Tyamzashe, A. A. Khumalo, Hamilton Masiza, Marks Radebe, Reuben
Caluza, Joshua Mohapeloa, Michael Moerane—have appeared.

Several outstanding songs exemplify the *makwaya* style. One is "*Nkosi Sikelel'
iAfrika* 'God Bless Africa'," composed in 1897 by a Johannesburg teacher, Enoch
Sontonga; S. E. R. Mqayi, the Xhosa national poet, later added more stanzas. In the
early 1900s, Reuben Caluza's Ohlange Institute Choir popularized this song, which
in 1925 became the anthem of the African National Congress, South Africa's most
active antiapartheid organization; in the 1990s, it was the national anthem of several
central and southern African countries. Though rhythmically stolid, its perceived
combination of melancholic yearning and spiritual grandeur made it a musical
embodiment of the thirst for freedom.

At least until the 1960s, *makwaya* must be considered popular music, because of
its distribution among choirs, civic and political organizations, unions, wedding parties, and community concerts. In evolving contexts, it supported the traditional
attachment of black South Africans to choral song. Reflecting the secular use of the
emotional and spiritual catharsis provided in sacred pieces (such as Methodist
hymns), it influenced other forms of vocal and instrumental music, including working-class choral forms—the sonorous *ingoma ebusuku* (Zulu) 'night music', more
recently known as *isicathamiya* 'sneaking up', and the lighter school songs, known as
mbholoho (Mthethwa 1980:24–26)—and South African ragtime and early jazz, plus
the rearrangement of indigenous folk songs for choral performance in four-part harmony.

INFLUENCES FROM THE UNITED STATES

Makwaya was not the only musical form or trend that in the late 1800s and early
1900s influenced the Western-educated African élite. Since the 1860s, blackface
minstrelsy had been popular with urban whites in South Africa; and as a representation (however distorted) of the performances of black Americans, it had an impact
on Anglicized black South Africans, who admired the achievements of Booker T.
Washington and other black American leaders. Many black South African leaders
(including John Dube, Solomon Plaatjie, Reuben Caluza, and Charlotte Manye
Maxexe) visited or received education in the United States.

No less important were the activities of the African Methodist Episcopal
Church, based in Philadelphia. With other black American denominations of the
very late 1800s, it sent missionaries to South Africa, where they set up schools and
churches, whose most important musical contribution was teaching and performing
Negro spirituals, an art form that delighted black South Africans, and stunned local
composers into recognizing what they might accomplish in Afro-Christian hymnody.
American performers, recordings in the first decade of the twentieth century, and
Tonic Sol-fa sheet music were also making black Americans' music available; and

coon songs, ragtime, and close-harmony quartet singing all made significant impressions on the Afro-Western cultural models of South Africa's black educated élite.

These trends came together in the tours Orpheus "Bill" McAdoo's Virginia Jubilee Singers made in Cape Town and other cities during the 1880s and 1890s (Erlmann 1991:21–53). McAdoo patterned his company after the Fisk Jubilee Singers and other black American troupes. By that time, black American performers had long since appropriated minstrelsy, which they infused with a representation of African-American culture. Their performances made a big impact on South African audiences, black as well as white; and their music helped revive the popularity of minstrelsy as a local genre. Amateur companies patterned after McAdoo's troupe sprang up among members of African civic and cultural organizations, and at secondary schools such as Lovedale and Healdtown in the Cape, and the Lyndhurst Road School in Kimberley. Notable among these companies were Kimberley's Diamond Minstrels and the Philharmonic Society, which included McAdoo's original pianist, Will Thompson, who had decided to stay in South Africa. Reflecting the revaluation of indigenous culture taking place among African intellectuals, the Philharmonic Society's programs featured several *makwaya* arrangements of traditional African folk songs. Another result was the formation of the South African Native Choir, patterned after McAdoo's company, but featuring an extensive selection of *makwaya* songs; in the 1890s, that choir toured Britain and the United States.

In Cape Town, the Virginia Jubilee Singers' appearances led to the emergence of the minstrel parades of the "Cape Coon Carnival," which became a permanent institution of coloured performances. Following the custom in which Cape Town became "the kingdom of the coloured man" for the duration of New Year's Day, coloured men's clubs began marching through the streets in American minstrel costume, performing for the amusement of riotous crowds a mix of minstrel and Afrikaans favorites. Before the 1970s, when the government quarantined the Coon Carnival in a football stadium, the parades gave Cape Town's best-known reed and brass jazzmen opportunities to display their talents.

Until about 1930, black South African urban popular music developed in mission schools, community and voluntary organizations, and neighborhood social events. Regionally, the most important centers that fostered the emergence of a new Afro-Western performative culture were in the Cape, among Xhosa-speaking élites in Queenstown, Port Elizabeth, and Cape Town itself, and at Lovedale and the other mission institutions. School concerts and community concerts included lively groups of "student coons," vocal quartets, choirs, solo balladeers, and "minstrels," who bore a closer resemblance to British "concert-parties," or to early vaudeville musical-variety shows, than to the blackface format. Missions and mission schools also sponsored brass bands of the type favored by evangelical ministries in Britain in the late 1800s. In addition, the parlors of many educated Cape Africans housed a piano, or a small harmonium or pedal organ, around which families gathered to sing hymns and popular ballads and "evergreens."

As American ragtime and jazz attained popularity in South Africa, mission-trained instrumentalists from popular "coon troupes," both coloured and Xhosa, came together to form some of South Africa's first jazz bands. Among the best known were the Blue Rhythm Syncopators of Queenstown, led by pianist Meekley "Fingertips" Matshikiza; it featured William "Sax-O-Wills" Mbali, one of the Cape's first professional tenor saxophone players and ballroom dancers. Bands, choirs, and variety troupes sprang up wherever there were missions, schools, and urban centers; and so, while coloureds and Cape Africans were leaders in early-twentieth-century Afro-Western musical performance, similar developments with a local cultural flavor occurred among the Zulu of Durban and Natal, and among the Tswana of

In the early 1900s, American ragtime, dixieland, and jazz became popular among westernizing coloureds and Africans, whether educated or not.

Rustenburg and Pretoria in the Transvaal. Developments in Kimberley reflected the community's multiethnicity, though even there the educated black élite was mainly Xhosa-speaking.

JOHANNESBURG

In 1886, the discovery of the world's largest known gold deposits, beneath a desolate ridge in the South African Republic of the Transvaal, upstaged the Kimberley lode. Again, work seekers from all over the subcontinent gravitated to the spot, soon to be the "Golden City" of Johannesburg, which by about 1900 sheltered at least fifty thousand whites, forty thousand urbanized blacks, and one hundred thousand black miners. To Johannesburg flocked educated African professionals, frustrated by smaller communities' limited opportunities, low pay, and isolation; by 1904, the census reported 25 percent of the permanent black population was literate. The range of regional, ethnic, class, and educational backgrounds that municipal regulation crowded together within a black community (and away from whites) created in turn a musical mix that became the basis for black show business in South Africa.

Like other towns in South Africa, turn-of-the-century Johannesburg was racially segregated as much by custom as by law. The city's atmosphere, duplicating on a larger scale that of Kimberley a quarter-century before, gave blacks opportunities to circulate more freely than in the older, settled towns of the Cape, Natal, and Transvaal. Some of the poorer residential areas on the eastern and western fringes of the city were racially mixed: Africans, coloureds, whites, Indians, and Chinese lived together. In addition to drinking houses frequented by blacks only, musical entertainment was available at many of the city's 118 unsegregated canteens. The harshness and insecurity of black life in early Johannesburg accompanied cultural disorientation. Musical performances became workshops in which musicians fashioned new models of urban African and African-Western culture, and devised new patterns of social identity and behavior. In the context of recreational socialization, interpersonal and community relationships formed and strengthened, and people enacted and celebrated the process of collective self-definition.

Probably the most familiar setting for informal music making was the shebeen, an unlicensed business (usually a private residence), whose owners illegally brewed and sold beer and liquor. The origins of this institution apparently go back to seventeenth-century Cape Town, where Dutch colonists sold liquor to black servants and slaves, and sometimes provided rooms to drink it in. The term *shebeen* apparently came from the speech of immigrant Irish vice police in early-twentieth-century Cape Town. Transvaal law decreed prohibition for blacks in 1896, but government-run distilleries produced cheap brandy for black workers. In addition to African home-brewed beer, the supply of strong drink led to the illegal sale of several near-lethal concoctions. Different shebeens attracted different kinds of patrons, as people sought each other's company on the basis of ethnic or geographical origins, occupational and class memberships, neighborhood and friendship ties, shared self-images and aspirations, and the forms of dance and music they implied.

So a group of Basotho migrants at a shebeen might hold an impromptu performance of young men's *mangae* songs or *mohobelo* dances, or listen to the improvisations of a concertina virtuoso; Zulu domestics and manual workers enjoyed guitar and violin duos, plus songs for walking and weddings; Shangaans (from Mozambique) displayed their (Portuguese-influenced) solo guitar styles; and the Bapedi excelled at accompanying melodies on the autoharp, or dancing in a circle, beating rhythms on rubber or oxhide stretched over the top of a 44-gallon petrol drum. Much of that music was neotraditional, as rural-born musicians discovered what they could do with trade-store instruments. The instruments themselves provided a natural vehicle for importing American, British, and even Afrikaans songs, rhythms, and styles of playing.

JAZZ, MARABI

For new arrivals from the countryside, the ability to incorporate black American and European elements and items into their performances expressed knowledge of, and a certain mastery over, the dominant exogenous culture and the new social environment. Africans returning home injected urban tunes, rhythms, and steps into country dances. Laborers who set their sights on permanent urban residence began buying American-style clothes, sending their families to church and school, and seeking popular music at neighborhood concerts and shebeens. All black people in the towns lived close together—well off and poor, educated and illiterate, Christian and animist, Zulu and Basotho, coloured and African. Ethnic musical traditions began to blend with Afro-Western and Western ones. An early generation of professional and semiprofessional black musicians, who by supplying musical modes of adaptation intended to earn good money, syncretized the new styles.

In the vanguard of that generation were solo "pianomen," primarily from the Cape, but not uncommonly from other towns in Natal, the Free State, and the Transvaal. In the early 1900s, American ragtime, dixieland, and jazz became popular among westernizing coloureds and Africans, whether educated or not. Queenstown, in the Cape midlands, produced so many leading players (like "Fingertips" Matshikiza), it earned the nickname "Little Jazz Town." Whether pianomen performed at school and community concerts and élite social affairs, or in rough canteens at railway junctions and in periurban shantytowns, they soon found they could lessen or cut their dependence on pay from menial jobs, provided they kept moving and played a variety of popular styles for diverse audiences. The shebeens belonged mostly to women, who had transformed into a profitable business their traditional skill at brewing. The "shebeen queens" often bought their own instruments, and vied for the services of popular pianists and organists, who attracted patrons to parties. In Johannesburg, their competition produced an unstable stylistic blend of Xhosa melodies, *tickey draai*, and ragtime. This was *thula n'divile* 'keep quiet, I've heard it', a three-chord harmonic format, which served as an exhortation for others to cease their noise, so the player might flaunt something new.

Whenever black people tried to create stable, ordered communities, with functioning social institutions and viable patterns of urban culture, the government moved in to destroy them. By the 1920s, authorities scheduled the "black spots" ("locations") for removal. Yet these places, which in Johannesburg included Doornfontein, Prospect Township, and Malay Camp–Vrededorp, and in Pretoria included Marabastad and Lady Selbourne, were centers of social and cultural inventiveness. Though slums, they were the settings for the emergence of professional black stage entertainment, and for the birth of an indigenous kind of jazz.

shebeen   Unlicensed bar, often a private home, where patrons gather to drink and perform neotraditional music

marabi   Hybrid music, dance form, and a social occasion that was both indigenous and urban

abaqhafi   "Street cowboys" who wandered the cities and played Zulu guitar songs

famo   A wild and risqué version of *marabi* that appeared among Basotho migrants

indunduma   A Zulu piano-vamp style of *marabi*

makwaya   Choral song that became a form of South African popular music until the 1960s

In the dance halls and shebeens, the pianomen's efforts at devising a musical formula that would please a diverse patronage led them to work into a repetitive three-chord version of American ragtime and jazz the melodies and rhythms of black ethnic groups. By the late 1920s, that music was known in the Transvaal towns as *marabi*, a term whose origins are uncertain, but whose incorporative flexibility and lively danceability gave listeners the sense of a music at once indigenous, urbanized, African, up to date, worldly. *Marabi* often develop a four-bar progression of polyphonic chords ending on the dominant: $I–IV–I_4^6–V^7$. In *marabi*, the use of a recurrent sequence of chords offset with varying melodic phrases simulates traditional choral part songs. "Fingertips" Matshikiza and his like were renowned *marabi* pianists, but in Johannesburg the most famous of all was Tebetjane, whose 1932 composition "*uTebetjana Ufana ne'Mfene* 'Tebetjane looks like a baboon'" became the emblem of the style. In accordance with African holistic concepts of performance, and the close identification of performance genres with their practitioners and social settings, *marabi* was not merely a hybrid instrumental music, but a dance form, a social occasion, and a category of participants (urbanizing proletarians). So pervasive a part of life did it become that music critic and jazz composer Todd Matshikiza (Fingertips's nephew) proclaimed it "the name of an epoch." True to its inclusive purpose, its rhythmic and chordal structure was rigid, and there was little of the "free" improvisation that characterized American jazz; but because it blended into the river of American honkytonk so many streams of indigenous music, it became the reservoir of a uniquely South African jazz.

Pianomen and pedal organists were not the only instrumentalists who spawned *marabi*: the brass and fife-and-drum bands of British forces sent to South Africa during the Boer War (1899–1902) had much impressed Africans. Later, African brass and reed players trained in the marching bands of the Native Military Corps and the Salvation Army began to form their own ensembles. They played at weddings and church festivals, and for women's neighborhood and religious organizations and the coins of outsiders seeking excitement in the "locations." Theirs was a process that added to European marches African polyrhythm and polyphonic improvisation. Soon, however, untrained bandsmen, especially Bapedi domestic servants exposed to brass by the Lutheran missions of the Transvaal, joined trained players. Their method was to repeat short segments of European tunes in combination with African melodies, worked out by trial and error on the new instruments, and orchestrated polyphonically by ear. During the 1920s and 1930s, *marabi*—including the famous *tamatie saus* (Afrikaans) 'ketchup', and the antipolice satire "Pick-up Van"—became staples of marching band repertories. In time, small ensembles of piano, brass, reed, violin, banjo, and drums began to play at shebeens and neighborhood social occasions, leading to the emergence of *marabi* dance bands like the Japanese Express.

Stylistic exchange between rural neotraditional African music on the one hand and *marabi* on the other took place in both directions. Rural dances (like Xhosa

mabokwe), neotraditional forms (like the Zulu guitar songs of roving *abaqhafi*, "street cowboys"), and incipient syncretic urban styles (like Xhosa *itswari* 'soirée' and *thula n'divile*), all flowed into *marabi*, which, in turn, contributed new rhythms and inventive, often deliberately comical, footwork. In Johannesburg, *famo*, a wild and risqué version of *marabi*, appeared among Basotho migrants and proletarians; combined with neotraditional Basotho dance, it became a staple of working-class entertainment in the towns and rural villages of the Orange Free State and Lesotho. Zulu guitar and violin players quickly assimilated into their walking, courting, and wedding songs *marabi*'s vamp. In Durban, workers danced to a Zulu piano vamp style of *marabi* called *indunduma* 'mine dumps'—a reference to Johannesburg, where people disappeared amid mountains of slag.

Indeed, for people trying either to maintain traditional family systems and codes of social behavior, or to construct new Afro-Western Christian ones, *marabi* represented the dangers and the depths of anomic urban immorality and hedonism; but the children of the "locations," loving the ragtime love songs and *marabi* favorites of the day, sneaked to the parties and dances with many a joy-seeking husband or wife. Rural-oriented traditionalists, urbanized elitists, and those trying to keep one foot in both social environments developed self-defining styles and occasions of performance.

JAZZ: THE "RESPECTABLE RESPONSE"

Through Christian preparatory schools, teachers' colleges and associations, membership in churches, urban professional employment, and even newspapers (such as *Isigidimi sama Xhosa*, *Ilanga lase Natal*, *Imvo Zabantsundu*, and *Tsala ea Bechuana*), educated African élites had long possessed social institutions and networks connecting rural areas, small towns, and "locations." By the 1920s, their culture was a century old. During the years between the world wars, several important developments occurred in it, in conscious opposition to ragtime, jazz, and *marabi*. First, a generation of *makwaya* composers arose, more innovative and influential than any before. Benjamin Tyamzashe enhanced the contribution of Xhosa folk song to *makwaya*. Joshua Mohapeloa, a talented tunesmith, used his facility with Tonic Sol-fa notation to arrange Basotho folk songs for Western four-part choral performance, and to compose choral songs that stretched and snapped the rigid rules of Western harmony to weld it to Basotho polyphony. A choir leader himself, Mohapeloa helped perfect the local method, whereby choirs are led rather than conducted: the leader sets up the foundation melody in the bass, and the other three parts enter above, in polyphonic relation to the bass (lead), though not necessarily to each other. For the representation of African part songs, Mohapeloa saw he could turn to advantage the rigidity and insufficiency of Tonic Sol-fa. While encouraging the free use of African tonality, ornamentation, timbre, and polyphonic "part agreement," choral leaders used Tonic Sol-fa as a skeletal sign of the general direction and organization of parts.

The greatest composer of *makwaya* was Reuben T. Caluza, of Natal (Erlmann 1991:181–236). His promotion of music as a fundraiser for the Ohlange Institute, a trade school, led him to experiment with a range of ensembles and styles. He went so far as to found student pennywhistle-and-drum bands, which paraded in the streets of small towns around Natal. More important was the Ohlange choir, whose performances under his direction became, before the Great War, major cultural events in Durban, Johannesburg, and other towns. Their performance of Enoch Sontonga's *Nkosi Sikelel' iAfrika* at early meetings of the South African Native National Congress (later the African National Congress) led to the adoption of that song as the ANC's organizational anthem. Caluza composed in Tonic Sol-fa dozens of songs, many of which had social and political themes, such as "*iLand Act*" (to protest the Land Act of

By the 1940s, ballroom and swing-jazz orchestras on the American big band model dominated black show business in the cities, especially Johannesburg.

1913), "Influenza" (to mourn deaths in the flu epidemic of 1918), and "*Ingoduso*" (to deplore a perceived loss of moral responsibility among young Zulu immigrants to Johannesburg). By variously combining indigenous Zulu melodies, ragtime, and hymnodic *makwaya*, he objectified three distinct categories of Afro-Western choral song: *isiZulu*, traditional folk songs arranged in four-part harmony; *imusic*, strongly Westernized "classical" *makwaya*; and *ukureka*, ragtime. In 1932, for His Master's Voice (London), he recorded more than one hundred twenty of his arrangements and compositions; Lovedale Press published several in Tonic Sol-fa. Caluza had no hesitation about performing for working-class audiences, or any audience that cared to hire him; and he was not, despite his exalted status, above composing a choral *marabi* or two. What apparently astonished audiences was his ability to synchronize harmoniously voices, onstage movements, and keyboard. He earned musical degrees at Hampton Institute (Virginia) and Columbia University (New York), and passed the later part of his musical career as director of the music school at Adams College (Amanzimtoti, Natal). His influence on popular composition and performance in Zulu was lasting and profound, from school concerts to élite and workers' choral competitions to jazz bands like J. C. P. Mavimbela's Rhythm Kings, which, in the late 1930s, specialized in swing-jazz arrangements of Caluza songs.

Another major development in élite performance was the development of polished semiprofessional variety song-and-dance companies (still called minstrels) out of the school and neighborhood amateur concerts of the 1920s. Minstrel companies like the Erie Lads, Darktown Negroes, Africans Own Entertainers, Hiver Hyvas, and Darktown Strutters, drew on British "concert-party" and black American vaudeville, made available through films, recordings, and sheet music. Their performers offered a mix of ragtime and dixieland vocals in African languages, American popular standards (like "Can't Help Lovin' Dat Man"), *makwaya*, step-dancing, tap-dancing, comic turns, and dramatic sketches—all wearing matching tuxedos.

At the same time, admiration for American jazz and big-band music, combined with a desire to upgrade the image of local entertainment created by the Japanese Express and other *marabi* bands, led to the formation of several black "society" jazz bands. Coloured dance bands of the 1920s, such as Rayner's Big Six and Sonny's Revellers, were the first to answer this need; but by the late 1930s, the Merry Blackbirds, Rhythm Kings, and the somewhat jazzier Jazz Maniacs, were providing the music for all-night concert and dance occasions at élite venues (such as the Bantu Men's Social Center and the Inchcape Hall's Ritz Palais de Danse). There, well-dressed, literate domestic servants and professionals immersed themselves in the turns of American ballroom dancing. Putting on evening dress to dance to the Jazz Maniacs' rendition of "Tuxedo Junction" or the Merry Blackbirds' ragtime favorite "MaDlamini" (a famous shebeen queen) was more than just good entertainment: it was a conscious effort to acquire the performative dimensions of (Western) "civilization" (especially its African cousin, black American show business), while projecting

FIGURE 2   Jazz at the Odin, 1950s. *Left to right:* Kippie Moeketsi, Banzi Bangani, Mackay Darashe, Elijah Nkonyane (trumpet), Ntemi Piliso.

FIGURE 3   Pinoccio Mokgaleng, founder of the Sophiatown Modern Jazz Club, and vocalist Dolly Rathebe, in the late 1950s.

oneself as an accomplished representative of it. Promoter and talent scout Griffiths Motsieloa brought the two forms of élite performance together in 1937, when, by teaming the Darktown Strutters with the Merry Blackbirds Orchestra, he created the Pitch Black Follies, a popular traveling concert and dance company.

By the 1940s, ballroom and swing-jazz orchestras on the American big band model dominated black show business in the cities, especially Johannesburg. Despite laws that did not recognize "musician" as a legitimate category of employment for blacks, dozens of such bands toured the country, often teaming up for concert and dance performances with variety troupes. Once begun, shows had to carry on until at least four or five A.M., since curfew laws and an absence of public transportation made it impossible for black concertgoers to go home at night. Some bands, like the Jazz Maniacs and Harlem Swingsters, avoided touring by securing regular engagements around Johannesburg. Few musicians, however, could manage exclusively on their musical earnings. For example, Wilson "King Force" Silgee, saxophonist and leader of the Jazz Maniacs, was for a lengthy period a "tea boy" in the Johannesburg municipal clerk's office. The Jazz Maniacs were among those bands who for many years refused to make recordings, stating that the flat fees of a few pounds per side weren't worth the effort, and helped competing bands copy their compositions and style. Others, however, especially the top vocal soloists and groups, viewed records as a useful medium for increasing their audience. It was common for people to attend shows expressly to hear their favorite recording artists perform current hits. In the late 1940s, The Band in Blue, starring virtuoso clarinet and alto saxophonist Kippie Moeketsi (figure 2), backed an all-black ensemble in Ike Brooks's musical variety film *Zonk* (unreleased, in private hands).

Among the most popular vocal groups were the male close-harmony quartets (patterned after the Mills Brothers and the Inkspots) such as the Manhattan Brothers, the African Inkspots, and the Woody Woodpeckers. Similar female soloists included Dolly Rathebe (figure 3), Dorothy Masuku, and Susan Gabashane. In the 1950s and early 1960s, female quartets, such as the Dark City Sisters and Miriam Makeba's Skylarks, sang jazz with a local flavor. Much of the jazz the singers and bands popularized was arrangements of American songs and local compositions in

As for *mbaqanga*, South Africa's own jazz, there is no more characteristic a composition than Miriam Makeba's "*Patha Patha* 'Touch Touch'."

the American swing idiom, with lyrics in African languages. Local music made its mark, however, in jazz orchestrations of African folk songs and popular *marabi*, and in the use of African rhythms in original compositions.

Many songs engagingly combined American and African melodic and rhythmic motifs. An important performative aspect of this process occurred in the late hours of live shows, when players would put away their American sheet music and "let go." A more *marabi*-based, African shebeen jazz took over; and the brass, reeds, and piano took improvised solo choruses over a pulsating beat. Not all audiences adored American popular culture, and many patrons demanded from the bandsmen a more local jazz idiom. Some bands, like the Chisa Ramblers, specialized in "backyard" party engagements, for which they supplied *marabi*.

From that kind of playing and the vocals that accompanied it arose *mbaqanga*, a Zulu name for a stiff corn porridge, which jazzmen regarded as their professional staple, a musical daily bread. The dance of the period was the *tsaba-tsaba*, a big-band successor to the *marabi*. The best-known song in this style was "*Skokiaan*" (named after a deadly drink), composed in the late 1940s by a Rhodesian, August Musurugwa, and first recorded by his African Dance Band of the Cold Storage Commission of Southern Rhodesia (later the Bulawayo Sweet Rhythm Band). This hit was eventually released as sheet music in seventeen European and African languages; in the United States, it topped the Lucky Strike Hit Parade in 1954, in a rendition by Louis Armstrong titled "Happy Africa." As for *mbaqanga*, South Africa's own jazz, there is no more characteristic a composition than Miriam Makeba's "*Patha Patha* 'Touch Touch'," the signature tune of a popular and playfully sexy dance of the 1950s.

As the example of *marabi* proves, much of what was African in local jazz was bubbling up from the music of migrants, urban workers, and people of the "location" streets—music performed in shebeens, in workers' hostels, in community halls, at backyard feasts, at weddings. At least as early as the Great War, Zulu workers arriving in Durban from smaller communities in Natal formed male choirs, modeled on church and school concerts, amateur coon variety shows (*isikunzi*), and Caluza's ensembles. The music of these choirs, a blend of ragtime and indigenous part singing, was first known as *ingoma ebusuku* 'night music', after all-night competitions among choirs. Performers wore matching blazers and sharply pressed trousers, and made synchronous movements with their arms, torsos, and bodies. Their styles of step dancing—*isicatamiya*, and later *cothoza 'mfana* (Zulu) 'sneak up, boy'—later became standard terms for the music and dance of Zulu workers' choirs (Erlmann 1991:156–174). By the 1940s, a range of styles within that idiom had evolved. The most traditional were the *mbombing* choirs, named after loud, high-pitched, choral yells, sung antiphonally with low-pitched parts, said to imitate the whine of bombs falling from airplanes in newsreels of World War II. The most sophisticated were the songs of Solomon Linda, a brilliant composer and arranger, whose Original Evening

Birds were the acknowledged champions of *isicatamiya*. Under the title "Wimoweh" (a mnemonic for the guitar vamp, which survived American transformation), Pete Seeger and the Weavers later rearranged and recorded his hit song "*Mbube* 'Lion'." Because of its popularity, *mbube* survived for many years as a term for a style of Zulu male singing.

The same rhythm that found its way to America in "Wimoweh" put a characteristic stamp on South African jazz through the interposition of *kwela*, a style of street jazz that sprang up in the 1940s. While several etymologies compete in explaining this term (which in its aspirated form, *khwela*, means 'to climb on' in both Zulu and Sotho), there is a clear association with petty criminality, youth gangs, and other forms of socially resistant street life. The central instrument of a *kwela* ensemble, the pennywhistle (a six-hole fippled metal recorder or flageolet), has antecedents in the *phalafala* and other indigenous aerophones. Its most noticeable early appearance in South Africa seems to have been with fife-and-drum corps of Scottish regiments, which paraded in Johannesburg and Pretoria during the Second Boer War. Early in the 1900s, groups of young Northern Sotho domestics and street toughs known as *amalaita* formed their own pennywhistle-and-drum bands, and on weekends marched in the streets. Later, the pennywhistle became the favored instrument of proletarian hustlers and crapshooters, who, whenever the police pickup van, known as a *kwela-kwela*, passed by, would hide their dice, and take out their pennywhistles for an innocent-looking jam session.

"OUR KIND OF JAZZ": *MBAQANGA*

During the 1940s and 1950s, for the coins of admiring passersby, aspiring young musicians (many only ten years old), formed street bands to play pennywhistles, acoustic guitars, and one-stringed washtub basses. Their music was *kwela*, a blend of American swing and the African melodies and guitar-vamp rhythms of the "locations." *Kwela* became a popular downscale version of *mbaqanga*, and eventually several of its most talented pennywhistle soloists found their way into recording studios. Since no system for paying royalties to black musicians existed in South Africa until 1964, they made little money; but they did achieve publicity. Famous pennywhistle virtuosos included Spokes Mashiyane (whose revenues from recording helped build Gallo into South Africa's largest recording company), and Little Lemmy Mambaso (who, when, in 1960, the black musical *King Kong* toured to London, played for Queen Elizabeth II). *Kwela* featured an ostinato vamp sequence of chords (C–F–C–G^7) on guitar, under a pennywhistle melody divided into an antiphonal AABB phrase pattern. This pattern also occurs in *mbaqanga*; its phrasing originates in traditional Nguni songs, which consist of a single musical sentence divided into two phrases (Kirby 1937:286–288). *Kwela* studio bands typically featured a soloist backed by four pennywhistles playing the theme in unison, plus bass and drums. In the early 1950s, Aaron "Jake" Lerole used such a unit to record his classic *kwela* hit, "Tom Hark," a song that made hundreds of thousands of pounds for Gallo, and became popular in Britain in a version by Ted Heath, a clarinetist. Many studio reed players got their start as pennywhistlers, and even the famous virtuosos eventually wound up in the studios playing saxophone *mbaqanga*. In the early 1990s, Mambaso and Lerole still made a living that way. Spokes Mashiyane said the simplicity of the pennywhistle allowed him greater freedom to bend and blend notes in the near-vocalized African manner. Improvised jazz solos on recordings such as "Kwela Kong" attest to Spokes' genius for making an aesthetic virtue out of technical limitations: he acrobatically shaded, warped, and vocalized a torrent of timbres and tones.

Black studio musicians had at first little respect for the street pennywhistlers, but the latter's popularity forced acceptance and encouraged musical exchange. By the

Under "separate-amenities" legislation, black and
white musicians could not perform together, or play
for multiracial audiences, without special permits.

late 1950s, a blend of *kwela*, *mbaqanga* and American big-band jazz, had emerged in
recordings such as "Baby Come Duze" by Ntemi Piliso and the Alexandra Allstar
Band. That form of *mbaqanga*, sometimes known as *majuba* (after the Jazz Maniacs'
recording of the same name), characterized South African jazz at its popular height.
American jazz was also popular, especially among sophisticates. In the United States,
the big bands were dying out, and jazz as a broadly popular music was in decline.

These developments influenced black South African jazzmen profoundly, and
the honor roll of local musical giants such as Kippie "Morolong" Moeketsi, Dollar
Brand, Mackay Davashe, Elijah Nkonyane, Sol Klaaste, Hugh Masekela, Jonas
Gwangwa, Chris MacGregor (a white pianist and leader of a multiracial band), and
Gideon Nxumalo is too lengthy to summarize here. Female singers (such as Miriam
Makeba, Dolly Rathebe, Abagail Khubeka, Peggy Phango, and Thandi Klaasens) and
close-harmony quartets (such as the Manhattan Brothers and LoSix) helped maintain
the popularity and compositional productivity of both *mbaqanga* and American-style
vocal jazz.

A series of jam sessions organized at the Odin Cinema by the Modern Jazz Club
in Sophiatown, a vigorous black suburb known as Johannesburg's "Little Harlem,"
epitomized and energized interest in American mainstream jazz. As in the United
States, smaller units, such as Mackay Davashe's Shantytown Sextet and the King
Force Quintet (Wilson Silgee's successor to the Jazz Maniacs), were replacing big
bands. Those ensembles played bebop *mbaqanga*, combining the melodic and rhythmic motifs and two-part, two-repeat phrasing of the latter with the virtuosic improvising of the former. Almost indistinguishable from their American counterparts were
the Jazz Epistles, featuring Dollar Brand on piano, Hugh Masekela on trumpet (figure 4), Jonas Gwangwa on trombone, and Kippie Moeketsi on clarinet and alto saxophone. Except for Moeketsi, who toured to London only with Mackay Davashe's Jazz
Dazzlers Orchestra and *King Kong* in 1960–1961, these players, and a good many
others of South Africa's most prominent musicians, fled from apartheid into exile,
where they enjoyed outstanding careers overseas. Most of the Jazz Epistles, Miriam
Makeba, all four of the Manhattan Brothers, drummer Louis Moholo, singer Letta
Mbuli, composer and author Todd Matshikiza, and countless other stars settled outside South Africa. Their decision to leave the country was not based on the declining
popularity of jazz. Despite their departure, the 1960s saw spirited developments in
South African jazz. During the first half of the decade, a series of major "Cold Castle"
jazz festivals, sponsored by South African Breweries in Soweto, helped focus urban
blacks' attention on established and rising vocalists and players.

BLACK SHOW BUSINESS UNDER APARTHEID

Voluntary exile was a response to increasingly restrictive conditions imposed by the
Nationalist Party government, which came to power in 1948 and set about imple-
menting a system of rigid measures to enforce the separation of the races. Under

FIGURE 4   A jazz concert in Sophiatown, 1950s; center stage, trumpeter Hugh Masekela.

"separate-amenities" legislation, black and white musicians could not perform together, or play for multiracial audiences, without special permits. To make way for white settlement, the government removed black suburbs close to urban centers, which had often served as centers of black cultural life. The residents relocated to distant new townships. In the late 1950s, Sophiatown was bulldozed out of existence—at its cultural and political apogee. In 1960, the musical *King Kong*, based on the downfall of black heavyweight boxing champion Ezekial "King Kong" Dhlamini, appeared. It was a result of collaboration between African performers and composers and white directors, choreographers, and producers. It featured the music of Todd Matshikiza, with arrangements by Stanley Glasser, Mackay Davashe's swinging Jazz Dazzlers Orchestra, Miriam Makeba, and the Manhattan Brothers' Nathan Mdledle in the leading roles, and a host of Johannesburg's top black performers. With both black and white audiences in Johannesburg, it was a big success; it served to define an era, in opposition to the government's good-fences-make-good-neighbors vision of apartheid. But when the show toured to London, many members of the cast chose to stay abroad, and returnees found the basis of black show business had severely eroded. Cut off from the city, the black communities like Soweto turned inward, and dissention and violence plagued concert and dance hall stages. Beginning in the 1960s, community halls, and even the black cinemas in Johannesburg, where African music was staged, instituted a no-dancing policy, lest physical high spirits lead to physical violence.

Frustrated in one direction, black popular musicians turned their energies in others. Neotraditionalists were still active, and electric amplification of their favored instruments provided opportunities for increased technical sophistication, a broader range of outside influences, and access to a wider popular audience. In the 1960s, the guitar became the dominant instrument in all Western popular music. In West and Central Africa, syncretic styles of guitar playing, such as highlife and Congo beat, dominated local scenes. In South Africa, a new electrified-guitar *mbaqanga* (accordion, violin, pennywhistle-cum-saxophone, backed by electric bass and trap drums) emerged, also known by the American loanword "jive." Musically, *mbaqanga* jive borrowed from the old *mbaqanga* and *tsaba-tsaba* to create a new up-tempo rhythm, played in 8/8 time on high hat, but with a strong internal feeling of 2/4 and syncopated accents on offbeats. The melodic theme was in the bass, which, with the back-up vocalists, became the lead instrument, representing the chorus in traditional vocal

This format became known as *simanjemanje* ("now-now things"), a form that at once celebrated and burlesqued Western manners, material culture, and indigenous heritage.

music. The lead guitar, saxophone, violin, accordion, and solo vocal took the upper parts in antiphonal fashion. The phrase structure was the familiar AABB repeat of the old *mbaqanga*. Hence, the sound of *mbaqanga* jive derived more from traditional and neotraditional African music than from the earlier, more Western and jazz-influenced *mbaqanga* of the 1950s. The leading figures in its innovation and development were Simon Nkabinde, a Swazi composer and vocalist (known as Indoda Mahlathini), and John Bhengu, a Zulu guitarist (known as Phuzhushukela).

The audience for this music was not the sophisticated, English-speaking, urbanized, American-jazz and popular-ballad fans of "Little Harlem," but the thousands of semiliterate domestic servants, industrial workers, and mineworkers who retained rural values. With the clearing of the "locations" under the group-areas legislation of the early 1950s, influx-control regulations reinforced the migrant-labor system, and denied most recent arrivals the right to bring their relatives, or to settle permanently in urban areas. In the same decade, the Land Acts of 1913, 1936, and 1945, which had reserved 87 percent of South Africa's territory for white ownership, uprooted and impoverished rural life. The remaining 13 percent became the basis for the infamous "Bantustans" or homelands, which South Africa began to declare independent, starting in 1963 with the Transkei. The government pursued on a new level the policy of preventing the formation of either a stable urban work force or a landed rural peasantry. By law, many black South Africans found themselves citizens of reserves they had never seen.

In such an atmosphere, urban workers turned their eyes from the ecological devastation, poverty, and hopelessness of their rural districts. In sound, text, and choreographic display, the music they preferred, *mbaqanga* jive, provided symbolic images of once independent African cultures, in which men and women possessed their full *ubuntu* (Zulu) 'humanity'. Indoda Mahlathini had a thrilling bass register, which he employed to develop the role of solo male "groaner" in front of a chorus of four female voices, the legendary Mahotella Queens. Mahlathini and his Queens developed a kind of variety show, which included fast changes among traditional dance movements in beads, feathers, and skins; athletic turns in shorts, sneakers, and baseball caps; and svelte ballads in evening dress. This format for *mbaqanga* became known as *simanjemanje* ("now-now things"), a form that at once celebrated and burlesqued Western manners, material culture, and indigenous heritage. Phuzushukela, who combined electrified Zulu guitar with bass, drums, saxophones, and all-male backup singers, dressed his band entirely in traditional Zulu leopard skins.

The texts of Mahlathini's songs created a vision of an autonomous rural African past, when people daily honored cohesive moral and political values, not just in the breach, but in the observance. The songs favorably compared these values to the supposed individualism and immorality of "now-now," but the comparison was less important than Mahlathini's presentation of forceful images of a heroic, independent African past, and of a self-sufficient African idyll. In the face of dependency and dehumanization, these images contributed to a sense of resistant nationalism and self-regard, and were less a mystification of African tradition than a mobilization of its remaining psychocultural resources. By the late 1960s, the major recording companies had recruited or formed dozens of *simanjemanje* ensembles, which sang in a variety of local languages, each with a groaner and a chorus. Until the mid 1970s, *simanjemanje* dominated sales of locally made recordings and the airwaves of the African-language services of the South African Broadcasting Corporation ("Radio Bantu"). Concerts and extended tours of groups like Mahlathini's, sponsored by their recording companies, were among the most frequent professional performance events for blacks. Educated Africans cared little for these events and preferred jazz or the rock and soul arriving from North America and England.

In 1954, the proceeds from a farewell concert for Father Trevor Huddleston, a social activist, went to set up, at Dorkay House in Johannesburg, a permanent home for the Union of Southern African Artists, a multiracial organization, which, in the "Dorkay Jazz" series of the late 1950s, first brought local jazz players and jazz singers to large white audiences, and produced *King Kong*. One Dorkay associate, Gibson Kente, a songwriter from the eastern Cape, who had studied social work at the Jan Hofmeyr School (Cape Town), took from *King Kong*'s success inspiration to start a theatrical company in Soweto. In 1963, his first production, *Manana, the Jazz Prophet*, introduced urban black audiences to musical theater with a mix of energetic dance-melodrama and solo and choral *mbaqanga*, backed by a swinging band. Over the years, his music style created an audience for theater in the black townships. The training he gave his cast produced a new generation of black theatrical performers, many of whom went on to create important companies and productions of their own. While he continued to produce major works, his disciples brought to international attention the energy of his music and dance. Mbongi Ngema, creator of *Sarafina!*, a success in 1988–1989, both in Johannesburg and on Broadway (New York), trained under him.

During the 1970s, township-jazz musical theater expanded to become the preeminent local showcase for new black talent. The *simanjemanje* style of *mbaqanga* or *mqhashiyo* (Zulu) 'fly off, like chips from the ax', as people then called it, continued to command a large following, rivaled only by imported Anglo-American popular hits, and by the latest and most professionally polished and talented of the *cothoz' mfana* or *isicatamiya* groups, Ladysmith Black Mambazo. People consider the leader of that group, Joseph Shabalala, a masterful composer and singer. Ladysmith Black Mambazo, who usually performed *a cappella* and in Zulu, were among the top-selling groups in South Africa, more than a decade before Paul Simon, an American musician, recruited them for his *Graceland* album and tour of 1986. In 1987, they won a Grammy, for best folk album (*Shaka Zulu*).

Another phenomenon of the late 1960s and 1970s whose popularity lasted two decades was the group Malombo, a unique fusion of the indigenous African musics of northern South Africa and progressive, "free" jazz and rock influences from North America. Malombo began with Philip Thabane on guitar, Abbie Cindi on flute, and Julian Bahula on African drums; but the band soon divided. For ten years, Thabane, the guiding genius of the group, and originator of its style, teamed up with Gabriel Mabee Thobejane, percussionist and dancer. They derived their vocals, melody, and percussion from the Northern Sotho, Amandebele, and Venda cultures of the Transvaal; and they took guitar arrangements and improvisatory style from such Americans as Wes Montgomery and John McLaughlin. Their music, though not explicitly political, came to occupy a special place in the vanguard of local progressive music, where it embodied a blend of African cultural nationalism and modernism known as the Black Consciousness Movement. Other groups that performed in the

Another innovator was Jonathan Clegg, a young white folk guitarist, who learned the Zulu language and Zulu traditional and neotraditional guitar playing.

Malombo style, such as Dashiki, were explicitly political; they played at rallies of the South African Students Organization. Curiously, Malombo established a loyal following among young white listeners. They probably spent more time touring in the United States than any other South African band. In the 1980s, Thobejane teamed up with Sakhile, an African jazz-fusion group, while Thabane recruited two young percussionists to carry on Malombo, who recorded their latest album, *Uhh!*, in New York and London (figure 5). The Malombo style, though a singular sensation in South African music, influenced other, more mainstream, jazz-fusion groups: Sakhile, Bayete, Amampondo, and Malopoets.

In the late 1970s, *simanjemanje*'s market dominance declined, as working-class listeners demanded a more worldly and less ethnically oriented music to accompany their political demands. The most successful new groups were local interpreters of popular international soul and reggae styles, though few could compete with Earth, Wind, and Fire; or with Bob Marley; or with Harold Melvin and the Blue Notes. "Wake Up Everybody," the last-named group's soul hit, was among the popular anthems of the Soweto Uprising of 1976–1977. Among the South African groups who managed to compete with the imports were soul-*mbaqanga* singers Babsi Mlangeni, Steve Kekana, Mparanyane, and the Soul Brothers. That blend of *mbaqanga* and American pop and soul led to the main musical developments and commercial successes in township music in the 1980s.

Among the most significant developments outside the "township soul" and the reggae mainstream was a revival of slow-tempo *marabi*, effected by pianist Dollar

FIGURE 5   The author, David Coplan, performing with Malombo; percussionist Gabriel Thobejane; guitarist Philip Thabane.

Brand (now Abdullah Ibrahim) on his album *Mannenburg*. His success inspired older jazz pioneers, such as Zakes Nkosi, Victor Ndlazilwane, and Ntemi Piliso, to return to the studio, and younger jazzmen, such as pianist Pat Matshikiza (Todd's nephew), guitarist Sandile Shange, and saxophonist Barney Rachabane, to record in the older style. Meanwhile, mainstream jazz musicians, such as Winston Mankunku Ngozi and Michael Makgalemele, helped revive the local popularity of American jazz, with arrangements of local melodies on landmark albums, *Yakhal' Inkomo* and *The Bull and the Lion*. At local festivals, a style of soul and jazz fusion with only few local characteristics attained considerable popularity, because of the musical excellence of representative groups such as the Drive, Spirits Rejoice, and the Jazz Messengers.

Another innovator was Jonathan Clegg, a young white folk guitarist, who, from fatherly mentors at Johannesburg's Wemmer Hostel for black migrant industrial workers, learned the Zulu language and Zulu traditional and neotraditional guitar playing. Among his close associates was young Sipho Mncunu, a domestic worker, dance-song composer, dance-team leader, and neotraditional guitarist from Zululand, with whom he formed Juluka, a group that combined Anglo-American folk with Zulu traditional and neotraditional music and instruments. A fine dancer and team leader, Clegg introduced multiracial Zulu dancing and stick fighting to South African audiences. Influenced by guitarist Phuzushukela, Juluka began their recording career in the Zulu *mbaqanga*-jive style, and soon evolved toward a more international form of Zulu rock. South African Broadcasting banned Juluka's recordings, stating that Clegg was insulting the Zulu people by claiming to play their music; but the ban did not prevent the Zulu monarch, King Zwelethini, from appointing Clegg a "royal minstrel." After the 1970s, Mncunu and Clegg split up, and Clegg achieved success with his new Zulu hard-rock ensemble, Savuka. Through statements, political songs, and leadership in the South African Musicians Association, Clegg maintained his good faith with the freedom movement in South Africa. He and his fellow members of Juluka and Savuka represented a new wave of musically bicultural black and white musicians, whose success signaled the emergence of a national South African popular culture.

The 1980s in South Africa saw an effloration of popular groups and musicians, fueled by the dramatic improvement in locally available electronic musical technology, and by a new international interest in African popular music. The styles described here maintained a particular following, and stars such as Ladysmith Black Mambazo, Jonathan Clegg, Mahlathini, Sakhile, and Ray Phiri's *mbaqanga*-rock band Stimela developed a diverse national audience. The most popular representatives of local music were the township funk-rock groups playing what people commonly call "bubblegum," a term that identifies the youthful, bouncy, top-40, party-music aspect of balladeers and funk-dance bands, though it suggests nothing of their stylistic innovations, or political lyrics and musical metaphors. The top township party-dance groups in the early 1990s were Brenda Fassie (with or without the Big Dudes), Steve Kekana, Chicco, Yvonne Chaka Chaka, Lazarus Kgakgudi, Condry Ziqubu, and Sipho "Hot Sticks" Mabuse. In the 1970s, it was the last, working with the group Harari, who developed the blend of South African rhythm and melody with "progressive" American rock music that became the basis for the most profound of the bubblegum artists. Since 1988, Chicco and Condry Ziqubu produced powerfully political songs about friends and relatives in exile, police brutality, and communal concerns like drunkenness and domestic violence. Sipho Mabuse's album *Chant of the Marching* was banned in South Africa. The music proved more experimental and inventive than many more "serious" listeners might have expected, and there was no music more danceable than the heavy-bass and synthesizer-bubblegum version of the old township rhythm.

> Township theater, with its music-and-dance component, remained the most potent form of the artistic expression of black South African social experiences and aspirations.

White South African bands kept current with international trends, and several, following the lead of Jonathan Clegg, blended local African influences into rock. Among Afrikaners, the popular social commentary of balladeer David Kramer led to the appearance of outré hard-rock and blues bands, such as the Kerkorrels and Gereformeerde Blues Band, who shocked conservative Afrikaner parents, but delighted their offspring.

The old traditions of choral dance music, continuing to flourish in performance among black South Africans, played an important role in the mobilization of the antiapartheid movement. The Congress of South African Trade Unions, and other major organizations, sponsored frequent cultural days and festivals, when amateur groups, through political dance and song, gave audiences emotional inspiration and unifying catharsis. Township theater, with its music-and-dance component, remained the most potent form of the artistic expression of black South African social experiences and aspirations. Meanwhile, the international focus on South Africa, and Paul Simon's Graceland project, gave greater recognition to South African performers. Celebrated artists in exile, such as Hugh Masekela and Miriam Makeba, revitalized their careers. In the early 1990s, these artists, plus Abdullah Ibrahim, returned home and achieved success in local tours.

REFERENCES

Andersson, Muff. 1981. *Music in the Mix.* Johannesburg: Ravan Press.

Coplan, David B. 1985. *In Township Tonight! South Africa's Black City Music and Theatre.* London and New York: Longman. Johannesburg: Ravan Press.

———. 1988. "Musical Understanding: The Ethnoaesthetics of Migrant Workers' Poetic Song in Lesotho." *Ethnomusicology* 32:337–368.

Erlmann, Veit. 1991. *African Stars.* Chicago: University of Chicago Press.

Kirby, Percival R. 1937 [1967]. "The Musical Practices of the Native Races of South Africa." In *Western Civilization and the Natives of South Africa*, ed. I. Schapera, 131–140. New York: Humanities Press.

Mthethwa, Bongani. 1980. "Zulu Children's Songs." In *Papers Presented at the Symposium on Ethnomusicology: Rhodes University, Grahamstown, October 10–11, 1980*, ed. Andrew Tracey, 23–25. Grahamstown: Rhodes University.

Performance in Madagascar
Mireille Rakotomalala

Streams of Influence
Musical Instruments
Religious Performance with Ancestors
Royal Music
Postcolonial Musical Life

The island of Madagascar, which the Republic of Malagasy occupies, is the third-largest island in the world, occupying some 600,000 square kilometers, and lying off the southeast coast of Africa. The history of the island is one of successive migrations. Data from the early period of settlement are even scarcer than for many other oral cultures, since archaeological evidence has been largely destroyed by the torrential rains of the wet season in areas of particular historical interest.

Though the exact chronology of arrivals remains mysterious, it is thought that the earliest colonies were established in approximately A.D. 500, probably by Austronesian-speaking settlers from the region now known as Indonesia. There are currently eighteen ethnic groups on the island. That early settlers following prevailing winds and currents, arrived directly and accidentally from Southeast Asia is a theory that has been largely discredited, because both Réunion and Mauritius—two islands directly in the path of the supposed voyage—were uninhabited until Europeans' arrival, much later. More likely is settlement via the coast of East Africa.

One theory of interaction between the earliest occupants of Madagascar and Africa proposes that communication occurred some time before A.D. 1000, the date established for Bantu migrations into the African rain forest. Before then, settlement of the rain forest may have been impossible until Africans had learned the adaptive strategies known to forest dwellers of Southeast Asia—strategies they presumably borrowed from the settlers of Madagascar.

STREAMS OF INFLUENCE

After the arrival of the original occupants, waves of new settlers arrived from the Middle East, Africa, and Europe. Islamic influence, arriving about A.D. 1500, has been credited with fostering conditions necessary for the development of hierarchical kingdoms among the Malagasy. Among these, the first and longest lasting were the state structures of the Sakalava, originating with the Maroserana dynasty in the southwest of the island. After Europeans had arrived, alliances between communities in the southwest and migrant people led to the establishment of the Volamena dynasty, which began the northward spread of dynastic influence and organization.

The music of the Malagasy Republic incorporates influences from Africa, Indonesia, Southeast Asia, Europe, and Arabia.

By the 1800s, the Sakalava kingdoms were dominating the west coast of the island—an influence that has lasted.

In the early 1700s, the Betsimisaraka began to organize on the east coast of the island, and under the command of a military chief named Ramaromanompo, united the ethnic groups along the coast into a confederacy, which lasted with varying degrees of cohesion for almost one hundred years, until it was subsumed by the third major kingdom of Madagascar, the Merina kingdom. Located in the interior of the island, the Merina kingdom coalesced in the late 1700s.

By the end of the 1800s, firearms had reached the Malagasy, changing the nature of indigenous conquest and expansion, but only the Merina had ironworkers capable of producing their own weapons. By 1820, the Merina had conquered much of Madagascar, controlled most of the major ports, and had developed a monarchy strong enough to force traders to conduct their business in the interior of the island, Merina country, rather than staying on the coasts, as they had previously done. During the reign of King Andrianampoinimerina (d. 1810), the only groups able to resist Merina expansion were the Sakalava kingdoms.

Musical exchanges

From an ethnomusicological point of view, the early history of Malagasy is important in consideration of A. M. Jones's proposal that the tuning of certain African instruments reveals evidence of an Indonesian–African relationship somewhere in African prehistory (1964). Because of the location of Madagascar and the apparent ethnic composition of the Malagasy, the island has been seen as a link between Southeast Asia and Africa, in confirmation of Jones's hypothesis. A comprehensive discussion of linguistic and musical evidence of early communication between Indonesia and Africa appears in Norma McLeod's "Musical Instruments and History in Madagascar" (1977).

Indeed, the music of the Malagasy Republic incorporates influences from Africa, Indonesia, Southeast Asia, Europe, and Arabia. The instruments found in the Malagasy Republic provide additional evidence of the successive but discontinuous immigrations of Austronesians and Africans. Oddly enough, there are no bronze instruments of Java present, though the Malagasy linguistic vocabulary contains originally Javanese words relating to the metals used in gamelans. The modern Malagasy language—in fact, an Austronesian language, which some scholars think to be most closely related to a language spoken in the interior of Borneo—appears to preserve certain Javanese linguistic traits that have disappeared in Java.

By 1800, a primary center for music and the other arts had become the royal courts of the three great kingdoms described above. Each court was renowned for the special genres of music it fostered: women's choirs, epic and shorter forms of poetry, and an operalike tradition. Beginning with the twentieth century, the influence of

Christian missionaries and French colonizers resulted in a degeneration of an art-music–folk-music distinction, until the two became virtually indistinguishable.

At present, the mixture of African and Southeast Asian influence is visible in all genres of music among the Malagasy, though some genres reflect one influence more strongly than others. Gilbert Rouget, for example, called the choral polyphony of the central island Merina, with its intervals of thirds and sixths and rapid rhythms, "oceanic" (1946:87), and found a more pronounced African influence among the Sakalava, with genres in call-and-response style, appearing more rhythmic than melodic (p. 88). Norma McLeod identifies two styles—one distinct to the Merina, the Vakinankaratra, and the Betsileo of the central highlands, and the other more typical of groups in the southern desert. Both styles demonstrate the polyphony mentioned by Rouget, and both show rhythms whose variability depends on whether the music is meant for dancing or singing. Of the difference between the two styles, McLeod says "songs in the high plateau area are set strophically. In the desert region, . . . litany is prominent with some examples of development into serial polyphony" (1980:547).

MUSICAL INSTRUMENTS

A Tsimihety myth exemplifies an important Malagasy belief about the origins of musical instruments: to enable men and women to entertain themselves, the creator god, Zanahary, gave them musical instruments; unaware of the blessing of these gifts, the people neglected them, and to punish this neglect, Zanahary transformed the men and women into dogs. The myth implies that musical instruments had a divine origin, as did the particular power of certain instruments to call ancestral spirits.

Another belief and practice concerns the Sakalava kings. To display the power of instruments, the kings hung them in front of royal huts, or at the entrance of royal villages.

A third example involves Andrianampomgatany, prince of the heavenly drums in the central highlands during the 1200s. He commanded the thunder and lightning of celestial rains. In his final words to his counselors and his children, he said, "If it happens that I must die, I would like to be buried here, at Fanongoavana, during the night. And I would like that the people of Imerina loosen their hair, without distinction of sex (a sign of mourning), for I have departed—I, the drum to which you have danced."

Instrumental taxonomy and symbolism

Musical instruments are known as objects that sound (*zavamaneo*), and musicians are those who play objects that sound (*mpitendry zavamaneo*). Instrumental terminology divides instruments into categories distinguished by techniques of playing, anthropo-morphic characterization, and symbolic associations (Rakotomalala 1986).

Terms to describe instrumental playing include *tsofina* 'to blow' (aerophones), *kapohina* 'to strike' (idiophones), *velezina* 'to beat' or 'to give life to' (membrane drums), and *tendrena* 'to play' (chordophones and keyboard instruments). Among the keyboard instruments, the accordion (*gorodao*) and the piano require specific techniques, modified by the Malagasy musicians to obtain desired tones.

Though anthropomorphism does not figure prominently in the Malagasy conception of instruments, the peoples of Madagascar often endow musical instruments with human structures. The part of the instrument that emits the sound is frequently called *vava* 'mouth'. The top part of the object, *loha* 'head', is the end of the neck of the stick zither or the topmost node of the tube zither, of which the *tongontra,* the *tsikatray*   Frame rattle constructed from a square frame of wood covered by rushes, and filled with seeds

atanatra   Xylophone that consists of planks of wood placed over the thighs of one of the players

n'lapa   Single-headed drums, one of which bears a resemblance to certain West African drums

FIGURE I   A drum (*langoro*) from Sakalava region (northwest), with an accordion in the background.

bottommost node, is shorter. *Vatany* 'resonator' or 'trunk' indicates the most important part of musical instruments, while the *vodony* 'buttock' is the inferior part of membrane drums.

The sacred drums include a *hazolahy reniny* 'wooden male mother' and a *hazolahy zanany* 'wooden male daughter'. The concept of motherhood represents femininity, fecundity, and longevity. Nevertheless, these are considered bisexual instruments, as are conchs, symbolizing the unity of male and female elements. The Malagasy represent the feminine element in forms of abundance, and the male element in forms of dynamism. People designate membranophones of different sizes by the opposition of adult and child or male and female. The term *ambaviny* 'female skin' denotes the drum on the left, played with fingers; the term *amdahiny* 'male skin' denotes the drum on the right, struck with a stick, a phallic symbol.

In certain regions, particularly among the Zafinaniry and Islamic (northwestern) peoples, several chordophones (*valiha vata, jejy, kabosa*) and drums are often decorated with various motifs. This decoration varies according to the region and the artistic sense of the musician or artisan. Tsimihety *valiha vasa* are characterized by motifs with white paint, representing cosmic life, including the crescent of the moon and the constellations. Zafimaniry chordophones show burnt engravings, with predominant geometric figures, especially subjects associated with fertility, such as the ibis (symbolizing prosperity) and the fish (symbolizing wealth). On the upper membrane of Bara or Vezo hoop drums (*langoro*), drawings often display magical symbols (figure 1).

Syncretism appears in the morphology, function, and name of the musical instruments of Madagascar. Regional traces manifest themselves separately or simultaneously; but in most cases, each object includes at least two superimposed traits.

Idiophones

Idiophones comprise a class of instruments made of naturally sonorous material, so the vibrating column is also the resonator, though often these instruments will have supplementary resonators for greater volume.

Struck tubes

These instruments are called variously *tsikaretika, raloba, kimbolo, karatsaka, farai, peripetika, tsipetrika,* or *volo* depending on their region of origin. In all regions, the instrument is composed of a bamboo tube several meters long, held horizontally. As in Africa, Asia, and the Americas, the tube can rest on the ground, or be held by forked sticks at belly level. In Madagascar, from two to more than ten players line up along the tube, striking it with small batons; different locations along the tube and different intensities of striking result in different tonal qualities.

Struck plank

This instrument, *kakanikakanika or rondro,* is a simple struck plank, often laid over a hollow mortar, which serves as a resonator. The plank is played by children in games, but also by adults, formerly to welcome the arrival of a village chief or a king.

Rattles

The tube rattle has many names, again depending on the region and ethnic group of origin; among these are *kritsakritsa, tsikiripika, tsakaiamba, voamaintilany, foray, kai-iamba,* and *doka.* The rattle is constructed from a piece of bamboo naturally closed at both ends, of which one end is pierced to allow the introduction of seeds; it is played most often with two hands, by men or women, frequently to emphasize the rhythms of dancing.

The *tsikatray* or *tsakaiamba* is a frame rattle constructed from a square frame of young wood covered by rushes, and filled with seeds; to serve as a handle, one or two of the sticks forming the frame may extend out beyond the frame's limits. The *kahemba, makasa, faray,* or *tsikatray* is a sewn rattle, made in the shape of a pyramid of leaves sewn together with thread and filled with seeds or rice. Sewn rattles in Madagascar are most often played simultaneously with a musical bow by a performer who holds the rattle with the fourth and fifth fingers of the same hand containing the stick with which he or she strikes the bow.

Scraped tube

This instrument, *tsikadraha* or *faray,* is a notched tube of bamboo. Scraped by a small stick, it accompanies dancing and the playing of other instruments.

Xylophones

The main xylophone among the Malagasy is the *atanatra* or *katikoky,* a freestanding xylophone consisting of planks of wood placed over the thighs of one of the players, usually a woman or a young girl; while the first player adds a melody, a second player sits to the side of the xylophone, playing an ostinato. This xylophone is played for religious ceremonies and entertainment.

Membranophones

Single-headed drums, *n'lapa,* are either sacred ('drum with a sacred peg', attaching the skin of the drum to the resonator) or secular ('drum with a simple peg'). The secular drum resembles certain drums in West Africa. It has three feet, made of clay; to accompany women's dancing during Islamic celebrations, chiefs or their designated representatives play it. The chief of each clan keeps the clan's sacred drum in the enclosure of the royal Sakalava tombs (*lapa*), and it is played during ceremonies of the royal tombs (*doany*).

Chordophones

Zithers

Zithers are a class of chordophones having neither a neck nor a yoke, of which nearly the entirety of the instrument is the resonator, with strings stretched the entire length of, and parallel to, the body. The body resonator may consist of a board, a round

The instrument for which Madagascar is best known is a tube zither, the *valiha*, from Sanskrit vadhya 'instrument of sacred music'. It originated in Indonesia in the pre-Islamic period (1100s to 1500s).

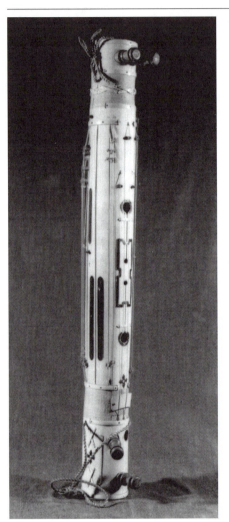

FIGURE 2   A *valiha* from the Merina region, in the area of the capital, Antanarivo.

stick, a tube, a lath, or a shallow box; supplementary resonators may be attached to the body.

Tube zithers

The instrument for which Madagascar is best known is a tube zither, the *valiha*, from Sanskrit *vadhya* 'instrument of sacred music' (figure 2). It originated in Indonesia in the pre-Islamic period (1100s to 1500s), from which more than five hundred words of Sanskritic origin remain in the Malagasy language. In the 1800s, it was considered an aristocratic instrument. In the time of the Merina monarchy, its presentation indicated consent to a pact.

Despite its Asian origin and Sanskritic name, the *valiha* is tuned like the West African *kora* (by thirds, using a heptatonic inventory of tones), but showing European influence. When Malagasy musicians tune their instruments, they never invoke the idea of absolute pitch; the tones are always a little higher or lower than the Western tempered octave. There exists no standard instrument: most of the time, the position of the strings varies with the performer.

The *valiha* usually accompanies sung poetry or laments. It can be accompanied by other *valiha*, by flutes, or even by electronically amplified instruments. It has several types: *valiha volo tototenany*, a bamboo idiochord of about seventeen strings; *valiha jihy vy*, a bamboo tube with sixteen to eighteen metal strings; *valiha bao*, a raffia tube (Tsimihety) with twenty to twenty-two strings, now obsolete; and *manibola*, a wooden tube (Bara) with eight to ten metal strings.

Raft zither

The raft zither, *valiha vero*, consists of ten bamboo tubes arranged progressively by length. A longitudinal notch on the body of each tube loosens fiber to form a string, raised with a piece of bamboo or calabash as a bridge. A bamboo plectrum activates the strings.

Board zither

This zither, *jejy vaotavo*, is similar to board zithers found in Africa. Originally, it had only three strings (of sisal), and its tuning is unknown. Late-twentieth-century models have twelve to sixteen metal strings, with a pentatonic or heptatonic inventory of tones. Considered an instrument of the lower classes in the 1800s, it has become associated with the *rija*, among the most important vocal genres in the narrative style of Malagasy culture. Fathers teach their sons how to play this instrument; to have the right to perform on it professionally, a man must have the blessing of a classificatory, not biological, grandfather (*raiamandreny*).

Stick zither

In Madagascar, the stick zither (figure 3) may or may not have a calabash resonator.

Both kinds consist of a stick with three small projecting platforms, or simple pegs, perpendicular to the stick, which can be used to "fret" the strings running over the platforms. Strings run over these projections and along the spine of the instrument, and are attached at the other end of the stick directly to the stick, which may be either arched or forked. If the instrument has a calabash resonator, it is held against the player's belly. It has a tonal range of about an octave, and is played solo or as vocal accompaniment.

Case zither (marovane)

This zither consists of a shallow, roughly rectangular resonator, of which one long side is straight while the opposite side is curved and slightly narrower (figure 4). On the straight side are small pegs of leather, which hold the steel strings; on the curved side are slots holding the strings. The chords of the instrument are strung on both sides of the resonator, often with twelve on one side and eleven on the other.

Lutes

A lute is a plucked stringed instrument, characterized by a hollow resonator from which a sometimes frettable neck extends. The strings of the lute run parallel to the neck, from one extreme (where they may be pegged for variable tuning), to the other end (where they often traverse a bridge, which helps transfer the vibrations of the string to the resonator).

Plucked lute

The oldest existing models of the Malagasy plucked lute (*kabosa*) are identical to the *qubuz,* played in Arabia from about A.D. 500 to about 1500. As the instrument of bards all over the Malagasy Republic, it often accompanies popular and satiric songs.

The resonator of the plucked lute—originally a calabash, a turtleshell, or hardwood, covered with goatskin—is in the 1990s wooden or metal. The original form was oval, but now can be rectangular. The neck is always long, and the strings consist of sisal, nylon, or steel. The strings vary in number with the region: highlands, four to six; northwest, two to five; south, three or four.

Bowed lute

This chordophone, *jejy,* appears either as a single- or multiple-stringed bowed lute. The single-stringed version is used in the south by the Tandroy griot farmers, who migrate northwestward during the planting season. They accompany recitativelike songs with a metal bell (*katasaha* or *katsa*). The bow is made of flexible wood and sisal fiber, to which they apply resin (*veheranga*).

The multiple-stringed version (*lokanga*) is played by the Bara and the Merina. The Bara use it in their magical and religious rites, and the Merina in the highlands use it in popular-theater performances. The number of strings varies from two to four.

Aerophones

Flutes

End-blown flute

Peoples of the northwest developed a six-hole, end-blown flute, *sababa,* similar to the Arabic *shabab.* In the highlands, it is known as *sodina*; in Indonesia, *suling.* It is most widely used in the central part of the country, where musicians are the most techni-

FIGURE 3   A stick zither from the highlands.

FIGURE 4   A case zither (*marovane*) from the south, southwest, north-central, and east coasts.

cally and musically accomplished in playing it. It is played in hocket with other flutes, or with drums for amusement outdoors.

Free-reed pipe

Made from a stalk of rice, the *farara* produces a strong, piercing sound, whose pitch depends mainly on the length of the pipe. Children in the highlands play it during their games. At harvesttime, however, to avoid attracting hailstorms, adults do not allow children to play it in rice fields. Each child blows one *farara* in turn, hocketing to produce an interlocking game and performance.

Panpipes

Made from flexible reeds, *fololtsy* are played by children guarding cattle. Each tube has a unique length, and having a set of several tubes allows players to produce a melody. The Vezo and people of the highlands play this instrument.

RELIGIOUS PERFORMANCE WITH ANCESTORS

Musical performances known as *doany, bilo, sandratse, sabo, osika,* and *tromba* have an important place in Malagasy life: they permit people to maintain communication with ancestors, intermediaries between the living people and the creator god. These performances are variable, but a certain structure is common to them: musical introduction, invocation to the spirits, manifestation of the spirits, thanksgiving, dances, and songs of the audience. Though music appears primarily at the beginning (to solicit the spirits) and at the end (for the closing section), it has a major role. The Malagasy believe each spirit has a favorite melody, by which the one who invokes spirits identifies them. An experienced musician must demonstrate his skill in his choice of melodies, for the spirits sometimes refuse to appear. The sounds are considered to have magic power, just as water and incense in these ceremonies do.

The musician plays for as long as necessary, until contact is established. During the performance, the audience is careful to do nothing to disturb the communication. This moment is important because it determines the quality of the rest of the event. With the arrival of the spirit and during the possession, all forms of sound cease, except the voice of the invoker, which has become that of the spirit. The concentration of the audience on the musician now moves toward the possessed, with an attentive silence in respect for the ancestor and his words. After some ritual movements, consisting of manipulation of different objects and signs toward the east, the imagined barriers between the participants disappear. The event closes in a communal feast, accompanied by dancing and singing.

Certain ancestral events, including the names of ancestors invoked and that of the Christian deity, show a syncretic character. Hymns are sung, though rarely.

The musical instrument for these events was originally the *valiha*, which the Malagasy consider their oldest instrument. Later, the case zither (*marovane*), the bowed lute (*lokanga*), or the accordion was substituted. Before the event, the instrument is purified with a special kind of clay (*tane fotsy*). The process of making the object sacred is a frequent act, for after the event, when the object is played as a virtuoso instrument, or serves for accompanying sung poetry, it becomes secular again.

Among other instruments used for religious purposes are the *angaroha* (a conch, used during the ceremony of the bath of the royal relics), the *katikoky* (a xylophone, played on the thighs by sterile young women who want to bear children), and *trotrobe* (calabashes, which become water drums when overturned on water and struck by women of Menave to invoke the *vazimba,* the first inhabitants of Madagascar).

ROYAL MUSIC

Oral traditions say that under the reign of Ralambo (1565–1610) the villagers of the central highlands organized competitions of singing and dancing for young girls. Over their shoulders, or fastened at their hips, the girls wore the *lamba,* a white scarf. They garnished their hair with flowers. By clapping hands and shouting exclamations, parents and friends encouraged each dancer or group of dancers. These competitions had the goal of strengthening communal life and maintaining peace among the villagers, for there was never a winner or a loser.

The elaborations of these games led progressively to their independence, in which form they became standing songs (*hira-tsangana*). Though little information remains of their contents, they were forerunners of the *hira-gasy.*

In Madagascar of the 1800s, through a series of political moves by which Andrianampoinimerina created alliances (including those of matrimony), Imerina became the most powerful indigenous kingdom. By means of a matrimonial alliance, *antsa* (sacred praise songs, dedicated to the sovereign) were introduced to the court. They arrived with the Princess Rambolamasonadro (of Sakalava origin), who demonstrated the performance by having thirty men and fifty women from her home perform. The king liked what he heard, and these performances were adopted as royal performances (Vig 1977).

For the duration of the Merina monarchy, *antsa* were performed at court. Radama I, the next monarch, sent his young students to the Mauritius Islands in 1824, with the goal of creating an official music. Queen Ranavalona I fostered the institutionalized development of art and culture. Royal singers were paid with cattle (or other livestock) and foodstuffs.

Theater

A popular form of theater, *hira-gasy* (figure 5), the genre most representative of the highlands, employs singing, dancing, and rhetoric, enlivened with improvisation. A troupe usually has about twenty members, all of one family, who have maintained the knowledge of the genre from generation to generation. In command of the troupe is the *reiamandreny* 'the oldest father and mother'. The oldest singer inherits command, but that does not hinder a theatrically competent woman from functioning as head of the troupe.

At the beginning of the reign of Radama I, the Malagasy were permitted to wear costumes in imitation of European courtly ladies and the military. European instruments—clarinets, trumpets, military drums, violins—were substituted for traditional instruments.

The performances offer critiques on daily life and marriage; with humor and spirit, they treat religion and politics. Their popularity was encouraged by the royalty, who considered them a means of transmitting messages to the people.

Music proved an important domain for the missionaries in their evangelical work, because it played an eminent political role among the monarchy, the missions, the social classes, and the people.

FIGURE 5 *Hira-gasy,* dance theater from the area of Antanarivo.

POSTCOLONIAL MUSICAL LIFE

Christian missionaries and music

In 1818, two Welsh mission families set up the first mission school in Madagascar, and by 1835, the Bible had been translated into Malagasy. By some accounts, the coming of Christianity was relatively untraumatic, since the endogamous social unit of the Malagasy, the *karazana*—what Maurice Bloch (1971) termed the *deme*—was compatible with the idea of congregation, and the sermon with traditional ideas of oratory. However, inevitable tension arose between traditional ideas of magic and ancestors and European culture as presented by Christian missionaries. From one monarch to the next, official royal attitude and policy changed in regard to missionary activity, until by the end of the 1800s, Christianity had nearly become a royal cult, and the London Missionary Society considered its efforts in Madagascar a success.

In addition to religious changes, the Europeans brought artisans, traders, and soldiers. Wooden dwellings began to be replaced by brick buildings, in some cases containing European furniture, and some of the Malagasy people began to dress in European fashions. The most important innovation brought by the missionaries was literacy, and soon an extensive literature was developing, in both Malagasy and Malagasy-French.

Thus, missionaries from the West left their traces in all areas of cultural and social life. Music proved an important domain for the missionaries in their evangelical work, because it was an activity for which the people had a predilection, and because it played an eminent political role among the monarchy, the missions, the social classes, and the people (both urban and rural). The period of missionization (1861–1920) is characterized by different conceptions of evangelization by Roman Catholics and Protestants, adaptations of hymns to indigenous musical traditions, and resistance to foreign songs and musical instruments.

For accompanying hymns, the English missionaries forbade traditional Malagasy musical instruments and gestures. The Jesuits, more indulgent, sought a compromise by accepting traditional musical elements for the Mass, but replacing traditional instruments with the harmonium. Urban people were generally receptive, but the missionaries' methods encountered resistance among the Betsileo, and local griots sang songs protesting missionization.

The Roman Catholics went so far as to teach Tonic Sol-fa and (later) musical composition. They sought to have musicians create compositions of a national character. The Betsileo of the rural area, however, countered with songs of a new genre, *zafindraona* 'popular religious song'. They took the texts of such songs from Christian scripture, but they took melodies and rhythms from Malagasy traditions. In the 1900s, this form experienced a resurgence, with a growing spirit of nationalism.

Trained in Western performance and composition, a musical élite emerged, assisting the missionaries in proselytization. Criteria for choosing choral directors were the ability to read notation and noble birth. The missionaries set up a royal choir, and composers were integrated into the court, where they obtained the king's patronage. As part of the elite, educated musicians committed themselves to devising musical forms dedicated to high society, and to creating examples of virtuosic Christian festivities in the form of oratorios and cantatas.

Elite theater

Soon after the Great War (1914–1918), when administrative and political structures of the French were in place in Madagascar, musicians imported a new form of expression, *kalon'ny fahiny,* that presented operas in which Malagasy artists were avidly curious and interested. The 1930s brought a flourishing of theatrical troupes, which tried to create a specifically Malagasy style within this genre. Celebrated composers, with the aid of poets, created operas drawn from legends on patriotic themes, or on daily life. The originality of the *kalon'ny* 'old songs' was judged by specific artists' performances, vocal techniques, and gestures.

These operas became a feature of the parties of high society, and the artists dressed appropriately: bow ties, silk dresses, and gaudy jewels became favorite attire. The modesty of the places where the events occurred contrasted with an affected appearance.

Women usually sang fluidly, in a high register, employing a nasal voice with ornamentation; men sang percussively, in a low register, excelling in rapid staccatos. Stylistic contrast between the women's line and the men's line produced a singular audio effect. Furthermore, one of the original elements of representation of these

One of the most important traits of Malagasy music is that it has always assimilated, then dominated, diverse currents of influence, to create new genres— all the while maintaining traditional forms.

singer-actors was gestures: performers accompanied each word with expressive hand movements, underscoring the textual sense and message.

Kalon'ny fahiny is now part of the classic repertory of Malagasy music. Students at the Université de Madagascar perpetuate the tradition by researching and staging examples of it.

Education and politics

After 1960, Malagasy musical life saw the introduction of music courses in schools and the appearance of music texts, the establishment of a symphony orchestra and an academy of music, and the certification of music teachers. Nevertheless, with a lack of official infrastructure and adequate funding, music struggles. Officials consider art to be simple entertainment, rather than an important factor in social and economic development.

In 1972, the political rise of a socialist régime began an upheaval in Malagasy society and culture. The régime discouraged musical genres and institutions the preceding government had favored. Artists from parts of the country that had earlier not received recognition emerged. Many sought inspiration in African music, then in vogue in Europe. On the west coast especially, new dances and music, with rhythms from Mozambique and other eastern and southern African countries, appeared.

For propaganda, in exchange for financial support, socialist politicians and official institutions obtained the services of singers and musicians. With the decline of the socialist régime, various genres reappeared. Private schools for teaching classical music, popular musics, and jazz multiplied. More intensive relations with foreign countries led to exchanges between local artists and artists from the West, particularly from anglophone countries.

Despite the intrusion of technology into musical events, regional music remains the principal source of inspiration, and becomes the reference for national cultural identity. One of the most important traits of Malagasy music is that it has always assimilated, then dominated, diverse currents of influence, to create new genres—all the while maintaining traditional forms.—translated by *Cornelia Fales*

REFERENCES

Bloch, Maurice. 1971. *Placing the Dead: Tombs, Ancestral Villages, and Kinship Organization in Madagascar.* London and New York: Seminar Press.

Jones, Arthur M. 1964. *Africa and Indonesia: The Evidence of the Xylophone and Other Musical and Cultural Factors.* Leiden: E. J. Brill.

McLeod, Norma. 1977. "Musical Instruments and History in Madagascar." In *Essays for a Humanist: An Offering to Klaus Wachsmann.* New York: Town House Press.

———. 1980. "Malagasy Republic." In *The New Grove Dictionary of Music and Musicians,* ed. Stanley Sadie. London: Macmillan.

Rakotomalala, Mireille. 1986. *Bibliographie critique d'intérêt ethnomusicologique sur la musique Malagasy.* Antananarive: Musée d'Art et d'Archéologie de Université de Madagascar.

Rouget, Gilbert. 1946. "Musique à Madagascar." In *Ethnographie et Madagascar* (Paris), 85–92.

Vig, Lars. 1977. *Croyances et mœrs des Malgaches,* trans. E. Fagereng. Antananarivo: TPL.

Glossary

Words beginning with special characters ae alphabetized according to pronunciation:

ɓ follows *b*
ɗ follows *d*
ə follows *e*
ɔ follows *o*
ʋ follows *v*

ORTHOGRAPHY

ε or ẹ = "eh" as in **bet**
ɔ or ọ = "aw" as in **awful**
ŋ or ṇ = "ng" as in **sing**
γ or yg = "ch" as in German **ach**
ʃ or ṣ = "sh" as in **shout**
ɓ = implosive "b"
ɗ = implosive "d"
! = click sound

ʹ = high tone
ˋ = low tone
˄ = high-low tone
˜ = nasalized sound

Page numbers in *italic* type indicate pages on which illustrations appear.

Abaluhya A subgroup of the Luhya cluster of peoples living in Kenya (304, 624)

abangarang (also *abaŋgaraŋ*) Berta song-accompanying lyre (565)

abaphakathi South African popular performers whose competence and versatility secured a free existence for them (762, 763)

abaqhafi "Street cowboys" who wandered South African cities and played Zulu guitar songs (708, 769)

abi Zaghawi old women's song praising camelmen (561)

aboakyere Festival of the Brong and Effutu of Ghana, in which local residents may criticize the chief (287)

abofoo Dance performed by Akan hunters to cleanse the hunter who killed the animal (286)

acculturation Assimilation of traits from one culture to another (10)

Achimota School Prestigious institution in Ghana where Ephraim Amu taught indigenous music (24, 25)

Acholi A people living in Uganda (224)

acoustic rules Constraints on the quality of sound produced by a voice or an instrument (168–77)

adaha Style of highlife that grew out of colonial military-band music (423)

adakem Struck box idiophone of West Africa (356)

adalo Colo kudu or waterbuck horn with lateral mouthhole and calabash bell (569)

àdàmọ̀ Yoruba pressure drum (474, 476, 481, 484)

adhan North African Muslim call to prayer (536)

adowa Dance of the G of Ghana that uses stamped bamboo tubes and a bell or rattle, utilizing a timeline (112, 113, 114)

adzida Kind of dance performance in Ghana (397, 398)

aerophone Musical instrument whose sound is produced by vibrating air, often a column of air (9)

afã An Anlo-Ewe cult (399)

Afã Ewe god of divination (462)

afãʋu Music of the *afã* cult of the Anlo-Ewe (399)

Afikpo A people living in Nigeria (117, 459)

African Fiesta A brass-heavy big band that became publicly acclaimed in Congo and Zaïre in the 1950s and 1960s (363, 424, 669)

African Jazz Joseph Kabasele's band, which defined and popularized Congo-Zaïre rumba (361, 362–63, 386, 424)

African Music Research Transcription Library Collection of African music begun in South Africa by Hugh Tracey (52)

African Music Society Newsletter Publication begun in South Africa by Hugh Tracey and later transformed into an academic journal (53)

African Musicology Journal founded at the University of Nairobi in the 1980s (13)

African Studies Institute at the University of Ife Creative-arts center that encouraged research in African music (39)

Afrikaans Language spoke by the Afrikaner people of South Africa (3, 761)

afrobeat Yoruba musical genre deriving in the late 1960s from highlife, jazz, and soul, and influential in *jùjú* and *fújì* (363, 482, 483–84)

afrodisco A disco-based style of African music, influenced in the 1980s by Angelique Kidjo (422)

afrojazz A style of jazz popular in Africa in the mid-1990s (428)

afroma A style of jazz popular in Africa in the mid-1990s (428, 436)

agbadza Dance in Ghana identified with the Anlo-Ewe people in rural and urban areas (35, 391, 397)

agbegijo Masquerade of the Yoruba people of Nigeria (461)

agbekor Energetic dance of the Anlo-Ewe of Ghana, employing intricate steps (289)

aggu (pl. *aggutan*) Tuareg griot of the artisanal caste, who performs music professionally (540, 546–47, 587)

agídìgbo (1) Large box-resonated Yoruba lamellophone that resembles a Cuban lamellophone; (2) Yoruba version of *konkoma* music, brought to Lagos by Ewe and Fanti migrant workers (317, 356, 461, 474, 476, 479)

agogo 'Iron bell', struck clapperless bell of the Yoruba of Nigeria that plays the timeline (461, 476, 481, 485)

Agona An Akan-speaking people of Ghana (463)

agudu amaro 'Those who have been away', emancipated Africans from Brazil and Cuba living in West Africa (401)

ahá Yoruba idiophone made from a gourd cut in half (475)

ahal A courtship gathering that features love songs, poetical recitations, jokes, and games of wit (576–77)

ahelli Nocturnal festival dance of Gourara, Algeria (543)

ahidus (also *haidous*) Berber dance of the middle and eastern High Atlas (543)

ahwash Berber dance of the western High Atlas (543)

Aïr Subgroup of the Tuareg, nomadic peoples of the Sahara and Sahel regions of Africa (443, 574)

Aizo A people living in Benin (37)

ajísáàrì Yoruba music customarily performed before dawn during Ramadan by young men associated with neighborhood mosques (484)

akadinda A xylophone of the Buganda in Uganda, having seventeen to twenty-two notes, played by several players, and associated with the court (312, 600, 601)

Akan A people speaking the Akan language in Ghana, West Africa (463–65)

Akim An Akan-speaking people of Ghana (463)

akpewu Music of the Ewe, dominated by the clapping of hands or wooden clappers (462)

Aksumite Empire (or **Axum**) A political structure centered in territory that has become the modern state of Ethiopia (147)

àkúbà Yoruba conga, based on Latin American prototypes (474, 476, 479)

akulavye A Mpyɛmɔ girls' secret society (309)

Akwamu An Akan-speaking people of Ghana (463)

Akwapim An Akan-speaking people of Ghana (463)

alaarinjo 'One who dances as he walks', a theatrical troupe that emerged from the *egungun* tradition (401)

aladura 'Owners of prayer', an indigenous Yoruba syncretic religious movement (5, 403–406)

algaita (also *algeita*) Oboe of the Hausa and other peoples in North Africa (313, 449)

Ali People living in Chad and the Central African Republic (267)

aliwen Nuptial song performed by women in the Ahaggar and Tassili-n-Ajjer regions of Algeria (592)

All-Eastern Nigeria Music Festival Event organized in 1951 for participation of the best choirs in Eastern Nigeria (14–15)

al-ʿūd Arab lute, used in recent times in Sudan (556, 571)

Alur A people of Uganda (601)

amadikh Tuareg panegyric poetry sung in praise of the prophet Muhammad (593)

amadinda Twelve-key log xylophone of the Ganda style in Uganda; two players sit on each side of it (218, 300, 312, 602)

amakonde[e]re Royal trumpet ensemble of the Buganda in Uganda (312, 602, 642)

Ambassadeurs Internationales, Les Name of Les Ambassadeurs after 1978, when it moved to the capital of Côte d'Ivoire (421)

Ambassadeurs, Les Twelve-piece band established by Salif Keita in Mali for combining modern urban pop with indigenous African instruments and Islamic vocals (365, 421)

Amhara Peoples who speak the Amharic language of Ethiopia (303, 599)

ammessad Berber singer-poet who performs for *ahidus* and *ahwash* (543)

analytical records Recordings in which each performer plays separately so that parts can be more easily transcribed (156)

angaroha Conch trumpet used during the ceremony of the bath of the royal relics in Madagascar (789)

anhemitonic Inventory of pitches with no semitones (minor seconds) (268)

Anlo-Ewe A subgroup of the Ewe-speaking people of the southeast coast of Ghana (222, 389–99)

anthropomorphization Attribution of human form or character, frequently to musical instruments (205)

anzad (also *anzhad*; *imzad*) Tuareg one-stringed fiddle (575–82, 590)

àpàlà Yoruba musical genre that originated in the Ijẹbu area, probably in the early 1940s (413, 474, 475–77, 485)

apesin Single-membrane cylindrical drum of the Yoruba of Nigeria (461)

apidan 'One who performs magic', a theatrical troupe that emerged from the *egungun* tradition (401)

apoo Festival of the Brong and Effutu of Ghana, in which participants may criticize the chief (287)

aquaquam Ecstatic liturgical dance performed in the Monophysite Christian Church of highland Ethiopia (603)

arabi Genre of Algerian popular music (545)

Aro-Chuku oracle Final arbiter for intertribal strife among the Igbo of Nigeria (458)

arokas Tuareg dance performed in the Agadez area of Niger (594)

art-composed music Often called classical music, and in Nigeria, school music and church music (232–53)

asafu A dance of the Fanti of Ghana that may be performed only by men belonging to the warrior company (112)

Asante (see **Ashanti**)

Asantehene Paramount ruler of a confederation of provincial chiefs in Ghana (464)

Asen An Akan-speaking people of Ghana (463)

asɛzaghu (also *asɔso*) Berta calabash rattle (565)

Ashanti An Akan-speaking people of Ghana (88–89, 463)

aṣíkò Yoruba dance-drumming style of early *jùjú*, performed mainly by Christian boys' clubs (478)

asonko Percussion logs played to accompany recreational music by the Akan of Ghana (465)

asoso Hand-held Sudanese rattle (555)

assakalabu (also *aghalabo*) Tuareg gourd upturned in a basin of water and struck with sticks (585, 586, 590–91)

atanatra Xylophone in Madagascar that consists of planks of wood resting on one of the players' thighs (784, 785)

atenteben Bamboo flute played by Akan peoples of Ghana (211, 465)

atitish Berta dried-fruit leg-tied rattle (565)

atonalism Musical style in which no single tonality is dominant and each tone receives equal weight (220)

atsiagbeko Genre of dancing performed in Ghana (397)

atumpan Asante single-headed barrel drums

played in pairs tuned a perfect fourth apart (106–107, 211, 316, 464)

aural perception Listening that allows into the conscious mind only a useful fraction of signals (165)

axatsevu Ewe music dominated by rattles (462)

ayidewoh Performer who dances at Igede funerals in Nigeria while singing in ways likened to a bird (111)

azan Muslim call to prayer (332, 333, 341, 342, 343)

Azande (1) A people living in the Central African Republic and Zaïre; (2) A people of southern Sudan, living south of the Bongo (299, 652–53)

azel (pl. *izlan*) Tuareg air composed for performance on the *anzad* (578)

azri Genre of modern Moroccan popular music (546)

ba tum-tum Gumuz women's vocal ensemble, accompanied with beating on gourds and clapping (564)

baakisimba National dance of the Baganda, most commonly performed for feasts (605)

baayii Hausa term for slaves (519)

BaBenzele A Pygmy people of Central Africa (117–18)

bajé Tumtum double-headed dance-accompanying drum (562)

bal (1) Berta one-pitched bamboo flute without fingerholes; (2) Ingassana nuptial and harvest-festival music (563, 565)

bal naggaro 'Flute drum', Berta flute-and-drum ensemble and its music (565)

bala A Mande xylophone with wooden keys fastened to a frame of gourd resonators (159, 364–65, 420, 446, 467, 489, 490, 495–98)

balabolo Basic Mandinka xylophone pattern (489, 490, 497)

balafon (see *bala*)

balangi Manding xylophone with fifteen to nineteen keys (446)

bali (also *baali*) Berta percussion sticks, carried over the right shoulder and struck with a cow horn (565–66)

Bamana (also **Bambara**) A northern Mande-speaking people of Mali (120–21, 445, 495)

bamba Masakin double-headed dance-accompanying drum (562)

Bambara A trade language of Senegal, developed from the Mande subfamily of the Niger-Congo family (2)

bambaro (also *bamboro*) Hausa and Songhai lamellophone (449)

BaMbuti A Pygmy people living in the Ituri forest of Zaïre (111, 117)

ban Small Mandinka kettledrum played with one stick (489)

Banda Culture group in the Central African Republic (267, 656)

bandiirii Hausa set of drums including a single-headed circular frame drum and a bowl-shaped drum (520, 521)

BaNgombe A Mongo people of Zaïre (119, 658)

bangwe Equiheptatonically tuned Sena zither (711)

Bankalawa A Plains Jawara people of northern Nigeria (289, 292)

Bantous, Les A brass-heavy big band that became publicly acclaimed in Congo and Zaïre in the 1950s and 1960s (424)

Bantu Group of more than five hundred languages in central and southern Africa (305–308, 635)

Baoulé An Akan-speaking people of Ghana (463, 465)

bappe Senegalese five-stringed plucked lute (444)

baroud (also *berzana*) North African men's dance with guns, climaxed by synchronized shooting toward the earth (544)

Barundi Kirundi-speaking people of Burundi (183)

bāsān-kōb (also *basamkub*) Five-stringed lyre of the Hadendowa of eastern Sudan (558, 560)

basarake Titled Nyamalthu men of the former Bauchi State in Nigeria (288)

Bassa A people of south-central Liberia (119)

bàtá Yoruba ensemble of conical, double-headed drums, associated with the thunder god Şango (404, 461, 471, 485)

bavugu !Kung bamboo stamping tubes (306, 307, 705)

baya Mandinka entertainment song that advises against deception or going behind another's back (512)

Bayete Internationally acclaimed South African pan-African-playing group of the mid-1990s (424, 778)

beboka BaAka singing, dancing, and drumming (689, 692, 693, 695)

begena (also *begana*) Amhara lyre with a box resonator (303–304, 600)

Bemba A people living in Zambia (112, 671)

bembe Yoruba double-headed drum incorporated into *aladura* churches (404, 413)

bendir Tunisian single-headed frame drum, used with *mizwid* to accompany canticles of praise (537, 541, 543)

benebene (also *beriberi*) Masakin five-stringed lyre of the Sudan (562)

benga The definitive popular music of Kenya, developed by the Luo of western Kenya (365, 427)

beni (1) Competitive associations in East Africa that used European instruments and stressed precision of movement; (2) Interethnic style of playing kazoos and moving associated with British marching bands from the Great War (1914–1918); (3) A synthesis of dance and competitive modes, influenced by colonial brass-band music in East Africa (150, 151, 426, 602–603, 626, 643)

bentere Gourd drums adopted by the Akan of Ghana from their northern neighbors (465)

bepha Collective visits by youthful performers sent by one chief to another among the Venda and Tsonga (708, 709)

berimbau Brazilian chordophone, possibly derived from the *mbulumbumba*, an Angolan gourd-resonated bow (435)

Berta A people living south of Ed Damazin in southernmost Blue Nile Province, Sudan (551–52, 564–68)

Bété A people of Côte d'Ivoire (287, 469)

Bibayak A Pygmy people of Gabon (256)

bimusical environment Social context where two traditions of music are present (34, 39)

bira Shona spirit-possession ceremony in which participants seek assistance from their deceased ancestors (434, 754–55)

bolo gbili Mandinka songs of praise whose musical and verbal allusions convey history and important myths (488–512)

bolon Manding and Fulɓe large three- or four-stringed arched harp, associated with war (444, 445)

bomboro Fulani lamellophone (449)

Bongo A people of southern Sudan, living north of the Azande (570)

boo Kpelle flute (467)

borii (also *bori*) Hausa groups organized around possession-trance performances (273, 290, 448, 450, 515–24, 528)

Bowu Vai male masquerader in Liberia (329)

bɔlo Berta one-pitched flute without finger-holes (565, 568)

bɔlo shuru Berta music played by a *bɔlo* flute ensemble (565, 568)

Bɔmdɔ Vai term for Muslim observance of Id al-Fitr (331)

braced bow A musical bow in which a thread (sometimes called a tuning noose) links the string to the bow, making the string vibrate in two sections (640, 702, 706)

bubblegum South African synthesized dance music, originating in the 1980s (431, 779)

budongo Basoga box-resonated lamellophone in southern Uganda (299–300)

bukhsa (1) Nuba gourd pot, struck with a thin stick for dancing; (2) Nuba set of small gourd trumpets (562)

bul (1) Colo long conical drum; (2) Colo young people's festival dance to the beat of drums (568–69)

buluŋ Berta cow horn, used to strike percussion sticks (565)

bumba meu boi 'Bull celebration,' a dramatic genre brought to Africa by Brazilians and Cubans (401)

bundu A mask of eastern Sierra Leone (119)

buta (also *buuta*) Hausa gourd rattle (273, 520, 521)

buusa Hausa term for blowing, including a musical instrument (519)

bwola An Achola musical ensemble (227)

bywoners White tenant farmers in South Africa who introduced the concertina, guitar, and violin (761)

ɓeli Vai men's secret society, Poro (328)

C-natural A Nigerian guitar-fingering pattern (353)

cabildos Cuban term for social brotherhoods of slaves (384)

call and response Structural form in which phrases performed by a soloist alternate with phrases performed by a choir or ensemble (10)

Cannon Stars Band of Bangui, Central African Republic, popular in the early 1980s (684)

Cape Coon Carnival Minstrel parades on New Year's Day in Cape Town, accompanied by jazz musicians (765)

caretta 'Fancy dance', Brazilian contredanse that influenced dancing in Yoruba *jùjú* (478)

cassuto Scrapers, particularly among Kumbundu-speakers of Angola (667, 668)

caste Rigid social class, one of which is designated for musicians in parts of West Africa (444)

cayaar A major class of Somali performance that includes dance-songs, often with topical subjects (615, 617–18, 621)

čēk (also *wau*) Colo poet-composer-singer (569)

cents Measurement of intervals based on the division of the octave into twelve hundred equal parts; a semitone spans a hundred cents (266)

chegbe Struck idiophone made of a bottle or kerosene can and played to accompany palm-wine guitar music (376)

chenepri Anyi drums, taller and slimmer than *atumpan* and played with L-shaped sticks (316)

Chewa A culture group of Malawi (227, 286)

Chichewa Language spoken in Malawi, Zambia, and parts of northern Mozambique (298)

chihumba Ovambo eight-stringed multiple-bow lute (714)

chilopa 'Blood sacrifice' among the Tumbuka of Malawi (277–78, 279, 283)

chimurenga 'Songs of liberation', *mbira*-derived songs related to the uprising in Zimbabwe, or to modern Shona political processes in Zimbabwe (364, 365, 432–33, 756–57)

chipendani Shona mouth-resonated braced bow with a thick handle carved onto the center of the bow (710, 752)

chisungu Nubility rite for Bemba girls in which scenes of grinding maize and collecting potatoes are enacted (286)

chivoti Flute of the coastal Bantu peoples of Kenya (624)

Chonyi A Migikenda culture group of Kenya (624)

Chopi A culture group of southern Africa (159, 709–10)

chordophone musical instrument whose sound comes from the vibrations of a stretched string (9)

chorumbal Transverse flute of the Fulɓe of The Gambia (445) *chuning* (from English *tuning*) Shona concept of pitch-based tuning that includes timbre and loudness (746)

Cinyanji Language spoken in Malawi, Zambia, and parts of northern Mozambique (298)

cisanji Small, board-shaped lamellophones in the Shiluba area of Zaïre (320, 670, 678–79)

Columbia Major recording label, which by the 1930s was distributing its products across Africa (417, 645)

Congo Success A brass-heavy big band that became publicly acclaimed in Congo and Zaïre in the 1950s and 1960s (424)

content analysis Principles that make a language grammatically functional (102–104)

Cool Stars Band from Bangui, Central African Republic of the early 1980s (684)

coro Horn of the Mbeere people of Mount Kenya (624)

crossrhythms Rhythms of two or more voices that create distinctively different and opposing patterns (33–34, 35, 47, 156)

dadɛwɛ 'Bush spirit' or nature divinity of the Vai Poro society (329)

daf Moroccan frame drum (541)

Dagbamba Culture group of northern Ghana (452–53)

dagomba Kru guitar style influenced by early highlife music of Ghana (353, 377–78)

Dajo A Sudanese people of the Nuba Mountains (562)

dako Community unit in Kru settlements, with territorial, dialect, and social identity (372–73)

dalūka Sudanese single-headed cup-shaped clay drum (554, 555, 556, 558, 562, 606)

dambatimbu Simplified versions of *mbira* songs used in learning (749–50)

dan Nyamalthu dance of the brave in the former Bauchi State in Nigeria (288)

Dan Southern Mande culture group in eastern Liberia (Gio) and western Côte d'Ivoire (Yacouba) (466)

dance ring A circular space defined by the placement of audience and dancers (287)

dandi Stick- and hand-beaten drum in an *mbira* ensemble, which plays improvisations (751)

dansi A non-Islamic popular music that developed in East Africa by the 1940s (426)

Daura Hausa state (291)

dayirigaba Dance of Nyamalthu or Terawa youths in the former Bauchi State in Nigeria (288)

dazoo Head of Poro activities in Vai communities (337)

Dei A people living in Liberia (467)

dende Venda braced gourd-resonated bow (709)

derbuka North African single-headed goblet-shaped drum (534, 535, 541, 546)

dhikr 'Remembrance', ecstatic ritual of the Sufi Islamic sect (344–45, 537, 550–51, 576–77, 593, 606)

diassare Senegalese five-string plucked lute (444, 445)

Digo A Mijikena people of Kenya (624, 627)

dilliara Songhai clarinet (449)

dingboku BaAka dance performed by a line of women related by residential camp or clan (690–91)

direct transcription Writing down music notation during live performances or from memory (154, 155)

djembe Wassoulou goblet-shaped drum (420)

dodecaphony Twelve-tone or serial composition technique, in which the composer assigns equal musical significance to each note (224, 226)

dodo Hausa masked dancer in northern Nigeria (289)

Dogon Speakers of a Gur language in the Boundiagara region of Mali (454)

donkilila la Singing often interspersed with words of praise in performance of the Mandinka of Sierra Leone (489, 497, 498, 505)

donno Hourglass drum adopted by the Akan from their northern neighbors (465)

doodo Songhai double-headed hourglass tension drum (449)

down the coast The area south and east of Liberia, including Fernando Po and other West African countries (374–75)

driven musical instrument One whose vibrating system is driven by continuous stimulation with a sustained tone (172–73)

drum recorder Machine invented by A. M. Jones to produce in real time a schematic representation of rhythm (254)

duma Gumuz small clay kettledrum (564)

dumbah (also *dumbak*) Arabic goblet drum, used in *taarab* orchestras of Zanzibar in the 1950s (427)

dùndún Yoruba double-headed, hourglass-shaped, pressure drum, can produce glides of speech; a symbol of pan-Yoruba identity (106–107, 404, 411, 413, 471, 472, 474, 477, 480, 484)

dunekpoe An Anlo-Ewe musical ensemble (397–98)

dunya 'World universe', term used at the ends of phrases in Maninka singing of praises (497)

duru Yoruba two-stringed plucked lute (460–61)

Duwa Mandinka song praising warriors (503–506, 509–11)

dyeli (also French *griot*) A professional musician among the Manding of Mali, often belonging to a specific caste (444)

dyo Bambara concept of a state of stability and nonchange (121)

Dyula A northern Mande-speaking people of Côte d'Ivoire; a trade language in West Africa (495)

d'aa (Vai) Islamic fortieth-day death feast (332, 334, 345)

d'aabo kulɛ 'Arabic voice', Vai stylistic designation for Qur'ānic recitation (330, 331, 342, 347)

d'ɔŋ (Vai) 'Song' (347)

ebenza Stick zither in the area of Nanga-Eboko in Cameroon (660)

Edi festival Observance that commemorates the heroine of Ife who saved the town (411–12)

Edo Culture group that includes the Bini and other related peoples of Nigeria (118, 459–60)

Efik An Ibibio-speaking people of Nigeria (107)

egungun Formal theatrical association for masquerades that reincarnates deceased ancestors in Nigeria (118, 119–20, 400, 410, 461)

ehti Zaghawi double-headed drum, one head struck with a stick and the other by hand (561)

ekine Mask of Calabar, Nigeria (119)

Ekiti One of the seven principal Yoruba peoples of Nigeria (400)

ekun iyawo Yoruba nuptial song, performed by brides the day before the wedding (411)

ekwe Igbo struck log idiophone (459)

elerun A Yoruba mask (119)

embaire Log xylophone of Uganda using fourteen slats with three players (299–300, 312)

emibala Drummed texts that accompany special songs addressed to specific spirits in turn (604)

endere A flute used in Uganda (218)

engalabi A long drum used in Uganda (218)

engoma A drum used in Uganda (218)

engwara Kazoos made from narrow conical sections of dried gourds and played for the *enswezi* cult performance (604)

enkana Lusoga lyre with a bowl-shaped calabash resonator (304)

ensasi A rattle used in Uganda (218)

enswezi Cult in southern Uganda whose music is marked by the use of four drums interlocking in fast triple rhythm (604)

entenga Buganda drum chime (312, 600, 601)

entongoli A lyre used in Uganda (218, 299)

Enugu Jazz Club Nigerian ensemble in which Okechukwu Ndubuisi performed and which met at the British Embassy (239–41)

Enugu Musical Society A choral group in Nigeria (239)

Enugu Operatic Society Nigerian group founded in 1960 to perform excerpts and occasionally full-scale operas and musicals (240–41)

equidistant heptatonic scale A seven-note pitch inventory in which all intervals are of equal size (489)

equipentatonic Pitch inventory with five equally spaced pitches to the octave (266–67, 268) *esime* The intensified rhythmic section in BaAka performance (690)

Espagnol Zambian guitar tuning, D–a–d–f♯–a–c♯′ (360)

ethnomusicology Study of music as culture, integrating the analysis of sound and behavior (13)

Eurocentrism Interpretation of events and situations with European assumptions and principles (57–58)

Ewe A Kwa-speaking people of Ghana and Togo (389–99, 461–63)

expandable moment A segment of performance conceived as a unit and subject to layering of sound (130–31)

Eyuphoro Mozambican band that became internationally popular in the 1980s (436)

ækänzam (pl. *iækänzaman*) Tuareg shallow frame drum (585, 591)

ætebel Large ceremonial kettledrum, symbol of Tuareg chieftainship (591)

* æzziker* (from **Arabic** *dhikr*) Tuareg ritual music sung recollecting Allah in mosques and improvised places of worship (593)

Falasha Jewish cultural group of Ethiopia (604)

famifami Yoruba short wooden trumpet, borrowed from the Hausa *famfami* (460)

famo A wild and risqué version of *marabi* that appeared among Basotho migrants (768, 769)

Fang A neo-Bantu-speaking people of Gabon (109–10)

fantaziya 'Fantasy', Maghrib spectacle involving choreographed movements by horses and men, accompanied by drums (544–45)

Fanti A Twi-speaking (Akan) people of Ghana and other West African coastal areas (89, 112, 211)

fao Gã rattles strung with nets of beads (463)

farara Free-reed rice-stalk pipe of Madagascar; it produces a strong, piercing sound (788)

fedefede Tumtum Nuba five-stringed lyre of the Sudan (562)

Fellani, Fellata (see **Fulɓe**)

fi fa gun Vocal slides, which usually appear at the beginning or end of Yoruba phrases (411)

fidao Vai ceremony of redemption held for the deceased (333, 345)

field recordings Recordings made by ethnomusicologists on location as people perform in various events (155–56)

field-rerecording technique Simha Arom's analytical method, based on musicians' reconstructions of a song through referential parts (254)

fieldwork Observation of musical performance, usually with recording, interviewing, and transcribing for later analysis (50–51)

figure-ground An image with background; in visual illusions, viewers may reverse the figure and ground (180–82)

fireman Guitar-fingering pattern associated with Kru styles (353, 377)

firqah An Egyptian kind of orchestra, whose style led to that of modern Egyptian film music (427, 645)

fission of the fundamental Separation of the fundamental pitch from the rest of the harmonic frequencies (185, 187–97)

fola Mandinka words of praise, often interspersed with instrumental playing (489, 498–99)

follay Songhai religious music (450)

fololtsy Panpipes made from flexible reeds and played by children guarding cattle in Madagascar (788)

Fon A people of the Republic of Benin (37, 461–62)

fontomfrom Genre of Akan music characterized by slow, dignified movements and played by royal orchestras (138, 227, 286, 316, 464)

Foulah (see **Fulɓe**)

Fouta Toro Region along the Senegal River; an important Muslim state in the 1700s and 1800s (313)

friction bow Instrument in which scraping a stick across notches carved into the bow indirectly vibrates the string (702)

fújì The most popular Yoruba musical genre of the early 1990s, using a lead singer, a chorus, and drummers, a development from *ajísáàrì* (414, 473, 474, 483, 484–87)

Fula, Fulani (see **Fulɓe**)

Fulɓe A pastoral people scattered throughout the western Sudan region (443–44)

Fulɓeni Hausa term for Fulɓe, used in the Central Sudanic and Voltaic clusters (443)

Fur A Sudanese people (561)

fusion of the fundamental Joining of the fundamental to the rest of the harmonic frequencies (186, 194–95, 197–99)

Gã A people of southeastern Ghana (102–103, 463)

gabay Somali poetry that deals with politics, war, peace, and social debate, and functions like editorials (613, 615, 616, 621)

gabusi Plucked lute of the Comoro Islands (351)

gagalo Three-meter stilts used by dancers at a Yoruba harvest festival in Nigeria in honor of the town's protector (118)

gagashi Long, end-blown trumpet of the Fulɓe in Togo (313)

gagra Higi dance that tests men's bravery (288)

gahu A genre of dancing in Ghana (397, 398)

Galambawa A people of northern Nigeria (289)

gambaré Soninke four-stringed plucked lute (463)

Ganda (also **Baganda**) Cultural group in Uganda (112)

ganga (pl. *gangatan*) (1) Tuareg drum; (2) double-headed cylindrical drum played in Niger to herald the beginning and end of Ramadan; (3) northern Nigerian double-headed cylindrical drums with a snare string (312, 313, 449, 536, 541, 584, 591, 592, 594)

gangan Fur cylindrical drum (561)

gángan Yoruba "talking drum" (475, 478, 479)

gano Traditional BaAka legends in which Komba, the creator god, is a friend and caretaker (690, 692)

garaya (also *gàraayàa*) Hausa two-stringed lute (273, 448, 520, 521)

gardagi Praise, satirical, or censorious Baggāra song (560)

Gay Gaieties A Zimbabwean all-female jazz band (433)

gaya 'Song', Gumuz responsorial genre, performed for deaths, epidemics, wars, and other special occasions (564)

Gbaya A people of the Central African Republic (257)

gbee-kee Kpelle single-stringed bow-lute (467)

gbegbetêle Kpelle multiple bow-lute (467)

gbèlee Kpelle lamellophone (467)

gbo Dan funeral lament (466)

geeraar Somali poetical genre distinguished from other genres by scansion, melody, topic, and function (612, 617)

geerewal Fulɓe ceremonial dance in which anklets add rhythmic sounds to performers' rapid hops (115)

Ge'z Liturgical language of the Christian church in Ethiopia (147)

gewel (pl. *awlu'be*) Name for a musician among the Wolof and Fulɓe of The Gambia and Senegal (444)

ghaita Moroccan oboe (536, 537, 541, 544)

Ghana Music Society Organization formed in 1958 for research, programming broadcasts on radio, and publishing results of music studies (31, 34, 35)

Ghorwane A large Mozambican band, with a lineup of three guitars, trumpet, sax, and percussion (429, 436)

gime Poems on religious themes and secular topics composed in Fulfulde (451)

gingiru Dogon four-stringed lute, made only by physicians and used to provide rhythm for the spirit to heal (112, 113, 454, 455)

Giriama A Mijikenda people of Kenya (624, 627)

gogeru Fulani one-stringed bowed lute (448)

goje (also *goge, gòjé*) (1) Hausa one-stringed bowed lute with resonating hole on the membrane, not the body; (2) Yoruba single-stringed bowed lute, made of a calabash and covered with skin (414, 448, 451, 460–61, 474, 475)

Gola A people of western Liberia (467)

Gold Coast Colonial name of the nation now known as Ghana (93)

Gold Coast Review Academic journal that provided a forum for literary and scientific contributions, including music (17)

goma Men's dance with slow, precise movements, using European accoutrements, including dark glasses (603) *gomboy* Dogon hourglass-shaped tension drum (455)

gome (also *gombay*) The earliest popular music of West Africa, believed to have developed in Freetown, Sierra Leone (419)

Gonja A cultural group of Ghana (222)

gonje Ghanaian one-string bowed lute (211)

gora Southern African musical bow in which the musician vibrates the string by blowing onto a feather attached to the bow (702, 703, 706)

gorodao Accordion in Madagascar that requires specific techniques by musicians to obtain desired tones (783)

gourd bow Musical bow that has as its resonator a gourd fastened to or held against the bow (702, 704)

Graceland Long-playing album released in 1986 featuring Paul Simon's crossover collaboration with South African musicians (364, 418, 431, 777, 780)

grammaticality System of rules governing a particular language (168)

graphic notation System of musical notation that utilizes a grid of horizontal and vertical lines (137)

Grebo A Kru-speaking people of southeastern Liberia (91, 468)

griot (French) West African musical specialist, usually a custodian of important historical and cultural knowledge (8)

griot-**model society** Socially despised professional musicians who work within a highly stratified social fabric (515, 518–19, 523–24, 544)

group bow A musical bow played by three individuals and known as *kambulumbumba* (704)

gubo Men's gourd-resonated bow of Zulu origin (320–21)

guedra (1) Moroccan pottery drum; (2) pottery-drum-accompanied dance performed in southern Morocco (543)

gugu Azande struck hollow-log idiophone (570)

gule wa mukulu A Chewa musical genre (227)

gullu Kasena-Nankani cylindrical double-headed drums, played in sets of four (455)

gumbri Gnawa three-stringed lute (537)

Gumuz A western Ethiopian people living in Sudan east of the Blue Nile (564)

gungonga Kasena-Nankani hourglass-shaped pressure drum, playable with flutes (455)

gurmi Hausa two-stringed plucked lute with a hemispherical calabash resonator (448)

gyile A xylophone used in Ghana (211)

gyilgo Gonja lamellophone (222, 457)

Ha Cultural group of Rwanda and Burundi (641)

habɔbɔ Voluntary association of the Anlo-Ewe in urban centers where music is a central part of the interaction (392–93, 396–98)

haddarat Moroccan female singer-instrumentalists (541)

hadj Pilgrimage to Mecca that devout Muslims are encouraged to make (330, 345, 536)

hakamma Baggāra female poets and bards (560)

hal Anlo-Ewe competitive musical performances, which often escalated into disruptive behavior from insults (389)

Ham (Jaba) A people of northern Nigeria (289)

Hamadsha Brotherhood in North Africa where members obtain healing through a dance (274)

Hannibal A small, independent British recording label (418)

harp, shelved type Harp found in a small area of Gabon and in southernmost Central African Republic (302, 662–63)

harp, spoon-in-the-cup type Baganda *ennanga*, found in the Great Lakes region of Africa (302)

harp, tanged type Azande *kundi* (302, 654, 655–56, 663)

Hausa A people of northern Nigeria and Ghana; their language is a trade language of the region (2, 447, 515)

Hawaiienne (French) 'Hawaiian' A tuning used by Masengo guitarists (360)

hawzi Musical genre popular in the Tell region of Algeria (545)

Haya A cultural group of Tanzania (637)

heavy-lift songs Kru mariners' songs for unloading ships and handling other hard jobs (371)

heello Youth-controlled Somali poetry, often treating political themes (614, 616, 618–20)

hees Somali work-accompanying songs, differentiated mainly by function and performers' sex (615, 616–17, 621)

Hehe A cultural group of Tanzania (635, 636, 640)

heptatonic equitonal scale Pitch inventory with seven pitches that are equally spaced within the octave (446, 746)

highlife Genre of West African popular music that originated in Ghana in the early 1900s featuring clarinets, trumpets, cornets, baritones, trombones, tuba, and parade drums (7, 227, 322, 377, 379, 477–78)

Higi A people of northern Nigeria (288–89)

Hima Pastoralists of western Uganda (311, 607)

hira-gasy Improvisatory theatrical form most representative of the Malagasy highlands (789, *790*)

His Master's Voice (HMV) London-based recording label, which by the 1930s was distributing its products across Africa (353, 361, 385, 417, 426, 645, 776)

hocket The distribution of a melody among several voices so that each voice performs only intermittent notes (456, 467, 563, 601)

hoddu Fulɓe three- to five-stringed lute (445)

hokke Berta harvest-festival songs and dances (565)

horde Fulani hemispherical gourd calabash held against the chest and struck with finger rings (446, 448, 449, 546)

hosho Shona seed-filled gourd rattle that accompanies singing, *mbira dzavadzimu* ensembles, and panpipes (432, 752)

Hottentots Old European name for pastoral peoples around the Cape of Good Hope, now known as Khoi and living in South Africa and Namibia (703, 761)

hymn Musical composition praising God or articulating religious faith (208)

Ibibio A people of Nigeria (459)

Ibo (see also **Igbo**) A cultural group of southern Nigeria (34–35)

idiophone Musical instrument whose principal vibrating substance is not a membrane, a string, or the air by the material of the instrument (10)

iduffu Haya large, circular frame drum used in a Moslem ritual dance, *kuzikiri* (637)

Ife Music Editions Publisher of selected works of famous educated and trained composers in Nigeria (237)

igba Igbo membranophone (459)

igbá Yoruba gourd held in both hands and struck with ringed fingers (475)

Igbo (see also **Ibo**) A cultural group of southern Nigeria (91–92, 458–59)

ijala Yoruba hunters' poetry that is sung and may also reproduce aspects of speech tone (136, 137)

ijala are ode Yoruba hunters' entertainment music (409)

Ijebu One of the seven principal subgroups of Yoruba peoples (89–91)

Ijo A culture group of Nigeria (459)

ikembe A plucked lamellophone of Burundi (172, 299)

Ile-Ife Religious center of the Yoruba peoples (411, 459)

ilugan (also *ilujan*, *ilaguan*) Tuareg spectacle involving choreographed movements of camels and men (545, 585, 592, 593)

imam Islamic teacher, doctor, scribe, musical leader, and interpreter of the Qur'ān (330)

imbutu Kumbu horn used as a chiefly emblem and considered the most sacred possession of the chiefdom (642)

imdyazn Professional musicians native to the eastern regions of Morocco (540)

impact notation Cinematographic technique that measures time between strikes on a drum (254)

impulsive instrument Plucked or struck instrument; between each impulse the sound rings and dies out (172–73)

imzad (also *anzad*) Tuareg bowed lute, played by women (541, 542–43, 575–76)

inanga Burundi trough zither of eight to twelve strings (164–206)

inanga chuchotée 'Whispered zither', Burundi musical genre in which the *inanga* is used (164–206)

indiki Zulu spirits in southern Africa (277)

indunduma Zulu piano-vamp style of *marabi* in South Africa (768, 769)

Ingassana Arabic name for ethnic groups inhabiting the Tabi Hills of Sudan (563)

inherent rhythms Rhythms that may be heard by a listener, but are not played as such by any of the performers (154, 155)

inside-outside Distinction often made in describing social order or musical performance in West Africa (130–31)

Institute of African Studies Institute in Ghana whose Music and Related Arts section was developed by J. H. Kwabena Nketia (25, 27, 32, 39)

International Folk Music Council International society of professional ethnomusicologists (31)

International Library of African Music Series of recordings of African music founded by Hugh Tracey in South Africa (54, 61)

iqamat Arabic isorhythmic musical patterns (222)

Irigwe A people of Nigeria (119)

isicat[h]amiya Step dancing of choirs that blended ragtime and indigenous part singing in South Africa (764, 772–73, 777)

isikunzi Amateur variety shows in South Africa (772)

isinyago Makua masks (119)

iskoki Hausa term for spirits (520)

Island Records Company whose Mango label signed Salif Keita, launching his international career on a monumental scale (364, 421)

Ituri Forest Large tropical forest in central Africa (652, 658)

iwi Yoruba musical genre associated with dead ancestors and often sung in a nasal falsetto (410)

iyá'lù (also *iya ilu*) Yoruba 'mother drum', principal instrument in a Yoruba drum ensemble (460, 472, 476)

izibongo Poetry of praise associated with chieftainship in groups of Ngoni descendants (320)

izli (pl. *izlan*) Berber songs performed for *ahidus* and *ahwash* (543)

Jabo A subgroup of the Kru-speaking peoples of Liberia (106, 468)

jabo Heavy brass rings given by Tuareg women to daughters and worn on the thighs until they give birth to a child (115)

jairo Mandinka general praise (499)

jali (pl. *jalolu*) Professional musicians among the Maninka of Guinea and Mandinka of Gambia (420, 444)

jalikumolu Miscellaneous commentary of the Mandinka (499)

jaliya-**type ensembles** Groups featuring a *jali* or professional singer (359, 366)

jamundiro Patronymic Mandinka praise that contains references to the past (499)

jangar (also *jaŋar*) Ingassana lyre (*303*, 564)

Jarawa A people of northern Nigeria (289)

jauje Hausa double-headed hourglass-shaped tension drum, reserved for royalty (449)

jazz bands Street bands in Kinshasha playing music unlike American jazz (385)

jejy Singly or multiply stringed bowed lute of Madagascar (787)

jeke Vai basket rattle (329, *334*)

jeli Man who specializes in singing praises, often employing the harp-lute for accompaniment (489, 490)

jeliklu Mandinka men who sing praises (489)

jelimuso Mandinka women who sing praises (489)

jènbe Conical drum with a single stretched-skin drumhead (489, 498)

jenge BaNgombe Pygmies' men's society, featuring masking (658)

jengsi Sisaala seventeen-keyed xylophones, normally played in pairs (457)

Jie A Karamojong people of Uganda (599)

jihad Arabic term for a holy war; several of these were fought in Africa in the past (314)

jiti Popular music in Zimbabwe, combining African drumming and European harmonies in responsorial form (755, 757)

jocho Popular music in Zimbabwe in the 1970s that showed little European influence (755, 757)

Johannesburg International Arts Alive Festival Musical festival established in 1992 to encourage experimental interchanges between international and local artists (431)

Johnny Walker Guitar-fingering pattern used in Nigeria (353)

Jola (Diola) A cultural group of the Cassamance region of Senegal (443, 445)

jongo Kasena-Nankani stamping dance (456)

Joobai Vai male masquerader (329)

jùjú (1) Yoruba tambourine; (2) Yoruba musical genre originating in Lagos around 1932 featuring a singer-banjoist, a *ṣ̀ẹ̀kẹ̀rẹ̀*, and a *jùjú* (322, 364, 377, 387, 423, 478–83)

Juluka South African musical duo formed by Johnny Clegg and Sipho Mchunu; it disbanded in 1985 (430, 779)

kàakàakii (also *kakaki*) Hausa long trumpet, made from thin brass or metal from a kerosene tin (313, 414, 448, 449, 524–25)

kabosa (also *kabosy*) Plucked lute of Madagascar that is identical to the *qubuz*, played in Arabia from about A.D. 500 to about A.D. 1500 (351, 367, 787)

kachacha Dance that involves a set of single-headed goblet-shaped drums and sometimes a two-note xylophone (678)

k'aho Hausa horn (449)

kakoxa Two-stringed bowed lute that took inspiration from the seventeenth- or eighteenth-century Iberian stringed instruments (668, 669, 677)

kalakiya Sudanese entertainment song, sung by men while drinking date wine (557)

kalangu Hausa double-headed hourglass-shaped tension drum, associated with butchers and recreation (448, 449)

kalela Zambian name of the genre *beni* (426)

kalenge Kasena-Nankani metal pails or large tins (455)

kalon'ny fahiny Operas in which Malagasy artists drew from legends on patriotic themes, or on daily life (791–92)

kamanja North African bowed lute, held vertically on the knee (535)

kambala Miri dance of initiation (563)

kamele ngoni Wassoulou six-stringed harp (420)

kànàngó Yoruba small hourglass-shaped drum, used singly or in sets of two or three to accompany *fújì* (485)

kang Colo small metal trumpet (569)

kanga Dajo trumpet, played in sets of four to six sizes and lengths (562)

Kano Chronicle A nineteenth-century manuscript (313)

kapohina 'To strike' (idiophones), term used to describe instrumental playing in Madagascar (783)

Karamojong A cultural group of Uganda (599, 605)

Karanga A Shona subgroup of Zimbabwe (709)

Karangu A people of Zimbabwe (106)

karimba A small *mbira*, often serving as a novice's instrument (624, 745)

karing'aringa Motor-engine flywheel that accompanies performance in the central highlands of Kenya (627)

karinyan Cylindrical iron bell suspended by a string from a finger of one hand and struck by an iron beater (489, 498)

Karoo Festival Afrikaans-language musical festival, which in the mid-1990s gained mass public appeal (431)

kā̀ Sudanese hand-held cymbals, played for *nōba* (552)

kasala Luba songs of mourning (217)

Kasena-Nankani A cultural group of northern Ghana (109, 455–56)

kawayawaya A central African friction bow (677)

kayamba A rectangular reed box, filled with stones or seeds and played in coastal communities of Kenya (624, 625, 627)

kazandik Miri five-stringed lyre of the Sudan (562)

kebele Dogon sistrum (455)

keleŋ Vai struck log idiophone (329)

kéleng Kpelle struck log idiophone (467)

kembe Lamellophone of the Mpyɛm5 (Nola District, Central African Republic) (299–300, 664)

kengai Vai women who supervise Sande musical activities; expert Vai dancers and singers (338, 339)

kente Cloth worn by royalty in Ghana (114)

kerân-non-koning Kpelle harp-lute (467)

kerona Fulɓe two-to-nine-stringed plucked lute (445)

kete (1) Asante master drum; (2) Yoruba globular cylindrical drum (461, 464)

kha:s Braced mouth-resonated bow played by Khoikhoi women (703)

Khoisan "Click" languages of southern Africa; speakers of any of these languages (702–703) *khomba*   A Tsonga "turning" dance to make women fertile (286, 287)

kiďa   Hausa term for drumming (519)

Kiganda   Language of the Baganda, a people of Uganda (210)

Kikuyu   A people of Kenya (109, 624–25)

kilumi   Akamba dance (624)

kinanda   Accordion, as known in the central highlands of Kenya (627)

kinesphere   The space within the reach around an individual (109)

kingi   Competitive association in East Africa that emphasized precision of movement and European instruments (602–603)

kinka   Anlo-Ewe genre of music and musical ensemble (397–98, 399)

kipango   Board zither in the Iranga District of Tanzania, with six strings and a gourd resonator at one end (640)

kirang   (1) Nuba conical drum; (2) Nuba stamping dance (562)

kirikiri   A name for Zaïrean rumba (423)

kiringoringo   A Kenyan boys' and girls' dance, accompanied by vocal and instrumental music (624)

Kirundi   Language spoken by the Barundi, a people of Burundi (202)

kishavi   A Taita dance (624)

Kisii   A cultural group of Kenya (624)

kisir   Nubian lyre (556, 557, 558)

kithara   Greek term for guitar (possibly via Arabic *qitara*) that appears in European texts from the thirteenth century (350)

Kituxe e os Acompanhantes   Angolan band that performs a mix of merengue, rumba, and rural Angolan styles (435)

kola   (1) Miri ceremonial earthen-pot drum; (2) Miri rainmaking festival (562)

kologo   Internal-spike lute of Ghana (367)

kolokua   Fur ensemble (two drums, end-blown flute, two side-blown antelope horns) that plays at harvesting and circumcision festivities (561)

Komba   BaAka creator god (690, 692)

kome   (1) Gumuz end-blown flute; (2) Gumuz ensemble for light recreation involving singing and dancing (564)

komo   Maninka secret society that uses wind instruments (445)

kòn-kpàla   Kpelle musical bow (467)

kondi   Azande and Moro lamellophone (570)

koni   Maninka four-stringed lute (445)

konîng   Kpelle triangular frame zither (467)

Konkoba   Mandinka songs praising farmers (503)

kónkoma   Kpelle lamellophone (467)

kóno   Kpelle hand-held struck log idiophone (467)

konting   Five-string plucked lute of the Mandinka of The Gambia (444, 445)

koŋgoma   Large lamellophone with three or four metal tongues and a box resonator (329, *334*, 356, 467)

kootsoo (also *kotsoo*)   Fulani or Hausa single-headed hourglass-shaped tension drum (449, 524–26)

kora   Manding harp-lute with nineteen or twenty-one strings that traditionally accompanies singing of praises and historical songs but has been incorporated into international styles (8, 158, 159, 161, 364–65, 420, 421–22, *437*, 444, 445, 489, 498)

Koranko   A northern Mande-speaking people of northern Sierra Leone (446, 488)

kori   Kasena-Nankani gourd drums, played in sets of two (455)

korro   Dogon struck log idiophone (455)

Kotafon   A cultural group of Benin (37)

Kɔlɔpɔɔ   Vai male masquerader (329)

kpáníngbá (also *kpaningbo, kpäningbä*)   Azande log xylophone, usually with twelve or fourteen keys (570)

kpanlogo   A fast dance of Ghana (211)

Kpelle   A southern Mande people of central Liberia and Guinea (124)

kpom kpom kpom   Igbo verbalization of the sound of knocking, employed by Ndubuisi in a composition (244)

kponingbo   A twelve- or thirteen-keyed log xylophone, accompanied by a struck hollow-log idiophone (*guru*) and a double-headed drum (656)

Kru   Liberian speakers of Kru or Krao, a language of the Kwa group, who worked on ships up and down the West African coast (370–82)

Krusbass   Yoruba two-finger guitar style in which all right-hand passages were played with the thumb and index fingers (353, 377, 478)

kuji   A Nyamlthu chief in the former Bauchi State in Nigeria (288)

kukuma   Hausa small one-stringed bowed lute (448)

kulɛ nyia   (Vai) 'Fine voice' (342, 347)

kuma   San raft zither (705)

kundi   (1) Bongo anthropomorphically carved harp, probably adopted from the Azande; (2) tanged harp in the region of the Central African Republic (302, 654, 570, 655–56)

!Kung   A subgroup of the San, living in southern Africa (305–307)

kuntigi   Hausa one-stringed plucked lute (448)

kuntiji   Songhai one-stringed bowed lute (450)

kuomboka   Lozi ceremony marked yearly by a procession of boats as the people migrate ceremonially to dry land (672, 712, 713)

kurbi (also *al-bakurbo*)   Five-stringed harp of the Baggāra of Darfur (560)

Kuria   A cultural group of Kenya (599)

kushaura   Leading mbira part, which plays melodic and higher notes (749, 750)

kutahiri   Circumcision celebrations in rural, coastal areas of Kenya (630, 631)

Kutin   A culture group of Cameroon (654)

kutiridingo   Conical drum from The Gambia, played with one stick and one hand (136)

kutsinhira   Following part on the *mbira* that emphasizes root movements of harmonic patterns (749)

kuvara   Of a disease, to mature, among the Tumbuka (277)

kuvina nthenda   Tumbuka term used when both patient and healer "dance their disease" (271)

kuyabilo   An Ila-Tonga musical genre (216)

Kuyate   Originally the name of Manding families of professional musicians in Mali (444)

kwadwom   An Akan genre of musical poetry in Ghana (218)

Kwahu   An Akan-speaking people of Ghana (463)

Kwanangoma College   Institution founded in Bulawayo, Zimbabwe, in 1961 to foster African musical scholarship (40)

kwasa kwasa   A name for Zaïrean rumba (386, 387, 423)

kwaya   'Choir'; term used in southern Africa (281)

kwela   A style of street jazz that sprang up in southern Africa in the 1940s and 1950s and featured pennywhistles, the precursor of *mbaqanga* (218, 219, 227, 296, 322, 387, 427, 430, 773)

Ladysmith Black Mambazo   South African band that achieved major international distribution partly as a result of the success of Paul Simon's album *Graceland* (418, 431, 777, 779)

lala   Sistrum with small pieces of round circular gourds threaded on a stick (446)

larakaraka   Acholi ensembles of struck calabashes (224)

'lawi   Algerian Saharan dance performed by men striking sticks or batons (544)

Leexo   Composed Somali poem played on the radio and credited with influencing political change (620)

lela ma sorek   'Children of the gourd', Miri slim tubular gourd trumpet ensemble (563)

leleng (also *lelɛŋ*)   Colo small kettledrum (569)

leng   Dinka small drum (569)

lenjengo   Recreational dance from The Gambia (136)

lesiba   Southern Sotho musical bow played by blowing air past a feather to vibrate the string (702, 707)

ligombo   Hehe narrow three-stringed trough zither with a gourd resonator at one end (641)

likembe   East African lamellophone, played in ensembles of up to fifteen, also known as *mbira* (295, 297, 299, 317, 320, 322, 608, 609, 678–79)

lilandi   A composite trumpet, made of seven to fourteen gourds and used in nuptial rituals in Tanzania (642)

Limba   A cultural group closely related to the Temne of Sierra Leone (445)

Lingala   Dominant language of Congo-Zaïre (385, 425)

linguistic rule   Any elemental constraint determined by, or having its origin in, the language of a text (167–68)

litungu   East African eight-stringed lyre (304, 625, 641)

lkmnža   Moroccan alto fiddle (541)

Lobi A cultural group of northeastern Côte d'Ivoire (456)

locations Black residential areas attached to towns in South Africa (762)

LoDagaa A subgroup of the Dagari-speaking people of Ghana (456–57)

longo A central African portable, gourd-resonated xylophone (656)

loor Dinka large drum (569)

Lozi Dominant cultural group of the Barotse kingdom of Zambia (113, 672–73, 711–13)

Lucazi (also **Luchazi**) A cultural group of eastern Angola and northwestern Zambia (150–51, 672–76)

Lugbara A cultural group of eastern Angola and northwestern Zambia (286)

Luhya A cultural group of Kenya (624–25)

luma Reed pipes popular among Ituri Forest Pygmies of central Africa (658)

maalmii Hausa Qur'ānic scholar-teacher (523)

Maasai A people of Kenya and Tanzania (109, 623)

maazo Head of women's secret society, Sande, among the Vai (340)

mabo A hunting-related dance that was one of the most popular BaAka dances of the late 1980s (689–90, 692)

madiaba Popular music in Kinshasa from 1988, based on a variant of the rumba (386, 387)

madīḥ Sudanese hymn praising Allah and the prophet Muhammad (550, 552–54)

madimba Central African gourd-resonated xylophones, probably deriving from southeast African models (668, 669)

magavhu Large gourd rattles worn on dancers' legs in Zimbabwe (752)

magu'da A woman specializing in celebratory ululation in West Africa (447)

Maguzawa A people of northern Nigeria (287, 289, 291)

mahobelo Choral singing of the Sotho peoples of southern Africa (707)

Mahodi Vai term for the Muslim observance of Mawlid (331, 345–46, 348)

mahon'era (also *mahonyera*) Zimbabwean basslike singing, primarily on roots of bichords, with yodeling (432, 750)

Mahotella Queens Female *mbaqanga* chorus, one of the most internationally celebrated South African groups of the 1990s (430, 776)

mai busa Performer on an aerophone in West Africa (447)

mainline Guitar-fingering pattern associated with Kru sailor styles (353, 359, 377)

majika Indigenous Mozambican rhythm that is the basis of *marrabenta* (436)

maka'di Generic term for players of membranophones, chordophones, and idiophones (447)

Makembe Band from Bangui, Central African Republic, popular in the early 1980s (684)

makhololo Venda rulers, as distinguished from common people (708)

Makonde A people of Mozambique (119, 606)

makossa Cameroonian style of urban music (387, 422, 682)

makwaya A music whose name is derived from the word *choir* and featuring songs, marching routines, and special costumes (33, 216–17, 227, 718, 755, 757, 763, 769–70)

malaila A genre performed in Zambia to honor a dead warrior (287)

malimba A Sena equiheptatonically tuned lamellophone (711)

Malinke A group of northern Mande-speakers of Mali, Guinea, and Côte d'Ivoire (114, 465)

malipenga Malawian name of the genre *beni* (426, 603)

mama jaliya Mandinka genealogical recitation (499)

mamokhorong A one-stringed Basotho violin, developed in South Africa (761)

Manden Speakers of northern Mande languages (488)

Manding Speakers of northern Mande languages (442, 445–46)

Mandingoes A group of northern Mande-speakers of Liberia (445)

Mandinka A people including the Manding, Malinke, Mandingo, and Maninka (136, 443)

mandjindji Bongo large, wooden, anthropomorphically carved trumpet (570)

Mangbetu Speakers of a Central Sudanic language in northeastern Zaïre (655, 658)

mangolologondo Makua loose-log xylophone with nine keys (638, 639)

mang'wanda Belt worn around the waist of Tumbuka dancers, whose movements make it produce a distinctive timbre (277)

Maninka A group of northern Mande-speakers in Guinea and Liberia (445)

manje-manje See *simanjemanje*

mansalingo Mandinka proverb (499)

manyanga Generic Swahili name for an array of shaken seed-filled rattles, mostly calabashes or coconuts (638)

Manza A people of Central African Republic (267)

manza Zande pentatonically tuned xylophone associated with royalty (656)

mapfuwe A dance of the Shona of Zimbabwe, used in making rain (753)

marabi A South African hybrid of indigenous and urban music, dance, and context (387, 430, 767–69)

marabout An itinerant Muslim cleric who possesses special powers (344)

Marari A people of Malawi (119)

Margi A people of northern Nigeria (289)

marimba Box-resonated xylophone played in the islands of Zanzibar and Pemba and on the nearby mainland (638–39)

maringa (1) Variant of the palm-wine-guitar style, using more strumming and incorporating West Indian rhythms; (2) Intertribal social dance, popular on the west coast of Africa from Sierra Leone to Zaïre (351, 377, 380–81, 386–88)

marok'i (female *marok'iya*) West African professional singer of praises (447)

marokaa (also *maroka*) Nigerian Hausa singers of praises (291, 515, 519–22, 524)

marrabenta Mozambican topical music, performed on three guitars and danced in a sexually suggestive style (436)

MASA (Marche des Arts et Spectacles Africains) Important musical trade fair held in Abidjan every other year (419–20)

masabe A Tonga dance (285)

Masakin A Sudanese people of the Nuba Mountains (562)

mashaira Swahili love poetry accompanied by *taarab* music (645)

mashave Foreign spirits that possess and afflict the Tonga of Zambia and the Shona of Zimbabwe (274, 745, 753)

mawak'i A West African professional male singer and/or composer (447)

mazamba A skin or cloth skirt, cut into many thin strips, that patients wear in northern Malawi (277)

mbalax (Wolof) 'percussion-based music' Senegalese popular music, mixing Cuban rhythms with *kora*-based traditional melodies, sung in a high-pitched style (365, 421–22)

mbaqanga A South African jazz idiom that took its name from a stiff corn porridge (364, 365, 430, 432, 433, 772, 773–74)

Mbem A people of Cameroon (110)

mbila Chopi word for a xylophone key and closely related to the term *mbira*, which designates a lamellophone (716)

mbila dzamadeza Venda twenty-seven-keyed lamellophone (709)

mbila mutondo Venda twenty-one-keyed xylophone (709)

mbira Shona plucked lamellophone, played singly or in ensembles (10, 136, 715–16, 744–50, 752–53, 756)

mbira dzavadzimu 'Mbira of the ancestral spirits', Zimbabwean lamellophone with twenty-two or more wide keys (153, 319, 429, 432, 433–35, 745–47, 752)

mbombing South African choirs with high-pitched yells imitating falling bombs as seen in newsreels of World War II (772)

mbongo Central Cameroonian Tikar raffia lamellophone (319)

mbube Style of Zulu male singing in South Africa (773)

mbulumbumba Angolan gourd-resonated bow, recognized in Brazil as the *berimbau* (435, 714)

m'dinga Gumuz large barrel drum (564)

mek Berta chief (565, 566)

melekket A system of musical notation invented by Ethiopian clerics in the mid-1500s (147–49, 151, *152*, 159)

melodic downdrift Basic melodic movement from high to low, characteristic of much African music (166)

melorhythmic codes Elements of musical sound, as defined by Lazarus Ekwueme (238)

membranophone Musical instrument whose sound comes from the vibrations of a stretched membrane (9–10)

Mende A people of western Liberia and eastern Sierra Leone (467)

mendzaŋ A central African xylophone (659, 660–61)

merengue A Haitian and Dominican ballroom dance, popular in Africa as a result of dissemination on gramophone records (317, 361, 384, 424, 435)

mganda Tanzanian name of the genre *beni* (426, 603)

mhito Shona small, stick-beaten drum that maintains a basic rhythm in an *mbira* ensemble (751)

microtones Intervals smaller than a minor second (220)

Mijikenda A cultural group of Kenya (624)

miko A transpositional technique in playing Baganda xylophones (36)

Milaji Vai term for the Muslim observance of Miraj (331, 345)

milo BaAka term for non-Pygmy dark-skinned Africans, whom the BaAka see as separate and distinct from themselves (688)

mime-dances Performances that imitate phenomena, sometimes symbolizing the relationship between people and their environment (117–18)

Miri A Sudanese people of the Nuba Mountains, living near Kadugli (561)

mirliton An object or membrane made to sound by the indirect action of the vibration of an instrument to which it is attached; its sound is often described as a buzz (263–64, 445, 454, 460, 673)

mizimu Tumbuka ancestral spirits (275, 278, 279, 283)

mizwid Tunisian bagpipe, used with *bendir* to accompany canticles of praise (537)

mnemonic Syllables that indicate relative pitch, rhythm, and timbre of rhythmic phrases (125)

mɔbeke Aka whistle of the Central African Republic (266, 267)

mokondi General BaAka name for dances involving spirits (692, 693)

molimo BaMbuti death ceremonies, which emphasize cooperation among surviving mortals (111)

molo Senegalese one-stringed plucked lute (289, 445, 448, 558)

móló Yoruba three-stringed lute, commonly used in *sákárà* ensembles during the 1920s and 1930s (474, 475, 789)

monochord Single-stringed instrument used to match pitches of instruments and determine tunings (255)

mora Temporal duration of a short vowel in poetry (125, 612)

moraic rhythm Rhythm created by the difference in length of short vowels and long vowels (167–68)

moshembe da Gumuz exorcism dance (564)

motengene Hip-swiveling, rib-rotating dance that is traditional among the Mbati Pygmies (682)

movement signature Element of movement that consistently marks a dance (109)

mɔi Sande Muslim version of a women's secret society among the Vai (337–38, 339–41, 348)

mphepo Spirit wind among the Tumbuka people of northern Malawi (275)

msam'at Algerian urban female professional singer-dancers (541)

msondo Cylindrical drum with pegged or tacked-on head that is played along the coast of Tanzania (637)

mu muraso 'In the blood', a musician in Burundi used this phrase to describe extraordinary ability for performance (164)

mucapata Lamellophone with a bell-type resonator that is probably of Cokwe or Cokwe-Mbangala invention (318, 679)

muchongolo A Tsonga dance representing warriors' actions in battle and featuring asymmetrical rhythms (710)

muchungwa A Kikuyu dance in which idiophones are attached to the dancers' legs (624)

mudzimu Ancestral spirits of the Shona of Zimbabwe (753)

mukanda Boys' age-grade circumcision schools established outside villages in central Africa (125–26, 309, 674, 723–25)

mukupela Drum played only at the royal death or installation in central Africa (670, 673)

muqaddam Muslim leader of a sect (344)

musakalunga 'Shiver dance' of the –Handa people of southwestern Angola (306)

musical bow Instrument having a string fastened with tension at each end of a curved stick, that can be plucked or struck (702)

Musiki Band from Bangui, Central African Republic, of the early 1980s (683–84)

musique moderne zaïroise Guitar-based music that emerged after the 1940s in the Brazzaville and Kinshasa area (386, 668, 669)

musu A spell or curse invoked with words alone or in combination with ritual acts among the Gã (103–104)

mutumba A Shona low-pitched, waist-high drum that plays a limited amount of variation (751)

muwashshah North African court poetry, developed in Spain and having strophic texts with instrumental refrains (535)

mvet Stick zither with idiochord strings lifted from the raffia; genre of oral literature in the central African region (654, 660)

mwanzele A Rabai dance in which brief rhythmic patterns regulate performances (624)

mwinjiro A Mbeere dance in which brief rhythmic patterns regulate performances (624)

myaso yakukuwa Lucazi or Luvale songs performed at night during circumcision ceremonies, accompanied by concussion sticks (674, 725)

nabona Kasena-Nankani side-blown ivory trumpets, usually played in sets of six or seven (455)

Nafali Vai male masquerader (329)

nagara Gumuz clay kettledrum, both *duma* and *sarma* (564, 568)

nagarit The emperor of Ethiopia's kettledrums, of which forty-four pairs played in his processions (601)

naggaro Berta drum (565)

nai An obliquely blown flute of Zanzibar (427)

Nangayivuza Individual for whom a healing cult in northern Burundi was named (202–206)

naqqāra Sudanese paired small kettledrums, played for *nōba* (552, 558–59, 565)

National Academy of Music Institution in Winneba, southern Ghana, founded to train teachers of music (25)

National Dance Company Troupe resident within the Institute of African Studies in Ghana (32, 39)

nations Term used in Brazil for slaves' social brotherhoods (384)

native airs Africanized hymns that came out of separatist African churches (406)

native blues A guitar-playing idiom practiced in interior villages (353)

native drama Dramatic tradition that grew out of the African-church movement in Nigeria (406)

nchimi Tumbuka diviner-healer (271, 278–81)

ncomane A Tsonga tambourine, played for exorcism-related rituals (711)

Ndebele A cultural group of southern Africa (114, 757)

ndere Senegalese five-stringed lute (445)

Ndogo A people of southern Sudan (570)

Ndubuisi bass Arpeggiated bass rhythmic pattern used pervasively by the Nigerian composer Ndubuisi (244, 245, 247)

né Mandinka bells in The Gambia (446)

neutral third The interval of a third that is larger than a minor third but smaller than a major third (740, 741)

nfir Moroccan trumpet (536)

nganga Musical bow of Fipa women, who live southeast of Lake Tanganyika (640)

Ngbaka-Manza A people of the Central African Republic (267)

ngodo Chopi dance cycles accompanied by large ensembles of xylophones (709)

ngoma (also *ng'oma*, *ngɛoma*) (1) East African performances that feature dancing with an emphasis on circular movements of the hips; (2) East African term for drums and performances; (3) 'Drum', a membranophone; a healing complex of central, southern, and parts of equatorial Africa (272, 274, 281, 312, 606, 637, 709, 712)

Ngoma Greek-owned recording studio in Kinshasa that began operating in the 1940s (359, 361, 385)

ngombi Faŋ term for the harp; stick zither outside the Bulu-Beti-Faŋ cluster (660, 663)

ngongi Double bells, which can be used only by royal ensembles of the Lozi and Nkoya of southern Africa (782)

Ngoni A cultural group of Malawi and Zambia (275, 276, 320)

ngorda Dance of the nobility of the former Bauchi State in Nigeria (288) *ngororombe* Shona panpipes played in ensemble in hocket for entertainment (711, 751–52)

ngoyo Bongo satirical song (570)

nguchu Mbeere dance whose performers use leg-tied bells (624)

ngulei-sîyge-nuu 'Song-raising-person', Kpelle solo singer (466)

Nguni A cultural group of South Africa and Namibia (45)

Nigerian Broadcasting Corporation Governmental agency that sponsors choirs of Nigerian-trained musicians (236)

Nigerian Institute of Music Institution founded at Onitsha in 1949 with the primary objective of promoting Nigerian music (14)

nihas (from Arabic *nahās* 'copper') Baggāra copper kettledrums, symbols of tribal power and sovereignty (561)

Nilotes Peoples of the northeast Sudan (599, 635)

njuga Swahili term that denotes a string of small iron bells that dancers wear around their ankles (638)

nkangala Women's mouth-resonated bow, of Zulu origin (*3*, 320–*21*, 430)

nkharamu The spirit of the lion among the Tumbuka people of northern Malawi (275, 276)

nkoni Bambara six- to nine-stringed harp-lute played by members of the hunter's society (445)

n'lapa Single-headed drums of Madagascar, one of which bears a resemblance to certain West African drums (784, 785)

nnawunta Ghanaian double bells (211)

nɔba (also *nawba*) Sudanese ceremonies of the Qādirīya brotherhood (551–52)

noggaara Sudanese cylindrical drum (554)

nono Gã clapperless iron bell (463)

notation Written use of a system of signs or symbols (146)

nsambi Central African multiple-bow lute (667)

Nsenga A subgroup of Maravi peoples of Malawi (286, 307–308, 673)

nsogwe Dance of the Nsenga and the Southern Chewa after the birth of a woman's first child (286)

ntahera Set of five or seven ivory trumpets associated with Akan royalty (465)

nthenda ya uchimi 'Disease of the prophets' that changes ordinary Tumbuka into diviner-healers (272, 278)

nuba North African suite of songs: (1) Moroccan, in five movements, each in one of five rhythmic modes and performed in a fixed order; (2) Algerian, in nine alternating instrumental and vocal movements; (3) Tunisian, in ten movements (534–35)

Nubians A cultural group, also known as the Barabra, of the Nubian desert in northeast Africa (555)

num The source of spiritual energy that the !Kung of southern Africa dance in order to boil (274)

nyama A kind of power of the Mandinka peoples of West Africa (499–500)

Nyamwezi A cultural group of Tanzania (637)

nyanga Nyungwe reed-pipe dances with one instrumental tune, within which singers improvise their parts (711)

nyanyuru Fulɓe and Tukulor one-stringed bowed lute (444, 445)

nyavikali Central African trumpets (673)

nyisi Metal idiophones tied around the waist and ankles for Tumbuka healing dances (277)

nzapa The Sango term for the Christian God in central Africa (690, 692–95)

nzumari Double-reed aerophone of the coastal Bantu peoples of Kenya (606, 624)

oba Edo king in Benin and Nigeria (459, 460)

OCORA (Office de Coopration Radiophonique) Organization that produced recordings of African music (54, 60)

Odeon Major recording label, which by the 1930s was distributing its products across Africa (417, 645)

odonso Guitar-playing idiom practiced in West African villages (353)

odurugya Notched flute made of cane husk and played at the Asantehene's court (465)

Ogboni A Yoruba secret society (459)

Ogede An Edo mask in Nigeria (118)

ògìdo Yoruba bass conga, based on Latin American prototypes (474, 478, 479)

ohonji (also *onkhonji*) Nkhumbi or Luhanda term for hunting bow or mouth-resonated musical bow, braced in the center, with the end pressed against the inside of the player's cheek (*306*, 714)

ohugua Guitar-playing idiom practiced in West African villages (353)

ohun orisa 'Voices of the deities', Yoruba stylized traditional singing (409–11)

O.K. Jazz Zaïrean band that achieved international renown in the 1960s (360–61, 386, 669)

OK Success A brass-heavy big band that became publicly acclaimed in Congo and Zaïre in the 1950s and 1960s (424)

ol-tnalan Set of bells worn on elaborate leather bands by Maasai Moran (638)

ollin aragiid Clapping-accompanied dancing in Halfa areas of Sudan and Kenuzi Nubian areas of Egypt (557)

Olodumare (or **Olorun**) The supreme being of the Yoruba people of Nigeria (400, 459)

omele Yoruba 'supporting drums', which play ostinatos designed to interlock rhythmically (472)

omolu Three pot drums and two pegged cylindrical wooden drums used to worship Omolu (461)

Omolu Yoruba god of water and fertility (461)

Omoluaiya festival Event designed to protect people from smallpox by invoking the deity Sopona (412)

omulanga Harpist for the ruler of Buganda in the area of Lake Victoria (600, 601)

omvʌk Note in the center of the xylophone where tuning begins, considered head of the family (660)

Ondo One of the seven principal Yoruba peoples of Nigeria (400)

onidan 'One who has tricks', a theatrical troupe that came out of the *egungun* tradition (401)

onomatopoeic vocalization Drummed or sung syllables that represent the rhythm and timbre of sounds depicted (125, 235)

oorlams Popular working-class musicians who were coloured or black Africans and served as cultural brokers in South Africa (762–63)

opim Guitar-playing idiom practiced in West African villages (353)

Orchestra Ethiopia Ethiopian ensemble founded in 1963 for the modern presentation of traditional music (150, 151)

Orchestra Makassy Tanzanian band joined by Remmy Ongala in 1964 (427)

Orchestra Matimila Tanzanian band joined by Remmy Ongala in 1981, after Orchestra Makassy had disbanded (427)

Orchestra Super Matimila Tanzanian band formed by Remmy Ongala in the 1990s (427)

oriki Yoruba poetry praising an individual, a deity, a town or even an inanimate object (218, 409, 410, 461, 472)

orile Yoruba poetry praising lineages, royal families, and ancient kingdoms (409)

orisa pipe Yoruba sung or semisung praises of any deity (410)

orisha (also *orisa*) Yoruba intermediate deities below the high god, Olodumare (273, 400, 460)

oro Yoruba secret society of night hunters, symbolized by the playing of a bullroarer (460, 461)

orutu Luo one-stringed lute-fiddle (625)

Os Zimbos (see **Zimbos, Os**)

oud A North African plucked lute with pear-shaped resonator; a short-necked plucked lute of Zanzibar (220, 427)

Oyo Yoruba kingdom, the most powerful coastal state that rose to prominence before 1500 (401, 459, 471)

ɔmade Igbo leopard society of eastern Nigeria (309)

pachanga Cuban dance made famous in Africa by Aragon and Johnny Pacheco (387, 422)

pagan Kenyan lyre with a box resonator (303–304)

palm-wine guitar style (also called **sea-breeze music**) Music played with a guitar and a bottle or hollowed-log idiophone (353, 376–79, 423)

pamploi Gã bamboo tubes (463)

Pathé-Marconi Major recording label, which by the 1930s was distributing its products across Africa (417)

Peda A people of Benin (37)

pele Performance of the Kpelle of Liberia that features singing, dancing, playing instruments, and speaking (128, 129–30)

pennywhistle A usually cheaply manufactured and sold metal whistle with several holes for fingering (296, 376, 379–80, 430, 719, 773)

pennywhistle jive An alternate name for *kwela* (430)

pentatonic Having pitch inventory of five tones to the octave (21, 268)

phata-phata Urban popular dance-song genre drawing from South African choral music (216–17)

pina (also *penah*) Gumuz gourd aerophone (564)

pluriarc Multiple-bow lute (445, 714)

poetics Examination of the poetry of songs by studying aesthetic systems and compositional procedures (104–105)

polyrhythm Simultaneous use of different rhythms (254–55)

pombeiros African-Portuguese traders (319, 668, 669, 679)

Poro General term for men's secret societies of West Africa (5, 125, 128, 129, 328–29)

pragmatic research Study aimed at rediscovering one's musical culture for immediate practical use (14)

praise-proverb mode In epic performance, a style exhibiting heightened melodic and rhythmic tension (498–99)

prempresiwa Large lamellophone with three or four metal tongues and a box resonator (356)

prescriptive transcription Notation that indicates to performers how to create specific musical sounds (154)

principle of harmonic equivalence Feature of Venda music where notes of the same harmonic series are substituted (709, 715, 728, 742)

Pullo, Pulo (see **Ful6e**)

Qaddiriyya Islamic brotherhood that traces its roots to Sufi sects of North Africa (344)

qarqabu (also *qarqaba*) North African instrument consisting of two pairs of iron castanets joined by a connecting bar, one pair held one in each hand (537)

qasaba Arab flute played by Tuareg herders in Algeria and Niger (542)

qasida North African solo vocal improvisation deriving from West Asian traditions (535, 550, 551)

qene Ethiopian Christian religious poetry chanted in Ge'ez (603)

qitara Arabic term for guitar (350)

quantitative time Time based on clocks, metronomes, or other forms of chronometry (128)

rabab North African two-stringed fiddle (534, 535)

rabi al-'awwal Third month of the Islamic Hijra calendar (345)

Radio Congo Belge pour les Indigènes Governmental station that opened in 1948 (385)

Radio Congo Belge First government-controlled station in Kinshasa, which opened in 1940 (385, 424)

Radio Congolia Privately owned radio station in Kinshasa, which began broadcasting in 1939 (385)

Radio-Léo Jesuit-owned radio station in Kinshasa, which broadcast 1937–1948 (385)

rai A North African Arabic style of cabaret music (422, 547)

Rail Band Guitar-based band that flourished in Mali in the late twentieth century (421)

Ramadan Islamic month of fasting (5, 330, 331, 515, 524–25)

ramkie Lute with three or four strings, played by southern Africans in Cape Town (351, 719, 761)

rara Speechlike singing initially associated with Esu, trickster deity of the Yoruba (409)

rika A tambourine of Zanzibar (427)

rimba Xylophone of the coastal Bantu people of Kenya (624)

riqq Arab tambourine, used Egypt and in Sudanese ceremonies of the Qādirīya brotherhood (552, 556, 571)

riti Wolof bowed lute with a holed gourd resonator (445)

rok'on fada Hausa state ceremonial music (450)

rommelpot European term for a Khoikhoi drum made by placing skins over a pot (703)

rongo Ndogo log xylophone with long gourd resonators (570)

rokoo Term for begging among the Hausa of Nigeria (519)

Royal College of Music School in London where many African musicians, including Ephraim Amu, studied (25)

rways Itinerant musicians of southern Morocco who perform Arab-Andalusian, European, Arab popular, and West African acculturated styles (541)

sababa Six-holed end-blown flute of Madagascar, similar to the Arabic *shabab* (787)

Sabanga A people of the Central African Republic (267)

sa'dawi Tunisian dance usually performed by women featuring hip movements and gestures with a hand-held scarf (543)

SADC Music Festival (Southern African Development Community Music Festival) A regionally cooperative festival, first held in October 1995 (428)

Sahel zone Dry borderland region between the savanna and the Sahara Desert (442)

sákárà (1) Yoruba single-membrane clay-bodied frame drum; (2) Yoruba musical genre for dancing and praising, performed and patronized mostly by Muslims (413, 474–75, 478, 485)

salsa A Latin American musical fusion of rhythm and blues, jazz, and rock, popular in Africa as a result of dissemination on gramophone records (416, 424)

samba Quadrangular, wooden frame drum introduced by Brazilian returnees to African churches (404)

sámbà Yoruba square drum, derived from Latin American or Caribbean models and associated with immigrant black Christians (478)

San A people of southern Africa (305–308, 659, 703–705)

Sandawe A cultural group of Tanzania (635)

Sande Generic term for women's secret societies in West Africa (5, 125, 126, 128, 129, 328–29)

sangoma Nguni healers (277)

sangwe Gumuz five-stringed lyre (564)

santur Mallet-hammered dulcimer or zither of North Africa and West Asia (220)

sapgba Vai conical single-headed drum (329)

sapeur Member of the Society of Ambienceurs and Persons of Elegance (424–25)

saransara Maguzawa feast with dancing in northern Nigeria (287)

sarewa Hausa four-holed flute, made of a reed or metal tube (449, 591)

sarma Gumuz large clay kettledrum (564)

sasa-ture Dance for chaotic social situations in the former Bauchi state, Nigeria (286, 287)

sasaa Vai gourd rattle (329, 338, 339, 340)

satandiro Mandinka extemporized vocal lines (499)

Savuka South African duo formed by Johnny Clegg after 1985 (431, 779)

Schnurpflockspannung (German) Cord-and-peg tension for fastening single-headed drums (314)

scotchi Competitive associations in East Africa that utilized bagpipes or locally made representations for performance (602–603)

sebiba Choreographed spectacle held at the oasis of Djanet, southeastern Algeria (544)

sefala (also *sefela*) Long, musical poetic narratives developed by Sotho veteran migrants on their travels to South African mines (218, 762)

ṣèkèrè (also *sekere*) Yoruba bottle-gourd rattle (461, 474, 478, 481, 483, 485)

ṣèlí (also *ṣèkèrè*) Yoruba tin cymbals with jingles, used to accompany *wákà* (474)

semantic coherence Textual unity in both plot and diction (168)

Semba Tropical Angolan national orchestra, founded after 1975 by the Ministry of Culture (435)

Senegambians People living west of the Mandinka in West Africa (443)

senhor de bomfim 'Lord of good fire', a genre brought to Africa by Brazilians and Cubans (401)

Sensacional Maringa da Angola Angolan fifteen-piece band that performs a mix of merengue, rumba, and rural Angolan styles (435)

Senufo A Gur-speaking cultural group of north-central Côte d'Ivoire (115, 453–54)

seŋ feŋ Vai term for instrumental performance (347)

seperewa (also *sanku*) Harp-lute of the Guinea Coast (22, 23, 351, 356, 367, 377, 465)

Serer A cultural group of north-central Côte d'Ivoire (443)

serkalla Miri stamping dance (562)

serndu Transverse flute of The Gambia (445)

sèsè Aesthetic quality of buzzing added to musical sounds by the Mandinka of Sierra Leone (489)

sha'bi Genre of Maghrib popular music (545)

shanbaal Carved wooden hand-held clappers played in southern Somalia (611)

Shango (also **Şango**) Yoruba god of thunder (274, 459, 461, 471)

shantu Hausa women's percussion tube (449)

shareero Coastal Somali six-stringed lyre (611)

shatam Sudanese small single-headed cup-shaped clay drum (556)

shebeen Unlicensed bar, often a private home, where patrons gather to drink and perform music (429, 766–67, 768)

shetani Spirits who possess and afflict Swahili-speaking people of East Africa (274)

shimolo Set of bells that Chagga male dancers of Tanzania wear on their backs (638)

Shirati Jazz Band founded by D. O. Misiani to play *benga* (427)

shiriri Luhiya one-stringed lute-fiddle (625)

Shona A people of Zimbabwe (307–308, 744)

simanjemanje (1) Urban dance-song type, drawing from South African choral music; (2) The soft female chorus that backs up a male "groaner" in South African *mbaqanga* (216–17, 430, 433, 776–77)

simbing Manding six- or seven-stringed arched harp that is smaller than the *bolon* (445)

sing'anga A Tumbuka local herbalist (271)

siŋar Ingassana gourd trumpet (563–64)

sistrum A shaken idiophone consisting of rattles attached to a stick or frame (446, 455)

skipping process A uniquely African way of producing harmony by singing a note and the next one after skipping one (740, 741)

Society for Ethnomusicology Professional society for the study of ethnomusicology, headquartered in the United States but open to interested persons worldwide (51, 65)

Society of Ambienceurs and Persons of Elegance Trend set by the Zaïrean musician Papa Wemba, who in the 1970s cultivated a style of dress reminiscent of 1950s Paris fashion and eighteenth-century dandyism (424)

son Traditional musical genre of Cuba, popular in Africa as a result of dissemination on gramophone records (385, 416, 424)

song mode Lyrical section of epic-style performance that exhibits a decreased melodic and rhythm tension (498–99)

Songhai A people of West Africa (447)

Soninke A group of Mande-speakers of northern Mali (445)

sorek A dance performed during the ritual harvest-festivals of the Miri of the Nuba Mountains in Sudan (463, 601)

soron Maninka harp-lute with nineteen or twenty-one strings (445)

soukous A name for Zaïrean rumba, featuring three guitar parts and a solo singer (227, 364, 365, 386, 387, 419, 423, 424, 682)

Southern African Development Community Cooperative forum that economically and culturally links twelve countries of southern Africa (428)

spectrogram Graphic representation of aspects of sound including pitch, rhythm, dynamics, and timbre (170–71)

speech surrogate Use of musical performance, often by instruments, to reproduce pitch and rhythm of speech (89, 105–107)

staff notation Notation utilizing the lines and spaces common to the representation of Western art music (157)

standard harmonic pattern Harmonic cycle for playing mbira that involves a succession of fifths (746–47)

Standard Bank Grahamstown Arts Festival Largest and most securely established musical festival in South Africa (431)

Sterns A small, independent British recording label (418)

subaŋ Character, reputation, social face as defined by the G people of Ghana (104–105)

suku-ba Vai professional Qur'ānic reciter (342, 346, 348)

Sunburst A Tanzanian jazz band that included native Tanzanians, African-Americans, and a Jamaican (645)

Sunjata Historic warrior revered in song by Mande peoples of West Africa (495–97)

Swahili An East African cultural group; a trade language that draws on the structures and vocabularies of Bantu languages and Arabic (2–3, 425–26, 635)

taar Northern Sudanese frame drum (556, 557)

taarab (Arabic 'joy, pleasure, delight') Popular coastal East African music that traditionally accompanied Swahili love-related poetry, often played at weddings (227, 415, 426, 427–28, 607, 631–32, 645–46)

tabla Sudanese small drum (555, 571)

tablature Notational system that places numbers or letters on a diagram that resembles the strings or keys of an instrument (158)

tahardent (1) Tuareg three-stringed lute, resembling the Mauritanian *tidinit;* (2) Tuareg musical genre that has become popular in Niger (540, 546, 575, 587–90, 593)

take Nyamalthu praise-name performance in the former Bauchi State in Nigeria (288)

takamba New Tuareg genre in which seated listeners respond to rhythms with undulating movements of the torso (588–89)

talawat Moroccan flute (541)

taletenga Idioglot reed pipe of the Akan of Ghana (465)

talk-men Kru sailors who served as interpreters for their ability with pidgin English (372)

Tallensi A people of Ghana (119)

tama Double-headed, hourglass-shaped tension drum of the Western Sudanic cluster (422, 446)

tambari Hausa large kettledrum with a resonator of wood, symbolizing royalty (448, 449)

tambing Ful6e transverse flute (445)

tambura (1) Sudanese usually six-stringed lyre; (2) Sudanese ritual organized by women, involving music-induced possession by spirits; (3) Sudanese large drum (554–55)

tamghra Berber dance performed for or by a bride and her attendants (543)

tan Dan dance-song (466)

ṭanbūr (also *ṭanbūra*) Sudanese-Arabic lyre (556, 571)

ṭar Sudanese frame drum, played for *nōba* (552)

tar North African frame drum with attached cymbals (534, 535, 541, 546)

ta'riya Moroccan clay cylindrical drum (541)

tarompet Western cornet played in *ngoma* performances (606)

tasabia (Arabic) String of prayer beads (344)

tatarizo A scraped bamboo idiophone of southern Tanzania (638)

tatûm Double bell in the border area of the Central African Republic and the Congo (311)

taẓammart (also *tasansagh* and *tasensigh*) Tuareg four-holed flute, made of a reed or metal tube (542, 591–92)

tazâwat Medium-sized kettledrum, played by women in the Azawagh region of Niger (541, 590–91)

tazengherit Tuareg ecstatic music and dance, performed especially at Tazruk and Hirafok oases, Ahaggar (594)

tazu ma sorek 'Songs of the gourd', Miri men's bawdy songs in hocket (563)

tbel Moroccan kettledrum (537, 540, 541, 543, 544)

tegennewt Algerian kettledrum, made from a wooden or enameled metal bowl and occasionally played by the Tuareg (541, 591, 594)

tehemmet Tuareg dance of Tassili-n-Ajjer, accompanied by songs, clapping, and one or more drums (593–94)

tehigelt Tuareg dance of Ahaggar, accompanied by songs, clapping, and one or more drums (593–94) *temja* Algerian six-holed wooden flute (543)

Temne A cultural group of Sierra Leone (445, 468)

tende (also *tindi*) Tuareg single-headed mortar drum (538, 545, 575, 582–87, 594)

tende n-ənnas Events where the mortar drum is played and that feature personalized references to camels (585–87)

tendrena 'To play', Malagasy verb used to denote playing chordophones and keyboard instruments (783)

tesîwit Pastoral Tuareg strophic poems sung solo to formulaic melodies or motifs (541, 579–81, 592)

text envelope An area of knowledge to be drawn upon that is larger than any single text (490–91)

tickey draai Dance accompanied by the guitar and popular until the 1940s in South Africa (351, 762–63, 767)

tidinit Mauritanian lute (540, 588)

Tijaniyya Islamic brotherhood that traces its roots to Sufi sects of North Africa (344)

timbila South African Chopi xylophones played in large ensembles (227, 429, 436, 709–10)

timbre Quality of sound that makes one voice or instrument sound different from another while producing identical pitches (135–37)

timbrh Raffia lamellophone of the Vute of central Cameroon (319)

timeline Any of several repeating rhythmic patterns underlying much West African ensemble music and usually played by a high-pitched struck idiophone, such as a double clapperless bell (310, 476)

tirtir Chadian circular dance performed by the Zaghawa and characterized by solemn hopping (561)

tobol Small drum played for the *sebiba* (544)

tom (1) Shilluk lyre; (2) Colo rain dance (568)

Tonic Sol-fa (also known as *solfège*) Verbal syllables that represent relative pitches (160, 224, 234–35)

toŋ ito Two double iron bells of the Central African flange-welded type, with a bow grip (654)

towo Wards of Anlo-Ewe towns in Ghana (389)

tɔmbɔ Vai word for dance (347)

tɔmbɔkɛ bɔɔniɛ-nu Vai troupe of Sande society young initiate dancers (338, 339)

trumba Gumuz trumpet of animal horn or aluminum (564)

tsaba-tsaba Urban popular dance-song genre, drawing from South African choral music (216, 322, 772, 775)

tshikona Venda music produced by an ensemble of one-pitch pipes played in hocket (708–709)

tshizambi Venda friction bow, obtained from the Tsonga (709)

tsikatray Frame rattle constructed from a square frame of wood covered by rushes and filled with seeds (784, 785)

tsofina 'To blow' (aerophones), Malagasy term denoting the playing of musical instrumentals (783)

tswawo Small gourd rattles worn on dancers' legs in Zimbabwe (752)

Tuareg Nomadic people of Algeria, Mali, and Niger (115–16, 537, 574)

TUBS Time Unit Box System of notation, developed in 1962 for teaching African drumming (157, *158*)

tuku Single-headed wooden goblet drum that accompanied music of the Kru of Liberia (374, 375)

tulon bololu 'Play songs', songs of the Mandinka of northern Sierra Leone (488, 490, 492–93, 503, 505, 507, 512)

tumble Fur bowl-shaped drum (561)

tumbuizo Genre of songs performed by women in Kenya, singing in Swahili (630, 631)

Tumbuka Language spoken by people of northern Malawi (771–83)

Tumtum A Sudanese people of the Nuba Mountains (562)

turu Daura dance, for which singers praise the royal ancestors (291)

túru Kpelle side-blown horn (467)

tusona Graphic configurations of dots circumscribed by lines of the Luchazi culture of Angola and Zambia (150–51)

Tutsi A cultural group of Rwanda and Burundi (108, 607)

Twi Language family spoken by Akan peoples in Ghana and Côte d'Ivoire (25)

tyi wara Bambara mask that comes from a narrative about a farmer of that same name (119, 120–21)

'ud North African four-stringed lute (534, 535)

'udi Swahili plucked lute of East Africa (351, 607)

Uganda Museum Site of major research and teaching program in ethnomusicology directed by Klaus Wachsmann (18)

ugubhu Zulu unbraced gourd-resonated musical bow more than a meter long (321, 706)

ujamaa Villages that served as resettlement habitats under President Nyerere's regime in Tanzania (634)

ulimba Makonde-Mwera type lamellophone with broad iron tongues with no bridge (317, 639)

umakhweyana Zulu gourd-resonated musical bow braced near the center (364, 706)

umkiki The Baggāra one-stringed fiddle, played to accompany *gardagi* (560)

umngqokolo A form of overtone singing performed by Xhosa women and girls in southern Africa (706)

umrhubhe A bow played by scraping a string with a stick in southern Africa (706)

umva Miri double-headed dance-accompanying drum (562)

University of Ibadan Unit of music research established in 1962 under the direction of Fela Sowande (39)

University of Nigeria (Nsukka) Department of music for teaching degree-qualifying courses in ethnomusicology (40)

urar (also *ural*) Berber ritual verses, sung usually by women at weddings and circumcision ceremonies (540, 541)

Utamaduni Tanzanian National Dance Troupe, founded in 1964 to amalgamate music styles in Tanzania (646)

Vai (Vey) Northern Mande-speakers of northwest Liberia (327–49, 467)

valiha Wire-stringed tube zither, the best-known instrument of Madagascar; also played in Tanzania (605, 786, 788)

valiha vero Malagasy raft zither that consists of ten bamboo tubes arranged progressively by length (786)

valimba A Sena xylophone in south-central Africa (711)

valimba (or *ulimba*) Gourd-resonated large xylophone of southern Malawi (322, 323, 711)

Vapostori A separatist church in Zimbabwe that forbids the use of African drums (755)

velezina 'To beat' or 'to give life to' (membrane drums), Malagasy term to denote instrumental playing (783)

vimbuza Tumbuka spirits (271–83)

vodoun (*vodun*) Deities of the people of Dahomey (273, 462)

voiced speech Speech marked by a periodic wave of a fundamental and partials (168–69)

vyanusi Tumbuka dance in which the spirit of the Ngoni comes out and transforms people (275, 276)

ʋufofo 'Drumming', Anlo-Ewe performance, including drumming, singing, dancing, and costuming (390)

ʋumegãwo 'Big men or women of the drum', persons who lead the hierarchy of urban Anlo-Ewe performing ensembles (390)

ʋuyɔyɔ Anlo-Ewe genre of performance that draws on rural musical practice (399)

Wagogo A people of central Tanzania (312, 604)

wákà Yoruba musical genre, adopted from the Hausa and usually performed by women (423, 474)

wala (Vai) Wooden boards on which Qur'ānic inscriptions are written (330)

wandindi Kikuyu single-stringed lute-fiddle, in which a string tuned a fourth below the others acts as a drone (625)

Wanyamwezi A cultural group of Tanzania (87, 317)

Wasa An Akan-speaking people of Ghana (463)

wasan bòorii Spirit-possession dance that occurs in many Hausa communities (290)

wasan maharba Dance in which hunters reenact personal experiences of going on hunts (288, 289)

wau (also *æk*) Colo poet-composer-singer (569)

waza (1) Berta conical trumpet; (2) Berta music played by a *waza* ensemble (564–67)

wedge-and-ring-tension drum   Drum with a wedge-tensioned girdle attached to leather lacings around its body   (665, *666*)

West African Cultural Society   Organization for preserving and promoting African culture, with branches in several countries   (32, 33)

whisper   Speech in which the vocal cords are loose and caught in the blast of air from the lungs, creating turbulent noise   (161–71)

Wolof   A cultural group of Senegal   (421, 444)

WOMAD (World of Music Arts and Dance)   Festival conceived by the British rock musician Peter Gabriel in 1980   (418)

word painting   Use of melody to depict a visual effect, a technique sometimes employed by Ndubuisi in his music   (249)

World Circuit   A small, independent British recording label   (418)

woyaya   A Pygmy dance accompanied by a twenty-four-pulse-unit pattern played on a percussion beam   (310)

wua   Kasena-Nankani two- or three-hole vertical flute, the most common melody-producing instrument of Ghana   (454, 455)

wule   Term for song among the Kpelle of Liberia; songs can be of various proportions   (131)

xalam (also *halam* or *khalam*)   Wolof five-stringed plucked lute   (366, 444, 445)

Xhosa   A cultural group of South Africa   (265–67, 306–307)

yaawn tashee   Predawn Ramadan procession during which musicians perform   (515)

yabon sarakai   Hausa court-praise music   (450)

Yalunka   A cultural group of Guinea and Sierra Leone   (446)

Yao   A cultural group of Tanzania   (119)

yaponsa (from the Ghanaian song "Yaa Amponsah")   Guitar-fingering pattern of Nigeria   (353)

Yavi   Vai male masquerader in Liberia   (329)

Yellow Blues   A Zimbabwean all-female jazz band   (433)

Yewe   Ewe god of thunder and lightning   (462)

yodeling   Rapid shifting between a singer's upper and lower registers   (307, 432, 635, 658, 705)

Yoruba   Dominant cultural group of southwest Nigeria   (400–401, 460–61)

ywok   Colo funeral and memorial dance   (568)

zabiya   Professional female singer in West Africa   (447)

zafindraona   'Popular religious song', musical genre of the rural Betsileo area of Madagascar   (791)

zagara   Tunisian dance performed by paired men brandishing swords   (544)

Zaghawa   A camel-breeding people of Darfur   (561)

Zaiko Langa Langa   Congo-Zaïre rumba band that in the 1970s popularized *soukous*   (424)

zajal   Popular North African court poetry, developed in Spain and having strophic texts with instrumental refrains   (535)

zammar   Moroccan double clarinet   (541)

Zanahary   Malagasy creator god, who gave human beings instruments to entertain themselves   (783)

zaowzaya   Mauritanian four-holed flute, made of acacia root or bark   (542)

zār   Northeast African curing ceremony involving singing, dancing, and drumming   (113, 273–74, 277, 554–55, 556, 604, 606)

zekete-zekete   Popular music from 1977 to 1987 in Kinshasa, based on a variant of the rumba   (386, 387)

zēmā   Ethiopian Christian chant liturgy   (147, 613)

zendani   Genre of Maghrib popular music, played and sung by urban female professionals at family festivals   (546)

zevu   Anlo-Ewe pot drum, adapted from pot drums of Nigeria   (399)

zeze   Generic Tanzanian term for bar zithers, bows, and lutes   (322, 640, 641)

zhita   Higi boys' inititiation ritual in northern Nigeria   (288)

zikr (see *dhikr*)

Zimbos, Os   Angolan band that performs a mix of merengue, rumba, and rural Angolan styles   (428, 435)

Zionists   A separatist church in Zimbabwe that employed African drums in its rituals   (755)

zlöö   'Praise song', a musical genre of the Dan of West Africa   (466)

zokela   An urban dance-music based in the Central African Republic city of Bangui   (681–87)

Zooba   Sande masked dancer who impersonates a male ancestor water-dwelling spirit   (329, 335–41)

zukra   Tunisian bagpipe, used to accompany a scarf dance   (543, 544)

Zulu   A cultural group of South Africa   (706–708)

A Guide to Publicatic
on African Music

Reference Works

Aning, Ben Akosa. 1967. *An Annotated Bibliography of Music and Dance in English-Speaking Africa.* Legon: Institute of African Studies.

Gaskin, Lionel John Palmer. 1965. *Select Bibliography of African Music.* London: International African Institute.

Gray, John. 1991. *African Music: A Bibliographical Guide to the Traditional, Popular, Arts, and Liturgical Musics of Sub-Saharan Africa.* New York and Westport, Conn.: Greenwood Press.

Greenberg, Joseph H. 1966. *The Languages of Africa.* Bloomington, Ind.: Research Center for the Language Sciences.

Guthrie, Malcolm. 1948. *The Classification of Bantu Languages.* London: International African Institute.

Merriam, Alan P. 1970. *African Music on LP.* Evanston, Ill.: Northwestern University Press.

Murdoc
Pittsbur

Murray,
Africa. (

Stone, I
African
Recordin
London

Thieme,
Annotat
Library

Tracey, I
Africa R
Internat

Varley, I
An Anno
Empire

General

Anderson, Lois Ann. 1971. "The Interrelation of African and Arab Musics: Some Preliminary Considerations." In *Essays in Music and History in Africa,* ed. Klaus P. Wachsmann, 143–169. Evanston, Ill.: Northwestern University Press.

Ankermann, Bernhard. 1901. "Die afrikanischen Musikinstrumente." *Ethnologisches Notizblatt* 3:I–X, 1–32.

Arom, Simha. 1976. "The Use of Play-Back Techniques in the Study of Oral Polyphonies." *Ethnomusicology* 20(3):483–519.

———. 1991. *African Polyphony and Polyrhythm,* trans. Martin Thom et al. Cambridge and Paris: Cambridge University Press and Editions de la Maison des Sciences de l'Homme.

———. 1992. "A Synthesizer in the Central African Bush: A Method of Interactive Exploration of Musical Scales." In *Für Gyorgy Ligeti: Die Referate des Ligeti- Kongresses Hamburg 1988,* ed. Peter Petersen, 163–178. Hamburg: Laaber-Verlag; Hamburger Jahrbuch für Musikwissenschaft, 11.

Ballanta, Nicholas George Julius. 1926. "Gathering Folk Tunes in the African Country." *Musical America* 44(23):3–11.

Bebey, F
Art, tran
Lawrenc

Blacking
of Africa
Hornbos

Bowdich
Superstiti
Ancient I
Paris: J. S

Carringt
London:

Collins, J
W. Foulsl

Curtin, P
Ideas and
Universit

Danielsor
East." In
by Peter I
Universit

Davidson
York: Tin

Erlmann, Veit. 1981. *Populäre Musik in Afrika.* Berlin: Staatliche Museen Preußischer Kulturbesitz. Veröffentlichungen des Museums für Völkerkunde Berlin, Neue Folge 53, Abteilung Musikethnologie 8.

Faruqi, Lois I. al. 1986. "Handashah al Sawt or the Art of Sound." In *The Cultural Atlas of Islam,* ed. Isma'il al Faruqi and Lois Lamya' al Faruqi, 441–479. New York: Macmillan.

————. 1986. "The Mawlid." *The World of Music* 28(3):79–89.

Finnegan, Ruth. 1970. *Oral Literature in Africa.* Nairobi: Oxford University Press.

Gibb, H. A. R. 1929. *Ibn Battuta, Travels in Asia and Africa.* London: Darf.

Hampton, Barbara. 1980. "A Revised Analytical Approach to Musical Processes in Urban Africa." *African Urban Studies* 6:1–16.

Herzog, George. 1934. "Speech-Melody and Primitive Music." *Musical Quarterly* 20(4):452–466.

Hornbostel, Erich M. von. 1928. "African Negro Music." *Africa* 1:30–62.

————. 1933. "The Ethnology of African Sound Instruments." *Africa* 6:129–154, 277–311.

Jones, Arthur M. 1971 [1959]. *Studies in African Music.* 2 vols. London: Oxford University Press.

————. 1964. *Africa and Indonesia: The Evidence of the Xylophone and Other Musical and Cultural Factors,* 2nd ed. Leiden: E. J. Brill.

————. 1976. *African Hymnody in Christian Worship: A Contribution to the History of Its Development.* Gwelo, Zimbabwe: Mambo Press.

Kauffman, Robert. 1980. "African Rhythm: A Reassessment." *Ethnomusicology* 24:393–415.

Kubik, Gerhard. 1962. "The Phenomenon of Inherent Rhythms in East and Central African Instrumental Music." *African Music* 1:33–42.

————. 1965. "Transcription of Mangwilo Xylophone Music from Film Strips." *African Music* 3(4):35–41.

————. 1972. "Transcription of African Music from Silent Film: Theory and Methods." *African Music* 5(1):28–39.

————. 1977. "Patterns of Body Movement in the Music of Boys' Initiation in South-East Angola." In *The Anthropology of the Body,* ed. John Blacking, 253–274. London: Academic Press.

————. 1985. "African Tone Systems—A Reassessment." *Yearbook for Traditional Music* 17:31–63.

————. 1986. "Stability and Change in African Musical Traditions." *The World of Music* 27:44–69.

Livingstone, David. 1857. *A Narrative of Dr. Livingstone's Discoveries in South-Central Africa.* London: Routledge.

Manuel, Peter. 1988. *Popular Musics of the Non-Western World.* New York: Oxford University Press.

Merriam, Alan P. 1959. "African Music." In *Continuity and Change in African Cultures,* ed. William R. Bascom and Melville J. Herskovits, 49–86. Chicago: University of Chicago Press.

————. 1964. *The Anthropology of Music.* Evanston, Ill.: Northwestern University Press.

————. 1972. *The Arts and Humanities in African Studies.* Bloomington: African Studies Program, Indiana University.

————. 1981. "African Musical Rhythm and Concepts of Time-Reckoning." In *Music East and West: Essays in Honor of Walter Kaufmann,* ed. Thomas Noblitt, 123–142. New York: Pendragon Press.

————. 1982. *African Music in Perspective.* New York: Garland.

Mudimbe, V. Y. 1988. *The Invention of Africa: Gnosis, Philosophy, and the Order of Knowledge.* Bloomington: Indiana University Press.

Mukuna, Kazadi wa. 1992. "The Genesis of Urban Music." *African Music* 7(2):72–74.

Murdock, George P. 1959. *Africa: Its People and Their Culture History.* New York: McGraw-Hill.

Nketia, J. H. Kwabena. 1962a. "The Hocket Technique in African Music." *Journal of the International Folk Music Council* 14:44–55.

————. 1962b. "The Problem of Meaning in African Music." *Ethnomusicology* 6(1):1–7.

————. 1974. *The Music of Africa.* New York: Norton.

————. 1982. "On the Historicity of Music in African Cultures." *Journal of African Studies* 9(3):1–9.

Nketia, J. H. Kwabena, and Jacqueline C. DjeDje. 1984. "Trends in African Musicology." In *Selected Reports in Ethnomusicology V: Studies in African Music* (UCLA), ix–xx.

Omibiyi, Mosunmola. 1973–1974. "A Model for the Study of African Music." *African Music* 5(3):6–11.

Rouget, Gilbert. 1985. *Music and Trance: A Theory of the Relations between Music and Possession,* trans. Brunhilde Biebuyck. Chicago: University of Chicago Press.

Serwadda, Moses, and Hewitt Pantaleoni. 1968. "A Possible Notation for African Dance Drumming." *African Music* 4(2):47–52.

Simon, Artur, ed. 1983. *Musik in Afrika.* Berlin: Museum für Völkerkunde.

Stapleton, Chris, and Chris May. 1990. *African Rock: The Pop Music of a Continent.* New York: Dutton.

Stone, Ruth M. 1985. "In Search of Time in African Music." *Music Theory Spectrum* 7:139–158.

Stone, Ruth M., and Verlon Stone. 1981. "Event, Feedback, and Analysis: Research Media in the Study of Music Events." *Ethnomusicology* 25(2):215–225.

Thompson, Robert Farris. 1974. *African Art in Motion.* Berkeley and Los Angeles: University of California Press.

Vansina, Jan. 1969. "The Bells of Kings." *Journal of African History* 10(2):187–197.

Wachsmann, Klaus P. 1964a. "Human Migration and African Harps." *Journal of the International Folk Music Council* 16:84–88.

———. 1964b. "Problems of Musical Stratigraphy in Africa." In *Colloques de Wégimont* 3:19–22.

———. 1966. "The Trend of Musicology in Africa." In *Selected Reports in Ethnomusicology* (UCLA), 1(1):61–65.

———. 1970. "Ethnomusicology in Africa." In *African Experience,* ed. John N. Paden and Edward W. Soja, 128–151. Evanston, Ill.: Northwestern University Press.

———, ed. 1971. *Essays on Music and History in Africa.* Evanston, Ill.: Northwestern University Press.

Wallaschek, Richard. 1893. *Primitive Music: An Inquiry into the Origin and Development of Music, Songs, Instruments, Dances, and Pantomimes of Savage Races.* London: Longmans, Green.

Waterman, Richard A. 1952. "African Influence on the Music of the Americas." In *Acculturation in the Americas,* vol. 2, ed. Sol Tax, 207–218. Chicago: University of Chicago Press.

Wegner, Ulrich. 1984. *Afrikanische Saiteninstrumente.* Berlin: Staatliche Museen Preußischer Kulturbesitz. Museum für Völkerkunde Berlin, Abteilung Musikethnologie, new series, 41.

West Africa

Agawu, Kofi. 1986. "'Gi Dunu,' 'Nyekpadudo,' and the Study of West African Rhythm." *Ethnomusicology* 30(1):64–83.

———. 1987. "The Rhythmic Structure of West African Music." *Journal of Musicology* 5(3):400–418.

———. 1990. "Variation Procedures in Northern Ewe Song." *Ethnomusicology* 34(2):221–243.

Akpabot, Samuel. 1972. "Theories on African Rhythm." *African Arts* (Los Angeles) 6(1):59–62, 88.

Ames, David W. 1973. "A Sociocultural View of Hausa Musical Activity." In *The Traditional Artist in African Societies,* ed. Warren d'Azevedo, 128–161. Bloomington: Indiana University Press.

Ames, David W., and Anthony V. King. 1971. *Glossary of Hausa Music in Its Social Contexts.* Evanston, Ill.: Northwestern University Press.

Amu, Ephraim. 1933. *Twenty-Five African Songs.* London: Sheldon Press.

Anyidoho, Kofi. 1982. "Death and Burial of the Dead: Ewe Funeral Folklore." M.A. thesis, Indiana University.

Arntson, Laura. 1992. "The Play of Ambiguity in Praise-Song Performance: A Definition of the Genre through an Examination of its Practice in Northern Sierra Leone." Ph.D. dissertation, Indiana University.

Avorgbedor, Daniel Kodzo. 1986. "Modes of Musical Continuity among the Anlo-Ewe of Accra: A Study in Urban Ethnomusicology." Ph.D. dissertation, Indiana University.

———. 1992. "The Impact of Rural-Urban Migration on a Village Music Culture: Some Implications for Applied Ethnomusicology." *African Music* 7(2):45–57.

Besmer, Fremont. 1972. *Hausa Court Music in Kano, Nigeria.* Ann Arbor, Mich.: University Microfilms.

———. 1974. *Kídàn Dárán Sállà: Music for the Muslim Festivals of Id al-Fitr and Id al- Kabir in Kano, Nigeria.* Bloomington: African Studies Program, Indiana University. Indiana University Monographs.

———. 1983. *Horses, Musicians, and Gods: The Hausa Cult of Possession-Trance.* South Hadley, Mass.: Bergin and Garvey.

Bird, Charles S., and Martha B. Kendall. 1980. "The Mande Hero." In *Explorations in African Systems of Thought,* ed. Ivan Karp and Charles S. Bird, 13–26. Bloomington: Indiana University Press.

Bird, Charles S., Mamadou Koita, and Bourama Soumaoro. 1974. *The Songs of Seydou Camara, Volume One: Kambili.* Bloomington: African Studies Center, Indiana University.

Bosman, William. 1967 [1705]. *A New and Accurate Description of the Coast of Guinea.* Facsimile of the 1705 (English) edition. London: Frank Cass.

Burton, Sir Richard Francis. 1966 [1893]. *A Mission to Gelele, King of Dahome.* London: Routledge and Kegan Paul.

Chernoff, John M. 1979. *African Rhythm and African Sensibility: Aesthetics and Social Action in African Musical Idioms.* Chicago: University of Chicago Press.

Collins, E. John. 1977. "Post-War Popular Band Music in West Africa." *African Arts* 10(3):53–60.

———. 1985. *Musicmakers of West Africa.* Washington: Three Continents.

———. 1986. *E. T. Mensah, King of Highlife.* London: Off the Record Press.

———. 1987. "Jazz Feedback to Africa." *American Music* 5(2):176–193.

———. 1989. "The Early History of West African Highlife Music." *Popular Music* 8(3):221–230.

Collins, E. John, and Paul Richards. 1982. "Popular Music in West Africa." In *Popular Music Perspectives,* ed. David Horn and Philip Tagg, 111—141. Goteborg, Exeter: International Association for the Study of Popular Music.

DjeDje, Jacqueline Cogdell. 1980. *Distribution of the One String Fiddle in West Africa.* Los Angeles: UCLA Program in Ethnomusicology, Department of Music.

————. 1982. "The Concept of Patronage: An Examination of Hausa and Dagomba One-String Fiddle Traditions." *Journal of African Studies* 9(3):116–127.

Duran, Lucy, et al. 1987. "On Music in Contemporary West Africa: Jaliya and the Role of the Jali in Present Day Manding Society." *African Affairs: Journal of the Royal African Society* 86(343):233–236.

Ekwueme, Lazarus. 1975–1976. "Structural Levels of Rhythm and Form in African Music with Particular Reference to the West Coast." *African Music* 5(4):105–129.

Euba, Akin. 1970. "New Idioms of Music-Drama among the Yoruba: An Introductory Study." *Yearbook of the International Folk Music Council* 92–107.

————. 1971. "Islamic Musical Culture among the Yoruba: A Preliminary Survey." In *Essays on Music and History in Africa,* ed. Klaus P. Wachsmann, 171–184. Evanston, Ill.: Northwestern University Press.

————. 1977. "An Introduction to Music in Nigeria." In *Nigerian Music Review,* no. 1, ed. Akin Euba, 1–38. Ife: Department of Music, University of Ife.

————. 1990. *Yoruba Drumming: The Dùndún Tradition.* Bayreuth: Bayreuth University. Bayreuth African Studies, 21–22.

Fiagbedzi, Nissio. 1976. "The Music of the Anlo: Its Historical Background, Cultural Matrix, and Style." Ph.D. dissertation, University of California, Los Angeles.

Gourlay, Kenneth A. 1982. "Long Trumpets of Northern Nigeria—In History and Today." *African Music* 6(2):48–72.

Hampton, Barbara L. 1992. "Music and Gender in Gã Society: Adaawe Song Poetry." In *African Musicology: Current Trends,* vol. 2, ed. Jacqueline Cogdell Djedje, 135–149. Los Angeles: University of California Press.

Harper, Peggy. 1970. "A Festival of Nigerian Dances." *African Arts* 3(2):48–53.

Herzog, George. 1945. "Drum-Signaling in a West African Tribe." *Word: Journal of the Linguistic Circle of New York* 1(3):217–238.

Keil, Charles. 1979. *Tiv Song.* Chicago: University of Chicago Press.

Kinney, Esi Sylvia. 1970. "Urban West African Music and Dance." *African Urban Notes* 5(4):3–10.

Knight, Roderic. 1972. "Towards a Notation and Tablature for the Kora." *African Music* 1(5):23–35.

————. 1974. "Mandinka Drumming." *African Arts* 7(4):25–35.

————. 1984a. "Music in Africa: The Manding Contexts." In *Performance Practice: Ethnomusicological Perspectives,* ed. Gerard Béhague, 53–90. Westport, Conn.: Greenwood Press; Contributions in Intercultural and Comparative Studies, 12.

————. 1984b. "The Style of Mandinka Music: A Study in Extracting Theory from Practice." In *Selected Reports in Ethnomusicology V. Studies in African Music,* ed. J. H. Kwabena Nketia and Jacqueline Cozdell Djedje, 3–66. Los Angeles: University of California.

Koetting, James. 1970. "Analysis and Notation of West African Drum Ensemble Music." *Selected Reports in Ethnomusicology,* ed. J. H. Kwabena Nketia and Jacqueline Cozdell Djedje, 1(3):115–146. Los Angeles: Institute of Ethnomusicology, University of California.

————. 1984. "Hocket Concept and Structure in Kasena Flute Ensemble Music." In *Selected Reports in Ethnomusicology V. Studies in African Music,* ed. J. H. Kwabena Nketia and Jacqueline Cozdell Djedje, 161–172. Los Angeles: University of California.

Ladzekpo, S. Kobla. 1971. "The Social Mechanics of Good Music: A Description of Dance Clubs among the Anlo Ewe-Speaking People of Ghana." *African Music* 5(1):6–22.

Little, Kenneth. 1965. *West African Urbanization: A Study of Voluntary Associations in Social Change.* Cambridge: Cambridge University Press.

Locke, David. 1982. "Principles of Offbeat Timing and Cross-Rhythm in Southern Eʋe Dance Drumming." *Ethnomusicology* 26(2):217–246.

————. 1987. *Drum Gahu.* Crown Point, Ind.: White-Cliffs Media.

Locke, David, and Godwin K. Agbeli. 1980. "A Study of the Drum Language in Adzogbo." *African Music* 6(1):32–51.

Mensah, Atta Annan. 1958. "Professionalism in the Musical Practice of Ghana." *Music in Ghana* 1(1):28–35.

Monts, Lester P. 1982. "Music Clusteral Relationships in a Liberian–Sierra Leonean Region: A Preliminary Analysis." *Journal of African Studies* 9(3):101–115.

Nketia, J. H. Kwabena. 1962. "The Problem of Meaning in African Music." *Ethnomusicology* 6:1–7.

————. 1963. *Drumming in Akan Communities of Ghana.* London: University of Ghana and Thomas Nelson.

————. 1973. "The Musician in Akan Society." In *The Traditional Artist in African Societies,* ed. Warren d'Azevedo , 79–100. Bloomington: Indiana University Press.

Nzewi, Meki. 1974. "Melo-Rhythmic Essence and Hot Rhythm in Nigerian Folk Music." *The Black Perspective in Music* 2(1):23–28.

Omibiyi, M. A. 1981. "Popular Music in Nigeria." *Jazzforschung* 13:151–168.

Parkin, David. 1969. "Urban Voluntary Associations as Institutions of Adaptation." *Man* 1(1):90–95.

Peil, Margaret. 1972. *The Ghanaian Factory Worker: Industrial Man in Africa.* Cambridge: Cambridge University Press.

Phillips, Ekundayo. 1953. *Yoruba Music.* Johannesburg: African Music Society.

Phillips, Ruth B. 1978. "Masking in Mande Sande Society Initiation Rituals." *Africa* 48:265–277.

Robertson, Claire. 1984. *Sharing in the Same Bowl: A Socioeconomic History of Women and Class in Accra.* Bloomington: Indiana University Press.

Smith, M. G. 1957. "The Social Functions and Meaning of Hausa Praise Singing." *Africa* 27:26–45.

———. 1959. "The Hausa System of Social Status." *Africa* 29:239–252.

Stone, Ruth. 1982. *Let the Inside Be Sweet: The Interpretation of Music Event among the Kpelle of Liberia.* Bloomington: Indiana University Press.

———. 1988. *Dried Millet Breaking: Time, Words, and Song in the Woi Epic of the Kpelle.* Bloomington: Indiana University Press.

Thieme, Darius. 1967. "A Descriptive Catalog of Yoruba Musical Instruments." Ph.D. dissertation, Catholic University of America.

Thompson, Robert F. 1966. "An Aesthetic of the Cool: West African Dance." *African Forum* 2(2):85–102.

———. 1974. *African Art in Motion: Icon and Act in the Collection of Katherine Coryton White.* Los Angeles: University of California Press.

Turay, A. K. 1966. "A Vocabulary of Temne Musical Instruments." *Sierra Leone Language Review* (Freetown) 5:27–33.

Ward, William Ernest. 1927. "Music in the Gold Coast." *Gold Coast Review* 3(2):199– 223.

Waterman, Christopher A. 1990. *Jùjú: A Social History and Ethnography of an African Popular Music.* Chicago: University of Chicago Press.

Yankah, Kwesi. 1983. "To Praise or Not to Praise the King: The Akan *Akpae* in the Context of Referential Poetry." *Research in African Literatures* 14(3):381–400.

———. 1985. "Voicing and Drumming the Poetry of Praise: The Case for *Aural·Literature.*" In *Interdisciplinary Dimensions of African Literature,* ed. Kofi Anyidoho et al., 137–153. Washington, D.C.: Three Continents Press.

Zemp, Hugo. 1967. *Musique Dan.* Paris: Mouton.

North Africa

Carlisle, Roxane. 1975. "Women Singers in Darfur, Sudan Republic." *The Black Perspective in Music* 3(3):253–268.

Daw, Ali al-, and Abd-Alla Muhammad. 1985. *Traditional Musical Instruments in Sudan.* Khartoum: Institute of African and Asian Studies, University of Khartoum.

———. 1988. *Al-mūsīqa al-taqlīdīya fi maġtamaʿa al-Berta* [*Traditional Music in al-Berta Society*]. Khartoum: Institute of African and Asian Studies, University of Khartoum.

Deng, Francis Mading. 1973. *The Dinka and Their Songs.* Oxford: Oxford University Press.

Erlmann, Veit. 1974. "Some Sources on Music in Western Sudan from 1300–1700." *African Music* 5(3):34–39.

Farmer, Henry George. 1924. "The Arab Influence on Music of the Western Soudan." *Musical Standard* 24:158–159.

———. 1939. "Early References to Music in the Western Sūdān." *Journal of the Royal Asiatic Society of Great Britain and Ireland,* part 4 (October):569–579.

Ismail, Mahi. 1970. "Musical Traditions in the Sudan." *La Revue Musicale* 288–289:87– 93.

Saada, Nadia Mécheri. 1986. "La musique de l'Ahaggar." Ph.D. dissertation, University of Paris.

Schmidt-Wrenger, Barbara. 1979. *Rituelle Frauengesänge der Tshokwe: Untersuchungen zu einem Säkularisierungsprozess in Angola und Zaire.* 3 vols. Tervuren: Musée Royal de l'Afrique Centrale.

Simon, Artur. 1989a. "Musical Traditions, Islam and Cultural Identity in the Sudan." In *Perspectives on African Music,* ed. Wolfgang Bender, 25–41. Bayreuth: Bayreuth African Studies, series 9.

———. 1989b. "Trumpet and Flute Ensembles of the Berta People in the Sudan." In *African Musicology: Current Trends,* ed. Jacqueline C. Djedje and William G. Carter, 1:183–217. Los Angeles: Crossroad Press; Festschrift J. H. K. Nketia.

———. 1991. "Sudan City Music." In *Populäre Musik in Afrika,* ed. Veit Erlmann, 165–180. Berlin: Museum für Völkerkunde.

Tucker, A. N. 1932. "Music in South Sudan." *Man* 32:18–19.

———. 1933a. "Children's Games and Songs in the Southern Sudan." *Journal of the Royal Anthropological Institute of Great Britain and Ireland* 63:165–187.

———. 1933b. *Tribal Music and Dancing in the Southern Sudan (Africa) at Social and Ceremonial Gatherings.* London: W. Reeves.

Wendt, Caroline Card. 1994. "Regional Style in Tuareg *Anzad* Music." In *To the Four Corners,* ed. Ellen Leichtman. Warren, Mich.: Harmonie Park Press.

East Africa

Abokor, Ahmed Ali. 1990. "Somali Pastoral Work Songs: The Poetic Voice of the Politically Powerless." M.A. thesis, Indiana University.

Anderson, Lois. 1967. "The African Xylophone." *African Arts / Arts d'Afrique* 1:46–49.

———. 1977. "The Entenga Tuned-Drum Ensemble." In *Essays for a Humanist: An Offering to Klaus Wachsmann*, 1–57. New York: Town House Press.

Campbell, C. A., and C. M. Eastman. 1984. "Ngoma: Swahili Adult Song Performance in Context." *Ethnomusicology* 28(3):467–494.

Cooke, Peter. 1970. "Ganda Xylophone Music: Another Approach." *African Music* 4(4).

———. 1990. "Report on Pitch Perception Carried Out in Buganda and Busoga (Uganda) August 1990." *ICTM Study Group* 33:2–6.

Cooke, Peter, and Martin Doornbos. 1982. "Rwenzururu Protest Songs." *Africa* 52(1):37–60.

DeVale, Sue Carole. 1984. "Prolegomena to a Study of Harp and Voice Sounds in Uganda: A Graphic System for the Notation of Texture." In *Selected Reports in Ethnomusicology*, vol. 5, ed. J. H. Kwabena Nketia and Jacqueline Cogdell DjeDje, 284–315. Los Angeles: University of California.

Giannattasio, Francesco. 1983. "Somalia: La Terapia Coreutico-Musicali del Mingis." *Culture Musicali* 2(3):93–119.

———. 1988a. "Strumenti Musicali." In *Aspetti dell' Espressione Artistica in Somalia,* ed. Annarita Puglielli, 73–89. Rome: University of Rome.

———. 1988b. "The Study of Somali Music: Present State." In *Proceedings of the Third International Congress of Somali Studies,* ed. Annarita Puglielli, 158–167. Rome: Il Pensiero Scientifico Editore.

Gnielinski, Anneliese von. 1985. *Traditional Music Instruments of Tanzania in the National Museum.* Dar es Salaam: National Museums. Occasional paper 6.

Gourlay, Kenneth A. 1972. *The Making of Karimojong Cattle Songs.* Nairobi: Institute of African Studies, University of Nairobi. Discussion paper 18.

Hartwig, Gerald W. 1969. "The Historical and Social Role of Kerebe Music." *Tanzania Notes and Records* 70:41–56.

Kavyu, Paul. 1978. "The Development of Guitar Music in Kenya." *Jazzforschung* 10:111–119.

Kimberlin, Cynthia. 1978. "The Baganna of Ethiopia." *Ethiopianist Notes* 2(2).

Kubik, Gerhard. 1967. "The Traditional Music of Tanzania." *Afrika* 8(2):29–32.

———. 1981. "Popular Music in East Africa since 1945." *Popular Music* 1:83–104.

Low, John. 1982a. "A History of Kenyan Guitar Music: 1945–1980." *African Music* 6(2):17–36.

———. 1982b. *Shaba Diary: A Trip to Rediscover the 'Katanga' Guitar Styles and Songs of the 1950's and '60's.* Vienna: Fohrenau. Acta Ethnologica et Linguistica, 54.

Martin, Stephen H. 1991a. "Brass Bands and the Beni Phenomenon in Urban East Africa." *African Music* 8(1):72–81.

———. 1991b. "Popular Music in Urban East Africa." *Black Music Research Journal* 11(1):39–53.

Omondi, Washington A. 1984. "The Tuning of the Thum, the Luo Lyre, A Systematic Analysis." In *Selected Reports in Ethnomusicology V. Studies in African Music* (UCLA), 263–281.

Ranger, T. O. 1975. *Dance and Society in Eastern Africa.* Berkeley and Los Angeles: University of California Press.

Roberts, J. S. 1968. "Popular Music in Kenya." *African Music* 4(2):53–55.

Shelemay, Kay Kaufman. 1983. "A New System of Musical Notation in Ethiopia." In *Ethiopian Studies Dedicated to Wolf Leslau,* ed. Stanislav Segert and Andras J. E. Bodrogligeti, 571–582. Wiesbaden: Otto Harrassowitz.

———. 1989 [1986]. *Music, Ritual, and Falasha History.* East Lansing: Michigan State University Press.

Wachsmann, Klaus P. 1971. "Musical Instruments in Kiganda Tradition and Their Place in the East African Scene." In *Essays on Music and History in Africa,* ed. Klaus P. Wachsmann, 93–134. Evanston, Ill.: Northwestern University Press.

Central Africa

Arom, Simha. 1967. "Instruments de musique particuliers à certaines ethnies de la République Centrafricaine." *Journal of the International Folk Music Council,* 19:104–108.

Blakely, Pamela A. 1993. "Performing Dangerous Thoughts: Women's Song-Dance Performance Events in a Hemba Funeral Ritual (Republic of Zaïre)." Ph.D. dissertation, Indiana University.

Brandel, Rose. 1961. *The Music of Central Africa.* The Hague: Martinus Nijhoff.

Carrington, John F. 1949. *A Comparative Study of Some Central African Gong-Languages.* Brussels: Institut Royal Colonial Belge.

Dehoux, Vincent, and Frédéric Voisin. 1992. "Analytic Procedures with Scales in Central African Xylophone Music." In *European Studies in Ethnomusicology: Historical Developments and Recent Trends,* ed. Max Peter Baumann et al., 174–188. Wilhelmshaven: Florian Noetzel; Intercultural Music Studies, 4.

———. 1993. "An Interactive Experimental Method for the Determination of Musical Scales in Oral Cultures: Application to the Xylophone Music of Central Africa." *Contemporary Music Review* 9:13–19.

Gansemans, Jos. 1978. *La musique et son rôle dans la vie sociale et rituelle Luba.* Tervuren, Belgium: Musée Royal de l'Afrique Centrale. Sciences Humaines, 95.

———. 1980. *Les instruments de musique Luba.* Tervuren, Belgium: Musée Royal de l'Afrique Centrale. Sciences Humaines, 103.

Gansemans, Jos, and Barbara Schmidt-Wrenger. 1986. *Zentralafrika.* Leipzig: Deutscher Verlag für Musik. Musikgeschichte in Bildern, 1, part 12.

Kubik, Gerhard. 1964. "Harp Music of the Azande and Related Peoples in the Central African Republic." *African Music* 3(3):37–76.

Laurenty, Jean Sébastien. 1960. *Les Cordophones du Congo Belge et du Ruanda-Urundi.* Tervuren: Musée Royale de l'Afrique Centrale.

———. 1962. *Les Sanza du Congo Belge.* Tervuren, Belgium: Musée Royale de l'Afrique Centrale.

———. 1968. *Les Tambours à fente de l'Afrique Centrale.* Tervuren, Belgium: Musée Royale de l'Afrique Centrale.

———. 1974. *La Systematique des aérophones de l'Afrique Centrale.* Tervuren: Musée Royale de l'Afrique Centrale.

Merriam, Alan P. 1973. "The Bala Musician." In *The Traditional Artist in African Societies,* ed. Warren d'Azevedo, 23–81. Bloomington: Indiana University Press.

Mukuna, Kazadi wa. 1973. "Trends of Nineteenth and Twentieth Century Music in the Congo-Zaïre." In *Musikkulturen Asiens, Afrikas und Ozeanien im 19. Jahrhundert,* ed. Robert Günther, 267–284. Regensburg: Gustav Bosse.

———. 1980. "The Origin of Zaïrean Modern Music: A Socio-economic Aspect." *African Urban Studies* 6:77–78.

Schweinfurth, Georg A. 1873. *In the Heart of Africa: Three Years' Travels and Adventures in the Unexplored Regions of Central Africa from 1868–1871.* London: S. Low, Marsten, Low, and Searle.

Voisin, Frédéric. 1994. "Musical Scales in Central Africa and Java: Modeling by Synthesis." *Leonardo Music Journal* 4:85–90.

Southern Africa

Adams, Charles R. 1974. "Ethnography of Basotho: Evaluative Expression in the Cognitive Domain Lipapali (Games)." Ph.D. dissertation, Indiana University.

Brown, Ernest Douglas. 1984. "Drums of Life: Royal Music and Social Life in Western Zambia." Ph.D. dissertation, University of Washington.

Berliner, Paul. 1978. *The Soul of Mbira: Music and Traditions of the Shona People of Zimbabwe.* Berkeley and Los Angeles: University of California Press.

Blacking, John. 1967. *Venda Children's Songs.* Johannesburg: Witwatersrand University Press.

———. 1985. "Movement, Dance, Music, and the Venda Girls' Initiation Cycle." In *Society and the Dance: The Social Anthropology of Process and Performance,* ed. Paul Spencer, 64–91. Cambridge: Cambridge University Press.

Colson, Elizabeth. 1969. "Spirit-Possession Among the Tonga of Zambia." In *Spirit Mediumship in Society in Africa,* ed. John Beattie and John Middleton, 69–103. London: Routledge and Kegan Paul.

Coplan, David B. 1985. In *Township Tonight! South Africa's Black City Music and Theatre.* London: Longman.

———. 1988. "Musical Understanding: The Ethnoaesthetics of Migrant Workers' Poetic Song in Lesotho." *Ethnomusicology* 32:337–368.

Erlmann, Veit. 1991. *African Stars: Studies in Black South African Performance.* Chicago: University of Chicago Press.

Johnston, Thomas. 1970. "Xizambi Friction-Bow Music of the Shangana-Tsonga." *African Music* 4(4):81–95.

———. 1971. "Shangana-Tsonga Drum and Bow Rhythms." *African Music* 5(1):59–72.

———. 1972. "Possession Music of the Shangana-Tsonga." *African Music* 5(2):10–22.

———. 1987. "Children's Music of the Shangana-Tsonga." *African Music* 6(4):126–143.

Joseph, Rosemary. 1983. "Zulu Women's Music." *African Music* 6(3):53–89.

Kauffman, Robert. 1969. "Some Aspects of Aesthetics in Shona Music of Rhodesia." *Ethnomusicology* 13(3):507–511.

———. 1972. "Shona Urban Music and the Problem of Acculturation." *IFMC Yearbook* 4:47–56.

Kirby, Percival R. 1937 [1967]. "The Musical Practices of the Native Races of South Africa." In *Western Civilization and the Natives of South Africa,* ed. Isaac Schapera, 131–140. New York: Humanities Press.

———. 1965. *The Musical Instruments of the Native Races of South Africa,* 2nd ed. Johannesburg: Witwatersrand University Press.

Kubik, Gerhard. 1964. "Harp Music of the Azande and Related Peoples in the Central African Republic." *African Music* 3(3):37–76.

———. 1971. "Carl Mauch's Mbira Musical Transcriptions of 1872." *Review of Ethnology* 3(10):73–80.

———. 1988. "Nsenga / Shona Harmonic Patterns and the San Heritage in Southern Africa." *Ethnomusicology* 32(2):39–76 (211–248).

———. 1989. "The Southern African Periphery: Banjo Traditions in Zambia and Malaŵi." *The World of Music* 31:3–29.

Kubik, Gerhard, Moya Aliya Malamusi, Lidiya Malamusi, and Donald Kachamba. 1987. *Malaŵian Music: A Framework for Analysis.* Zomba, Malaŵi: University of Malaŵi, Department of Fine and Performing Arts.

Malamusi, Moya Aliya. 1984. "The Zambian Popular Music Scene." *Jazzforschung* 16:189–195.

Marshall, Lorna. 1969. "The Medicine Dance of the !Kung Bushmen." *Africa* 39(4):347–381.

McLeod, Norma. 1977. "Musical Instruments and History in Madagascar." In *Essays for a Humanist: An Offering to Klaus Wachsmann.* New York: Town House Press.

Mthethwa, Bongani. 1980. "Zulu Children's Songs." In *Papers Presented at the Symposium on Ethnomusicology: Rhodes University, Grahamstown, October 10–11, 1980,* ed. Andrew Tracey, 23–35. Grahamstown: Rhodes University.

Rycroft, David. 1961. "The Guitar Improvisations of Mwenda Jean Bosco." *African Music* 2(4):81–98.

———. 1962. "The Guitar Improvisations of Mwenda Jean Bosco (Part II)." *African Music* 3(1):86–102.

———. 1971. "Stylistic Evidence in Nguni Song." In *Essays on Music and History in Africa,* ed. Klaus P. Wachsmann, 213–241. Evanston, Ill.: Northwestern University Press.

Tracey, Andrew. 1971. "The Nyanga Panpipe Dance." *African Music* 5(1):73–89.

Tracey, Hugh. 1970. *Chopi Musicians: Their Music, Poetry, and Instruments.* London and New York: International African Institute, Oxford University Press.

Tsukada, Kenichi. 1988. "Luvale Perceptions of Mukanda in Discourse and Music." Ph.D. dissertation, Queen's University of Belfast.

———. 1990. "*Kukuwa* and *Kachacha:* Classification and Rhythm in the Music of the Luvale of Central Africa." In *People and Rhythm,* ed. Tetsuo Sakurai, 229–276. Tokyo: Tokyo Shoseki. In Japanese.

———. 1991a. "*Mukanda* Rites and Music: A Study of Initiation Rites in Central Africa." In *Ritual and Music,* vol. 2, ed. Tomoaki Fujii, 177–228. Tokyo: Tokyo Shoseki. In Japanese.

———. 1991b. "*Kalindula* in *Mukanda:* The Incorporation of Westernized Music into the Boys' Initiation Rites of the Luvale of Zambia." In *Tradition and Its Future in Music,* ed. Yoshihiko Tokumaru et al., 547–551. Tokyo: Mita Press.

Turner, Victor. 1968. *The Drums of Affliction: A Study of Religious Processes among the Ndembu of Zambia.* Oxford: International African Institute.

Westphal, E. O. J. 1978. "Observations on Current Bushmen and Hottentot Musical Practices." *Review of Ethnology* 5(2–3):9–15.

Zenkovsky, S. 1950. "Zar and Tambura as Practiced by the Women of Omdurman." *Sudan Notes and Records* 31:65–85.

A Guide to Recordings of African Music

Catalogs and Audiographies

Catalogue of Zonophone West African Records by Native Artists. 1929. Hayes, Middlx.: British Zonophone Company.

Merriam, Alan P. 1970. *African Music on LP: An Annotated Discography.* Evanston, Ill.: Northwestern University Press.

Tracey, Hugh. 1973. *Catalogue: The Sound of Africa Series.* Roodepoort, South Africa: International Library of African Music.

General

Africa Dances. 1980. Authentic Records, ARM 601C Authentic. Audiocassette.

Courlander, Harold, and Alan P. Merriam. 1957. *Africa South of the Sahara.* Folkways Records FE 4503. 2 LP disks.

Discover a Whole New World of Music. 1991. Newton, N. J.: Shanachie Records 9101, CD 124. Compact disc.

Hood, Mantle. 1969. *Africa East and West.* Los Angeles: Institute of Ethnomusicology, University of California. IER 6571.

Kronos Quartet and Judith Sherman. 1992. *Pieces of Africa.* Elektra / Nonesuch 979275–2. Compact disc.

Tracey, Hugh. 1953. *The Guitars of Africa.* London LB-829. Music of Africa, 5. LP disk.

West Africa

Adé, Sunny. 1976. *Synchro System Movement.* African Songs AS26. LP disk.

———. 1982. *Juju Music.* Island Records CID 9712. Compact disc.

Aingo, George Williams. 1992. *Roots of Highlife–1927.* Heritage HT CD 17. Compact disc.

Ames, David. 1964. *The Music of Nigeria, Hausa Music,* vol.1. Bärenreiter- Musicaphon Records BM 30 SL 2306. LP disk.

———. 1976? *Nigeria III: Igbo Music.* Bärenreiter-Musicaphon Records BM 30 SL 2311. LP disk.

Amoaku, W. K. 1978. *African Songs and Rhythms for Children.* Folkways Records FC 7844. LP disk.

Arom, Simha. 1975. *The Music of the Peuls.* EMI Odeon. LP disk.

Bebey, Francis. 1978. *Francis Bebey: ballades africaines: guitare.* Paris: Ozileka 3306. LP disk.

———. 1984. *Akwaaba.* Tivoli, N. Y.: Original Music OMCD 005. Compact disc.

Camara, Ladji. 1993. *Les ballets africains de Papa Ladji Camara.* Lyrichord. LP disk.

Dairo, I. K., and his Blue Spots. 1962. *Elele Ture.* Decca NWA 5079.

Dieterlen, Germaine. 1957. *Musique Dogon Mali.* Ocora OCR 33. LP disk.

———. 1966. *Musique Maure Mauritania.* OCR 28. LP disk.

Diamonds, Black. 1971? *Songs and Rhythms from Sierra Leone.* New Rochelle, N. Y.: Afro Request SRLP 5031. LP disk.

Duran, Lucy. 1985. *Jaliya / Malamini Jobarteh and Dembo Konte.* London: Stern's Africa. LP disk.

———. 1990. *Boubacar Traoré: Mariama.* London: Stern's Africa 1032. LP disk.

Forster, Till. 1987. *Musik der Senufo, Elfenbeinkuste.* Berlin: Musikethnologische Abteilung, Museum für Völkerkunde MC 4. 2 LP disks.

Freire, João. 1992. *Travadinha: The Violin of Cape Verde.* Buda Records 92556–2. Compact disc.

Işola, Haruna. 1959. "Hogan Bassey." Decca WA 3120. 78-rpm, 10-inch disk.

Jenkins, Jean. 1985. *Sierra Leone: Musiques traditionnelles.* Paris: OCORA 558- -549. LP disk.

Johnson, Kathleen. 1983. *Rhythms of the Grasslands: Music of Upper Volta,* vol. 2. Los Angeles: Elektra / Asylum / Nonesuch 72090. 2. LP disk.

Kouyate, Tata Bambo. 1989. *Tata Bambo Kouyate.* London: Globestyle ORB 042. LP disk.

Kroo Young Stars Rhythm Group. 1953. *O Gi Te Bi.* Decca DKWA 1335. LP disk.

Leigh, Stuart. 1981. *Music of Sierra Leone: Kono Mende Farmer's Songs.* Folkways Records FE 4330. LP disk.

Maal, Baaba. 1991. *Baayo*. New York: Island Records, Mango Records 162 539907–2. Compact disc.

Rouget, Gilbert. 1971. *Musique Malinke, Guinée*. Paris: Vogue LDM 30 113. LP disk.

———. 1981. *Sénégal: musique des Bassari*. Paris: Chant du Monde LDX 74 753. LP disk.

Okie, Packard, ed. 1955. *Folk Music of Liberia*. Folkways Records FE 4465.

Weka-Yamo, Aladji, and Ayivi Go Togbassa. 1992. *Togo: Music from West Africa*. Rounder CD 5004. Compact disc.

Stone, Ruth M., and Verlon L. Stone. 1972. *Music of the Kpelle of Liberia*. Folkways FE 4385. LP disk.

Zemp, Hugo. 1971. *Musique Guère: Côte d'Ivoire*. Paris: Vogue LD 764. LP disk.

North Africa

Atiya, Aziz S. 1960. *Coptic Music*. Folkways Records. LP disk.

Deng, Francis M. 1976. *Music of the Sudan: The Role of Song and Dance in Dinka Society*. Folkways Records FE 4301–03. 3 LP disks.

Duvelle, Charles. 1966. *Musique maure*. Paris: OCORA OCR 28. LP disk.

Gottlieb, Robert. N.d. *Sudan I: Music of the Blue Nile Province: The Gumuz Tribe*. Cassel: Bärenreiter Musicaphon BM 30L 2312. LP disk.

———. N.d. *Sudan II: The Ingessana and Berta Tribes*. Cassel: Bärenreiter Musicaphon BM 30L 2313. LP disk.

Guignard, Michel. 1975. *Mauritanie: Musique traditionnelle des griots maures*. SELAF / ORSTOM (Collection Tradition Orale) CETO 752–3. 2 LP disks.

Laade, Wolfgang. 1962. *Tunisia*, vol. 2, "Religious Songs and Cantillations." Folkways Records FW 8862. LP disk.

Lortat-Jacob, Bernard, and H. Jouad. 1979. *Berbères du Maroc: ahwach*. Collection du Centre National de la Recherche Scientifique du Musée de l'Homme LDX 74705. LP disk.

Lortat-Jacob, Bernard, and Gilbert Rouget. 1971. *Musique berbère du haut atlas*. Paris: Disques Vogue LD 786. LP disk.

Musiciens du Nil. 1988. Paris: OCORA D559006. Compact disc.

Pacholczyk, Jozef M. 1976. *Andalusian Music of Morocco*. Tucson, Ariz. Ethnodisc ER 45154. LP disk.

Schuyler, Philip. N.d. *The Music of Islam and Sufism in Morocco*. Bärenreiter- Musicaphon BM 30 SL 2027. LP disk.

———. 1977. *Morocco: Arabic Tradition in Moroccan Music*. UNESCO Collection. EMI Odeon 3C 064-18264.

Simon, Artur. 1980a. *Musik der Nubier / Nordsudan (Music of the Nubians / Northern Sudan)*. Berlin: Musikethnologische Abteilung, Museum für Völkerkunde MC 9. 2 LP disks.

———. 1980b. *Dikr und Madih. Gesänge und Zeremonien: Islamisches Brauchtum im Sudan*. Berlin: Museum Collection MC 10.

Yassin, H. M., and Amel Benhassine. 1986. *Sounds of Sudan, Vol. 3: Mohamed Gubara*. London: Record World Circuit, WCB 005. LP disk.

Yurchenco, Henrietta. 1983. *Ballads, Wedding Songs, and Piyyutim of the Sephardic Jews of Tetuan and Tangier, Morocco*. 1983. Folkways Records FE 4208. LP disk.

East Africa

Abana Ba Nasery. 1992. *!Nursery Boys Go Ahead! The Guitar and Bottle Kids of Kenya*. Green Linnet GLCD 4002. Compact disc.

African Acoustic. 1988. Tivoli, N.Y.: Original Music OMA 110C. Audiocassette.

Boyd, Alan. 1985. *Music of the Waswahili of Lamu, Kenya*. Folkways Records, FE 4093–4095. 3 LP disks.

Burundi Drums: Batimbo-Musiques et Chants. 1992. Auvidis, Playa Sound PS 65089. Audiocassette.

Graebner, Werner. 1989. *Nyota: Black Star and Lucky Star Musical Clubs*. Globestyle CDORBD 044. Compact disc.

———. 1990. *Zein Musical Party: Mtindo Was Mombasa / The Style of Mombasa*. Globestyle CDORBD 066. Compact disc.

Kenya: Musiques du Nyanza. 1993. Paris: OCORA C 560022/23. 2 compact discs.

Mandelson, Ben, and Werner Graebner. 1990. *Mombasa Wedding Special: Maulidi and Musical Party*. Global Style CDORBD 058. Compact disc.

The Nairobi Sound. 1982. Brooklyn, N.Y.: Original Music OMA 101C. Audiocassette.

Nzomo, David. 1976. *Gospel Songs from Kenya: Kikamba Hymns*. Folkways FR 8911. LP disk.

Roberts, John Storm. 1988? *The Kampala Sound: 1960s Ugandan Dance Music*. Tivoli, N. Y.: OMA 109C. Audiocassette.

Songs the Swahili Sing: Classics from the Kenya Coast. 1980. Brooklyn, N.Y.: Original Music OMA 103C. Audiocassette.

Ssalongo, Christopher Kizza, and Peter Cooke, arr. and ed. 1988. *The Budongo of Uganda*. Edinburgh: K and C Productions KAC 1001. Audiocassette.

The Tanzania Sound. 198-. Tivoli, N.Y.: Original Music OMA 106C. Audiocassette.

Tanzania Yetu. 1985. Terra 101. London: Triple Earth Records. LP disk.

Central Africa

Arom, Simha. 1965. *Ba-Benzélé.* UNESCO Collection. Bärenreiter Musicaphon BM 30 L 2303. LP disk.

———. 1980. *Anthologie de la Musique des Pygmées Aka.* Paris: OCORA 558.526.27.28. 3 LP disks and notes.

———. 1992. *République Centrafricaine: Banda Polyphony.* UNESCO/Auvidis D 8043. Compact disc.

Arom, Simha, and G. Dournon-Taurelle.1971. *Musiques Banda: République Centrafricaine.* Disques RA 558.526–528. LP disk.

Bourgine. Caroline. 1991. *Congo: Cérémonie du Bobé.* OCORA W 560010.

Dehoux, Vincent. 1992. *Centrafrique: Musique Gbáyá—Chants à penser.* Paris: OCORA C 580008.

Fernandez, James W. 1973. *Music from an Equatorial Microcosm: Fang Bwiti Music from Gabon Republic, Africa, with Mbira Selections.* Folkways Records FE 4214. LP disk.

Gabon: pygmées bibayak et chantres des bapounou et des fang. 1980. Paris: OCORA 4.504.515. Audiocassette.

Gansmans, Jos. 1981. *Zaïre: musique des Salampasu.* Paris: OCORA 558.597. LP disk.

Jangoux, Jacques. 1973? *Music of Zaïre: Peoples of the Ngiri River.* Folkways Records FE 4241–4242. 2 LP disks.

Kisliuk, Michelle. 1992. *Mbuti Pygmies of the Ituri Rain Forest.* Recordings by Colin Turnbull and Frances S. Chapman. Smithsonian / Folkways CDSF 40401. Compact disc.

Mouquet, Eric, and Michel Sanchez. 1992. *Deep Forest.* Compact disk. Sony Music Entertainment (France) / Columbia Records DAN 4719762.

Papa Wemba: Le voyageur. 1992. Filament Music Publishers/WOMAD, Real World CD RW 20. Compact disc.

Roots of O.K. Jazz: Zaïre Classics 1955–56. 1993. Cramworld Crammed Discs Craw 7. Compact disc.

Sallée, Pierre. 1968? *Gabon: musiques des Mitsogho et des Batéké.* Paris. OCORA 84. LP disk.

Zaïre: musiques urbaines à Kinshasa. 1987. Paris: OCORA 559.007. LP disk.

Zaïre: la musique des Nande. Geneva. 1991. VDE-Gallo CD-652. Compact disc.

Southern Africa

Barkaak, Odd Are, and Pearson Likukela. *Kuomboka Music [Zambia].* Nayuma Museum. Audiocassette.

Chimurenga Songs: Music of the Revolutionary People's War in Zimbabwe. 1988. Harare, Zimbabwe: Gramma Records L4VZ5. Audiocassette.

Chiweshe, Stella. 1990. *Stella Chiweshe: Ambuya?* Newton, N. J.: Shanachie 65006. Compact disc.

D'Gary. *Malagasy Guitar: Music from Madagascar.* 1992. Newton, N. J.: Shanachie 65009. Compact disc.

Dube, William (William Dube Jairos Jiri Sunrise Kwela Band). 1980. *Take Cover.* Bulawayo, Zimbabwe: Teal Record Company ZIM 32. LP disk.

Erlmann, Veit. 1986. *Zulu Songs of South Africa.* Lyrichord LLST 7401. LP disk.

———. 1988. *Mbube Roots: Zulu Choral Music from South Africa, 1930's–1960's.* Rounder CD5025. Compact disc.

Gesthuisen, Birger, and Henry Kaiser. 1992. *A World Out of Time: Henry Kaiser and David Lindley in Madagascar.* Shanachie 64041. Compact disc.

Hanna, Marilyn, ed. 1985. *Ephat Mujuru: Master of Mbira from Zimbabwe.* Lyrichord LLST 7398. LP disk.

Hallis, Ron, and Ophera Hallis. 1980. *Music from Mozambique.* Folkways Records FE 4310. LP disk.

Homeland 2: A Collection of Black South African Music. 1990. Rounder CD 5028. Compact disc.

Kachamba, Donald, Moya Aliya Malamusi, Gerhard Kubik, and Stuwadi Mpotalinga. *Malawi: Concert Kwela.* Le Chant du Monde CDM LDX 274972. Compact disc.

Kivnick, Helen, and Gary Gardner. 1987. *Let Their Voices Be Heard.* Rounder Records 5024. LP disk.

Kubik, Gerhard. 1981. *Mukanda na makisi—Circumcision school and masks.* Berlin: Museum für Völkerkunde MC 11. LP disk and notes.

Kubik, Gerhard, and Moya Aliya Malamusi. 1989. *Opeka nyimbo: Musician-Composers from Southern Malaŵi.* Museum für Völkerkunde, Musikethnologische Abteilung. Museum Collection MC 15. Two LP disks and notes.

Laade, Wolfgang. 1991. *Zimbabwe: The Ndebele People.* Westbury, N. Y.: Koch International, Jecklin-Disco JD 654-2. LP disk.

Mapoma, Isaiah Mwesa. 1971. *Inyimbo: Songs of the Bemba People of Zambia.* Tucson, Ariz.: Ethnodisc ER 12103. LP disk.

Mazai Mbira Group. 1989?. Harare, Zimbabwe: Gramma Records L4AML. Audiocassette.

Mujuru, Ephat. 1980? *Rhythms of Life.* Lyrichord LLCT 7407. Audiocassette.

Project Grassworks. 1990. *Sounds Sung by South African Children.* Athlone: Grassroots Educare Trust. Audiocassette.

Randafison, Sylvestre, and Jean-Baptiste Ramaronandrasana. 1989. *Madagascar: Le valiha.* Harmonia Mundi Playa Sound PS 65046. Compact disc.

Tchiumba, Lilly. 1975. *Angola: Songs of My People.* Monitor Records MFS 767.

Tracey, Hugh. 1956. *International Library of African Music.* Roodepoort, South Africa.

Tracey, Hugh, and John Storm Roberts. 1989a. *Siya Hamba!* Tivoli, N. Y.: Original Music OMCD 003. LP disk.

———. 1989b. *From the Copperbelt: Zambian Miners' Songs.* Tivoli, N. Y.: Original Music OMCD 004. Compact disc.

Wood, Bill. 1976. *Music of Lesotho.* Folkways Records FE 4224. LP disk.

A Guide to Films and Videos

GENERAL

Katsumori, Ichikawa, prod. 1990. *The JVC Video Anthology of World Music and Dance.* Tokyo: JVC, Victor Company of Japan.Vols. 17, 18, and 19. Videocassettes.

WEST AFRICA

Chevallier, Laurent, and Nicole Jouve. 1991. *Djembefola.* New York: Interama. 16mm.

Cohen, Hervé. 1991. *Sikambano: The Sons of the Sacred Wood.* Paris: Les Films du Village. Videocassette.

Haas, Philip. 1990? *Seni's Children.* New York: Milestone Film and Video. Videocassette.

Hale, Thomas A. 1990. *Griottes of the Sahel: Female Keepers of the Songhay Oral Tradition in Niger.* University Park: Pennsylvania State University. Videocassette.

Holender, Jacques. 1991. *Juju Music!* New York: Rhapsody Films.

Knight, Roderic. 1992a. *Jali Nyama Suso: Kora Player of the Gambia.* Tivoli, N. Y.: Original Music. Videocassette.

———. 1992b. *Music of the Mande.* Tivoli, N. Y.: Original Music. Videocassette.

Locke, David. 1990. *A Performance of Kpegisu by the Wodome-Akatsi Kpegisu Habobo.* Tempe, Ariz.: White Cliffs Media. Videocassette.

Marre, Jeremy. 1983. *Konkombe: Nigerian Pop Music Scene.* Newton, N. J.: Shanachie Records. Videocassette.

Rossellini, Jim. 1983. *Dance of the Bella.* Venice, Calif.: African Family Films. Videocassette.

NORTH AFRICA

Guindi, Fadwa El. 1990. *El Moulid: Egyptian Religious Festival.* Los Angeles: El Nil Research. Videocassette, 16mm.

Llewellyn-Davies, Melissa, and Elizabeth Fernea. 1978. *Saints and Spirits.* Chicago: Films Incorporated Video. Videocassette.

Marre, Jeremy. 1991 [1983]. *The Romany Trail: Part I, Gypsy Music into Africa.* Newton, N. J.: Shanachie Records.

Mendizza, Michael, and Philip D. Schuyler. 1983. *The Master Musicians of Jabjouka.* New York: Alegrías Productions.

Wickett, Elizabeth. 1990. *For Those Who Sail to Heaven.* New York: Icarus Films. Videocassette, 16mm.

EAST AFRICA

Hawkins, Richard, and Suzette Heald. 1988. *Imbalu: Ritual of Manhood of the Bagisu of Uganda.* London: Royal Anthropological Institute, University of Manchester, Media Support and Development Centre.

Woodhead, Leslie. 1991. *The Mursi: Nitha.* New York: Granada Television. Videocassette.

CENTRAL AFRICA

Villers, Violaine de. 1992. *Mizike Mama.* New York: Interama. 16mm.

SOUTHERN AFRICA

Gavshon, Harriet. 1992. *A Stranger in a Strange Land: Paul Simon in South Africa.* Johannesburg: Free Film-Makers. Videocassette.

Hallis, Ron, and Ophera Hallis. 1989. *Music of the Spirits.* El Cerrito, Calif.: Flower Films. Videocassette.

———. 1992. *Chopi Music of Mozambique and Banguza.* El Cerrito, Calif.: Flower Films. Videocassette, 16mm.

Marshall, John, Robert Gardner, and Lorna Marshall. 1989. *The Hunters.* Chicago: Films Incorporated Video. Videocassette.

Morell, Karen, and Steven Friedson. *Prophet Healers of Northern Malawi.* 1990. Seattle: African Encounters PC-45. Videocassette.

May, Deborah. 1991. *We Jive Like This.* New York: Filmakers Library. Videocassette.

Poschl, Rupert, and Ulrike Poschl. 1990. *Vimbuza-Chilopa: A Spirit Possession Cult among the Tumbuka of Malawi.* University Park: Pennsylvania State University, Audio-Visual Services. Videocassette.

ACKNOWLEDGMENTS

This compact disc was edited and mastered at the Archives of Traditional Music at Indiana University in Bloomington, Indiana. All recordings are reproduced with the permission of the original collectors and copyright holders.

Archives of Traditional Music Staff:
Gloria J. Gibson, Director
Peter Alyea, Sound Restoration and Mastering
Daniel B. Reed, Selection and Editing
Mary Russell Bucknum
Marilyn Graf
Suzanne Mudge
Jonathan Cargill
Judge Wilkinson, Indiana University Advanced Research and Technology Institute

---

Notes on the Audio Examples

---

1. Kpelle *Woi-mene-pele* epic excerpt (4:27)
   Performed by Kulung of Koloboi and a chorus from Yilataa
   Instruments: struck beer bottles

   Recorded by Ruth and Verlon Stone on 31 March 1976 in Totota, Liberia

2. Ethiopian *Lidet* (Christmas) celebration (3:08)
   Performed by priests and *debteras* of the Holy Trinity Church of Addis Ababa
   Instruments: *tsenatsel* (sistrum) and *kebaro* (liturgical drum)

   Recorded by Kay Kaufman Shelemay on 1 June 1974 in Addis Ababa, Ethiopia

3. *Inanga Chuchotée* (whispered *inanga*) (4:12)
   Performed by Joseph Torobeka, *inanga* (trough zither) and voice

   Performed on 19 August 1986 in Bujumbura, Burundi
   Collected by Cornelia Fales

4. Vai call to prayer (5:07)
   Performed by Muhammad Manobala, voice

   Recorded by Lester P. Monts in 1987–1988 in Bulumi, Liberia

5. Palm-wine highlife song (2:56)
   Performed by Koo Nimo and band; Koo Nimo, guitar and lead voice
   Additional instruments: one pair of struck wooden sticks, one goblet-shaped drum, and one *apremprensemma* (bass sanza)

   Recorded by David B. Coplan on 19 December 1970, in Kumasi, Ghana

6. Anlo-Ewe *kinka* drumming (2:16)
   Performed by the Avenor Youth Association
   Instruments: one *atsimevu* (master drum), one *bombalagboba* (submaster drum), one *sogo* (response drum), one *kidi* (response drum), one *kagaŋ* (ostinato drum), several *axatsɛ*(s) (shakers), and single- and double-slit bells

   Recorded by Daniel Avorgbedor on 29 January 1989 in Accra, Ghana

7. Anlo-Ewe *kinka* songs (2:13)
   Performed by the Avenor Youth Association
   Instruments: one *atsimevu* (master drum), one *bombalagboba* (submaster drum), one *sogo* (response

drum), one *kidi* (response drum), one *kagaŋ* (ostinato drum), several *axatsɛ*(s) (shakers), and single- and double-slit bells

Recorded by Daniel Avorgbedor on 29 January 1989 in Accra, Ghana

8. Maninka *Mansareh* praise song (*balabolo*) including "*Nyin min nyama, nyama*" (5:44)
Performed by Pa Sanasi Kuyateh, *bala* (frame xylophone with gourd resonators, played with rubber-tipped mallets; rattles are attached to the hands); Hawa Kuyateh, *karinyan* (cylindrical iron bell struck with iron beater) and solo voice; Nimeh Kaleh, Sayo Kaleh, Mariama Kaleh and others, chorus

Recorded by Laura Arntson on 20 January 1988 in Sukurala, Sierra Leone

9. *Bala* pattern of Maninka *Mansareh bolo* (0:51)
Performed by Pa Sanasi Kuyateh, *bala*

Recorded by Laura Arntson on 27 January 1988 in Sukurala, Sierra Leone

10. Maninka *Duwa* praise song (1:15)
Performed by Pa Sanasi Kuyateh, *bala;* Hawa Kuyateh and Nimeh Kaleh, voices

Recorded by Laura Arntson on 9 February 1988 in Sukurala, Sierra Leone

11. Tuareg *Tihadanaren* (1:57)
Performed by Bouchit bint Loki, *anzad* (bowed lute)

Recorded by Caroline Card Wendt on 16 December 1976 in Tamanrasset, Algeria

12. Tuareg *takɔmba* song "*Khadisia*" (1:32)
Performed by Hattaye ag Muhammed, *tahardent* (plucked lute) and voice

Recorded by Caroline Card Wendt on 20 May 1977 in Agadez, Algeria

13. Basoga *lusoga* song "*Enyhonyhi kolojo*" 'Thieving birds' (4:00)
Performed by Silagi Kirimungo and his family group of semiprofessional farmer-musicians
Instruments: one *akadongo* (lamellophone), one *embaire* (xylophone), 4 *enkwanzi* (panpipes), one *akalere* (notched flute with four finger holes), one *ndingidi* (tube fiddle), one long drum, one "Uganda" drum, one rattle

In this song, Silagi sings about the hard work of turning swamps into productive rice paddies. He compares the many birds that steal his rice just as it is ripening with the many relatives and friends who come to scrounge some rice once it is harvested.

Recorded by Peter Cooke on 10 September 1990 in Bukoona village, Busoga, eastern Uganda

14. Baganda *akadinda* song "*Gganga aluwa*" 'Gganga escaped with his life' (2:26)
Performed by Sheikh Burukan Kiwuuwa and his group of royal *akadinda* musicians
Instrument: *akadinda* (large xylophone played by six musicians)

This *akadinda* song was known to many of the former palace ensembles of the *kabaka* of Buganda. It celebrates the rough justice meted out to Gganga, a young page of the palace who was caught sexually molesting the Princess Nassolo. The song was probably composed by the king's harpist.

Recorded by Peter Cooke on 25 September 1987 in Kidinda Village, Mpigi, Buganda, Uganda

15. Somali *caayar "dhaanto,"* excerpt 1 (2:45)
Performed by Cabdillaahi Xirsi "Baarleex," Xasan Maxamed Faarax, and mixed chorus, voices

Recorded by John William Johnson on 29 May 1987 in Muqdishow, Somalia

16. Somali *caayar "dhaanto,"* excerpt 2 (0:16)
Performed by Cabdillaahi Xirsi "Baarleex," Xasan Maxamed Faarax, and mixed chorus, voices.

Recorded by John William Johnson on 29 May 1987 in Muqdishow, Somalia

17. Popular song "*Motike*" 'Orphans' (2:02)
Composed and arranged by Kaida Mongana
Performed by Zokela Original
Kaida Mongana, lead voice; Maurice Kpamanda, bass

First recorded by the band in the early 1980s, but still circulated on homemade cassettes for sale in Bangui kiosks by small entrepreneurs; one of these cassettes, purchased by Michelle Kisliuk in 1992, is the source of this selection.

(The distortion on this selection was on the original tape and is a common characteristic of cassettes recorded on makeshift equipment in Africa and copied informally for sale by street vendors.)

18. "*Makala*," a song performed during a BaAka (pygmy) hunting dance called *Mabo* (2:30)
Performed by approximately thirty-five singers, three of whom, young women named Kwanga, Mbouya, and Ndami, lean close to the mic; their voices stand out from the rest of the group.
Instruments: two *(ba)ndumou* (drums)

Recorded by Michelle Kisliuk in December 1988 in a temporary BaAka camp outside Bagandou village, Lobaye prefecture, Central African Republic

19. BaAka of Dzanga perform a song during the *eboka ya nzapa* 'god dance' in the style of neighboring Bolamba pygmies (2:12)
Instrument: one drum

Recorded by Michelle Kisliuk in 1992 in Dzanga, a forest settlement in the Bagandou region (within the borderlands of Central African Republic and the Republic of the Congo)

20. Shona *Munyonga mbira* song, "*Tongore*"* (2:25)
Performed by James Masango, *mbira* (plucked lamellophone)

Recorded by John E. Kaemmer on 13 February 1972, in Bondiya, Zimbabwe (then Rhodesia).

21. Shona ancestral spirit song, "*Nyama musango*"* (2:45)
Performed by Elias Kunaka and Kidwell Mudzimirema (Mharadzirwa), wide *mbiras* (plucked lamellophones)

Recorded by John E. Kaemmer on 10 July 1973, in Jirira, Zimbabwe (then Rhodesia)

*The buzzing sound on these recordings is intentional. *Mbira* musicians attach metal rattles to their instruments to create this desired effect (for explanation see Kaemmer, MUSIC OF THE SHONA OF ZIMBABWE in this volume)

Index

ORTHOGRAPHY

ɛ or ẹ   = "eh" as in **bet**
ɔ or ọ   = "aw" as in **awful**
ŋ or ṇ   = "ng" as in **sing**
γ or yg = "ch" as in German **ach**
ʃ or ṣ   = "sh" as in **sh**out
     ɓ   = implosive "b"
     ɗ   = implosive "d"
     !   = click sound

ʹ   = high tone
ˋ   = low tone
˄   = high-low tone
˜   = nasalized sound